Windows 8
IN DEPTH

Brian Knittel

Paul McFedries

que®

800 East 96th Street,
Indianapolis, Indiana 46240 USA

WINDOWS 8 IN DEPTH

ISBN-10: 0-7897-5012-0

ISBN-13: 978-0-7897-5012-9

Library of Congress Cataloging-in-Publication data is on file.

Printed in the United States of America

First Printing: October 2012

Trademarks

All terms mentioned in this book that are known to be trademarks or service marks have been appropriately capitalized. Que Publishing cannot attest to the accuracy of this information. Use of a term in this book should not be regarded as affecting the validity of any trademark or service mark.

Warning and Disclaimer

Every effort has been made to make this book as complete and as accurate as possible, but no warranty or fitness is implied. The information provided is on an "as is" basis. The authors and the publisher shall have neither liability nor responsibility to any person or entity with respect to any loss or damages arising from the information contained in this book.

Bulk Sales

Que Publishing offers excellent discounts on this book when ordered in quantity for bulk purchases or special sales. For more information, please contact

> **U.S. Corporate and Government Sales**
>
> **1-800-382-3419**
>
> **corpsales@pearsontechgroup.com**

For sales outside of the U.S., please contact

> **International Sales**
>
> **international@pearsoned.com**

Editor-in-Chief
Greg Wiegand

Executive Editor
Rick Kughen

Development Editors
Todd Brakke
Rick Kughen

Managing Editor
Sandra Schroeder

Senior Project Editor
Tonya Simpson

Copy Editor
Bart Reed

Indexer
Larry Sweazy

Proofreader
Debbie Williams

Technical Editor
Karen Weinstein

Publishing Coordinators
Cindy Teeters
Romny French

Book Designer
Anne Jones

Compositor
Bronkella Publishing

CONTENTS AT A GLANCE

CONTENTS

ABOUT THE AUTHORS

Brian Knittel is a software developer, consultant, and writer. He has authored or coauthored many of Que's best-selling Windows books, including Que's leading Windows books, *Special Edition Using Microsoft Windows* and *Windows 7 In Depth*. Brian is also the author of *Windows XP Under the Hood* and *Windows 7 and Vista Guide to Scripting, Automation, and Command Line Tools*. In addition, Brian coauthored *Upgrading and Repairing Microsoft Windows* with Scott Mueller.

Paul McFedries is the author of more than 75 computer books that have sold more than 4 million copies worldwide. His recent titles include the Sams Publishing books *Microsoft Windows 7 Unleashed* and *Microsoft Windows Home Server 2011 Unleashed* as well as the Que Publishing books *Tweak It and Freak It: A Killer Guide to Making Windows Run Your Way*, *Formulas and Function: Microsoft Excel 2010*, and *Build It. Fix It. Own It: A Beginner's Guide to Building and Upgrading a PC*. Paul is also the proprietor of Word Spy (www.wordspy.com), a website devoted to tracking new words and phrases as they enter the English language.

DEDICATION

To my mother, who didn't go to Burning Man this year but is still as feisty as ever.

—Brian

To Karen, who gives new meaning to the phrase better half.

—Paul

ACKNOWLEDGMENTS

It's an honor to work with a highly respected publisher like Que. We are grateful to our editor-in-chief, Greg Wiegand, and executive editor, Rick Kughen, who played matchmaker and shepherd and brought together a great team to write and produce this book. We thank Rick and Todd Brakke for their guidance and editing, Bart Reed for amazing attention to detail in copy editing, and Tonya Simpson for keeping everyone on track and making the production process seem effortless. Don't let those job descriptions fool you—at Que at least, titles such as "development editor" and "copy editor" don't begin to describe the breadth of the contributions that each team member makes to each book.

We'd also like to acknowledge the support of our technical editor, Karen Weinstein, who meticulously checked every detail and tried every procedure. Then, there is an entire army of people who labor largely unseen and unthanked—the people who do the real work—the editorial, indexing, layout, art, proofing, and other production staff at Que. And finally, thanks to everyone from the marketing and sales folks at Que to the booksellers who ensured that this book made it from the printing press to your hands.

Brian also wishes to thank Maureen Maloney at Waterside Productions for great work in taking care of the legal mumbo-jumbo part of the book business.

WE WANT TO HEAR FROM YOU!

As the reader of this book, *you* are our most important critic and commentator. We value your opinion and want to know what we're doing right, what we could do better, what areas you'd like to see us publish in, and any other words of wisdom you're willing to pass our way.

We welcome your comments. You can email or write to let us know what you did or didn't like about this book—as well as what we can do to make our books better.

Please note that we cannot help you with technical problems related to the topic of this book.

When you write, please be sure to include this book's title and authors as well as your name and email address. We will carefully review your comments and share them with the author and editors who worked on the book.

Email: feedback@quepublishing.com

Mail: Que Publishing
          ATTN: Reader Feedback
          800 East 96th Street
          Indianapolis, IN 46240 USA

READER SERVICES

Visit our website and register this book at quepublishing.com/register for convenient access to any updates, downloads, or errata that might be available for this book.

Introduction

Welcome

We shall not cease from exploration
And the end of all our exploring
Will be to arrive where we started
And know the place for the first time.
—T. S. Eliot

Thank you for purchasing or considering the purchase of *Windows 8 In Depth*. Windows 8 is Microsoft's bold attempt to create an operating system that works well on a variety of devices, from desktop PCs to smartphones. Rather than take Apple's approach of having one OS for desktops/notebooks (OS X) and a second OS for tablets/smartphones (iOS), Microsoft has engineered Windows 8 to run basically the same on all four types of devices. To accomplish this, Microsoft has created an entirely new interface and an entirely new style of program that can be manipulated and controlled using the keyboard, mouse, fingers, or a stylus.

The main Windows 8 vehicle is the app, a new style of program that does away with menus, toolbars, ribbons, dialog boxes, and other familiar interface elements. Apps run full-screen (although a second app can be docked beside a running app) and make features available through *application bars* that are usually hidden but can be summoned with a right-click or swipe gesture. Apps are generally simplified, secure versions of existing apps.

All apps reside on the new Start screen, which displays each app as a *tile*, a rectangular object that shows the app name and icon. Many of these are *live tiles* that show the latest information from the app, including recent email messages in Mail, recent instant messages in Messages, the current slide show in Photos, stock data in Finance, and many more.

Windows 8, in short, shows us that the evolution of Windows is taking a big turn in a new direction, toward a new way of interacting with computers.

Now, despite all the new features, if you're used to Windows 7, you'll find that almost everything you know about Windows 7 still applies to Windows 8—you just have to learn new routes to reach old places. In this book, we show you not only how to use all the new features, but also how to quickly and easily navigate to the parts of Windows that you're already familiar with.

If you're moving up from XP, though, you're in for *big* changes almost everywhere you look. In addition to the changes that we just described, you'll find that even the traditional Windows desktop is dramatically different. This book will get you up to speed with the new desktop taskbar, new File Explorer, and vastly improved home networking. You'll be glad you made the move. Windows 8 leaves XP in the dust, adding more than a decade's worth of innovation and improvement in speed, ease of use, and reliability.

If you're moving up from Vista, you'll be *very* pleasantly surprised at the improvements. Let's face it, Vista was slow and the frequent User Account Control prompts were annoying. That's been taken care of and then some! Windows 8 is blazingly fast where Vista was slow and ponderous. You'll be happy to see, as you read through our book, that managing Windows is easier than it was in Vista, and the Homegroup networking feature is a huge plus.

This book covers the three primary versions of Windows 8: Windows 8, Windows 8 Pro (which includes advanced features such as virtualization, encryption, Remote Desktop hosting, and group policy), and Windows 8 Enterprise (which includes additional features for enterprise IT support). There is a sibling to Windows 8 called Windows RT that runs on low-power ARM processor-based tablets. It omits many Windows 8 features and settings, and doesn't permit the installation of desktop software. We talk a bit about Windows RT in Chapter 35, "Windows 8 on Mobile Devices," and it shares many of Windows 8's apps and setup screens, but we don't explicitly cover Windows RT in this book.

Why This Book?

Windows has been evolving, mostly incrementally, since 1985. Each new version has new features. Some you can figure out on your own, but some require explanation. Some features, such as networking, are easy enough to use, but are very complex underneath, and setting them up can involve making complex technical decisions. In some cases years may go by between the times that you use some management tool, and your human Random Access Memory may need refreshing. Computer books come to the rescue for all of these needs, giving step-by-step instructions, helpful advice, and detailed reference material for the future.

And although usually the path from one version of Windows to the next is smooth and straight, every so often there is a big bump in the road. The first was with Windows 95, where the Start button appeared and the right mouse button suddenly became very important. The next bump was Windows XP, which marked the move from MS-DOS to the Windows NT operating system kernel, to a security system for files, and to a whole new way of managing Windows. It's happened again with Windows 8. The Start button is gone, and you now have to use Windows 8's arcane "gestures" and tools to get anywhere.

The new "Windows 8–style" Start screen and app interface are touted as intuitive and easy to use, but they're *not*, at least at first. At first, they will seem frustrating and opaque, unless you have guidance. Many of the shortcuts and tricks that give you easy ways to do things are hidden, and almost impossible to guess. We found that out for ourselves as we worked with Windows 8 daily, for months, as we wrote this book. We didn't have anyone's guidance then, but you do now. In this book, we'll show you how to manage the Windows 8 interface without a struggle.

In addition to getting you through the steep parts of the Windows 8 learning curve, we'll also give you the benefit of our combined 45+ years of experience working with, writing about, and even writing software for, Microsoft Windows. We know what parts of using and managing Windows are confusing. We know the easy ways to do things. We've seen just about every bug and glitch, have been through just about every ugly scenario one can come up with, and have made just about every mistake that one can make. Therefore, we can spare you having to repeat some of them.

You might also appreciate that in this book, we can be honest with you. We don't work for Microsoft, so we can tell you what we really feel about the product: the good, the bad, and the downright ugly. If we say something's great, it's because we think it is, and if we hate something, we'll tell you, and we'll try to show you how to avoid it.

Our book addresses both home and business computer users. As we wrote, we imagined that you, our reader, are a friend or co-worker who's familiar enough with your computer to know what it's capable of, but might not know the details of how to make it all happen. So we show you, in a helpful, friendly, professional tone. We make an effort not just to tell you *what* to do, but why you're doing it. If you understand how Windows and its component parts work, you can get through rough patches: diagnosing problems, fixing things that the built-in wizards can't fix, and otherwise solving problems creatively.

And, if you're looking for power-user tips and some nitty-gritty details, we make sure you get those too. We try to make clear what information is essential for you to understand and what is optional for just those of you who are especially interested.

However, no one book can do it all. As the title says, this book is about Windows 8, which runs on desktop computers, notebooks, and mobile devices (tablets) that have an Intel-compatible processor. Our coverage of the new "Windows 8–style" interface, Start screen, apps, and setup panels *should* apply to ARM-processor tablets that run a scaled-down operating system called Windows RT; however, much of this book won't apply to those devices, and if you have one, you may want to get a book that specifically addresses Windows RT.

We also don't have room to cover how to set up or manage the various Microsoft Server operating systems, called Windows Server 2012, Windows Server 2008, and so on, or how to deploy or manage Windows 8 using tools that are provided only with those operating systems. For these topics, you'll need to consult a Windows Server book.

Because of space limitations, only one chapter is devoted to coverage of Windows 8's numerous command-line utilities, its batch file language, Windows Script Host, and Windows PowerShell. For that (in spades!), you might want to check Brian's book *Windows 7 and Vista Guide to Scripting, Automation, and Command Line Tools*, which is equally applicable to Windows 8.

Even when you've become a Windows 8 pro, we think you'll find this book to be a valuable source of reference information in the future. Both the table of contents and the very complete index will provide easy means for locating information when you need it quickly.

How Our Book Is Organized

Although this book advances logically from beginning to end, it's written so that you can jump in at any location, quickly get the information you need, and get out. You don't have to read it from start to finish. (Remember, the index at the back of the book is your best friend.)

If you're new to Windows 8, however, we do recommend that you read Chapter 3, "Your First Hour with Windows 8," and Chapter 4, "Using the Windows 8 Interface," in their entirety. Windows 8 has new ways of doing things that aren't necessarily intuitive and obvious. Reading these two chapters may save you *hours* of frustration.

This book is broken down into six major parts. Here's the scoop on each one:

Part I, "Starting Out with Windows 8," introduces Windows 8's new user interface, shows you how to install Windows 8 on a new computer or upgrade an older version of Windows to Windows 8. In addition, we take you on a one-hour guided tour that shows you the best of Windows 8's new features, and we walk you through making essential settings and adjustments that will help you get the most out of your computer. Consider this the Windows 8 version of "freshman orientation."

In Part II, "Using Windows 8," we cover the new "Windows 8–style" user interface and apps, managing documents and files, starting and stopping applications, searching for files and media, printing, and using the included desktop accessories and accessibility tools. In other words, this section covers all of the routine, day-to-day stuff. However, it's very important material: Windows 8 does many things differently, and using it can be frustrating and confusing, especially if you don't know the basic tricks and techniques.

Part III, "Multimedia and Imaging," covers the Windows 8 bells and whistles, including the Media Player and Media Center programs, imaging devices, using a document scanner, faxing, and all the other media tools that ship with Windows 8.

In Part IV, "Windows 8 and the Internet," we help you set up an Internet connection, then move on to cover Windows 8's Internet tools. The final chapter shows you how to diagnose Internet connection problems.

Any home or office with two or more computers needs a local area network (LAN) to easily transfer and back up files, share printers, and use a shared, high-speed Internet connection. In Part V, "Networking," we walk you through setting up a network in your home or office, and show you how to take advantage of it in day-to-day use. We also show you how easy it is to share a DSL or cable Internet connection with all your computers at once, show you how to network with other operating systems, and, finally, help you fix it when it all stops working.

Part VI, "Maintaining Windows 8," covers system configuration, maintenance, and troubleshooting. We tell you how to work with the huge assortment of Windows 8 management tools, show you various useful tweaks and customizations, take you through some hard disk management techniques, give you advice on troubleshooting and repairing problems, show you how to manage software and hardware, and give you the details on editing the Windows Registry. And for real power users, we show how to use and tweak the command-line interface.

When Windows was introduced more than two decades ago, computer viruses, online fraud, and hacking were only starting to emerge as threats. Today (thanks in great part to *gaping* security holes in previous versions of Windows), computer threats are a worldwide problem, online and offline. In Part VII, "Security," we provide a 360-degree view of the ways in which Windows 8 protects you and your data. Here you'll find out both what Windows 8 will do to help you, and what you must do for yourself. We cover protection against viruses and spyware, data loss and theft, hackers and snoops, and fraud and spam—in that order.

Part VIII, "Windows on the Move," shows you how to get the most out of Windows 8 when either you or your computer, or both, are on the go. We show you how to use a touch or pen interface on a Windows 8 tablet or other mobile PC, how to use wireless networking safely, how to get the most out of your laptop or tablet PC when traveling, and how to connect to remote networks. We also show you how to use Remote Desktop to reach and use your own computer from anywhere in the world.

Appendix A, "Virtualization," explains how to use Microsoft's Hyper-V virtualization technology to run other operating systems side-by-side with Windows 8, or to run Windows 8 within some other operating system. This can be an excellent alternative to setting up a dual-boot system. And, finally, Appendix B, "Command-Line Utilities," takes you through a tour of various Windows 8 command-line utilities.

Conventions Used in This Book

Special conventions are used throughout this book to help you get the most from the book and from Windows 8.

Text Conventions

Various typefaces in this book identify terms and other special objects. These special typefaces include the following:

Type	Meaning
Italic	New terms or phrases when initially defined
`Monospace`	Information that appears in code or on screen in command-line tools

All Windows book publishers struggle with how to represent command sequences when menus and dialog boxes are involved. In this book, we separate commands using a comma. Yeah, we know it's confusing, but this is traditionally how Que's books do it, and traditions die hard. So, for example, the instruction "Choose Edit, Cut" means that you should open the Edit menu and choose Cut. Another, more complex example is "Select Control Panel, System and Security, Change Battery Settings."

Key combinations are represented with a plus sign. For example, if the text calls for you to press Ctrl+Alt+Delete, you would press the Ctrl, Alt, and Delete keys at the same time. The letterless

"Windows Logo" key is very useful in Windows 8. In a key combinations it will appear as, for example, "Windows Logo+X."

Special Elements

Throughout this book, you'll find Notes, Tips, Cautions, Sidebars, Cross-References, and Troubleshooting Notes. Hopefully, they'll give you just the tidbit you need to get through a tough problem, or the one trick that will make you the office hero. You'll also find little nuggets of wisdom, humor, and lingo that you can use to amaze your friends and family, or that may come in handy as cocktail-party conversation starters.

tip

We specially designed these tips to showcase the best of the best. Just because you get your work done doesn't mean you're doing it in the fastest, easiest way possible. We show you how to maximize your Windows experience. Don't miss these tips!

note

Notes point out items that you should be aware of, but you can skip them if you're in a hurry. Generally, we've added notes as a way to give you some extra information on a topic without weighing you down.

caution

Pay attention to cautions! They could save you precious hours in lost work.

Something Isn't Working

Throughout the book we describe some common trouble symptoms and tell you how to diagnose and fix problems with Windows, hardware, and software.

We Had More to Say

We use sidebars to dig a little deeper into the more esoteric features, settings, or peculiarities of Windows. Some sidebars are used to explain something in more detail when doing so in the main body text would've been intrusive or distracting. Sometimes, we just needed to get something off our chests and rant a bit. Don't skip the sidebars, because you'll find nuggets of pure gold in them (if we do say so ourselves).

We designed these elements to call attention to common pitfalls that you're likely to encounter.

Finally, cross-references are designed to point you to other locations in this book (or other books in the Que family) that provide supplemental or supporting information. Cross-references appear as follows:

➡ *For information on using the charms,* **see** *"Navigating the Start Screen with a Touch Interface,"* *p. 98*.

Let's get started!

1

MEET WINDOWS 8

An Overview of Windows 8

In the first paragraph of a book about Windows, it's traditional to describe how this newest version is a straightforward evolutionary advance over the previous version, with some nifty new features that we can't wait to tell you about; but otherwise, Windows N is basically Windows $(N\text{-}1)\text{+}1$.

Well, that's not going to happen here.

With Windows 8, we have a decidedly more complex picture to paint. There are new ways of doing things. There is a surprising learning curve. Many things that you thought you knew how to do easily have become difficult or impossible—or so it seems at first. There are actually easy ways to do almost everything, but you might never discover them unless you have someone show you the ropes. In other words, we have a brand-new, untamed beast here.

The underpinnings of Windows 8 do represent that expected evolutionary step forward from Windows 7. All the stability and performance of Windows 7 is there, and then some: startup and shutdown times have been significantly improved yet again, device drivers are ever more reliable thanks to the automatic crash report data that Microsoft has been collecting for years now, tools such as Windows Explorer (now called File Explorer) have been revamped and extended, there's built-in support for Internet connections through cellular data providers, and so on.

But on the surface, it's a different story. What you see in Windows 8 is more than just a layer of rectangular and square icons pasted over the screen, as seen in Figure 1.1. Windows 8 is Microsoft's attempt to change the entire set of expectations you bring to a computer. In a way, Windows 8 says to you, "This is the way the world is going, and you're starting down that road right now, whether you want to or not." This is sort of obnoxious, but it's also sort of realistic and helpful. If your experience of Windows 8 is like ours, you'll constantly waver back and forth between these two interpretations.

Figure 1.1
The new Start screen features "tiles" that represent either Windows 8–style apps or traditional Windows desktop applications.

Here's one way Windows 8 will change your expectations: Windows 8 is the first version that has a deep relationship with the Internet and online "cloud" services. Now that most computers have an Internet connection virtually all the time, from almost anywhere, it was finally time to implement features that have only been talked about before:

- One logon name and password identifies you to multiple computers and a host of online services.

- Your preferences—screen backgrounds, application settings, bookmarked websites, memorized passwords for other systems, and so on—can follow you to any computer you use.

- You can have access to your documents, photographs, and other media on any computer you use.

- Applications, music, movies, and other items you've purchased online can be available on any computer you use.

- "Any computer you use" can really be *any* computer: laptops, desktops and tablets, at your home, your office, or in other people's homes and offices.

On the Cloud

The term *cloud* comes from early engineering drawings of computer networks, where straight lines and boxes represented one's own network cables and server computers, and a cloud, drawn as a child might draw one, represented a network that was owned and managed by someone else, whose details were unknown and unimportant. Data went into the cloud, and data came out of the cloud somewhere else, and how that was accomplished wasn't a big concern. A cloud thus represented something opaque but useful.

Now, "the cloud" refers to disk storage services and data-processing services reachable over the Internet. They exist physically somewhere, but international security concerns aside, we don't really care where they are. We just want to be able to see our Instagram pictures wherever we are. And that's the fundamental shift: we no longer think about where our data is; we just expect it to be where *we* are.

If this is real, can you see how it might change your expectations? In the Windows XP days, it was an accomplishment to copy a file from one computer to another over a network. It won't be long before you start thinking, "Copy? You have to *do* something? It doesn't just go there by itself?"

Another way that Windows 8 will change your expectations is through its touch interface. If you're using a tablet or if your computer has a touch-screen monitor, you'll be able to interact with Windows using your fingertip (or a pen-like stylus, but a finger is what most people will be using). The keyword to look out for is *multitouch*, which means that the screen can distinguish the location of several fingertips at once—up to ten, on some models.

Finger-pointing is more than just a major preoccupation of politicians; it turns out to make a very intuitive and natural way of communicating your intentions to a computer. Anyone who's used an Apple iPhone or iPad can attest to this. We all can point and click and drag with a mouse now, but few of us remember how odd it felt at first. Pointing and poking and dragging with a fingertip comes naturally, and once you experience it, it's very hard to go back. (If you don't believe me, go look at a standard computer monitor owned by anyone with an iPhone, and notice all the greasy fingerprints on it. They can't help themselves.)

The third major change in Windows 8 is found in the new Start screen and the "Windows 8" interface, and this is where people's feelings about Windows 8 start to diverge. Microsoft's stated goal was simple: to bring the full-screen, minimalistic user interfaces seen on smartphones and popular tablets (that is, specifically, on Apple's iOS and Google's Android) to the desktop. Microsoft's new mantra is "content over chrome," meaning that you want to be looking *through* the computer screen at pictures and text and movies, and not so much *at* the screen with its buttons and sliders and text entry fields and dialog boxes and window title bars and so on. And indeed, for graphic and web interface designers, simple is the new black. The trend toward simpler interfaces and away from skeuomorphism (for example, trying to make items such as dialog box buttons really look like real-world physical buttons) is widespread.

> ### 🔍 note
>
> The new interface design scheme was universally called Metro while Windows 8 was under development. You'll see that term used still, as in "Metro app," although in August 2012 Microsoft frantically backtracked on that name and came up with the names "Windows 8 interface" and "Windows 8 apps" to avoid touchy trademark issues with Metro AG, a large German firm. The name Metro was catchy, but more importantly it gave a name to a style that first *appeared* in Windows 8, but isn't *tied* to Windows 8. What is Microsoft going to call these apps when Windows 9 comes out? Will they still be called Windows 8 apps? How ridiculous would that be? But if the design scheme doesn't change, it would be just as ridiculous to change the name to "Windows 9 app" just because... well, never mind that now.
>
> Although we can't imagine why Microsoft let itself get into this mess, we have to go along with it. We'll refer to the new design as "Windows 8 style" when that wording seems appropriate. We might say "Windows 8 interface" and "Windows 8 app" here and there. What we mean by these is the new interface design and the new style of application program. We'll use the term *desktop* to refer to the older Windows interface and its applications.

This sounds great, but things are more complex than that. We've spent 25 years working with overlapping windows on our computers. Now we're supposed to be better off viewing one window at a time? Not so quick. The simple full-screen interface that makes a smartphone or a tablet so easy to use can seem clumsy and oddly claustrophobic on a desktop computer with a 21" screen.

So why is Microsoft pushing this so hard? There are other motivations:

- Consumers have been gradually moving away from bulky desktop computers toward portables (laptops) for some time. And, people have literally stampeded Apple stores to buy iPads, sometimes ditching even their laptops in the process. It's not certain yet whether tablets will be an adjunct to or a replacement for laptops and desktop computers, but they're selling like hotcakes. Consumers want smaller, lighter devices. Those devices need simpler interfaces on their smaller screens, and less graphical gimmickry, to extend the usable time of a battery charge.

- People are buying small software applications called "apps" by the gazillion (that's the technical term). It's hard to get consumers to spring for a $200 word processing package, but they'll buy $2 apps like candy.

- It's easier to develop and maintain one operating system for all of these devices, as Microsoft is doing with Windows 8, than Apple is doing with its OS X and iOS.

- If you have one OS for all these devices, people can use those apps on any computer they use (they *expect* to now). What's more, you'll be able to sell apps to that chunk of the population that doesn't have a tablet yet (cha-ching!) and after they've used them for a while, they'll want to go buy a tablet (cha-CHING!).

So, as they say, "There's money in them thar hills," and this may be the real reason for Microsoft's not-so-gentle insistence that you, the Windows 8 user, deal with the Start screen every time you turn around.

Now, regardless of whether the full-screen simple app eventually takes over the entire computer world, at present, most computer software still uses the old overlapping window, keyboard and mouse, "cluttered desktop" paradigm that's been around since the 1980s. Microsoft understands that, and Windows 8 is fully capable of running traditional Windows applications on the traditional desktop screen.

What's problematic is that Microsoft has decided that the two models be kept separate from each other, so you can either view a single Windows 8–style app or view your cluttered desktop with multiple windows, but you can't interact with both at the same time. (The lone exception being a two-monitor setup where you have the Start screen on one monitor and the desktop on the other; see Chapter 28.) There's more: Microsoft also decided that the full-screen world is where things are going, and *you* need to get with the program, so they removed the venerable Start button. You have to use the tiled Start screen virtually every time you want to start a program or change tasks.

➡ *To learn more about using Windows 8 with two or more monitors,* **see** *"Running Windows 8 with Multiple Monitors," **p. 673**.*

If you work primarily with desktop applications such as Microsoft Word, Outlook, and Open Office, this has the consequence of throwing you back and forth between these two "world views" pretty frequently, and the effect is not entirely pleasant. The back and forth flipping of the screen is accompanied by back and forth feelings about Windows 8 itself. Until you've learned and integrated a few new touch gestures, and keyboard and mouse tricks, it can be intensely frustrating. In one minute it will seem joyously intuitive and a real pleasure to use, and in the next you may find yourself wondering, "Do they hate me? Is that why they made it work this way?" Or, saying "Hey Microsoft, what do you think of *this* gesture?"

This is where Windows 8 falls short. These feelings arise because in some areas, Windows 8 is at cross-purposes with itself. It has to be a straightforward successor to a long line of Windows versions, because there are about a billion people who use it daily and depend on it to get their jobs done and their lives organized, and yet it also wants to be a radical departure from the past. It's half touch, immersive experience, and "content over chrome," and half mouse, menu, and keyboard. Windows 8 has one figurative foot firmly in the past and one in the world of *Star Trek*. It's up to you to bridge the gap, and it has a disconcerting way of constantly reminding you about the gap. Whereas Windows 7 was reliable, efficient, and, crucially, stayed out of your way, Windows 8 manages to be reliable, efficient, and yet somehow is in your face all the time, which is precisely what the new interface model is trying to eliminate.

So, are we saying we hate it? No, not at all. We just have some criticisms. Is it any good? Yes, it is, it just takes some getting used to. And we show you ways to get around the limitations so that you'll see more of its good side than its bad.

Microsoft is right, we do have to get used to doing things in new ways. But it does feel forced at times. Let's just say that we can see where Microsoft is going with this, and it's going to be an interesting ride getting there.

Should I Get Windows 8?

In our last book, when we posed the same question about Windows 7, the answer was absolutely clear, for virtually everyone: "Yes! Run, don't walk."

The answer isn't absolute in this case. It depends on what you have now and what you want to do:

■ If you're getting a tablet computer such as the Microsoft Surface, you're going to be getting Windows 8 (or Windows RT, as we'll discuss shortly) no matter what, but even if you had an option, Windows 8 would be the right choice. This is where it shines.

■ If you're buying a new laptop, Windows 8's faster startup, reduced power consumption, online services, and slicker ways of working with wireless and cellular Internet make pretty compelling arguments for going with Windows 8, even if the device doesn't have a touchscreen.

■ If you're going to buy a new computer and it has a multitouch monitor, or you can get one for it, you should probably opt for Windows 8. With a keyboard, mouse, *and* a touchscreen, you'll be able to interact with the computer in whatever way feels best to you.

■ If you are willing to buy a multitouch monitor for an existing computer that runs Windows 7 (at a cost of $200 or more), we suggest that you go to a computer store and play with Windows 8 a bit, before you consider upgrading to Windows 8. If the Windows 8–style apps appeal to you, and if you spend most of your time at the computer doing just one thing at a time, you'll probably like Windows 8 enough to make upgrading worthwhile. The price of the Windows 8 Upgrade is pretty low. Check online for special deals from Microsoft.

■ If you don't have a multitouch monitor, and you don't want to buy one, again, go to a computer store and play with Windows 8. Do use a touchscreen so that you don't get distracted by how frustrating and hard it is to *guess* how to work Windows 8 without touch. (We'll teach you how.) Focus on the new look. If you like it a lot, and if the Windows Store and its plethora of free and cheap apps and games appeals to you, then an upgrade from Windows 7 to Windows 8 may make sense for you. And if you're not willing to spend the big bucks on a multitouch monitor, consider investing in a multitouch mouse (such as the Microsoft Touch Mouse), which will give you many of the same advantages at a fraction of the price.

■ If you've read this far without getting an answer, the news isn't good. If you use your computer primarily to run complex applications such as Word, Excel, AutoCAD, and the like, and you tend to have lots of windows open at once, you probably won't find that Windows 8 is a big enough improvement to make it worth putting up with its insistence that you're going to do things the "new way" or else. We show you tricks and tweaks that let you reproduce a pretty close approximation to the Windows 7 desktop, but that just lets you break even. You need some positives: Windows 8's online account services (syncing your stuff between multiple computers and the cloud), super fast startup and shutdown, and perhaps the thought of playing *Angry Birds* when the boss isn't looking. These may well be enough to tip the balance for you.

■ If you are running Windows XP on a computer that's more than 5 years old, don't upgrade it. It's not going to live that much longer anyway. If your XP computer is relatively new, see Chapter 2, "Installing or Upgrading Windows 8," for Windows 8's requirements to see if you might be able to upgrade. However, you'll be doing an essentially clean install and will have to reinstall all applications from scratch. It's probably not worth it.

No matter which of these scenarios describes you, if you do move to Windows 8 you can have a very positive experience *if* you know its essential techniques and tricks. What's surprising and frustrating about Windows 8 is that so many of its touch, mouse, and keyboard interactions are difficult or impossible to guess, and these are *precisely* the things you need to know so that you don't end up tearing your hair out. Luckily for you, you bought this book. The first few chapters of *Windows 8 In Depth* will get you past the hurdle of learning these things.

Windows 8 Versions

For a long time, we got one new version of Windows every 3 years or so. It was called Windows Some Number: Windows 1, Windows 2, Windows 3, Windows 3.1, Windows 95, Windows 98, and Windows 666 (well, technically it was called Windows Me). There was just one one-size-fits-all version: Windows.

In parallel, the New Technology product line, written from scratch, without MS-DOS underneath it, spawned Windows NT Workstation and Windows 2000 Professional. NT was stable and much more secure than Windows 3 and 9x, although its user interface always lagged by about 3 years. That was due mostly to the difficulty and expense of developing and maintaining two completely separate Windows. Still, it was revered in the business world where reliability matters more than appearance.

Microsoft finally, thankfully, closed the book on the original Windows code when they released Windows XP, so now it's NT for everybody. However, they kept the home/business split. We got Windows XP Home Edition and Windows XP Professional. They were really the same product, but Home Edition lacked a few features found in Professional. Home Edition was sold to the more price-sensitive home computer market. Professional was used by enthusiasts who wanted more to play with, and in the business world where XP was managed through corporate networks by Windows Server. There was also Windows XP Media Center Edition, which was XP Professional sold to home users, with an additional application that let Windows record TV shows and drive a TV as its monitor.

When Vista came out, Microsoft decided to split things up even further, fractionating Windows into six distinct editions. Windows 7 was also sold in six editions. Microsoft has retreated somewhat with Windows 8. The Windows 8 family has just four siblings and two cousins. Figure 1.2 shows the Windows lineage from XP through 8.

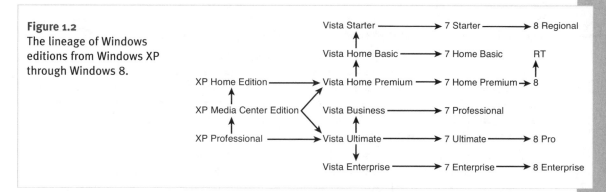

Figure 1.2
The lineage of Windows editions from Windows XP through Windows 8.

The editions are as follows:

- **Windows 8**—All of the features a consumer would be interested in, but lacking enough that motivated users might pay to upgrade to the Pro edition.

- **Windows 8 Pro**—Adds disk encryption, the ability to connect to enterprise servers, and additional features, as listed in Table 1.1.

- **Windows 8 Enterprise**—This is Windows 8 Ultimate sold through Microsoft's Volume Licensing channels to large business customers. The primary difference between Pro and Enterprise is how it's licensed for use on desktops, in virtual machines, and on Terminal Services (remote desktop) servers. In addition, there are a few networking and management tools that can be applied to a Windows 8 Enterprise computer by the organization's IT department, as listed in Table 1.1.

- **Windows 8 For China and other regional editions sold in a few other developing markets**— The only reduced functionality is that the regional language is fixed and add-on language packs can't be installed.

- **Windows RT**—Strictly speaking, Windows RT is not Windows 8, but a version for tablets that use the ARM low-power microprocessor rather than the Intel and AMD chips that drive desktop PCs. It has all of the new Windows 8 interface components, and it runs desktop versions of Microsoft Office applications that are preinstalled by Microsoft. However, you can't install or run any other traditional Windows applications on it.

- **Windows 8 Embedded**—You may not have heard of this one, but like its predecessors, Windows 8 is licensed to hardware manufacturers to embed in devices such as vending machines, digital music players, ATMs, anesthesia respirators, and so on. You may have interacted with Windows Embedded and never known it, unless the device was crashed with a Blue Screen of Death. (Which I've actually seen on those huge electronic billboards a couple of times. And that's not the most embarrassing thing that can happen. I was driving through Palo Alto, California a few years ago, in the heart of Silicon Valley, and saw an electronic billboard whose message was obscured by a 10-foot tall dialog box saying, "Your subscription to Norton Antivirus has expired.")

Besides these various editions, N-, E-, K-, and KN-suffixed editions are sold in specific markets. These are missing a few of the usual preinstalled applications, as a way of resolving antitrust troubles. (For example, Microsoft had to remove Windows Media Player and fork over 784 million dollars to buy the letter *N* from the European Commission.) If you have one of these flavors, you need only download the missing application(s) from Microsoft.com to get rid of the distinction.

Just to be clear, this book covers Windows 8, Windows 8 Pro, and Windows 8 Enterprise. If you have Windows RT, or Windows 8 Embedded, our coverage of the new Windows 8 interface may be applicable to you, but we also talk about many features that your edition of Windows won't have. And in our coverage of Windows 8 Enterprise, we focus on the features that you can use and manage yourself as an end user. We don't cover features that are controlled entirely by network managers from the Windows Server operating system.

There appear to be a lot of versions to choose from, but thankfully you can usually narrow it down to one or two. In a corporate setting, your IT department will select the Pro or Enterprise edition for you. In Europe or Korea, the N and KN flavors will be the only ones available. If you do have a choice to make, it will be between Windows 8 and Windows 8 Pro. Now, if you're interested enough in Windows versions to be reading this section, you've probably already done plenty of research online already, so we'll keep this brief. Table1.1 lists the *primary* feature differences between the editions.

Table 1.1 Primary Differences in the Feature Sets of Windows 8, Windows 8 Pro, and Windows 8 Enterprise

Feature	Windows 8	Windows 8 Pro	Windows 8 Enterprise
Windows Media Center	$	$	
Presentation Settings		✓	✓
Remote Desktop host		✓	✓
Boot from VHD file		✓	✓
Hyper-V Virtual Machine Manager		✓	✓
BitLocker and BitLocker To Go (whole-drive encryption of storage)		✓	✓
Encrypted File System (file-level encryption)		✓	✓
Domain network member		✓	✓
Manageable by Group Policy		*	*
AppLocker (restriction of runnable apps by IT managers)		*	*
Boot from USB drive (Windows To Go)			✓
DirectAccess (automatic VPN to the office)			*
Installation of Windows 8–style apps outside the Windows Store			*

$ Feature available for download at an additional cost.

* Only when joined to a Windows Domain network. Feature is not user configurable, but is controlled entirely by network managers.

Windows 8 comes in both 32-bit and 64-bit versions. This is a significant decision to make, because you can't change back and forth between 32-bit and 64-bit versions; you'll be stuck with the choice and will have to do a complete, clean install to change. If you're not sure which to choose, here are some pointers:

- The 32-bit versions can use only up to 3GB of RAM (program memory) in your computer, even if you have more installed. This can seriously slow you down if you edit video or use huge image-editing programs such as Adobe Photoshop. The 64-bit versions can take advantage of, well, as much RAM as you can stuff in.

- The 32-bit versions can run antique MS-DOS and 16-bit Windows 3.1 applications directly. The 64-bit versions can't. If you need to use applications that are that old on a computer that runs 64-bit Windows, you'll have to run them in a virtual machine that runs a 16- or 32-bit version of Windows or MS-DOS. We discuss this in Appendix A, "Virtualization."

- The 64-bit versions of Windows 8 Pro and Enterprise include Microsoft's Hyper-V virtual machine manager (VMM). If you want to run virtual machines on 32-bit Windows 8 Pro or Enterprise (or any variety of plain Windows 8), you'll have to install VMware, VirtualBox, or another VMM.

- If you have devices in or connected to your computer that were manufactured before 2008, you might not be able to find 64-bit device drivers for them. Most equipment made since then has 32- and 64-bit support.

At the time that Windows Vista was released in January 2007, 64-bit versions of Windows were still considered exotic, and device driver support lagged. Now, virtually all new computers ship with 64-bit Windows preinstalled.

Upgrading Windows

You can upgrade an existing installation of Windows Vista and Windows 7 to Windows 8, with applications, settings, and personal data (user accounts and files), subject to the restrictions listed in Table 1.2. If you're moving up from Windows XP (and if your old Windows XP computer is capable of running Windows 7), you can get an upgrade (read: cheaper) Windows 8 license, but you'll have to do a clean install. This means your files and documents will be available, but your settings will be lost and you'll have to reinstall your application programs if you want to use them in Windows 8. It's probably not worth doing; it's better to get a new computer.

Table 1.2 lists the upgrade paths that Microsoft supports.

Table 1.2   Windows Upgrade Paths

From...	To... 8	8 Pro	Users/Files	Keeping... Settings	Applications
XP Home	✓	✓	+		
XP Professional		✓	+		
Vista Home Basic	✓	✓	✓	*	
Vista Home Premium	✓	✓			
Vista Business		✓	✓	*	
Vista Ultimate		✓	✓	*	
7 Home Basic	✓	✓	✓	✓	✓
7 Home Premium	✓	✓	✓	✓	✓
7 Professional		✓	✓	✓	✓
7 Ultimate		✓	✓	✓	✓
8		✓	✓	✓	✓

+ Upgrade allowed only if XP SP3 is installed.

* Settings copied only if Vista SP1 or SP2 is installed.

When you're upgrading, although you can choose what edition of Windows you want to install, you can't change between 32-bit and 64-bit versions. Doing so requires a clean install.

➡ *To learn more about upgrading,* **see** *"Upgrading to Windows 8," **p. 37.***

What's New in Windows 8?

In the previous sections we mentioned that Windows 8 is unlike any previous version of Windows. The departure is in some ways more radical than the one from Windows 3.1 to Windows 95, when the Start button and taskbar first appeared. In the following sections we'll review the ways that Windows 8 differs from its predecessors both on the screen and under the covers.

A Tale of Two Windows: The Start Screen Versus the Desktop

The most obvious difference between Windows 8 and its predecessors is that once you've logged on, you're shown the new Start screen (refer to Figure 1.1), which represents applications (apps) with various sized *tiles* rather than icons. Touching or clicking on a tile opens the app. Tiles don't necessarily display just static images and text: *live tiles* can display dynamic information such as the date, time, weather forecast, and the arrival of new email messages.

Apps are divided into two completely separate categories: first, there are Windows 8–style apps, which are full screen in nature, and can only be obtained by visiting the Windows Store (which is itself an app).* Second, there are traditional Windows "desktop-type" applications, such as Windows Notepad, Microsoft Word, and the Control Panel. You can install your favorite traditional Windows applications just as you did in the past.

> **🔍 note**
>
> * This is true for home users anyway. In a corporate environment, system managers can preinstall locally developed Windows 8–style apps—so-called Line of Business apps—when they install Windows on a managed computer.

If you open the tile for a Windows 8–style app, it expands to fill the screen. You can have at most two of these apps displayed per attached monitor. If you open a desktop app, the Windows 8 interface draws away and reveals the familiar Windows desktop behind it, the taskbar, the recycle bin, and so on (see Figure 1.3). All that's missing is the Start button. To start a new application, it appears that you have to go back to the Start screen. I say *appears* because there are actually several ways to start Windows applications from the desktop, which we'll cover in Chapter 3, "Your First Hour with Windows 8," and Chapter 4, "Using the Windows 8 Interface."

> ➡ *To learn more about the Windows 8–style interface,* **see** *"Taking a Tour of the Windows 8 Interface," p. 93.*

Touch-a Touch-a Touch-a Touch Me!

Our apologies to *The Rocky Horror Picture Show*, but Windows 8 just begs to be touched, prodded, and poked. The Start screen and the Windows 8–style interface only truly make sense the first time you interact with Windows 8 as it was meant to be used: on a tablet or on a desktop computer with a multitouch monitor. Scrolling, selecting, and manipulating objects on the screen feels completely natural and intuitive, even pleasurable.

Figure 1.3
The Windows 8 desktop is mostly familiar territory, but the missing Start button is maddening for desktop fans.

This isn't to say that Windows 8 is useless without a touch screen. You can definitely use Windows 8 with just a keyboard and mouse. In fact, if you're a good typist, you may actually prefer to keep your fingers on the keyboard most of the time. The trick here is that it's not immediately apparent just what you should *do* with the mouse and keyboard to get Windows 8 to do what you want. The familiar buttons and icons are gone, replaced with "secret" mouse hotspots and Windows Logo key shortcuts. Lucky for you, we show you these secrets in Chapters 3 and 4, and you'll have them committed to memory in no time.

 To learn more about using Windows 8 with a keyboard and mouse, **see** *"Navigating the Start Screen,"* **p. 98**.

Windows 8 Apps

Windows 8–style apps use a very simplified user interface. As we discussed earlier in the chapter, the mantra is "content over chrome," meaning, show the user what he or she wants to see, not a bunch of graphical gimmickry. The new "Don't-Call-It-Metro" look is simple and clean, with large type, not so many words, and plain interface objects that don't try to look like something they aren't. Figure 1.4 shows an example. The days of the etched, 3-D dialog box pushbutton that looks like brushed stainless steel are numbered.

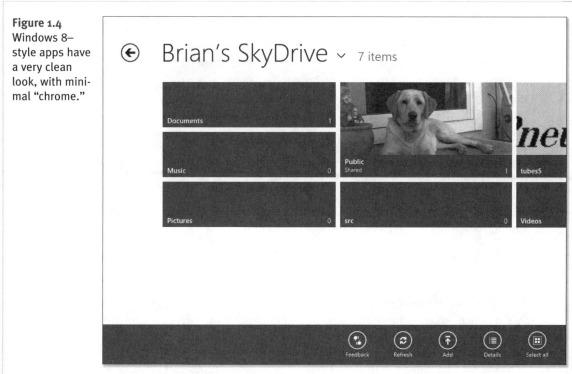

Figure 1.4
Windows 8–style apps have a very clean look, with minimal "chrome."

➡️ *To learn more about using Windows 8 apps, **see** "Working with Running Apps," **p. 104**.*

Charmed, I'm Sure

At any time you can pull in from the right side of the screen a panel that has five icons: Search, Share, Start, Devices, and Settings. These are called the *charms*. The charms offer services related to whatever app is displayed on the screen at the time. Share lets you send photos, links, or other data via email or to your Twitter followers or Facebook friends. Search lets you search an app's data, or your computer's hard disk, or the programs and settings on the Start screen. Settings lets you adjust the app, or your computer itself. Start takes you to the Start screen. Devices lets you print and otherwise send information through hardware.

The charms are readily available. With touch, you pull in the charms by swiping your finger in from the right edge of the screen toward the middle. With a keyboard, you simply press Windows Logo+C. With the mouse, you point the mouse cursor to the very bottom-right corner of the screen and wait a moment. (See what we meant about things being simple but not at all obvious? Each of these techniques takes but a moment; however, you'd never guess what to do just from looking at the screen.)

Online User Accounts

One new and very useful feature in Windows 8 is the ability to use your online Microsoft account name as your Windows logon name. This could be something like yourname@live.com or whatever email address you use to create the Microsoft account.

If you elect to use your Microsoft account on Windows 8, Windows will automatically sync your Windows preferences over the Internet: your chosen background screens, colors and pictures, your account password and passwords you use to connect to shared network and Internet resources, Ease of Access and language settings, apps and app settings, preferences you set in File Explorer (discussed in the next section) and some other tools, and so on will all be stored on Microsoft's servers and will follow you to any Windows 8 computer you sign on to, provided it has an Internet connection.

 note

You can't just walk up to any Windows 8 computer and sign in using your Microsoft account logon name; the computer's owner has to set up an account for you by entering your Windows account name. This person doesn't, however, need to know your password.

 To learn more about creating a Microsoft account, **see** *"Setting Up User Accounts,"* **p. 68.**

File Explorer Ribbon

The venerable, aged Windows Explorer has a new name, File Explorer (a sensible change, if you ask us), and a whole new look, including a ribbon interface to replace the traditional File/Edit/View drop-down menu system that was originally designed by IBM and cultivated in every version of Windows from 1.0 through 7. (Back in the late 1980s, in fact, IBM's user interface design manual was required reading for all Windows developers. This is why menu organization was so consistent from one Windows application to another, at least early on.)

In place of a menu there is now a graphical toolbar whose contents change depending on what you've selected below it. It works well, but it takes some getting used to. Gone are the days that you could just look through all of a program's menus to see what's possible. Microsoft says their research shows that people actually do "discover" more functions and features with a ribbon interface than with a traditional menu system. I'm not so sure. There are probably things in there now that nobody will ever discover, because they appear only if you select three different files in three different folders, on a Saturday afternoon, around teatime.

 To learn more about the new File Explorer, **see** *"Navigating the Windows 8 Folder Windows,"* **p. 152.**

The Windows Store

Windows 8–style apps can only be purchased from the Windows Store, Microsoft's online marketplace for free and paid apps from both Microsoft and a myriad other vendors. There, presumably, apps are vetted for viruses and malicious intent before they're released upon the public. This marketplace is relatively new, but the number of available apps is growing rapidly. *Angry Birds* was an early arrival, and although Games is clearly going to be one of the biggest sections of the Store, we expect that the range and quantity of apps will eventually match that of the iPhone/iPad world.

These apps can be used on the purchaser's desktop computers as well as on tablets, thus adding to their appeal (and market base).

At least, Microsoft is making a huge bet that this is the case. After watching the success of Apple's "Buy it from us or, well... there is no *or*—you have to buy it from us" software marketing model for the iPhone and iPad, Microsoft has decided that this is the way of the future, starting with Windows 8. Having one OS for the desktop and mobile worlds, a touch interface, and integrated cloud connectivity makes sense from the technical and usability perspectives—and makes us geeks happy—but a healthy slice of an ever-growing stream of revenue from software that *other* people are climbing over each other to build? This makes the suits in Redmond weak in the knees. Here, at last, we find the reason for Windows 8.

➡ *To learn more about the Windows Store,* **see** *"Store,"* **p. 142**.

🔍 **note**

During Windows 8's development period there was a persistent rumor that on Windows 8, you would not be able to install older software that you already owned, that you would have to buy everything from the Store. This is false: you call still install any *desktop* software you want, from any source, past, present or future. Only Windows 8–style apps *have* to be acquired through Microsoft.

And, even this restriction has some loopholes: Software developers can build, test, and use Windows 8 apps of their own devising, to their heart's content, although only on their own computers. And enterprise IT departments can pre-install locally developed Windows 8 apps on Windows 8 computers that they deploy in their organizations. The ability to create these so-called "line-of-business" apps that will run on both desktops and mobile devices should add to Windows 8's appeal in the business world.

Management Tools

Managing Windows has always been somewhat of a challenge because it's complex, and it's not something most of us do every day. When the management tools are switched around, then, it can be pretty taxing. Have no fear: there is not a whole lot that is new in the way that you manage Windows 8. New, straightforward Windows 8–style panels let you mange new Windows 8–style features, but they've usurped little that was familiar from previous versions of Windows. (The significant exception is a new way to set up user accounts.)

The top of the Windows 8 Settings charm (the People app version is shown in Figure 1.5) lists items that you can change in the current active app, while the lower part has icons for basic PC functions such as Power, Volume, and network connections. The Change PC Settings item displays a detailed, but very straightforward list of management items.

Chapter 3 takes you on a quick tour of the new Windows 8 management tools. We cover the new and old-style management tools in detail throughout the book. If there's a particular topic that interests you, the index should lead you straight to it.

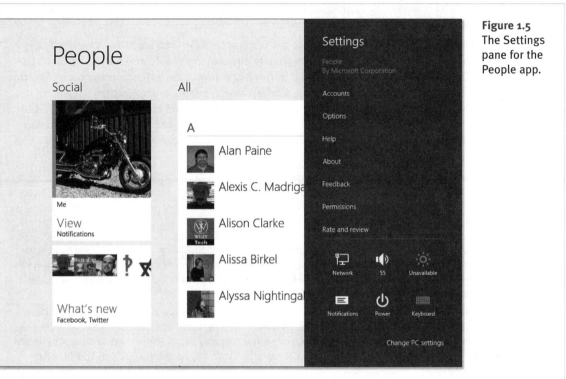

Figure 1.5
The Settings
pane for the
People app.

Installation and Setup

Windows 8's installation and setup process is much like that in Windows 7. The install process is smooth and fast due to a deployment technology that copies an "image" of a fully installed Windows system onto your hard disk rather than copying and configuring files piecemeal. (One downside for hardcore operating system geeks, though, is that you can't select the drive letter that will be assigned to the new copy of Windows. It's going to be drive C: no matter what. If you have other hard disks in your system, they will be assigned letters other than C: when Windows 8 boots.)

One notable change is that when Windows 8 has been installed, you're taken on a quick tour of the new Windows 8 user interface, including touch gestures if your computer has a touchscreen. (You also see this tour when you log on to a new account for the first time.) This is to make your initial exposure to Windows 8 a little less confusing and frustrating. (We think it takes more than just a few minutes to get your bearings, which is why we wrote Chapter 3.)

➡ *To learn more about installing Windows 8, **see p. 27**.*

Storage Spaces

Storage Spaces offers a completely new, sensible approach to adding disk space to a personal computer. Instead of having to deal with separate disk drives, you can choose to simply "pool" them.

If your first disk fills up, you add another and Windows combines the added free space with your existing disk volume. You don't have to keep track of what data is stored on which drive, Windows does that. You just see one big drive. Makes sense, yes?

You can have Storage Spaces present the entire combined storage space of your disks, or you can dedicate some space to storing redundant information to help recover from a physical disk failure. If you wish, you can choose to use added disks the old way, separately.

 *To learn more about growing your hard disk storage, **see** "Working with Storage Spaces," p. 601.*

Improved Web Browsing with Internet Explorer 10

Windows 8 ships with Internet Explorer 10, which offers much better HTML5 support, a much faster JavaScript engine to make interactive websites snappier, and it takes advantage of your computer's graphics processor to significantly speed up the rendering (drawing) of complex web pages. It's more secure as well, due to features such as Windows 8's High Entropy Address Space Layout Randomization, which randomizes the location of sensitive system code modules. This makes them moving targets for malicious code that tries to exploit bugs in known program locations.

There are actually two faces to Internet Explorer 10 in Windows 8: the desktop version sports the now-familiar multitabbed interface and menu bar. There is also a Windows 8–style version that uses the new simplified user interface. You can try them both and choose which one suits you best.

 *To learn more about IE 10, **see** "Using Internet Explorer 10," p. 17.*

Faster Startup

One thing you're sure to notice about Windows 8 is that it starts up and shuts down faster than previous versions of Windows. If you have it installed on a solid state disk (SSD), bootup is *amazingly* fast.

Microsoft has tuned up the techniques it used to speed up Windows 7's boot time. It keeps a list of which operating files get read in during startup, in which order, and uses at least one core of a multicore CPU to read those files into memory as quickly as possible, so they're loaded even before they're needed. And, it defers the loading of nonessential services and subsystems until after the logon screen is up, so that you can start logging on while Windows is still putting itself together.

This was done in Windows 7, too, but Windows 8 has another trick up its sleeve: kernel hibernation. As you may know, hibernation is a way of putting the computer to sleep by writing the contents of memory to disk before shutting off the power entirely. When you power it back up, the computer reads the stored data back into memory and takes up where it left off. To speed startup in Windows 8, when you do a normal, power-off shutdown, Windows ignores all of the memory used by applications, but hibernates the Windows kernel—just a few hundred MB, so this takes almost no time at all. When you power on the next time, the kernel is restored intact, saving the time it would take to load and configure it from scratch. The logon screen follows in short order, then the rest of Windows loads in the normal manner. This shaves several seconds off the startup time.

One consequence of this is that the loaded copy of the Windows kernel can stick around for a long time—months perhaps. It's stable enough to do that, but, if you use the Power icon's Restart option, Windows does a true restart, discarding everything in memory and reloading everything from scratch.

Secure Boot

Secure Boot is a new feature that protects your computer from malware that takes control of your computer at the moment it boots up, before Windows' security system kicks in. This kind of malware can sneak in on a USB thumb drive, or appear in a virus that infects the disk's Master Boot Record, the first code that's executed after the BIOS self-test has finished.

When Windows 8 is installed on a computer that has a Unified Extensible Firmware Interface (UEFI) BIOS on its motherboard, you (or your organization's IT department, or your computer's manufacturer) can lock down the system so that only an authorized, unmodified, digitally signed operating system can boot.

In fact, to earn a Windows 8 logo sticker, computer vendors are required to ship computers with Secure Boot enabled. To install an alternative operating system such as a version of Linux, you may need to disable Secure Boot in the computer's BIOS settings. Alternatively, your OS vendor may be able to supply a digitally signed copy that is recognized by the BIOS in your computer.

Integrated Cellular Data Connections

Windows 8 includes built-in support for Internet connectivity using 3G or 4G mobile broadband (cellular) networks. This is an obvious feature for tablets, letting Microsoft's Surface compete with the iPad, but it's also available for laptop computers that have a SIM card and 3G or 4G data modem either built in or added on. In past versions of Windows, mobile connectivity required third-party software, but this is now built into Windows 8. Windows can determine from the SIM card which mobile carrier you use, and can help you get additional broadband accessories from your carrier through the Windows Store.

In addition, Windows can help meter your Internet usage through a mobile broadband connection so that you don't exceed your data plan's cap.

Life Without the Start Menu

Working without the familiar Start menu takes some getting used to. As we mentioned earlier in this chapter, if someone doesn't show you the ropes, your first experience with Windows 8, especially if there is no touchscreen, is likely to be wildly frustrating. We've been there, and we will show you how to keep your sanity, and even learn to love Windows 8 in Chapters 3 and 4.

Here, we just want to give some basic reassurance.

One thing to remember is that Windows 8 is all about *searching* and *prioritizing*.

You might find that you miss the hierarchy of programs in the Start menu, which lets you dig down through sensible categories to find what you were looking for. (Well, they start out as sensible categories. After a few years when your Start menu has 50 or 100 items in it, they're not so sensible.)

In this new world, you *search* for what you want by typing the first few letters of its name while you're at the Start screen. This takes just a fraction of a second. It's much quicker than poking around with the mouse.

Then, you *prioritize* the Start screen by moving tiles for your most-used apps to the first page. Then, you can start up a favorite application with one poke of your finger, or one click.

The same holds for the desktop. *Pin* your favorite programs to the taskbar, so that you don't need to locate them more than once. Don't try to navigate the old Control Panel; instead, *search* it.

This is so easy, once you remember to do it.

The second thing to remember is that there are keyboard and mouse shortcuts for almost everything important. Searching, File Explorer, the charms, the Desktop, and almost all Windows management tools are always just *two keystrokes* or *one mouse click* away, *if* you know the right keys to press or the right place to click.

You'll learn them quickly.

And then, Windows 8 starts to be fun.

2

INSTALLING OR UPGRADING WINDOWS 8

Windows 8 System Requirements

Personal computing is governed by two inexorable, and not unrelated, "laws":

Moore's Law—Processing power doubles every 18 months (from Gordon Moore, cofounder of Intel).

Parkinson's Law of Data—Data expands to fill the space available for storage (from the original Parkinson's Law: Work expands to fill the time available).

These two observations help explain why, when the computers we use are becoming increasingly powerful, our day-to-day tasks never really seem all that much faster. The leaps in processing power and memory are being matched by the increasing complexity and resource requirements of the latest programs. Therefore, the computer you're using today might be twice as muscular as the one you were using a year and a half ago, but the applications you're using are twice the size and require twice as many resources.

Windows fits neatly into this scenario. With each new release of Microsoft's flagship operating system, the hardware requirements become more stringent, and our computers' processing power is taxed a little more. Windows 8 is no exception. Even though Microsoft spent an enormous amount of time and effort trying to shoehorn Windows 8 into a minimal system configuration, you need a reasonably powerful computer if you don't want to spend most of your day cursing the dreaded hourglass icon. The good news is that Windows 8's hardware requirements are nowhere near as onerous as many people believed they would be. In fact, most midrange or better systems purchased in the past year or two should run Windows 8 without a problem.

The next few sections present a rundown of the system requirements you need to meet in order to install and work with Windows 8. Note that we give the minimum requirements, as stipulated by Microsoft, as well as a set of "reasonable" requirements that we believe you need to make working with Windows 8 more or less pleasurable.

Processor Requirements

Windows 8 desktop minimum: 1GHz modern processor

This is a true *minimum* requirement because these days you'd be hard pressed to even find a PC with a 1GHz processor. There are plenty of cheap PCs available running old Intel Core 2 Duo CPUs at 1.8GHz and AMD Athlon processors at 2.0GHz. But for adequate Windows 8 performance, you need at least a midrange processor, which means an Intel Core i3 or i5, or an AMD Phenom II X3 or X4, running at 2.5–3.0GHz. Faster is better, of course, but only if money is no object. Moving up to an Intel i7 or AMD FX-series chip running at 3.2GHz or even 3.8GHz might set you back a few hundred dollars, but the performance improvement won't be all that noticeable. You'd be better off investing those funds either in extra memory (discussed later) or in a quad-core processor.

Memory Requirements

Windows 8 minimum: 1GB (32-bit Windows) or 2GB (64-bit Windows)

You can run 32-bit Windows 8 on a system with 1GB of RAM, but the performance will be quite slow. Admittedly, we've been running beta versions of Windows 8, which are always slower than release versions because they contain debugging code and are works-in-progress as far as optimization goes. However, we believe that, for most people, 2GB is a more realistic minimum for day-to-day work on 32-bit systems. If you regularly have many programs running at the same time, if you use programs that manipulate digital photos or videos, or if you do extensive work with large files such as databases, 3GB should be your RAM goal on a 32-bit system.

 note

What does *quad-core* mean? It describes a CPU that combines four separate processors, each with its own cache memory, on a single chip. (The cache memory is an on-board storage area that the processor uses to store commonly used bits of data. The bigger the cache, the greater the performance.) This enables the operating system to perform four tasks at once without a per-formance hit. For example, you could work in your word proces-sor or spreadsheet program in the foreground using one proces-sor, while the other processors take care of a background File History backup, virus check, and print operation. Current exam-ples of quad-core processors are the Intel Core i5 and i7, and the AMD FX-series and Phenom II X4.

note

That "32-bitness" of 32-bit Windows means these systems can address a maximum of 4GB RAM (because 2 raised to the power of 32 is 4,294,967,296 bytes, which is the same as 4GB). However, if you install 4GB on your motherboard and then check the amount of system memory, you might see only 3198MB (3.12GB). What's going on here? The problem is that some devices require a chunk of system memory to operate. For example, the memory on the video card must be mapped to an area in system memory. To allow for this, 32-bit versions of Windows set aside a chunk of the 4GB address space for devices. This means the maximum amount of RAM available to your programs will always be 3.12GB.

Note, however, that if you're running a 64-bit version of Windows 8, you should seriously consider upgrading your system RAM. The conventional wisdom is that because 64-bit machines deal with data in chunks that are twice the size of those in 32-bit machines, you need twice the memory to see the full benefit of the 64-bit advantage. Therefore, if you'd normally have 1GB of RAM in a 32-bit machine, opt for 2GB in your 64-bit computer. However, the real reason 64-bit versions of Widows are superior to 32-bit versions for many people is that 64-bit systems can address memory far beyond the 4GB maximum of 32-bit systems. These days, 64-bit machines installed with 8GB or even 16GB of RAM are becoming commonplace. It's unlikely you need double-digit gigabytes of RAM, but you won't regret getting an 8GB system, which offers plenty of room for your programs and data to roam.

Finally, consider the speed of the memory. Older DDR2 (double data rate) memory chips typically operate at between 200MHz and 533MHz. The latest DDR3 chips operate at between 1066MHz and 2800MHz, which is a substantial speed boost that improves Windows 8 performance noticeably.

Storage Requirements

Windows 8 hard disk free space minimum: 16GB (32-bit Windows) or 20GB (64-bit Windows)

The disk space requirements depend on which version of Windows 8 you're installing, but count on the new OS requiring at least 16GB free space to install. The OS will use perhaps another few gigabytes for the storage of things such as the paging file, System Restore checkpoints, Internet Explorer temporary files, and the Recycle Bin, so 32-bit Windows 8 will require at least 20GB of storage, and 64-bit Windows at least 24GB.

These days, of course, it's not the operating system that usurps the most space on our hard drives; it's the massive multimedia files that now seem to be routine for most of us. Multimegabyte digital photos and spreadsheets, and even *multigigabyte* database files and digital video files, are not unusual. Fortunately, hard disk storage is dirt cheap these days, with most disks costing less—often *much* less—than a dime a gigabyte.

Note, too, that the type of hard drive can affect performance. For desktop systems, an older drive that spins at 5,400RPM will be a significant performance bottleneck. Moving up to a 7,200RPM drive will help immeasurably, and a 10,000RPM (or even 15,000RPM) drive is even better if you don't mind the extra expense. You should also look for Serial Advanced Technology Attachment (SATA) drives that boast throughput rates of 6GBps. Look for a SATA drive with a 32MB or 64MB cache.

If having a ton of storage space isn't a priority for you, consider opting for a solid-state hard drive (SSD). These 2.5-inch drives are made from solid-state semiconductors, which means they have no moving parts. As a result, SSDs are much faster than regular hard drives, last longer, use less power, weigh less, and are completely silent. The downside is price. This is still newish (although no longer bleeding-edge) technology, so expect to pay around a dollar a gigabyte.

Finally, you should also bear in mind that one of Windows' longstanding features is the ability to burn data to recordable optical discs (CDs, DVDs, and Blu-ray discs). To take advantage of this, your system requires an optical disc burner, at the very least one that supports both the DVD-RW and DVD+RW disc formats (that is, a DVD±RW drive).

Graphics Requirements

Windows 8 graphics memory minimum: DirectX 9 video card with WDDM driver; 1024×768 resolution for Windows 8 apps; 1366×768 resolution for snapping apps

Windows 8's interface is graphics intensive, but it will be smart enough to adopt a less intensive interface based on what your PC can handle. Whether Windows 8 holds back on the visual bells and whistles depends on whether you have a separate graphics card (as opposed to an integrated motherboard graphics chip), the capability of the card's graphics processing unit (GPU), and how much graphics memory the card has onboard:

- If Windows 8 detects a low-end card, it defaults to the Windows Classic theme, which offers a Windows 2000–like interface.

- If Windows 8 detects a card with medium-range capabilities, it uses the Aero theme, but without the Glass effects (such as transparency).

- If Windows 8 detects a high-end card, it defaults to the full Aero Glass interface.

To get the beautiful Aero Glass look as well as the new 3D and animated effects, your system should have a graphics processor that supports DirectX 9, Pixel Shader 2.0 (in hardware, not as a software emulation), and 32 bits per pixel, and comes with a device driver that supports the Windows Display Driver Model (WDDM). (If you purchase a new video card, look for the Windows 8 Capable or Windows 8 Pro Ready logo on the box. If you just need to upgrade the driver for an existing graphics card, look for "WDDM" in the drive name or description.)

Note that some games and programs might require a graphics card compatible with DirectX 10 or higher for best performance.

The amount of onboard graphics memory you need does not depend on the resolution you plan to use. For example, even a card running at HD (1920×1080) resolution only requires a bare minimum of 8MB of graphics memory to display an image, whereas a card running at a whopping 2560×1600 resolution only really needs 16MB. However, factor in features such as triple buffering (rendering images while the current image is displayed) and high-end game features (such as rendering textures), and basically the more graphics memory you can afford, the better.

Hardware Requirements for Various Windows 8 Features

Windows 8 is a big, sprawling program that can do many things, so it's not surprising that there is a long list of miscellaneous equipment you might need, depending on what you plan to do with your system. Table 2.1 provides a rundown.

Table 2.1 Equipment Required for Various Windows 8 Tasks

Task	Required Equipment
Using the Internet	For a broadband connection: A cable or DSL modem and a router for security.
	For a dial-up connection: A modem, preferably one that supports 56Kbps connections.
Networking	For a wired connection: A network adapter, preferably one that supports Gigabit Ethernet (1Gbps) connections, a network switch or hub, and network cables.
	For a wireless connection: A wireless adapter and wireless access point that support IEEE 802.11n. Ideally, the access point will double as a router to provide wireless Internet access.
Multi-touch	A tablet PC or a PC with a touch-sensitive screen.
Photo editing	A USB slot for connecting the digital camera. If you want to transfer the images from a memory card, you need the appropriate memory card reader. Memory card readers are built in to most newer desktop and laptop computers, but if yours doesn't have one, you can purchase an external memory card reader.
Document scanning	A document scanner or an all-in-one printer that includes scanning capabilities.
Faxing	A modem that includes fax capabilities.
Ripping and burning CDs	For ripping: A CD or DVD drive.
	For burning: A recordable CD drive.
Burning DVDs	A recordable DVD drive.
Video editing	An internal or external video-capture device, or an IEEE 1394 (FireWire) port.
Videoconferencing	A webcam or a digital camera that has a webcam mode.
BitLocker	A PC with Trusted Platform Module (TPM) 1.2.
Listening to digital audio files	A sound card or integrated audio, as well as speakers or headphones. For the best sound, use a subwoofer with the speakers.
Listening to radio	A radio tuner card.
Watching TV	A TV tuner card (preferably one that supports video capture). A remote control is useful if you are watching the screen from a distance.

Preparing Your System: A Checklist

Installing a new operating system—especially one that makes relatively radical changes to your system, as Windows 8 does—is definitely a "look before you leap" operation. Your computer's operating system is just too important, so you shouldn't dive blindly into the installation process. To make sure that things go well, and to prevent any permanent damage in case disaster strikes, you need to practice "safe" installing. This means taking some time beforehand to run through a few precautionary measures and to make sure your system is ready to welcome Windows 8. To that end, the next few sections run through a checklist of items you should take care of before firing up the Setup program.

Check Your System Requirements

Before getting too involved in the Setup process, you need to make sure your computer is capable of supporting Windows 8. Go back over the system requirements we outlined earlier to make sure your machine is Windows 8 ready.

Back Up Your Files

Although the vast majority of Windows 8 installations make it through without a hitch, there's another law that software (particularly complex operating system software) always seems to follow: Murphy's Law (that is, if anything can go wrong, it will). Windows 8 Setup has a Smart Recovery option that should get you out of most jams, but you should still make backup copies of important files, in case Smart Recovery is, for once, just not smart enough. At the very least you should back up your data files, which are both precious and irreplaceable.

Clean Up Your Hard Disk

To maximize the amount of free space on your hard disk (and just for the sake of doing some spring cleaning), you should go through your hard disk with a fine-toothed comb, looking for unnecessary files you can delete.

The easiest route here is to use the Disk Cleanup utility. In most recent versions of Windows, open File Explorer, display the Computer folder, right-click drive C (or whatever drive contains the Windows system files), click Properties, and then click Disk Cleanup. Chapter 25, "Managing Hard Disks and Storage Spaces," offers more details about the Disk Cleanup utility.

 To learn more about Disk Cleanup, **see** *"Deleting Unnecessary Files," p. 595.*

Check and Defragment Your Hard Disk

Windows 8 Setup uses CHKDSK to give your hard disk a quick once-over before settling down to the serious business of installation. Sure, a "quick once-over" is better than nothing, but you should be more thorough. Specifically, use your version of Windows' Check Disk program to give your hard disk a "surface" scan. The surface scan checks your hard disk for physical imperfections that could lead to trouble down the road. In most recent versions of Windows, open File Explorer, display the Computer folder, right-click drive C (or whatever drive contains the Windows system files), click Properties, click the Tools tab, and then click Check Disk. When the Check Disk interface appears, activate the Scan For and Attempt Recovery of Bad Sectors check box and then click Start.

Don't forget to do a virus check if you have antivirus software. Viruses have been known to wreak havoc on the Windows 8 Setup program (in addition to their other less-endearing qualities, such as locking up your system and trashing your hard drive).

When that's done, you should next defragment the files on your hard drive. This action ensures that Setup will store the Windows 8 files with optimal efficiency, which will improve performance and lessen the risk of corrupted data. In most recent versions of Windows, open File Explorer, display the Computer folder, right-click drive C (or whatever drive contains the Windows system files), click Properties, click the Tools tab, and then click Defragment Now.

Create a System Image Backup and a System Repair Disc

If you're upgrading to Windows 8 from Windows 7, you should prepare for the worst by creating both a system image backup and a system repair disc.

The worst-case scenario for an operating system upgrade is a system crash that renders your hard disk or system files unusable. Your only recourse in such a case is to start from scratch with either a reformatted hard disk or a new hard disk. This usually means that you have to reinstall Windows 7 and then reinstall and reconfigure all your applications. In other words, you're looking at the better part of a day or, more likely, a few days, to recover your system. However, Windows 7 has a feature that takes most of the pain out of recovering your system. It's called a *system image* backup, and it's actually a complete backup of your Windows 7 installation. It takes a long time to create a system image (at least several hours, depending on how much stuff you have), but it's worth it for the peace of mind. Here are the steps to follow to create the system image:

1. On your Windows 7 PC, select Start, type **backup**, and then click Backup and Restore in the search results.

2. Click Create an Image. The Create a System Image Wizard appears.

3. The wizard asks you to specify a backup destination. You have three choices. (Click Next when you're ready to continue.)

   ■ **On a Hard Disk**—Select this option if you want to use a disk drive on your computer. If you have multiple drives, use the list to select the one you want to use.

   ■ **On One or More DVDs**—Select this option if you want to use DVDs to hold the backup.

   ■ **On a Network Location**—Select this option if you want to use a shared network folder. Either type the UNC address of the share or click Select, and then either type the UNC address of the share or click Browse to use the Browse for Folder dialog box to select the shared network folder. Type a username and password for accessing the share, and then click OK.

4. The system image backup automatically includes your internal hard disk in the system image, and you can't change that. However, if you also have external hard drives, you can add them to the backup by activating their check boxes. Click Next. Windows Backup asks you to confirm your backup settings.

5. Click Start Backup. Windows Backup creates the system image.

6. When the backup is complete, click Close.

The second half of your Windows 7 recovery system is the system repair disc, which is a CD or DVD that enables you to boot to the disc and then restore your system using the system image backup you just created. Here's how you go about creating a system repair disc:

1. On your Windows 7 PC, select Start, type **system repair**, and then click Create a System Repair Disc in the search results. The Create a System Repair Disc dialog box appears.

2. Insert a blank recordable CD or DVD into your burner. If the AutoPlay dialog box shows up, close it.

3. If you have multiple burners, use the Drive list to select the one you want to use.

4. Click Create Disc. Windows 7 creates the disc (it takes a minute or two) and then displays a particularly unhelpful dialog box.

5. Click Close and then click OK.

Eject the disc, label it, and then put it someplace where you'll be able to find it later on.

Installing Windows 8

The installation process for Windows 8 is probably the easiest—and, certainly, the least interactive—Windows install to date. Upgrading takes just a few mouse clicks, and even a clean install is a simple affair, although it does come with some welcome tools for managing partitions.

After the Setup program boots from the install media, it copies a file named boot.wim (located in the \sources subfolder on the Windows 8 install media) into RAM. This file is a scaled-down OS called the Windows Preinstallation Environment (Windows PE) that boots after a few seconds, so the rest of the install takes place in GUI mode. Windows PE begins by displaying the Windows Setup dialog box shown in Figure 2.1, which acts as kind of a Welcome screen for Windows PE.

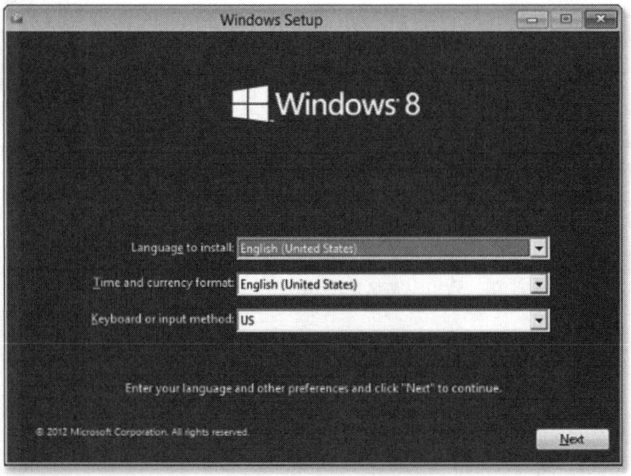

Figure 2.1
This dialog box is the first stop in the Windows 8 installation process, which uses a GUI for all user interaction.

Click Next, and then click Install Now to get the install underway. At this point, you are running in the Windows PE OS. The next major screen asks for your Windows 8 product key; then the installer displays the license agreement and asks whether you accept its terms. The install program next asks you what type of installation you want to perform. You have two choices, as shown in Figure 2.2:

- **Upgrade**—Click this choice to upgrade Windows 8 over your existing operating system. Note, however, that this option does *not* preserve data such as your user accounts and Windows settings. If you want to preserve your data, you must run the upgrade from within your current Windows installation. See the next section for more details.

- **Custom**—Click this choice to install a clean version of Windows 8. This is the install that we cover in this section.

> **tip**
>
> When Windows PE is running, you can display the command line at any time by pressing Shift+F10.

Figure 2.2
You can install Windows 8 either as an upgrade or as a clean (or custom) version.

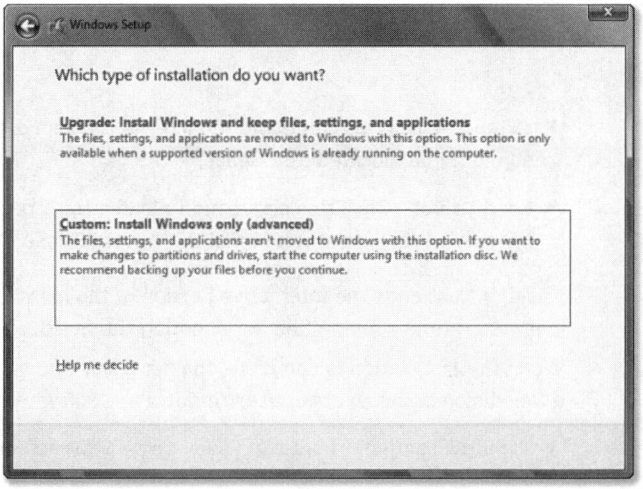

If you choose the Custom option, you come to the most interesting part of the setup process. The installer begins by showing you a list of your system's available partitions, and you click the one on which you want to install Windows 8. The real install fun begins if you click the Drive Options (Advanced) link, which appears for only unformatted partitions. It displays a few extra commands, as you can see in Figure 2.3

Depending on the partition, one or more of the following commands become available:

- **Delete**—Click this command to delete the selected partition.

- **Format**—Click this command to format the selected partition. Note that the installer formats the partition using NTFS.

- **New**—Click this command to create a new partition out of the selected unallocated disk space. This displays a spin box that you can use to set the partition size. Click Apply to create the new partition.

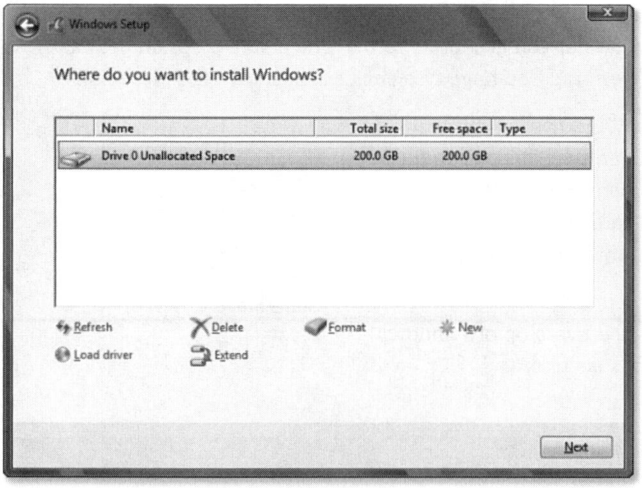

Figure 2.3
The installer gives you a number of options for manipulating the partition on which you want to install Windows 8.

- **Extend**—Click this command to increase the size of the selected partition by extended it into adjoining unallocated disk space.

- **Load Driver**—Click this command to load a third-party device driver for the selected partition. Note that Windows 8 can install the drivers from a CD, DVD, or USB Flash drive.

Clicking Next ends the interactive portion of the installation. From here on, the installer handles everything from copying files to rebooting the machine without prompting you.

When the installation is complete, the Set Up Windows dialog box appears and you're taken through a few dialog boxes to configure Windows 8. Configuration chores include the following:

- Typing a computer name and selecting a Start screen background (see Figure 2.4)

- Deciding whether you want to use express settings (to set up Windows 8 with a default configuration) or customize the install yourself (we recommend the customization path)

- Deciding whether you want to turn on network sharing

- Selecting options for Windows Update and Windows SmartScreen (Windows 8's anti-phishing tool)

- Selecting the type of information you want to send to Microsoft

- Deciding whether you want to check online for solutions to problems and choosing the information you want to share with your apps

- Deciding whether you want to sign in to your PC using a Microsoft account or a local user account (we recommend a Microsoft account to get the most out of Windows 8)

Figure 2.4
Part of the Windows 8 configuration process includes typing a name for your computer and choosing a Start screen background.

Upgrading to Windows 8

The good news is that not only can you upgrade to Windows 8 from Windows 7, Windows Vista, and even Windows XP, but that upgrade will only set you back $40 for the online download (it's $70 at retail). The bad news is that upgrading isn't straightforward, not even close. For starters, if you're thinking of making the move from a 32-bit version of Windows 7, Vista, or XP to 64-bit Windows 8, you can't do it as an upgrade. Instead, you need to install the full version of Windows 8 and then restore your personal files from a backup, reinstall your applications, and reconfigure your Windows settings.

Also, each earlier version of Windows has its own upgrade quirks, as the next few sections show.

Upgrading from Windows 7

You can upgrade to Windows 8 from any version of Windows 7, but there are a few things to keep in mind for each version of Windows 8:

- **Windows 8**—You can only upgrade to Windows 8 (the basic version of Windows 8) from the Starter, Home Basic, or Home Premium version of Windows 7.

- **Windows 8 Pro**—You can upgrade to Windows 8 Pro from any version of Windows 7 except Enterprise.

- **Windows 8 Enterprise**—You can only upgrade to Windows 8 Enterprise from Windows 7 Professional or Windows 7 Enterprise.

In all cases, the Windows 8 installer enables you to transfer your current Windows 7 settings, your Windows 7 user accounts and personal data, as well as any applications that are compatible with Windows 8. When you run the install from within Windows 7, you eventually see a dialog box that asks what you want to preserve during the upgrade, as shown in Figure 2.5. Note that in this case you can preserve just your personal data (user accounts and personal files), everything (your personal data, your Windows settings, and your apps), or nothing.

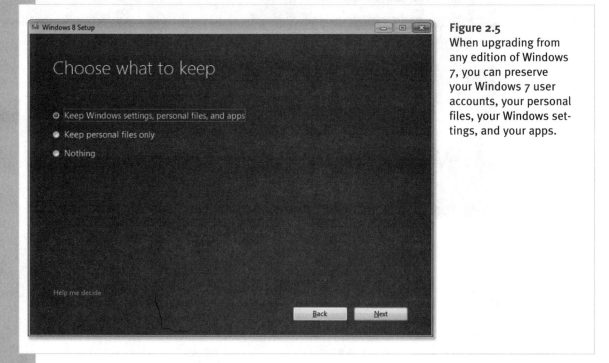

Figure 2.5
When upgrading from any edition of Windows 7, you can preserve your Windows 7 user accounts, your personal files, your Windows settings, and your apps.

Upgrading from Windows Vista

You can upgrade to Windows 8 from any version of Windows Vista, but the data that gets preserved depends on what Service Pack you have installed:

- **Windows Vista with no Service Pack installed**—If you're still running the original version of Windows Vista, you'll only be able to transfer your user accounts and their associated files.

- **Windows Vista with Service Pack 1 or later**—If you've installed at least one Vista Service Pack, then you'll be able to transfer not only your user accounts and personal files, but also your current Windows settings.

When you run the install from within Vista, you eventually see a dialog box that asks what you want to preserve during the upgrade. Figure 2.6 shows the dialog box that appears if you're running Windows Vista with Service Pack 1 or later. Note that in this case you can preserve just your personal data (user accounts and personal files) or both your personal data and your Windows settings.

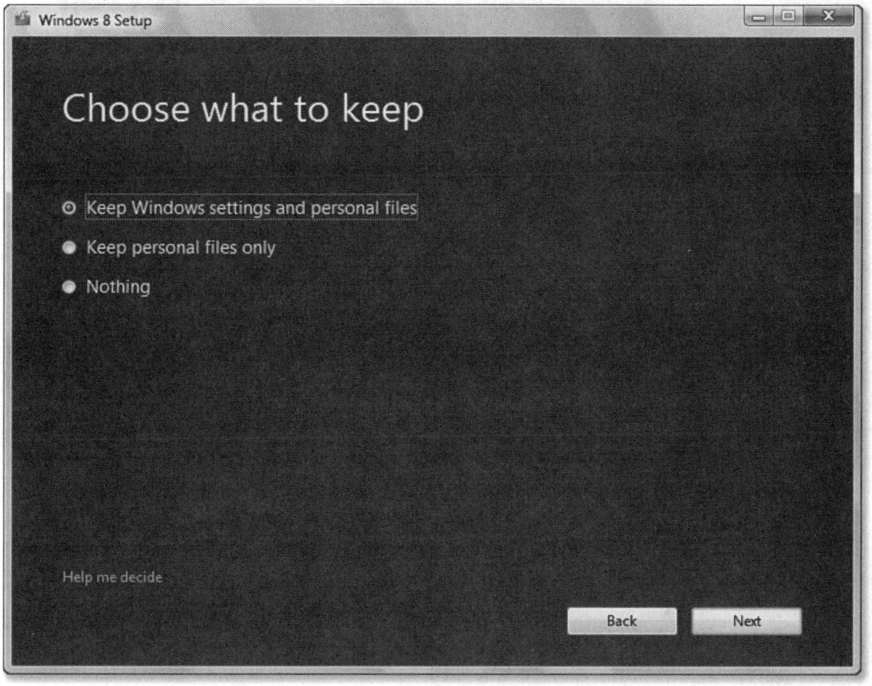

Figure 2.6
When upgrading from Windows Vista Service Pack 1 or later, you can preserve your Vista user accounts, your personal files, and your Windows settings.

Upgrading from Windows XP

Not surprisingly for an operating system that first saw the light of day more than 11 years before Windows 8, Windows XP offers the least attractive upgrade path to Windows 8.

For starters, you must have Service Pack 3 installed, or it's no upgrade for you! Also, even with Service Pack 3 installed, when you run the install, you eventually see the dialog box shown in Figure 2.7. This dialog box means that the only thing that Windows 8 can preserve for you is your XP user accounts and personal files. To preserve even that pittance, be sure to leave the Keep Personal Files option activated.

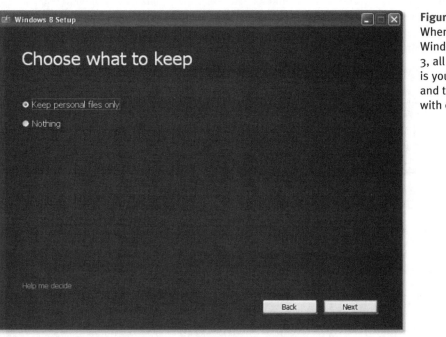

Figure 2.7
When upgrading from Windows XP Service Pack 3, all you can preserve is your XP user accounts and the files associated with each account.

Running the Upgrade

To preserve your data (whether it's apps, settings, or user profile data), you need to launch the Windows 8 Setup program from within your current version of Windows. (In other words, don't boot to the install media and then run Setup.)

When you launch the installer, you usually see the Get the Latest dialog box, shown in Figure 2.8. For the best chance of a successful upgrade, we recommend installing the latest updates. The installer then asks what you want to transfer to Windows 8 (as we described in the previous three sections). From there, the installer checks your system to see if you need to make any adjustments before proceeding. (For example, if your notebook PC is running on batteries, the installer will prompt you to switch to AC power before it will let you continue the install.)

Figure 2.8
When you launch the
Windows 8 Setup pro-
gram from within a previ-
ous version of Windows,
the program asks if you
want the latest updates.

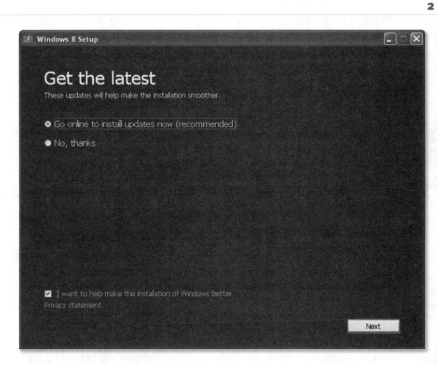

Dual- (and Multi-) Booting Windows 8

The last thing you need to mull over before getting down to the nitty-gritty of the Setup program
is whether you want to run Windows 8 exclusively or "dual-boot" with another operating system.
Dual-booting means that when you start your computer, you have the option of running Windows
8 or some other operating system, such as Windows 7 or XP. It's even possible to multi-boot, which
means having the choice of three or more operating systems at startup.

Windows 8 keeps track of which operating systems are installed on your PC by using a data store
called the Boot Configuration Data (BCD). Earlier Windows versions that are compatible with the
BCD are Windows 7 and Windows Vista. This means that if you have a system currently running
either Vista or Windows 7, when you install Windows 8, the BCD will automatically set up a dual-
boot configuration. Actually, we should say that Windows 8 sets up the automatic dual-boot *provided* you do two things:

- Install Windows 8 to a separate partition on your hard disk or to a separate hard disk connected
  to your PC.

- You install Windows 8 after you install the earlier OS.

For versions of Windows prior to Vista that aren't compatible with the BCD store, the BCD lumps
everything together under the rubric "Earlier Version of Windows," and it uses the legacy BOOT.INI
file to store the boot data from these older operating systems.

You might be surprised to hear that the BCD is actually quite configurable. We show you the details a bit later in this chapter (see "Customizing the Boot Configuration Data").

The next two sections show you how to dual- and multi-boot Windows 8 with various other systems.

Dual-Booting Windows 8

Assuming your PC has the earlier version of Windows already installed, follow these steps to install Windows 8 for dual-booting with the other OS:

1. Boot to the Windows 8 install media and then follow the initial prompts to launch the installation, enter your product key, and accept the license agreement.

2. When you get to the Which Type of Installation Do You Want? dialog box (see Figure 2.2, earlier in this chapter), be sure to click the Custom option.

3. Click the partition you want to use to install Windows 8. Remember, be sure to choose a partition other than the one where your current version of Windows is installed. This will be the partition with System shown in the Type column, as you can see in Figure 2.9.

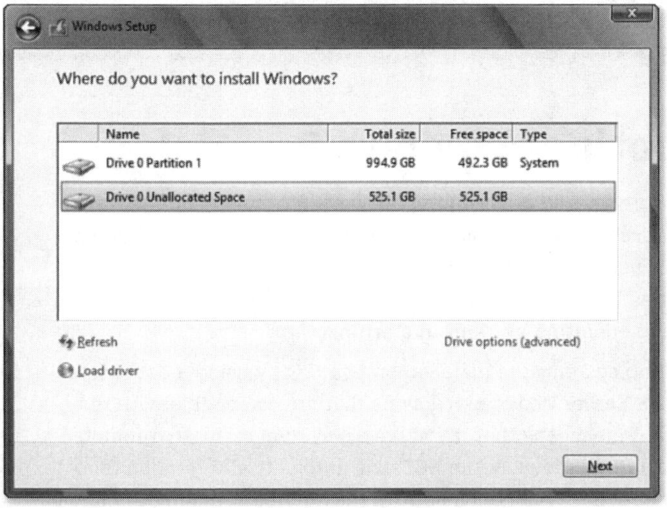

Figure 2.9
When installing Windows 8, be sure to select a partition other than the one where your current version of Windows is loaded.

4. Follow the install steps we outlined earlier to complete the Windows 8 installation (see "Installing Windows 8").

Multi-Booting with Three or More Operating Systems

For maximum OS flexibility, you want to have three or more systems available on your machine so that you can multi-boot among them. Depending on the operating systems you want to use, this isn't all that much more work than setting up a dual-boot system.

If you're installing only Windows operating systems, you need only keep the following two points in mind for foolproof multi-booting:

- Install each operating system to its own partition on your hard disk or to its own hard disk connected to your PC.

- Install the operating systems in release date order, with the oldest operating first and Windows 8 last. For example, if you want to multi-boot Windows XP, Windows 7, and Windows 8, install XP, then Windows 7, then Windows 8.

If you want to multi-boot other operating systems, such as Linux, then your best bet is a third-party boot manager program or the boot manager that comes with the OS (such as any of the boot managers that come with Linux distributions).

Using Windows Boot Manager

Now that your system can boot to one or more operating systems other than Windows 8, you need to know how to control your OSs. You do this using the Windows Boot Manager, which is a menu of the operating systems installed on your PC.

By default, Windows Boot Manager appears automatically when you start your PC. However, you can also invoke Windows Boot Manager from within Windows 8 itself by following these steps:

1. Press Windows Logo+I to open the Settings pane and then click Change PC Settings.

2. Click the General tab.

3. Under the Advanced Startup heading, click Restart Now. The Choose an Option screen appears.

4. Click Use Another Operating System. The Choose an Operating System screen appears, which is the Windows 8 version of Windows Boot Manager.

The screen you see depends on your dual-boot setup. For example, if you're dual-booting with Windows 7 or Windows Vista (or both), you see a screen similar to the one shown in Figure 2.10.

If you're dual-booting with Windows XP or earlier, you see a screen similar to the one shown in Figure 2.11. Again, notice that the BCD simply refers to the legacy OS as "Earlier Version of Windows."

If you invoke Windows Boot Manager at startup and you do nothing at this point, Windows Boot Manager will automatically boot the default OS—usually Windows 8—after 30 seconds. Otherwise, you click the operating system you want to boot.

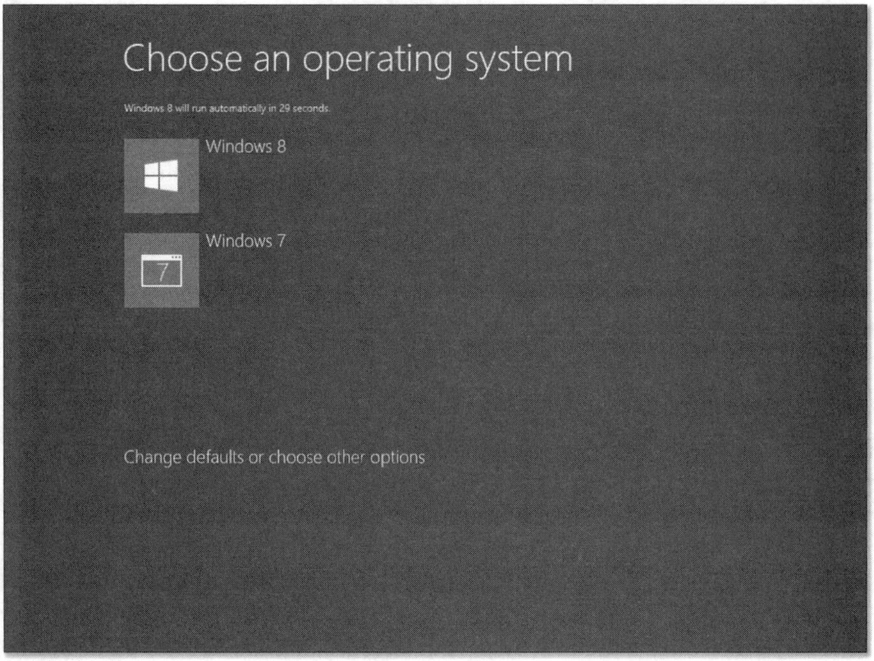

Choose an operating system

Windows 8 will run automatically in 29 seconds.

Windows 8

Windows 7

Change defaults or choose other options

Figure 2.10
If you're dual-booting Windows 8 with either (or both) Windows 7 or Windows Vista, you use this startup screen to choose which operating system you want to load.

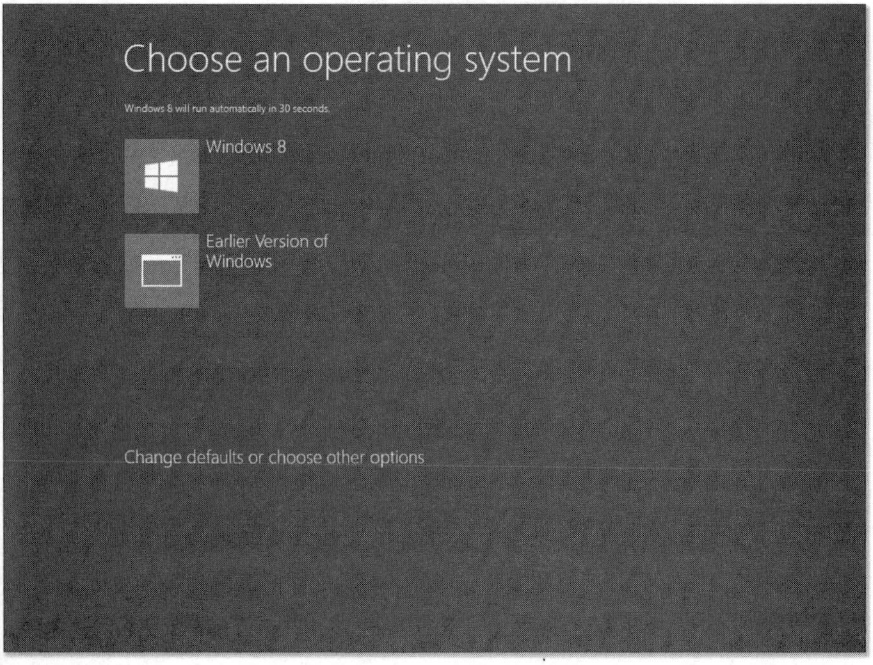

Choose an operating system

Windows 8 will run automatically in 30 seconds.

Windows 8

Earlier Version of Windows

Change defaults or choose other options

Figure 2.11
If you're dual-booting Windows 8 with Windows XP or earlier, you use this startup screen to select an operating system to boot.

Customizing the Boot Configuration Data

As we mentioned earlier, the specifics of the Windows Boot Manager menu are determined by the BCD, which offers the following features:

- It can be used with both BIOS-based systems and EFI-based systems. BCD creates a common store for both types of operating systems.

- It supports *boot applications*, which refers to any process that runs in the boot environment that the Windows Boot Manager creates. The main types of boot applications are Windows 8 partitions, legacy installations of Windows, and startup tools. In this sense, Windows Boot Manager is a kind of miniature operating system that displays an interface (the Windows Boot Manager menu) that lets you select which application you want to run.

- Boot options are scriptable. The BCD exposes a scripting interface via a Windows Management Instrumentation (WMI) provider. This enables you to create scripts that modify all aspects of the BCD.

Windows 8 gives you five methods to modify some or all the data in the BCD store:

- Windows Boot Manager

- The Startup and Recovery feature

- The System Configuration Utility

- The BCDEDIT command-line utility

- The BCD WMI provider

> **note**
>
> We don't discuss the BCD WMI provider in this book. To get more information, see the following page:
> http://msdn.microsoft.com/en-us/library/windows/desktop/aa362639(v=vs.85).aspx

Using Windows Boot Manager to Modify the BCD

You can use the Windows Boot Manager to modify just a couple of BCD options: the default operating system and the maximum time the Windows Boot Manager menu is displayed. Here are the steps to follow:

1. Display the Windows Boot Manager, either at startup or from within Windows 8.

2. Click Change Defaults or Choose Other Options. (If you invoked Windows Boot Manager from within Windows 8, this command is called Just Change Defaults.)

3. To change the time that elapses before Windows Boot Manager selects the default OS, click Change the Timer and click the time you want to use (5 Minutes, 30 Seconds, or 5 Seconds).

4. To change the default OS, click Choose a Default Operating System and then click the OS you want to use as the default.

5. Click the Back arrow to return to the Choose an Operating System screen.

6. Click the operating system you want to boot.

Using Startup and Recovery to Modify the BCD

You can modify a limited set of BCD options using the Startup and Recovery dialog box: the default operating system, the maximum time the Windows Boot Manager menu is displayed, and then maximum time the Windows 8 startup recovery options are displayed. Here are the steps to follow:

1. In the Start screen or Run dialog box (press Windows Logo+R), type **systempropertiesadvanced** and then press Enter. The System Properties dialog box appears.

2. In the Advanced tab, click the Settings button in the Startup and Recovery group. Windows 8 displays the Startup and Recovery dialog box, shown in Figure 2.12.

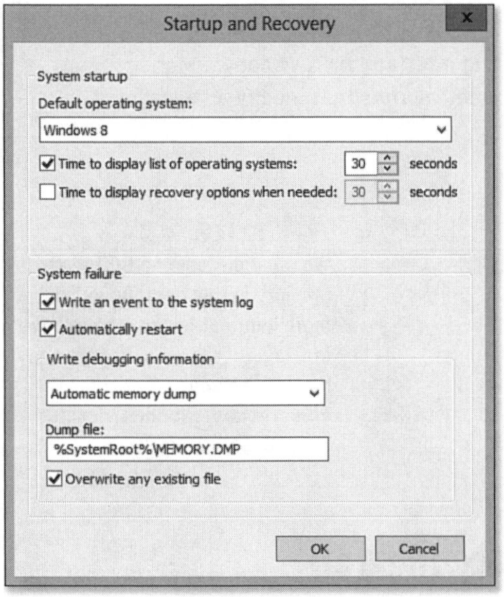

Figure 2.12
Use the Startup and Recovery dialog box to modify some aspects of the Boot Configuration Data.

3. Use the Default Operating System list to click the operating system that Windows Boot Manager highlights by default at startup. (In other words, this is the operating system that runs automatically if you do not make a choice in the Windows Boot Manager screen.)

4. Use the Time to Display List of Operating Systems spin box to set the interval after which Windows Boot Manager launches the default operating system. If you don't want Windows Boot Manager to select an operating system automatically, deactivate the Time to Display List of Operating Systems check box.

5. If Windows 8 is not shut down properly, Windows Boot Manager displays a menu of recovery options at startup. If you want the default options selected automatically after a time interval, activate the Time to Display Recovery Options When Needed check box and use the associated spin box to set the interval.

6. Click OK in all open dialog boxes to put the new settings into effect.

Using the System Configuration Utility to Modify the BCD

For more detailed control over the BCD store, you can modify the data by using the System Configuration Utility. To start this program, follow these steps:

1. In the Start screen or Run dialog box (press Windows Logo+R), type **msconfig** and then press Enter.

2. If you see the User Account Control dialog box, either click Continue or type an administrator password and click Submit. The System Configuration window appears.

3. Select the Boot tab, shown in Figure 2.13.

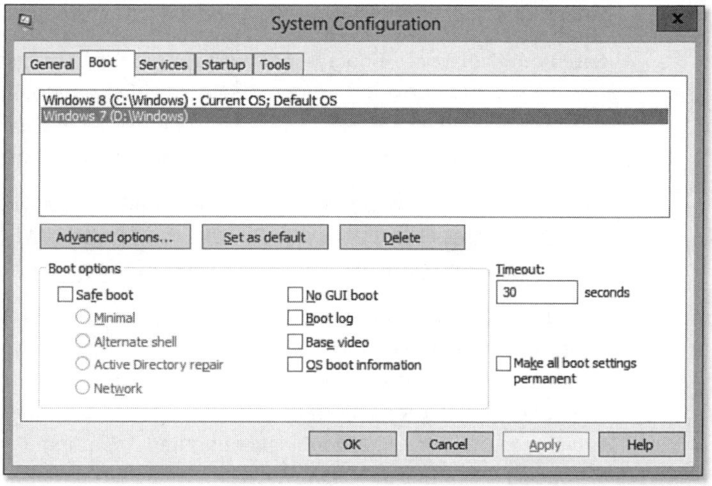

Figure 2.13
In the System Configuration Utility, use the Boot tab to modify the BCD store.

The large box near the top of the tab displays the operating systems on the current computer. You see "Current OS" beside the operating system you're running now; you see "Default OS" beside the operating system that's set up as the default. (Note, however, that the Boot tab does *not* include an entry for any legacy OS—that is, Windows XP or earlier—that you have installed.) There are four main tasks you can perform:

- Click the Set as Default button to set the highlighted operating system as the default for the Windows Boot Manager menu.

- Use the Timeout text box to set the maximum time that Windows Boot Manager waits before selecting the default OS.

- Use the check boxes in the Boot Options group to set the following startup options for the currently highlighted Windows 8 install:

  Safe Boot: Minimal—Boots Windows 8 in *Safe mode*, which uses only a minimal set of device drivers. Use this switch if Windows 8 won't start, if a device or program is causing Windows 8 to crash, or if you can't uninstall a program while Windows 8 is running normally.

Safe Boot: Alternate Shell—Boots Windows 8 in Safe mode but also bypasses the Windows 8 GUI and boots to the command prompt instead. Use this switch if the programs you need to repair a problem can be run from the command prompt or if you can't load the Windows 8 GUI.

> ### 🔍 note
>
> The shell loaded by the /safeboot:minimal(*alternateshell*) switch is determined by the value in the following Registry key: HKEY_LOCAL_MACHINE\SYSTEM\CurrentControlSet\SafeBoot\AlternateShell
>
> The default value is CMD.EXE (the command prompt).

Safe Boot: Active Directory Repair—Boots Windows 8 in Safe mode and restores a backup of the Active Directory service (this option applies only to domain controllers).

Safe Boot: Network—Boots Windows 8 in Safe mode but also includes networking drivers. Use this switch if the drivers or programs you need to repair a problem exist on a shared network resource, if you need access to email or other network-based communications for technical support, or if your computer is running a shared Windows 8 installation.

No GUI Boot—Tells Windows 8 not to load the VGA display driver that is normally used to display the progress bar during startup. Use this switch if Windows 8 hangs while switching video modes for the progress bar, or if the display of the progress bar is garbled.

Boot Log—Boots Windows 8 and logs the boot process to a text file named ntbtlog.txt that resides in the %SystemRoot% folder. Move to the end of the file and you might see a message telling you which device driver failed. You probably need to reinstall or roll back the driver (see Chapter 26, "Troubleshooting and Repairing Problems"). Use this switch if the Windows 8 startup hangs, if you need a detailed record of the startup process, or if you suspect (after using one of the other Startup menu options) that a driver is causing Windows 8 startup to fail.

> ### 🔍 note
>
> %SystemRoot% refers to the folder into which Windows 8 was installed. This is usually C:\Windows.

Base Video—Boots Windows 8 using the standard VGA mode: 640×480 with 256 colors. This is useful for troubleshooting video display driver problems. Use this switch if Windows 8 fails to start using any of the Safe mode options, if you recently installed a new video card device driver and the screen is garbled, if the driver is balking at a resolution or color depth setting that's too high, or if you can't load the Windows 8 GUI. After Windows 8 has loaded, you can reinstall or roll back the driver, or you can adjust the display settings to values that the driver can handle.

OS Boot Information—Displays the path and location of each device driver as it loads, as well as the operating system version and build number, the number of processors, the system memory, and the process type.

- Click the Advanced Options button to display the BOOT Advanced Options dialog box shown in Figure 2.14:

Number of Processors—In a multiprocessor system, specifies the maximum number of processors or cores Windows 8 can use. Activate this check box if you suspect that using multiple processors is causing a program to hang.

Maximum Memory—Specifies the maximum amount of memory, in megabytes, that Windows 8 can use. Use this value when you suspect a faulty memory chip might be causing problems.

PCI Lock—Activate this check box to tell Windows 8 not to dynamically assign hardware resources for PCI devices during startup. The resources assigned by the BIOS during the POST are locked in place. Use this switch if installing a PCI device causes the system to hang during startup.

Debug—Enables remote debugging of the Windows 8 kernel. This sends debugging information to a remote computer via one of your computer's ports. If you use this switch, you can use the Debug Port list to specify a serial port, IEEE 1394 port, or USB port. If you use a serial port, you can specify the transmission speed of the debugging information using the Baud Rate list; if you use an IEEE 1394 connection, activate Channel and specify a channel value; if you use a USB port, type the device name in the USB Target Name text box.

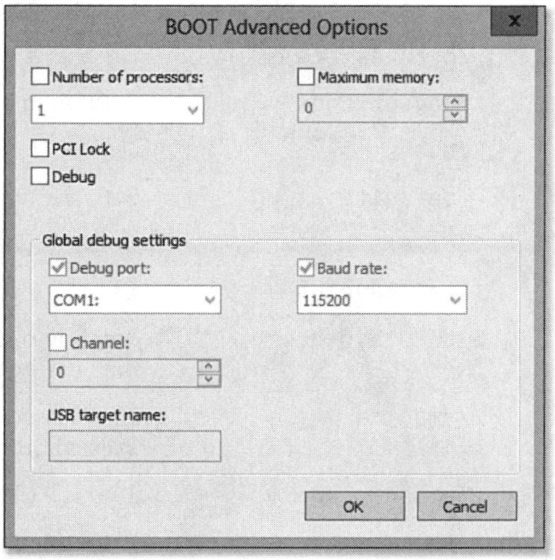

Figure 2.14
In the Boot tab, click Advanced Options to display the dialog box shown here.

Using BCDEDIT to Customize the Startup Options

The System Configuration Utility makes it easy to modify BCD store items, but it doesn't give you access to the entire BCD store. For example, the Boot tab doesn't list any legacy boot items on your system, and there are no options for renaming boot items or changing the order in which the boot items are displayed in the Windows Boot Manager menu. For these tasks, and indeed for every possible BCD task, you need to use the BCDEDIT command-line tool.

Note that BCDEDIT is an Administrator-only tool, so you must run it under the Administrator account (not just any account in the Administrators group). The easiest way to do this is by running a Command Prompt session with elevated privileges, as described in the following steps:

1. Press Windows Logo+X. A menu of power user commands appears.

2. Click Command Prompt (Admin). The User Account Control dialog box appears.

3. Either click Yes or type an administrator password and click Yes. The Command Prompt window appears.

Table 2.2 summarizes the switches you can use with BCDEDIT.

Table 2.2   Switches Available for the BCDEDIT Command-Line Tool

Switch	Description
/bootdebug	Toggles boot debugging for a boot application on and off
/bootems	Toggles Emergency Management Services for a boot application on and off
/bootsequence	Sets the one-time boot sequence for the boot manager
/copy	Makes a copy of an entry
/create	Creates a new entry
/createstore	Creates a new and empty BCD store
/dbgsettings	Sets the global debugger settings
/debug	Toggles kernel debugging for an operating system entry
/default	Sets the default entry
/delete	Deletes an entry
/deletevalue	Deletes an entry value
/displayorder	Sets the order in which Boot Manager displays the operating system entries
/ems	Enables or disables Emergency Management Services for an operating system entry
/emssettings	Sets the global Emergency Management Services settings
/enum	Lists the entries in the BCD store
/export	Exports the contents of the BCD store to a file
/hypervisorsettings	Sets or displays the hypervisor debugger settings, which are similar to the Debug options described in the previous section
/import	Restores the BCD store from a backup file created with the /export switch
/set	Sets an option value for an entry
/store	Specifies the BCD store to use

Switch	Description
/timeout	Sets the Boot Manager timeout value
/toolsdisplayorder	Sets the order in which Boot Manager displays the Tools menu
/types	Displays the data types required by the /set and /deletevalue commands.
/v	Displays all entry identifiers in full, instead of using well-known identifiers

To help you understand how BCDEDIT works, let's examine the output that appears when you run BCDEDIT with the /enum switch on a system that dual-boots Windows 8 and Windows 7:

```
Windows Boot Manager
--------------------
identifier              {bootmgr}
device                  partition=\Device\HarddiskVolume1
description             Windows Boot Manager
locale                  en-US
inherit                 {globalsettings}
integrityservices       Enable
default                 {current}
resumeobject            {14d214f2-caf4-11e1-b73a-83d46d071b71}
displayorder            {current}
                        {14d214ef-caf4-11e1-b73a-83d46d071b71}
toolsdisplayorder       {memdiag}
timeout                 30

Windows Boot Loader
-------------------
identifier              {current}
device                  partition=C:
path                    \Windows\system32\winload.exe
description             Windows 8
locale                  en-US
inherit                 {bootloadersettings}
recoverysequence        {14d214f4-caf4-11e1-b73a-83d46d071b71}
integrityservices       Enable
recoveryenabled         Yes
allowedinmemorysettings 0x15000075
osdevice                partition=C:
systemroot              \Windows
resumeobject            {14d214f2-caf4-11e1-b73a-83d46d071b71}
nx                      OptIn
bootmenupolicy          Standard
```

```
Windows Boot Loader
-------------------
identifier              {14d214ef-caf4-11e1-b73a-83d46d071b71}
device                  partition=D:
path                    \Windows\system32\winload.exe
description             Windows 7
locale                  en-US
inherit                 {bootloadersettings}
recoverysequence        {14d214f0-caf4-11e1-b73a-83d46d071b71}
recoveryenabled         Yes
osdevice                partition=D:
systemroot              \Windows
resumeobject            {14d214ee-caf4-11e1-b73a-83d46d071b71}
nx                      OptIn
```

Here's another example from a system that dual-boots with Windows XP:

```
Windows Boot Manager
--------------------
identifier              {bootmgr}
device                  partition=D:
description             Windows Boot Manager
locale                  en-US
inherit                 {globalsettings}
integrityservices       Enable
default                 {current}
resumeobject            {bdf44e81-cad5-11e1-b38b-cbbdd9e7fb08}
displayorder            {ntldr}
                        {current}
toolsdisplayorder       {memdiag}
timeout                 30

Windows Legacy OS Loader
------------------------
identifier              {ntldr}
device                  partition=D:
path                    \ntldr
description             Earlier Version of Windows

Windows Boot Loader
-------------------
identifier              {current}
device                  partition=C:
path                    \Windows\system32\winload.exe
description             Windows 8
locale                  en-US
inherit                 {bootloadersettings}
recoverysequence        {bdf44e83-cad5-11e1-b38b-cbbdd9e7fb08}
integrityservices       Enable
```

```
recoveryenabled          Yes
allowedinmemorysettings  0x15000075
osdevice                 partition=C:
systemroot               \Windows
resumeobject             {bdf44e81-cad5-11e1-b38b-cbbdd9e7fb08}
nx                       OptIn
bootmenupolicy           Standard
```

As you can see, this BCD store has four entries: one for Windows Boot Manager, one for a legacy Windows install (on partition C:), and two for Windows 8 installs (on our test machine, partitions D: and G:). Notice that each entry has an Identifier setting, and these IDs are unique to each entry. All IDs are actually 32-digit globally unique identifiers (GUIDs), such as the one shown earlier for the first Windows Boot Loader item:

```
14d214f4-caf4-11e1-b73a-83d46d071b71
```

The other entries have GUIDs as well, but by default BCDEDIT works with a collection of well-known identifiers, including the following (type **bcdedit id /?** to see the complete list):

- **bootmgr** — The Windows Boot Manager entry

- **ntldr** — An entry that uses a legacy operating system loader (NTLDR) to boot previous versions of Windows

- **current** — The entry that corresponds to the operating system that is currently running

- **default** — The entry that corresponds to the Windows Boot Manager default operating system

- **memdiag** — The Windows Memory Diagnostics entry (deprecated in Windows 8)

If you want to see the full GUIDs for every entry, add the /v (verbose) switch:

```
bcdedit /enum /v
```

It would take dozens of pages to run through all the BCDEDIT switches, so we'll just give you a few examples so you can get a taste of how this powerful utility operates.

Making a Backup Copy of the BCD Store

Before you do any work on the BCD store, you should make a backup copy. That way, if you make an error when you change something in the BCD, you can always restore the backup copy to get your system back to its original state.

You create a backup copy using the /export switch. For example, the following command backs up the BCD store to a file named bcd_backup in the root folder of drive C:

```
bcdedit /export c:\bcd_backup
```

If you need to restore the backup, use the /import switch, as in this example:

```
bcdedit /import c:\bcd_backup
```

Renaming an Entry

The names that Windows Boot Manager assigns to the boot applications leave a lot to be desired. For a legacy operating system entry, for example, the default Legacy (pre-Longhorn) Microsoft Windows Operating System name is overly long and not particularly descriptive. A simpler name, such as Windows XP Pro or Windows 2000, would be much more useful. Similarly, all Windows 8 installs get the same name: Microsoft Windows, which can be quite confusing. Names such as Windows 8 Home Premium and Windows 8 Ultimate would be much more understandable.

To rename an entry using BCDEDIT, use the following syntax:

```
bcdedit /set {id} description "name"
```

Here, replace *id* with the entry identifier (the GUID or the well-known identifier, if applicable) and replace *name* with the new name you want to use. For example, the following command replaces the current name of the legacy operating system entry (ntldr) with Windows XP Pro:

```
bcdedit /set {ntldr} description "Windows XP Pro"
```

> **⊙ tip**
>
> GUIDs are 32-character values, so typing them by hand is both time-consuming and error-prone. To avoid this, first run the `bcdedit /enum` command to enumerate the BCD entries, and then scroll up until you see the GUID of the entry with which you want to work. Pull down the system menu (click the upper-left corner of the window or press Alt+Spacebar), select Edit, Mark, click-and-drag over the GUID to select it, and then press the Enter key to copy it. Begin typing your BCDEDIT command, and when you get to the part where the identifier is required, pull down the system menu again and select Edit, Paste.

Changing the Order of the Entries

If you'd prefer that the Boot Manager menu entries appear in a different order, you can use BCDEDIT's `/displayorder` switch to change the order. In the simplest case, you might want to move an entry to either the beginning or the end of the menu. To send an entry to the beginning, include the `/addfirst` switch. Here's an example:

```
bcdedit /displayorder {a8ef3a39-a0a4-11da-bedf-97d9bf80e36c} /addfirst
```

To send an entry to the end of the menu, include the `/addlast` switch instead, as in this example:

```
bcdedit /displayorder {current} /addlast
```

To set the overall order, include each identifier in the order you want, separated by spaces:

```
bcdedit /displayorder {current} {a8ef3a39-a0a4-11da-bedf-97d9bf80e36c} {ntldr}
```

Installing Windows 8 Components

Like a hostess who refuses to put out the good china for just anybody, Windows 8 doesn't install all of its components automatically. Don't feel insulted; Windows is just trying to go easy on your hard disk. The problem, you see, is that some of the components that come with Windows 8 are software behemoths that will happily usurp acres of your precious hard-disk land. In a rare act of digital politeness, Windows bypasses these programs (as well as a few other nonessential tidbits) during a typical installation. If you want any of these knickknacks on your system, you have to tell Windows 8 to install them for you.

The good news about installing features is that Windows 8 makes it easy to add any of those missing pieces to your system without having to dig out the installation media (wherever it may be) or (shudder) trudge through the entire Windows installation routine. That's because when Windows 8 was foisting itself upon your PC, it was thoughtful enough to also deposit the files necessary to install the features on your hard drive. They reside in a special folder in a compressed format so they don't take up much room. You must tell Windows 8 to decompress them, which sounds hard, but it's not. You just have to follow these steps:

1. Press Windows Logo+W to open the Settings search pane, type **features**, and then click Turn Windows Features On or Off. The Windows Features dialog box appears, as shown in Figure 2.15.

Figure 2.15
The Windows Features dialog box helps you add the bits and pieces that come with Windows 8.

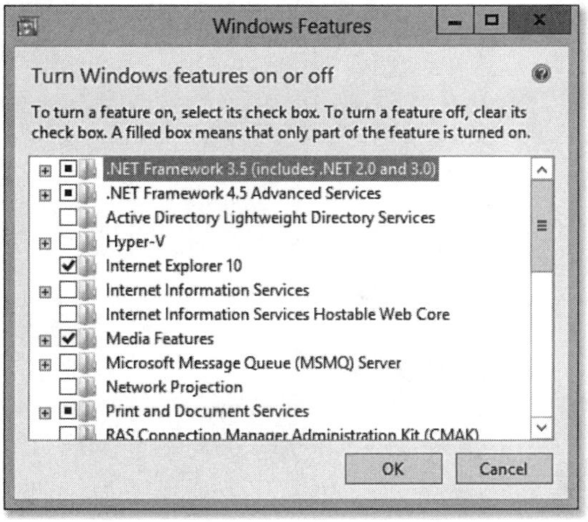

2. If a component has a plus sign (+), it means it has multiple subcomponents. Click the plus sign to see those subcomponents.

3. Activate the check box beside the component you want to install.

4. Click OK. Windows 8 installs the feature.

3

YOUR FIRST HOUR WITH WINDOWS 8

The First Things to Do After Starting Windows 8

If you just installed Windows 8, or have just purchased a new computer that came with Windows 8 already installed, you're probably itching to use it. This chapter is designed to help get you off to a good start. We're going to take you and your computer on a guided tour of Window 8's new and unusual features, and walk you through making some important and useful settings. Here's our itinerary:

- A quick tour of Windows 8's important features

- Setting up user accounts

- Personalizing system settings to make using Windows 8 more comfortable and effective

- Transferring information from your old computer

- Setting up Internet access and automatic updates

- Logging off and shutting down

Our hope is that an hour or so invested in front of your computer following us through these topics will make you a happier Windows user in the long run.

At the end of the chapter, we have some additional reference material. If you're moving to Windows 8 from Windows XP, you will almost certainly want to read the final sections. If you have previously used Windows

Vista, 7, or 8, you may want to just quickly scan the last sections just to know what's there. It might come in handy at some point in the future.

A Quick Tour of Windows 8's Important Features

This section discusses some of the most important features and the most significant differences between Windows 8 and its predecessors. It would be best if you read this while seated in front of your computer and follow along. That way, when you run into these features and topics later in this book and in your work with Windows, you'll already have "been there, done that" at least once. We'll start with the Lock screen, which you'll see after you finish installing Windows 8 or when you turn on a new Windows 8 computer for the first time.

The Lock and Sign On Screens

When Windows starts, you see the Lock screen, which displays just a picture, the time, and the date. Click anywhere on the screen with your mouse or, if you have a touch screen, touch it and slide your finger upward. (This gesture is called a swipe.) The Lock screen slides up and out of view to reveal the Sign On screen, shown in Figure 3.1, which has a large icon (*tile*) for each person (*user*, in computer parlance) who has been authorized to use the computer. Press Tab, or touch or click your account's tile to sign on.

By default, Windows will prompt you for a password, as in previous versions. There are other ways to sign on, using setup options we'll describe shortly. They are as follows:

- **Password**—Enter your password and press Enter, or click or touch the right arrow button to complete the logon process.

- **Picture Password**—Make your pre-set three gestures on the sign-on picture. To make a gesture, touch a point on the picture, drag your finger or the mouse pointer to another point, and release.

- **PIN**—Type your four-digit PIN code using your keyboard or the touch screen keyboard.

The first time you sign on (and only the first time), it may take a minute or two for Windows to prepare your *user profile*, the set of folders and files that holds your personal documents, email, pictures, preference settings, and so on. During that first sign-on delay, Windows will present you with a little animation that shows how to display the *charms*, which take the place of the old Windows Start button.

> **note**
>
> If you're using Windows 8 in a corporate setting and your computer was set up for you, some of the steps in this chapter won't be necessary, and they may not even be available to you. Don't worry—you can skip over any parts of this chapter that have already been taken care of, don't work, or don't interest you.

> **note**
>
> If you just purchased a new computer, the first screen you see might be from the tail end of the installation process described in the previous chapter. Your computer's manufacturer set it up this way so that you could choose settings such as your local time zone and keyboard type. If you do see something other than the Lock or Sign On Welcome screen, scan back through Chapter 2, "Installing or Upgrading Windows 8." If you recognize the screen you see in one of that chapter's illustrations, carry on from there.
>
> If Windows jumps right up to the Start screen, your computer's manufacturer set up Windows not to require an initial logon. In that case, skip to the following section in this chapter, where we show you how to set up a user login.

Figure 3.1
The Sign On
screen is the
starting point
for logging on.

If you have difficulty hearing or seeing the Windows screen, use the icon at the lower-left corner of the Sign On screen to display a list of accessibility options. These include Narrator, which reads the screen aloud, Magnifier, which enlarges the display, and High Contrast, which makes menu and icon text stand out more clearly from the background. You can select any of these items what will make Windows easier for you to use. You can press the left Alt key, the left Shift key, and the PrintScreen key together to toggle High Contrast.

Once you're signed on, you can use the Windows Logo+U keyboard shortcut to open the Ease of Access Center anytime.

The Start Screen

When you've signed on, Windows 8 displays the Start screen, shown in Figure 3.2. This window replaces the old Windows Start menu, and it's the gateway to everything that you do in Windows 8. Removing the Start menu has been a controversial move; however, if you think of it as an enlarged start menu that just happens to fill the screen, it's really not *such* a big change. We talk more about the Start screen in Chapter 4, "Using the Windows 8 Interface." Here, we just want to point out a few things, and you may want to follow along with your copy of Windows as we go:

- You can bring up the Start screen at *any time* by pressing the Windows logo key.

- The large icons on the Start screen are called *tiles*. Some of them, such as the Calendar and Finance apps, display live, updated data.

Figure 3.2
The Start screen replaces the old Windows Start menu. It scrolls left and right, and you can also zoom and shrink its contents.

- The screen scrolls sideways. You can move it with the keyboard (PgUp and PgDn keys), with the mouse (horizontal scrollbar at the bottom), or using your finger, if you have a touchscreen. Just touch the screen and slide it left or right. You can also zoom in and out using Ctrl++ and Ctrl+- on the keyboard, or by touching the screen with two fingers and squeezing them toward each other or spreading them apart.

- Personalizing the Start screen is the key to making Windows 8 easy to use. Pin your favorite applications (*apps*) and folders to the Start screen. Drag tiles around so that the things you do most often appear on the first page of the Start screen. Right-click them or touch-and-hold to make them larger or smaller.

- Right-click the desktop (or drag your finger up from the bottom edge of the screen) and select All Apps to view an extended app list.

- Touch or click the Desktop icon to display the familiar Windows desktop and taskbar (familiar, except that the Start button is gone). In Windows 8, instead of clicking Start, you press the Windows Logo key to get back to the Start screen.

Windows 8–Style Apps (Don't Call It Metro)

The Start screen can list icons for standard Windows applications, such as Microsoft Word and the old familiar Notepad, favorite folders, and new Windows 8–style apps, which are full-screen applications that have a simplified, clean graphical user interface without the traditional menu or window title bar. This new graphical style was called "Metro" during Windows 8's development, but Microsoft has now named it "Windows 8." In this book, when we refer to "Windows 8 style," we're referring to this new full-screen graphical look and the apps that use it.

To see how this looks, touch or click the Weather app. If there is a prompt asking if it's OK to use your location, click Allow. Scroll the display horizontally using any of the methods we described in the previous section. (We'll get you out of the Weather app in the next section.)

The new style of apps takes some getting used to because they have no menu bar, nor the window title bar that in previous versions of Windows had a close box, the application title, and minimize and maximize buttons. We tell you how to manage without these elements in Chapter 4. For now, let's go on to introduce the charms.

Charmed, I'm Sure

Windows 8 has a set of icons called *charms* that can slide into view over any screen. They're shown in Figure 3.3. The charms are search, share information with others, display the Start screen, print, and change settings. We talk about the charms in more detail in Chapter 4. For now, let's just emphasize the most important points.

Figure 3.3
The charms are available at any time, and their functions vary depending on what you were doing when you brought them up.

There are three ways to display the charms: press Windows Logo+C, move the mouse cursor into the very top-right or bottom-right corner of the screen and let it sit there a moment, or, on a touch screen, swipe your finger in from the right edge of the screen.

> 🌀 **tip**
>
> If you're a keyboard user, Windows Logo+C is the easiest method to use.

The charms are context sensitive. This means that what they can do varies depending on what you were doing on the screen before you brought them up. For example, on the Start screen, the Search charm searches for the names of apps, Control Panel settings, and files. In the Maps app, however, the Search charm searches for locations and the names of businesses. On the Start screen, the Devices charm lets you add a second monitor but in Windows 8–style apps that can print, it lets you choose a printer.

To return to the Start screen now, press and release the Windows Logo key, or on a touch screen, display the charms and touch Start. This is an important point: You don't close Windows 8–style apps when you're finished using them; you simply return to the Start screen.

The Touch Tour

If your computer has a touch interface, there are several gestures you can make with one or two fingers that make quick work of navigating through Windows. (Yes, we've all been making certain finger gestures at our computers for years, but this is different.)

In the section "Navigating the Start Screen with a Touch Interface" in Chapter 4, we list the touch gestures in detail. Here, we just want to show you some basic navigation moves. Follow these steps:

1. At the start screen, touch the Desktop tile and keep your finger on it. Drag it to another location on the screen and release it. This is *dragging*.

2. Tap the Desktop icon. This is the same as a mouse click.

3. Touch your finger to the far-right edge of the screen and quickly drag it back toward the middle about an inch. This is a *swipe*, and it should bring up the charms bar. (On the keyboard, Windows Logo+C does the same thing.) Touch Start to return to the Start screen.

4. Swipe from the bottom edge of the screen up toward the middle, or from the top down toward the middle. Just swipe an inch or so. This displays the *app bar*. (On the keyboard, Windows Logo+Z does the same thing.)

   New Windows 8–style apps don't have menus. The charms and the app bar replace the menu. Use this gesture whenever you feel lost in an app, especially in the Windows 8–style Internet Explorer app.

5. Touch the Maps app and, if necessary, let Windows read your location. Bring up its app bar (swipe up from the bottom edge) and change the Map Style. Bring up the charms (swipe in from the right edge) and use Search to find your hometown. You may need to tap the search box at the top to get the Touch Keyboard to appear.

6. Touch the Bing app.

7. Swipe your finger from the left edge of the screen toward the center (just an inch or two) to flip between running apps. You should be flipping between Maps, Bing, and the desktop.

8. Swipe in from the left again, but this time don't release, and then swipe back out to the left edge. Windows should display a panel with tiles for the other running apps at the top, and the Start menu at the bottom. This is called the *switcher*. Touch Bing.

9. Open the switcher again. Drag the Maps tile to the right an inch or two and hold it there, with your finger on the screen. Bing should slide to the right. Drop the Maps tile in the open space. This is called a *snap*, and it lets you view two Windows 8–style apps at the same time. (Note, however, that you can't snap an app unless your screen resolution is set to at least 1366×768.) You can't change the division of space between the two apps. You can just drag the divider bar to the right side of the screen, or off the screen entirely. Drag the divider left off the screen.

10. Finally, drag your finger from the top edge of the screen down to the bottom. The current app should shrink and disappear. This closes the app. Microsoft says you don't need to close Windows 8–style apps in routine use, but you can use this gesture when an app is having problems and needs to be killed.

If you practice this a few times, you'll quickly get a feel for using the touch interface.

Important Keyboard Shortcuts

If you're not using a touch screen, you'll find it *much* easier to use Windows 8 if you memorize a few keyboard shortcuts. These are the most important to learn:

Keyboard	Displays
Windows Logo	Start screen
Windows Logo+C	Charms
Windows Logo+D	Desktop
Windows Logo+X	Pop-up menu of Windows management tools
Windows Logo+Z	App bar

If you memorize just these five shortcuts, you'll be way ahead of the game! We'll cover many more in "Navigating the Start Screen with a Keyboard" in Chapter 4.

There are also useful keyboard shortcuts to switch between apps. Alt+Tab cycles through traditional desktop applications and Windows 8–style apps.

Windows Logo+Tab displays a panel on the left side of the screen that lets you choose between Windows 8–style apps and the Start screen. Hold the Windows Logo key down after you release Tab. You can then press Tab again to select an app, or you can click an icon with the mouse.

> **tip**
>
> Almost all traditional Windows applications have keyboard shortcuts for their menus. If you know them, you can save a lot of time by typing commands instead taking your hands off the keyboard to use the mouse. But if you can't see these shortcuts, you'll never learn them. To tell Windows to show menu shortcuts, go the Ease of Access Center, as described in Chapter 8, "Accessories and Accessibility," under the heading "Ease of Access Center (in Control Panel)." Then select Make the Keyboard Easier to Use and check Underline Keyboard Shortcuts and Access Keys.

The Desktop, or Who Moved My Start Menu?

New Windows 8–style apps run full-screen, entirely overlaying the Start screen. On the other hand, older-style Windows applications with overlapping, sizable windows run on the familiar Windows desktop. Standard Windows applications run here, along with the Command Prompt, Control Panel, Computer Management, and so on.

If you click the Desktop tile on the Start screen (or press Windows Logo+D), you'll see the traditional desktop. However, you'll see that something's different. In every version of Windows from Windows 95 through Windows 7, the route to Windows applications and settings was through the Start menu. In Windows 8, there is no Start menu on the desktop view.

The Start menu has been superseded by the Start screen, which, as we suggested earlier, is best considered to be just a screen-filling version of the Start menu. The full-screen/desktop flip-flop may seem annoying at first, but we have three suggestions for making the change smoother and maybe even sensible:

- When you want to start a desktop program that doesn't have an icon pinned to the taskbar, suppress the instinct to click. Instead, display the Start screen with the Windows Logo key and then type the first few letters of the program's name. (If you don't have a keyboard, bring up the Start screen and select the Search charm.)

- Pin your favorite apps to the Start screen: after you've found an app by searching, right-click it and select Pin to Start Screen. Then drag your favorite apps to the first page of the Start screen.

- On the desktop, pin your favorite applications to the taskbar. Once the application is running, right-click its taskbar icon and select Pin This Program to Taskbar.

- Memorize the keyboard shortcuts listed in the previous section!

If you still feel that you can't live without the Start menu, and especially its hierarchical lists of software manufacturers, categories, and applications, here are some tricks you can use:

- To create a poor-man's Start menu, right-click the desktop, select New, Shortcut, and then enter the following path: `C:\ProgramData\Microsoft\Windows\Start Menu\Programs`. Click Next. Give this shortcut the name All Programs and click Finish. Right-click the icon for the shortcut on the desktop and select Pin to Start. Press the Windows Logo key to display the Start screen. Drag the Start Menu tile to the first page of the Start screen.

- Third-party software developers have created Start menu replacements. Check out lee-soft.com/vistart, classicshell.sourceforge.net, and www.8startbutton.com.

Keep in mind, however, that if you use one of these dodges to tweak your own computer, and you avoid learning how to use the new Start screen, you may find yourself stumped when you eventually have to use someone else's computer.

Windows Explorer Is Now Called File Explorer

To continue our tour, let's take a quick look at Windows Explorer... oops, we mean File Explorer. It has a new name and a ribbon bar in place of a menu. To open File Explorer, touch the Desktop tile or press Windows Logo+D. By default, File Explorer is pinned to the taskbar. Just click the icon to open it. You should see the Libraries window, as shown in Figure 3.4.

(If there is no File Explorer icon in your taskbar, go back to the Start screen, type the word **explorer**, and select File Explorer under Apps. Right-click the File Explorer icon in the taskbar [or touch and hold], and then select Pin This Program to Taskbar.)

Figure 3.4
File Explorer sports a new name and a new ribbon interface.

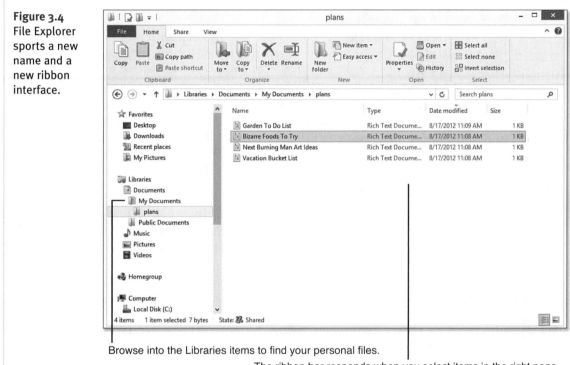

Browse into the Libraries items to find your personal files.

The ribbon bar responds when you select items in the right pane.

In the left pane, you can select the major categories Favorites, Libraries, Homegroup (if one is set up on your network—more on that in Chapter 18, "Creating a Windows Network"), Computer, and Network. Open the Libraries list to see Documents, Music, Pictures, and Videos. Inside each of these library categories you'll find the My ____ and Public ____ folders, which contain your personal files and files shared with all users, respectively.

Collectively, all of these various categories display what the old separate My Documents, My Computer, and other links displayed in earlier versions of Windows.

As you select items in the right pane, the ribbon bar changes to show actions that you can perform on the selected object(s). Oddly, the ribbon does not respond appropriately when you select items in the *left* pane.

Search Before You Look

Here's one of the most important tips we can give you for Windows 8: Although there are usually many ways to get to the same thing in Windows, the *fastest* way usually is to *let Windows find it for you.*

When you're at the Start screen, you can simply type letters or words associated with the Control Panel item, app, setting, or file that you're looking for. You don't even have to open the Search charm. Just start typing.

Windows will find and list apps, files, or Control Panel settings much faster than you could ever get to them by poking around with the mouse or by scrolling through the tiles on the Start screen. If your computer doesn't have a keyboard, go to the Start screen, open the charms, select Search, tap inside the Search box, and then type using the Touch keyboard.

The same applies to the Control Panel and any File Explorer screen. It's usually *much* faster and easier to type a few letters of the name of what you're looking for than to hunt, click, and dig using the mouse. Don't remember what the Control Panel app is called? No worries, just type a related word or words. Chances are, the item you want will appear in the search results under Settings.

Getting to the Management Tools

With the Start button and Start menu gone, it may seem difficult at first to get to the tools you need to use to manage Windows. Remember, you can simply search for any desired management tool or setting by typing its name or a word that describes it at the Start screen. This will usually do the trick.

You can also open any management tool directly. We'll give you the required steps all through this book as we describe specific tasks; however, it's worth mentioning the quickest methods here. Many of these tools can be found by expanding the Start menu using the "All Apps" command button, but there are usually quicker paths. Tables 3.1 and 3.2 list quick ways to get to these tools using a keyboard and using touch, respectively.

Table 3.1   Keyboard Shortcuts to Management Tools

To Get To:	Follow These Steps:
Administrative Tools	Go to the Start screen, open the Settings charm (Windows Logo+C or Windows Logo+I), select Tiles, and then set Show Administrative Tools to Yes. Now, go back to the Start screen and scroll it to the right.
Command Prompt	Press Windows Logo+X, and then select Command Prompt.
Computer Management	Press Windows Logo+X, and then select Computer Management.
Computer Properties	Open File Explorer, select Computer in the left pane, click Computer at the top and then System Properties in the ribbon.
Control Panel	Press Windows Logo+X and select Control Panel, or go to the desktop, open charms, and select Settings, Control Panel.

To Get To:	Follow These Steps:
Devices and Printers	Open Control Panel and select View Devices and Printers. Easier, though, to search for **printers** at the Start screen and select Settings.
Elevated Command Prompt	Press Windows Logo+X, and then select Command Prompt (Admin).
Network and Sharing Center	Go to the desktop, right-click the network icon, and select Open Network and Sharing Center.
System Tools	At the Start screen, press Windows Logo+Z, select All Apps, and then scroll the Start screen to the right.

Table 3.2 Touch Shortcuts to Management Tools

To Get To:	Follow These Steps:
Administrative Tools	At the Start screen, open the Settings charm, select Tiles, and then set Show Administrative Tools to Yes. Now, go back to the Start screen and scroll it to the right.
Command Prompt	At the Start screen, open the Search charm and type **command** or **cmd**.
Computer Management	At the Start screen, open the Search charm and type **manag**.
Computer Properties	Open File Explorer, select Computer in the left pane, click Computer at the top and then System Properties in the ribbon.
Control Panel	Go to the desktop, open the Settings charm, and then select Control Panel.
Devices and Printers	At the Start screen, open the Search charm and type **printers**.
Elevated Command Prompt	At the Start screen, open the Search charm and type **cmd**. Touch and swipe down on the Command Prompt result to display the app bar, and then select Run As Administrator.
Network and Sharing Center	Go to the desktop, touch and hold the network icon, and select Open Network and Sharing Center.
System Tools	At the Start screen, slide the bottom app bar up, select All Apps, and then scroll the Start screen to the right.

If your computer doesn't have a keyboard, use the Search charm to search for these tools by name. If you need to run the tool with elevated privileges, touch and swipe down on the item in the search results, and then select Run As Administrator.

By the way, in the Control Panel, the View By drop-down item lets you instantly switch back and forth between the Category view

note

The Back button is found all over the place in Windows 8. It can come in handy, so make a mental note to remember to look for it as you use various Control Panel options, File Explorer, setup wizards, and so on.

and an icon view that resembles the Windows 9x Control Panel. In this book, our instructions will refer to the Category view unless we state otherwise.

Before proceeding, be sure View By is set to Category.

Setting Up User Accounts

On a computer that's joined to a corporate Windows domain network, the network servers take care of authorizing each user, and accounts are created by network managers.

On home and small office computers, it's best to set up a separate account for each person who will use the computer. Having separate user accounts keeps everyone's stuff separate: email, online purchasing, preferences and settings, documents, and so on. Although it's certainly possible for everyone to share one account, having separate accounts often turns out to be more convenient than sharing. A Computer Administrator user can create, delete, and otherwise manage user accounts.

Microsoft Versus Local Accounts

On a computer that has Internet access, you can create two types of user accounts: *Microsoft accounts* and *local accounts*. A local account is what we had in previous versions of Windows. You can assign a logon name and password. Information about each account stays on the computer. If you set up accounts for yourself on two different computers, your password on the two machines would not necessarily be the same, your individual preferences would have to be set up separately on both computers, and so on.

If you use a Microsoft account (formerly called a Windows Live account) to sign on to Windows 8, Windows uses Microsoft's online services to securely back up certain information from the account to Microsoft's servers "in the cloud," which means "in some big data center somewhere—we don't really know where, but it works." Your Microsoft account email address and password are used to sign on. If you use the same Microsoft account to sign on to another Windows 8 computer, your information follows you—your password, preferences, purchased apps, and so on. It's pretty spiffy. (Documents, music, and so on don't follow you automatically, but you can use the SkyDrive app or other online data services for that.)

For this to work, the computer has to have a working Internet connection when you log on for the first time, so that Windows can check your password. Also, it's best if the computer has an always-on Internet connection, so that your information can be backed up as you work. If the Internet connection goes down later, you can still log on. Windows remembers your last-used password.

You can change any account from a Windows account to a local account, and vice versa. If you switch to a local account, settings

tip

If you have trouble finding a setting, check this book's index, which should lead you to instructions for finding the correct links in the Control Panel or elsewhere. You can also use the Search box at the top of the Control Panel window.

tip

If you want to transfer user accounts and files from an older computer to your Windows 8 computer using the Windows Easy Transfer program, described later in this chapter, do that first and then come back to this section to set passwords on each of the transferred accounts.

you change and purchases you make from that point forward won't follow you from computer to computer. You can switch back to an online account anytime.

In addition, you can choose between Computer Administrator and Standard User types. A Computer Administrator can change any setting as well as view any file on the computer (even someone else's). A Standard User can't change Windows settings that involve networking or security, and can view other people's files only if they've chosen to share them.

The first account set up on your computer during installation and finalization is always a Computer Administrator account. At this point on our tour, let's add user accounts for other people who will be using your computer.

Create New Accounts

Go to the Start screen and open the charms by pressing Windows Logo+C or sliding your finger in from the right edge of the screen toward the middle. Select Settings, Change PC Settings, Users. You should see information about your own account in the right panel. Under Other Users, you can see the + icon labeled Add a User, as shown in Figure 3.5.

If you want to create a new Microsoft account for someone, either he must have already set up his account online at live.microsoft.com or he must be present to set up a new account while you're adding him to your computer.

To create a new user account, click Add a User and then perform one of the following procedures:

- To set up a Microsoft account, if the person has already created a Microsoft account online, enter his Microsoft Account email address.

  If he has an email account already, but hasn't set up a Microsoft account yet, type in his email address and click Next. You or he will need to select and type in a password and then enter his name and location information. Click Next, and then enter security information that will be used only to recover the account if the user forgets his password. Click Next, and then enter demographic information and the "captcha." Click Next and then Finish to create the online account.

  If the person doesn't have an email address, you can create one by clicking Sign Up for a New Email Address and then proceeding as just explained. This will let you create a new email address on one of Microsoft's free online email services at the same time you set up the online account.

 tip

If you purchased a computer with Windows 8 preinstalled, the manufacturer might have set Windows up to skip the Welcome screen logon process entirely. There actually is a user account set up for you, and when you start Windows it automatically logs on to that one account.

If you expect to have other people use your computer, go ahead and create more user accounts now, and we'll show you how to make the Welcome screen work later in the chapter, under "Just One User?"

tip

If you want maximum protection against viruses and other malware, reserve that first Computer Administrator account for management work only, and then create a Standard User account for yourself for day-to-day use.

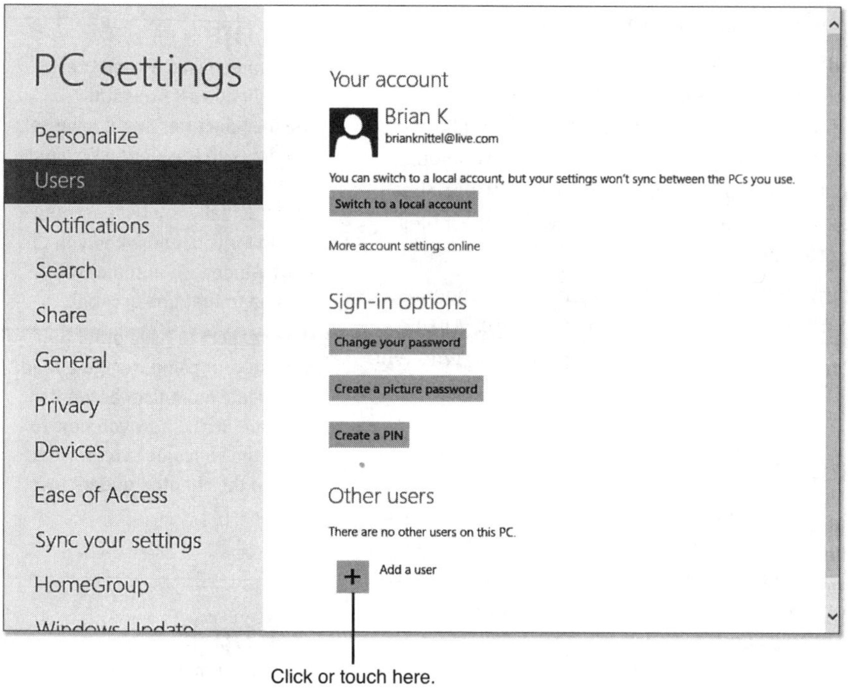

PC settings

Personalize

Users

Notifications

Search

Share

General

Privacy

Devices

Ease of Access

Sync your settings

HomeGroup

Windows Update

Your account

Brian K
brianknittel@live.com

You can switch to a local account, but your settings won't sync between the PCs you use.

Switch to a local account

More account settings online

Sign-in options

Change your password

Create a picture password

Create a PIN

Other users

There are no other users on this PC.

+ Add a user

Click or touch here.

Figure 3.5
Add a new user account from the Users panel in PC Settings.

- If you want to create a local account, and not use Microsoft's online account system, select Sign In Without a Microsoft Account, Local Account.

  Enter a username, consisting of letters and numbers. Choose a password and enter it twice as indicated. Enter a hint that will remind the user what his password is, but won't give a clue to anyone else. (This can be hard to come up with!) Click Next and then Finish.

This new Windows 8–style panel creates all new users as standard users. If you want them to be administrators, you must use the old Control Panel, as we'll discuss shortly.

Change Account Settings

To change the settings shown in Figure 3.5 for your own account, use the Users panel described in the previous section. You can do the following:

- Change between a local and Microsoft account.

- Change your password.

 tip

A Microsoft account user actually has a local user account on the computer, and Windows just checks online to update the password and settings. The account is given a goofy name along the lines of brian_ooo. If you want your computer's Microsoft accounts to have predictable, useful names, create accounts as local accounts first. Then, have the users sign on and change them to Microsoft accounts.

 note

Before logging on to any new accounts for the first time, see the "Configuring a Default User Profile" section at the end of this chapter.

- Create a picture password. You can select a picture to use instead of a password to sign in. You draw three lines on the picture with your mouse or fingertip, gestures that only you know.

- Create a PIN. You can select a four-digit number to use instead of a password to sign in. This PIN works only at the computer screen, not over the network.

If you're using a Microsoft account, you can control what information is backed up on Microsoft's servers using the Sync Your Settings panel. Two settings on that panel that have significant privacy implications are Passwords and Browser. If Password and Browser Sync are turned on, Windows may upload to Microsoft's servers the names of websites you visit and the passwords you use to log on to them. You can be assured that in the U.S., this information is available to government agencies upon subpoena without any notification to you and maybe even without a judge's warrant. You may also wonder what happens if Microsoft's servers get hacked by criminals or governments.

Oddly, to change other aspects of a user account, you have to use the old Control Panel. To do this, press Windows Logo+X and select Control Panel, or from the desktop, open the Settings charm and select Control Panel. Under User Accounts and Family Safety, select Change Account Type. This displays the Manage Accounts screen, as shown in Figure 3.6.

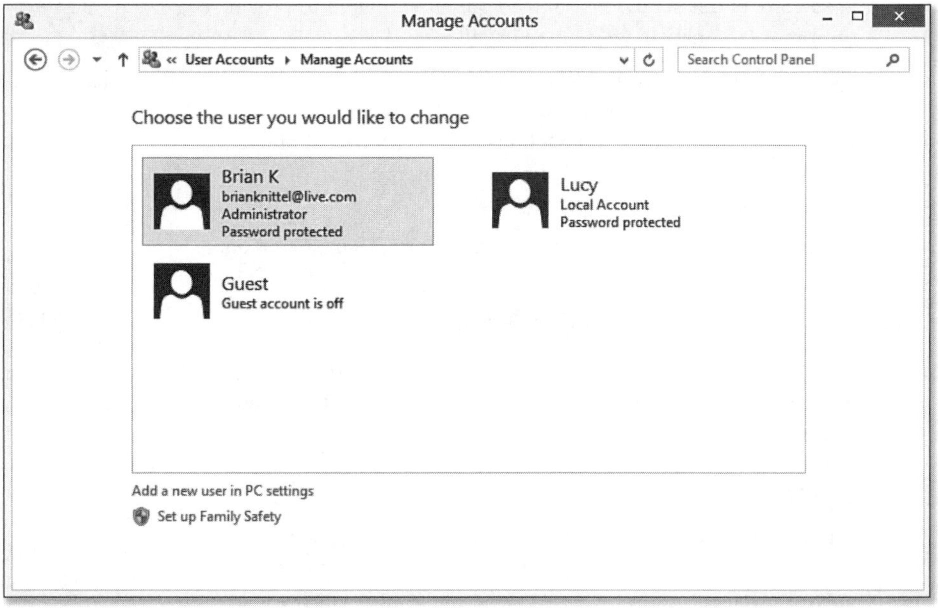

Figure 3.6
To change many aspects of your user accounts, you must use the old-fashioned Manage Accounts window.

Manage Accounts

« User Accounts ▸ Manage Accounts

Search Control Panel

Choose the user you would like to change

Brian K
brianknittel@live.com
Administrator
Password protected

Lucy
Local Account
Password protected

Guest
Guest account is off

Add a new user in PC settings

Set up Family Safety

Click an account icon to perform any of several tasks, including the following:

- **Change the account name**—Click to edit the account's username. (Note: If the user has already logged on, this does not change the name of the user's profile folder in the \Users folder. If this doesn't make sense to you right now, don't worry about it.)

- **Create a password or change the password**—Click to create or change the user's password. This applies only to a local account, not a Microsoft account. We *strongly* recommend that you set a password on every user account, or at the very least on *every* Administrator account.

- **Change the picture**—Click to select a different picture to appear on the Sign On screen. You can select one of the pictures supplied by Microsoft or click Browse for More Pictures to locate one of your own images.

- **Set up Family Safety**—Click to control when this user can use the computer as well as what games and applications the user can use.

- **Change the account type**—Click to change the account type from Administrator to Standard User, or vice versa.

- **Delete the account**—Click to delete the account. You can elect to keep or delete the account's files (documents, pictures, and so on).

> **tip**
>
> Before logging on to other accounts for the first time, see "Configuring a Default User Profile" at the end of this chapter.

In this window, you can also select and enable the Guest account. The Guest account is a Standard User account that requires no password, and it should be enabled only if you want to provide a computer to guests in your home or office.

At this point on our tour of Windows 8, we recommend that you take a moment to add a user account for each person who will be using your computer. Definitely set a password on each Administrator account. We recommend that you set a password on each Standard User account as well.

After you add your user accounts, continue to the next section.

Before You Forget Your Password

If you use a Microsoft (online) account, as discussed in the previous section, and you forget your password, you can go online to reset your password and regain access to your computer accounts—*if* you can get to your email. If you can't, you may be out of luck.

And if you use a local account and forget your account's password, you could be in serious trouble. On a corporate domain network, you can ask your network administrator to save you. However, on a home computer or in a small office, forgetting your password is serious. It can put your encrypted files at risk,

> **tip**
>
> If you are in a home or small office environment, have more than one computer, and plan on setting up a local area network, we suggest you read about the Homegroup feature in Chapter 18. It really simplifies file sharing on Windows. If you don't want to use it, though, but you do want to share files and printers, create local accounts for every one of your users on each of your computers using the *same name and same password* for each person on each computer. This makes it possible for anyone to use any computer, and it makes it easier for you to manage security on your network.

and you could lose any passwords that you've stored for automatic use on websites. (Do you even remember them all?)

You can use another Computer Administrator account to change the password on your own account, but if you can't remember the password to any Computer Administrator account, you'll really be stuck. You'll most likely have to reinstall Windows, and all of your applications, and you'll be *very* unhappy.

There is something you can do to prevent this disaster from happening to you. You can create a password reset disk *right now* and put it away in a safe place. A password reset disk is linked to your account and lets you log in using data physically stored on the disk. It's like a physical key to your computer. Even if you later change your account's password between making the disk and for-getting the password, the reset disk will still work to unlock your account.

So, make a password reset disk now! Here's how. You need a blank, formatted floppy disk, recordable CD, removable USB thumb drive, or other such removable medium. Follow these steps:

1. Press Windows Logo+X and select Control Panel, or go to the desktop, open the Settings charm, and select Control Panel.

2. In the Control Panel's search box, type **password**. Then, select Create a Password Reset Disk.

3. When the wizard appears, click Next.

4. If necessary, select a removable disk drive from the list and click Next.

5. Enter your current password and click Next.

6. Follow the wizard's instructions. When the wizard finishes writ-ing data, click Next and then click Finish.

The disk will now contain a file called userkey.psw, which is the key to your account. (You can copy this file to another medium, if you want.) Remove the disk, label it so that you'll remember what it is, and store it in a safe place.

You don't have to re-create the disk if you change your password in the future. The disk will still work regardless of your password at the time. However, a password disk works only to get into the account that created it, so each user should create one.

If you forget your password and can't log on, see "After You Forget Your Password" toward the end of this chapter.

Just One User?

If you are the only person who is going to use your computer, there is a setting you can use so that Windows starts up and goes directly to your desktop without asking you to log on. You may find that your computer does this anyway; some computer manufacturers turn on this setting before they ship the computer to you. Technically, a password is still used; it's just entered for you automatically.

 caution

A password reset disk, or rather the file userkey.psw that's on it, is as good as your password for gaining access to your com-puter, so store the reset disk in a safe, secure place. By "secure," we mean something like a locked drawer, filing cabinet, or safe deposit box.

note

Be absolutely sure to create a password reset disk for at least one Computer Administrator account on your computer.

note

Each user should create his or her own password reset disk. In theory, a Computer Administrator could always reset any other user's password, but that user would then lose his or her encrypted files and stored pass-words. Better to have a password reset disk for *every* user account.

We recommend that you don't use this automatic logon option. Without a password, your computer or your Internet connection could be abused by someone without you even knowing it. Still, in some situations it's reasonable to change this setting—for example, if your computer manufacturer set your computer up this way, you can disable it. Or you may want to use the feature in a computer that's used in a public place or in an industrial control setting. To change the startup setting, follow these steps:

1. Press Windows Logo+R, type `control userpasswords2`, and press Enter.

2. To require a logon, check Users Must Enter a Username and Password to Access This Computer and then click OK.

   Alternately, to make Windows go to the desktop automatically, uncheck Users Must Enter a Username and Password to Access This Computer and click OK. Then, type the username and password of the account you want to log on automatically and click OK.

The change takes effect the next time Windows starts up.

Downloading Critical Updates

The next thing to do is download critical security updates from Microsoft. If you don't have an Internet connection yet, follow the instructions in Chapter 14, "Getting Connected." When you have a working Internet connection, go to the Start menu, open the charms, and then select Settings, Change PC Settings, Windows Update, Check for Updates Now.

This panel might say that updates are available and that it will install them automatically. That's fine, but if you'd like to install them immediately, you must jump through some hoops. Go to the Start screen, open the Search charm, and type **updates**. Under Settings, select Install Optional Updates. Then, click the link that gives the number of critical, important, and optional updates available. Check the updates you'd like to install from each category. Then, click Install and wait for the process to complete before continuing the tour. If Windows has to restart, log on and immediately return to Windows Update to see whether any *additional* updates are available. It's essential that you get all security fixes installed before proceeding.

Personalizing Windows 8

For the next part of your first hour with Windows 8, we want to help you make changes to some settings that make Windows easier to use and understand. So, let's tear through them.

You might to change the screen background from the picture you chose during installation or set up a screen saver. Let's start personalizing Windows by adjusting these settings.

Personalize Screen Settings

Now we're ready to make a couple of quick selections to the settings that control the Windows appearance. To do this, go to the desktop using the Start menu tile or Windows Logo+D. Right-click the desktop anywhere but on an icon or in the taskbar, and then select Personalize. You can select a *theme*, which is a collection of desktop and sound settings, and/or you can customize individual settings, such as the desktop background and screen saver, by clicking the icons at the bottom of the window.

Resolution and Multiple Monitors

You change the display's physical settings through a different window. View the desktop, right-click the desktop, and select Screen Resolution.

Click the Resolution value, and drag the slider up or down to set the resolution of your monitor. If Windows looks a little blurry, especially on an LCD monitor, it could be that Windows guessed too low a resolution. Drag the resolution button up to set it to the exact native resolution of your LCD monitor; then click Apply to check the setting. If it works, click OK to keep it. (If the type is too small to read, don't worry; we'll get to the fix for that shortly.)

> **note**
> You can put those unused computer processor cycles to better use than making the Windows logo swim around your screen. Several worthy screen-saver alternatives actually might help find a cure for cancer or eavesdrop on ET phoning home. Our favorites can be found at http://boinc.berkeley.edu.

If you have two or more monitors attached to your computer, Windows should have offered you the option of extending your desktop onto all of them. If not, follow these steps:

1. Next to Multiple Displays, select Extend These Displays, and then click Apply.

2. Click the Identify button, and drag the numbered icons in the Screen Resolution pane so that they are in the same arrangement as your monitors. Click Apply again.

Font Size

If you have trouble reading the type on the screen, at the bottom of the Screen Resolution window select Make Text and Other Items Larger or Smaller, and then select either Medium or Larger. Click Apply to check the setting.

ClearType Tuner

Finally, if you have an LCD monitor, use the nifty ClearType Tuner tool to ensure that the text displayed on your monitor is sharp and easy to read. Here's what to do:

1. Go to the Start screen and search for **cleartype**. Under Settings, select Adjust ClearType Text.

2. Be sure that Turn On ClearType is checked, and then click Next. Follow the wizard's instructions to select the text layout that looks best to you.

3. When the wizard has finished, click the small icon at the top of the Control Panel's left margin to restore the web layout, and then close it.

> **note**
> On the desktop, the old Show Desktop icon that parks all applications in the taskbar is now the unlabeled rectangle at the far right.

Now, we'll make some other adjustments to the desktop.

Tune Up the Taskbar

You might want to take a moment now to add taskbar icons for the programs you use frequently. Personally, I always add icons for the Command Prompt, File Explorer, and Microsoft Word, but you might have other favorites. To add an application's icon, search for the app on the Start screen, and then right-click it or press and hold it. In the App command bar, select Pin to Taskbar.

Important Adjustments and Tweaks

You're probably familiar with Internet Explorer, Microsoft's web browser. The other Explorer you need to know about is File Explorer, the program behind the desktop itself, and the one that you use to browse the contents of your Documents, Pictures, and other folders. By default, it hides some information about files, and we want to give you the option of seeing that hidden information.

Disable Hide Extensions for Known File Types

By default, File Explorer hides the file extension at the end of most filenames: this is the `.doc` at the end of a Word document, the `.xls` at the end of an Excel spreadsheet, or the `.exe` at the end of an application program. Hiding the extension makes it more difficult for you to accidentally delete it when renaming the file, but we think it also makes it more difficult to tell what a given file is. It can also make it easier to fall for ruses, as when someone sends an email virus in a file named `payroll.xls.exe`. If Explorer hides the `.exe` part, you might fall for the trick and think the file is just an Excel spreadsheet.

To make File Explorer show filenames in all their glory, follow these steps:

1. Go to the desktop and open File Explorer.

2. At the top, select View, and then select Options in the ribbon.

3. Select the View tab. In the Advanced Settings list, find Hide Extensions for Known File Types and uncheck it.

4. This one is optional: If you're curious about Windows' internal files and folders and plan on investigating them, under Hidden Files and Folders, also select Show Hidden Files and Folders. You can change this setting after you finish looking around.

5. Click OK.

Set Internet Explorer's Home Page

By default, whenever you open Internet Explorer, it immediately displays a Microsoft website or a website specified by your computer manufacturer. Personally, I prefer to have Internet Explorer open to a blank page because I rarely start my browsing in the same place twice. You also might want to select a different home page, one that *you* want to visit rather than one selected by some company's marketing department. To take control of IE's startup page, follow the steps under "Changing the Home Page," p. 319 in Chapter 15.

You might want to download and install a different web browser entirely. Safari, Chrome, Firefox, and Opera are popular alternatives to IE.

Set Internet Explorer's Search Providers

Internet Explorer has a search tool built right in to the URL address box. If you type something that doesn't look like a URL and press Enter, IE sends the text to an Internet search engine and displays the result. This saves you from having to open the search engine page first, typing the search text, and then waiting for the results.

By default, IE sends you to Microsoft's own search engine, called Bing. (Or, your computer manufacturer might have specified a different default search engine.) Again, we suggest that you take control and tell IE which search engine *you* want to use. You can use Bing, of course, but you can also select a different default site. To change the default search site, follow the instructions under "Searching the Web," p. 310 in Chapter 15.

That's the end of our list of "must-do" Windows settings. You can, of course, change hundreds of other things, which is why we went on to write Chapters 4 through 39.

> ## note
> Normally, you must go through most of these same setup steps for each user account on your computer. At the end of this chapter, under "Configuring a Default User Profile," we show you how you can do all of your setup, tweaking, and adjusting just once, and have your finely tuned setup be the default setup for all of your computer's user accounts.
>
> If that sounds interesting, skip ahead to the end of the chapter now, *before* you or anyone else logs on to any other account on your computer.

Transferring Information from Your Old Computer

If you have set up a new Windows 8 computer rather than upgrading an old one, you probably have files you want to bring over to your new computer. Windows has a tool called Windows Easy Transfer that will help you do that. The next several sections show you how to use it. (Corporate network managers can use a program called the User State Migration Tool, but it's beyond the scope of this book.)

Windows Easy Transfer

The Windows Easy Transfer program lets you copy documents and preference settings from an older computer running Windows 8, 7, Vista, or XP to a new computer running Windows 8. You can also use this tool to preserve your data if you plan to reformat or replace your hard disk. You can use several different means to transfer the data:

- If you can plug both computers into the same local area network (LAN), the transfer can occur directly over the network.

> ## note
> Be aware that Windows Easy Transfer doesn't transfer your application programs. Some third-party programs, such as LapLink PCMover, do purport to transfer applications, but we can't vouch for them.
>
> By default, if you elect to copy Shared Items, Windows Easy Transfer *will* copy data stored outside the usual My *Whatever* folders on *all* of your hard drives; that is, everything except the \Windows, \Program Files, and \Program Data folders.

- If you don't have a network but both of your computers have Ethernet network adapters, you can connect them using an Ethernet crossover cable. (See "Connecting Just Two Computers" in Chapter 18.) Then, you can use the network transfer method.

- You can connect the two computers using a special Easy Transfer USB cable, which you can buy for about $30 U.S.

- You can elect to copy data using a Flash drive; a removable, external USB, FireWire, or SATA hard disk; or a network folder.

- The system doesn't make it easy to use a recordable CD or DVD drive. If you have a small enough amount of data to copy, you could, however, use the "external drive" method, save the user data file on your hard disk, and then burn this to a DVD or CD.

The wizard is self-explanatory, so we won't give you step-by-step instructions here. However, we do have some pointers that might make the process smoother and easier to follow.

The process goes like this:

- First, copy the Windows Easy Transfer program to your old computer. Then, run the program on your old computer.

- If you're using a direct network connection or an Easy Transfer cable, start up the Easy Transfer program on your new computer as well, select the user accounts and files you want to copy, and the program goes to town.

- If you're using a flash drive, an external disk, or a shared folder, select the user accounts and files you want to transfer. The program will create one big file containing all the user data. Then take this file to the new computer and run the Easy Transfer program there. Tell it where the big file is. The program will re-create the selected user accounts and documents from the data stored in the file.

Now, we'll give you some tips for each of these stages.

> **⚠ caution**
>
> Passwords are *not* set up for user accounts copied by the transfer program, even though the Users control panel makes it seem that they are. Be sure to read the section "Setting Password" that follows shortly.

> **⊚ tip**
>
> The Windows Easy Transfer program and our instructions here refer to an *old computer* and a *new computer*. However, you can use them to save your user accounts and files and then restore them on the *same computer*. You might do this if you want to install a fresh copy of Windows 8 on a new or erased hard disk. Use Windows Easy Transfer to save your user files on an external disk, set up Windows on a clean hard disk, and then run the program again to restore your files. Again, this doesn't save your application software, but it does preserve user accounts and files.

Copying the Easy Transfer Program

If your old computer is running the *same version* of Windows 8 as your new computer, you already have the program on both machines. Start at your *old* computer. At the Start screen, search for the word **easy** and select Windows Easy Transfer. Follow the instructions from there.

Otherwise, you have to get the transfer program into your old computer.

If you have a Windows 8 setup DVD handy, you can save some time using this trick: start at your *old* computer, log on as a Computer Administrator user, and insert the Windows 8 setup DVD. If an AutoPlay dialog box pops up, select Open Folder or Browse Files; otherwise, open File Explorer, browse into Computer, your DVD drive, and folder \support\migwiz. Double-click the migsetup or migsetup.exe icon. Follow the instructions from there. When you later run the transfer program on your *new* computer, tell it that the program is already installed on the old computer.

If you don't have a setup DVD or if you don't want to use it, you'll need a USB Flash drive, a removable external USB, FireWire, or SATA hard drive that works with both your new and old computer, or network access to a shared folder. Start at your *new* computer. At the Start screen, search for the word **easy** and select Windows Easy Transfer. Follow the instructions and then select I Need to Install It Now to copy the program onto your removable drive. Then, take that drive over to your old computer. Be sure to log on using a Computer Administrator account. Find and double-click the Windows Easy Transfer shortcut on the removable drive.

Selecting a Transfer Method

As previously mentioned, you can use a direct network connection, an Easy Transfer USB cable, or some sort of disk medium that can carry a file from your old computer to your new computer.

The direct network connection and the Easy Transfer cable methods are the easiest; because they let the old computer talk directly to the new computer, you don't have to worry about having enough room on the external disk for all of the files you'll transfer, and it saves you a few steps.

However, the external disk method is just fine, too, and it's the only method you can use if the old and new computers are physically the same computer—that is, if you want to store your user accounts and documents while you perform a fresh installation of Windows 8.

You can also use the external disk method if you want to use a recordable DVD or CD to transfer your data. (Remember, though, that a DVD can only hold 4GB to 5GB of data, and a CD can only hold about 700MB. Is that enough room for all of your files?) To use these media, have the transfer program save your information to the old computer's hard disk. Then, burn a DVD or CD with the file that the transfer program creates. By default, this file is named Windows Easy Transfer - Items from old computer.MIG.

Selecting Accounts and Content

The Windows Easy Transfer program lets you select which user accounts to copy and, if you want to get picky, decide which files to copy from each account, as shown in Figure 3.7. By default, the program will transfer all accounts and all files and folders under each account (that is, Documents, Pictures, and so on). In addition, the Shared Items entry copies the files under \Users\Public on Windows 8, 7, and Vista or under \Documents and Settings\All Users on Windows XP, as well as *all other folders on all of your hard drives* except \Windows, \Program Files, and \Program Data. The total amount of data to be copied is displayed under the list of accounts.

> ## 🌊 tip
>
> Under each user account, you can click Customize to select categories of documents and file types to copy, or not copy. Click Customize and then Advanced to select folders and files on an individual basis.

Figure 3.7
Select which user accounts to copy. Shared Items copies all shared user files plus all other folders on all of your hard drives.

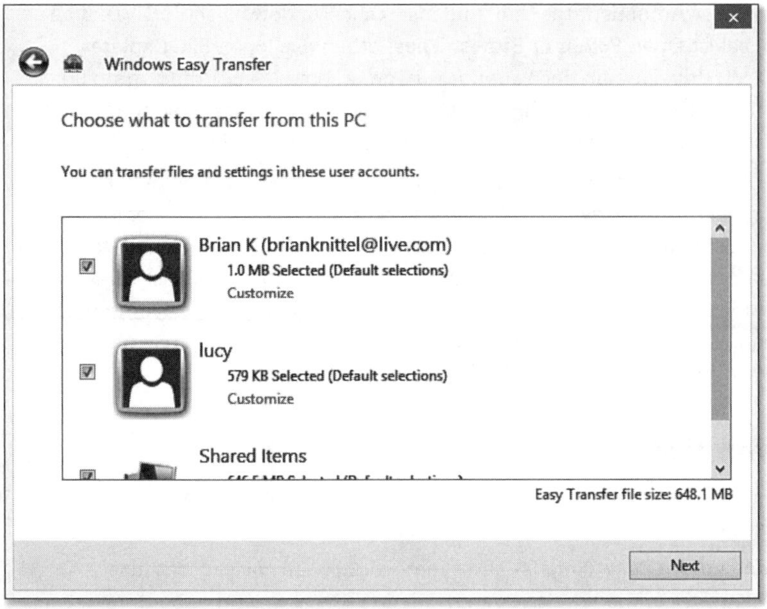

If you use a direct network or Easy Transfer cable connection, you'll make these selections from the *new* computer. Note that there is an Advanced Options link under the list of user accounts. If you click this, you can select alternate names for the user accounts that are copied. It makes sense to do this if you already have accounts with the same names on the new computer.

And if your old computer has multiple hard drives, click Advanced Options and then click the Map Drives tab to select which drives on the new computer to use for data from your old computer.

If you use the external disk method to transfer accounts, you'll select which accounts to copy when you run the Easy Transfer program on the *old* computer. You won't have the option to set Advanced Options there; you're just deciding what to store in the big data file. When you later run the transfer program on your new computer, you'll see the account list again. This time, you can select Advanced Options, and you can rename the accounts or change drive letters if necessary.

Running Easy Transfer on the New Computer

If you're using an external disk to transfer your data, when the transfer program instructs you to, unplug the external disk from the old computer and plug it into the new one. To run the Windows Easy Transfer program on your new computer, at the Start screen, search for the word **easy**, and select Windows Easy Transfer. Follow the instructions it presents. The program will help you locate the transfer file that was stored on the external disk.

> **tip**
> You can also start the transfer program by locating and double-clicking the `.mig` file that the old computer created on your external disk or in a shared folder; this will automatically start up the transfer program.

Viewing The Transfer Report

When the process is complete, the Easy Transfer program will display a window that lets you browse through the list of user accounts, documents, and program settings it copied. Another tab lets you see the list of application programs it detected on your old computer. You can use this list as a reminder of what to install on your new computer.

To view this transfer report again later on, at the Start screen search for the word **easy** and then select Windows Easy Transfer Reports.

Setting Passwords

When the old computer's user accounts have been copied to your new computer, the Users control panel makes it appear that these accounts have passwords set. However, they *do not*. No password will be required when these accounts are selected from the Welcome screen. Windows will prompt the users to create one the first time they log on. Therefore, it's a good idea to use the Users control panel to set a password for each transferred account right after you finish with the Windows Easy Transfer program—otherwise, the user accounts are unprotected.

Also, once you've copied accounts to your new computer, you might want to log on and create password reset disks for them, as described previously under "Before You Forget Your Password."

You might then want to jump back to "Change Account Settings," earlier in this chapter, to tune up the settings for each added user account.

How the Heck Do I Shut This Thing Off?

We end our tour and setup marathon by showing you how to log off and turn off your computer.

Shutdown and logoff options have changed yet again. (Remember the ribbing we Windows users got from Mac users because we had to click Start to stop? It's going to get only a little better now.)

Here are the log off and shutdown options:

- **To make the computer sleep, shut down, or restart**—Open the charms by swiping or by pressing Windows Logo+C. Select Settings, Power and then select Sleep, Shut Down, or Restart.

- **To log off**—Go to the Start screen, click your name in the upper-right corner, and select Sign Out.

- **To switch users**—Go to the Start screen, click your name in the upper-right corner, and select another user name.

Sleep is a great way to save energy if you're leaving your computer for more than 10 minutes or so and plan to come back. However, if the computer loses power, Windows will not have a chance to shut down properly, and you could lose data if you hadn't saved your documents. You can tell Windows that if you leave the computer "asleep" for some time, automatically turn the computer back on, save its memory to disk, and then really power itself off. This is called *hibernation*. When you turn the computer back on, it'll take a bit longer to restart, but it's still usually faster than a cold Windows startup.

> **⚠ caution**
> Always use Shut Down before you unplug your computer.

To set up automatic hibernation, go to the Start screen and search for **sleep**. Under Settings, select Change When the Computer Sleeps, Change Advanced Power Settings. Scroll down to Sleep and expand the list to view Hibernate After. Change the time from Never to, say, 120 minutes (2 hours) and then click OK.

This ends our tour. To close the book, so to speak, go to the Start screen, open the charms, and select Settings, Power and Shut Down. Watch Windows power off. When it's finished shutting down, press your computer's power button briefly and see how fast it powers back up.

> **note**
>
> When you shut down Windows 8, it closes all running applications and services, but it actually hibernates the Windows kernel. When you start up again, the kernel loads nearly instantly, speeding up the boot time by several seconds.

> **tip**
>
> On desktop computers, Hibernate isn't shown as an option on this Shut Down menu because the automatic hibernate-after-sleep mechanism, called *Hybrid Sleep*, is enabled by default. If you disable Hybrid Sleep in the Advanced Power Settings control panel, Hibernate will appear as an option on this Shut Down menu. On laptops, Hibernate should appear on the Shut Down menu because Hybrid Sleep is disabled by default.

More Than You Wanted to Know

In the rest of this chapter, we cover some more advanced topics that some of you might want to know about and some of you won't. Feel free to skim the rest of the chapter and read just what interests you. You're probably itching to start poking around with Windows 8 now anyway, and you can always come back to these items later on if the need arises.

Now, let's go on to learn where Windows 8 stores your documents, music, and so on, and how this differs from Windows XP and earlier versions of Windows.

After You Forget Your Password

Forgetting the password to your computer account is an unpleasant experience. If this happens to you, take a deep breath. You might recover from this. Here are the steps to try, in order of preference:

1. If you are using a Microsoft account, use another computer and open a web browser to go to account.live.com/password/reset.

2. If you created a password reset disk, as described earlier in the chapter in the section "Before You Forget Your Password," you're in good shape. Follow the instructions in the next section, "Using a Password Reset Disk."

3. If you are a member of a domain network, contact the network administrator to have him or her reset your password. The administrator *might* be able to recover any encrypted files you created.

4. Log on using a different Computer Administrator account and use the User Accounts control panel to change your primary account's password.

5. If you don't remember the password to any Administrator account, or you can't find someone else who does, you're in big trouble. Programs are available that can break into Windows and reset one of the Computer Administrator account's passwords. It's a gamble—there's a chance these programs might blow out your Windows installation. Still, if you're in this situation, you probably will want to risk it. Here are some programs you might look into:

   ■ Windows Key (www.lostpassword.com) creates a Linux boot disk, which pokes through your NTFS disk volume, finds the Windows security Registry file, and replaces the administrator's password so that you can reboot and log on.

   ■ Active@ Password Changer (www.password-changer.com) works on a similar principle, booting up in Free-DOS from a CD or floppy disk. The program finds the security Registry file on your Windows installation and deletes the password from selected accounts.

   ■ You can download several free password-reset programs from the Internet. The ones we tested did not work with Windows 8. (We would try to get one of the for-sale products if possible and would attempt a free program only if we were *really* desperate.)

6. If you need to retrieve only files, you can remove the hard drive and install it in another Windows computer as a *secondary* drive. Boot it up, log on as an Administrator, and browse into the added drive. You probably need to take ownership of the drive's files to read them. (If the hard drive is encrypted with BitLocker, this technique won't work either.)

7. If you get this far and are still stuck, things are pretty grim. You'll need to reinstall Windows using the Clean Install option, which will erase all your user settings. Then, as an Administrator, you can browse into the \Users folder to retrieve files from the old user account folders. Again, you'll need to take ownership of the files before you can give yourself permission to view or copy them.

If you are not a member of a domain network, you can avoid all this by creating a password reset disk ahead of time.

> ### ⚠ caution
> If you have to resort to option number four (logging on as an administrator and changing your primary account's password), you will lose any stored website passwords linked to your account and, worse, any files that you encrypted using Windows file encryption (a feature found on Windows 8 Pro and Enterprise only). There will be absolutely *no way* to recover the encrypted files.

> ### ⚠ caution
> The existence of such programs that allow you to reset passwords should raise your eyebrows. The fact is that with physical possession of your computer, people can get into it. However, these break-in tools won't work if your hard drive is encrypted with BitLocker, a feature available in the Pro and Enterprise editions.

Using a Password Reset Disk

If you have lost your password but have a password reset disk that you made earlier, you can use it to log on. Just attempt to sign on using the Welcome screen. When the logon fails, click Reset Password. Then, follow the Password Reset Wizard's instructions to change your password and store the password reset disk away for another rainy day. You don't need to remake the disk after using it.

Accessing the Real Administrator Account

In Windows NT, 2000, and XP, there was an account named Administrator that was, by definition, a Computer Administrator account. You may have noticed that it's nowhere to be seen in Windows 8.

Actually, it's still there, but hidden. There's a good reason for this. It's disabled by default and hidden on the Welcome screen and even in Safe Mode, and it requires no password to log on. This was done to provide a way to recover if you somehow manage to delete the last (other) Computer Administrator account from your computer. In this case, Windows will automatically enable the Administrator account so that you can log on (without having to remember a password) and re-create one or more Computer Administrator accounts, or turn a Standard User into an Administrator. (You would then immediately log off and use the restored regular account.)

This is a good fail-safe scheme, and we recommend that you leave it set up this way. Still, if for some reason you want to set a password on the Administrator account or use it directly, here's how:

1. At the desktop, press Windows Logo+X and select Computer Management.

2. Select Local Users and Groups and then open the Users list.

3. Right-click Administrator and select Properties. Uncheck Account Is Disabled and click OK.

4. Log off or switch users; then log on as Administrator (which now appears on the Welcome screen).

5. Press Ctrl+Alt+Del, and then click Change a Password.

6. We strongly urge you to click Create a Password Reset Disk and make a password reset disk for the Administrator account, as described earlier in this chapter. Be sure to store it in a secure place.

7. Back at Change a Password, leave the old password field blank and enter a new password as requested. Press Enter when you finish.

Now, the Administrator account is accessible and secured.

If you're worried that the default, disabled, passwordless Administrator account is a security risk, remember that by default it can't be accessed unless all other Administrator accounts have been deleted, and only an Administrator user could manage to do that. Therefore, a non-administrator can't do anything personally to get to Administrator. If you enable the Administrator account, then, yes, you really *must* set a password on the account.

> **caution**
> When you are logged on using the real Administrator account, User Account Control is bypassed, and all privileged programs run with elevated privileges.

Configuring a Default User Profile

As you saw in this chapter, it can take quite a bit of time to tune up a user account and set it up "just so." There are taskbar icons to add, things to change in File Explorer and Internet Explorer, and potentially dozens of other applications to configure. It's bad enough doing this once, but if you have many accounts on your computer and you want them all to be set up more or less the same way (at least initially), you're looking at a *lot* of setup time.

Fortunately, you can do this just once and have Windows use your settings as the base settings for other accounts. You can set up one account as you want it and copy that account's profile to the Default user profile so that all future accounts start with a copy of your finely tuned setup. The trick is that you have to do this before other users have logged on to the computer for the first time. It's also best to do this after setting up, but before really using, your own account.

To use this technique to set up nicely pre-tweaked accounts on your computer, follow these steps:

1. Log on to a Computer Administrator account and set it up just as you want all the accounts to look. (Of course, other users can change things after they log on; you're just setting up their account's initial look and feel.)

   In addition to setting preferences, you can add icons to the desktop and taskbar, documents to the Documents folder, and favorites to the Favorites list in Internet Explorer. You can also delete marketing junk installed by Microsoft or your computer manufacturer.

2. Create a new local Computer Administrator user account named **xyz**. Don't bother setting a password for it.

3. Restart Windows, and then log in using the new xyz account. Don't bother making any changes.

4. Go to the desktop and open File Explorer. At the top, select View, Options, Change Folder and View Options. Select the View tab and select Show Hidden Files and Folders. Click OK.

5. In the left pane, right-click Computer and select Properties, Advanced System Settings.

6. In the middle User Profiles section, click Settings.

7. Select the entry for the account that you originally logged on to and set up. Click Copy To, and then click Browse.

8. In the Browse for Folder dialog box, open the drive that Windows is installed on, dig into Users, and select Default. Click OK to close the Browse for Folder dialog box; then click OK to close the Copy To dialog box.

9. When prompted, click Yes to overwrite the original default profile.

10. When the copying finishes, close all the windows and log out.

11. Log back in to the original account.

12. Press Windows Logo+X and select Control Panel, Change Account Type.

13. Select account xyz, and then select Delete the Account, Delete Files, Delete the Account.

Now, when any other user logs on for the first time, his or her user profile will be created with the settings, files, and icons exactly as you set them.

For the advanced management guru, we point out that there are at least six ways to manage user accounts. They are as follows:

- From the Settings charm, Change PC Settings, Users. (This is the only way to set up an online Microsoft account.)

- Computer Management, Local Users and Groups.

- Control Panel, User Accounts.

- From the command line, `control userpasswords2`.

- Also from the command line: `net user`, `net group`, `net localuser`, `net localgroup`.

- Using Windows Management Instrumentation objects in a scripting language such as VBScript.

All of which provide completely different ways of doing almost the same things, because new ways keep getting added but none are ever taken away.

If You're Moving to Windows 8 from XP

If you somehow avoided using Windows Vista and Windows 7, and you're moving straight from Windows XP to Windows 8, you have more than 10 years of catching up to do. In this section, I'll go through a few things that are going to be fairly big changes for you.

Control Panel Wordiness

The first time you open the Control Panel (Windows Logo+X, then select Control Panel) you may be shocked to see that it reads like a Russian novel. There is so much text, and as you poke around, you see that many links lead to the same place. Why? We mentioned it earlier in the chapter: Search. You're meant to find things by searching now, not by poking around. All those words saying the same things different ways make it more likely that the search function will find what you're looking for.

Where's My Stuff? The User Profile Structure

Windows 8, 7, and Vista store your documents, music, and pictures in a different folder layout than did Windows XP and earlier versions of Windows.

Each user's personal files are stored in a folder with the same name as the user account name inside folder \Users. In some cases, Windows adds other letters or numbers to the user name to create a unique folder name.

This folder is called a *user profile*, and it contains not only your personal documents but also some hidden files that contain your personal Windows Registry data (which contains information used by Windows and application programs), temporary files used by Internet Explorer, and so on. Another folder inside \Users is named Public, and this folder can be used by any of the computer's users. It's a place to put files that you want to share with anyone else.

In Windows 8, you *can't* store your own files inside \Program Files, \Windows, or the root (top) folder of the drive on which Windows is installed, although you can create folders there and put files in the new folders.

The directory structure looks like this:

```
C:\
    Windows
    Program Data
    Program Files
    Program Files (x86)
    Users
        myname
        yourname
        .
        .
        .
        Default
        Public
```

Here's a brief tour:

- The Windows and Program Files folders have the same purpose as older versions of Windows—to hold Windows and application programs, respectively. On 64-bit versions of Windows, the Program Files (x86) folder holds 32-bit applications.

- The Program Data folder is hidden, so you won't see it unless you elected to show hidden files earlier in the chapter in the section "Disable Hide Extensions for Known File Types." In it, the Start Menu subfolder contains shortcuts to programs that end up on the Start screen. This was folder \Documents and Settings\All Users\Start Menu on Windows XP.

- The Users folder contains user profiles, the Public folder (which contains the rest of what was \Documents and Settings\All Users in Windows XP), and the Default user profile, which is discussed in "Configuring a Default User Profile," earlier in this chapter.

- A user profile folder for a given account is created only when the user logs on for the first time. The hidden Default folder is copied to create the new profile.

The user profile folder for the account named "myname" is c:\Users\myname, the folder for the account named "yourname" is c:\Users\yourname, and so on.

Inside each user's profile folder is a series of subfolders, which are listed in Table 3.3.

Table 3.3   User Profile Folders

Folder Name	Purpose
AppData (hidden folder)	Per-user application data. Subfolders Local, LocalLow, and Roaming are used to separate data that will never leave this computer from data that should be copied back to a central server if the account is on a corporate network with roaming profiles.
Contacts	Address book data.
Desktop	Files and shortcuts that appear on the desktop.
Documents	On Window 8, its name is displayed in File Explorer as My Documents or *Username's* Documents; but in reality, the folder is named just Documents.
Downloads	Files downloaded from the Internet.
Favorites	Favorites links for Internet Explorer.
Links	Shortcuts to important Windows folders.
Music	Personal folder for music files.
Pictures	Personal folder for images.
Saved Games	Data saved by games.
Searches	Saved search queries.
Videos	Personal folder for multimedia files.

These folders are organized differently than in Windows XP, but correctly written application programs won't need to know about the differences; Windows has mechanisms to provide to programs the paths to these various folders based on their function rather than their location. Still, for those applications whose programmers "wired in" the old XP structure, Windows 8 has a mechanism to let them run without problems, as we'll show you in the next section.

Profile Compatibility Junction Points

Windows 8 setup creates *junction points* and *symbolic links* in the Windows drive that provide a measure of compatibility with applications that were hard-wired to expect the Windows XP user profile structure. Junction points and symbolic links are special "virtual" folders that point to other, real folders. When a program attempts to examine files in the virtual folder, Windows shows it the files in the real folder. If older applications attempt to read from folder \Documents and Settings, for example, Windows shows them the contents of \Users.

You should ignore these special link folders; don't delete them, and to the extent possible, forget that they exist. They are hidden system files by default, so you only see them, in fact, when you instruct File Explorer or use the dir command-line tool to display both hidden and system files.

Compatibility and Virtualization

In previous versions of Windows, applications could store files inside the \Program Files and \Windows folders, and they often took advantage of this to store common data that was shared among all users. The same was true for the Registry, a database of user and setup information—programs frequently stored information in the HKEY_LOCAL_MACHINE Registry section.

To make Windows more secure, user programs are no longer allowed to store files or Registry data in these areas unless their setup programs explicitly change Registry security settings to permit it. (And this has to happen while the program is being installed under elevated privileges.)

Most of the applications that ship with Windows are subject to these restrictions. Try it yourself—open Notepad, type a few words, and try to save a file in \Program Files. You can't. Any application that Windows deems as "modern" or "should know better" is entirely blocked from saving information in these protected areas. (Technically, the presence of a *manifest file* in the program's folder or inside the program file itself is what tells Windows that the program is "modern.")

Older programs, however, expect to write in these privileged directories and Registry areas. Therefore, to maintain compatibility, Windows 8 gives them an assist called *file and Registry virtualization*. What happens is that if an older program attempts to create a file in one of the protected folders or Registry areas and access is blocked, and the program is not running with elevated permissions and the file doesn't have a manifest file, Windows stores the file or Registry data in an alternate, safer location. Whenever an older program tries to read a file or Registry data from a protected location, Windows first checks the alternate location to see whether it had been shunted there earlier and, if so, returns the data from that location.

Thus, the application doesn't actually store information in the secure locations but thinks it has.

Why are we explaining this to you? There are two reasons:

- One consequence of virtualization is that older programs that try to share data between users can't. Each user will see only his or her private copy of the files that should have been stored in a common place. For example, in the "high score" list in a game, each user may see only his or her own name and scores. This may also cause problems with programs that track licensing or registration.

- If you go searching for files in File Explorer or the command-line prompt, you won't see the files that got virtualized where you expected them to be because explorer.exe and cmd.exe have manifests—they don't get the virtualization treatment, so they see only the files stored in their intended locations.

The first problem can't be helped; the older programs just have to be redesigned and replaced. Knowing that virtualization occurs, you can work around the second problem by knowing where to look.

Files intended for \Windows or \Program Files (or any of their subfolders) will be placed into \Users\username\AppData\Local\VirtualStore\Windows or ...\Program Files, respectively.

Registry data intended for HKEY_LOCAL_MACHINE will be shunted to HKEY_CURRENT_USER\Software\Classes\VirtualStore\Machine.

> 🔍 **note**
>
> Some Registry keys are not virtualized in any case. For example, most keys under HKEY_LOCAL_MACHINE\Software\Microsoft\Windows will not be virtualized; attempts to write data in this key or most of its subkeys will simply fail. This prevents rogue applications from creating startup program Run entries.

3

User Account Control

Windows NT, 2000, and XP had the necessary structure to secure the operating system against viruses and hackers. The way Windows security works, any program that a user runs gains the privileges associated with the user's logon account; this determines what folders the user can save files in, what settings the user can change, and so on. Computer Administrator accounts have the capability to change any system setting, change any security setting, change any file, install any software, or modify Windows itself. In effect, software run by a Computer Administrator account could do *anything*.

Unfortunately, in Windows XP, all user accounts were by default created as Computer Administrator accounts, and it took a lot of effort and training to work with Windows any other way. So, for most home and small office users, Windows security was entirely bypassed. One consequence of this was that tens of millions of Windows computers became infected with spam-sending and otherwise malicious software, unbeknown to their owners.

Windows Vista, 7, and now 8 have tightened up security through several means, including these:

- The disk on which Windows is installed uses the NTFS disk formatting system so that access to files and folders can be tightly controlled.

- As initially installed, the security system is actually used and ensures that users do not have the ability to randomly create, delete, or modify files in the Windows program folders. This protects Windows not only from accidents but also from rogue software.

- Programs and system control panels that can make changes that have security implications use a special feature called User Account Control to ensure that changes can't be made without you knowing it.

This latter part is what we want to talk about and show you now.

As mentioned earlier, Windows programs run with the permissions associated with a user account. Permissions include things such as the ability to create or modify files in each folder, change settings on features such as networking and hard disk management, install software and hardware device drivers, and so on. Computer Administrator accounts can do any of these things.

What changed starting with Windows Vista is that programs run even by users with Administrator accounts *don't* automatically get all those privileges. The potential is there, but by default, programs run with a reduced set of privileges that lets them modify files in the user's own folders but *not* in the Windows folder or the Program Files folder. Likewise, by default, programs run even by a Computer Administrator cannot change networking settings, install applications, install device drivers, or change system software services.

Instead, you have to take a special step to run a program with *elevated privileges*—that is, with the full complement of Computer Administrator privileges. On Windows Vista, when *any* privileged program was run, you had to respond to a dialog box to confirm that you did intend to run it. It was fairly intrusive and annoying. On Windows 8, as we'll explain shortly, this mechanism is still there, but Windows requires this sort of confirmation in fewer circumstances.

What is important is that when this "go or no go" dialog box is displayed, it's displayed by Windows in a secure way, from a deep, protected part of Windows, and there is no way for rogue software to bypass it, block it, or fake your approval. Thus, there is no way for rogue software to install itself *without your consent*. This is called *User Account Control (UAC)*.

If you are logged on using a Computer Administrator account, Windows just asks you to consent to running the program. However, if you logged on using a Standard User account, Windows *can still run the administrative program*—the UAC prompt asks you to select the username and enter the password of a Computer Administrator account.

All this makes Windows more secure *and* usable. It makes it safer to let people have and use Computer Administrator accounts. And, it is now reasonable to set up Standard User accounts for everyday use, for anyone, and especially for people whom you'd rather not be asked to judge which programs should run—for example, children or non-computer-literate employees. Should they actually need to change some setting that brings up a UAC prompt, you can simply reach over their shoulders, type in a privileged account name and password, let them make the one change, and poof!—they're back to being a limited-privilege user.

Of course, this type of intervention is required only for programs that involve security-related settings.

A program can be run with elevated privileges in three ways:

- Some applications are "marked" by their developers as *requiring* elevated privileges. These programs display the UAC prompt whenever you try to run them.

- You can right-click *any* program's icon and select Run As Administrator. Generally, you need to do this only if you attempt some task and are told that you don't have permission. This can happen, for instance, if you try to delete some other user's document from the printer's queue.

- If you have an old program that you find doesn't work correctly with UAC, right-click its icon and select Properties. On the Shortcut tab, click the Advanced button, check Run As Administrator, and then click OK. This will make the program run with elevated privileges every time you run it.

The New Taskbar

The taskbar at the bottom of the desktop shows an icon for each running application. This much hasn't changed since Windows 95. You might also recall the Quick Launch bar from previous versions of Windows, which had little icons you could use to start up commonly used programs with a single click.

In Windows 8, the Quick Launch bar and the taskbar have been combined and enhanced, and now there is just one set of icons: they represent applications that *are* running and those that represent programs you *could* run. This new arrangement might seem strange at first, but it's actually pretty handy, and we think you'll like it a lot. (And if it seems vaguely familiar, it might be because the Apple Mac has worked this way for more than a decade.)

Take these actions to see the taskbar in action:

- Go to the desktop and click the blue *e* icon for Internet Explorer. (If it's not present on your computer, use another of the icons.)

  When you click the icon for an application that isn't running, Windows starts it.

- Click the blue *e* icon two more times.

  When you click the icon for an application that's already running, Windows hides or brings up the application's window, in alternation.

- Right-click the blue *e* icon and select Internet Explorer.

  This opens up another, separate instance of the application.

- Click the blue *e* icon.

  When you click the icon for an application that has more than one instance open, Windows displays thumbnail views of the various windows so you can select which one you want to use.

In practice, you won't have to think about it. When you want to use a program, you just click its icon, and you get it, whether it was already running or not.

You can also easily organize the icons on the taskbar:

- You can drag the icons around to reorder them any way you want.

- To put an application in the taskbar permanently, start it, and then select Pin This Program to Taskbar. You can also right-click an icon on the Start screen and select Pin to Taskbar.

- To remove an icon, right-click and select Unpin This Program from Taskbar. (Use this technique to get rid of icons that some application installers insist on putting on the taskbar, whether you want them or not.)

Jumplists

Another neat feature of the taskbar is the jumplist. Remember the old Recent Documents list from previous versions of Windows? This feature is now part of the taskbar, and recently used documents are automatically linked to the icons for the applications that opened them.

Right-click the taskbar's Internet Explorer icon, for example, and you'll see a list of recently visited websites. Right-click Microsoft Word or WordPad or Notepad, and you'll see the last several documents you saved using those programs. It's all very intuitive and natural. (However, it only works with applications that know about this feature. Older applications may not create a jumplist.)

 tip

If you want to keep a website or document in the jumplist permanently, right-click it and select Pin to This List. If you no longer want it pinned, right-click it and select Unpin from This List.

USING THE WINDOWS 8 INTERFACE

Taking a Tour of the Windows 8 Interface

When Microsoft was designing Windows 8, one of their guiding principles was "content before chrome." That is, Windows 8's new interface gives top priority to content—apps and app data—and either hides or eliminates chrome—menus, tabs, controls, icons, and so on. That way, when most new users first come face-to-face with the Windows 8 interface, whether it's the Start screen or a Windows 8 app, they usually don't have a clue how to proceed. The lack of chrome makes for a pleasing, uncluttered screen, but it also means that you get no clues that tell you how to proceed. The most common scenario we've seen is for a new user to click a Start screen tile to open an app (which seems like the obvious thing to do), and then have no idea how to get back to the Start screen. Veteran Windows users try pressing Alt+Tab, but that doesn't work. Esc? No, sorry. Alt+F4? Ah, that does it!

It's this guesswork that makes Windows 8 so frustrating at first, so the goal of this chapter is to replace guesswork with knowledge. That is, you learn exactly how the Windows 8 interface works, what shortcuts you can use to make it easier, and what customizations you can apply to make it your own.

Let's begin with a tour of the Windows 8 interface. Figure 4.1 shows the Windows 8 Start screen. Note that, for technical reasons, we shot this screen at 1,024×768, so the entire Start screen doesn't quite fit. If you're running Windows 8 at a higher resolution, your Start screen will not only fit, but will have a much different arrangement.

Tiles

User Account Tile

Figure 4.1
The Windows 8
Start screen.

Desktop

Live Tile

The default Start screen has four main features:

- **Tiles**—The rectangles you see each represent an app on your PC, and you click a tile to open that app. With the exception of the Desktop tile (discussed in this list), all the default Start screen tiles represent Windows 8 apps.

- **Live tiles**—Many of the Start screen tiles are "live" in the sense that they display often-updated information instead of the app icon. For example, the Weather tile shows the current weather for your default location; the Mail and Messaging tiles display recent email and instant messages; and the Calendar tile shows your upcoming events.

- **Desktop**—Arguably one of the biggest controversies surrounding Windows 8 is the relegation of the desktop to just another app, represented on the Start screen by the Desktop tile. This is controversial because most Windows users will still use desktop programs most of the time, so getting to the desktop not only requires an extra step, but it's also harder to work with because the Start button is gone. We'll show you some ways to work around these limitations a bit later in this chapter (see "Bypassing the Start Screen").

■ **User account tile**—Clicking this tile gives you access to several account-related tasks (see Figure 4.2), such as locking your PC, signing out of your account, and switching users.

Figure 4.2
Click your user account tile for quick access to some account features and commands.

The Start screen certainly demonstrates Microsoft's commitment to content over chrome, because there's nary a menu, button, or command to be seen. Obviously, however, there's not much you can do with a computer without such interface elements (just ask any new Windows 8 user!), so where's the chrome? For the most part, it resides in two hidden interface elements: the app bar and the Charms menu, which we discuss in the next two sections.

The App Bar

You can hunt around all you like, but you won't find menu bars, toolbars, or taskbars anywhere in Windows 8's new interface. The only "bar" you'll (eventually) see is a new interface element called the *app bar* (or sometimes *application bar*), which contains app-related commands, features, controls, and settings. In any new Windows 8 screen—the Start screen, the Apps screen, a Windows 8 app screen, and so on—you display the app bar by using one of the following techniques:

■ Right-click the screen.

■ Press Windows Logo+Z.

■ If you're using a touchscreen, swipe up from the bottom edge of the screen (or swipe down from the top edge).

App bars are *context sensitive*, meaning that what you see when the app bar slides into view depends on what you right-clicked (or what is currently selected if you press Windows Logo+Z or swipe from the bottom or top edge). For example, Figure 4.3 shows the app bar that appears when you right-click the Start screen (or when you press Windows Logo+Z or swipe from the bottom or top edge with nothing selected). In this case, you see just the All Apps button, which you click to display the Apps screen and view all your installed apps.

Figure 4.3
The Start screen's app bar.

The App Bar

However, if you right-click a Start screen tile (or swipe down on a tile if you're using a touchscreen), the app bar that appears contains a few extra commands related to just that tile, as shown in Figure 4.4 (we'll talk about these commands later in this chapter).

note

To dismiss the app bar without doing anything, right-click the same object, press either Esc or Windows Logo+Z, or repeat the swipe gesture that you used to invoke the app bar.

Figure 4.4
A Start screen tile's app bar.

You see yet another version of the app bar when you invoke it within a Windows 8 app. For example, as you can see in Figure 4.5, bringing up the app bar in the Weather app displays *two* elements: one along the bottom of the screen and another along the top. Some apps display two app bars, whereas in others only a single app bar appears, either at the top of the screen or at the bottom. (This lack of consistent app bar placement is yet another maddening element of the new interface.)

Figure 4.5
The Weather app's two app bars.

The Charms Menu

The other piece of the Start screen chrome that you need to know about is the Charms menu, which you invoke by using one of the following techniques:

- Move the mouse pointer to the top-right or bottom-right corner of the screen, and then when the Charms icons appear, move the pointer straight down to display the full Charms menu.

- Press Windows Logo+C.

- If you're using a touchscreen, swipe left from the right edge of the screen.

Figure 4.6 shows the Charms menu. Note, too, that Windows also displays a box showing the current date and time, the Network icon, and the Power icon.

The Charms menu offers the following items (yes, they're called charms; we don't know why):

- **Search**—Click this charm to search your PC; see "Searching via the Start Screen," later in this chapter.

- **Share**—Click this charm to use a Windows 8 app (such as Mail) to send a file or some app data to a friend.

  ⮕ *To learn about the Share charm, **see** "Sharing Windows 8 App Data," **p. 147**.*

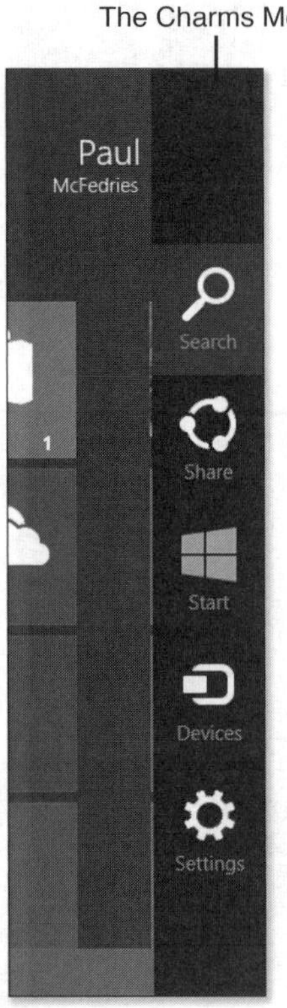

The Charms Menu

Figure 4.6
The Windows 8 Charms menu.

- **Start**—Click this charm to return to the Start screen.

- **Devices**—Click this charm to open a screen that shows you all the major devices and hardware doodads attached to your computer.

  ➡ *To learn about the Devices charm,* ***see*** *"Viewing Your Devices,"* ***p. 668***.

- **Settings**—Click this charm to configure various Windows 8 options and settings.

  ➡ *To learn about the Settings charm,* ***see*** *"Working with the PC Settings App,"* ***p. 557***.

Navigating the Start Screen

If the lack of chrome on the Start screen makes it hard to figure out what to do with Windows 8, it also makes it hard to figure out how to navigate Windows 8. With no traditional navigational aids such as scrollbars and tabs in sight, how do you get around the Start screen? The next three sections provide the answers to that question.

Navigating the Start Screen with a Mouse

It turns out that the Start screen *does* have a scrollbar after all, it's just that, like the rest of the Windows 8 chrome, it's hidden by default. To see the scrollbar, move the mouse pointer to the bottom of the screen, as shown in Figure 4.7.

The Start screen scrollbar works like a traditional horizontal scrollbar. That is, to scroll the Start screen right or left, you use any of the following techniques:

 note

If you're running Windows 8 at a high enough resolution that you can see the entire Start screen, then the scrollbar doesn't appear when you move your mouse to the bottom of the screen.

- Drag the white scroll box right and left.

- Click the scroll arrows that appear on the left and right edges of the scrollbar.

- Click between the scroll box and the scroll arrows.

Figure 4.7
Move the mouse pointer to the bottom of the screen to reveal the scrollbar.

The Scrollbar   Semantic Zoom Button

Note that all Windows 8 apps are also oriented horizontally and come with their own horizontal scrollbars, so you can use these same techniques to navigate any Windows 8 app.

For our money, however, the scrollbar is a really inefficient way to navigate the Start screen or a Windows 8 app. A much faster and more elegant method is to use your mouse's scroll wheel (if it has one):

- Turn the wheel forward to scroll the screen to the right.

- Turn the wheel backward to scroll the screen to the left.

What about the Semantic Zoom button pointed out earlier in Figure 4.7? That's a new Windows 8 feature that enables you to quickly "zoom out" of the Start screen (or a Windows 8 app) to get a bird's-eye view of the screen. For example, Figure 4.8 shows the Start screen after the Semantic Zoom icon has been clicked. With most Windows 8 apps, instead of a simple lower magnification, invoking Semantic Zoom displays a list of the app's main sections—a welcome technique to know because many apps have eight or ten sections!

Figure 4.8
Invoking
Semantic
Zoom in the
Start screen
gives you a big
picture view of
the tiles.

Navigating the Start Screen with a Keyboard

Everyone's talking about the new touch features in Windows 8, but you'd be surprised just how many new keyboard shortcuts there are. We'll get to those in a second, but for now you should know that you *can* navigate the Start screen using the keyboard. Here's how:

1. Press Tab. Windows 8 selects the user account tile. If you want to select a command from this tile, press Spacebar, use the up and down arrow keys to select the command, and then press Enter.

2. Press Tab again. Windows 8 selects the first app tile.

3. Use the arrow keys to select the app you want to run.

4. Press Enter. Windows 8 launches the selected app.

Besides this technique, Windows 8 also offers a huge number of Windows Logo key–based short-cuts that enable you to not only navigate the Windows 8 interface quickly, but also let you easily invoke many Windows 8 features and programs. Table 4.1 provides the complete list.

Table 4.1 Keyboard Shortcuts for Navigating Windows 8

Press this:	To do this:
Windows Logo	Switch between the Start screen and the most recent Windows 8 app
Windows Logo+B	Switch to the Desktop app and activate the taskbar's Show Hidden Icons arrow
Windows Logo+C	Display the Charms menu
Windows Logo+D	Switch to the Desktop app
Windows Logo+E	Run File Explorer
Windows Logo+F	Display the Files search pane
Windows Logo+H	Display the Share pane
Windows Logo+I	Display the Settings pane
Windows Logo+K	Display the Devices pane
Windows Logo+L	Lock your computer
Windows Logo+M	Switch to the desktop and minimize all windows
Windows Logo+O	Turn the tablet orientation lock on and off
Windows Logo+P	Switch to a second display
Windows Logo+Q	Display the Apps search pane
Windows Logo+R	Open the Run dialog box
Windows Logo+T	Switch to the desktop and cycle through the taskbar icons
Windows Logo+U	Open the Ease of Access Center
Windows Logo+W	Display the Settings search pane
Windows Logo+X	Display a menu of Windows tools and utilities
Windows Logo+Z	Display the app bar
Windows Logo+=	Open Magnifier and zoom in
Windows Logo+-	Zoom out (if already zoomed in using Magnifier)
Windows Logo+.	Snap the current Windows 8 app
Windows Logo+,	Temporarily display the desktop in the Desktop app
Windows Logo+Enter	Open Narrator
Windows Logo+PgUp	Move the current Windows 8 app to the left-hand monitor
Windows Logo+PgDn	Move the current Windows 8 app to the right-hand monitor
Windows Logo+PrtSc	Capture the current screen and save it to the Pictures folder
Windows Logo+Tab	Switch between running Windows 8 apps

tip

Two other keyboard shortcuts that are important for navigating the Start screen are Ctrl+- (hyphen), which invokes the Semantic Zoom feature, and Ctrl++ (plus), which turns off Semantic Zoom.

Navigating the Start Screen with a Touch Interface

We used to always say that Windows was built with the mouse in mind. After all, the easiest way to use screen elements such as the Start menu, the taskbar, toolbars, ribbons, and dialog boxes was via mouse manipulation. In Windows 8, however, most of these screen elements are gone (or appear only in the Desktop app). Yes, as you saw earlier, you can still use your mouse to display the app bar, the Charms menu, and to scroll the screen, but what if you're using a computer that doesn't even have a mouse? We're talking of course about the tablet PC, a device that is basically just a glass screen with no mouse or keyboard in sight (excluding the cover/keyboard of the Microsoft Surface).

For tablet PCs that come with no input devices, it's now safe to say that Windows 8 was built with *touch* in mind. That is, instead of using a mouse or keyboard to manipulate Windows 8, you use your fingers to touch the screen in specific ways called *gestures*. (Some tablet PCs also come with a small pen-like device called a *stylus,* and you can use the stylus instead of your finger for some actions.)

What are these gestures? Here's a list:

- **Tap**—Use your finger (or the stylus) to touch the screen and then immediately release it. This is the touch equivalent of a mouse click.

- **Double-tap**—Tap and release the screen *twice,* one tap right after the other. This is the touch equivalent of a mouse double-click.

- **Tap and hold**—Tap the screen and leave your finger (or the stylus) resting on the screen until the shortcut menu appears. This is the touch equivalent of a mouse right-click, and it works most often in desktop apps, not Windows 8 apps.

- **Swipe**—Quickly and briefly run your finger along the screen. This usually causes the screen to scroll in the direction of the swipe, so it's roughly equivalent to scrolling with the mouse wheel. You also use the swipe to display some of the Windows 8 interface elements: swipe up from the bottom edge of the screen (or down from the top edge) to display the app bar; swipe left from the right edge to display the Charms menu; swipe down on a tile to select it.

- **Slide**—Place your finger on the screen, move your finger, and then release. This is the touch equivalent of a mouse click and drag, so you usually use this technique to move an object from one place to another. However, this is also ideal for scrolling, so you can scroll the Start screen or a Windows 8 app horizontally by sliding your finger right and left on the screen, making this technique the touch equivalent of clicking and dragging the scroll box.

- **Pinch**—Place two fingers apart on the screen and bring them closer together. This gesture zooms out on whatever is displayed on the screen, such as a photo. On the Start screen, use the pinch gesture to invoke the Semantic Zoom feature.

- **Spread**—Place two fingers close together on the screen and move them farther apart. This gesture zooms in on whatever is displayed on the screen, such as a photo. On the Start screen, use the spread gesture to turn off Semantic Zoom.

■ **Turn**—Place two fingers on the screen and turn them clockwise or counterclockwise. This gesture rotates whatever is displayed on the screen, such as a photo.

You can also use touch to enter text by using the onscreen touch keyboard, shown in Figure 4.9. To display the keyboard in a Windows 8 app, tap inside whatever box you'll be using to type the text; in a Desktop app, tap the Keyboard icon that appears in the taskbar.

🔍 **note**

If you don't see the Keyboard icon in the taskbar, tap and hold the taskbar to display the short-cut menu, tap Toolbars, and then tap Touch Keyboard.

Figure 4.9
To type on a tablet PC, use the touch keyboard.

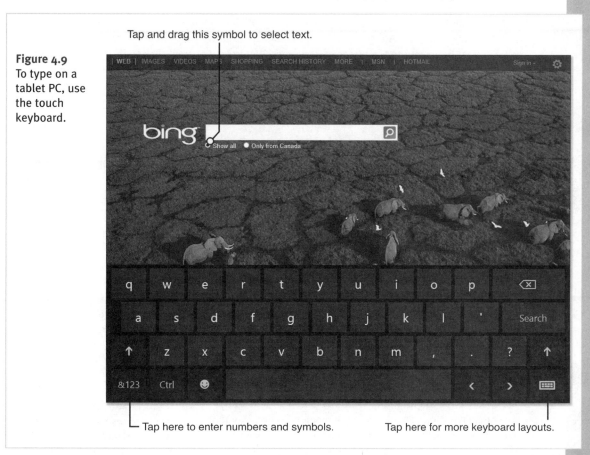

Tap and drag this symbol to select text.

Tap here to enter numbers and symbols.

Tap here for more keyboard layouts.

As pointed out in Figure 4.9, you can tap the key in the bottom-right corner to see a selection of keyboard layouts, including the one shown in Figure 4.9, a split keyboard, and a writing pad for inputting handwritten text using a stylus (or, in a pinch, a finger). There's also a full keyboard available, but you have to follow these steps to enable it:

1. Swipe left from the right edge to display the Charms menu.

2. Tap Settings to open the Settings pane.

3. Tap Change PC Settings to open the PC Settings app.

4. Tap General.

5. Tap the Make the Standard Keyboard Layout Available switch to On.

➡ *To learn more about using the touch keyboard,* **see** *"Touch Keyboard," p. 841.*

Working with Running Apps

One of the ironies of Windows 8 is that, at least as far as the new interface goes, there no longer seems to be any windows. After all, when you launch a Windows 8 app, it doesn't appear inside a "box." So what happened to the windows that gave Windows its name? The truth is that Windows 8 apps do technically appear in a window, it's just that by default these windows take up the entire screen. You see this for yourself over the next three sections as we take you through various techniques for manipulating running apps.

Snapping an App

One way that you can take advantage of the hidden "windowness" of Windows 8 apps is to show two Windows 8 apps onscreen at the same time. So, for example, you could display your Finance app stock watchlist while simultaneously surfing the Web, or watch what your Facebook friends are up to while also shopping in the Windows Store.

You do this by *snapping* the current Windows 8 app to the left or right side of the screen. This means that the app shrinks down to about a quarter of its normal width and parks itself on the left or right side of the screen, and then the next app takes up the rest of the screen. Figure 4.10 shows the Finance app snapped to the left side of the screen, while the Internet Explorer app covers the rest.

How you snap a Windows 8 app depends on whether you're using a regular PC or a tablet PC:

- **Regular PC**—Move the mouse pointer to the top of the screen, where it changes to a hand, and then click and drag the hand down. As you drag, the Windows 8 app shrinks down to a small window. (This is what we mean when we say that Windows 8 apps have a hidden "windowness.") Now drag the smaller window all the way to the left or right side of the screen and then release the mouse button. An easier method is to move the mouse pointer to the top-left corner to display the list of running apps, move the pointer over the app you want to snap, right-click it, and then click either Snap Left or Snap Right.

note

You can't snap an app unless your screen resolution is set to at least 1366×768.

 tip

Another way to snap the current Windows 8 app is to press Windows+. (period). If you hold down the Windows key and tap . (period) repeatedly, Windows 8 cycles the app through snap left, snap right, and full screen.

Figure 4.10
You can display two Windows 8 apps at the same time by snapping an app to the left or right side of the screen.

■ **Tablet PC**—Place your finger at the top edge of the screen, and then slide down until the Windows 8 app shrinks down to a window. Keep dragging your finger to the left or right side of the screen and then release your finger.

Switching Between Running Apps

If you have multiple Windows 8 apps going, Windows 8 gives you two ways to switch between them using a mouse:

■ Position the mouse pointer in the top-left corner of the screen. Windows responds by showing you a thumbnail version of the next running app (see Figure 4.11); click to switch to that app. If you want to cycle through the apps, leave the mouse pointer in the top-left corner and keep clicking.

Figure 4.11
Move the mouse pointer to the top-left corner of the screen to see a thumbnail of the next running app.

- Move the mouse pointer into the top-left corner of the screen and when the thumbnail of the next app appears, slide the mouse pointer straight down. Once you get below the next app, Windows 8 displays a list of all running Windows 8 apps, as shown in Figure 4.12. Click the app you want to use. Notice, too, that the list of running Windows 8 apps includes the Start screen at the bottom, and you can click that to return to the Start screen.

Figure 4.12
Move the mouse pointer to the top-left corner of the screen and then slide it down to see a list of your up-and-running Windows 8 apps.

Here are the techniques to use to switch between Windows 8 apps using a tablet PC:

- To switch to the next running app, slide to the right from the left edge of the screen. Your finger drags in a thumbnail of the next app, and when you release your finger from the screen the app fills up the screen.

- To see the list of running Windows 8 apps, slide in from the left edge again, but this time when you see the next app appear under your finger, reverse course and slide your finger back to the left edge of the screen. As soon as your finger hits the ledge, the app disappears and you see the list of running apps, and you then tap the one you want.

tip
You can also switch to another Windows 8 app using the keyboard. For example, you can quickly switch between the current Windows 8 app and the Start screen by pressing the Windows Logo key. You can also hold down the Windows key and then tap Tab. When you do this, Windows 8 displays the list of running Windows 8 apps. With the Windows key held down, keep pressing Tab until the app you want is highlighted, then release the Windows key.

Shutting Down an App

Generally speaking, you don't have to worry about shutting down Windows 8 apps because when they don't have the focus they use very few system resources. However, if you're having trouble with a Windows 8 app, or if you just want to make it easier to switch between the other running apps, then you need to know how to shut down a Windows 8 app. How you do this depends on whether you're using a regular PC or a tablet PC:

- **Regular PC**—Move the mouse pointer to the top of the screen, where it changes to a hand, and then click and drag the hand down. As you drag, the Windows 8 app window shrinks down to a thumbnail window. Keep dragging the window all the way to the bottom of the screen, and then release the mouse button. Alternatively, move the mouse pointer to the top-left corner to display the list of running apps, move the pointer over the app you want to close, right-click it, and then click Close. If all that just feels like a bit too much work, you can also just press Alt+F4 to close the current Windows 8 app.

- **Tablet PC**—Place your finger at the top edge of the screen, and then slide down until the Windows 8 app window shrinks down to a thumbnail window. Keep dragging your finger to the bottom of the screen, and then release your finger.

Working with Notifications

If you're a Windows old-timer, then you're certainly all too familiar with the notification area in the taskbar, which displays banners whenever Windows or an application has information for you. Those notifications are still available in the Desktop app, but now they only work for desktop programs. Windows 8 and all Windows 8 apps use a new notification system. For example, you might add an appointment to the Calendar app and ask the app to remind you about it, and that reminder appears as a notification. Similarly, someone might send you a text message, and the Messaging app displays the text as a notification.

These notifications appear briefly in the upper-right corner of the screen. For example, Figure 4.13 shows the notification that appears when you insert a USB flash drive. In this case, Windows 8 is wondering what you want to do with the drive.

> **tip**
>
> Notifications appear for only a few seconds. To keep a notification onscreen indefinitely, move your mouse pointer over the notification.

To handle the notification, click it. Windows 8 then takes you to the app that generated the notification. If the notification was generated by Windows 8 itself, it displays more information. In the flash drive example, Windows 8 displays a list of options similar to the one shown in Figure 4.14.

Figure 4.13
Notifications appear in the upper-right corner of the screen.

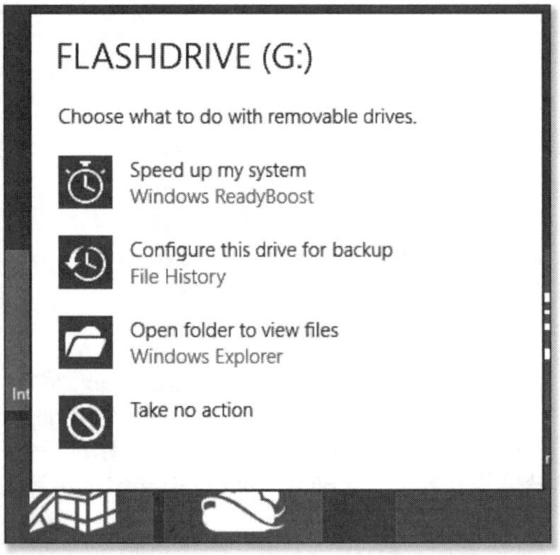

Figure 4.14
Click a notification, and Windows 8 either displays more information, as shown here, or switches to the app that generated the notification.

Searching via the Start Screen

If you use your PC regularly, there's an excellent chance that its hard drive is crammed with thousands, perhaps even tens of thousands, of files that take up hundreds, perhaps even thousands, of gigabytes. That's a lot of data, but it leads to a huge and growing problem: finding things. Everyone wants to have the proverbial information at their fingertips, but these days our fingertips tend to fumble around more often than not, trying to locate not only documents and other data we've created ourselves, but also apps, Windows settings, and that wealth of information that exists "out there" on the Web, in databases, and so on.

Windows 8 attempts to solve this problem by combining *all* search operations into a single interface element called the Search pane. Using this deceptively simple pane with its single text box, Windows 8 lets you search for apps by name, for Windows 8 settings and features, for documents, for app data, and more.

To get to the Search pane, display the Charms menu and click Search. (You can also use some shortcut methods, which we'll discuss as well.) Figure 4.15 shows the Search pane that appears.

Figure 4.15
The Windows 8 Search pane.

The Search pane consists of a text box followed by a collection of icons. Here's what they do:

- **Apps**—Click this icon to search for an app by name. Note, too, that app searching is the default in Windows 8, so you can initiate an app search from the Start screen just by typing your search text.

- **Settings**—Click this icon to search for a setting that's available either in the PC Settings app or the Control Panel. Note that this is a search that includes metadata (specifically, descriptions embedded in each setting), so you don't have to search for a specific setting name. To display the Search pane with Settings preselected, press Windows Logo+W.

- **Files**—Click this icon to search through your user account libraries. To display the Search pane with Files preselected, press Windows Logo+F.

- **Within apps**—The rest of the Search pane icons represent individual Windows 8 apps that implement a search contract. When you select one of these icons, you're doing a search within that app. For example, click Internet Explorer to search the Web using Bing; click Maps to search for a location; or click Music to search for bands, songs, or albums.

As you type, Search displays the results that match your search text, as shown in Figure 4.16. When you see the item you want, click it.

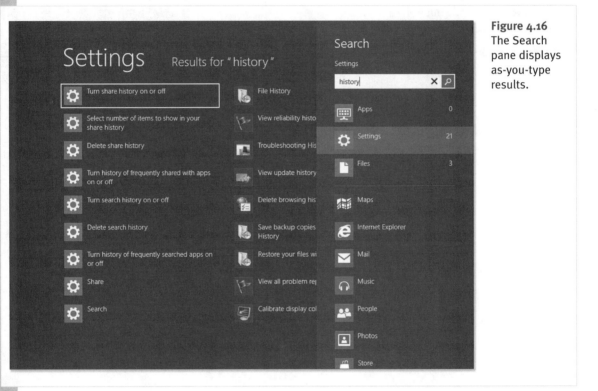

Figure 4.16
The Search pane displays as-you-type results.

To learn how to customize Start screen searching, **see** "Customizing Search," **p. 566.**

Customizing the Start Screen

The Start screen, with its live tiles and easy access (just press the Windows Logo key), is meant to be a kind of automatically and frequently updated bulletin board that tells you what's going on in your life: your latest messages, your upcoming appointments, the music you're listening to, the weather, the latest news and financial data, and so on. The key phrase here is "*your* life," meaning that it's unlikely the default configuration of the Start screen will be a reflection of who you are, what you do, and how you use Windows 8. Fortunately, the default Start screen layout isn't set in stone, so you're free to customize it by resizing and moving tiles, grouping tiles, adding new tiles, and much more. The next few sections provide the details.

Resizing a Tile

The Start screen tiles come in two sizes: small, as seen with the Internet Explorer and Store tiles, and large, as seen with the Mail and Calendar tiles. The large size is useful for tiles that are live, because the tile has more room to display information. However, if you've turned off the live tile for an app (see "Turning Off a Live Tile," later in this chapter), then the large tile size now seems like a waste of screen real estate, so you might prefer to use the smaller size. Similarly, if your turn on the live tile for an app that's using the smaller tile, you might see only limited information in the tile. For example, when the Mail app is small, it only shows the number of new messages you have, compared to showing you a preview of the new messages when the tile is larger.

Whatever the scenario, you can resize a tile by right-clicking it (or swiping down on it if you're using a tablet PC) to display the app bar and then clicking Smaller (if the tile is currently large; see Figure 4.17) or Larger (if the tile is currently small).

Figure 4.17
Right-click (or swipe down on) a tile and then click Smaller or Larger.

Moving a Tile

One of the problems many new users have with the Windows 8 Start screen is the slight delay that occurs when they try to find the app they want to launch. This is particularly true when you have many live tiles on the go, because you no longer see the app name in each tile, just the app icon. If this is the case with just the default Start screen tiles displayed, it's only going to get worse once you start adding more tiles (see "Pinning a Program to the Start Screen," later in this chapter).

One way to reduce this problem is to rearrange the Start screen in such a way that it helps you locate the apps you use most often. For example, you could place your favorite apps on the left side of the screen, or you could arrange similar apps together (for example, all the media-related apps).

Here are the techniques to use to move an app tile:

- **Regular PC**—Use your mouse to click and drag the tile and then drop it on the new location.

- **Tablet PC**—Use your finger (or a stylus) to tap and drag the tile and then drop it on the new location.

Creating an App Group

If you examine the default Start screen, you notice a gap between the four "lifestyle" apps (News, Sports, Travel, and Finance) on the right, and the rest of the apps on the left. This gap tells you that these two sections of the Start screen represent special collections of apps called *app groups*. You can make the Start screen much easier to navigate and apps much easier to find by creating your own groups of related apps. You can also apply a name to your groups, which makes the Start screen even easier to work with.

Follow these steps to create an app group:

1. Drag the first tile you want to include in the group to the left side of the Start screen until you see a vertical bar appear, as shown in Figure 4.18, and then drop the tile. Windows 8 creates a new group on the left side of the Start screen.

The vertical bar indicates a new group.

Figure 4.18
Drag the first group tile to the left side of the screen until you see the vertical bar.

2. For each tile you want to include in the group, drag it to the left side of the screen and then drop it inside the new group.

3. Press Ctrl+- (hyphen) or pinch the screen to zoom out.

4. If you want your group to appear elsewhere in the Start screen, drag the group to the position you prefer.

5. Right-click the group and then click Name Group. Windows 8 displays a dialog box for naming the group, as shown in Figure 4.19.

6. Type the name you want to use and then click Name.

7. Click the screen. Windows 8 zooms back in and your new group is done.

The New App Group

Figure 4.19
Right-click the group and then click Name group to give your new group a name.

The name now appears at the top of the group. Rename the group at any time by repeating steps 5–7.

Turning Off a Live Tile

As we mentioned earlier, the Start screen offers a kind of aerial view of what's happening in your life, and it does this by displaying live content—called *tile notifications*—on many of the tiles. That seems like a good idea in theory, but much of that live content is not static. For example, if you have multiple email messages waiting for you, the Mail tile continuously flips through previews of each unread message. Similarly the News and Finance tiles constantly flip through several screens of content.

This tile animation ensures that you see lots of information, but it can be distracting and hard on the eyes. If you find the Start screen is making you *less* productive instead of more, you can tone down the Start screen by turning off one or more of the less useful live tiles. You do that by right-clicking a tile (or swiping down on the tile if you're a tablet user) and then clicking Turn Live Tile Off.

 tip

If you'd like to see no live content for a minute or two, you can temporarily turn off all live tiles. From the Start screen, display the Charms menu and then click Settings (or just press Windows Logo+I), click Tiles, and then click Clear.

tip

You can clear tile notifications automatically when you sign out or when you restart or shut down Windows 8. In the Start screen (or the Run dialog box; press Windows Logo+R), type **gpedit.msc** and then press Enter to open the Local Group Policy Editor. Open the User Configuration, Administrative Templates, Start Menu and Taskbar branch, double-click the Clear History of Tile Notifications on Exit policy, select Enabled, and then click OK.

Pinning a Program to the Start Screen

One of the significant conveniences of the Start screen is that the apps you see can all be opened with just a single click or tap. Contrast this with the relatively laborious process required to launch just about any other program on your PC: right-click the Start screen (or swipe up from the bottom edge on a tablet), click All Apps, scroll through the Apps screen to find the program you want to run, and then click it. Alternatively, you can start typing the name of the program and then click it when it appears in the Apps search screen.

Either way, this seems like a great deal of effort to launch a program, and it's that much worse for a program you use often. You can avoid all that extra work and make a frequently used program easier to launch by pinning that program to the Start screen.

Follow these steps to pin a program to the Start screen:

1. Use the Apps screen or the Apps search screen to locate the program you want to pin.

2. Right-click the program tile (or, on a tablet PC, swipe down on the tile) to display the app bar.

3. Click Pin to Start. Windows 8 adds a tile for the program to the Start screen.

 tip

If you have a folder that you open frequently, you can pin that folder to the Start screen. Click Desktop, click File Explorer in the taskbar, and then open the location that contains the folder you want to pin. Click the folder and then select Home, Easy Access, Pin to Start.

Pinning a Website to the Start Screen

If you have a website that you visit often, you can use the Internet Explorer app to pin the website to the Start screen. This means that you can surf to that site simply by clicking its Start screen tile.

Follow these steps:

1. On the Start screen, click Internet Explorer.

2. Navigate to the website you want to pin.

3. Click the Pin Site icon, which is the pushpin that appears to the right of the address bar, as pointed out in Figure 4.20.

4. Click Pin to Start.

5. Edit the website name, if needed.

6. Click Pin to Start. Windows 8 adds a tile for the website to the Start screen.

 note

To remove a tile from the Start screen, right-click it (or, on a tablet PC, swipe down on the tile) and then click Unpin from Start. Windows 8 removes the tile from the Start screen.

Displaying the Administrative Tools on the Start Screen

Windows 8 comes with a set of advanced programs and features called the administrative tools. We cover many of these tools in this book, including Performance Monitor, Resource Monitor, and Services (all covered in Chapter 23, "Windows Management Tools") as well as Disk Cleanup, Defragment and Optimize Drives, and Computer Management (all covered in Chapter 25, "Managing Hard Disks and Storage Spaces").

➡ *For a rundown of all the administrative tools,* **see** *"Reviewing the Control Panel Icons," p. 507.*

Figure 4.20
Surf to the website and then click Pin to Start.

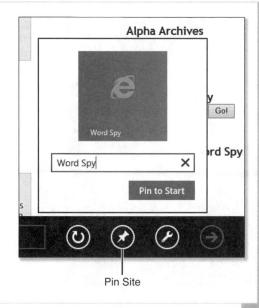

Pin Site

Some of these tools are relatively easy to launch. For example, you can press Windows Logo+X to display a menu that includes Event Viewer, Disk Management, Computer Management, and a few other administrative tools (see Figure 4.21). However, the rest of these tools are difficult to access in Windows 8. For example, to run Defragment and Optimize Drives, you display the Charms menu, click Search, click Settings, type **defrag**, and then click Defragment and Optimize Your Drives in the search results. Other administrative tools aren't even accessible via an apps or settings search, so instead you need to know the tool's filename. For example, to run the System Configuration utility, you type **msconfig** and then press Enter.

This extra effort isn't that big of a deal if you only use the administrative tools once in a while. If you use them frequently, however, all those extra steps are real productivity killers. Instead, configure Windows 8 to display the administrative tools as tiles on the Start screen by following these steps:

1. Display the Charms menu and then click Settings to display the Settings pane. (You can also press Windows Logo+I.)

2. Click Tiles. The Start settings pane appears.

3. Click the Show Administrative Tools switch to Yes.

4. Click the Start screen. The administrative tools appear as tiles on the Start screen, as shown in Figure 4.22.

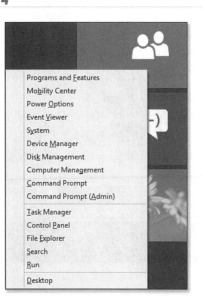

Figure 4.21
Press Windows Logo+X to display this handy menu of power user tools, which includes a few of the administrative tools.

Figure 4.22
The administrative tools displayed as Start screen tiles.

Adding Shutdown and Restart Tiles to the Start Screen

While the Start screen does offer a few productivity improvements—at-a-glance info with live tiles, one-click app launching, as-you-type searching—there are a few tasks that are maddeningly (and, in our view, unnecessarily) inefficient. We're thinking in particular of shutting down and restarting your PC. To perform these tasks using a mouse, you must display the Charms menu, click Settings to open the Start settings pane, click Power, and then click Shut Down or Restart. Yes, you can always go directly to the Settings pane by pressing Windows Logo+I, but then you have to switch back to the mouse to continue. It's just inefficient either way.

If you want to apply the one-click ease of a Start screen tile to shutting down and restarting your PC, we'll show you how you can do just that. The basic idea is to create shortcut files that perform the shut down and restart tasks, and then pin those shortcuts to the Start screen.

So let's begin with the steps required to create the shortcuts:

1. Click the Desktop tile (or press Windows Logo+D) to display the desktop.

2. Right-click the desktop and then select New, Shortcut. The Create Shortcut dialog box appears.

3. Type `shutdown /s /t 0`. This command shuts down your PC. Note that the last character in the command is the number zero.

4. Click Next. Windows 8 prompts you to name the shortcut.

5. Type the name you want to use. The name you type is the name that will appear on the Start screen.

6. Click Finish.

7. For the restart shortcut, repeat steps 2–6, except in step 3 type `shutdown /r /t 0` (again, the last character is a zero).

To help differentiate between these two shortcut files, follow these steps to apply a different icon to each file:

1. Right-click a shortcut and then click Properties. The shortcut's Properties dialog box appears.

2. Click Change Icon. Windows 8 warns you that the shutdown command contains no icons.

3. Click OK. The Change Icon dialog box appears.

4. Click the icon you want to use and then click OK to close the Change Icon dialog box.

> **tip**
>
> Although the `Shell32.dll` file contains plenty of shortcut icons, you can also try two other files:
>
> - `%SystemRoot%\system32\pifmgr.dll`
> - `%SystemRoot\explorer.exe`
>
> Press Enter after you type each location to see the icons.

5. Click OK to close the Properties dialog box.

6. Repeat steps 1–5 to apply a new icon to the other shortcut file.

Finally, pin the shortcuts to the Start screen by right-clicking each shortcut and then clicking Click Pin to Start.

Customizing the Start Screen Background

If you're coming to Windows 8 from an earlier version of Windows, you're probably familiar with the desktop background (or *wallpaper*, as we old-timers still sometimes call it), particularly the fact that you can create a custom desktop background using an image from your Pictures library. This remains a quick way to give your PC a personal look and feel (because you can still customize the background used by the Desktop app).

Alas, that bit of eye candy isn't available for the Windows 8 Start screen, which offers no mechanism for applying a custom photo or other image as its background. All you can do is tweak the color scheme, as follows:

1. Display the Charms menu and then click Settings to display the Settings pane. (You can also press Windows Logo+I.)

2. Click Change PC Settings. The PC Settings app appears.

3. Click Personalize.

4. Click Start Screen. The PC Settings app displays the Start Screen tab, as shown in Figure 4.23.

5. Click the background pattern you want to use (see Figure 4.23). Windows 8 applies the new pattern.

6. Click the color scheme you want to use. Windows 8 applies the new colors.

> **tip**
>
> A faster (if slightly unintuitive) method for getting to the Start Screen tab is to click your user account tile, click Change Account Picture, and then click Start Screen.

Figure 4.23
Use the Start
Screen tab to
customize the
background
pattern and
color scheme.

Start Screen Preview

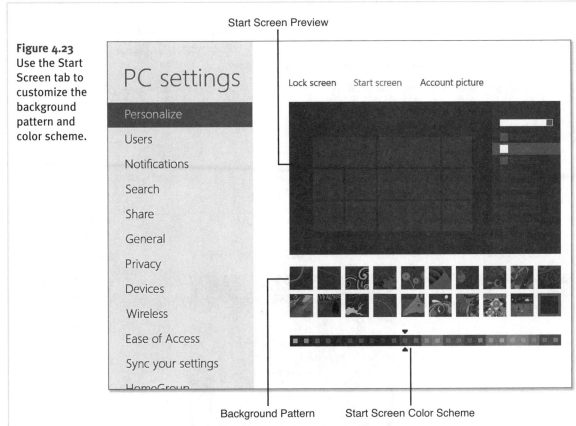

Background Pattern   Start Screen Color Scheme

Customizing the Lock Screen

The Lock screen is the screen that appears before you sign on to Windows 8 (or, if your PC has multiple user accounts, it's the screen that appears before you select which account to sign on). You have three ways to invoke the Lock screen:

- Turn on or restart your PC.

- Sign out of your user account (by clicking your user account tile and then clicking Sign Out).

- Lock your PC (by clicking your user account tile and then clicking Lock, or by pressing Windows Logo+L).

In other words, the Lock screen comes up relatively often when you use Windows 8, so you might as well get the most out of it by customizing it to suit how you work. The next three sections take you through these customizations.

Customizing the Lock Screen Background

If you use the lock screen frequently, you might prefer to view a background image that is different from the default image. To choose a different lock screen background, follow steps 1 to 4 to display the Lock Screen tab and then click one of the default images:

1. Display the Charms menu and then click Settings to display the Settings pane. (You can also press Windows Logo+I.)

2. Click Change PC Settings. The PC Settings app appears.

3. Click Personalize.

4. Click Lock Screen. The PC Settings app displays the Lock Screen tab, as shown in Figure 4.24.

Figure 4.24
Use the Lock Screen tab to customize the background image displayed on the Lock screen.

5. Choose a new background image either by clicking one of the supplied images or by clicking Browse and then using the file picker screen to choose an image from your Pictures library.

> 🔍 **note**
> Another way to apply one of your own images as the Lock screen background is to launch the Photos app, display the image you want to use, right-click the screen, and then select Set As, Lock Screen.

Controlling the Apps Displayed on the Lock Screen

As you learn in Chapter 31, "Protecting Windows from Viruses and Spyware," locking your computer is a useful safety feature because it prevents unauthorized users from accessing your files and your network. When you lock your PC, Windows 8 displays the Lock screen, which includes the current date and time, an icon that shows the current network status, and an icon that shows the current power state of your computer (that is, either plugged in or on battery). By default, Windows 8 also includes Lock screen icons for apps that have had recent notifications. For example, the Mail app shows the number of unread messages, the Messages app shows the number of new text messages, and the Calendar app shows upcoming appointments. The Lock screen also shows any new notifications that appear for these apps.

 To learn more about locking your computer, ***see*** *"Locking Your Computer," **p. 734**.*

If you lock your computer frequently, you can make the Lock screen even more useful by adding icons for other apps that support notifications. Here are the steps to follow:

1. Display the Charms menu and then click Settings to display the Settings pane. (You can also press Windows Logo+I.)

2. Click Change PC Settings. The PC Settings app appears.

3. Click Personalize.

4. Click Lock Screen. The PC Settings app displays the Lock Screen tab.

5. Under Lock Screen Apps, click +. Windows 8 opens the Choose an App window.

6. Click the app you want to add to the lock screen.

7. Under Choose an App to Display Detailed Status, click the icon (or click + if no app is currently selected).

8. Click the app you want to use. Windows 8 puts the new settings into effect, and the apps appear in the Lock screen the next time you use it.

Disabling the Lock Screen

The Lock screen is one of those innovations that seems like a good idea when you first start using it, but then quickly loses its luster the more you come across it. In the case of the Lock screen, the problem is that it forces you to take the extra step of dismissing it before you can sign on:

- **Regular PC**—Press any key or click the screen

- **Tablet PC**—Swipe up

If you've had to perform this extra task one too many times, and if you don't find the Lock screen all that useful anyway, you can disable it. This means you don't see the Lock screen when you start or lock your PC. Instead, Windows 8 takes you directly to the sign-on screen.

Follow these steps to disable the Lock screen:

1. In the Start screen (or the Run dialog box; press Windows Logo+R), type **gpedit.msc** and then press Enter. The Local Group Policy Editor appears.

2. Open the Computer Configuration, Administrative Templates, Control Panel, Personalization branch. The Personalization policies appear.

3. Double-click the Do Not Display the Lock Screen policy. The policy details appear.

4. Click Enabled.

5. Click OK. Windows 8 puts the new policy into effect.

> **caution**
>
> In Chapter 31, we show you how to require that users press Ctrl+Alt+Delete before they log on, which is a helpful security precaution. However, if you configure your PC to require Ctrl+Alt+Delete, then Windows 8 ignores the Do Not Display the Lock Screen policy setting.

Bypassing the Start Screen

The Windows 8 Start screen is a bold and innovative move on Microsoft's part, and now no one can accuse the company of resting on its considerable laurels. Microsoft is clearly looking to a future where computing is just as often performed on a tablet or a smartphone as on a traditional PC. But it's important to understand that Microsoft, unlike Apple, is *not* gearing up for the so-called post-PC world where *all* computing is done on mobile devices. Microsoft is still very much pro-PC, and as evidence you need look no further than the existence of the Desktop app in Windows 8. Although it's jarring and disorienting to switch between the new interface and the Desktop app, Microsoft understands that most people will need to use both environments for the foreseeable future, so Windows 8 stands with a foot in both camps.

However, it's entirely possible that a subset—perhaps even a very *large* subset—of Windows 8 users will find that they have little or no use for the new elements of the Windows 8 interface: the Start screen and the Windows 8 apps it houses. Those people might find that they spend the overwhelming bulk of their time in the familiar environs of the Desktop app, with only occasional forays into Start screen territory.

If your Windows 8 experience is similar, then you've no doubt come across the basic flaw in this plan: the Desktop app isn't a great place for day-to-day Windows tasks because there's no longer a Start button, launching programs takes a bit of work, and Windows 8 often opens files in Windows 8 apps instead of desktop programs.

Well, we've got your back on this one because there *are* ways to make the desktop a more pleasant place to work and play. The next few sections show you the details.

Booting Directly to the Desktop

If there's one question we get asked most often about Windows 8, it's this: "How can I bypass the Start screen and boot directly to the desktop?" No other question comes close, and it's yet another indication that many folks are going to spend time using the Desktop app more than any other Windows feature.

The bad news is that Windows 8 doesn't offer any built-in option that you can set to boot directly to the desktop. There's no setting, no Registry value, no group policy. We experimented with various startup and logon tweaks, but we found them to be flaky and slow. Then we discovered an interesting fact about the Start screen. When Windows 8 first loads and displays the Start screen, pressing Enter automatically loads whatever app's tile is in the upper-left corner of the screen. In a default layout, this is the Mail app. If you create a new app group on the left side of the Start screen, as we described earlier, pressing Enter will launch whatever app is in the upper-left corner of that group.

So one obvious solution here is to move the Desktop tile to the upper-left corner of the Start screen and then press Enter as soon as the Start screen appears.

That works, but we're really looking for a way to bypass the Start screen entirely. You can try timing your Enter keypress to just before the Start screen appears, but that doesn't always work. Instead, when you're at the sign-on screen, type your user account password, and then press and *hold down* Enter. This just sends a series of Enter keypresses to Windows, and eventually one of them triggers the Desktop tile and you sign on directly to the Desktop. Elegant? No, not even close, but it works.

Accessing Start Menu Items from the Taskbar

As we mentioned earlier, perhaps the biggest problem with using Windows 8's Desktop app is the lack of a Start button. How are you supposed to get at the accessories, the system tools, and other Start menu goodies if there's no Start button in sight? Utilities are available that re-create the Start button for you (see, for example, Stardock; www.stardock.com/products/start8/), but you can get the next best thing by configuring the taskbar to give you access to the Start menu items.

Here are the steps to follow:

1. On the Start screen, click the Desktop tile (or press Windows Logo+D). The desktop appears.

2. Right-click an empty section of the taskbar and then select Toolbars, New Toolbar. The New Toolbar – Choose a Folder dialog box appears.

3. Click an empty section of the address bar, type the following folder path, and then press Enter:

   `C:\ProgramData\Microsoft\Windows\Start Menu`

4. Click Select Folder. Windows 8 adds the Start Menu folder as a taskbar toolbar.

As you can see in Figure 4.25, this new toolbar places Start menu items just a few clicks away.

Pinning a Program to the Taskbar

We showed you earlier in this chapter how to pin an app to the Start screen for one-click access. That's great if you spend most of your time in the new interface, but it doesn't do you much good if you're a dedicated desktop denizen. Accessing the Start menu items from the taskbar, as we described in the previous task, is great, but it can take a few clicks to launch some items, so it's not the most efficient way to start those programs you use frequently.

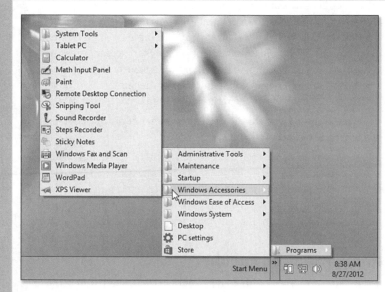

Figure 4.25
Add the Start Menu folder as a taskbar toolbar for easy access to many Start menu items.

A better way to go is to pin your favorite programs to the Desktop app's taskbar, which puts those programs just a click away.

You can pin a program to the taskbar either from the Start screen or from the desktop. First, here's the Start screen method:

1. Use the Apps screen or the Apps search screen to locate the desktop program you want to pin. (Note that this technique doesn't work with Windows 8 apps.)

2. Right-click the program tile. (On a tablet PC, swipe down on the tile to display the app bar.)

3. Click Pin to Taskbar. Windows 8 adds an icon for the program to the taskbar.

Here's how to pin a running desktop program to the taskbar:

1. Launch the program you want to pin.

2. Right-click the running program's taskbar icon. (On a tablet PC, tap and hold the program's taskbar icon.)

3. Click Pin This Program to Taskbar. Windows 8 adds an icon for the program to the taskbar.

Finally, if you displayed the Start Menu toolbar as described in the previous section, you can also follow these steps to pin a Start Menu item to the taskbar:

1. Add the Start Menu toolbar to the taskbar as described in the previous section.

2. Click the Start Menu toolbar arrows.

3. If necessary, open the submenu that contains the program you want to pin to the taskbar. For example, if the program is in the Accessories submenu, select Programs, Windows Accessories.

4. Click and drag the program icon to any empty section of the taskbar.

5. When you see the Pin to Taskbar banner, drop the icon. Windows 8 adds an icon for the program to the taskbar.

 tip

Windows 8 displays the taskbar icons left to right in the order you pinned them. To change the order, click and drag a taskbar icon to the left or right and then drop it in the new position.

Using Desktop Programs as the Defaults

We mentioned earlier that it's jarring to switch between the Start screen and desktop interfaces because they're just so drastically different. Unfortunately, Windows 8 often forces this transition by using many Windows 8 apps as the default programs for certain file types. For example, if you double-click a JPEG file in File Explorer, Windows 8 opens it in the Photos app. Similarly, double-click an MP3 file and Windows 8 plays the song using the Music app.

Fortunately, with a bit of work you can configure Windows 8 to open these and other file types using desktop programs. Here are the steps to follow:

1. Press Windows Logo+X to display the power tool list.

2. Click Control Panel.

3. In the Search box, type **set program**.

4. In the search results, click Set Your Default Programs. The Set Default Programs window appears.

5. Click a desktop program that you want to use for opening one or more file types. For example, to change how Windows opens MP3 files, click Windows Media Player.

6. Click Choose Defaults For This Program. The Set Program Associations window appears.

7. Select the check box beside each file type that you want to associate with this program. For example, in Figure 4.26 you can see that we're working with Windows Media Player and that we've selected the .mp3 check box.

8. Click Save. Windows 8 associates the program with the file types you selected.

9. Repeat steps 5–8 to set the defaults for your other desktop programs.

10. Click OK.

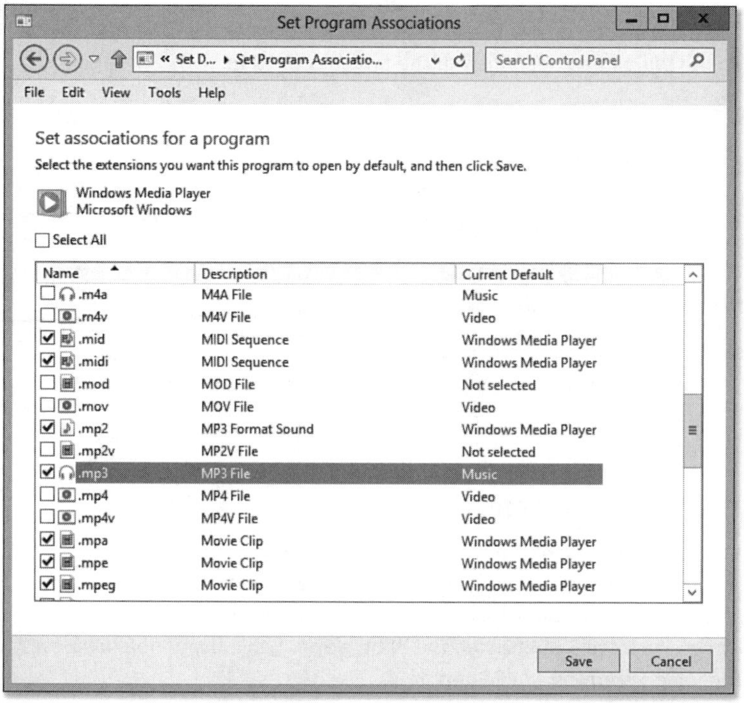

Figure 4.26
Use the Set Program Associations window to associate file types with a desktop program.

5

WINDOWS 8 APPS AND THE WINDOWS STORE

The Windows 8 Apps

When we discussed the new Windows 8 interface in Chapter 4, "Using the Windows 8 Interface," we mentioned that one of Microsoft's fundamental design principles for the interface is "content before chrome." That is, the Windows 8 interface is characterized by an overall style that places content front and center, and where chrome—including menus, scrollbars, and icons—is either hidden most of the time or eliminated altogether.

That principle applies to Windows 8 apps as well, which for the most part adhere to the following guidelines:

- **Clean layout**—Windows 8 app interfaces are characterized by a generous amount of open space, so you won't find lots of graphical knick-knacks such as lines, boxes, and borders. These interfaces are also visually simple, so you won't find color tricks such as gradients and blurs. The result is that the content gets some room to breathe.

- **Uncluttered interface**—Windows 8 apps have lots of white (or black or green or whatever) space surrounding the content. Most Windows 8 apps achieve this look by not leaving commands, navigational aids, and other features displayed full-time. Instead, apps "leverage the edge" by placing commands and features in the app bar (which can be accessed by swiping from the top or bottom edge) or the Charms menu (which can be accessed by swiping from the right edge).

- **Typography conveys hierarchy**—Traditional programs use boxes and lines to separate sections and establish interface hierarchies. Windows 8 apps use typographical indicators—particularly text size, weight, and color—to convey boundaries and hierarchies. For example, Figure 5.1 shows a typical file picker screen, which makes good use of typography to provide a great deal of information.

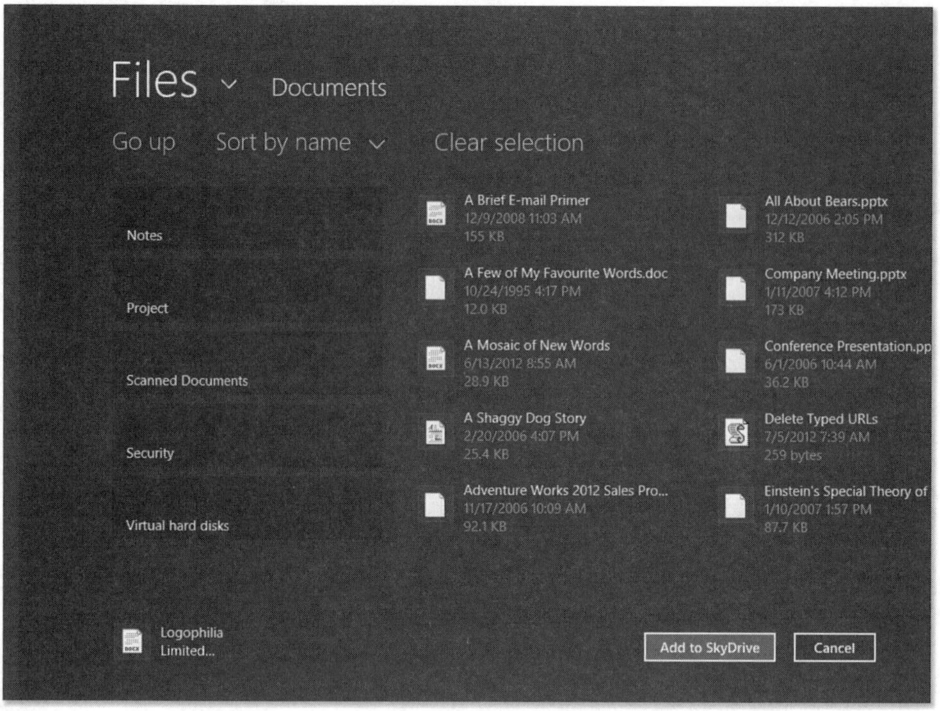

Figure 5.1
Windows 8 apps use consistent typographical conventions to convey boundaries and hierarchies.

- **Direct content interaction**—In most Windows 8 apps, you manipulate the content itself by performing taps, drags, zooms, and swipes directly on an item. Wherever possible, a Windows 8 app doesn't offer separate controls for manipulating content.

Another unique characteristic of Windows 8 apps is that they can work with *contracts*, which are common background services and features that an app can use and that offer a consistent interface to the user. More than a dozen contracts are available to Windows 8 apps, but the following are the four you'll use most often:

- **Search**—Available from the Charms menu, this contract implements in-app searches. For example, tapping the Search charm from within Internet Explorer runs a Bing search on whatever text you enter. You can also use the Search charm to find a location from within the Maps app.

- **Settings**—Available from the Charms menu, this contract displays the app's Settings pane, which can include links to program options and information.

■ **Printing**—Available via Devices in the Charms menu, this contract displays a list of devices—both local (that is, connected directly to your PC) and remote (that is, on your network)—that you can use to print content in the current app.

■ **Share**—Available from the Charms menu, this contract enables you to send app data to another person, either via the Mail app, or to a social network via the People app. See "Sharing Windows 8 App Data," later in this chapter.

Calendar

Calendar is Windows 8's scheduling app, enabling you to create events for meetings, appointments, get-togethers, and all-day tasks such as conferences and vacations. By default, Calendar displays events from three calendars (see Figure 5.2):

■ Your personal calendar associated with your Microsoft account. These events appear with a blue background.

■ A Birthdays calendar that displays birthdays from contacts associated with your Microsoft account as well as contacts from any other online accounts connected to your Microsoft account (such as Facebook). Birthdays appear with a light purple background.

■ A Holidays calendar that shows prominent holidays from your location (for example, a U.S. Holidays calendar if you're located in the United States). Holidays appear with a dark purple background.

> **note**
>
> To change the colors of the calendars, press Windows Logo+I (or display the Charms menu and click Settings) and then click Options to open the Options pane. For each calendar, click the current color and then use the color picker to choose the color you want. Note, too, that you can also use the Options pane to hide a particular calendar by clicking its Show switch to Hide.

You can also add other accounts to Calendar. Press Windows Logo+I (or display the Charms menu and click Settings) and then click Accounts to open the Accounts pane. Click Add an Account, click Exchange or Google, and then fill in the details.

To change the calendar view, right-click the screen and then click one of the three views: Day, Week, or Month. Whichever view you choose, note that you navigate by clicking the Next and Previous arrows, pointed out in Figure 5.2. (If you don't see these arrows, move your mouse over the Calendar screen.) If you're using a touchscreen, you can also navigate the Calendar view by swiping right and left.

To add an event, either click the day of the event in Month view or click the time the event occurs (on the day it occurs) in Week or Day view.

Click these arrows to navigate the current Calendar view.

Figure 5.2
By default,
the Calendar
app shows
you personal
events, birth-
days, and
holidays.

Bing

This app takes you directly to a Bing search screen, where you can perform web searches without having to load the Internet Explorer app. The Bing app displays search results as tiles that show the web page name and address and a brief description of the page.

Camera

If your PC or tablet has a built-in or connected camera, you can use the Camera app to take a photo or record a video:

- **Photo**—To take a photo, click the Camera app on the Start screen, and then click on the screen where you see the picture to take the photo.

- **Video**—Click the Camera app on the Start screen; then, to record a video, first click the Video Mode icon to activate it (that is, give the icon a white background). Click the screen to start the recording, and then click the screen again to stop.

In both cases, you can click to activate the Timer icon, which gives you a 3-second countdown before Camera takes the photo or begins recording the video.

Photos and videos you shoot with the Camera app are stored in your user account's Pictures library, in the Camera Roll folder.

Finally, you can also click Camera Options to configure various settings, which vary depending on your camera. For example, you can choose a photo resolution and audio input device for video recording, and you can turn on video stabilization (if your camera supports it).

Desktop

Desktop is perhaps the simplest of the apps in that it does just one thing: displays the Windows 8 desktop. (You can also get there by pressing Windows Logo+D.) The Desktop app has no app bar, and if you open the Charms menu and click Settings, the pane that appears gives you links for Control Panel, Personalization, and PC Info (which displays the System window).

Finance

The Finance app is Windows 8's one-stop shop for business, economic, and investing news and statistics, gathered by Bing Finance. The main Finance app screen is divided horizontally into eight sections:

- **Today**—The top story of the day as well as recent values of market indices such as the Dow and the NASDAQ.

- **Indices**—Current values and daily, weekly, monthly, or yearly charts for four market indices: Dow, S&P 500, NASDAQ, and Russell 2000 (see Figure 5.3).

Figure 5.3
The Indices section of the main Finance app screen.

- **News**—The latest news stories from the world of finance.

- **Watchlist**—A list of stocks that you're watching. Note that you only see this section if you've added at least one stock. To add a stock to your list, right-click the screen, click Watchlist in the app bar, click Add (+), type the company name or stock symbol, and then click the stock you want in the list that appears.

- **Market Movers**—The stocks with the highest percentage gains and losses on the day, as well as the most actively traded stocks. NASDAQ stocks are displayed by default, but you can see other exchanges by clicking Market Movers and then clicking NYSE or AMEX.

- **Across the Market**—Recent values for various currencies, bonds, commodities, and exchange-traded funds.

- **Rates**—Recent rates for mortgages, savings accounts, and credit card accounts.

- **Fund Picks**—Lists of top-performing mutual funds in various categories.

> **note**
>
> By default, Finance shows you information tailored to your current Windows 8 regional setting. To see news and data from a different region, press Windows Logo+I (or display the Charms menu and click Settings), click Settings, and then use the Display Content From list to choose the location you want. Restart Finance to put the new setting into effect.

You can also see extra news and data from various categories by right-clicking the screen and using the app bar to click a category: Today, Watchlist, News, Rates, Currencies, World Market, or Best of Web.

Internet Explorer

The Internet Explorer app is a vastly scaled-down version of desktop Internet Explorer. Besides standard web browsing (that is, typing a new address, clicking links, and using the Back and Forward buttons to navigate your session history), you can only do the following with the Internet Explorer app:

- **Select a frequent site**—When you click inside the Address box, Internet Explorer displays a list of the websites you've visited most often, as shown in Figure 5.4. Click one of those tiles to surf to that site.

- **Pin a site**—Rather than storing favorites, as in desktop Internet Explorer, the Internet Explorer app enables you pin a site, which you do by clicking the Pin Site icon to the right of the Address box and then clicking Pin to Start. This not only adds the site to the Pinned section of the browser (this section appears to the right of the Frequent section when you click within the Address box), but it also adds a tile for the site to the Start screen.

- **Add a tab**—To load a page into a new tab, right-click the screen and then click New Tab (+), or press Ctrl+T. To load a link into a new background tab, hold down Ctrl as you click the link; to load a link into a new foreground tab, hold down Shift and Ctrl as you click the link. To shut down a tab, right-click the screen and then click the Close (X) button in the top-right corner of the tab.

Figure 5.4
The Internet Explorer app maintains a list of sites you've visited often.

- **Browse privately**—To start a surfing session where Internet Explorer doesn't store your browsing history (addresses visited, page data, cookies, and so on), right-click the screen, click Tab Tools (the ellipsis icon), and then click New InPrivate Tab.

That, we're sorry to say, is about it. There are a few (a very few) options you can configure by pressing Windows Logo+I and then clicking Internet Options. What about security, you ask? The Internet Explorer app runs in enhanced protected mode by default, so it's super-secure right out of the box, although that also means it doesn't support add-ons and other interface extensions.

 *To learn about enhanced protected mode, **see** "Understanding Internet Explorer's Advanced Options," p. 753.*

Mail

The Mail app is an extremely simple mail client that offers only the most basic functionality: sending messages, responding to messages (Reply, Reply to All, or Forward), moving messages to different folders (although you need to create new folders online), and deleting messages.

To create a new message, click New (+) and then use the screen that appears to fill in the message details. Click Attachments to add a file attachment; click More Details to add a Bcc field and a

Priority list; and when the cursor is inside the message field, you can right-click to see the available formatting options, as shown in Figure 5.5. Click More to insert a bulleted or numbered list, as well as to undo or redo an operation.

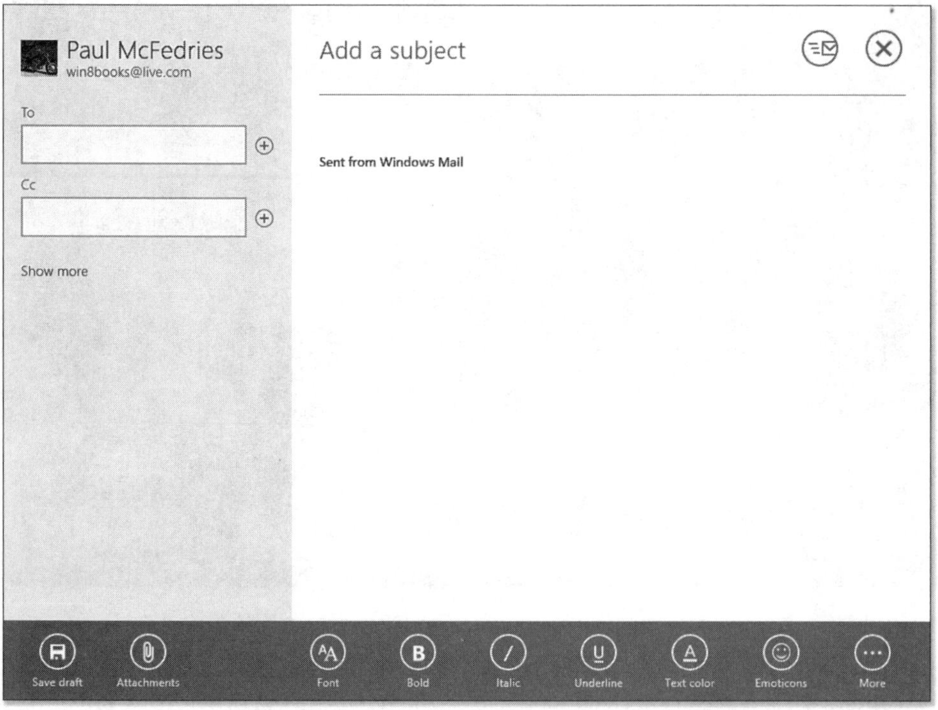

Figure 5.5
Right-click when using the message field to see these formatting options.

You can also add other accounts to Mail. Press Windows Logo+I (or display the Charms menu and click Settings) and then click Accounts to open the Accounts pane. Click Add an Account, click Hotmail, Exchange, or Google, and then fill in the account details.

Maps

The Maps app is a simple mapping program. Besides enabling you to peruse the map, the Maps app also offers the following features, most of which require the app bar, as shown in Figure 5.6:

- **Search for a location**—Display the Charms menu, click Search, and then type the address or name of the location you want.

- **Display your current location**—In the app bar, click My Location to have the map zero in on your present location. (If this doesn't work, see the steps that follow this list.)

- **Get directions to a location**—In the app bar, click Directions and then specify a starting point (the default is your current location) and a destination.

- **Change the map view**—In the app bar, click Map Style and then click Road View or Aerial View (that is, satellite view).

- **Show current traffic conditions**—In the app bar, click Show Traffic to overlay traffic data on the map. Routes shown in green have good traffic, whereas routes shown in shades of orange have heavy traffic (the deeper the orange, the heavier the traffic).

Figure 5.6
The Maps app and its app bar.

To get the most out of Maps, you should make sure your Windows 8 PC has the Windows Location platform turned on:

1. Press Windows Logo+W to open the Settings search pane.

2. Type **location**.

3. In the search results, click Location Settings. The Location Settings window appears.

4. Activate the Turn On the Windows Location Platform check box (it it's not checked already) and then click Apply.

You also need to give Maps (and other apps) permission to use your location. From the Start screen, press Windows Logo+I (or display the Charms menu and click Settings), click Change PC Settings, click Privacy, and then make sure the Let Apps Use My Location switch is On.

Messaging

You use the Messaging app to exchange instant messages with your friends. By default, your "friends" are the contacts associated with your Microsoft account's Messenger service. However, you can also connect your Microsoft account to your Facebook account and exchange instant messages with Facebook friends who are online.

To start a new conversation, right-click the screen and then click New to open the People app. Click Online Only to see who's available to chat, click a contact, and then click Select. As you can see in Figure 5.7, the main part of the screen shows the current conversation, and the left side shows a list of your current conversations. Messaging also lets you know about new messages by displaying a notification when a message arrives, and by using its live Start screen tile to display recent messages.

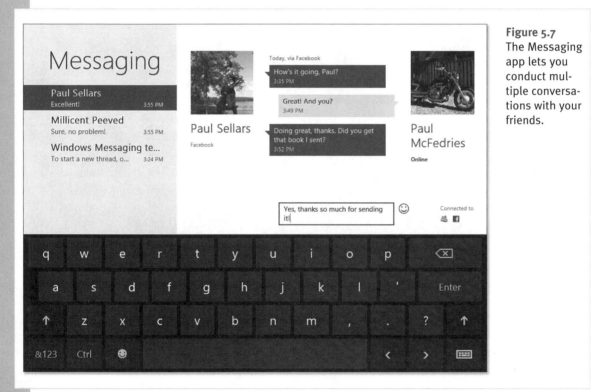

Figure 5.7
The Messaging app lets you conduct multiple conversations with your friends.

If you want to change your status, right-click the screen, click Status, and then click an option: Online, Invisible, or Not Connected.

Music

You use the Music app to play the music that's on your PC, or to purchase new songs or albums. The main Music screen is divided into four sections:

- **My Music**—This section displays tiles for several of your albums, plus an extra tile that includes a Play All Music button. To see all your music, click My Music. To listen to an album, click it and then click Play. Once you have an album open, you can also click a song and then click Play to hear just that song. Click Add to Now Playing to show the current music in the Now Playing tile (discussed next).

- **Now Playing**—This section offers previews of upcoming music. Click a tile and then click Preview Top Songs to hear snippets from the album. This section also includes a large Now Playing tile that tells you what's currently playing in the app.

- **Xbox Music Store**—This section offers several tiles for newly released albums. You can also click Xbox Music Store to see a complete list of new music organized by genre.

- **Most Popular**—This section offers several tiles for the most popular albums. You can also click Most Popular to see a complete list of popular music organized by genre.

In both the Xbox Music Store and Most Popular sections, click an album to open it (see Figure 5.8) and then click Preview to get a taste. If you like what you hear, click Buy Album. Alternatively, if you only want a particular song, click it and then click Buy Song.

 note

To purchase music, you need to have enough Microsoft Points in your account. If you don't have enough, the Music app will let you know and offer a Buy Points button that you can click to purchase more points. You can also press Windows Logo+I (or display the Charms menu and click Settings), click Account, and then click either Microsoft Points (to purchase points) or Redeem Code (if you have a Microsoft Points gift card).

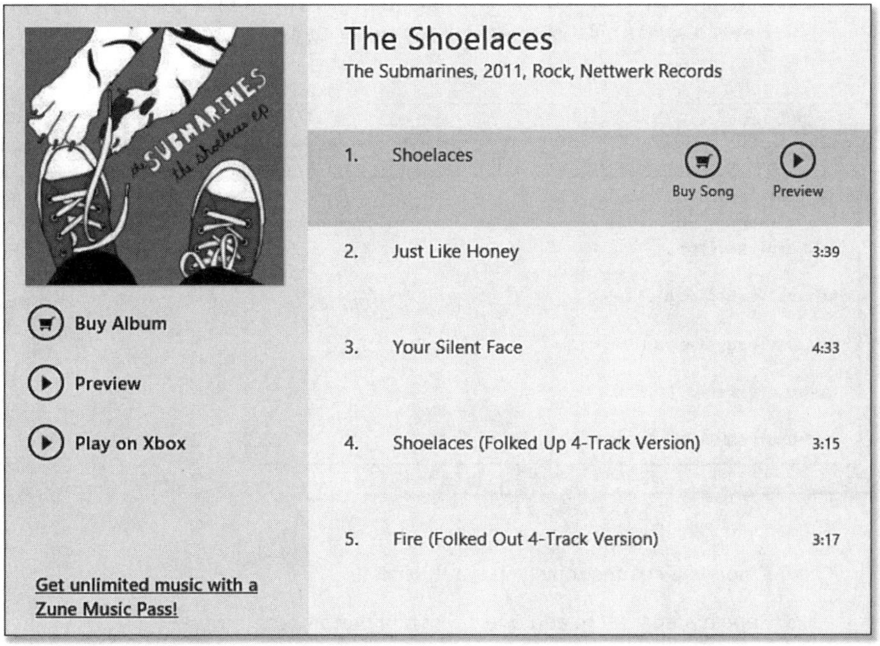

Figure 5.8
When you open an album, you can either buy the entire album or just a song.

The Shoelaces
The Submarines, 2011, Rock, Nettwerk Records

1.	Shoelaces	Buy Song	Preview
2.	Just Like Honey		3:39
3.	Your Silent Face		4:33
4.	Shoelaces (Folked Up 4-Track Version)		3:15
5.	Fire (Folked Out 4-Track Version)		3:17

Buy Album

Preview

Play on Xbox

Get unlimited music with a Zune Music Pass!

If you can't find what you want in the Music app (and you probably can't), use the Search contract to find what you're looking for. Display the Charms menu, click Search, and then type the name of the band, album, or song.

News

The News app offers the latest news stories from various categories, which are listed on the main News screen and include World, Technology, Business, Entertainment, Politics, and Sports. The main screen also includes a Top Story section and a section related to news from your region. To see a list of the sources used by the News app, right-click the screen and then click Sources. In the Sources screen, you can also click a source to see articles from just that media outlet.

Most usefully, the News app includes a My News screen that enables you to display articles on those news topics that most interest you. Here's how you set up the My News screen:

> **🔍 note**
>
> By default, News shows you stories tailored to your current Windows 8 regional setting. To see articles from a different region, press Windows Logo+I (or display the Charms menu and click Settings), click Settings, and then use the Display Content From list to choose the location you want. Restart News to put the new setting into effect.

1. In the News app, right-click the screen and then click My News. The News app opens the My News screen.

2. If you have no sections added, click Add a Section (+). Otherwise, right-click the screen and then click Add a Section.

3. Use the Add a Section text box to begin typing the news topic you want to follow. As you type, News displays a list of matching topics, as shown in Figure 5.9.

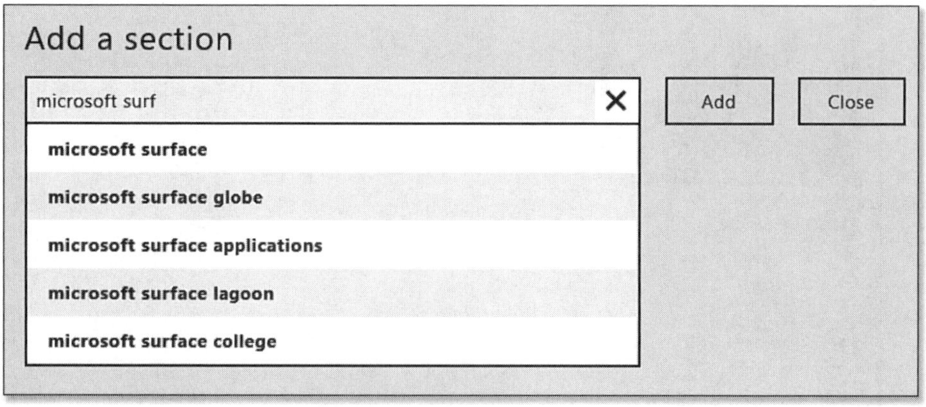

Add a section

| microsoft surf | ✕ | | Add | | Close |

microsoft surface

microsoft surface globe

microsoft surface applications

microsoft surface lagoon

microsoft surface college

Figure 5.9
Type the news topic you want to add as a section in the My News screen.

4. When you see the topic you want, click it.

5. Repeat steps 2–4 to add other sections that interest you.

People

The People app may be the most ambitious of the default Windows 8 apps. Why? First, it's a competent contacts manager that can store a wide variety of information about each person, including name, company name, email address, web address, street address, phone number, and job title. More significantly, People acts as the social networking hub for your Windows 8 PC. Not only does People automatically connect to the social network associated with your Microsoft account, but it can also connect that account to other social networks, including Facebook, Twitter, and LinkedIn (see Figure 5.10). To add a social network account, click Add More Accounts and then click the account type. From there, you log in to your social network and give permission for your Microsoft account to access your social network profile.

Figure 5.10
You can use the People app to connect your Microsoft account to a number of social networking accounts, including Facebook, Twitter, and LinkedIn.

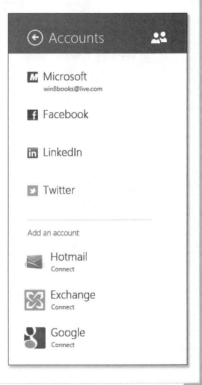

Once you're connected to other social networks, your contacts from those networks—for example, your Facebook friends, LinkedIn connections, and the people you follow on Twitter—now appear in the People section of the app. You have various ways to view and interact with these contacts. To do this, you use the two main headings at the top of the People app screen (if you don't see these headings, right-click the screen and then click Home):

- **All**—Displays a list of all your contacts. To view information about a contact and see that person's latest social network activity, click the contact in the All section. The screen that appears enables you to view the person's profile, view the latest updates, and see the latest photos.

- **Social**—Displays links to your social networks. To see the latest updates (tweets, Facebook posts, and so on), click the What's New link. Note, too, that you can interact with these updates. For example, you can like or comment on a Facebook post, and you can favorite, retweet, or reply to a tweet. To see notifications from your social networks, Twitter mentions and direct messages, and similar items related to you, click the Me link.

> **tip**
>
> To disconnect a social network from your Microsoft account, click Connected To in the upper-right corner to open the Accounts pane, click the account you want to disconnect, and then click Manage This Account Online. Windows 8 switches to Internet Explorer and loads the account's settings page. Click Remove This Connection Completely and then click Remove when asked to confirm.

Photos

The Photos app is the Windows 8 home for all your photos, both on your PC and in your social networks. The main Photos screen is divided into the following five sections:

- **Pictures Library**—Click this tile to see a list of the subfolders in your Pictures library, then click a subfolder to see its images.

- **Facebook**—If you've connected your Facebook account to your Microsoft account, click this tile to see a list of the albums on your Facebook profile.

- **SkyDrive Photos**—Click this tile to see the images in your SkyDrive's Pictures folder.

- **Flickr**—If you have a Flickr account, click this tile to connect to that account and display your Flickr albums.

- **Devices**—Click this tile to view the photos on your connected devices. For this to work, each device must be running the SkyDrive software, available from http://skydrive.com/windows.

In each case, once you open a folder you can scroll left and right through the images, or you can click an image to view it full-screen and then use the left and right arrow keys to navigate the rest of the photos. You can also right-click the screen and then click Slide Show to view the images in the current folder as an automatic slide show.

> **tip**
>
> If there are any sections of the Photos app you never use, you can hide them. Press Windows Logo+I (or display the Charms menu and click Settings) to open the Settings pane, and then click Settings. Click the switch to Off for each section you want to hide.

SkyDrive

SkyDrive is a simple file uploader that enables you to send files from your PC to your SkyDrive:

1. Click the SkyDrive folder you want to use as the upload destination.

2. Right-click the screen and then click Add.

3. Use the file picker screen to select the file you want to upload.

4. Click Add to SkyDrive. The SkyDrive app uploads the file.

Sports

The Sports app is loaded with sports-related news, stats, and standings. The main Sports app screen is divided horizontally into four sections:

- **Top Story**—The top sports story of the day.

- **News**—The latest news stories from the world of sports.

- **Schedule**—Upcoming games in whatever major sports are currently playing.

- **Favorite Teams**—A list of the teams you're watching. To add a team to your list, click Add (+), type the team name, and then click the team you want in the list that appears. You can then click the team to get extra information related to that team, including news (see Figure 5.11), schedules, results, individual stats, team stats, and the team roster.

Figure 5.11
Add your favorite teams to the Sports app to get great extra news and stats related to those teams.

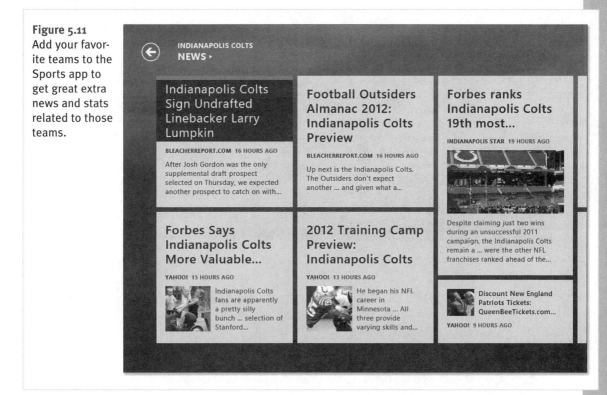

note

By default, Sports shows you information tailored to your current Windows 8 regional setting. To see sports news and data from a different region, press Windows Logo+I (or display the Charms menu and click Settings), click Settings, and then use the Display Content From list to choose the location you want. Restart Sports to put the new setting into effect.

You can also see extra news and data from various leagues by right-clicking the screen and using the app bar to click a league (such as NFL, NBA, MLB, or NHL).

Store

You use the Store app to access the online Windows Store and browse and purchase new Windows 8 apps for your Windows 8 PC. The main Store screen is divided into a number of app categories, including Spotlight, Games (see Figure 5.12), Social, Entertainment, Photo, Lifestyle, and Tools.

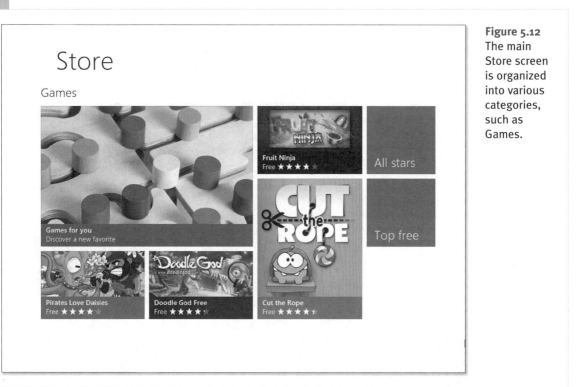

Figure 5.12
The main Store screen is organized into various categories, such as Games.

In each category, you have four choices:

- Click an app tile to see that app's details.

- Click New Releases to see a list of the latest apps added to the category.

- Click Top Free to see a list of the most popular free apps in the category.

- Click the category name to see a complete list of the apps in the category. From there, you can filter the apps by price (for example, Free or Paid), and you can sort the apps (for example, by highest rating or by newest).

Clicking an app displays the app's details, including its user rating, price, description and features, user reviews, permissions, and more. See also "Installing Apps from the Windows Store," later in this chapter.

Travel

The Travel app is designed to help you research travel destinations and then book your trip once you've decided where to go. On the research front, the main Travel app screen is divided horizontally into four sections:

- **Today**—The top travel destination of the day.

- **Featured Destination**—Several tiles displaying travel destination chosen by the editors of Bing Travel. You can also click More to see an additional list of destinations.

- **Panoramas**—360-degree images from various locations.

- **Articles**—News articles about locations and travelling.

When you click a destination, the Travel app displays a screen devoted to that location (see Figure 5.13), which includes an overview, maps, weather, the recent currency exchange rate, photos and panoramas, lists of attractions, hotels, and restaurants, and travel guides.

Figure 5.13 Each destination screen offers lots of information of interest to potential travelers.

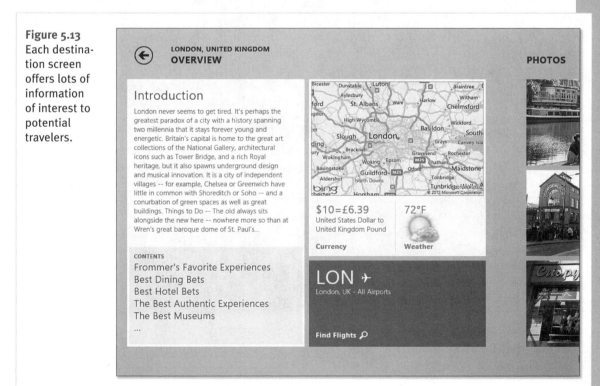

You can also see more destination and travel stories by right-clicking the screen and then clicking Destinations or Best of Web.

When you're ready to book your trip, right-click the screen and then click Flights to book your airline tickets, and click Hotels to set up your accommodations.

Video

You use the Video app to play the digital videos that are on your PC, to purchase or rent movies, or to purchase TV show episodes. The main Video screen is divided into four sections:

- **My Videos**—This section displays tiles for several of your videos. To see all your videos, click My Videos. To view a video, click it and the playback begins immediately. Move the mouse to display the playback controls (see Figure 5.14), which include the Pause/Play button, Fast Forward and Rewind buttons, and a scrubber to scroll through the video. You can also right-click the screen to see similar controls (Pause/Play, Previous, and Next) as well as a Repeat button that, when activated, starts playback from the beginning once the video ends.

Figure 5.14
Move the mouse during video playback to see the controls.

- **Spotlight**—This section offers previews of upcoming movies and TV shows. This section also includes a Now Playing tile that shows you what's currently playing in the app.

- **Movies Store**—This section offers several tiles for newly released movies. You can also click Movies Store to see a complete list of movies organized by various categories (Featured, New Releases, Top Selling, Genres, and Studios). Click a movie and then click Buy/Rent to purchase or rent the movie.

- **Television Store**—This section offers several tiles for new TV shows. You can also click Television Store to see a complete list of TV shows organized by various categories (Featured, Last Night's Shows, Free TV, Top Selling, Genres, and Networks). Click a show, display the show's seasons, and then click a season. You can buy the entire season or click an episode and purchase just that episode.

Weather

The Weather app is a straightforward weather forecast program. When you first start the app, it might ask if it can use your location. If it's your local forecast you're after, click Allow and you're pretty much done. You can also add other places to the Weather app:

1. Right-click the Weather app screen and then click Places. The Places screen appears.

2. Click Add (+). Weather prompts you to enter the city name.

3. Start typing the name of the city you want to add.

4. When you see the name of the city in the list that appears, click it. Weather adds the city to the Places screen.

Games

You use the Games app to view your Xbox LIVE profile and activity and to purchase games for Windows 8 or Xbox. The main Games screen is divided into six sections:

- **Xbox LIVE profile**—This section displays your Xbox LIVE profile data, and also enables you to view your achievements and edit your profile.

- **Friends**—This section displays a list of your Xbox LIVE friends.

- **Spotlight**—This section offers previews of upcoming games.

- **Game Activity**—This section lists your active games.

> **note**
>
> To purchase or rent movies or TV shows, you need to have enough Microsoft Points in your account. If you don't have enough, the Video app will let you know and offer a Buy Points button that you can click to purchase more points. You can also press Windows Logo+I (or display the Charms menu and click Settings), click Account, and then click either Microsoft Points (to purchase points) or Redeem Code (if you have a Microsoft Points gift card).

> **tip**
>
> To make a city the default (that is, the city that appears on the Weather app's live tile and that appears first when you launch the Weather app), display the Places screen, right-click the city, and then click Set as Default. Alternatively, if you want to add a second Weather app tile to the Start screen, display Places, right-click the city, click Pin, and then click Pin to Start.

- **Windows Game Store**—This section offers several tiles for newly released Windows games. You can also click Windows Game Store to see a complete list of Windows games organized by various categories. In addition, you can filter the games list by genre. Click a game and then click Buy to purchase the game.

- **Xbox 360 Game Store**—This section offers several tiles for newly released Xbox games. You can also click Xbox Game Store to see a complete list of Xbox games organized by various categories. In addition, you can filter the games list by genre. Click a game and then click Buy Game for Xbox to purchase the game.

Installing Apps from the Windows Store

Windows 8 comes with quite a few apps, but it doesn't cover every base, not by a long shot. If there's an app that you need, you can obtain the app yourself and then install it on your PC. Here are the steps to follow to install an app from the Windows Store:

1. On the Start screen, tap Store. The Windows Store appears.

2. Open the app that you want to install. See the "Store" section, earlier in this chapter, to learn how to navigate the Windows Store.

3. If it's a paid app, tap the price; otherwise, tap Install. Windows 8 displays a message that it's installing the app (see Figure 5.15).

Figure 5.15
The Store app lets you know that it's currently installing the app.

Uninstalling Windows 8 Apps

If you have an app that you no longer use, you can free up some disk space and reduce clutter on the Start screen by uninstalling that app. Here's how it works:

1. Use the Start screen or the Apps screen to locate the Windows 8 app that you want to uninstall. To display the Apps screen, switch to the Start screen, right-click or swipe up from the bottom edge, and then tap All Apps.

2. Right-click or swipe down on the app tile. Windows 8 displays the app bar.

3. Click Uninstall. Windows 8 asks you to confirm.

4. Click Uninstall. Windows 8 removes the app.

Sharing Windows 8 App Data

In these days of ubiquitous social networking, we are immersed in a world of sharing: happenings, links, information, and much more. You can enhance your social contacts and share more of your life with other people by using Windows 8's Share feature to send data. For example, you can send a photo, alert a person about a web page, or let someone know about some cool music.

First, here are the general steps to follow to use the Share feature:

1. Using an app, open or select the file you want to share.

2. Press Windows Logo+C or swipe left from the right edge of the screen. The Charms menu appears.

3. Tap Share. The Share pane appears and displays a list of apps you can use to share the data.

4. Tap the app you want to use to send the selected item.

5. Fill in any data that's required to send the item and then initiate the send. In Mail, for example, you type the recipient's address, add a subject line, and then tap Send.

For a more specific example, here are the steps to follow to post a website link to Facebook or Twitter (assuming you've linked one or both of these social networks to your Microsoft account):

1. Use the Internet Explorer app to open the website you want to share.

2. Press Windows Logo+C or swipe left from the right edge of the screen. The Charms menu appears.

3. Tap Share. The Share pane appears and displays a list of apps you can use to share the link.

4. Tap People. Windows 8 displays a new social network message that includes a link to the website (see Figure 5.16).

5. Use the list to select Facebook or Twitter.

6. Type a message introducing or describing the link.

7. Tap the Send button. Windows 8 posts the link to the social network.

> **note**
>
> Several other Windows 8 apps support sharing data to Facebook and Twitter. For example, you can use the Music app to open an album—which could be one of your own albums or an album in the Music Store—and then post information about the artist to your friends or followers. You can also use the Video app to share information about a movie or TV show, the Store app to share a link to an app in the Windows Store, and the Maps app to share a map or directions to a location.

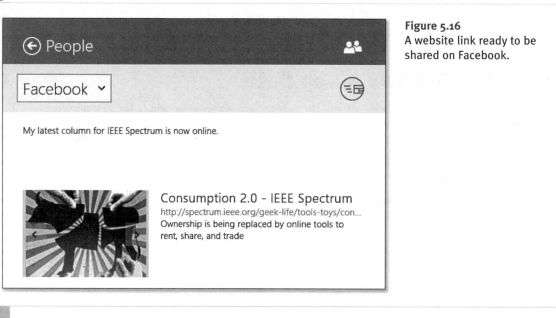

Figure 5.16
A website link ready to be shared on Facebook.

To customize app sharing, press Windows Logo+I (or display the Charms menu and click Settings), click Change PC Settings, and then click the Share tab. You can configure the following options:

- **Show Apps I Use Most Often at the Top of the App List**—Leave this switch On to have Windows 8 float your most frequently used sharing apps to the top of the list that appears in the Sharing pane.

- **Show a List of How I Share Most Often**—Leave this switch On to see a list of the share methods you use most often.

- **Items in List**—Use this list to control the size of the list of frequent sharing methods. You can also click Clear List to remove everything from the list and start over.

- **Use These Apps to Share**—If there are apps you never use to share, you should click their switches to Off in this section to remove them from the Sharing pane.

MANAGING FILES AND SEARCHING

Understanding File Types

To get the most out of this chapter, you need to understand some background about what a file type is and how Windows 8 determines and works with file types. The next couple of sections tell you everything you need to know to get you through the rest of the chapter.

File Types and File Extensions

One of the fictions that Microsoft has tried to foist on the computer-using public is that we live in a "document-centric" world. That is, that people care only about the documents they create and not about the applications they use to create those documents. This is actually not all that far from the truth if you only use the new Windows 8 interface because Windows 8 apps are designed to hide their interface elements, so you see only the document (whatever it might be) that's currently onscreen.

However, for the rest of us who spend the majority of our time in the Desktop app, this notion of a document-focused computing world is pure hokum. The reality is that applications are still too difficult to use and the capability to share documents between applications is still too problematic. In other words, you can't create documents unless you learn the ins and outs of an application, and you can't share documents with others unless you use compatible applications.

Unfortunately, we're stuck with Microsoft's worship of the document and all the problems that this worship creates. A good example is the hiding of file extensions. As you learn in Chapter 24, "Tweaking and Customizing

Windows," Windows 8 turns off file extensions by default, and this creates a whole host of problems, from the confusion of trying to determine a file type based on a teensy icon, to not being able to edit extensions, to not being able to save a file under an extension of your choice. You can overcome all these problems by turning on file extensions, as we show later.

➥ *To learn how to activate file extensions,* ***see*** *"Turning On File Extensions," **p. 572**.*

Why does the lack of file extensions cause such a fuss? Because file extensions determine the file type of a document. In other words, if Windows 8 sees that a file has a `.txt` extension, it concludes the file uses the Text Document file type. Similarly, a file with the extension `.bmp` uses the Bitmap Image file type.

The file type, in turn, determines the application that's associated with the extension. If a file has a `.txt` extension, Windows 8 associates that extension with Notepad, so the file will always open in Notepad. Nothing else inherent in the file determines the file type; therefore, at least from the point of view of the user, the entire Windows 8 file system rests on the scrawny shoulders of the humble file extension.

This method of determining file types is, no doubt, a poor design decision. For example, there is some danger that a novice user could render a file useless by imprudently renaming its extension. Interestingly, Microsoft seems to have recognized this danger and programmed a subtle behavior change into recent versions of Windows (Windows Vista and later): when file extensions are turned on and you activate the Rename command (click the file and then press F2), Windows displays the usual text box around the entire filename, but it selects *only* the file's primary name (the part to the left of the dot), as shown in Figure 6.1. Pressing any character obliterates the primary name, but leaves the extension intact.

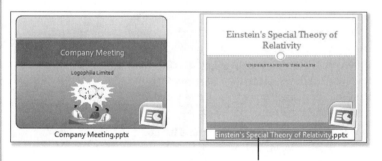

Figure 6.1
When you activate the Rename command with file extensions turned on, Windows selects just the file's primary name.

Windows selects just the primary name.

Despite the drawbacks that come with file extensions, they lead to some powerful methods for manipulating and controlling the Windows 8 file system, as you see in the rest of this chapter.

File Types and the Registry

As you might expect, everything Windows 8 knows about file types is defined in the Registry. (See Chapter 29, "Editing the Windows Registry," for the details on understanding and using the

Registry.) Open the Registry Editor (in the Start screen, type **regedit**, press Enter, and enter your UAC credentials) and examine the HKEY_CLASSES_ROOT key. Notice that it's divided into two sections:

■ The first part of HKEY_CLASSES_ROOT consists of dozens of file extension subkeys (such as .bmp and .txt). There are well over 400 such subkeys in a basic Windows 8 installation, and there could easily be two or three times that number on a system with many applications installed.

■ The second part of HKEY_CLASSES_ROOT lists the various file types associated with the registered extensions. When an extension is associated with a particular file type, the extension is said to be *registered* with Windows 8.

 note

HKEY_CLASSES_ROOT also stores information on ActiveX controls in its CLSID subkey. Many of these controls also have corresponding subkeys in the second half of HKEY_CLASSES_ROOT.

To see what this all means, take a look at Figure 6.2. Here, we've selected the .txt key, which has txtfile as its Default value.

Figure 6.2
The first part of the HKEY_CLASSES_ROOT key contains subkeys for all the registered file extensions.

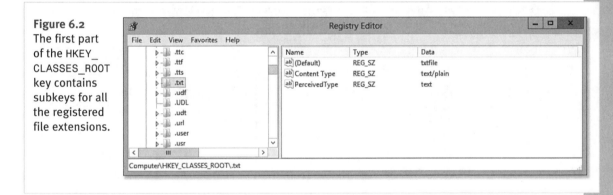

That Default value is a pointer to the extension's associated file type subkey in the second half of HKEY_CLASSES_ROOT. Figure 6.3 shows the txtfile subkey associated with the .txt extension. Here are some notes about this file type subkey:

■ The Default value is a description of the file type (Text Document, in this case).

■ The DefaultIcon subkey defines the icon that's displayed with any file that uses this type.

■ The shell subkey determines the actions that can be performed with this file type. These actions vary depending on the file type, but Open and Print are common. The Open action determines the application that's associated with the file type. For example, the Open action for a Text Document file type is the following:

```
%SystemRoot%\system32\NOTEPAD.EXE %1
```

 note

The %1 at the end of the command is a placeholder that refers to the document being opened (if any). If you double-click a file named memo.txt, for example, the %1 placeholder is replaced by memo.txt, which tells Windows to run Notepad and open that file.

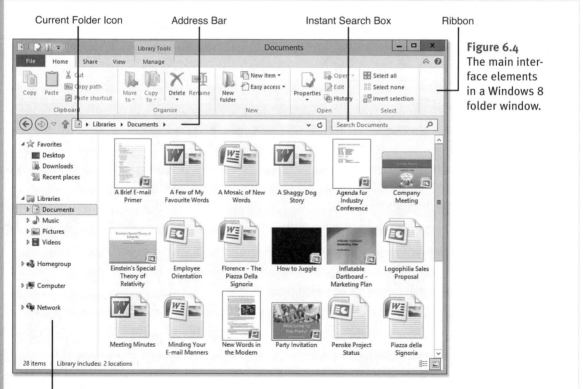

Figure 6.3
The second part of HKEY_CLASSES_ROOT contains the file type data associated with each extension.

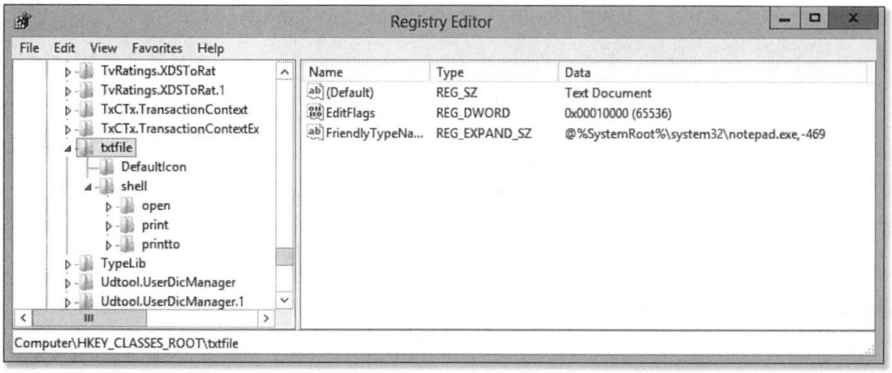

Navigating the Windows 8 Folder Windows

Let's take a quick tour of the interface features you'll find in Windows 8's folder windows. Figure 6.4 shows a typical example of the species, the Documents library.

Current Folder Icon   Address Bar   Instant Search Box   Ribbon

Figure 6.4
The main interface elements in a Windows 8 folder window.

Navigation Pane

Folder Navigation

Windows 8 implements drives and folders as hierarchies that you navigate up, down, and even across. As you can see in Figure 6.4, the address bar doesn't show any drive letters or backslashes. Instead, you get a hierarchical path to the current folder. The path in Figure 6.4 has three items, separated by right-pointing arrows:

- **Current folder icon**—This icon represents the current folder. You'll see a bit later that you can use this icon to navigate to your computer drives, your network, the Control Panel, your user folder, and more.

- **Libraries**—This represents the second level of the sample hierarchy. In the example, this level represents all the libraries associated with the current user account. (A *library* is a virtual folder that displays the contents of one or more folders on your system.)

- **Documents**—This represents the third level of the sample hierarchy. In the example, this level represents all the folders and files that reside in the user's Documents library.

 tip

If you miss the old pathname way of looking at folders, you can still see drive letters and backslashes in Windows 8 by clicking an empty section of the Address bar. To return to the hierarchical path, press Esc.

 tip

To copy the full path name (drive, folders, and filename) of the selected file, select Home, Copy Path.

This is a sensible and straightforward way to view the hierarchy, which is already a big improvement over earlier versions of Windows. However, the real value here lies in the navigation features of the Address bar, and you can get a hint of these features from the nickname that many people have applied to the Address bar: the *breadcrumb bar*.

Breadcrumbing refers to a navigation feature that displays a list of the places a person has visited or the route a person has taken. The term comes from the fairy tale of Hansel and Gretel, who threw down bits of bread to help find their way out of the forest. This feature is common on websites where the content is organized as a hierarchy or as a sequence of pages.

Windows 8 implements breadcrumb navigation not only by using the address bar to show you the hierarchical path you've taken to get to the current folder, but also by adding interactivity to the breadcrumb path:

- You can navigate back to any part of the hierarchy by clicking the folder name in the address bar. For example, in the path shown in Figure 6.4, you could jump immediately to the top-level hierarchy by clicking Libraries in the path.

- You can navigate "sideways" to any part of any level by clicking the right-pointing arrow to the right of the level you want to work with. In Figure 6.5, for example, you see that clicking the arrow beside the current folder icon displays a list of the other navigable items, such as Computer, Network, and Control Panel. Clicking an item in this list opens that folder.

Click the arrow to see
the items in that level.

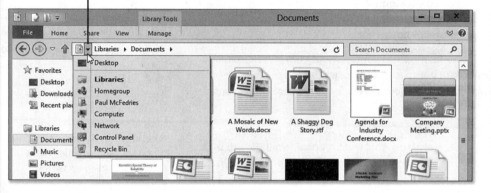

Figure 6.5
Breadcrumb
navigation: In
the Address
bar, click a
folder's arrow
to see a list of
the navigable
items in that
folder.

Instant Search

The next major element in the Windows 8 folder window interface is the Instant Search box, which appears to the right of the address bar in all folder windows. Search is everywhere in Windows 8, and we go into it in much more detail later in this chapter (see "Desktop Searching"). For folder windows, however, the Instant Search box gives you a quick way to search for files within the current folder. Most of us nowadays have folders that contain hundreds or even thousands of documents. To knock such folders down to size in Windows 8, you need only type all or part of a filename, and Windows 8 filters the folder contents to show just the matching files, as shown in Figure 6.6. Windows 8 also matches those files that have metadata—such as the author or tags—that match your text.

The Ribbon

Windows 8's version of the venerable File Explorer file management program comes with a new ribbon interface that replaces the menu bar and toolbar in previous versions. As with all ribbons, File Explorer's is divided into several tabs: File, Home, Share, and View. Also, when you open certain folders or activate certain features, the ribbon sprouts extra contextual tabs that display commands related to the folder or feature. For example, in Figure 6.6 you can see that when you run a search, File Explorer adds the Search Tools contextual tab to the ribbon. Note, too, that because the search was run in the music library, Figure 6.6 also shows a Music Tools contextual tab.

The Navigation Pane

The Navigation pane appears on the left side of each folder window, and it offers quick links to the major sections of your system, including your libraries, Homegroup, Computer, and Network. The Favorites section offers access to a few common folders, including Desktop, Downloads, and Recent Places (folders that you've visited recently).

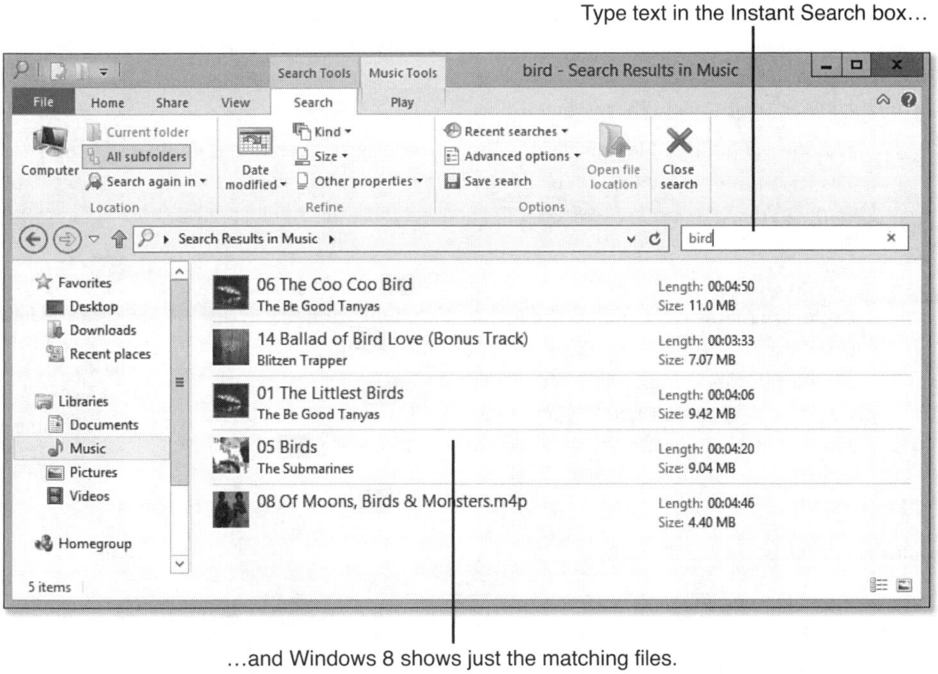

Type text in the Instant Search box…

Figure 6.6
With Instant
Search,
Windows 8
displays just
those files with
names or meta-
data that match
your search
text.

…and Windows 8 shows just the matching files.

tip
The Favorites section is fully customizable. For example, you can add a link to one of your own favorite folders by clicking and dragging that folder and dropping it inside the Favorites section. You can also rename links (right-click a link
and then click Rename) and remove links you don't use (right-click a link and click Remove).

Basic File and Folder Chores: The Techniques Used by the Pros

Now that you're familiar with Windows 8's folders, it's time to put them through a workout. The
next few sections take you through a few basic file and folder chores, including selecting, moving
and copying, and renaming.

Selecting Files with Check Boxes

In this chapter, you learn about quite a few substantive elements in the Windows file system:
metadata, searching, grouping, filtering, and more. All of these are fairly sophisticated and useful
technologies. However, sometimes it's the small, mundane elements that make your life with an
operating system easier and more efficient. In this section, you learn about one of our favorites of
Windows 8's many small but quite useful tweaks: a technique that affects the way you select files.

When you need to select multiple, noncontiguous objects, the easiest method is to hold down the Ctrl key and click each item you want to select. However, when we use this technique to select more than a few files, we *always* end up accidentally selecting one or more files that we don't want. It's not a big deal to deselect these extra files, but it's one of those small drains on productivity that bugs us (and many other users).

Windows 8 offers a file-selection technique that promises to eliminate accidental selections. With this technique, you use a check box to select individual files and folders. To activate this feature, display File Explorer's View tab and then activate the Item Check Boxes check box.

As you can see in Figure 6.7, when you turn on this feature, Explorer creates a column to the left of the folder contents in Details view. When you point at a file or folder, a check box appears in this column, and you select an item by activating its check box. You don't need to hold down Ctrl or use the keyboard at all. Just activate the check boxes for the files and folders you want to select.

> **tip**
> Bonus technique: You can also select all the items in the folder quickly by clicking the check box that appears at the top of the Name column.

Activated check boxes remain visible.

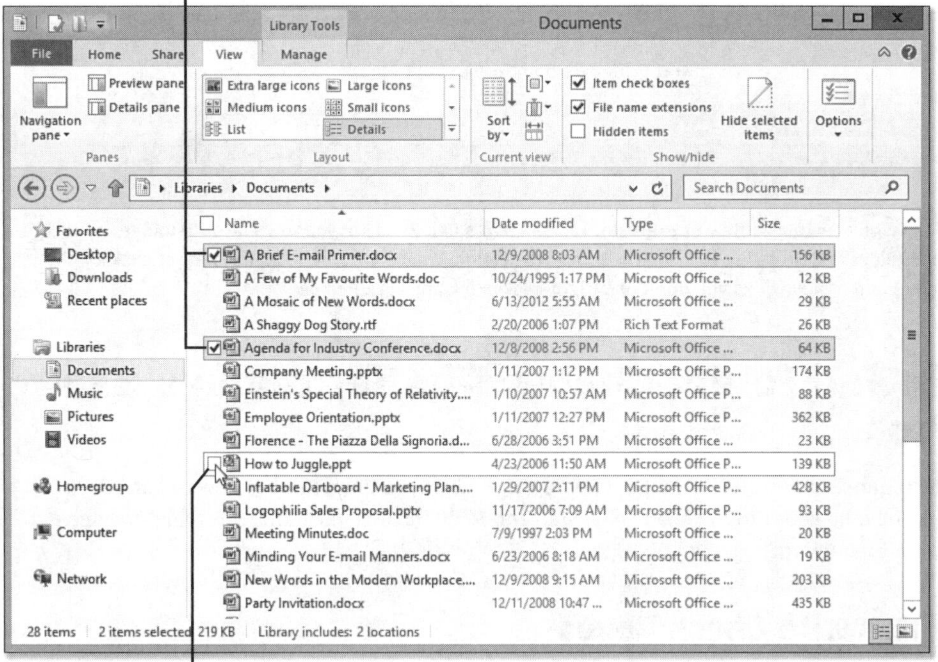

Figure 6.7
In Windows 8, you can select files and folders using check boxes.

A check box appears when you point at an item.

Understanding Size on Disk

To see the total size of the objects in the current selection, right-click the selection and then click Properties. Windows 8 counts all the files, calculates the total size as well as the total size on the disk, and then displays this data in the property sheet that appears.

What's the difference between the Size and Size on Disk values? Windows 8 stores files in discrete chunks of hard disk space called *clusters*, which have a fixed size. This size depends on the file system and the size of the partition, but 4KB is typical. The important thing to remember is that Windows 8 always uses full clusters to store all or part of a file. For example, suppose that you have two files, one that's 2KB and another that's 5KB. The 2KB file will be stored in an entire 4KB cluster. For the 5KB file, the first 4KB of the file will take up a whole cluster, and the remaining 1KB will be stored in its own 4KB cluster. Therefore, the total size of these files is 7KB, but they take up 12KB on the hard disk.

Resolving File Transfer Conflicts

When you move or copy a file into the destination folder, it sometimes happens that a file with the same name already resides in that folder. In earlier versions of Windows, you'd see a dialog box asking whether you want to replace the existing file, and you'd click Yes or No, as appropriate. Unfortunately, Windows didn't give you much information to go on to help you make the choice. Windows 8 takes a step in the right direction by displaying the Replace or Skip Files dialog box instead. Figure 6.8 shows an example.

Figure 6.8
This dialog box appears if a file with the same name already exists inside the destination folder.

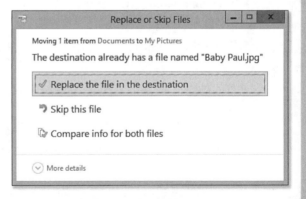

This dialog box gives you the following choices:

- **Replace the File in the Destination**—Click this option if you want the file you are copying (or moving) to replace the existing file.

- **Skip This File**—Click this option if you want Windows 8 to not copy (or move) the file, so the original remains in the destination folder.

- **Compare Info for Both Files**—Click this option to see more information about both files, including a thumbnail, the last modified date, and the size. Activate the check box for the version you want to keep and then click Continue. Note, too, that you can keep *both* files by activating both check boxes and then clicking Continue. In this case, the existing file remains as is, and the file being copied or moved is placed in the folder with (2) appended to the filename.

Expert Drag-and-Drop Techniques

You'll use the drag-and-drop technique throughout your Windows career. To make drag-and-drop even easier and more powerful, here are a few pointers to bear in mind:

- **"Lassoing" multiple files**—If the objects you want to select are displayed in a block within the folder list, you can select them by dragging a box around the objects. This is known as *lassoing* the objects.

- **Drag-and-scroll**—Most drag-and-drop operations involve dragging an object from the contents area and dropping it on a folder in the Folders list (be sure to display the Folders list first). If you can't see the destination in the Navigation pane, drag the pointer to the bottom of the pane. Windows Explorer will scroll the pane up. To scroll the pane down, drag the object to the top of the pane.

- **Drag-and-open**—If the destination is a subfolder within an unopened folder branch, drag the object and hover the pointer over the unopened folder. After a second or two, File Explorer opens the folder branch.

- **Inter-window dragging**—You can drag an object outside of the window and then drop it on a different location, such as the desktop.

- **Drag between Explorers**—Windows 8 lets you open two or more copies of File Explorer (select File, Open New Window). If you have to use several drag-and-drop operations to get some objects to a particular destination, open a second copy of File Explorer and display the destination in this new window. You can then drag from the first window and drop into the second window.

- **Canceling drag-and-drop**—To cancel a drag-and-drop operation, either press Esc or click the right mouse button. If you're right-dragging, click the left mouse button to cancel.

Taking Advantage of the Send To Command

For certain destinations, Windows 8 offers an easier method for copying or moving files or folders: the Send To command. To use this command, select the objects you want to work with, right-click the selection, and then click Send To in the shortcut menu. You see a submenu of potential destinations, as shown in Figure 6.9.

Note that the items in this menu (except the disk drives) are taken from the following folder that contains shortcut files for each item:

`%UserProfile%\appdata\roaming\Microsoft\Windows\SendTo`

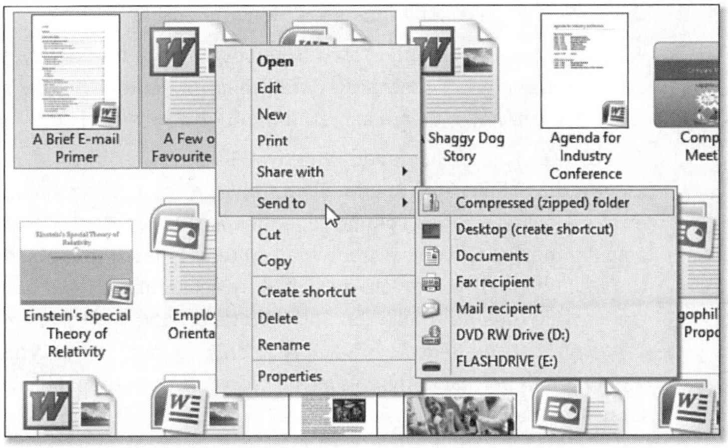

Figure 6.9
The Send To command offers a
menu of possible destinations.

This means that you can customize the Send To menu by adding,
renaming, and deleting the shortcut files in your SendTo folder.

Click the destination you want, and Windows 8 sends the object
there. What do we mean by *send*? We suppose that *drop* would
be a better word because the Send To command acts like the drop
part of drag-and-drop. Therefore, Send To follows the same rules
as drag-and-drop:

- If the Send To destination is on a different disk drive, the
  object is copied.

- If the Send To destination is on the same disk drive, the object
  is moved.

> **note**
>
> The user profile folder for a user is
> the following:
>
> %SystemDrive%\Users*User*
>
> Here, %SystemDrive% is the drive
> on which Windows 8 is installed
> (such as C:), and *User* is the per-
> son's username. Windows 8 stores
> the user profile folder for the cur-
> rent user in the %UserProfile%
> environment variable.

Forcing a Move or Copy

As with a drag-and-drop operation, you can force the Send To command to copy or move an
object. To force a move, hold down Shift when you select the Send To command. To force a
copy, hold down Ctrl when you select the Send To command. To force a shortcut, hold down
Shift and Ctrl when you select the Send To command.

The Recycle Bin: Deleting and Recovering Files and Folders

In our conversations with Windows users, we've noticed an interesting trend that has become more
prominent in recent years: people don't delete files as often as they used to. We're sure that the
reason for this is the absolutely huge hard disks that are offered these days. Even entry-level systems come equipped with 250GB or 500GB disks, and terabyte-sized drives are no longer a big deal.

Unless someone's working with digital video files, even a power user isn't going to put a dent in these massive disks any time soon. So, why bother deleting anything?

Although it's always a good idea to remove files and folders you don't need (it makes your system easier to navigate, it speeds up defragmenting, and so on), avoiding deletions does have one advantage: you can never delete something important by accident.

Just in case you do, however, Windows 8's Recycle Bin can bail you out. The Recycle Bin icon on the Windows 8 desktop is actually a frontend for a collection of hidden folders named Recycled that exist on each hard disk volume. The idea is that when you delete a file or folder, Windows 8 doesn't actually remove the object from your system. Instead, the object moves to the Recycled folder on the same drive. If you delete an object by accident, you can go to the Recycle Bin and return the object to its original spot. Note, however, that the Recycle Bin can hold only so much data. When it gets full, it permanently deletes its oldest objects to make room for newer ones.

It's important to note that Windows 8 bypasses the Recycle Bin and permanently deletes an object under the following circumstances:

- You delete the object from a removable drive.

- You delete the object from the command line.

- You delete the object from a network drive.

> **tip**
>
> If you're absolutely sure you don't need an object, you can permanently delete it from your system (that is, bypass the Recycle Bin) by selecting it and pressing Shift+Delete.

Setting Some Recycle Bin Options

The Recycle Bin has a few properties you can set to control how it works. To view these properties, right-click the desktop's Recycle Bin icon and then click Properties. Windows 8 displays the Properties dialog box sheet shown in Figure 6.10.

Figure 6.10
Use this property sheet to configure the Recycle Bin to your liking.

Here's a rundown of the various controls:

- **Recycle Bin Location**—Choose the Recycle Bin you want to configure: you see an icon for each of the hard drive partitions on your computer.

- **Custom Size**—Enter the size of the Recycle Bin. The larger the size, the more disk space the Recycle Bin takes up, but the more files it will save.

- **Do Not Move Files to the Recycle Bin**—If you activate this option, all deletions are permanent.

- **Display Delete Confirmation Dialog**—For the first time in Windows history, Windows 8 does *not* ask for confirmation when you delete an object. If you miss the prompt, or if you just want to be super careful about deletions, activate this check box.

> **tip**
> You can clean out your Recycle Bin at any time by right-clicking the desktop's Recycle Bin icon and then clicking Empty Recycle Bin. The Recycle Bin contents can also be purged using Windows 8's Disk Cleanup utility.

Click OK to put the new settings into effect.

Recovering a File or Folder

If you accidentally delete the wrong file or folder, you can return it to its rightful place by using the following method:

1. Open the desktop's Recycle Bin icon, or open any Recycled folder in File Explorer.

2. Select the object you want to restore.

3. Click the Manage tab and then click Restore the Selected Items. (You can also right-click the file and then click Restore.)

Undoing a File or Folder Action

If deleting the file or folder was the last action you performed in File Explorer, you can recover the object by selecting the Edit, Undo Delete command (or by pressing Ctrl+Z). Note, too, that Windows 8 enables you to undo the ten most recent actions.

File Maintenance Using the Open and Save As Dialog Boxes

One of the best-kept secrets of Windows 8 is the fact that you can perform many of these file maintenance operations within two of Windows 8's standard dialog boxes:

- **Open**—In most applications, you display this dialog box by selecting the File, Open command, or by pressing Ctrl+O.

- **Save As**—You usually display this dialog box by selecting File, Save As. Or, if you're working with a new, unsaved file, by selecting File, Save, or by pressing Ctrl+S.

Here are three techniques you can use within these dialog boxes:

- To perform maintenance on a particular file or folder, right-click the object to display a shortcut menu like the one shown in Figure 6.11.

- To create a new object, right-click an empty section of the file list, and then click New to get the New menu.

- To create a new folder within the current folder, click the New Folder button.

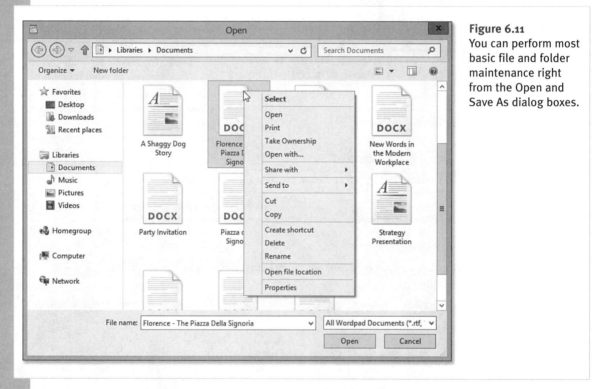

Figure 6.11
You can perform most basic file and folder maintenance right from the Open and Save As dialog boxes.

Metadata and the File Explorer Property System

We mentioned earlier that Windows is gradually lessening the importance not only of drive letters, but also specific file locations. As an example of the latter, note that file libraries are really virtual folders that can consist of multiple locations.

If file location will become less important, what can you use to take its place as a basis for file organization? Content seems like a pretty good place to start. After all, it's what's inside the documents that really matters. For example, suppose you're working on the Penske account. It's a pretty good bet that all the Penske-related documents on your system actually have the word *Penske* inside them somewhere. If you want to find a Penske document, a file system that indexes document content sure helps because then you need only do a content search on the word *Penske*.

However, what if a memo or other document comes your way with an idea that would be perfect for the Penske account, but that document doesn't use the word *Penske* anywhere? This is where purely content-based file management fails because you have no way of relating this new document with your Penske documents. Of course, you could edit the new document to add the word *Penske* somewhere, but that's a bit kludgy and, in any case, you might not have write permission on the file. It would be far better if you could somehow identify all of your documents that have "Penskeness"—that is, that are directly or indirectly related to the Penske account.

This sounds like a job for metadata, and that's fine because metadata is nothing new in the Windows world:

- Digital photo files often come with their own metadata for things such as the camera model and image dimensions, and some imaging software enables you to apply tags to pictures.

- In Windows Media Player, you can download album and track information that gets stored as various metadata properties: Artist, Album Title, Track Title, and Genre, to name just a few.

- The last few versions of Microsoft Office have supported metadata via the File, Properties command.

- For all file types, Windows displays in each file's property sheet a Summary tab that enables you to set metadata properties such as Author, Comments, and Tags.

In Windows 8, metadata is an integral part of the operating system. With the Windows Search engine, you can perform searches on some or all of these properties (see "Desktop Searching," later in this chapter). You can also use them to group and filter files (see "Grouping and Filtering with Metadata," later in this chapter).

To edit a document's metadata, Windows 8 gives you two methods:

- In File Explorer, select View, Details Pane. In the Details pane that now appears on the right side of the window, click the property you want to edit. Windows 8 displays a text box in which you can type or edit the property value. For example, Figure 6.12 shows a photo's Title property being edited. Click Save when you're done.

- Right-click the document and click Properties to display the property sheet, and then click the Details tab. This tab displays a list of properties and their values. To edit a property, click inside the Value column to the right of the property.

note

By default, in most folder windows, Windows 8 displays the Tags and Type properties in Windows Explorer's Details view. (Specialized folders such as Music, Pictures, and Videos display other properties in Details view.) To toggle a property's column on and off, right-click any column header and then click the property. Click More to see a complete list of the available properties.

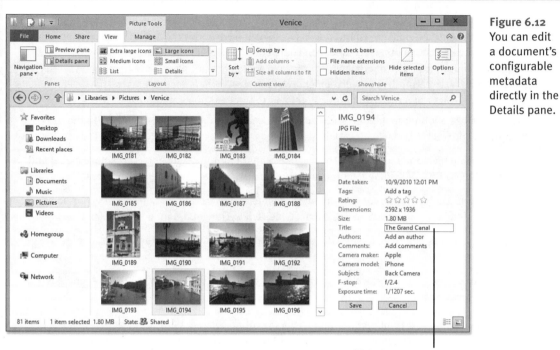

Figure 6.12
You can edit a document's configurable metadata directly in the Details pane.

Click the property you want to edit.

Desktop Searching

One of Microsoft's goals in Windows 8 was to make search a truly useful tool that provides complete results quickly. Did it succeed? For the most part, yes. As you saw in Chapter 4, "Using the Windows 8 Interface," searching via the new interface (particularly app searching) is as easy as just typing what you're looking for.

➥ *For the details on searching the new Windows 8 interface,* **see** *"Searching via the Start Screen," p. 108.*

If you're a dedicated Desktop app user, however, then we're sad to report that searching has taken a step backward in Windows 8. In Windows 7 you could quickly search your system by clicking the Start button and then typing a search string. The Start menu would then generate a list of programs with names that include the typed characters, a list of your user account documents with content or metadata that include the typed characters, and a list of other data—such as contacts, email messages, and sites from Internet Explorer's Favorites and History lists—with content or metadata that include the typed characters.

That was extremely convenient and fast, but with the dismissal of the Start button in Windows 8, that convenience and speed went along with it. The good news is that, as you see in the next section, you can still run relatively quick and powerful searches from the desktop, as long as you know where to start.

Desktop searching remains powerful in Windows 8 because it still uses the Windows Search service, which starts automatically each time you load Windows 8. On the downside, it can still take Windows 8 a long time to search, say, all of drive C. However, that's because Windows Search does *not* index the entire drive. Instead, it just indexes your documents, your offline files (local copies of network files), and your email messages. If you're searching for one of these types of files, Windows 8 searches are lightning quick.

Note that you can control what Windows Search indexes and force a rebuild of the index by opening File Explorer, clicking inside the Search box to display the Search pane in the ribbon, and then selecting Advanced Options, Change Indexed Locations. (You can also open Control Panel and click Indexing Options.) This displays the dialog box shown in Figure 6.13. To customize the search engine, you have two choices:

- **Modify**—Click this button to display the Indexed Locations dialog box, which enables you to change the locations included in the index. Activate the check box for each drive or folder you want to include.

- **Advanced**—Click this button to display the Advanced Options dialog box, which enables you to index encrypted files, change the index location, specify the file types (extensions) you want to include in or exclude from the index. You can also click Rebuild to re-create the index.

> ⚠ **caution**
>
> Windows Search takes a *long* time to index even a relatively small amount of data. If you're asking Windows Search to index dozens of gigabytes of data, wait until you're done working for the day and let the indexer run all night.

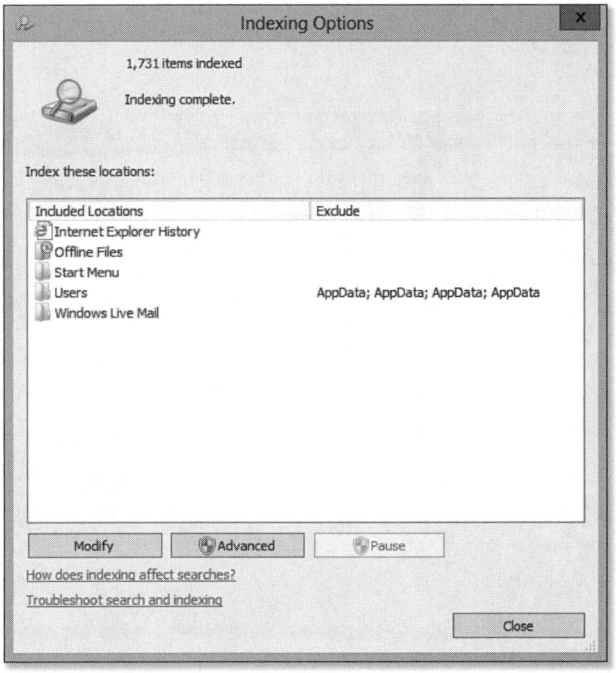

Figure 6.13
Use the Indexing Options dialog box to control the Windows Search engine.

As-You-Type Searches with Instant Search

We mentioned earlier that as-you-type searching, while still alive and well in the new Windows 8 interface, is no longer possible through the Start button. That's the bad news. The good news is that you can still perform desktop-based as-you-type searches in any folder by using the Search box that appears in every Explorer window.

What gets searched depends on several things:

- If you just want to search within a particular folder, display that folder before clicking inside the Search box. By default, Windows searches within subfolders as well. To turn that off, click All Subfolders in the ribbon's Search tab.

- If you want to search your entire computer, either display the Computer folder and then run the search or click inside the Search box and then click the Computer button that appears in the ribbon's Search tab.

- If you want to search your user account, click the arrow next to the current folder icon in the Address bar (see Figure 6.5, earlier in this chapter), click your user account in the list, and then run the search. This is as close as you can get to emulating Start button searches in the Windows 8 desktop.

tip

In a folder window, you can access the Search box via the keyboard by pressing Ctrl+E.

Whatever location you choose, as you type, Explorer displays those files in the location with names or metadata that matches your search text, as shown in Figure 6.14.

Type your search text here.

	Figure 6.14 As-you-type searching using the Explorer window's Search box.

Using Advanced Query Syntax to Search Properties

When you run a standard text search from any Search box, Windows looks for matches not only in the filename and the file contents, but also in the file metadata: the properties associated with each file. That's cool and all, but what if you want to match only a *particular* property. For example, if you're searching your music collection for albums that include the word *Rock* in the title, a basic search on *rock* will also return music where the artist's name includes *rock* and the album genre is Rock. This is not good.

To fix this kind of thing, you can create powerful and targeted searches by using a special syntax— called Advanced Query Syntax (AQS)—in your search queries.

For file properties, you use the following syntax:

property:value

Here, *property* is the name of the file property you want to search on, and *value* is the criteria you want to use. The property can be any of the metadata categories used by Windows. For example, the categories in a music folder include Name, Track, Title, Artists, Album, and Rating. Right-click any column header in Details view to see more properties such as Genre and Length, and you can click More to see the complete list.

Note, too, that Windows will immediately recognize a property as soon as you type it (followed by a colon) and will then display a list of the unique property values, as shown in Figure 6.15. You then click a value to complete the search string.

Type a property name to display
that property's unique values.

Figure 6.15
As-you-type searching using the Explorer window's Search box.

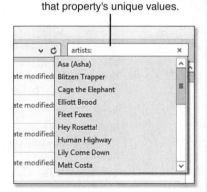

Here are a few things to bear in mind when constructing AQS strings:

- If the property name is a single word, use that word in your query. For example, the following code matches music where the Artists property is Coldplay:

  artists:coldplay

- If the property name uses two or more words, remove the spaces between the words and use the resulting text in your query. For example, the following code matches pictures where the Date Taken property is August 23, 2012:

```
datetaken:8/23/2012
```

- If the value uses two or more words and you want to match the exact phrase, surround the phrase with quotation marks. For example, the following code matches music where the Genre property is Alternative & Punk:

```
genre:"alternative & punk"
```

- If the value uses two or more words and you want to match both words in any order, surround them with parentheses. For example, the following code matches music where the Album property contains the words Head and Goats in any order:

```
album:(head goats)
```

- If you want to match files where a particular property has no value, use empty braces, [], as the value. For example, the following code matches files where the Tags property is empty:

```
tags:[]
```

You can also refine your searches with the following operators and wildcards:

> Matches files where the specified property is greater than the specified value. For example, the following code matches pictures where the Date Taken property is later than January 1, 2012:

```
datetaken:>1/1/2012
```

>= Matches files where the specified property is greater than or equal to the specified value. For example, the following code matches files where the Size property is greater than or equal to 10,000 bytes:

```
size:>=10000
```

< Matches files where the specified property is less than the specified value. For example, the following code matches music where the Bit Rate property is less than 128 (bits per second):

```
bitrate:<128
```

<= Matches files where the specified property is less than or equal to the specified value. For example, the following code matches files where the Size property is less than or equal to 1024 bytes:

```
size:<=1024
```

.. Matches files where the specified property is between (and including) two values. For example, the following code matches files where the Date Modified property is between August 1, 2012 and August 31, 2012, inclusive:

```
datemodified:8/1/2012..8/31/2012
```

* Substitutes for multiple characters. For example, the following code matches music where the Album property includes the word *Hits*:

```
album:*hits
```

? Substitutes for a single character. For example, the following code matches music where the Artists property begins with Blu and includes any character in the fourth position:

```
artists:blu?
```

For even more sophisticated searches, you can combine multiple criteria using Boolean operators:

AND (or +) Use this operator to match files that meet *all* of your criteria. For example, the following code matches pictures where the Date Taken property is later than January 1, 2012 and the Size property is greater than 1,000,000 bytes:

```
datetaken:>1/1/2012 AND size:>1000000
```

OR Choose this option to match files that meet *at least one* of your criteria. For example, the following code matches music where the Genre property is either Rock or Blues:

```
genre:rock OR genre:blues
```

NOT (or –) Choose this option to match files that do not meet the criteria. For example, the following code matches pictures where the Type property is not JPEG:

```
type:NOT jpeg
```

Saving Searches

After taking all that time to get a search just right, it would be a real pain if you had to repeat the entire procedure to run the same search later. Fortunately, Windows 8 takes pity on searchers by enabling you to save your searches and rerun them anytime you like. After you run a search, you save it by clicking the Save Search button in the ribbon's Search tab. In the Save As dialog box that appears, type a name for the search and click Save.

note

The Boolean operators AND, OR, and NOT must appear in all-uppercase letters in your query.

Windows 8 saves your searches in the Searches folder, appropriately enough, and also adds each saved search to the Favorites section of the Navigation bar, so you can rerun a saved search with just a click.

Grouping and Filtering with Metadata

Metadata is a useful file system element, but people might not be motivated to apply metadata to their documents unless they can be convinced that metadata is worth the short-term hassle. The Windows programmers seem to understand this because they built two file-management techniques into File Explorer, both of which become more powerful and more useful the more metadata you've applied to your files. These techniques are grouping and filtering.

Grouping Files

Grouping files means organizing a folder's contents according to the values in a particular property. In the Windows 8 version of File Explorer, select the ribbon's View tab and then click Group By. This displays a list of the properties you can use for the grouping. Clicking one of these properties groups the files according to the values in that property. Figure 6.16 shows the Pictures folder grouped by the values in the Type property.

Click here to select a group.

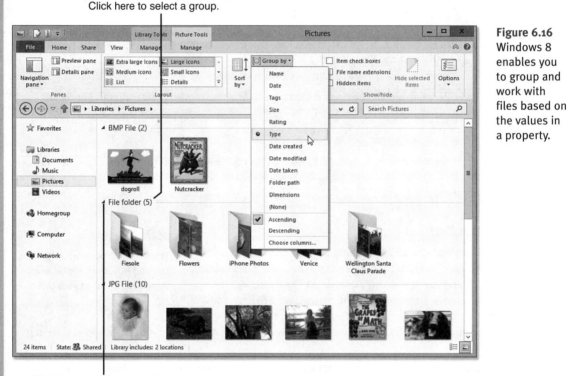

Click here to collapse a group.

Figure 6.16
Windows 8 enables you to group and work with files based on the values in a property.

As Figure 6.16 shows, Windows 8 enhances the grouping feature with two new techniques:

- You can select all the files in a group by clicking the group title.

- You can collapse the group (that is, show just the group title) by clicking the arrow to the left of the group title. (You can collapse all the groups by right-clicking any group title and then clicking Collapse All Groups.)

Filtering Files

Filtering files means changing the folder view so that only files that have one or more specified property values are displayed. Returning to the Type property example, you could filter the folder's files to show only those where Type was, say, JPG Image or File Folder.

In Details view, when you pull down the list associated with a property's header, you see an item for each discrete property value, along with a check box for each value. To filter the files, activate the check boxes for the property values you want to view. For example, in Figure 6.17 we've activated the check boxes beside the BMP File and JPG File values in the Type property, and only those two types appear in the folder.

Activate the check boxes to filter the files.

Figure 6.17
You can filter a folder to show only those files that have the property values you specify.

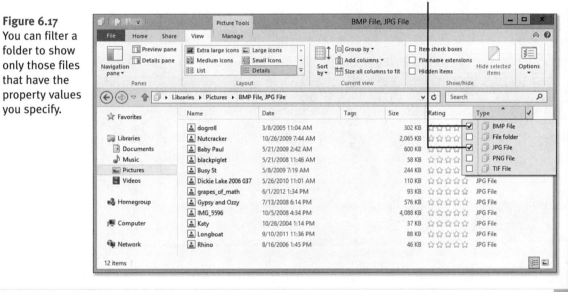

7

DEVICES AND PRINTERS

Windows Printing Primer

In most cases, installing and using a printer with Windows is nearly effortless. Just plugging the printer into your computer is usually enough. Installation and setup is automatic and silent. Within a few seconds you can start printing from whatever programs you use, without thinking any more about it. It doesn't always go quite this smoothly, though, so we've devoted this chapter to the ins and outs of installing and using a printer in Windows 8.

Windows gives you control over the printing system through the Devices and Printers window, which is part of the old Control Panel. Here are the easiest ways to get there:

- Right-click the very bottom-left corner of the screen and click Control Panel. Then, under Hardware and Sound, click View Devices and Printers.

- At the Start screen, type **printers**, and then under Settings, select Devices and Printers.

 note

To print from a Windows 8–style app, open the charms and select Devices. If the app can print (not all of them can) the installed printers will be listed under Devices. Select the printer you want to use.

Figure 7.1 shows the Devices and Settings window with all but the Printers section closed. Here, you can see icons for four print devices:

- The Brother printer, which is installed directly on the computer. You can see that the printer is being shared with others on the network by the icon with two faces.

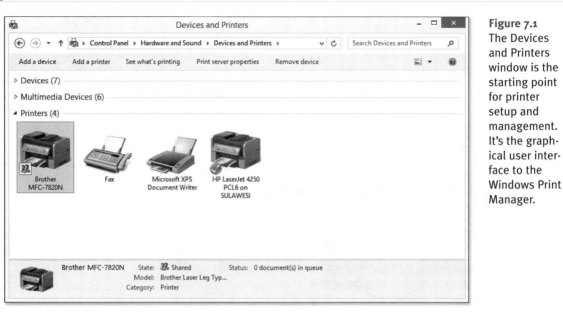

Figure 7.1
The Devices and Printers window is the starting point for printer setup and management. It's the graphical user interface to the Windows Print Manager.

- The HP printer, which is connected to a computer named Sulawesi. It is being used through the network. The check mark shows that it's the default printer.

- The Microsoft XPS Document Writer, which is not a printer in the physical sense. XPS is a type of electronic document format comparable to Adobe's Acrobat (PDF) format. It lets any computer view and/or print a document without needing to have the application that created it. If you select XPS Document Writer as the "printer" in any of your applications, the program's print function will create an XPS document file that you can then send to other people.

- The Fax printer. If your computer has a modem with fax capability, or if your organization has a network fax server, the Fax printer lets you send faxes directly from your applications without having to first print a hard copy and then feed it through a fax machine or scanner. Instead, you simply select the Fax printer from inside your application and use the normal print function.

Initially, the task ribbon shows just two tasks: Add a Device and Add a Printer. If you click one of the printer icons, additional items appear: See What's Printing, Manage Default Printers, Print Server Properties, and Remove Device.

You will probably find that the first time you log on to Windows 8, one or more printer icons are already present. These may include any or all of the following:

- Icons for any printer(s) you have attached to your computer, which were detected by Windows and set up automatically.

- Icons for any printer(s) shared by computers attached to your network. Windows might discover and add these automatically. On a corporate network, they might be installed for you by your network administrator.

- The XPS Document Writer icon, and if you have a fax modem installed, the Fax icon.

In the next section, we show you how to add new printers icons that don't appear automatically. The subsequent sections tell you how to manage your printers.

 After your printer is installed, if you want to let other users on your network use it, **see** *"Sharing Printers" on* **p. 480.**

Installing and Configuring a Printer

The basic game plan for installing and configuring a printer is as follows:

- Read your printer's installation manual and follow the instructions for Windows 7 or 8. If there are none, read the instructions for Windows Vista, XP, or 2000.

- Plug in the printer. Most newer printers are detected when you plug them into the USB or parallel port. Your printer might be found and then configure itself automatically.

- If the printer doesn't configure itself, you can run the Add New Printer Wizard (or use a setup program, if one is supplied with your printer). We'll go over this procedure in detail in the next section.

- If you want, set print defaults pertaining to two-sided printing, scaling, paper source, halftone imaging, ink color, and paper orientation. These will be the default print settings that every Windows application starts with when you select this printer.

- Share the printer and specify its share name so that other network users can use your printer.

- If you are on a network and want to control who gets to use your printer, set custom access permissions.

- Right-click the icon for the printer you'll be using most often and select the Default Printer option. This way, your printer will be preselected as the printer of choice when you use the Print function of Windows applications.

We discuss these topics in the following sections.

> ### ⚡ caution
> Some printer manufacturers ask you to install their driver software *before* you plug in and turn on the printer for the first time. *Heed their advice!* If you plug the printer in first, Windows may install incorrect drivers. (If this happens to you, unplug the printer, delete the printer icon, run the manufacturer's setup program, and try again.)

> ### 🔍 note
> You can select a network printer as your default printer even if you move from one network to another (as you might with a laptop that you use at work and at home). Windows 8 is supposed to remember which printer is the default printer on each network you use.

Adding a New Printer

How you go about adding a new printer depends on how you'll be connecting to it:

- If your printer is connected directly to your computer with a USB, parallel, or serial printer cable, you are installing a *local printer*. Installing a local printer is covered in the next section.

- If you want to use a printer that's shared by another computer on your network, you still need to set up a printer icon on your own computer. This is called installing a *network printer*, and it's covered under "Using Printers on the Network" in Chapter 21, "Using a Windows Network."

- A printer that's physically connected to the network itself and not cabled to another computer is called a *local printer on a network port*, which is somewhat confusing, or a *network-attached printer*, which makes a little more sense. We'll cover the installation of these in Chapter 21 as well. If you're in a hurry, try the standard Add Printer procedure we describe in the next section. Windows is pretty smart about finding and using network-attached printers.

Installing a Local Printer

In most cases, Windows will detect and set up a printer that's directly attached to your computer with no help at all. In some cases, though, you might have to help. This section will help you in such instances. The procedures vary, depending on how the printer is connected to your computer:

- Parallel printer port

- USB

- Network, wireless, or Bluetooth

- Serial port. (If you still have a serial port printer, you are a true retro-computing geek and I love you.)

Here's the basic game plan, which works with most printers. You must be logged on using a Computer Administrator account. Follow these steps:

1. Read the printer's installation instructions specific to Windows 8 or 7. If there are none, look for Windows Vista, XP, or 2000 instructions. You may be instructed to install software *before* connecting the printer to your computer for the first time. This is especially important if your printer connects via USB.

> **🔍 note**
>
> If you have an old printer that has a parallel connector and no USB connector, and your new computer has no parallel port, you can purchase a USB-to-Parallel (also called IEEE-1284) adapter cable. These cost about $20 at a local computer store (less online). Alternatively, you can get a network parallel print server device, or add a parallel port to your computer, but the adapter cable is the easiest way to go.

2. If the printer uses a cable, connect the printer to the appropriate port on your computer according to the printer manufacturer's instructions.

3. Locate the type of connection that your printer uses in the following list, as directed:

   - **Parallel port**—Connect the printer to your computer's parallel port. Windows *should* detect and install the printer. If it doesn't, see the next section.

- **USB**—Install any driver programs provided by your manufacturer, and then connect the printer's USB cable to your computer. Windows will detect it and automatically start the Add a Device Wizard. Follow the instructions onscreen to finish installing the printer.

- **Network, wireless, or Bluetooth**—If your printer can be directly attached to your network, connect it and then click Add a Printer in the Devices and Printers window. If Windows finds the printer, select it and click Next. Otherwise, follow the printer manufacturer's specific instructions.

  If you are using a wireless network or Bluetooth, be sure that your computer's wireless or Bluetooth adapter is turned on and enabled. On some laptops these are switched off by default to conserve power.

- **Infrared**—Be sure your printer is turned on and within range of your computer's infrared eye. Also, make sure your computer's infrared (IrDA) interface is turned on and enabled in software. Windows should detect the printer automatically and create an icon for it.

- **Serial port**—Some antique laser and daisywheel printers use a serial data connection. (If you're still using one of these, I like you already.) The next section describes how to set up a serial printer.

If Windows can't automatically detect the make and model of your printer, it will ask you to assist in selecting the appropriate type. If you can't find your printer's make and model in the list of choices, see "What to Do If Your Printer Isn't Listed."

If the Printer Isn't Found

If your printer isn't found automatically using the options in the preceding section, you have to fake out Plug and Play and go the manual route. To do so, follow these steps:

1. Open the Devices and Printers window as described at the beginning of this chapter. At the top of the Devices and Printers window, select Add a Printer.

2. If your printer does not appear within 20 seconds or so, click The Printer That I Want Isn't Listed. Select Add a Local Printer or Network Printer with Manual Settings and then click Next. Select Use an Existing Port.

3. Select the port to which the printer is connected. The choices are as follows:

   - **LPT1:, LPT2:, LPT3:**—These are parallel port connections. Most computers have only one parallel port connection, LPT1. The higher-numbered ports will still appear in the list even if your computer doesn't have them—so be careful.

   - **COM1: through COM4:**—If you know your printer is of the serial variety, it's probably connected to COM1 or COM2. If COM1 is tied up for use with some other device, such as a modem, use COM2.

   - **File**—If you select this port, when you subsequently print a document, you will be prompted for the name of a file into which the printer commands will be stored. The main use for this option is with a PostScript printer driver, to create a file for submission to a print shop.

- **BTH001**—This is for printing to a wireless Bluetooth printer if you have one connected to your computer.

- **Create a New Port**—This is used to make connections to printers that are directly connected to your LAN and are to be controlled by your computer. Its use is covered in Chapter 21.

After selecting the correct port, click Next.

4. Select the manufacturer and model of your printer in the next dialog box, as shown in Figure 7.2. You can quickly jump to a manufacturer's name by pressing the first letter of the name, such as *H* for HP. Then use the up- and down-arrow keys to home in on the correct one.

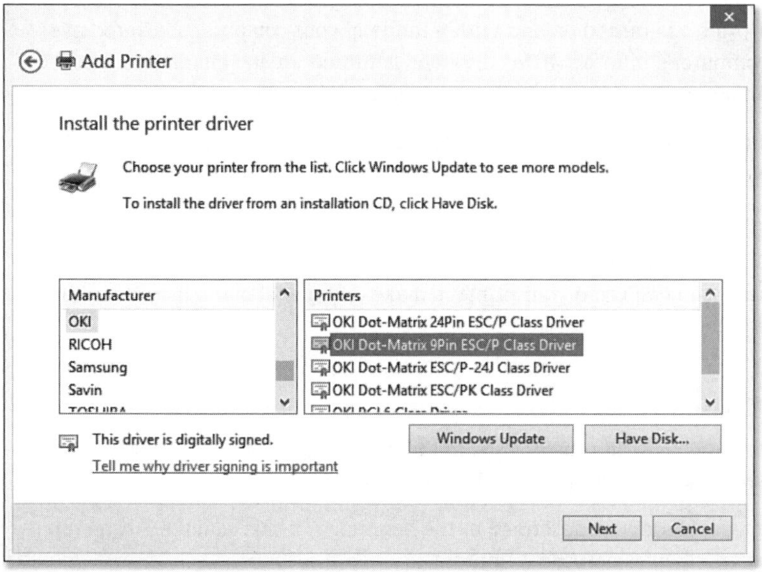

Figure 7.2
Choose the make and model of your printer here.

If you can't find the appropriate model, you have three choices:

- If you have an Internet connection, click Windows Update to see if Microsoft has a driver available. This might well work.

- Get the manufacturer's driver on a floppy disk or CD-ROM or download it via the Internet, open or run the downloaded file to expand its files, and then click Have Disk. Locate the driver (look for an INF file, the standard type for driver setup programs) and click OK.

- Choose a similar, compatible model and risk getting less-than-perfect output. This option can often be successful with dot-matrix printers and *older* inkjet and laser printers, but is less likely to work with modern cheap inkjet or laser printers that have no internal processing "smarts."

➡ *For more information on dealing with unlisted printers, see the next section, "What to Do If Your Printer Isn't Listed."*

If the wizard finds that the appropriate driver is already installed on your machine, you can elect to keep it or replace it. It's up to you. If you think the replacement is newer and will be better, go for it. By contrast, if no driver is listed on the machine, you may be prompted to install it or insert a disk from the vendor. On the whole, manufacturer-provided drivers tend to be newer and better than the default ones provided with Windows.

When you have selected a printer manufacturer and model, click Next.

5. By default, the printer will be named using its full model name. You can change or shorten this if you wish. Then, click Next.

6. By default, the printer will not be shared on your network. You can elect to share the printer, and you can adjust the sharing name if you wish. It's best to keep the share name to no more than 31 characters. To help other users identify the printer, you can also type in a location and a comment.

If you do not want to share the printer, click Do Not Share This Printer. Then, click Next.

7. If you want this printer to be your default (primary) printer, check Set As the Default Printer.

If you want to be sure the printer is working, click Print a Test Page; otherwise, click Finish.

A User Account Control prompt may appear, confirming that you want to install the driver.

When you're finished, the icon for the printer appears in your Devices and Printers window.

> **note**
>
> If the driver software isn't "signed" with digital proof that it came from the manufacturer that it says it came from, Windows may warn you. Permit the software to be installed only if you *know* that it came directly from a reputable manufacturer. If it came from a website other than the manufacturer's, you probably do *not* want to trust it. On a corporate network you may be prevented from installing any unsigned drivers.

➡ *If you later want to share the new printer with other users on your network, **see** "Sharing Printers," **p. 480.***

If you have just set up a printer that's connected to a serial (COM) port, right-click the printer's icon and select Printer Properties. Select the Ports tab, highlight the correct COM port line (which should be checked), and click Configure Port. Select the proper data transfer rate in bits per second (baud rate), data bits, parity, stop bits, and flow control. For *most* serial printers, these settings should be 9600, 8, None, 1, and Xon/Xoff, respectively. Finally, click OK to save the changes.

If your printer is set up and working now, you can skip ahead to the section 'Changing a Printer's Properties."

What to Do If Your Printer Isn't Listed

If your printer isn't detected with Plug and Play and isn't listed in the printer manufacturer and model selection list discussed in the previous section, you'll have to find a driver elsewhere.

First, your printer probably came with a CD-ROM containing driver software. In the Add Printer dialog box (refer to Figure 7.2), click Have Disk and then click Browse to find the Windows 8, 7, or Vista driver files for your printer. If there are separate folders for 64-bit and 32-bit drivers, choose the one appropriate for your copy of Windows. Select the appropriate INF file and click OK.

The Windows Update button lets Windows download additional printer drivers from Microsoft, and this may well obtain the correct driver for you.

If Windows Update doesn't help, your next step should be to visit the printer manufacturer's website. Check out their Product Support section, and look for a way to locate and download drivers. If you can find an appropriate driver, follow the manufacturer's instructions for downloading it. It will probably come as a compressed or executable file that has to be expanded or run, and this will put the installation files into a folder on your hard drive. You can then use the Have Disk feature (discussed earlier) to point Windows to this folder. If there is no downloadable Windows 8, 7, or Vista driver set, you could try a Windows XP driver; however, this is a gamble. A 32-bit XP driver is unlikely to work on a 64-bit version of Windows 8.

> **tip**
>
> Use the Internet to see whether other people have run in to the same problem and have found a solution. For instance, you might use Google to search for "Windows 7 8 *printer driver manufacturer model*," substituting in the manufacturer's name and model number. However, do *not* download a driver from some random site: it could be infected with a virus. Download drivers *only* from the manufacturer's website or a credible corporate or institutional website.

If neither Microsoft nor the manufacturer provides a driver, hope is fading. Still, some off-brand printers or models are designed to be compatible with one of the popular printer types, such as the Apple LaserWriters, HP LaserJets, or one of the Epson series. Also, many printer models are very similar and can use the same driver (with mostly correct results). Check the product manual or manufacturer's website to see if your printer supports an *emulation mode*. This might help you identify an alternative printer model, and you can try its driver.

Assuming that you have obtained a printer driver, follow these instructions to install it:

1. If you obtained a driver by downloading it from the Internet, run the downloaded file. This will either install the driver directly or "expand" or "unzip" a set of files into a location on your hard disk. Take note of the location.

2. Follow steps 1 through 4 in the preceding section.

3. Click the Have Disk button.

4. You're now prompted to insert a disk. Click the Browse button. If you downloaded the driver, locate the folder in which the driver files were expanded or unzipped. If you have a CD, insert the CD, wait a few moments, and then browse to the driver files on the CD.

   The wizard is looking for a file with an .inf extension, which is the standard file extension the installer setup file provided with all drivers. You may have to hunt around a bit to find a folder with drivers for Windows 8, 7, Vista, or XP.

5. When you have located the folder with INF files, click OK. You might have to choose a printer model from a list if multiple options exist.

6. Continue through the wizard dialog boxes, as explained in the previous section.

Changing a Printer's Properties

Every printer has several sets of preference and properties dialog boxes, each with enough settings to choke a horse. Different printers have different features, and your particular printer's driver will dictate the particular set of options available to you. The following sections describe the most general and common options. Those relating to network printer sharing are covered in Chapter 21.

The different sets of printer properties and preferences each serve a different purpose. If you right-click a printer's icon in Devices and Printers, you will see these choices:

- **Printing Preferences**—These are the default settings that each application will start with when you use an application's Print function. These include paper size, page orientation, and paper source. Although most applications let you make changes for an individual document, if you find that you have to keep adjusting the same settings every time you print, change the printer's Printing Preferences. This way, each application starts with those selections as the default.

  Preferences are *per-user* settings. Each computer user can set his or her own printing preferences.

- **Printer Properties**—These are settings that apply to the printer itself, most of which tell Windows how to communicate with the printer, what capabilities and optional features it has, and so on. Printer properties also include settings that determine the initial Printing Preferences for each user.

- **Properties**—This one is useless. It's just there because of the way that Devices and Printers is organized. (It *is* useful for other device types, however.) This takes a little getting used to, because in previous versions of Windows, to configure a printer you would right-click its icon and select Properties. In Windows 8, you have to use the other three choices just mentioned.

When you select a printer's icon, the Print Server Properties selection appears at the top of the Devices and Printers window. This leads to settings that apply to all printers used by the computer, including paper size and form definitions.

These groups of settings are described in the following sections.

Printing Preferences

If you find yourself having to change the same page setup settings nearly every time you go to print something, you can save yourself time by changing the settings in the Printing Preferences dialog box. These settings are used as the defaults whenever you select a printer in one of your applications.

To change your personal printing preferences for a particular printer, open Devices and Printers as described at the beginning of this chapter. Right-click the printer icon and select Printing Preferences. The number of tabs and the choices they offer vary widely from printer to printer. Table 7.1 describes them in general terms.

Table 7.1 Printing Preferences Tabs

Tab	What It Controls
Layout	Landscape or portrait paper orientation, the number of pages placed on each sheet, and so on
Paper/Quality	The bin or feed slot to use, paper size, type, and so on
Effects	Page resizing, watermarks, and so on
Finishing	Stapling, duplexing (two-sided printing), collating, binding, and so on
Advanced	Printer features, color management, and, in some cases, paper and layout choices
Services	Links to manufacturer web pages and online services

🌐 tip

If the Layout tab is not present, you should be able to set the default page orientation on the Paper/Quality or Effects tabs.

If your printer's preferences dialog box looks like the one shown in Figure 7.3, you must click the unlabeled icon to change the orientation. You may run into this especially if you're using a Hewlett-Packard printer that is shared by a Windows 7 computer. We have no idea why HP made such an important setting so unobvious, and we haven't yet seen this on the HP drivers that come with Windows 8.

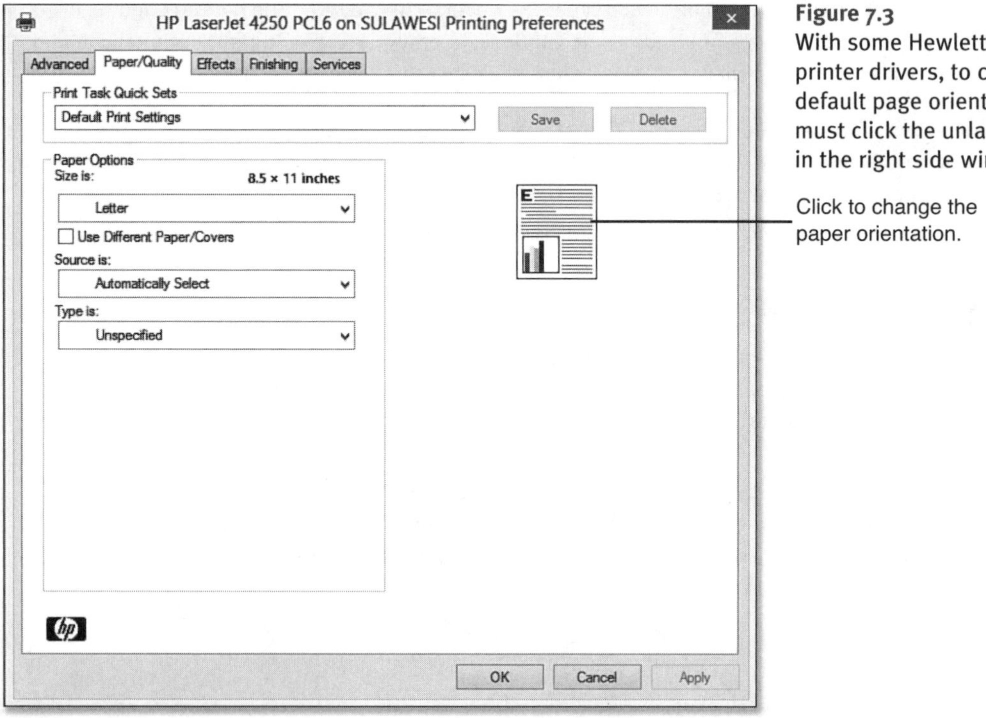

Figure 7.3
With some Hewlett-Packard printer drivers, to change the default page orientation, you must click the unlabeled icon in the right side window.

Click to change the paper orientation.

If you want to change a printer's default preferences for *all* users, view its Printer Properties, as described in the next section, and click Printing Defaults on the Advanced tab. This brings up what looks like the Printing Preferences dialog box, but these settings will become the default settings for *all* users. Users can then customize their printing preferences from that starting point.

Printer Properties

To make changes to a printer driver or its physical connection to your computer, or to define some of the default settings that will be supplied to every user, open Devices and Printers as described at the beginning of this chapter. Right-click the printer icon and select Printer Properties. (That's *Printer Properties*, not just plain *Properties*.) This displays a dialog box like the one shown in Figure 7.4.

Figure 7.4
A typical printer's Printer Properties dialog box.
The settings available vary among printers.
Some have more or fewer tabs.

A printer's Properties dialog box can have any of several tabs. Table 7.2 shows the general breakdown. Again, the tabs you'll see can vary depending on the capabilities of your printer.

🐾 tip

Each time you add a printer, Windows creates an icon for it in the Devices and Printers window. Although each is called a printer, it is actually just a "pointer" to the printer, much the way a shortcut represents a document or application on the Windows desktop. A given *physical* printer can have multiple icons, each with different default settings. For example, one could be set to print in landscape orientation on legal-size paper, whereas another printer could default to portrait orientation with letter-size paper. Of course, you can always adjust these settings when you go to print a document, but that can get tedious. If you create multiple printer icons for the same printer, with different, descriptive names, you can choose a setup just by selecting the appropriate printer icon.

Table 7.2 Printer Properties Tabs

Tab	What It Controls
General	This tab lists the name, location, model number, and features of the printer. From this tab, you can print a test page. You also can click the Preferences button to change your personal printing preferences (the same settings described in the previous section). Some color printers may have settings for paper quality and color control as well as buttons for maintenance functions on this tab.
Sharing	On this tab, you can alter whether the printer is shared with other network users and what the share name is.
Ports	On this tab, you can select the printer's connection port, add and delete ports, and in some cases configure the physical connection itself. This tab also lets you set up additional ports for network-connected printers.
Advanced	This tab controls time availability, printer priority, driver changes, spooling options, and advanced printing features such as booklet printing and page ordering. The first two settings are pertinent to larger networks and should be handled by a server administrator.
	Booklet printing is worth looking into if you do lots of desktop publishing. Using this option, you can print pages laid out for stapling together small pamphlets.
	The New Driver button on the Advanced tab lets you replace the current driver with a better one, should this be necessary.
	The Printing Defaults button lets you set the default printing properties supplied to each user.
Color Management	On this tab, you can set optional color profiles on color printers, if this capability is supported.
Security	This tab lets you control who has access to print, manage printers, or manage documents from this printer.
Device Settings	The settings on this tab vary greatly among printers. For example, you can set paper size in each tray, tell Windows how much RAM is installed in the printer, and substitute fonts.
About	Lists the printer's driver components.
Utilities	This tab, if present, might contain options for inkjet nozzle cleaning, head cleaning, head alignment, and so on.
Bluetooth	This tab, if present, contains information about your Bluetooth printer and connection in case you need to troubleshoot connection problems.

➡ *For more details about printer sharing, printer pooling, and other server-related printing issues,* **see** *Chapter 21.*

Print Server Properties

To define paper sizes or forms, or to change the location of the spooling folder used to hold data being sent to the printer, in the Start screen, type **printer**. Then from Settings, select Devices and

Printers. Select any printer icon and then select Print Server Properties up near the top of the window.

The Print Server Properties dialog box is covered in Chapter 21 because it's mainly a networking topic.

Removing a Printer

You might want to remove a printer setup for several reasons:

- The physical printer has been removed from service.

- You don't want to use a particular network printer anymore.

- You have several definitions of a physical printer using different default settings, and you want to remove one of them.

- You have a nonfunctioning or improperly functioning printer setup and want to remove it and start over by running the Add Printer Wizard.

In any of these cases, the approach is the same:

1. Be sure you are logged on with Administrator privileges.

2. Open the Devices and Printers window, as described at the beginning of this chapter.

3. Be sure nothing is in the printer's queue. You have to cancel all jobs in the printer's queue before deleting the printer. If you don't, Windows will try to delete all jobs in the queue for you, but it isn't always successful.

4. Right-click the printer icon you want to delete, and then choose Remove Device.

5. Windows will ask you to confirm that you want to delete the printer. Click Yes. The printer icon or window disappears from the Devices and Printers window.

> **tip**
>
> The removal process removes only the printer icon in the Devices and Printers window. The related driver files and font files are *not* deleted from your hard disk. Therefore, if you ever want to re-create the printer, you don't have to insert discs or respond to prompts for the location of driver files. On the other hand, if you are having problems with the driver, deleting the icon and then reinstalling the printer won't delete the bad driver. Use the New Driver tool on the Advanced tab of the Properties dialog box to solve the problem in this case.

Printing from Your Applications

To print from Windows 8–style apps, use the Devices charm.

On the desktop, most Windows applications have a Print menu item. The traditional place for the Print selection was always on the File menu, thanks to IBM's Common User Access initiative, which has provided structure and continuity in program menus for over 25 years. In applications that use Microsoft's ribbon interface, it could be anywhere. Microsoft Word 2007, for example, put it in an unlabeled round button in the upper-left corner. Word 2010 put it in the File ribbon. Good luck guessing where it will be in the next...oh, but, I digress.

The Print menu selection usually displays a Print dialog box that lets you select a printer. There is usually a button next to the printer selection list labeled Properties. This button lets you change the orientation of the printing on the page, the paper source, and so on. The settings are the same as discussed in "Printing Preferences" in this chapter, except, here, you're changing the settings just for one particular document in one application

If an application doesn't provide a way to select a specific printer, then the default printer is used. To choose which printer you'd like to use as the default, open the Devices and Printers window, right-click a printer's icon, and select Set As Default Printer. A green check mark appears to show which printer is the default.

When you print from a Windows application, it generates commands and data that tell the printer to form letters and images on a page. Applications generally produce these much faster than a printer can consume them, so the work is done in two separate steps. As an application generates print commands, the Windows Print Spooler service "spools" the output. Here, *spooling* refers to a process where the output of an application is stored on disk or in RAM and then fed to an output device at the device's own pace. The application then turns its attention back to you while the Print Spooler plays back the list of commands to the printer. The Print Spooler can coordinate individual printouts (called *jobs*) from possibly several applications and users at once, and feeds the output to the assigned printer(s) one at a time. We talk about managing queued print jobs in the next section.

> **tip**
>
> You don't always have to print from an application. As a shortcut, in many cases you can simply right-click a document's icon in File Explorer and select Print. You won't have the option of setting any print options; your Printing Preference settings are used. The document type must also have an association linking the filename extension (for example, `.doc` or `.bmp`) to an application that can open and print files this way. The Control Panel entry Programs, Make a File Type Always Open in a Specific Program governs these associations.

No Output from Printer

If your application says it has printed something but nothing comes out of the printer, open the Devices and Printers window, as described at the beginning of this chapter, and work through the following checklist:

- First, check that you printed to the correct printer. Check to see whether your default printer is the one from which you are expecting output. If you're on a LAN, you can easily switch default printers and then forget that you made the switch.

- Right-click the printer icon and select See What's Printing. In the window that opens, select Printer, and if Pause Printing is checked, uncheck it. On the same menu see if the option Use Printer Offline appears. If it does and it's checked, uncheck it.

- Check to see whether the printer you've chosen is actually powered up, loaded with paper, and ready to roll. Be sure its "online" or "ready" light is lit up.

- If you're using a network printer, check whether the station serving the printer is powered up and ready to serve print jobs.

- Check the cabling (unless, of course, it is a wireless printer). Is it tight?

- Does the printer need ink, toner, or paper? Are any error lights or other indicators on the printer itself flashing or otherwise indicating an error, such as a paper jam?

- Are you printing from an MS-DOS application? You may need to use the `net use` command to redirect an LPT port to your Windows printer. See "Printing from MS-DOS Applications" in Chapter 30, "Command-Line and Automation Tools."

- If all else fails, turn the printer off and back on. If that doesn't help, restart Windows. It's sad that we have to suggest this, but it sometimes does bring a zombie printer back to life.

Printer Produces Garbled Text

If your printed pages contain a lot of garbled text or weird symbols, check the following:

- You might have the wrong driver installed. Run the print test page and see whether it works. Open the Devices and Printers window, right-click the printer's icon, select Printer Properties, and in the General tab click Print Test Page. If that works, you're halfway home. If it doesn't, try removing the printer and reinstalling it. Right-click the printer icon in the Devices and Printers window and choose Delete. Then add the printer again and try printing.

- Some printers have emulation modes that might conflict with one another. Check the manual. You may think you're printing to a PostScript printer, but the printer could be in an HP emulation mode; in this case, your driver is sending PostScript commands, and the printer is expecting PCL, or vice versa.

Printing Offline

You can print from applications even if your printer is turned off or disconnected. You might do this while traveling, for instance, if you don't want to drag a 50-pound laser printer along in your carry-on luggage. (It's hard to get them through security.)

If you try this, however, you'll quickly find that the Print Manager will beep, pop up messages to tell you about the missing printer, and otherwise make your life miserable. To silence it, open the Devices and Printers window, as described at the beginning of this chapter. Right-click your printer's icon and select See What's Printing. Then, in the window that opens, click Printer, Use Printer Offline. The printer's icon will turn a light-gray color to show that it has been set for offline use, and Windows will now quietly and compliantly queue up anything you "print." It just won't try to send it to the printer.

Just don't forget that you've done this, or else nothing will print out even when you've reconnected your printer. You'll end up yelling at your unresponsive printer, when it's only doing what it was told. When you've reconnected the printer, repeat the preceding steps and uncheck Use Printer

Offline. This is a nifty feature, but it's available only for local printers, not printers shared by other computers.

Working with the Printer Queue

After you or other users on your computer or on the network have sent print jobs to a given printer, an entry appears in its print queue window until the printer has absorbed the last of the data for the printout. There are several ways you can view a printer's queue window:

- Open Devices and Printers, as described at the beginning of this chapter, right-click the printer's icon, and select See What's Printing.

  Alternatively, double-click the icon. If it's a network printer shared by another computer, you'll then have to click See What's Printing.

- For a local printer attached to your computer, when there are active jobs, an icon appears in the desktop's notification area, near the clock. Hover the mouse pointer over it to see the number of documents waiting to print. Right-click it and select the printer's name to display the queue.

> **tip**
>
> You can drag a printer's icon from the Devices and Printers window to your desktop for easy access.

- If you wish, you can drag a printer icon from the Devices and Printers window onto your desktop to create a shortcut to the queue window.

Figure 7.5 shows a sample printer's queue window. The window displays the status of the printer (in the title bar) and the documents that are queued up, including their size, status, owner, pages, date submitted, and so on.

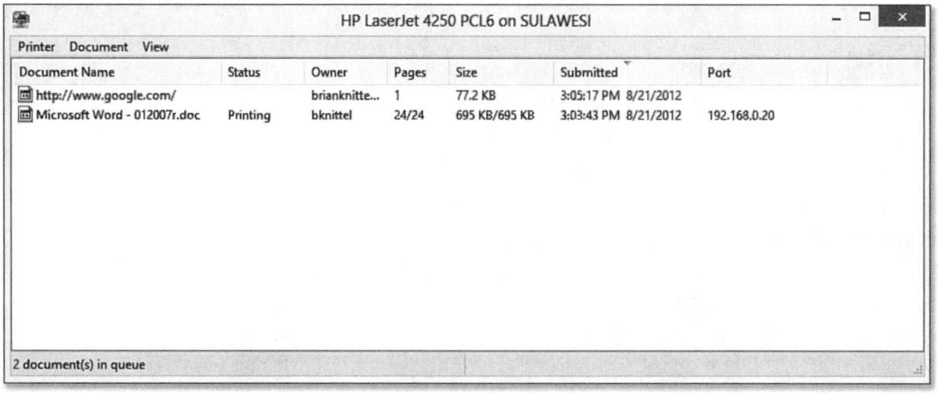

Figure 7.5
A printer's queue window showing one job printing and one pending.

If you're looking at the print queue for a printer that's shared by another computer on your network, the screen won't update itself very frequently. Press F5 or select View, Refresh to see the most up-to-date information.

Deleting a File from the Queue

After sending a document to the queue, you might change your mind about printing it, or you might want to reedit the file and print it again later. To remove a job from the queue, view the printer's queue window, right-click the document you want to delete, and choose Cancel. Alternatively, choose Document, Cancel from the menu. The document is then removed from the printer's queue window.

If you're trying to delete the job that's currently printing, it might take a while to disappear from the list.

By default, all users can pause, resume, restart, and cancel the printing of their own documents. To manage documents printed by other users, your user account must have the Manage Documents privilege for the printer. If Windows says you don't have permission to perform some function, such as deleting a document from the queue or changing printer settings, in most cases you can right-click the document or printer and select Run As Administrator to perform the operation with elevated privileges. From the pop-up menu, select the task you were trying to perform and then try again.

Alternatively, a Computer Administrator user can edit the printer's Security properties to give your account Manage Documents permission. We discuss this shortly.

Canceling All Pending Print Jobs on a Given Printer

To cancel *all* pending and active print jobs on a printer, open the Devices and Printers window, double-click the printer icon, and choose Printer, Cancel All Documents. A confirmation dialog box appears to confirm this action.

If you have a printer's queue window open, you can also select Printer, Cancel All Documents from that window's menu.

Pausing, Resuming, and Restarting the Printing Process

If you need to, you can pause the printing process for a particular printer or even just a single document print job. You can do this to give other jobs a chance to print first, or if you just want to adjust or quiet the printer for some reason.

To pause an individual print job, in the printer's queue window, right-click the document name and choose Pause. The word *Paused* then appears on the document's line under Status. The printer may not stop immediately. First, Windows won't stop sending data until it has reached the end of a page. Second, the printer may have one or more pages already in its memory, and it will finish printing

> ### ⊛ tip
> Pausing an individual document lets other documents later in the queue proceed to print, essentially moving them ahead in line. To stop the printer entirely, you must pause the printer.

those unless you take the printer offline. Third, Windows may go on and start sending pages for the next job in the print queue. When you're ready to resume printing, right-click the job in question and choose Resume.

In some situations, you might need to pause *all* the jobs on your printer so that you can add paper to it, alter the printer settings, or just quiet the printer while you take a phone call. To pause all jobs, open the printer's queue window and choose Printer, Pause Printing. (Again, the printer may not stop immediately; it will continue to print any pages already in its memory.) To start the printer up again, uncheck Pause Printing.

If you need to (because of a paper jam or other botch), you can restart a printing document from the beginning. Just right-click the document and choose Restart.

Advanced Printer Management

In Chapter 21, we describe some advanced printer management topics that apply mostly to printers that you are sharing on a network.

 To control who has permission to use and/or manage a printer, **see** *"Setting Printer Permissions,"* **p. 481.**

 To change the disk drive on which Windows stores (spools) printer data that's waiting to be sent to printers, **see** *"Changing the Location of the Spool Directory,"* **p. 483.**

 To connect multiple printers to one queue in a high-print-volume environment, **see** *"Printer Pooling,"* **p. 483.**

In addition, Windows 8 comes with a printer management tool that's part of the Windows Management Console system. It's intended primarily for network administrators who sometimes have to manage dozens of printers spread around an office. We won't go into great detail on this tool here because it's fairly self-explanatory, but we'll show you how it works.

To run the tool, go to the Start screen and type **admin**. Click on Settings and select Administrative Tools. Then, double-click Print Management. You might need to confirm the User Account Control prompt or enter an Administrator password, because this tool requires elevated privileges.

The left pane lets you choose views that include lists of all the printers installed on the local computer (or on a domain network), all printers that have documents pending, and so on. You can also create custom "filters" to select only printers with specific attributes.

Under the Print Servers section, the local computer is listed, and you can right-click the "Print Servers" title to add the names of other computers on your network (or named print server devices). You can use this feature to build a single panel that lists all your organization's printers. Print servers that you add to this list will remain in the list the next time you run the printer management tool.

XPS Print Output

Windows 8 includes support for a document file type called XPS, which stands for XML Paper Specification. An XPS file represents printed output. The idea is that you can view an XPS file on any computer that has an XPS viewer program, without having to have a copy of the application that created the document. For example, you can view the XPS version of a Microsoft Word document without needing to have a copy of Word. If this sounds suspiciously like Adobe's PDF file format, you're right. XPS is Microsoft's attempt to create a universal electronic document format. It does work well, but it's not been widely adopted. It's telling that Microsoft has added PDF output capability to Microsoft Word, Excel, and other Office applications.

You can generate XPS documents by following these steps:

1. Edit and format a document in one of your applications. Be sure to save the document in the application's native format, so that you can come back and change it later. You can't edit an XPS file.

2. Use the application's Print function. Select the Microsoft XPS Document Writer printer. Click Print.

3. When the Save the Print Output As dialog box appears, select a location and name for the XPS document.

You can now distribute the XPS document to others to view and print as desired.

Windows 8, 7, and Vista have built-in XPS document viewers. On these versions of Windows, just double-click an XPS file to open and view it.

You can download XPS support for Windows XP from Microsoft.com; search for "Microsoft XPS Essentials Pack." This tool requires the .NET Framework, so you may need to download and install that program as well. There are also XPS viewers for Apple's iOS and OS X, Linux, and other UNIX-like operating systems.

Faxing

If your computer has a fax-capable modem installed, you can use it to send and receive faxes. All Windows 8 editions come with fax software built in.

To send a fax from Windows 8, set up the fax service as described in Chapter 12, "Scanning and Faxing." Then create a document using your favorite application, click Print, and select Fax as the printer. Windows will ask you for the fax phone number and make the call—no paper is involved. The fax service can even add a cover sheet to your document on the way out. You can attach additional documents to an outgoing fax; there's no need to send a group of documents in several separate phone calls.

We cover faxing in detail in Chapter 12.

ACCESSORIES AND ACCESSIBILITY

A Boatload of Useful Tools

Tools. Better yet, *power tools*. Do those words make you start to drool? Are you a tool freak, always looking for the latest gadget that will both (a) simplify your life and (b) prove that you truly are cooler than anyone else in the room? If that's you, I predict you'll become an app junkie, and will soon be spending more time scouring the Windows Store than actually working. (After all, your reasoning goes, if you find the right tool, you'll recover the time and money many times over.)

Or do you see tools as just the means to an end? Do you look *through* the computer screen at what you're working on, rather than *at* it? If that's you, you seek simplicity, and you just want to get on with the job.

Whichever "type" you are, what if I told you that those simple, forgettable accessories and apps that come with Windows—some of which have been there since the late 1980s—are worth more than you think? We're going to give them a quick review, to remind you that they're there, to show you some interesting tips, and to show that they're actually more useful than you may remember. At the end of the chapter, we cover additional accessibility tools that can make Windows easier to use.

Of course, as the years go by, the Windows Store is sure to bring forth a deluge of new tools and gadgets, at least two or three of which you'll find you can't imagine life without. But it's still worth knowing about the basics, the ones that you can count on being there on every copy of Windows you encounter.

note

Personally, I find that I use some of these accessories all day, every day: Notepad for writing quick notes to myself and for editing scripts, batch files and other types of programs, and Calculator for those odd little math problems. I use Character Map at least once a week to find that odd little symbol that I *know* is in one of my fonts somewhere, but can't remember where. You may have a few favorites of your own. If you scan through this chapter, you may find a new favorite, and you might find a few uses and capabilities that will surprise you.

Gadgets Are Gone

If you used Windows Vista or Windows 7, you may have used some of the desktop tools that Microsoft called "Gadgets" in Windows 7 and "Sidebar" in Windows Vista. These included a graphical clock, calendar, news headline feed, a CPU tachometer, and more. There was also an online Windows Live Gallery where you could download other Gadgets. On Windows 8, Start screen tiles and apps replace the Gadgets, and the Windows Store replaces the Windows Live Gallery.

The Sidebar system was removed from Windows 8 for two reasons. For one thing, as we mentioned, Start screen "live" tiles can do the same things that the Gadgets did—although, the Gadgets lived on the desktop where they were always visible and available, whereas nobody will spend their day looking at the Start screen. But nonetheless, Windows 8–style apps can fill the place of the Gadgets.

The primary reason that the Gadgets are gone is that security risks were discovered in the Sidebar system's design, making it possible for malicious third-party Gadgets to take control of your computer. In July 2012, Microsoft shut down the Windows Live Gallery and issued a security bulletin describing how to disable Gadgets on existing Windows 7 and Vista systems (see the accompanying Caution). Gadgets were originally slated to be provided with Windows 8, but the Sidebar infrastructure was pulled out after the vulnerabilities were discovered.

> **caution**
>
> As of the time this was written, Microsoft has not disabled the existing Sidebar system on Windows 7 and Vista computers via Windows Update, but they do recommend that you stop using it, or at least stop using any third-party Gadgets. For details, search Microsoft.com for Microsoft Security Advisory 2719662, or see http://bit.ly/PI7OCP.

Apps as Accessories

Windows 8 comes with a number of preinstalled apps that you could consider to be part of the same family as the preinstalled desktop accessories. And the Windows Store app is a gateway to potentially thousands of other downloadable apps, both free and paid. Perhaps as an incentive for you to start looking at the Windows Store, some apps that should really have been preinstalled require you to search for and download them, such as the Remote Desktop app, a free Windows 8 version of the Remote Desktop Connection program that lets you connect to and control other computers. The Desktop version of this is preinstalled; the Windows 8–style version you have to download. We'll briefly touch on that app in Chapter 39, "Remote Desktop and Remote Access."

The apps that are standard on all copies of Windows 8 are covered in Chapter 5, "Windows 8 Apps and the Windows Store." In this chapter, we cover the standard Desktop-style accessories. Later in the chapter, we cover the Accessibility Tools.

Desktop Accessories

A number of standard-issue accessories live in Windows 8's Desktop world. Some of them may be familiar to you from previous versions of Windows, but as mentioned at the start of the chapter, it's worth browsing through the list so that you are reminded of what's available. They're actually pretty useful. You can start them in several ways:

- From the Start screen, type the first few letters of the accessory's name and select it from Apps.

- Display the app bar by right-clicking the Start screen or dragging up from the bottom and then select All Apps. Accessories will be listed on the Start screen under Windows Accessories, Windows Ease of Access, and Windows System.

  (There are a bunch of Administrative Tools you can see if you go to the Start screen, open the charms, select Settings, Tiles, and then set Show Administrative Tools to Yes. These are really maintenance tools, not day-to-day accessories, so they're covered elsewhere in this book.)

- Some accessories can be started quickly if you know the accessory's program filename. Just press Windows Logo+R followed by the name, or type the name into a Command Prompt window. In the descriptions that follow, we'll list the filename for each command that can be run this way. (The technical scoop is this: the filename technique works only for those commands whose program file is in a folder that's listed in the PATH environment variable.)

We'll also try to offer an obscure, helpful tidbit about each accessory, just to prove that they're more interesting than they seem.

By the way, some of the accessories are covered in other chapters, as follows:

- **Remote Desktop Connection**—Covered in Chapter 39, "Remote Desktop and Remote Access." Program name: mstsc.

- **Windows Fax and Scan**—Covered in Chapter 12, "Scanning and Faxing." Program name: wfs.

- **Windows Media Player**—The topic of Chapter 9, "Windows Media Player."

Calculator

If you last looked at the calculator in Windows XP, take another look. It's now four calculators in one. Click its View menu to select one of four personalities:

- **Standard**—A basic four function calculator.

- **Scientific**—Adds log and trigonometric, "nth power," and "nth-root," functions to the Standard calculator.

- **Programmer**—Performs arithmetic and bitwise functions on 8-bit to 64-bit integers in binary, octal, decimal, or hexadecimal. There are no floating-point functions. In this calculator, 1/3 = 0.

- **Statistics**—Performs statistical functions such as mean, mean square, and standard deviation on groups of numbers.

Check View, History to display a "tape" that shows previous calculations.

Program name: calc (works with Windows Logo+R; in the Start screen or at the command prompt, type **calc**)

What you may not have known: The View menu provides access to unit conversions, date calculations, and worksheets to calculate mortgages, leases, and, strangely, fuel economy.

Character Map

Character Map lets you quickly find obscure or interesting typographic symbols. You can select any of your computer's installed fonts from the list at the top and then scroll through the font's characters. Highlight a symbol and click Select to add a character to the text box, then click Copy to put those symbol(s) onto the Clipboard. Then, you can paste them into another application. If the application accepts Rich Text Format through the Clipboard, the pasted text will come through in the selected font—otherwise, you get the characters in the applications ambient font.

Program name: charmap (works with Windows Logo+R; in the Start screen or at the command prompt, type **charmap**)

What you may not have known: By default, Character Map displays fonts by their Unicode (16-bit) numerical value, and *all* of the font's symbols are listed. But only some applications accept Unicode characters and values. Many applications only accept local (regional) Windows encodings, where just 8 bits (or 256 numbers) are used to represent a subset of the font's symbols. If you check Advanced View, you can display various encodings. When an 8-bit encoding is selected, the status bar at the bottom of Character Map shows the Unicode value followed by the 8-bit value. For example, when you've selected the Windows: Western character mapping used in the U.S., you can see that the Em Dash symbol is 2014 (hexadecimal) in Unicode, but 97 (hexadecimal) in the Windows encoding (see Figure 8.1). Character 97 might be something else in other encodings.

If you get the wrong characters when you use Copy and Paste to move characters in Character Map into an application, check Advanced View, set the Character Set to Windows: Western, clear out Characters to Copy, and start over.

Alternatively, you can put symbols into an application by character number: hold down the Alt key and type the *decimal* representation of the number on the numeric keypad. The decimal representation is shown at the right side of Character Map's status bar.

You can also use the Programmer version of the Calculator to do the hexadecimal-to-decimal conversion, but it's easier to just go to Google and type something like **0x2014 in decimal**. Put 0x (zero x) in front of any hexadecimal number to do the conversion.

Figure 8.1
Character Map's advanced view.

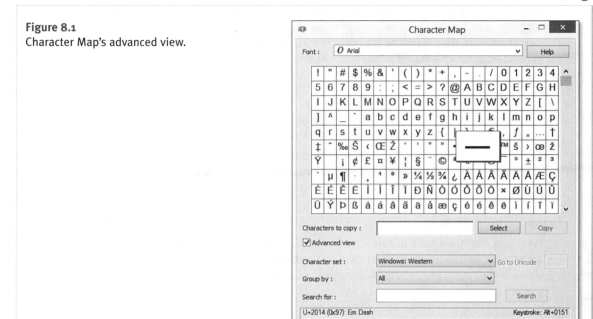

Math Input Panel

The Math Input Panel (MIP) lets you sketch out mathematical equations and then paste them into programs that support the Mathematical Markup Language (MathML). The accessory is useful if you have a program that accepts MathML, such as the built-in equation editor in Microsoft Word 2007 and later, math formatting add-ons such as MathType from Design Science (dessci.com), or symbolic math programs such as Mathematica, Maple, and MathCAD.

The MIP works better with a stylus and a touch-sensitive screen than with your fingers or a mouse, although you can make do with those. It takes some trial and error to train yourself to draw symbols the way the MIP expects them. It's quite a trial, actually.

To enter an equation, open the MIP, and then draw the letters and symbols in the large lower portion of the MIP window, just as you would on paper. As you write, Windows typesets and displays its interpretation in a second window. You can't edit anything in the result window. You have to edit your input. If Windows gets a symbol wrong (and it does, frequently), touch Select and Correct, then touch the symbol you drew. You may be able to select the right symbol from the pop-up list. If that doesn't help, touch Erase and then rub out the symbol you drew. Touch Write, and try again. When you're satisfied with the result, touch Insert. If the cursor is in an application that can accept MathML, it will be pasted in automatically. Otherwise, you may have to manually paste in the equation. When you close the MIP window, it will minimize itself to the notification area of the taskbar.

What you might not have known: I found as I wrote this that if your cat faces away from the computer screen and you scratch her head, her tail draws equations. Most of them are unsolvable. (Bonus question: Use Mathematica to calculate how long it would take for Schrödinger's cat to come up with Schrödinger's equation by chance alone.)

Notepad

The simple Notepad accessory is surprisingly useful for typing quick notes to yourself as well as for editing scripts and batch files, web page HTML files, programs, configuration files, and so on.

I use it so often myself that I always install a shortcut batch file named n.bat on my computers so I don't have to type out **notepad** all the time; I can just type the letter **n**. We show you how to do this in Chapter 30, "Command-Line and Automation Tools," under "Batch File Tips."

Program name: notepad (works with Windows Logo+R; in the Start screen or at the command prompt, type **notepad**)

What you might not have known: If you turn Word Wrap off in the Format menu, you can use the Ctrl+G keyboard shortcut to jump to a specific line in the file, by number. This is really handy when you're editing programs or Windows Script Host scripts. Error messages usually tell you on which line the error occurred. Ctrl+G takes you right to the broken program statement.

Paint

Paint was revamped between Windows XP and Windows 7, and now sports a ribbon interface (see Figure 8.2). It's still a bitmap graphics tool, meaning that you can't grab and resize various elements in your drawing. Once they're put into the screen, they stay where they are. However, it's still a useful tool for creating simple graphics, and for touching up graphics made in other programs.

If you're new to ribbon interfaces, it can take some getting used to. The trick is to notice the small downward arrows in each of the sections of the ribbon. These lead to more detailed choices. The other tricky thing is that, on the Home menu, usually Color 1 and Color 2 mean "foreground" and "background"—the colors laid down by drawing and erasing, respectively. When you're drawing shapes, Color 1 is used for the shape's edges, and Color 2 is used to fill in the middle of the shape. To control whether shapes have an outside line and/or a fill color, use the unlabeled icons at the right side of the Shapes ribbon section.

You can still set the image's desired dimensions using the familiar File, Properties menu item.

The new Paint can read and write files in Windows Bitmap (BMP), JPEG, GIF, TIFF, and PNG formats. If you don't know which to use, here's a short description of each format, along with some pros and cons:

- **BMP**—The Windows Bitmap format stores images with all detail preserved. There are three BMP formats: 16 Color, 256 Color, and 24-bit color. The 16 and 256 Color formats can record only that many distinct colors in the whole image. If there is a larger variety of colors, Windows degrades the image. (You may see *dithering*, which looks like someone sprinkled salt or pepper on the image, or *posterizing*, where large swaths of the image are the same color; a sort of paint-by-numbers effect.)

Figure 8.2
Paint comes
with a snazzy
ribbon
interface.

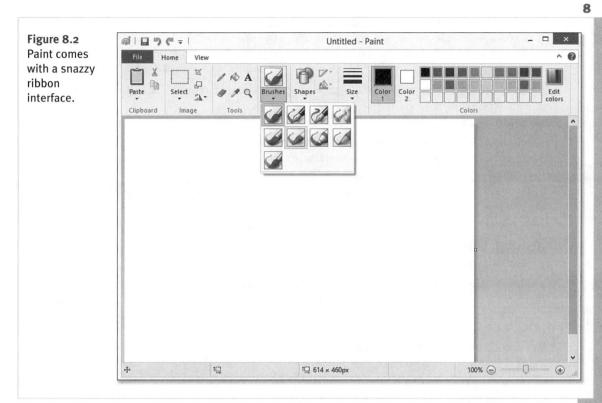

- **TIFF**—TIFF format preserves all colors, and the saved file size can be much smaller than BMP due to lossless compression. The downside of TIFF is that not every application can display it. It's not used to store images for web pages, but is great for pasting into Word documents or storing scanned images.

- **GIF**—This format uses lossless compression and is widely supported by web browsers and email clients. It's suitable mostly for drawings in color or black-and-white where there are relatively few distinct colors.

- **PNG**—This format is similar to GIF and is used primarily for web page graphics, when it's used at all. It was created to circumvent a patent on software used to create the GIF format (which is a rather funny, sad story, but I don't have room to digress). GIF is still the most widely used format for drawings and small graphics.

- **JPEG (JPG)**—JPEG is a highly compressed, lossy format that's appropriate only for photographic images of natural (real-world) scenes. *Lossy* means that the image degrades with each edit-and-save iteration. JPEG does a terrific job of reducing the amount of storage needed to hold pictures by eliminating fine detail that our brains tend to overlook, so to speak (for example, fine gradations in color in a section of an image where brightness and darkness are changing rapidly). It's a very poor format for drawings and text because the JPG format blurs sharp edges.

If you're editing and saving photographs, use JPG to get smaller file sizes. If you're editing a graphic to put on a web page, try GIF, and try PNG or JPG if you end up with bad color dithering. If you're storing drawings or computer images that you'll later put into documents, use TIFF rather than BMP.

Program name: mspaint (works with Windows Logo+R; in the Start screen or at the command prompt, type **mspaint**)

What you may not have known: When you drag or paste a selected part of a picture and drop it, you'll see that the background pixels in the selection get copied too. If you check Transparent Background under Select on the Home panel, when you paste or drop a selection on another part of the screen, Paint drops only those copied or dragged pixels that are *not* the background color (Color 2). If you set Color 2 before you paste, you'll be able to control which color gets ignored in the pasting process.

Snipping Tool

The Snipping Tool lets you grab a portion of the computer screen and paste it into a document. It's useful for taking notes while you're working with your computer, especially to extract information from websites that don't let you easily select text or graphics from the displayed pages. You can simply pick up the interesting part of the page, and paste it into a Word or WordPad document as an image. It's also helpful if you create how-to manuals that involve computer programs. Note that this tool saves bitmap images, not editable or pasteable text, when you use it to snip text off the screen. Think of it as a type of scanner.

To use it, start the Snipping Tool and select New. Then, before you select the portion of the screen you want to capture, choose the shape you'd like to snip. Here are your options:

- **Free-form**—Use the cursor to encircle the exact portion of the screen that you want

- **Rectangular**—Drag the cursor to select a rectangular portion of the screen

- **Window**—Click the cursor in an open window to capture the entire window (including its frame and menu)

- **Full-screen**—Captures the entire screen. This is like pressing Shift+PrintScrn, but you get to draw on the captured image before you save it.

When you've selected the snipping region, the Snipping Tool window expands to show the captured image. You can draw on it with the Pen Tool, shade sections with the Highlighter Tool, and erase portions with the—you guessed it—Eraser Tool. You can paste whatever the Snipping Tool shows directly into another program, or you can save the result as in an image file in GIF, JPEG, PNG, or HTML format. (The HTML format is actually saved with an .mht extension and contains the image as a MIME enclosure. It's very strange.)

Program name: snippingtool (works with Windows Logo+R; in the Start screen or at the command prompt, type **snippingtool**)

Steps Recorder

The Steps Recorder records a movie of your entire computer screen (or screens, if you have more than one monitor) while you perform some task. It saves the recording of what happened on the screen so that you or anyone else can later play it back. The finished product isn't very elegant, but it can be useful if you want to create a tutorial of how to perform a computer task or to document a software bug. What it creates is a slideshow of the steps you take while you're recording: every mouse click, keyboard entry, and window movement is recorded.

To create a recoding, start the Steps Recorder and then click Start Record. Perform the task you want to document. You can use the following tools:

- Click Pause Record if you have to stop to think about things, or if you need to, say, open another window to look up information that doesn't pertain to what you're recording. Close the window and then click Resume Record.

- If you want the slideshow to explain something on the screen, click Add Comment. Use the mouse to drag a box around a part of the screen that you want to call attention to, then type a message into the text box. Click OK to continue recording the slideshow.

Click Stop Recoding when you're done. Save the recording using the Save menu item. This creates a ZIP file that contains the slideshow in MHTML format. You can send the ZIP file to someone else, who can open it and then open the MHTML file inside it to view the recording. The top of the recording contains links that let you view the recording step by step, or view it as a slideshow. To view a Steps Recorder slideshow, it's best to click Pause, then use Next and Previous to step through the recording manually.

Program name: psr (works with Windows Logo+R; in the Start screen or at the command prompt, type **psr**)

What you may not have known: The Steps Recorder is really useful if you're having a problem with a software program. Record yourself performing the task that's vexing you, review the recording, and if it does a good job of illustrating the problem, send it to a tech support person. They may be able to tell you if you're doing something wrong, or they may see evidence of a bug that needs fixing.

Sticky Notes

Sticky Notes is a slick computer simulacrum of the ubiquitous Post-it Note pad. Run the Sticky Notes accessory, and a yellow square appears on the screen. Type into it. Move it around, make it larger or smaller. Click + to make another one. Click x to tear it off the screen and throw it away. There is no need for a Save button because they... well, they stick. That's it.

Program name: stikynot (works with Windows Logo+R; in the Start screen or at the command prompt, type **stikynot**)

What you may not have known: 6,000,000,000 Post-it notes are used and thrown away each year, so just think how much this app could save in paper, energy, and water pollution if everyone used it.

Sound Recorder

Sound Recorder does just as you might expect: it records sound from your computer's microphone input. Before you start, select the input channel and recording volume level. To do this, right-click the speaker (Sound) icon at the right end of the taskbar and select Recording Devices. If you're recording voice, you can click Configure and use the Set Up Microphone Wizard to set a good recording volume level. Otherwise, watch the level indicator in the Sound dialog box to look for a good signal: you want the bar to be bouncing in the middle of the meter, not near the top of the meter.

When the volume level is set, start the Sound Recorder tool and click Start Recording. When you're done, click Stop Recording and save the resulting Windows Media Audio (WMA) file. To start a new recording, you have to close the Sound Recorder and open it again. If you click Resume Recording, you'll add to the recording you first made.

Program name: soundrecorder (works with Windows Logo+R; in the Start screen or at the command prompt, type **soundrecorder**)

What you may not have known: This tool is just barely adequate for the task. If you're serious about recording audio, get a third-party tool such as Audacity (audacity.sourceforge.net/download).

Windows Journal

Windows Journal presents a window that looks like college ruled paper, in which you can draw and print text. (It's great with a stylus, and not too bad with a finger on a touchscreen.) It's a nifty note-taking tool, and a great one to know about if you have a touchscreen monitor, or a tablet or "pad"-type computer. There are times when pen and paper are exactly what you need, and this one won't leak ink into your shirt pocket. Also, this tool lets you take notes by hand and later convert your handwriting to text.

The first time you run it, it will ask if you want to install the Journal Note Writer printer driver. This driver sets up a virtual printer that lets *other* applications print into the file format that Journal uses, so that you can view, open, and mark up output from any other programs in Window Journal. If you select No and change your mind later, you can install it from Journal's Tool menu. If you select Yes and change your mind, you can remove the printer icon from the Devices and Printers window.

Journal's features are pretty "discoverable" by poking around its menus. Here are some tips for the less obvious things:

- Each whole stroke of the stylus (or your finger or the mouse) is stored separately, and can be selected, moved, or deleted independently.

- To convert handwriting to text, click the Select tool button. It looks like a loop of rope. Draw completely around the writing you want to convert, and then click Actions, Convert Handwriting to Text.

- File, Save and File, Save As save files in the Journal application's file format. You can save a document as a Journal Template, which makes it available as a starting point for future documents.

- File, Export lets you save pages as MHTML or TIF image files.

Program name: journal (works with Windows Logo+R; in the Start screen or at the command prompt, type **journal**).

What you may not have known: You can use Windows Journal as a sketching tool even if you don't have touch or stylus input. Just use the mouse and hold down the left button to draw.

WordPad

On Windows 8, WordPad looks like a stripped-down version of Microsoft Word 2010, complete with a ribbon bar. It's a decent, if *very* basic word processor that supports any variety of fonts, text coloring, and background shading as well as left, right, and hanging paragraph indents, paragraph alignment, bulleted and numbered lists, image embedding, and generic OLE object embedding.

It's actually a good introduction to ribbon bar applications, because in this rather singular case, it's simple, pretty intuitive, and well organized. About the only flaws are a couple of obscure symbols in the ribbon's Paragraph section. Just hover the mouse over them to see what they do. The program's options are set in the View menu, just as they are with the new File Explorer. (Which is odd, because options are set on the File menu in all of the Microsoft Office programs. The best advice we can give on that score is to learn to enjoy playing hide-and-seek.) You can set tab stops by dragging the mouse in the ruler at the top of the page.

Program name: wordpad (works with Windows Logo+R; in the Start screen or at the command prompt, type **wordpad**).

What you may not have known: The new WordPad saves files in formats that are compatible with most other word processing programs: Rich Text Format (.rtf) and Office Open XML (.docx) are both native formats for Microsoft Word. Use either of these formats if you want to trade documents with Office users. WordPad can read documents created by Microsoft Word, too; however, it just might not display all the document's fancy formatting. Tables and page headers and footers, for example, don't show up correctly. And if you save a Word document, the undisplayed formatting will be lost permanently. Most Apple programs and almost all publishing programs can read .rtf files, too. OpenDocument Text (.odt) format is compatible with Star Office, a free open-source office productivity suite (www.openoffice.org).

XPS Viewer

XPS is Microsoft's universally unpopular response to the universally popular Adobe PDF page description file format. You can print from any application using the Microsoft XPS Document Writer virtual printer, which creates a file that has all the text, graphics, and font information needed to display the "printed" page. The XPS Viewer can then display the file exactly as it would have looked on paper. XPS Viewer programs come with Windows 8, 7, and Vista, and can be downloaded for Windows XP. Also, third-party viewers are available for Apple's OS X and Linux.

What you may not have known: On Windows 8, as it's initially installed, the .xps file extension is associated with the Windows 8–style Reader application. I personally don't like the Reader app. If you want to use the Desktop (windowed) version of the XPS reader, you have to change a setting. Here's how: open the Control Panel using Windows Logo+X, or by searching from the Start screen. Select Programs, Make a File Type Always Open in a Specific Application. Scroll down and select .XPS, click Change Program, then click XPS Viewer.

Accessibility Tools

Windows can be made more accessible to people with varying hearing, movement, sight, and cognitive abilities. The following is a list of the various accessibility tools:

- **Ease of Access Center**—In the Control Panel, the Ease of Access Center lets you control a large number of settings and features that make Windows more accessible.

- **Ease of Access**—In the Windows 8–style PC Settings app, Ease of Access lets you control a few of the accessibility options, but oddly enough, not all of them. For the rest you have to go through the Ease of Access Center in the Control Panel.

- **Magnifier**—The Magnifier accessory lets you see an enlarged version of a portion of the screen.

- **Narrator**—The Narrator uses a synthesized voice to speak aloud the contents of the screen.

- **Speech Recognition**—Speech Recognition lets you use a computer without touching it. This topic is covered in Chapter 13, "More Windows 8 Media Tools."

- **On Screen Keyboard**—The On Screen Keyboard lets you type by clicking on the screen with a mouse, or if you have a touch-sensitive screen by touching the screen. The On Screen Keyboard is similar to Windows 8's Touch Keyboard, which is discussed in Chapter 4, but it uses much smaller on-screen buttons for the keys. Its layout exactly matches a standard PC keyboard.

- **Welcome (logon) screen**—The icon at the lower-left corner of the Welcome screen opens a panel that lets you turn on various accessibility settings. The Narrator starts reading the contents of this panel aloud when you open it. The Welcome screen is discussed in Chapter 3, "Your First Hour with Windows 8."

All but the last three tools are described in the following sections.

Ease of Access Center (in Control Panel)

The Ease of Access Center controls the full gamut of Windows accessibility settings and tools. The easiest ways to open it are as follows:

- Use the Windows Logo+U keyboard shortcut.

- Search at the Start screen for **ease**. Select Settings, Ease of Access Center.

- Open the Control Panel, select Ease of Access, and then Ease of Access Center.

The Ease of Access Center lists a number of accessibility settings. By default, the Narrator reads the options aloud. See the Narrator section that follows for some tips on using Windows through the Narrator. You may need to scroll down the window to see all the choices, which are listed here:

- **Get Recommendations to make your computer easier to use**—Starts a wizard that lets you describe your limitations in eyesight, hearing, and so on. Windows adjusts itself in response.

- **Start Magnifier, Start On-Screen Keyboard, Start Narrator**—These items start accessibility tools that are described in the following sections.

- **Set up High Contrast**—Makes the screen display white text on a black background. By default, you can also toggle High Contrast mode by pressing the left Alt key, the left Shift key, and the PrintScrn key together.

- **Use the computer without a display**—Turns on the Narrator, which reads the screen aloud. You can also turn on the Narrator by pressing the Windows Logo+Enter keyboard shortcut.

- **Make the computer easier to see**—Enables High Contrast and other visual aids.

- **Use the computer without a mouse or keyboard**—Enables the On Screen Keyboard and speech recognition.

- **Make the mouse easier to use**—Enables high-visibility mouse pointers, cursors, and other mouse-positioning options.

- **Make the keyboard easier to use**—Lets you use keyboard shortcuts even if you can press only one key at a time (the Sticky Keys feature) or if you tend to repeatedly strike keys (Filter Keys). You can also enable Caret Browsing, which puts a cursor on the screen in some applications. You can then move the cursor around to select text and web page links and then press Enter to activate the selected link.

- **Use text or visual alternatives for sounds**—Tells Windows to flash the screen rather than beep to get your attention (Sound Sentry) and enables additional text captions on dialog boxes.

- **Make it easier to focus on tasks**—Enables some of the previously mentioned accommodations and lets you disable distracting animations and increase the time that notifications stay on the screen.

- **Make touch and tablets easier to use**—Enables a keyboard shortcut and lets you adjust touch screen sensitivity.

> ⚙ **tip**
>
> You can use the Make Touch and Tablets Easier to Use window to assign an accessibility tool to the Windows Logo+Volume Up keyboard shortcut.

The Magnifier, Narrator, and Speech Recognition accessories are described later in this chapter.

Ease of Access (in PC Settings)

You can find a limited version of the Ease of Access Center on the Windows 8–style PC Settings panel. To open it, view the charms by typing Windows Logo+C, by pointing the mouse at the bottom-right corner of the screen, or by dragging in toward the center from the right edge of the screen. Select Settings, Change PC Settings, Ease of Access.

This panel lets you enable two accommodations: High Contrast and Make Everything on Your Screen Bigger (affects Windows 8–style apps only). You can also adjust an accessibility shortcut, increase the time that notifications are shown, and thicken the cursor.

Magnifier

The Magnifier tool enlarges the contents of the Windows screen so you see an enlarged version of a small portion of it. You can move the display around to see the whole screen, a bit at a time. Magnifier is unusual in that it works on both the Desktop and Windows 8 screens.

To open the Magnifier, use the Ease of Access Center (the control panel version) or just type the Windows Logo+= key combination, and then press the Windows logo key and the = key at the same time to increase magnification.

A Magnifier's control box appears to let you adjust the way the tool works. If you see just a magnifying glass icon (somewhere) on the screen, click it to restore the control box, and then make one of the following choices:

- Click the Windows Logo key and the + or – icon to zoom in or out, respectively.

- Click Views to change how the Magnifier works. In the Full Screen view, the screen is expanded and the zoomed portion moves to follow the mouse pointer. In the Lens view, you drag a box around, and it shows a zoomed view of what's underneath it. In Docked view, the upper part of the screen shows a magnified version of the lower part of the screen. The zoomed part follows the mouse pointer.

- Click the gear-shaped icon to change Magnifier's settings. You can enable Color Inversion to make the magnified portion have higher contrast.

Whenever Magnifier is in operation, you can use the following hot keys:

- Windows+= and Windows++ (that is, Windows logo key and either + or =) increases the magnification.

- Windows+- (Windows logo key and -) decreases the magnification.

- Ctrl+Alt+Space temporarily zooms out so that you can see what part of the full screen you're looking at.

- Other shortcuts let you switch the view mode. The Views menu lists these.

Program name: magnify (works with Windows Logo+R; in the Start screen or at the command prompt, type `magnify`)

Narrator

Narrator is a screen reader application that describes the contents of the Windows screen in a synthesized voice. To activate it, use the Windows Logo+Enter keyboard shortcut. Alternatively, search the Start screen for **narrator** and select it from the Apps list.

By default, Narrator reads the contents of any window when you activate it—that is, when it becomes the topmost window. It will also describe what's under the mouse pointer as you move it. As Narrator reads menus and dialog box controls, the input focus follows along so that you can press the spacebar to trigger the most recently described pushbutton, check box or radio button, or you can type to enter text into the most recently described input field.

Be forewarned, though, that check boxes work as toggles. If you trigger a check box that's already checked, you will *uncheck* it. So, for example, if you press spacebar after Narrator says "Always read this section aloud" and the box was already checked, you will turn the option *off*. Just press the spacebar again to toggle it back on.

When Narrator is active, its icon appears in the Desktop's taskbar. You can click that icon to open the Narrator's Settings window, where you can change the voice and navigation options as well as fine-tune what sorts of events Windows will describe, from pop-up warnings to keystrokes. If you change the voice to Microsoft David, increase the speed two ticks, and raise the pitch all the way, you'll get something close to NPR's Ira Glass.

Program name: narrator (works with Windows Logo+R; in the Start screen or at the command prompt, type **narrator**)

9

WINDOWS MEDIA PLAYER

Getting to Know Media Player

Windows Media Player (WMP) is your computer's one-stop media shop, with support for playing digital music, audio CDs, digital videos, and recorded TV shows; ripping music from CDs; burning files to disc; synchronizing with external audio devices; and much more. (Actually "one-stop" isn't quite accurate. In Windows 8, you must use Windows Media Center to play DVD movies and listen to Internet radio.) Windows 8 ships with version 12 (technically, version 12.084) of this popular program (see Figure 9.1), which is essentially the same version as the one that came with Windows 7 (which was version 12.076). To launch the program, switch to the Start screen, type **media**, and then click Windows Media Player in the search results.

> **note**
>
> If you're running Windows 8 on a tablet powered by an ARM processor, you can search high and low and you won't find Windows Media Player. That's because the version of Windows 8 that runs on ARM processors—Windows RT—doesn't include Media Player.

Navigating the Library

WMP organizes its media library by category, and by default it displays the Music category at startup. However, you can change to a different category (Music, Videos, Pictures, Recorded TV, Other Media, or Playlists) using either of the following techniques:

- Use the Navigation pane (pointed out in Figure 9.1) to click the category you want, if it's displayed. (See "Customizing the Navigation Pane," later in this chapter, to learn how to add more views to the Navigation pane.)

- Drop down the Library tab list (see Figure 9.2) and then click the category you want.

Navigation Pane

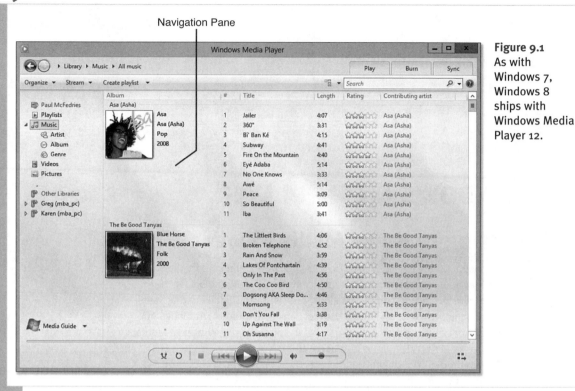

Figure 9.1
As with
Windows 7,
Windows 8
ships with
Windows Media
Player 12.

The path information beside the Select a Category list tells you the name of the current category, folder, and view, as pointed out in Figure 9.2.

Current Folder

Current Category   Current View

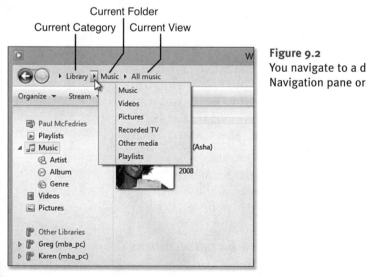

Figure 9.2
You navigate to a different category using either the Navigation pane or the Library list.

By default, WMP opens in the Music category's All Music view, which groups songs according to the values in the `Album Artist` property and then by the values in the `Album` property. WMP also offers several other Music views based on media metadata. Here's a sampling:

- **Artist**—Stacks the albums using the values in the Album Artist property

- **Album**—Groups the albums alphabetically using the values in the Album property

- **Genre**—Stacks the albums using the values in the Genre property

- **Year**—Groups the albums by decade using the values in the Date Released property

- **Rating**—Stacks the albums using the values in the Rating property

Three of these views—Artist, Album, and Genre—are available in the Navigation pane. For the rest, drop down the Music list (see Figure 9.3) and then click the view you want.

Figure 9.3
Drop down the folder list to see all the views available in that folder.

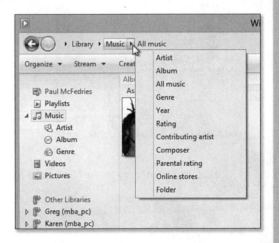

Of course, you get a different set of views for each category. For example, you can view items in the Videos category by actors, genre, and rating, and you can view items in the Recorded TV category by series, genre, actors, and rating. In each category, you can see even more views by clicking the folder list in the path.

Customizing the Navigation Pane

The Navigation pane is a handy way to get around the WMP interface, but by default it includes only a few categories and even fewer views. If you have sections of the library that you use frequently, you can make WMP easier to use by adding those sections to the Navigation pane. Here's how it's done:

1. Select Organize, Customize Navigation Pane. WMP opens the Customize Navigation Pane dialog box, shown in Figure 9.4.

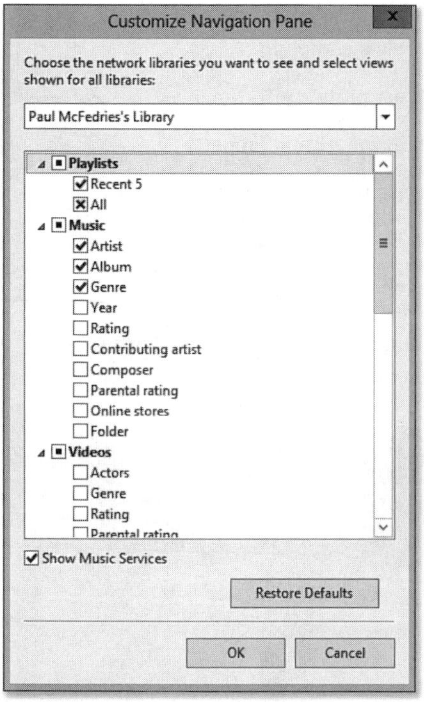

Customize Navigation Pane   X

Choose the network libraries you want to see and select views
shown for all libraries:

Paul McFedries's Library   ▼

▲ ▪ **Playlists**   ∧
  ☑ Recent 5
  ☒ All
▲ ▪ **Music**   ≡
  ☑ Artist
  ☑ Album
  ☑ Genre
  ☐ Year
  ☐ Rating
  ☐ Contributing artist
  ☐ Composer
  ☐ Parental rating
  ☐ Online stores
  ☐ Folder
▲ ▪ **Videos**
  ☐ Actors
  ☐ Genre
  ☐ Rating
  ☐ Parental rating   ∨

☑ Show Music Services

                          Restore Defaults

              OK   Cancel

Figure 9.4
Use the Customize Navigation Pane dialog box to control which
categories and views you see in the Navigation pane.

2. To add a category to the Navigation pane, activate its check box.

3. Use the check boxes within each category to control the views that appear in the Navigation
   pane.

4. Click OK.

Syncing Media Devices

When you insert a WMP-compatible media device, WMP recognizes it and automatically displays
the device, its total capacity, and its available space in the Sync tab's List pane, as shown in
Figure 9.5.

To create a list of items to add to the device, display the album,
song, or whatever in the Contents pane; click and drag the item;
and then drop it inside the Sync List. WMP automatically updates
the available storage space in the device as you drop items in the
Sync List. You can also click and drag the items within the Sync
List to control the order.

 tip

You can "preshuffle" the media
files before starting the sync.
Pull down the Sync List button
and click Shuffle List.

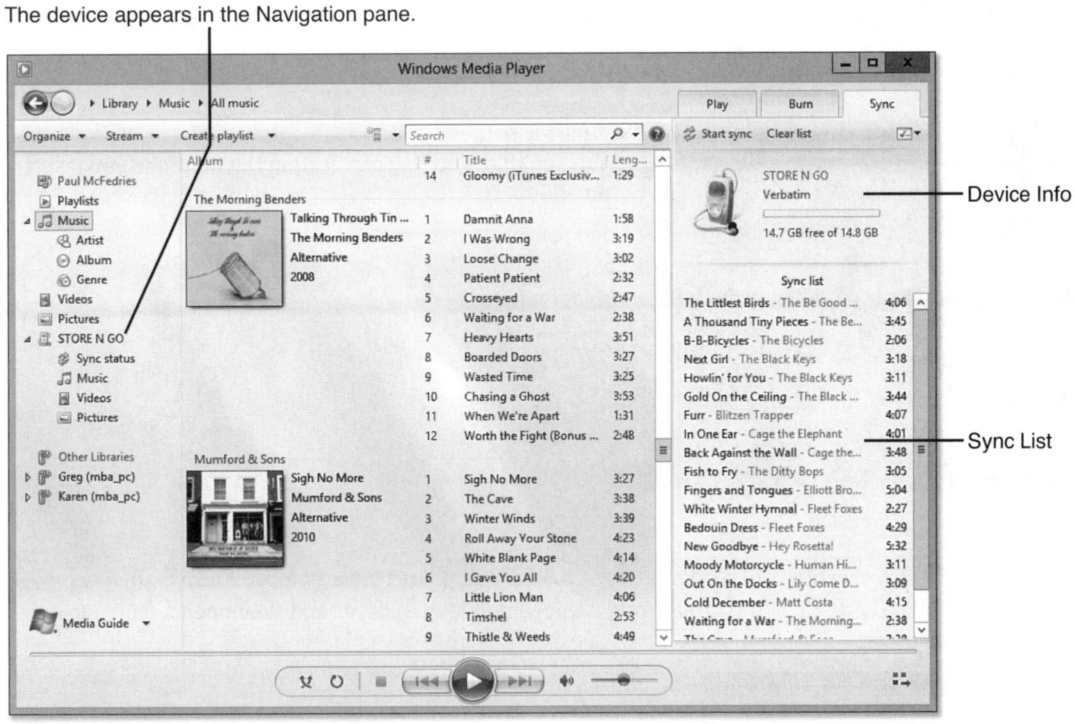

The device appears in the Navigation pane.

Device Info

Sync List

Figure 9.5
When you insert a media device, information about the device appears in the Sync tab's List pane.

When you're ready to add the item, click Start Sync. WMP switches to the device's Sync Status folder to display the progress of the sync.

WMP supports two-way synchronizing, which means that not only can you sync files from your PC to a media device, but you also can sync files from a media device to your PC. This is handy if you've purchased music directly to the device or uploaded media to the device using a different application.

To sync from a media device to your PC, you open a view on the media device, find the files you want to sync, and then click and drag them to the Sync List. Alternatively, just click Start Sync to synchronize everything on the device with WMP.

Playing Media Files

Windows 8 gives you many indirect ways to play media files via Windows Media Player. Here's a summary:

- Open File Explorer, find the media file you want to play, and then double-click the file.

note

To control the media file types that are associated with Windows Media Player, switch to the Start screen, type **default**, and then click Default Programs. In the Default Programs window, click Set Your Default Programs, click Windows Media Player, and then click Choose Defaults for This Program. Activate the check boxes for the file types that you want to open automatically in Windows Media Player. If you don't want Windows Media Player to handle a particular file type, deactivate its check box.

- Insert an audio CD in your computer's optical drive. The first time you do this, Windows 8 displays an AutoPlay notification that asks you what you want to do when you insert an audio CD (see Figure 9.6). Click the notification and then click Play Audio CD.

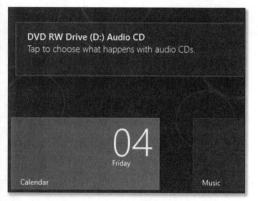

Figure 9.6
You see this AutoPlay notification the first time you insert an audio CD.

- If you have a memory card reader, insert a memory card (such as a CompactFlash card or a MultiMedia Card). Click the drive when it appears in Media Player and then open a media folder from the drive.

- Download media from the Internet.

- You can also open files directly from Media Player by pressing Alt, pulling down the File menu, and selecting either Open (to launch a media file from your computer or from a network location) or Open URL (to launch a media file from the Internet).

tip

Many of today's keyboards are *media enhanced*, which means they come with extra keys that perform digital media functions such as playing, pausing, and stopping media, adjusting the volume, and changing the track. In addition, here are a few Windows Media Player shortcut keys you might find useful while playing media files:

Ctrl+P—Play or pause the current media

Ctrl+S—Stop the current media

Ctrl+B—Go to the previous track

Ctrl+Shift+B—Rewind to the beginning of the media

Ctrl+F—Go to the next track

Ctrl+Shift+F—Fast forward to the end of the media

Ctrl+H—Toggle shuffle playback

Ctrl+T—Toggle repeat playback

Ctrl+1—Switch to the Library window

Ctrl+2—Switch to the Skin window

Ctrl+3—Switch to the Now Playing window

Alt+1—Display video size at 50%

Alt+2—Display video size at 100%

Alt+3—Display video size at 200%

F7—Mute sound

F8—Decrease volume

F9—Increase volume

Setting Media Player's Playback Options

Windows Media Player comes with several options you can work with to control various aspects of the playback. To see these options, select Organize, Options. The Player tab, shown in Figure 9.7, contains the following settings:

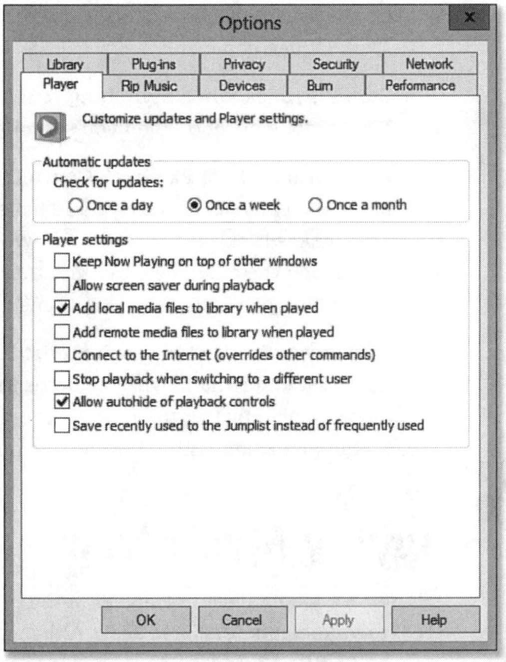

Figure 9.7
Use the Player tab to configure Windows Media Player's playback options.

- **Check for Updates**—Use these options to determine how often Windows Media Player checks for newer versions of the program.

- **Keep Now Playing on Top of Other Windows**—When this check box is activated, WMP's Now Playing window stays on top of other windows. This is useful if you want to access Windows Media Player's playback controls while working in another program.

- **Allow Screen Saver During Playback**—When this check box is activated, the Windows 8 screensaver is allowed to kick in after the system has been idle for the specified number of minutes. If you're watching streaming video content or a recorded TV show, leave this check box deactivated to prevent the screensaver from activating.

- **Add Local Media Files to Library When Played**—When this check box is activated, Windows Media Player adds files that you play to the library. For example, if you play a downloaded MP3 file, Windows Media Player adds it to the library. Note that, by default, Windows Media Player doesn't add media from removable media and network shares to the library (see the next setting).

- **Add Remote Media Files to Library When Played**—When this check box is activated, Media Player adds music files to the library that you play from removable media, such as a CompactFlash card, as well as from shared network folders. Note that you won't be able to play these items unless the removable media is inserted or the network share is available.

- **Connect to the Internet**—When this check box is activated, Windows Media Player always connects to the Internet when you select a feature that requires Internet access, such as the Media Guide (windowsmedia.com). This connection occurs even if you have activated the File menu's Work Offline command.

- **Stop Playback when Switching to a Different User**—When this check box is activated, Media Player stops playing when you switch to a different user account.

- **Allow Autohide of Playback Controls**—When this option is activated, the Now Playing window hides the playback controls if you haven't done anything within the window after a few seconds. This makes it easier to view the Now Playing art or visualization, and you get the controls back by moving the mouse pointer into the window. If you find this a hassle, deactivate this option to display the playback control full time.

- **Save Recently Used to the Jumplist Instead of Frequently Used**—When this check box is deactivated, Media Player populates its taskbar jumplist with a Frequent section that lists the media you've played the most. If you deactivate this option, Media Player replaces the jumplist's Frequent section with a Recent section, which shows the media you've played most recently.

Copying Music from an Audio CD

Windows Media Player comes with the capability to copy (*rip* in the vernacular) tracks from an audio CD to your computer's hard disk. Although this process is straightforward, as you'll see, there are several options you need to take into account *before* you start copying. These options include the location of the folder in which the ripped tracks will be stored, the structure of the track filenames, the file format to use, and the quality (bit rate) at which you want to copy the tracks. You control all these settings in the Rip Music tab of the Options dialog box (select Organize, Options to get there).

Selecting a Location and Filename Structure

The Rip Music to This Location group displays the name of the folder that will be used to store the copied tracks. By default, this location is `%UserProfile%\Music`. To specify a different folder (for example, a folder on a partition with lots of free space), click Change and use the Browse for Folder dialog box to choose the new folder.

The default filenames that Windows Media Player generates for each copied track use the following structure:

```
Track_Number Song_Title.ext
```

Here, *Track_Number* is the song's track number on the CD, *Song_Title* is the name of the song, and *ext* is the extension used by the recording format (such as WMA or MP3). Windows Media

Player can also include additional data in the filename, such as the artist name, the album name, the music genre, and the recording bit rate. To control which of these details the name incorporates, click the File Name button in the Rip Music tab to display the File Name Options dialog box, shown in Figure 9.8. Activate the check boxes beside the details you want in the filenames, and use the Move Up and Move Down buttons to determine the order of the details. Finally, use the Separator list to choose which character to use to separate each detail.

Figure 9.8
Use the File Name Options dialog box to specify the details you want in the filename assigned to each copied audio CD track.

Choosing the Recording File Format

Prior to version 10, Windows Media Player supported only a single file format: WMA (Windows Media Audio). This is an excellent music format that provides good quality recordings at high compression rates. If you plan to listen to the tracks only on your computer or on a custom CD, the WMA format is all you need. However, if you have an MP3 player or other device that may not recognize WMA files (although most do, unless you're one of the zillions with an iPod, iPhone, or iPad), you need to use the MP3 recording format. Windows Media Player 12 supports the following formats:

- **Windows Media Audio**—This is Windows Media Player's default audio file format. WMA compresses digital audio by removing extraneous sounds that are not normally detected by the human ear. This results in high-quality audio files that are a fraction of the size of uncompressed audio.

- **Windows Media Audio Pro**—This version of WMA can create music files that are smaller than regular WMA and therefore are easier to play on mobile devices that don't have much room.

- **Windows Media Audio (Variable Bit Rate)**—This version of WMA is a bit "smarter" in that it changes the amount of compression depending on the audio data: if the data is more complex, it uses less compression to keep the sound quality high; if the data is less complex, it cranks up the compression.

- **Windows Media Audio Lossless**—This version of WMA doesn't compress the audio tracks at all. This gives you the highest possible audio quality, but it takes up much more space (up to about 400MB per CD).

- **MP3**—This is a popular format on the Internet. Like WMA, MP3 compresses the audio files to make them smaller without sacrificing quality. MP3 files are generally about twice the size of WMA files, but more digital audio players support MP3 (although not many more, these days).

- **WAV**—This is an uncompressed audio file format that is compatible with all versions of Windows, even going back to Windows 3.0.

Use the Format list in the Rip Music tab to choose the encoder you want to use. Note that if you select any Windows Media Audio format, the Copy Protect Music check box becomes enabled. Here's how this check box affects your copying:

- If Copy Protect Music is activated, Media Player applies a license to each track that prevents you from copying the track to another computer or to any portable device that is SDMI compliant (SDMI is the *Secure Digital Music Initiative*; see www.sdmi.org for more information). Note, however, that you are allowed to copy the track to a writeable CD. So this is the route to take if you'll be lending out a music CD that you created, and you don't want the borrower to illegally copy any of the tracks.

- If Copy Protect Music is deactivated, there are no restrictions on where or how you can copy the track. As long as you're copying tracks for personal use, deactivating this check box is the most convenient route to take.

> **tip**
> Another way to access the format list is to click the audio CD in Media Player and select Rip Settings, Format.

Specifying the Quality of the Recording

The tracks on an audio CD use the CD Audio Track file format (`.cda` extension), which represents the raw (uncompressed) audio data. You can't work with these files directly because the CDA format isn't supported by Windows 8 and because these files tend to be huge (usually double-digit megabytes, depending on the track). Instead, the tracks need to be converted into a Windows 8–supported format (such as WMA). This conversion usually involves compressing the tracks to a more manageable size. However, because the compression process operates by removing extraneous data from the file (that is, it's a *lossy* compression), there's a tradeoff between file size and music quality. That is, the higher the compression, the smaller the resulting file, but the poorer the sound quality. Conversely, the lower the compression, the larger the file, but the better the sound quality. Generally, how you handle this tradeoff depends on how much hard disk space you have to store the files and how sensitive your ear is to sound quality.

The recording quality is usually measured in kilobits per second (Kbps; this is called the *bit rate*), with higher values producing better quality and larger files, as shown in Table 9.1 for the Windows Media Audio format.

Table 9.1   WMA Ripping Bit Rates and the Disk Space They Consume

Kbps	KB/Minute	MB/Hour
32	240	14
48	360	21
64	480	28
96	720	42
128	960	56
160	1,200	70
192	1,440	84
256	1,920	112
320	2,400	140

To specify the recording quality, use the Audio Quality slider in the Rip Music tab. Move the slider to the right for higher quality recordings, and to the left for lower quality.

Copying Tracks from an Audio CD

After you've made your recording choices, you're ready to start ripping tracks. Here are the steps to follow:

1. Insert the audio CD. Windows Media Player displays a list of the available tracks.

2. Activate the check boxes beside the tracks you want to copy.

3. Click Rip CD.

> **tip**
>
> Another way to select the recording quality is to click the audio CD in Media Player, and then select Rip Settings, Audio Quality.

Copying Tracks to a Recordable CD or Device

In addition to copying music to your computer from a CD, Windows Media Player can also perform the opposite task: copying media files from your computer to a recordable CD or portable device.

Creating a Playlist

Most people find recording is easiest if it's done from a *playlist*, a customized collection of music files. Here's how to create a new playlist:

1. Click Create Playlist. Windows Media Player adds the new playlist.

2. Type a name for the playlist and press Enter.

3. For each song you want to include in the new playlist, either drag it from the library and drop it on the playlist in the Navigation pane, or right-click the song, click Add To, and then click the playlist in the menu that appears.

After your playlist has been created, you can view, play, or edit the list by clicking it in the Navigation pane.

Recording to a CD or Device

Here are the steps to follow to burn music files to a recordable CD or portable device:

1. Insert the recordable CD or attach the portable device.

2. Click Burn in the Windows Media Player taskbar. The Burn List appears on the right side of the window.

3. For each playlist or song you want to burn, drag it from the library to the Burn List pane.

4. Click Start Burn.

Streaming Your Media Library

If you've spent a great deal of time ripping audio CDs, downloading music files, adding other media to your library, and organizing the library, you probably do not want to repeat all that work on another computer. If you have a wired or wireless network, however, you can take advantage of the library work you have done on one computer by sharing—or *streaming*—that library through your local homegroup. This enables any other homegroup user to include your media in their Media Player library. This also applies to other user accounts on your computer. Those users can sign on and then access your shared library. Your shared library is also available to other media devices on the network, such as an Xbox 360 or a networked digital media receiver.

➡️ *To learn how to create and join a local homegroup,* **see** *"Setting Up a Homegroup," **p. 407**.*

To activate media streaming, select Stream, Turn On Media Streaming with Homegroup. This displays the Share With Other Homegroup Members dialog box, shown in Figure 9.9. For Pictures, Videos, and Music, select Shared in the Permissions list. Click Next and then click Finish.

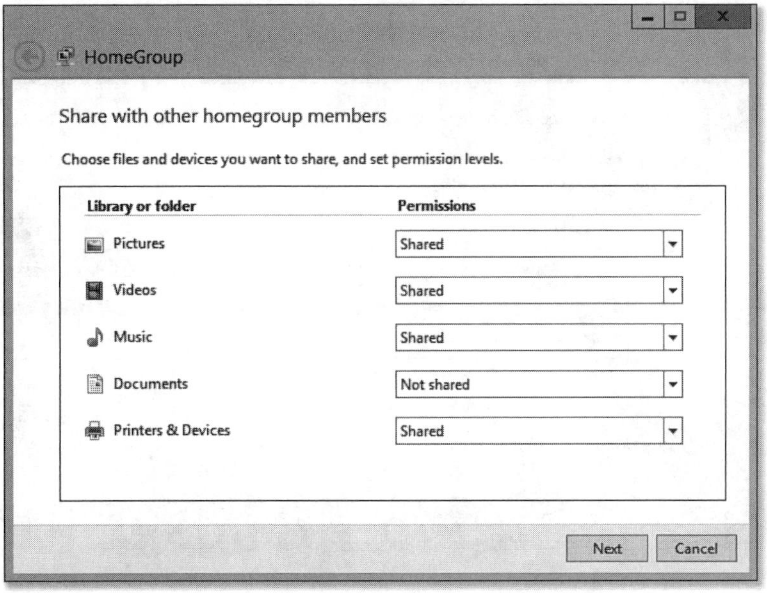

Figure 9.9
You can stream your Media Player library's pictures, videos, and music with your homegroup.

Windows 8 now displays the Media Streaming Options window, shown in Figure 9.10. The large box in the middle lists the network computers and devices that Media Player has detected. In each case, click an icon and then either activate or deactivate the Allowed check box. If you allow an item, you can also click Customize to specify exactly what you want to share based on star ratings and parental ratings. To return to the Media Streaming Options window in the future, open Media Player and select Stream, More Streaming Options.

note
You can also allow network devices to control your local Media Player, which enables those devices to add music and other media to your library. To set this up, click Stream and then click Allow Remote Control of My Player. In the Allow Remote Control dialog box, click Allow Remote Control on This Network.

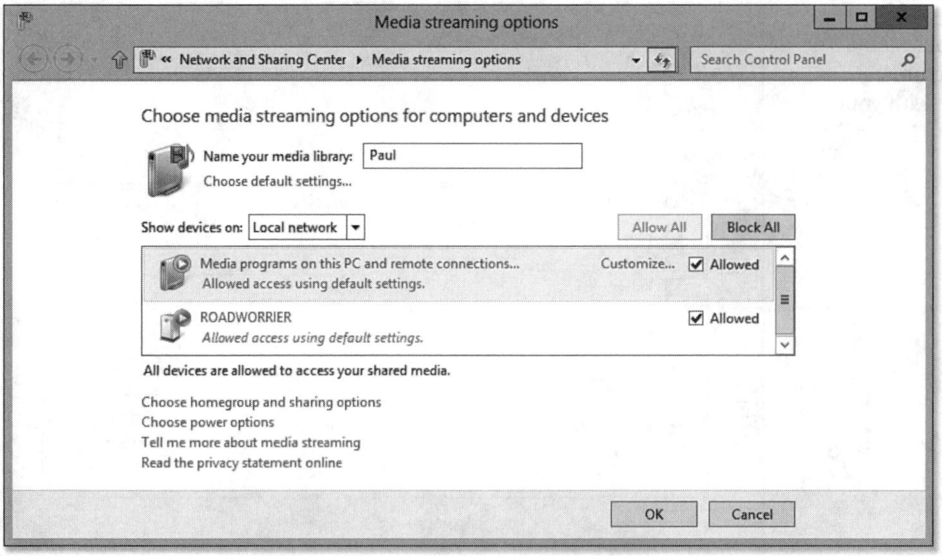

Figure 9.10
Use the Media Streaming Options window to allow or deny other network devices access to your Media Player library.

WINDOWS MEDIA CENTER

Windows 8 and Windows Media Center

For many years, Microsoft has pitched Windows Media Center as the application that turns your computer into a home entertainment hub. You can connect your PC to your TV, stereo system, and other entertainment components, and then use Windows Media Center to stream movies, photos, music, and more from your PC to your external entertainment devices. With the right equipment, you also can use Windows Media Center to record TV shows.

That sounds like a great thing, and it's certainly more than the Windows 8 Video app can do, so you'd think that Windows Media Center would be a Windows 8 centerpiece. Alas, the saga of the relationship between Windows 8 and Windows Media Center is an epic tale, full of the requisite sound and fury, signifying, well, we're not really sure. We do know how the story ends, however, and we're not spoiling anything by telling you the ending up front: Media Center is *not* part of any Windows 8 edition.

The reasons why not take up a significant chunk of that epic tale, but the basic problem is that, as you see in the next section, Media Center comes with fairly hefty system requirements, far more than anything else that Windows 8 offers. In the past, Microsoft handled these extra requirements either by creating different editions of Windows (such as Windows XP Media Center Edition) or by including Media Center only in certain editions of Windows (such as the Home Premium and Ultimate editions of Windows 7 and Windows Vista). With Windows 8, however, Microsoft was determined to greatly simplify its editions, and it succeeded in that regard by offering just two editions for the consumer desktop: Windows 8 and Windows 8 Pro. Microsoft felt there was no place for Media Center in either edition, so it dropped the program from standard installs.

So, given all that and given Media Center's omission from Windows 8, why are we writing about it? Because Media Center is still around, just that it's now an add-on, and how you get it depends on which version of Windows 8 you're running:

- **Windows 8 Pro**—Microsoft is offering a Windows 8 Media Center Pack, which you can purchase and install via the Add Features wizard.

- **Windows 8**—Microsoft is offering a Windows 8 Pro Pack, also available through the Add Features Wizard.

In both cases, you end up with a new edition of Windows 8 installed on your PC: Windows 8 Pro with Media Center. What about cost? If you take advantage of Microsoft's $40 upgrade offer for Windows Pro, which is available until January 31, 2013, you get a free product key that you can use to install Media Center. Outside of that, the price of both the Windows 8 Media Center Pack and the Windows 8 Pro Pack were not set as this book went to press, but Microsoft has stated the price would be "in line with marginal costs."

Here are the steps to follow to get Media Center on your Windows 8 PC:

1. Press Windows Logo+W to open the Settings search pane.

2. Type **add features** and then click Add Features to Widows 8 in the search results. User Account Control asks you to confirm.

3. Click Yes or enter your Windows 8 administrator account credentials. The Add Features to Windows 8 Wizard appears. If you already have a product key for Media Center, skip to step 6.

4. Click I Want to Buy a Product Key Online. The wizard takes you online where you can purchase a product key for either the Windows 8 Media Center Pack (if you're currently running Windows 8 Pro) or the Windows 8 Pro Pack (if you're currently running Windows 8).

5. If necessary, repeat steps 1–3 to return to the Add Features to Windows 8 Wizard.

6. Click I Already Have a Product Key. The wizard prompts you to enter your add-on product key.

7. Type the product key and then click Next. The wizard asks you to accept the license.

8. Activate the I Accept the License Terms check box, and then click Add Features. Windows 8 updates your PC with Media Center.

Media Center Hardware Requirements

Media Center requires a fair amount of firepower to sling all those video and audio bits around, plus you'll need some extra equipment to take full advantage of all the Media Center features. Here's the list:

- A powerful graphics card for smoothly displaying and buffering moving images, particularly DVDs, live TV, and recorded TV. Video memory is crucial here, so don't skimp: your graphics card should have at least 256MB of onboard RAM, or even 512MB for high definition (HD) video.

- Video output jacks that are compatible with the video input jacks on your TV, assuming you want to display Media Center content on a nearby set. For standard video, this usually means component (red, green, and blue), composite (yellow, red, and white), or S-Video connections; for HD, you need component connection or an HDMI (High-Definition Multimedia Interface) jack on your PC (see Figure 10.1) and an HDTV.

Figure 10.1
A PC that includes output jacks for HDMI HD digital video and S/PDIF digital audio.

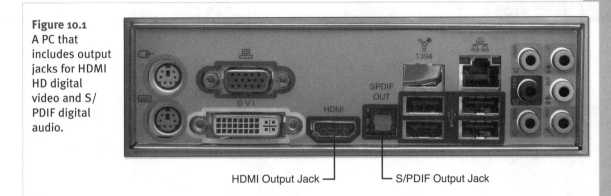

HDMI Output Jack —   — S/PDIF Output Jack

- Audio output jacks that are compatible with the audio input jacks on your TV stereo system. For standard audio, this might mean the red and white jacks associated with composite output, or the S/PDIF (Sony/Philips Digital Interface Format) jack associated with digital audio (see Figure 10.1).

- A huge hard drive for storing ripped DVD movies and recorded TV shows. Depending on how many movies and TV shows you plan on keeping, a 1TB hard drive should be your minimum, particularly if you're recording HD video. To be safe, a 2TB drive is probably a better choice.

- An internal or external TV tuner that captures the television signal from a cable, satellite, standard definition (SD) TV, or HDTV source. Again, the jacks on both ends of the connection must be compatible, meaning component, composite, or S-Video for SD, or HDMI for HD.

- A hardware encoder for real-time recording of TV shows from a cable, satellite, SDTV, or HDTV source.

- A Media Center–compatible remote control (see Figure 10.2) and an infrared (IR) sensor connected to your computer to accept and interpret IR signals from the remote, which enables you to control Media Center from a distance.

Figure 10.2
To control your PC from the comfort of your couch, you'll need a remote control designed to work with Media Center.

Connecting Your PC to Other Media Devices

As its name implies, Media Center is meant to act as a kind of hub for your home entertainment center. In a basic setup, you connect your computer to your TV and you can then use Media Center to play DVDs or downloaded movies, listen to music, watch digital slide shows, view TV listings, and even record TV programs.

A more space-age approach is to set up a wireless network and add an *extender*—such as an Xbox 360 game console—that enables you to stream movies, music, tunes, and TV to other devices on the network, even if they reside in another room or floor of your house. Beyond that, you can also connect speakers, a video projector, game controllers, and more, as shown in Figure 10.3.

There are many ways to configure a Media Center PC as an entertainment hub, but the simplest and most common is to connect the PC to a TV, which enables you to "watch" what's on the PC using the TV instead of a regular computer monitor. In particular, it means that whatever you do with the Media Center program—watch a DVD, run a digital slide show, and so on—appears on the TV.

How you connect your computer to the TV depends on the configuration of both, but there are two basic concepts you need to know:

- You attach one end of a cable to a port on your computer's video card and the other end to an input port in back of your TV.

- The video card port and the TV port either must be the same type or you can get an adapter (such as a DVI-to-HDMI adapter).

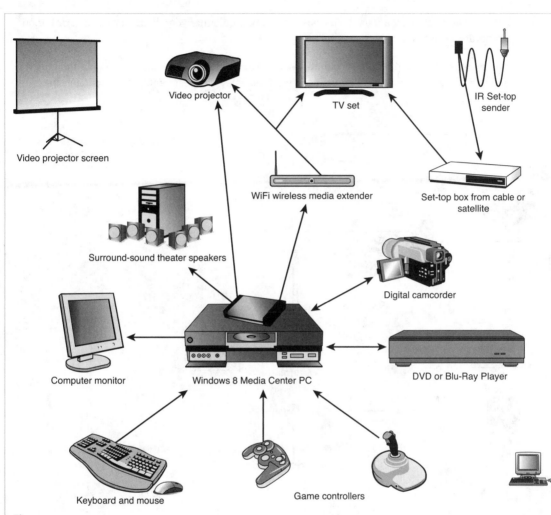

Figure 10.3
A Media Center PC can serve as the entertainment hub for your home or office.

For example, if you have a newer HDTV and PC, you most likely need an HDMI cable. If your equipment's a bit older, you most likely need component cables or an S-Video cable instead. Even older than that and you'll most likely be using a cable with RCA connectors, which are the red, white, and yellow jacks that used to be commonly used with audiovisual equipment.

Looking at things the other way around, you might want to use Media Center to watch TV and record programs. In this case, you also need to connect your TV set-top box to your computer:

- You attach one end of a coaxial cable to the output port (usually labeled *Cable Out* or *Out to TV*) in back of your set-top box, and the other end to a port on your computer.

- The computer connection must be a coaxial cable port on either your computer's video card or on a separate TV tuner device.

Of course, depending on the number of devices you want in your entertainment hub and the types of connections those devices require, your wiring duties may be considerably more complex, as shown in Figure 10.4.

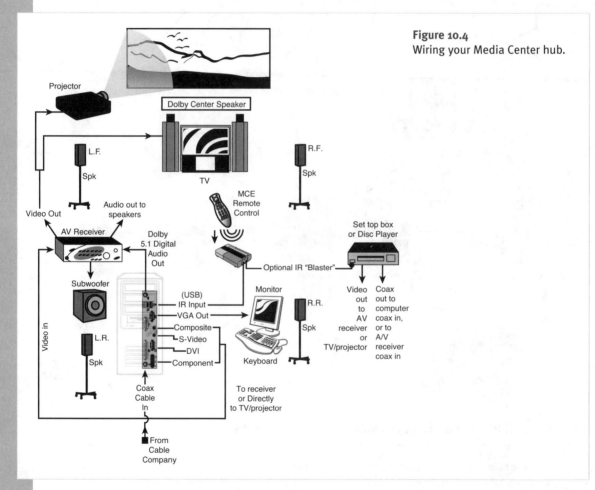

Figure 10.4
Wiring your Media Center hub.

Touring the Windows Media Center Interface

Once you've got your devices wired, you start Media Center by typing **media** in the Start screen and then clicking Windows Media Center. The first time you launch Media Center, the program leads you through a series of configuration screens, some of which are optional. By judiciously skipping the unimportant parts of the process, you can get through it in just a few minutes. For even faster service, click Continue and then click Express to let Media Center handle the details.

Figure 10.5 shows the Media Center Start page that appears after you've handled the program's initial setup chores.

Figure 10.5
The Media
Center Start
page.

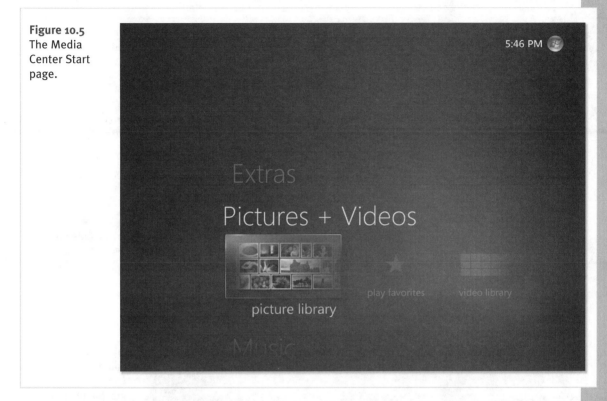

Media Center's Start page displays a list of the main tasks you can perform, which include the following:

- **Pictures + Videos**—Access your user account's Pictures and Videos libraries. Second-level tasks here are Picture Library, Play Favorites, and Video Library.

- **Music**—Work with music and radio. Second-level tasks are Music Library (a list of the music files on your system), Play Favorites, Radio (listen to radio either through a tuner or via the Internet), and Search (search your system for music).

- **Now Playing**—The currently playing slide show, movie, or other media.

- **Movies**—Work with DVD movies. Second-level tasks are Movie Library (a list of the DVD movies you've watched), Search, Play DVD, and Netflix (use Media Center to access your unlimited membership Netflix account).

 tip

The Play Favorites task plays a slide show of those images in your Pictures library that you've rated at four or five stars. Unfortunately, by default the task also includes unrated images in the slide show, which kind of defeats the point. To fix this, click Play Favorites to start the show, right-click the screen, click Settings, and then deselect the Unrated check box. Click Save to put the new setting into effect.

- **TV**—Watch TV and work with your TV tuner. Second-level tasks are Internet TV (TV shows streamed over your Internet connection), Guide (what's on and when), Search, Recorded TV (a list of TV shows you've recorded to your hard disk), and Live TV Setup (configuring TV options).

- **Sports**—Get sports information. Second-level tasks are Scores (the latest scores in various leagues), Players (stats for players that you add), and Leagues (settings for the types of stats and info you want to see for each league).

- **Tasks**—Run other Media Center features. Second-level tasks are Shut Down (close Media Center), Settings (configure Media Center), Sync (synchronize content with an external device), Add Extender (add networked devices—such as Xbox 360—to view your content on those devices), and Media Only (locks Media Center in full-screen mode).

- **Extras**—Features you can add to the Media Center interface. Second-level tasks are Extras Library (extras that you've installed in Media Center) and Extras Gallery (a list of extras that you can install).

To navigate the Media Center interface, move your mouse within the Media Center window to display the controls shown in Figure 10.6. You click the Back button to return to the previous Media Center screen; if you're several layers deep in the Media Center hierarchy, you can click the Start button to return to the Media Center Start page. You use the playback icons to control your Media Center slide shows, music, DVDs, and other playing media.

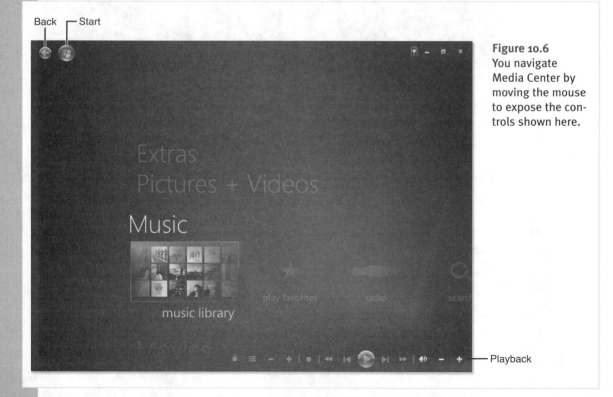

Back   Start

Playback

Figure 10.6
You navigate Media Center by moving the mouse to expose the controls shown here.

Some Useful Media Center Techniques

Media Center's interface feels a bit clunky nowadays, but it does make the program straightforward to use. To get the most out of Media Center, however, you need to know a few tips and techniques that make the program easier to use and more flexible. The next few sections take you through a few of our favorites.

Rating Pictures via the Keyboard

You saw earlier that you can use the Play Favorites task to run a slide show of the four- and five-star rated images in your Pictures library. You normally rate a picture by displaying it using the Picture Library task, right-clicking the picture, and then clicking the star that corresponds to the rating you want to assign. This technique is fine if you only have to rate a picture or two, but if you're looking at rating dozens, it can become quite tedious. Fortunately, you can configure Media Center to enable keyboard (and remote control) shortcuts for ratings: press 0 for no stars, 1 for one star, 2 for two stars, and so on. Follow these steps to set this up:

1. In the Media Center Start page, select Tasks, Settings. The Settings page appears.

2. Click Pictures to display the picture settings.

3. Click Ratings to open the Ratings page.

4. Select the Let Me Use Shortcut Keys to Set Ratings check box.

5. Click Save to put the new setting into effect.

Setting Up a Custom Slide Show

You can start a photo slide show in Media Center by using the Picture Library to open the folder containing the photos you want to view and then clicking the Play button. By default, Media Center displays each photo in order for 12 seconds, and employs a pan-and-zoom effect, where Media Center moves the photo along the screen while simultaneously magnifying the photo. These are reasonable options for most of us, but Media Center offers several options for customizing your slide shows. Here's how to set them up:

> **tip**
>
> If you're already watching a slide show, you can jump directly to the Settings page by right-clicking the screen and then clicking Settings.

1. In the Media Center Start page, select Tasks, Settings to open the Settings page.

2. Click Pictures to display the picture settings.

3. Click Slide Shows to open the slide show settings.

4. Configure the following options:

   - **Show Pictures in Random Order**—Select this check box to display the images in no particular order.

- **Show Picture Information**—Select this check box to display the name of each photo, the date it was taken, and its rating.

- **Show Song Information**—Select this check box to display the song title, album title, artist, and album cover for the currently playing song.

- **Use Pan-and-Zoom**—Deselect this check box to turn off the pan-and-zoom effect.

- **Show Pictures For**—Use this text box to decide how long you want Media Center to display each photo.

- **Slide Show Background Color**—Use this list to choose a background color on which to display the photos.

5. Click Save to put your custom slide show settings into effect.

Setting Parental Controls

If you have children who share your computer, or if you're setting up a computer for the kids' use, it's wise to take precautions regarding the media content that they can access. Fortunately, Media Center offers parental controls that can block TV shows, movies, and DVDs based on their rating. Any media that has a higher rating requires a code to view.

Follow these steps to set up parental controls in Media Center:

1. In the Media Center Start page, select Tasks, Settings. The Settings page appears.

2. Click General to display the general settings.

3. Click Parental Controls. Media Center prompts you to create an access code that you'll use to display blocked content.

4. Type a four-digit code, and then retype the code. Media Center displays the Parental Controls page.

5. To block TV programs based on ratings, click TV Ratings, select the Turn On TV Blocking check box, and use the Maximum Allowed TV Rating list to select a rating. (Any program with a rating higher than the one you select requires the four-digit code to view.) For more specific control, click Advanced, click Yes when Media Center prompts you to save, and then use the lists in the Advanced TV Ratings page to set specific settings such as Offensive Language and Sexual Content. Click Save.

6. To block movies and DVDs based on ratings, click Movie/DVD Ratings, select the Turn On Movie Blocking check box, and use the Maximum Allowed Movie Rating list to select a rating. (Any movie with a rating higher than the one you select requires the four-digit code to view.) Click Save.

Media Center Keyboard Shortcuts

If you have a wireless keyboard, you can control Media Center from afar using a large set of keyboard shortcuts, which we list in Table 10.1.

Table 10.1   Media Center Keyboard Shortcuts

Press...	To do this...
General Keyboard Shortcuts	
Windows Logo+Alt+Enter	Return to the Start page.
Backspace	Go back to the previous page.
Ctrl+D	Display the shortcut menu.
Alt+Enter	Toggle full screen.
Controlling Audio	
F8	Mute the volume.
F9	Turn down the volume.
F10	Turn up the volume.
Ctrl+Shift+C	Toggle closed captioning.
Ctrl+M	Display the Music Library.
Ctrl+Shift+P	Play a song.
Ctrl+Shift+S	Stop playing a song.
Ctrl+P	Pause or resume a song.
Ctrl+B	Replay a song.
Ctrl+F	Skip to the next song.
Ctrl+Shift+F	Fast forward a song.
Ctrl+R	Rip a CD.
Controlling TV	
Ctrl+O	Display recorded TV.
Ctrl+G	Display the Guide.
Ctrl+T	Display live TV.
Ctrl+R	Record a TV show.
Ctrl+P	Pause or resume recorded TV or live TV.
Ctrl+Shift+S	Stop recording or playing a TV show.
Ctrl+Shift+P	Resume playing a TV show.
Ctrl+Shift+B	Rewind recorded TV or live TV.
Ctrl+Shift+F	Fast forward recorded TV or live TV.

Table 10.1   Continued

Press...	To do this...
Ctrl+B	Skip back.
Ctrl+F	Skip forward.
Page Up	Display the next channel.
Page Down	Display the previous channel.
Controlling Radio	
Ctrl+A	Go to Radio.
Ctrl+P	Pause or resume the radio.
Ctrl+Shift+S	Stop the radio.
Ctrl+Shift+P	Resume playing the radio.
Ctrl+B	Skip back.
Ctrl+F	Skip forward.
Viewing Pictures	
Ctrl+I	Display the Pictures library.
Enter	Zoom a picture in Picture Details.
Ctrl+Shift+P	Play a slide show.
Ctrl+Shift+S	Stop a slide show.
Ctrl+P	Pause a slide show.
Up or Left Arrow	Display the previous picture.
Down or Right Arrow	Display the next picture.
Playing Videos	
Ctrl+E	Display the Videos library.
Ctrl+Shift+P	Play a video.
Ctrl+P	Pause a video.
Ctrl+Shift+S	Stop a video.
Ctrl+Shift+B	Rewind a video.
Ctrl+Shift+F	Fast forward a video.
Ctrl+B	Skip back.
Ctrl+F	Skip forward.
Playing DVDs	
Ctrl+Shift+M	Display the DVD menu.
Ctrl+Shift+P	Play the DVD.
Ctrl+P	Pause the DVD.
Ctrl+Shift+S	Stop the DVD.

Press...	To do this...
Ctrl+Shift+B	Rewind the DVD.
Ctrl+Shift+F	Fast forward the DVD.
Ctrl+B	Display the DVD's previous chapter.
Ctrl+F	Display the DVD's next chapter.
Arrow keys	Change the DVD angle.
Ctrl+Shift+A	Change the DVD audio selection.
Ctrl+U	Change the DVD subtitles selection.

Archiving Recorded TV on Your Network

When you record TV in Windows Media Center, the program stores the resulting files—which use the Microsoft Recorded TV Show file type with the `.dvr-ms` extension—in the following folder:

`%SystemDrive%\Users\Public\Recorded TV`

If you have Windows Home Server and you want to stream your recorded TV shows to Windows Media Connect programs and to devices on your network, you need to move or copy the Recorded TV files to Windows Home Server's `Recorded TV` share.

This extra step is a pain, particularly because Recorded TV files are often multigigabyte affairs that can take quite a while to transfer. A better solution is to record TV shows directly to Windows Home Server. In early versions of Windows Home Server, this wasn't as simple as tweaking a folder value, because by default Media Center has no such setting. It was possible to work around this problem by modifying some Media Center services and Registry settings, but it was a hassle.

Fortunately, it's a hassle that's now history. Windows Home Server 2011 comes with a Windows Media Center Connector feature, which adds a Home Server menu item to the Media Center interface. The Home Server menu item includes a tile called TV Archive that enables you to configure Media Center to record TV shows directly to the server.

Assuming you've installed Windows Media Center Connector, follow these steps to configure TV archiving in Media Center:

1. In Windows Media Center, select Home Server and then click TV Archive.

2. Click Settings. Media Center shows the TV archiving settings, as shown in Figure 10.7.

3. If you want Media Center to archive all your TV shows—that is, shows you've already recorded and shows you record in the future—to Windows Home Server's `Recorded TV` share, activate the Archive All Recordings Automatically check box.

> ## 🔊 caution
> Recording a TV show is incredibly bandwidth intensive, so the modification in this section stretches your home network to its limit. Therefore, although it's possible to record shows to Windows Home Server on a 100Mbps wired or 54Mbps wireless connection, for best results, you really should do this only on a network that uses 1Gbps wired or 802.11n (248Mbps) wireless connections.

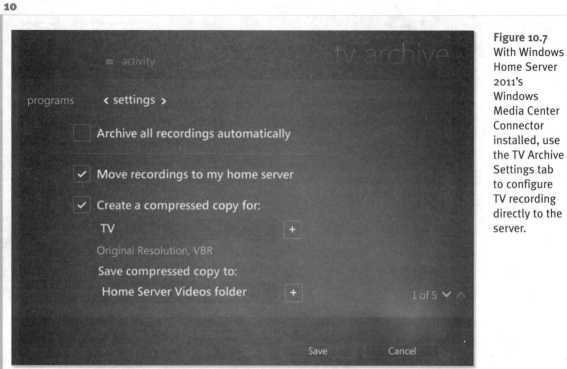

Figure 10.7
With Windows Home Server 2011's Windows Media Center Connector installed, use the TV Archive Settings tab to configure TV recording directly to the server.

4. If you want Media Center to record TV shows directly to Windows Home Server's Recorded TV share, activate the Move Recordings to My Home Server check box.

5. If you want Media Center to also create a compressed version of each recorded TV show, activate the Create a Compressed Copy For check box and then choose a format and location:

- **Create a Compressed Copy For**—Use this list to choose one of the following three formats: TV (uses the original resolution of the recording); Windows Mobile (320×240, 500Kbps bitrate); or Zune (720×480, 1,500Kbps). Note that in all cases, the resulting file uses the Windows Media Audio/Video (.wmv) format.

> **note**
> Actually, it's not really accurate to say that if you activate the Move Recordings to My Home Server check box, Media Center records TV shows "directly" to the server. Instead, Media Center creates a temporary copy of the recorded TV show locally and it then moves that copy to the server.

- **Save Compressed Copy To**—Use this list to select a location for the compressed copies. The default is Home Server Videos folder, and you should leave that as is if you want your compressed copies on the server. Otherwise, you can choose either Public Videos Folder or Let Me Use a Different Folder. (The latter requires a path to the save location.)

6. Click Save to put the new settings into effect.

If you left the Archive All Recordings Automatically check box deactivated, you can select which of your existing recordings get archived to the server. In Media Center, select the Home Server item and then click the TV Archive tile. You have two choices from here, as follows:

- **Series**—Click this tab to see a list of your recorded TV series. Activate the check box beside each series that you want to archive.

- **Programs**—Click this tab to see a list of your recorded TV programs. Activate the check box beside each program that you want to archive.

Click Save to put the settings into effect. Remember that how your existing series and programs are archived depends on the options you configured in the Settings tab:

- If you activated the Move Recordings to My Home Server check box, your selected series and programs are moved to the server's `Recorded TV` share.

- If you activated the Create a Compressed Copy for Server check box, Media Center creates compressed copies of your selected series and programs and then stores the copies in the server's `Videos` share.

WINDOWS AND IMAGING DEVICES

Connecting Imaging Devices

Windows 8 can work with both digital cameras and document scanners and often identifies them by a single generic name—*imaging devices*—because both produce image files. Windows 8 comes with support for a variety of cameras and scanners, so getting your images from out here to in there has never been easier, as you see in this chapter.

To install an imaging device, you have two choices:

- If the device is Plug and Play–compatible (as the vast majority are these days), just connect the device and turn it on. Windows 8 should recognize the device and install the appropriate drivers.

- If Windows 8 doesn't recognize your imaging device, press Windows Logo+W to open the Settings search pane, type **scanner**, and then click View Scanners and Cameras. In the Scanners and Cameras window that appears, click Add Device and then click Yes when User Account Control asks you to confirm. This starts the Scanner and Camera Installation Wizard. Click Next in the initial dialog box to see a list of scanner and digital camera manufacturers and models. Find your camera or scanner in this list, click Next, and follow the instructions on the screen.

- If you still can't access your image device, install the device software. Any scanner or digital camera worth its salt comes with software for setting up the device. If the first two options don't work, try installing the software.

After you connect the imaging device, you might see a notification like the one shown in Figure 11.1. To set the AutoPlay default for the device, select the notification and, in the option list that then appears, select the action you want Windows 8 to take whenever you connect the device (see Figure 11.2).

Apple iPhone
Tap to choose what happens with this device.

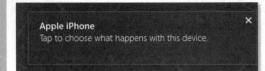

Figure 11.1
You might see a notification similar to this when you connect your imaging device.

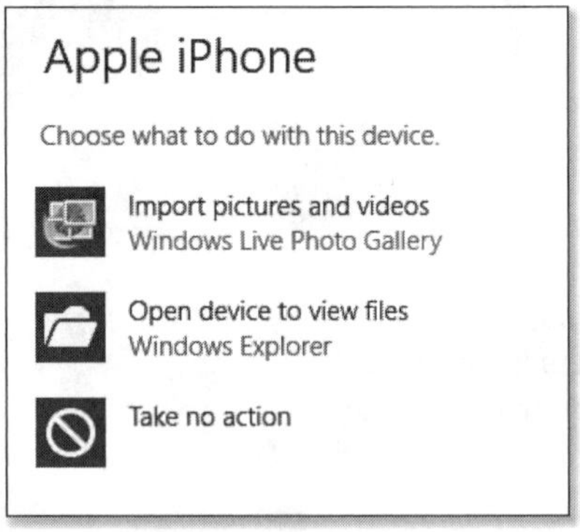

Apple iPhone
Choose what to do with this device.
Import pictures and videos
Windows Live Photo Gallery
Open device to view files
Windows Explorer
Take no action

Figure 11.2
Click the notification and then click the AutoPlay default action you want Windows 8 to take each time you insert the device.

Testing an Installed Scanner

If you installed a scanner, you can test it using these steps:

1. Press Windows Logo+W to open the Settings search pane.
2. Type **scanner**, and then click View Scanners and Cameras to open the Scanners and Cameras window.
3. Double-click the device. User Account Control asks you to confirm.
4. Click Yes or enter your administrative credentials. Windows 8 opens the device's property sheet.
5. Display the General tab.
6. Click the Test Scanner button. Ideally, you then see the Test Successful dialog box, which tells you that your scanner successfully completed the diagnostic text. If the scanner fails the test, double-check the scanner-PC connection. If that seems fine, try reinstalling the scanner's device driver or see whether an updated driver is available from the manufacturer.
7. Click OK.

Configuring Device Events

The imaging device might support one or more *events*, which are actions taken on the device. For example, most scanners support "push" scanning, in which you press a button on the scanner to initiate the scanning process. Windows 8 recognizes the pressing of the scan button as an event, and you can configure Windows 8 to specify which scanning program loads and scans the current image. If your scanner supports this and other events, you can tell Windows how you want these events handled by following these steps:

1. Press Windows Logo+W to open the Settings search pane.

2. Type **scanner**, and then click View Scanners and Cameras to open the Scanners and Cameras window.

3. Double-click the device. User Account Control asks you to confirm.

4. Click Yes or enter your administrative credentials. Windows 8 opens the device's property sheet.

5. Display the Events tab, shown in Figure 11.3.

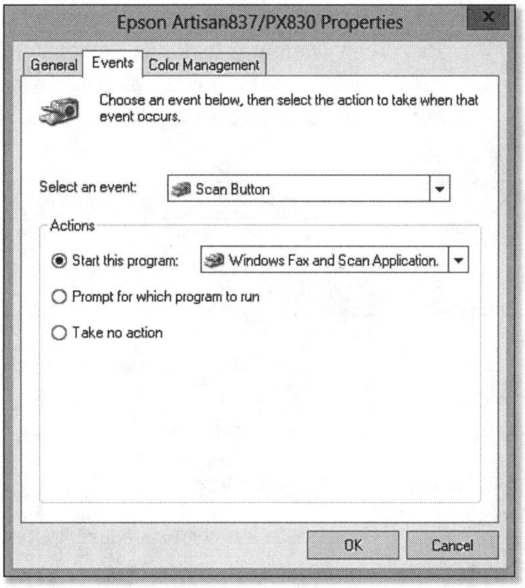

Figure 11.3
Open the image device's property sheets, and then use the Events tab to configure events such as pressing the scan button.

6. Use the Select an Event list to choose which event you want to configure.

7. Use the Actions group to choose the action you want Windows 8 to take whenever the event occurs:

   ■ **Start this program**—Select this option to have Windows 8 automatically launch a program whenever it detects the event. Use the list to choose the program you want to use. For example, if you're configuring the scan event for a scanner, you can choose to run Windows Fax and Scan.

- **Prompt for which program to run**—Select this option to have Windows 8 ask you what to do each time it detects the event.

- **Take no action**—Select this option to have Windows 8 ignore the event.

8. Repeat steps 6 and 7 to configure other events as needed.

9. Click OK.

Accessing Media on a Memory Card

Most digital cameras store images using a storage device called a *memory card*. These miniature memory modules come in many different shapes and sizes, including CompactFlash cards, MultiMedia cards, Memory Sticks, SecureDigital cards, and more. They're handy because after you transfer your images to your computer, you can wipe the card and start all over again. Although you usually get at the card's images by connecting the camera directly to your computer, as described in the previous section, there are devices called memory card readers into which you can insert one or more memory cards and then connect the unit to the computer.

Windows 8 treats each slot in a memory card reader as a disk drive, and they show up in File Explorer's Computer folder as Removable Disk drives. You're then free to insert a memory card and browse its contents directly, as described in the next section. In Figure 11.4, you see four Removable Disk drives created by a card reader—D:, E:, F:, and G:—and only drive D has a card inserted.

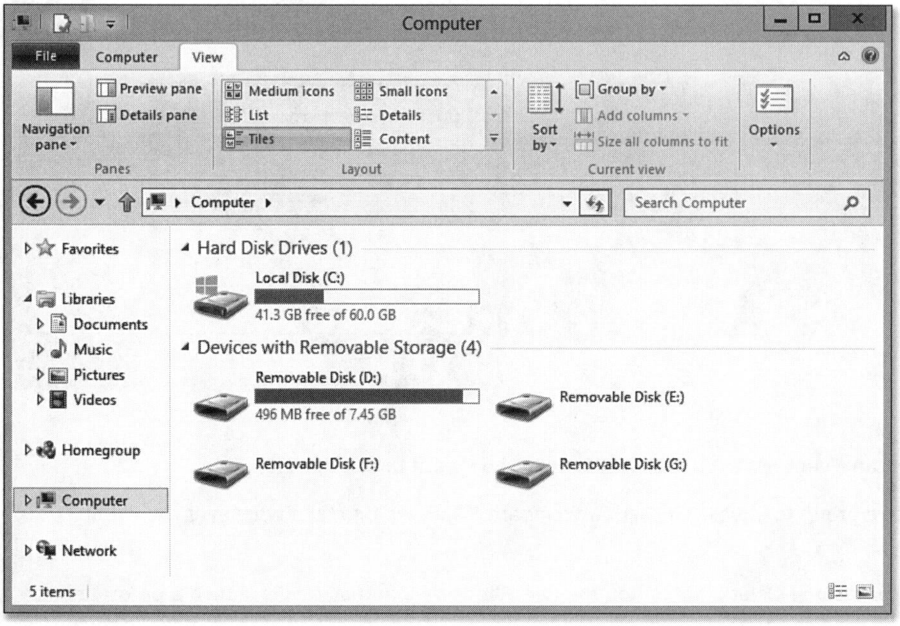

Figure 11.4
When you insert a memory card, Windows 8 creates a few temporary removable disk drives for the reader's slots.

Importing Photos from a Digital Camera

Although you can certainly leave your photos on your digital camera, at least until space becomes an issue, you can get more out of them if you transfer some or all of them to your computer hard drive. That's because once they're on your computer, you can edit the photos, email them to friends or family, publish them to the Web, or simply store them for safekeeping.

Viewing Digital Camera Images

One of Windows 8's nicer features is the capability to interface directly with a digital camera—whether it's a standalone camera or a smartphone camera—using File Explorer. This is possible because Windows 8 treats whatever the camera uses to store the digital photos as an honest-to-goodness folder. This means you can open the folder and work with the images yourself.

To do this, press Windows Logo+E or launch File Explorer and click Computer. As shown in Figure 11.5, you see a Portable Devices section that includes an icon for your digital camera.

Figure 11.5
Connect your digital camera and an icon appears for it in the Computer folder's Portable Devices section.

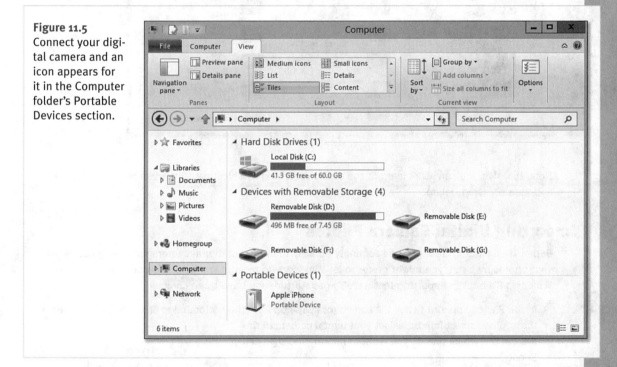

Now double-click the camera icon (although bear in mind that this technique also applies to memory cards). Windows 8 connects to the camera and displays the folders the camera uses for storage:

- **Removable storage**—Open this folder if your pictures are stored on a memory card that you plug into the camera.

■ **Internal storage**—Open this folder if your pictures are stored on a hard drive or similar internal storage device.

Open the folders to get to your pictures (you may have to wade through a few levels of subfolders). Windows 8 displays the images "thumbnail style," as shown in Figure 11.6. To copy an image from the camera to your hard disk, click and drag the image and drop it onto the Pictures library.

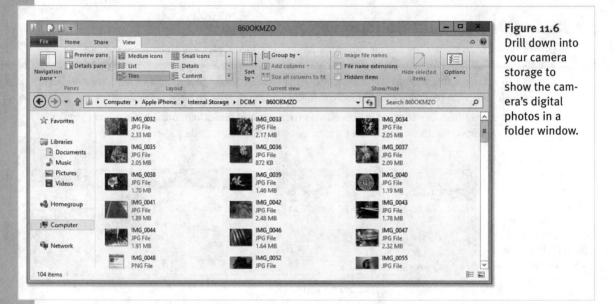

Figure 11.6
Drill down into your camera storage to show the camera's digital photos in a folder window.

Note, too, that you can also clear out the camera's photos by selecting all the images (press Ctrl+A) and then pressing Delete.

Importing Digital Camera Photos

Rather than wading through the seemingly endless hierarchy of digital camera storage to copy your photos by hand, you might prefer to let Windows do most of the work. You do that by using Windows 8's built-in importing features. To get started, you have three choices:

■ In the Photos app, right-click the screen (or swipe up from the bottom edge of the screen) to open the app bar, select Import, select your digital camera in the list, choose which photos you want to import, and then select Import.

■ Open File Explorer and then click Computer to open the Computer folder. Right-click the camera and then click Import Pictures and Videos.

■ If you've downloaded Microsoft's Photo Gallery program, launch the program (in the Start screen, type **photo**, and then

> **note**
>
> If you've just connected your camera and you're seeing the notification shown earlier in Figure 11.1, click the notification. If you have Photo Gallery installed, you can then click Import Pictures and Videos.

click Windows Live Photo Gallery). In the Home tab, click Import, use the Import Pictures and Videos dialog box to select the camera you want to use, and then click Import.

For the second and third methods, Windows 8 offers up the Import Pictures and Videos dialog box, shown in Figure 11.7.

Figure 11.7
Use this dialog box to get your Windows 8 digital camera import underway.

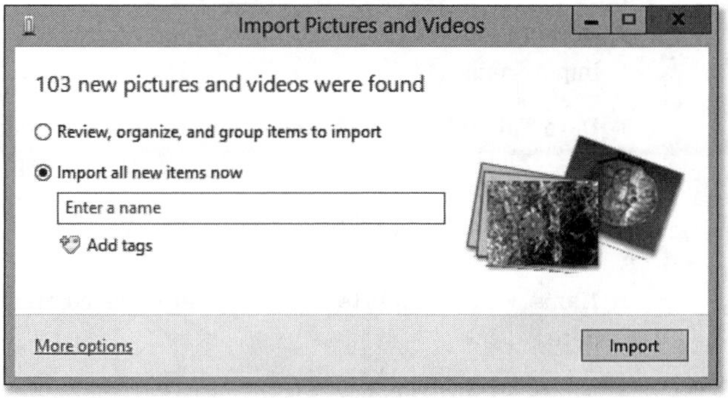

Import Pictures and Videos

103 new pictures and videos were found

○ Review, organize, and group items to import

◉ Import all new items now

Enter a name

🏷 Add tags

More options   Import

The next few sections take you through the details of the import process.

Configuring the Import Settings

When you need to import images from a device such as a digital camera, you can always connect the camera and then open the camera using the icon that appears in the Computer window, as we described earlier. You can then move or copy the image from the camera to your PC using the standard cut (or copy) and paste techniques.

The only problem with that approach is that you end up with photos that use the existing filenames of the images. This is a problem because most cameras supply images with cryptic filenames, such as IMG_1083. These nondescriptive names can make it more difficult to find and work with images, particularly if you use the Details view in the Pictures folder.

To work around this problem, the Import Pictures and Videos dialog box asks you to enter an import name for your photos, which can be a word or a short phrase. Windows 8 uses the import name as follows:

- It creates a subfolder in the Pictures folder, and the name of the new subfolder is today's date followed by the import name. For example, if today is August 23, 2013, and the import name is Scotland Vacation, then the new subfolder will have the following name:

    2013-08-23 Scotland Vacation

- It gives the file the same name as the import name, with the number 001 after it, like so:

    Scotland Vacation 001.jpg

If you're importing several images from your digital camera, then the number gets incremented for each image: 002, 003, and so on.

Even better, Windows lets you customize the folder name using any of the following variations (where in each case *Name* is the import name that you supply):

- **Date Imported + Name**—This is the default folder name.

- **Date Taken + Name**—This folder name combines the date the photos were taken with the import name.

- **Date Taken Range + Name**—This folder name combines the date the first photo was taken, the date the last photo was taken, and the import name. Here's an example:

  2013-08-09 - 2013-08-23 Scotland Vacation

- **Name + Date Imported**—This folder name combines the import name followed by the import date.

- **Name + Date Taken**—This folder name combines the import name followed by the photo date.

- **Name + Date Taken Range**—This folder name combines the import name followed by the photo date range.

- **Name**—This folder name uses just the import name.

- **None**—This option bypasses the subfolder altogether and imports the photos directly to the Pictures folder.

You can also customize the filename using these variations (where, again, *Name* is your import word or phrase):

- **Name**—This filename uses just the import name followed by 001, 002, and so on.

- **Original File Name**—The filename is the internal name supplied by the camera.

- **Original File Name (Preserver Folders)**—The filename is the internal name supplied by the camera. If the camera storage uses subfolders, those subfolders are included in the import.

- **Name + Date Taken**—The filename combines the import name followed by the date the photo was taken.

- **Date Taken + Name**—The filename combines the date the photo was taken with the import name.

To configure these and other import settings, click More Options in the Import Pictures and Video dialog box. Windows 8 opens the Import Settings dialog box, shown in Figure 11.8.

Follow these steps to configure custom photo import names and set a few other useful importing options:

1. If you want to import photos to a different folder, click Browse beside the Import Images To list, use the Browse For Folder dialog box to choose the folder, and then click OK.

Figure 11.8
Use the Import Settings dialog box to configure custom import folder and file names and other import tweaks.

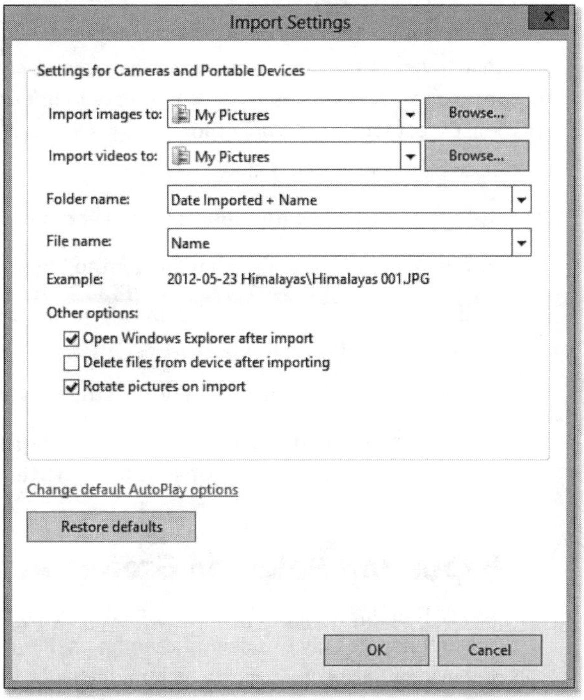

2. If you'll also be importing videos from your camera, you can select a custom import folder by clicking Browse beside the Import Videos To list.

3. In the Folder Name list, choose the format you want to use for the destination folder name.

4. In the File Name list, choose the format you want to use for the imported filenames.

5. By default, Windows 8 opens the destination folder once the import is complete. If you'd rather skip this part of the import, deactivate the Open File Explorer After Import check box.

6. If you always clear the storage in your digital camera after you import the images, you can have the Import Pictures and Videos tool do this for you automatically by activating the Delete Files from Device after Importing check box.

7. By default, Windows 8 rotates photos automatically during the import. If you'd rather handle this chore by hand, deactivate the Rotate Pictures on Import check box.

8. Click OK to put the new settings into effect and return to the Import Pictures and Videos dialog box.

From here, you must decide whether you want to import all the pictures from the camera or import only selected groups of photos. The next two sections explain the difference.

Importing Everything from the Camera

By far the easiest way to handle the import is to import everything at once. We should mention here that "everything" doesn't necessarily mean all the photos on your camera. This is certainly true the first time you import from the camera, but subsequent runs of the Import Pictures and Videos tool will detect and import only those images you haven't imported previously.

To import everything, follow these steps:

1. In the Import Pictures and Videos dialog box, select the Import All New Items Now option.

2. Use the text box to type a name for the import.

3. If you want to add tag metadata to your photos, click Add Tags and then type your tags, separating each with a semicolon (;).

4. Click Import. Windows 8 imports all the new photos to your hard drive.

5. During the import, if you want Windows 8 to delete the photos from the camera when the import is complete, activate the Erase After Importing check box.

Importing Selected Groups of Photos

Rather than importing all new photos from your camera, you might prefer to be a bit more selective and import only a subset of the photos. For example, if you have photos of a wedding and the groom's earlier bachelor party, you might want to import those separately! By default, Windows 8 organizes camera photos into groups based on the photo dates, so you can use this fact to import photos into different folders by giving each group you want to import its own import name.

Follow these steps to import selected groups of photos:

1. In the Import Pictures and Videos dialog box, select the Review, Organize, and Group Items to Import option.

2. Click Next. Windows 8 presents your photos in groups by date.

3. Use the Adjust Groups slider to set the interval Windows 8 uses to separate the groups based on the time each photo was taken. The default is 4 hours, meaning that Windows 8 creates groups at 4-hour intervals. You can choose an interval in hours (between 0.5 hours and 23 hours) or days (between 1 day and 30 days).

4. If you only want to import a group or two, deactivate the Select All check box to deactivate all the group check boxes.

5. For each group you want to import, activate the group's check box and type a name for the group. You can also click Add Tags to import the group with tag metadata.

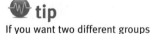 **tip**

If you want two different groups to import to the same folder, give them the same import name.

6. Click Import. Windows 8 starts importing the selected photos.

7. During the import, if you want Windows 8 to delete the photos from the camera when the import is done, activate the Erase After Importing check box.

Burning Photos to an Optical Disc

Although it carries with it the faint scent of the old fashioned, you can copy a selection of photos to a recordable optical (CD or DVD) disc—a process called *burning*. You can then send the disc to a friend or relative to share your photos.

If you have a CD or DVD burner—that is, a CD or DVD drive capable of recording data to a disc—attached to your computer (almost all new computers come with one), Windows should recognize it and be ready to burn at will.

Selecting an Optical Disc Format

Before getting to the burning steps, you need to decide which disc format you want to use. You have two choices:

- **Mastered**—This format requires that you burn photos to the disc in a single operation. That is, you first gather all the photos you want to copy to the disc, and then you run the burn. Mastered optical discs are compatible with most optical drives and CD or DVD players. For discs that can be rewritten with new data (such as CD-R, CD-RW, DVD-R, and DVD-RW), you can burn a new set of photos to the disc in each session. Keep in mind that you can't delete individual photos from a mastered CD-R or DVD-R disc, but you can delete individual photos from a mastered CD-RW or DVD-RW disc.

- **Live File System**—This is a Universal Disk Format (UDF) that treats the optical disc just like a USB flash drive. This means you can copy files to the disc anytime you like, delete one or more files, and use the disc just like a removable drive. While a recording session is open, you can only use the disc on your PC. To use the disc on another PC, you must close the session. Live File System discs are only compatible with optical drives on computers that are running Windows XP or later.

 note

Optical discs that can be rewritten in multiple recording sessions—such as CD-R, CD-RW, DVD-R, and DVD-RW discs—are known as *multisession discs*. Optical discs that can only be written to once—such as CD-ROM and DVD-ROM discs—are known as *single-session discs*.

Burning a Mastered Disc

If you want to use the optical disc in a CD or DVD player, or on an older computer, you should burn a mastered disc. Here are the steps to follow:

1. Insert a blank optical disc into your optical drive. Windows 8 reads the disc and then displays a notification asking what you want to do with blank discs.

2. Click the notification, and then click Burn Files to Disc. Windows 8 displays the Burn a Disc dialog box, shown in Figure 11.9.

3. Type a disc title.

4. Select the With a CD/DVD Player option.

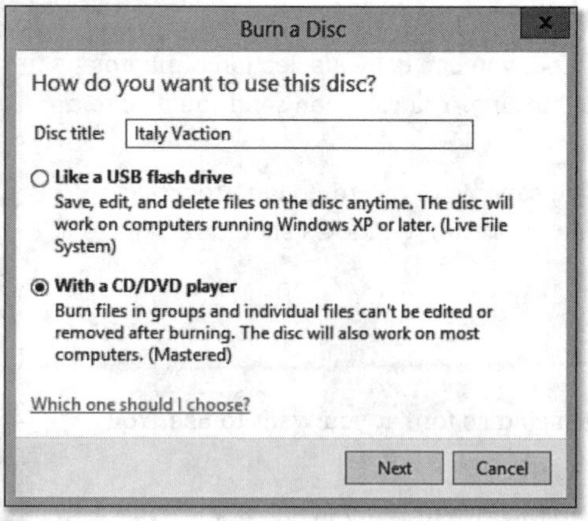

Figure 11.9
Use the Burn a Disc dialog box to initialize the optical disc.

Burn a Disc

How do you want to use this disc?

Disc title: Italy Vaction

○ **Like a USB flash drive**
Save, edit, and delete files on the disc anytime. The disc will work on computers running Windows XP or later. (Live File System)

◉ **With a CD/DVD player**
Burn files in groups and individual files can't be edited or removed after burning. The disc will also work on most computers. (Mastered)

Which one should I choose?

[Next] [Cancel]

5. Click Next. Windows opens the drive.

6. In File Explorer, open a folder that contains one or more of the photos you want to burn.

7. Select the photos you want to burn and then drag them to the disc. You can also select the photos, right-click any selected item, click Send To, and then click the optical drive.

8. Repeat steps 6 and 7 until you've selected all the photos you want to burn.

9. Click Computer and then right-click the disc.

10. Click Burn to Disc. The Burn to Disc wizard appears.

11. Adjust the title, select a recording speed, and then click Next. Windows burns the files to the disc and then ejects the disc.

12. Click Finish.

> **tip**
> If you don't want Windows 8 to automatically eject the disc once the mastered burn is complete, you can turn off this setting. In File Explorer, click Computer, right-click the optical drive, and then click Properties. In the drive's Properties dialog box, deactivate the Automatically Eject the Disc After a Mastered Burn check box, and then click OK.

Closing a UDF Session

As we mentioned earlier, if you use the Live File System format, Windows 8 sets up a UDF recording session that enables you to leave the disc in the drive and add or delete files at will, just like a USB flash drive. However, while the session is open, you cannot use the disc on another computer, so you must close the session when you are done with the disc.

By default, Windows 8 automatically closes the current session when you eject a disc. If you prefer to control when the session is closed by hand, follow these steps to turn off automatic session closing:

1. In File Explorer, click Computer.

2. Right-click the optical drive and then click Properties. The drive's Properties dialog box appears.

3. Click the Recording tab.

4. Click Global Settings. Windows 8 displays the Global Settings dialog box shown in Figure 11.10.

Figure 11.10
Use the Global Settings dialog box to control automatic UDF session closing.

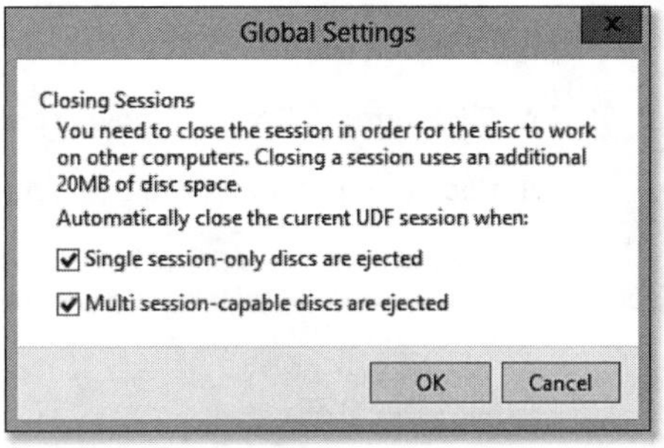

> **Global Settings**
>
> Closing Sessions
> You need to close the session in order for the disc to work on other computers. Closing a session uses an additional 20MB of disc space.
> Automatically close the current UDF session when:
> ☑ Single session-only discs are ejected
> ☑ Multi session-capable discs are ejected
>
> OK   Cancel

5. If you don't want Windows 8 to automatically close the current session when you eject a single-session disc, deactivate the Single Session-Only Discs Are Ejected check box.

6. If you don't want Windows 8 to automatically close the current session when you eject a multis-ession disc, deactivate the Multi Session-Capable Discs Are Ejected check box.

7. Click OK to put the new settings into effect and return to the optical drive's Properties dialog box.

8. Click OK.

Burning a Live File System Disc

If you want to burn the disc using the Live File System, you first have to initialize the disc by following these steps:

1. Insert a blank optical disc into your optical drive. Windows 8 reads the disc and then displays a notification asking what you want to do with blank discs. If you see the Burn a Disc dialog box, instead, skip to Step 3.

2. Click the notification, and then click Burn Files to Disc. Windows 8 displays the Burn a Disc dialog box, shown earlier in Figure 11.9.

3. Type a disc title.

4. Select the Like a USB Flash Drive option.

5. Click Next. Windows formats the disc to make it ready to receive files, which may take a while, depending on the disc and the speed of your burner. You know the task is complete when you see an AutoPlay notification asking what you want to do with removable drives.

With that done, you're ready to burn your photos by following these steps:

1. In File Explorer, open a folder that contains one or more of the photos you want to burn.

2. Select the photos you want to burn to the disc.

3. Click the Share tab.

4. Click Burn to Disc. Windows copies the files to the disc.

5. Click Computer and then examine the disc to see how much free space you have left.

6. Repeat steps 1 to 5 until you've sent all the files you want to the disc.

7. Click Computer.

8. Click the disc.

9. Click the Drive tab and then click Close Session. Windows 8 closes the recording session.

10. Click Eject. Windows 8 spits out the disc.

Sending Photos to a Printer

Printing a picture—particularly a digital photo—is a bit different from printing a text document because in most cases you want to choose a different print layout, depending on the size of the image and the size of the print you want. For that reason, Windows 8 includes a special photo-printing feature that makes it easy to get your photo hard copies. Here's how it works:

1. Open the Pictures folder.

2. Select the pictures you want to print.

3. Click the Share tab's Print button. Windows 8 displays the Print Pictures dialog box.

4. If you have more than one printer, use the Printer list to select the printer you want to use.

5. Use the Paper Size list to select the size of the paper you're using.

6. Use the Quality list to select the printout quality: Photo or Best Photo (the latter is higher quality, but it uses more ink).

7. Use the Paper Type list to select the paper you're using.

8. Use the Select a Layout list on the right to select the print size you want. When you select a different layout, the Print preview box shows you what your printed images will look like (see Figure 11.11).

9. Click Print. Windows 8 sends your image (or images) to the printer.

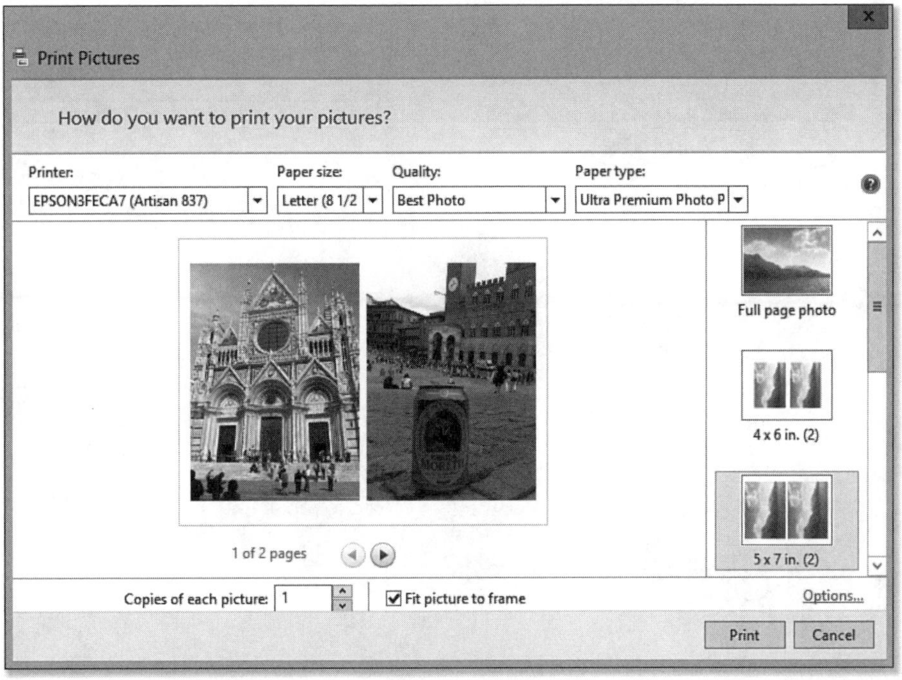

Figure 11.11
Use this dialog
box to set up your
photo-printing
options.

SCANNING AND FAXING

Introducing Windows Fax and Scan

Windows Fax and Scan (WFS) is a built-in tool that lets you do the following:

- Send and receive faxes using a fax modem connected to a telephone line. On a corporate network, WFS can also let you send faxes through a shared Fax Server.

- Scan images, drawings, and documents using a scanner or a multi-function (all-in-one) printer that has scanning capability.

Although you can use it to scan pictures, WFS is designed primarily to scan documents. If your main goal is to scan your photograph library, you're probably better off using the Windows Photo Gallery tool, which is a free download from microsoft.com.

You don't need to have both a scanner and a fax modem to take advantage of WFS. The program does let you use both together, but it can be useful even if you have just one or the other.

> **🔍 note**
>
> If your computer doesn't already have a modem, you can easily buy and install an inexpensive internal or USB external fax modem. If you have Internet-based telephone service, contact your phone service provider to see whether your line can carry fax signals. In a corporate setting, check to see whether your organization uses digital telephone wiring before you try to hook up a dial-up modem. Digital phone lines can damage your modem.

Installing Fax and Scanner Hardware

If your scanner or fax device is not already installed, follow the manufacturer's recommendations to install the fax or scanner hardware before you use Windows Fax and Scan. Use Windows 8 drivers and software, if available, but Windows 7 or Vista drivers should work, too.

Installing a Fax Modem

Many modems require you to install the manufacturer's driver software before you attach the modem for the first time. Internal and USB external modems will then self-install when you plug them in. For an external serial-port modem, you might need to type Windows Logo+X (or right-click the very bottom-left corner of the screen), select Control Panel, and then click Add a Device under Hardware and Sound.

Once the modem is installed, follow the instructions in the next section to configure the fax service.

Installing a Scanner

A scanner or multifunction printer that is connected via USB or FireWire should self-install when you connect it. Your manufacturer may suggest that you install their software before you plug in the device for the first time.

For network-attached scanners and all-in-one printers, install the manufacturer's software first. It will then find the device on your network.

If you are given a choice between installing either TWAIN or WIA drivers for your scanner, install WIA (Windows Imaging Architecture) drivers. TWAIN drivers may support more advanced scanner features, such as transparency adapters and dust/scratch removal, found on some models, but they are not compatible with Windows Fax and Scan. Some scanners install both types of drivers; that's fine.

Configuring the Fax Service

To set up your system to send and/or receive faxes with a fax modem, go to the Start screen. If there is no tile for Windows Fax

 tip

If you try to install driver software and you get a message saying that it won't work on your version of Windows, be sure that you are using the right 32-bit or 64-bit version to match Windows. If that's not the problem, right-click the installer program, select Properties, select the Compatibility tab, and then set the compatibility mode to Windows 7. If the installer first unzips files, then runs a second installer, you'll have to locate and then perform this compatibility trick on the second installer program.

 note

If you have an all-in-one printer, it most likely will *not* work as a fax modem device for Windows Fax and Scan. Instead, its software should set up two printer devices: one for printing, and one for faxing. A multifunction device *should* be able to scan, though, using Windows Fax and Scan.

 note

Windows Fax and Scan won't help you scan slides or transparencies. For that, you'll need to use third-party software or software provided with your scanner. You'll likely also need to install TWAIN drivers for that software to run the transparency adapter hardware.

and Scan, right-click the Start screen and select All Apps (or just type **fax** at the Start screen). Then, select Windows Fax and Scan.

Click Fax at the bottom of the left pane. Next, click the New Fax button on the toolbar (refer to Figure 12.1). The Fax Setup dialog box appears. The first time you do this, Windows will walk you through the process of setting up the faxing software, using these steps:

> **tip**
>
> If you'll be using WFS frequently, pin it to your Start screen. Here's how: At the Start screen, type **fax**. Right-click Windows Fax and Scan and select Pin to Start. You can also pin it to the desktop's taskbar.

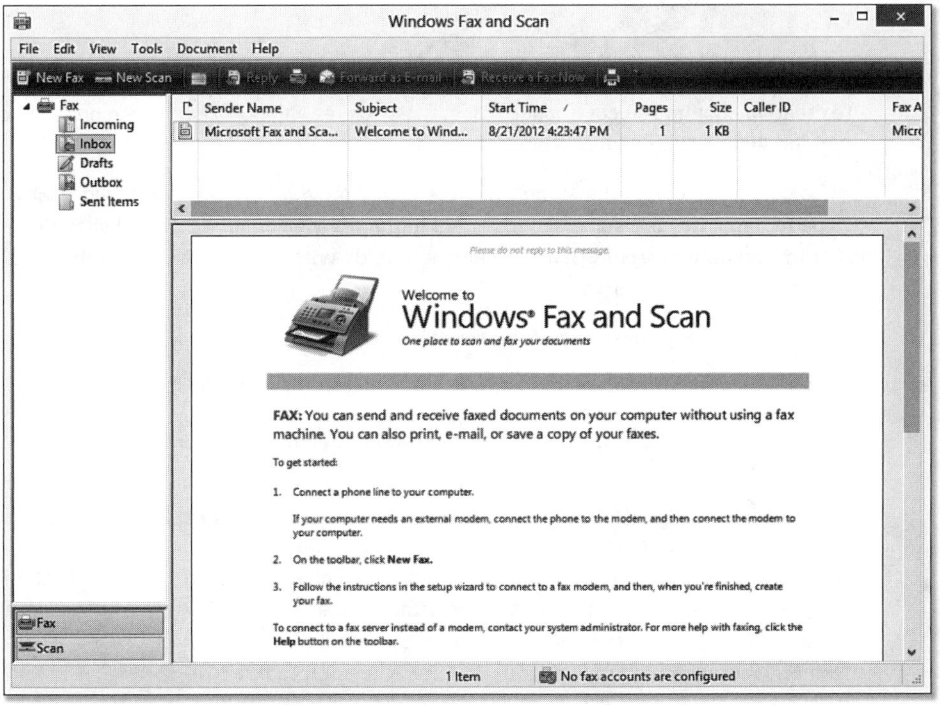

Figure 12.1
Windows Fax and Scan lets you scan and/or fax documents. (You probably guessed that.)

1. Select Connect to a Fax Modem. On the next screen, enter a name for the modem or keep the default name, Fax Modem. Click Next to continue.

2. Choose how you wish to receive faxes from the following choices:

   - **Answer Automatically**—Choose this option if you have a dedicated fax line and want the fax modem to pick up every incoming call.

   - **Notify Me**—Choose this option if you share the telephone line with voice calls. Windows will pop up a notification when there is an incoming call, and you can tell Windows whether or not to answer it and receive an incoming fax.

   - **I'll Choose Later**—Choose this option if don't want the computer to answer incoming calls.

3. A New Fax dialog box appears. Close it.

4. Click Tools, Sender Information. Enter your name, address, and telephone number information. This will later be used in fax cover sheets. Click OK when you're done.

5. Click Tools, Fax Settings, and then click the More Options button. Enter your preferred incoming fax number or company name in the TSID (Transmitting Subscriber Identification) box. This text is printed at the top of every fax you send and appears on the screen and receive log of the fax machine you call. Enter the same information in the CSID (Called Subscriber Identification) box. This is displayed on the screen and transmit log of fax machines that call you. Click OK.

That sets up the basic fax service. You can go on to create customized cover pages if you wish.

Creating a Customized Cover Page

To create a customized cover page, click Tools, Cover Pages. Existing personalized cover pages (if any) are listed. Then take one of the following actions:

- To customize one of the standard cover pages provided by Microsoft, click Copy, select a cover page template, and select Open. Then, highlight the copied entry and click Rename. Give it a new name, but be sure that the name still ends with .cov. Press Enter and then click Open to personalize the cover page.

- To create a new cover page from scratch, click New.

- To modify one of your existing cover pages, select it and click Open.

In each case, this opens the Fax Cover Page Editor, shown in Figure 12.2.

Use the Insert menu to place text, fields, and simple shapes. Fields are automatically replaced with information from the sending document and sending user, whereas literal text is fixed for all time. Use the Format menu to align objects, adjust spacing, center the page, or change the order of overlapping objects. Use the View menu to show or hide menus and grid lines (grid lines are hidden by default, but can be useful in aligning design elements). Use the File menu to print or save your cover page. Cover pages are saved with the .cov file extension and are saved in your Documents\Fax\Personal CoverPages folder by default.

To make your personalized cover page available to all users, you must copy the cover page file to \ProgramData\Microsoft\ Windows NT\MSFax\Common CoverPages\xx-xx, where xx-xx is a code that specifies your geographic region and language. Moving the file to there is a bit tricky. Follow these steps:

1. Create a cover page and save the cover page file in the default location (your Personal CoverPages folder). Test it by sending it in a fax, to be sure that it looks the way you want it to. After you're sure that it's correct, proceed to the next step.

> **tip**
>
> When you insert a field name and associated field, they're selected as a group and they will move as a group. If you want to move one of the components separately, click somewhere in the cover page away from any items. Then, move the desired item.
>
> To move several items at once, hold the Shift key down and click each of them and then drag them. You can also click the Select icon (leftmost on the toolbar) and drag a box around the items you want to move.

Figure 12.2
Creating a cover page with the Fax Cover Page Editor.

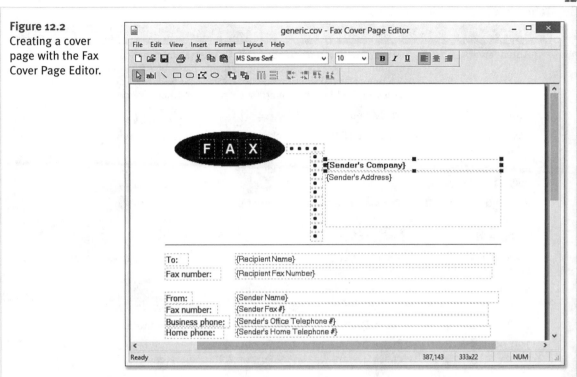

2. Go to the Desktop and click the File Explorer icon in the taskbar. (If it's not there, type Windows Logo+X and select File Explorer). Browse into Libraries, Documents, Fax, Personal CoverPages. Locate the cover page file, right-click it, and select Cut.

3. Click in File Explorer's address bar (the box where Libraries ▶ Documents ▶ Fax ▶ Personal Cover Pages is displayed). Type **c:\programdata** and press Enter. Then double-click, in turn, Microsoft, Windows NT, MSFax. Windows will say you don't have permission to view MSFax. Click Continue to grant yourself permission and continue into Common Coverpages and then into the regional folder, which is en‑US for U.S. English (but might be different on your computer).

4. Right-click in the folder's contents pane and select Paste. In the User Account Control dialog box, click Continue to paste the file into this folder.

The cover page will now be available to all users on your computer.

Changing Fax Settings

To change your computer's fax settings after the initial setup described in the previous sections, open Windows Scan and Fax and select Fax in the left pane. Then, use the menu options listed in Table 12.1 to change fax settings.

Table 12.1 Fax Service Settings

Setting	Menu Selection
Autoanswer	Tools, Fax Settings, General tab. To answer automatically, check Check Allow...to Receive, select Automatically Answer After, and set to 1 ring. To be prompted to answer, check Allow...to Receive, and select Manually Answer. To block incoming faxes, uncheck Check Allow...to Receive.
Cover Page Data	Tools, Sender Information.
Fax arrival/complete sounds	Tools, Fax Settings, Tracking tab, Sound Options button.
Fax complete/failed popups	Tools, Fax Settings, Tracking tab.
Fax send progress popup	Tools, Fax Settings, Tracking tab.
Multiple fax devices	Tools, Fax Accounts.
Personal cover pages	Tools, Cover Pages. To share a customized cover page with other users on your computer, see the previous section.
Redialing on busy/no answer	Tools, Fax Settings, Advanced tab.
TSID/CSID strings	Tools, Fax Settings, General Tab, More options button.
TSID/Page # on header	Tools, Fax Settings, Advanced tab. The Include Banner in Sent Faxes check box enables sending your TSID and the page number at the top of every sent fax page.

Sending Faxes from Windows Fax and Scan

To send a fax, in most cases you will start by creating a document using a word processing application such as Microsoft Word or the built-in WordPad application. You can fax from *any* application that can print. To send a document as a fax, open the application's Print menu and select the printer named Fax. When you click Print, Windows will pop up a dialog box in which you specify the recipients for the fax, as shown in Figure 12.3. A printed version of your document will appear as the first "attachment" of this new fax.

If you want to send more than one document in the same fax call, use the Print menu to print the first document and then add the other documents as attachments, as we describe shortly.

You can also open Windows Fax and Scan, click New Fax, and manually construct an entire fax.

Select Recipients

To send a fax to a recipient not on your Contacts list, enter the fax number in the To field. If you want to enter more than one recipient, use a semicolon to separate multiple fax numbers.

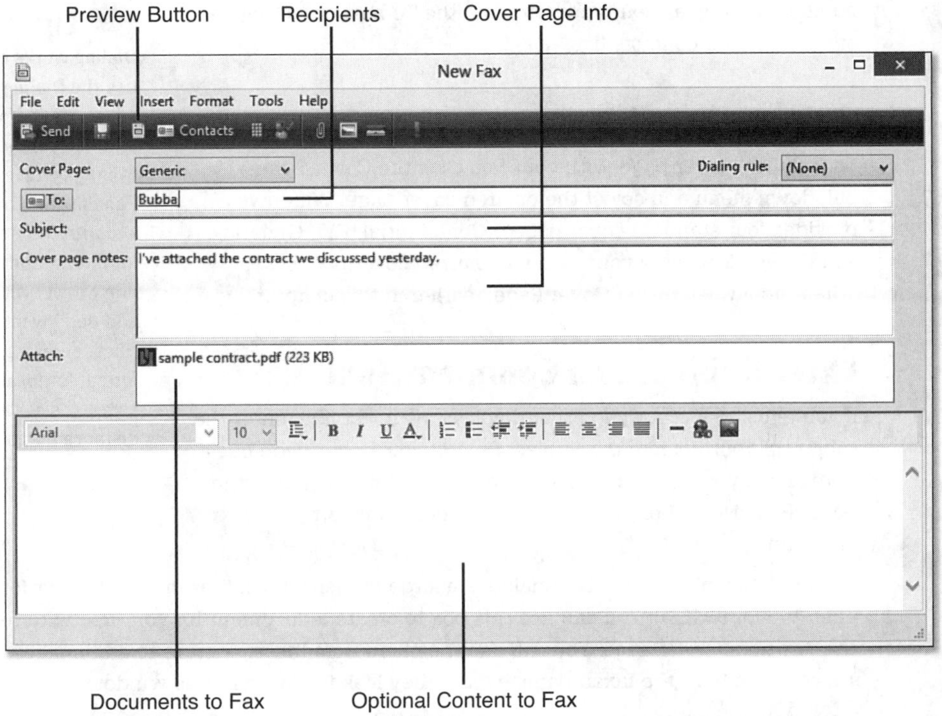

Preview Button   Recipients   Cover Page Info

Figure 12.3
You can send
a fax by print-
ing to the Fax
printer, but you
can also cre-
ate one from
scratch by
clicking New
Fax.

Documents to Fax   Optional Content to Fax

To send a fax to someone in your Contacts list, or to create and save a new contact, click the To but-ton. Then, select one or more entries from the list of contacts and click the To-> button to add them to the recipient list.

If a contact has a fax number listed, you might need to add the area code or country code to the number to enable Windows Fax and Scan to make the call correctly. Use the same information as you would provide for a standalone fax machine.

If you have selected contacts that have no associated fax number, the name will appear in red in the fax recipient list. Double-click these names and enter their fax number on the Home or Work tab.

Select a Dialing Rule

In many cases you will send faxes to recipients outside your own area code. You can have Windows automatically figure out which fax numbers need to be preceded by an area code and which can be dialed as a 7-digit number by selecting a dialing rule at the right side of the New Fax window. If no rule is listed, select New Rule and follow the instructions to set your current location and area code. When you see My Location in the Dialing Rules list, highlight it and select Properties. Change My Location to your actual city name, and then save the change.

If you travel to a different area code with your computer, select the appropriate location from the Dialing Rule list or select New Rule to create a new one.

Alternatively, you can select No Rule, and Windows will dial numbers exactly as you type them into the To box, or as they're entered in your contacts list.

Select a Cover Page

To include a cover page with your fax, click the Cover Page pull-down menu and select the desired cover page. Windows provides four standard cover pages: Confidential, FYI, Generic, and Urgent. To create your own customized cover pages, see "Creating a Customized Cover Page" earlier in this chapter.

Enter Subject and Comment Text

If you're using a cover page that displays a subject line, enter the subject of your fax into the Subject field. If your cover page has a Notes field, you can add a paragraph or two of comments in the Cover Page Notes box. These text fields don't support complex formatting.

> **tip**
>
> Dialing works best if you always use the Dialing Rule system, or never use it. If you want to use it, enter all contact fax numbers in (333) 555-1212 format for U.S./Canada/Mexico numbers and +*countrycode number* format for international numbers. If you don't travel with your computer and don't want to use numbering rules, enter numbers in 555-1212 format for local numbers and 1-333-555-1212 format for long-distance numbers.

At the bottom of the New Fax dialog is a large text entry box that includes a text-formatting toolbar (refer to Figure 12.3). You can use this box to create a document for your fax, with full formatting, and any number of pages. You can use the menu item Insert, Picture to add images, which will get scaled down to fit the faxed page, even if they look too large in this window.

You won't be able to save whatever you create here, however. Once it's faxed, it's gone. I recommend that rather than use this input area, create a document in a word processor or WordPad, and then save and print it from there.

If you leave the large input area blank, the fax will consist just of the optional cover page and any attachment documents you add in the next step.

Add Other Documents to the Fax

To send a previously scanned document, a word processing file, PDF file, or other printable file in the fax, click Insert, File Attachment. Navigate to the file and click Open. The file will be converted to fax pages when the fax is sent. You must have an installed application capable of printing this file.

You can insert any number of attachments here, to construct a single fax from multiple components.

Add Scanned Pages

You can scan pages and directly add them to your fax. Place the pages you want to scan into your scanner's Automatic Document Feeder (ADF) or place one sheet on its platen. Click Insert, Pages

> **tip**
>
> You can use your scanner like a standard fax machine using this technique. Open Windows Scan and Fax, select New Fax, fill in the recipient list, and then click Insert, Pages from Scanner. What makes this beat a standard fax machine is that Windows keeps a copy of every fax it sends. This can come in really handy.

from Scanner. The pages are scanned automatically and show as an attachment. If your scanner does not have an automatic feeder, remove the first page after scanning it, insert the next page, and repeat the process until all pages have been scanned. Each scanned page is inserted as a TIFF file.

Preview the Fax

After typing and inserting all the information needed into the fax, click View, Preview to see a preview of the fax. Alternatively, click the Preview icon, which is just to the right of the Save icon on the toolbar. Attachments are converted into text or graphics, as appropriate. Use the Zoom Level pull-down menu to select a magnification for review.

Uncheck View, Preview (or click the Preview icon again) to return to the normal fax-editing mode.

Send the Fax

To send the fax, click Send. The fax is placed in the Windows Fax and Scan program's Outbox folder until transmission is complete. After the fax is transmitted, the fax is placed in the Sent Items folder.

You can view any previously sent fax by viewing this folder in Windows Fax and Scan. To print a copy of a sent fax, right-click it in the fax list and select Print. To resend, right-click it and select Forward As Fax.

Monitoring Outgoing Faxes

After you click Send, a pop-up window appears, displaying the status of the current fax and previous fax events. At the end of the fax transmission, a notification is also displayed over the system tray. You can turn these notifications off if you find them annoying—see "Changing Fax Settings," earlier in this chapter.

Can't Detect a Dial Tone

If the fax modem doesn't detect a dial tone, Windows won't send the fax. Make sure the RJ-11 telephone cable is properly connected to the fax modem and to the phone jack. Some fax modems use a pair of RJ-11 ports, one for the phone line and one to permit a telephone to share the line when the modem is not in use. Make sure you connect your telephone cables to the correct ports. A good way to start troubleshooting is to unplug the phone cable from your modem and plug it into a regular telephone. Be sure the phone gets a dial tone.

Receiving Faxes

To configure Windows Fax and Scan to receive a fax automatically, select Tools, Fax Settings, and then make sure that the option Allow the Device to Receive Fax Calls is enabled, Automatically Answer After radio is selected, and the number of rings is set to 1. The computer will now answer any incoming call on the telephone line connected to its modem, just like a standard fax machine.

If you configure Windows Fax and Scan to receive faxes manually, a notification appears when an incoming call is detected. If you are expecting a fax, click the notification balloon to have the modem pick up the call.

Incoming faxes are received and saved to the Inbox.

During the reception, the Review Fax Status window displays the status of the incoming fax. Click Close to close the window after receiving the fax.

Printing Received Faxes Automatically

If you want received faxes to print automatically, click Tools, Fax Settings. On the General tab, click More Options. In the When a Fax Is Received section, open the Print a Copy To pull-down menu and select a printer. When you receive a fax, the fax will automatically print on the specified printer.

Scanning Documents with Windows Fax and Scan

To start Windows Fax and Scan, go to the Start screen. If there is no tile for Windows Fax and Scan, right-click the Start screen and select All Apps, or you can just type **fax** at the Start screen. Then, select Windows Fax and Scan.

Click the Scan button in the bottom of the left pane to switch to the Scan view.

You can later change the scanner's settings for any individual photo or document, but it helps to predefine the settings you use most frequently as the defaults. We discuss this in the next section.

> **tip**
>
> If you'll be using WFS frequently, pin it to your Start screen. Here's how: At the Start screen, type **fax**. Right-click Windows Fax and Scan and select Pin to Start. You can also pin it to the desktop's taskbar.

Editing Scan Profile Defaults

Before you scan your first documents, take a moment to configure the program's scan settings. Click Tools, Scan Settings. The dialog box lists the default settings, known as scan profiles, for different types of scans. As initially installed, there will be two: Photo (color) and Documents (grayscale, like old movies).

The Photo setting is the default scan profile. If you plan to scan printed documents more often than color photos, click the Documents profile name and then click the Set as Default button. This will make this profile the one to be used with your scanner's "one-button scanning" feature, if it has one.

To edit the default scan resolution or other settings for a profile, select the profile, and then click Edit. Figure 12.4 illustrates the settings for a typical Documents profile.

From this dialog box, you can select the scanner (if you have more than one installed), the profile name, the paper source (such as flatbed or automatic document feeder [ADF]), the paper size, the color format (black and white, grayscale, or color), the file type (JPEG, BMP, TIFF, or PNG), and the scan resolution, brightness, and color. Make the changes you want to the profile and click Save Profile to replace the current settings with your changes.

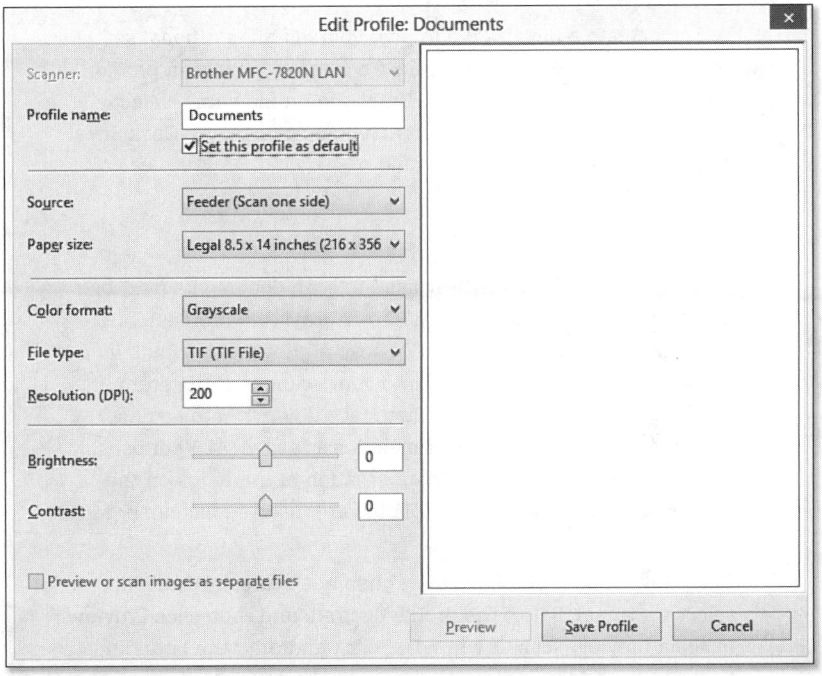

Figure 12.4
Editing the Documents
scan profile.

Edit Profile: Documents

Choosing the Right Settings

What resolution should you use? If you're going to send the scan as a fax, 300dpi matches the Very Fine (best quality) black-and-white document resolution setting supported by standard fax machines. However, for most faxing applications, 200dpi is adequate. Use a higher resolution, such as 600dpi, if you are scanning a photo for printing on a high-quality color inkjet or laser printer or for publishing use. For images that you plan to email or use on a web page, try 75dpi to 96dpi. This will produce a smaller image that is better suited for displaying on a computer screen. Set the File Type to TIF.

For color photographs, set the Color Format to Color. For black-and-white pictures or faded documents, set the Color Format to Grayscale. For typed documents and for pencil or pen-and-ink line drawings, try Black and White. This produces the smallest scan file, but thin lines might drop out...try it and see.

Under File Type, the TIFF format produces the best quality but can produce rather large files (often too large to email). If you are scanning photographs and want to save disk space, use JPEG. BMP can be used by applications that do not support other file types, but BMP files are very large. For black-and-white scans, use the TIFF format. JPEG is *not* a good choice—it can cause blurriness and weird image distortions in black-and-white scans.

Creating a New Scan Profile

You can create a new profile to give yourself an additional set of default settings to choose from. To create a new scan profile, click Tools, Scan Settings, Add. Enter the profile name, select the paper source, and make other changes as needed. Click Save Profile to save the new scan profile.

Scanning Images

Windows Fax and Scan is best used to scan documents (text or drawings using the black-and-white or grayscale profiles), but you can use it to scan pictures. To scan a photo with Windows Fax and Scan, insert the photo into your scanner. If the scanner is a flatbed design, insert the photo face down (photo against the cover glass). If the scanner includes a feeder (ADF) or uses a sheet-fed design, see the documentation or markings on the scanner to determine whether photos are inserted face up or face down.

Click New Scan. If you have more than one scanner installed, select a scanner. Select the profile desired, and then click Preview to see a preview scan. If you wish, click and drag the bounding boxes to the edges of the photo, or crop the photo as desired. If the photo is too bright or too dark, adjust the Brightness slider. Adjust the Contrast slider if the photo is too flat (contrast too low) or too harsh (contrast too high). To see the results of the changes, click Preview again. When you are satisfied with scan quality, click Scan.

A scanning progress bar appears, and the scanned image is displayed in the workspace after being saved to disk.

You can select items in the Fax and Scan workspace list and right-click to choose various actions such as View, Print, Send To (for faxing), Rename, and Move to Folder.

 tip

The preset resolution for a new scan profile is 200dpi. To match the dpi of current Windows desktops, we recommend 96dpi for viewing or emailing. Use a resolution of at least 200dpi or more for profiles intended for printing or faxing. See the sidebar "Choosing the Right Settings" for specific resolution recommendations for different types of documents and destinations.

tip

Fax and Scan doesn't let you drag and drop files, which is sort of annoying. It's sometimes easier to work with scanned files using File Explorer. You'll find the files under Documents, inside the Scanned Documents folder.

Slow Scanning Speed

If a USB 2.0–based scanner is very slow, make sure you have connected the scanner to a USB 2.0 (also known as Hi-Speed USB) port. Some front-mounted USB ports support only USB 1.1 speeds. If you have connected the scanner to an external USB hub, try connecting the scanner directly to a USB port on the computer.

Emailing and Faxing Scans

To fax a scanned document or photo without switching to the Fax view, select the item you want to fax and click Document, Forward as Fax. The New Fax dialog box appears. If you want to fax more than one scanned image (or set of images), click Insert, File Attachment and then locate the additional image(s). You'll find them under Documents inside the folder Scanned Documents.

➡ *For more information,* **see** *"Sending Faxes from Windows Fax and Scan,"* **p. 260.**

If you have a standalone email program (such as Outlook) installed, it's easy to email a scanned document or photo. Just open Windows Fax and Scan, click Scan, and locate the image file. Select the item you want to email, and click Document, Forward as Email. Enter the recipient(s), message, and other information, and click Send to send the scan. Be aware, though, that really large scanned image files might get rejected as too large by the email system. You may need to reduce the size of images before you can email them. (You can use any number of image editing programs to create reduced-resolution copies of your pictures. The free Windows Photo Gallery program can do it. You can download this program from microsoft.com.)

If you use a web-based email service, this won't work. You'll have to compose an email and use your email system's Add Attachment feature to upload the image files. You can find them under Documents inside the folder Scanned Documents.

MORE WINDOWS 8 MEDIA TOOLS

Controlling the Volume

Controlling the volume of your audio is crucial. During playback, you might want to turn the volume down if you're in a public place where you don't want to disturb others nearby. If you have no such worries, you might want to crank up a particularly good audio CD. During recording, setting the right input levels can make the difference between recording high-quality audio and distorted noise. Windows 8 gives you the tools to set these volume levels, equalize the volume, and more.

Controlling the Overall System Volume

The *system volume* is the volume that Windows uses for all things audio on your computer: the sounds that Windows itself makes (warning beeps, the sign-on and sign-off tones, and so on) and the sounds that waft from your applications (such as music from Media Player and the new-mail notification from Windows Live Mail).

Windows 8 offers two methods for controlling the system volume:

- If you're hanging out in the Start screen, press Windows Logo+I to open the Settings pane, click the speaker icon, and then drag the slider up or down to set the volume.

- If you're on the desktop, click the Volume icon in the taskbar's notification area to open the volume control, shown in Figure 13.1. Use your mouse to drag the slider to the volume level you prefer, or click Mute to get the sounds of silence.

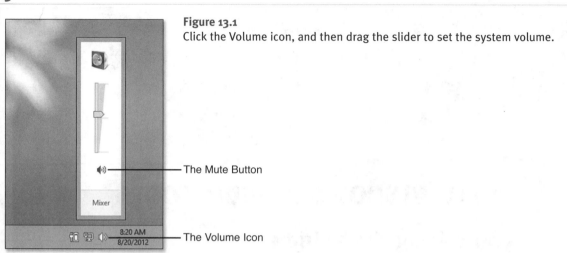

Figure 13.1
Click the Volume icon, and then drag the slider to set the system volume.

The Mute Button

The Volume Icon

Controlling an Application's Volume

Controlling the system volume is the easiest way to get the sound level you need, but in many cases it's not the best way. For example, suppose you're waiting for an important email message, so you set up Windows Live Mail to play a sound when an email message comes in. Suppose further that you're also using Windows Media Player to play music in the background. If you get a phone call, you want to turn down or mute the music. If you mute the system volume, you mute the music playback but you also mute other system sounds, including Windows Live Mail's audio alerts. So, while you're on the phone, there's a good chance that you'll miss that important message you've been waiting for.

The Windows 8 solution to this kind of problem is called *per-application volume control*. This means that Windows 8 gives you a volume control slider for every running program and process that is a dedicated sound application (such as Media Player or Media Center) or is currently producing audio output. In our example, you'd have separate volume controls for Windows Media Player and Windows Live Mail. When that phone call comes in, you can turn down or mute Windows Media Player while leaving the Windows Live Mail volume as is, so there's much less chance that you'll miss that incoming message.

Figure 13.2 shows the Volume Mixer window that appears when you right-click the Volume icon in the taskbar notification area and then click Open Volume Mixer. The Device section on the left has a slider that controls the speaker volume, so you can use it as a systemwide volume control. The rest of the window contains the *application mixer*, which includes sliders and mute buttons for individual programs.

> ## 🔍 note
> How long an application's slider remains in the Volume Mixer window depends on how often the application accesses the audio stack. If a program just makes the occasional peep, it will appear only briefly in the Volume Mixer and then disappear. If a program makes noise fairly often, it remains in the Volume Mixer for much longer. So, for example, if you receive email messages all day, you should always see the Windows Live Mail icon in the Volume Mixer.

Figure 13.2
Windows 8 uses per-application volume control to enable you to set the volume level for each program that outputs audio.

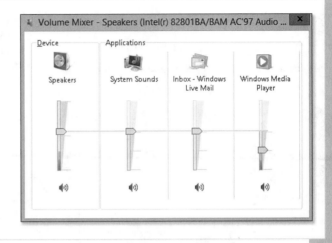

Note, too, that when you move the speaker volume slider, the program sliders move along with it. That's a nice touch, but what's even nicer is that the speaker volume slider preserves the relative volume levels of each program. So if you adjust the speaker volume to about half its current level, the sliders in the application mixer also adjust to about half of their current level.

The volume control also remembers application settings between sessions. So, if you mute Solitaire, for example, it will remain muted the next time you start the program.

Determining the Devices That Appear in the Volume Control

By default, the output device you see in the volume control is whatever device your system is currently using to play sounds. If you regularly switch from, say, your PC's built-in or external speakers to a headset, you might want to display both in the volume control so that you can make adjustments to them at the same time.

To choose the volume control devices, right-click the Volume icon in the taskbar notification area, then click Volume Control Options. In the Volume Control Options dialog box that appears, activate the check box beside each device you want to add to the volume control, as shown in Figure 13.3.

Balancing Your Headphones

Many of us have one ear that doesn't hear as well as the other. In this situation, adjusting the system volume or an application's volume is problematic because turning up the sound enough to hear things in your bad ear can make those sounds too loud in your good ear.

Windows can help by enabling you to balance the sound in each ear. That is, you can turn up the sound for your bad ear and/or turn down the sound for your good ear. Here's what you do:

1. Right-click the Volume icon in the taskbar notification area and then click Playback Devices. Windows 8 displays the Sound dialog box with the Playback tab selected.

2. In the list of playback devices, click your headphones.

Figure 13.3
Use the Volume Control Options dialog box to select which sound output devices you want to appear in the volume control.

3. Click Properties.

4. Click the Levels tab.

5. Click Balance. Windows displays the Balance dialog box shown in Figure 13.4.

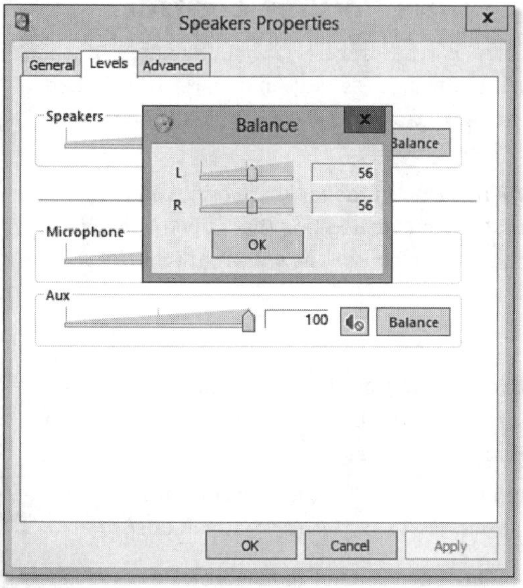

Figure 13.4
Use the Balance dialog box to adjust the headphone volume for each ear.

6. Drag the L (left) and R (right) sliders to the volume levels you prefer. (In some cases, instead of L you see the number 1, and instead of R you see the number 2.) If you're not sure whether the balance is correct, run Media Player and start playing some music, then try balancing the headphones.

7. Click OK in each of the open dialog boxes to put the new levels into effect.

Equalizing the Volume

You might find that wide fluctuations in volume can make sounds—particularly speech—much harder to perceive. You can compensate by turning on the Loudness Equalization enhancement for your computer's speakers or your headphones, which makes all sounds that emanate from your computer equally loud.

Follow these steps to turn on Loudness Equalization:

1. Right-click the Volume icon in the taskbar notification area and then click Playback Devices. Windows 8 displays the Sound dialog box with the Playback tab selected.

2. In the list of playback devices, click the sound device you want to adjust.

3. Click Properties. Windows 8 opens the Properties dialog box for the device.

4. Click the Enhancements tab.

5. Activate the Loudness Equalization check box, as shown in Figure 13.5.

6. Click OK in each of the open dialog boxes to put the new levels into effect.

Figure 13.5
With the Loudness Equalization feature on the job, sounds such as speech will be easier to discern.

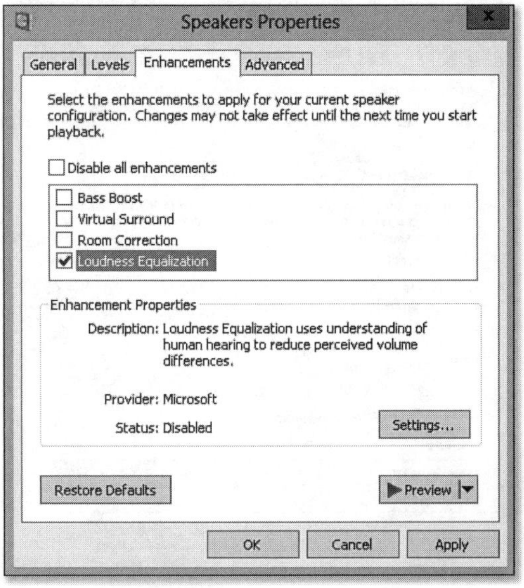

Setting the Default Output Device

Windows 8 is happy to let you have more than one audio playback device installed on your system. For example, you might have your PC connected to desktop speakers, headphones, and a home theater receiver; however, you might want to set up one of these devices as the default. To do this, right-click the taskbar notification area's Volume icon and then click Playback Devices to open the Sound dialog box with the Playback tab selected. Click the device you want to use, and then below click Set Default.

Assigning Sounds to Events

As you work with Windows 8, you hear various sounds emanating from your speakers. These sounds always correspond to particular events. There's the odd two-note beat when you connect a device; there's the short, sharp shock of a sound when a warning dialog box pops up; and there's the nice and perhaps all-too-familiar chime when a new email message arrives.

If you're getting tired of the same old sounds, however, Windows 8 lets you customize what you hear by assigning different WAV files to these events. You can also assign sounds to a couple of dozen other events. This section shows you how it's done.

The sounds assigned to various Windows 8 events comprise a sound scheme. To view the current scheme, press Windows Logo+W, type **sounds** in the Start screen, and then click Change System Sounds in the search results. (If you're on the desktop, you can also right-click the Volume icon and then click Sounds.) Windows 8 opens the Sound dialog box with the Sounds tab displayed, as shown in Figure 13.6.

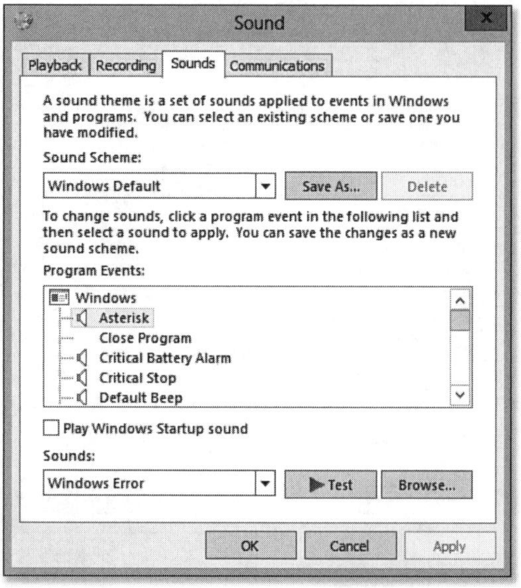

Figure 13.6
Use the Sounds tab in the Sound dialog box to change the current Windows 8 sound scheme.

Here's a rundown of the various controls in the Sounds tab:

- **Sound Scheme**—This drop-down list displays the currently selected sound scheme. (Windows 8 ships with just two schemes: Windows Default and No Sounds.)

- **Program Events**—This list displays a number of Windows 8 events, including four that apply to the various types of dialog boxes displayed by Windows 8 and Windows applications: Asterisk, Critical Stop, Exclamation, and Question. If an event has a sound icon beside it, this means a WAV file is currently assigned to that event.

- **Sounds**—This drop-down list shows you the name of the WAV file assigned to the currently highlighted event. You can use the Browse button to select a different WAV file (or just use the Name drop-down list to select a WAV file from Windows 8's Media subfolder).

- **Test**—Click this button to try out the WAV file shown in the Sounds list.

You can use three methods to work with sound schemes:

- To change the current sound scheme, select items in the Program Events list and use the Sounds list to change the associated WAV file.

- To use a different sound scheme, select it from the Sound Scheme drop-down list.

- To create your own sound scheme, first associate WAV files with the various system events you want to hear. Then click Save As, enter a name for the new scheme, and click OK.

Recording Sounds with the Sound Recorder

If you have a system capable of recording sounds from a microphone (most desktops or laptops are), you can have hours of fun creating your own Windows Media Audio (WMA) files. Preserving silly sounds for posterity is the most fun, of course, but you can also create serious messages and embed them in business documents or for use as a Windows Live Movie Maker narration track.

Setting Up the Microphone

Before you start recording, you need to set up your microphone, particularly the volume levels for recording. Follow these steps:

1. Press Windows Logo+W, type **microphone**, and then click Set Up a Microphone. Windows 8 runs the Microphone Setup Wizard, shown in Figure 13.7.

2. Select the option that best describes your microphone and then click Next. The wizard displays a dialog that tells you about the proper placement and use of your microphone.

3. Click Next. The wizard displays some text for you to read.

4. Read the text into the microphone using your normal speaking voice, and then click Next when you're done.

5. Click Finish. The wizard completes the configuration of your microphone.

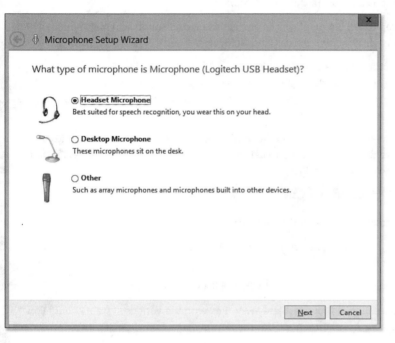

Figure 13.7
The Microphone Setup Wizard takes you step-by-step through the microphone configuration.

Recording a WMA File

To get started with Sound Recorder, type **sound** in the Start screen and then click Sound Recorder in the search results. When you're ready to begin recording, here are the steps to follow:

1. With your microphone ready, click the Start Recording button.

2. Speak (yell, sing, whatever) into the microphone. Sound Recorder shows you the length of the file as you record.

3. When you're done, click the Stop Recording button. Sound Recorder pauses the recording and displays the Save As dialog box.

4. If you're not done with your recording, click Cancel, click Resume Recording, and then click Stop Recording again.

5. Select a location, type a filename, and then click Save.

Controlling Your Computer with Speech Recognition

If due to injury or age you find that using a mouse and keyboard is too time-consuming, too difficult, or too frustrating, you may think you're out of luck—because how else are you supposed to control your computer? Fortunately, there *is* another way: voice commands. Using the Speech Recognition feature, you can speak commands into a microphone, and Windows will do your bidding.

Does it really work? Actually, most of the time, yes—it really does. Windows 8 has very good voice-recognition technology, and as long as you're in a relatively quiet room and speak clearly, Windows will recognize actions such as click, double-click, and select; commands such as Save, Copy, and Close; keystrokes such as Backspace, Delete, and Enter; and screen features such as Minimize, Scroll, and Back.

To get started, you need a system with a built-in mic or the ability to attach a microphone to your computer. A microphone that's part of a headset is easiest to use, but you can also use a standalone microphone that sits on your desk.

With your microphone attached to your computer, your next task is to configure the Speech Recognition feature (if you configured your microphone earlier, you can skip through steps 2 to 6):

> ## tip
>
> One of Speech Recognition's handiest tricks you can use is to say "Show numbers," which then overlays a number over everything in the current window that can be clicked. You can then state the number of the item you want and then say "OK," and Speech Recognition will "click" that item for you *and* tell you the correct command name.

1. In the Start screen, type **speech** and then click Speech Recognition. The Speech Recognition box appears. From here, click Start Speech Recognition. Then the Set Up Speech Recognition Wizard appears.

2. Click Next. The wizard asks what type of microphone you have.

3. Make your selection (Headset Microphone, Desktop Microphone, or Other) and then click Next. The wizard displays a screen that tells you about the proper placement of your microphone.

4. After you've read the text and made the necessary adjustments, click Next. The wizard now displays some text for you to read aloud.

5. Read the text in your normal voice, and then click Next. The wizard lets you know that your microphone is set up and ready for use.

6. Click Next. Now, the wizard asks whether it can examine your documents to look for words that it should learn.

7. This is a good idea, so select Enable Document Review and click Next. Now, the wizard wants to know how you want to activate speech recognition.

8. The easiest route here is to select Use Voice Activation Mode, which means you can start Speech Recognition by saying "Start listening" and stop Speech Recognition by saying "Stop listening." (If you choose Use Manual Activation Mode instead, you must manually activate Speech Recognition each time by pressing Windows Logo+Ctrl or by clicking the microphone icon in the Speech Recognition window.) Click Next. The wizard suggests that you print the Speech Reference Card, which contains a list of useful commands.

9. If you want to print the card, click View Reference Card and then click the Print button in the Help window that appears.

10. Return to the Set Up Speech Recognition Wizard (if you printed the card in the previous step) and then click Next. The wizard wonders whether you want to start Speech Recognition automatically each time you start your computer.

11. This is a good way to go, so leave the Run Speech Recognition at Startup check box activated and click Next. The wizard now offers to take you through a Speech Recognition tutorial, which enables you to practice the voice commands.

12. The tutorial is definitely worthwhile, so click Start Tutorial.

13. When you're done, click Finish.

> **tip**
>
> If you no longer want Speech Recognition to run at startup, press Windows Logo+W to open the Settings search pane, type **speech,** and then select Speech Recognition. In the Speech Recognition window, select Advanced Speech Options, and then deselect the Run Speech Recognition at Startup check box.

With all that out of the way, you can start using Speech Recognition, which appears as a small window at the top of the desktop. You speak your commands, and Speech Recognition will either carry them out or will say "What was that?" if it doesn't recognize what you said. In Figure 13.8, I've just said "Open Run," and not only has Speech Recognition opened the Run dialog box but it has also echoed the command in its window.

Figure 13.8
Speech Recognition at work: say "Open Run" to open the Run dialog box.

GETTING CONNECTED

Going Worldwide

In this chapter, you'll find information about choosing an Internet service provider (ISP), making the connection through a modem or other link, installing and configuring your system, and making your system safe and secure. This chapter tells how to select an Internet connection technology and connect a single computer to the Internet. However, this isn't your only option. You can take any one of several routes:

- If your computer is part of an existing local area network (LAN) with Internet access, you can skip this chapter entirely because Internet access comes as part and parcel of your LAN connection. In fact, if you are part of a corporate LAN, it is most likely a violation of your company's security policy to establish your own independent connection.

- If you have or are willing to set up a LAN for your home or office, you can provide Internet access to all your computers through one connection. You should read Chapter 19, "Connecting Your Network to the Internet," and decide whether you want to connect to the Internet through a LAN. Use the instructions in this chapter to set up the initial connection, and Chapter 19 tells you how to share it with the rest of your workgroup.

  (If you don't already have a network, and you have two or more computers, you should seriously consider creating one. Chapter 18, "Creating a Windows Network," tells you how.)

- If you have already selected your ISP and connection technology, you can skip the introductory sections of this chapter and go right to "Installing a Modem for Dial-Up Service" or "Installing a Network Adapter for Broadband Service," later in this chapter.

- If you need to make a clean start with the Internet, read on!

Connection Technologies

Not long ago, you had but one choice to make for your Internet connection: which brand of modem to buy. Now options abound, and you can choose among several technologies, speeds, and ISP types. In the last decade high-speed (broadband) DSL and cable digital service have largely replaced dial-up modem service, but in some regions dial-up and satellite services remain the only options.

Let's take a look at the basic Internet connection technologies that are appropriate for an individual user or workgroup, in increasing order of performance and usability. After describing each one, we'll show you roughly what each costs to set up and use.

Analog Modem

Standard, tried-and-true dial-up modem service requires only a telephone line and a modem in your computer. Its downside is that it ties up a telephone line while you're online. Furthermore, if you have call waiting, the "beep" that occurs when someone calls while you're online can make the modem drop its connection. To avoid these hassles, many people order an additional phone line just for the modem, and this adds to the monthly expense.

The data transfer speed provided by dial-up service is adequate for general web surfing—that is, reading text and viewing pictures. That is, as long as the websites you visit were designed by people who understand the technology and made them usable at dial-up speeds. Dial-up is completely unsuitable for viewing video. In other words, forget about YouTube.

To use standard dial-up Internet service, you need a modem and a telephone cable. Modems come in internal, external, USB, and PC Card varieties from dozens of manufacturers. At one time, desktop computers made for home use almost always came with a modem preinstalled. This is no longer the case, so you will likely have to buy one. Modern laptops may or may not come with a built-in modem.

ISDN

Integrated Services Digital Network (ISDN) is a special digital-only telephone service that can carry two independent voice or data conversations over one telephone wire. ISDN service is actually a different type of telephony; you can't plug an ordinary telephone into an ISDN line. ISDN modems can carry data at 64Kbps or 128Kbps, depending on whether you use one or two of its channels to connect to your ISP. Although ISDN Internet service is still available in some areas, we don't recommend it as an Internet connection option. Dial-up is nearly as fast as ISDN. If you need greater speed, and you can't get DSL or cable service, satellite and wireless service are better options.

DSL

Digital Subscriber Line (DSL) service sends a high-speed digital data signal over regular telephone wires. In most cases, DSL signals can be sent over the same telephone wire that serves your telephone, at the same time. This means that you can usually get DSL service installed without needing an extra telephone line. The most common DSL service is called *asymmetric*, or *ADSL*, because it receives data at 128Kbps to 6000Kbps but sends at a lower rate. (This is fine because most web surfing involves sending a very small request and receiving a large amount of data.)

DSL has at least one Achilles' heel: its availability is restricted by your distance from the telephone company's central office, and it isn't available when the distance is more than a couple of miles (as the wires run, not as the crow flies). DSL's reach can be extended by optical fiber lines and special equipment, but this is expensive for the telephone companies to install. DSL might never make it into rural areas.

DSL modems come in two varieties: external units connect to your computer through a network adapter or a USB cable, whereas internal units plug right into your computer. If your ISP uses external adapters, before you buy a network adapter, check with your DSL provider, because often one is included in the installation kit. In addition, before you decide to pay extra to get service for multiple computers, read Chapter 19 to see how all your computers can share a single connection.

Some external DSL modems include a connecting-sharing router that lets you share the Internet connection with several computers over a wired or wireless network. If your modem includes a router, you just need to connect your computers to the router, and you don't really need this chapter at all. Instead, see Chapter 19.

Cable Modem

Your local television cable company may provide cable modem Internet service, which sends high-speed data signals through the same distribution system it uses to carry high-quality TV signals.

Cable modem service has none of the distance limitations of DSL. One early criticism of cable service was that data speeds could drop during high-use times, such as the early evening, because everyone in a given neighborhood shares a single network "pipe." That may have been true when cable service was first introduced, but cable vendors seem to have built up their networks considerably, and this seems to happen less frequently now. Surveys show that cable subscribers usually get several times the download speed of DSL subscribers.

Cable modems generally are external devices that connect to your computer through a network adapter or a USB cable. Before you buy a network adapter, though, check with your ISP; one might be included in the installation kit. Some ISPs charge extra to lease the modem. The price of a cable modem is $30–$60 new and about $1 on eBay, so leasing one from your cable company isn't such a great deal. Also, if you have more than one computer and your cable ISP wants to charge you for extra connections, read Chapter 19 to see how all your computers can use a router to share a single connection.

> **🔍 note**
>
> DSL varieties include asymmetric, symmetric, high-speed, and DSL over ISDN, so you might run into the acronyms SDSL, ADSL, HDSL, and IDSL, or the collective xDSL. For this chapter, these distinctions are unimportant, so we just call it DSL.

> **🔍 note**
>
> If you consider DSL service, shop around before you buy. The signal has to come over your local phone company's wiring, but you can usually select among several Internet service providers that have a presence in the phone company central office that serves your neighborhood. The availability of different speeds and different pricing options can vary from neighborhood to neighborhood, so you have to check with the different ISPs by giving them your street address to find out what's available.

Some cable companies now provide a cable modem that includes a built-in connection-sharing router that lets you share the Internet connection with several computers over a wired or wireless network. If your modem includes a router, you just need to connect your computers to the router, and you don't really need this chapter at all. Instead, see Chapter 19.

Satellite Service

Satellite Internet service uses microwave signals and small (roughly 2-foot-diameter) dish antennas to connect to an orbiting communication satellite. You should consider only *bidirectional* satellite service, which uses the satellite dish for both sending and receiving. Satellite's one advantage is that it's available where DSL and cable haven't yet reached, wherever there's a good view of either the southern sky in the Northern Hemisphere or the northern sky in the Southern Hemisphere. The disadvantages are numerous: installation requires the abilities of both a rocket scientist and a carpenter, the equipment and service plans can be expensive, you'll have to sign a long-term contract to get discounts on installation and equipment, the system slows when many people are using it, you can lose the signal entirely when it's raining or snowing, and if you download more than your monthly quota allows, you'll be punished by having your download speed cut to a crawl for the remainder of the month. Despite all this, many people beyond the reach of cable and DSL say that satellite service beats dial-up, and it's worth the hassle.

Satellite service requires you to purchase a receiving dish antenna, a receiver, and a USB or network adapter to connect the setup to your computer. Your ISP should furnish these devices. For unidirectional satellite service, you also need to have a phone line near your computer.

Installing a satellite dish is difficult, and it's best to hire a professional dish installer for this task. (Our executive editor, Rick Kughen, installed his himself and says "About halfway through the ordeal, I decided that I really wished I had paid the $199 installation fee.") Some satellite providers offer free installation, however, so you might not have to get dirty installing your own or pay big bucks to have someone else do it.

After the dish is installed and aligned, installing the satellite modem is not terribly tricky, but the procedure is specific to the type of hardware you're using. Therefore, unfortunately, we have to leave you at the mercy of the manufacturer's instruction manual, and can't provide specific instructions in this book.

Wireless and Cellular Service

Wireless Internet service is available in most major metropolitan areas and even in some remote areas, through cellular telephone providers. Three types of service are available:

- **Fixed-antenna wireless service**—The wireless modem connects to a small whip or dish antenna, and data transfer rates typically are more than 1Mbps using setups with a fixed antenna.

- **Wireless modems for laptops**—With this type of service, you connect a small plug-in PC Card or USB wireless modem unit to your computer. The modem has a built-in radio, and it establishes a data connection through the cellular network. Windows 8 is the first version of Windows that has built-in software for this type of data service.

- **Tethered data service through a cell phone**—Some cell phones let you connect a data cable from the phone to your computer. The telephone provides the radio and modem components.

Fixed-antenna wireless is similar to satellite service. You must purchase a receiving antenna, a receiver, and a USB or network adapter to connect the setup to your computer. Your ISP should furnish these devices. You might also have to pay for professional installation. When the network connection is set up, you can use it on a single computer or share it using a router, as described in Chapter 19.

The other two options are portable, and serve only a single computer. You may be able to find data plans that let you buy service on a day-by-day basis rather than committing to a long-term service contract. This can be very cost effective when you travel. Because the setup and usage steps are specific to each provider, we can't provide instructions in this chapter.

Choosing a Technology

With all the options potentially available to Windows users for Internet access, making a choice that fits your needs and limitations can become a bit confusing. Research the options that local and national ISPs provide, and then start narrowing them. Table 14.1 summarizes the costs and speeds of several ways for a single computer user to access the Internet (excluding ISDN and wireless service). The prices shown are typical costs for the service in question after applying the usual discounts and special offers.

Table 14.1   Internet Connection Options for the Individual User

Method	Approximate Cost (per Month)	Approximate Setup and Equipment Cost	Time Limits in Hours (per Month)	Availability	Download Speed
Analog modem	$10*–25	$50	10 to unlimited	Worldwide	33Kbps–56Kbps
DSL	$30 and up	$100	Unlimited	Limited but growing	312Kbps–6Mbps
Cable modem	$30–50	$100	Unlimited	Limited but growing	1Mbps–100Mbps
Satellite	$50–150	$150–800	25 and up	Almost worldwide	400Kbps—12Mbps

Remember that you have several costs to factor in:

- The cost of hardware required to make the connection

- The cost of installation and setup

- The monthly ISP cost for Internet service

- The cost of telephone lines, if you order a separate line just for Internet access

- The savings you'll get if you can drop separate dial-up service accounts and extra phone lines for high-speed service that you can share

In addition, if you travel frequently, ask any prospective ISP to tell you if they provide free dial-up or wireless hot spot Internet service when you're on the road. These costs can add up quickly if you select an ISP that makes you pay extra for this service.

For more information on selecting an Internet technology and to help choose an ISP, check out these sites:

- For information on DSL and cable, see www.dslreports.com.

- For information on satellite service in North and Central America, check out www.dish.com, www.starband.com, www.hughesnet.com and www.exede.com. I don't have any direct experience with these providers, but Exede advertises download speeds up to 12Mbps. If that is true, it's terrific. Satellite services are often resold through regional companies. For example, my ISP sonic.net resells satellite service. You might get better customer support if you buy through a regional ISP.

- For information on wireless service, see www.mobilebroadbandnetwork.com or contact your area's cellular providers.

Choosing Equipment

You need to purchase equipment that is compatible with the particular type of Internet service you'll be using. Your computer might have come with a modem preinstalled; therefore, if you will be using dial-up service, you might not have to make any decisions. If you will be buying new connection hardware, here are some points to consider:

- Broadband service requires a modem that your ISP will either provide, sell, or lease (rent) to you. Typically, DSL modems are given to you as part of the deal, but cable providers want to ding you every month—and it adds up! You can get a new or used DSL or cable modem independently, and very cheaply, but be sure it will be compatible with the equipment your ISP uses. In addition, broadband modems connect via Wi-Fi, USB, or through an Ethernet network adapter. If your service needs a network adapter, and your computer doesn't already have an Ethernet adapter, be sure to get one that's compatible with Windows 8 or 7.

- If you want to share your Internet connection with other computers via a LAN, read Chapter 19 before making any hardware purchases; you'll find information on some special hardware setups.

- Above all, be sure any hardware you have to plug directly into the computer (that is, a modem or LAN adapter) appears in the Windows Compatibility Center list (www.microsoft.com/windows/compatibility). All brand-new equipment should be compatible with Windows 8 and Windows 7, but something you buy used might not be. Check the list before you make any purchases.

- For dial-up service, choose a modem that is compatible with the fastest service level your ISP provides. Your ISP should be using V.90 modems for 56Kbps service. Some ISPs support the

V.92 call-waiting protocol. If you have a modem that supports this feature, ask prospective ISPs whether they support it and whether there's an additional charge.

Installing a Modem for Dial-Up Service

Before installing a dial-up modem, first install any driver software that came with the product. Follow the manufacturer's instructions to install a Windows 8 or Windows 7 driver, using the 32-bit or 64-bit version, as appropriate, for your copy of Windows.

For an internal modem on a desktop computer, shut down Windows, turn off the power, pop open your PC's case, and insert the modem card into a free expansion slot inside the computer. An external USB modem simply plugs into the USB port on your computer. For an external serial modem, cable it to a serial port on your PC and then connect the external power supply.

 note

When you have your modem set up, skip ahead to the next section, "Configuring a Dial-Up Internet Connection."

➡ *For more information about installing new hardware, **see** Chapter 28, "Managing Your Hardware."*

If you're using an older serial modem, you might need to set up its driver manually by following these steps:

1. Press Windows Logo+R, type **telephon.cpl**, and then press Enter. (You can also get here through the Control Panel, by searching for the phrase *Phone and Modem*.)

2. Select the Modems tab. If Windows has already detected your modem, its name appears in the Modems tab. If the correct modem type is listed, skip to step 7.

   If no modem is listed, click the Add button to run the Add Hardware Wizard.

3. Click Next. Windows scans your computer's COM (serial) ports and determines the type of modem you have. If this is successful, Windows tells you. In this case, continue with step 6.

4. If Windows detects your modem incorrectly, go back to the Modem list, select the incorrectly identified modem, click Change, and then locate the manufacturer and model of your modem in the dialog box. If you find the correct make and model, select them and click OK. If your modem came with a driver disk for Windows 8 or Windows 7, click Have Disk and locate the installation file for the modem.

   If your modem isn't listed, try to download the proper driver from Windows Update or from the modem manufacturer (using another Internet-connected computer, of course). You also might try selecting a similar model by the same manufacturer.

5. After you select the modem type, click OK and then Next.

6. Click Finish to complete the installation.

7. Select the Dialing Rules tab.

8. Select My Location and click Edit.

9. Enter the General tab information for your current location, as shown in Figure 14.1.

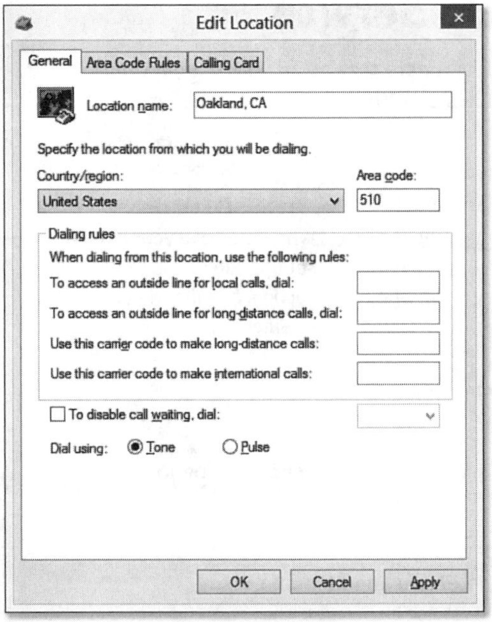

Figure 14.1
In the Edit Location dialog box, you can record the dialing instructions for your current location. The important settings are Country/Region, Area Code, codes for outside lines (if you are on a corporate phone system), and Disable Call Waiting.

10. Enter a name for your location—for example, "home," the name of your city, or another name to distinguish the current telephone dialing properties. Set the country, area code, and dialing rules information.

For example, if your telephone system requires you to dial a 9 to make an outside local call, enter **9** in the box labeled To Access an Outside Line for Local Calls, Dial. Make a corresponding entry for long-distance access.

If your telephone line has call waiting, check To Disable Call Waiting, Dial and choose the appropriate disable code.

We assume here that your ISP access number is a local call in the same area code. If this is not the case, you might want to fill in the Area Code Rules tab for the ISP access number. (If you don't know the number yet, don't worry; you can come back and fix it later.)

11. Click OK.

Now your modem is installed and you can continue with "Configuring a Dial-Up Internet Connection," next.

Configuring a Dial-Up Internet Connection

Windows can quickly walk you through setting up the connection from your modem to your ISP. In this section, we show you how to set up the connection the first time, and how to modify it later on if that should be necessary. The subsequent sections tell you how to use the connection to get on the Internet.

Creating a New Dial-Up Connection

To set up a new connection to your dial-up Internet service, follow these steps:

1. Go to the desktop, right-click the network icon at the bottom-right corner of the taskbar, and select Open Network and Sharing Center. (You can also get there from the Control Panel by searching for the word *Sharing*.)

2. Select Set Up a New Connection or Network. Select Connect to the Internet and click Next. Click Dial-Up.

3. Fill in the information provided by your ISP. The first field asks for the local access telephone number for your ISP. Enter the local number, optionally preceded by any other codes needed to dial the call. For instance, in the United States, if you enter an area code, you must first enter a **1**, then the area code, as shown in Figure 14.2. You can enter parentheses or dashes (-) between the parts of the number, if you want; the modem ignores them. You will have to fix this later anyway, as discussed shortly.

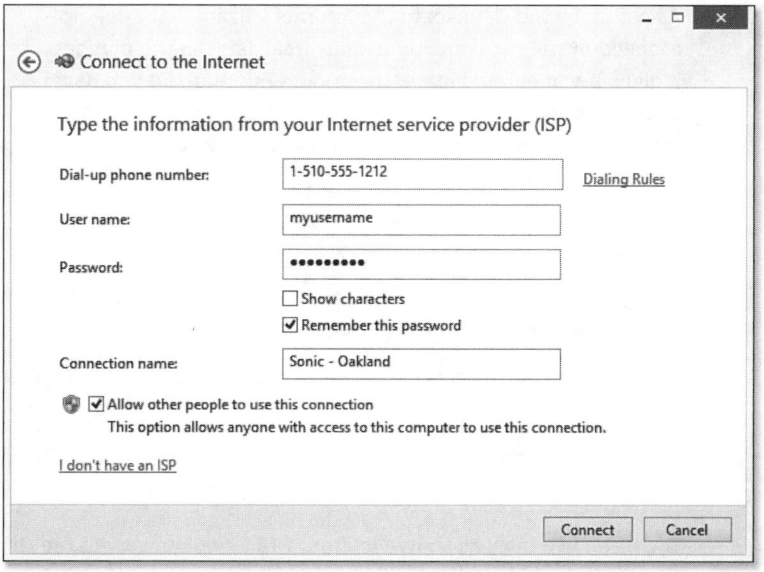

Figure 14.2
When prompted, enter the local access number and the username and password provided by your ISP.

The next fields record your username and password. You can check Show Characters to verify that you are typing the password correctly.

Check Remember This Password unless you want Windows to prompt you for it every time you connect. If other people who use your computer use the same ISP account, check Allow Other People to Use This Connection.

4. The last field asks for a connection name. Type in a name that will help you identify what the connection is used for. The name of your ISP is always good. If you will be traveling, you'll probably accumulate several of these dial-up connections, one for each location you visit, so it would be helpful to add the location to the name, as in "Sonic-Oakland."

5. Click Connect. Windows immediately dials your ISP. Check to be sure that the connection works before proceeding. If it doesn't, click Skip and continue anyway.

caution

Be sure to use a local number. Your ISP will not help pay your phone bill if you choose a toll number by mistake!

note

If you have ISP access numbers for different cities that you travel to, see "Managing Multiple Internet Connections," later in this chapter, for a way to make dialing easier.

The last step in setting up a dial-up Internet connection is to clean up the new connection's settings, such as the area code and call waiting control. We'll do that in the next section.

Adjusting Dial-Up Connection Properties

As set up by the Connect to the Internet Wizard, your dial-up connection will not correctly handle area codes in the number it dials. If you entered just a seven-digit number and you never intend to travel with your computer, you don't have to worry about this. However, if the number has an area code, or you travel, you'll have to fix this.

You have several ways to view and change a connection's properties. Here are the easiest:

tip

You can instantly view your list of dial-up connections by clicking the Network icon in the taskbar or in the Settings charm, as described in the next section.

- If you're at the desktop, click the network icon in the taskbar, right-click the new connection name, and select View Connection Properties.

- If you're at the Start screen, open the charms, select Settings, Network, right-click the new connection name, and then select View Connection Properties.

- If you're viewing the Network and Sharing Center, select Change Adapter Properties, right-click the new connection icon, and select Properties.

You'll see five tabs, as shown in Figure 14.3, which we will run through in the order in which they appear. Only a few settings ever need to be changed for an ISP connection:

Figure 14.3
A dial-up connection's
Properties dialog box lets
you change dialing rules, set
network parameters, manage
the security options, and manage networking and sharing
options.

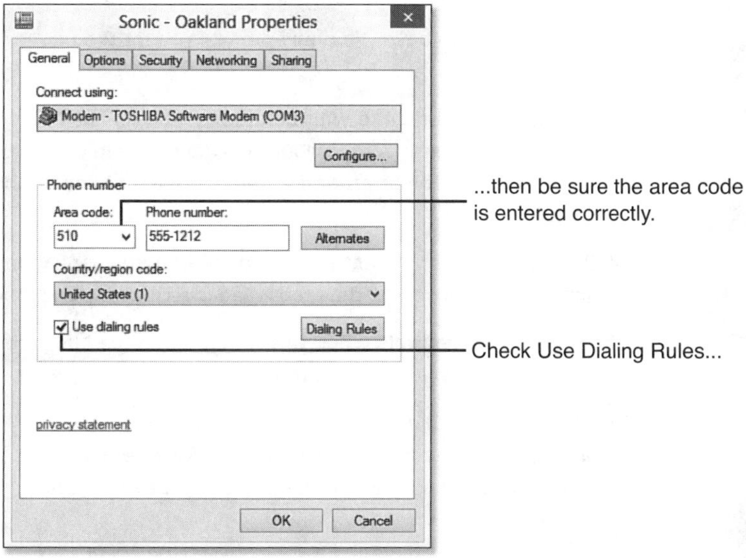

...then be sure the area code
is entered correctly.

Check Use Dialing Rules...

- The General tab lists modem properties and the ISP telephone number. The following two set-tings are the most important ones to examine and, if necessary, change:

  - If you travel with your computer, or the dial-up number has an area code, check Use Dialing Rules and be sure that the ISP's area code is shown correctly in its own box and is not entered in the same box as the phone number. Figure 14.3 shows how it should look.

    Then, click Dialing Rules to be sure that your local area code is set correctly.

  - If your telephone line has call waiting service, click Dialing Rules. Check To Disable Call Waiting, Dial; then select the code used by your telephone company. In most parts of the U.S., this is ***70**. Click OK twice to return to the connection properties dialog box.

  - If you have multiple modems, you can choose at the top of this tab which one to use for this particular connection. (If you select more than one modem, Windows will attempt to use them simultaneously. Don't do this unless your ISP offers "modem binding" service.)

  - Using the Configure button for the modem, you can set the maximum speed used to commu-nicate from the computer to the modem. For *external* modems connected via a COM port, if you don't have a special-purpose high-speed serial port, you might want to reduce this speed from the default 115200 to 57600.

  - Using the Alternates button for the telephone number, you can add multiple telephone num-bers for your ISP, which will be automatically tried, in turn, if the first doesn't answer.

- On the Options tab, you can configure the following dialing and redialing options:

  - You can elect to have Windows prompt you for the phone number of your ISP each time you connect.

  - You can select a time to wait before hanging up the line when no activity occurs. By doing so, if you pay an hourly rate to your ISP, you can help cut costs by having your computer disconnect itself from the Internet if it detects that you haven't been using your connection for a set amount of time.

  - To maintain a permanent (or *nailed-up*) dial-up connection, check Redial If Line Is Dropped and set the disconnect time to Never. (Do this only with the consent of your ISP.)

- The Security tab controls whether your password can be sent in unencrypted form. It's okay to send your ISP password unsecured.

- The Networking tab determines which network components are accessible to the Internet connection. If you're dialing in to a standard ISP, be *sure* to leave File and Printer Sharing unchecked.

- The Sharing tab allows other network users to connect through your computer's Internet connection. You'll learn more about Internet Connection Sharing in Chapter 19.

> ### ⦿ tip
>
> If you want to rename a dial-up connection, you have to go about it an odd way: right-click the network icon in the desktop's taskbar, select Open Network and Sharing Center, and then select Change Adapter Settings. Right-click the icon for your dial-up connection and select Rename.

Click OK to save your changes.

Making and Ending a Dial-Up Connection

If you use a dial-up connection with an analog modem, after you've set up an icon for your ISP, making the connection is a snap. You use this same procedure if you use a broadband connection with Point-to-Point Protocol over Ethernet (PPPoE) that requires you to log on:

1. Click the Network icon in your taskbar, or open the charms and then select Settings, Network.

2. Select the appropriate connection from the list, as shown in Figure 14.4, and click Connect.

3. Windows displays a connection dialog box (see Figure 14.5). If you previously let Windows remember the password, you can simply skip ahead to step 4.

   Otherwise, enter the password assigned by your ISP. You can check Save This User Name... if you want to use this information the next time you dial, and you can select Anyone Who Uses This Computer if it's OK for other people on this computer to use your dial-up account.

Figure 14.4
Open the Networks panel to start a dial-up connection.

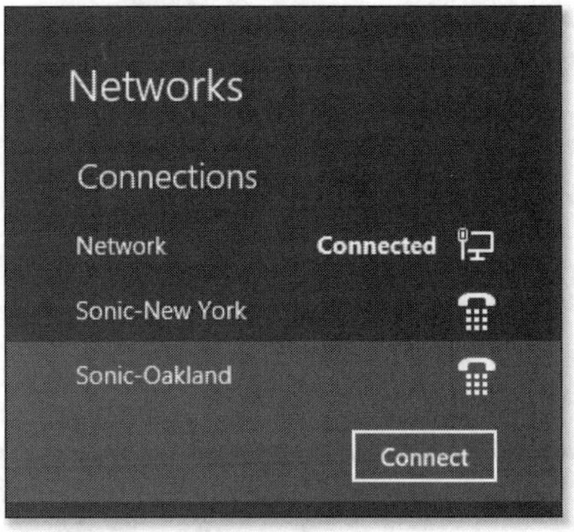

Figure 14.5
Enter your password, if necessary, double-check the number Windows is about to call, and then click Dial.

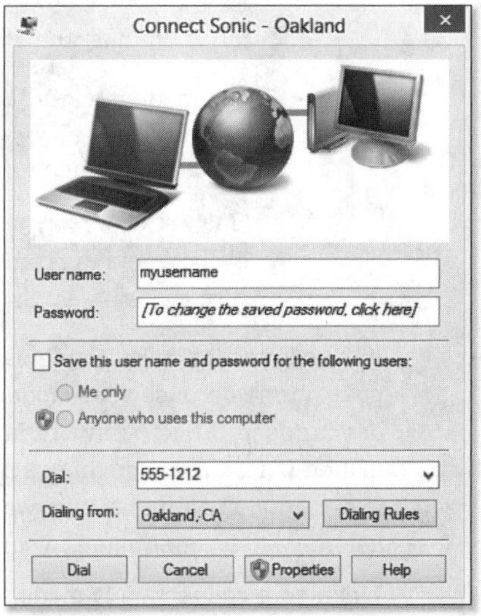

4. For a dial-up connection only, Windows shows you exactly how it's going to dial the number. Double-check that the prefix and area code are correct. You might need to click Properties to correct your current location (Dialing From) and/or Dialing Rules if the prefix or area code isn't correct.

5. Click Dial to make the connection.

Windows then dials your ISP and establishes the connection.

Modem Doesn't Dial ISP

If you attempt to connect to your ISP, but the modem doesn't make an audible attempt to connect, there are several possible solutions:

- Your phone line might not be correctly plugged into the modem. Be sure the phone cable is plugged into the correct jack on the modem.

- The phone line might not be working. Try an extension phone in the same wall jack to see if there's a dial tone.

- The modem might be working, but its speaker volume might be turned down (this has fooled me more than once!), or it may have no speaker at all. Some external modems have volume knobs. You can set the volume on an internal modem by opening Control Panel, Hardware and Sound, Device Manager. Expand the Modems option in the tree to view all your modems, right-click the modem in the tree, and select Properties. Select the Modem tab and adjust the volume control.

- The modem might have a hardware problem. Open the modem properties, as described in the previous paragraph. View the Diagnostics tab and click Query Modem. After 5–15 seconds, you should see some entries in the Command/Response list. If an error message appears instead, your modem is not working properly. If it's an external modem, be sure it's powered up. It may help to update the modem's driver software.

If the connection fails, Windows displays a (usually) sensible message explaining why: there was no dial tone because your modem is unplugged, there was no answer at the ISP or the line is busy, or your user ID and password failed. In the last case, you get three tries to enter the correct information before Windows hangs up the phone. Your ISP might require you to enter the account name information in an unintuitive way. (EarthLink, for example, at one time required you to put **ELN** before your account name.) Your ISP's customer support people can help you straighten this out.

When your connection is made, you should be able to browse websites, check your email, and so on.

Can't Reach Any Websites

If your Internet connection seems to be established correctly, but you can't reach any websites, turn to Chapter 17, "Troubleshooting an Internet Connection," for the nitty-gritty details.

Hanging Up a Dial-Up Connection

When you finish using your Internet connection, click the Network icon in the taskbar to view the Networks panel, shown earlier in Figure 14.4. Click the name of your Internet connection and then click Disconnect. Windows will hang up the connection.

Installing a Network Adapter for Broadband Service

If you are going to use cable or DSL Internet service, the following sections should help you get the service installed and working. To start with, you will need to connect your computer to your cable or DSL modem. A very few DSL and cable modems use a USB connection and can just be plugged into your computer this way.

---

tip

If a professional installer comes to configure your computer and wants to add software to it, you should know that Windows has all the software it needs to use cable or DSL service—there is no *need* for them to install any additional software on your computer. I initially try to refuse to let them. What they're after is installing a modified version of Internet Explorer that carries their brand name and steers you toward their websites. However, they also sometimes want to install customer support and antivirus software. You can decide if you want this or not. They may say it's up to you to set things up for yourself if you refuse it. You can always uninstall their stuff after they've left.

In any case, take thorough notes of what the installer does. Don't hesitate to ask questions—you have a right to know exactly what the installer is doing to your computer. And be sure to test the setup before the installer leaves.

Most DSL and cable service providers require an Ethernet network adapter for use by their modems. Virtually every new computer today has an Ethernet adapter built in, ready to use. If not, your ISP will supply and install one for you.

If you want to purchase or install the network adapter yourself, install it according to the manufacturer's instructions. This process will go something like this:

- For an internal adapter in a desktop computer, shut down Windows, unplug the computer, and install the card. Then, power up the computer and log on.

- For a laptop computer, if you have to install a plug-in PCMCIA (PC Card) adapter, you don't need to shut down Windows. Just plug in the card.

The Plug and Play system should take care of the rest for you. The driver software will in all likelihood install itself automatically.

After installation, confirm that the network adapter is installed and functioning by following these steps:

1. At the desktop, right-click the very bottom-left corner of the screen and then select Device Manager. (Alternatively, from the Start screen, type **manager**, select Settings, and then select Device Manager.)

2. The list should show only "first-level" items. Under Network Adapters, you should see no items listed with an exclamation mark icon superimposed.

caution

When your network adapter is working and connected to your DSL or cable modem, Windows will pop up a box asking you, "Do you want to turn on sharing between PCs and connect to devices on this network?" If you connected directly to the cable or DSL modem that does not have a built-in router, you must select No, Don't Turn On Sharing. This way, Windows knows to block network services that let hackers break into your computer. If you are connecting to a connection-sharing router, either standalone or built in to your broadband modem, it's okay to select Yes, Turn On Sharing. We talk about this in detail in Chapter 19.

If the network adapter appears and is marked with a yellow exclamation point, follow the network card troubleshooting instructions in Chapter 22, "Troubleshooting Your Network."

If you're using cable Internet service, skip ahead to the "Configuring a PPPoE Broadband Connection" section.

Installing Filters for DSL Service

For DSL service with self-installation, you will be provided with filters, small boxes that plug into your telephone jacks. Then the cord from your phone plugs into the filter. The filters block the DSL signal from reaching your telephones and answering machines. You need to identify every phone jack that is connected to the line your DSL service uses, and install a filter on every jack but the one that plugs into your DSL modem. If you need to plug a phone into the same jack that the DSL modem uses, use a dual jack adapter that has a filter on the side that connects to the phone. This adapter will have jacks clearly labeled "Phone" and "DSL."

 tip

If a jack is unused, you don't need to plug a filter in it, but it's a good idea to put a label over the jack indicating that it carries the DSL signal. This way, you'll remember to add a filter if you ever do plug in a phone or other device to this jack.

Alternatively, the service installer might connect your telephone line to a device called a *splitter* outside the house and will install a separate cable to bring the DSL signal to your computer. These devices separate the high-frequency DSL carrier signal from the normal telephone signal before it enters your house.

Now, skip ahead to the "Configuring a PPPoE Broadband Connection" section of this chapter.

Configuring a High-Speed Connection

If you're using an Ethernet network adapter to connect your computer to a DSL or cable Internet service, the installer might set up your computer for you. "Self-install" providers give you a set of instructions specific to your service. We can give you a general idea of what's required.

If your broadband service uses a network adapter (that is, an Ethernet adapter) to connect to a cable or DSL modem, you *must* take the following steps to secure your computer from hackers.

1. Right-click the network icon in the taskbar and then click Open Network and Sharing Center.

2. Under View Your Active Networks, there should be an entry named Network, and at the right, after Connections, should be the name of your Ethernet adapter, as shown in Figure 14.6.

   Be sure that the label under the network name says Public Network, *not* Private Network. Because the connection hooks up directly to the Internet, it *must* be designated as a Public network.

   If the label says Private Network, click the network icon in the taskbar, right-click the network name in the Connections list, select Turn Sharing On or Off, then select No, Don't Turn On Sharing or Connect to Devices.

Figure 14.6
The Network and Sharing Center must label the connection to the broadband modem as a Public Network.

Public/Private Label

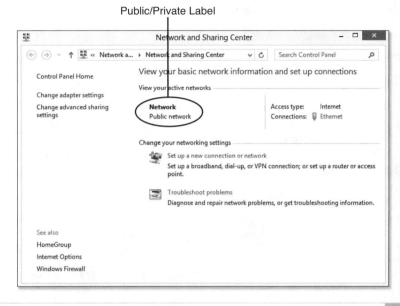

3. Now, for additional insurance, back in the Network and Sharing Center, select Change Adapter Settings. Locate the icon for the Ethernet adapter that goes to your DSL or cable modem, right-click it, and select Properties.

4. Under This Connection Uses the Following Items, uncheck File and Printer Sharing for Microsoft Networks and then uncheck Client for Microsoft Networks.

5. If your ISP requires you to set a specific IP address for the network adapter, highlight Internet Protocol Version 4 (TCP/IPv4) and click Properties. Check Use the Following IP Address and then enter the IP address, subnet mask, and default gateway provided by your ISP. You may also be instructed to enter DNS server addresses. Most of the time, this is not necessary.

6. Click OK.

After the adapter has been configured and attached to the DSL or cable modem with a network cable, you configure the connection. The procedure you should use depends on whether your ISP uses PPPoE or an always-on connection. The following sections describe these procedures.

Configuring a PPPoE Broadband Connection

Most DSL and some cable Internet providers use a connection scheme called *Point-to-Point Protocol over Ethernet (PPPoE)*. This technology works a lot like a standard dial-up connection, but the "call" takes place through the DSL circuit or TV cable instead of over a voice connection. Windows has PPPoE software built in, but the setup process varies from provider to provider; yours should give you clear instructions.

If you perform the procedure manually, after you've connected your network adapter to the broadband modem, you'll follow these steps:

1. Go to the desktop, right-click the network icon in the taskbar, and select Open Network and Sharing Center.

2. Click Set Up a New Connection or Network. Select Connect to the Internet and click Next. If Windows says you are already connected to the Internet, click Set Up a New Connection Anyway. If Windows asks, "Do you want to use a connection that you already have?", click No, Create a New Connection and then click Next.

3. Select Broadband (PPPoE).

4. Enter the username and password assigned by your ISP. You might want to check Show Characters before you enter the password, to make sure you enter it correctly.

5. Check both Remember This Password and Allow Other People to Use This Connection.

6. Click Connect.

At this point, you're prompted to sign on. The procedure for signing on and off is exactly the same as for dial-up Internet service. This is described earlier in this chapter, under "Making and Ending a Dial-Up Connection," so we won't repeat the instructions here. We will repeat one tip, though: remember to click the network icon on the taskbar whenever you want to start or stop your Internet connection.

Setting Up Dynamic IP Addressing (DHCP)

In most cases, your ISP will use the DHCP protocol to configure client network adapters. This is the default setting for all newly installed network adapters.

Some ISPs require you to give them the *MAC address* of your network adapter. This is an identification number built into the hardware that uniquely identifies your particular network adapter. To find this number, follow these steps:

1. From the desktop, right-click the network icon in the taskbar and select Open Network and Sharing Center. (Alternatively, from the Start screen, search for **center** and select Network and Sharing Center under Settings.)

> **note**
>
> Some ISPs give you a disc with installation software that does the next setup procedure for you. I intensely dislike this practice: Who knows what other software—including adware and "customer support" spyware—they're installing? Personally, I lie to them, tell them I'm installing the connection on a Macintosh or Linux computer that can't use their software, and ask for the information needed to perform the setup manually. Sometimes this works, and sometimes it makes life difficult. For instance, one major ISP I've worked with requires you to set up the service account through a special website, so if you want to shun its software, you need Internet access to set up your Internet access.

> **note**
>
> Installing a network adapter to connect to a broadband modem doesn't give you a LAN—it's just a way of connecting to the modem. If you want to set up a LAN in addition to an Internet connection, see Chapters 18 and 19.

2. Select Change Adapter Settings. Locate the icon for the network adapter that leads to your cable or DSL modem. This might be Ethernet (or Ethernet 2 if you've installed an extra adapter). If you have multiple adapters and can't tell which is which, unplug the network cable from all but the one that goes to the modem and then look for the one that doesn't say "Disconnected."

3. Right-click the icon and select Status, Details. Find the line titled Physical Address. It will be followed by six pairs of numbers and letters, as in 00-03-FF-B9-0E-14. This is the information to give to your ISP.

Alternatively, you might be instructed to set your computer's name to one your ISP provides. To do this, follow these steps:

1. Log on using an Administrator account. Right-click the very bottom-left corner of the screen and select System. Alternatively, from the Start screen, search for System under Settings.

2. In the Computer Name, Domain, and Workgroup Settings section, click Change Settings. On the Computer Name tab, click the Change button.

3. Enter the computer name as supplied by your ISP. Click More and enter the domain name speci-fied by your ISP.

When you close all these dialog boxes by clicking OK, you need to let Windows restart. When it restarts, your Internet connection should be up and running.

Setting Up a Fixed IP Address

In some cases, your ISP will require you to set your LAN adapter to a fixed IP address. This might be required with either PPPoE or "always-on" service. To set the address, follow these steps:

1. Right-click the network icon on the right side of the taskbar, and then click Open the Network and Sharing Center window.

2. Under View Your Active Networks, click the Connections name. In the Status window, select Properties to open the Local Area Connection Properties dialog box.

3. Select the Networking tab, select the Internet Protocol (either Version 6 or Version 4, depending on the IP provided by your ISP), and click the Properties button.

4. Select Use the Following IP Address and then enter the IP address, subnet mask, and default gateway information provided by your ISP, as shown in Figure 14.7.

5. Select Use the Following DNS Server Addresses, and enter the two DNS addresses provided by your ISP.

6. Click OK to return to the Local Area Connection Properties dialog box.

When you have completed this procedure, return to the PPPoE setup steps. Alternatively, if you have always-on service, open Internet Explorer to test-drive your new connection.

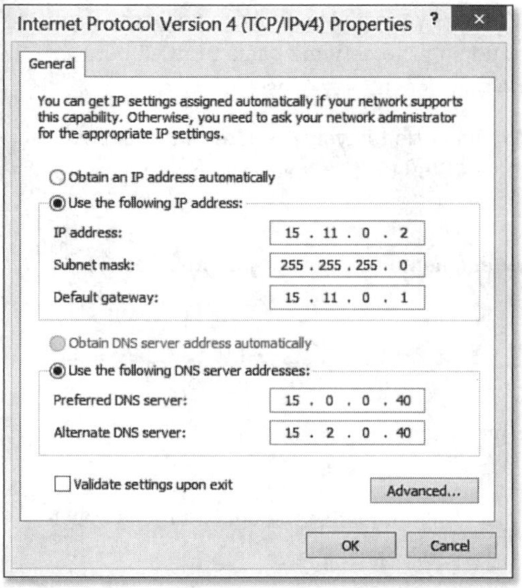

Internet Protocol Version 4 (TCP/IPv4) Properties   ?   ×

General

You can get IP settings assigned automatically if your network supports this capability. Otherwise, you need to ask your network administrator for the appropriate IP settings.

○ Obtain an IP address automatically
● Use the following IP address:

IP address: 15 . 11 . 0 . 2

Subnet mask: 255 . 255 . 255 . 0

Default gateway: 15 . 11 . 0 . 1

○ Obtain DNS server address automatically
● Use the following DNS server addresses:

Preferred DNS server: 15 . 0 . 0 . 40

Alternate DNS server: 15 . 2 . 0 . 40

☐ Validate settings upon exit   Advanced...

OK   Cancel

Figure 14.7
Here you can add the network address, subnet mask, and DNS information supplied by your ISP.

Changing the Default Connection

If you use dial-up Internet service, Windows may dial your ISP automatically when you start a program such as Internet Explorer. If you don't want Windows to dial automatically, or if you have defined multiple dial-up connections, you can tell Windows which, if any, of the connections you want it to dial.

To change the default settings, follow these steps:

1. From the Start screen, search for **internet options**, select Settings, and then select Internet Options. Alternatively, in the desktop version of Internet Explorer, press and release the Alt key and then choose Tools, Internet Options.

2. Select the Connections tab and highlight the dial-up connection you want to use for Internet browsing (see Figure 14.8).

3. If you use a standalone computer or a portable computer that sometimes has Internet access via a LAN, select Dial Whenever a Network Connection Is Not Present.

   If you want to use the modem connection even while you're connected to a LAN, you can select Always Dial My Default Connection.

   Finally, if you don't want Windows to ever dial automatically and you prefer to make your connection manually, you can choose Never Dial a Connection.

4. If you have actually changed the default dial-up connection, click Set Default.

5. Click OK.

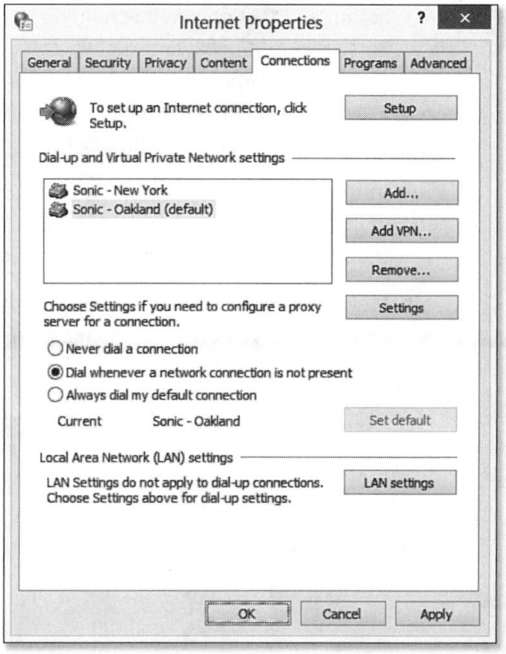

Figure 14.8
In the Internet Properties dialog box, you can specify which dial-up connection to use automatically when an Internet application is started.

Managing Multiple Internet Connections

Life would be so simple if computers and people just stayed put, but that's not the way the world works anymore. Portable computers now account for more than half of the computers sold in the United States. Managing Internet connections from multiple locations can be a little tricky.

We talk a bit more about the ins and outs of traveling with your computer in Chapter 36, "Wireless Networking," and Chapter 37, "Computing on the Road," where the topics are wireless and remote networking.

The issue comes up with plain Internet connectivity as well, so let us share some tips:

- If you use a LAN Internet connection in the office and a modem connection elsewhere, follow the instructions in the previous section "Changing the Default Connection" to tell Windows to "dial whenever a network connection is not present."

- If you use different file-sharing networks in different locations, see "Multiple LAN Connections," in Chapter 37.

- If you use a dial-up ISP with different local access numbers in different locations, life is a bit more difficult. It would be great if Windows would let you associate a distinct dial-up number with each dialing location, but it doesn't—dialing location settings just adjust the area code and dialing prefixes.

The solution is to make separate connection icons for each location's access number. After you set up and test one connection, go to the Network and Sharing Center, select Change Adapter Settings, right-click your dial-up connection icon, and select Create Copy. Rename the icon using the alternate city in the name; for example, I might name my icons Sonic-Oakland, Sonic-Freestone, and so on. Finally, right-click the icon, select Properties, and set the appropriate local access number and dialing location.

In this case, it's best to tell Windows never to automatically dial a connection (as shown earlier in "Changing the Default Connection") because it will not know which of several connections is the right one to use; it might dial a long-distance number without you noticing.

- Moving around from one network to another or one ISP to another can also cause major headaches when you try to send email. For more information on this topic, see "Email and Network Connections" in Chapter 37.

USING INTERNET EXPLORER 10

Understanding Web Page Addresses

Let's begin by examining that strange creature, the World Wide Web address, officially known as a *Uniform Resource Locator (URL)*. A web page's address usually takes the following form:

http://*host.domain/directory/file.name*

- **host.domain**—The domain name of the host computer where the page resides.

- **directory**—The host computer directory that contains the page.

- **file.name**—The page's filename. Note that most web pages use the extensions .html and .htm.

Here are some notes about URLs:

- The *http* part of the URL signifies that HTTP (Hypertext Transfer Protocol) is the TCP/IP protocol to use for communication between the web browser and the web server. HTTP is the protocol for standard web pages. Other common protocols are *https* (Secure Hypertext Transfer Protocol; secure web pages), *ftp* (File Transfer Protocol; file downloads), and *file* (for opening local files within the browser).

- Most web domains use the www prefix and the com suffix (for example, www.mcfedries.com). Other popular suffixes are edu (educational sites), gov (government sites), net (networking companies), and org (not-for-profit sites). Note, too, that most servers don't require the www prefix (for example, mcfedries.com).

- Directory names and filenames are case sensitive on most web hosts (those that run UNIX servers, anyway).

Tips and Techniques for Better Web Surfing

Surfing web pages with the desktop version of Internet Explorer is straightforward and easy, but even experienced users might not be aware of all the ways they can open and navigate pages. Here's a review of all the techniques you can use to open a web page in desktop Internet Explorer:

- **Type a URL in any Address bar**—Internet Explorer and all Windows 8 folder windows have an Address bar. To open a page, type the URL in the Address bar and press the Enter key.

- **Type a URL in the Run dialog box**—Press Windows Logo+R, type the URL you want in the Run dialog box, and click OK.

Fixing Run URL Problems

When you type a URL in the Run dialog box, you must include the "www" portion of the address. For example, typing **microsoft.com** won't work, but typing **www.microsoft.com** will. If the URL doesn't have a "www" component—for example, support.microsoft.com—you must add "http://" to the front of the address.

- **Select a URL from the Address bar**—Internet Explorer's Address bar doubles as a drop-down list that holds the last few addresses you entered.

- **Use the Open dialog box for remote pages**—Press Ctrl+O to display the Open dialog box, type the URL, and click OK.

- **Use the Open dialog box for local pages**—If you want to view a web page that's on your computer, display the Open dialog box, enter the full path (drive, folder, and filename), and click OK. Alternatively, click Browse, find the page, click Open, and then click OK.

- **Select a favorite**—Press Ctrl+I to open the Favorites list and then click the site you want to open.

- **Click a Favorites bar button**—If you've displayed the Favorites bar (right-click an empty section of the title bar and then click to activate the Favorites Bar command), click a button to navigate to that site.

- **Click a web address in a Windows Mail message**—When Windows Mail recognizes a web address in an email message (that is, an address that begins with http://, https://, ftp://, www., and so on), it converts the address into a link. Clicking the link opens the address in Internet Explorer. Note, too, that many other programs are "URL aware," including the Microsoft Office suite of programs.

After you've opened a page, you usually move to another page by clicking a link: either a text link or an image. However, there are more techniques you can use to navigate to other pages:

- **Open a link in another window**—If you don't want to leave the current page, you can force a link to open in another Internet Explorer window by right-clicking the link and then clicking Open in New Window. You can open a new window for the current page by pressing Alt+F and then selecting New Window, or by pressing Ctrl+N.

> **tip**
>
> You can also hold down the Shift key and click a link to open that link in a new browser window.

- **Retrace the pages you've visited**—To return to a page you visited previously in this session, either click Internet Explorer's Back button or press Alt+Left Arrow. After you go back to a page, you move ahead through the visited pages by clicking the Forward button or pressing Alt+Right Arrow. Note, too, that if you click and hold either the Back or Forward button, Internet Explorer displays a list of pages you've visited in the current session, as shown in Figure 15.1.

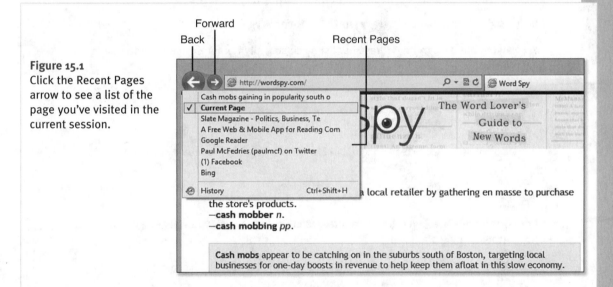

Figure 15.1
Click the Recent Pages arrow to see a list of the page you've visited in the current session.

- **Return to the start page**—When you launch Internet Explorer without specifying a URL, you usually end up at Bing, the default start page (http://www.bing.com/; note, however, that many computer manufacturers change the default start page). You can return to this page at any time by clicking the Home button in the toolbar or by pressing Alt+Home.

- **Use the History list**—Press Ctrl+H to open the Favorites Center with the History tab displayed to see a list of the sites you've visited over the past 20 days. (You can also press Ctrl+Shift+H to display the History tab pinned to the left side of the browser window.) Just click a URL to go to a site. The items you see in the History list are based on the contents of the %UserProfile%\ AppData\Local\Microsoft\Windows\History folder. See "Using the Handy History List," later in this chapter, for more on the History list.

Taking Advantage of the Address Bar

Internet Explorer's Address bar (and the Address bars that appear in all Windows 8 folder windows) appears to be nothing more than a simple type-and-click mechanism. However, it's useful for many things, and comes with its own bag of tricks for making it even easier to use. Here's a rundown:

- Internet Explorer maintains a list of the last few URLs you typed into the Address bar. To access this list, press F4 and then use the Up Arrow and Down Arrow keys to select an item from the list.

Clearing the Address Bar List

One way to clear the Address bar list is to clear the history files. You do this by selecting Tools, Safety, Delete Browsing History (or by pressing Ctrl+Shift+Del), activating the History check box, and then clicking Delete. If you prefer to preserve the history files, note that Internet Explorer stores the last 50 typed URLs in the following Registry key:

```
HKCU\Software\Microsoft\Internet Explorer\TypedURLs
```

You can therefore clear the Address bar list by closing all Internet Explorer windows and deleting the settings url1 through url50 in this key. Here's a script that does so:

```
Option Explicit
Dim objWshShell, i
Set objWshShell = WScript.CreateObject("WScript.Shell")
For i = 1 to 50
    objWshShell.RegDelete "HKCU\Software\Microsoft\Internet Explorer\
  ➥TypedURLs\url" & i
Next 'i
objWshShell.Popup "Finished deleting typed URLs", , "Delete Typed URLs"
```

Note that if there are fewer than 50 addresses in the history list, you will get a Windows Script Host error stating the following:

```
Unable to remove registry key "HKCU\Software\Microsoft\Internet
➥\Explorer\TypedURLs\urln,
```

Here, *n* is one greater than the number of history items found in the list. You can safely ignore the message; the script removed all the history items from the list.

- To edit the Address bar text, press Alt+D to select it.

- The Address bar's AutoComplete feature monitors the address as you type. If any previously entered addresses match your typing, they appear in a list. To choose one of those addresses, use the Down Arrow key to select it and then press the Enter key. The quickest way to use AutoComplete is to begin typing the site's domain name. For example, if you want to bring up http://www.microsoft.com/, start typing the **microsoft** part. If you start with the full address, you have to type **http://www.** or just **www.**, and then one other character.

- Internet Explorer assumes that any address you enter is for a website. Therefore, you don't need to type the http:// prefix because Internet Explorer adds it for you automatically.

- Internet Explorer also assumes that most web addresses are in the form http://www.*something*.com. Therefore, if you simply type the *something* part and press Ctrl+Enter, Internet Explorer will automatically add the http://www. prefix and the .com suffix. For example, you can get to the Microsoft home page (http://www.microsoft.com) by typing **microsoft** and pressing Ctrl+Enter.

- Some websites use frames to divide a web page into multiple sections. Some of these sites offer links to other websites but, annoyingly, those pages appear within the first site's frame structure. To break out of frames, drag a link into the Address bar.

- The Internet Explorer Address bar also doubles as a search box, which means you can simply type your search text and then press Enter. To ensure Internet Explorer runs a search rather than trying to load a URL, either click the Search icon in the Address bar or add a question mark (**?**) and a space before your search text (you can press Ctrl+E to add the question mark and space automatically) and then press Enter.

> **tip**
>
> You can also set up a custom URL prefix and suffix that Internet Explorer uses when you press Ctrl+Shift+Enter (instead of Ctrl+Enter). Select Tools, Internet Options, display the General tab, and then click Languages to open the Language preferences dialog box. If you don't want Internet Explorer to automatically add the www prefix, activate the Do Not Add 'www' to the Beginning of Typed Web Addresses check box. Use the Suffix text box to enter the domain suffix you want added automatically, such as .org or .ca. Click OK.

Creating a Shortcut to a URL

Another way to navigate websites via Internet Explorer is to create shortcuts that point to the appropriate URLs. To do this, use either of the following techniques:

- Copy the URL to the Clipboard, create a new shortcut (open the folder in which you want to store the shortcut and then select Home, New Item, Shortcut), and then paste the URL into the Type the Location of the Item text box.

- You can create a shortcut for the currently displayed page by using the page icon that appears to the left of the address in the Address bar. Drag this icon and drop it on the desktop or on whatever folder you want to use to store the shortcut.

- You can create a shortcut for any hypertext link by dragging the link text from the page and dropping it on the desktop or within a folder. When Windows asks you to confirm, click OK.

After your shortcut is in place, you can open the website by launching the shortcut's icon.

> **tip**
>
> If you have a site that you use frequently, create a shortcut for it on the taskbar. This is called *pinning* the site to the taskbar. The easiest way to do this is to navigate to the site, click and drag the site's icon from the Address bar, and then drop it on the taskbar.

> ## 🔵 tip
>
> Internet shortcuts are simple text files that use the URL extension. They contain only the address of the Internet site, as in the following example:
>
> ```
> [InternetShortcut]
> URL=http://www.microsoft.com/
> ```
>
> If you need to make changes to that address, it's possible to edit the shortcut by opening the URL file in Notepad.

Working with Tabs

Internet Explorer supports *tabbed browsing*, in which each open page appears in its own tab within a single Internet Explorer window. You can open dozens of tabs in each window, which makes surfing multiple sites easy. One of the nicest features of tabs is that Internet Explorer supplies each tab with its own execution thread, which means that you can start a page loading in one tab while reading downloaded page text in another tab. You can also specify multiple home pages that load in their own tabs when you start Internet Explorer (see "Changing the Home Page," later in this chapter).

Opening a Page in a New Tab

Tabs are only as useful as they are easy to use, and Internet Explorer does a good job of making tabs simple. One way that it does this is by giving you a satisfyingly wide variety of methods to use for opening a page in a new tab. There are six in all:

- **Hold down Ctrl and click a link in a web page**—This creates a new tab and loads the linked page in the background.

🔧 Switching to a New Tab Automatically

Opening a page in the background in a new tab when you Ctrl+click a link is useful if you want to keep reading the current page. However, we find that most of the time we want to read the new page right away. If you have a fast connection, the page loads quickly enough that the delay between clicking and reading is usually minimal. In such cases, you can tell Internet Explorer to switch to the new tab automatically when you Ctrl+click a link. Select Tools, Internet Options to open the Internet Options dialog box, display the General tab, and then click Tabs. In the Tabbed Browsing Settings dialog box, activate the Always Switch to New Tabs When They Are Created check box and then click OK in the open dialog boxes.

- **Use the middle mouse button (if you have one) to click a link in a web page**—This creates a new tab and loads the linked page in the background.

- **Type the page URL in the Address bar and then press Alt+Enter**—This creates a new tab and loads the page in the foreground.

- **Click the New Tab button (or press Ctrl+T) to display a blank tab**—Type the page URL in the Address bar and then press the Enter key. This loads the page in the foreground.

Displaying the New Tab Button

To see the New Tab button, you must configure Internet Explorer to display the tabs on a separate row of the interface. Right-click an empty section of the Internet Explorer title bar and then click to activate the Show Tabs on a Separate Row command.

- **Click and drag a web page link or the current Address bar icon and drop it on the New Tab button**—This creates a new tab and loads the page in the foreground.

- **Click a link in another program**—This creates a new tab and loads the linked page in the foreground.

Figure 15.2 shows Internet Explorer with several tabs open.

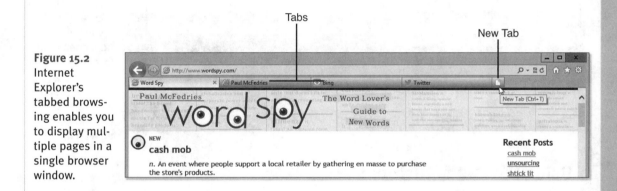

Figure 15.2
Internet Explorer's tabbed browsing enables you to display multiple pages in a single browser window.

To close a tab, Internet Explorer gives you five choices:

- Hover the mouse pointer over the tab and then click the tab's Close Tab button.

- Select the tab and then press Ctrl+W.

- Right-click the tab and then click Close Tab.

- To close every tab except one, right-click the tab you want to keep open and then click Close Other Tabs.

- Click the tab using the middle mouse button (if you have one).

Navigating Tabs

When you have two or more tabs open, navigating them is straightforward:

- With your mouse, click the tab of the page you want to use.

- With your keyboard, press Ctrl+Tab to navigate the tabs from left to right (and from the last tab to the first tab); press Ctrl+Shift+Tab to navigate the tabs from right to left (and from the first tab to the last tab).

Unfortunately, Internet Explorer has only so much room to the right of the command bar, so it can display only a limited number of tabs. Internet Explorer does reduce the tab width as you add more tabs, but the width can shrink only so far if the tabs are to remain useable. On a 1024×768 screen, Internet Explorer can display a maximum of nine tabs. If you open more tabs than Internet Explorer can display, Internet Explorer adds two new buttons to the tab strip, as shown in Figure 15.3. Click Scroll Tab List Backward to display the previous unseen tab and click Scroll Tab List Forward to display the next unseen tab.

Scroll Tab List Backward

Scroll Tab List Forward

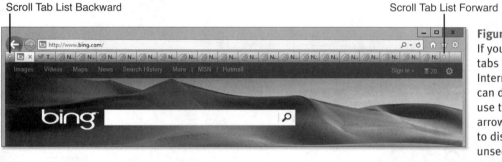

Figure 15.3
If you have more tabs open than Internet Explorer can display, use the double-arrow buttons to display the unseen tabs.

Using the Handy History List

You saw earlier (in "Tips and Techniques for Better Web Surfing") how you can click the Back and Forward buttons to follow your own footsteps on the World Wide Web. However, Internet Explorer wipes those lists clean when you exit the program. What do you do when you want to revisit a site from a previous session? Happily, Internet Explorer keeps track of the addresses of all the pages you perused for the last 20 days.

The names and addresses of these pages are stored in the History list, and you can view it by clicking the Favorites Center button and then clicking History (alternatively, you can press Ctrl+H). To bring a site into view, follow these steps:

1. Click the day or week you want to work with. Internet Explorer displays a list of the domains you visited on that day or during that week.

2. Click the domain of the website that contains the page you want to see. Internet Explorer opens the domain to reveal all the pages you visited within that site, as shown in Figure 15.4.

3. Click the name of the page you want.

Figure 15.4
The History list keeps track of all the web addresses you called on in the last 20 days.

Pin the Favorites Center

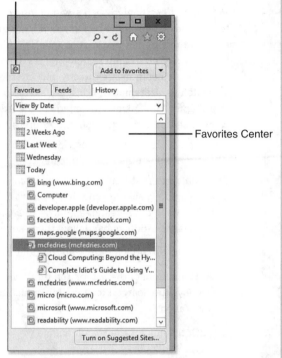

Favorites Center

If you have a large History list, you might have trouble finding the page you want. To help, click the drop-down list at the top of the History list to display a menu with the following choices:

- **By Date**—Click this item to sort the History list by the date you visited each page (this is the default sort order).

- **By Site**—Click this item to sort by the site names.

- **By Most Visited**—Click this item to sort the History list by popularity, with the pages you visited most often at the top.

- **By Order Visited Today**—Click this item to show only the pages you visited today, sorted in the order you visited them (with the most recent at the top).

- **Search History**—Click this item to search the History list. Internet Explorer searches not only the site and page names, but also the page text (via local copies of each page stored in the Temporary Internet Files folder).

tip

If you want to revisit a number of sites, it's a hassle to reopen the Favorites Center repeatedly. You can tell Internet Explorer to leave the Favorites Center open by clicking the Pin the Favorites Center button, pointed out in Figure 15.4. Alternatively, press Ctrl+Shift+H to pin the Favorites Center and display the History list at the same time.

Searching the Web

Veteran surfers, having seen a wide range of what the Web has to offer, usually prefer to tackle it using a targeted approach that enables them to find information quickly. This means using one or more of the Web's many search engines. It's usually best to deal with a search engine site directly, but Internet Explorer offers some default searching options. For example, you saw earlier in this chapter (in "Taking Advantage of the Address Bar") that you can run searches directly from the Address bar.

 tip

In some cases you may only want to search for text within the currently displayed web page. To do that, press Ctrl+F and use the Find bar to enter your search text and then click Next.

Enter your search terms in the Address bar and then press Enter or click Search (you can also press Alt+Enter to open the results in a new tab).

By default, Internet Explorer initially submits the search text to the Bing search engine. (The default search engine is also the one that Internet Explorer uses for the Address bar AutoSearch.) If you want access to other search engines—or *search providers*, as Internet Explorer insists on calling them—via the Address bar, follow these steps:

1. Click the drop-down arrow on the right side of the Address box.

2. At the bottom of the list, on the right, click Add. The Internet Explorer Gallery page appears and displays the Search Providers tab, which has links to various search engines, including Google and Yahoo!.

3. Click the link for the search engine you want to add. Internet Explorer displays the search engine's details.

4. Click Add to Internet Explorer. The Add Search Provider dialog box appears.

tip

You can change the default search engine at any time. Select Tools, Manage Add-ons, and then click Search Providers. Click the search engine you want to use and then click Set as Default. Click Close to put the new setting into effect.

5. If you want Internet Explorer to use this search engine as the default, activate the Make This My Default Search Provider check box.

6. Click Add.

To use the new search engine, drop down the Address bar list to see a list of the search engines, and then click the one you want to use, as shown in Figure 15.5.

Figure 15.5
Drop down the
Address bar list and
then click a search
engine icon to use
that service for
searching.

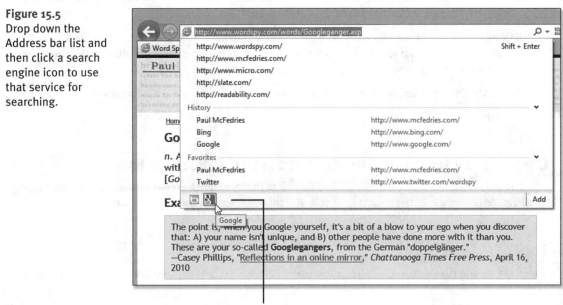

Search providers appear here.

The Favorites Folder: Sites to Remember

The sad truth is that much of what you'll see on the Web will be utterly forgettable and not worth a second look. However, there are all kinds of gems out there waiting to be uncovered—sites you'll want to visit regularly. Instead of memorizing the appropriate URLs, jotting them down on sticky notes, or plastering your desktop with shortcuts, you can use Internet Explorer's handy Favorites feature to keep track of your choice sites.

The Favorites feature is really just a folder (you'll find it in your %UserProfile% folder) that you use to store Internet shortcuts. The advantage of using the Favorites folder as opposed to any other folder is that you can add, view, and link to the Favorites folder shortcuts directly from Internet Explorer.

Adding a Shortcut to the Favorites Folder

When you find a site you'd like to declare as a favorite, follow these steps:

1. Click the Favorites Center button (alternatively, you can press Alt+Z) and then click Add to Favorites. The Add a Favorite dialog box appears.

 tip

The quickest route to the Add a Favorite dialog box is to press Ctrl+D. If you want to avoid the dialog box and place the favorites directly on the Favorites bar, press Alt+Z and then click Add to Favorites Bar.

2. The Name text box displays the title of the page. The title is the text that will appear when you view the list of your favorites later. Feel free to edit this text if you like.

3. Internet Explorer enables you to set up subfolders to hold related favorites. If you don't want to bother with this, skip to step 4. Otherwise, click the New Folder button to display the Create a Folder dialog box, type a folder name, and then click Create.

4. Use the Create In list to select the folder in which you want to store the favorite.

5. Click Add.

Opening an Internet Shortcut from the Favorites Folder

The purpose of the Favorites folder, of course, is to give you quick access to the sites you visit regularly. To link to one of the shortcuts in your Favorites folder, you have two choices:

- In Internet Explorer, the Favorites list contains the complete list of your Favorites folder shortcuts. To link to a shortcut, click the Favorites Center button, click Favorites (see Figure 15.6), and then select the shortcut you want.

tip

You can quickly display the Favorites list by pressing Ctrl+I.

tip

Internet Explorer offers two methods for quickly adding a site to the Favorites list. Both of these methods work only when you position the Favorites Center on the left side of the Internet Explorer window. Therefore, before using either of these methods, you must click the Pin the Favorites Center button.

- If the current page has a link to the site you want to save, click and drag the link to the Favorites list. ◈
- If you want to save the current page instead, click and drag the icon from the Address bar to the Favorites list.

- If you added a site to the Favorites bar (pointed out in Figure 15.6), display the Favorites bar (right-click an empty section of the title bar and then click to activate the Favorites Bar command) and then click the favorite you want.

Maintaining Favorites

When you have a large number of favorites, you need to do some regular maintenance to keep things organized. This involves creating new subfolders, moving favorites between folders, changing URLs, deleting unused favorites, and more. Here's a summary of a few maintenance techniques you'll use most often:

- To change the URL of a favorite, display the Favorites list, find the item you want to work with, and right-click it. In the contextual menu, click Properties and then use the properties sheet to adjust the URL.

Figure 15.6
In the Favorites Center, the Favorites list displays the contents of your Favorites folder.

- To move a favorite, display the Favorites list, find the item you want to work with, and then drag the item to another spot on the menu (or into a submenu).

- To delete a favorite, display the Favorites list, find the item you want to work with, right-click it, and then click Delete.

- To sort the favorites alphabetically, pull down the Favorites menu, right-click any favorite or folder, and then click Sort By Name.

Sharing Favorites with Other Browsers

Many users like to run Internet Explorer along with another browser such as Firefox, Chrome, or Safari on their machines. Unfortunately, these browsers store saved sites differently: Internet Explorer uses *favorites*, whereas Firefox, Chrome, and Safari use *bookmarks*. However, Internet Explorer has a feature that enables you to either export favorites to a bookmark file or import bookmarks as favorites. Here's how to do it:

1. In Internet Explorer, press Alt to display the menu bar and then select File, Import and Export. The Import/Export Settings Wizard makes an appearance.

2. Select Export to a File and then click Next.

3. Click to activate the Favorites check box and then click Next. The wizard asks you which Favorites folder you want to export.

4. Click the folder and then click Next. The wizard prompts you to enter the path to the `bookmark.htm` file.

5. Type or select the path, and then click Export. The wizard exports the favorites and then displays a dialog box to let you know when it's complete.

6. Click Finish.

Working with RSS Feeds

Some websites—particularly blogs—regularly add new content. That makes for a dynamic and interesting site (depending on the content, of course), but it does mean that you have to check the site often if you want to keep up with the latest information. You can avoid this hassle altogether by turning the tables and having the site tell you when it has posted something new. You can do this if the site supports a feature called *Real Simple Syndication*, or *RSS*, which enables you to subscribe to the feed that the site sends out. That feed usually contains the most recent data posted to the site.

RSS feeds are XML files, so you cannot read them directly. Instead, you need a *feed reader* program or website that can interpret the RSS content. However, Internet Explorer has this capability built in, so you can subscribe to and read RSS feeds from the comfort of your desktop.

Navigating to a site that has one or more feeds available enables the View Feeds icon in Internet Explorer's Command bar. (If you don't see the Command bar, right-click an empty section of the title bar and then click to activate the Command Bar command.) Pull down the View Feeds list (or press Alt+J) to see a list of the site's feeds, as shown in Figure 15.7.

Figure 15.7
If a site offers one or more RSS feeds, Internet Explorer's View Feeds button becomes enabled.

Why would a site have multiple feeds? There are two main reasons:

- The site offers a single feed in multiple formats. The three main formats are RSS 1.0, RSS 2.0, and Atom. Internet Explorer supports all three formats, so in this case it doesn't matter which one you choose.

- The site offers multiple content feeds. For example, some blogs offer separate feeds for posts and comments.

Click the feed you want to view, and Internet Explorer displays the feed content, as shown in Figure 15.8.

Figure 15.8
Select the feed you want and Internet Explorer displays the feed content.

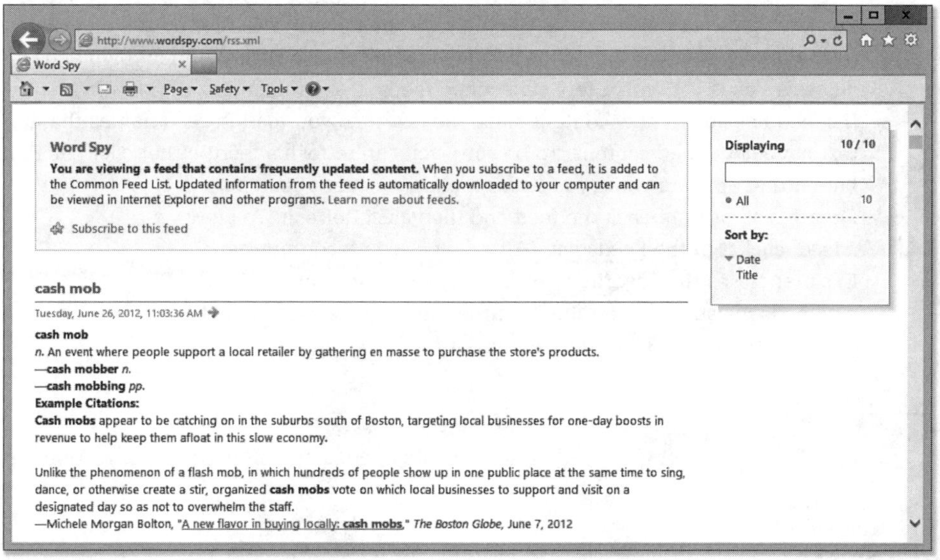

Subscribing to a Feed

Simply viewing a site's RSS feed is only marginally useful. To get more out of a feed, you need to subscribe to it, which tells Internet Explorer to check the feed for new content automatically and download that content to your computer, which makes the feed part of what Microsoft calls the *RSS Feed Store*. (The default update schedule is once per day.) You then use the Feeds list in the Favorites Center to view the content of your subscribed feeds (see "Reading Feeds," next).

To subscribe to a feed, follow these steps:

1. Display the feed you want to subscribe to.

2. Click the Subscribe to This Feed link. The Subscribe to This Feed dialog box appears.

3. The Name text box displays the title of the feed, which is the text that appears when you later view the Feed list. You can edit this text if you like.

4. Internet Explorer enables you to set up subfolders to hold related feeds. If you don't want to bother with this, skip to step 4. Otherwise, click the New Folder button to display the Create a Folder dialog box, type a folder name, and then click Create.

5. Use the Create In list to select the folder in which you want to store the feed.

6. Click Subscribe.

Reading Feeds

Because, by definition, a feed contains content that updates regularly, you'll want to stay on top of your feeds and peruse them for new content as often as you can.

To view feeds via the Favorites Center, click the Favorites Center button and then click Feeds. (Immediately after you subscribe to a feed, you can also click the View My Feeds link.) Figure 15.9 shows a Feeds list with a few subscribed feeds. If the feed name appears in bold type, it means the feed has added new content since the last time you read it; feed names that appear in regular text have not added content. To be sure, you can refresh a feed: either click the Refresh This Feed button that appears when you hover the mouse over a feed (see Figure 15.9) or right-click the feed and then click Refresh. To view a feed, click it in the Feeds list. (After you click a feed, Internet Explorer closes the Favorites Center. If you're going through several feeds, be sure to keep the Favorites Center onscreen by first clicking the Pin the Favorites Center button.)

 tip

You can display the Feeds list quickly by pressing Ctrl+G.

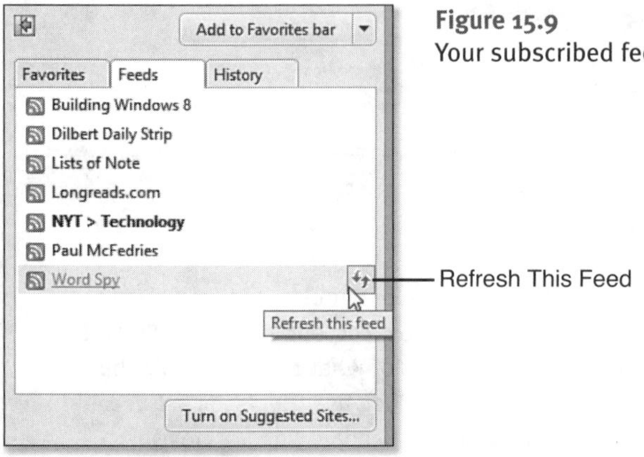

Figure 15.9
Your subscribed feeds appear in the Favorite Center's Feeds list.

Refresh This Feed

Setting the Feed Update Schedule

Most websites that offer a feed will update it at the same time as, or soon after, the site posts new content. The frequency with which this occurs varies widely: once a day, once a week, several times a day, or even several times an hour.

By default, Internet Explorer checks for an updated feed once per day. Checking once a day is a reasonable schedule for sites that post new content once or twice a day or every couple of days. However, it's not an efficient schedule for feeds that update much more or much less frequently. For example, if a feed updates only once a week, it's wasteful for Internet Explorer to check the feed every day. On the other hand, if a feed updates many times during a day, you might not see a time-sensitive post until it is too late or you might face a daunting number of posts to read. You can make a feed more efficient or easier to read by setting up a custom refresh schedule that suits the feed. Here are the steps to follow:

1. Click Favorites Center and then click Feeds to display the Feeds list.

2. Right-click the feed you want to work with and then click Properties. (If Internet Explorer displays the feed, you can also click the View Feed Properties link.) Internet Explorer displays the Feed Properties dialog box.

3. Click the Use Custom Schedule option. Internet Explorer activates the Frequency list.

4. Use the Frequency list to select the update schedule you prefer: 15 minutes, 30 minutes, 1 hour, 4 hours, 1 day, 1 week, or Never.

5. Click OK.

🌐 tip

If you want to use the same schedule for all your feeds, the easiest way to do so is to change the default schedule. If you have the Feed Properties dialog box open, click the Settings button that appears beside the Use Default Schedule option. Otherwise, click Tools and then click Internet Options to display the Internet Options dialog box. Click the Content tab and then click Settings in the Feeds group. Use the Default Schedule list to click the interval you want to use and then click OK in all open dialog boxes. Note that this only affects those feeds where you've selected the Use Default Schedule option. Feeds where you have selected the Use Custom Schedule option are not affected.

Customizing Internet Explorer

Internet Explorer is chock full of customization options that enable you to set up the program for the way you work and surf. The rest of this chapter examines what we think are the most useful of Internet Explorer's long list of customization features.

Controlling the Web Page Cache

In the same way that a disk cache stores frequently used data for faster performance, Internet Explorer also keeps a cache of files from web pages you've visited recently. The cache is maintained on a per-user basis and is located in the following folder:

```
%UserProfile%\Local\Microsoft\Windows\Temporary Internet Files
```

Internet Explorer uses these saved files to display web pages quickly the next time you ask to see them or while you are offline.

To control the cache, select Tools, Internet Options and display the General tab. Use the following buttons in the Browsing History group:

■ **Delete Files**—Clicking this button displays the Delete Browsing History dialog box. (You can also display the dialog box by selecting Tools, Safety, Delete Browsing History.) Make sure the Temporary Internet Files and Website Data check box is activated and then click Delete to clean out the Temporary Internet Files folder.

■ **Settings**—Clicking this button displays the Website Data Settings dialog box, shown in Figure 15.10.

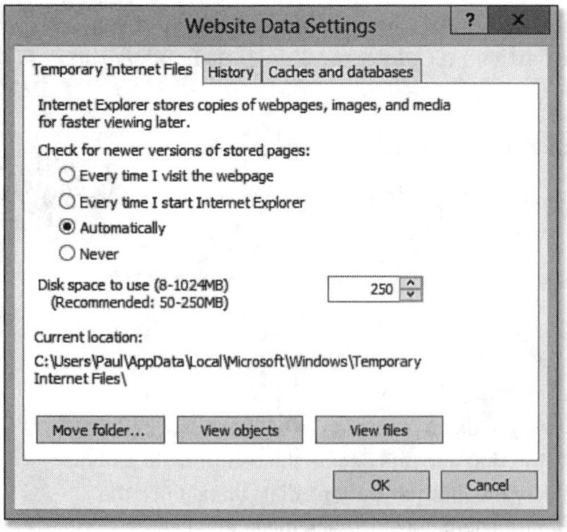

Figure 15.10
Use this dialog box to control how the Internet Explorer cache works.

You have the following options in the Website Data Settings dialog box:

■ **Check for Newer Versions of Stored Pages**—Activate an option in this group to determine when Internet Explorer checks for updated versions of cache files. If you have a fast connection and you want to be certain that you're always seeing the most current data, activate the Every Time I Visit the Webpage option.

note
No matter which cache update option you choose, you can view the most up-to-date version of a page at any time by pressing F5 or by clicking the Refresh button.

■ **Disk Space to Use**—Use this spin box to set the size of the cache as a percentage of the hard disk's capacity. A larger cache speeds up website browsing but also uses more hard drive space.

■ **Move Folder**—Click this button to change the folder used for the cache. For example, you could move the cache to a partition with more free space so that you can increase the cache size, or to a faster hard drive to improve cache performance. Note that you must restart your computer if you move the cache folder.

■ **View Objects**—Click this button to display the Downloaded Program Files folder, which holds the Java applets and ActiveX controls that have been downloaded and installed on your system.

■ **View Files**—Click this button to display the Temporary Internet Files folder.

Setting Internet Explorer Options

You had a brief introduction to the Internet Options dialog box in the previous section. However, this dialog box is loaded with useful options and settings that enable you to control dozens of aspects of Internet Explorer's behavior and look. These include cosmetic options such as the fonts and colors used by the program, but also more important concerns, such as your home page and the level of security that Internet Explorer uses. To display these options, you have several ways to proceed:

- In Internet Explorer, click Tools (the gear icon; you also can press Alt+X), and then click Internet Option. Alternatively, press Alt and then select Tools, Internet Options.

- In the Start screen, press Windows Logo+W to open the Settings search pane, type **internet options**, and then press Enter.

- In Control Panel, display all the icons and then click Internet Options. (If you're using the Category view, select Network and Internet, Internet Options.)

Whichever method you use, you see the Internet Options dialog box. The next few sections discuss the details of some of the controls in this dialog box.

Changing the Home Page

In Internet Explorer, the *home page* is what the browser views when you start a new session. The default home page is usually Bing.com, but most computer manufacturers substitute their own pages.

To change the home page, open the Internet Options dialog box (see "Setting Internet Explorer Options"), display the General tab, and then click one of the following buttons:

- **Use Current**—For this button, first navigate to the page you want to use. Then open the Internet Options dialog box and click Use Current to change the home page to the current page. If you'd rather open Internet Explorer with a blank page, type **about:blank** in the text box and click Use Current.

- **Use Default**—Click this button to revert to Internet Explorer's default home page.

- **Use New Tab**—Click this button if you'd prefer to launch Internet Explorer without loading a home page.

Internet Explorer also gives you an easier way to set the current page as your home page. Navigate to the page, right-click the Home button, and then click Add or Change Home Page. In the Add or Change Home Page dialog box that appears, activate the Use this Webpage as Your Only Home Page option and then click Yes.

Even better, Internet Explorer also enables you to specify *multiple* home pages. When you launch Internet Explorer or click the Home button, Internet Explorer loads each home page in a separate tab. This is a great feature if you regularly open several pages at the start of each browsing session. You can use two methods to specify multiple home pages:

- Display the Internet Options dialog box and click the General tab. In the Home Page list box, type the address of each page on a separate line. (That is, type one address, press Enter to start a new line, and then type the next address.)

- Navigate to the page you want to add, click the drop-down arrow beside the Home button, and then click Add or Change Home Page. In the Add or Change Home Page dialog box that appears,

activate the Add This Webpage to Your Home Page Tabs
option and then click Yes.

Configuring the Page History

In the Internet Options dialog box (see "Setting Internet Explorer
Options"), the General tab's Browsing History group also controls
various options related to the History folder (refer to the "Using
the Handy History List" section, earlier in this chapter):

- **Delete**—Clicking this button displays the Delete Browsing
  History dialog box. (You can also display the dialog box by
  selecting Tools, Safety, Delete Browsing History.) Activate the
  History check box and then click the Delete button to remove
  all URLs from the History folder.

- **Settings**—Clicking this button displays the Website Data Settings dialog box, shown earlier in
  Figure 15.10. Display the History tab and then use the Days to Keep Pages in History spin box to
  set the maximum number of days that Internet Explorer stores a URL in its History list. Enter a
  value between 1 and 999. If you do not want Internet Explorer to keep any pages in the History
  folder, enter **0**.

Setting More General Options

In the Internet Options dialog box (see "Setting Internet Explorer Options"), the General tab also
boasts four buttons at the bottom:

- **Colors**—Click this button to display the Colors dialog box, where you can deactivate the Use
  Windows Colors check box to set the default text and background colors used in the Internet
  Explorer window. You can also use the Visited and Unvisited buttons to set the default link colors. Finally, activate the Use Hover Color check box to have Internet Explorer change the color of
  a link when you position the mouse pointer over it. Use the Hover button to set the color.

- **Languages**—Click this button to display the Language
  Preference dialog box, which enables you to add one or more
  languages to Internet Explorer. This makes it possible for
  Internet Explorer to handle pages in foreign languages. You
  can also use this dialog box to set up relative priorities for the
  designated languages.

- **Fonts**—Click this button to display the Fonts dialog box,
  which enables you to determine how web page fonts appear
  within Internet Explorer.

- **Accessibility**—Click this button to display the Accessibility
  dialog box. From here, you can tell Internet Explorer to ignore

note

If Internet Explorer currently
displays all the tabs you want to
use as your home pages, right-
click the Home button and then
click Add or Change Home Page.
In the Add or Change Home Page
dialog box that appears, activate
the Use the Current Tab Set as
Your Home Page option and then
click Yes.

tip

To change the size of the fonts
Internet Explorer uses, press
Alt+V, select Text Size, and then
choose a relative font size from
the submenu (for example,
Larger or Smaller). If you have a
mouse with a wheel button, hold
down Ctrl while pressing and
turning the wheel. This changes
the onscreen text size on the fly.

the colors, font styles, and font sizes specified on any web page. You can also specify your own style sheet to use when formatting web pages.

Understanding Internet Explorer's Advanced Options

In the Internet Options dialog box (see "Setting Internet Explorer Options"), the Advanced tab has a huge list of customization features (see Figure 15.11). Many of these settings are obscure, but many others are extremely useful for surfers of all stripes. This section runs through all of these settings.

Figure 15.11
In the Internet Options dialog box, the Advanced tab contains a long list of Internet Explorer customization settings.

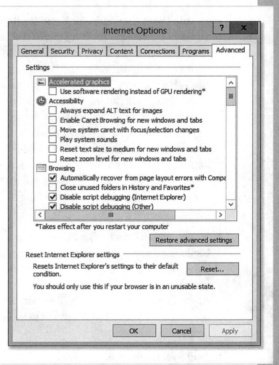

Accelerated Graphics

The Accelerated Graphics section has a single check box named Use Software Rendering Instead of GPU Rendering. Normally you want to leave this check box deactivated to take advantage of the hardware acceleration features of your video card's graphics processing unit (GPU). However, if you're having trouble viewing graphics on a particular site—particularly streaming video or full-screen video—then you might be able to solve the problem by activating this check box to let the CPU render graphics instead of the GPU.

Accessibility

The Accessibility group has six options:

- **Always Expand ALT Text for Images**—Most webmasters define a text description for each image they include on a page. If you tell Internet Explorer not to show images (see the later discussion of the Show Pictures check box), all you see are boxes where the images should be, and each box contains the text description (known as *alt text*, where *alt* is short for *alternate*). Activating this check box tells Internet Explorer to expand the image box horizontally so that the alt text appears on a single line.

- **Enable Caret Browsing for New Windows and Tabs**—Activate this check box to switch Internet Explorer into caret browsing mode. You normally navigate a web page using the mouse to click links and scroll the screen. The keyboard comes into play occasionally for scrolling (with Page Down and Page Up keys) and rarely for selecting links (with the Tab key). However, many people find the mouse difficult to use and would prefer to navigate a web page the same way they navigate a word processing document: using the Left and Right Arrow keys to navigate characters, the Up and Down Arrow keys to navigate lines, and Ctrl+arrow key to navigate words (with the Left and Right Arrow keys) or paragraphs (with the Up and Down Arrow keys), and so on. This is called *caret browsing* (where *caret* is a fancy term for a vertical cursor).

 note

To activate a link when caret browsing, navigate the cursor inside the link text (Internet Explorer adds a box around the link text), and then press Enter.

- **Move System Caret with Focus/Selection Changes**—Activating this check box tells Internet Explorer to move the system caret whenever you change the focus. (The *system caret* is a visual indication of what part of the screen currently has the focus. If a text box has the focus, the system caret is a blinking, vertical bar; if a check box or option button has the focus, the system caret is a dotted outline of the control name.) This is useful if you have a screen reader or screen magnifier that uses the position of the system caret to determine what part of the screen to read or magnify.

- **Play System Sounds**—Activate this check box to reinstate Internet Explorer's sounds, such as the "click" that plays then you select a link and the sound Internet Explorer plays when it displays the notification bar.

- **Reset Text Size to Medium for New Windows and Tabs**—Activating this check box tells Internet Explorer to return the Text Size value to Medium when you open a new window or tab. This is useful if you find that you only have to enlarge the text size for a few sites.

- **Reset Zoom Level for New Windows and Tabs**—Activating this check box tells Internet Explorer to return the Zoom value to 100% when you open a new window or tab. This is useful if you find that you have to zoom in on only a few sites.

Browsing

Here are the options in the Browsing group:

- **Automatically Recover from Page Layout Errors with Compatibility View**—If you leave this check box activated, Internet Explorer automatically fixes any page layout problems that occur by switching to Compatibility mode.

- **Close Unused Folders in History and Favorites**—When you activate this check box, Internet Explorer keeps unused folders closed when you display the History list and the Favorites list. That is, if you open a folder and then open a second folder, Internet Explorer automatically closes the first folder. This makes the History and Favorites lists easier to navigate, so it's usually best to leave this option activated. You need to restart Internet Explorer if you change this setting.

- **Disable Script Debugging (Internet Explorer)**—This check box toggles the script debugger (if one is installed) on and off within Internet Explorer only. You should have to activate this option only if you're a page designer and you have scripts in your pages that you need to debug before uploading them to the Web.

- **Disable Script Debugging (Other)**—This is similar to the Disable Script Debugging (Internet Explorer) option, except that it toggles the script debugger (again, if one is installed) on and off within any application other than Internet Explorer that can display web content (such as Windows Mail).

- **Display a Notification About Every Script Error**—If you activate this check box, Internet Explorer displays a dialog box to alert you to JavaScript or VBScript errors on a page. If you leave this option deactivated, Internet Explorer displays an error message in the status bar. To see the full error message, double-click the status bar message. Only script programmers will need to enable this option and, even then, only when they're debugging scripts. Many websites are poorly programmed and contain script errors. Therefore, enabling this option means that you'll have to deal with lots of annoying dialog boxes as you surf.

- **Display Accelerator Button on Selection**—With this check box activated, when you select text in a web page, Internet Explorer displays an Accelerator button above the selected text. Click that button to see the installed accelerators (such as Blog with Windows Live and Define with Encarta). You must restart Internet Explorer if you change this setting.

- **Enable Automatic Crash Recovery**—When this check box is activated, Internet Explorer attempts to reopen the current tab set if the program crashes. This is welcome behavior, particularly if you regularly have a large bunch of tabs on the go. You must restart Internet Explorer if you change this setting.

- **Enable Flip Ahead**—If you activate this check box, Internet Explorer enables its Flip Ahead feature, which predicts which page you are most likely to view next based on your browsing history (which, yes, gets sent to Microsoft for analysis).

- **Enable FTP Folder View (Outside of Internet Explorer)**—When you activate this option and you access an FTP (File Transfer Protocol) site, press Alt and then select Tools, FTP in File Explorer to display the contents of the site using the familiar Windows folder view. This makes it easy to drag and drop files from the FTP site to your hard disk, and possibly to perform other file maintenance chores, depending on what permissions you have at the site.

- **Enable Suggested Sites**—When you enable this check box, you can click Internet Explorer's Suggested Sites button to see a list of what Internet Explorer thinks are sites that are similar to the current site (and so might interest you).

- **Enable Third-Party Browser Extensions**—With this check box activated, Internet Explorer supports third-party extensions to its interface. For example, the Google toolbar is a third-party extension that integrates the Google search engine into Internet Explorer as a toolbar. If you deactivate this check box, third-party extensions don't appear and can't display. Deactivating this check box is a good way to turn off some (but, unfortunately, not all) of those annoying third-party toolbars that install themselves without permission. You need to restart Internet Explorer if you change this setting.

- **Enable Visual Styles on Buttons and Controls in Webpages**—With this check box activated, Internet Explorer applies the current Windows 8 visual style to all web pages for objects such as form buttons. If you deactivate this check box, Internet Explorer applies its default visual style to all page elements.

- **Enable Websites to Use the Search Pane**—When you enable this check box, you allow websites to display content using the old Search pane, which has been disabled since Internet Explorer 7. We have no idea why anyone would want to do this. If you do change this setting, you must restart Internet Explorer.

- **Go to an Intranet Site for a Single Word Entry in the Address Bar**—When you activate this setting, Internet Explorer treats single-word entries in the address bar as intranet addresses; if you leave this setting deactivated, Internet Explorer treats single-word entries in the address bar as search queries.

- **Notify When Downloads Complete**—If you leave this check box activated, Internet Explorer leaves the Notification bar onscreen after the download finishes (see Figure 15.12). This enables you to click either Run to launch the downloaded file or Open Folder to display the file's destination folder. If you deactivate this check box, Internet Explorer closes the Notification bar as soon as the download is complete.

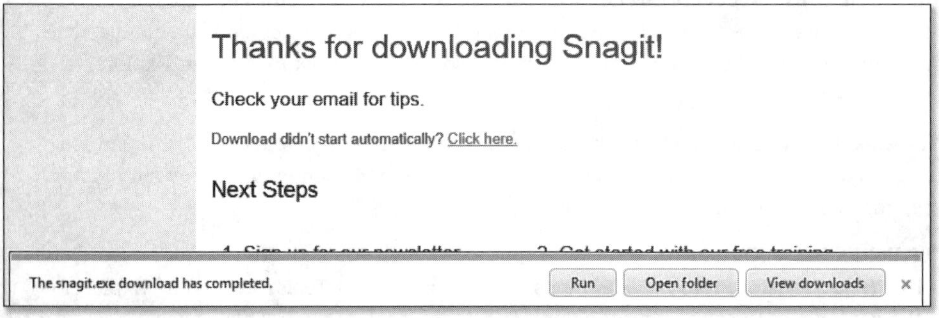

Thanks for downloading Snagit!

Check your email for tips.

Download didn't start automatically? Click here.

Next Steps

1. Sign up for our newsletter

The snagit.exe download has completed.   Run   Open folder   View downloads   ✕

Figure 15.12
When Internet Explorer completes a file download, it leaves the Notification bar onscreen to help you deal with the file.

- **Reuse Windows for Launching Shortcuts (When Tabbed Browsing Is Off)**—With this check box enabled and tabbed browsing turned off, Windows looks for an already-open Internet Explorer window when you click a web page shortcut (such as a web address in a Windows Mail email message). If a window is open, the web page loads there. This is a good idea because it prevents Internet Explorer windows from multiplying unnecessarily. If you deactivate this option, Windows always loads the page into a new Internet Explorer window.

- **Show Friendly HTTP Error Messages**—With this check box enabled, Internet Explorer intercepts the error messages (for, say, pages not found) generated by web servers and replaces them with its own messages that offer more information as well as possible solutions to the problem. If you deactivate this option, Internet Explorer displays the error message generated by the web server. However, we recommend deactivating this option because webmasters often customize the web server error messages to be more helpful than the generic messages reported by Internet Explorer.

- **Tell Me If Internet Explorer Is Not the Default Browser**—If you leave this check box activated, Internet Explorer checks at startup whether it's the default browser on your system and lets you know if it's not. If you have another browser set up as the default and you don't want to be pestered with these messages each time you run Internet Explorer, deactivate this setting.

- **Underline Links**—Use these options to specify when Internet Explorer should format web page links with an underline. The Hover option means that the underline appears only when you position the mouse pointer over the link. Many websites use colored text, so it's often difficult to recognize a link without the underlining. Therefore, we recommend that you activate the Always option.

- **Use Inline AutoComplete in the Internet Explorer Address Bar and Open Dialog**—This check box toggles the Address bar's inline AutoComplete feature on and off. When inline AutoComplete is on, Internet Explorer monitors the text that you type in the Address bar. If your text matches a previously typed URL, Internet Explorer automatically completes the address by displaying the matching URL in the Address bar. It also displays a drop-down list of other matching URLs. When inline AutoComplete is off, Internet Explorer displays only the drop-down list of matching URLs.

Controlling AutoComplete

If you want to prevent Internet Explorer from displaying the drop-down list of matching URLs, display the Content tab and click the Settings button in the AutoComplete group to display the AutoComplete Settings dialog box. Deactivate the Address Bar check box. Note that Internet Explorer's AutoComplete feature also applies to web forms. That is, AutoComplete can remember data that you type into a form—including usernames and passwords—and automatically enter that data when you use the form again. You can control the web form portion of AutoComplete by using the other check boxes in the Use AutoComplete For section of the AutoComplete Settings dialog box.

- **Use Inline AutoComplete in File Explorer and Run Dialog**—Activate this check box to extend AutoComplete to the File Explorer address bar and to the Run dialog box.

- **Use Most Recent Order When Switching Tags with Ctrl+Tab**—If you activate this check box, pressing Ctrl+Tab (or Ctrl+Shift+Tab) switches between tabs in the order you most recently viewed them.

- **Use Passive FTP (for Firewall and DSL Modem Compatibility)**—In a normal FTP session, Internet Explorer opens a connection to the FTP server (for commands) and then the FTP server opens a second connection back to the browser (for data). If you're on a network with a firewall, however, it will not allow incoming connections from a server. With passive FTP, the browser establishes the second (data) connection itself. Therefore, if you're on a firewalled network or are using a DSL modem and you can't establish an FTP connection, activate this check box.

- **Use Smooth Scrolling**—This check box toggles a feature called *smooth scrolling* on and off. When you activate this check box to enable smooth scrolling, pressing the Page Down or Page Up key causes the page to scroll down or up at a preset speed. If you deactivate this check box, pressing the Page Down or Page Up key causes the page to jump instantly down or up.

> **tip**
> When reading a web page, you can scroll down one screen by pressing the spacebar. To scroll up one screen, press Shift+Spacebar.

HTTP 1.1 Settings

The check boxes in the HTTP 1.1 Settings branch determine whether Internet Explorer uses the HTTP 1.1 protocol:

- **Use HTTP 1.1**—This check box toggles Internet Explorer's use of HTTP 1.1 to communicate with web servers. (HTTP 1.1 is the standard protocol used on the Web today.) You should deactivate this check box only if you're having trouble connecting to a website. This tells Internet Explorer to use HTTP 1.0, which might solve the problem.

- **Use HTTP 1.1 Through Proxy Connections**—This check box toggles on and off the use of HTTP 1.1 only when connecting through a proxy server.

International

To understand the options in the International group, you need a bit of background on how Internet Explorer's SmartScreen Filter watches out for phishing sites. Besides checking a global database of known phishing sites, the SmartScreen Filter also analyzes the site content to look for known phishing techniques (that is, to see whether the site is "phishy"). The most common of these is a check for *domain spoofing*. This common scam also goes by the names *homograph spoofing* and the *lookalike attack*. Internet Explorer also supports Internationalized Domain Names (IDN), which refers to domain names written in languages other than English, and it checks for *IDN spoofing*, domain name ambiguities in the user's chosen browser language.

Phishers often resort to IDN spoofing to fool users into thinking an address is legitimate. For example, instead of the address ebay.com, a phisher might use εbαy.com (with the Greek letters ε (epsilon) and α (alpha) in place of *e* and *a*). Almost all the world's characters have a Unicode value, but Internet Explorer is usually set up to recognize only a single language (such as English). If it comes across a character it doesn't recognize, it works around the problem by converting all Unicode values into an equivalent value that uses only the ASCII characters supported by the domain name system.

This conversion uses a standard called *Punycode*. If the domain name uses only ASCII characters, the Punycode value and the Unicode value are the same. For a domain such as εbαy.com, the Punycode equivalent is xn--by--c9b0.com (the xn-- prefix always appears; it tells you that the domain name is encoded). Internet Explorer encodes the domain to this Punycode value, displays the Punycode domain in the Address bar, and then surfs to the site. Internet Explorer also displays a message in the Notification bar telling you that the address contains characters it doesn't recognize. In other words, an IDN spoofing site is less likely to fool users because the URL that appears in the status bar and the address no longer looks similar to the URL of the legitimate site.

The options in the International group enable you to control aspects of this encoding process and related features (you need to restart Internet Explorer if you change any of these settings):

- **Always Show Encoded Addresses**—Activate this check box to tell Internet Explorer to display the encoded Punycode web addresses in the status bar and Address bar. If you're not worrying about IDN spoofing, you can deactivate this check box to see the Unicode characters instead.

- **Send IDN Server Names**—When activated, this check box tells Internet Explorer to encode addresses into Punycode before sending them for domain resolution.

- **Send IDN Server Names for Intranet Addresses**—When activated, this check box tells Internet Explorer to encode intranet addresses into Punycode before sending them for resolution. Some intranet sites don't support Punycode, so this setting is off by default.

- **Send UTF-8 URLs**—When activated, this check box tells Internet Explorer to send web page addresses using the UTF-8 standard, which is readable in any language. If you're having trouble accessing a page that uses non-English characters in the URL, the server might not be able to handle UTF-8, so deactivate this check box.

- **Show Notification Bar for Encoded Addresses**—When activated, this check box tells Internet Explorer to display the following Notification bar message when it encodes an address into Punycode: "This Web address contains letters or symbols that cannot be displayed with the current language settings."

Multimedia

The options in the Multimedia branch toggle various multimedia effects on and off:

- **Enable Alternative Codecs in HTML5 Media Elements**—When this option is turned on, Internet Explorer allows HTML5 media to use alternative codecs to play the media. If you're having trouble playing media in Internet Explorer, the first thing you should check is that this setting is activated. You must restart Internet Explorer if you change this setting.

- **Enable Automatic Image Resizing**—If you activate this check box, Internet Explorer automatically shrinks large images so that they fit inside the browser window. This is useful if you're running Windows 8 with a small monitor or at a relatively low resolution, and you're finding that many website images don't fit entirely into the browser window.

- **Play Animations in Webpages**—This check box toggles animated GIF images on and off. Most animated GIFs are unwelcome annoyances, so you'll probably greatly improve your surfing experience by clearing this check box. If you turn this option off and you want to view an animation, right-click the box and then click Show Picture. Changing this setting requires you to restart Internet Explorer.

- **Play Sounds in Webpages**—This check box toggles web page sound effects on and off. Because the vast majority of web page sounds are extremely bad MIDI renditions of popular tunes, turning off sounds will save your ears.

- **Show Image Download Placeholders**—If you activate this check box, Internet Explorer displays a box that is the same size and shape as the image it is downloading.

- **Show Pictures**—This check box toggles web page images on and off. If you're using a slow connection, turn off this option and Internet Explorer will show only a box where the image would normally appear. (If the designer has included alt text, that text will appear inside the box.) If you want to view a picture when you've toggled images off, right-click the box and select the Show Picture option.

Security

The Security branch has many options related to Internet Explorer security:

- **Allow Active Content from CDs to Run on My Computer**—Leave this check box deactivated to prevent active content such as scripts and controls located in CD-based web pages to execute on your computer. However, if you have a CD-based program that won't function, you might need to activate this check box to enable the program to work properly. You must restart Internet Explorer if you change this setting.

- **Allow Active Content to Run in Files on My Computer**—Leave this check box deactivated to prevent active content such as scripts and controls located in local web pages to execute on your computer. If you're testing a web page that includes active content, activate this check box so that you can test the web pages locally. You must restart Internet Explorer if you change this setting.

- **Allow Software to Run or Install Even If the Signature Is Invalid**—Leave this check box deactivated to avoid running or installing software that doesn't have a valid digital signature. If you can't get a program to run or install, consider activating this check box.

- **Always Send Do Not Track Header**—When activated, this setting tells Internet Explorer to send the Do Not Track (DNT) header on all HTTP and HTTPS requests. The DNT header tells the server that you don't want to be tracked. If you deactivate this check box, Internet Explorer only sends the DNT header when you're using InPrivate Browsing mode or when you're using a Tracking Protection List. You must restart Internet Explorer if you change this setting.

- **Check for Publisher's Certificate Revocation**—When this option is activated, Internet Explorer examines a site's digital security certificates to see whether they have been revoked.

- **Check for Server Certificate Revocation**—If you activate this option, Internet Explorer also checks the security certificate for the web page's server. Changing this setting requires you to restart Internet Explorer.

- **Check for Signatures on Downloaded Programs**—If you activate this check box, Internet Explorer checks for a digital signature on any program that you download.

- **Do Not Save Encrypted Pages to Disk**—If you activate this option, Internet Explorer won't store encrypted files in the Temporary Internet Files folder.

- **Empty Temporary Internet Files Folder When Browser Is Closed**—With this option activated, Internet Explorer removes all files from the Temporary Internet Files folder when you exit the program.

- **Enable DOM Storage**—This option is activated by default, and it allows Internet Explorer to use the Document Object Model (DOM) to store website data on your computer. DOM storage is similar to cookie data, except that DOM storage spans multiple tabs and windows. DOM storage consists of both *session storage*, where data is saved only for the current browser session, and *local storage*, where data never expires and you can store up to 10MB of data. DOM storage is superior to cookies, so in most cases you should leave this setting activated. If you're worried that having up to 10MB of site data on your computer represents a security or privacy risk, you can disable this option.

- **Enable Enhanced Protection Mode**—Activate this check box to use the new Enhanced Protected Mode features in Internet Explorer 10. These new features include using 64-bit processes (which prevent attackers from planting malicious code on your system), preventing Internet Explorer from accessing your user account data unless you grant explicit permission for it to do so, and preventing Internet Explorer from accessing certain corporate intranet data. Many add-ons aren't compatible with Enhanced Protected Mode, so this setting is turned off by default. If you're not worried about add-on compatibility, you should turn on this setting for safer browsing. Changing this setting requires you to restart Internet Explorer.

- **Enable Integrated Windows Authentication**—With this check box activated, Internet Explorer uses Integrated Windows Authentication (formerly known as Windows NT Challenge/Response Authentication) to attempt to log on to a restricted site. This means the browser attempts to log on using the current credentials from the user's network domain logon. If this doesn't work, Internet Explorer displays a dialog box prompting the user for a username and password. You must restart Internet Explorer if you change this setting.

- **Enable Memory Protection to Help Mitigate Online Attacks**—When activated, this check box enables Data Execution Prevention (DEP) for Internet Explorer. DEP prevents malicious code from executing in protected memory locations. This check box is disabled in Internet Explorer 10, so you can't turn off DEP for Internet Explorer.

- **Enable Native XMLHTTP Support**—With this check box activated, Internet Explorer works properly with sites that use the XMLHTTPRequest API to transfer XML data between the browser and a server. This API is most commonly used in Ajax-powered sites. Ajax (Asynchronous JavaScript and XML) is a web development technique that creates sites that operate much like desktop programs. In particular, the XMLHTTPRequest API enables the browser to request and accept data from the server without reloading the page.

- **Enable SmartScreen Filter**—This setting toggles the SmartScreen Filter on and off.

- **Use SSL 2.0**—This check box toggles support for the Secure Sockets Layer Level 2 security protocol on and off. This version of SSL is currently the Web's standard security protocol.

- **Use SSL 3.0**—This check box toggles support for SSL Level 3 on and off. SSL 3.0 is more secure than SSL 2.0 (it can authenticate both the client and the server), but isn't currently as popular as SSL 2.0.

- **Use TLS 1.0**—This check box toggles support for Transport Layer Security (TLS) 1.0 on and off. This is a relatively new protocol, so few websites implement it.

- **Use TLS 1.1**—This check box toggles support for TLS 1.1 on and off.

- **Use TLS 1.2**—This check box toggles support for TLS 1.2 on and off.

- **Warn About Certificate Address Mismatch**—When activated, this option tells Internet Explorer to display a warning dialog box if a site is using an invalid digital security certificate. You must restart Internet Explorer if you change this setting.

- **Warn If Changing Between Secure and Not Secure Mode**—When activated, this option tells Internet Explorer to display a warning dialog box whenever you enter and leave a secure site.

- **Warn If POST Submittal Is Redirected to a Zone That Does Not Permit Posts**—When activated, this option tells Internet Explorer to display a warning dialog box if a form submission is sent to a site other than the one hosting the form.

WINDOWS 8 INTERNET COMMUNICATIONS

Working with Email

If software programs can have inferiority complexes, the Mail app that ships with Windows 8 would be a prime candidate. After all, despite its prominence on the Windows 8 Start screen, Mail might just be the most underwhelming email client ever created. You can literally use the fingers of one hand to count the tasks you can perform with Mail: send new messages, read incoming messages, reply to a message, forward a message, and move a message to a different folder. Yes, that's the complete list.

Obviously Microsoft is aiming Mail at beginners, (very) light email users, and people who prefer to use the Hotmail web interface. For the rest of us, the Mail app is clearly not a serious email tool.

So in this section we talk about Windows Live Mail (which we'll call just Mail from here on), the successor to the Windows Mail and Outlook Express clients that shipped with earlier versions of Windows. You can download Mail from download.live.com.

Once the program is installed, you can launch it by selecting the Windows Live Mail tile on the Start screen.

Setting Up Mail Accounts

If you haven't yet started Mail—and therefore haven't yet defined your first mail account—or if you have multiple accounts and need to set up the others, this section shows you how to do it within Mail.

Specifying Basic Account Settings

Here are the steps to follow to set up an email account with just the basic settings (which should be enough to get most accounts up and running):

1. Start the process using one of the following techniques:

   ▪ Start Mail for the first time.

   ▪ In Mail, select the Accounts tab and then click Email.

2. In the Add Your Email Accounts dialog box, type the email address and password for the account and then type your *display name*, which is the name that appears in the From field when you send a message.

3. If you're adding a non-web account (that is, not a Hotmail, Gmail, or similar account that Mail can configure automatically), activate the Manually Configure Server Settings check box.

4. Click Next. If you're adding a web account, Mail should configure it automatically, so you're done. If Mail can't perform the automatic configuration, or if you're adding a non-web account, you see the Configure Server Settings dialog box.

 note

The data for your incoming and outgoing mail servers should have been supplied to you by your ISP when you set up your account. If not, or if you can't find the data, contact the ISP's tech support department.

5. Specify your incoming mail server data:

   ▪ **Server Type**—Use this list to select the incoming mail server type, such as POP or IMAP.

   ▪ **Server Address**—Type the domain name for your incoming mail server (such as pop.provider.com).

   ▪ **Port**—Type the port number used by the incoming mail server.

   ▪ **Requires a secure connection**—Activate this check box if your provider requires that incoming mail be sent over a secure connection.

   ▪ **Authenticate Using**—Select the authentication type used by your mail provider.

   ▪ **Logon User Name**—Type the username assigned to your account by your mail provider.

6. Specify your outgoing (SMTP) mail server data:

   ▪ **Server Address**—Type the domain name for your outgoing mail server (such as smtp.provider.com).

   ▪ **Port**—Type the port number used by the outgoing mail server.

   ▪ **Requires a secure connection**—Activate this check box if your provider requires that outgoing mail be sent over a secure connection.

- **Requires Authentication**—Activate this check box if your mail provider requires authentication before it will send your messages. (See "Enabling SMTP Authentication," later in this chapter, for more details.)

7. Click Next.

8. Click Finish.

When the wizard completes its labors, your new account appears in the list of accounts on the left side of the Mail window. To make changes to your accounts, select File, Options, Email Accounts to open the Accounts dialog box, shown in Figure 16.1. The next few sections use this dialog box, so you might want to leave it open for now.

Figure 16.1
Your Internet email accounts are listed in the Mail section of the Accounts dialog box.

Setting the Default Account

If you have more than one account, you should specify one of them as the default account. The default account is the one Mail uses automatically when you send a message. To set the default account, select it in the Mail group and then click Set as Default.

Specifying Advanced Account Settings

Although the basic account settings that you specify during the account setup process suffice in most cases, many accounts require a more advanced setup. For example, you might prefer to use a different reply address or to leave copies of your messages on the server.

 note

It *is* possible to send a message using any of your accounts. However, sending a message using anything other than the default account requires an extra step. See "Sending Messages," later in this chapter.

To work with the advanced settings, select an account in the Mail group and then click Properties. The Properties dialog box that appears contains a number of tabs, and most of the controls in this dialog box are straightforward. The next four sections take you through some of the other options and show how useful they can be.

Using a Different Reply Address

It's occasionally useful to have replies sent to a different address. For example, if you're sending a message requesting feedback from a number of people, you might prefer that the return messages go to a colleague or assistant for collating or processing. Similarly, if you send a work-related message from a personal account, you might want replies sent to your work account.

To specify a different reply address, display the General tab in the account's properties sheet, and then type the address in the Reply Address text box.

Enabling SMTP Authentication

With spam such a never-ending problem, many ISPs now require *SMTP authentication* for outgoing mail, which means that you must log on to the SMTP server to confirm that you are the person sending the mail (as opposed to some spammer spoofing your address). If your ISP uses authentication, display the Servers tab in the account's properties sheet and then activate the My Server Requires Authentication check box. By default, Mail logs you on using the same username and password as your incoming mail server. If your ISP has given you separate logon data, click Settings, activate the Log On Using option, type your account name and password, and click OK.

Specifying a Different SMTP Port

For security reasons, some ISPs insist that all their customers' outgoing mail route through the ISP's SMTP server. This usually isn't a problem if you're using an email account maintained by the ISP, but it can lead to problems if you're using an account provided by a third party (such as your website host):

- Your ISP might block messages sent using the third-party account because it thinks you're trying to relay the message through the ISP's server (a technique often used by spammers).

- You might incur extra charges if your ISP allows only a certain amount of SMTP bandwidth per month or a certain number of sent messages, whereas the third-party account offers higher limits or no restrictions at all.

- You might have performance problems because the ISP's server takes much longer to route messages than the third-party host.

You might think that you can solve the problem by specifying the third-party host's SMTP server in the account settings. However, this doesn't usually work because outgoing email transmits by default through port 25; when you use this port, you must also use the ISP's SMTP server.

To work around this, many third-party hosts offer access to their SMTP server via a port other than the standard port 25. To configure an email account to use a nonstandard SMTP port, display the Advanced tab in the account's properties sheet, and then use the Outgoing Mail (SMTP) text box to type the port number specified by the third-party host.

Checking the Same Account from Two Different Computers

In today's increasingly mobile world, it's common to have to check the same email account from multiple devices. For example, you might want to check your business account using not only your work computer but also your home computer or your notebook while traveling or using a smartphone or other portable device while commuting.

That's not a problem with web-based accounts, but with it is with POP accounts because, unfortunately, after you download a message, the server deletes it from the server and you can't access it from any other device. If you need to check mail on multiple devices, the trick is to leave a copy of the message on the server after you download it. That way the message will still be available when you check messages using another device.

To tell Mail to leave a copy of each message on the server, display the Advanced tab in the account's properties sheet and activate the Leave a Copy of Messages on Server check box. You can also activate the following options:

- **Remove from Server After X Day(s)**—If you activate this check box, Mail automatically deletes the message from the server after the number of days specified in the spin box.

- **Remove from Server When Deleted from 'Deleted Items'**—If you activate this check box, Mail deletes the message from the server only when you permanently delete the message from your system.

Here's a good strategy to follow:

- On your main computer, activate the Leave a Copy of Messages on Server check box *and* the Remove from Server After *X* Days check box. Set the number of days long enough so that you have time to download the messages using your other devices.

- On all your other devices, activate only the Leave a Copy of Messages on Server check box.

This strategy ensures that you can download messages on all your devices, but it prevents messages from piling up on the server.

> **note**
>
> Other occasions could arise when you prefer to leave messages on the server temporarily. For example, if you're on the road, you might want to download the messages to a notebook or to some other computer that you're using temporarily. By leaving the messages on the server, you can still download them to your main computer when you return to the office or to your home. Similarly, you might want to download your messages into another email client for testing purposes or for taking advantage of features in that client not found in Mail.

Handling Incoming Messages

Incoming email messages are stored in your mailbox on your ISP's server until you use an email client such as Mail to retrieve them. The easiest way to do that is to let Mail check for and download new messages automatically. Several settings within the Options dialog box control this feature. Select File, Options, Mail and make sure that the General tab is displayed, as shown in Figure 16.2.

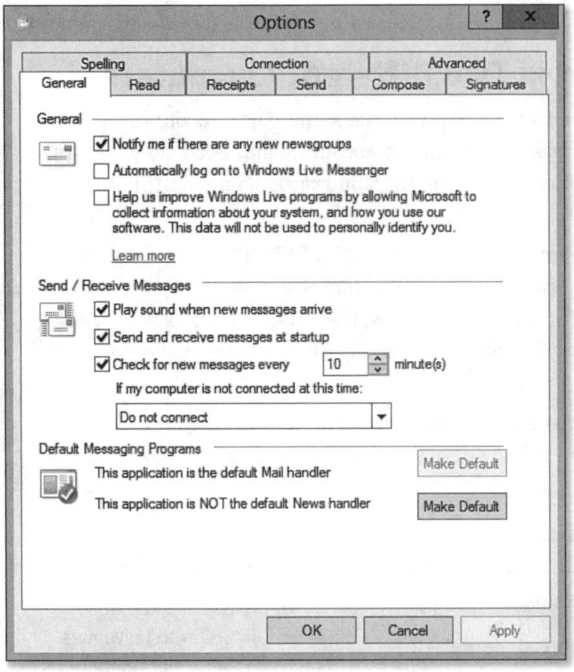

Figure 16.2
The General tab contains options related to retrieving messages.

Here are the settings related to retrieving messages:

- **Play Sound When New Messages Arrive**—When you activate this option, Mail plays a sound whenever it downloads one or more messages. If multiple messages arrive, Mail plays the sound only once. This is useful only if you don't get very many messages and if you leave Mail running in the background while maintaining a connection to the Internet. The sound is either annoying or redundant in any other scenario, so consider deactivating this check box.

- **Send and Receive Messages at Startup**—When this check box is activated, Mail connects with the server to check for waiting messages as soon as you start the program. It also sends any messages that are waiting in the Outbox folder. Note that if your computer has no current connection to the Internet, Mail attempts to establish one. This is true even if you select Do Not Connect in the If My Computer Is Not Connected at This Time list (described later). If you prefer to stay offline at startup, deactivate this check box.

tip

It's possible to change the sound that indicates the arrival of a new message. Right-click the Volume icon in the notification area and then click Sounds. In the Program Events list, select New Mail Notification and then click Browse to choose the sound file you want Mail to play when it delivers new messages.

- **Check for New Messages Every X Minute(s)**—With this option activated, Mail automatically checks for new messages using the interval specified in the spin box. You can enter a time between 1 and 480 minutes.

- **If My Computer Is Not Connected at This Time**—If you activate the Check for New Messages Every X Minute(s) check box, use the following list to specify what Mail should do if your computer is not connected to the Internet when the time comes to check for new messages:

   Do Not Connect—Choose this option to prevent Mail from initiating a connection.

   Connect Only When Not Working Offline—Choose this option to tell Mail to connect only when the program is in online mode.

   Connect Only When Working Offline—Choose this option to tell Mail to connect only when the program is in offline mode.

   If you elect not to have Mail check for new mail automatically, you can use any of the following techniques to check the server by hand:

note

To put Mail in offline mode, select the Home tab and click the Work Offline command. To return to online mode, select Home, Work Online.

- **To receive messages on all your accounts**—Select the Home tab and then click the top half of the Send/Receive button.

- **To receive messages on only a single account**—Select the Home tab, click the bottom half of the Send/Receive button to drop down the list, and then click the account.

tip

A quick way to send and receive messages on all your accounts is to press F5.

Processing Messages

Each new message that arrives is stored in the Inbox folder's message list and appears in a bold font. To view the contents of any message, select it in the message list; Mail displays the message text in the reading pane. If you find the reading pane too confining, you can open the selected message in its own window by double-clicking it.

When you have a message selected, you can do plenty of things with it (in addition to reading it, of course). You can print it, save it to a file, move it to another folder, reply to it, delete it, and more. Most of these operations are straightforward, so we'll just summarize the basic techniques here:

- **Dealing with attachments**—If a message has an attachment, you'll see a paper clip icon in the Inbox folder's Attachment column, as well as in the upper-right corner of the preview pane. You have two choices:

   Open the attachment—In the reading pane, double-click the attachment icon.

   Save the attachment—In the reading pane, right-click the attachment icon and then click Save As.

- **Moving a message to a different folder**—Later in this chapter, we'll show you how to create new folders you can use for storing related messages. To move a message to another folder, use your mouse to drag the message from the Inbox folder and then drop it on the destination folder.

- **Printing a message**—To print a copy of the message, select File, Print.

- **Replying to a message**—Mail gives you two reply options:

  Reply—This option sends the reply to only the person who sent the original message. Mail ignores any names in the Cc line. To use this option, select Home, Reply or press Ctrl+R.

  Reply all—This option sends the reply not only to the original author, but also to anyone else mentioned in the Cc line. To use this option, select Home, Reply to All or press Ctrl+Shift+R.

- **Forwarding a message**—You can forward a message to another address by using either of the following commands:

  Forward—Select Home and click the top half of the Forward button (or press Ctrl+F). Mail inserts the full text of the original message into the body of the new message and appends a greater than sign (>) to the beginning of each line.

  Forward as Attachment—Select Home, click the bottom half of the Forward button, and then click Forward as Attachment. In this case, Mail packages the original message as an attachment, but it makes no changes to the message. The user who receives the forwarded message can open this attachment and view the original message exactly as you received it.

- **Deleting a message**—To get rid of a message, select it in the folder and then press Delete (or Ctrl+D) or click the Home tab's Delete button. Note that Mail doesn't really delete the message. Instead, it just moves it to the Deleted Items folder. If you change your mind and decide to keep the message, open the Deleted Items folder and move the message back to the folder it came from. To remove a message permanently, open the Deleted Items folder and delete the message from there.

Setting Read Options

To help you work with your correspondence, Mail has a number of options related to reading messages. To view them, select File, Options, Mail to open the Options dialog box, and then display the Read tab, as shown in Figure 16.3.

Here's a review of the controls in this tab:

- **Mark Message Read After Displaying for X Second(s)—** Deactivate this check box to prevent Mail from removing the boldfacing while you're reading a message. Alternatively, you can use the spin box to adjust how long it takes Mail to remove the bold (the maximum is 60 seconds).

- **Automatically Expand Grouped Messages**—When you group messages by conversation (by selecting the View, Conversations, On command), Mail displays only the first message in the group and includes a plus sign (+) to its left. You have to click the plus sign to see the other messages in the conversation. If you prefer to see all the messages in the conversation automatically, activate this check box.

> **note**
> You can also toggle the marking of read messages via the Home tab by clicking the Unread/Read button. Alternatively, you can press Ctrl+Q.

> **note**
> You can ask Mail to display only unread messages by selecting the View, Filter Messages, Hide Read Messages command. Select View, Filer Message, Show All Messages to return to the regular view.

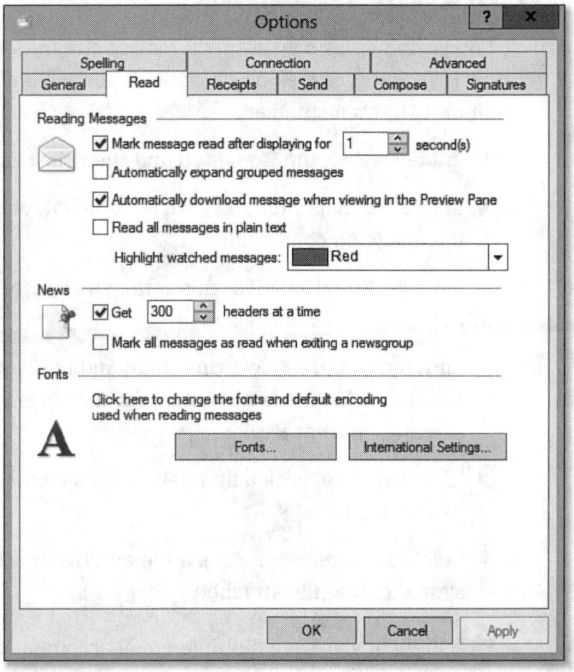

Figure 16.3
Use the Read tab to set various properties related to reading messages.

- **Automatically Download Message When Viewing in the Preview Pane**—When you're working with a web-based email account (such as Hotmail), deactivate this check box to prevent Mail from downloading message text when the message header is selected. When you're ready to receive the text, press the spacebar.

- **Read All Messages in Plain Text**—Activate this check box to convert all HTML messages to plain text, which helps to thwart web bugs and malicious scripts.

- **Highlight Watched Messages**—Use this list to specify the color that Mail uses to display messages marked as watched. To mark a message as watched, select it and then click Home, Watch.

- **Fonts**—Click this button to display the Fonts dialog box, which displays a list of the character sets installed on your computer. For each character set, you can specify a proportional and fixed-width font, as well as a font size and encoding. You can also specify which character set to use as the default.

- **International Settings**—Click this button to display the International Read Settings dialog box. Activate the Use Default Encoding for All Incoming Messages option to apply the encoding shown in the Default Encoding box to all your messages.

Sending Messages

Composing a basic message in Mail is straightforward, and it isn't all that much different from composing a letter or memo in WordPad. You have a number of ways to get started, not all of them well known. Here's a summary:

- In Mail, select the Home tab and then click Email Message in the New group, or press Ctrl+N.

- In Internet Explorer, press Alt+F to pull down the File menu, select Send, and then choose one of the following commands:

  Page by E-mail—Select this command to create a new message with the current web page as the content of the message.

  Link by E-mail—Select this command to create a new message with a URL shortcut file attached. This file is a shortcut for the current website that the recipient can click to load that site into Internet Explorer.

- In a web page, click a mailto link. This creates a new message addressed to the recipient specified by the link.

- In File Explorer, right-click a file and then click Send To, Mail Recipient. This creates a new message with the file attached.

From here, if you have multiple email accounts, use the From list to select the account from which you want to send the message. Use the To field to enter the address of the recipient; click Show Cc and Bcc and then use the Cc field to enter the address of a recipient that you want to receive a copy of the message; use the Bcc field to enter the addresses of any recipients you want to receive blind copies of the message. Note that in each field you can specify multiple recipients by separating the addresses with a semicolon (;).

Use the Subject field to enter a brief description of the message, and then use the box below the Subject field to enter your message. To send your message, you have two choices:

- **Click Send (or press Alt+S)**—This tells Mail to send the message out to the Internet right away.

- **Select Options, Send Later**—This command tells Mail to store the message in the Outbox folder. If you choose this route, Mail displays a dialog box telling you that your message is stored in the Outbox folder. Click OK. When you're ready to send the message, select the Home, Send/Receive, All Email Accounts command.

Taking Control of Your Messages

Mail offers many more options for composing messages than the simple steps outlined in the previous section. Here's a summary of the other features and techniques you can use to modify your outgoing messages (note we're assuming here that you have a new message window open):

- **Choosing the message format**—By default, new messages use the HTML format, which means you can format the message text, add images, and use any of the formatting options found on the

Message and Insert tabs. Remember, however, that not all systems will transfer the HTML formatting (although most will). If you need to send an unadorned message, select Message, Plain Text and then click OK when Mail asks you to confirm.

- **Setting the message priority**—In the Message tab, select either High Importance or Low Importance in the Delivery group.

- **Asking for a read receipt**—If you want to know when your recipient opens your message, display the Message tab and then activate the Read Receipt check box in the Delivery group. Note, however, that as a privacy precaution, many people don't allow read receipts to be sent.

> **tip**
> Another way to attach a file to a message is to drag the file from File Explorer and drop it in the body of the message.

- **Attaching a file**—Select Message, Attach File, use the Open dialog box to select a file, and then click Open. Mail adds an Attach box below the Subject line and displays the name and size of the file. To remove the attachment, click it in the Attach box and then press Delete.

- **Inserting an image into the message**—To insert an image file into the message, select Insert, Single Photo. In the Insert Picture dialog box that appears, select the image file and click Open. Mail inserts the picture into the message.

- **Inserting a signature**—A *signature* is text that appears at the bottom of a message. Most people use a signature to provide their email and web addresses, their company contact information, and perhaps a snappy quote or epigram that reflects their personality. If you've defined a signature (see the next section), you can insert it into the body of the message at the current cursor position by selecting Insert, Signature. If you've defined multiple signatures, select the one you want from the submenu that appears.

> **tip**
> You might be tempted to email a photo by selecting it in File Explorer and then selecting Share, Email. That works, but Mail inserts the image as a photo album that must be viewed online rather than as a file attachment. If this happens, convert the image to an attachment by clicking the album to select it, displaying the Format tab, and then clicking Attach Photos to This Message (the paperclip icon) in the Album Styles gallery.

- **Requesting a read receipt**—To ask the recipient to send you a read receipt, activate the Message, Read Receipt check box. Note that you can also set up Mail to request a read receipt for all outgoing messages. In the Mail window, select File, Options, Mail and then display the Receipts tab. Activate the Request a Read Receipt for All Sent Messages check box, and then click OK. (Of course, *asking* for a read receipt is one thing, but actually *receiving* one is quite another. Unless the recipient's email client is set up to automatically send read receipts when requested, the decision on whether to send a read receipt is up to the recipient, and most people opt not to send them.)

Creating a Signature

As we mentioned in the previous section, a signature is a few lines of text that provide contact information and other data. Mail enables you to define a signature and append it to the bottom of every outgoing message (you can also insert it by hand in individual messages). Follow these steps to define a signature:

1. In the main Mail window, select File, Options, Mail to open the Options dialog box.

2. Display the Signatures tab.

3. Click New to add a new signature to the Signatures list.

4. The default name for each new signature (such as Signature #1) is not very informative. To define a new name, click the signature, click Rename, type the new name, and then press Enter.

5. You now have two choices:

   ■ **Type the signature text by hand**—Activate the Text option and type your signature in the box provided.

   ■ **Get the signature from a text file**—Activate the File option and enter the full path to the file in the box provided. (Alternatively, click Browse to choose the file from a dialog box.) In this case, note that if the file is in HTML format, the recipient might not see your signature correctly if their email client doesn't support HTML or (more likely these days) the recipient has opted to view all messages in plain text.

6. If you want Mail to add the signature to all of your messages, activate the Add Signatures to All Outgoing Messages check box.

7. If you'd rather use the signature only on original messages, leave the Don't Add Signature to Replies and Forwards check box activated.

8. Mail adds the default signature automatically if you activated the Add Signatures to All Outgoing Messages check box. To set a signature as the default, select it in the Signatures list and then click Set as Default.

9. To associate a signature with one or more accounts, select the signature in the Signatures list and then click Advanced. In the Advanced Signature Settings dialog box, activate the check box beside each account with which you want to associate the signature. Click OK.

10. Click OK to put the signature options into effect.

Setting Send Options

Mail offers a number of options for sending email. Select File, Options, Mail and display the Send tab in the Options dialog box that appears, as shown in Figure 16.4.

Here's a quick rundown of the options in the Sending group:

■ **Save Copy of Sent Messages In the 'Sent Items' Folder**—When this check box is activated, Mail saves a copy of each message you send in the Sent Items folder. It's a good idea to leave this option checked because doing so gives you a record of the messages you send.

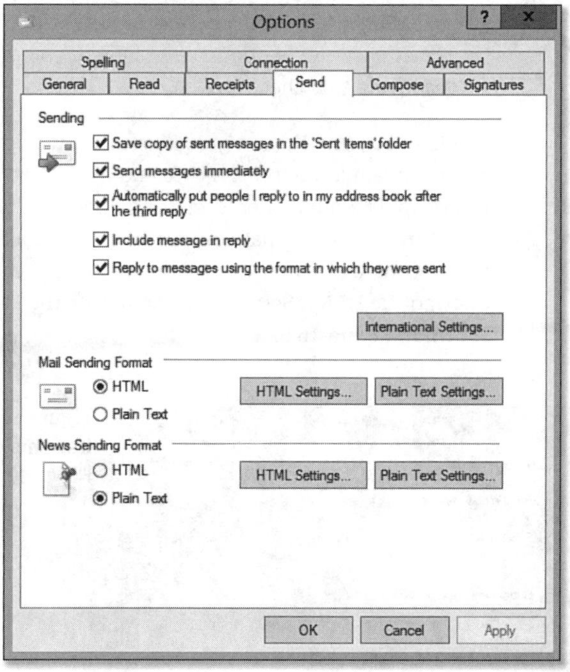

Figure 16.4
Mail's options for sending email.

- **Send Messages Immediately**—When you activate this check box, Mail passes your message to the SMTP server as soon as you click the Send button. If you deactivate this option, clicking the Send button when composing a message only stores that message in the Outbox folder. This is useful if you have a number of messages to compose and you use a dial-up connection to the Internet. That is, you could compose all your messages offline and store them in the Outbox folder. You could then connect to the Internet and send all your messages at once.

- **Automatically Put People I Reply to in My Address Book After the Third Reply**—When you activate this option, after you reply to a person for the third time, Mail adds the recipient's name and email address to the Contacts list. If you find that this only serves to clutter your Contacts list with names you'll never or rarely use, deactivate this check box.

- **Include Message in Reply**—When you enable this check box, Mail includes the original message text as part of the new message when you reply to or forward a message. This is a good idea because including the original message text serves as a reminder to the original author of what you're responding to.

tip

Including the original message text in replies is useful, but you should rarely have to include the entire reply. It's good email etiquette to delete unnecessary parts of the original message. Keep only the text that directly applies to your response.

- **Reply to Messages Using the Format in Which They Were Sent**—When you activate this check box, Mail automatically selects either the HTML or Plain Text sending format, depending on the format used in the original message. If you prefer to always use your default sending format, deactivate this check box.

The Mail Sending Format group contains two option buttons that determine whether your messages contain formatting: HTML and Plain Text. If you activate the HTML button, Mail enables you to apply a number of formatting options to your messages. In effect, your message becomes a miniature web page that you can format in much the same way that you would format a web page. Note, however, that only recipients who have an HTML-enabled mail client can see the formatting. Clicking the HTML Settings button beside the HTML option displays the HTML Settings dialog box, shown in Figure 16.5.

Figure 16.5
Use this dialog box to work with settings associated with the HTML sending format.

Here's a synopsis of the available options:

- **Encode Text Using**—SMTP supports only 7-bit ASCII data, so binary messages or messages that include full 8-bit values (such as foreign characters) must be encoded. This list determines how (or whether) Mail encodes message text:

  None—Tells Mail not to encode the text.

  Quoted Printable—Use this encoding if your messages have full 8-bit values. This encoding converts each of these characters into an equal sign (=) followed by the character's hexadecimal representation. This ensures SMTP compatibility. (Note that most 7-bit ASCII characters are not encoded.)

  Base 64—Use this encoding if your message contains binary data. This encoding uses the Base64 alphabet, which is a set of 64 character/value pairs: *A* through *Z* is 0 through 25; *a* through *z* is 26 through 51; 0 through 9 is 52 through 61; + is 62 and / is 63. All other characters are ignored.

- **Allow 8-Bit Characters in Headers**—When this check box is activated, characters that require 8 bits—including ASCII 128 or higher, foreign character sets, and double-byte character sets—will be allowed within the message header without being encoded. If you leave this check box deactivated, these characters are encoded.

- **Indent Message on Reply**—When you enable this check box and reply to a message, Mail displays the original message indented below your reply.

- **Automatically Wrap Text at X Characters, When Sending**—This spin box determines the point at which Mail wraps text onto a new line. Many Internet systems can't read lines longer than 80 characters, so you shouldn't select a value higher than that. Note that the Quoted Printable and Base 64 encoding schemes require 76-character lines, so this option is available only if you select None in the Encode Text Using list.

If you activate the Plain Text option instead, Mail sends your message as regular text, without any formatting. Clicking the Plain Text Settings button displays the Plain Text Settings dialog box, shown in Figure 16.6.

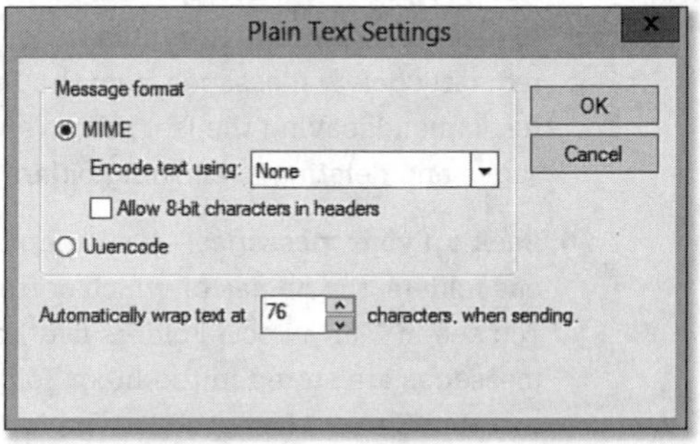

Figure 16.6
Use this dialog box to work with settings associated with the Plain Text sending format.

This dialog box includes many of the same options as the HTML Settings dialog box shown earlier. Here's what's different:

- **MIME**—MIME stands for *Multipurpose Internet Mail Extensions*, the standard encoding format for text-based messages. Each of the encoding options we discussed earlier is MIME based.

- **Uuencode**—This is an older encoding format used primarily when sending binary files to newsgroups.

Maintaining Mail

For the most part, Mail is a set-it-and-forget-it application. After the program and your accounts have been set up, you can go about your email business without worrying about Mail itself. However, to ensure trouble- and worry-free operation, here's a list of a few maintenance chores you should perform from time to time:

- **Remove clutter from your inbox**—Few things in business life are more daunting and frustrating than an inbox bursting at the seams with a huge list of new or unprocessed messages. To prevent this from happening, you should regard the Inbox folder as a temporary holding area for all your incoming messages. Periodically, you should perform the following routine to keep your Inbox clean:

  If a message doesn't require a response, file it or delete it. By "file it," we mean move the message to another folder. You should have folders set up for all major recipients, projects, customers, and categories that you deal with.

If a message requires a response and you can answer it without further research or without taking a lot of time, answer it immediately and then either delete or file the message.

If a message requires a response but you can't send a reply right away, move the message to a folder designated for messages that require further action. You can then handle those messages later in the day when you have some time.

- **Clean out your Deleted Items folder**—This folder is a good safeguard to help you recover accidentally deleted messages. However, after a while, it's extremely unlikely that you'll need to recover a message from this folder. Therefore, you should regularly delete messages from the Deleted Items folder. We recommend leaving the last month's worth of deleted messages and deleting everything older.

- **Back up your messages**—Mail keeps your messages in various folders, the names of which correspond to the names you see in Mail's Local Folders list. For example, the Inbox messages are stored in the Inbox folder. Each message uses the Mail E-mail Message file type (`.eml` extension). Together these folders constitute the Mail message store, which you can find in the following folder:

```
%UserProfile%\AppData\Local\Microsoft\Windows Live
Mail\
```

You should include the contents of this folder in your backups and run those backups regularly.

- **Back up your accounts**—If you have multiple accounts, re-creating them on a new system or in the event of a crash can be a lot of work. To lessen the drudgery, make backups of your accounts by saving them to Internet Account Files (`.iaf` extension). In Mail, select File, Options, Email Accounts, select an account, and then click Export. In the Export dialog box, choose a location and then click Save.

- **Back up your Mail data**—Your defined Mail rules, signatures, and settings are stored in the following Registry key:

```
HKCU\Software\Microsoft\Windows Live Mail\
```

Regularly export this key to save this important Mail data.

tip

Before moving the message to whatever you've designated as your "action items" folder, be sure to mark the message as unread. That way you'll be able to see at a glance whether there are items in that folder and how many there are.

tip

You can change the location of the message store. In Mail, select File, Options, Mail, display the Advanced tab, and click Maintenance. Click the Store Folder button and, in the Store Location dialog box, click Change. Use the Browse for Folder dialog box to choose the new location and click OK. Note, too, that the following Registry setting holds the Mail store location:

```
HKCU\Software\Microsoft\
Windows Live Mail\Store
Root
```

tip

Mail stores the data for each account in a file named `account{ID}.oeaccount`, where *ID* is a unique 32-digit identifier. An even easier way to back up your accounts is to include these account files in your backup. You can find these files in the same folder as your message store:

```
%UserProfile%\AppData\
Local\Microsoft\Windows
Live Mail\
```

■ **Compact your message store database**—Although Mail keeps your email data in regular folders and `.eml` files, it keeps track of those folders and files using a database file named `Mail.MSMessageStore`. When you delete messages, Mail removes the corresponding data from the message store database, which results in gaps within the file. To remove these gaps and reduce the size of the file, Mail is set up to compact the database from time to time. Specifically, Mail compacts the database every hundredth time you shut down the program. If you want the database compacted more often, select File, Options, Mail to display the Advanced tab and then click Maintenance. Activate the Compact the Database on Shutdown Every *X* Runs check box, and use the spin box to set the compaction interval you prefer.

Filtering Incoming Messages

If you're someone who receives a lot of email, you know it can take up to two or three hours to get through the hundreds of messages you receive every day. This is by no means unusual. Most people find that email now takes up massive chunks of each day.

To help ease the crunch, Mail offers *message rules*, and you can set up and configure these rules to handle incoming messages for you automatically. Of course, these rules are limited in what they can do, but what they *can* do isn't bad:

■ If you'll be out of the office for a few days or if you'll be on vacation, you can create a rule to send out an automatic reply that lets each sender know you received the message but won't be able to deal with it for a while.

■ If you have multiple email accounts, you can set up a rule to redirect incoming messages into separate folders for each account.

■ You can create a rule to redirect incoming messages into separate folders for specific people, projects, or mailing lists.

■ If you receive unwanted messages from a particular source (such as someone who is harassing you or someone who sends you an excessive number of jokes), you can set up a rule to automatically delete those messages.

Here are the steps to follow to create a message rule:

1. Select the Folders, Message Rules command. One of two things will happen:

   ■ If this is the first time you're creating a rule, Mail displays the New Mail Rule dialog box.

   ■ If you already have at least one rule, the Message Rules dialog box appears with the Mail Rules tab displayed. In this case, click New to open the New Mail Rule dialog box.

2. In the Select One or More Conditions list, activate the check box beside the rule condition you want to use to pick out a message from the herd. Mail adds the condition to the description text box. You're free to select multiple conditions.

3. The condition shown in the rule description will probably have some underlined text. You need to replace that underlined text with the specific criterion you want to use (such as a word or an address). To do that, click the underlined text, type the criterion in the dialog box that appears, and click Add. Most conditions support multiple criteria (such as multiple addresses or multiple words in a Subject line), so repeat this step as necessary. When you're done, click OK. Mail updates the rule description with the text you entered, as shown in Figure 16.7.

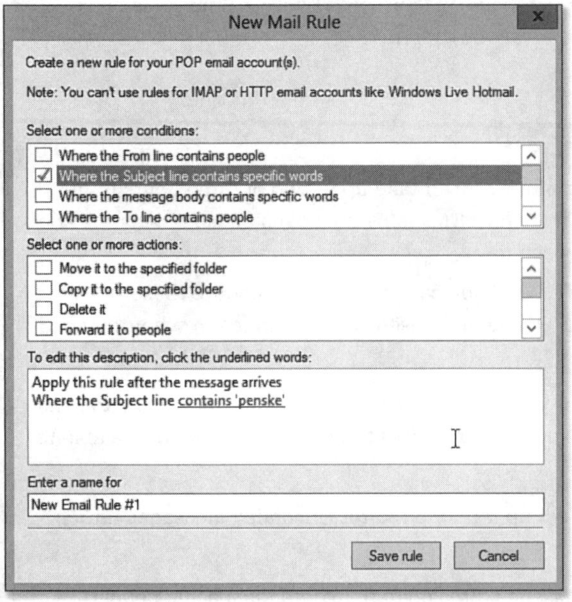

New Mail Rule

Create a new rule for your POP email account(s).

Note: You can't use rules for IMAP or HTTP email accounts like Windows Live Hotmail.

Select one or more conditions:

- ☐ Where the From line contains people
- ☑ Where the Subject line contains specific words
- ☐ Where the message body contains specific words
- ☐ Where the To line contains people

Select one or more actions:

- ☐ Move it to the specified folder
- ☐ Copy it to the specified folder
- ☐ Delete it
- ☐ Forward it to people

To edit this description, click the underlined words:

Apply this rule after the message arrives
Where the Subject line contains 'penske'

Enter a name for

New Email Rule #1

Save rule   Cancel

Figure 16.7
Click underlined text in the rule description to edit the text to the criterion you want for your rule.

4. If you selected multiple conditions, Mail assumes that all the conditions must be true before invoking the rule (Boolean AND). If you need only one of the conditions to be true (Boolean OR), click and in the rule description, activate the Messages Match Any One of the Criteria option, and click OK.

5. In the Select One or More Actions list, activate the check box beside the action you want Mail to take with messages that meet your criteria. You might have to click underlined text in the rule description to complete the action. You can select multiple actions.

tip

If you add multiple words or phrases to a rule criterion, you can make that criterion use Boolean operators such as AND, OR, and NOT. To do this, click the Options button in the dialog box that appears in step 3. To make an AND criterion, activate Message Matches All of the *X* Below (where *X* depends on the condition—for example, *words* or *people*); to make an OR criterion, activate Message Matches Any One of the *X* Below; to make a NOT criterion, activate Message Does Not Contain the *X* Below.

6. Use the Enter a Name For text box to type a descriptive name for the rule.

7. Click Save Rule. Mail drops you off at the Mail Rules tab of the Message Rules dialog box.

Whichever method you used, here are a few notes to bear in mind when working with the list of rules:

- **Toggling rules on and off**—Use the check box beside each rule to turn the rule on and off.

- **Setting rule order**—Some rules should be processed before others. For example, if you have a rule that deletes messages from annoying people, you want Mail to process that rule before sending out a vacation reply. To adjust the order of a rule, select it and click either Move Up or Move Down.

- **Modifying a rule**—To make changes to a rule, you have two choices: If you just want to edit the rule's underlined values, select the rule and use the rule description box to click the underlined values you want to change; if you want to make more substantial changes to a rule, select it and click Modify.

- **Applying a rule**—If you want to apply a rule to existing Inbox folder messages or to messages in a different folder, click Apply Now to open the Apply Mail Rules Now dialog box. Select the rule you want to apply (or click Select All to apply them all). To choose a different folder, click Browse. When you're ready, click Apply Now.

- **Deleting a rule**—Select the rule and click Remove. When Mail asks whether you're sure, click Yes.

> **⚑ caution**
>
> If you've defined multiple rules, problems can occur if you have two or more rules that apply to an incoming message, but the first of those rules moves the message to another folder. In such cases, Mail will often display an error message saying that it can't process more rules. To avoid this error, add the action Stop Processing More Rules to the initial rule.

Finding a Message

Although you'll delete many of the messages that come your way, it's unlikely that you'll delete all of them. Over time, you'll probably end up with hundreds (or more likely thousands) of messages stored throughout various folders. What happens if you want to find a particular message? Even if you curmudgeonly delete everything that comes your way, your Sent Items folder will eventually contain copies of the hundreds or thousands of missives you've sent out. What do you do if you want to find one of those messages?

For both incoming and outgoing messages, Mail offers a decent Find Message feature that can look for messages based on addresses, subject lines, body text, dates, and more.

Simple Searches

Mail comes with an Instant Search box that appears above the message list. If you're not fussy about what part of the message Find uses to look for a particular word, and if you already know which folder holds the message you want, you can use the Instant Search box for quick-and-dirty searches. Here are the steps to follow:

1. Use the folders list to select the folder in which you want to search.

2. Click inside the Instant Search box (or press Ctrl+E).

3. Type the text you want to use as the search criteria. Instant Search looks for the search text in the From, To, and Subject fields as well as the body of each message.

Advanced Searches

If you want to search specific message fields, if you want to specify different criteria for each field, or if you want to include specialized criteria (such as the message date or whether a message has attachments), you have to use the full-fledged Find Message feature. To try it out, select the Folders, Find, Message command (or press Ctrl+Shift+F). Figure 16.8 shows the Find Message dialog box that appears. Use the following controls to set the search criteria:

- **Browse**—Select the folder to search. If you want the search to include the subfolders of the selected folder, leave the Include Subfolders check box activated.

- **From**—Type one or more words that specify the email address or display the name of the sender you want to find.

- **To**—Type one or more words that specify the email address or display the name of the recipient you want to find.

- **Subject**—Type one or more words that specify the Subject line you want to find.

- **Message**—Type one or more words that specify the message body you want to find.

- **Received Before**—Select the latest received date for the message you want to find.

- **Received After**—Select the earliest received date for the message you want to find.

- **Message Has Attachment(s)**—Activate this check box to find only messages that have attached files.

- **Message Is Flagged**—Activate this check box to find only messages that have been flagged.

> **note**
>
> When entering your search criteria, you can enter partial words, single words, or multiple words. If you include multiple words, Instant Search matches only messages that contain *all* the words. If you want to search for an exact phrase, place quotation marks around the phrase. Finally, note that the search is not case sensitive.

> **note**
>
> As with Instant Search, the individual Find Message criteria match only those messages that contain *all* the words you enter, match only whole words, and are not case sensitive. Note, too, that Find Message looks only for messages that match all the criteria you enter.

Figure 16.8
Use the Find Message dialog box to look for specific messages in a folder.

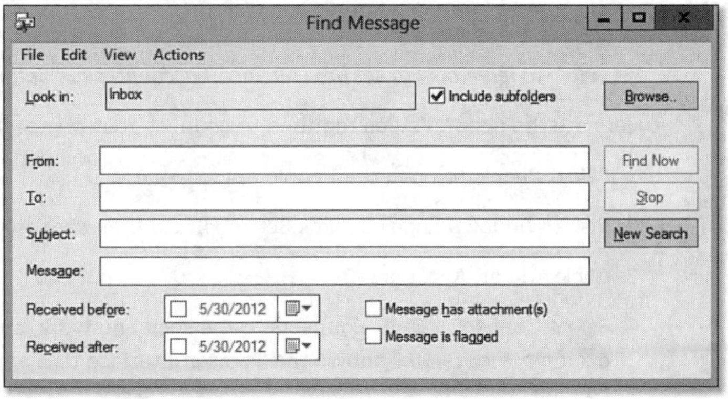

After you define your search criteria, click Find Now. If Mail finds any matches, it displays them in a message list at the bottom of the dialog box. From there, you can open a message or use any of the commands in the menus to work with the messages (reply, forward, move to another folder, delete, and so on).

Setting Up Social Networks with the People App

For many years you could confidently claim email as the most popular Internet service. That's still technically true, because most people who have Internet access have an email account, and according to The Radicati Group, there were more than three billion email accounts worldwide at the end of 2011. Even taking into account people with multiple addresses, that's still a lot of accounts. But these days nobody even talks about email, not even to complain about message overload or the influx of spam. Now all anyone talks about is social networking, "friend" has become a verb, and a billion souls call Facebook home.

Microsoft has read the social writing on the wall, and in response they've baked social tools into some of the default Windows 8 apps. This is particularly true of the People app, which enables you to connect your Microsoft account to one or more social networks, including Facebook, Twitter, and LinkedIn. The People app live tile then shows notifications from your connected networks, and you can open People to see your friends' status updates, exchange messages, and view your own social posts.

Connecting to a Social Network

As we said, the People app is your gateway to working with social networks on Windows 8. Through the People app you can connect to a half dozen networks, including Facebook, Twitter, LinkedIn, and Google. In each case, you are giving permission for your Microsoft account to use data from and post data to the social network account. So, of course, it means you must be using a

Microsoft account to sign in to Windows 8 before you can connect to any social network using the People app.

➡️ *To learn how to set up a Microsoft account, **see** "Setting Up User Accounts," **p. 68**.*

Here are the general steps required to connect your Microsoft account to a social network:

1. Select People to open the People app.

2. Press Windows Logo+C, click Settings, and then click Accounts.

3. Click Add an Account.

4. Select Connect. People connects to the social network, and the network's interface appears. For example, Figure 16.9 shows the Twitter interface that appears.

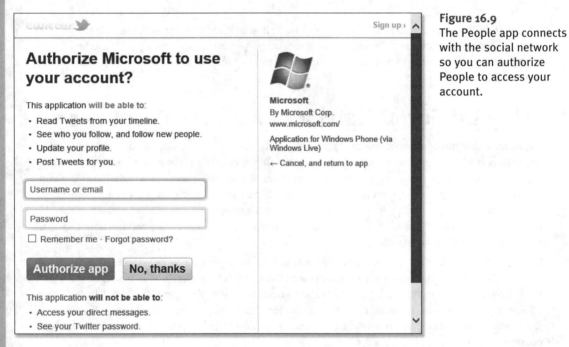

Figure 16.9
The People app connects with the social network so you can authorize People to access your account.

5. Enter your username and password for the network. If the network offers an option for remembering your login data, be sure to activate it (assuming you're the only person who uses your Windows 8 account).

6. Click the button that submits the forms. This is your authorization that People can access your social network account.

7. Click Done.

Once you've connected a network or two, your friends (or, in the case of Twitter, the people you follow) appear in the All section of the People app. You can now perform the following tasks:

- **Send a message to a contact**—Click the contact in the All list, and then click Send Email or Send Message (that is, an instant message).

- **See a contact's updates**—Click the contact in the All list, and then scroll right to the What's New box.

- **Interact with a contact's update**—Click the contact in the All list, scroll right to the What's New box, and then click the update. This enables you to perform tasks such as like or comment on a Facebook post and retweet or favorite a Twitter update.

- **See a contact's photos**—Click the contact in the All list, and then scroll right to the Photos box.

- **See information about a contact**—Click the contact in the All list, and then click All Info.

- **Map a contact's location**—Click the contact in the All list, and then click Map Address.

- **See updates from all your contacts**—Click the What's New tab.

- **See your own posts, notifications, and photos**—Click the Me tab. The What's new box contains your latest posts, the Notifications box contains the latest messages from your social networks, and the Photos box contains your recent photos.

Editing a Connection's Settings

When you authorize your Microsoft account to connect with your social network account, you are actually giving permission for several things, depending on the network. For example, in most cases you're giving permission to access your friend list and to send updates to the network on your behalf. However, some networks offer even more fine-grained control. Facebook, for example, has a half a dozen sharing settings that you can turn on or off separately.

Follow these steps to adjust your settings for a social network connection:

1. Select People to open the People app.

2. In the upper-right corner of the screen, select Connected To. People displays a list of your connected accounts.

3. Select the social network account you want to edit. Windows 8 opens Internet Explorer and displays the settings for the connection. Figure 16.10 shows the settings for a Facebook connection.

4. Use the check boxes to activate or deactivate the sharing options.

5. Select Save.

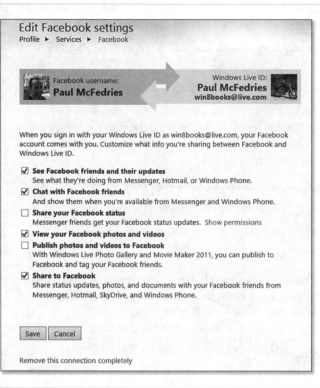

Figure 16.10
You can tweak your connection settings to choose exactly what you want to share between your Microsoft account and a social network, such as Facebook.

Removing a Connection

If you find the People app is getting a bit crowded and a bit overwhelmed with updates, consider removing any social networks that you don't use all that often. Here's how:

1. Select People to open the People app.

2. In the upper-right corner of the screen, click Connected To. People displays a list of your connected accounts.

3. Click the social network account you want to remove. Windows 8 switches to Internet Explorer and displays the settings for the connection.

4. Click Remove This Connection Completely. Windows 8 asks you to confirm.

5. Click Remove.

TROUBLESHOOTING AN INTERNET CONNECTION

It's Great When It Works, But...

Browsing the Internet is great fun and very useful. Just watch as I instantly transfer millions of dollars from my secret Swiss bank account to... wait a minute, what's a "404 Server Not Found Error"? What's going on? Did the DSL go out? Is the IRS closing in on me? Help! Where's my money?

If you've used the Internet for any length of time, this scene might seem all too familiar (give or take a Swiss bank account). Using the Web today is an amazingly user-friendly experience that would have astounded people just 20 years ago, yet we can't escape that it's a staggeringly complex system. If something goes wrong at any step along the way between your fingertips and a server in cyberspace, the whole system comes to a crashing halt. Where do you begin to find and fix the problem?

In this chapter, we'll show you the basic strategies to use when tracking down Internet problems, and we'll briefly discuss some of the diagnostic tools available to help you pinpoint the trouble.

Troubleshooting Step by Step

A functioning Internet connection depends on an entire chain of hardware and software components that reaches all the way from your keyboard to a computer that might be halfway around the world. Troubleshooting is a real detective's art, and it's based more on methodical tracking down of potential suspect problems than intuition. If something goes wrong, you have to go through each component, asking "Is *this* the one that's causing the problem?"

Windows 8 comes with network-troubleshooting capabilities that, in *some* cases, can identify and repair problems automatically. If you encounter Internet connection problems—especially problems using high-speed broadband Internet service—try these steps:

1. At the Desktop, right-click the network icon at the right end of the taskbar and select Open Network and Sharing Center. If there is a problem with your Internet connection, Windows displays a yellow exclamation point icon in the taskbar, as shown in Figure 17.1.

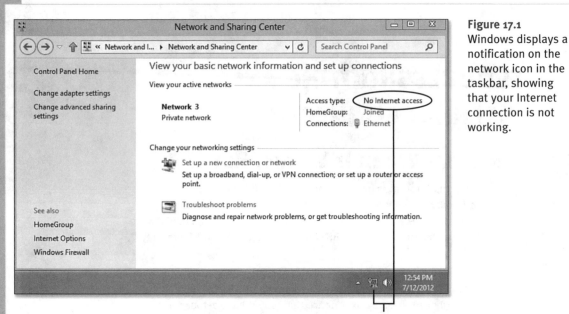

Figure 17.1
Windows displays a notification on the network icon in the taskbar, showing that your Internet connection is not working.

Indications That Internet Connectivity Has Been Lost

2. Double-click the red X.

3. If Windows displays a message indicating that it might be able to repair the problem, click Repair.

4. If that does not solve the problem, go back to the Network and Sharing Center. At the bottom of the page, click Troubleshoot Problems, and then click Internet Connections. Click Advanced, Run As Administrator, and then click Next. Follow the troubleshooting wizard's prompts from there.

If the wizard's diagnosis is "The DNS server isn't responding," and if you connect to the Internet through a shared connection using a router, this most likely means that your connection sharing router can't connect to the Internet. The problem is either with the router, your cable or DSL modem, or its connection to the Internet. Use Internet Explorer to connect to your sharing router, as described later in the chapter under "Identifying Network Hardware Problems." If you can bring up the router's setup web page, the router itself is working, so your best bet is to contact your ISP for further assistance.

5. If this does not fix the problem, and if your computer connects to the Internet through a wireless or wired Ethernet connection, go back to the Network and Sharing Center. Click Troubleshoot Problems and select Network Adapter. Again, click Advanced, Run As Administrator, and then click Next.

If the problem occurred because your computer failed to obtain its network settings from a router, this procedure will often work. In many cases, though, you'll need to locate the problem yourself, using good, old-fashioned Sherlock Holmes–style deductive reasoning. For example, let's assume you are having trouble using a certain website. Here are some scenarios:

- You can view some of its pages but not others, or you see text displayed but not the streaming video or sound.

    In this case, you know that your Internet connection itself is fine because something *does* appear. The problem, then, is that the video or sound application isn't working. You might want to check the index to see whether we discuss the application in this book. You might also check the application's built-in help pages. If the application was one that you downloaded or purchased, check the manufacturer's website for support information or an updated software version.

- Nothing on this particular site is responding. In this case, see if you can view any other website. Try www.google.com, www.quepublishing.com, your ISP's website, or your local newspaper's website.

    If you get a response from even one other website, again, your Internet connection is fine. The problem is most likely with the site you're trying to use or with your ISP. Check to be sure that Internet Explorer isn't set up to block access to the site you're interested in. (See Chapter 15, "Using Internet Explorer 10," for more help on this topic.)

- You can't view any web pages on any site. If this is the case, you know that your Internet connection itself is at fault. This chapter can help you find out what's wrong.

To that end, Figures 17.2 and 17.3 show flowcharts to help direct you to the source of the problem. The first chart is for broadband or LAN Internet connections; the second is for dial-up connections to an ISP. If you're having Internet connection trouble, follow the appropriate flowchart for your type of connection. The endpoints in each flowchart suggest places to look for trouble. I discuss these in the sections that follow.

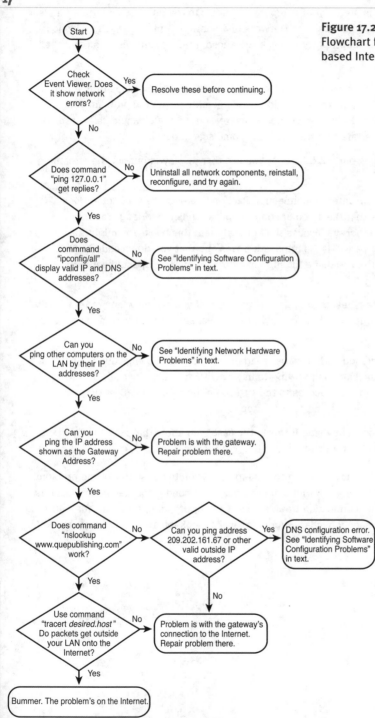

Figure 17.2
Flowchart for diagnosing broadband or LAN-based Internet connection problems.

Figure 17.3
Flowchart for diagnosing dial-up
Internet connection problems.

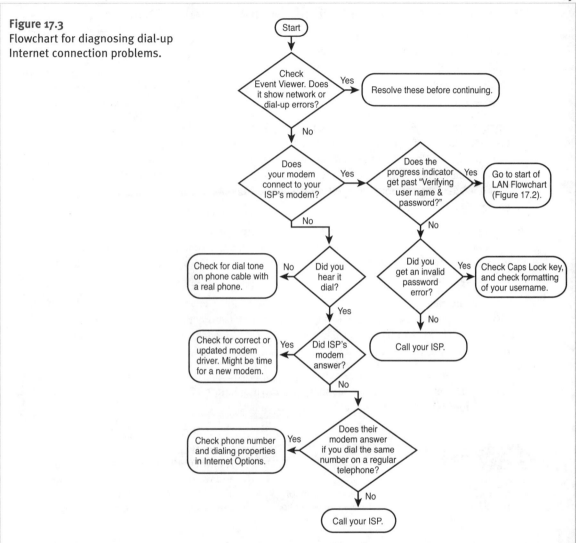

Identifying Software Configuration Problems

Software configuration problems can easily be the cause of Internet connection problems, and it's
fairly simple to determine that this is the problem—you can't make any Internet connection whatsoever, although the Device Manager says your network card or modem seems to be working correctly.
The potential problems depend on the type of Internet connection you use.

Troubleshooting a Cable or DSL Modem Connection

If your computer connects *directly* to a cable or DSL modem, you might have one or two network cards installed in your computer, depending on whether your computer is doing the job of sharing the high-speed connection on your LAN.

To check for the proper settings, follow these steps:

1. Open a Command Prompt window by pressing Windows Logo+X and selecting Command Prompt. Type **ipconfig /all** and press Enter. Be sure that the IP address and DNS information for the network card that connects to your high-speed modem are accurate. Your ISP's tech support people can help you confirm this.

> 🔍 **note**
>
> If you have DSL or cable service but your computer connects to a connection sharing router and the *router* connects to the DSL or cable modem, don't follow these instructions. Instead, see "Identifying Network Hardware Problems" later in this chapter.

2. If your DSL provider requires you to "sign on" before using the Internet, you'll be using a sort of "dial-up" connection, except that the connection is made digitally over the DSL network. This is called Point-to-Point Protocol over Ethernet, or PPPoE. You set up this connection using the Broadband (PPPoE) option, as described in Chapter 14, "Getting Connected."

   If this is the case, and if you use a LAN adapter to connect to your DSL modem, the IP address displayed for the LAN adapter is used only to communicate with your DSL modem. Be sure to check with your ISP to be certain that this computer-to-modem connection is configured correctly; if it's not, you won't be able to make the connection to your ISP.

   Use the Connection icon to connect to your ISP. You can get to it quickly from the Desktop by left-clicking the network icon in the taskbar (as shown in Figure 17.4). Click the name of the connection for your Internet service, and then click Connect.

Network Icon for Ethernet Connection

Network Icon for Wireless Connection

Figure 17.4
The Network icon on the taskbar, for wired and wireless connection types. A left click displays the connection list. A right click lets you open the Network and Sharing Center.

When the logon process has completed, `ipconfig /all` should show a "dial-up" connection with a different IP address. This is your real, public Internet address for the duration of the connection.

3. If you're sharing your computer's high-speed connection with your home or office LAN using two network cards in your computer, be sure you've enabled sharing on the correct connection. The connection to check as "shared" is the one that connects to your high-speed DSL or cable modem. The LAN-side connection is not the shared connection and should have an IP address of 192.168.0.1. Internet connection sharing is described in Chapter 19, "Connecting Your Network to the Internet."

Troubleshooting a LAN Connection

If you connect to the Internet via a wired or wireless connection on your LAN, the first question is, can you communicate with other computers on your LAN? To test this, you should use the `ping` command.

Open a Command Prompt window by pressing Windows Logo+X and selecting Command Prompt. Type the command **ipconfig** and press Enter. The output of `ipconfig` lists a number called a *gateway address*. To test the connection to your gateway, type **ping** followed by the gateway address and then press Enter. For example:

```
ping 192.168.0.1
```

This tests the connection to the computer or router that is sharing its Internet connection. If **ping** says "Request timed out" or "Transmit failed" instead of listing four successful replies, you have a LAN problem that you need to fix first.

If you are using a wireless network connection, be sure your wireless connection is working correctly, that you are connected to the correct wireless network, and that you have the correct network key entered. Chapter 22, "Troubleshooting Your Network," is devoted to LAN troubleshooting.

If you can communicate with other computers on the LAN but not the Internet, can anyone else on your LAN access the Internet? If no one can, the problem is in your LAN's connection to the Internet. If your LAN uses Windows' built-in Internet Connection Sharing (ICS), go to the sharing computer and start diagnosing the problem there. Otherwise, follow these steps:

1. Open a Command Prompt window and type `ipconfig /all` to view your TCP/IP settings. The output appears similar to that shown in Listing 17.1. (The Tunnel Adapter entries are not important here and are not shown.)

> **tip**
>
> Windows has a diagnostic and repair function that resets all the software components of a LAN connection, including the DHCP address assignment. This often solves LAN problems. To use it, open the Network Connections page, find your LAN or wireless connection, right-click it, and select Diagnose. If a problem is identified, follow the instructions or select the Reset option.

> **note**
>
> If you have a laptop, see if yours has a little slide or pushbutton switch that turns the internal wireless adapter on and off. It's easy for that switch to get turned off.

Listing 17.1   Output from the `ipconfig /all` Command

```
Windows IP Configuration
     Host Name . . . . . . . . . . . . .: MyComputer
     Primary Dns Suffix  . . . . . . . .:
     Node Type . . . . . . . . . . . . .: Hybrid
     IP Routing Enabled. . . . . . . . .: No
     WINS Proxy Enabled. . . . . . . . .: No
Ethernet adapter Local Area Connection:
     Connection-specific DNS Suffix  . .:
     Description . . . . . . . . . . . .: Intel PCI Fast Ethernet Adapter
     Physical Address. . . . . . . . . .: 00-03-FF-D0-CA-5F
     DHCP Enabled. . . . . . . . . . . .: Yes
```

```
Autoconfiguration Enabled . . . . . .: Yes
Link-local IPv6 Address . . . . . .: fe80::8014:cfc7:9a98:cdfe%10(Preferred)
IPv4 Address. . . . . . . . . . . .: 192.168.1.106(Preferred)
Subnet Mask . . . . . . . . . . . .: 255.255.255.0
Lease Obtained. . . . . . . . . . .: Sunday, October 7, 2012 7:22:23 PM
Lease Expires . . . . . . . . . . .: Sunday, October 14, 2012, 7:22:21 PM
Default Gateway . . . . . . . . . .: 192.168.1.1
DHCP Server . . . . . . . . . . . .: 192.168.1.1
DHCPv6 IAID . . . . . . . . . . . .: 252182567
DHCPv6 Client DUID. . . . . . . . .: 00-01-03-01-37-F2-EB-C2-38-3C-40-F3-02-38
DNS Servers . . . . . . . . . . . .: 192.168.1.1
NetBIOS over Tcpip. . . . . . . . .: Enabled
```

Within the output, check the following:

- The DNS suffix search list and the connection-specific DNS suffix should be set correctly for your ISP's domain name or your company's domain name. (This is helpful but not crucial.) It can also be left blank.

- The IP address should be appropriate for your LAN. If you're using ICS, the number will be 192.168.0.*xxx*. If you're using a hardware connection-sharing device, the number might be different.

- If your IP address appears to be 169.254.*xxx*.*yyy*, the sharing computer or router was not running when you booted up your computer, or it is no longer set up to share its connection. Get the sharing computer or router restarted and then skip to step 2.

- The default gateway address should be the IP address of your router or sharing computer, usually something similar to 192.168.0.1 or 192.168.1.1.

- The default gateway address and your IP address should be identical for the first few sets of numbers, corresponding to those parts of the subnet mask that are set to 255. That is, both might start with 192.168.0 or 192.168.1.

- If your computer gets its IP address information automatically, DHCP Enabled should be set to Yes. If your computer has its IP address information entered manually, no DHCP server should be listed.

- If you're using connection sharing, the DNS server address will be 192.168.0.1. Otherwise, the DNS server numbers should be those provided by your ISP or network administrator. Some routers substitute their own address as the DNS server address and do DNS lookups themselves, as in the example shown here.

- If your computer gets its settings automatically or uses a shared connection, continue with the next two steps.

2. Be sure the master router or sharing computer is running. Then, in the Network Connections window, right-click your Local Area Connection icon and select Diagnose. This might lead you through solving the problem. Alternatively, view the Network and Sharing Center and select Troubleshoot Problems from the task list. Select Internet Connections and then repeat the process, selecting Network Adapter.

3. Repeat the `ipconfig` command and see whether the correct information appears now. If it does, you're all set. If not, the master computer or the router is not supplying the information described previously and needs to be set correctly before you can proceed.

These steps should take care of any software configuration problems. If none of these steps indicates or solves the problem, check that your network or modem hardware is functioning correctly.

Identifying Network Hardware Problems

If you suspect hardware as the source of your Internet connection problems, check the following:

- Log on using an account with Administrator privileges. Right-click the very bottom-left corner of the screen and select Computer Management. Select Device Manager. Look for any yellow exclamation point (!) icons in the device list. If your network adapter is marked with this trouble indicator, you must solve the hardware problem before continuing. If the device needs an updated driver, see "Updating Device Drivers" in Chapter 28, "Managing Your Hardware," for more information.

- Also within Computer Management, check the Event Viewer for any potentially informative error messages that might indicate a hardware problem.

- Use `ipconfig` on each of your computers to check that all the computers on your LAN have the same gateway and network mask values, and similar but distinct IP addresses.

- If your LAN has indicator lights on the network cards and hubs, open a Command Prompt window and type

  `ping -t x.x.x.x`

  where `x.x.x.x` is your network's default gateway address. (This might be something similar to 192.168.0.1.) This forces your computer to transmit data once per second. Confirm that the indicator lights blink on your LAN adapter and the hub, if you have one. This test might point out a cabling problem.

- If your hub or LAN card's indicator doesn't flash, you might have a bad LAN adapter, the wrong driver might be installed, or you might have configured the card incorrectly. You can stop the `ping` test by typing Ctrl+C when you're finished checking.

If you use a hardware-connection-sharing router for a broadband (DSL or cable) connection, your router might provide further assistance. To access the router, follow these steps:

1. Open a Command Prompt window: press Windows Logo+X, then select Command Prompt.

2. Type the command **ipconfig** and press Enter.

3. Note the gateway address. It will be something along the lines of 192.168.0.1.

4. Open Internet Explorer. In the Address bar, type **http://** followed by the gateway address. This will look something like **http://192.168.0.1**.

5. You are prompted to enter the administrative username and password for your router. Each manufacturer has a default name and password, which you can find in the router's user's manual. You might also have changed it when you installed it. (You might try username `admin` and password `admin`.)

6. Most routers have a Status menu item that displays the status of the router's Internet connection. If it says that it can't connect, you might have an incorrect PPPoE username or password entered. Or it might have dropped the connection. In this case, there might be a Connect button you can click, or you might want to just power off and then power on the router.

If you use a dial-up Internet connection, the next section can help you diagnose modem problems.

Troubleshooting Internet Problems with Windows TCP/IP Utilities

If you think you are connected to your ISP but you still can't communicate, you can use some of the command-line tools provided with Windows to trace TCP/IP problems. (TCP/IP is the network language or protocol used by the Internet.)

To run the command-line utilities, first open a Command Prompt window by right-clicking the very bottom-left corner of the screen and selecting Command Prompt. Then, type in the commands as we describe them later. If you're not familiar with a particular command-line utility, type the command name followed by /**?**, as in this example:

```
ping /?
```

Now, let's go through some of the TCP/IP diagnostic and command-line utilities provided with Windows.

 note

If you're a UNIX devotee, you'll find these utilities familiar, if not identical, to their UNIX counterparts. If you're new to TCP/IP networking or debugging, you might find these utilities a little unfriendly. (Welcome to the world of networking.)

ipconfig

`ipconfig` is one of the most useful command-line utilities provided with Windows because it displays the current IP address information for each of your computer's network adapters and active dial-up connections. On networks that assign addresses automatically, `ipconfig` can tell you what your computer's IP address is, if you ever need to know it.

Within an open Command Prompt window, the command `ipconfig` prints the following information (of course the IP, subnet, and gateway information `ipconfig` provides will be different for your computer, and you might see a dial-up connection listed instead of a LAN adapter):

```
Windows IP Configuration
Ethernet adapter Local Area Connection:
    Connection-specific DNS Suffix   . :
    Link-local IPv6 Address . . . . . : fe80::8014:cfc7:9a98:cdfe%10
    IPv4 Address. . . . . . . . . . . : 192.168.15.106
    Subnet Mask . . . . . . . . . . . : 255.255.255.0
    Default Gateway . . . . . . . . . : 192.168.15.1
```

(You can ignore the Tunnel Adapter information; this is part of the Version 6 Internet Protocol system, which is used only on large, managed corporate networks.)

If you type the command

```
ipconfig /all
```

Windows displays additional information about your network settings, including the information shown in Table 17.1.

Table 17.1   Information Displayed by `ipconfig/all`

Setting	What It Means
Host Name	The name you gave your computer.
Primary DNS Suffix	The Internet domain to which your computer belongs. (You might temporarily belong to others as well while using a dial-up connection.) This might be blank; it is not a problem.
Node Type	The method that Windows uses to locate other computers on your LAN when you use Windows Networking. This usually is Hybrid or Broadcast.
DNS Suffix Search List	Alternative domain names used if you type just part of a hostname and the default domain does not provide a match.
Connection-specific DNS Suffix	The domain name for this particular connection. This is most applicable to dial-up connections.
DHCP Enabled	If set to Yes, this adapter is set to receive its IP address automatically. If set to No, the address was set manually.
DNS Servers	IP addresses of domain name servers.

`ipconfig` displays most of the information that can be set in the Network and Dial-Up Connection Properties dialog box, but it shows their real-world values. This makes it an invaluable "first stop" when troubleshooting any network problem. If you determine that an Internet connection problem lies in your equipment somewhere (because you cannot access any Internet destinations), typing **ipconfig /all** can tell you whether your network setup is correct. You need this information at hand before calling your ISP for assistance.

ping

If you try to browse the Internet or share files with other computers on your LAN and get no response, it could be because the other computer isn't receiving your data or isn't responding. After `ipconfig`, `ping` is the most useful tool to determine where your Internet connection or your network has stopped working.

tip

You can type **ping** $x.x.x.x$, replacing $x.x.x.x$ with the default gateway address or the address of any other operational computer on the Internet or your network (if applicable), and in an instant, you will know whether your dial-up or high-speed modem, computer, network hardware, and cabling are operating properly. If echoes come back, the physical part of your network is functioning properly. If they don't, you can use `tracert` and other tools (explained later in this chapter) to see why.

Here's how it works:

1. The `ping` command sends a few packets of data to any computer you specify.

2. The other computer should immediately send these packets back to you.

3. `ping` lets you know whether the packets come back.

Therefore, `ping` tests the low-level communication between two computers. If `ping` works, you know that your network wiring, TCP/IP software, and any routers in between you and the other computer are working. `ping` takes several options that can customize the type and amount of output it reports back to you. Three especially useful variations of these options exist; the first two are

```
C:\ > ping hostname
```

where *hostname* is the name of one of the computers on your network, and

```
C:\ > ping nnn.nnn.nnn.nnn
```

where *nnn.nnn.nnn.nnn* is a computer's numeric IP address, as discovered by `ipconfig`. That is, you can ping a computer either by its name or by its IP address. These variations transmit four packets to the host or IP address you specify and tell you whether they return. This command returns the following information:

```
C:\> ping www.mycompany.com
Pinging sumatra.mycompany.com [202.222.132.163] with 32 bytes of data:
Reply from 202.222.132.163: bytes=32 time<10ms TTL=32
Reply from 202.222.132.163: bytes=32 time<10ms TTL=32
Reply from 202.222.132.163: bytes=32 time<10ms TTL=32
Reply from 202.222.132.163: bytes=32 time<10ms TTL=32
```

In this example, the fact that the reply packets came back tells us that the computer can communicate with www.mycompany.com. It also tells us that everything in between my computer and mycompany.com is working.

The third useful variation is to add the `-t` option. This makes `ping` run endlessly once per second until you press Ctrl+C. This is especially helpful if you're looking at indicator lights on your network hub, changing cables, and so on. The endless testing lets you just watch the screen to see whether any changes you make cause a difference.

note

It's not uncommon for one packet of the four to be lost; when the Internet gets congested, sometimes ping packets are discarded as unimportant. If any come back, the intervening networks are working. It's also not unusual for the name that appears after "Pinging" to be different from what you typed. Some computers have alternative names.

`ping` is a great quick test of connectivity to any location. If the `ping` test fails, use `tracert` to tell you where the problem is. `ping` is a good, quick tool to use to discover whether an Internet site is alive. (However, some large companies have made their servers not respond to `ping` tests. For example, `ping www.microsoft.com` doesn't work ever, even with a good Internet connection. It's not just that Microsoft got tired of being the first site everyone thought of to test their Internet connections; malicious people also can use `ping` to suck up all of a company's Internet bandwidth.)

tracert

The `tracert` command is similar to `ping`: it sends packets to a remote host and sees whether packets return. However, `tracert` adds a wrinkle: it checks the connectivity to each individual router in the path between you and the remote host. (Routers are the devices that connect one network to another. The Internet itself is the conglomeration of a few million networks all connected by routers.) If your computer and Internet connection are working but you still can't reach some or all Internet sites, `tracert` can help you find the blockage.

In the output of `tracert`, the address it tests first is your local network's gateway (if you connect to the Internet via a high-speed connection or a LAN) or the modem-answering equipment at your ISP's office (if you're using a dial-up connection). If this first address responds, you know that your modem, LAN, or broadband connection is working. If the connection stops after two or three routers, the problem is in your ISP's network. If the problem occurs farther out, there might be an Internet outage somewhere else in the country.

Here's an example that shows the route between my network and the fictitious web server www.fictitious.net. Typing

```
C:\ > tracert www.fictitious.net
```

returns the following:

```
Tracing route to www.fictitious.com [204.179.107.3]
over a maximum of 30 hops:
1   <10 ms  <10 ms   <10 ms   190.mycompany.com [202.201.200.190]
2   <10 ms  <10 ms    10 ms   129.mycompany.com [202.201.200.129]
3    20 ms   20 ms    20 ms   w001.z216112073.sjc-ca.dsl.cnc.net [217.112.73.1]
4    10 ms   10 ms    10 ms   206.83.66.153
5    10 ms   10 ms    10 ms   rt001f0801.sjc-ca.concentric.net [206.83.90.161]
6    10 ms   20 ms    20 ms   us-ca-sjc-core2-f5-0.rtr.concentric.net [205.158.11.133]
7    10 ms   20 ms    10 ms   us-ca-sjc-core1-g4-0-0.rtr.concentric.net [205.158.10.2]
8    10 ms   20 ms    20 ms   us-ca-pa-core1-a9-0d1.rtr.concentric.net [205.158.11.14]
9    10 ms   20 ms    20 ms   ATM2-0-0.br2.pao1.ALTER.NET [137.39.23.189]
10   10 ms   20 ms    20 ms   125.ATM3-0.XR1.PAO1.ALTER.NET [152.63.49.170]
11   10 ms   10 ms    20 ms   289.at-1-0-0.XR3.SCL1.ALTER.NET [152.63.49.98]
12   20 ms   20 ms    20 ms   295.ATM8-0-0.GW2.SCL1.ALTER.NET [152.63.48.113]
13   20 ms   20 ms    20 ms   2250-gw.customer.ALTER.NET [157.130.193.14]
14   41 ms   30 ms    20 ms   www.fictitious.com [204.179.107.3]

Trace complete.
```

> **tip**
>
> As mentioned at the start of the chapter, when your Internet connection is working, run `tracert` to trace the path between your computer and a few Internet hosts. Print and save the listings. Someday when you're having Internet problems, you can use these listings as a baseline reference. It's very helpful to know whether packets are stopping in your LAN, in your ISP's network, or beyond when you pick up the phone to yell about it.

You can see that between my computer and this web server, data passes through 13 intermediate routers owned by two ISPs.

I should point out a couple of `tracert` oddities. First, notice in the example that on the command line I typed www.fictitious.net, but `tracert` printed www.fictitious.com. That's not unusual. Web servers sometimes have alternative names. `tracert` starts with a reverse name lookup to find the *canonical* (primary) name for a given IP address.

You might run into another glitch as well. For security reasons, many organizations use firewall software or devices, which block `tracert` packets at the firewall between their LAN and the Internet. In these instances, `tracert` will never reach its intended destination, even when regular communications are working correctly. Instead, you'll see an endless list that looks similar to this:

```
14      *       *       *     Request timed out.
15      *       *       *     Request timed out.
16      *       *       *     Request timed out.
```

This continues up to the `tracert` limit of 30 probes. If this happens, just press Ctrl+C to cancel the test. If `tracert` could reach routers outside your own LAN or PC, your equipment and Internet connection are fine—and that's all you can directly control.

Third-Party Utilities

In addition to the utilities provided with Windows, you can use some third-party tools to help diagnose your connection and gather Internet information. I describe some web-based utilities and a commercial software package.

WhatIsMyIP

If you are using an Internet router or Windows Internet Connection Sharing, your network uses one "public" IP address to communicate with the Internet, using a mechanism called Network Address Translation (NAT). The public address is different from the private one assigned to your computer. It's not always easy or convenient to find out your public IP address from your router. Solution: just open whatismyip.com in your web browser and you'll see your public address in a flash.

➡ To find out how NAT works, **see** "NAT and Internet Connection Sharing," **p. 418**.

Speed Check

Ever wondered how to find the real-world transfer rate of your Internet connection? There are several speed test websites that you can use, but we like www.speedtest.net and www.dslreports.com, where you need to click Tools and then Speed Tests. You'll only get valid results if you perform the test while your computer and other computers on your network are sitting idle, not downloading or streaming content.

Reverse tracert

As discussed earlier, the `tracert` program investigates the path that data you send through the Internet takes to reach another location. Interestingly, data coming back to you can take a different path, depending on the way your ISP has set up its own internal network.

It's handy to know the path data takes coming to you. If you record this information while your Internet connection is working and subsequently run into trouble, you can have a friend perform a `tracert` to you. (You need to give him your IP address, which you can find using the `ipconfig` command.) If the results differ, you might be able to tell whether the problem is with your computer, your ISP, or the Internet.

You can visit www.traceroute.org for a list of hundreds of web servers that can perform a `traceroute` test from their site to you. Don't be surprised if the test results take a while to appear; these tests can take a minute or longer.

CREATING A WINDOWS NETWORK

Creating or Joining a Network

For about the cost of a trip to the movies, you can set up a network that will let everyone trade music, videos, and documents, use the same printer and Internet connection, and back up files, almost effortlessly. It's not as hard or expensive as you may think. Once you've done the planning and shopping, you should be able to get a network up and running in an hour or two.

This chapter should give you all the information you need. Then, check out Chapter 19, "Connecting your Network to the Internet," and if you have computers with older versions of Windows or other operating systems, Chapter 20, "Networking with Other Operating Systems."

If you're just adding a computer to an existing Ethernet network, you can skip ahead to the section "Installing Network Adapters." If you're joining an existing wireless network, see "Joining a Wireless Network" in Chapter 36.

> ### 🔍 note
>
> If you have high-speed Internet service and your ISP provided you with a router when you started your service, you already have the makings of a network. If you want to share files and printers, perform backups, and so on, you just need to make sure that your router is set up securely, and you may need to change a few settings in Windows. You can skip ahead to "Installing Network Adapters," later in this chapter, to see how to do this.

Planning Your Network

You must plan your network around your own particular needs. What do you expect from a network? The following tasks are some you might want your network to perform:

- Share printers, files, optical (Blu-ray, DVD, and CD) drives, music and videos

- Share an Internet connection

- Provide wireless Internet access to laptops and mobile devices

- Receive faxes directly in one computer and print or route them to individuals automatically

- Provide access to another network at another location

- Provide remote access so that you can reach your LAN from elsewhere, via a modem or via the Internet

- Host a website

- Operate a database server

- Play multiuser games

You should make a list of your networking goals. You need to provide adequate capacity to meet these and future needs, but you also don't need to overbuild.

Instant Networking

If your goal is simply to share printers, files, and maybe an Internet connection among just a few computers that are fairly close together, here's a recipe for instant networking. Get the following items at your local computer store, or at an online shop such as buy.com, compusa.com, or newegg.com. Big office supply and consumer electronics stores are also a good bet if a sale or rebate offer is available.

- One 10/100BASE-T Ethernet network adapter for each computer that doesn't already have network interface. These cost $5–$15 for internal PCI cards, and $10–$40 for PCMCIA or USB adapters. Get a "featured" or "sale price" internal PCI card for a desktop, or PC Card or USB adapter for a notebook. But, check before you buy: virtually all computers these days have an Ethernet or wireless adapter built-in.

- A Wireless-N router with a built-in four-port switch for $20–$90. I recommend using a wireless router even if you aren't setting up a shared Internet connection, and even if you don't yet have any devices that use wireless networking. However, if you're sure you won't ever want to use a wireless connection, you can instead buy a four- or eight-port "10/100 Ethernet Switch." You need one port for every computer you want to hook up.

- One CAT-5 patch cable for each computer that doesn't have a wireless adapter. You'll place the switch or router next to one of the computers, so you'll need one 4-foot cable. The other cables need to be long enough to reach from the other computers to the switch. These cables can be very inexpensive online, and tend to be overpriced in big-box stores.

When you have these parts, skip ahead to the "Installing Network Adapters" section, later in this chapter. If you get a wireless router, be *sure* to set up WPA2 wireless security, even if you aren't going to use the wireless part right away. We describe how to do that under "Setting Up a New Wireless Network" on page 395.

On the other hand, if you need access to large databases, want fast Internet connectivity, or require centralized backup of all workstations, you need to plan and invest more carefully. We discuss some of the issues you should consider in the next section.

Are You Being Served?

If you're planning a network of more than just a few computers, you need to make a big decision: whether or not to use Windows Server. The Server versions provide a raft of networking services that Windows 8 doesn't have, but you must learn how to configure and support them.

Table 18.1 lists the primary trade-offs between the regular desktop versions of Windows and Windows Server.

 note

When we talk about Windows Server here, we mean the *business* Server versions. There was a product called Windows Home Server, but it's meant just to let you back up files across the network.

Table 18.1 Primary Differences Between Desktop Versions of Windows and Windows Server

Desktop Windows	Windows Server
Allows file sharing connections for up to 20 other computers.	Unlimited connections, but there are client licensing fees.
Cost is low.	Requires an extra computer, a copy of Windows Server, and possibly additional fees for Client Access Licenses. The added costs will easily exceed $1,000. For example, a copy of Windows Server Foundation, which can serve 25 clients, costs about $425, and you have to buy a computer on which to run it.
Configuration is simple.	Complex to configure and administer.
Each computer must be administered separately (setting up user accounts, for instance).	Administration is centralized.
Managing file security can be difficult when you have more than one user per computer.	Centralized user management eases the task of managing file security.
Two levels of user security: "standard" and "administrator."	Extremely fine-grained control of what each user can and cannot do.
Only one signed-in user can work at a time.	Supports multiple simultaneous users via Remote Desktop and/or "Thin Client" devices, subject to client access license fees.
Fax modem can't be shared with other computers.	One fax modem and phone line can be shared by multiple computers.
Rudimentary remote access, connection sharing, and WAN support are provided.	These features are more sophisticated.

For me, manageability is the main issue. As you add more and more users, centralized management becomes more and more important. If you have a network of ten or more computers, we recommend using at least one copy of Windows Server.

You can certainly use Server with smaller networks, too. Reasons for doing so include these:

- You want join your network to a Server domain somewhere else. This is often the case in a business's branch office.

- You want to support multiple simultaneous remote dial-in, or virtual private network (VPN) users. (Alternatively, you could buy inexpensive VPN routers or software to handle this.)

- You want to exercise strict security controls, support multiple signed-in users on one computer, restrict your users' ability to change system settings, or use automatic application installation.

- You want to take advantage of advanced networking services such as Group Policy, DHCP, DNS, WINS, and so on.

If you decide you need or want Windows Server, you should get a book dedicated to that OS and a big box of Alka-Seltzer before you go any further.

When to Hire a Professional

You've probably heard this old adage: "If you want something done right, do it yourself!" It is true, to a point. Sometimes, though, the benefit of hiring someone else outweighs the pleasure of doing it yourself.

For a home network, you should definitely try to set it up yourself. Call it a learning experience, get friends to help, and, if you run into problems, a high-school-aged neighbor can probably get them straightened out in 15 minutes. As long as you don't have to run wires through the wall or construct your own cables, you should be able to manage this job even with no prior networking experience. When something is called "Plug and Play" now, it really is.

The balance tips the other way for a business. If you depend on your computers to get your work done, getting them set up should be your first concern, but keeping them working should be your second, third, and fourth. When your business is hanging in the balance, you should consider the cost of computer failure when you're deciding whether it's worth spending money on setup and installation. Hiring a good consultant and/or contractor will give you the following:

- An established relationship. If something goes wrong, you'll already know whom to call, and that person will already know the details of your system.

- A professional installation job.

- The benefit of full-time experience in network and system design without needing to pay a full-time salary.

- Documentation that describes how your network is set up.

- Time you can spend doing something more productive than installing a network.

If you do hire someone else to build your network, you should check out that person's references first, and stay involved in the process so that you understand the choices and decisions that are made.

Choosing a Network and Cabling System

For a simple home or small office network, you can choose among four types of network connections:

- **10/100BASE-T Ethernet over CAT-5 cables**—These cables look like telephone cables, with a fatter version of a telephone modular connector at each end. This networking scheme is dirt cheap and ultra-reliable.

- **802.11n or -g wireless networking**—Wireless (Wi-Fi) networking sends data over a radio signal, so no cabling is necessary. It's easy to set up, but it can't be used over long distances, and in some buildings the signal might not go as far or as fast as the advertising leads you to believe it will.

- **Phoneline or powerline networking**—You can purchase network adapters that send data signals between your electrical outlets, or between telephone jacks that are wired to the same phone extension. In most cases, though, you may be better off using wireless.

- **1000Mbps (Gigabit) Ethernet over CAT-5E cables**—These cables look like CAT-5 cables, but they are capable of carrying the higher-speed signals required by Gigabit Ethernet. The higher speed is great, but only worth the extra cost if you routinely back up hard disks or copy huge video files over your network, *and* if the devices you're copying to and from can keep up with gigabit speeds. (Many can't.) We talk more about this in the following sections. You'll often see Gigabit Ethernet referred to in computer specs as 10/100/1000Mbps.

For most homes and offices, a combination of 10/100 Ethernet and wireless is a winning combination, but any of these four options will provide perfectly adequate performance.

In the following sections, we go over each type in a little more detail. Then, we discuss additional network features you might want to consider, such as printing and Internet connectivity.

10/100BASE-T Ethernet

10/100BASE-T Ethernet networks use unshielded twisted-pair cabling (commonly called UTP or CAT-5 cable) run from each computer to a device called a switch or router, as shown in Figure 18.1.

note

You might have heard these connecting boxes called *hubs*. Hubs and switches do the same job of passing data between the network's computers, but hubs use an older technology. All "hubs" made in recent years are actually switches, so we'll use the term *switch* in this chapter.

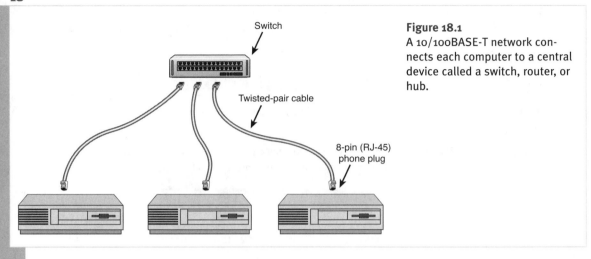

Switch

Twisted-pair cable

8-pin (RJ-45)
phone plug

Figure 18.1
A 10/100BASE-T network connects each computer to a central device called a switch, router, or hub.

tip

Most home routers, which are used to share a broadband Internet connection and to establish a wireless network, include a switch, and most people can base their network on one of these.

Whether or not you're going to set up a shared broadband Internet connection, we recommend that you buy a wireless Internet Connection Sharing router instead of a plain switch, just to get the wireless networking and DHCP services it provides (more on that later in the chapter). On sale, these routers can cost no more than a plain switch. I've even seen ads for $20 routers with a $20 mail-in rebate. See Chapter 19 for advice about hardware-connection-sharing devices.

The 10/100 part of the name means that the equipment can run at 100Mbps, but it can automatically slow down to 10Mbps if it's connected to older 10BASE-T equipment.

The cables look like telephone cables, and the connectors look like fat versions of telephone modular plugs, but it's a dangerous comparison, because the electrical properties of the cables and connectors are specifically tuned for networking, and ordinary telephone cabling *will not work*.

These networks require that you use cable designated "CAT-5" or better. They have labels on the wire that state this clearly. CAT-5, CAT-5E, and CAT-6 are all fine. You can buy premade network cables in lengths of 3–50 feet, or you can buy bulk cable and attach the connectors yourself. We discuss this more in the "Installing Network Wiring" section, later in this chapter. All cable connectors and data wall jacks have to be CAT-5 certified as well.

A cable is run from each computer to a switch, which routes the signals between each computer. You need to get a switch that has at least as many ports (sockets) as you have computers, plus a spare or two. 10/100BASE-T switches cost roughly $5–$10 per port.

tip

Multiple switches can be connected if your network grows beyond the capacity of your first switch. Therefore, you can add on instead of entirely replacing your original equipment.

No 10/100 Base-T cable can be more than 100 meters (328 feet) in length. To extend farther than that, you have to add an additional switch in the middle of a longer cable run, or use fiber optic cabling.

10/100BASE-T network interface cards (NICs) are available for as little as $5 each (if you catch a sale) and are made by dozens of companies. Most generic-brand, cheap-o NICs are based on one of a handful of standard circuit chips, so they'll usually work just fine, even if they're not listed in the Windows Compatibility Center at www.microsoft.com/windows/compatibility.

Overall, 10/100BASE-T networking is as inexpensive as it gets—hooking up three computers will set you back between $20 and $75. It's easy to set up, and it's very reliable. On the down side, though, you do need to run those wires around.

802.11n and 802.11g Wireless (Wi-Fi) Networking

One way to build a network without switches, cables, connectors, drills, swearing, tools, or outside contractors is to go wireless. Blocks of radio frequencies in the 2.4GHz and 5GHz bands are reserved for close-range data communications, and standardized products from cordless telephones to computer networking devices take advantage of this. Prices have fallen to the point that wireless connectivity is competitive with wired networks, even before the installation cost savings are factored in.

There are two common types of wireless equipment, titled 802.11g (or *Wireless-G*) and 802.11n (or *Wireless-N*) after the industry standard documents on which they're based.

802.11g equipment operates at up to 54Mbps and is compatible with older 802.11b (11Mbps) equipment. Some manufacturers offer Wireless-G equipment that operates at up to 108Mbps, but you get this speed boost only if you buy all your equipment from the same manufacturer (and even then, you need to read the packaging carefully to see if the double-speed function will work with the particular parts you're buying). Wireless-G can transmit data about 100 feet indoors and up to 300 feet outdoors—at most. And at these longer distances, lower signal strengths will result in data errors, so the equipment will switch down to lower data speeds.

The newer standard for wireless networking is 802.11n (Wireless-N). It offers higher speeds—up to 150Mbps—and greater range than Wireless-G. Here's the skinny on Wireless-N:

> **note**
>
> Add-on adapters come in three styles: internal PCI cards for desktop computers; external adapters that you connect to a USB socket; and thin, credit-card-sized PCMCIA (PC Card) adapters for laptops. You may not need to add one, though, because most modern computers already have a 10/100 or 10/100/1000 Ethernet adapter built in, with a socket on the back of the computer box.

> **tip**
>
> If your network is small and/or temporary, you can run network cables along walls and desks. Otherwise, you probably should keep them out of the way and protect them from accidental damage by installing them within the walls of your home or office. If you use in-wall wiring, the work should be done by someone with professional-level skills.

> **note**
>
> Some additional terminology: *Wi-Fi* is an industry term that doesn't mean anything in particular, but it's kind of catchy. It's used to refer to any variant of 802.11 wireless networking. Wireless local area networks are often called *WLANs*.

- Wireless-N, -G and -B equipment is compatible, and can be used together on the same network. That is, a -G network adapter in a computer can talk with a -N router, and vice versa. However, they'll communicate with each other at the lower -G speed. Older -B equipment can be used, too, but again, at the lower -B speed.

- Furthermore, having -G or -B equipment on the network can drag down the speed as much as 25%, even for -N devices talking to -N, if the older devices are transmitting at the same time.

- Wireless-N signals should travel about twice as far as Wireless-G: about 200 feet indoors, and about 600 feet outdoors. However, this applies only when an -N device is talking to another -N device. Getting a Wireless-N router won't improve reception for a distant Wireless-G or -B device.

- Wireless-N can operate in the 2.4GHz frequency band and the 5GHz band. Only "dual-radio" routers can operate at both frequencies at once, however. Single-radio routers have to switch back and forth, slowing performance if both frequencies are used at the same time. The 5GHz band tends to work better than 2.4GHz at shorter distances. At 5GHz, the signal can't travel as far, but there tends to be less interference from neighboring networks, cordless phones, and so on.

Whichever version you use, Wi-Fi networking products typically have the following features:

- An actual throughput up to about half the advertised speed.

- Available for both desktop and laptop computers, in PCI, PCMCIA (PC Card), and USB formats.

- A cost of $25–$70 per adapter.

- The ability to be bridged to a wired LAN through a device called an access point, router, bridge, or base unit, costing $20 and up. (That's not a typo: $20, if you catch a good sale. $40 to $150 is more typical without a sale.)

- Usually don't work well between floors of a multistory building.

Figure 18.2 shows a typical family of wireless products: a wireless access point (Ethernet bridge), a wireless router that can also share a DSL or Internet connection, an internal wireless network adapter for desktop computers, and a PCMCIA adapter for laptops.

Phoneline and Powerline Networking

HomePNA Alliance devices send network data by transmitting radio signals over your existing telephone wiring, using a network adapter that plugs in to a telephone jack (see Figure 18.3). These devices don't interfere with the normal operation of your telephones; the extra signal just hitchhikes along the wires.

Figure 18.2
Typical wireless networking equipment. Clockwise from upper left: access point, router with Internet Connection Sharing capability, PCI adapter, PCMCIA adapter. (Photo used by permission of D-Link.)

Figure 18.3
Phoneline networking uses existing household telephone wiring to carry a radio frequency signal between networked computers.

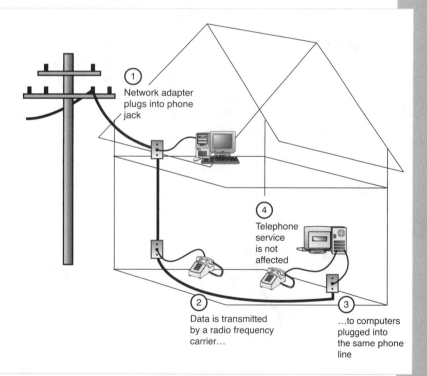

① Network adapter plugs into phone jack

④ Telephone service is not affected

② Data is transmitted by a radio frequency carrier…

③ …to computers plugged into the same phone line

Phoneline networking is intended primarily for home use. The products are relatively inexpensive—about $50 per computer—and don't require you to string cables around the house. They're very convenient, and their signal will usually go much farther than a wireless networking signal. However, they have some disadvantages:

- All your adapters must be plugged into the same telephone line. Therefore, the same extension must be present at a phone outlet near each of your computers. If you need to call in a wiring contractor to add a phone extension, you haven't saved much over a regular wired network.

- "Access point" devices, used to link a standard wired-networked computer to your phoneline or powerline network, are relatively rare.

- 10Mbps is fine for sharing an Internet connection or printers, but you'll find that it's too slow to back up a chock-full hard disk over your network—it could take days!

> **tip**
>
> If you use phoneline networking, be certain to get only HomePNA 2.0–compatible adapters or better. This will ensure that your equipment operates at least at 10Mbps and will work with other manufacturers' products.

Without a hardware access point, it's difficult to use a hardware Internet Connection Sharing device or to add standard wired computers to your network. However, Windows 8 can manage it in software, if necessary. We discuss this later in this chapter under "Bridging Two Network Types."

HomePlug (HomePlug Powerline Alliance) adapters work in a similar fashion, sending signals through your electrical wiring, and are plugged into a wall socket. These also provide 10Mbps performance, and they are more flexible than the phoneline system because you don't need a phone jack near your computers—just a nearby electrical outlet. Powerline networking can't cross the utility company's transformers, so it usually works only within a single home or office.

In addition, you can get HomePlug devices called *bridges*, which are specifically designed to link a wired network to the powerline network, for about $80. You can use one of these to easily add a shared Internet Connection Sharing router or mix in wired computers. Figure 18.4 shows how this would look in a typical home network.

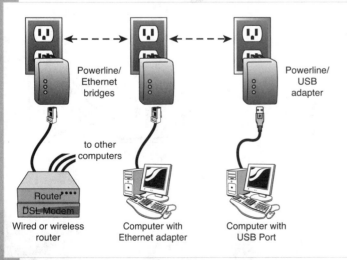

Figure 18.4
Typical powerline networking setup, showing HomePlug adapters and bridges.

Powerline/Ethernet bridges

Powerline/USB adapter

to other computers

Router

DSL Modem

Wired or wireless router

Computer with Ethernet adapter

Computer with USB Port

1000Mbps Ethernet (Gigabit Ethernet)

Ultra-high-speed Gigabit Ethernet networking is probably overkill for most home and small office networks, but it's sometimes found in the corporate world and in fields such as medical imaging and video editing. Gigabit speed can also help if you back up your hard disk over your network from one computer to another, or copy large video files. The adapter cost is so low that many new PCs and all Macs now come with 10/100/1000Mbps Ethernet adapters built in as standard equipment.

It sounds great at first, but here are some things to consider:

- It won't speed up your Internet connection (unless, perhaps, you have Fiber-to-the-Home service), and it won't improve the streaming of HD video within your home. Standard 100Mbps Ethernet will do just fine for these applications.

- You will only realize a speed benefit when a large amount of data is moving between two devices that both have gigabit connections *and* when both can actually feed data to the network at a high speed.

- If you have to buy a Gigabit Ethernet adapter for a computer (that is, if the adapter built into the computer's motherboard is only 10/100Mbps), it only makes sense to go gigabit if you can install a PCI-e adapter. Regular PCI cards can't move data to and from the CPU fast enough to make gigabit worthwhile.

- Most consumer/small office network-attached storage (disk) devices are way too slow internally to benefit from gigabit connections. You *should* see a benefit when backing up to or copying files to or from another Windows computer's shared drive.

If you want to use Gigabit Ethernet, you need to use CAT-5E or CAT-6 certified connectors and cabling; CAT-5 gear *might* work (and then only if all four wire pairs inside the cable are connected on all of your cables), but don't chance it. You should use only commercially manufactured patch cables or professionally installed wiring.

> **🔍 note**
>
> Most wireless cable/DSL-sharing routers have built-in switches that run at only 10 or 100Mbps. If you use a connection-sharing router, plug your computers into a gigabit (10/100/1000Mbps) switch using CAT-6 cables and then connect the switch's "cascade" port to your cable/DSL-sharing router. Otherwise, your computers will only talk at 100Mbps maximum.

Mixed Networking

If you are updating an existing network or are connecting two separate types of networks, you should consider several things.

If you have some existing 10Mbps-only devices and want to add new 100Mbps devices without upgrading the old, you can buy a new dual-speed (10/100) switch, which connects to each computer at the maximum speed its adapter permits. Read the specifications carefully. You want a switch that's labeled "N-way autosensing." Be sure to use CAT-5 certified cables to connect to the 100Mbps devices.

Additional Networking Functions

Besides sharing files between computers, you can do several other things with a network. In the next few sections, we outline some additional features you might want to include in your network.

Printing and Faxing

You can share with the network any printer connected to a Windows computer with a standard USB or parallel printer cable. Other computers can then reach the printer through the network, as long as the host computer is turned on. However, if you need to put a printer farther than about 10 feet away from a networked computer, beyond the reach of a standard printer cable, you have three choices:

- Get a really long cable and take your chances. The electrical signal for a USB or parallel printer connection is not supposed to be extended more then 10 feet (but I've gotten away with 25 feet in the past). Buy a high-quality shielded cable. You might get data errors (bad printed characters) with this approach.

- Alternatively, you can buy a "print server" module, which connects to the printer on one side and to a network cable on the other, for about $40. Network supply catalogs list myriad such devices. Some of the newer DSL/cable-sharing routers and wireless access points have a print server built in.

- Use a network-capable printer and connect it directly to your network. Some printers have Ethernet or wireless networking capability built in. For some printers, you can buy an add-on network printer module.

The latter two approaches are very nice because any computer can "talk" directly to the printer. It doesn't require you to leave one computer turned on all the time. With standard printer sharing, the computer that "owns" the printer must be turned on in order for other computers to use the printer.

If several people on your network need to send or receive faxes, you might want to set up a network-based faxing system. Unfortunately, Windows 8 does not let you share your fax modem with other users on your network, as Windows Server does. If you want to share a single fax line with several users on your network, you have to use a third-party solution. The easiest approach is to use a "network-ready" all-in-one printer/scanner/fax unit. If you shop for one of these, be sure that its faxing features are network compatible.

Third-party software products are available that can give network users shared access to a fax modem. The former gold standard product was Symantec's WinFax Pro, but it has been discontinued, and most of the products still on the market seem to be oriented toward large corporations. For a small office network, you might consider products such as Snappy Fax Network Server from www.snappysoftware.com or ActFax from www.actfax.com.

> **🔍 note**
>
> I have an all-in-one laser printer/scanner/fax/copier, and anyone on the network can use it to print, send faxes, or scan documents. I love that part, and I got a great deal on it, but its manual paper feed is terrible. Lesson learned: read reviews before you buy!

Providing Internet Connectivity

One of the best reasons for having a network is to share high-speed Internet service. It's far less expensive, and far safer security-wise, to have one connection to the Internet for the entire LAN than to let each user fend for himself or herself. In fact, many DSL and cable Internet providers now supply preconfigured routers when you start your service—if that's the case for you, you may only need to configure your computers to use the shared connection, as we'll discuss later in this chapter under "Configuring a Peer-to-Peer Network."

Windows 8 has a built-in Internet Connection Sharing feature that lets a single computer use a dial-up, cable, or DSL modem and make the connection on behalf of any user on your LAN. You can also use an inexpensive hardware device called a *router* to make the connection. I strongly prefer the hardware devices over Windows Internet Connection Sharing. This topic is important enough that it gets its own chapter. If you want to share an Internet connection on your network, you should read Chapter 19 before you buy any equipment.

You should also study Chapter 33, "Protecting Your Network from Hackers and Snoops," and pay close attention to the section titled "Network Security Basics" to build in proper safeguards against hacking and abuse. This is especially important with full-time cable/DSL connections.

Providing Remote Access

You also can provide connectivity to your network from the outside world, either through the Internet or via a modem. This connectivity enables you to access your LAN resources from home or out in the field, with full assurance that your network is safe from outside attacks. Chapter 37, "Computing on the Road," covers dial-up and VPN network access, and Chapter 39, "Remote Desktop and Remote Access," covers Remote Desktop.

If you need to access your network from outside and you aren't planning to have a permanent direct Internet connection, you might want to plan for the installation of a telephone line near one of your Windows 8 computers so that you can set up a dedicated modem line for incoming access.

Connecting to a Remote Network

You can tie your network to a network in another location so that you and the other network's users can share files and printers as if you were all in the same room. Windows Server has many features to support this, but you can also do it with smaller networks without Windows Server. There are two straightforward ways to do this: by getting routers that have built-in Virtual Private Networking (VPN) support and by using a software service. For a hardware approach, Linksys, Asus, Trendnet, and other manufacturers sell inexpensive routers with VPN capability. The router in one office is set up as the VPN "host" or server, and the routers in other offices are set up to connect to that. This ties the separate networks together. For a software solution, check out the Hamachi product from logmein.com. You can tie individual computers into a VPN, or you can set up one computer on each network to act as a "gateway."

Installing Network Adapters

If you're installing a new network adapter in your computer, follow the manufacturer's instructions for installing the product for Windows 8. If there are instructions for Windows 7 or Vista, but not Windows 8, those instructions should work. And if there are no instructions at all, just follow these steps:

1. If you have purchased an internal card, shut down Windows, shut off the computer, unplug it, open the case, and install the card in an empty slot. Close the case and then restart Windows.

   If you are adding a PCMCIA or USB adapter, be sure you're logged on with a Computer Administrator account, plug it in while Windows is running, and skip ahead to step 3.

    tip

   If you've never worked inside your computer, jump ahead to Chapter 28, "Managing Your Hardware," for advice and handy tips.

2. When you're back at the Windows login screen, log in using a Computer Administrator account. Windows displays the New Hardware Detected dialog box when you log in.

3. In most cases, Windows should already have the software it needs to run your network adapter. If Windows cannot find a suitable driver for your adapter, it might ask you to insert the driver CD-ROM that your network card's manufacturer should have provided. It may also offer to get a driver from Windows Update. If you have an Internet connection up at this time, this online option is very useful.

   If you are asked, insert the requested disk and click OK. In the unlikely event that Windows says that it cannot locate an appropriate device driver, try again, but this time click the Browse button. Locate a folder named Windows 8, Windows 7, or Windows Vista (or some reasonable approximation) and click OK. If both 32-bit and 64-bit folders are listed, be sure to choose the version that matches your version of Windows.

   note

   The exact name of the folders containing device drivers varies from vendor to vendor. You might have to poke around a little on the disk to find the right folder.

4. After Windows has installed the card's driver software, it automatically configures and uses the card. Check the Device Manager, as described in the next section, to see whether the card is installed and functioning. Then you can proceed to "Installing Network Wiring," later in this chapter.

➡ *For more-detailed instructions about installing drivers,* ***see*** *Chapter 28.*

Checking Existing Adapters

If your adapter was already installed when you set up Windows 8, it should be ready to go. Follow these steps to see whether the adapter is already set up:

1. Right-click the very bottom-left corner of the screen and select Device Manager. Expand the Network Adapters section by clicking the triangular arrow icon to the left of its name.

2. Look for an entry for your network card. If it appears and does not have a yellow exclamation point (!) icon to the left of its name, the card is installed and correctly configured. In this case, you can skip ahead to "Installing Network Wiring."

   If an entry appears but has a yellow exclamation point icon by its name, the card is not correctly configured.

3. If no entry exists for the card, the adapter is not fully plugged into the motherboard, it's damaged, or it is not Plug and Play capable. Be sure the card is installed correctly. If you can't get it to appear, replace it.

> **🔍 note**
>
> If you see an exclamation point icon in the Network Adapters list, skip ahead to Chapter 26, "Troubleshooting and Repairing Problems," for tips on getting the card to work before you proceed. Here's a tip: network adapters are really inexpensive, so if you're having trouble with an old adapter, just go get a new one.

Installing Multiple Network Adapters

You might want to install multiple network adapters in your computer in the following situations:

- You simultaneously connect to two or more different networks with different IP addresses or protocols. You'd use a separate adapter to connect to each network.

- You want to share a broadband cable or DSL Internet connection with your LAN without using a hardware-sharing router. We strongly recommend using a hardware router, as we discuss in Chapter 20, but you can also do this using one adapter to connect to your LAN and another to connect to your cable or DSL modem.

- You have two different network types, such as phoneline and Ethernet, and you want the computers on both LAN types to be able to communicate. You could use a hardware bridge or access point, but you could also install both types of adapters in one of your computers and use the Bridging feature to connect the networks. We discuss bridging later in this chapter.

We suggest you use the following procedure to install multiple adapters:

1. Install, configure, and test the first adapter. (If you're doing this to share an Internet connection, install and configure the one you'll use for the Internet connection first. Be sure you can connect to the Internet before you proceed.)

2. On the Start screen, right-click the very bottom-left corner and select Control Panel. Select Network and Internet, Network and Sharing Center. Click Change Adapter Settings on the left side of the window. Select the icon for the network adapter—it will likely be named Ethernet—and choose Rename This Connection in the ribbon bar. (Or right-click the icon and select Rename.) Change the connection's name to something that indicates what it's used for, such as "Connection to Cable Modem" or "Office Ethernet Network."

3. Write the name on a piece of tape or a sticky label and apply it to the back of your computer above the network adapter or to the edge plate of the network card.

4. Install the second adapter. Configure it and repeat steps 2 and 3 with the new connection icon. Rename this connection appropriately—for example, "LAN" or "Wireless Net"—and label the adapter socket.

If you follow these steps, you'll be able to easily distinguish the two connections instead of needing to remember which connection icon is which.

Installing Network Wiring

When your network adapters are installed, the next step is to get your computers connected. Installing wiring can be the most difficult task of setting up a network. How you proceed depends on the type of networking adapters you have:

- If you're using wireless adapters, of course, you don't need to worry about wiring. Lucky you. You can just skip ahead to "Installing a Wireless Network," later in this chapter.

- If you're using phoneline networking, plug a standard modular telephone cable into each phone-line network adapter and connect them to the appropriate wall jacks. The adapter must be plugged directly into the wall jack, and then additional devices such as modems, telephones, and answering machines can be connected to the adapter. Remember that each of the phone jacks must be wired to the same telephone line. Then skip ahead to the "Configuring a Peer-to-Peer Network" section, later in the chapter.

- If you're using a powerline networking adapter, follow the manufacturer's installation instructions. If you're using a powerline bridge, plug the bridge into a wall socket and connect it to your computer or other networked device with a CAT-5 patch cable. Follow the manufacturer's instructions for configuring the adapter's security features. You should enable encryption if it's available. Then skip ahead to the "Configuring a Peer-to-Peer Network" section, later in the chapter.

If you're using wired Ethernet adapters, you need to decide how to route your wiring and what type of cables to use. The remainder of this section discusses Ethernet wiring.

Cabling for Ethernet Networks

If your computers are close together, you can use prebuilt patch cables to connect your computers to a switch or router. (The term *patch cable* originated in the telephone industry—in the old days, switchboard operators used patch cables to connect, or "patch," one phone circuit to another.) You can run these cables through the habitable area of your home or office by routing them behind furniture, around partitions, and so on. Just don't put them where they'll be crushed, walked on, tripped over, run over by desk chair wheels, or chewed by pets.

> **tip**
>
> As you install each network card and plug in the cables, you should see a green light turn on at the switch or router, and at the network adapter. These lights indicate that the network wiring is correct.

If the cables need to run through walls or stretch long distances, you should consider having them installed inside the walls with plug-in jacks, just like your telephone wiring. We discuss this topic later in this section. Hardware stores sell special cable covers that you can use if you need to run a cable where it's exposed to foot traffic, as well as covers for wires that need to run up walls or over doorways.

Switch Lights Do Not Come On

If one or more UTP switch link lights do not come on when the associated computers are connected, the problem lies in one of the cables between the computer and the switch. Which one
is it? To find out, do the following:

1. Move the computer right next to the switch. You can leave the keyboard, mouse, and monitor behind. Just plug in the computer, turn it on, and use a commercially manufactured
   or known-to-be-working patch cable to connect the computer to the switch. If the light
   doesn't come on regardless of which switch connection socket you use, you probably have
   a bad network card.

2. If you were using any patch cables when you first tried to get the computer connected, test
   them using the same computer and switch socket. This trick might identify a bad cable.

3. If the LAN card, switch, and patch cables are all working, the problem is in whatever is
   left, which would be your in-wall wiring. Check the connectors for proper crimping and
   check that the wire pairs are correctly wired end to end. You might need to use a cable
   analyzer if you can't spot the problem by eye. These devices cost about $75. You connect
   a "transmitter" box to one end of your cabling, and a "receiver" to the other. The receiver
   has four LEDs that blink in a 1-2-3-4 sequence if your wiring is correct.

General Cabling Tips

You can determine how much cable you need by measuring
the distance between computers and your switch location(s).
Remember to account for vertical distances, too, where cables run
from the floor up to a desktop, or go up and over a partition or wall.

Keep in mind the following points:

- We refer to "CAT-5" here, but if you're using 1000Mbps
  Ethernet, you must use CAT-5E or CAT-6 cable and connectors.

- Existing household telephone wire probably won't work. If the
  wires inside the cable jacket are red, green, black, and yellow:
  no way. The jacket must have CAT-5 (or higher) printed on it. It
  must have color-matched twisted pairs of wires; usually each
  pair has one wire in a solid color and the other white with colored stripes.

- You must use CAT-5-quality wiring and components throughout,
  and not just the cables. Any jacks, plugs, connectors, terminal blocks, patch cables, and so on
  also must be CAT-5 certified.

> **caution**
>
> If you need to run cables through
> the ceiling space of an office
> building, you should check with
> your building management to
> see whether the ceiling is listed
> as a plenum or air-conditioning
> air return. You might be required
> by law to use certified plenum
> cable and follow all applicable
> electrical codes. Plenum cable
> is formulated not to emit toxic
> smoke in a fire.

- If you're installing in-wall wiring, follow professional CAT-5 wiring practices throughout. Be sure not to untwist more than half an inch of any pair of wires when attaching cables to connectors. Don't solder or splice the wires.

- When you're installing cables, be gentle. Don't pull, kink, or stretch them. Don't bend them sharply around corners; you should allow at least a 1-inch radius for bends. To attach cables to a wall or baseboard, use only special cable staples or rigid cable clips that don't squeeze the cable, as shown in Figure 18.5. Your local electronics store or hardware store can sell you the right kind of clips.

note

If you really want to get into the nuts and bolts, so to speak, of pulling your own cable, a good starting point is Frank Derfler and Les Freed's *Practical Network Cabling* (Que, 1999; ISBN 078972247X).

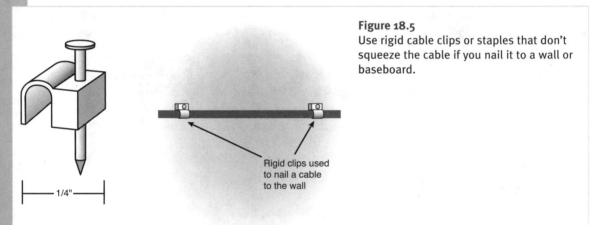

Figure 18.5
Use rigid cable clips or staples that don't squeeze the cable if you nail it to a wall or baseboard.

Rigid clips used to nail a cable to the wall

1/4"

- Keep network cables away from AC power wiring and away from electrically noisy devices such as arc welders, diathermy machines, and the like. (I've never actually seen a diathermy machine, but I hear they're trouble.)

Wiring with Patch Cables

If your computers are close together and you can simply run prefabricated cables between your computers and switch, you've got it made. Buy CAT-5 (or better) cables of the appropriate length online or at your local computer store. Just plug (click) them in, and you're finished. Figure 18.1 shows how to connect your computers to the switch.

If you have the desire and patience, you can build custom-length cables from crimp-on connectors and bulk cable stock. Making your own cables requires about $75 worth of tools, though, and more detailed instructions than we can give here. Making just a few cables probably doesn't make buying the tools worthwhile. Factory-assembled cables are also more reliable than homemade ones because the connectors are attached by machine. They're worth the extra few dollars.

For the ambitious or parsimonious reader, Figure 18.6 shows the correct way to order the wires in the connector.

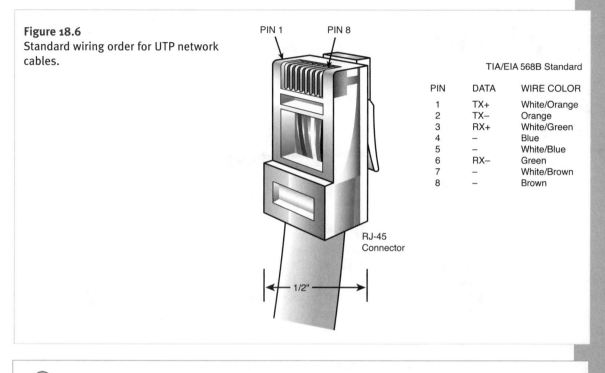

Figure 18.6
Standard wiring order for UTP network cables.

PIN 1   PIN 8

TIA/EIA 568B Standard

PIN	DATA	WIRE COLOR
1	TX+	White/Orange
2	TX–	Orange
3	RX+	White/Green
4	–	Blue
5	–	White/Blue
6	RX–	Green
7	–	White/Brown
8	–	Brown

RJ-45
Connector

1/2"

🔍 note

The modular plugs used in Ethernet networking are often called *RJ-45 connectors*. To pick a technical nit here, the connector used in networking is really called an *8P8C connector*. The "true telephone RJ-45" connector is slightly different, and not compatible. If you're buying RJ-45 connectors, just make sure that the package says that they're for networking use.

Installing In-Wall Wiring

In-wall wiring is the most professional and permanent way to go. However, this often involves climbing around in the attic or under a building, drilling through walls, or working in an office telephone closet. Hiring someone to get the job done might cost $30–$75 per computer, but you'll get a professional job.

In-wall wiring is brought out to network-style modular jacks mounted to the baseboard of your wall. These RJ-45 jacks look similar to telephone modular jacks, but are wider. You need patch cables to connect the jacks to your computers and switch, as shown in Figure 18.7.

〰️ tip

Look in the Yellow Pages under "Telephone Wiring," and ask the contractors you call whether they have experience with network wiring.

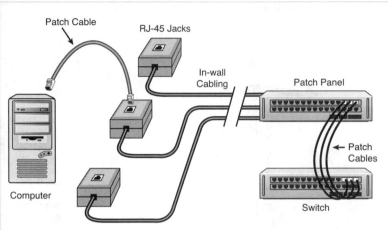

Figure 18.7
Connect your computers and switch to the network jacks using short patch cables.

Connecting Just Two Computers

If you're making a network of just two computers (say, to copy files from an old to a new computer), you might be able to take a shortcut and eliminate the need for a network switch or additional special hardware. If you want to add on to your network later, you can always add the extra gear then.

If you are connecting two computers, simply run a special cable called an *Ethernet crossover cable* from one computer's network adapter to the other, and you're finished. This special type of cable reverses the send and receive signals between the two ends and eliminates the need for a switch. You can purchase an Ethernet crossover cable from a computer store or network supply shop, or you can make one, as shown in Figure 18.8.

> 🔍 **note**
> Microsoft is encouraging the use of a special USB cable for use by the Windows Easy Transfer program, for people who don't have a network. However, you can just as easily (and much less expensively) use an Ethernet crossover cable.

> 〰️ **tip**
> Be sure that your crossover cable is labeled as such. It won't work to connect a computer to a switch, and you'll go nuts wondering what's wrong if you try. Factory-made models usually have yellow ends. (When I make them myself, I draw three rings around each end of the cable with a permanent-ink marker.)
>
> If you have a cable that you're not sure about, look at the colors on the little wires inside the clear plastic connectors at the two ends. Considering just the colors on the wires, without regard to whether the colors are solid or striped:
>
> - If you can see that each color is in the exact same position at both ends of the cable, in the arrangement "AABCCBDD," you have a standard Ethernet patch cable.
>
> - If a pair of wires that is together at one end of the cable is split apart at the other end (that is, if one end has the pattern AABCCBDD and the other has BBACCADD), you have an Ethernet crossover cable.
>
> - If the pairs of wire are arranged symmetrically around the center of the connector (that is, if the pattern is ABCDDCBA), the cable is a telephone cable and *not* an Ethernet cable. You can't use this type of cable for networking.

Figure 18.8
Wiring for a UTP crossover cable. The cable reverses the send and receive wires so that two network cards can be directly connected without a switch. Note that the green pair and orange pair are reversed across the cable.

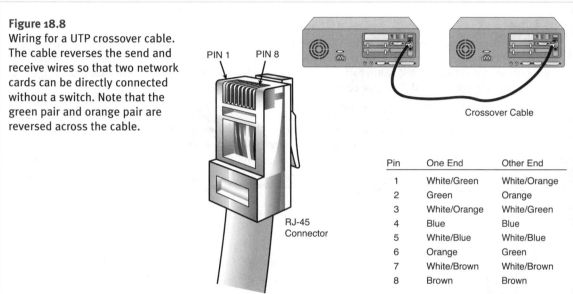

Pin	One End	Other End
1	White/Green	White/Orange
2	Green	Orange
3	White/Orange	White/Green
4	Blue	Blue
5	White/Blue	White/Blue
6	Orange	Green
7	White/Brown	White/Brown
8	Brown	Brown

Connecting Multiple Switches

You might want to use more than one switch to reduce the number of long network cables you need if you have groups of computers in two or more locations. For example, you can connect the computers on each "end" of the network to the nearest switch, and then connect the switch to a main switch. Figure 18.9 shows a typical arrangement using this technique.

Figure 18.9
You can connect groups of computers with multiple switches to reduce the number of long cables needed. Use the cascade port on the remote switches to connect to the central switch.

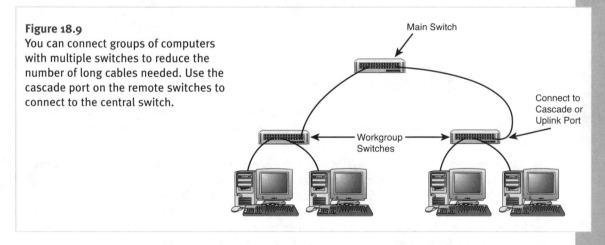

> ### 🔍 note
>
> A switch's *uplink* or *cascade* port is a connector designed to be connected to another switch or hub. Some switches have a separate connector for this purpose, whereas others make one of their regular ports do double-duty by providing a pushbutton that turns the last switch port into a cascade port. Still others handle this automatically. Refer to your switch's manual to see what to do with your particular hardware.

If you need to add a computer to your LAN and your switch has no unused connectors, you don't need to replace the switch. You can just add a switch. To add a computer to a fully loaded switch, unplug one cable from the original switch to free up a port. Connect this cable and your new computer to the new switch. Finally, connect the new switch's cascade port to the now-free port on the original switch, as shown in Figure 18.10.

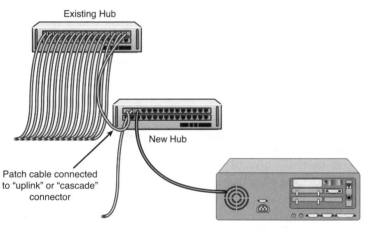

Figure 18.10
You can expand your network by cascading switches. The instructions included with your switch describe how to connect two switches using a patch cable. Some switches have a dedicated uplink port, whereas others have a pushbutton that turns a regular port into an uplink port.

Installing a Wireless Network

If you are using a wireless router, you need to configure wireless security and networking options after installing your network adapters. You need to do this even if you are just using it for its wired Ethernet connections, and don't plan on using its wireless capability.

You really do have to worry about wireless network security. In my home, I can pick up signals from four separate wireless networks: mine, the house next door's, and two others (I can't tell whose they are). It's not uncommon to find that you can receive signals from several neighbors. And people do actually drive around with laptops in their car, looking for free Internet access. To protect against both freeloaders and hackers, one or two protection techniques are used: *encryption*, which scrambles data, and *authentication*, which certifies that a given computer should be allowed to connect to the network. You can use either encryption alone, or both encryption and authentication.

Wireless Network Setup Choices

To be able to distinguish your network's signal from others and to secure your network, you will be asked to make the following choices when you set up a wireless network:

- **An SSID (Service Set Identifier)**—A short name that you give your network, up to 32 characters in length. This could be your last name, your company name, your pet's name, or whatever makes sense to you.

- **A security type**—The authentication method that your network uses to determine whether or not a given computer should be allowed to connect. For home and small office use, the choices are as follows, in order of increasing security:

  - **No Authentication (open)**—No authentication is performed; any computer can connect to the network.

  - **WPA-Personal**—A method that uses a passphrase to validate each computer's membership in the network. The passphrase also serves as an encryption key. Like WEP, it has been found to be insecure. Don't use it unless your wireless router can't use WPA2 and its software can't be upgraded

  - **WPA2-Personal**—An improved version of WPA-Personal. This is the best choice for home and small office networks.

On corporate networks, other security types are sometimes used: 802.1X, WPA-Enterprise, and WPA2-Enterprise. These systems use a network server, smart card, or software certificate to validate network membership.

- **An encryption type**—The encryption method used to secure network data against eavesdropping. The options available depend on the security (authentication) type selected. The choices, in increasing order of security, are as follows:

  - **None**—No data encryption is performed. This option is available only when the security type is set to No Authentication.

  - **WEP**—Data is encrypted using the WEP protocol, using a 40-, 128-, or 256-bit key. WEP encryption can easily be broken by a hacker.

  - **TKIP**—An encryption method that can be used with any of the WPA security types. A better choice is, however, is AES.

  - **AES**—An improved encryption method that can be used with any of the WPA security types. AES is more secure and may offer faster network transmission. This is the best choice for home and small office networks.

- **An encryption key**—The key used to encrypt and decrypt data sent over the network. The different encryption methods use keys of different lengths. Longer (more bits) is better.

- For WEP encryption, Windows 8 supports 40-bit and 128-bit security. A 128-bit WEP key must be exactly 26 hexadecimal digits—that is, the numerals 0 through 9 and the letters A through F. It could look something like this: `5e534e503d4e214d7b6758284c`. You can Google "Random WEP Key Generator" if you want help coming up with one.

  A 40-bit key consists of exactly ten hexadecimal digits. Windows 8 will let you join an existing 40-bit WEP network but not create a new one.

  Some routers and some earlier versions of Windows let you enter a WEP key as a text phrase, but the text method was not standardized, and was pretty much guaranteed not to work across brands of wireless routers and access points, so it has been abandoned.

- For WPA or WPA encryption, enter a passphrase: a word or phrase using any letters or characters, of eight or more letters—the more the better, up to 63. The passphrase is case sensitive and can contain spaces, but must not begin or end with a space. You might use two random words separated by punctuation symbols (for example, something like "topiary#clownlike").

- The encryption key should be kept secret because, with it, someone can connect to your network, and from there get to your data and your shared files. (I usually write it on a sticky note that I put on the bottom side of the router.)

- **A channel number**—The channel number selects the frequency used to transmit your network's data. The channels used in North America are usually 1, 6, and 11. The other channels overlap these and can interfere with each other. For double-bandwidth Wireless-N, the choices are 3 and 11. The preferred channel numbers are different in other countries.

  Some wireless routers select a channel automatically. If you have to choose one, see the tips under "Getting Maximum Wireless Speed," later in this chapter.

Why are there so many different security methods? Because thieves, like rust, never sleep, and it seems that as soon as a new, safer method is standardized, someone figures out a way to break it. WEP stands for Wired-Equivalent Privacy, but that turned out to be a bit too optimistic—a determined person can break WEP security in as little as a minute. WPA (which stands for Wi-Fi Protected Access) uses an improved encrypting scheme, and can deter most attacks, but it, too, turns out to be crackable. WPA2 is a further improvement upon that, and it's the best option we have at present. It should deter even the most determined hacker (although I suspect that it wouldn't keep the National Security Agency scratching its collective head for too long, if you know what I mean).

Finally, one more bit of nomenclature: If you have a router or access point, you are setting up what is called an *infrastructure network*. Windows 8 has a wizard to help you choose the correct settings. We'll go through this in the next section.

> **note**
>
> If you don't use a router, but just want to create a wireless network between two or more computers, you are creating an *ad hoc* network. We focus on infrastructure networks in this chapter because using a router makes it easier to network with wired-in computers and also to share an Internet connection. The news isn't good; the capability to easily create them was removed from Windows 8. We talk about this in Chapter 36 under "Ad Hoc Networks and Meetings."

Which methods should you use to set up your network? On a home or small office network, you're limited by the least capable of the devices on your network—your weakest link. So, use the strongest encryption method and the longest key that is supported by *all* of the devices and computers on your network. This means that if you have even one computer that doesn't support WPA, you need to use WEP, and if you have even one computer that doesn't support 256-bit keys, you have to use a 128-bit key. If you have a router, access point, or network adapter that doesn't support WPA, it's worth checking to see if you can update its internal software (firmware) or drivers to support this stronger encryption method.

> **🔍 note**
>
> Windows 8, 7, Vista, and XP with Service Pack 3 all have built-in support for WPA2. If your router doesn't support WPA2 or WPA, you might be able to install updated firmware to get it. If that's not possible, a new wireless router shouldn't set you back more than $40 to $90.

Setting Up a New Wireless Network

If you're setting up a new wireless network using a wireless router or access point, the hardest part of the job is setting up security and Internet access settings in the router itself. There are three ways to configure a new router:

- Using a setup program provided by the router's manufacturer on a CD or DVD. This is usually the quickest and easiest method, because the setup program knows exactly how to configure your router. If you have high-speed Internet service, the setup program may also be able to set up the router to connect to your Internet service at the same time. (The next two options don't do that.)

- If your router supports Wi-Fi Protected Setup (WPS), use the Set Up a Network Wizard provided with Windows 8. If your router has an eight-digit numeric PIN code printed on the bottom, or if it has a pushbutton labeled WPS, you can use this wizard.

- Manually, by connecting to the router using a web browser.

We give general instructions for these three setup methods in the following sections. The manufacturer's instructions might be more detailed.

Whichever method you use, as mentioned in the previous section, you need to select up to five things to set up a wireless network: an SSID (name), security type, encryption type, encryption key, and possibly a channel number. A setup program or the Set Up a Network Wizard in Windows 8 might help you make these selections automatically.

> **⚙ tip**
>
> Before you get started, you might want to check the router manufacturer's website to see if a firmware update is available. (*Firmware* is the software built into the device.) Firmware updates are usually issued when serious bugs have been found and fixed, so it's definitely worth checking. Update the firmware following the manufacturer's instructions before you start using the network because the update process sometimes blows out any settings you've made in the router, and you'll have to start over as if it was new.

Using the Manufacturer's Setup Program

The easiest way to set up a wireless router is using a program provided by the manufacturer. Connect one of your computers to the wireless router using an Ethernet cable, and then run the program from the manufacturer's CD or DVD.

The setup program will typically suggest default settings for the router, which you may change. As mentioned previously, select WPA2 security unless your router or one or more of your computers don't support it.

You should write the final settings down, especially the security key. The setup program will then install the settings in the router. When your computers detect the new wireless network, you can connect to it and type in the security key.

If the router doesn't set up Internet service, see "Setting Up Internet Service" after the other setup methods are described.

Using the Set Up a Network Wizard

If your router supports the Wi-Fi Protected Setup (WPS) automatic configuration scheme, Windows 8 can set up the router for you automatically. You'll need the router's eight-digit PIN number to use this method. The PIN might be printed on a label on the bottom of the router, or you might be able to find out what the PIN is by connecting to the router using a web browser. We'll tell how to do this shortly. Also, this method works only on a router that has all of its factory-default settings and hasn't yet been configured. (If you have a used WPS-capable router, you may be able to use its setup web page to restore its factory-default settings.)

To use the Set Up a Network Wizard, follow these steps:

1. Connect your computer to one of the LAN ports on your wireless router using an Ethernet cable, and then power up the router. Wait 60 seconds or so before proceeding. If you are prompted about turning on sharing, select Yes, Turn On Sharing and Connect To Devices. This indicates that you are on a trusted, private network.

2. Go to the Desktop. Right-click the Network icon in the taskbar and select Open Network and Sharing Center, as shown here:

   Notice that a network name is listed at the top of the window, as shown in Figure 18.11. If under that it says "Private network," proceed to step 3. If it says "Public network," click (not right-click) the network icon in the taskbar. The Network pane will slide in. Right-click the network name, select Turn Sharing On or Off, then select Yes, Turn On Sharing and Connect to Devices.

3. Under Change Your Networking Settings, select Set Up a New Connection or Network. Highlight Set Up a New Network and click Next.

4. Wait for your wireless router to appear in the dialog box. When it does, select it and click Next.

   If it doesn't appear within 90 seconds, it might not be WPS capable, or it may already have been configured. If so, skip ahead to the next section, "Configuring Manually."

Figure 18.11
To use the wizard to set up a wireless router, the network location must say "Private network."

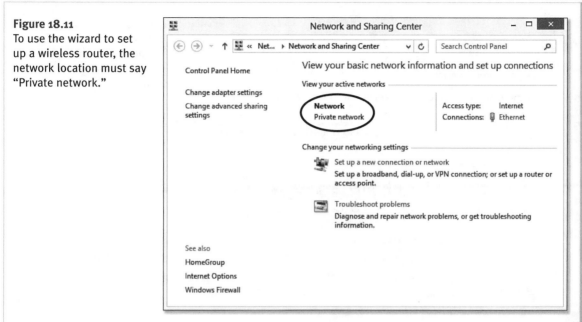

5. Enter the PIN code printed on your router and click Next. If the PIN is not printed, see if you can get it out of the router. Follow steps 2 through 5 in the section titled "Configuring Manually" to get into the router. See if any of its setup screens display the WPS PIN number. (On one router I tested, I found this under Wireless, Wi-Fi Protected Setup.)

6. Click the downward pointing arrow next to Change Passphrase, Security Level and Encryption Type. Adjust the network name if you wish, as shown in Figure 18.12. You may also change the passphrase if you wish.

   If not all of your computers support WPA2 security, you can downgrade the security level to WPA or WEP, but we *strongly* recommend against this. (See the discussion earlier in this chapter under "Wireless Network Setup Choices.")

   When the settings are made, click Next.

7. The wizard will configure the router, and will eventually display the security key. Write this down and keep a copy of it in a safe place. (If your location is secure, you can write in on a sticky note and attach it to the router itself, being sure not to block any ventilation holes.)

   We suggest that you also click Print These Network Settings. If you don't have a printer set up, select Microsoft XPS Document Writer and save the resulting file in your Documents library.

When you've followed these steps, your computers can all attach to the wireless network, using the network key that you or the wizard selected. If you need to set up Internet service as well, see "Setting Up Internet Service" after the following section.

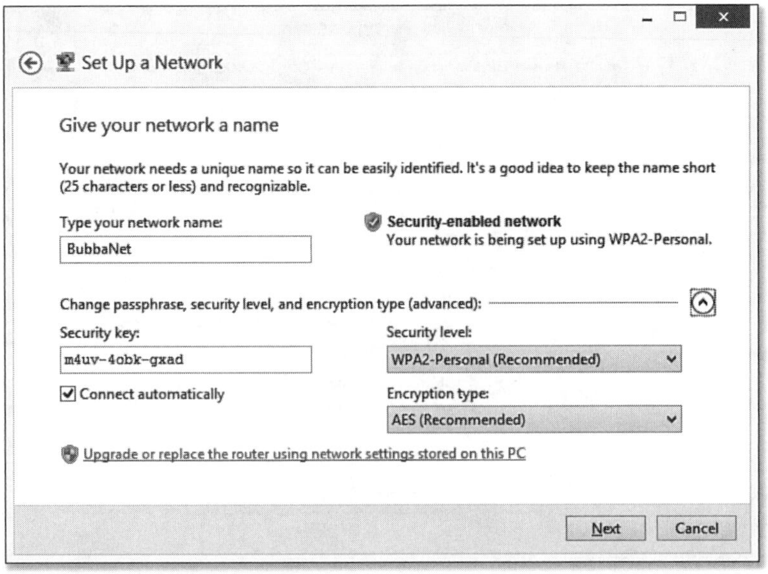

Figure 18.12
The Set Up a Network Wizard lets you change the default network name and security settings.

Configuring Manually

If you have to configure your router manually, your best bet is to follow the manufacturer's instructions. We can't give you specific instructions here, but we can give a general outline of the process:

1. Connect your computer to one of the LAN ports on your wireless router using an Ethernet cable, and then power up the router. Wait 60 seconds or so before proceeding. If you are prompted to turn sharing on or off, turn sharing on.

2. Right-click the very bottom-left corner of the screen and select Command Prompt. Type the command `ipconfig` and press Enter.

3. Look for the heading that reads something like "Ethernet Adapter Ethernet," and under that, look for the Default Gateway setting. It should be 192.168.0.1 or 192.168.1.1 (or something similar).

4. Open Internet Explorer, and in the Address bar, type **http://** followed by the default gateway numbers (for example, **http://192.168.0.1**) and press Enter.

5. Log on to the router using its administrative username and password. In many cases, you can leave admin for both the username and password, but this varies by manufacturer. You'll have to read the instruction manual or search the Web to find the default password for your router.

   You may wish to change the default password as your first step. If you do change it, be sure to write the new password down and store it in a secure place.

6. Use the router's web page menus to locate the Wireless Configuration page. Enter a network name (SSID), select a security type, and enter a key.

7. Use the appropriate "save settings" button or menu choice, wait 30 seconds, and try to have one of your other computers connect to the router using a wireless adapter, following the instructions under "Joining an Existing Wireless Network" in this chapter).

Once other computers can connect successfully, if the computer you used for setup has a wireless adapter, you can disconnect the Ethernet cable. Ethernet connections are faster and more reliable than wireless, though, so use wired connections whenever it's convenient to do so.

When your computer can connect to the wireless router, you can have the router establish an Internet connection for you.

Setting Up Internet Service

Once your wireless network is working and your computers can connect to the wireless router, you will probably want to have the router share a high-speed Internet connection.

If you used the manufacturer's setup program to configure your router, it might have set this up for you already. If you have to set up the Internet side of your router manually, try to follow the manufacturer's instructions. We can give you only general instructions here.

To set up shared Internet service, view to the router's setup web pages by following steps 2 through 5 in the preceding section, "Configuring Manually." Locate the router's wide area network (WAN) or Internet setup web pages. Many routers have a button that you can click to run an Internet setup wizard; otherwise, you'll have to set up the connection manually.

In general terms, there are three ways to connect:

- If your wireless router's WAN (Internet) port is connected to a network that already has a full-time Internet connection, choose the router's "direct connection" option.

- If you use cable Internet service, most likely you'll select the DHCP option. You may have to enter a specific hostname supplied by your cable company. Other cable ISPs key off your network adapter's MAC address, so you may have to call the ISP to inform them of the router's MAC address. This is usually printed on the bottom of the router.

- If you use DSL service, most likely you'll select the PPPoE option. You'll have to enter a username and password.

Your ISP should help you get the Internet connection working, or at least they should provide you with the information you need to get it working.

See Chapter 19 for more detailed instructions on connecting your LAN to the Internet.

Getting Maximum Wireless Speed

802.11n wireless networking supports speeds of up to 150Mbps, which is a huge improvement over older 801.11g and 802.11b equipment. However, you won't get the maximum possible speed if any of these conditions exist:

- There are other nearby networks using radio channels that overlap your network.

- You have older Wireless-G or -B equipment on the same network as -N (perhaps an old laptop or TiVo).

- You are using the insecure WEP or WPA security protocol (perhaps because you have older equipment that doesn't support WPA2).

- You are using the WPA2/TKIP security setting.

- Your router is not using the legal maximum transmitting power.

The following sections tell you how to fix these conditions.

Eliminate Overlapping Channels

The 2.4GHz band used by wireless gear supports 11 to 14 radio frequency channels so that you don't have to share radio bandwidth with your neighbors. The surprising fact is that many of these channels overlap each other to a large extent—a given channel overlaps about two and a half channels on either side. If your neighbor's wireless router is using channel 1, and you set your router to use channel 2, there can still be considerable interference, and both networks will be slowed down if you're both using them at the same time.

To avoid this, right-click the very bottom-left corner of the screen and select Command Prompt. Type **netsh wlan show networks mode=bssid** and press Enter. This will list each neighboring network, its signal strength (as a percentage of something—what, I don't know), and its channel. Examine the list, ignoring your own network. Select a channel for your network that doesn't conflict with at least the strongest of your neighbors' networks.

In the U.S., Canada, and Mexico, if you are using Wireless-G, or a standard 20MHz bandwidth Wireless-N router, try to select from channels 1, 6, and 11 only. Try to pick a channel that's five channels away from any strong neighboring signals.

If you are using a double-rate 40MHz bandwidth 2.4GHz Wireless-N router, use either channel 3 or 11. In Europe and elsewhere, find out what channels are recommended in your region.

Set your router to use this channel. Your other wireless devices will automatically catch on within minutes.

You could also repeat this exercise in the 5GHz band, if your router supports it. Many more channels are available, and there's much less overlap between them. Use a channel several numbers away from any neighboring 5GHz networks.

Tune Up Wireless Security

If you want to get the best Wireless-N performance, use the WPA2/AES security setting on your router. This just requires a setting change on the router. The connecting devices will work it out on their own.

If you have some equipment that doesn't support WPA2, you'll get maximum performance if you set up to use a separate, lower-speed network, as described in the next section.

Separate Your -N and -G/-B Networks

Wireless-N, -G, and -B equipment can all interoperate; however, having lower-speed equipment can slow down the performance of higher-speed equipment when both are transmitting at the same time, and even for several seconds afterward. If you have mixed equipment, there are two ways to get peak speed on your Wireless-N network:

- Use a two-radio (simultaneous dual-band) router. Set up different network names (SSIDs) for the two frequency bands. Set all of your Wireless-N equipment to use the 5GHz network, and all of your -B and -G equipment to use the 2.4GHz network. This requires a two-radio router, however, and 5GHz signals don't have the same reach as 2.4GHz.

- Alternatively, use two routers: a Wireless-N router for your -N gear, and an inexpensive -N or -G router for your other gear.

To set this up, configure the first Wireless-N router as your primary wireless network. Choose a clear channel, as described previously, and give it a network name (SSID) like "MyWirelessN." Set it up with WPA2/AES security.

Configure the other router as an access point. This turns off its routing features and turns it into a simple "repeater." Most routers can be set up this way; check the instructions. Select a channel that doesn't conflict with your other router. (For example, in the U.S., if your main router is set for channel 1, set this one to channel 6 or 13.) Give it a distinct SSID name, like "MyWirelessG." Set up WPA2/AES security if the router and your -G and -B devices support it. Position it at least 6 feet away from the other router. Now, just plug this device's WAN port into one of your first router's LAN ports. Have your slower devices connect to this alternative network name.

Use the Right Security Settings

For most routers, you'll get maximum throughput only if you have wireless security shut off entirely, or set to use WPA2/AES security. We don't recommend turning security off, unless you have a really good reason to do so (for example, if the network is for random passersby and guests to use, and is separated from your Windows file sharing network by a router).

Otherwise, be sure to set the router for WPA2/AES rather than WEP, WPA, or WPA2/TKIP. If your router doesn't support WPA2, get one that does. If you have network clients that don't support WPA2 (my old TiVo falls in this category), consider setting up a separate network for those devices, as discussed in the previous section.

Bump Up the Power?

Around the world, countries have differing regulations for the allowed frequencies and maximum power that unlicensed transmitters such as wireless routers can use. To play it safe, most routers are shipped with settings that adhere to the lowest common denominator, which means that your router might be operating at a lower power than is legally permissible in your area. It can be worth checking your router's advanced wireless settings to see if there is a setting for the regulatory domain (operating region) or the transmitter power.

The rules for the maximum-allowed power are esoteric, and the allowed wattage depends on the frequency band and the efficiency (gain) of the antenna used. For *most* antennas, in North America the maximum 2.4GHz power is 100mW. You might bump the power up to 60mW to see if this improves your data speed. It might not. (And for many routers, much more than 60mW could shorten the life of the router and actually degrade the signal.) If increasing the power doesn't improve your data speed, put it back to the original setting.

Configuring a Peer-to-Peer Network

When you're sure that the wired or wireless physical connection between your computers is set up correctly, you're ready to configure Windows 8. With today's Plug and Play network cards and with all the needed software built in to Windows, this configuration is a snap.

If your computer is part of a Windows Server domain network, which is often the case in a corporate setting, skip ahead to "Joining a Windows Domain Network."

Configuring the TCP/IP Protocol

After your network adapters are all installed—and, if you're using a wired network, cabled together—you need to ensure that each computer is assigned an *IP address*. This is a number that uniquely identifies each computer on the network. These numbers are assigned in one of the following ways:

- If you have an Internet-sharing router, or if one of your computers shares its Internet connection using Windows Internet Connection Sharing, or if you are on a corporate LAN running Windows Server, each computer will be assigned an IP address automatically—they're doled out by the Dynamic Host Configuration Protocol (DHCP) service that runs on the router or in the sharing computer. This is why I recommend using a router even if you aren't setting up a shared Internet connection.

  By default, Windows sets up new network adapters to receive an address this way. If your network fits into this category, you don't have to change any settings, and you can just skip ahead to the section "If You Have a Shared Internet Connection."

- Each computer can be given an address manually, which is called a *static address* as opposed to a dynamic (automatic) one. If you are not going to use a router or a shared Internet connection, you should set up static addressing. We tell you how shortly.

- If no static settings are made but no DHCP server exists on the network, Windows automatically assigns IP addresses anyway. Although the network will work, this is not an ideal situation and can slow Windows down. The setup steps shown in the following two sections let you avoid having IP addresses be assigned this way.

If you're setting up a new computer on an existing network, use whatever scheme the existing computers use; check their settings and follow suit with your new one. Otherwise, use either of the schemes described in the following two sections.

If You Have No Shared Internet Connection

If you're setting up a new network from scratch, and you do not have a connection-sharing computer, router, or wireless access point, you should use static addressing.

For most home and small office networks, the following static address scheme should work fine:

IP Address	192.168.1.11 for your first computer, 192.168.1.12 for your second computer, 192.168.1.13 for your third, and so on.
	We strongly suggest that you keep a list of your computers and the addresses you assign to them.
Subnet Mask	255.255.255.0
Default Gateway	(Leave blank)
Preferred DNS Server	(Leave blank)
Alternate DNS Server	(Leave blank)

Follow these steps on each computer to ensure that the network is set up correctly:

1. Go to the Desktop and right-click the Network icon that appears at the right end of the taskbar. Select Open Network and Sharing Center. (You can also get here from the Control Panel.) At the left side, select Change Adapter Settings. Right-click the Ethernet or Wireless Connection icon that corresponds to your LAN connection and select Properties.

2. Scroll to the bottom of the list box and select Internet Protocol Version 4 (TCP/IPv4). Click Properties.

3. Change the settings in the Properties dialog box. Figure 18.13 shows an example, but you must use the address values appropriate for your computer and your network.

> **tip**
>
> If your computer will move back and forth between a network that uses automatic configuration and a network that uses static settings—say, between work and home—select Obtain an IP Address Automatically. A tab named Alternate Configuration will appear. Select the Alternate Configuration tab and configure the static settings. Windows will use these static settings only when a DHCP server is not present.

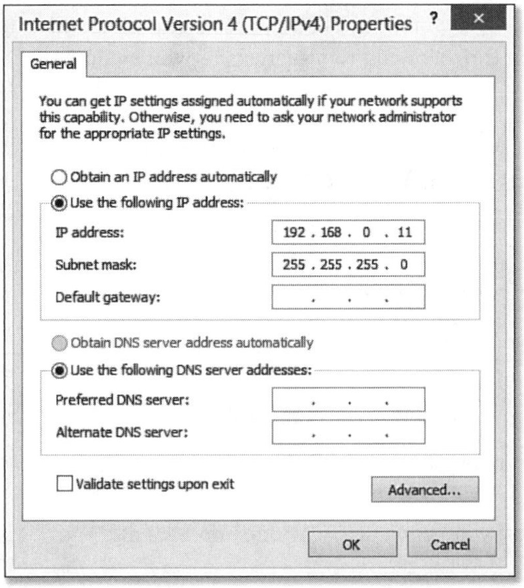

Figure 18.13
Make IP address settings within the Internet Protocol Version 4 (TCP/IPv4) Properties dialog box.

If You Have a Shared Internet Connection

As mentioned previously, if you plan to share an Internet connection with all the computers on your network, you should read Chapter 19 first. Keep the following tips in mind:

- If you will use Windows Internet Connection Sharing, first set up the one computer that will be sharing its connection, as described in Chapter 19, and then set up networking in your other computers.

- All the computers, including the one sharing its Internet connection, should have their Ethernet connections set to Obtain an IP Address Automatically and Obtain DNS Server Address Automatically (see Figure 18.13).

- If you will be using a hardware router, configure the router first, following the manufacturer's instructions. Enable its DHCP feature. If you can, set the starting DHCP IP address to 100 so that numbers from 2 to 99 can be used for computers with static settings. Also, if your ISP has provided you with a static IP address for your router, be sure to enter your ISP's DNS server addresses in the router's setup screens so it can pass them to your computers.

Now that your new network connection is set up, be sure to set the correct file-sharing option, as described in the next section. This is a critical part of Windows networking security.

> **🔍 note**
>
> If you add a shared Internet connection later, go to every one of your computers, bring up the TCP/IPv4 Properties dialog box shown in Figure 18.13 again, and select Obtain an IP Address Automatically and Obtain DNS Server Address Automatically. Otherwise, the shared connection will not work.

Enabling and Disabling Sharing

When you connect to a new network for the first time, Windows 8 automatically disables file and printer sharing through the connection, to protect you from hackers. You can then manually enable or disable sharing on the network. The choice you make determines the Windows Firewall settings that are applied and the networking features that will be available.

Two choices are available:

- When you connect to a *private* network, you can choose to *enable* sharing. A private network is one where you trust the other computers on the network. That is, you trust the *people* using the other computers. File and printer sharing is enabled, as is Network Discovery, which makes your computer visible to other users and makes their computers visible to you. It's also possible to join a homegroup, which we discuss shortly.

- When you connect to a *public* network, you must *disable* sharing. A public network is one where you don't trust the other users or computers, for example, on any direct connection to a cable or DSL modem, on networks and Internet connections in hotels, Internet cafes, airports, clients' offices, dorms, and anywhere else where you don't want random people poking into your computer. File and printer sharing and Network Discovery are disabled on this network connection.

  Here's a good rule of thumb: If you don't *need* to use file sharing and printer sharing in a given location, disable sharing on the connection.

> ## ⚠ caution
>
> Any connection that leads directly to the Internet without your own firewall or router in between *must* have sharing turned off and be designated a public network, to protect your computer from the hackers and bad software "out there." This holds no matter how you make the connection: plug-in Ethernet, wireless, dial-up, or a direct connection to a cable or DSL modem.

Microsoft changed the way this setting is made going from Windows 7 to Windows 8. In Windows 7, you were prompted to select the network's location: Public, Home, or Work. In Windows 8, you enable or disable sharing.

By default, sharing is disabled when you first connect to a new network. That is, when you move your computer from one network to another, Windows will detect the change and turn off sharing. To change the sharing setting, follow these steps:

1. Move the pointer to the bottom-right corner of the screen and click the Settings (gear-shaped) charm. When the Settings panel slides into view, click the network icon.

2. Right-click the name of your network connection and select Turn Sharing On or Off.

3. If you are on a network that you trust, select Yes, Turn On Sharing and Connect to Devices. Otherwise, on a public network, select No.

Setting Your Computer Identification

After you've configured your network, the next step is to make sure that each of the computers on your network is a member of the same domain or workgroup.

If you are part of a Windows domain-type network, your system administrator will give you the information you need to set your computer identification.

If you are setting up your own network without Windows Server, right-click the very bottom-left corner of the screen and select System on each of the computers on your network. Does each have a different full computer name, and the same workgroup name? If so, you're all set.

If not, click Change Settings, click the Network ID button, and prepare to answer the wizard's questions. Click Next on the wizard's first screen. You are asked to select the option that best describes your computer:

- This Computer Is Part of a Business Network; I Use It to Connect to Other Computers at Work.

- This Computer Is a Home Computer; It's Not Part of a Business Network.

Which one you choose makes a significant difference. If you choose the "Home Computer" option, the wizard sets up your computer for peer-to-peer networking with the workgroup name WORKGROUP and then finishes.

If you are on a business network with Windows Server, see "Joining a Windows Domain Network" in this chapter.

caution

You must be sure that every computer on your network uses the same workgroup name if you want them to be able to easily share files and printers.

Configuring Windows Firewall

It is a good idea to check that Windows Firewall is set up correctly; otherwise, you could end up exposed to Internet hacking, or you could find that your network is so locked down that you can't use file and printer sharing. Windows Firewall is discussed in more detail in Chapter 33.

If your Windows 8 computer is connected to a domain network, your network manager will set up a firewall "profile" that controls security when you are connected to the corporate network. You shouldn't be able to change these settings. Your network manager will also probably configure another "default" profile to protect you when you are disconnected from the corporate network, such as when you are traveling or using your computer at home.

In this section, we assume that you are managing your own computer and that your network is not protected by a professionally installed firewall. As a home or small office user, go through this quick checklist of steps to confirm that your network will function safely:

1. At the Start screen, type the word **fire** and, under that, click Settings. In the search results, select Check Firewall Status.

2. You should see that you are connected to a private network, and within the Private Networks box, you should see that Windows Firewall is on. If it's not, and you haven't installed an alternate Internet security program that has a replacement firewall, at the left select Turn Windows Firewall On or Off. In both the Private and Public sections, be sure that Turn On Windows Firewall is selected and that Notify Me When Windows Firewall Blocks a New Program is checked.

In general, Block All Incoming Connections doesn't need to be checked. You can check it in the Public profile section to get the strongest security, but you might not be able to use some Internet services such as FTP (file transfer), telephone, and voice/video chat.

These are the default settings, but it's best to check them to be sure.

File and Printer Sharing Without a Router

If you are setting up a small network of computers that connect with each other through an Ethernet switch or hub but not a router, you'll run in to a problem with the Windows Network Location feature. Windows uniquely identifies each network that your computer joins by the Media Access Control address (MAC address), a physical hardware identification number, of the network adapter at the network's TCP/IP gateway address. On a computer without a router, Windows automatically assigns IP addresses; however, there is no gateway address, so no MAC address to examine, so Windows cannot tell this network from any other network. It will call the network an unidentified network and will not let you enable file or printer sharing on it.

You can solve this problem in either of two ways:

- Use an inexpensive DSL/modem connection sharing router instead of a switch, and just don't connect its WAN port to a DSL or cable modem. You can get these used on eBay or Craigslist for just a few dollars.

- Assign IP addresses to each of your computers manually, using addresses like 192.168.0.2, 192.168.0.3, and upward. (Skip 192.168.0.1 in case you eventually do add a router). In each computer, when you assign an IP address using the dialog box shown in Figure 18.13, enter the IP address of one of the *other* computers as the gateway address. This is clunky, but it works. The other computer must be turned on for your computer to be able to identify the network and enable sharing.

Setting Up a Homegroup

Windows 7 and 8 have a networking feature called HomeGroup that can make sharing files, folders, printers, and music/video media very easy. What a homegroup does is let each user decide whether or not to share specific categories of documents, music, video, printers, and so on, or even specific folders and files. Every user on every computer in the homegroup can see the items, once shared, without worrying about passwords or usernames. It's all just there, organized, and easy to get to.

HomeGroup networking works by setting up a password that is used to join each computer to the group. Any user on any of the member computers can see any of the group's shared folders and printers.

> ### 🔍 note
>
> It's "HomeGroup" here and "homegroup" almost everywhere else in this chapter because the genius lawyers at Microsoft want people to use the trademarked word HomeGroup when we talk about the product feature, but to use homegroup when we talk about a group of computers that *use* the feature. Got that?

Is a homegroup right for you? Consider these points to decide whether or not to use this feature:

- The HomeGroup feature works only with Windows 7 and 8 computers. (Although, computers running Windows Vista, XP, Mac OS, Linux, and so on can still share with a homegroup, and use folders and printers shared by a homegroup, if you take the additional steps discussed under "Using Windows Vista and XP with a Homegroup," in Chapter 20.)

- Within a homegroup, you can't decide individually which other users can see your shared stuff and which users can't. Anybody who can use a computer that's a member of the homegroup can use the content that you decide to share.

  What you *can* control is whether to share your stuff or not, and whether the other users can just view and use your stuff, or modify, delete, and add to it.

If you don't need to control access on a person-by-person basis, then a homegroup is definitely a convenient thing to set up. If a homegroup isn't right for you, skip ahead to the next section, "Alternatives to Using a Homegroup." It's easy to change your mind later on, so don't worry too much about this.

To set up a homegroup, log on to one of your Windows 8 computers and perform the following steps:

1. At the Start Screen, type **home**. Under that, click Settings. Then, in the search results, select Homegroup.

2. Click Create.

3. Select which types of *your* content you want to share with everyone else in the homegroup, as shown in Figure 18.14. Check Pictures, Documents, Music, and/or Videos to let other users see your files. Check Printers and Devices to share your computer's printer(s) with other computers in the group. (You can easily change these selections later, as we discuss in Chapter 21, "Using a Windows Network.")

4. Scroll down to the bottom of the list of settings, if necessary, to view the Password listed in the Membership section. Jot this down. You'll need it to join your other Windows 8 computers to the homegroup. Upper- and lowercase matter, by the way.

   If you want to use a different HomeGroup password than the one Windows chose, you can, and now is the time to change it. On the Start screen, type **home** and, under that, click Settings. In the search results, select Change HomeGroup Password. Then, click Change the Password.

 note

If you have a computer that is part of a domain network when you connect at work, you can still join it to your homegroup at home. You'll be able to use folders and printers shared by other computers in the homegroup, but you won't be able to share any of your computer's folders with the group.

note

If you are signed on to Windows 8 with a Microsoft (online) account when you set up your homegroup, and then use that same account to sign on to another computer on your network, the HomeGroup password will be automatically filled in for you when you go to enroll this new computer into the group. HomeGroup passwords are one of the things that Windows 8 syncs between the computers you use. (It's an odd thing for Microsoft to have done, because HomeGroup passwords are a "per-computer" rather than a "per-user" attribute.)

Figure 18.14
Select the types of files you want to share with everyone else in the homegroup. This selection applies only to your own files—other users get to choose for themselves what they want to share.

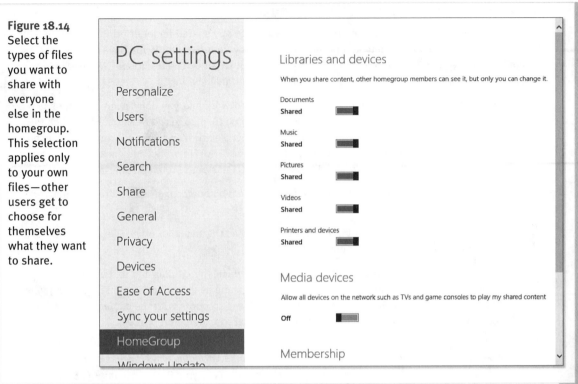

5. You or another computer owner can now go to another Windows 8 computer on your network, log on, and repeat this process. This time, instead of "Create," you'll be able to join the existing homegroup.

On Windows 7, go to the Control Panel. Select Homegroup and Sharing Options, then Join Now.

Repeat step 5 with any other Windows 7 or 8 computers that you want to join to the homegroup.

Each user on each computer will have to log on and decide which of their materials they want to share with the homegroup. Until they do, their names won't appear in the HomeGroup listing in File Explorer. We talk about this in the section "Sharing With a Homegroup" in Chapter 21.

tip

If you forget the password, go to the Start screen, type **home** and, under that, click Settings. Select HomeGroup and scroll down to the Membership section.

note

If you have computers running Windows XP, Vista, Mac OS, Linux, or other OSs, read Chapter 20, "Networking with Other Operating Systems," to see how to make it easier to share files and printers with these other OSs.

Alternatives to Using a Homegroup

HomeGroup security gives anyone in the group access to any shared folder or printer. If you need to restrict access to shared folders and printers on a user-by-user basis, or if you have computers that don't run either Windows 7 or 8, you might instead want to set up the traditional Windows file sharing scheme. There are two ways you can configure traditional sharing:

■ If you have OSs other than Windows 7 or 8 on your network and you don't need per-user security, you can turn off Password Protected Sharing. To do this, go to the Desktop. Right-click the network icon at the right end of the taskbar and select Network and Sharing Center. At the left, select Change Advanced Sharing Settings. Scroll down to All Networks and click the down arrow to open the list. Scroll down more and select Turn Off Password Protected Sharing.

This makes any shared folder or printer available to anybody who can connect to your network, with no passwords required at all.

If you have computers running Windows XP, Vista, Mac OS, Linux, or other OSs, read Chapter 20 for more information on sharing with these OSs.

■ If you need to control in detail which users can use which shared files and folders, leave Password Protected Sharing turned on (which is the same as disabling Simple File Sharing was on Windows XP). You will have to set up the same user accounts with the same passwords on each of your computers so that people can access shared folders and printers.

➡ *For more information on Password Protected Sharing, including ways it works differently on Windows 8 than previous versions of Windows,* **see** *"Configure Passwords and File Sharing," p. 802.*

Wrapping Up

This completes the procedure for setting up Windows networking on one Windows 8 computer. After you have configured, connected, and—if required to—restarted each of your computers, right-click in the extreme bottom-left corner of the screen and select File Explorer. Look for the Network and Homegroup items at the left edge of the Window, as shown in Figure 18.15.

If your network is up and running, and Network Discovery is enabled, you should see one icon for every computer you've connected. Double-click any icon to see what that computer is sharing with the network.

➡ *If you don't see other computers in the Network window,* **see** *Chapter 22, "Troubleshooting Your Network."*

If you set up a homegroup, the Homegroup list will have an entry for each user who has elected to share files. There may be entries for the other users on your own computer, as well as users on other computers. Shared printers *should* already be listed in your Devices and Printers Control Panel applet, automatically, although if you have one or more printers that are not connected via USB cables, you may have to take additional steps to share them.

Figure 18.15
File Explorer
has links at the
left edge that
let you explore
your network,
and your home-
group, if you
have one.

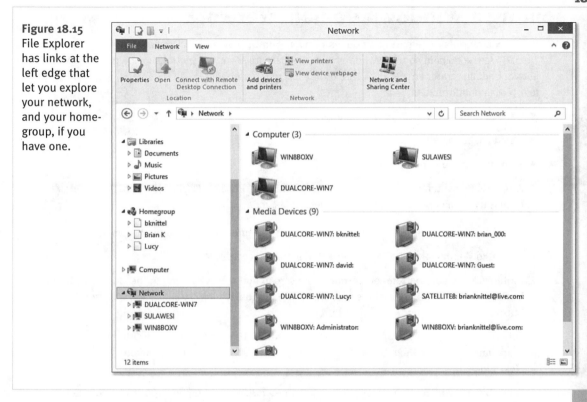

You're almost done. You have just a little more reading do to:

- You'll certainly be connecting to the Internet, and when you do, you risk exposing your network to the entire world. Refer to Chapter 33 to find out what risks you'll be exposed to and what you can do to protect your LAN. If you use Internet Connection Sharing or a connection-sharing router, you're in pretty good shape. But in any case, going through Chapter 33 carefully is very important.

- Read Chapter 21 to learn how to get the most out of your Windows network.

- See Chapter 37 for instructions on enabling remote access to your computer and network.

- See Chapter 20 for information about networking with Macs, UNIX, Linux, and older versions of Windows, as well as installing advanced networking services.

Joining a Windows Domain Network

If your computer is to be part of a domain network run by a version of Windows Server, it has to be "joined" to the domain so that Windows will delegate its security functions to the network. Your network administrator should take care of this for you. If you have to do it yourself, you will need four pieces of information:

- The name to be given to your computer.

- The domain name for your network.

- Your domain logon name and password.

- Any specific configuration information for the Internet Protocol (TCP/IP). In most cases, it is not necessary to make any changes in the default settings.

Use the following procedure to make your computer a member of your network domain:

1. Log on to Windows with a Computer Administrator account.

2. Right-click the very bottom-left corner of the screen and select System. In the Computer Name, Domain, and Workgroup settings section, click Change Settings. Then, click the Network ID button.

3. Select This Computer Is Part of a Business Network; I Use It to Connect to Other Computers at Work, and then click Next. Select My Company Uses a Network with a Domain, and then click Next twice.

4. Enter the network login name, password, and network domain name supplied by your network administrator. Then click Next.

5. If the network administrator prepared the domain to accept your computer, a box will pop up saying "An account for this computer has been found...." Click Yes.

6. You will be prompted for the credentials for an account that has domain administrator privileges. An administrator may have to assist you here.

7. The next prompt asks, "Do you want to enable a domain user account to this computer?" You have two choices:

   - If you want your domain account to be able to manage hardware, software, and files on your own computer, select Add the Following Domain User Account and then enter your domain logon name and domain name. Click Next. Select Administrator and then click Next.

   - If you want to manage your computer using your original "local" account, select Do Not Add a Domain User Account, and then click Next.

8. Click Finish. Click OK to close the System Properties dialog and then click Restart Now.

When your computer has been joined to the domain and restarted, the login process may be slightly changed. If the Welcome screen says Press Ctrl+Alt+Del to Sign In, type this key combination. (Hold down the Ctrl and Alt keys, press the Del key, and then release all of the keys.)

The first time you sign in, the icon for your original non-domain ("local") account will still appear. If an icon for your domain account does not appear, click the left arrow and select Other User. Then, enter the username and password for your domain account.

Bridging Two Network Types

A Windows 8 computer can connect or bridge two different network types through software, letting the devices on both networks communicate with each other. This can eliminate the need to buy a hardware device to connect two disparate networks (although it only works when your Windows 8 computer is turned on). Figure 18.16 shows an example of what bridging can do. In the figure, one Windows 8 computer serves as a bridge between an Ethernet LAN and a phoneline LAN.

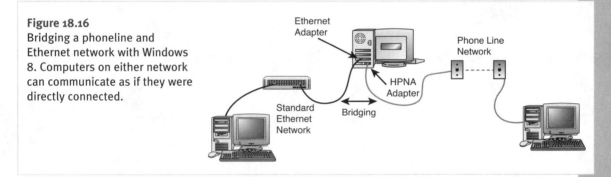

Figure 18.16
Bridging a phoneline and Ethernet network with Windows 8. Computers on either network can communicate as if they were directly connected.

Bridging is similar to routing, but it's more appropriate for small LANs because it's easier to configure and doesn't require different sets of IP addresses on each network segment. Technically, bridging occurs at the physical level of the network protocol stack. Windows forwards network traffic, including broadcasts and packets of all protocol types received on either adapter, to the other. In effect, it creates one larger network.

To enable bridging in your Windows 8 computer, install and configure two or more network adapters, as described under "Installing Multiple Network Adapters," earlier in this chapter. However, don't worry about setting up the Internet Protocol (TCP/IP) parameters for either of the adapters yet. Then do the following:

1. Go to the Desktop screen. At the right end of the taskbar, right-click the network icon and select Open Network and Sharing Center. (You can also get there via the Control Panel entry by selecting View Network Status and Tasks). In the left panel, select Change Adapter Settings.

2. Select the icons you want to bridge by clicking the first, holding down the Ctrl key, and clicking the second.

3. Right-click one of the now-highlighted icons and select Bridge Connections.

4. A new icon named Network Bridge appears. Select this new icon and, if you want, rename it appropriately—for example, "Ethernet to Phoneline Bridge."

5. Double-click the new Network Bridge icon. Select Internet Protocol (TCP/IP) and configure your computer's TCP/IP settings. You must do this last because any TCP/IP settings for the original two adapters are lost.

When you've created a bridge, your two network adapters function as one and share one IP address, so Microsoft disables the "network properties" of the individual network adapters. You must configure your computer's network properties with the Network Bridge icon.

Remember that the connection between the two networks depends on the computer with the bridge being powered on.

You can remove the bridge later by right-clicking the Network Bridge icon and clicking Delete.

CONNECTING YOUR NETWORK TO THE INTERNET

Sharing an Internet Connection

The previous chapter shows how to create an inexpensive local area network (LAN) to tie your computers together. With a network in place, a single high-speed Internet connection can serve all of the computers in your home or office, or you can share a modem connection made from one designated Windows computer.

A shared Internet connection can actually provide better protection against hackers than can an individual connection, because a shared connection has to funnel through a router device or a software service that blocks outside attempts to connect to your computers—except on your terms. In this chapter, we show you how to set this up.

> **note**
>
> You should also read Chapter 33, "Protecting Your Network from Hackers and Snoops," for more details on protecting your network from hacking.

Ways to Make the Connection

When you're using a single computer, you use its analog modem or a broadband cable, DSL, or satellite modem to connect to your ISP as needed. To share your Internet connection on a network, you can designate one computer running Windows to make the connection, or you can use an inexpensive hardware device called a *connection-sharing router* or *residential gateway* to serve as a bridge between your network and a cable, DSL, or dial-up modem. Whichever method you choose, the designated computer or router automatically establishes the Internet connection any time anybody on your network needs it.

As an overview, Figure 19.1 shows five ways you can hook up your LAN to an Internet service provider (ISP). Throughout this chapter, we'll refer to these as schemes A through E. They are as follows:

A. Internet Connection Sharing (ICS) with an analog dial-up connection—In this scenario, Windows automatically dials your ISP from one computer whenever anyone on the LAN wants to connect to the Internet. This is called *demand-dialing*. (By the way, the modem doesn't have to be an external one, like in the figure; it can be an internal modem.)

B. ICS with a broadband DSL or cable modem—The computer that hosts the shared connection has two network adapters. One connects to a broadband modem; the other connects to your other computers.

 note

One disadvantage of schemes A and B is that the one "sharing" computer must be turned on before anyone else can use the Internet connection.

C. Sharing router with a broadband connection—You can use a small hardware device that can cost as little as $20 to do the same job as ICS. It could even be free: many ISPs now provide a router as a standard part of broadband Internet service. The advantage of using a router is that you don't have to leave a particular Windows computer turned on for other users to reach the Internet. It is also more secure because a separate device is shielding Windows from the Internet.

Some ISPs give you a box that combines a broadband modem with a router in one box. That's fine. What matters is that there is a router in between the Internet and your computers. This is still scheme C, not D.

D. Service with multiple directly connected computers—This is the setup that some cable ISPs recommend for a home with more than one computer, but it is a *bad idea*. You can't use this method and also use file and printer sharing. Use scheme B, C, or E instead. See "Special Notes for Cable Service," later in this chapter, for more information.

E. Routed (Multiple IP Address) Service—Some ISPs provide what's called *routed* Internet service through DSL, cable, Frame Relay, optical fiber, or other technologies. There's usually an extra charge for this type of service because it provides a separate public IP address to each computer on the LAN. This has some advantages that we discuss later, but it also incurs a risk of exposing your network to hackers, unless you're vigilant in setting it up.

Now let's look at the issues involved in having a single ISP connection serve multiple computers.

Managing IP Addresses

Connecting a LAN to the Internet requires you to delve into some issues about how computers are identified on your LAN and on the Internet. Each computer on your LAN uses a unique network identification number called an *IP address* that is used to route data to the correct computer. As long as the data stays on your LAN, it doesn't matter what numbers are used; your LAN is essentially a private affair.

Figure 19.1
Five ways to connect your LAN
to the Internet.

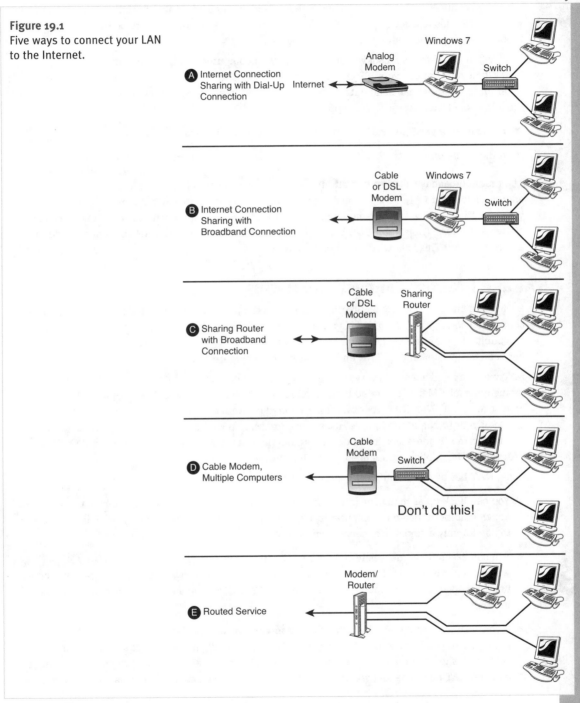

When you connect to the Internet, though, those random numbers can't be used to direct data to you; your ISP has to assign a *public* IP address to you so that other computers on the Internet can properly route data to your ISP and then to you.

Now, when you establish a solo connection from your computer to the Internet, this isn't a big problem. When you connect, your ISP assigns your computer a temporary public IP address. Any computer on the Internet can send data to you using this address. When you want to connect a LAN, though, it's not quite as easy. Two approaches are used:

- You can get a valid public IP address for each of your computers.

- You can use *one* public IP address and share it among all the users of your LAN.

The first approach is called *routed* Internet service because your ISP assigns a set of consecutive IP addresses for your LAN—one for each of your computers—and routes all data for these addresses to your site. This is shown in scheme E in Figure 19.1. The second approach uses a technique called *Network Address Translation (NAT)*, in which all the computers on your LAN share one IP address and connection. This is how schemes A through C work.

NAT and Internet Connection Sharing

Microsoft's Internet Connection Sharing system and the popular devices called *residential gateways*, *connection-sharing routers*, or *wireless routers* use NAT to establish all Internet connections using one public IP address. The computer or device running the NAT service mediates all connections between computers on your LAN and the Internet (see Figure 19.2).

NAT works a lot like mail delivery to a large commercial office building, where there's one address for many people. Mail is delivered to the mail room, which sorts it and delivers it internally to the correct recipient. With NAT, your router is assigned one public IP address, and all communication between your LAN and the Internet uses this address. The NAT service takes care of changing or translating the IP addresses in data packets from the private, internal IP addresses used on your LAN to the one public address used on the Internet.

Using NAT has several significant consequences:

- You can hook up as many computers on your LAN as you want. Your ISP won't care, or even know, that more than one computer is using the connection. You save money because you need to pay for only a single-user connection.

- You can assign IP addresses inside your LAN however you want. In fact, all the NAT setups we've seen provide DHCP, an automatic IP addressing system, so virtually no manual configuration is needed on the computers you add to your LAN. Just plug a computer in, and it's on the Internet.

- If you want to host a website, VPN, or other service on your LAN and make it available from the Internet, you have some additional setup work to do. When you contact a remote website, NAT knows to send the returned data back to you, but when an unsolicited request comes from outside, NAT has to be told where to send the incoming connection. We discuss this later in the chapter.

Figure 19.2
A NAT device or program carries out all Internet communications using one IP address. NAT keeps track of outgoing data from your LAN to determine where to send responses from the outside.

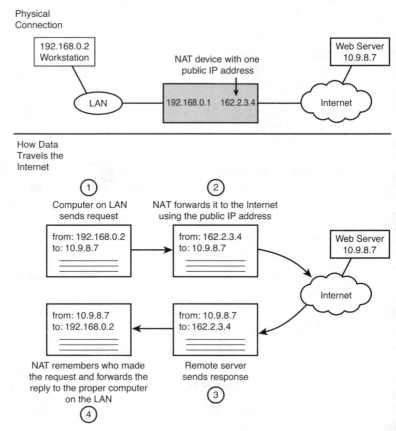

- NAT serves as an additional firewall to protect your LAN from probing by Internet hackers. Incoming requests, such as those to read your shared folders, are simply ignored if you haven't specifically set up your connection-sharing service to forward requests to a particular computer.

- Some network services can't be made to work with NAT. For example, you might not be able to use some audio and video chat services. These programs expect that the IP address of the computer on which they're running is a public address. Windows ICS and some hardware-sharing routers can sometimes work around this problem using the Universal Plug and Play (UPnP) protocol, which is discussed later in the chapter.

- A hardware connection-sharing router might provide you with better security than Windows ICS because, as special-purpose devices, their software is simpler and less likely to be buggy than Windows. Also, when used along with Windows Firewall, you have *two* separate lines of defense against hackers instead of just one.

Starting with Windows 98, Microsoft has provided a NAT service through its ICS feature. It's a built-in part of Windows. Given the choice between using Windows' ICS service and buying an external hardware router, we recommend that you use a router, for two reasons:

- First, to use ICS, you have to leave one of your Windows computers turned on so that other computers can reach the Internet. Connection-sharing routers have to be left on, too, but they consume very little power compared to what a PC sucks up.

- More important, connection-sharing routers provide better security than using Windows alone. With the hardware router, a hacker would have to break through the router and *then* break into Windows.

If you decide to use a router, look at the products made by Linksys, D-Link, SMC, and Netgear. You can find them at computer stores, office supply stores, and online. On sale you can pick one up for $20 or less. Wireless versions that include an 802.11n or 802.11g wireless networking base station as well as a switch for wired Ethernet connections don't cost that much more.

More advanced (and expensive) versions include additional features such as a built-in print server and virtual private networking (VPN) service.

The next section discusses issues that are important to business users. If you're setting up a network for your home, you can skip ahead.

Special Notes for Wireless Networking

If you're setting up a wireless network, you *must* enable WEP or WPA encryption to protect your network from unexpected use by random strangers. People connecting to your wireless network appear to Windows to be part of your own LAN and are trusted accordingly.

 To learn more about setting up a secure wireless network, **see** *"Installing a Wireless Network,"* **p. 392.**

If you really want to provide free access to your broadband connection as a public service, provide it using a second, unsecured wireless router plugged into your network, as shown in Figure 19.3. Use a different channel number and SSID from the ones set up for your own wireless LAN. Set up filtering in this router to prevent Windows file-sharing queries from penetrating into your own network. See "Scheme E—Routed Service Using a Router," later in this chapter, for the list of ports you must block.

(And remember that someone might use your connection to send spam or attack other networks. If the FBI knocks on your door some day, don't say we didn't warn you.)

Special Notes for Cable Service

Some cable ISPs can provide you with multiple IP addresses so you can connect multiple computers directly to your cable modem, without a router. This is scheme D in Figure 19.1. It's a very simple setup, but we strongly urge you *not* to use this type of service. You can't take advantage of file and printer sharing on such a network.

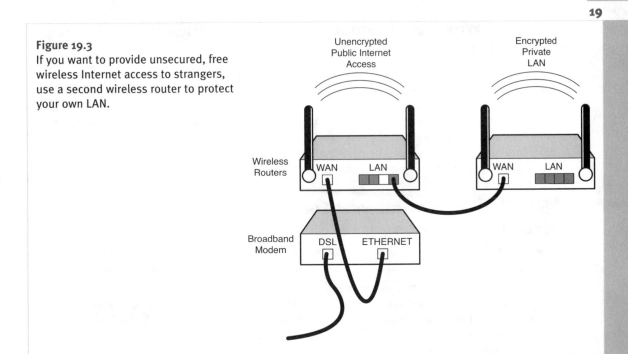

Figure 19.3
If you want to provide unsecured, free wireless Internet access to strangers, use a second wireless router to protect your own LAN.

Unencrypted
Public Internet
Access

Encrypted
Private
LAN

Wireless
Routers

WAN   LAN

WAN   LAN

Broadband
Modem

DSL   ETHERNET

(Now, some ISPs provide you with a combination modem and router in one box. That would be fine; there's still a router in place, and you have scheme C. What we're talking about here is a plain cable modem without a router.)

If you want to take full advantage of having a LAN in your home or office, use scheme C instead. Simply add an inexpensive connection-sharing router—at a cost of less than $40, as mentioned previously—and you'll get *all* the benefits of a LAN without the risks of a direct connection.

Configuring Your LAN

In the following sections, we describe how to set up each of the connection schemes diagrammed in Figure 19.1. If you're still in the planning stages for your network, you might want to read all the sections to see what's involved; this might help you decide what configuration you want to use. If your LAN is already set up and your Internet service is ready to go now, just skip ahead to the appropriate section.

> **⚏ caution**
> The "scheme D" setup requires you to connect your cable modem directly to your LAN, without any firewall protection between the Internet and your computers. If you do this, you *have* to disable file and printer sharing on each computer. In Windows 8 parlance, you must designate your network a *public network*. If you don't, you would expose all your computers to a *severe* security risk.

Scheme A—Windows Internet Connection Sharing with a Dial-Up Connection

The ICS feature provided with Windows can share modem or broadband connections that require a sign-on procedure. The connection is made automatically whenever any user on the network tries to access the Internet; this is called *demand-dialing*. With some sort of broadband connectivity almost universally available now, very few people use a shared analog connection, so we won't describe this technique in detail. If you *do* need to use a shared dial-up connection, here is the basic procedure: Create a standard dial-up connection on one computer, and follow the instructions under Scheme B to share it. The procedure is almost exactly the same.

Scheme B—Windows Internet Connection Sharing with a Broadband Connection

This section shows how to set up the Internet connection method illustrated in Figure 19.1 as scheme B.

The procedure for configuring a shared high-speed cable or DSL Internet connection with Windows ICS is very similar to that for setting up a shared dial-up connection. To prepare, be sure to install and test your DSL or cable connection on the computer you'll use to host the shared connection, as described in Chapter 14. It's essential that you have this working before you proceed to set up your LAN and the shared connection.

> ### tip
>
> If your broadband service uses a LAN adapter instead of USB to connect your computer to the DSL or cable modem, you'll be installing two LAN adapters in this computer: one for the LAN and one for the modem. We suggest that you install them one at a time. Install the one you'll use for your broadband connection first. From the Network and Sharing Center, select Change Adapter Settings, right-click the network adapter's icon, click rename, and then rename it DSL Modem Connection or Cable Internet Connection, or some other name that indicates what it's used for, as shown in Figure 19.4. Configure and test the Internet connection. Then install the network adapter that you'll use to connect to your LAN. Rename this connection LAN Connection or leave it as Ethernet or Wireless. This will help you later in the setup process, when you need to know which connection goes to your ISP.

Verify that the broadband Internet connection is labeled as a public network. To do this, follow these steps:

1. Go to the Desktop and right-click the small network icon at the right end of the taskbar. Select Open Network and Sharing Center.

2. In the Network and Sharing Center window, be sure that your Internet connection's location is labeled "Public Network."

3. If your broadband connection is not active, left-click the network icon in the taskbar. Click the network name, and then select Connect.

Figure 19.4
Install and rename your network adapters one at a time, indicating what purpose they'll serve. "DSL Modem Connection" or "LAN Connection" is much more informative than "Ethernet #2."

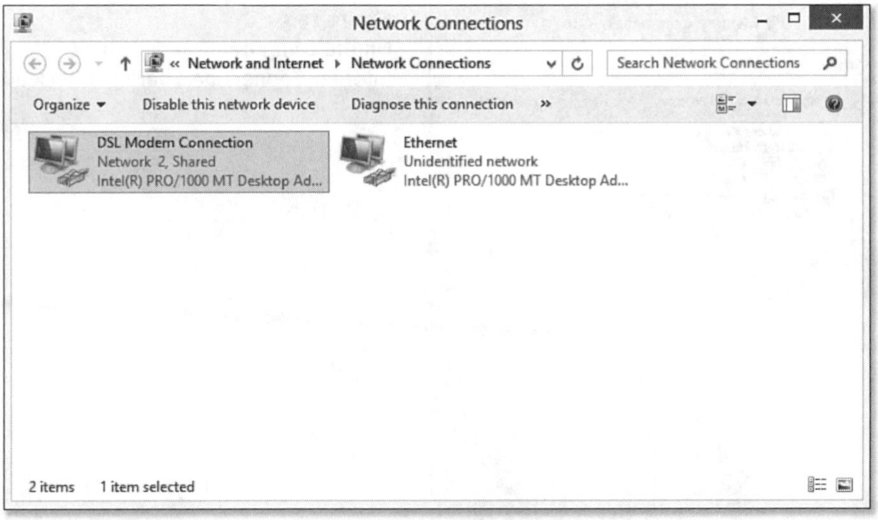

When your broadband connection is configured correctly and is working, follow these steps:

1. Go to the Desktop and right-click the network icon at the right end of the taskbar. Select Open Network and Sharing Center. Select Change Adapter Settings.

2. Locate the icon that corresponds to your broadband connection.

   If you have cable Internet service, this will probably be a network adapter. Earlier, we suggested that you rename it something like "Internet Connection," or it may still be labeled "Ethernet." If you use DSL service that requires a username and password to sign on, locate the connection icon that you set up for your ISP; it might be named "Broadband Connection." Right-click this icon and select Properties.

3. Choose the Sharing tab. Check all the boxes, as shown in Figure 19.5.

4. Select the Networking tab. In the list of components used by the connection, be sure that *only* Internet Protocol Version 6 (TCP/IPv6), Internet Protocol Version 4 (TCP/IPv4), and QoS Packet Scheduler, if present, are checked. This will prevent file sharing from being exposed to the Internet. (Windows Firewall will do that, too, but it doesn't hurt to be extra safe.)

5. Click OK.

6. Click Windows Firewall in the Network and Sharing window. Make sure Windows Firewall is On.

7. Restart Windows and try to view any web page (such as www.google.com). If it doesn't appear, you'll have to resolve the problem before proceeding. You should check the appropriate connection icon to be sure it's still configured correctly for your ISP.

Now, follow the instructions under "Configuring the Rest of the Network," in this chapter, to set up your other computers.

Figure 19.5
On the computer that will share its connection, enable Internet Connection Sharing. Check all the boxes.

Scheme C—Connection Sharing Router with a Broadband Connection

This section shows how to set up the Internet connection method illustrated in Figure 19.1 as scheme C.

Your router's manufacturer will provide instructions for installing and configuring it. If you're using cable or DSL Internet service, you'll connect your broadband modem to the router using a short Ethernet patch cable. Then you'll connect the router to your LAN using one of the two methods shown in Figure 19.6. Alternatively, your ISP may provide you a single device that has both a modem and a router in it.

You then configure the router, telling it how to contact your ISP and what range of IP addresses to serve up to your LAN. Every device will use a different procedure, so you will have to follow the manufacturer's instructions.

If your ISP uses PPPoE to establish a connection, you need to enable PPPoE and store your logon and password in the router. Most DSL service works this way. If your DSL provider does use PPPoE, you should enable the router's auto-sign-on feature, and you can optionally set up a "keepalive" value that will tell the modem to periodically send network traffic even if you don't, to keep your connection active all the time.

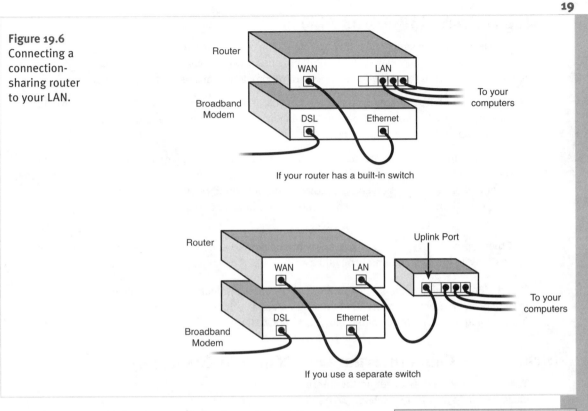

Figure 19.6
Connecting a connection-sharing router to your LAN.

If your router has a built-in switch

If you use a separate switch

If you use cable Internet service and your ISP didn't provide you with a special hostname that you had to give to your computer, your ISP probably identifies you by your network adapter's MAC (hardware) address. You *might* find that your Internet connection won't work when you set up the router. One of your router's setup pages should show you its MAC address. You can either call your ISP's customer service line and tell them that this is your new adapter's MAC address, or configure the router to "clone" your computer's MAC address—that is, copy the address from the computer you originally used to set up your cable connection. Your router's setup manual should tell you how to do this.

As you are configuring your router, you might want to enable Universal Plug and Play, discussed next in this chapter.

You might also opt for even better hacker protection by having your router filter (block) Microsoft file and printer sharing data. This is usually done on an advanced setup screen labeled Filtering. See "Scheme E—Routed Service Using a Router," later in this chapter, for the list of ports that you must block.

When the router has been set up, go to each of your computers and follow the instructions under "Configuring the Rest of the Network" in this chapter.

> **⚠ caution**
> Be sure to change the factory-supplied password of your router after you install it. (And write the password somewhere in the router's manual, or put it on a sticky label on the bottom of the router.) Also, be sure to disable outside (Internet) access to the router's management screens.

Using Universal Plug and Play

If you use a hardware connection-sharing router, you might want to consider enabling a feature called Universal Plug and Play (UPnP). UPnP provides a way for software running on your computer to communicate with the router. Specifically, UPnP provides a means for the following:

- The router to tell software on your computer that it is separated from the Internet by NAT. This may let some software—the video and audio parts of most instant messaging programs, in particular—have a better chance of working.

- Software running on the network to tell the router to forward expected incoming connections to the correct computer. Online messaging programs often require this. When the computer on the other end of the connection starts sending data, the router would not know to send it to your computer. UPnP lets UPnP-aware application programs automatically set up forwarding in the router.

- Other types of as-yet-undeveloped hardware devices to announce their presence on the network so that Windows can automatically take advantage of the services they provide.

To use UPnP, you must enable the feature in your router. It's usually disabled by default. If your router doesn't currently support UPnP, you might have to download and install a firmware upgrade from the manufacturer. Most routers now do support UPnP.

Scheme D—Cable Internet with Multiple Computers

This section shows how to set up the Internet connection method illustrated in Figure 19.1 as scheme D. As mentioned earlier in the chapter, you *cannot* safely use file and printer sharing with this setup. Use this setup only if you don't want file and printer sharing and just want to have several computers with Internet access.

In this configuration, follow your ISP's instructions for setting up each computer separately. The only unusual thing here is that the computers plug into a switch or hub, and the switch or hub plugs into the cable modem—otherwise, each computer is set up exactly as if it was a completely separate, standalone computer with cable Internet service.

> **🔊 caution**
>
> If you use this scheme, on each Windows 8, 7, and Vista computer, you must set the network location for the connection that goes to your switch and cable modem to Public Network. If you have computers running Windows XP, be sure that Windows Firewall is enabled and that file and printer sharing is disabled.

To verify that the network location is set to Public Network on Windows 8, follow these steps:

1. Go to the Desktop and right-click the network icon at the right end of the taskbar. Select Open Network and Sharing Center.

2. Check that the label under your network connection is labeled Public Network. If it's not, click the network location label and select Public Network.

If you later decide that you want to use file and printer sharing, *do not* simply set the network location to Private, or enable file and printer sharing, or create a Homegroup. Instead, set up a shared connection using scheme B or C.

Scheme E—Routed Service Using a Router

This section shows how to set up the Internet connection method illustrated in Figure 19.1 as scheme E.

Some ISPs will sell you service that provides multiple, fixed IP addresses. This is the case for Frame Relay service and, in some cases, higher-priced business-class DSL or cable service. You should really have a good reason for going this way, beyond just wanting to connect multiple computers—it's not as secure as a single shared connection. A good reason might be that you want the reliability of Frame Relay service or you need fixed IP addresses to host web, email, or other Internet-based services on several different computers.

For this type of service, if you are using a cable, DSL, satellite, or Frame Relay modem with a built-in router, your ISP will help you configure your network. In this setup, you will be provided with a fixed list of IP addresses, which you'll have to parcel out to your computers. Your ISP should help you install all of this, but we can give you some pointers.

First of all, it is *absolutely essential* that your router be set up to protect your network. You must ensure that at least these three items are taken care of:

- The router must be set up with filters to prevent Microsoft file-sharing service (NetBIOS and NetBT) packets from entering or leaving your LAN. In technical terms, the router must be set up to block TCP and UDP on port 137, UDP on port 138, and TCP on ports 139 and 445. It should "drop" rather than "reject" packets, if possible. This helps prevent hackers from discovering that these services are present but blocked. Better to let them think they're not there at all.

- Be *absolutely* sure to change your router's administrative password from the factory default value to something hard to guess, with uppercase letters, lowercase letters, numbers, and punctuation. Don't let your ISP talk you out of this. Also, you should let them know what the new password is so they can get into the router from their end, if needed.

- Disable SNMP access, or change the SNMP read and read-write "community names" to something other than the default. Again, use something with letters, numbers, and punctuation.

> **◉ tip**
>
> We *strongly* urge you to ask your ISP to set up filtering in your router for you, to block all Windows networking services.

> **▲ caution**
>
> If your router is not properly configured to filter out NetBIOS traffic, your network will be exposed to hackers. This is absolutely unacceptable. If you're in doubt, have your ISP help you configure the router. Also, after setting things up, visit www.grc.com and use the ShieldsUP pages there to be sure your computers are properly protected. For more information about network security, see Chapter 33.

Second, either your ISP will set up your router to automatically assign network addresses using DHCP, or you will have to manually set up a fixed IP address for each computer, using the IP address, network mask, gateway address, and DNS server addresses supplied by your ISP.

If you will be making the settings manually, make a list of the names of each of your computers and the IP addresses you want to assign. Follow these steps on each computer that is to get manual settings:

1. Go to the Desktop and right-click the network icon at the right end of the taskbar. Select Open Network and Sharing Center, and then select Change Adapter Settings.

2. Right-click Ethernet or Wireless and select Properties.

3. Select the Networking tab, select Internet Protocol Version 4 (TCP/IPv4), and then click Properties.

4. In the General tab, click Use the Following IP Address. Then enter an IP address and the other information provided by your ISP. The required settings are the IP address, subnet mask, default gateway, and DNS server(s). Click OK.

If your ISP supplies you with Internet Protocol Version 6 (TCP/IPv6) settings, repeat the previous steps, except select Internet Protocol Version 6 (TCP/IPv6) in step 3.

Making Services Available

You might want to make some internal network services available to the outside world through your Internet connection. You would want to do this in these situations:

- You want to host a web server using Internet Information Services (IIS).

- You want to enable incoming VPN access to your LAN so you can securely connect from home or afield.

- You want to enable incoming Remote Desktop access to your computer.

If you have set up routed Internet service with a router (scheme E in Figure 19.1), you don't have to worry about this because your network connection is wide open and doesn't use NAT. As long as the outside users know the IP address of the computer hosting your service—or its DNS name, if you have set up DNS service— you're on the air already.

Otherwise, you have either Windows Firewall, NAT, or both in the way of incoming access. To make specific services accessible, you need to follow one of the sets of specific instructions in the next few sections, depending on the type of Internet connection setup you've used. Skip ahead to the appropriate section.

> **caution**
>
> Make absolutely sure that Windows Firewall is turned on, to protect your network from hackers. For more information on network security, see Chapter 33.

> **note**
>
> If you're interested in being able to reach your computer over the Internet using Remote Desktop, see Chapter 39, "Remote Desktop and Remote Access," which is entirely devoted to the subject.

Enabling Access with Internet Connection Sharing

When you are using Microsoft's Internet Connection Sharing feature, you need to execute two steps to provide outside access to a given service supplied by a computer on your network. First, you must tell the connection-sharing system (ICS) which computer on your network is to receive incoming connection requests for a particular service. Then, on the computer that provides the service, you must tell Windows Firewall to let these requests through.

On the computer that is providing the service itself, you must tell Windows Firewall to allow incoming connections to the service by following these steps:

1. Go to the Start screen and type **firewall**. Select the Settings icon in the Search panel. At the left, select Windows Firewall.

2. Click Advanced Settings. In the left pane, click Inbound Rules. Locate the service that this computer is providing, and find the line for the Private profile. If the service is listed with Yes in the Enabled column and Allow in the Action column, you can proceed to configure the computer that is sharing its Internet connection.

3. If the service isn't already listed, click New Rule in the right pane. Click Port, click Next, select TCP or UDP, and enter the specific port number or port number range required by the service. Table 19.1 lists common services, port numbers, and protocols. (For the FTP and DNS services, you have to make two entries.) Alternatively, you could add a new rule and select Program, to enable *all* incoming connections to an application.

4. Click Next and click Allow the Connection.

5. Click Next and leave all three check boxes (Domain, Private, Public) checked.

6. Click Next. For the rule name, enter the name of the service you're enabling, add an optional description, and click Finish.

Table 19.1 Common Services and Port Numbers

Service	Protocol	Port
Domain Name Service (DNS)	TCP and UDP	53
FTP Server	TCP	20 and 21
Internet Mail Server (SMTP)	TCP	25
Post-Office Protocol Version 3 (POP3)	TCP	110
Remote Desktop	TCP	3389
Secure Shell (SSH)	TCP	22
Secure Web Server (HTTPS)	TCP	443
Symantec PCAnywhere	TCP	5631
Telnet Server	TCP	23
Web Server (HTTP)	TCP	80

Next, you must instruct the computer that is sharing its Internet connection to forward incoming requests to the designated computer. On the computer that physically connects to the Internet, follow these steps:

1. Go to the Desktop and right-click the network icon at the right end of the taskbar. Select Open Network and Sharing Center, and then select Change Adapter Settings.

2. Right-click the icon for the shared Internet connection and select Properties. View the Sharing tab and, in the Internet Connection Sharing section, click Settings.

3. The Advanced Settings dialog box opens. Check the Service entry for each service for which you want to permit access and for which you have servers on your LAN. The most common ones to select are Remote Desktop, FTP Server, and Web Server, if you have set up IIS.

4. When you select a check box, the Service Settings dialog box appears. Enter the IP address of the computer that is hosting this service, if your LAN uses fixed IP addresses. If your LAN uses automatically assigned addresses from ICS, you can enter the computer's name, and the software will locate the correct computer. Click OK to save the settings.

note

If you want to use an incoming VPN connection, you must set it up on the computer that is sharing its Internet connection. ICS can't forward VPN connections to other computers.

5. If the service you want to use isn't listed, you need to find out what TCP and/or UDP ports the service communicates with. You have to search through the service software's documentation or on the Internet to find these port values.

   To add an unlisted service, click Add. Enter the name of the service or the IP address of the computer that is hosting this service and then add the port number. Generally, you'll want to use the same number for the port number the public sees (external port) and the port number used on the LAN (internal port). Check TCP or UDP and then click OK.

   If the service you're adding uses more than one protocol type or port number, you'll have to make multiple entries.

When you've enabled the desired services, incoming requests using the selected service ports will be forwarded to the appropriate computer on your LAN. Windows Firewall will know to let these services through.

Enabling Access with a Sharing Router

If you use a connection-sharing router on your LAN, you need to follow a somewhat different procedure to enable outside access to services on your network.

You must still open Windows Firewall on the computer(s) providing services, as described in the first six-step procedure in the previous section. Then you must use a manufacturer-specific procedure to set up forwarding for services that you want to expose to the Internet.

One difficulty with these devices is that you must forward services by IP address, not by computer name, and, normally, you will have set up computers to obtain their IP addresses automatically. This makes the computers moving targets, because their IP address could change from day to day.

So, you have to make special arrangements for the computers on your LAN that you want to use to host services. On your router's setup screens, make a note of the range of IP addresses that it will hand out to computers requesting automatic (DHCP) configuration. Most routers have a place to enter a starting IP address and a maximum number of addresses. For instance, the starting number might be 2, with a limit of 100 addresses. For each computer that will provide an outside service, pick a number between 2 and 254 that is *not* in the range of addresses handed out by the router, and use that as the last number in the computer's IP address. We recommend using address 250 and working downward from there for any other computers that require a static address.

To configure the computer's network address, follow the instructions under "Port Forwarding with a Router" in Chapter 39, with these changes:

- The material in Chapter 39 shows instructions for setting up Remote Desktop, with protocol TCP port 3389. You'll need to use the protocol and port numbers for the service you're enabling.

- Use a static IP address ending with .250 for the first computer you set up to receive incoming connections. Use .249 for the second computer, and work downward from there. Be sure to keep a list of the computers you assign static addresses to as well as the addresses you assign.

For services that use TCP/UDP in unpredictable ways, you must use another approach to forwarding on your LAN. Some services, such as Windows Live Messenger, communicate their *private*, internal IP address to the computer on the other end of the connection; when the other computer tries to send data to this private address, it fails. To use these services with a hardware router, you must enable UPnP, as described earlier in the chapter.

Other services use network protocols other than TCP and UDP, and most routers can't be set up to forward them. Incoming Microsoft VPN connections fall into this category. Some routers have built-in support for Microsoft's PPTP protocol. If yours has this support, your router's manual will tell you how to forward VPN connections to a host computer.

Otherwise, to support nonstandard services of this sort, you have to tell the router to forward *all* unrecognized incoming data to one designated computer. In effect, this exposes that computer to the Internet, so it's a fairly significant security risk. In fact, most routers call this targeted computer a *DMZ host*, referring to the notorious Korean no-man's-land called the Demilitarized Zone and the peculiar danger one faces standing in it.

To enable a DMZ host, you want to use a fixed IP address on the designated computer, as described in the previous section. Use your router's configuration screen to specify this selected IP address as the DMZ host. The configuration screen for my particular router is shown in Figure 19.7; yours might differ.

Now, designating a DMZ host means that this computer is fully exposed to the Internet, so you must protect it with a firewall of some sort. On this computer, you *must* set its network location to Public, and it can't participate in file sharing or a homegroup.

You should also set up filtering in your router to block ports 137–139 and 445. Figure 19.8 shows how this is done on my Linksys router; your router might use a different method.

> **◉ tip**
>
> It's not a bad idea to enable filtering for these ports even if you're not using a DMZ host. It's *essential* to do this if you set up a DMZ host.

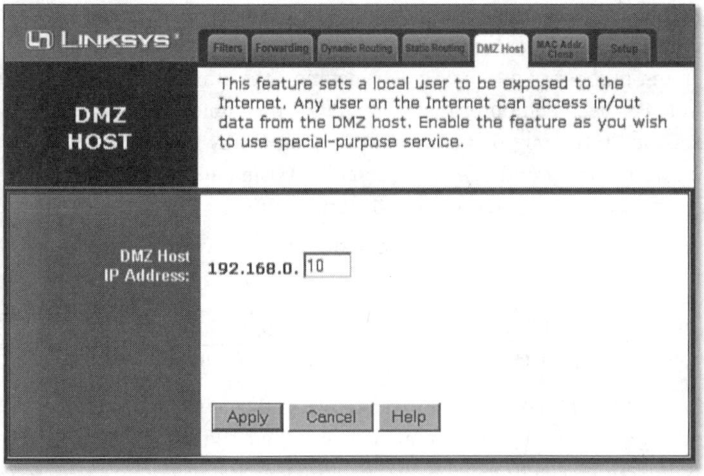

Figure 19.7
Enabling a DMZ host to receive all unrecognized incoming connection requests. This is an option of last resort if you can't forward incoming connections any other way.

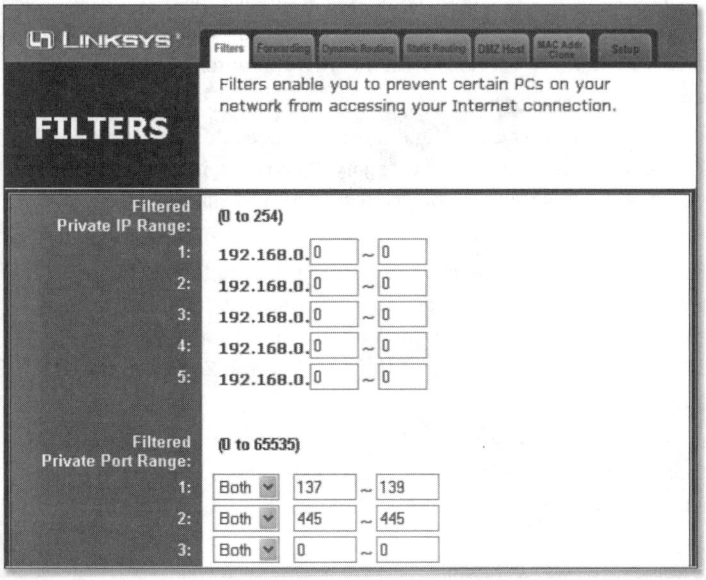

Figure 19.8
Configuring filters to block Microsoft file-sharing services.

NETWORKING WITH OTHER OPERATING SYSTEMS

Mix and Match with Windows and Macs

It's easy enough to plug a couple Windows 8 computers together and call it a network, but real-life networks are seldom so simple, even at home. Networks usually have a mix of operating systems, and Windows often has to be coaxed into getting along with them.

On a real-life LAN with multiple OSs, it's not enough that computers be capable of coexisting on the same network cable at the same time. They need to actually work *with* each other, or *internetwork*, so that users of these various systems can share files and printers. At best, this sharing should occur without anyone even knowing that alternative platforms are involved. Achieving this kind of seamlessness can range from effortless to excruciating.

Save the Heartache—Buy a Network Appliance

One way to avoid *most* of the hassles of internetworking is to buy a *network appliance*, also called *network-attached storage (NAS)*: a small server computer that "speaks" all the networking languages you need (UNIX, Macintosh, or whatever). These devices can cost less than $200 and can put terabytes of storage on your network for anyone to access. They tend to be very easy to set up, and a few even provide Internet Connection Sharing, wireless connectivity, an email server, a firewall, and a web server all in the same box. Products for the home and small office are made by Axentra (www.axentra.com), Cisco (www.linksysbycicso.com), D-Link (www.dlink.com), Buffalo Technology (www.buffalotech.com), LG (www.lg.com), and several other companies.

Additionally, Acer, Hewlett-Packard, Niveus, Velocity, and others made NAS devices based on a Microsoft software package called Windows Home Server (WHS). Microsoft has pulled the plug on the WHS product line, but, at the time this was written, there was the potential that Windows Server 2012 Foundation Edition might take its place. If products based on Foundation appear, they have the potential to provide a great backup and file-sharing solution. They "speak" only SMB, but Macs and Linux can use them, too.

If you're shopping for such a network appliance, be very careful to check what format it uses on its disks and what maximum file size it supports. Some devices support a maximum file size of only 2GB or 4GB, depending on the disk format and internal software used. Such a device might be okay for storing documents and photos, but it will be incapable of storing complete movies and computer backup files, many of which run 6GB in size or more—often way more. Other devices use proprietary networking drivers and/or proprietary disk formats. Personally, I'd only use a NAS device that uses standard file access protocols (SMB, NFS, and so on) *and* a disk format that can be read by Windows or Linux, so that if the hardware box were to die, I could at least put its hard disk into my desktop computer and extract its contents.

If a network appliance isn't in the cards, you need to get your computers to interoperate directly. This chapter shows you how to get computers running Windows, Mac OS X, UNIX, and Linux to play together nicely.

Windows 8 and 7 have some networking features that weren't in older versions, and some features have been removed. With respect to internetworking, this list provides a summary of the most significant changes since Windows Vista and XP:

- Windows 8 and 7 behave differently from previous versions of Windows when Password Protected Sharing is turned off. This is discussed later in the chapter under "Password Protection and Simple File Sharing."

- The NetBEUI network protocol is not available under Windows 8 and 7. This could impact you if your network includes computers running Windows XP, or—heaven forbid—earlier versions. We'll discuss this in more detail when we talk about networking with older versions of Windows later in this chapter.

- The Link Level Discovery Protocol (LLDP) is relatively new to Windows. LLDP lets Windows eke out a map of the connections between your computers and the other hardware on your network. LLDP support is available for Windows XP via a download, and is included in all the more recent versions. It's also in Server 2003 and later Server editions. Connections to computers running older versions of Windows will not be diagrammed on the network map. Computers running Linux and Mac OS X won't appear, either, unless you add a third-party program such as Open LLDP (at http://openlldp.sourceforge.net). Some commercial network-mapping applications (such as LANsurveyor at www.solarwinds.com) also have a Mac LLDP responder.

- Microsoft no longer provides out-of-the-box support for Novell NetWare (a corporate networking system). Novell Corporation has a NetWare client that works on Windows 8, but its installation and use is beyond the scope of this book.

However, although some things change, other things stay the same. You probably won't be surprised to learn that the Network Browser service (the relatively obscure software component responsible for collecting the list of names of the computers on your network, the list upon which the old Network Neighborhood display was based) is still present—and still works only when it feels like it.

In addition to covering internetworking issues, this chapter discusses some of the advanced and optional networking features provided with Windows 8. These features are not needed for "vanilla" Windows networks, but they are used for the more complex networks found in corporate environments.

Internetworking with Windows 7, Vista, and XP

Windows 8's file and printer sharing services work quite well with Windows 7, Vista, XP, and the various Windows Server versions. All of these OSs were intended from the start to work well with the TCP/IP network protocol favored by Windows 8.

For all practical purposes, Windows 8 and Windows 7 networking are virtually identical. There are no compatibility issues to worry about, other than the Network Location issue (discussed in Chapter 18, "Creating a Windows Network," in the section "Network Location Settings").

If your network has computers running older versions of Windows, the differences in OSs may show up in these areas:

- **Default networking protocols**—You might have configured older computers to use the NetBIOS or SPX/IPX protocol as the primary networking protocol. Windows 8 requires that you use TCP/IP. And, it's best if you use *only* TCP/IP.

- **LLDP mapping**—By default, Windows XP computers did not come with support for LLDP, and without it, these computers will appear as "orphans" on the network map display. You can download and install an LLDP add-on for XP if you wish.

- **Password Protected Sharing (Simple File Sharing)**—Windows can provide username/password security for shared files and folders. Windows 8, 7, Vista, and XP also have a "passwordless" option.

■ **HomeGroup networking**—Windows 8 and 7 let you join your computers into a homegroup, which simplifies file sharing security. A homegroup member can still share files and printers with older versions of Windows, but there are some subtleties that we explain in this chapter.

We cover these topics in the next four sections.

Setting TCP/IP as the Default Network Protocol

When freshly installed, Windows XP was set up to use the TCP/IP network protocol for file and printer sharing by default. If your network previously included Windows 95, 98, Me, 2000, or NT computers, you might have changed the network protocols to simplify internetworking with the older operating systems.

Because newer versions of Windows support only TCP/IP, you need to make sure that TCP/IP is enabled on your Windows XP computers. Also, Windows networking works much more reliably when every computer on the network has the exact same set of protocols installed. You should ensure that TCP/IP is the *only* installed network protocol.

> 🔍 **note**
>
> If your computer is connected to a corporate network, your network administrator will make all necessary changes for you.

Follow these steps on all your computers that run Windows XP Home Edition or XP Professional:

1. Log on using a Computer Administrator account.

2. Click Start, Control Panel, Network and Internet Connections; then click the Network Connections icon.

3. Right-click the Local Area Connection icon and select Properties.

4. Look in the list of installed components and make sure that Internet Protocol (TCP/IP) is listed. If not, click Install, select Protocols, click Add, and select Internet Protocol (TCP/IP). If your network uses manually assigned (static) IP addresses, configure the Internet Protocol entry just as you configured your Windows 7 computers.

5. Look in the list of installed components for the NWLink IPX/SPX or NetBEUI protocols. Select these entries and click Uninstall.

6. Click OK to close the Local Area Connection Properties dialog box.

7. From the menu in the Network Connections window, select Advanced, Advanced Settings. Select the Adapters and Bindings tab.

8. In the top list, select Local Area Connection. In the lower list, make sure that Internet Protocol (TCP/IP) is checked under both File and Printer Sharing for Microsoft Networks and Client for Microsoft Networks.

9. Click OK to close the dialog box.

After checking all your computers, restart *all* your computers if you had to make changes on *any* of them.

Password Protection and Simple File Sharing

On small Windows networks (that is, networks that aren't managed by a Windows Server computer using the Domain security model), each computer is separately responsible for managing usernames and passwords. Before Windows XP, this made it difficult to securely share files across the network—you had to create accounts for each of your users on every one of your computers, using the same password for each user on each computer.

Windows XP introduced a concept called Simple File Sharing that, when enabled, entirely eliminated security for file sharing. All network access was done in the context of the Guest user account, regardless of the remote user's actual account name. Essentially, anyone with physical access to your network could access any shared file. This made it much easier for other people in your home and office to get to each other's files. (And, horrifyingly, everyone on the Internet could also get at your files, until XP Service Pack 2 came out.)

Windows 8, 7, and Vista also include Simple File Sharing, although it's now called Password Protected Sharing. And, the effect of disabling and enabling the feature is reversed on the two newer operating systems. Table 20.1 shows the settings and the results.

Table 20.1   File Sharing Settings

Windows 8, 7, Vista Password Protected Sharing	XP Professional Simple File Sharing	Account and Password
On	Unchecked	Required
Off	Checked	Not required

This setting is not always changeable. In Windows XP Home Edition, Simple File Sharing is always checked and cannot be turned off. In all other versions of Windows, it can be turned on or off, except if the computer is a member of a domain network. In this case, passwords are always required.

Finally, Windows 8 and 7 have a new twist in the way that security works when Password Protected Sharing is turned off. On Vista and XP, when passwords are not required, *all* incoming network access uses the Guest account. Thus, anyone on the network can access any file in a shared folder if the file can be accessed by the user account Guest or by the user group Everyone.

But on Windows 8 and 7, the following happens when a remote user attempts to use a folder or file shared by a Windows 8 or 7 computer with Password Protected Sharing turned off:

- If the remote user's account matches an account in the Windows 8 or 7 sharing computer *and* that account has a password set, that account is used for file access.

- If the remote user's account matches an account in the sharing computer but that account has no password set, then the Guest account is used.

- If the remote user's account matches no account in the sharing computer, the Guest account is used.

This might seem convoluted, but it is actually a very useful change. First of all, this change was necessary to support the new HomeGroup feature. All homegroup member computers use a special, password-protected account named HomeGroupUser$ to access other member computers, and this change lets it work whether Password Protected Sharing is turned on or off. Second, it gives you the *option* of giving designated users additional access privileges, without requiring you to set up a full-blown security scheme.

We know this has probably given you a headache by now. You probably just want to know how to get at the library of pictures stored on your old computer. In the end, however, it can be pretty easy to decide how to set things up, based on how concerned you need to be about security.

To see how to set up your network, decide which of the following three categories best describes your environment:

- **My computer is part of a corporate domain network.**

   In this case, accounts and passwords are always required. Your network administrator sets these up. Use the Security tab on any folder that you share to select the users and groups to which you want to grant access.

- **Ease of use is my priority, and network security is not a great concern.**

   In this case, turn off Password Protected Sharing on your Windows 8, 7, and Vista computers, and enable Simple File Sharing on any Windows XP Professional computers. This lets anyone on the network access any shared folder.

   You must make sure that a firewall is set up to block File and Printer Sharing access over your Internet connection. Use a connection-sharing router, Windows Firewall, or a third-party firewall program to do this. If you have a wireless network, you must enable WPA or WEP security.

- **Security is important to me; I want specific control over which individual users can use specific shared files and folders.**

   In this case, turn on Password Protected Sharing on your Windows 8, 7, and Vista computers as well as disable Simple File Sharing on any XP Professional computers. Do not share sensitive resources from any computer that runs Windows XP Home Edition (or do not use XP Home Edition at all). Do not create a homegroup.

   On every computer that does share sensitive folders or printers with the network, you need to create an account for every user who needs access to the shared folders or printers. For each user, be sure to create an account with the same name and the same password as on that user's own computer.

To change the Simple File Sharing setting on Windows XP Professional, follow these steps:

1. Log on as a Computer Administrator.

2. Click Start, My Computer.

> **🔊 tip**
>
> If you change your password on any computer, it's a good idea to make the same change on every computer where you have an account. This way, you won't be asked to supply your password whenever you use network resources.

> **🔍 note**
>
> All these rules about whether a password is required are interpreted by the computer that is *sharing* a folder or printer. When any version of Windows *uses* a folder or printer shared by another computer, *that* computer sets the rules for requiring a password. For example, XP Home Edition never requires an account or password when someone wants to use its shared folders, but it can still use password-protected shared resources shared by, say, Windows 8 or even a Windows domain server.

3. Press and release the Alt key to display the menu. Select Tools, Folder Options and then select the View tab.

4. Scroll to the bottom of the Advanced Settings list. Simple File Sharing is the last entry in the list. Check or uncheck the entry as desired.

More discussion of file-sharing password arrangements can be found in Chapter 18, "Creating a Windows Network," and in Chapter 33, "Protecting Your Network from Hackers and Snoops."

Using Windows Vista and XP with a Homegroup

If you have two or more Windows 7 or 8 computers, you can set up a homegroup (as described in Chapter 18) to simplify sharing libraries, folders, and printers. The HomeGroup system is based on regular Windows file sharing, so computers running other operating systems can also participate in your network.

The easiest way to make XP and Vista fit in with a homegroup is to disable password protected sharing on all your computers. (Password protected sharing is discussed in the previous section.) Here are the instructions for doing this on various versions of Windows:

- **Windows 8 and 7**—Click Start (in Windows 8, right-click Start at the bottom-left corner of the screen), and then click Control Panel, View Network Status and Tasks (under Network and Internet), Change Advanced Sharing Settings. Scroll down, and in the All Networks section (which you might need to expand), select Turn Off Password Protected Sharing, and then click Save Changes.

- **Windows Vista**—Click Start, Control Panel, Set Up File Sharing (under Network and Internet). Click the circular icon with the down arrow to the right of Password Protected sharing, click Turn Off Password Protected Sharing, and then click Apply. You might need to confirm a user account control prompt.

  (A better alternative: upgrade the computer to Windows 8 or 7).

- **Windows XP Professional**—Log on as a computer administrator. Click Start, My Computer. In the menu, select Tools, Folder Options and then select the View tab. Scroll the list down to the bottom, check Simple File Sharing, and then click OK.

- **Windows XP Home Edition**—No adjustments are necessary.

Now Windows 8 and 7 computers will connect to other Windows 8 and 7 computers using the special HomeGroupUser$ account, but all other combinations will use the Guest account. This means you need to make sure that resources are shared so that "Everyone" can use them. In particular, the file security settings for the shared folder and its contents must be set so that Everyone has read or read and write permission.

To ensure that this happens, use the following procedures when you're sharing folders on various versions of Windows:

- **Windows 8 and 7**—Right-click a folder or library and select Share With, Share with Homegroup (View), or Share with Homegroup (View and Edit). Then, right-click it again and select Share With, Specific People. Type or select Everyone in the drop-down list, and then click Add. If you want other users to be able to change the contents of the folder, next to Everyone, click the word

Read in the Permissions column and select Read/Write. Click Share to finish.

- **Windows Vista**—Right-click a folder and select Share. Type or select Everyone in the drop-down list and then click Add. If you want other users to be able to change the contents of the folder, next to Everyone, click the word Reader in the Permissions column and select Contributor. Click Share to finish.

- **Windows XP Professional or Home Edition**—Right-click a folder and select Sharing and Security. Select Sharing This Folder and click Apply. Select the Security tab. Under Group or User Names, if there is an entry for Everyone, select it; otherwise, click Add, type **Everyone**, press Enter, and select the entry for Everyone. In the lower section (in the Allow column), Read & Execute, List Folder Contents, and Read should be checked. If you would like to let other network users modify the contents of the folder, check Modify. Click OK to finish.

> **caution**
>
> If you give Everyone permission to change files, you must be sure that your network is secured. If you have a wireless network, you must have it set up so that it has WEP or WPA security enabled (that is, so that a password or key is required to use the network). If you connect to the Internet, you must be sure that Windows Firewall or a third-party firewall product is set up to block Windows file sharing. If you don't secure your network, "Everyone" means "anyone in the world," and that's a recipe for disaster.

If you want to use passwords to protect access to shared folders, you should leave password-protected sharing turned on. There are two ways in which you can deal with the Windows Vista and XP computers:

- Set up accounts on every computer using the same account name and password for each person, on each computer. This will give you complete control over who has access to which folders shared by Windows 8, 7, Vista, and XP Professional. (Per-user security is not available on folders shared by XP Home.)

- Set up a single account that you'll use for file sharing, perhaps named *share*, on every computer, with the same password on every computer. Use this account when you set the permissions on shared folders, and use this account when Windows asks for an account and password when you connect to another computer.

If you share your printer, it's enough just to enable sharing. By default, all versions of Windows enable Everyone to print to every installed printer, so anyone on the network should be able to print to any shared printer without the security settings needing to be changed.

Internetworking with UNIX and Linux

The UNIX operating system, originally developed in the 1970s at AT&T's Bell Laboratories as a platform for internal software development and as a "workbench" for programmers, is still evolving and growing. Today, hundreds of millions of people use UNIX or UNIX-like OSs every day, sometimes without even knowing it, on everything from iMacs to Androids, laptops to mainframes, routers to space probes, and... well, the list goes on and on.

This section looks at ways to network Windows 8 with UNIX-type OSs. Although many of the examples involve Linux, most of the examples can be translated to almost any UNIX-type OS. And because typing "UNIX-like" is already getting tiresome, from here on, we sometimes write just "UNIX," but we always mean "UNIX and/or Linux and/or Mac OS X."

Samba

Samba is an open source (free) software suite available on most UNIX-like OSs. The Samba server program makes it possible for UNIX computers to share folders and printers that Windows users can access, and the Samba client tools let UNIX users access folders and printers shared by Windows computers. Samba is included with Apple's OS X, which is how Macs get their Windows file-sharing capability. The names of the Samba programs start with the letters smb, which stands for Server Message Block. This is the name of the network protocol on which Windows file sharing is based.

> **note**
>
> You can get more information about Samba and download a version for most UNIX systems from www.samba.org. Most Linux distributions include a version of Samba and install it by default. For a good Samba introduction and reference, check out *The Official Samba-3 HOWTO and Reference Guide* (Prentice Hall, 2005, ISBN 0131882228).

Samba Client Tools

To access file services shared by Windows computers from UNIX, you must know exactly what resources are available from a given host on the network. Samba includes a command-line program called smbclient for just that purpose. This application enables you to list available Windows shares and printers from within UNIX. For example, the command smbclient -L //lombok lists all the folders and printers shared by the computer named lombok.

When you know the name of the desired shared folder, the smbmount command enables you to mount the Windows share on the local (UNIX) file system. The command

```
smbmount //lombok/shareddocs /mnt/winshare -U brian
```

mounts the SharedDocs folder shared by computer lombok to the local directory /mnt/winshare. The -U switch tells smbclient what username to use when trying to mount the share. You are prompted for a password.

You also can use a Windows printer from a UNIX client, but the procedure is complex and beyond the scope of this chapter. Some Linux distributions include a GUI print configuration tool to simplify the process. In any case, we recommend that you read the SMB How-To at http://en.tldp.org/HOWTO/SMB-HOWTO.html.

> **note**
>
> If the Windows computer is running Windows 8 or 7 with Password Protected Sharing turned off, you can specify any nonexistent account name to gain access using the Guest account. If you specify a valid account name, you will gain access using this account. This differs from previous versions of Windows where, if Password Protected Sharing is turned off, the Guest account is used no matter what. Password Protected Sharing is discussed earlier in the chapter under "Password Protection and Simple File Sharing."

Samba Server Tools

Samba also includes tools and servers to make your UNIX system look just like a Windows-based network server; this capability lets your Windows computers use files and printers shared by UNIX systems.

The parameters for configuring Samba in a server capacity are contained in the file /etc/smb.conf on the UNIX host. The default file included with Samba has comments for every parameter to explain each one. Configuring the Samba server is beyond the scope of this book. However, we can offer a few pointers:

- Some OSs, such as Mac OS X, include a GUI tool to configure Samba file sharing. These tools make the job a lot easier.

- If you have to set up file sharing by hand, read the documentation and FAQs for your Samba version before starting the setup procedure. A good place to start is http://en.tldp.org/HOWTO/SMB-HOWTO.html.

- Configure Samba for user-specific passwords with the `security` option. You need to set up UNIX user accounts for each of your Windows users. Alternatively, you can set up a single UNIX account that all Windows user will share. Windows users would need to supply the selected username and password when they use UNIX shares.

    Set `encrypt passwords = yes` in `smb.conf`. You also need to set up a user and password file for Samba's use, which is usually specified with the `smb.conf` entry `smb passwd file = /etc/smbpasswd`. Your Samba documentation explains how to do this.

- Alternatively, you can use share-level security without a password. This makes Samba behave similar to a Windows host with Password Protected Sharing turned off. However, in this case, you *must* take care to prevent SMB access to your UNIX computer from the Internet. To be precise, you must be sure that TCP port 445 is blocked.

When you have finished editing the `smb.conf` file, you can test to see that the syntax is correct by using the Samba program `testparm`. `testparm` checks `smb.conf` for internal "correctness" before you actually use it in a production environment.

Printing to UNIX Queues from Windows

You can configure Samba to offer standard Windows shared printer service. As an alternative, Windows 8 has built-in support to send output to UNIX-based printers using the Line Printer Remote (LPR) protocol. You can install a standard Windows printer whose output is directed to a UNIX system and can use this printer just as you would any local or networked Windows printer.

 *For instruction on connecting to an LPR-based printer from Windows, **see** "Using UNIX and LPR Printers," p. 468.*

Printing to Windows Printers from UNIX

You can install software on Windows 8 to let UNIX users print to any local printers shared Windows. This is the receiving end of the LPR protocol, and it's called Line Printer Daemon (LPD) Print Service.

To install this service on a Windows host, log on as a Computer Administrator and follow these steps:

1. Right-click the very bottom-left corner of the screen and select Control Panel. Under Programs, select Turn Windows Features On or Off. (Alternatively, press Windows Logo+R, and then type **optionalfeatures** and press Enter.

2. Scroll through the list of features and open Print and Document Services.

3. Check LPD Print Service and then click OK.

Carriage Returns and Line Feeds Are Mangled

If you send plain-text files from UNIX machines to Windows printers using lpr and Print Services for UNIX and you find that carriage returns and line feeds are mangled (for example, line feeds are inserted where just carriage returns were present in text that should have been overprinted), you need to disable the translation of both newlines and carriage returns, or just carriage returns, by adding a value to the Registry. Follow these steps:

1. Find the key HKEY_LOCAL_MACHINE\System\CurrentControlSet\Control\Print\ Printers*printername*\PrinterDriverData, where *printername* is the name of the shared printer the UNIX user is using.

2. Select the key PrinterDriverData and choose Edit, New, DWORD Value. Enter the name **Winprint_TextNoTranslation** and set the value to **1**.

3. To prevent the server from replacing CR with CR+LF but still have it replace LF with CR+LF, add the DWORD value **Winprint_TextNoCRTranslation** with the value **1**.

4. After making either of these additions, go to Computer Management, view Services, right-click TCP/IP Print Server, and select Restart.

➡ *For instructions and warnings about using the Registry editor,* **see** *"Using Regedit," p. 701.*

Some Windows printer drivers do not correctly implement overprinted lines. You might find that these lines are now correctly stacked on top of each other, but only the text from the topmost line is visible. You might need to use the binary mode flag (-o l) in your lpr command and add a form feed to the end of your file.

If you later decide to undo the Registry change, you can remove the value item or set its value to **0** and then restart the LPD service.

Services for NFS and Subsystem for UNIX-Based Applications

Windows 8 Enterprise edition includes Services for NFS, a network client that enables Windows to attach to servers using the NFS file-sharing protocol commonly used in UNIX environments, and the Subsystem for UNIX-Based Applications (SUA), a software package that enables POSIX-compliant UNIX applications to run within Windows. These services are used primarily in enterprise settings. To install either of these features, open the Control Panel and select Turn Windows Features On or

Off. (Alternatively, press Windows Logo+R, type **optionalfeatures**, and then press Enter.) Then, check the boxes next to the desired features.

In Windows 7, these features were available in the Professional, Enterprise, and Ultimate editions. In Windows 8, they are available in the Enterprise edition only. Microsoft has indicated that it intends to drop SUA from the next version of Windows.

Internetworking with Macintosh

The Apple Macintosh is arguably *the* computer of choice in the music, graphic arts, design, and publishing worlds. Although Macs used to live pretty much in a world apart, it's common now for both Macs and Windows computers to need to coexist on the same network. However, Macs normally use a proprietary file sharing system called AppleTalk File Protocol (AFP), whereas Windows computers use a protocol called Server Message Block (SMB).

To link Macs and PCs on a network, either the Macs must learn to "speak" SMB or the Windows computers must speak AFP. Both solutions are possible. On a corporate network based on Windows Server, your network administrator can install a component called Services for Macintosh (SFM), which speaks AFP to make Windows-based resources visible to Macs as well as resources shared by Macs visible to Windows users. The process of installing and configuring SFM is not complicated, but it needs to be done by the administrator of a Windows Server computer; as such, it's beyond the scope of this book.

Microsoft appears to have lost interest in providing support for Mac users in the home and small office. Fortunately, Apple has stepped up and provided Windows-compatible networking support as a standard part of OS X. You can also add Windows networking support to older Mac OS computers. We cover these options in the next several sections. First, though, let's talk about other issues that come up when Windows and Macs need to work together.

Compatibility Issues

If you share files between Macs and Windows computers on your network, you need to be aware of some compatibility issues.

Resource Data Issues

The first issue arises because Mac files actually consist of two separate parts, called *forks*:

- The data fork, which contains data, document text, program code, and so on

- The resource fork, which in applications contains language-specific strings and dialog box layouts for programs, and in documents contains the association information that links a document to the application that created it

The two parts can be read and written to completely independently. It's as if each Mac file is composed of two bundled but separate files.

Windows also supports this concept. On Windows, the separate parts are called *streams* rather than forks. But, for reasons unknown, they're not used for Mac file sharing. When a Mac file is copied to a Windows shared folder, the resource fork data is stored in a separate hidden file. If the Mac file is named `special.doc`, the resource data is put into a file named `._special.doc`. It's invisible unless you enable the display of hidden files in File Explorer.

The problem is that if you move, edit, or rename the main document or application file in Windows, the resource file might be left behind or end up with the wrong name. Then, on the Mac side, the Mac will no longer know what application to use to open the document—and in the case of an application program, the application will not run. Therefore, it's best not to store Mac applications on Windows shares if they will be renamed or moved.

Mac Files Have Lost Application Associations

After a Windows user edits a shared file and a Mac user tries to open the file, the Mac Finder may say it can't find the application required to open the document. What happened is that the file's resource fork was stripped out when the file was edited in Windows, so the file's Type and Creator codes are missing. The Mac user should drag and drop the file onto the application's icon or manually locate the application, and then resave the file. This will restore the association for future edits.

The Type and Creator codes can also be set using a Mac resource editor. However, resource editing is tricky and best not done unless it's an emergency.

Type and Creator codes are case sensitive. MSWD is not the same as mswd. Case can often cause confusion if you must restore the codes after they were stripped on a trip through Windows or DOS.

Filename Compatibility Issues

Mac filenames can have up to 255 characters and can contain any character except the colon (:).

Windows permits filenames up to 256 characters in length but has a longer list of unacceptable characters: the colon (:), backslash (\), forward slash (/), question mark (?), asterisk (*), quotation mark ("), greater-than symbol (>), less-than symbol (<), and pipe symbol (¦).

Therefore, for files that will be shared, it's best to avoid all of these characters when you name files on your Mac.

Application Concurrency Issues

When a Mac application is installed on a shared folder stored on a Windows computer, an "Unable to Open File" error occurs on Macs when more than one Mac user attempts to run the application concurrently.

> ### "Unable to Open File" Error Occurs on Macs
>
> Some Mac programs fail to open their application executable files in the proper file-sharing mode. You can patch the problem by using a resource editor program on the Mac:
>
> 1. Obtain a copy of ResEdit from www.resexcellence.com, which is a terrific resource (pun intended) for all things resource related. For novice users, a better resource editor program is File Buddy, from SkyTag Software (www.skytag.com).
>
> 2. Start ResEdit or File Buddy. Select File, Get Info. In the dialog box that appears, you can select the application.
>
> 3. Put a check in the Shared check box.
>
> 4. If you're using ResEdit, quit the application and choose Yes to save the changes. In File Buddy, click OK.

Working with Mac OS X

Mac OS X comes with Windows-compatible networking support built in, via the Samba software mentioned earlier in the chapter. This means that Macs running OS X can connect directly to drives and folders shared by Windows computers. You don't even need to use the command line; the Mac GUI manages the Samba client and server components for you.

Using Windows Shared Files on the Mac

On OS X 10.5 and later editions, you can easily browse folders shared by Windows computers from any Finder window. In the left pane, under Shared, you can select a Windows computer from the list of detected computers and then browse into its shared folders, as shown in Figure 20.1.

 note

This section shows you how to use Windows shared files from your Mac, and how to share files from your Mac for use by Windows. To see how to set up file sharing on Windows, see Chapter 21, "Using a Windows Network."

When you select a remote computer, OS X attempts to connect to the computer using your Mac account's username and password so that it can display a list of available shared folders. If this fails, you can use a different account by clicking the Connect As button that appears in the upper-right corner of the Finder window. We discuss accounts in the next section, "Selecting a Windows Account."

If you are using OS X 10.4 or earlier, or if the Windows computer does not appear in the list of local computers that the Finder displays under Shared, there is an alternative way to connect. Select the Finder and choose Go, Connect to Server. The dialog box shown in Figure 20.2 appears.

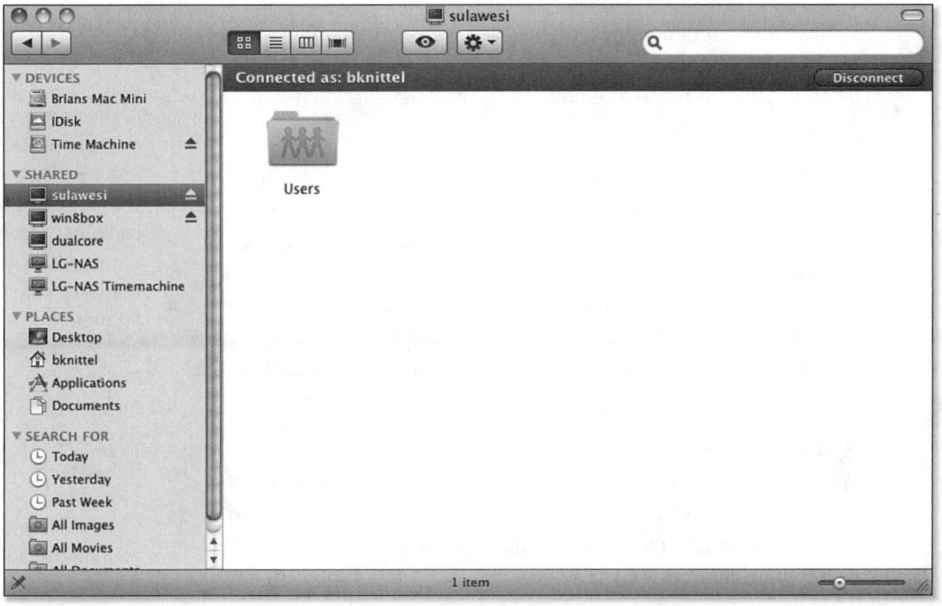

Figure 20.1
The Finder in OS X 10.5 and later lets you easily select and connect to both Mac and Windows computers.

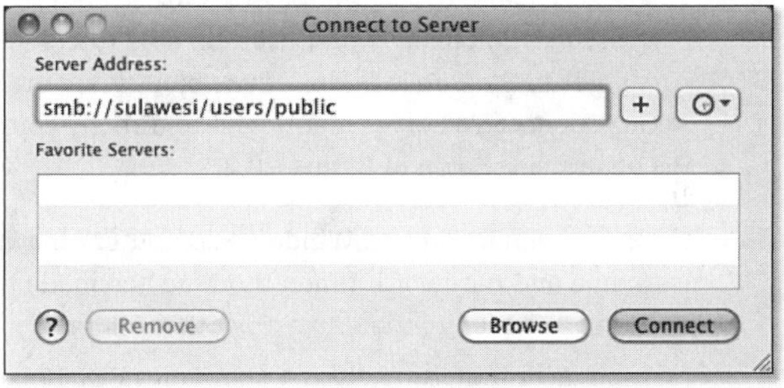

Figure 20.2
The Connect to Server dialog box lets a Mac OS X computer connect directly to a folder shared by Windows. Enter **smb:** followed by the share's UNC path, or click Browse.

You can enter the UNC name of the shared folder directly, in the format smb://*computername*/*sharename*, where *computername* is the name of the Windows computer or its IP address, and *sharename* is the name of the shared folder. For example, the Public folder on a computer named sulawesi could be entered as smb://sulawesi/users/public, or using the computer's IP address, as something like smb://192.168.0.12/users/public. Click Connect to proceed.

You can click the + button to add the path to the Favorites list. You also can click the Browse button to select from a list of detected Mac and Windows computers.

Selecting a Windows Account

Whichever connection method you use, when you connect, a login dialog box might appear. If you're connecting to a Windows 8 computer on a home or small office network, the following applies:

- If Password Protected Sharing is enabled, or to access files that are shared only to specified user accounts, choose Connect As Registered User. Enter a username and password that is valid on the Windows 8 computer. (On a home or small office workgroup network, you can ignore the Workgroup or Domain entry, if it appears. Fill in just the Name and Password entries.) You will connect with the file and folder access rights associated with this account.

- If you have disabled Password Protected Sharing, select Connect As Guest; alternatively, enter the username Guest with no password. (Actually, you can enter any *invalid* username, with any password.) This gives you the file and folder access rights granted to Everyone.

In most cases, using Guest access means that you will have access only to the shared folder \Users\Public, but no other shared folders, unless the person who shared the other folders explicitly granted rights to Everyone. You likely won't even be able to view the list of users folders inside \Users so that you can get to the Public folder. If you can't view the contents of the Users folder, use the Finder's Go, Connect To Server menu item to directly connect to folder smb://*computername*/Users/Public, as shown in Figure 20.2.

If you are connecting to a Windows computer on a Windows domain network, enter a valid domain username and password. When the Mac has made the network connection, the shared folder is displayed in a Finder window like any other folder.

To disconnect from the network share on OS X 10.5 or later, click the Eject button next to the computer's name under Shared in the Finder window. On OS X 10.4, drag the shared folder desktop icon to the trash or locate it in the Finder and click the Eject button.

Now, recall the point we made earlier about Mac files having two parts, or *forks*. If you copy a file from a Mac to a shared Windows folder, Windows might create an extra hidden file to contain the resource information for the file. The resource file's name will consist of a period and an underscore followed by the name of the main file. Windows users need to move and rename these files together; otherwise, Mac users will receive errors when they try to access the files.

> **🔍 note**
>
> If you are using a Microsoft (online) account with Windows 8, the username for networking is not the email address you use when you sign on. To find the real name of your Windows computer account, right-click the very bottom-left corner of the screen and select Command Prompt. At the bottom of this window will appear something like this: c:\users\bknittel>. The word after users is your account name (in this example, it's bknittel). Use this name when you try to connect from your Mac to a shared Windows folder.

> **🔍 note**
>
> When a Mac user opens a Window share, the Finder creates a file named .DS_Store and sometimes also one named ._.DS_Store. These hold Mac desktop information. Windows users should ignore these files, just as Mac users should ignore the file desktop.ini.

Using Windows Printers on the Mac

If you are using a Mac, to use a printer that is shared by a Windows computer, follow these steps:

1. On the Windows computer, when you share the printer, be sure to use a share name that's no more than 12 letters long. If you use a longer name, the printer might not appear in the list of printers on the Mac.

2. On the Mac, open System Preferences and select Print & Fax.

3. If the page is locked, click the lock icon and enter an administrator's credentials.

    Click the + button to add a printer.

    On OS X 10.4, at the bottom of the Printer Browser dialog box, click More Printers.

4. At the top of the next Printer Browser dialog box, select Windows (on OS X 10.5 and later) or Windows Printing (on OS X 10.4), and underneath, select the appropriate Windows workgroup name. In the computer list, choose the name of the computer that is sharing the printer you want to use.

5. In the Connect To dialog box, enter a username and password that is valid on the Windows computer. (See the previous section, "Selecting a Windows Account.") If you turned off Password Protected Sharing on Windows 8, you can select Connect As: Guest (or enter username Guest with no password).

> **🔍 note**
>
> In our testing we found that there could be delays of up to a couple of minutes between printing a document from the Mac and having the Windows printer start up.

6. Select the desired shared printer in the list. Open the Print Using list (on OS X 10.5 and later) or the Printer Model list (on OS X 10.4), and then select the correct printer manufacturer name and model. Finally, click Add.

This adds the Windows printer to the list of available printers on your Mac.

Using Mac Shared Files on Windows

Mac OS X computers can share folders with Windows computers over the network, thanks to the Samba file server software that is installed as part of OS X.

To enable Windows-compatible file sharing on OS X 10.5 (Leopard) or later, follow these steps:

1. Open System Preferences and select Sharing. If the panel is locked, click the lock icon and enter an administrative password.

2. If File Sharing is not checked, check it. Select folders to share, and for each selected folder, choose the user accounts that can access the share. This much is standard for file sharing on the Macs. The next step lets you use these same folders from Windows computers.

tip

To save yourself a world of pain, create user accounts on your Mac and Windows computers using the same account names (short names, in Mac parlance) and passwords on both types of computers. From the Windows side, you cannot use or even see a list of the folders or printers shared by the Mac unless you are using a Windows account that matches up with one on the Mac and that has been enabled on the Sharing page. If you want to use Microsoft (online) accounts on Windows 8, create local Windows accounts first, using the same account names as you use on your Macs, and then turn those Windows accounts into Microsoft accounts. We discuss this in Chapter 3, "Your First Hour with Windows 8," under "Creating User Accounts."

3. Click Options and then check Share Files and Folders Using SMB (Windows), as shown in Figure 20.3.

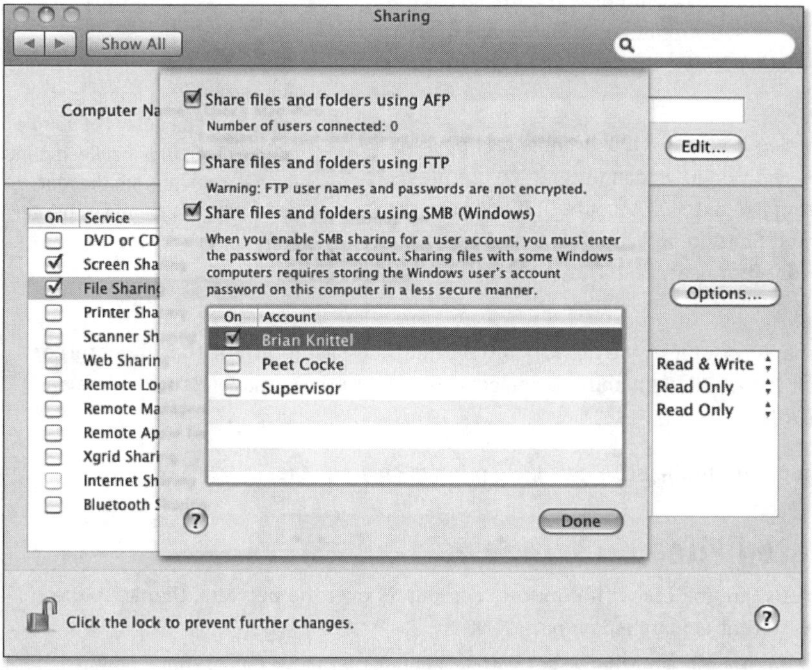

Figure 20.3
Enable Windows-compatible file sharing from the Options button on the System Preferences Sharing page.

To enable Windows-compatible file sharing on OS X 10.4 (Tiger), follow these steps:

1. Open System Preferences and select Sharing. Check Windows Sharing.

2. Click the Accounts button and check the names of the accounts that you want to permit to be used for Windows Sharing connections.

3. Click Show All and select Accounts.

On Windows, you can use Mac shared folders just as you use folders shared from any Windows computer. Macs appear in the list of available computers in the Network folder, and you can open the shared folders from those icons.

You can also specify a Mac shared folder directly using its UNC pathname. By default, OS X 10.5 shares users' Public folders, with share names based on each user's full name. For example, the path to my Public folder might be *computername*\brian knittel's public folder. OS X 10.4 shares users' entire home directories by default, using each user's short name. Therefore, on OS 10.4, my home directory's UNC path might be *computername*\ bknittel.

> ### 🔍 note
>
> When you open the Network folder icon for a Mac running OS X 10.4, or use the net view command to view the items shared by a Mac running OS X 10.4, you will see only shared folders and printers that you have permission to use.

Using Mac Shared Printers on Windows

After enabling Windows Sharing in System Preferences, you can share your Mac's printer(s) with Windows users by selecting Show All and then clicking Print and Fax. View the Sharing tab, click Share These Printers with Other Computers, and check the printers that you want to make available to others.

To use a printer shared from a Mac on Windows, follow these steps:

1. Set up accounts on both the Mac and on Windows, using the same account name and the same password on both computers.

2. On the Mac, enable SMB File Sharing on the Mac as described in the previous section, "Using Mac Shared Files on Windows." Then, enable Printer Sharing on the System Preferences Sharing page. Select the printer that you want to use from Windows.

3. Follow the strange procedure described next.

The strange bit is that you must trick Windows into using a PostScript printer driver, no matter what type of printer the Mac is really sharing. The Mac accepts only PostScript printer codes and converts the PostScript to the appropriate codes for its installed printer.

To connect to the Mac printer from Windows, follow these steps:

1. Press Windows Logo+X, then select Control Panel, View Devices and Printers, Add a Printer, The Printer That I Want Isn't Listed. Then, click Add Bluetooth, Wireless or Network Discoverable Printer and click Next.

2. Wait for the desired Mac printer to appear in the list. Double-click it. If requirements 1 and 2 from the previous list aren't met, the printer won't appear.

   It also won't appear if the Mac is on a different subnet than the Windows computer. In this case, click Cancel. Repeat the process but this time select Select a Shared Printer by Name, and then enter the printer share name as *ipaddress**sharename*, where *ipaddress* is the IP address of the Mac and *sharename* is the name of the Mac printer.

3. When the message "The server for the printer does not have the correct printer driver installed" appears, click OK.

4. In the Manufacturer list, select HP. In the Printers list, if the Mac printer is a color printer, select HP Color LaserJet 2800 Series PS. If the Mac printer is a black-and-white printer, select HP LaserJet 2300 Series PS. Then click OK.

Installing Optional Network Components

Windows 8 comes with some networking features or services that are not used in most networks but can be essential in others. We don't cover these features in great detail because your network manager will probably install them for you if they're used on your LAN.

Table 20.2 describes the optional features. Not every component is available on every version of Windows 8.

To enable any of the components, press Windows+X, then select Programs and Features, Turn Windows Features On or Off. Check the box next to each desired feature and then click OK.

Table 20.2   Windows 8 Optional Networking Features

Category/Component	Description
Web and Application Services	
Internet Information Services and Internet Information Services Hostable Web Core	IIS is a full-featured web server. IIS can also be used by software developers as a platform for peer-to-peer applications, which is why certain IIS components are provided with all versions of Windows 8 and 7. If you install an application that requires IIS, the application's installer will most likely configure it for you. This category also includes an FTP server.
Windows Communication Foundation HTTP Activation	The HTTP Activation system can be used by .NET application software to run services on demand. This component is enabled by the application program(s) as needed. (This selection is located under Microsoft .NET Framework 3.5.)
Microsoft Message Queue (MSMQ) Server	MSMQ Server is a tool used primarily in distributed database applications. It is provided with Windows 8 and 7 primarily for use by software developers who are writing and testing such applications.
Management and Monitoring Tools	
Simple Network Management Protocol (SNMP)	SNMP is a remote monitoring and measurement tool used by some network-management systems.
WMI SNMP Provider	This allows Windows Management Instrumentation (WMI) applications to access SNMP data.
Telnet Client	This enables you to connect computers and network devices using a command-line interface. This service has significant network security risks and should not be enabled unless required by a network administrator.

Table 20.2   Continued

Category/Component	Description
Telnet Server	This enables you or an administrator to log on to your computer remotely using only a command-line interface.
TFTP Client	This can be used to retrieve files from a TFTP server. This tool is used primarily to test network boot servers or to retrieve network device firmware.
Networking Services	
Internet Printing Client	This provides support for network- or Internet-hosted printers or printing services using the Internet Printing Protocol (IPP).
LPD Print Service	This service lets UNIX computers send print output to your Windows computer's shared printers.
LPR Port Monitor	This enables you to send print output to network-connected printers or UNIX servers. (IPC, LPD, and LPR are found in the Print and Document Services list.)
RAS Connection Manager Administration Kit (CMAK)	This tool enables network managers to create predefined dial-up and VPN network connections for enterprise users.
RIP Listener	This service is used to listen for network routing information in large networks. Don't install it unless it's required by your network administrator.
Simple TCP/IP Services	This suite of services performs simple functions for testing purposes, such as echoing data to a remote computer and generating a stream of data. Don't install these services unless you're instructed to do so by a network administrator. Hackers can use them to tie up your network with pointless traffic.

The Reliable Multicast Protocol is installed using a different procedure from that used to install the other services listed in Table 20.2. If required, it can be installed for a specific network adapter using these steps:

1. Right-click at the bottom-left corner of the screen, and then click Control Panel, View Network Status and Tasks (under Network and Internet), Change Adapter Settings.

2. Right-click a network adapter and select Properties.

3. Click Install. Select Protocol and then click Add.

4. Select Reliable Multicast Protocol and click OK.

The Hosts File

If you have an office LAN, especially one with mixed and matched computers, you probably, like me, have a chart of computer names and IP addresses posted on your wall—not just computers, but routers, firewalls, monitored devices, and all manner of devices. (Who knows? Your next espresso machine may have an Ethernet port on it.)

On a corporate or enterprise LAN, the LAN administrators enter each device into the organization's domain name system (DNS) so that you can type a command such as `ping firewall` instead of needing to type `ping firewall.mycompany.com` or, worse, something like `ping 192.168.56.102`.

On a home or small office LAN, though, you probably don't have your own domain name server. The hosts file is the answer to this annoying situation. You can add entries to the file `\windows\system32\drivers\etc\hosts` to associate names with IP addresses. The Windows domain name lookup software looks first in the hosts file before consulting the network, so you can add entries for your own workgroup's computers and devices, regardless of OS.

The format is simple, but editing it is a bit tricky. The hosts file has become a target for adware hackers, who put fake entries in it to hijack your web browser.

To edit it, right-click the very bottom-left corner of the screen or press Windows Logo+X, select Command Prompt (Admin), and confirm the User Account Control prompt. Then, when the Command Prompt window opens, type **notepad \windows\system32\drivers\etc\hosts** and press Enter.

Add lines to the file, listing IP addresses at the left margin, followed by some whitespace (tabs or spaces), followed by one or more names. You can enter simple names or full domain names. Simple names are assumed to belong to your own domain.

My hosts file looks like this:

```
127.0.0.1        localhost
192.168.56.1     router
192.168.56.45    macmini
```

The first entry is the default entry shipped with Windows. `localhost` stands for "my own computer" and is used for internal testing of the network software.

I added the second entry myself to give a name to my network's wireless router. I can now configure the router by typing //**router** into Internet Explorer, instead of needing to look up at that sheet on the wall and type a bunch of numbers.

Finally, there's an entry for my Mac computer, `macmini`. This way, I can view its web server's home page from Internet Explorer using `http://macmini` instead of needing to remember its IP address.

This file also serves as a sort of documentation of my network because it records important IP addresses. One thing you must watch out for, though, is that Windows checks this file before using the real DNS system to look up names. If you put a name in your LAN's (or the Internet's) DNS system and the computer's IP address later changes, your hosts file will be incorrect. It's best to use this file only for machines that are in nobody's DNS system.

USING A WINDOWS NETWORK

Windows Was Made to Network

Most homes and offices have more than one computer, and you'll quickly find that as days go by, you end up using most or all of them. You'll download a file, and a few days later, when you want to use that file... where is it? You hardly need to ask: if you're searching for the file on the computer you're using now, nine times out of ten it will turn out to be on some other computer. This is not just a fact of life, it's a law of nature. But with a network, you can easily access any file and any printer, on any computer, from your own, thus short-circuiting the law—for a while at least. A network also lets everyone in your home or office share printers and an Internet connection, thus saving you time and money.

In traditional desktop apps at least, using files and printers on the network is exactly the same as using files and printers on your own hard drive. The "look and feel" are identical. The only new tasks you have to learn are how to find resources shared by others and how to make your own computer's resources available to others on the network. In Windows 8–style apps, you can easily print to networked printers. For files and folders, you're stuck using local hard disk folders unless the app allows you to browse through arbitrary folders.

By the way, we'll use the word *resource* frequently in this chapter. When we say *resource*, we mean a shared folder or printer on someone else's computer, which you can access through the LAN or the Internet. *The American Heritage Dictionary* defines a resource as "an available supply that can be drawn upon when needed." That's actually a perfect description of a network resource: it's there for you to use—provided that you can find it and that you have permission.

Windows networks work pretty much the same way whether they're in your home, in a small office, or in a large corporate setting. Big "domain" networks managed by computers running Windows Server software, though, may have some additional features. The following are some notable differences you might see on a domain network:

- The network administrator can set up *roaming profiles* so that your settings, preferences, Documents folder, and so on are centrally stored on the network and are available to you on any computer on your LAN or even at other network sites.

- Active Directory (AD) gives you added search functions to find users and printers on your network. These search functions appear as added icons and menu choices that only AD network computers have.

- The network administrator might use *policy* functions to limit your access to applications, Windows features, and settings. If you are on a domain or AD network and can't find an option mentioned in this chapter, ask your network manager if its use has been restricted.

If you are using a home or small office workgroup network, don't feel left out. Because a workgroup typically has fewer than ten computers, the searching and corporate-style management functions provided by AD simply aren't necessary.

Using Shared Folders in Windows 8

Windows lets you share folders and their contents with other network users. Users within your network can see the folders and, if permission settings allow it, access the files in them just as they would any file on their own hard drive. In this section, we show you how to use files and folders shared by other users. Later in the chapter, you'll learn how to share folders on your own computer.

In the following sections, we'll be using the Desktop view unless we say otherwise. To go to the desktop, press Windows Logo+D or select Desktop from the Start screen.

Browsing Through a Homegroup

Start by clicking the taskbar's File Explorer icon to open File Explorer. If your computer is a member of a homegroup, on the left side of the File Explorer window you'll see the title "Homegroup." Under this are entries for each user's account, on each of the homegroup computers. Anyone who has elected to share materials with the homegroup—and whose computer is turned on—will be listed here.

⮕ *If you can't or don't want to use a homegroup, skip ahead to "Browsing a Network's Computers," p. 458. To see how to set up a homegroup for your Windows 8 and 7 computers, see "Setting Up a Homegroup," p. 407.*

The Homegroup list will include accounts for any additional users on your own computer, as well as the users on other computers.

You can open these entries to see what files and folders are being shared, as shown in Figure 21.1. It doesn't matter whether the other user's materials are stored in another account on your computer or are on another computer on your network; it works the same way regardless. You can only see materials that users elected to share.

Figure 21.1
If your computer is a member of a homegroup, you can view the materials shared by other members of your group in File Explorer.

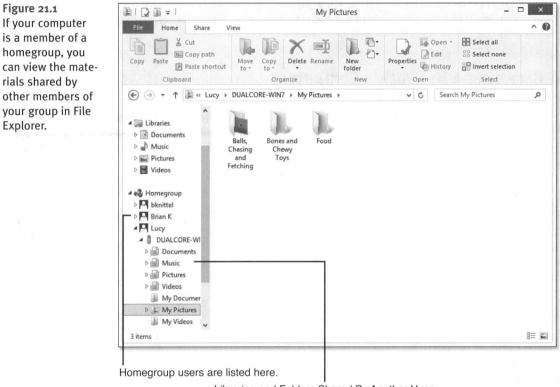

Homegroup users are listed here.

Libraries and Folders Shared By Another User

If the other user gave the homegroup permission to make changes to the folder, you'll be able to edit, delete, and rename files and add new files. Otherwise, you'll just be able to view, read, print, and play the files. If you want to make changes in this case, just drag a copy from the other user's folder into one of your own folders, or onto your desktop.

 To learn how you can share your files with the group, **see** *"Sharing with a Homegroup," p. 475.*

Regardless of whether or not you have a homegroup set up, you can browse through files and folders shared by any networked computer using the Network list, as described next.

tip
You can bookmark a network computer or a shared folder so that you can easily come back to it later. To do this, browse to locate the computer or folder as just described. Then, in the window's left pane, right-click Favorites and select Add Current Location to Favorites.

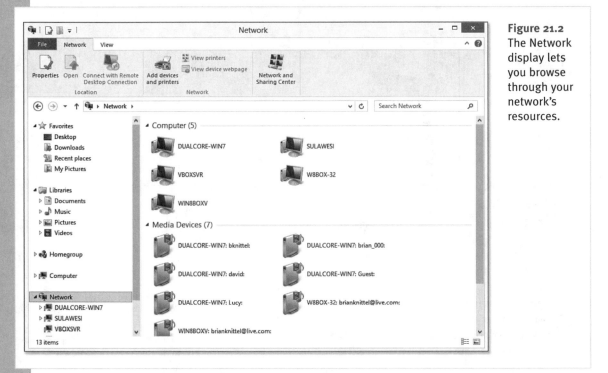

note

Computers whose workgroup or domain name is different from yours might take longer to appear, but all computers on your computer's same network subnet should eventually show up. On a corporate network, computers on other subnets and those separated by firewalls will not appear. You can still use their resources, by typing their share names directly in UNC format as described later in the chapter under "Network Power User Topics."

Browsing a Network's Computers

In any File Explorer window (for example, in the Computer or Documents window), the left pane contains an item titled Network. If you open this item, you'll see icons for every active computer on your network. (On a corporate network you will see only computers on your local subnet.) You'll see a screen like the one shown in Figure 21.2.

Figure 21.2
The Network display lets you browse through your network's resources.

The Network window shows computers with shared folders, shared Media Center libraries, and network hardware. You can browse into any of the folder icons to locate shared files and folders you want to use.

tip

It can take time and effort to dig down to the network, so if there is a particular shared file or folder that you use frequently, use one of these methods to retain quick access to it:

- **Create a shortcut**—Hold down the Alt key while you drag the file or folder into your desktop. You can leave the shortcut there, or move it to some other convenient location.

- **Create a bookmark**—Browse to locate a computer or folder. In the File Explorer window's left pane, right-click Favorites and select Add Current Location to Favorites.

- **Create a Start window tile**—Right-click a folder or application icon and select Pin to Start.

In addition, you can add a network location to one of your libraries, as discussed later under "Network Power User Topics."

When you browse into other Windows 8, 7, and Vista computers, you will notice that the entire \users folder structure is shared, with the name Users. This folder contains everyone's user profiles and documents, and is shared by default. What preserves everyone's privacy and security is that each user must give other users (or other groups, or everyone) permission to read a folder or file in order for them to even see that it exists. This scheme makes it much simpler to control which items you share, simply by changing the security settings on the files and folders themselves. We'll talk more about this later in the chapter, under "Sharing Resources."

On Windows 8 and 7 computers, the Public folder is shared "in place," meaning it's found inside the Users share, and is not shared separately under its own name as it was on Windows XP. The Public Folder Sharing option in the Advanced Sharing Settings page controls whether remote users can have access to the Public folder.

When you browse into Windows Vista and XP computers, the Public user profile is shared separately, under the name Public or Shared Documents. Shared user profiles will be shared individually as separate shares.

> **note**
>
> Remember, for all folders shared by Windows 8, 7, Vista, and Windows Server 2008 computers, to even see that a folder or file exists inside a shared folder, you must have permission to read the file or view the folder's contents. In folders shared by other operating systems, you may be able to see the presence of files and folders that you don't have permission to read.

> **tip**
>
> If you're using Windows 8 Pro or Enterprise edition, you can make a shared folder's contents available even when you're disconnected from the network. For instructions, see the "Offline Files" section in Chapter 37, "Computing on the Road."

Viewing a Computer or Shared Folder Directly Using Its UNC Path

If you know the Universal Naming Convention (UNC) pathname of a shared folder on a specific computer, you can instantly view its files by typing the UNC path into the Address box at the top of any File Explorer window. You can type a path that includes just computer name, a computer name followed by a folder's share name, or a longer path that specifies subfolders or a file within the shared folder.

For example, suppose you want to see the folders shared by a computer named "laptop." Open a File Explorer window by pressing Windows Logo+X and selecting File Explorer. Click in the Address box, and the "breadcrumb" path will disappear. Then, type `\\laptop` and press Enter. This displays all of laptop's shared folders, without you having to browse your way there. Likewise, you can see the files shared by a user whose account is named "lucy" on that computer using `\\laptop\users\lucy`.

We talk more about UNC pathnames later in the chapter, in the section "Understanding the Universal Naming Convention."

Searching the Network

If there is a particular file you'd like to find, but you don't know where it is, browsing through the network isn't a particularly easy way to find it. However, you can quickly locate shared folders and files by name and by content using the Search box at the upper-right corner of any File Explorer window.

To begin a search, open any File Explorer window (for example, by typing Windows Logo+X and selecting File Explorer). Then follow the instructions under the next several headings to find files, computers, or printers.

Searching for Files or Folders

You can search a particular network computer for files and folders, by name and by content, using these steps:

1. Open a File Explorer window and select Network in the left pane.

2. Expand the Network list and click the name of a computer.

   Alternatively, you can just type the computer's UNC name into File Explorer's address window.

3. Type all or part of the desired filename, or a word or phrase to be found in the file, in the Search box.

This will locate files and folders within the contents of all shared folders on that computer, but only those that you have permission to view.

 To learn more about searching for files on Windows 8, ***see*** *"Desktop Searching," **p. 164.***

To search all the shared folders and libraries in a homegroup, the steps are similar:

1. Open a File Explorer window and select Homegroup in the left pane.

2. Type all or part of the desired filename, or a word or phrase to be found in the file, in the Search box.

This searches all of the libraries you and others have shared, on all computers that are turned on and connected to the network.

On an Active Directory network, the domain administrator can choose to list, or *publish*, some shared folders in the directory; they might contain important resources that the company wants to make widely accessible and easy to find. See "Searching Active Directory," later in the chapter, for more information. If you are trying to find a particular shared folder but it has not been explicitly published in the directory, you're out of luck; there's no other way to find it besides browsing through the network's computers or searching specific computers as described earlier in this section.

Searching for Computers

To search for a computer by name, select the word *Network* in the File Explorer window's left pane and type all or part of a computer name in the Search box. Windows will display an icon for each matching computer.

You can explore any of the listed computers to view its shared folders or printers; if you delve into the shared folders, you can open or copy the available files as you find them.

Searching for Printers

Searching for printers is possible only on an Active Directory network. In a large corporate network, hundreds or thousands of network printers might be scattered over a large area. Find Printers lets an AD network user find just the right type of printer using a powerful query form. This feature is handy if you're a business traveler using the network in an unfamiliar office, or if you're in such a large office setting that you aren't familiar with all the printing resources on your network.

To search AD for a printer, open File Explorer and select Network in the left pane. In the ribbon, click Search Active Directory and select Printers from the Find drop-down list. You can leave the scope set to Entire Directory, or you can select a subdomain next to the word *In*.

You can search for printers in three ways: by name and location, by printer capabilities, or by more advanced attributes. To find all the printers in the directory, leave the form blank, as shown in Figure 21.3, and click Find Now. To search for printers with capabilities such as double-sized printing or color, select the Features tab, select the desired features, and then click Find Now.

> **tip**
>
> On an Active Directory network, view the entire directory the first time you use Find Printers. This will give you an idea of how location and printer names are organized in your company. If too many names are listed, you can click Clear All to clear the search listing and then restrict your search using a location name that makes sense for your network. For example, if your company has put floor and room numbers such as "10-123" in the Location column, you could restrict your search to printers on the tenth floor by searching for "10-" in Location.

Figure 21.3
You can search Active Directory for a printer based on location or capabilities (features) that you require.

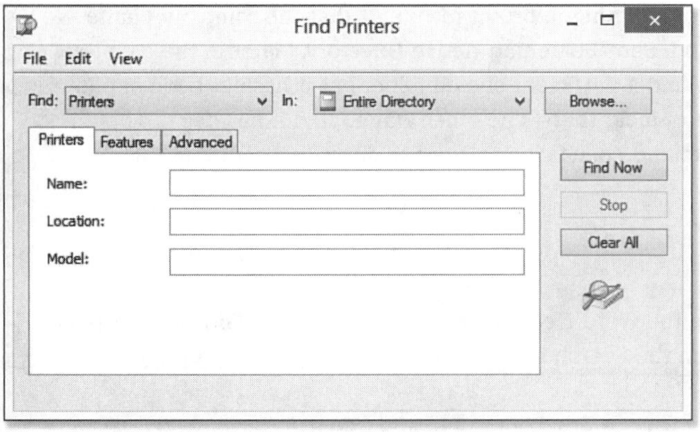

Searching Active Directory

On an enterprise domain-type network, Active Directory contains information on many more objects than just users, computers, and printers. It includes shared folders, organizational units, policy settings, certificate templates, containers (business groupings), foreign security principals, remote storage services, RPC services (used for advanced client/server software applications), and trusted domains. It can also contain information for other objects defined by your own organization. Most of this information is used only by domain administrators to configure Windows networks over vast distances; however, you can search for anything and can specify your qualifications based on more than 100 different criteria.

To make an AD search, select Network in the left pane File Explorer and select Search Active Directory. The AD search tool appears, as shown in Figure 21.4. To start, select one of several search categories in the Find drop-down list. You can use a quick form-based search for any of the most useful objects.

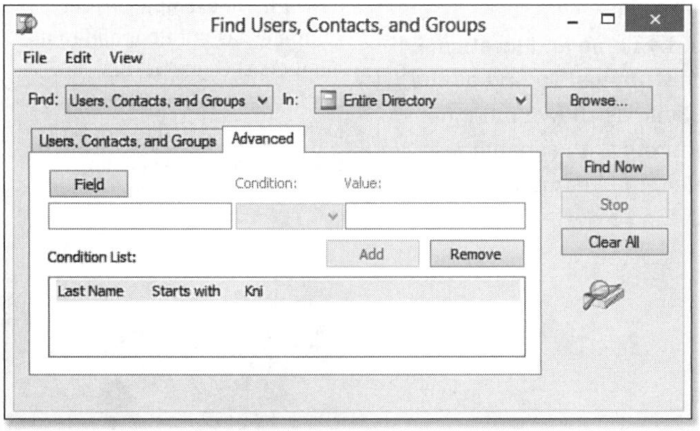

Figure 21.4
Using the Active Directory search tool, you can use a simplified form for any of several categories of directory objects, or you can use the Advanced tab to construct queries using any of the available fields.

You can also use the Advanced tab to build specific queries such as "Last Name Starts with *Kni*," as shown in Figure 21.4. This is the full-blown search system, and here you have 53 fields to choose from when searching for users—everything from A to Z (Assistant to ZIP Code) if you need it.

If you choose Find: Custom Search, you have the whole gamut of fields in the entire catalog of AD objects to choose from, and in the Advanced tab, you can enter Lightweight Directory Access Protocol (LDAP) queries directly for submission to the AD service. This is the native query syntax for Active Directory, and it's available here mostly for system debugging.

 note

For a brief introduction to LDAP queries, you might visit technet.microsoft.com and search for "LDAP Query Basics."

Security and File Sharing

Windows 8 and 7 computers only let network users see the presence of files and folders that they actually have permission to use, based in most cases on their username and password. It's worth explaining just how that permission is determined. It's not that difficult a topic, but it's complicated by the fact that there are several different ways that permissions are calculated by Windows networking, depending on settings and the versions of Windows you encounter.

note

In the following discussion, we refer to "files," but the issues are the same for both the files and folders inside any shared folder.

Two levels of security are involved when Windows grants a user access to a file over a network: permission settings on the file itself, which would apply if the user logged on at the computer directly, and "network permissions," which act as additional *restrictions* when a file is accessed over the network but don't grant any additional *permissions* that a user wouldn't have if he or she tried to access the file while logged in directly to the computer. We'll explain why this is done shortly. Let's look at file permissions first.

File Permissions and Networking

File permissions determine who can read, modify, write to, or delete a file or folder based on their user account. Files and folders stored on a disk formatted with the NTFS file system (which is always used on the disk that contains Windows 8) can have these permission settings applied on a user-by-user basis as well as by membership in groups such as Administrators and even Everyone. When you log on to a computer, these settings determine which files you can look at and which you can change.

➡ *For more information about file permissions,* **see** *"Setting Security Permissions on Files and Folders," **p. 775**.*

When you access a file over a network, this permission system still applies. What can get confusing is, how does the remote computer determine who you are? The answer to that question depends on the versions of Windows you and it are running, and on several settings. Here are some scenarios you might encounter. Go down through the list to find the first scenario that describes your situation, and stop there. In the following discussion, "the remote computer" refers to a computer on the network that has a file you want to use, and "you" and "your computer" are trying to get to that file.

- If your computer and the remote computer are members of a domain network, your user account is recognized by all computers on the network. You'll get access to the file if its permission settings grant access to your account, or to groups to which you belong.

- If your computer and the remote computer are members of a homegroup, and if you left enabled the Advanced Sharing setting Allow Windows to Manage Homegroup Connections, as it is by default, your computer will connect to all other homegroup computers using the built-in user account HomeGroupUser$, which is a member of group HomeUsers. Whenever you share a library, folder, or file with your homegroup, Windows sets permissions on that library, folder, or file so that the HomeUsers group has Read or Read and Write access. In this way, all users in the homegroup get the same access rights to the shared resources.

- If the remote computer runs Windows 8, 7, or Vista with Password Protected Sharing turned on, or XP Professional with Simple File Sharing disabled, or Windows Server in a domain that your computer is not a member of, the remote computer will check to see whether it has an account set up with the same name and password as the account you are using on your computer. If so, it will grant you access to files based on rights set for that account name. If the account name or password doesn't match, your computer will prompt you to enter an account name or password that *is* valid on the remote computer.

- If both your computer and the remote computer run Windows 8 or 7, and the remote computer has Password Protected Sharing turned off, a rule unique to these versions of Windows applies:

  If the remote computer has an account with the same name as your account, and that account has a password set, you will be given access to a file based on privileges set for your account on the remote machine.

- If none of the preceding scenarios apply, the remote computer attempts to access the file using the Guest account. You'll be able to use only files that are readable and/or writable by Everyone or Guest.

Phew! We know this looks like a big mess, but it actually boils down to just two alternatives: a remote computer either will use a specific account to access files, in which case you can get to the files that this account can see, or it will use the Guest account, in which case you only can get to files that are marked as usable by Everyone or Guest.

Another point to remember is that files stored on removable media typically don't use the NTFS format, and don't have any per-user permission settings. Floppy disks and flash media formatted with the FAT or ExFAT file systems are readable and writable by everyone, and CD/DVD-ROMs are readable by everyone who connects to the computer. Network permissions, described next, do apply.

Network Permissions

The preceding permission scheme applies equally to files accessed over the network and files accessed directly by logging in to a computer. When you share a folder or drive with the network, though, you can assign privileges, again based on user and group names, that act like a filter for the file permissions we just discussed. A network user gets only the privileges that are listed in *both* file permissions *and* network permissions. Figure 21.5 shows how this works.

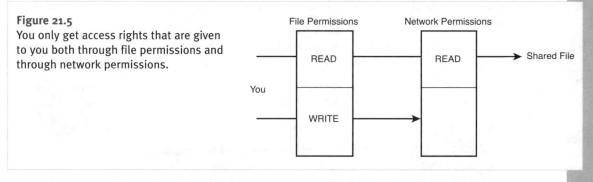

Figure 21.5
You only get access rights that are given to you both through file permissions and through network permissions.

Another way to look at this is, a network user *loses* any permissions that are *omitted* from the network permission list. This can be used in complex ways, but mostly only two situations are used:

- If you share a folder and set its network privilege list to give Read access, but not Write access, to Everyone, then users get Read access *if* their user account gives them permission, but *nobody* gets to modify its files over the network.

- If you set the network permissions so that Everyone has both Read and Write permissions, then users get exactly what they'd get if they tried to use the file while logged on directly—no more, no less.

These are the two ways Windows sets up network permissions when you share folders using the techniques we describe later in the chapter.

Using Printers on the Network

Whether you're part of a large corporation or a small workgroup, or even if you're a home user with just two computers, network printing is a great time and money saver. Why connect a printer to each computer when it will spend most of its time idle? By not having to buy a printer for each user, you can spend the money you save more constructively on faster, higher-quality, and more interesting printers. You might add a color photo-quality printer or a transparency maker to give your network users more output choices.

Because the software comes with Windows 8, and you can hook computers together for about the cost of a movie ticket, printer sharing alone is a good enough reason to install a network.

Later in the chapter, we describe how to share a printer attached to your computer; right now, let's look at using a printer that has already been shared elsewhere on the network.

Windows can directly attach to printers shared by any computer that supports Microsoft Networking services, which includes any version of Windows released since 1993, OS/2, Mac OS X, as well as UNIX and UNIX-like operating systems running the Samba service. Windows can also connect to networked printers that use the LPR or other TCP/IP protocols.

Using a Shared Printer

To use a shared printer, you have to set up an icon for the printer in your Devices and Printers window. The easiest way to do this is to browse or search your network for shared printers by following these steps:

1. Go to the desktop and open File Explorer from the taskbar, or press Windows Logo+X and select File Explorer.

2. In the left pane, click Network. Locate the computer that is sharing the printer you want to use. (On a large network, you can use the Search box to help find it.) Double-click the computer icon.

3. Double-click the icon for the printer you wish to use.

4. Windows will try to get the printer's driver software from the computer that is sharing the printer. Click Install Driver if you trust the owner of the other computer. You will also need to approve a User Account Control prompt. Windows may automatically locate and install a driver if the driver software is "signed" (that is, certified as having come directly from the stated manufacturer without any modification). However, if you can't trust the other computer, click Cancel. Then use the procedure that immediately follows this one so that you can select your own driver software.

5. When the process finishes, view the new printer in the Devices and Printers window, using either of these methods:

   - Press Windows Logo+X and select Control Panel. Then, under Hardware and Sound, select View Devices and Printers.

   - At the Start screen or in the Search charm, type **printers**, and then under Settings, select Devices and Printers.

If you want to verify that the printer will actually work for you, right-click the printer icon and select Printer Properties. Click Print Test Page to ensure that the network printer is working correctly.

If you will use this printer most or all of the time, right-click the printer's icon and select Set As Default Printer.

That's all there is to it. You can now use this printer just like any other Windows printer, so the printer-management discussion in Chapter 7, "Devices and Printers," applies to network printers too. The only difference is that the remote computer's administrator might not have given you management privileges for the printer, so you might not be able to change the printer's properties or delete print jobs created by other users.

> **note**
>
> Don't make any changes to the printer's Printer Properties settings without the permission of the printer's owner.

An alternative way to add a printer is with the Add Printer Wizard, using these steps:

1. Open Devices and Printers as described in step 5 of the previous procedure, and at the top, select Add a Printer.

2. Windows displays a list of networked printers that it knows about, such as ones that it finds shared within the same workgroup. If the printer you want to use is listed, select it, click Next, and then proceed with step 4.

3. If the printer you want to connect to isn't listed, click (drumroll, please) The Printer That I Want Isn't Listed.

    You're then presented with another dialog box, where you can type the location and name of the printer to which you want to connect. If you know its network name already, click Select a Shared Printer by Name and enter the share name into the Name box in UNC format—for example, \\kevins\LaserJet. Click Next to finish installing the printer. If you don't know the name, click Browse, and you'll be able to dig into your network to find the printer.

4. After you've identified and selected the shared printer, click Next. If a suitable printer driver is not found automatically, Windows will prompt for one. Select the printer's manufacturer and model number from the displayed lists. If the printer model isn't listed, click Windows Update to see if the driver can be downloaded. Otherwise, follow the steps under "What to Do If Your Printer Isn't Listed" in Chapter 7.

5. Follow any additional instructions to finish setting up the printer.

Again, as noted previously, you can now use this printer like any other Windows printer, and if you will use it most or all of the time, you may want to make it your default printer.

Using Printers over the Internet with IPP

The Internet Printing Protocol (IPP) sends output to printers over the Internet. Some companies and service bureaus provide this sort of service. If you need to connect to an IPP-based printer, follow these steps:

1. Press Windows Logo+X and select Control Panel. Select Programs, Turn Windows Features On or Off. Click the + sign next to Print and Document Services. Check Internet Printing Client (if it's not already checked) and then click OK. You only need to perform this step once.

2. In the still-open Control Panel window, click the Back button, and then select View Devices and Printers, Add a Printer. Immediately click The Printer That I Want Isn't Listed.

3. Click Select a Shared Printer by Name, enter the URL supplied by the print service provider, and then click Next.

4. You might be prompted to select the printer manufacturer and model number. The print service provider will tell you which model to select.

5. You might also be prompted to enter a username and password, which will also be supplied by the service provider. By default, Windows will use your current logon name, domain, and password.

 tip

If you use a printing service while traveling, remember to delete the printer from your Printers folder when you leave town; you don't want to accidentally send a report to Katmandu after you've returned to Kalamazoo.

When the new printer icon is installed, you have a fully functional Windows printer. You can view the pending jobs and set your print and page preferences as usual, as long as you're connected to the Internet (or the LAN, in a service establishment).

Using UNIX and LPR Printers

In the UNIX world, most shared printers use a protocol called LPR/LPD.

➡ *For more information about UNIX printing, **see** "Internetworking with UNIX and Linux," **p. 440**.*

The LPR protocol is also used outside of UNIX. Manufacturers such as Hewlett-Packard make direct network-connected printers that accept the LPR protocol, and many companies sell small LPR-based print server devices that can attach to your printer as well. You can connect one of these printers to your LAN, configure its TCP/IP settings to match your LAN, and immediately print without running a cable from a computer to the printer. This way, you can place a printer in a more convenient place than can be reached by a 10-foot printer cable. Better yet, you can use these networked printers without requiring a Windows computer to be left turned on to manage it.

To have Windows send output to an LPR print queue or device, follow these steps:

1. Press Windows Logo+X and select Control Panel. Select Programs, Turn Windows Features On or Off. Click the + sign next to Print and Document Services. Check Internet Printing Client (if it's not already checked) and then click OK. You only need to perform this step once.

2. In the still-open Control Panel window, click the Back button, and then select View Devices and Printers, Add a Printer. Immediately click The Printer That I Want Isn't Listed.

3. Select Add a Printer Using a TCP/IP Address or Hostname and click Next.

4. Enter the IP address or hostname of the UNIX or print server, and the name of the print queue on that server.

5. If Windows fails to determine what type of printer you are connecting to, click Cancel and then repeat the process. This time, set Device Type to TCP/IP Device and uncheck Query the Printer and Automatically Select the Device to Use. After you click Next, manually select the manufacturer and printer model. (If the appropriate driver is not listed, you might be able to get it by clicking Windows Update.) Then, click Next to proceed with the printer installation.

> ### 🔍 note
>
> If you enter the wrong IP address, hostname, or print queue name, right-click the printer's icon and select Printer Properties. Select the Ports tab, highlight the LPR port, and click Delete Port. Click Add Port and then enter the correct information. When the new port has been added, check the box next to its name.

Because an LPR printer is considered a local printer, you can share it with others on your network. Your computer will talk directly to the printer, while other computers will connect through yours. Alternatively, they can each connect to it directly, as you did.

Using Other Network-Connected Printers

Windows 8 can use other types of network-connected printers as well. Some printer models come with a built-in network connection (either wired or wireless), and others have a network adapter option. You can also buy network printer servers, which are small boxes with a network connector and one to three printer-connection ports. These devices let you locate printers in a convenient area, which doesn't need to be near a computer.

The installation procedures for various printer and server models vary. Your networked printer or print server has specific installation instructions. You have a choice about how the printer will be shared on your network:

- You can install the network-to-printer connection software on *one* of your Windows computers and then use standard Windows printer sharing to make the printer available to the other computers on your network.

- You can install the printer's connection software on *each* of your computers.

With the first method, you guarantee that print jobs will be run "first come, first served" because one computer will provide a single queue for the printer. Another plus is that you have to do the software setup only once; it's much easier to set up the additional workstations to use the standard Windows shared printer. The one computer must be left on for others to use the printer, however.

With the second method, each computer contacts the printer independently. If more than one user attempts to print at the same time, the "winner" will be chosen by the printer at random while the other users wait. However, no computers need to be left on because each workstation contacts the printer directly.

You can use either method. The first one is simplest and is best suited for a busy office. The second method is probably more convenient for home networks and small offices.

Network Power User Topics

This section presents some Windows networking techniques that can let you get the most out of your network. You can scan through this section for any tips that might be helpful in your home or office.

Backing Up Your Computer over the Network

You can back up the contents of your hard disk, or the attached external drives on your computer, to another computer's hard disk over the network. On all Windows 8 versions, you can back up to a shared network folder using the built-in Windows backup programs discussed in Chapter 32, "Protecting Your Data from Loss and Theft."

You can also back up files over the network using command-line tools. We give an example of this at the end of this chapter in the "Managing Network Resources Using the Command Line" section.

Finally, most third-party backup programs let you back up to a network location.

Adding a Network Folder to a Library

You can actually link other people's shared folders right into one of your own libraries so that their content appears and is searchable along with your own, although doing so is not quite as simple as you might hope, and doing so can make opening the Library folder take a long time. If you really do want to do this, use the following procedure:

1. View one of your libraries (for example, your Documents library) in File Explorer.

2. In the ribbon bar's Home tab, select Properties. Then, under the list of locations, click Add.

3. In the Include Folder in Documents window, locate the folder you want to add, from one of two places:

   ■ If the folder you want to add belongs to another user on your own computer, select Computer in the left pane, drill down into c:\users, then into the other user's profile folder, until you locate the folder you want to add.

   ■ If the folder you want to add is on another computer, select Network in the left pane, double-click the computer's name, and then double-click the shared folder. (To get to a folder shared by one of the computer's users, double-click the Users share.) Then, drill down to the folder you want to add to your library.

   Don't dig into the Homegroup list. Most of the items listed in the Homegroup list are libraries. You need to locate the actual folder that went into the other user's library, in one of the two locations just mentioned.

4. When you have located the desired folder, click it and then click Include Folder.

   This works like a charm if the folder on the remote computer is indexed on that computer. If it's not indexed there, Windows will not allow you to add the folder to your library. There are three ways you can get around this:

   ■ Have the person who owns the remote computer index the shared folder. To do this, he has to open his Control Panel, search for the word *Index*, and then select Change How Windows Searches. From there, he can add the shared folder to the indexing list.

   ■ Right-click the shared folder and select Always Available Offline. This makes copies of all of the remote folder's contents, including subfolders, on your hard disk. This may not be practical if the remote folder has a lot of data.

   ■ Trick Windows into including the remote folder using what's called a *symbolic link*, a folder name that appears to be on your own hard disk but actually redirects Windows to get content from another location. The procedure is documented in Windows 8's online help. To find it, type **help** in the Start screen and then in Apps click Help and Support. In Windows Help and Support, search for "Libraries: How to Add or Remove a Folder," open the article with that title, scroll to the bottom, and select To Add a Network Folder That Isn't Indexed to a Library.

Be aware, though, that if you add a folder from another computer to one of your own libraries, Windows may take a long time to display your library if the other computer is not running and connected to the network.

Sharing and Using an Entire Drive

Shared folders don't have to be subfolders. Computer owners can share the *root folder* of a disk drive, making the entire drive available over the network. This is especially useful with DVD, CD, floppy, and USB disk drives. For example, if an entire DVD-ROM drive is shared, you can access the data disc in it from any computer on the network.

Just so you know, Windows automatically shares your entire hard drive with the special name C$. (Any other hard drives would also be shared as D$, E$, and so on.) These shares don't show up when you browse the network—the dollar sign at the end tells Windows to keep the name hidden. Oddly enough, they don't appear if you view the drive's Sharing properties either. You can only see them if you type **net share** at the command prompt. And, you can't use these shares on a home/small office workgroup network; they can be accessed only by the "true" Administrator account on a domain network.

However, you can get around this by sharing the root (top-level) folder of one of your drives using a share name of your own choosing. For example, you could right-click your DVD drive in the File Explorer window and then share the drive using the name dvd, using the instructions for sharing a folder found later in the chapter. Then, on another computer, you can map a drive letter to the shared disc, using the instructions under "Mapping Drive Letters," also found later in this chapter.

 tip

You can use this technique to install software on a computer that has no working CD/DVD drive but does have a working network connection. Just put the disc into a computer that does have a working drive, and share that drive.

Understanding the Universal Naming Convention

You can specify folders and files on your own hard disk using a full pathname and filename in the MS-DOS filename syntax that looks like this:

```
c:\folder\subfolder\filename
```

Similarly, you can specify printers, folders, and files on a network using a syntax called the *Universal Naming Convention*, or *UNC*, which looks like this:

```
\\computername\sharename\subfolder\filename
```

Notice that a UNC name uses backslashes, not forward slashes like an Internet URL. Anywhere a Windows application lets you enter a pathname or filename, you can also enter a UNC name.

For example, I might have a folder on my hard disk named C:\users\brian\documents\plans. If I want to give officemates the use of these business documents, I might share that folder with the share name plans. My computer is named Ambon, so the UNC name for this folder will be \\ambon\plans.

If a spreadsheet file named to do list.xls exists in this folder, on my computer its full path and filename would be C:\users\brian\documents\plans\to do list.xls. A user on another computer can refer to this same file by its UNC name, \\ambon\plans\to do list.xls.

A share name is a sort of "shortcut" to a real folder on the remote computer's hard disk. It can be anywhere in the folder structure on the disk. It doesn't have to be a top-level folder. When users on the network access a shared folder, they can't see "up" into the higher-level folders.

If the computer whose files you want to use is on a corporate LAN using Active Directory or is part of a distant company network, the computer name part of a UNC name can be specified as in the following:

```
\\ambon.mycompany.com\docs\to do list.xls
```

If you know only a remote computer's IP network address, you can use it as the computer name, as in this example:

```
\\192.168.0.10\docs\to do list.xls
```

> **🔍 note**
>
> Elsewhere in this chapter, we use UNC names such as \\server\ folder as a generic sort of name. By server, we mean the name of the computer that's sharing folder. It doesn't have to be a Windows Server; it can be any computer on your network. You need to use your network's actual computer names and shared folder names.

Shared printers are also given share names, and are specified by their UNC path. For example, if I share my HP LaserJet 4V printer, I might give it the share name HPLaser, and it will be known on the network as \\ambon\HPLaser. Here, it's not a folder, but rather a printer. You can't tell this from the name, but Windows keeps track of the type of resource.

Mapping Drive Letters

If you frequently use the same shared network folder, you can make it a "permanent houseguest" of your computer by *mapping* the network folder to an unused drive letter on your computer—one of the letters after your hard drive's usual C: and the DVD-ROM drive's usual D:. Mapping gives you several benefits:

- The mapped drive appears along with your computer's other real, physical drives in the Computer view for quick browsing, opening, and saving of files.

- Access to the shared folder is faster because Windows maintains an open connection to the sharing computer.

- MS-DOS applications can use the shared folder through the assigned letter. Most legacy DOS applications can't accept UNC-formatted names such as \\server\shared\subfolder\file, but they can use a path such as I:\subfolder\file.

- If you need to, you can map a shared folder using an alternative username and password to gain access rights that you might not have with your current Windows login name.

To map a drive, follow these steps:

1. Open File Explorer. In the ribbon, select Easy Access, Map As Drive.

2. Select an unused drive letter from the drop-down list, as shown in Figure 21.6. You can pick a drive letter that has some association for you with the resource you'll be using: E for Editorial,

S for Sales—whatever makes sense to you. I usually start with Z: and work backward from there if I map more than one drive.

Figure 21.6
You can select any unused drive letter to use for the drive mapping.

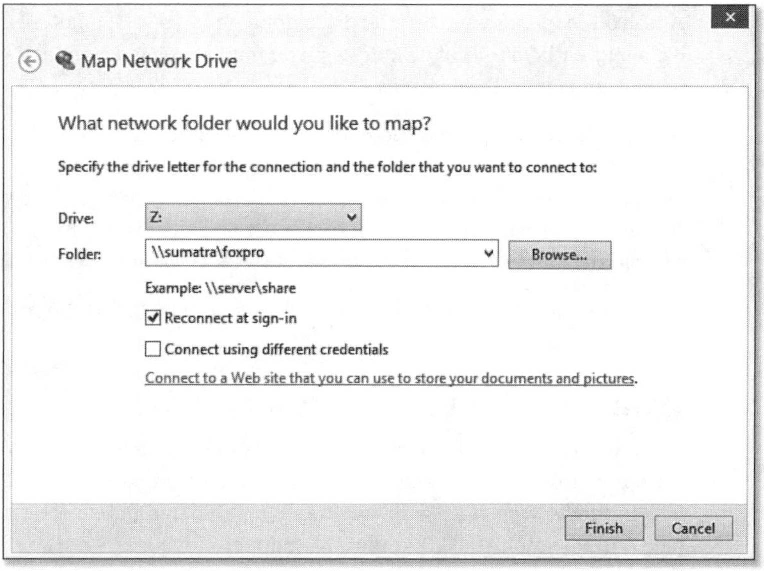

3. Select the name of the shared folder you want to assign to the drive letter. You can type the UNC-formatted name, if you know it already—for example, \\servername\sharename.

   Alternatively, you can click Browse to poke through your network's resources and select the shared folder, as described earlier in this chapter. Find and select the desired shared folder, and then click OK.

4. You have two options:

   ■ If you want this mapping to reappear every time you log in, check Reconnect at Logon. If you don't check this box, the mapping will disappear when you log off.

   ■ If your current Windows username and password don't give you permission to use the shared resource, or if your username isn't recognized at the other computer, select Connect Using a Different Username. (This works only if usernames are actually used on the networked computer. If it always grants access via the Guest account, as discussed under "File Permissions and Networking," earlier in this chapter, it doesn't matter what account information you supply.)

5. Click Finish.

note
You must use the same username for *all* connections to a given computer. If you have other drive letters already mapped to the other computer with your original username, you have to unmap those drives before you can make a drive mapping with a different username.

6. If you selected Connect Using a Different Username, Windows prompts you for a username and password. Enter them, and then click OK.

After you map a drive letter, the drive appears in your Computer list along with your local disk drives. You might notice a couple of funny things with these drives:

- If you haven't accessed the network drive for 20 minutes or so, it might turn gray, indicating that the network connection to the remote computer has been disconnected. When you use the drive again, Windows will reconnect and the drive entry will turn black.

- If the remote computer (or you) really goes offline, a red X appears through the drive.

> **tip**
>
> If you're using Windows 8 Professional or Enterprise edition, you can make the drive's contents available even when you're disconnected from the network. For instructions, see the "Offline Files" section in Chapter 37, "Computing on the Road."

Mapping a Drive to a Subfolder

When you're setting up a drive mapping, as described in the previous section, and you use the Browse button to select a shared folder, you may notice that Windows lets you delve into the shared folders themselves. If you drill down into a subfolder and select it as the location to use in mapping a drive letter, you'll find that the mapped drive starts at the subfolder. That is, the subfolder becomes the mapped drive's "root directory," and you can't explore upward into the shared folder that contains it. You can map a drive letter to a subfolder using the GUI method described in the preceding section, or using the net use command-line utility described later.

This feature is most useful for administrators in setting up scripts to map drives based on a user's login name. For example, mail might be stored in subfolders of \\server\mail according to username. Mapping drive M: to the folder \\server\ mail\%username% lets each user get at his or her mail (directly) via the same folder M:\, and discourages users from poking around in other people's mail folders.

> **tip**
>
> Once administrators have configured this sort of drive mapping, each user can configure his or her mail program to get mail from drive M:, and the same configuration will work for everyone.

Sharing Resources

In this section, we'll show you how to share folders and printers with other users on your network. You can elect to share your files with others in several different ways:

- If your computer is part of a homegroup, you can share your libraries with the homegroup. Other users will be able to see anything you save in a shared library.

- You can move files to a folder under \Users\Public, which is called the Public user profile. Here, anyone can access them automatically without you having to do anything else but enable sharing on the Public folder, as described shortly.

- You can elect to share any folder anywhere within your own user profile; the files or folders can reside anywhere within your own profile folder, which is found under \Users on the hard disk. Other network users will be able to find those files by browsing into your computer's Users share name.

- You can create new, separate folders on your hard disk and share them under their own share names.

In the past, it was common to create separate folders and share them independently. To some extent this makes it easier for other users to locate shared folders, because each folder has its own name. On Windows 8 and 7, Microsoft suggests "sharing in place," using any of the first three methods. These are easier to set up, but it's perhaps a bit harder on people who want to find those shared materials because they have to dig into the Users folder. Any of the methods are acceptable, though; it really just depends on how you prefer to organize your files.

The next sections describe how to share folders these various ways.

note

On a large corporate LAN, most important network resources, shared folders, and printers are set up and tightly controlled by network managers. You might not be able to share resources from your own computer, although in many companies you can, and it's useful to know how to do this so that you can easily give co-workers access to files that you use in common.

On a home or office work-group network, any Computer Administrator user can set up and manage file and printer sharing.

Sharing with a Homegroup

If your computer is a member of a homegroup, you can share the entire contents of any of your libraries so that the other members of the homegroup can see and use files in your libraries. Use the following procedure:

1. At the desktop, right-click the network icon in the taskbar and select Open Network and Sharing Center, Homegroup, or you can open the Control Panel and select Choose Homegroup and Sharing Options.

2. Select Change What You're Sharing with the Homegroup.

3. Set the drop-down list box next to each library name to Shared or Not Shared, as shown in Figure 21.7. When you're done, click Next and then Finish.

When you change a library's setting from Not Shared to Shared, the libraries will be shared *read-only*. All other homegroup members can see, view, play, and print any of the files in your shared libraries, but they can't change, delete, rename, or add to them.

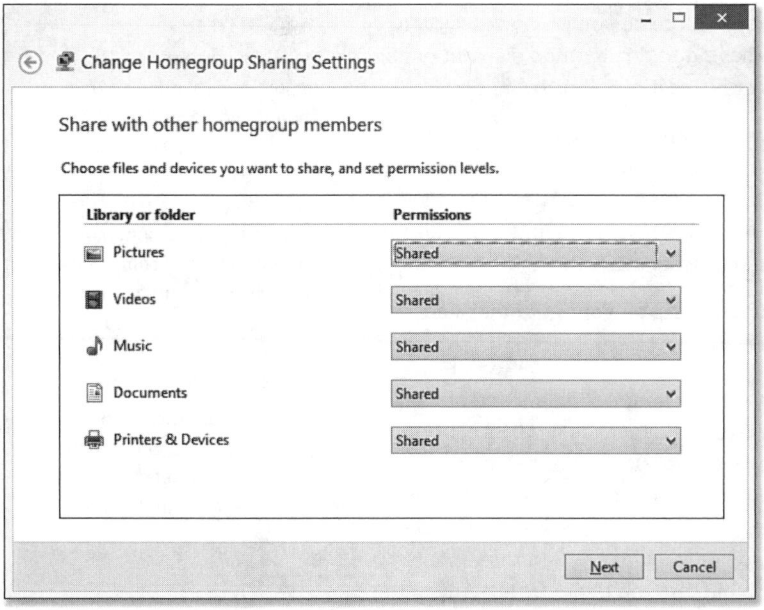

CHAPTER

21

Figure 21.7
You can change your mind about sharing or not sharing your libraries and printers with the homegroup at any time.

Setting Permissions for HomeGroup Sharing

If you want to let other users add to or change the files in any of your libraries, or if you want to enable or prevent access to a specific library, folder, or individual file, use this procedure:

1. Locate the library, folder, or file in File Explorer, right-click its icon, and select Share With.

2. Select one of these choices:

   - **Stop Sharing**—Keeps everyone else out of the library, file, or folder.

   - **Homegroup (view)**—Lets everyone else in the homegroup read but not change, rename, delete, or add to the file(s).

   - **Homegroup (view and edit)**—Lets all other homegroup users not only view but also make changes to the selected library, folder, or file. This includes adding new files, deleting files, and so on.

   - **Specific people**—Enables you to choose access levels for individual users. This may not work quite as you might guess, as we'll explain next.

note

The first time you share a new folder, use one of the two Share With Homegroup options. This makes the folder appear in the Homegroup listing on everyone else's computer. *Then*, if you want to customize access for specific people, right-click again and select Share With Specific People to make adjustments.

Editing Permissions for Specific People

The fourth choice, Specific People, lets you set permissions for yourself, for the homegroup, for Everyone, and for individual user accounts, using the permissions list shown in the File Sharing dialog box (see Figure 21.8).

Figure 21.8
You can control the type of access to a shared library, folder, or file that is granted to your homegroup, and in some cases to specific user accounts.

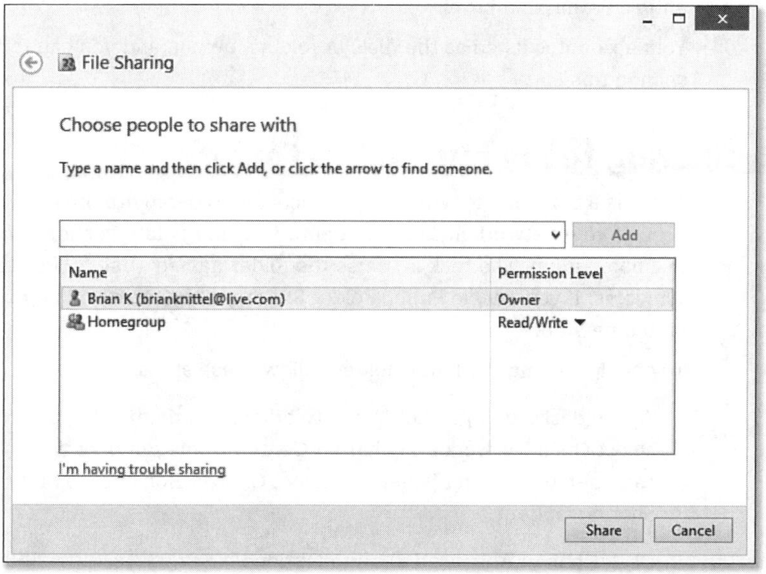

Any entries you add for individual users *won't* apply when other users in your homegroup try to use the shared resource, because member computers always use a common built-in account. Only the permissions for the Homegroup entry matter. Entries for individual user names only affect access from computers that aren't members of the homegroup, and from computers not running Windows 8 or 7. And whether a specific account or the Guest account will be used depends on that complex list of situations we provided under "File Permissions and Networking," earlier in this chapter.

If you have computers on your network that run older versions of Windows, and therefore can't be members of the homegroup, you can give their users easy access to your shared files in either of two ways:

- If you turn off Password Protected Sharing on your computer, add the group name Everyone to the permission list. The other computers will get access to the files this way.

- If you want to leave Password Protected Sharing turned on for your computer, either create accounts for each of the other computers' users on your computer, using their account names and passwords, or create a single user account named, for example, "sharing" on your computer, assign a password to it, and have all of the other users use this account when they connect over the network. Add this account to the permissions list and then grant it Read or Read/Write access.

To change the permissions granted to a user or group listed in the File Sharing dialog box, shown in Figure 21.8, change the entry in the Permission Level column to Read, Read/Write, or Remove, which removes the entry from the list. To add a new entry, select a name from the drop-down list next to the Add button and then click the Add button. You can then change the new entry's Permission Level.

Your account is listed as the file's or folder's owner, and you can't change this entry.

> **🔍 note**
>
> If you add Everyone to the list, the permissions you give to it will set the minimum access level granted to, well, everyone. Specifically, if you grant Everyone Read/Write access, this trumps any other settings in the list. *Anyone* will be able to change the files.

Sharing the Public Profile Folder

There is a very simple way to share files and folders with other users if your network includes computers running older versions of Windows that can't participate in a homegroup. The trick is to use the folder named \Users\Public on the drive that contains Windows. If you enable Public Folder Sharing, this folder will be readable and writable by everyone on the network.

To enable sharing the Public folder, follow these steps:

1. At the desktop, right-click the network icon in the taskbar and select Open Network and Sharing Center, Homegroup, or you can open the Control Panel and select Choose Homegroup and Sharing Options.

2. Click Change Advanced Sharing Options.

3. Scroll down and click the button that opens the All Networks section. Under Public Folder Sharing, select Turn On Sharing. Then click Save Changes.

This makes the folder available to anyone who can connect to your computer over the network. Next, you must make it possible for people to connect. You can do this in either of two ways:

> **〜 tip**
>
> In most previous versions of Windows, the public folder was listed in the [My] Computer display as "Shared Documents." On Windows 8, you can get to its subfolders in your libraries, where they're labeled Public Documents, Public Pictures, and so on. You can also browse into c:\users\Public under Computer.

- Leave Password Protected Sharing turned on. Each of the other users on the network will need an account on your computer. You can create individual accounts, or you can create a single account, set a password on it, and have all the other users use that name and password when they go to use your computer's shared folder Users\Public. (The folder's full UNC name is *computername*\Users\Public, with the actual name of your computer substituted in place of *computername*.)

> **🔺 caution**
>
> If you use this second option, be careful only to let trustworthy people connect to your network. If you have a wireless network, you *must* have WEP or WPA security enabled on it.

- In the Change Advanced Sharing Options screen, turn Password Protected Sharing off. Now, *anyone* who can connect to your network will be able to read and write files in your computer's shared folder Users\Public.

Once the Public folder has been shared, you must move or copy files or folders that you want to share into the Public folder structure.

Sharing Your Own Folders in Place

To share a folder that's inside your user profile (for example, a folder inside your Documents folder) without sharing an entire library, just right-click the folder or file in any File Explorer and select Share With.

The entire \Users directory structure is shared by default on Windows 8, so all that's necessary is to let Windows change your file's or folder's permissions so that network users can see it. This is called "sharing in place." Just follow the steps:

1. Locate your file or folder in File Explorer. Right-click it and select Share With.

2. If your computer is a member of a homegroup, select one of the two Homegroup options, as outlined previously under "Setting Permissions for HomeGroup Sharing." This makes the folder appear in everyone else's Homegroup listing. If you want to customize access to the folder, right-click it again, select Share With, Specific People, and proceed as described under "Editing Permissions for Specific People."

   Otherwise, if the Homegroup options don't appear, select Specific People and then proceed as described under "Editing Permissions for Specific People."

If you later want to stop sharing this file or folder, right-click and select Share With, Nobody.

Sharing Folders Independently

To share a folder that isn't inside your user profile folder, follow these steps:

1. Locate the folder in File Explorer, or to share an entire drive, select the name of the DVD-ROM, floppy, USB, or hard drive from the list in the Computer section.

2. Right-click the folder's or drive's icon and choose Share With.

3. If your computer is a member of a homegroup, proceed as outlined previously under "Setting Permissions for HomeGroup Sharing." Be sure to select one of the two Homegroup options first, even if you intend to customize access for specific users or change the share name later.

4. If your computer is not a member of a homegroup, or if you want to grant access to non-home-group computers, select Specific People and proceed as described previously under "Editing Permissions for Specific People."

5. If you want to customize the share name or select specific users with which to share the folder, after you've finished sharing using the preceding steps, right-click the folder's or drive's icon again, select Properties, and select the Sharing tab. Click Advanced Sharing and correct the

---

tip

If you move files from your own private folders into the Public folders using File Explorer, it will automatically update the files' permissions settings as it moves or copies them, so that network users can work with them. If you use Command Prompt tools to move files, permissions are not modified, and the file will likely not be readable or writable by network users. You may need to manually add group Everyone to the files' permissions list.

share name as desired. You can also enter a comment that will appear when people browse to this folder over the network, if you wish.

You can use the Permissions button to limit the access users have to the shared files when they're using them over the network. A file's Security settings control each user's access to the file, even if the Sharing Permissions settings give everyone read/write permission. Sharing Permissions just let you *further restrict* access by unchecking boxes in the Allow column.

6. Click OK to close the dialog box.

If you later want to stop sharing the folder or drive, follow these steps:

1. Locate the folder or drive in File Explorer. Right-click it and select Properties.

2. Select the Sharing tab and then click Advanced Sharing.

3. Uncheck Share This Folder and then click OK.

Alternatively, you can locate the folder, right-click it, and select Share With, Nobody. However, this not only removes the share, it may also change file permissions.

> ### 〰️ tip
> You can prevent other users from seeing your shared folder when they browse the network by adding a dollar sign to the end of the share name, as in `mystuff$`. They must know to type this name to use the shared folder. This technique alone does *not* prevent anyone from seeing your files if they know the share name.

> ### 🔍 note
> If you are canceling sharing of an entire drive, you may notice that the administrative share C$, D$, or other, is not listed. You can safely uncheck Share This Folder, and the administrative share will not be canceled.

🔧 File Is in Use by Another User

If you go to edit a file in a folder you've shared on the network, and receive an error message indicating that the file is in use by another user, you can find out which remote user has the file open by using the Shared Folder tool in Computer Management, as described later in this chapter under "Monitoring Use of Your Shared Folders."

You can wait for the remote user to finish using your file, or you can ask that person to quit. Only in a dire emergency should you use the Shared Folder tool to disconnect the remote user or close the file. Possible reasons why you might do this are that the remote user's computer has crashed but your computer thinks the connection is still established, and that the remote user is an intruder.

Sharing Printers

You can share any of your "local" printers so that other people on the network can use them. A local printer is any printer that is directly cabled to your computer, or to which you connected via the network using LPR or other direct network protocols.

To be sure that printer sharing is enabled, do the following (you should only need to do this once):

1. Right-click the network icon in the taskbar and select Open Network and Sharing Center. Alternatively, open the Control Panel and select View Network Status and Tasks.

2. Look to see what type of network you're attached to. If your network is labeled Public Network, and you really are connected to a public network (for example, in a cafe, hotel, or school), you should *not* enable file and printer sharing—this would expose your computer to hackers. If the label says Public Network but you really are on a safe, protected home or office network, click the Network icon in the taskbar, right-click your network connections' name, and select Turn Sharing On or Off, Yes, Turn On Sharing and Connect to Devices. The Network and Sharing Center should now label the connection as Private.

3. At the left, click Change Advanced Sharing Settings.

4. Under File and Printer Sharing, make sure Turn On File and Printer Sharing is selected. If it isn't, select it and click Save Changes; otherwise, click Cancel. This will take you back to the Network and Sharing Center.

5. If your computer is part of a homegroup, select Homegroup under See Also. If Printers isn't listed as being shared, select Change What You're Sharing With the Homegroup, set Printers & Devices to Shared, and click Next and then Finish.

Now you can share any printer that is attached to your computer. To share a printer, follow these steps:

1. Open the Control Panel using Windows Logo+X, or go to the Desktop, open the Settings charm, and select Control Panel. Then under Hardware and Sound, select View Devices and Printers.

2. In the Printers section, right-click a printer that you'd like to share and select Printer Properties. This selection is near the middle of the right-click menu; you don't want the last entry labeled just "Properties."

3. Select the Sharing tab.

4. If Share This Printer isn't already checked, check it. Windows will fill in a share name for the printer. If you like, you can shorten or simplify it.

5. Click OK.

Other people on your network can now use your printer by following the instructions earlier in the chapter under "Using a Shared Printer."

In most cases, that's all you need to do. In some cases, you might wish to change some of the advanced settings described in the next few sections, but these are optional.

Setting Printer Permissions

If you have a workgroup network and have disabled Password Protected Sharing, or if you have set up a homegroup, you don't need to worry about setting permissions for printers: anyone can use your shared printer. If you're on a domain network or have chosen to use detailed user-level permissions on your workgroup network, you can control access to your shared printers with security attributes that can be assigned to users or groups, as shown in Figure 21.9 and described next:

Permission	Lets the User or Group...
Print	Send output to the printer.
Manage this printer	Change printer configuration settings as well as share or unshare a printer.
Manage documents	For the CREATOR OWNER entry, this permission lets a user suspend or delete his or her own print jobs. For other users and groups, this permission lets the user cancel or suspend *other* users' print jobs.
Special permissions	Don't bother with this entry; it just controls whether a user can change the permission settings.

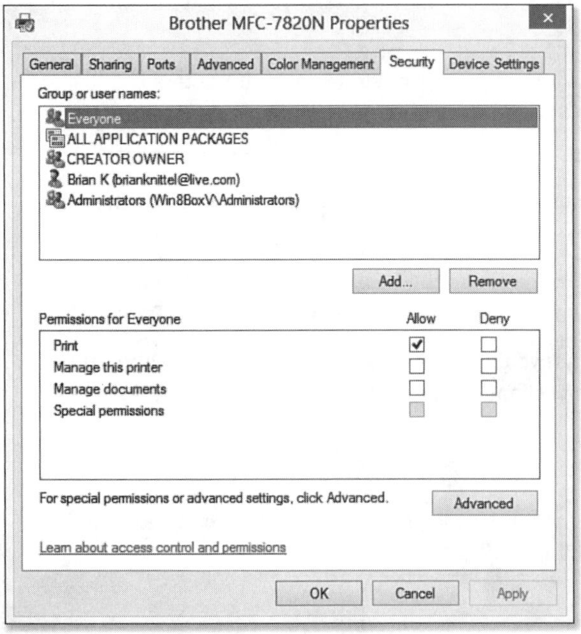

Figure 21.9
The Security tab lets you assign printer-management permissions for users, groups, and the creator of each print job.

You don't have to change any of the default permission settings, unless you want to restrict the use of the printer to just specific users on your network. If this is the case, open Devices and Printers, right-click the printer whose settings you want to change, and select Printer Properties. View the Security tab. Select the group Everyone and then click Remove. Next, click Add to add specific users or groups, and then give them Print permission. (You could also give someone Manage This Printer or Manage Documents permission, if you want to let that person change the printer's settings or delete other users' print jobs.)

Don't change the CREATOR OWNER entry, however. It should have the Manage Documents permission checked so that each user can delete his or her own print jobs from the queue.

Changing the Location of the Spool Directory

When jobs are queued up to print, Windows stores the data it has prepared for the printer in a folder on the computer that's sharing the printer. Data for your own print jobs and for any network users will all end up on your hard drive temporarily. If the drive holding your Windows folder is getting full and you'd rather house this print data on another drive, you can change the location of the spool directory.

To change the location of the Windows print spooler folder, follow these steps:

1. Open the Devices and Printers window.

2. Click any printer. Then, in the upper task menu, click Print Server Properties.

3. Select the Advanced tab and click Change Advanced Settings.

4. Enter a new location for the Spool Folder and click OK.

Printer Pooling

If your network involves heavy-duty printing, you might find that your printers are the bottleneck in getting your work done. One solution is to get faster printers, and another is to add multiple printers. However, if you have two printers shared separately, you'll have to choose one or the other when you print, and you'll almost certainly encounter bank-line syndrome: the other line always seems to move faster.

The way around this problem is to use printer pooling. You can set up one printer queue that sends its output to two or more printers. The documents line up single-file, and the printers take jobs from the front of the line, first come, first served.

To set up pooled printers, follow these steps:

1. Buy identical printers—at least, they must be identical from the software point of view.

2. Set up and test one printer and then configure network sharing for it.

3. Install the extra printer(s) on the same computer as the first. If you use network-connected printers, you need to add the necessary additional network ports.

4. View the first printer's Printer Properties dialog box and select the Ports tab. Mark Enable Printer Pooling and check the ports for the additional printers. Then, delete the printer icons for the second and subsequent printers. You should be left with one icon for the pool.

That's all there is to it; Windows passes print jobs to as many printers as you select on the Ports tab.

Managing Your Network

When you select Network in the left pane of the File Explorer window, the ribbon lists some tasks that can help you manage your network:

- **Network and Sharing Center**—Opens the Network and Sharing Center window, from which you can change homegroup settings, manage network adapters, and run automatic network trouble-shooting wizards.

- **Add Devices and Printers**—Opens a wizard to connect to a locally attached, Bluetooth, wireless, or networked printer.

- **Add a Wireless Device**—Opens a wizard to assist in adding a wireless device such as a wireless printer or network card.

If you click a computer or server name in the *right* pane (not the left), additional computer-specific task options appear in the ribbon:

- **Open**—Lets you browse the computer's shared folders and printers.

- **Connect with Remote Desktop Connection**

- **View Printers**—Lets you browse just the computer's or server's shared printers.

Windows provides additional tools that you can use to monitor the use of the files you're sharing as well as command-line tools that you can use to manage network resources that you use and share.

Monitoring Use of Your Shared Folders

If you've shared folders on your LAN, you might want to know who's using them. For example, you might need to know this information if someone were editing a file in your shared folder. If you tried to edit the same file, you'd be told by your word processor that the file was "in use by another." But by whom?

The Computer Management tool can help you. Press Windows Logo+X, select Computer Management, and open the Shared Folders item in the left pane. The Sessions and Open Files sections can show you who is using your shared folders as well as which files they currently have open. In an emergency, you can right-click and disconnect a user or close an open file with the Delete key. (This is a drastic measure and is sure to mess up the remote user, so use it only when absolutely necessary.)

Managing Network Resources Using the Command Line

You can perform drive mappings and printer selections with the command line just as easily as from the GUI. If you find yourself repeating certain network and file operations day after day, it makes sense to try to automate these processes by putting commands into batch files.

The net command comes to us virtually unchanged since the original PC network software developed by Microsoft and IBM debuted in 1984. There are so many variations of the net command that

I think of them as separate commands: net view, net use, net *whatever*. Each net command contains a word that selects a subcommand or operation type.

Interestingly, the net command not only can manage and explore your network, it also can start and stop Windows services and create user accounts and groups. You can get online help listing all the net subcommands by typing **net /?**, and you can get detailed help by typing ***net command /?***, where *command* is any one of the net subcommands.

The net use command makes and disconnects drive mappings as well as establishes printer redirection for console (command-line) applications. The basic command is as follows:

```
net use drive sharename
```

The following example maps drive letter Q to the shared folder \\abalone\book:

```
net use q: \\abalone\book
```

You can't replace the shared folder attached to an already mapped drive, so you should try to delete a previous mapping before trying to make a new one:

```
net use q: /delete
net use q: \\abalone\book
```

⊛ tip

If the drive mapping didn't exist beforehand, the /delete command will print an error message. That's fine if you're typing commands directly in the Command Prompt window. If you perform drive mapping in a batch file, the error message would be disconcerting. You can prevent it from appearing by issuing the command this way:

```
net use q: /delete >nul 2>nul
```

NUL is a special filename to Windows; it's basically a black hole for data. Directing all output to NUL makes sure that the command doesn't display anything.

Here is an example of a batch file that performs a simple computer-to-computer backup of some important files. Let's say I want to back up the folder C:\book, and all of its subfolders, from my computer to a shared folder on another computer named abalone. I could put the following commands into a file named backup_book.bat:

```
@echo off
net use q: /delete 1>nul 2>nul
net use q: \\abalone\book
xcopy c:\book q: /e /r /c /y
net use q: /delete
```

The `net use` command also maps network printers to the legacy DOS printer devices LPT1, LPT2, and LPT3. The following command lets MS-DOS applications send output to a network printer, by redirecting the LPT1 device:

```
net use lpt1: \\server\printername
```

The following command cancels redirection:

```
net use lpt1: /delete
```

TROUBLESHOOTING YOUR NETWORK

When Good Networks Go Bad

As part of my software consulting work, I end up doing a fair bit of network support for my clients. And every time I get a call from a client with a network problem, I cringe. I never know whether it's going to take 10 minutes or a week to fix. Sometimes the problem isn't so bad; I've fixed more than one "broken" computer by turning it on. If such an easy fix doesn't present itself immediately, though, a bit of a cold sweat breaks out on my forehead. The problem could be anything. How does one even start to find a nasty problem in the maze of cards, wires, drivers, and hidden, inexplicable system services? And it's difficult enough debugging the stuff that belongs there. What if viruses, adware, or rootkits are messing up the works?

Well, if you work for a corporation with a network support staff, of course the answer to any of these questions is to call the help desk and then take a refreshing walk around the block while someone else sweats over your network. It's great if you can get that kind of support. If you want to (or have to) go it alone, though, the good news is that some tools provided with Windows can help you find the problem. After discussing trouble-shooting in general, this chapter shows you how to use these tools.

In reading this chapter, you probably won't find the solution to any particular network problem you're having. I can't really help you solve any one specific problem here, but I can show you some of the tools available to help you identify the source of a problem you might have.

Getting Started

In years of helping clients and friends with hardware, software, and network problems, what I've noticed is that the most common—and most frustrating—way people report a problem is to say "I can't..." or "The computer won't...." Unfortunately, knowing what *doesn't* happen isn't helpful at all. I always have to ask, "What happens when you *try*?" The answer to that question usually gets me well on the way to solving the problem. The original report usually leaves out important error messages and symptoms that can identify the problem. If you can get someone to express a problem in terms of what *is* happening, rather than what isn't, you'll go from "My online banking doesn't work" to something like "The website says my password is invalid" or "Windows says that I don't have any network connections." This leads from the vague toward something you can grapple with.

Extending that principle, as you work on a problem, pay as much attention to what *does* work as to what doesn't. Knowing what isn't broken lets you eliminate whole categories of problems. For example, check to see whether a problem affects just one computer or all the computers on your home or office network. If other computers can manage the task that one computer is having trouble with, you know that the problem is located *in that one computer*, or in its connection to the others.

The following are some other questions I always ask:

- Does the problem occur all the time or just sometimes?

- Can you reproduce the problem consistently? If you can define a step-by-step procedure to reproduce the problem, can you reduce it to the shortest, most direct procedure possible?

- Has the system ever worked, even once? If so, when did it stop working, and what happened just before that? What changed?

These questions can help you determine whether the problem is fundamental (for example, due to a nonfunctioning network card) or interactive (that is, due to a conflict with other users, with new software, or confined to a particular subsystem of the network). You might be able to spot the problem right off the bat if you look at the scene this way. If you can't, you can use some tools to help narrow down the problem.

Generally, network problems fall into one or more of these categories:

- Application software

- Network clients

- Name-resolving services

- Network protocols

- Addressing and network configuration

- Driver software

- Network cards and hardware configuration

- Wiring/hubs

If you can determine which category a problem falls in, you're halfway to finding the culprit. At that point, diagnostic tools and good, old-fashioned deductive reasoning come into play. That, and random plugging and unplugging of things.

You might be able to eliminate one or more categories right away. For example, if your computer can communicate with some other computers but not all of them, and your network uses a central hub, you can deduce that at least your computer's network card and the wiring from your computer to the hub are working properly.

 tip
You might also peruse Chapter 17, "Troubleshooting An Internet Connection," for tips on diagnosing network problems specific to the Internet (TCP/IP) protocol.

Windows comes with some diagnostic tools to help you narrow down further the cause of a network problem. In the rest of this chapter, we outline these tools and suggest how to use them.

Troubleshooters and Diagnostic Tools

Each diagnostic tool described in this section serves to test the operation of one or more of the categories mentioned in the preceding section. The tools are discussed in roughly the order you should try them.

Some tools can be used to find problems in any of the many networking components. These tools quickly identify many problems.

The Network and Sharing Center

The Network and Sharing Center is the first place to start diagnosing a network problem because it can quickly take you to Windows network troubleshooters, status displays, and network settings. There are several ways to bring up the Network and Sharing Center. Here are two easy ways:

- From the Desktop, right-click the small network icon located in the right corner of the taskbar near the time of day. Select Open Network and Sharing Center.

- From the Start screen, type the word **sharing**. Click Settings and then select Network and Sharing Center from the search results.

Either method brings up the window shown in Figure 22.1.

Under View Your Active Networks, Windows displays information about any active network and/or direct Internet connections. For example, in Figure 22.1, you can see that I am attached to a LAN, through the network adapter named Ethernet. The network location is set to Private, which means that file and printer sharing are allowed. The network can reach the Internet, and the computer is a member of a homegroup.

 *If you want to use file sharing and/or the HomeGroup feature, your network location must be "Private Network." For more information, **see** "Setting Up a Homegroup," **p. 407**.*

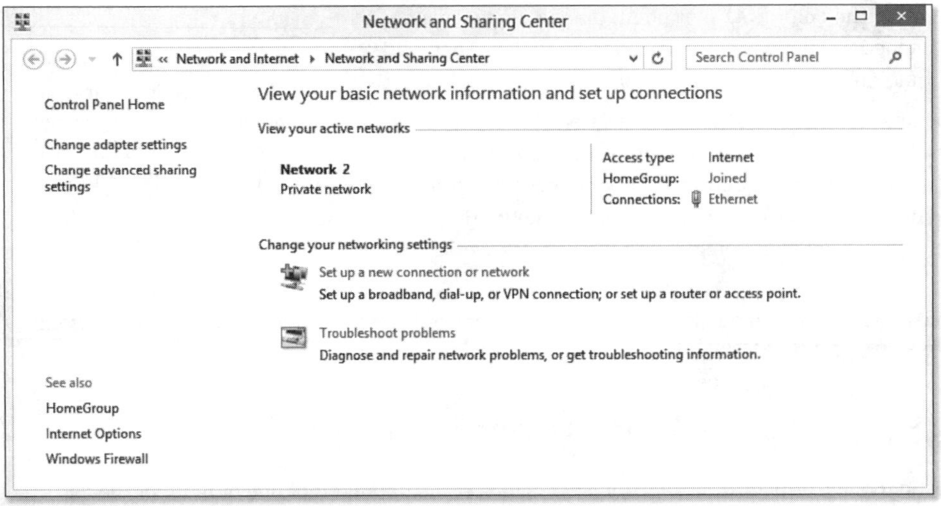

Figure 22.1
The Network and Sharing Center gives you a quick overview of your network and Internet status and leads to other diagnostic and setup tools.

This window leads to several other useful tools:

- To see whether various networking features are turned on or off, click Change Advanced Sharing Settings.

- To let Windows try to diagnose your network problem, click Troubleshoot Problems. Then select a troubleshooter for the particular problem you're having (see "Network Troubleshooters," later in the chapter, for a description of these tools).

- To check or modify the settings for one of your network adapters, click Change Adapter Settings.

- To check or change your homegroup settings, click HomeGroup in the lower-left portion of the window.

- To see if your computer can find other computers on your network, click Network and Internet in the Windows address bar, at the top of the window. We discuss this next.

If you're having problems with file and printer sharing, the first thing to check is the Network window.

Network

The Network window lets you determine whether your computer can "see" other computers on your network that are sharing files, printers, or media. Use any of these methods to view the Network window:

- From the desktop, click the File Explorer icon pinned to the taskbar. Then, click Network at the left.

- From the Start screen, type **network**, and then select Network from the search results.

- Right-click the very bottom-left corner of the screen and select Control Panel. Click the green Network and Internet title. Then click View Network Computers and Devices.

The window that appears should look something like Figure 22.2, except that the names of the computers on your network will be different. My network also includes a router (gateway) device, which also appears in this display because its Universal Plug and Play (UPnP) feature has been enabled.

> **note**
>
> Other computers will appear only if your Network Location setting is Private Network, which is set in the Network and Sharing Center window. Otherwise, file and printer sharing is disabled.

Figure 22.2
The Network view shows other computers your computer knows about.

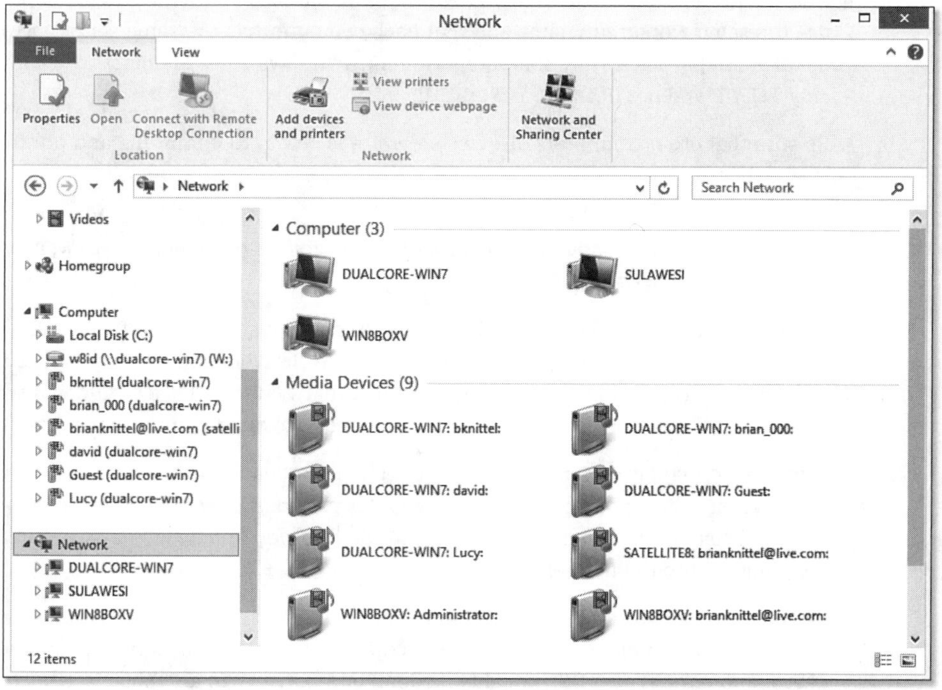

If you see at least one other computer besides your own displayed here, your computer's network cabling, network adapter, and drivers are working correctly. In addition, both your computer and the computers shown are running the Network Discovery service and/or file sharing.

If other computers don't appear, check the following:

- If your network is protected from the Internet by a firewall or a router, be sure that the Network Location is shown as Private Network. Check the Network and Sharing Center, as discussed in the previous section. If it's set to Private, left-click the network icon in the taskbar. Right-click the name of your LAN connection (usually Ethernet or Wireless), and then select Turn Sharing On or Off. Select Yes, Turn On Sharing and Connect to Devices.

■ If your computer is directly connected to the Internet in a public place such as a school or an Internet cafe, it's not safe to enable file sharing. Your network type is Public, and file sharing should be disabled. Other computers should not appear in the Network list.

➡ *For more information,* **see** *"Take Care When You Share,"* **p. 850**.

If a computer that you want to connect to is powered up, connected to the network, and is correctly configured, but still doesn't appear in the Network list, try these procedures:

■ Wait 10 minutes, and then press the F5 key. Other computers may appear this time.

■ Check each of the computers in your workgroup and make sure that each computer is set to use the same workgroup name and that each computer has the same set of network protocols installed. In particular, any computers running Windows 98 or Me must be reconfigured to use only TCP/IP and not IPX/SPX or NetBEUI.

■ Be sure that other computers' firewall software is set up to permit file and printer sharing on the local subnet.

➡ *For information about networking with older versions of Windows,* **see** *"Networking with Other Operating Systems,"* **p. 433**.

If you are having trouble with file and printer sharing with some or all of your other computers, and this screen didn't identify the problem, go back to the Network and Sharing Center and click Change Advanced Sharing Settings. This displays settings that Windows uses with home/work (private) networks and public networks, respectively. The settings are divided into three parts:

■ **Private**—Settings used for a network connection that leads to home or office networks. A network can be a home or work network, even if it provides Internet access, as long as a router or firewall is placed between the network and the Internet, and as long as you trust all the computers plugged into the network.

■ **Public**—Settings used for network connections that lead directly to networks in an insecure environment. A public network could be a direct Internet connection (for example, a connection plugged in directly to a DSL or cable modem) or a network in a public place such as a hotel or cafe, where you do not trust the other computers.

■ **All Networks**—Settings used on all network connections. These settings control file-sharing and media-sharing security options.

The first two sections are location-dependent settings, and the settings in the third section are location independent. The default settings are listed in Tables 22.1 and 22.2.

Table 22.1 Location-Dependent Advanced Sharing Settings

Setting	Private Default	Public Default	Description
Network Discovery	On	Off	When off, other computers will not appear on the network map and your computer will not appear on other computers' maps.
File and Printer Sharing	On	Off	When off, *your* computer will not share its files and/or printers with other computers. You can still use files and printers shared by *other* computers.
HomeGroup Connections	Windows	—	By default, Windows manages the user account and password used for HomeGroup sharing. For more information, see "Setting Up a Homegroup," in Chapter 18. HomeGroup connections are available on private networks only.

Table 22.2 Location-Independent Advanced Sharing Settings

Setting	Default	Description
Public Folder Sharing	On	When off, the Public user folder will not be shared. When on, it is shared and anyone can store or change files in it. (This setting applies only when File and Printer Sharing is turned on.)
Media Streaming	On	Leads to options that control how music and video are shared with networked media-playing devices and computers.
File Sharing Connections	128-bit	By default, encrypted network connections use a strong key.
Password Protected Sharing	On	When on, other users must have a user account and password to use shared files and printers that are not accessed via a homegroup. When off, other users who don't have an account on your computer, or who have an account with no password, will be granted access to shared files and printers via the Guest account. (For more information, see "Configure Passwords and File Sharing" in Chapter 33.)

Network Troubleshooters

Windows 8 has a set of network repair tools called *troubleshooters* that are said (by Microsoft) to be capable of recognizing and diagnosing more than 100 network problems. We're skeptical of claims like this; but, on the other hand, it takes only a few seconds to let these tools examine your network and offer whatever advice they can, so it's absolutely worth a crack.

There are several different network troubleshooters, each dealing with different categories of problems. You have two ways of getting to them that look very different, but actually just run the same set of tools.

The quickest way to start them is to right-click the network icon at the right end of the taskbar and select Troubleshoot Problems. This runs some basic network adapter tests, prompts you to select the type of problem you're experiencing, and then runs the appropriate troubleshooting programs. We won't describe this further; it's self-explanatory once you've started the process.

You can also access the individual troubleshooters directly: open the Network and Sharing Center as described earlier in this chapter. Click Troubleshoot Problems. Then, select one of the network troubleshooters from the list:

- **Internet Connections**—Select this if you are having a problem reaching the Internet in general, or even one particular website.

- **Shared Folders**—Select this if you can't access a network shared folder whose name you know.

- **HomeGroup**—Select this if you are having problems accessing a homegroup.

- **Network Adapter**—Select this if you are having general problems accessing the Internet and/or network resources and suspect a hardware problem.

- **Incoming Connections**—Select this if other computers can't connect to your computer's shared files or to other programs or services that you want to make available on your computer (for example, Remote Desktop, a web server, and so on).

- **Connection to a Workplace Using DirectAccess**—Select this if you can't access your corporate network over the Internet via the DirectAccess virtual private networking feature.

Windows displays a box that says "Identifying the problem..." and then displays a results window that explains what was found to be wrong, what Windows did about it (if anything), what the outcome was, and where to go for more assistance.

If the diagnostics tool doesn't solve your network problem, check Windows Firewall to be sure it isn't blocking a desired network service.

> **tip**
>
> Whichever troubleshooter(s) you use, if the word *Advanced* appears on the first screen, click it and select Run As Administrator and also check Apply Repairs Automatically.

> **note**
>
> The troubleshooters aren't good at determining that nothing is actually wrong with their particular area of concern. If a troubleshooter says that it can't find a problem, it might mean that there is no problem with that specific topic. Try another troubleshooter.

Windows Firewall

Another configuration setting that could prevent file and printer sharing from working correctly is Windows Firewall. To ensure that file and printer sharing isn't blocked, open the Windows Firewall window. The quickest way is to type **firewall** at the Start screen, select Settings, and then select Windows Firewall.

Windows Firewall filters network activity based on the type of network to which you're attached. For both private and public networks, the Windows Firewall State should be On, and Incoming Connections should be set to Block All Connections to Apps That Are Not on the List of Allowed Apps.

Click Allow an App or Feature Through Windows Firewall to view the settings. File and Printer Sharing should be checked in the Private column, but *not* in the Public column. Core Networking should be checked in both columns.

> For more information about configuring the firewall, **see** "Configuring Windows Firewall," p. 406.

If the firewall settings appear to be correct, the next step is to check Windows Event Viewer, to see whether Windows has left a record of any network problems there.

Event Viewer

Event Viewer is another important diagnostic tool and one of the first to check because Windows often silently records useful information about problems with hardware and software in an Event Log. To check, open the Event Viewer, using one of these two methods:

- Press Windows Logo+X and select Event Viewer.

- At the Start screen, search for **event**, click Settings, and then click View Event Logs.

Start by selecting Custom Views, Administrative Events in the left pane. This provides a view of all significant management events from all of the various Windows events logs (and there are a lot of them!). Look for anything that might mention a networking error.

If nothing useful appears there, select Windows Logs, and then examine the System, Application, and Security logs in turn. Finally, open Applications and Services Logs, Microsoft, Windows, and under any of the network-related categories, view the Operational and Admin logs.

Event Viewer displays Event Log entries, most recent first, on the right (see Figure 22.3).

Figure 22.3
Event Viewer might display important diagnostic information when you have network problems.

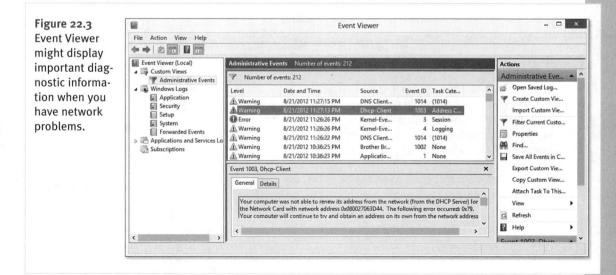

Log entries for serious errors are displayed with a red X in a circle; warnings appear with a yellow ! in a triangle. Informational entries (marked with a blue *i*) usually don't relate to problems. Double-click any error or warning entries in the log to view the detailed description and any associated data recorded with the entry. The Warning entry in Figure 22.3 indicates that my computer couldn't acquire a network address in a reasonable amount of time. It turns out that my router had come unplugged.

These messages are usually significant and informative to help diagnose network problems; they might indicate that a network card is malfunctioning, that a domain controller for authentication or a DHCP server for configuration can't be found, and so on. The Source column in the error log indicates which Windows component or service recorded the event. These names are usually fairly cryptic. Table 22.3 lists a few of the more common nonobvious ones.

Table 22.3 Network Sources of Event Log Entries

Source	Description
Application Popup	Can come from any system utility; these warning messages are usually significant.
Atapi	IDE hard disk/CD-ROM controller.
Browser, bowser	Name resolution system for Client for Microsoft Networks.
Dhcp-Client	Network address assignment service client.
DNS Client Events	Network name lookup client.
Dnsapi	DNS client component.
Dnscache	DNS client component.
MrxSmb	Client for Microsoft Networks.
NetBT	Client for Microsoft Networks.
RasClient, RasMan	Dial-up networking.
Time Service	Computer clock synchronization service.

If you're at a loss to solve the problem, even with the information given, check the configuration of the indicated component, or remove and reinstall it to see whether you can clear up the problem.

➡ *To learn more details about the Event Log,* **see** *"Event Viewer,"* **p. 529.**

> **tip**
>
> A problem with one network system usually causes other problems. Therefore, the oldest error message in a closely timed sequence of errors is *usually* the most significant, with subsequent errors just a result of the first failure. Because the Event Log is ordered "most-recent first," you might get the most useful information down a bit from the top of the list.

Device Manager

Hardware problems with your network card will most likely be recorded in the Event Log. If you suspect that your network card is the culprit, and nothing is recorded in the Event Log, check the Device Manager.

You have two easy ways to open the Device Manager:

- Right-click the very bottom-left corner of the screen and select Device Manager.

- At the Start screen, type **manager**, click Settings, and then click Device Manager.

Any devices with detectable hardware problems or configuration conflicts appear with a yellow ! icon when you display the Device Manager. If no yellow icons appear, you don't have a *detected* hardware problem. This doesn't mean that you don't have a problem, but the odds are slim that your network card is the problem.

If devices are shown with ! icons, double-click the device name to see the Windows explanation of the device status and any problems. A device that you've told Windows not to use (disabled) will have a red X on it; this is generally not a problem.

> ⊚ **tip**
>
> The real cause of your problem might reveal itself at system startup time rather than when you observe the problem. Reboot your system and note the time. Then reproduce the problem. Check the Event Log for messages starting at the reboot time.

➡ *For more detailed instructions and tips on device troubleshooting, **see** Chapter 26, "Troubleshooting and Repairing Problems."*

Testing Network Cables

If your computer can't communicate with any other computer on your LAN, and the Device Manager doesn't indicate a faulty network card, you *might* have a wiring problem. Wiring problems can be the most difficult to solve because it's difficult to prove that data is leaving one computer but not arriving at another. The ping program, discussed later in this chapter, can help with this problem.

➡ *To learn how you can use the ping command to diagnose Internet-related problems, as opposed to LAN problems, **see** "ping," p. 361.*

If your computer is not properly wired into the LAN or is connected through a wireless network, in many cases Windows will display an offline icon right on the system tray and indicate that your network card is disconnected. It might not, though, so you shouldn't take a lack of this kind of message to mean that no wiring problems exist.

If your network uses CAT-5 or CAT-6 cabling plugged into a hub, there's usually a green LED indicator on each network card and at each port on the hub. Be sure that the lights are on at each end of your network cable and those for the other computers on your LAN.

You also can use inexpensive (about $75) cable-test devices that check for continuity and correct pin-to-pin wiring order for UTP wiring. They come as a set of two boxes. One gets plugged into each end of a given cable run, and a set of blinking lights tells you whether all four wire pairs are connected and in the correct order. It's nice to have one of these if you install your own network cabling and/or make your own patch cables.

Checking Network Configuration

If hardware isn't at fault, you might have a fundamental network configuration problem. Often the Event Log and Device Manager give these problems away, but if they don't, you can use another batch of tools to check the computer's network configuration.

ipconfig

If your computer can't communicate with others on your LAN, after you check the Event Log and Device Manager, use the `ipconfig` command-line utility to see whether your computer has a valid IP address. Check other computers on the LAN, too, to ensure that they do as well.

Open a Command Prompt window by typing **cmd** at the Start screen and then selecting Command Prompt. Type the following command and press Enter:

ipconfig /all

The results should look something like this:

```
Windows IP Configuration
    Host Name . . . . . . . . . . . . : myvpc-hb
    Primary Dns Suffix  . . . . . . . : mycompany.com
    Node Type . . . . . . . . . . . . : Hybrid
    IP Routing Enabled. . . . . . . . : Yes
    WINS Proxy Enabled. . . . . . . . : No
Ethernet adapter Local Area Connection:
    Connection-specific DNS Suffix  . :
    Description . . . . . . . . . . . : Intel 21140-Based PCI Fast Ethernet Adapter
    Physical Address. . . . . . . . . : 00-03-FF-DD-CA-5F
    DHCP Enabled. . . . . . . . . . . : Yes
    Autoconfiguration Enabled . . . . : Yes
    Link-local IPv6 Address . . . . . : fe80::ed10:dff9:693c:803d%8(Preferred)
    IPv4 Address. . . . . . . . . . . : 192.168.15.108(Preferred)
    Subnet Mask . . . . . . . . . . . : 255.255.255.0
    Lease Obtained. . . . . . . . . . : Friday, October 20, 2006 5:55:11 PM
    Lease Expires . . . . . . . . . . : Friday, October 27, 2006 5:55:23 PM
    Default Gateway . . . . . . . . . : 192.168.15.1
    DHCP Server . . . . . . . . . . . : 192.168.15.1
    DHCPv6 IAID . . . . . . . . . . . : 201327615
    DNS Servers . . . . . . . . . . . : 192.168.15.1
    NetBIOS over Tcpip. . . . . . . . : Enabled
```

(Unless you're troubleshooting IPv6 Teredo connections, ignore the parts that mention Tunnel Adapters.)

The most important items to look for are the following:

- **Host Name**—This should be set to the desired name for each computer. If you can correspond with some computers but not others, be sure that the ones that don't work are turned on and correctly named. Make sure you don't have two computers with the same name, and that none of the computer names is the same as the workgroup name.

- **IP Address**—This should be set appropriately for your network. If your LAN uses Internet Connection Sharing (ICS), the address will be a number in the range 192.168.0.1 through 192.168.0.254. If your LAN has a connection-sharing router, the IP address will *usually* use numbers starting with 192.168.*x*, where *x* is a number between 0 to 100.

  If your IP address starts with the numbers 169.254, your computer is set for automatic configuration but no DHCP server was found, so Windows has chosen an IP address by itself. This is fine if your LAN uses this automatic configuration system; perhaps you've just connected a few computers so you can share files and printers. However, if you expected to get Internet access through your network—that is, if you use ICS or a hardware Internet connection router, or you have a more complex network with a DHCP server—this is a serious problem. Restart the connecting-sharing computer or the router and then restart your computer and try again.

> 🔍 **note**
>
> To learn more about IP addressing, network masks, and configuration, visit http://support.microsoft.com and search for article number 164015, "Understanding TCP/IP Addressing and Subnetting Basics."

- **Network Mask**—This is usually 255.255.255.0, but other settings are possible. All computers on the same LAN should have the same network mask.

Each computer on the same LAN should have a similar valid IP address and the same network mask. If they don't, check your network configuration. The built-in Windows Repair function may also be used to help fix problems with DHCP-based (automatic) IP address assignment.

System

You can check a computer's identification and workgroup or domain membership setup from the System window. Perform one of the following actions to open this window:

- At the Desktop, click the File Explorer icon in the taskbar. Click Computer in the left pane, and then click System Properties in the ribbon bar at the top.

- Right-click the very bottom-left corner of the screen and select System.

- At the Start window, type **system**, click Settings, and then click System.

Look at the bottom of the screen for the computer name and domain or workgroup name, as shown in Figure 22.4.

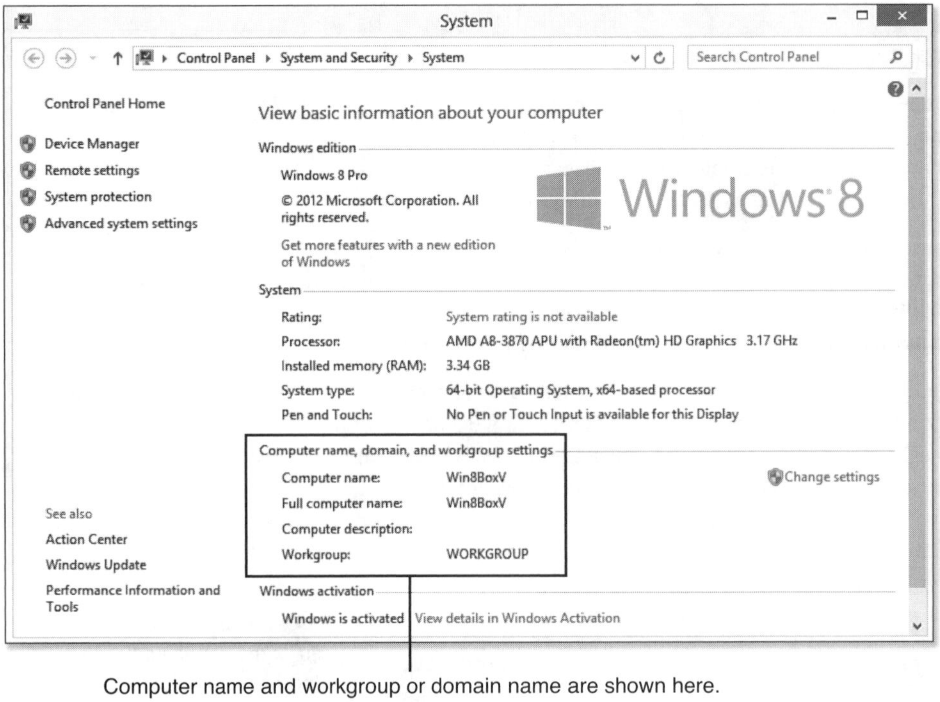

Figure 22.4
Your computer's name and workgroup or domain membership are displayed at the bottom of the System window.

Computer name and workgroup or domain name are shown here.

On a home/small office Workgroup network, the workgroup name should be the same on all computers on your workgroup LAN. All of the computer names *must* be different from each other.

On a corporate Windows domain network, you should see your computer's name displayed as part of a Windows domain name (for example, my computer named bribox might be called bribox.mycompany.com on a domain network) and the domain name displayed separately. Your domain name might not include .com. It might say .local instead or use a different ending. In any case, be sure that your computer is actually a domain member. If the word *Workgroup* appears instead, your computer is not a domain member and will not be able to use domain logins or some domain resources.

> **note**
>
> None of your computers can use the workgroup or domain name as its computer name. For example, if your workgroup is MSHOME, you can't also name a computer MSHOME. If you find this on one of your computers, change that computer's name.

Network Connections

You can manually check all installed network protocols and services and their configuration by viewing Network Connections and viewing the properties for Local Area Connection. To view this screen, open the Network and Sharing Center as discussed at the start of this chapter and click Change Adapter Settings. Right-click your Ethernet icon (or the appropriate wireless connection icon) and select Properties.

Confirm that each required protocol is installed and correctly configured. In general, the settings on each computer on your LAN should match, except that the IP address differs (usually only in the last of its four dot-separated numbers). If your LAN uses automatic IP address configuration, use the `ipconfig` command, described earlier, to check the settings.

Testing Network Connectivity with `ping`

`ping` is the fundamental tool for testing TCP/IP network connectivity. Because most networks today use the Internet (TCP/IP) protocol for file and printer sharing services, as well as for Internet access, most Windows users can use the `ping` test to confirm that their network cabling, hardware, and the TCP/IP protocol are all functioning correctly. `ping` sends several data packets to a specified computer and waits for the other computer to send the packets back. By default, it sends four packets and prints the results of the four tests.

To see whether the network can carry data between a pair of computers, use the `ipconfig` command (described previously) to find the IP address of the two computers. Then, on one computer, in the open Command Prompt window, type the following command:

```
ping 127.0.0.1
```

This command tests the networking software of the computer by sending packets to the special internal IP address 127.0.0.1. This test has the computer send data to itself. It should print the following:

```
Reply from 127.0.0.1: bytes=32 time<10ms TTL=128
Reply from 127.0.0.1: bytes=32 time<10ms TTL=128
Reply from 127.0.0.1: bytes=32 time<10ms TTL=128
Reply from 127.0.0.1: bytes=32 time<10ms TTL=128
```

If this doesn't, the TCP/IP protocol itself is incorrectly installed or configured; check the computer's IP address configuration, or, if that seems correct, remove and reinstall the Internet Protocol from the Ethernet connection icon in Network Connections. (I have to say, in more than 15 years of working with PC networks, I've never seen this test fail.)

If your computer can send data to itself, go to a second computer on your LAN. Find its IP address by running `ipconfig` on that computer. Go back to the first computer and type the `ping` command again, using the address of the second computer, as in this example:

```
ping 192.168.0.23
```

Of course, you should use the other computer's real IP address in place of 192.168.0.23. You should get four replies, as before:

```
Reply from 192.168.0.23: bytes=32 time<10ms TTL=32
Reply from 192.168.0.23: bytes=32 time<10ms TTL=32
Reply from 192.168.0.23: bytes=32 time<10ms TTL=32
Reply from 192.168.0.23: bytes=32 time<10ms TTL=32
```

These replies indicate that you have successfully sent data to the other machine and received it back.

If, on the other hand, the ping command returns Request timed out, the packets either didn't make it to the other computer or were not returned. In either case, you have a problem with your cabling, network adapter, or the TCP/IP protocol setup.

You can use ping to determine which computers can send to which other computers on your LAN or across wide area networks (WANs) or the Internet. ping should also work when given a computer's IP address or its network name.

> **note**
>
> If you enter a computer name, and ping can't determine the computer's IP address, the problem isn't necessarily a wiring problem—it could be that the DNS or WINS name lookup system is not working correctly. Try using an IP address with ping in this case to help determine what the problem really is.

Diagnosing File and Printer Sharing Problems

If the test in the previous section doesn't point to a problem—that is, if basic network connectivity is fine but you're still having problems with file or printer sharing—the next step depends on whether you have a workgroup or domain-type network.

If you're on a domain network, it's time to call your network administrator for assistance. He or she has more training and experience in network troubleshooting than we can impart in the space allowed here.

If you're on a home or small office workgroup network, there are a few things you might try. Here are some tips:

- Did you make sure that file sharing is enabled on each of your computers?

- Do your Windows 8 computers say Private as their network location? Do your Windows 7 and Vista computers say Home or Work? The Public setting blocks file sharing.

    On Windows XP, there is no network location setting. Instead, open Windows Firewall, view the Exceptions list, and make sure that File and Printer Sharing is checked.

- If you use Internet Connection Sharing, restart the computer that's sharing your Internet connection and wait a minute or two after it's booted up. Then, restart your other computers. This may help. The ICS computer needs to be up and running *before* any other computers on your LAN start up.

- If you can see the folders shared by another computer but can't move any files into them, or edit files in them, then your network is fine—you just have a permissions problem. On the computer that is sharing the folders, be sure that the folders are shared so that remote visitors can change files.

    For more information on shared folders, **see** *"Using Shared Folders," p. 456.*

If the *sharing* computer has Password Protected Sharing enabled (or has Simple File Sharing turned off, if the computer is running XP), the owner of the other computer should check to see that your user account has permission to read and/or modify the files in the shared folder. In the folder or files' Security properties, check to see that your user account is listed or that the group you're in (for example, Users or Everyone) has the necessary permissions.

→ *File permissions are discussed in the "Setting Security Permissions on Files and Folders" section, **p. 775**.*

In Windows 8 and 7, Password Protected Sharing works differently than it does on Vista and XP. If you can't access a file over the network that you know you could access if you were logged on directly at the sharing computer, that computer might be using the Guest account to access the file instead of yours.

→ *For more information on Password Protected Sharing, **see** "Configure Passwords and File Sharing" on **p. 802**.*

One way you can tell whether this feature is causing your problem is to log on at the sharing computer, right-click [My] Computer, and then select Manage. At the left, open the Shared Folders item and select Sessions. Try to access the problem file or folder from across the network. You should see an entry for the networked computer. If the username is Guest, you will only be able to read or write files that group Everyone can read or write. See Chapter 33 for a discussion about the way Password Protected Sharing works in various situations

WINDOWS MANAGEMENT TOOLS

Managing Windows

Our goal in this book is to help you plumb the true depths of Windows 8, and our premise is that this goal can't be met by toeing the line and doing only what the Help system tells you. Rather, we believe you can reach this goal only by taking various off-the-beaten-track routes that go beyond Windows orthodoxy.

The topics in this chapter illustrate this approach quite nicely. The tools we discuss—Control Panel, Group Policy Editor, Microsoft Management Console, and Services—aren't difficult to use, but they put an amazing amount of power and flexibility into your hands. We discuss them in depth because you'll be using these important tools in other chapters of the book. However, you can scour the Windows 8 Help system all day long and you'll find only a few scant references to these tools. To be sure, Microsoft is being cautious because these *are* powerful tools, and the average user can wreak all kinds of havoc if these features are used incorrectly. However, your purchase of this book is proof that you are not an average user. So, by following the instructions in this chapter, we're sure you'll have no trouble at all using these tools.

We begin with an in-depth look at Control Panel: understanding it, navigating it, and customizing it to suit your needs.

Controlling Windows 8 with Control Panel

Control Panel is a folder that contains a large number of icons—the Classic view of a default Windows 8 setup contains about 50 icons, but depending on your system configuration, even more icons could be available. Each of these icons deals with a specific area of the Windows 8 configuration: hardware, applications, fonts, printers, multimedia, and much more.

Opening an icon displays a window or dialog box containing various properties related to that area of Windows. For example, launching the Programs and Features icon enables you to install or uninstall third-party applications and to activate or deactivate Windows 8 components.

Touring the Control Panel Window

You have three main ways to launch Control Panel:

- On the Windows 8 Start screen, type **control**, and then click Control Panel in the search results.

- Press Windows Logo+R to open the Run dialog box, type **control**, and then press Enter.

- Press Windows Logo+X and then click Control Panel.

By default, Windows 8 displays the Control Panel in Category view, shown in Figure 23.1, which displays icons for eight different categories (System and Security, Network and Internet, and so on), as well as two or three links to common tasks under each category icon.

 tip

If you prefer the All Control Panel Items window, but you find that the Small Icons view makes the icons *too* small, you can make it a tad easier to manage by switching to the Large Icons view, which still enables you to see every icon if you enlarge or maximize the Control Panel window. In the View By list, click Large Icons.

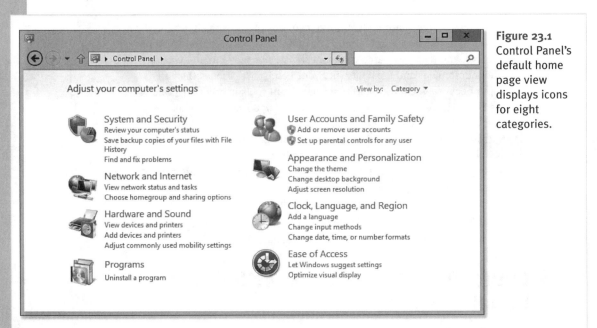

Figure 23.1
Control Panel's default home page view displays icons for eight categories.

Category view is designed to help novice users, but even power users quickly get used to its layout. However, if you feel that it just delays you unnecessarily, you can switch to the classic Small Icons view by selecting Small Icons in the View By list. This opens the All Control Panel Items window, as shown in Figure 23.2.

Figure 23.2
Switch Control Panel to the Small Icons view to see all the icons in one window.

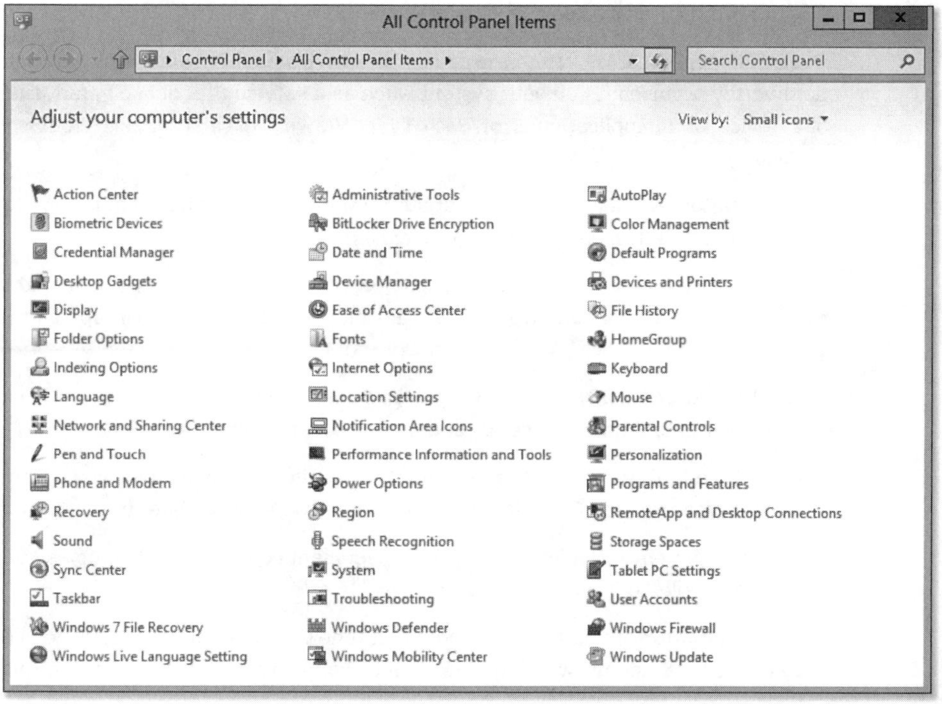

All Control Panel Items

▸ Control Panel ▸ All Control Panel Items ▸

Search Control Panel

Adjust your computer's settings   View by: Small icons ▾

- 🚩 Action Center
- 🔲 Biometric Devices
- 🗝 Credential Manager
- 🖥 Desktop Gadgets
- 🖥 Display
- 📁 Folder Options
- 🗂 Indexing Options
- 🌐 Language
- 📶 Network and Sharing Center
- ✏ Pen and Touch
- 📠 Phone and Modem
- 🔄 Recovery
- 🔊 Sound
- 🔄 Sync Center
- ☑ Taskbar
- 🔄 Windows 7 File Recovery
- 🌐 Windows Live Language Setting

- 🛠 Administrative Tools
- 🔐 BitLocker Drive Encryption
- 🕐 Date and Time
- 🖨 Device Manager
- 🕑 Ease of Access Center
- 🅰 Fonts
- 🗝 Internet Options
- 📍 Location Settings
- 🖥 Notification Area Icons
- ■ Performance Information and Tools
- 🔌 Power Options
- 🌐 Region
- 🎤 Speech Recognition
- 🖥 System
- 🖥 Troubleshooting
- 🛡 Windows Defender
- 🖥 Windows Mobility Center

- 🖥 AutoPlay
- 🖥 Color Management
- 🖥 Default Programs
- 🖨 Devices and Printers
- 🗂 File History
- 🏠 HomeGroup
- ⌨ Keyboard
- 🖱 Mouse
- 🔲 Parental Controls
- 🖥 Personalization
- 🖥 Programs and Features
- 🖥 RemoteApp and Desktop Connections
- 🖥 Storage Spaces
- 🖥 Tablet PC Settings
- 🔲 User Accounts
- 🛡 Windows Firewall
- 🖥 Windows Update

Reviewing the Control Panel Icons

To help you familiarize yourself with what's available in Control Panel, this section offers summary descriptions of the Control Panel icons found in a standard Windows 8 installation when using either the Large or Small Icons view. Note that your system might have extra icons, depending on your computer's configuration and the programs you have installed.

- **Action Center**—Displays a list of your computer's current security issues and hardware and software problems.

- **Administrative Tools**—Displays a window with more icons, each of which enables you to administer a particular aspect of Windows 8:

   Component Services—Displays the Component Services window, which you can use to investigate Component Object Model (COM) and Distributed COM (DCOM) applications and services.

   Computer Management—Enables you to manage a local or remote computer. You can examine hidden and visible shared folders, set group policies, access Device Manager, manage hard disks, and much more.

   Defragment and Optimize Drives—Enables you to defragment your hard drives and set a defragmentation schedule. See "Defragmenting Your Hard Disk" in Chapter 25, "Managing Hard Disks and Storage Spaces."

Disk Cleanup—You use this tool to remove old and unneeded files from your system. See "Deleting Unnecessary Files" in Chapter 25.

Event Viewer—Enables you to examine Windows 8's list of *events*, which are unusual or noteworthy occurrences on your system, such as a service that doesn't start, the installation of a device, or an application error. See "Event Viewer" in Chapter 22, "Troubleshooting Your Network."

iSCSI Initiator—Displays the iSCSI Initiator property sheet, which enables you to manage connections to iSCSI devices such as tape drives.

Local Security Policy—Displays the Local Security Settings snap-in, which enables you to set up security policies on your system. See "Policing Windows 8 with Group Policies," later in this chapter.

ODBC Data Sources ODBC—Enables you to create and work with *data source names*, which are connection strings that you use to connect to local or remote databases.

Performance Monitor—Runs the Performance Monitor, which enables you to monitor various aspects of your system. See "Using the Performance Monitor," later in this chapter.

Print Management—Displays the Print Management console, which enables you to manage, share, and deploy printers and print servers.

Resource Monitor—Enables you to view real-time data related your computer's CPU, memory, hard disk usage, and networking. See "Using the Resource Monitor," later in this chapter.

Services—Displays a list of the system services available with Windows 8. System services are background routines that enable the system to perform tasks such as network logon, disk management, Plug and Play, Internet connection sharing, and much more. You can pause, stop, and start services, as well as configure how services load at startup. For the details, see "Controlling Services," later in this chapter.

System Configuration—Opens the System Configuration utility. In Chapter 2, "Installing or Upgrading to Windows 8," see the "Using the System Configuration Utility to Modify the BCD" section, and in Chapter 26, "Troubleshooting and Repairing Problems," see the "Disabling Startup Services" section.

System Information—Displays a summary of your computer's hardware and software resources.

Task Scheduler—Runs the Task Scheduler console, which enables you to run programs or scripts on a schedule.

Windows Firewall with Advanced Security—Enables you to control every aspect of Windows 8's bidirectional firewall. See "Configuring Windows Firewall" in Chapter 33, "Protecting Your Network from Hackers and Snoops."

Windows Memory Diagnostic—Runs the Windows Memory Diagnostics Tool, which checks your computer's memory chips for problems. See "Running the Memory Diagnostics Tool" in Chapter 26.

Windows PowerShell ISE—Loads the Windows PowerShell Integrated Scripting Environment for creating and running PowerShell scripts. To learn about PowerShell, see the "Windows PowerShell" section in Chapter 30, "Command-Line and Automation Tools."

■ **AutoPlay**—Opens the AutoPlay window, which enables you to configure AutoPlay defaults for various media.

■ **Biometric Devices**—Enables you to configure biometric devices on your PC, such as a fingerprint reader.

■ **BitLocker Drive Encryption**—Turns on and configures BitLocker, which encrypts your Windows 8 system drive to protect it from unauthorized viewing. In Chapter 32, "Protecting Your Data from Loss and Theft," see "Encrypting a Disk with BitLocker."

■ **Color Management**—Enables you to configure the colors of your monitor and printer to optimize color output.

■ **Credential Manager**—This new tool enables you to store and work with usernames and passwords for servers, websites, network shares, and other secure resources.

■ **Date and Time**—Enables you to set the current date and time, select your time zone, and set up an Internet time server to synchronize your system time. You can also display extra clocks to monitor other time zones (see "Displaying Multiple Clocks for Different Time Zones" in Chapter 24, "Tweaking and Customizing Windows").

■ **Default Programs**—Displays the Default Programs window, which enables you to change the programs associated with Windows 8's file types.

■ **Desktop Gadgets**—Enables you to add and remove gadgets to and from the Windows 8 desktop. See Chapter 8, "Accessories and Accessibility."

■ **Device Manager**—Launches Device Manager, which enables you to view and work with your system devices and their drivers. See "Troubleshooting Device Problems" in Chapter 26 for more information.

■ **Devices and Printers**—Displays a list of the major devices connected to your computer.

■ **Display**—Enables you to change the size of the screen text and perform other display-related tasks.

■ **Ease of Access Center**—Enables you to customize input (the keyboard and mouse) and output (sound and display for users with special mobility, hearing, or vision requirements).

■ **File History**—You use this feature to save previous versions of your personal files to an external hard drive or network share. See "Activating File History" in Chapter 32.

■ **Folder Options**—Enables you to customize the display of Windows 8's folders, set up whether Windows 8 uses single- or double-clicking, work with file types, and configure offline files.

■ **Fonts**—Displays the Fonts folder, from which you can view, install, and remove fonts.

- **HomeGroup**—Enables you to join a homegroup, which is Windows 8's user-account-free networking technology. In Chapter 18, "Creating a Windows Network," see "Setting Up a Homegroup."

- **Indexing Options**—Enables you to configure the index used by Windows 8's new search engine.

- **Internet Options**—Displays a large collection of settings for modifying Internet properties (how you connect, the Internet Explorer interface, and so on).

- **Keyboard**—Enables you to customize your keyboard, work with keyboard languages, and change the keyboard driver.

- **Language**—Enables you to add languages to Windows 8.

- **Location Settings**—Enables you to enable or disable location services.

- **Mouse**—Enables you to set various mouse options and to install a different mouse device driver.

- **Network and Sharing Center**—Displays general information about your network connections and sharing settings. See "The Network and Sharing Center" in Chapter 22.

- **Notification Area Icons**—Gives you access to notification area customization options. In Chapter 24, see the section "Taking Control of the Notification Area."

- **Parental Controls**—Enables you to restrict computer usage for other users of the computer.

- **Pen and Touch**—Displays the Pen and Input Devices dialog box, which enables you to configure your tablet PC's digital pen.

- **Performance Information and Tools**—Displays the performance rating for your computer.

- **Personalization**—Offers a large number of customization options for the current Windows 8 theme: glass effects, colors, desktop background, screensaver, sounds, mouse pointers, and display settings.

- **Phone and Modem**—Enables you to configure telephone dialing rules and to install and configure modems.

- **Power Options**—Enables you to configure power management properties for powering down system components (such as the monitor and hard drive), defining low-power alarms for notebook batteries, enabling sleep and hibernation modes, and configuring notebook power buttons.

- **Programs and Features**—Enables you to install and uninstall applications, add and remove Windows 8 components, and view installed updates.

- **Recovery**—Enables you to recover your system by restoring it to an earlier working configuration.

- **Region**—Enables you to configure international settings for country-dependent items such as numbers, currencies, times, and dates.

- **RemoteApp and Desktop Connections**—Enables you to create and work with remote programs and desktops.

- **Sound**—Enables you to control the system volume, map sounds to specific Windows 8 events (such as closing a program or minimizing a window), and specify settings for audio, voice, and other multimedia devices.

- **Speech Recognition**—Enables you to configure Windows 8's speech recognition feature.

- **Storage Spaces**—Enables you to pool multiple hard drives into a single storage area. In Chapter 25, see "Working with Storage Spaces."

- **Sync Center**—Enables you to set up and maintain synchronization with other devices and with offline files.

- **System**—Displays basic information about your system, including the Windows 8 edition, system rating, processor type, memory size, computer and workgroup names, and whether Windows 8 is activated. Also gives you access to Device Manager and settings related to performance, startup, System Protection, Remote Assistance, and the Remote Desktop.

- **Tablet PC Settings**—Displays settings for configuring handwriting and other aspects of your tablet PC.

- **Taskbar**—Enables you to customize the taskbar. In Chapter 24, see "Customizing the Taskbar for Easier Program and Document Launching" for more information.

- **Troubleshooting**—Displays a collection of tasks related to troubleshooting various aspects of your system.

- **User Accounts**—Enables you to set up and configure user accounts.

- **Windows 7 File Recovery**—Gives you access to the backup tools from Windows 7. In Chapter 32, see "Creating a System Image Backup."

- **Windows Defender**—Launches Windows Defender, Windows 8's antispyware program. See "Making Sure Windows Defender Is Turned On" in Chapter 31, "Protecting Windows from Viruses and Spyware."

- **Windows Firewall**—Enables you to configure Windows Firewall. See "Managing Windows Firewall" in Chapter 32.

- **Windows Live Language Setting**—Enables you to set the language to use with Windows Live programs.

- **Windows Mobility Center**—Displays Windows 8's Mobility Center for notebooks.

- **Windows Update**—Enables you to configure Windows 8's Windows Update feature, check for updates, view update history, and set up a schedule for the download and installation of updates.

> 🔍 **note**
>
> You'd think that with about 50 icons in a default Control Panel, Microsoft isn't in the business of *removing* icons. However, there are a few that have been relegated to the dustbin of Windows history. The following Windows 7 icons are gone from the Windows 8 version of Control Panel: Windows PowerShell Modules (replaced by Windows PowerShell ISE), Backup and Restore (now Windows 7 File Recovery), Getting Started, Location and Other Sensors (replaced by Location Settings), Region and Language (replaced by separate icons for Region and for Language), Taskbar and Start Menu (replaced by Taskbar), and Windows CardSpace.

Understanding Control Panel Files

Many of the Control Panel icons represent *Control Panel extension* files, which use the .cpl extension. These files reside in the %SystemRoot%\System32 folder. When you open Control Panel, Windows 8 scans the System32 folder looking for CPL files, and then displays an icon for each one.

The CPL files offer an alternative method for launching individual Control Panel dialog boxes. The idea is that you run control.exe and specify the name of a CPL file as a parameter. This bypasses the Control Panel folder and opens the icon directly. Here's the syntax:

```
control CPLfile [,option1 [, option2]]
```

> *CPLfile*—The name of the file that corresponds to the Control Panel icon you want to open (see Table 23.1, later in this chapter).
>
> *option1*—This option is obsolete and is included only for backward compatibility with batch files and scripts that use Control.exe for opening Control Panel icons.
>
> *option2*—The tab number of a multitabbed dialog box. Many Control Panel icons open a dialog box that has two or more tabs. If you know the specific tab you want to work with, you can use the option2 parameter to specify an integer that corresponds to the tab's relative position from the left side of the dialog box. The first (leftmost) tab is 0, the next tab is 1, and so on.

 note

If the dialog box has multiple rows of tabs, count the tabs from left to right and from bottom to top. For example, if the dialog box has two rows of four tabs each, the tabs in the bottom row are numbered 0 to 3 from left to right, and the tabs in the top row are numbered 4 to 7 from left to right.

Also, note that even though you no longer use the *option1* parameter, you must still display its comma in the command line.

For example, to open Control Panel's System icon with the Hardware tab displayed, run the following command (using the Run command or the Command Prompt):

```
control sysdm.cpl,,2
```

Table 23.1 lists the various Control Panel icons and the appropriate command line to use. (Note, however, that some Control Panel icons—such as Taskbar and Start Menu—can't be accessed by running Control.exe.)

Table 23.1 Command Lines for Launching Individual Control Panel Icons

Control Panel Icon	Command	Dialog Box Tabs
Action Center	control wscui.cpl	N/A
Administrative Tools	control admintools	N/A
Date and Time	control timedate.cpl	3
Personalization	control desk.cpl	1
Ease of Access Center	control access.cpl	N/A
Folder Options	control folders	N/A

Control Panel Icon	Command	Dialog Box Tabs
Fonts	control fonts	N/A
Game Controllers	control joy.cpl	N/A
Internet Options	control inetcpl.cpl	7
Keyboard	control keyboard	N/A
Mouse	control mouse	N/A
Network Connections	control ncpa.cpl	N/A
Pen and Touch	control tabletpc.cpl	3
Phone and Modem	control telephon.cpl	N/A
Power Options	control powercfg.cpl	N/A
Printers	control printers	N/A
Programs and Features	control appwiz.cpl	N/A
Region	control intl.cpl	3
Scanners and Cameras	control scannercamera	N/A
Sound	control mmsys.cpl	4
System	control sysdm.cpl	5
Tablet PC Settings	control tabletpc.cpl	3
User Accounts	control nusrmgr.cpl	N/A
Windows Firewall	control firewall.cpl	N/A

Easier Access to Control Panel

Control Panel is certainly a useful and important piece of the Windows 8 package. It's even more useful if you can get to it easily. In this section, we show you a few methods for gaining quick access to individual icons and the entire folder.

Access to many Control Panel icons is scattered throughout the Windows 8 interface, meaning that there's more than one way to launch an icon. Many of these alternative methods are faster and more direct than using the Control Panel folder. Here's a summary:

- **Action Center**—Click (or right-click) the Action Center icon in the notification area and then click Open Action Center.

- **Administrative Tools**—You can display these tools as a menu on the main Start screen. To learn how, see "Displaying the Administrative Tools on the Start Screen" in Chapter 4, "Using the Windows 8 Interface."

> **note**
>
> If you find your Control Panel folder is bursting at the seams, you can trim it down to size by removing those icons you never use. You can do this in a number of ways in Windows 8, but the easiest is probably via group policies. See "Removing an Icon from Control Panel" later in this chapter.

- **Date and Time**—Right-click the clock in the notification area and then click Adjust Date/Time.

- **Device Manager**—Press Windows Logo+X and then click Device Manager.

- **Personalization**—Right-click the desktop and then click Personalize.

- **Event Viewer**—Press File Logo+X and then click Event Viewer.

- **Fonts**—In File Explorer, open the %SystemRoot%\Fonts folder.

- **Internet Options**—In Internet Explorer, select Tools, Internet Options.

- **Network and Sharing Center**—Right-click the Network icon in the notification area and then click Open Network and Sharing Center.

- **Notification Area Icons**—Click the Show Hidden Icons arrow in the notification area and then click Customize.

- **Power Options**—Click the Power icon in the notification area and then click More Power Options. Alternatively, press Windows Logo+X and then click Power Options.

- **Programs and Features**—Press Windows Logo+X and then click Programs and Features.

- **Sound**—Right-click the Volume icon in the notification area and then click Sounds.

- **System**—Press Windows Logo+X and then click System. Alternatively, in File Explorer, click Computer, and then click System Properties.

- **Taskbar**—Right-click an empty section of the taskbar and then click Properties.

- **Troubleshooting**—Right-click the Action Center icon in the notification area and then click Troubleshoot a Problem.

- **Windows Update**—Right-click the Action Center icon in the notification area and then click Open Windows Update.

In Windows 8, you can also jump directly to some Control Panel tasks by searching the settings. If you know the task you want to run, press Windows Logo+W to open the Settings search pane, and then type a word or short phrase that exemplifies the task. As a demonstration, in Figure 23.3 we've typed **personalization** in the search box. As you can see, the search results include items such as Change the Theme, Change Desktop Background, and Adjust Screen Resolution. These just happen to be the task links that appear under the Appearance and Personalization heading in Control Panel's Category view (refer to Figure 23.1). If you were to click Appearance and Personalization in Control Panel, the subsequent screen's task links would include many more of the results you see in Figure 23.3.

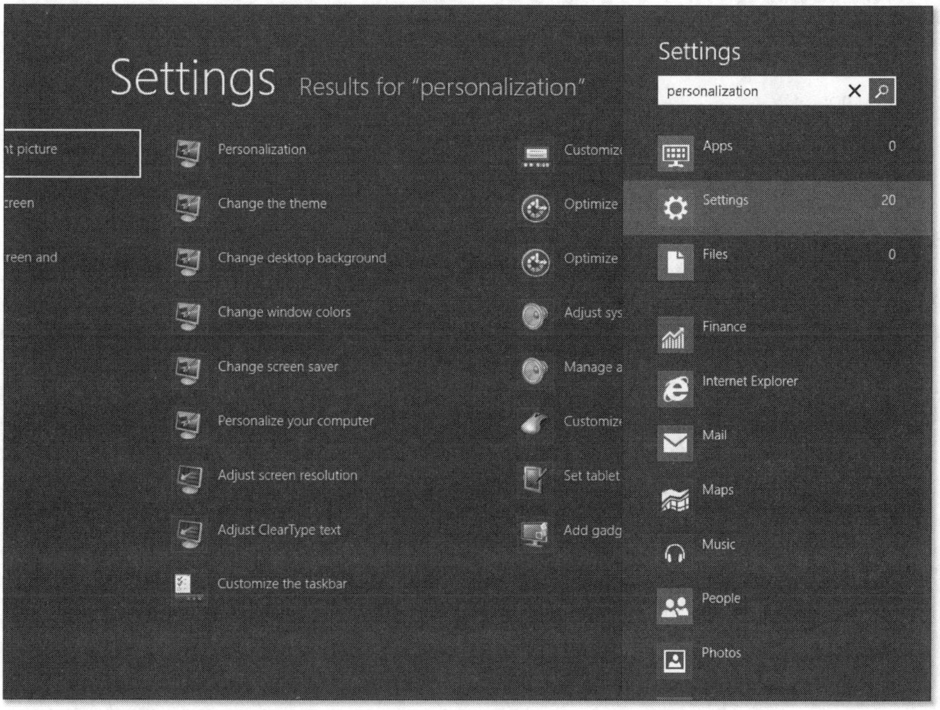

Figure 23.3
You can use the Settings search pane to search for and link directly to most Control Panel tasks.

Policing Windows 8 with Group Policies

You've seen in many places throughout this book that you can perform some pretty amazing things by using a tool that's about as hidden as any Windows power tool can be: the Local Group Policy Editor. That Microsoft has buried this program in a mostly untraveled section of the Windows landscape isn't the least bit surprising, because in the wrong hands the Local Group Policy Editor can wreak all kinds of havoc on a system. It's a kind of electronic Pandora's box that, if opened by careless or inexperienced hands, can loose all kinds of evil upon the Windows world.

Of course, none of this doom-and-gloom applies to you, dear reader, because you're a cautious and prudent wielder of all the Windows power tools. This means that you'll use the Local Group Policy Editor in a safe, prudent manner, and that you'll create a system restore point if you plan to make any major changes. We knew we could count on you.

As you see in this section, the Local Group Policy Editor isn't even remotely hard to use. However, it's such a powerful tool that it's important for you to know exactly how it works, which will help ensure that nothing goes awry when you're making your changes.

Understanding Group Policies

Put simply, *group policies* are settings that control how Windows works. You can use them to customize the Windows 8 interface, restrict access to certain areas, specify security settings, and much more.

Group policies are mostly used by system administrators who want to make sure that novice users don't have access to dangerous tools (such as the Registry Editor) or who want to ensure a consistent computing experience across multiple machines. Group policies are also ideally suited to situations in which multiple users share a single computer. However, group policies can be useful on single-user standalone machines, as you see in various sections of this book.

Local Group Policy Editor and Windows Versions

The power of the Local Group Policy Editor is aptly illustrated not only by the fact that Microsoft hides the program deep in the bowels of the system, but most tellingly by the fact that Microsoft didn't even offer the Local Group Policy Editor in some Windows versions. For Windows 8, the Local Group Policy Editor is not available in Windows RT and Windows 8 (that is, the basic version of Windows 8), but it is available in Windows 8 Pro and Windows 8 Enterprise. This tool was also removed from Windows XP Home, Windows Vista Home Basic, Windows Vista Home Premium, Windows 7 Home Basic, and Windows 7 Home Premium. In other words, those Windows versions that Microsoft expects novices to be using are the same Windows versions where Microsoft doesn't even include the Local Group Policy Editor, just to be safe.

Of course, plenty of experienced users use these Windows versions, mostly because they're cheaper than high-end versions such as Windows 8 Pro. So what's a would-be policy editor to do when faced with having no Local Group Policy Editor?

The short answer is, don't sweat it. That is, although the Local Group Policy Editor does provide an easy-to-use interface for many powerful settings, it's not the only way to put those settings into effect. Most group policies correspond to settings in the Windows Registry, so you can get the identical tweak on any basic Windows system by modifying the appropriate Registry setting instead. In this book, we've tried to augment group policy tweaks with the corresponding Registry tweak, just in case you don't have access to the Local Group Policy Editor.

---

tip

Understanding that most group policies have parallel settings in the Registry is all fine and dandy, but how on earth are you supposed to know which of the Registry's thousands upon thousands of settings is the one you want? The old method was to export the Registry to a REG file, make the change in the Local Group Policy Editor, export the Registry again, and then compare the two files. *Way* too much work (and impossible if all you have to work with is a basic Windows version)! You can also try filtering the policies as described later (see "Filtering Policies"). Fortunately, Microsoft has Excel workbooks that list every single group policy value and give the corresponding Registry setting. Links to the different reference workbooks for Vista, Windows 7, and Windows 8 (among others) can be found here: www.microsoft.com/en-us/download/details.aspx?id=25250

Given a setting that you can tweak using either the Local Group Policy Editor or the Registry Editor (and assuming you're running a version of Windows that comes with the Local Group Policy Editor), which tool should you choose? We highly recommend using the Local Group Policy Editor, because (as you'll see next) it offers a simpler and more straightforward user interface, which means it saves time, and you'll be much less likely to make an error.

Launching the Local Group Policy Editor

As we've said, you make changes to group policies using the Local Group Policy Editor, a Microsoft Management Console snap-in. To start the Local Group Policy Editor, you have two choices:

- In the Windows 8 Start screen, type **gpedit.msc**, and then click gpedit in the search results.

- Press Windows Logo+R to open the Run dialog box, type **gpedit.msc**, and then press Enter.

Figure 23.4 shows the Local Group Policy Editor window that appears. (The word *Local* refers to the fact that you're editing group policies on your own computer, not on some remote computer.)

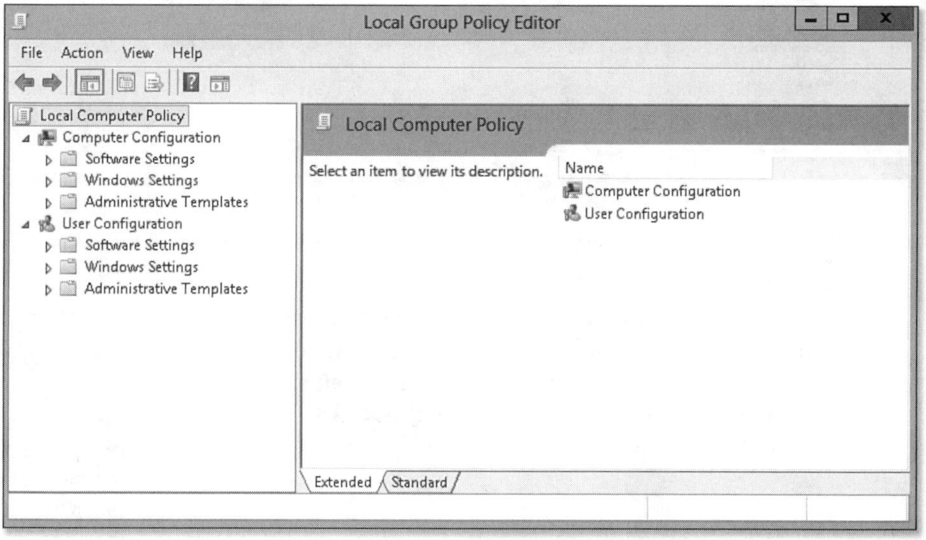

Figure 23.4
You use the Local Group Policy Editor to modify group policies on your PC.

Working with Group Policies

The Local Group Policy Editor window is divided into two sections:

- **Left pane**—This pane contains a tree-like hierarchy of policy categories, which is divided into two main categories: Computer Configuration and User Configuration. The Computer

Configuration policies apply to all users and are implemented before the logon. The User Configuration policies apply only to the current user and, therefore, are not applied until that user logs on.

- **Right pane**—This pane contains the policies for whichever category is selected in the left pane.

The idea, then, is to open the tree's branches to find the category you want. When you click the category, its policies appear in the right pane. For example, Figure 23.5 shows the Local Group Policy Editor window with the User Configuration, Administrative Templates, Control Panel category selected.

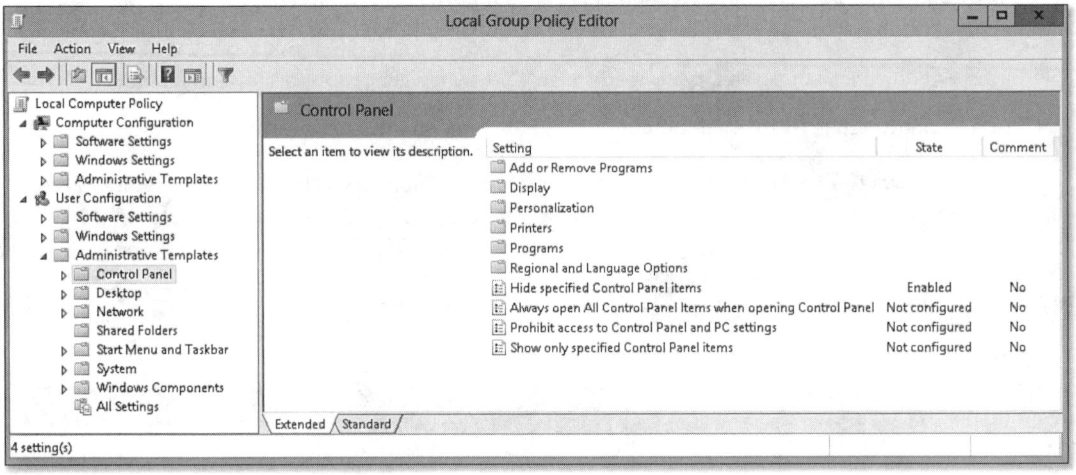

Figure 23.5
When you select a category in the left pane, the category's policies appear in the right pane.

In the right pane, the Setting column tells you the name of the policy, and the State column tells you the current state of the policy. Click a policy to see its description on the left side of the pane, as shown in Figure 23.6. If you don't see the description, click the Extended tab.

tip

Windows comes with another tool called the Local Security Policy Editor, which displays only the policies found in the Local Group Policy Editor's Computer Configuration, Windows Settings, Security Settings branch. To launch the Local Security Policy Editor, display the Start screen, type **run**, click Run (or press Windows Logo+R to open the Run dialog box), type **secpol.msc**, and then press Enter. As you might expect, this snap-in isn't available in the Windows Home editions.

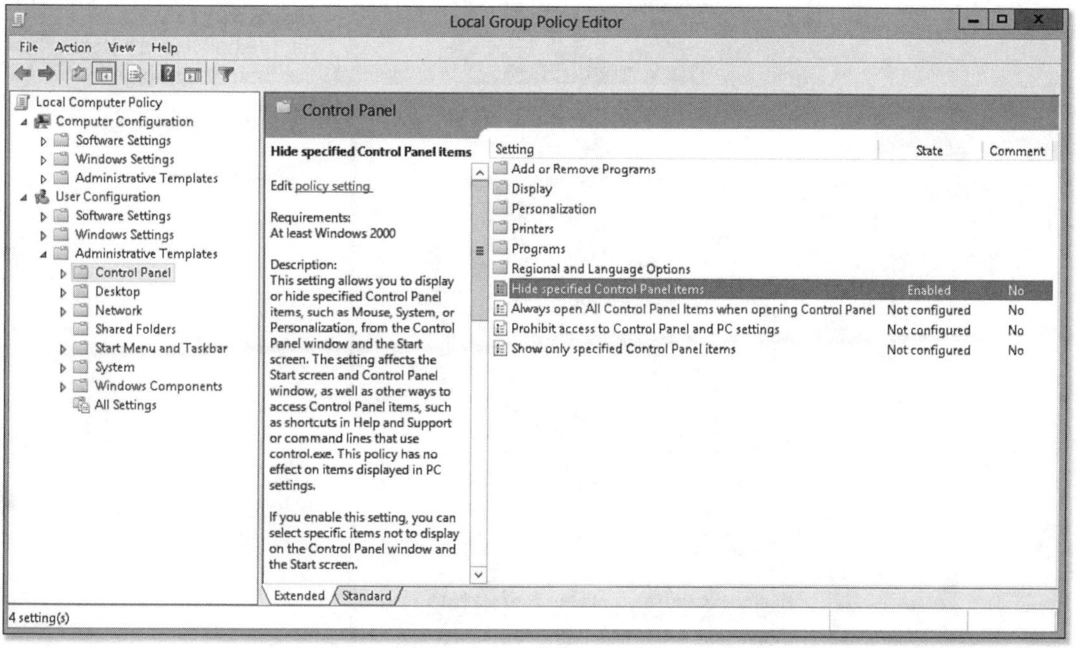

Figure 23.6
Click a policy to see its description.

Configuring a Policy

To configure a policy, double-click it. The type of window you see
depends on the policy:

- For simple policies, you see a window similar to the one shown
  in Figure 23.7. These kinds of policies take one of three states:
  Not Configured (the policy is not in effect), Enabled (the policy
  is in effect and its setting is enabled), and Disabled (the policy
  is in effect but its setting is disabled).

> **note**
>
> Take note of the Supported On
> value in the dialog box. This
> value tells you which versions of
> Windows support the policy.

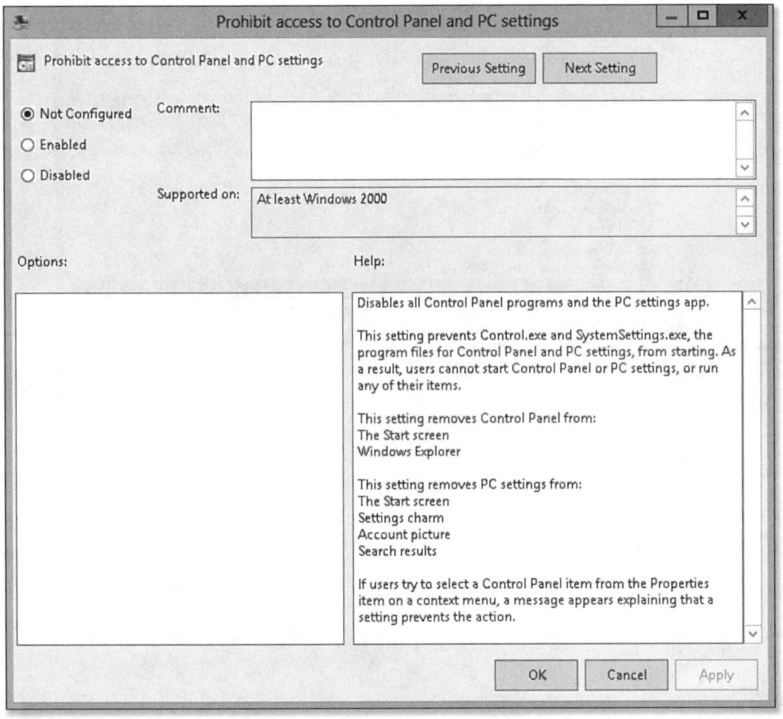

Figure 23.7
Simple policies are Not Configured, Enabled, or Disabled.

- Other kinds of policies require extra information when the policy is enabled. For example, Figure 23.8 shows the window for the Hide Specified Control Panel Items policy (described in detail later in the "Removing an Icon from Control Panel" section). When the Enabled option is activated, one or more controls in the Options box become enabled. In this case, the Show button becomes enabled and you click it to specify which Control Panel items you want to hide.

Filtering Policies

We've been saying for years that the Local Group Policy Editor desperately needs a search feature. There are nearly 3,000 policies and they're scattered around dozens of folders. Trying to find the policy you need by rooting around in the Local Group Policy Editor is like trying to find a particularly small needle in a particularly large haystack.

Fortunately, although the Windows 8 version of the Local Group Policy Editor still isn't searchable (unless you export it to a text file by selecting Action, Export List), it does come with two features that make it quite a bit easier to track down a wayward policy:

- The two Administrative Templates branches (one in Computer Configuration and the other in User Configuration) each come with a new sub-branch called All Settings. Selecting this branch displays a complete list of all the policies in that Administrative Templates branch. (Almost all non-security-related policies are in the Administrative Templates branches, so that's why they get singled out for special treatment.)

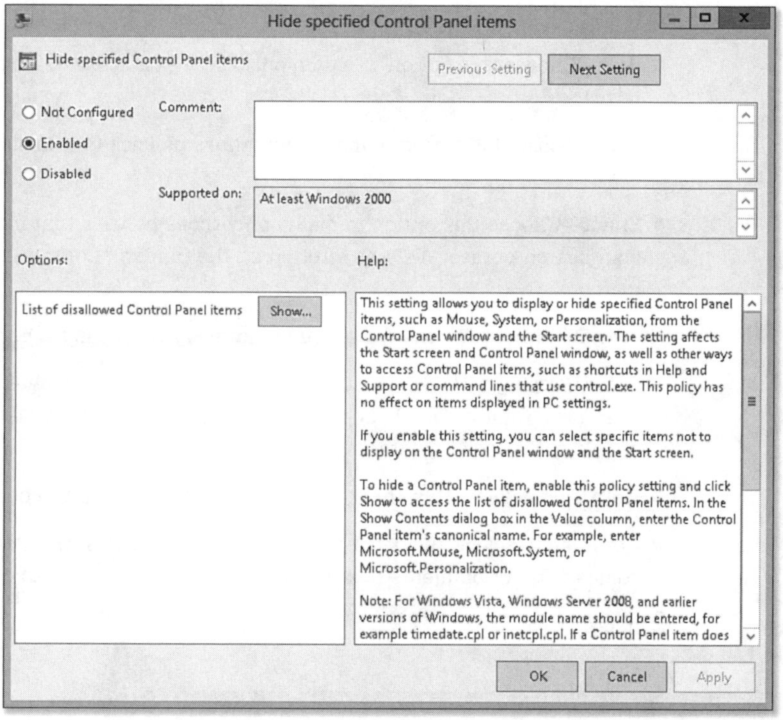

Figure 23.8
More complex policies also require extra information, such as a list of folders to display in the Places bar.

- A beefed-up filtering feature that's actually useful for cutting the vastness of the policy landscape down to size.

In combination, these two features make it much easier to find what you're looking for. The basic idea is that you select the All Settings branch that you want to work with and then set up a filter that defines what you're looking for. Local Group Policy Editor then displays just those policies that match your filter criteria.

To show you how this works, let's run through an example. Suppose we want to find the Hide Specified Control Panel Items policy shown earlier in Figure 23.8. Here's how we'd use a filter to locate it:

1. Select the User Configuration, Administrative Templates, All Settings branch.

2. Select Action, Filter Options to open the Filter Options dialog box.

3. Make sure the Enable Keyword Filters check box is activated.

4. Use the Filter for Word(s) text box to type a word or phrase that should match the policy you're looking for. In our example, we know that "Control Panel" is part of the policy name, so we'll use that as the filter text.

5. Use the associated drop-down list to choose how you want the policy text to match your search text:

- **Any**—Choose this option to match only those policies that include at least one of your search terms.

- **All**—Choose this option to match only those policies that include all of your search terms in any order.

- **Exact**—Choose this option to match only those policies that include text that exactly matches your search phrase. We'll be filtering on the phrase "Control Panel," so we'll use an exact match.

6. Use the Within check boxes to specify where you want the filter to look for matches:

- **Policy Setting Title**—Select this check box to look for matches in the policy name. In our example, "Control Panel" is part of the policy name, and it's a relatively unique term, so it should suffice to only filter on the title, as shown in Figure 23.9.

- **Help Text**—Select this check box to look for matches in the policy description.

- **Comment**—Select this check box to look for matches in the Comments text. (Each policy comes with a Comments box that you can use to add your two-cent's worth about any policy.)

7. Click OK.

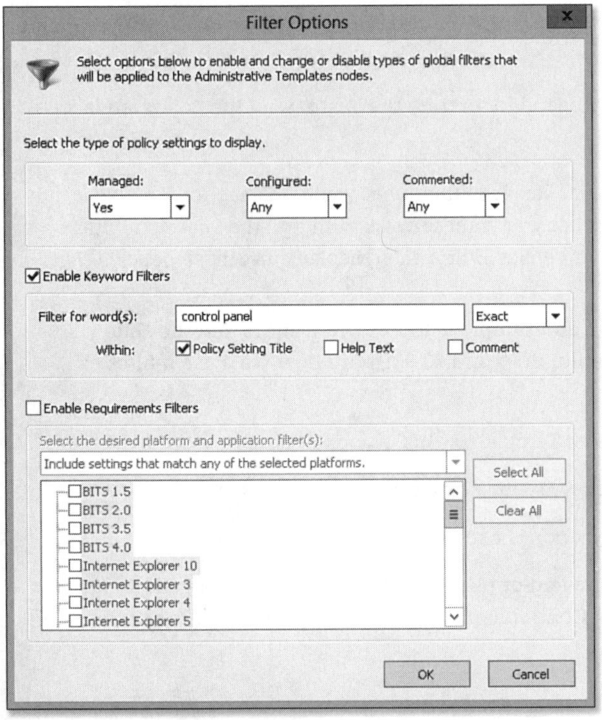

Figure 23.9
In the Windows 8 Local Group Policy Editor, you can use the Filter Options dialog box to find the policy you need.

With your filter in place, select Action, Filter On (or click to activate the Filter button in the toolbar). The Local Group Policy Editor displays just those policies that match your filter settings. For example, Figure 23.10 shows the results when the filter in Figure 23.9 is turned on. As you can see, the Hide Specified Control Panel Items policy is among the results.

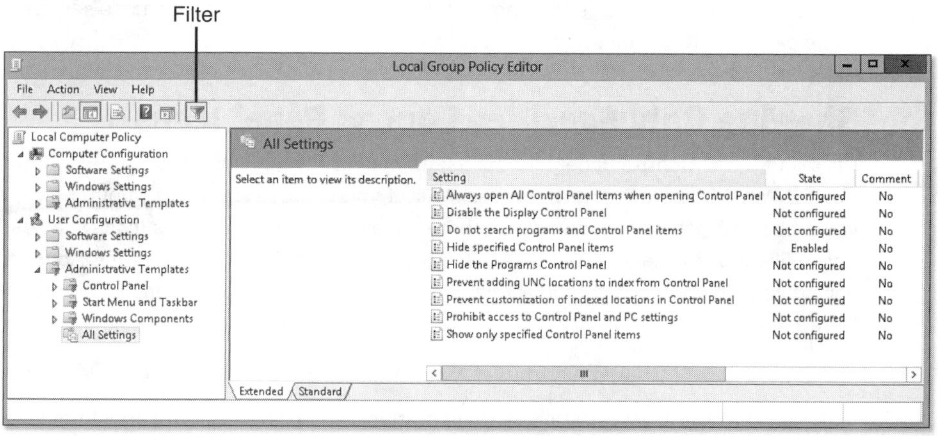

Figure 23.10
The results when the filter set up in Figure 23.6 is turned on.

Group Policy Examples

Although there are plenty of examples of group policies in action throughout this book, I'm a firm believer that you can't get enough of this powerful tool. With that in mind, the next few sections take you through a few of our favorite policies.

Removing an Icon from Control Panel

You can gain a bit more control over the Control Panel by configuring it not to display icons that you don't ever use or that aren't applicable to your system. Here's how it's done:

1. Open the Local Group Policy Editor window, as described earlier in this chapter.

2. Select the User Configuration, Administrative Templates, Control Panel branch.

3. Double-click the Hide Specified Control Panel Items policy.

4. Click the Enabled option.

5. Click the Show button. The Show Contents dialog box appears.

6. For each Control Panel icon you want to hide, type the icon name and press Enter.

7. Click OK to return to the Hide Specified Control Panel Items dialog box.

8. Click OK. Windows 8 puts the policy into effect.

To perform the same tweak in the Registry, open the following key:

`HKCU\Software\Microsoft\Windows\CurrentVersion\Policies\Explorer`

Add a DWORD value named `DisallowCpl` and set it equal to 1. Also create a new key named `DisallowCpl`, and within that key create a new String value for each Control Panel icon you want to disable. Give the settings the names 1, 2, 3, and so on, and for each one set the value to the name of the Control Panel icon you want to disable.

Showing Only Specified Control Panel Icons

Disabling a few Control Panel icons is useful because it reduces a bit of the clutter in the All Control Panel Items window. However, what if you want to set up a computer for a novice user and you'd like that person to have access to just a few relatively harmless icons such as Display and Personalization? In that case, it's *way* too much work to disable most of the icons one at a time. A much easier approach is to specify just those few Control Panel icons you want the user to see. Here's how:

1. Open the Local Group Policy Editor window, as described earlier in this chapter.

2. Select the User Configuration, Administrative Templates, Control Panel branch.

3. Double-click the Show Only Specified Control Panel Items policy.

4. Click the Enabled option.

5. Click the Show button. The Show Contents dialog box appears.

6. For each Control Panel icon you want to show, type the icon name and press Enter.

7. Click OK to return to the Show Only Specified Control Panel Items dialog box.

8. Click OK. Windows 8 puts the policy into effect.

To perform the same tweak in the Registry, open the following key:

`HKCU\Software\Microsoft\Windows\CurrentVersion\Policies\Explorer`

Add a DWORD value named `RestrictCpl` and set it equal to 1. Also create a new key named `RestrictCpl`, and within that key create a new String value for each Control Panel icon you want to show. Give the settings the names 1, 2, 3, and so on, and for each one set the value to the name of the Control Panel icon you want to show.

> ### Other Control Panel Policies
>
> While you've got the Local Group Policy Editor up and running, consider the other two Control Panel–related policies that appear in the User Configuration, Administrative Templates, Control Panel branch:
>
> **Always Open All Control Panel Items When Opening Control Panel**—If you enable this policy, Control Panel is always displayed in the All Control Panel Items window, and the user can't change to the Category view. If you disable this policy, Control Panel is always displayed in the Category view, and the user can't change to the All Control Panel Items window.
>
> **Prohibit Access to Control Panel and PC settings**—If you enable this policy, users can't access Control Panel at all.

Customizing the Windows Security Window

When you press Ctrl+Alt+Delete while logged on to Windows 8, you see the Windows Security window, which contains the following items, as shown in Figure 23.11:

- **Lock**—Click this button to hide the desktop and display the Lock screen. To return to the desktop, you must enter your Windows 8 user account password. This is useful if you're going to leave Windows 8 unattended and don't want another person accessing the desktop. However, Windows 8 offers a faster way to lock the computer: press Windows Logo+L.

- **Switch User**—Click this button to switch to a different user account while also leaving your current user account running.

- **Sign Out**—Click this button to display the sign-on screen, which lets you log on using a different user account.

- **Task Manager**—Click this button to open Task Manager.

Of these four commands, all but Switch User are customizable using group policies. So if you find that you never use one or more of those commands, or (more likely) if you want to prevent a user from accessing one or more of the commands, you can use group policies to remove them from the Windows Security window. Here are the steps to follow:

1. Open the Local Group Policy Editor window, as described earlier in this chapter.

2. Open the User Configuration, Administrative Templates, System, Ctrl+Alt+Del Options branch.

3. Double-click one of the following policies (ignore the Remove Change Password policy, which isn't supported in Windows 8):

   - **Remove Lock Computer**—You can use this policy to disable the Lock item in the Windows Security window.

   - **Remove Task Manager**—You can use this policy to disable the Task Manager item in the Windows Security window.

   - **Remove Logoff**—You can use this policy to disable the Sign Out item in the Windows Security window.

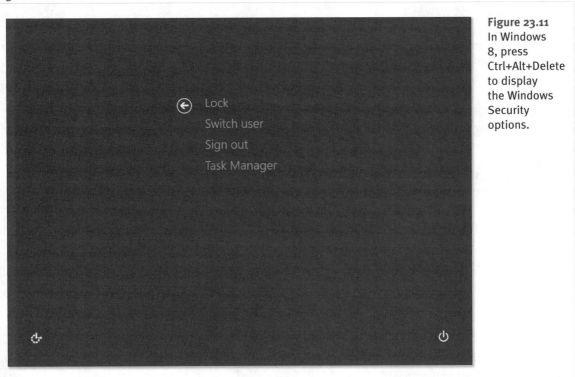

Figure 23.11
In Windows
8, press
Ctrl+Alt+Delete
to display
the Windows
Security
options.

4. In the policy dialog box that appears, click Enabled and then click OK.

5. Repeat steps 3 and 4 to disable all the buttons you don't need.

Figure 23.12 shows the Windows Security window with the three buttons removed.

To perform the same tweak using the Registry, launch the Registry Editor and open the following key:

```
HKCU\Software\Microsoft\Windows\CurrentVersion\Policies\System
```

Change the value of one or more of the following settings to 1:

```
DisableLockWorkstation
DisableTaskMgr
```

To remove the Log Off button via the Registry, open the following key:

```
HKCU\Software\Microsoft\Windows\CurrentVersion\Policies\Explorer
```

Change the value of the NoLogoff setting to 1.

Switch user

Figure 23.12
You can use group policies to remove most of the buttons in the Windows Security window.

Enabling the Shutdown Event Tracker

When you run the Shut Down command, Windows 8 proceeds to power down without any more input from you (unless any running programs have documents with unsaved changes). That's usually a good thing, but you might want to keep track of why you shut down or restart Windows 8, or why the system itself initiates a shutdown or restart. To do that, you can enable a feature called Shutdown Event Tracker. With this feature, you can document the shutdown event by specifying whether it is planned or unplanned, selecting a reason for the shutdown, and adding a comment that describes the shutdown.

Here are the steps to follow to use a group policy to enable the Shutdown Event Tracker feature:

1. Open the Local Group Policy Editor window, as described earlier in this chapter.

2. Navigate to the Computer Configuration, Administrative Templates, All Settings branch.

3. Double-click the Display Shutdown Event Tracker policy.

4. Click Enabled.

5. In the Shutdown Event Tracker Should Be Displayed list, select Always.

6. Click OK.

Now when you run the Shut Down command, you see the dialog box shown in Figure 23.13. Use the list to select the reason for the shutdown and then click Continue.

Figure 23.13
The Shut Down Windows dialog box appears with the Shutdown Event Tracker feature enabled.

To enable the Shutdown Event Tracker on systems without the Local Group Policy Editor, open the Registry Editor and dig down to the following key:

HKLM\Software\Policies\Microsoft\Windows NT\Reliability

Change the value of the following two settings to 1:

ShutdownReasonOn
ShutdownReasonUI

Configuring the Microsoft Management Console

The Microsoft Management Console (MMC) is a system administration program that can act as a host application for a variety of tools. The advantage of MMC is that it displays each tool as a *console*, a two-pane view that has a tree-like hierarchy in the left pane (this is called the *tree pane*) and a *taskpad* in the right pane that shows the contents of each branch (this is called the *results pane*). This gives each tool a similar interface, which makes it easier to use the tools. You can also customize the console view in a number of ways, create custom taskpad views, and save a particular set of tools to reuse later. These tools are called *snap-ins* because you can "snap them in" (that is, attach them) as *nodes* to the console root.

This section gives you an overview of the MMC and shows you a few techniques for getting the most out of its often-useful tools.

Reviewing the Windows 8 Snap-Ins

When you work with the MMC interface, what you're really doing is editing a Microsoft Common Console Document, an .msc file that stores one or more snap-ins, the console view, and the task-pad view used by each snap-in branch. You learn how to create custom MSC files in this chapter, but you should know that Windows 8 comes with a large number of predefined MSC snap-ins, and we've summarized them in Table 23.2.

Table 23.2   The Default Windows 8 Snap-Ins

Snap-In	File	Description
ActiveX Control	N/A	Launches the Insert ActiveX Control Wizard, which enables you to choose an ActiveX control to display as a node. (We haven't been able to find a good use for this one yet!)
Authorization Manager	azman.msc	Used by developers to set permissions on applications.
Certificates	certmgr.msc	Enables you to browse the security certificates on your system.
Component Services	comexp.msc	Enables you to view and work with Component Object Model (COM) services.
Computer Management	compmgmt.msc	Contains a number of snap-ins for managing various aspects of Windows 8. You can examine hidden and visible shared folders, set group policies, access Device Manager, manage hard disks, and much more.
Device Manager	devmgmt.msc	Enables you to add and manage your system hardware.
Disk Management	diskmgmt.msc	Enables you to view and manage all the disk drives on your system.
Event Viewer	eventvwr.msc	Enables you to view the Windows 8 event logs.

Table 23.2 Continued

Snap-In	File	Description
Folder	N/A	This item enables you to add a folder node to the root to help you organize your nodes.
Group Policy Object Editor	gpedit.msc	Enables you to work with group policies.
IP Security Monitor	N/A	Enables you to monitor Internet Protocol (IP) security settings.
IP Security Policy Management	N/A	Enables you to create IP Security (IPSec) policies.
Link to Web Address	N/A	Adds a node that displays the contents of a specified web page.
Local Users and Groups	lusrmgr.msc	Enables you to add, modify, and delete user accounts.
NAP Client Configuration	napclcfg.msc	Enables you to configure Network Access Protection (NAP) for a computer.
Performance Monitor	perfmon.msc	Enables you to monitor one or more performance counters.
Print Management	printmanagement.msc	Enables you to view and manage either local printers or network print servers.
Resultant Set of Policy	rsop.msc	Shows the applied group policies for the current user.
Security Configuration and Analysis	N/A	Enables you to open an existing security database, or build a new security database based on a security template you create using the Security Templates snap-in.
Security Templates	N/A	Enables you to create a security template where you enable and configure one or more security-related policies.
Services	services.msc	Enables you to start, stop, enable, and disable services.
Shared Folders	fsmgmt.msc	Enables you to monitor activity on your shared folders.
Task Scheduler	taskschd.msc	Enables you to schedule programs, scripts, and other items.
TPM Management	tpm.msc	Enables you to configure and work with Trusted Platform Module (TPM) security devices.
Windows Firewall with Advanced Security	wf.msc	Presents an advanced Windows Firewall interface.
WMI Control	wmimgmt.msc	Enables you to configure properties related to Windows Management Instrumentation.

Launching the MMC

To get the MMC onscreen, you have two choices:

- To start with a blank console, either display the Start screen or press Windows Logo+R to open the Run dialog box, type **mmc**, and then press Enter.

- To start with an existing snap-in, either display the Start screen or press Windows Logo+R to open the Run dialog box, type the name of the .msc file you want to load (see Table 23.2), and then press Enter.

Figure 23.14 shows a blank MMC window. We show you how to add snap-ins to the console in the next section.

Figure 23.14
The Microsoft Management Console ready for customizing.

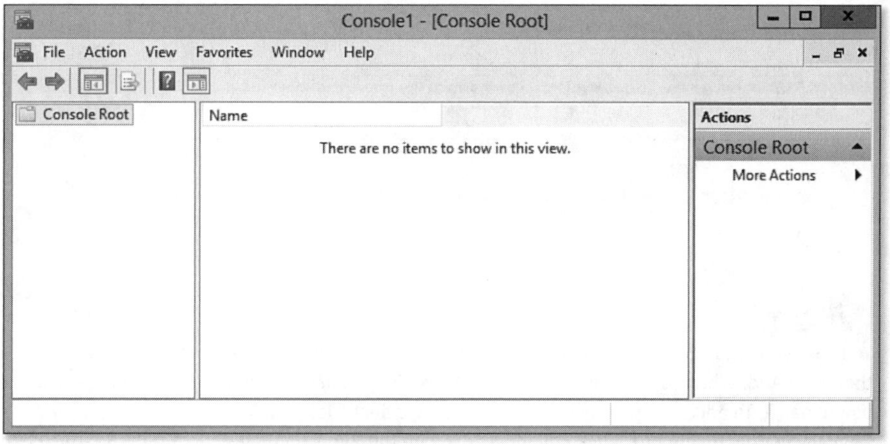

Adding a Snap-In

You start building your console file by adding one or more snap-ins to the console root, which is the top-level MMC container. (Even if you loaded the MMC by launching an existing snap-in, you can still add more snap-ins to the console.) Here are the steps to follow:

1. Select File, Add/Remove Snap-In (or press Ctrl+M). The MMC displays the Add or Remove Snap-Ins dialog box, shown in Figure 23.15.

2. In the Available Snap-ins list, select the snap-in you want to use.

3. Click Add.

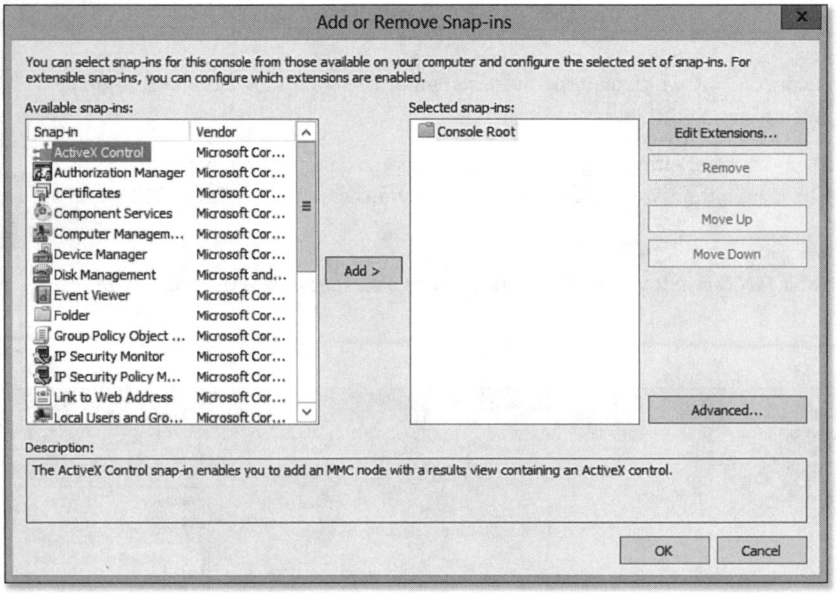

Figure 23.15
You use the Add or Remove Snap-Ins dialog box to populate the MMC with snap-in nodes.

tip

You can help organize your snap-ins by adding subfolders to the console root. In the list of snap-ins, select Folder and then click Add. When you return to the MMC, right-click the new subfolder and then click Rename to give the subfolder a useful name. To add a snap-in inside this subfolder, select File, Add/Remove Snap-In (or press Ctrl+M) to open the Add/Remove Snap-In dialog box. Click Advanced, activate the Allow Changing the Parent Snap-in check box, and then click OK. In the new Parent Snap-In list that appears, choose the subfolder you added. See Figure 23.17, later in this section, for some sample subfolders.

4. If the snap-in can work with remote computers, you see a dialog box similar to the one shown in Figure 23.16. To have the snap-in manage a remote machine, select Another Computer, type the computer name in the text box, and then click Finish.

5. Repeat steps 2–4 to add other snap-ins to the console.

6. Click OK.

Figure 23.17 shows the MMC with a custom console consisting of several snap-ins and subfolders.

note

In Figure 23.17, the items in the Web Pages subfolder are based on the Link to Web Address snap-in, which is a special snap-in that displays the current version of whatever web page you specify. When you add the snap-in, the MMC runs the Link to Web Address Wizard. Type the web page address (either an Internet URL or a path to a local or network page), click Next, type a name for the snap-in, and then click Finish.

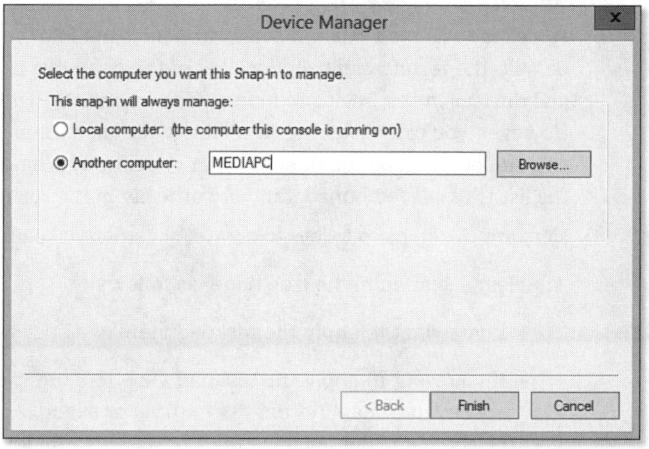

Figure 23.16
Some snap-ins can manage remote computers as well as the local machine.

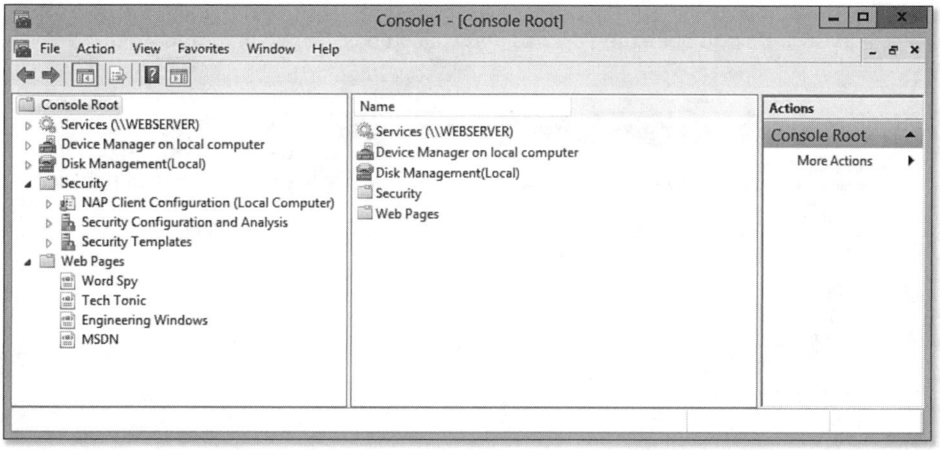

Figure 23.17
The MMC with a custom console.

Saving a Console

If you think you want to reuse your custom console later on, you should save it to an .msc file. Here are the steps to follow:

1. Select File, Save (or press Ctrl+S) to open the Save As dialog box.

2. Type a filename for the console.

3. Select a location for the console file.

4. Click Save.

tip

By default, MMC assumes you want to save your console file in the Administrative Tools folder. However, if you want to be able to launch your console file from the Start screen or the Run dialog box, you should save it in the %SystemRoot%\System32 folder, along with the predefined snap-ins.

Creating a Custom Taskpad View

A *taskpad view* is a custom configuration of the MMC results (right) pane for a given snap-in. By default, the results pane shows a list of the snap-in's contents—for example, the list of categories and devices in the Device Manager snap-in and the list of installed services in the Services snap-in. However, you can customize this view with one or more tasks that run commands defined by the snap-in, or any program or script that you specify. You can also control the size of the list, whether the list is displayed horizontally or vertically in the results pane, and more.

Here are the steps to follow to create a custom taskpad view:

1. Select a snap-in in the tree pane, as follows:

   - If you want to apply the taskpad view to a specific snap-in, select that snap-in.

   - If you want to apply the taskpad view to a group of snap-ins that use the same snap-in type, specify one snap-in from the group. For example, if you want to customize all the folders, select any folder (such as the Console Root folder); similarly, if you want to customize all the Link to Web Address snap-ins, select one of them.

2. Select Action, New Taskpad View to launch the New Taskpad View Wizard.

3. Click Next to open the Taskpad Style dialog box, shown in Figure 23.18.

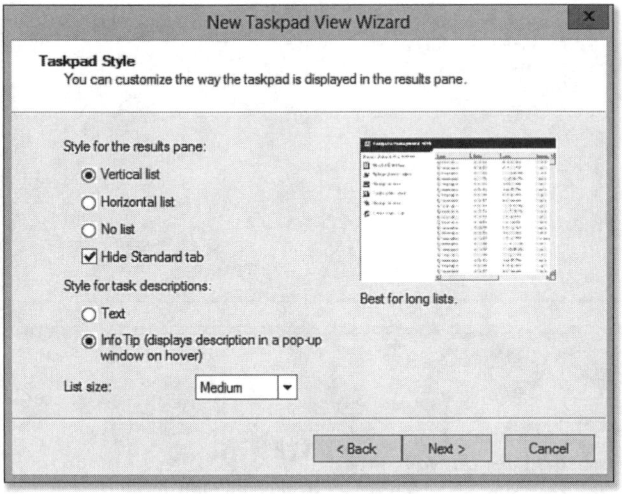

Figure 23.18
Use the New Taskpad View Wizard to create your custom taskpad view.

4. Use the following controls to set up the style of taskpad you want:

   - **Style for Results Pane**—Select an option for displaying the snap-in's results: Vertical List (this is best for lists with a large number of items), Horizontal List (this is best for web pages or lists with a large number of columns), or No List (choose this option if you want only tasks to appear in the results pane).

- **Hide Standard Tab**—After you create the new taskpad view, the MMC displays two tabs in the results pane: The Extended tab shows your custom taskpad view, and the Standard tab shows the default view. To keep the option of displaying the default view, deactivate the Hide Standard Tab dialog box.

- **Style for Task Descriptions**—When you add descriptions for your tasks later on, you can have the MMC display each description either as text below the task link or as an InfoTip that appears when you hover the mouse over the task link.

- **List Size**—Choose the size of the list: Small (good if you add lots of tasks), Medium (this is the default), or Large (good if you have few or no tasks).

5. Click Next. The Taskpad Reuse dialog box appears.

6. The wizard assumes you want to apply the new taskpad view to all snap-ins of the same type. If you only want to apply the taskpad view to the current snap-in, select the Selected Tree Item option.

7. Click Next. The Name and Description dialog box appears.

8. Type a name and optional description for the taskpad view, and then click Next. The final wizard dialog box appears.

9. If you don't want to add tasks to the new view, deactivate the Add New Tasks to This Taskpad After the Wizard Closes check box.

10. Click Finish. If you elected to add tasks to the view, the New Task Wizard appears.

11. Click Next. The Command Type dialog box appears.

12. Select one of the following command types:

    - **Menu Command**—Select this option to create a task that runs an MMC or snap-in menu command.

    - **Shell Command**—Select this option to create a task that runs a program, script, or batch file.

    - **Navigation**—Select this option to create a task that takes you to another snap-in that's in your MMC Favorites list.

> **note**
>
> To add a snap-in to the MMC Favorites list, select the snap-in in the tree pane and then select Favorites, Add to Favorites.

13. Click Next.

14. How you proceed from here depends on the command type you selected in step 12:

    - **Menu Command**—In the Menu Command dialog box, first select an item from the Command Source list. Choose Item Listed in the Results Pane to apply the command to whatever item is currently selected in the results pane; choose Node in the Tree to select a command based on an item in the MMC tree pane.

■ **Shell Command**—In the Command Line dialog box, use the Command text box to specify the path to the program executable, script, or batch file that you want the task to run. You can also specify startup parameters, the Start In folder, and a Run window type.

■ **Navigation**—In the Navigation dialog box, select the items from the MMC Favorites list.

15. Click Next. The Name and Description dialog box appears.

16. Edit the task name and description, and then click Next. The Task Icon dialog box appears, as shown in Figure 23.19.

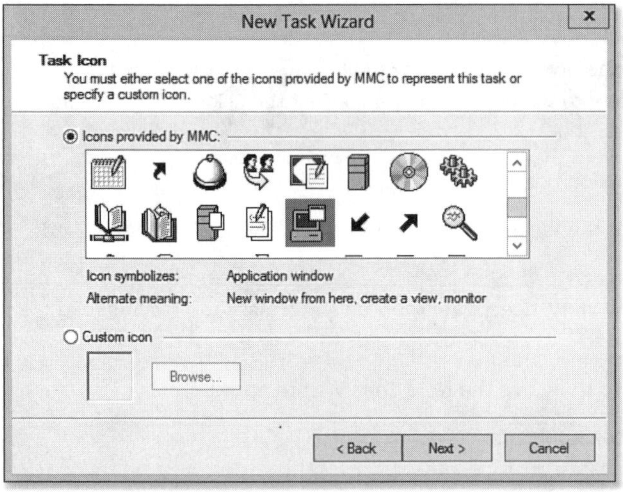

Figure 23.19
Use the Task Icon dialog box to choose an icon to display with your task.

17. Click Next. The final New Task Wizard dialog box appears.

18. If you want to add more tasks, activate the When I Click Finish, Run This Wizard Again check box.

19. Click Finish.

20. If you elected to add more tasks, repeat steps 11–19, as needed.

Figure 23.20 shows the MMC with a custom taskpad view applied to a Link to Web Address snap-in.

> **note**
>
> To make changes to a custom taskpad view, right-click the snap-in and then click Edit Taskpad View.

Figure 23.20
A custom task-pad view.

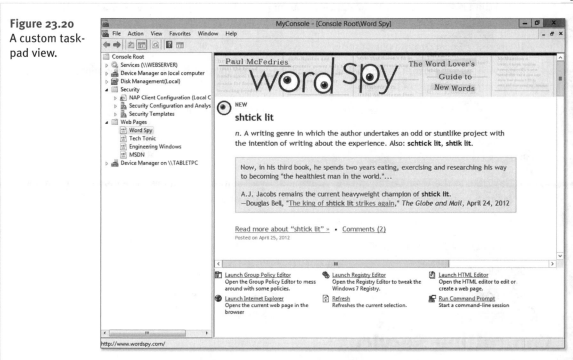

Controlling Snap-Ins with Group Policies

If you share Windows 8 with other people, you can control which snap-ins they're allowed to use, and you can even prevent users from adding snap-ins to the MMC.

The latter is the simpler of the two options, so let's begin with that. The MMC has an *author mode* that enables you to add snap-ins to it. If you prevent the MMC from entering author mode, you prevent users from adding snap-ins. You can do this using a group policy. Note, too, that this policy also prevents users from entering author mode for those snap-ins that can be opened directly (from the Start menu Search box, from the Run dialog box, from the command line, from Administrative Tools, and so on). Here are the steps to follow:

1. Open the Local Group Policy Editor, as described earlier in this chapter in the section "Launching the Group Policy Editor."

2. Navigate to the User Configuration, Administrative Templates, Windows Components, Microsoft Management Console branch.

3. Double-click the Restrict the User from Entering Author Mode policy.

4. Activate the Enabled option.

5. Click OK.

Rather than blocking off the MMC entirely, you might prefer to allow users access only to specific snap-ins. Here are the steps to follow:

1. Open the Local Group Policy Editor.

2. Navigate to the User Configuration, Administrative Templates, Windows Components, Microsoft Management Console branch.

3. Double-click the Restrict Users to the Explicitly Permitted List of Snap-Ins policy.

4. Activate the Enabled option.

5. Click OK.

6. Navigate to the User Configuration, Administrative Templates, Windows Components, Microsoft Management Console, Restricted/Permitted Snap-Ins branch.

7. Double-click a snap-in that you want users to access.

8. Activate the Enabled option.

9. Click OK.

10. Repeat steps 7–9 for each snap-in that you want users to access.

Controlling Services

Windows 8 comes with a long list of programs called *services* that operate behind the scenes and perform essential tasks either on their own or in support of other programs or Windows features. These services are background routines that enable the system to perform tasks such as logging on to the network, managing disks, collecting performance data, and writing event logs. Windows 8 comes with more than 160 installed services, which is a Windows record.

You won't have to interact with services very often, but when they do come up, you'll be glad to have this section's tools in your Windows 8 toolbox. For example, although services usually operate behind the scenes, you may need to pause, stop, and start services, as well as configure how services load at startup. The first few sections in this chapter show you the various methods you can use to perform these service tasks.

Controlling Services with the Services Snap-In

The standard interface for the Windows 8 services is the Services snap-in, which you can load by using any of the following techniques:

- Display either the Start screen or the Run dialog box, type **services.msc**, and press Enter.

- In Control Panel, display the All Control Panel Items window, click Administrative Tools, and then click Services.

- Press Windows Logo+X, click Computer Management, and then select the Services and Applications, Services branch.

The Services snap-in that appears displays a list of the installed services, and for each service, it displays the name of the service and a brief description, the current status of the service (Running, Paused, or blank for a stopped service), the service's startup type (such as Automatic or Manual), and the name of the system account the service uses to log on at startup. When you select a service, the Extended tab of the taskpad view shows the service name and description and offers links to control the service status (such as Start, Stop, or Restart). Figure 23.21 shows an example.

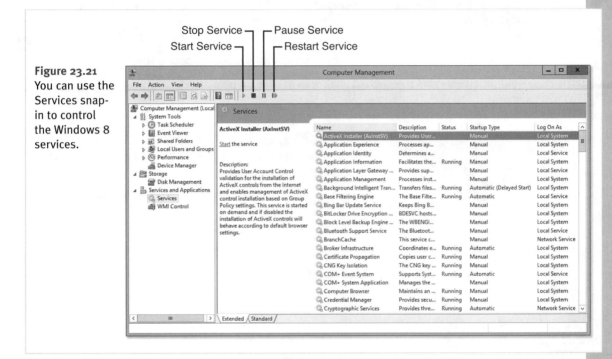

Figure 23.21
You can use the Services snap-in to control the Windows 8 services.

To change the status of a service, select it and then use one of the following techniques:

- To start a stopped service, either click the Start link in the task-pad or click the Start Service toolbar button.

- To stop a running service, either click the Stop link in the task-pad or click the Stop Service toolbar button.

- To pause a running service, either click the Pause link in the taskpad or click the Start Service toolbar button. (Note that only a few services support the Pause task.)

- To resume a paused service, either click the Restart link in the taskpad or click the Restart Service toolbar button.

note

If a service is started but it has no Stop link and the Stop toolbar button is disabled, this means the service is essential to Windows 8 and can't be stopped. Examples of essential services include DCOM Server Process Launcher, Group Policy Client, Plug and Play, Remote Procedure Call (RPC), and Security Accounts Manager.

> ## 📡 caution
>
> It's possible that a service might be dependent on one or more other services, and if those services aren't running, the dependent service will not work properly. If you stop a service that has dependent services, Windows 8 also stops the dependents. However, when you restart the main service, Windows 8 may not start the dependent services as well. You need to start those services by hand. To see which services depend on a particular service, double-click that service to open its property sheet, and then display the Dependencies tab. Dependent services are shown in the list titled The Following System Components Depend on This Service.

To change the way a service starts when you boot Windows 8, follow these steps:

1. Double-click the service you want to work with to open its property sheet. Figure 23.22 shows an example.

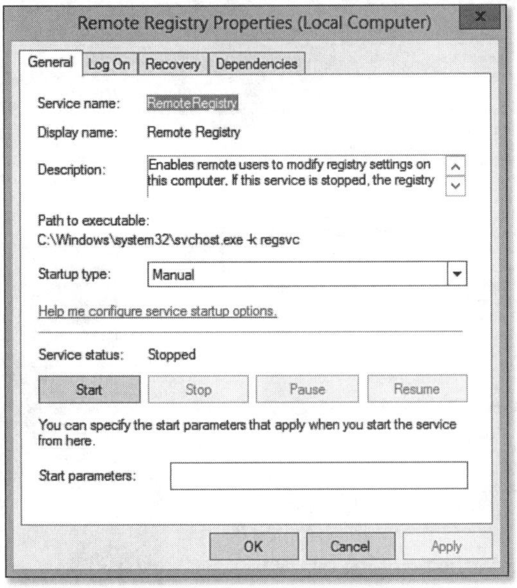

Figure 23.22
You use a service's property sheet to control its startup type.

2. In the General tab, use the Startup Type list to select one of the following types:

   - **Automatic**—The service starts automatically when Windows 8 boots. The service is started before the logon screen appears.

   - **Automatic (Delayed Start)**—The service starts automatically when Windows 8 boots, but not until you log on.

> ## 🔍 note
>
> If the Startup Type list is disabled, this means the service is essential to Windows 8 and must be started automatically when the system boots.

- **Manual**—The service does not start when Windows 8 boots. You must start the service yourself.

- **Disabled**—The service does not start when Windows 8 boots, and you can't start the service manually.

3. Click OK.

tip

If you make changes to service startup types and you find your system is unstable or causing problems, the best thing to do is return each service to its default startup type.

Controlling Services at the Command Prompt

If you regularly stop and start certain services, loading the Services snap-in and manually stopping and then restarting each service can be time-consuming. A better method is to take advantage of the NET STOP and NET START command-line tools, which enable you to stop and start any service that isn't disabled. If a service can be paused and restarted, you can also use the NET PAUSE and NET CONTINUE commands to control the service. Each of these commands uses the same syntax:

```
NET STOP Service
NET START Service
NET PAUSE Service
NET CONTINUE Service
```

Service is the name of the service you want to control. Use the same value that appears in the Name column of the Services snap-in. If the name contains a space, surround the name with quotation marks.

Here are some examples:

```
net start Fax
net stop "Disk Defragmenter"
net pause "Windows Audio"
net continue "Windows Time"
```

You can combine multiple commands in a batch file to easily control several services with a single task.

tip

To see a list of the currently running services, open a command-line session and enter the command net start without the *Service* parameter.

Controlling Services with a Script

If you want to automate service control, but you also want to control the startup type, you need to go beyond the command line and create scripts that manage your services. Windows Management Instrumentation (WMI) has a class called Win32_Service that represents a Windows service. You can return an instance of this class to work with a specific service on Windows 8. After you have the service object, you can query its current status with the State property, determine whether the service is running with the Started property, and return the service's startup type with the StartMode property. You can also change the service state using the StartService, StopService, PauseService, and ResumeService methods.

Listing 23.1 presents a script that uses most of these properties and methods.

➡ *To learn how to run scripts,* **see** *"Windows Script Host," **p. 723.***

Listing 23.1 A WMI Script That Toggles a Service's State Between Started and Stopped

```
Option Explicit
Dim strComputer, strServiceName, intReturn
Dim objWMI, objServices, objService
'
' Get the WMI service
'
strComputer = "localhost"
Set objWMI = GetObject("winmgmts:{impersonationLevel=impersonate}!\\" & _
    strComputer & "\root\cimv2")
'
' Specify the service name
'
strServiceName = "Remote Registry"
'
' Get the service instance
'
Set objServices = objWMI.ExecQuery("SELECT * FROM Win32_Service " & _
                "WHERE DisplayName = '" & strServiceName & "'")
For Each objService In objServices
    '
    ' Save the service name
    '
    strServiceName = objService.DisplayName
    '
    ' Is the service started?
    '
    If objService.Started Then
        '
        ' Can it be stopped?
        '
        If objService.AcceptStop Then
            '
            ' Attempt to stop the service
            '
            intReturn = objService.StopService
            '
            ' Check the return value
            '
            If intReturn <> 0 Then
                '
                ' Display the error message
                '
```

```
                    WScript.Echo "ERROR: The " & strServiceName & " service " & _
                                "failed to stop. The return code is " & intReturn
                Else
                    '

                    ' Display the current state
                    '

                    WScript.Echo "The " & strServiceName & " service is now " & _
                                objService.State
                End If
            Else
                '

                ' Display the error message
                '

                WScript.Echo "ERROR: The " & strServiceName & " service " & _
                            "cannot be stopped."
            End If
        Else
            '

            ' Attempt to start the service
            '

            intReturn = objService.StartService

            ' Check the return value
            '

            If intReturn <> 0 Then
                '

                ' Display the error message
                '

                WScript.Echo "ERROR: The " & strServiceName & " service " & _
                            "failed to start. The return code is " & intReturn
            Else
                '

                ' Display the current state
                '

                WScript.Echo "The " & strServiceName & " service is now " & _
                            objService.State
            End If
        End If
    End If
Next
'

' Release the objects
'

Set objWMI = Nothing
Set objServices = Nothing
Set objService = Nothing
```

This script gets the WMI service object and uses its `ExecQuery` method to return an instance of the `Win32_Service` class by using the `WHERE` clause to look for a specific service name. That name was earlier stored in the `strServiceName` variable. In the `For Each...Next` loop, the script first checks to see whether the service is currently started by checking its `Started` property:

- If the `Started` property returns `True`, the service is running, so we want to stop it. The script then checks the service's `AcceptStop` property, which returns `False` for essential Windows 8 services that can't be stopped. In this case, the script returns an error message. If `AcceptStop` returns `True`, the script attempts to stop the service by running the `StopService` method.

- If the `Started` property returns `False`, the service is stopped, so we want to start it. The script attempts to start the service by running the `StartService` method.

The `StopService` and `StartService` methods generate the return codes shown in Table 23.3.

Table 23.3 Return Codes Generated by the `StartService` and `StopService` Methods

Return Code	Description
0	Success
1	Not supported
2	Access denied
3	Dependent services running
4	Invalid service control
5	Service cannot accept control
6	Service not active
7	Service request timeout
8	Unknown failure
9	Path not found
10	Service already stopped
11	Service database locked
12	Service dependency deleted
13	Service dependency failure
14	Service disabled
15	Service logon failed
16	Service marked for deletion
17	Service no thread
18	Status circular dependency
19	Status — duplicate name
20	Status — invalid name

Return Code	Description
21	Status — invalid parameter
22	Status — invalid service account
23	Status — service exists
24	Service already paused

For both the `StopService` and `StartService` methods, the script stores the return code in the `intReturn` variable and then checks to see whether it's a number other than 0. If so, the script displays an error message that includes the return code; otherwise, the script displays the new state of the service (as given by the `State` property).

Making Windows Shut Down Services Faster

If it seems to take Windows forever to shut down, the culprit might be all those services that it has running because Windows has to shut down each service one by one before it can shut down the PC. In each case, Windows waits a certain amount of time for the service to close, and if it hasn't closed in that time, Windows kills the service. It's that waiting for services to shut themselves down that can really bring the shutdown process to its knees.

However, most services shut down as soon as they get the command from Windows. So although it's polite of Windows to give some services a bit of extra time, it's really wasted time because in most cases Windows is just going to have to kill those slow services anyway. So in that case, you should configure Windows 8 to tell it to kill services faster. Here's how:

1. Select Start, type **regedit**, and then press Enter. The Registry Editor appears.

2. Navigate to the following key:

   `HKEY_LOCAL_MACHINE\SYSTEM\CurrentControlSet\Control`

3. Double-click the `WaitToKillServiceTimeout` setting.

4. Reduce the value to `1000`.

5. Click OK.

Resetting a Broken Service

If Windows 8 is acting erratically (or, we should say, if it's acting more erratically than usual), the problem could be a service that's somehow gotten corrupted. How can you tell? The most obvious clue is an error message that tells you a particular service isn't running or couldn't start. You can also check the Event Viewer for service errors. Finally, if a particular feature of Windows 8 is acting

> **tip**
>
> You can also reduce the amount of time that Windows 8 waits before killing any running applications at shutdown. In the Registry Editor, navigate to the following key:
>
> `HKEY_CURRENT_USER\Control Panel\Desktop`
>
> Double-click the `WaitToKillAppTimeout` setting. (If you don't see this setting, select Edit, New, String Value, type **WaitToKillAppTimeout**, and click OK.) Change the value to `5000` and click OK.

funny and you know that a service is associated with that feature, you might suspect that service is causing the trouble.

To fix the problem (hopefully!), you can reset the broken service. The procedure involves the following four general steps:

1. Find out the name of the service that is (or that you suspect is) broken.

2. Delete the service.

3. Load a backup copy of the system hive into the Registry.

4. Copy the service from the backup hive copy to the service's actual Registry location.

To begin, follow these steps to determine the name of the service:

1. Open the Services snap-in, as described earlier in this chapter.

2. Double-click the service you want to reset.

3. In the General tab, locate the Service Name value.

4. Click OK.

Next, follow these steps to delete the service:

1. Select Start, type **command**, right-click Command Prompt in the results, click Run as Administrator, and then enter your User Account Control credentials. Windows 8 opens an Administrator Command Prompt session.

2. Type the following (where *service* is the service name that you noted in the previous set of steps):

   ```
   sc delete service
   ```

3. Press Enter. Windows 8 attempts to delete the service.

If the deletion works properly, you see the following message:

```
[SC] DeleteService SUCCESS
```

Note that you need the Command Prompt again a bit later, so leave the session open for now.

Now follow these steps to load a fresh copy of the system hive:

1. Select Start, type **regedit**, press Enter, and then enter your User Account Control credentials to open the Registry Editor.

2. Select the HKEY_LOCAL_MACHINE key.

3. Select File, Load Hive to open the Load Hive dialog box.

4. Open the system backup file:

   ```
   %SystemRoot%\system32\config\RegBack\SYSTEM.OLD
   ```

> **note**
>
> If the deletion isn't successful, double-check the service name. If you're sure you have the name right, try deleting the service using the Registry Editor instead. Open the Registry Editor, navigate to the HKEY_LOCAL_MACHINE\System\CurrentControlSet\Services key, and then locate the service. Right-click the service and then click Delete.

5. Click Open. The Registry Editor prompts you for a key name.

6. Type **reset** and click OK.

You now have the backup copy of the system hive loaded into the HKLM\reset key. Now you complete the operation by copying the service from this backup. Here are the steps:

1. Return to the Command Prompt.

2. Type the following (where *service* is the service name you noted in the first set of steps):

   ```
   reg copy hklm\reset\controlset001\services\service
   ➥hklm\system\currentcontrolset\services\service /s /f
   ```

3. Press Enter. Windows 8 copies the backup version of the service to the original Registry location.

4. Reboot your PC to put the change into effect.

Monitoring Performance

Performance optimization is a bit of a black art in that every user has different needs, every configuration has different operating parameters, and every system can react in a unique and unpredictable way to performance tweaks. That means if you want to optimize your system, you have to get to know how it works, what it needs, and how it reacts to changes. You can do this by just using the system and paying attention to how things look and feel, but a more rigorous approach is often called for. To that end, the next few sections take you on a brief tour of Windows 8's performance-monitoring capabilities.

Viewing Your Computer's Performance Rating

Windows 8 scales aspects of your system up or down to suit its hardware home. With games, for example, Windows 8 enables certain features only if the hardware can support them. Other features scaled for the computer's hardware are TV recording (for example, how many channels can it record at once?) and video playback (for example, what is the optimal playback size and frame rate that doesn't result in dropped frames?).

The tool that handles all of this, not only for Windows 8 itself but also for third-party programs, is the Windows System Assessment Tool, or *WinSAT*. This tool runs during setup, and again whenever you make major performance-related hardware changes to your system. It focuses on four aspects of your system performance: graphics, memory, processor, and storage. For each of these subsystems, WinSAT maintains a set of metrics stored as an *assessment* in XML format. Windows 8 needs to examine only the latest assessment to see what features the computer can support. Note, too, that third-party programs can use an application programming interface that gives them access to the assessments, so developers can tune program features depending on the WinSAT metrics.

Five metrics are used:

- **Processor**—This metric determines how fast the system can process data. The Processor metric measures calculations per second processed.

- **Memory (RAM)**—This metric determines how quickly the system can move large objects through memory. The Memory metric measures memory operations per second.

- **Graphics**—This metric determines the computer's capability to run a composited desktop like the one created by the Desktop Window Manager. The Graphics metric expresses frames per second.

- **Gaming Graphics**—This metric determines the computer's capability to render 3D graphics, particularly those used in gaming. The Gaming Graphics metric expresses effective frames per second.

- **Primary Hard Disk**—This metric determines how fast the computer can write to and read from the hard disk. The Primary Hard Disk storage metric measures megabytes per second.

In addition to WinSAT, Windows 8 comes with the Performance Rating tool that rates your system based on its processor, RAM, hard disk, regular graphics, and gaming graphics. The result is the Windows Experience Index base score.

To launch this tool, press Windows Logo+W to open the Settings search pane, type **performance**, and then click Performance Information and Tools in the search results. In the Performance Information and Tools window, if you see a button named Rate This Computer, click that button to run the initial assessment.

As you can see in Figure 23.23, Windows 8 supplies a subscore for each of the five categories and calculates an overall base score. You can get a new rating (for example, if you change performance-related hardware) by clicking the Re-run the Assessment link.

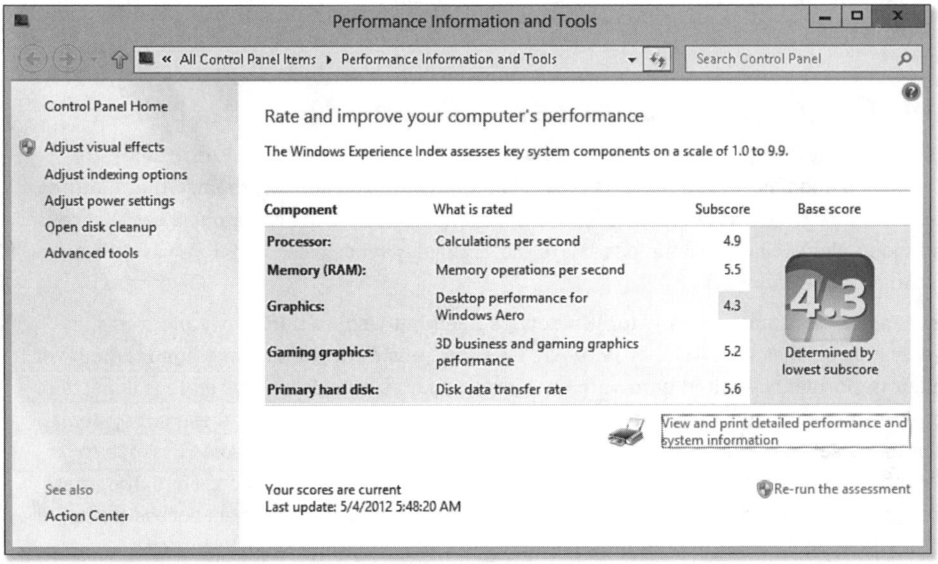

Figure 23.23
Windows 8 calculates a Windows System Performance Rating based on five categories.

Interpreting the ratings is a bit of a black art, but we can tell you the following:

- In general, the higher the rating, the better the performance.

- The lowest possible value is 1.0.

- The highest possible value is 9.9 (up from 7.9 in Windows 7 and 5.9 in Windows Vista, which is a reflection of hardware improvements over the past few years).

- The base score takes a weakest-link-in-the-chain approach. That is, you could have nothing but 5.0 scores for everything else, but if you get just 1.0 because your notebook can't do gaming graphics, your base score will be 1.0.

Monitoring Performance with Task Manager

The Task Manager utility is excellent for getting a quick overview of the current state of the system. To get it onscreen, press Ctrl+Alt+Delete to open the Windows Security screen and then click the Task Manager link. Once Task Manager shows up, click More Details to expand the window.

The Processes tab, shown in Figure 23.24, displays a list of the programs, services, and system components currently running on your system.

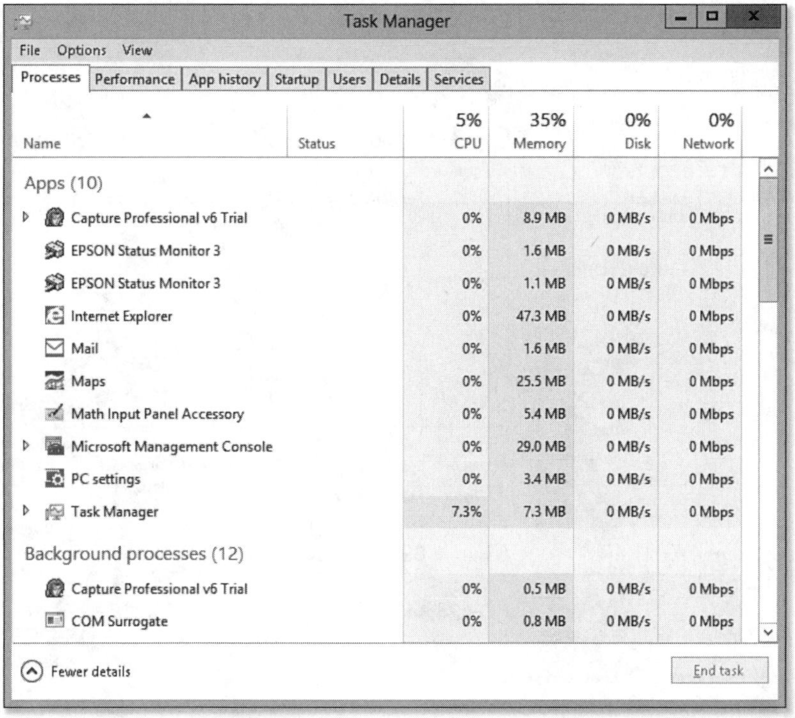

> **tip**
> To bypass the Windows Security screen, either press Ctrl+Shift+Esc or right-click an empty section of the taskbar and click Task Manager.

Figure 23.24
The Processes tab lists your system's running programs and services.

In addition to the name and status of each process, you see four performance measures:

- **CPU**—The values in this column tell you the percentage of CPU resources that each process is using. If your system seems sluggish, look for a process consuming all or nearly all the resources of the CPU. Most programs will monopolize the CPU occasionally for short periods, but a program that is stuck at 100 (percent) for a long time most likely has some kind of problem. In that case, try shutting down the program. If that doesn't work, click the program's process and then click End Process. Click the Yes button when Windows 8 asks whether you're sure that you want to do this.

- **Memory**—This value tells you approximately how much memory a process is using. This value is less useful because a process might genuinely require a lot of memory to operate. However, if this value is steadily increasing for a process that you're not using, it could indicate a problem and you should shut down the process.

- **Disk**—This tab shows the total hard disk I/O transfer rate (disk reads and writes in megabytes per second).

- **Network**—This tab shows the total network *data transfer rate* (data sent and received in megabits per second).

The Performance tab, shown in Figure 23.25, offers a more substantial collection of performance data.

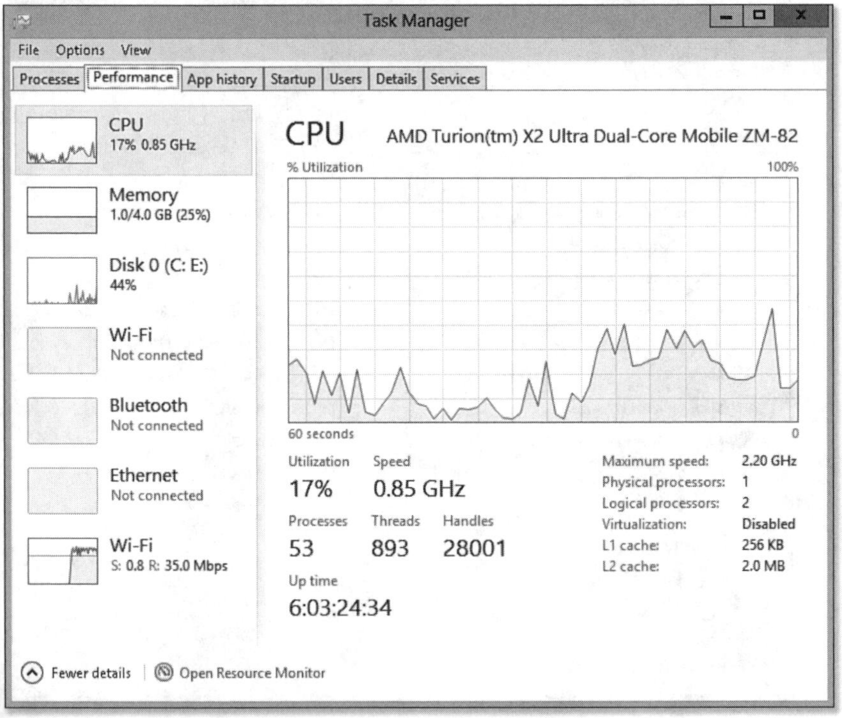

Figure 23.25
The Performance tab lists various numbers related to your system's memory components.

Click the items on the left—CPU, Memory, Disk, and various network interfaces—to see one or more graphs that show current activity, as well as several values related to the system component. Here's what they mean:

- **CPU: Utilization**—This is the current value and the graphed values over time for the CPU usage, which is the total percentage of CPU resources that your running processes are using.

- **CPU: Speed**—The current clock speed of the CPU. Compare this to the Maximum Speed value on the right.

- **CPU: Processes**—The number of processes currently running.

- **CPU: Threads**—The number of threads used by all running processes. A *thread* is a single processor task executed by a process, and most processes can use two or more threads at the same time to speed up execution.

- **CPU: Handles**—The number of object handles used by all running processes. A *handle* is a pointer to a resource. For example, if a process wants to use a particular service offered by a particular object, the process asks the object for a handle to that service.

- **CPU: Up Time**—The number of days, hours, minutes, and seconds that you have been logged on to Windows 8 in the current session.

- **Memory: Memory Usage**—A graph of the current amount of memory in use compared the total amount of memory in the system over time.

- **Memory: Memory Composition**—The current proportion of used to unused memory.

- **Memory: In Use**—The total amount of RAM currently being used by the system.

- **Memory: Available**—The amount of physical RAM that Windows 8 has available for your programs. Note that Windows 8 does not include the system cache (see the Memory: Cached value, later in this list) in this total.

- **Memory: Committed**—The minimum and maximum values of the page file. What is a page file? Your computer can address memory beyond the amount physically installed on the system. This nonphysical memory is *virtual memory* implemented by setting up a piece of your hard disk to emulate physical memory. This hard disk storage is actually a single file called a *page file* (or sometimes a *paging file* or a *swap file*). When physical memory is full, Windows 8 makes room for new data by taking some data that's currently in memory and swapping it out to the page file.

- **Memory: Cached**—The amount of physical RAM that Windows 8 has set aside to store recently used programs and documents. This is called the *system cache*.

- **Memory: Paged Pool**—This value is the amount of virtual memory, in megabytes, that Windows 8 has allocated to the process in the *paged pool*—the system memory area that Windows 8 uses for objects that can be written back to the disk when the system doesn't need them. The most active processes have the largest paged pool values, so it's normal for this value to increase over time. However, it's unusual for any one process to have a significantly large paged pool value. You can improve performance by shutting down and restarting such a process.

- **Memory: Non-paged Pool**—This value is the amount of virtual memory, in megabytes, that Windows 8 has allocated to the process in the *non-paged pool*—the system memory area that Windows 8 uses for objects that must remain in memory and therefore can't be written back to the disk when the system doesn't need them. Because the non-paged pool takes up physical RAM on the system, if memory is running low, processes that require a lot of non-paged pool memory could generate lots of page faults and slow down the system. Consider closing some programs to reduce memory usage.

- **Disk: Active Time**—The percentage utilization of the hard disk, both over time (the Active Time graph) and current (the Active Time value).

- **Disk: Disk Transfer Rate**—The rate over time at which data is transferred through the hard disk system in kilobytes per second.

- **Disk: Average Response Time**—The average time in milliseconds that the hard disk takes to respond to read and write requests.

> **note**
>
> A *page fault* occurs when a process requests a page from virtual memory and the system can't find the page. (A *page* is an area of virtual memory used to transfer data between virtual memory and a storage medium, usually the hard disk.) The system then either retrieves the data from another virtual memory location (this is called a *soft page fault*) or from the hard disk (this is called a *hard page fault*). Unfortunately, Task Manager doesn't give you any data on page faults. For this, you need to use Performance Monitor, as described later in the "Using the Performance Monitor" section.

- **Disk: Read Speed**—The current speed in kilobytes per second at which the system is reading data from the hard disk.

- **Disk: Write Speed**—The current speed in kilobytes per second at which the system is writing data to the hard disk.

- **Network: Throughput**—The speed over time in kilobits per second at which network data is passing through whatever network interface you selected.

- **Network: Send**—The current speed in kilobits per second at which the network interface is sending data.

- **Network: Receive**—The current speed in kilobits per second at which the network interface is receiving data.

Here are two notes related to the Memory values that will help you monitor memory-related performance issues:

- If the Memory: Available value approaches zero, this means your system is starving for memory. You might have too many programs running or a large program is using lots of memory.

- If the Memory: Cached value is much less than half the total memory installed, this means your system isn't operating as efficiently as it could because Windows 8 can't store enough recently used data in memory. Because Windows 8 gives up some of the system cache when it needs RAM, close down programs you don't need.

In all of these situations, the quickest solution is to reduce the system's memory footprint by closing either documents or applications. For the latter, use the Processes tab to determine which applications are using the most memory and shut down the ones you can live without for now. The better, but more expensive, solution is to add more physical RAM to your system. This decreases the likelihood that Windows 8 will need to use the paging file, and it enables Windows 8 to increase the size of the system cache, which greatly improves performance.

Using the Resource Monitor

The revamped Task Manager should serve most of your performance-monitoring needs. However, Windows 8 comes with another tool for monitoring your system yourself: the Resource Monitor. You load this tool by opening Control Panel, opening the Administrative Tools, and then opening Resource Monitor. Figure 23.26 shows the window that appears.

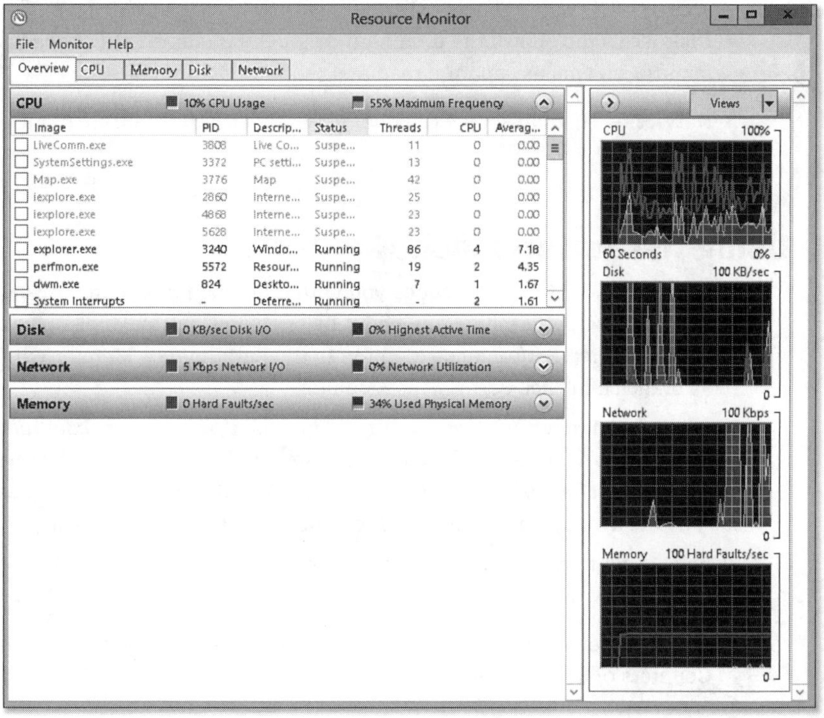

Figure 23.26
The Resource Monitor enables you to monitor various aspects of your system.

The Resource Monitor is divided into five tabs:

- **Overview**—This section shows a couple of basic metrics in four categories—CPU, Disk, Network, and Memory—as well as graphs that show current activity in each of these categories. To see more data about a category (as with the CPU category in Figure 23.26), click the downward-pointing arrow on the right side of the category header.

- **CPU**—This section shows the CPU resources your system is using. In two lists, named Processes and Services, you see for each item the current status (such as Running), the number of threads used, the CPU percentage currently being used, and the average CPU percentage. You also get graphs for overall CPU usage, service CPU usage, and CPU usage by processor (or by core).

- **Memory**—This tab displays a list of processes; for each one it shows the average number of hard memory faults per minute, the total memory committed to the process, the *working set* (the number of kilobytes resident in memory), the amount of *shareable* memory (memory that other processes can use if needed), the amount of *private* memory (memory that is dedicated to the process and cannot be shared), and a breakdown of how the PC's physical memory is currently allocated.

 note

A *memory fault* does not refer to a physical problem; instead, it means that the system could not find the data it needed in the file system cache. If the system finds the data elsewhere in memory, it is a *soft fault*; if the system has to go to the hard disk to retrieve the data, it is a *hard fault*.

- **Disk**—This tab shows the total hard disk I/O transfer rate (disk reads and writes in bytes per minute), as well as separate read and write transfer rates.

- **Network**—This tab shows the total network *data transfer rate* (data sent and received in bytes per minute).

Using the Performance Monitor

The Performance Monitor provides you with real-time reports on how various system settings and components are performing. You load it by opening Control Panel, opening the Administrative Tools, and then opening Performance Monitor. In the Performance Monitor window, open the Monitoring Tools branch and click Performance Monitor.

Performance Monitor displays real-time data using *performance counters*, which are measurements of system activity or the current system state. For each counter, Performance Monitor displays a graph of recent values over a time space (the default time space is 100 seconds) as well as statistics such as the average, maximum, and minimum values over that span.

By default, Performance Monitor doesn't show any counters. To add one to the Performance Monitor window, follow these steps:

1. Right-click anywhere inside the Performance Monitor and then click Add Counters. The Add Counters dialog box appears.

2. To use the Available Counters list, click the downward-pointing arrow beside a counter category (such as Memory, Paging File, or Processor). A list of available counters appears.

3. Select the counter you want to use. (If you need more information about the item, activate the Show Description check box.)

4. If the counter has multiple instances, they appear in the Instances of Selected Object list. Click the instance you want to use.

5. Click Add.

6. Repeat steps 2–5 to add any other counters you want to monitor.

7. Click OK.

The counter appears at the bottom of the window (see Figure 23.27). A different-colored line represents each counter, and that color corresponds to the colored lines shown in the graph. Note, too, that you can get specific numbers for a counter—the most recent value, the average, the minimum, and the maximum—by clicking a counter and reading the boxes just below the graphs. The idea is that you should configure Performance Monitor to show the processes you're interested in (page file size, free memory, and so on) and then keep it running while you perform your normal chores. By examining the Performance Monitor readouts from time to time, you gain an appreciation of what is typical on your system. If you encounter performance problems, you can check Performance Monitor to see whether you've run into any bottlenecks or anomalies.

Figure 23.27
Use
Performance
Monitor to
keep an eye on
various system
settings and
components.

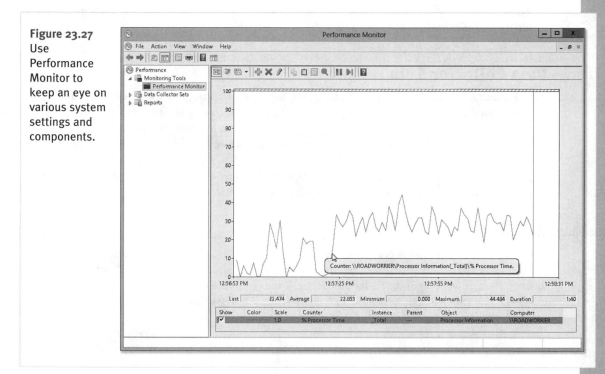

Performance Monitor has a few new features that make it easier to use and a more powerful diagnostics tool:

- If you're using a counter with a significantly different scale, you can scale the output so that the counter appears within the graph. For example, the graph's vertical axis runs from 0 to 100; if you're displaying a percentage counter, the Scale value is 1.0, which means the graph numbers correspond directly to the percentages (50 on the graph corresponds to 50%). If you're also show-ing, say, the Commit Limit counter, which shows values in bytes, the numbers can run in the billions. The Commit Limit counter's Scale value is 0.00000001, so the value 20 on the graph cor-responds to 2 billion bytes.

- You can save the current graph as a GIF image file: right-click the graph and then click Save Image As.

- You can toggle the display of individual counters on and off. You do this by toggling the check boxes in the Show column.

- You can change the duration of the sample (the number of seconds of data that appear on the chart). Right-click the chart, click Properties, click the General tab, and then modify the Duration value. You can specify a value between 2 and 1,000 seconds.

- You can see individual data points by hovering the mouse over a counter. After a second or two, Performance Monitor displays the counter name, the time and date of the sample, and the coun-ter value at that time (refer to Figure 23.27).

Data Collector Sets

A *data collector* is a custom set of performance counters, event traces, and system-configuration data that you define and save so that you can run and view the results any time you need them. You can configure a data collector set to run for a preset length of time or until the set reaches a speci-fied size. You can also configure a data collector to run on a schedule. For example, you could run the data collector every hour for 15 minutes from 9 a.m. to 5 p.m. This enables you to benchmark performance and analyze the results not only intraday (to compare performance at different times of the day) but also interday (to see whether performance is slowing over time).

Reports

This section holds the reports created by each data collector set. These are .blg files, and you can see the results by clicking the report and then switching to Sysmon view (click the Chart icon in the toolbar). Alternatively, open the folder that contains the report file in File Explorer (the default save location is %SystemDrive%\perflogs) and double-click the report file.

TWEAKING AND CUSTOMIZING WINDOWS

Working with the PC Settings App

Microsoft spent countless hours and untold millions of dollars testing and retesting the Windows 8 user interface (UI) in its usability labs. It's important, however, to remember that Windows 8 is an operating system designed for the masses. With an installed base running in the hundreds of millions, it's only natural that the Windows UI would incorporate lots of lowest-common-denominator thinking. So, in the end, you have an interface that most people find easy to use most of the time; an interface that skews toward accommodating neophytes and the newly digital; an interface designed for a typical computer user, whoever the heck that is.

In other words, unless you consider yourself a typical user (and your purchase of this book proves otherwise), Windows 8 in its right-out-of-the-box setup won't be right for you. Fortunately, you'll find no shortage of options and programs that will help you remake Windows 8 in your own image, and that's just what this chapter shows you how to do. After all, you weren't produced by a cookie cutter, so why should your operating system look like it was?

Having said that, we should also point out that the litmus test of any interface customization is a simple question: does it improve productivity? We've seen far too many tweaks that fiddle uselessly with some obscure setting, resulting in little or no improvement to the user's day-to-day Windows experience. This may be fine for people with lots of time to kill, but most of us don't have that luxury, so efficiency and productivity must be the goals of the customization process. (Note that this does not preclude aesthetic improvements to the Windows 8 interface. A better-looking Windows provides a happier computing experience, and a happier worker is a more productive worker.)

Although you still tweak many Windows settings using Control Panel as well as advanced tools such as the Local Group Policy Editor and the Registry Editor, the customize tool of choice in the new Windows 8 interface is the PC Settings app. To get this app running, follow these steps:

1. Move the mouse pointer to the top-right or bottom-right corner of the screen to display the Charms menu. You can also coax the Charms menu out of hiding by pressing Windows Logo+C. If you're using a tablet, swipe left from the right edge of the screen.

2. Click Settings to open the Settings pane. A more direct route to the Settings pane is to press Windows Logo+I.

3. Click Change PC Settings. This launches the PC Settings app, which appears in Figure 24.1.

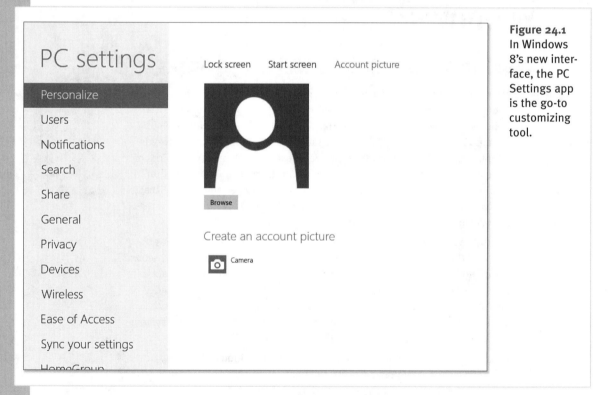

Figure 24.1
In Windows 8's new interface, the PC Settings app is the go-to customizing tool.

The left side of the PC Settings screen displays a long list of tabs, each of which represents a different customization category. Here's a summary:

- **Personalize**—Click this tab to customize the Windows 8 Lock screen and Start screen (see Chapter 4, "Using the Windows 8 Interface") as well as your user account picture (see "Changing Your User Account Picture," later in this chapter).

- **Users**—Click this tab to work with your user account—for example, giving your account a new password (see "Changing a Password," later in this chapter) and setting up a picture password (see "Creating a Picture Password," later in this chapter) and adding other user accounts to your PC.

- **Notifications**—Click this tab to control notifications as a whole, as well as individual app notification (see "Customizing Notifications," later in this chapter).

- **Search**—Click this tab to control your search history and to toggle searching on and off for specific apps (see Chapter 4).

- **Share**—Click this tab to customize Windows 8's app-sharing options (see Chapter 5, "Windows 8 Apps and the Windows Store").

- **General**—Click this tab to see a hodgepodge of settings, including the time zone, app switching, the spell checker, and language preferences. The General tab is also home to Refresh Your PC, Reset Your PC, and the advanced startup options (see Chapter 26, "Troubleshooting and Repairing Problems").

- **Privacy**—Click this tab to set your Windows 8 privacy options.

- **Devices**—Click this tab to see a list of devices on your system (see Chapter 28, "Managing Your Hardware").

- **Wireless**—Click this tab to see a list of wireless devices connected to your PC, as well as put your PC into airplane mode (see Chapter 36, "Wireless Networking").

- **Ease of Access**—Click this tab to adjust the Windows 8 accessibility settings.

- **Sync Your Settings**—Click this tab to specify how you want to sync settings with other devices through your Microsoft account (see "Synchronizing Your Settings Between Devices," later in this chapter).

- **HomeGroup**—Click this tab to configure your homegroup sharing options (see Chapter 18, "Creating a Windows Network").

- **Windows Update**—Click this tab to check for new updates (see Chapter 27, "Managing Your Software").

Changing Your User Account Picture

When you install Windows 8, the setup program takes you through several tasks, including choosing a username and password. However, it doesn't ask you to select a picture to go along with your user account. Instead, Windows 8 just supplies your account with a generic illustration. (If you're running Windows 8 under a Windows Live account, then your Windows 8 user picture is whatever image your Windows Live account uses.) This picture appears in the top-right corner of the Start screen, the sign-on screen, and the Users section of the PC Settings screen. So rather than using the default illustration, you might prefer to use a photo or other artwork. In that case, you can configure your user account to use another picture, which can either be an existing image or a new shot taken with your webcam.

For an existing image, you can use any picture you want, as long as it's in one of the four image file types that Windows 8 supports: Bitmap, JPEG, GIF, or PNG. Here are the steps to follow:

1. In the PC Settings app, click Personalize.

2. Click the Account Picture subtab.

3. Click Browse. A file chooser screen appears.

4. Click Files and then click the folder that contains the image you want to use.

5. Click the image.

6. Click Choose Image. Windows 8 applies the new picture to your user account.

Alternatively, if your computer comes with a webcam or you have a similar camera attached to your PC, you can use the camera to take your account picture. Follow these steps:

1. In the PC Settings app, click Personalize.

2. Click the Account Picture subtab.

3. Click Camera to open the Camera app.

4. Compose your shot, and then click the screen to take the picture.

5. Click and drag the account picture box to set the image area, and then click OK. (Alternatively, if you're not happy with the result, click Retake to try again.)

If you prefer to use a short video (up to 5 seconds) instead, follow steps 1 to 3 and then click the Video Mode button to switch to video mode, click the screen to begin recording, and then click the screen again when the recording is complete. Click OK to set the video as your account picture.

〰️ **tip**

If you change your account picture again, the Account Picture subtab displays a thumbnail of your old picture, so you can revert to the previous image just by clicking it in the subtab. If you change your account picture frequently, the subtab maintains thumbnails of your last five account pictures. If you find that you never use these thumbnails, you can remove then from the subtab by right-clicking any thumbnail and then clicking Clear History. To control these thumbnails individually, use File Explorer to navigate to the following folder:

%UserProfile%\AppData\Roaming\Microsoft\Windows\AccountPictures

Changing a Password

Assigning a password to each user account is good practice because otherwise someone who sits down at the PC can sign in using an unprotected account. However, it's not enough to just use any old password. You can improve the security of Windows by making each password robust enough that it's impossible to guess and is impervious to software programs designed to try different password combinations. Such a password is called a *strong* password. Ideally, you want to build a password that provides maximum protection while still being easy to remember.

Lots of books will suggest absurdly fancy password schemes (we've written some of those books ourselves), but you really need to know only three things to create strong-like-a-bull passwords:

- **Use passwords that are at least eight characters long**—Shorter passwords are susceptible to programs that just try every letter combination. You can combine the 26 letters of the alphabet into about 12 million five-letter word combinations, which is no big deal for a fast program. If you bump things up to eight-letter passwords, however, the total number of combinations rises to 200 *billion*, which would take even the fastest computer quite a while. If you use 12-letter passwords, as many experts recommend, the number of combinations goes beyond mind-boggling: 90 *quadrillion*, or 90,000 trillion!

- **Mix up your character types**—The secret to a strong password is to include characters from the following categories: lowercase letters, uppercase letters, numbers, and symbols. If you include at least one character from three (or, even better, all four) of these categories, you're well on your way to a strong password.

- **Don't be too obvious**—Because forgetting a password is inconvenient, many people use meaningful words or numbers so that their password will be easier to remember. Unfortunately, this means that they often use extremely obvious things such as their name, the name of a family member or colleague, their birth date, their social security number, or even their username. Being this obvious is just asking for trouble.

Whether you want to assign a password to another user account or change an existing password to one that's stronger or easier to remember, you can use the PC Settings app to change an existing password.

First, here are the steps follow to change the password on your main Windows 8 user account:

1. In the PC Settings app, display the Users tab.

2. Click Change Your Password to display the Change Your Password screen, shown in Figure 24.2.

3. Use the Old Password text box to type your old password.

> **tip**
>
> How will you know whether the password you've come up with fits the definition of *strong*? One way to find out is to submit the password to an online password complexity checker. (If you're the least bit paranoid about these things, consider submitting a password that's only similar to the one you want to use.) We recommend Microsoft's (www.microsoft.com/security/pc-security/password-checker.aspx), but a Google search on "password complexity checker" will reveal many others.

Change your password

Paul McFedries
win8books@live.com

Can't access your account?

New password   ●●●●●●●●●

Re-enter password   ●●●●●●●●●

[Next]   [Cancel]

Figure 24.2
Use the Change Your Password screen to update the password for your main Windows user account.

Click and hold this icon to temporarily reveal the password characters.

4. Use the New Password and Re-enter Password text boxes to type and then re-type the new password. If you're not sure whether you typed a password correctly (and you're sure no one can see your screen), click and hold the Display Characters icon (pointed out in Figure 24.2) to temporarily display the password.

5. Click Next.

6. Click Finish. Windows 8 updates the user account password.

Here are the steps to follow to add or change the password on a secondary Windows 8 user account:

1. Sign in as the user you want to work with.

2. In the PC Settings app, display the Users tab.

3. Click Change Your Password to display the Change Your Password screen. If the account has no password, click Create a Password, instead, and skip to step 5.

4. Use the Current Password text box to type the old password and then click Next.

5. Use the New Password and Re-enter Password text boxes to type and then re-type the new password.

6. Type a password hint. Make the hint useful enough to jog your (or the user's) memory, but vague enough that it doesn't make the password easy to guess.

7. Click Next.

8. Click Finish. Windows 8 updates the user account password.

Creating a Picture Password

As you learned in the previous section, if you're serious about your tablet's security, then you should have configured your Windows 8 user account with a strong password. This means a password that is at least eight characters long, and uses at least one character from at least three of the following four sets: lowercase letters, uppercase letters, numbers, and symbols. However, the stronger the password you use, the more cumbersome it is to enter using a touch keyboard.

If you find that it's taking you an inordinate amount of time to sign in to Windows 8 using your tablet's touch keyboard, you can switch to a picture password instead. In this case, your "password" is a series of three gestures—any combination of a tap, a straight line, and a circle—that you apply to a photo. Windows 8 displays the photo at startup, and you repeat your gestures, in order, to sign in to Windows.

However, in the same way that you shouldn't choose a regular account password that is extremely obvious (such as the word "password" or your username), you should take care to avoid creating an obvious picture password. For example, if you're using a photo showing three faces, then an obvious picture password would be a tap on each face. A good picture password not only uses all three available gestures, but also uses them in ways that aren't obvious.

> **⚠ caution**
>
> The biggest drawback to using a picture password is that it's possible for a malicious user to view and possibly even record your gestures using a camera. Unlike a regular text password where the characters appear as dots to prevent someone from seeing them, your gestures have no such protection.

Follow these steps to create a picture password on your Windows 8 tablet:

1. In the PC Settings app, display the Users tab.

2. Tap Create a Picture Password. Windows 8 prompts you for your account password.

3. Type your password and then tap OK. The Welcome to Picture Password screen appears.

4. Tap Choose Picture. A file chooser screen appears.

5. Select the picture you want to use and then tap Open. The How's This Look? screen appears.

6. Drag the picture so that the image is positioned where you prefer.

7. Tap Use This Picture. The Set Up Your Gestures screen appears.

8. Use your finger or a stylus to draw three gestures. As you complete each gesture, Windows 8 replays it briefly on the screen, as shown in Figure 24.3.

Set up your gestures

Draw three gestures on your picture. You can use any combination of circles, straight lines, and taps.

Remember, the size, position, and direction of your gestures — and the order in which you make them — become part of your picture password.

1 2 3

Start over   Cancel

Figure 24.3
After you draw each gesture, Windows 8 replays the gesture on the screen.

9. Repeat the gestures to confirm.

10. Tap Finish. The next time you sign in to Windows 8, you'll be prompted to enter your picture password gestures.

To ensure you've memorized your picture password, you should practice signing out from your account and then signing back in using the picture password a few times.

If you forget the gestures in your picture password, tap Switch to Password in the sign-in screen to sign in with your regular password. To get a reminder of your picture password gestures, open the PC Settings app, display the Users tab, tap Change Picture Password, type your user account password, and tap OK. In the Change Your Picture Password screen, tap Replay, then tap the picture to see each gesture.

Customizing Notifications

An app notification is a message that appears in the upper-right corner of the screen when an application has information to impart. This could be a new text message or email, or a message letting you know some operation has completed.

App notifications can be useful if you want to know what's going on in another app without having to switch to that app. However, app notifications can also distract you from your current work by focusing your attention elsewhere. That is, not only do you take your eye off your current task to view the notification, but the notification message itself might cause you to begin thinking about the content of the message.

If you find that a certain app is particularly distracting (either in its frequency or its content), you can tell Windows 8 to no longer display notifications for that app. Similarly, you might prefer to turn off all app notifications for a while if you don't want to be disturbed.

Many people find that the most distracting thing about app notifications is not the notifications themselves, but the sound that Windows 8 plays as it displays them. So another alternative is to leave notifications on, but disable the sound.

Follow these steps to customize app notifications:

1. In the PC Settings app, click Notifications. The Notifications settings appear, as shown in Figure 24.4.

Figure 24.4
Use the Notifications screen to customize app notifications.

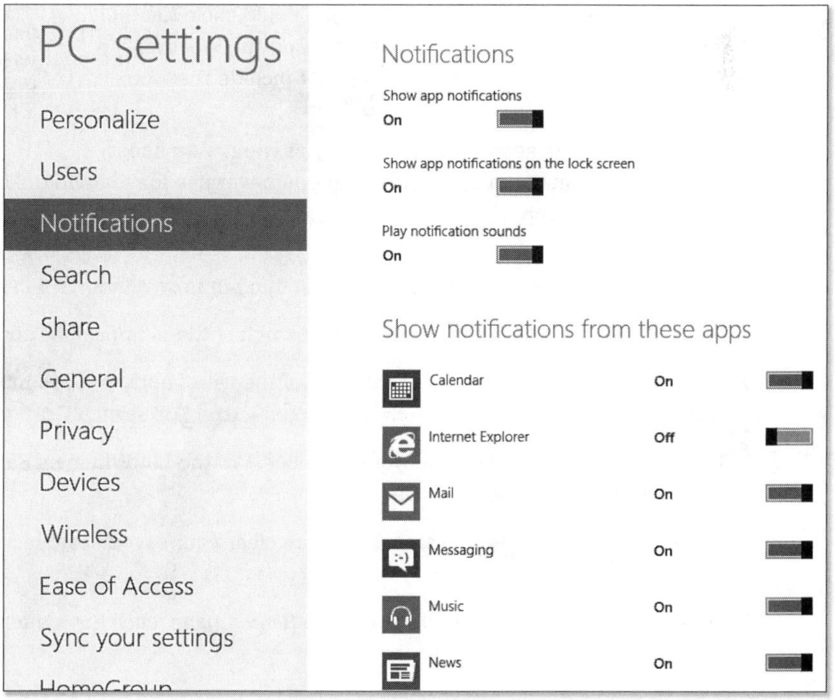

2. If you don't want to see any notifications, click Show App Notifications to Off.

3. If you don't want to see any notifications in the Lock screen, click Show App Notifications On the Lock Screen to Off.

4. If you don't want to hear the notification sound, click Play Notification Sounds to Off.

5. In the Show Notifications from These Apps section, click the switch to Off for each app you want to prevent from showing notifications.

Customizing Search

As you learned in Chapter 4, Windows 8 introduces a new search system that enables you to search for a particular term across multiple apps. For example, if you are currently using the Internet Explorer app and you bring up the Search pane, you could use it to run a search for Indianapolis using the Bing search engine. Without leaving the Search pane, you could also click Maps to search for Indianapolis in the Maps app; you could click Weather to see the current weather in Indianapolis using the Weather app, or click Mail to search for messages that include the word *Indianapolis*.

 tip

If you just want to disable app notifications for a while, there's a faster way to do it. Press Windows Logo+I to open the Settings pane, click the Notifications icon, and then click the amount of time you want to hide notifications (1 Hour, 3 Hours, or 8 Hours). The Notifications icon now appears with a clock inside to indicate that app notifications are hidden.

If you want to turn app notifications back on before the time interval is complete, press Windows Logo+I and then tap the Notifications icon.

This makes it easy to search just the apps you want. To make it even easier, you can remove any apps that you never use for searching. For example, if you never search the Finance app, you can remove it from the Search pane to make it easier to find and select the rest of the apps.

Here are the steps to follow to customize searching in new Windows 8 interface:

1. In the PC Settings app, click Search. The Search settings appear, as shown in Figure 24.5.

2. If you want Windows 8 to float to the top of the list of apps you use most often for searching, leave the Show the Apps I Search Most Often at the Top switch On.

3. If you want Windows 8 to save your searches, tap the Let Windows Save My searches as Future Search Suggestions switch to On.

4. If you activate the switch in step 3, you can clear your saved searches at any time by clicking Delete History.

5. For each app you don't want to see in the Search pane, click the switch beside the app to Off.

Synchronizing Your Settings Between Devices

You can run Windows 8 using either a local user account or a Microsoft account. Using the latter enables you to store data online, connect social networks such as Facebook and Twitter, and access services such as the Windows Store for purchasing apps.

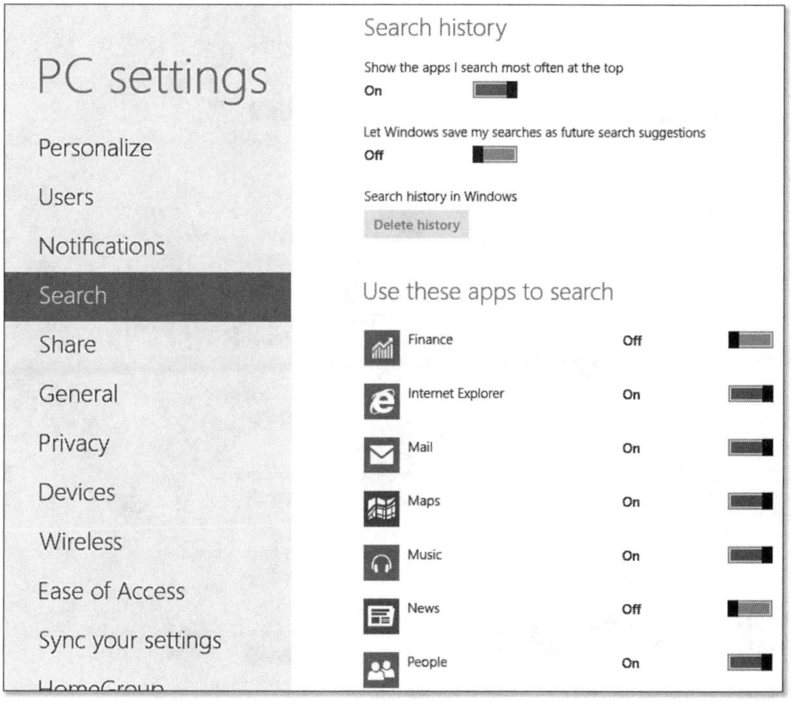

Figure 24.5
Use the Search screen to customize searches in the new Windows 8 interface.

However, arguably the most useful feature of using a Microsoft account is that you can use it to synchronize your settings across multiple devices. If besides your Windows 8 desktop computer you also have a Windows 8 notebook, a Windows 8 tablet, and a Windows 8 phone, using the same Microsoft account on each device means you can synchronize data between them. You can sync customizations (such as the user account picture and screen backgrounds), system settings (such as languages and regional settings), Internet Explorer data (such as favorites and history), app settings, and more. This gives you a consistent interface across your devices, and consistent data so you can be more productive.

Follow these steps to customize how Windows 8 synchronizes your settings across devices:

1. In the PC Settings app, click Sync Your Settings. The Sync Your Settings screen appears, as shown in Figure 24.6.

2. If you don't want your settings synced at all, click the Sync Settings On This PC switch to Off.

3. Under Settings to Sync, click the switch to Off beside each type of setting you don't want to include in the sync.

4. If you're using a metered Internet connection that only allows you so much data and you don't want to sync while using that connection, click the Sync Settings Over Metered Connections switch to Off.

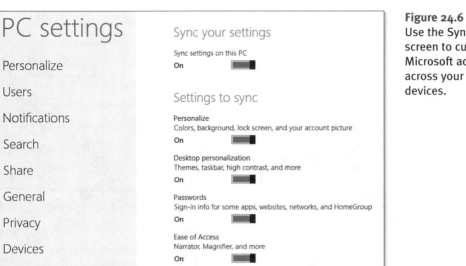

Figure 24.6
Use the Sync Your Settings screen to customize Microsoft account syncing across your Windows 8 devices.

5. By default, Windows 8 doesn't sync when you're roaming with a metered connection. This is wise (because roaming charges can be hideously expensive) so double-check that the Sync Settings Over Metered Connections Even When I'm Roaming switch is Off.

Customizing File Explorer

Although we're sure you have countless more important things to do with your precious time, at least some of your Windows 8 face time will be spent dealing with files, folders, and other Windows "f-words." These file system maintenance chores are the unglamorous side of the digital lifestyle, but they are, regrettably, necessary for the smooth functioning of that lifestyle.

This means that you'll likely be spending a lot of time with File Explorer over the years, so customizing it to your liking will make you more efficient and more productive, and setting up File Explorer to suit your style should serve to remove just a bit of the drudgery of day-to-day file maintenance. This section takes you through a few of our favorite File Explorer customizations.

note

Not syncing over a metered Internet connection is a good idea, but you have to tell Windows 8 when you're using a metered connection. To do this, press Windows Logo+I to open the Settings pane, click the network icon, right-click your Internet connection, and then click Set as Metered Connection.

Customizing the Ribbon

File Explorer's new ribbon interface is a great way to expose all the program's functionality, but it can sometimes be hard to locate the command you want to use. Also, some commands take several clicks because you must first click the tab, then drop down a list, and only then click the command.

If you have commands that you use frequently, you can put them within easy reach by adding them to the Quick Access Toolbar. Because the Quick Access Toolbar is always visible, any of its commands can be launched with just a single click.

The easiest way to go about this is to add one or more of the default commands. Click the Customize Quick Access Toolbar arrow (pointed out in Figure 24.7). The commands with check marks beside them are already on the Quick Access Toolbar, so click any of the other commands (such as Undo or Rename) to add it.

Figure 24.7
Click the Customize Quick Access Toolbar arrow and then click a command.

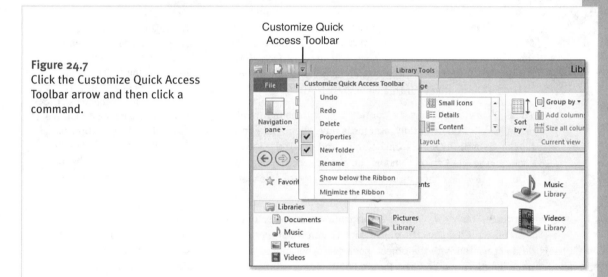

To add any command to the Customize Quick Access Toolbar, first open the tab that contains the command you want to add. Right-click the command and then click Add to Quick Access Toolbar.

Getting More Room for the Quick Access Toolbar

By default, the Quick Access Toolbar appears at the top of the File Explorer window in the title bar. Unfortunately, whenever File Explorer displays a Tools tab, it truncates the Quick Access Toolbar to show only seven icons. To work around this problem, right-click the Quick Access Toolbar and then click Show Quick Access Toolbar Below the Ribbon. This moves the toolbar below the ribbon, so you always see all of its commands.

Changing the View

The icons in File Explorer's content area can be viewed in no less than *eight* different ways, which seems a tad excessive to us, but Windows has never been about restraint when it comes to interface choices. To see a list of these views, display the View tab and then click the More arrow that appears in the lower-right corner of the Layout gallery. You get four choices for icon sizes: Extra Large Icons (shortcut key: Ctrl+Alt+1), Large Icons (Ctrl+Alt+2; see also Figure 24.8), Medium Icons (Ctrl+Alt+3), and Small Icons (Ctrl+Alt+4). You also get four other choices:

- **List**—This view divides the content area into as many rows as will fit vertically, and it displays the folders and files alphabetically down the rows and across the columns. For each object, File Explorer shows the object's icon and name. The shortcut key for this view is Ctrl+Alt+5.

- **Details**—This view displays a vertical list of icons, where each icon shows the data in all the displayed property columns (such as Name, Date Modified, Type, and Size). See "Viewing More Properties," later in this chapter, to learn how to add to these columns. You can also choose this view by clicking the Details icon in the lower-right corner, as pointed out in Figure 24.8. The shortcut key for this view is Ctrl+Alt+6.

> **tip**
>
> The default property columns you see depend on the template that the folder is using. To change the folder template for a folder not already part of a library, right-click the folder, click Properties, and then display the Customize tab. In the Optimize This Folder For list, choose the type you want: General Items, Documents, Pictures, Music, or Videos.

- **Tiles**—This view divides the content area into as many columns as will fit horizontally, and it displays the folders and files alphabetically across the columns and down the rows. For each object, File Explorer shows the object's icon, name, file type, and (for files only) size. The shortcut key for this view is Ctrl+Alt+7.

- **Content**—This view displays a vertical list of objects, and for each object it displays the object's icon, name, last modified date, size (files only), and any metadata associated with the object, such as author names and tags; the album name, genre, and track length (for music; see Figure 24.8); and the dimensions and date taken (for photos). The shortcut key for this view is Ctrl+Alt+8.

Viewing More Properties

Explorer's Details view is the preferred choice for power users because it displays a great deal of information in a relatively compact format. (The Content view also provides lots of information, but each object takes up quite a bit of space, and the object properties that you see aren't customizable.) Details view also gives you a great deal of flexibility. For example, here are some techniques to you can use when working with the Details view:

- You can change the order of the property columns by dragging the column headings to the left or right.

- You can sort on a column by clicking the column heading.

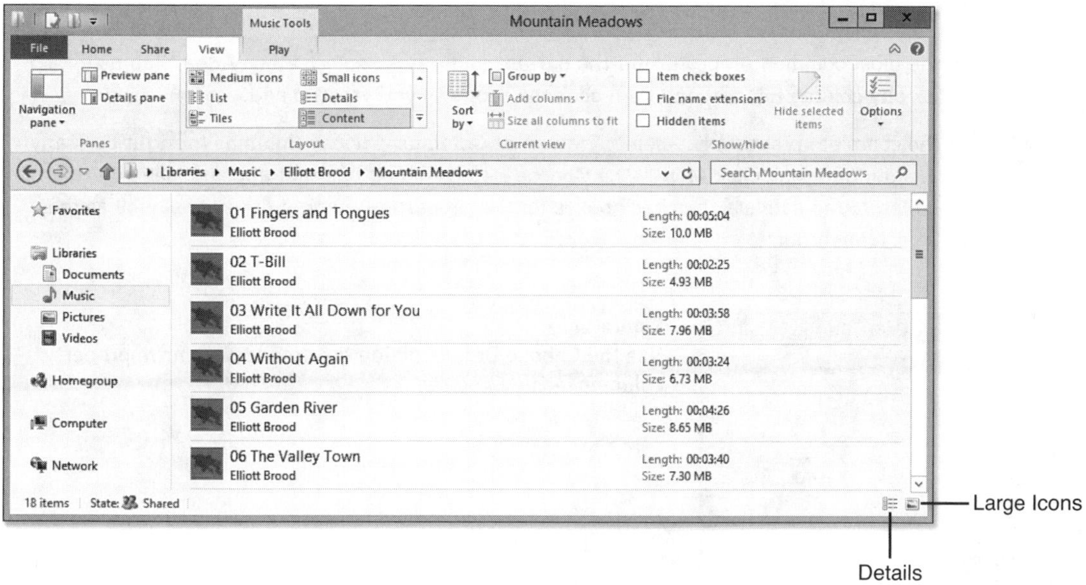

Large Icons

Details

Figure 24.8
File Explorer's Content view.

- You can adjust the width of a column by pointing the mouse at the right edge of the column's heading (the pointer changes to a two-headed arrow) and dragging the pointer left or right.

- You can adjust the width of a column so that it's as wide as its widest data by double-clicking the right-edge of the column's heading.

In addition, the Details view is informative because it shows you not only the name of each file, but also other properties, depending on the folder:

- **Documents**—Name, Date Modified, Type, and Size

- **Pictures**—Name, Date, Tags, Size, and Rating

- **Videos**—Name, Date, Type, Size, and Length

- **Music**—Track Name, Contributing Artists, Album Title, Track Number, and Track Title

These are all useful, to be sure, but Explorer can display many more file properties. In fact, there are nearly 300 properties in all, and they include useful information such as the dimensions of a picture

> **tip**
> To adjust all the columns so that they're exactly as wide as their widest data, right-click any column header and then click Size All Columns to Fit.

file, the bit rate of a music file, and the frame rate of a video file. To see these and other properties, you have two choices:

- To see the most common properties for the current folder type, select View, Add Columns (or right-click any column header) and then click the property you want to add.

- To see the complete property list, select View, Add Columns, Choose Columns (or right-click any column header and then click More). The Choose Details dialog box that appears (see Figure 24.9) enables you to activate the check boxes for the properties you want to see, as well as rearrange the column order.

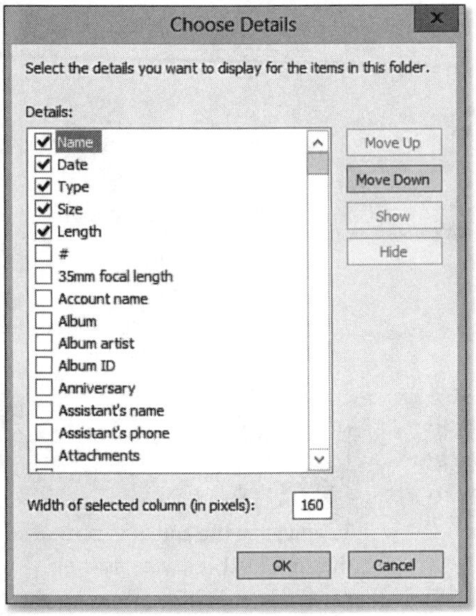

Figure 24.9
Use the Choose Details dialog box to add or remove property columns in File Explorer.

Turning On File Extensions

Microsoft figures that, crucial or not, the file extension concept is just too hard for new users to grasp. Therefore, right out of the box, File Explorer doesn't display file extensions. This may not sound like a big whoop, but not being able to see the extension for each file can be downright confusing. To see why, suppose you have a folder with multiple documents that use the same primary name. This is a not uncommon scenario, but it's also a fiendish one because it's often difficult to tell which file is which.

For example, Figure 24.10 shows a folder with 18 different files, all apparently named Project. Windows unrealistically expects users to tell files apart just by examining their icons. To make matters worse, if the file is an image, Windows 8 shows a thumbnail of the image instead of an icon. (This happens in thumbnail

> **note**
> Not being able to recognize a JPEG or a text file isn't a huge deal in the larger scheme of things, but it *is* a huge deal if you can't recognize a file type that could lead to trouble. I'm talking here about executable files, batch files, Registry files, and script files that could harbor malicious code that an imprudent double-click would unleash.

views such as Tiles, Medium Icons, and Large Icons.) The result is that in Figure 24.10 it's impossible to tell at a glance which image is a GIF, which is a JPEG, and so on.

Figure 24.10
With file extensions turned off, it's tough to tell one file from another.

The need to become an expert in Windows iconography is bad enough, but it gets worse. Not being able to see file extensions also leads to two other problems:

- **You can't rename extensions**—For example, suppose you have a text file named index.txt and you want to rename it to index.html to make it a web page file. Nope, sorry, you can't do it with file extensions hidden. If you try—that is, if you click the file, press F2 to choose the Rename command, and then type **index.html**—you just end up with a text file named index.html.txt.

- **You can't save a document under an extension of your choice**—Similarly, with file extensions turned off, Windows 8 forces you to save a file using the default extension associated with an application. For example, if you're working in Notepad, every file you save must have a .txt extension. If you create your own web pages, for example, you can't rename these text files with typical web page extensions such as .htm, .html, .asp, and so on.

You can overcome all these problems by turning on file extensions. To do that, display the View tab and then activate the File Name Extensions check box. Figure 24.11 shows the Project files with extensions in full display.

> **tip**
> There is a way to get around the inability to save a document under an extension of your choice. In the Save As dialog box, use the Save as Type list to select the All Files option, if it exists. You can then use the File Name text box to type the filename with the extension you prefer to use.

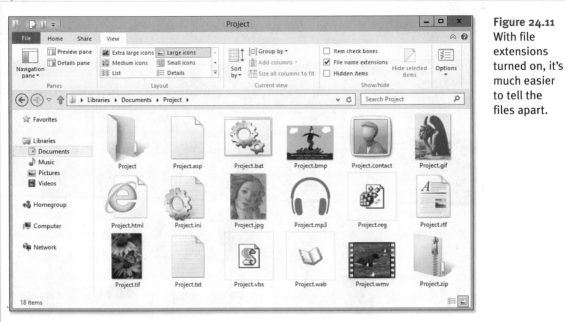

Exploring the View Options

File Explorer's view boasts a large number of customization options that you need to be familiar with. To see these options, you have two choices:

- In File Explorer, select View, Options.
- Press Windows Logo+W, type **folder**, and then click Folder Options in the search results.

Either way, the view options can be found, appropriately enough, on the View tab of the Folder Options dialog box, as shown in Figure 24.12.

Here's a complete list of the various items in the Advanced Settings list:

- **Always Show Icons, Never Thumbnails**—Activate this check box to prevent File Explorer from displaying file thumbnails. This can speed up the display of some folders that are heavy on pictures and other "thumbnail-able" file types.

- **Always Show Menus**—Activating this item restores the menu bar. Note that this has no effect in folder windows because in those windows the menu bar has been replaced by the ribbon. However, it does display the menu bar in other File Explorer windows, most notably Control Panel.

- **Display File Icon on Thumbnails**—When this check box is activated, File Explorer superimposes the file type icon on the lower-right corner of each file's thumbnail. This is usually a good idea because the extra icon allows you to figure out the file type at a glance. However, if you find the icon getting in the way of the thumbnail image, deactivate this setting.

Figure 24.12
The View tab has quite a few options for customizing File Explorer.

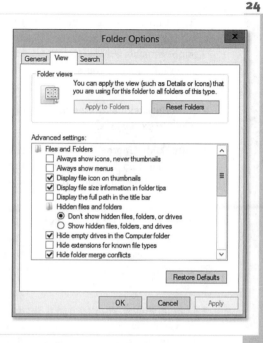

- **Display File Size Information in Folder Tips**—When this setting is activated and you hover your mouse pointer over a folder icon, File Explorer calculates the size of the files and subfolders within the folder, and displays the size in a pop-up banner. This is useful information, but if you find that your system takes too long to calculate the file size, consider deactivating this setting.

- **Display the Full Path in the Title Bar**—Activate this setting to place the full pathname of the current folder in the File Explorer title bar. The full pathname includes the drive, the names of the parent folders, and the name of the current folder.

- **Hidden Files and Folders**—Windows 8 hides certain types of files by default. This makes sense for novice users because they could accidentally delete or rename an important file. However, it's a pain for more advanced users who might require access to these files. You can use these options to tell File Explorer which files to display:

  Don't Show Hidden Files, Folders, or Drives—Activate this option to avoid displaying objects that have the Hidden attribute set.

  Show Hidden Files, Folders, and Drives—Activate this option to display the hidden files.

> 🔍 **note**
>
> If you activate the Display File Size Information in Folder Tips setting, you must also activate the Show Pop-Up Description for Folder and Desktop Items setting, described later.

> 🔍 **note**
>
> Files are hidden from view by having their Hidden attribute activated. You can work with this attribute directly by right-clicking a visible file, clicking Properties, and then toggling the Hidden setting on and off.

- **Hide Empty Drives in the Computer Folder**—When this setting is activated, File Explorer does not include empty drives in the Computer folder. This is potentially confusing (because you might attach a drive and wonder why it doesn't show up in the Computer folder) and not all that sensible (because you're just as likely to want to work with an empty drive as a non-empty one), so consider deactivating this option.

- **Hide Extensions for Known File Types**—Deactivating this setting is an alternative way to display file extensions.

- **Hide Folder Merge Conflicts**—When this option is activated, File Explorer doesn't pester you about merging folders when data that you're copying or moving includes a folder that already exists in the destination. If you always want to know when a folder merge is taking place, deactivate this option.

- **Hide Protected Operating System Files**—This setting is activated by default, and it tells Windows 8 to hide files that have the System attribute activated. This is not usually a problem because you rarely have to do anything with the Windows system files. However, if you do need to see one of these files, deactivate this setting. When Windows 8 asks whether you're sure, click Yes.

- **Launch Folder Windows in a Separate Process**—Activating this setting tells Windows 8 to create a new thread in memory for each folder you open. This makes File Explorer more stable because a problem with one thread won't crash the others. However, this also means that File Explorer requires far greater amounts of system resources and memory. Activate this option only if your system has plenty of memory (at least 2GB).

- **Restore Previous Folder Windows at Logon**—If you activate this setting, Windows 8 notes which folders you have open when you log off. The next time you log on and display the desktop, Windows 8 displays those folders again. This is a very useful option if you normally have one or two particular folder windows open all day long: It saves you having to reopen those folders each time you start Windows 8.

- **Show Drive Letters**—If you deactivate this check box, File Explorer hides the drive letters in the Computer folder and in the address bar when you open a drive.

Renaming Drives for Easier Access

If you hide drive letters, File Explorer displays drive names such as Local Disk. This isn't particularly useful, so consider renaming your drives with monikers that are meaningful (some examples: System Drive, Data Partition, and DVD Drive). Right-click the drive and then click Rename. Note that you must enter administrator credentials to perform this operation.

- **Show Encrypted or Compressed NTFS Files in Color**—When this setting is activated, File Explorer shows the names of encrypted files in a green font and the names of compressed files in a blue font. This is a useful way to distinguish these from regular files, but you can deactivate it if you prefer to view all your files in a single color. Note that this only applies to files on NTFS partitions because only NTFS supports file encryption and compression.

- **Show Pop-Up Description for Folder and Desktop Items**—Some icons display a pop-up banner when you point the mouse at them. For example, the default desktop icons display a pop-up banner that describes each icon. Use this setting to turn these pop-ups on and off.

- **Show Preview Handlers in Preview Pane**—When this check box is activated, File Explorer includes controls for previewing certain types of files in the Reading pane. For example, when you display a video file in the Reading pane, File Explorer includes playback controls such as Play, Pause, and Stop.

- **Show Status Bar**—This option toggles the status bar on and off.

- **Use Check Boxes to Select Items**—Activate this check box to add check boxes beside each folder and file. You can then select objects by activating their check boxes.

- **Use Sharing Wizard**—When this check box is activated, Windows 8 uses a simplified file and folder sharing method called the Sharing Wizard. Power users will want to disable the Sharing Wizard.

- **When Typing into List View**—These options determine File Explorer's behavior when you open a folder and begin typing:

  Automatically Type into the Search Box—Activate this option to have your typing appear in the Search box.

  Select the Typed Item in the View—Activate this option to jump to the first item in the folder with a name that begins with the letter you type.

Customizing the Taskbar for Easier Program and Document Launching

In the Windows 8 Desktop app, the taskbar acts somewhat like a mini-application. The purpose of this "application" is to launch other programs, display a button for each running program, and to enable you to switch from one program to another. Like most applications these days, the taskbar also has its own toolbars that, in this case, enable you to launch programs and documents.

Improving Productivity by Setting Taskbar Options

The taskbar comes with a few options that can help you be more productive either by saving a few mouse clicks or by giving you more screen room to display your applications, so let's start there. Follow these steps to set these taskbar options:

1. Right-click the taskbar and then click Properties. The Taskbar Properties dialog box appears with the Taskbar tab displayed, as shown in Figure 24.13.

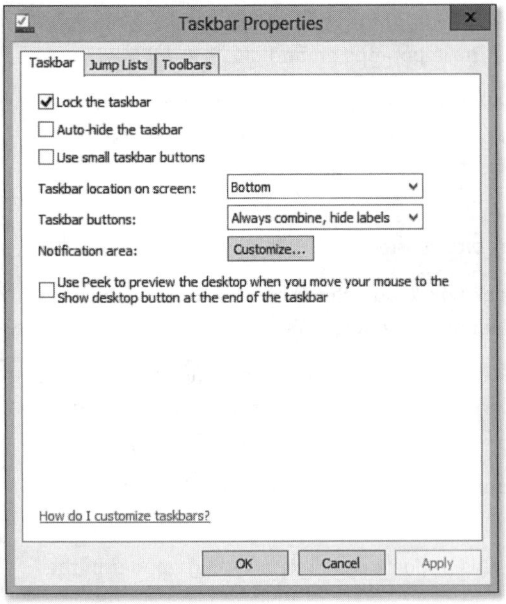

Figure 24.13
Use the Taskbar tab to set up the taskbar for improved productivity.

2. Activate or deactivate the following options, as required, to boost your productivity:

- **Lock the Taskbar**—When this check box is activated, you can't resize the taskbar and you can't resize or move any taskbar toolbars. This is useful if you share your computer with other users and you don't want to waste time resetting the taskbar if it's changed by someone else.

> **tip**
> You can also toggle taskbar locking on and off by right-clicking an empty section of the taskbar and then clicking Lock the Taskbar.

- **Auto-Hide the Taskbar**—When this check box is activated, Windows 8 reduces the taskbar to a thin, blue line at the bottom of the screen when you're not using it. This is useful if you want a bit more screen room for your applications. To redisplay the taskbar, move the mouse pointer to the bottom of the screen. Note, however, that you should consider leaving this option deactivated if you use the taskbar frequently; otherwise, auto-hiding it will slow you down because it takes Windows 8 a second or two to restore the taskbar when you hover the mouse pointer over it.

- **Use Small Taskbar Buttons**—Activate this check box to shrink the taskbar's program buttons. This not only reduces the overall height of the taskbar (so you get more room for the desktop and your programs) but it also enables you to populate the taskbar with more buttons.

3. Use the Taskbar Location on Screen list to choose where you want to situate the taskbar: Bottom, Left, Right, or Top. For example, if you want to maximize the available screen height, move the taskbar to one side or the other.

4. Use the Taskbar Buttons list to choose how you want Windows 8 to group taskbar buttons when an application has multiple windows open (or an application such as Internet Explorer has multiple tabs open):

- **Always Combine, Hide Labels**—Choose this option to have Windows 8 always group similar taskbar buttons.

- **Combine When Taskbar Is Full**—Choose this option to have Windows 8 only group similar taskbar buttons when the taskbar has no more open space to displays buttons.

- **Never Combine**—Choose this option to have Windows 8 never group similar taskbar buttons.

5. If you don't want to use Windows 8's Peek feature, for some reason, deactivate the Use Peek to Preview the Desktop... check box.

6. Click OK.

> **note**
>
> Peek is Windows 8's answer to the perennial question, "Why should I put anything on my desktop if I can't see it?" If you have Peek activated, hover your mouse pointer over the right edge of the taskbar, and Windows 8 temporarily turns your open windows transparent so that you can see the desktop. Slip the mouse pointer off the preview button and your windows rematerialize. Nice!

Pinning a Favorite Program to the Taskbar

In Chapter 4, you learned that you can pin an icon for your favorite program to the Start screen. That's great if you spend time in the Start screen, but it's not much of a productivity booster if you spend most of your time in the Desktop app. And by far the biggest problem with the Windows 8 desktop is that the old Start menu is gone, so launching programs is a real hassle. You also learned in Chapter 4 how to access Start menu items from the taskbar, but that solution requires several clicks to launch a program. We live in a "multiple clicks bad, one click good" world, so what you really need is a faster way of launching programs while working in the Desktop app.

That way is, of course, the taskbar, which offers two examples—the Internet Explore and File Explorer icons—that are pinned to the taskbar and hence require but a single click to launch.

If you're coming to Windows 8 from Windows Vista (or even XP), you might think of these icons as being glorified Quick Launch toolbar icons, but there's a big difference: in Windows 8, when you click one of these icons, it turns into its own running program icon! In other words, a separate icon doesn't show up on the taskbar; instead, Windows 8 puts a frame around the icon to indicate that its program is running.

So how can you get in on this one-click action for your own programs? You can pin those program to the taskbar. You have four choices:

- In File Explorer, right-click a program's icon or a program's shortcut and then click Pin to Taskbar.

- In the Start screen, use the Apps screen or Apps Search pane to find the Desktop program you want to pin, right-click that program, and then click Pin to Taskbar.

- If the program is already running, right-click its taskbar icon and then click Pin This Program to Taskbar.

- In File Explorer, drag a program's icon or a program's shortcut to an empty section of the taskbar and then drop it.

If you decide later that you no longer want a program pinned to the taskbar, right-click the program's taskbar icon and then click Unpin This Program from Taskbar.

Pinning a Destination to a Program's Jump List

A useful feature of the Windows 8 taskbar is the *jump list*, which is a menu of program commands, the most recently used files, and other features that appears when you right-click a program's taskbar icon. For example, the Internet Explorer jump list includes a Frequent list of often-viewed sites, and the Media Player jump list includes a list of frequently played music and the command Play All Music.

Most jump lists also include a hidden section that enables you to pin your favorite destinations to the jump list. Here, "destinations" depends on the application: for Internet Explorer, it's websites; for File Explorer, it's folders; for Media Player, it's media (a song, an artist, or whatever); for just about any other application, it's documents you create in that application.

Pinning a destination to its program's jump list is a handy way to launch that destination because all you have to do is right-click the taskbar icon and then click the pinned icon at the top of the jump list. Windows 8 offers a couple of ways to pin a destination to its program's jump list:

- If the destination already appears in the program's jump list, right-click the destination and then click Pin to This List. You can also hover the mouse over the destination and then click the Pin to This List icon that appears to the right of the destination (pointed out in Figure 24.14).

- Drag the destination to its program's taskbar icon (or to an empty section of the taskbar) and then drop it.

Figure 24.14 shows the Internet Explorer jump list with a few sites pinned at the top.

If you decide later that you no longer want a destination pinned to the program's jump list, click the program's taskbar icon, right-click the pinned destination, and then click Unpin from This List. You can also hover the mouse over the pinned destination and then click the Unpin from This List icon that appears to the right of the destination.

 tip

Once you've pinned a program to the taskbar, you can use that icon to open documents that aren't normally associated with the program. You normally do this by right-clicking the document, clicking Open With, and then selecting the other program. In Windows 8, however, you can hold down Shift, click and drag the document, and drop it on the program's taskbar icon.

 tip

By default, jump lists show only the ten most recently used destinations. If you'd like to see more (or even fewer) recent items, you can customize that number. To do this, right-click the taskbar, click Properties, and then click the Jump Lists tab. Use the Number of Recent Items to Display in Jump Lists spin button to set the number of items you prefer (the maximum is 60) and then click OK.

tip

To add a website to Internet Explorer's jump list, either drag an item from the Favorites list and drop it on the Internet Explorer taskbar icon, or navigate to the site, drag the address bar icon, and drop it on the Internet Explorer taskbar icon.

Figure 24.14
Each program jump list includes a Pinned area where you can tack up your favorite program destinations.

Pin to This List

Using the Windows Key to Start Taskbar Programs

We're a big fan of the super-duper Windows 8 taskbar because it offers the easiest way to launch our favorite desktop programs: just click the icon. However, even that easy-as-pie method is ever-so-slightly inconvenient when your hands are busy typing. It would be a tad more efficient if you could launch taskbar icons from the comfort of your keyboard.

But wait, you can! In Windows 8, you can use the Windows Logo key and the numbers across the top of your keyboard (*not* the ones on the numeric keypad) to press taskbar icons into service without having to reach all the way over to the mouse.

The trick here is that Windows 8 numbers the pinned taskbar icons starting at 1 for the leftmost icon, 2 for the icon to its right, and so on. The first nine icons are numbered from 1 to 9 (again, left to right), and if there's a tenth icon it's numbered as 0. To select a particular pinned taskbar icon from the keyboard, hold down the Windows Logo key and press the corresponding icon number on the top row of the keyboard. For example, on most Windows 8 systems, File Explorer is the second pinned taskbar icon from the left, so you can start it by pressing Windows Logo+2.

> **note**
>
> Bear in mind that when Windows 8 numbers the taskbar icons, it only looks at the pinned icons. For example, suppose you start a program and then decide later to pin some other program to the taskbar. That pinned icon will be the fifth icon on the taskbar, but it will be the fourth *pinned* icon, so you'd launch it by pressing Windows Logo+4.

Taking Control of the Notification Area

The notification area (sometimes called by its old name, the *system tray*) on the right side of the taskbar has been a fixture on the Windows landscape since Windows 95, and for most people it's either really useful or it's a complete waste of otherwise useful taskbar space. You're more likely to fall into the latter camp if your notification area in earlier versions of Windows was bristling with icons, as shown in Figure 24.15.

Figure 24.15
An out-of-control notification area.

Horror stories of notification areas threatening to take over the taskbar must have inspired Microsoft to rein in the bloat, so they modified the notification area in Windows 7, and the same modifications are used in Windows 8. Now, no matter how many of your installed programs try to run roughshod over the notification area, you'll always see *only* the following icons: Volume, Network, Action Center, and Power (if you have a portable PC). Bliss!

That doesn't mean all your other notification area icons are gone for good—they're just permanently hidden, although in two different ways:

- Some icons are visible, but to see them you have to click the upward-pointing arrow on the left side of the notification area (see Figure 24.16).

- Some icons are completely hidden, but you do see any notification messages displayed by those icons.

Figure 24.16
In Windows 8, you must click the arrow to see your other notification area icons.

This setup simplifies things considerably and gives you more taskbar breathing room, but there are times when it's not so convenient. For example, if you frequently control a program by right-clicking its tray icon, you either have that extra click to get at the icon, or you can't get at it at all. Fortunately, you can customize the notification area to show an icon right in the tray, hide it in the extra menu, or remove it completely and see just its notifications. Here's how:

1. Click the notification area arrow and then click Customize. The Notification Area Icons window appears, as shown in Figure 24.17.

2. For each icon, use the Behaviors list to choose one of the following options:

- **Show Icon and Notifications**—Choose this option to add the icon to the main notification area.

- **Hide Icon and Notifications**—Choose this option to shuffle the icon off to the notification area's extra menu.

- **Only Show Notifications**—Choose this option to completely remove the icon from the main notification area. Windows 8 will still display the icon's notifications, however.

3. Click the Turn System Icons On or Off link. The System Icons window appears, as shown in Figure 24.18.

4. In the Behaviors columns, select Off for each system icon you don't use.

5. Click OK in each open window.

If you have zero use for the notification area, you can disable it entirely by following these steps:

1. In the Start screen (or the Run dialog box; press Windows Logo+R), type **gpedit.msc**, and then press Enter. The Local Group Policy Editor appears.

> **note**
> These steps require the Group Policy Editor, which is available only with Windows 8 Pro and Windows 8 Enterprise. If you're not running one of these versions, we'll show you how to perform the same tweak using the Registry.

Figure 24.18
Use the System Icons window to specify which system icons appear in the notification area.

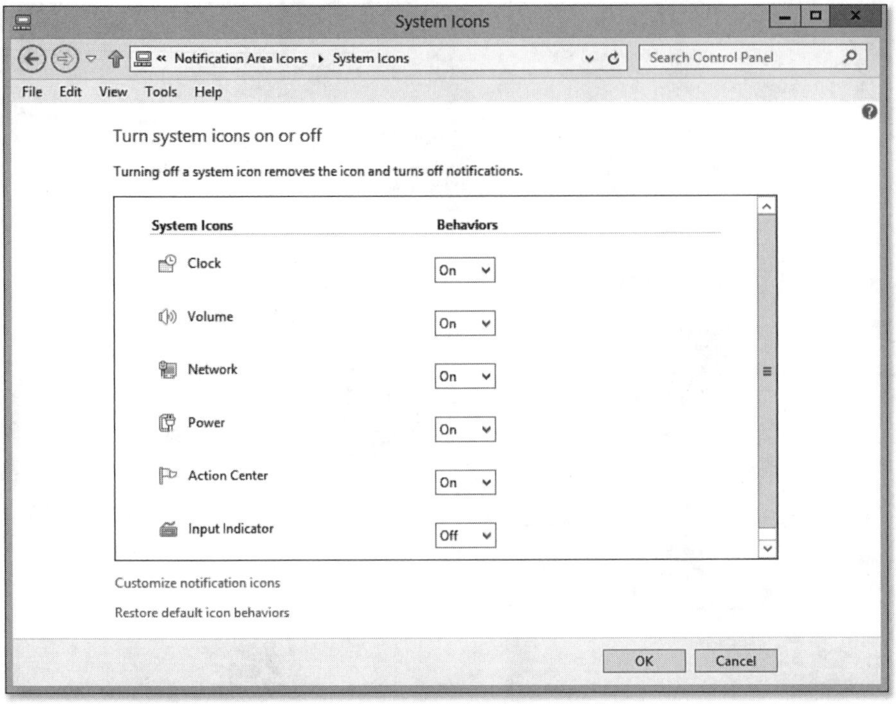

2. Open the User Configuration branch.

3. Open the Administrative Templates branch.

4. Click the Start Menu and Taskbar branch.

5. Double-click the Hide the Notification Area policy, click Enabled, and then click OK.

6. Double-click the Remove Clock from the System Notification Area policy, click Enabled, and then click OK.

7. Log off and then log back on to put the policy into effect.

If you prefer (or need) to implement this policy via the Registry, first open the Registry Editor (click Start, type **regedit**, press Enter, and enter your UAC credentials). Navigate to the following key:

HKCU\Software\Microsoft\Windows\CurrentVersion\Policies\Explorer

(If you don't see the Explorer key, click the Policies key, select Edit, New, Key, type **Explorer**, and press Enter.)

Now follow these steps:

1. Select Edit, New, DWORD (32-bit) Value.

2. Type **NoTrayItemsDisplay** and press Enter.

3. Press Enter to open the NoTrayItemsDisplay setting, type **1**, and then click OK.

4. Select Edit, New, DWORD (32-bit) Value.

5. Type **HideClock** and press Enter.

6. Press Enter to open the HideClock setting, type **1**, and then click OK.

7. Log off and then log back on to put the policies into effect.

Displaying Multiple Clocks for Different Time Zones

If you have colleagues, friends, or family members who work or live in a different time zone, it's often important to know the correct time in that zone. For example, you wouldn't want to call someone at home at 9 a.m. your time if that person lives in a time zone that's three hours behind you. Similarly, if you know that a business colleague leaves work at 5 p.m. and that person works in a time zone that's seven hours ahead of you, you know that any calls you place to that person must occur before 10 a.m. your time.

If you need to be sure about the current time in another time zone, you can customize Windows 8's date and time display to show not only your current time, but also the current time in the other time zone. Follow these steps:

1. Click the time in the notification area, and then click Change Date and Time Settings to display the Date and Time dialog box.

2. Click the Additional Clocks tab. Figure 24.19 shows a completed version of this tab.

3. Activate the first Show This Clock check box.

4. Use the Select Time Zone list to click the time zone you want to display in the additional clock.

5. Use the Enter Display Name text box to type a name for the clock.

6. Repeat steps 4 and 5 for the second clock.

7. Click OK.

To see the clocks, click the time to display a fly-out similar to the one shown in Figure 24.20.

> **tip**
>
> After you customize Windows 8 with the extra clocks, you normally click the time in the notification area to see the clocks. However, if you just hover the mouse pointer over the time, Windows 8 displays a banner that shows the current date, your current local time, and the current time in the other time zones.

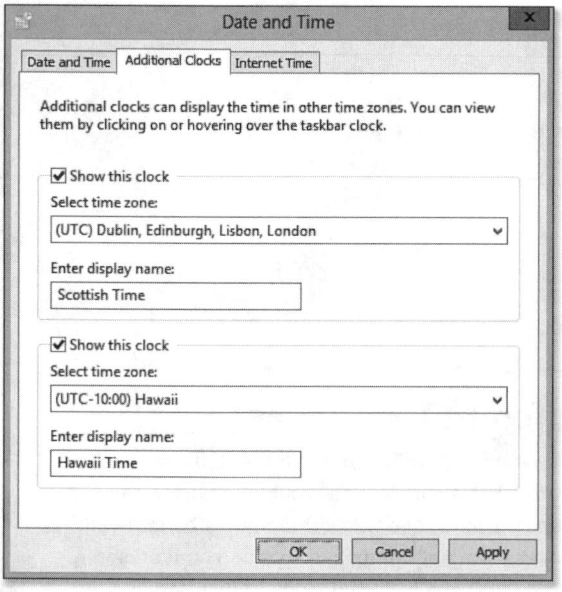

Figure 24.19
Use the Additional Clocks tab to add one or two more clocks for different time zones in Windows 8.

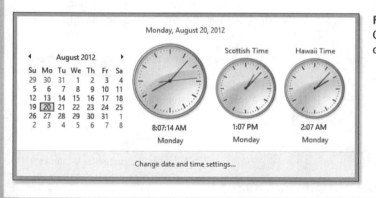

Figure 24.20
Click the time to see your additional clocks.

Displaying the Built-in Taskbar Toolbars

Windows 8 taskbar comes with four default toolbars:

- **Address**—This toolbar contains a text box into which you can type a local address (such as a folder or file path), a network address (a UNC path), or an Internet address. When you press Enter or click the Go button, Windows 8 loads the address into File Explorer (if you entered a local or network folder address), an application (if you entered a file path), or Internet Explorer (if you entered an Internet address). In other words, this toolbar works just like the address bar used by File Explorer and Internet Explorer.

- **Links**—This toolbar contains several buttons that link to predefined Internet sites. This is the same as the links toolbar that appears in Internet Explorer.

- **Touch Keyboard**—This toolbar (displayed by default on a tablet PC) contains just a single icon: the Touch Keyboard icon, which, when clicked, displays the onscreen touch keyboard.

- **Desktop**—This toolbar contains all the desktop icons, as well as an icon for Internet Explorer and submenus for your user folder and the following folders: Public, Computer, Network, Control Panel, and Recycle Bin.

Unlocking the Taskbar

You can adjust the size of a toolbar by clicking and dragging the toolbar's left edge. However, this won't work if the taskbar is locked. To unlock the taskbar, right-click an empty section of the taskbar and then click Lock the Taskbar to deactivate it.

To toggle these toolbars on and off, right-click an empty spot on the taskbar and then use either of the following techniques:

- Click Toolbars and then click the toolbar you want to work with.

- Click Properties, click the Toolbars tab, activate the check box of the toolbar you want to work with, and then click OK.

Setting Some Taskbar Toolbar Options

After you've displayed a toolbar, you can set a number of options to customize the look of the toolbar and to make it easier to work with. (Note that you need to unlock the taskbar to see these options; right-click the taskbar and then click to deactivate the Lock the Taskbar option.) Right-click an empty section of the toolbar and then click one of the following commands:

- **View**—This command displays a submenu with two options: Large Icons and Small Icons. These commands determine the size of the toolbar's icons. For example, if a toolbar has more icons than can be shown given its current size, switch to the Small Icons view.

- **Show Text**—This command toggles the icon titles on and off. If you turn on the titles, it makes it easier to decipher what each icon does, but you'll see fewer icons in a given space.

- **Show Title**—This command toggles the toolbar title (displayed to the left of the icons) on and off.

Creating New Taskbar Toolbars

In addition to the predefined taskbar toolbars, you can create new toolbars that display the contents of any folder on your system. For example, if you have a folder of programs or documents that you launch regularly, you can get one-click access to those items by displaying that folder as a toolbar. Here are the steps to follow:

1. Right-click an empty spot on the toolbar and then click Toolbars, New Toolbar. Windows 8 displays the New Toolbar dialog box.

2. Select the folder you want to display as a toolbar. (Alternatively, click New Folder to create a new subfolder within the currently selected folder.)

3. Click Select Folder. Windows 8 creates the new toolbar.

MANAGING HARD DISKS AND STORAGE SPACES

Dealing with Hard Disk Errors

Our hard disks store our programs and, most important, our precious data, so they have a special place in the computing firmament. They ought to be pampered and coddled to ensure a long and trouble-free existence, but that's rarely the case, unfortunately. Just consider everything that a modern hard disk has to put up with:

- **General wear and tear**—If your computer is running right now, its hard disk is spinning away at probably 7,200 revolutions per minute. That's right, even though you're not doing anything, the hard disk is hard at work. Because of this constant activity, most hard disks simply wear out after a few years.

- **The old bump-and-grind**—Your hard disk includes *read/write heads* that are used to read data from and write data to the disk. These heads float on a cushion of air just above the spinning hard disk platters. A bump or jolt of sufficient intensity can send them crashing onto the

> **note**
>
> I should say that your hard disk is *probably* spinning away as I speak. Windows 8 is actually configured out of the box to put your hard disk to sleep after 20 minutes of inactivity, so your hard disk may be resting. If you want to change the hard disk sleep interval (personally, I turn it off on my machines to improve performance), press Windows Logo+W to open the Settings search pane, type **power**, and then select Power Options in the search results. Select the power plan you want to use, click Change Plan Settings, and then click Change Advanced Power Settings, open the Hard Disk branch, open the Turn Off Hard Disk After branch, and then set the interval you prefer.

surface of the disk, which could easily result in trashed data. If the heads happen to hit a particularly sensitive area, the entire hard disk could crash. Notebook computers are particularly prone to this problem.

- **Power surges**—The current supplied to your PC is, under normal conditions, relatively constant. It's possible, however, for massive power surges to assail your computer (for example, during a lightning storm). These surges can wreak havoc on a carefully arranged hard disk.

So, what can you do about this? In previous versions of Windows, you had basically two choices:

- Wait until Windows recognized a disk error (for example, when you tried to open a corrupted file). In this case, Windows would run a program called Check Disk (actually, its command-line equivalent called chkdsk) that scanned your hard disk for problems and could repair them automatically.

- Run the Check Disk program yourself on a regular schedule (say, once a month or so) or when you suspected a hard disk error.

In both cases, Windows would not be able to run Check Disk right away on the Windows volume (usually drive C) because it had files in use. Instead, Windows would schedule Check Disk to run during the next boot. (Windows would be able to run Check Disk immediately on any other volume.)

The major downside to all this was that Check Disk would have to take the Windows volume offline to scan and repair it. That wasn't a big deal for a small hard disk, but with drive capacities getting into the hundreds and then thousands of gigabytes, these disk scans were taking forever. And the more full the volume was (technically, the more files it stored), the longer the check would take, sometimes several hours for extremely large disks with tons of files. Windows 7 improved things a bit by making Check Disk itself faster, but Microsoft realized it was facing a losing battle, and that hard disk size would easily outpace any performance improvements they could squeeze out of Check Disk.

The solution to this dilemma is a feature of Windows 8's NTFS file system called *self-healing*, where certain disk errors can be fixed on-the-fly without having to take the entire volume offline. This feature was introduced in Windows Vista, where it applied to only a few relatively rare errors, but in Windows 8 Microsoft has significantly increased the number of problems that can be self-healed. This means that many drive errors will get fixed behind the scenes without you even knowing an error occurred (and, more importantly, without having to take the Windows volume offline).

> **note**
>
> Although most hard disks consist of a single storage area, you'll see later in this chapter that you can split a hard disk into multiple storage areas, and these areas are called *volumes* (see "Dividing Your Hard Drive into Two Volumes"). A volume is also known as a *logical drive*, so we'll often refer to a volume as a hard drive in this chapter and throughout the book.

Hard Drive Health States

From a hard drive point of view, the main difference between Windows 8 and its predecessors is that Windows 8 now maintains a running assessment of the current health of the drive. Specifically, Windows 8 always sees your hard drive as currently in one of the five following states:

- **Healthy**—This state means that your hard drive is online and currently has no errors or corruption. When you open the Action Center's Maintenance section (press Windows Logo+W, type **action**, and then select Action Center), the Drive Status value shows "All drives are working properly," as you can see in Figure 25.1.

Figure 25.1
Action Center's
Drive Status
when your
hard drives are
healthy.

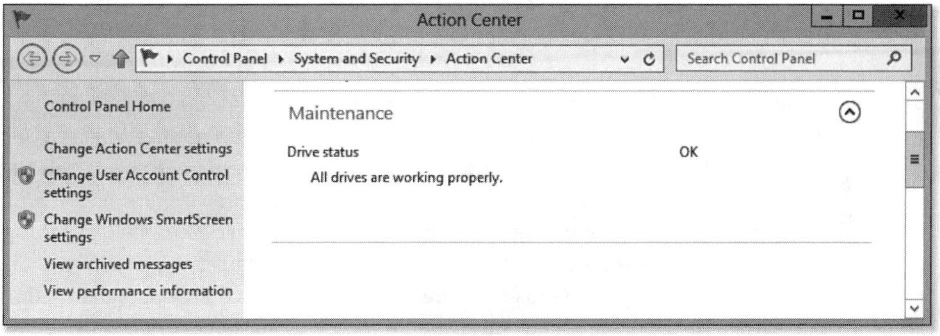

- **Self-healing**—This state means that Windows 8 has detected an error and is in the process of repairing it using NTFS self-healing. This transient state lasts a very short time and you see no indication either on the desktop or in the Action Center.

- **Error verification**—This state means that Windows 8 has detected a possible hard drive error that it can't self-heal. We say "possible" because some problems that appear to be hard drive corruption are actually intermittent memory errors. Rather than just escalating the health status to the next level, Windows 8 runs a new feature called the *spot verification service*, which attempts to verify that the error is a drive-related one. This is also a transient state that lasts a very short time.

- **Scan required**—This state means that the spot verification service has confirmed the hard drive error and the system now needs to scan the hard drive. That scan is scheduled to run during the next automatic maintenance window. However, as you can see in Figure 25.2, the Action Center shows a "Scan drive for errors" message, and you can run the scan immediately by clicking the Run Scan button. The drive remains online and you can work normally while the scan runs. During the scan, Windows 8 logs the error, determines the precise fix required, and escalates the health status to the next level.

➡ *To learn about the automatic maintenance window, **see** "Setting the Automatic Maintenance Schedule," **p. 655**.*

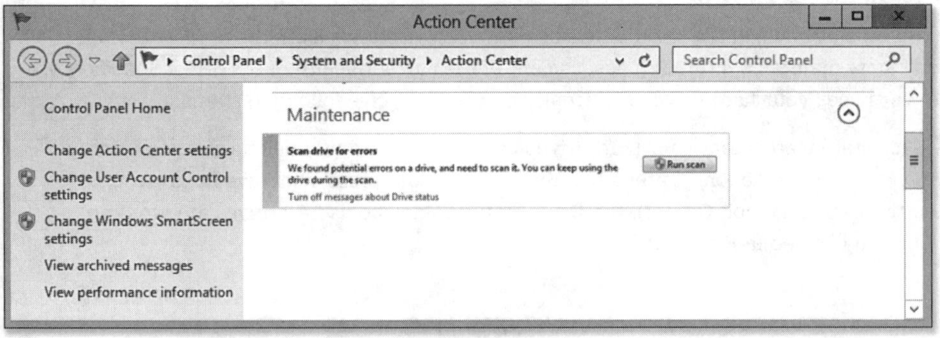

Figure 25.2
Action Center shows "Scan drive for errors" when Windows 8 detects a hard drive error.

■ **Restart required**—This state occurs after the drive scan has logged the error and determined the repair that's required, which Windows 8 calls a *spot fix*. The notification area displays a "Restart to repair drive errors" message, and the same message appears in the Action Center, as shown in Figure 25.3. You can click Restart to begin the spot fix process. Because the full hard drive has already been scanned and the needed fix has already been determined, repairing the hard drive adds only a few seconds to the restart. Note that the restart is *required* to repair the system volume (which must go offline to effect the repairs), but is actually *optional* for non-system drives. Windows 8 displays the restart message for all drives so that users don't have to take any direct action to repair the drive. However, for non-system drives, advanced users can initiate the repair manually without a restart, as we describe in the next section.

Figure 25.3
Action Center shows "Restart to repair drive errors" when Windows 8 is ready to fix a hard drive problem.

Repairing a Drive Manually

On a multivolume system, when Windows 8 is ready to spot fix a drive and it alerts you that a restart is required, it is unfortunately vague as to which drive requires the repair. If you'd rather not restart at this time, you can check the drives yourself and, if the repair is required on a non-system drive, you can run the repair manually to avoid the restart. Follow these steps:

1. On the desktop, open File Explorer and then select Computer.

2. Right-click the first hard drive (this is usually drive C, which is almost always the system volume; look for the Windows logo on the drive icon) and then click Properties. The drive's Properties dialog box appears.

3. Display the Tools tab.

4. Click the Check button. One of two things will happen:

   ■ You see the message "You don't need to scan this drive." This means the drive is in the Healthy state, so no repair is necessary. Repeat steps 2–4 to check the next drive.

   ■ You see the message "Repair this drive," as shown in Figure 25.4. If this is the system volume, you need to restart your computer to repair the drive. Otherwise, continue with step 5.

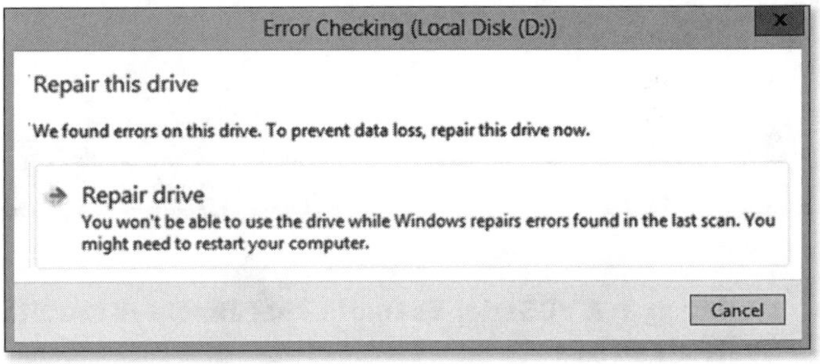

Figure 25.4
Check each hard drive until you see this message.

5. Click Repair Drive. Windows 8 repairs the non-system volume and returns its status to Healthy.

Checking Free Disk Space

Hard disks with capacities measured in the hundreds of gigabytes are standard even in low-end systems nowadays, and multi-terabyte hard disks are now commonplace. This means that disk space is much less of a problem than it used to be. Still, you need to keep track of how much free space you have on your disk drives, particularly the %SystemDrive% (usually the C: drive), which usually stores the virtual memory page file.

One way to check disk free space is to view the Computer folder using either the Tiles view (see Figure 25.5), the Content view (which include the free space and total disk space with each drive icon), or the Details view (which includes columns for Total Size and Free Space). Alternatively, right-click the drive in File Explorer and then click Properties. The disk's total capacity, as well as its current used and free space, appear in the General tab of the disk's property sheet.

Listing 25.1 presents a VBScript procedure that displays the status and free space for each drive on your system.

➡ *To learn how to run scripts,* ***see*** *"Windows Script Host," **p. 723**.*

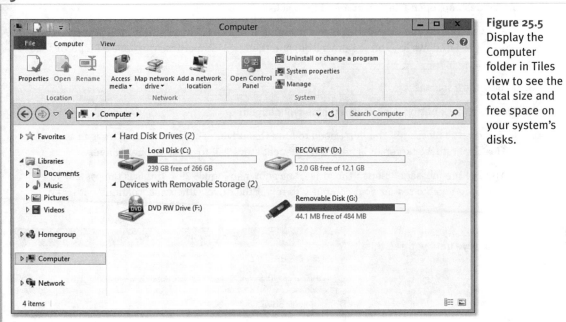

Figure 25.5
Display the Computer folder in Tiles view to see the total size and free space on your system's disks.

Listing 25.1 A VBScript Example That Displays the Status and Free Space for Your System's Drives

```
Option Explicit
Dim objFSO, colDiskDrives, objDiskDrive, strMessage

' Create the File System Object
Set objFSO = CreateObject("Scripting.FileSystemObject")

' Get the collection of disk drives
Set colDiskDrives = objFSO.Drives

' Run through the collection
strMessage = "Disk Drive Status Report" & vbCrLf & vbCrLf
For Each objDiskDrive in colDiskDrives

    ' Add the drive letter to the message
    strMessage = strMessage & "Drive: " & objDiskDrive.DriveLetter & vbCrLf

    ' Check the drive status
    If objDiskDrive.IsReady = True Then

        ' If it's ready, add the status and the free space to the message
        strMessage = strMessage & "Status: Ready" & vbCrLf
        strMessage = strMessage & "Free space: " & objDiskDrive.FreeSpace
```

```
        strMessage = strMessage & vbCrLf & vbCrLf
    Else

        ' Otherwise, just add the status to the message
        strMessage = strMessage & "Status: Not Ready" & vbCrLf & vbCrLf
    End If
Next


' Display the message
Wscript.Echo strMessage
```

This script creates a `FileSystemObject` and then uses its `Drives` property to return the system's collection of disk drives. Then a `For Each...Next` loop runs through the collection, gathering the drive letter, the status, and, if the disk is ready, the free space. It then displays the drive data, as shown in Figure 25.6.

Figure 25.6
The script displays the status and free space for each drive on your system.

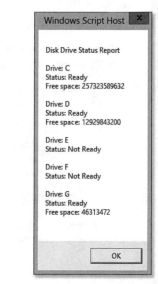

Deleting Unnecessary Files

If you find that a hard disk volume is getting low on free space, you should delete any unneeded files and programs. Windows 8 comes with a Disk Cleanup utility that enables you to remove certain types of files quickly and easily. Before discussing this utility, let's look at a few methods you can use to perform a spring cleaning on your hard disk by hand:

- **Uninstall programs you don't use**—With the new Windows Store handily located on the Start screen, it's easier than ever to download new software for a trial run. Unfortunately, that also means it's easier than ever to have unused programs cluttering your hard disk. Uninstall these and other rejected applications.

■ **Delete downloaded program archives**—Your hard disk is also probably littered with ZIP files or other downloaded archives. For those programs you use, you should consider moving the archive files to a removable medium for storage. For programs you don't use, you should delete the archive files.

■ **Archive documents you don't need very often**—Our hard drives are stuffed with ancient documents that we use only rarely, if at all: old projects, business records from days gone by, photos and videos from occasions held long ago, and so on. You probably don't want to delete any of this, but you can free up hard disk space by archiving those old documents to removable media such as an external hard drive or a flash drive.

After you've performed these tasks, you should next run the Disk Cleanup utility, which can automatically remove some of the preceding file categories, as well as several other types of files, including downloaded programs, Internet Explorer cache files, the hibernation files, Recycle Bin deletions, temporary files, file system thumbnails, and offline files. Here's how it works:

1. On the desktop, open File Explorer and then select Computer.

2. Right-click the drive you want to clean up and then click Properties. The drive's Properties dialog box appears.

3. Click Disk Cleanup. Disk Cleanup scans the drive to see which files can be deleted.

4. Click Clean Up System Files. Disk Cleanup displays an expanded list of file types, as shown in Figure 25.7

> ### 🔊 tip
> Windows 8 also offers a faster route to the Disk Cleanup window. In the Start screen or the Run dialog box (select Windows Logo+R), type `cleanmgr /d drive`, where *drive* is the letter of the drive you want to work with (for example, `cleanmgr /dc`), and then press Enter.

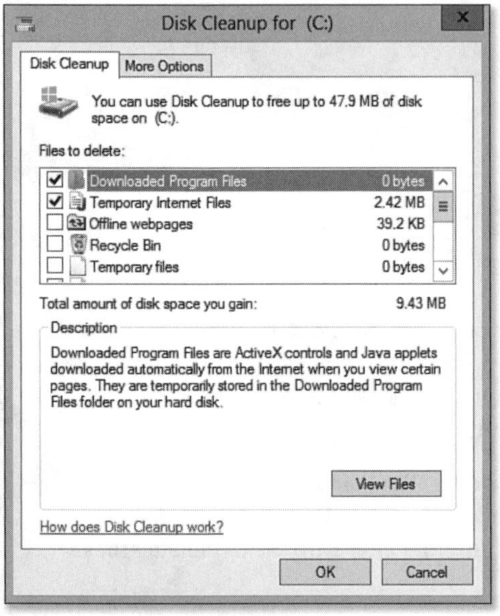

Figure 25.7
Disk Cleanup can automatically and safely remove certain types of files from a disk drive.

5. In the Files to Delete list, activate the check box beside each category of file you want to remove. If you're not sure what an item represents, select it and read the text in the Description box. Note, too, that for most of these items you can click View Files to see what you'll be deleting.

6. Click OK. Disk Cleanup asks whether you're sure that you want to delete the files.

7. Click Yes. Disk Cleanup deletes the selected files.

Saving Disk Cleanup Settings

It's possible to save your Disk Cleanup settings and run them again at any time. This is handy if, for example, you want to delete all your downloaded program files and temporary Internet files at shutdown. Display the Start screen (or open the Run dialog box), type the following command, and then press Enter:

```
cleanmgr /sageset:1
```

Note that the number 1 in the command is arbitrary: you can enter any number between 0 and 65535. This launches Disk Cleanup with an expanded set of file types to delete. Make your choices and click OK. What this does is save your settings to the Registry; it doesn't delete the files. To delete the files, use the Start screen or the Run dialog box to type the following command and then press Enter:

```
cleanmgr /sagerun:1
```

You can also create a shortcut for this command, add it to a batch file, or schedule it with the Task Scheduler.

Defragmenting Your Hard Disk

Windows 8 comes with a utility called Defragment and Optimize Drives that's an essential tool for tuning your hard disk. The job of Defragment and Optimize Drives is to rid your hard disk of file fragmentation.

File fragmentation is one of those terms that sounds scarier than it actually is. It simply means that a file is stored on your hard disk in scattered, noncontiguous bits. This is a performance drag because it means that when Windows 8 tries to open such a file, it must make several stops to collect the various pieces. If a lot of files are fragmented, it can slow even the fastest hard disk to a crawl.

Why doesn't Windows 8 just store files contiguously? Recall that Windows 8 stores files on disk in clusters, and that these clusters have a fixed size, depending on the disk's capacity. Recall, too, that Windows 8 uses a file directory to keep track of each file's whereabouts. When you delete a file, Windows 8 doesn't actually clean out the clusters associated with the file. Instead, it just marks the deleted file's clusters as unused.

To see how fragmentation occurs, let's look at an example. Suppose that three files—FIRST.TXT, SECOND.TXT, and THIRD.TXT—are stored on a disk and that they use up four, three, and five clusters, respectively. Figure 25.8 shows how they might look on the disk.

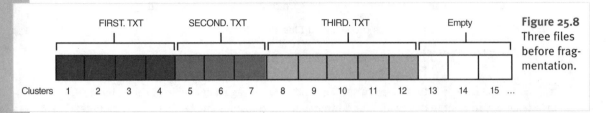

Figure 25.8
Three files before fragmentation.

If you now delete SECOND.TXT, clusters 5, 6, and 7 become available. But suppose that the next file you save—call it FOURTH.TXT—takes up five clusters. What happens? Well, Windows 8 looks for the first available clusters. It finds that 5, 6, and 7 are free, so it uses them for the first three clusters of FOURTH.TXT. Windows continues and finds that clusters 13 and 14 are free, so it uses them for the final two clusters of FOURTH.TXT. Figure 25.9 shows how things look now.

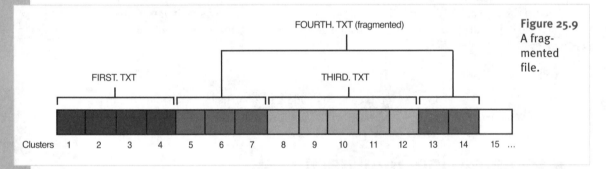

Figure 25.9
A fragmented file.

As you can see, FOURTH.TXT is stored noncontiguously—in other words, it's fragmented. Although a file fragmented in two pieces isn't that bad, it's possible for large files to split into dozens of blocks.

Running the Defragment and Optimize Drives Tool

The good news with Windows 8 is that it configures Defragment and Optimize Drives to run automatically—the default schedule is once a week during the maintenance window. This means you should never need to defragment your system manually. However, you might want to run a defragment before loading a particularly large software program.

Before using Defragment and Optimize Drives, you should perform a couple of housekeeping chores:

- Delete any files from your hard disk that you don't need, as described in the "Deleting Unnecessary Files" section earlier in this chapter. Defragmenting junk files only slows down the whole process.

- Open Action Center and check your hard drive's status as described earlier in this chapter (refer to "Dealing with Hard Disk Errors"). Run a scan or repair if the drive status is anything but Healthy.

Follow these steps to use Defragment and Optimize Drives:

1. In the Start screen, press Windows Logo+W to open the Settings search pane, type **defrag**, and then click Defragment and Optimize Your Drives in the search results. Alternatively, in File Explorer, open the Computer folder, right-click the drive you want to defragment, click Properties, display the Tools tab in the dialog box that appears, and then click the Optimize button. Either way, the Optimize Drives window appears, as shown in Figure 25.10.

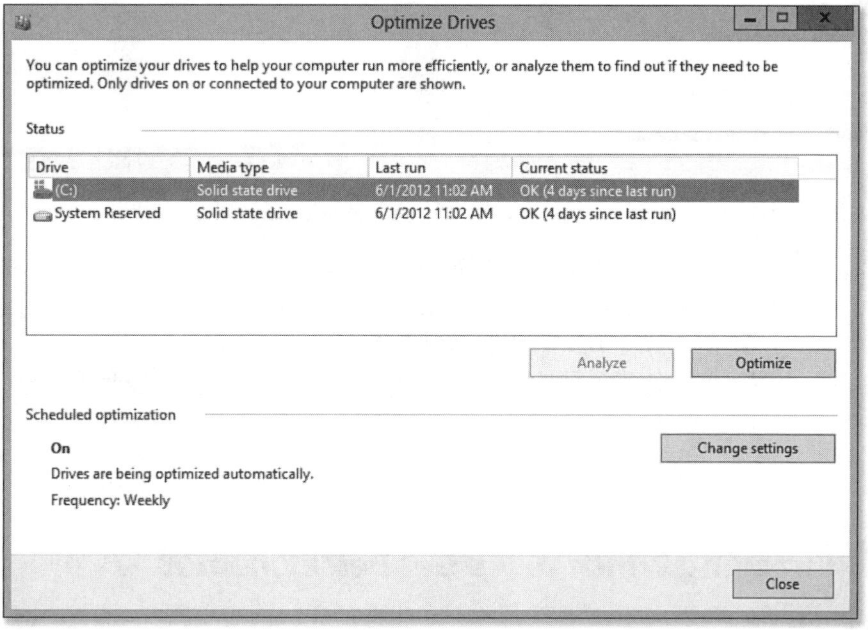

Figure 25.10
Use Defragment and Optimize Drives to eliminate file fragmentation and improve hard disk performance.

2. Click the disk you want to defragment.

3. Click Optimize. Windows 8 defragments your hard drives.

4. When the defragment is complete, click Close.

Changing the Optimization Schedule

If you want to run Defragment and Optimize Drives on a different day, at a different time, more often or less often, follow these steps to change the default schedule:

> **tip**
> In some cases, you can defragment a drive even further by running Defragment and Optimize Drives on the drive twice in a row. (That is, run the defragment, and when it's done immediately run a second defragment.)

1. In the Start screen, press Windows Logo+W to open the Settings search pane, type **defrag**, and then click Defragment and Optimize Your Drives in the search results.

2. Click Change Settings to display the Optimize Drives: Optimization Schedule dialog box, shown in Figure 25.11.

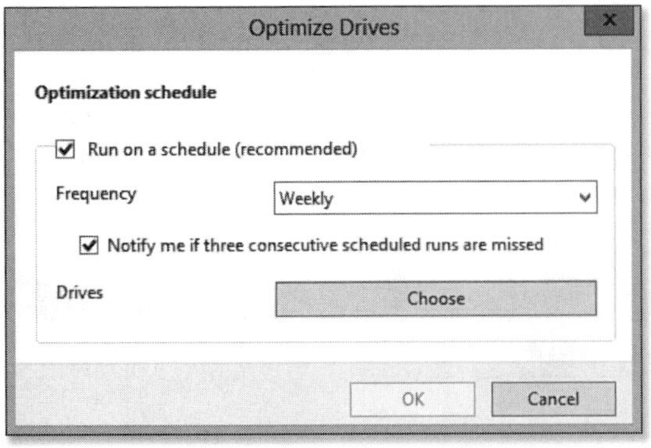

Figure 25.11
Use this dialog box to set up a custom defrag schedule.

3. Make sure that the Run on a Schedule check box is activated.

4. Use the Frequency list to select the defragment frequency: Daily, Weekly, or Monthly.

5. It's probably best to leave the Notify Me If Three Consecutive Scheduled Runs Are Missed check box activated. This lets you know if Windows 8 has not been able to optimize your drives in a while because your computer has not been idle during the maintenance window.

6. Click OK to return to the Optimize Drives window.

7. Click Close.

Changing Which Disks Get Defragmented

Defragment and Optimize Drives also has a feature that enables you to select which disks get worked on when the program performs its weekly (or whatever) defragment. This is useful if you have many hard drives or volumes on your system and you'd like to restrict the ones that Defragment and Optimize Drives works on to speed things up.

Follow these steps to specify which disks get defragmented:

1. In the Start screen, press Windows Logo+W to open the Settings search pane, type **defrag**, and then click Defragment and Optimize Your Drives in the search results.

2. Click Change Settings to display the Optimize Drives: Optimization Schedule dialog box.

3. Click Choose to display the Optimize Drives dialog box, shown in Figure 25.12.

4. Deactivate the check box beside any disk you don't want defragmented.

5. If you want Defragment and Optimize Drives to stop adding new disks to the defragment list, deactivate the Automatically Optimize New Disks check box.

6. Click OK to return to the second Optimize Drives dialog box.

7. Click OK to return to the first Optimize Drives dialog box.

8. Click Close.

Figure 25.12
Use this dialog box to choose which disks get defragmented.

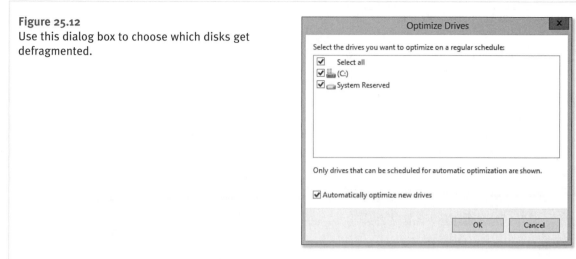

Working with Storage Spaces

Multiple-terabyte (TB) hard drives are becoming routine sights. However, if anything our data is expanding at an even faster rate as we download and rip music, TV shows, movies, and other massive media files. Nowadays, media collections that take up 10 or 20TB are not at all unusual.

In previous versions of Windows, the only simple way to store 10TB of data was to purchase five 2TB hard drives and split the data across the drives. This is not a great solution because it's difficult both to allocate storage efficiently and to find the file you need. Unfortunately, higher-end solutions such as RAID (Redundant Array of Inexpensive Disks) are complex to implement.

Windows 8 solves this problem by offering a new feature called *storage spaces*. This feature enables you to combine two or more USB, SATA, or SAS drives into a single storage pool and then create a storage space—that is, a virtualized hard drive—from that pool. You can then use that space just as you would a regular hard drive.

There are two other key characteristics of storage spaces:

- **Resiliency**—This means that the storage space protects your data should a hard drive in the storage pool fail. *Mirroring* is usually the best choice here, and you can select either two-way (which creates a second copy of each file and requires at least two drives) or three-way (which creates three copies and requires at least three drives). You can also use *parity* resiliency, where Windows 8 stores information about the data within a storage space, which enables Windows 8 to reconstruct that data in the event of a failure. Because of the overhead of maintaining this extra information, parity resiliency is best suited for spaces that mostly consist of large files that aren't updated very often (such as digital movies and recorded TV shows).

- **Logical size**—You can specify a logical storage space size that is larger than the current physical capacity. For example, if you have five 2TB drives, you can still create a storage space with a logical size of, say, 20TB. Windows 8 will then alert you when you need to add more drives to the storage space.

Follow these steps to create a storage pool:

1. Connect the USB, SATA, or SAS drives you want to use.

2. In the Start screen, press Windows Logo+W. The Settings search pane appears.

3. Type **storage** and then click Storage Spaces in the search results. The Storage Spaces window appears.

4. Click Create a New Pool and Storage Space, and when User Account Control asks you to confirm, click Yes or enter administrative credentials. Windows 8 displays a list of drives you can use to create the storage pool, as shown in Figure 25.13.

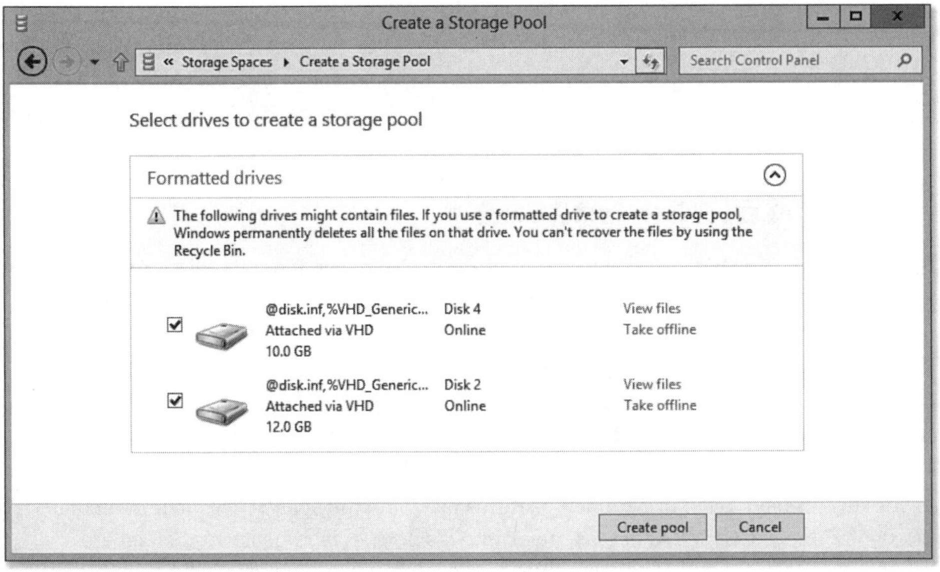

Figure 25.13
Use this dialog box to choose which disks are included in the storage pool.

5. Click the check box beside each drive you want to use and then click Create Pool.

6. Type a name for the storage pool and select a drive letter.

7. Select a resiliency type.

8. Type the logical size you want for the storage pool.

9. Click Create Storage Space. Windows 8 pools the hard drives and creates the storage space.

To add a drive to the storage space, follow steps 1 to 4, click Add Drives, activate the new drive's check box, and then click Add Drives.

Managing Your Disks

You've seen so far that Windows 8 takes a number of steps to relieve you of the burden of managing your hard disks and other drives:

- Windows 8 monitors your hard disk for errors, automatically repairs corruption that can be self-healed, scans other errors automatically during the maintenance window, and prompts you to restart your PC to conduct spot fix repairs.

- Windows 8 optimizes your drives automatically once a week (or whatever schedule you choose).

- Storage spaces enable you to easily combine multiple drives into a single storage area of any size where data can span the drives and is protected by resiliency.

We all want to use Windows for productive, creative, or playful pursuits, so anything that relieves us of the burden of routine maintenance is welcome in our books. Still, there are many disk-related chores that are not covered by this list and that are not automated in any way, so they require you to "lift up the hood" and work on your disks yourself.

Your interface for these tasks is the Disk Management snap-in, which you can get onto the desktop using any of the following techniques:

- In the Start screen or the Run dialog box, type **diskmgmt.msc** and press Enter.

- Press Windows Logo+W, type **disk**, and then click Create and Format Hard Disk Partitions.

- Press Windows Logo+X and then click Disk Management.

You end up at the Disk Management window, which looks similar to the one shown in Figure 25.14. The top half of the window presents a list of volumes on your system and provides data about each volume, including its name, file system, status, capacity, and free space (actual and percentage). The bottom half of the window offers a graphic display of the volumes.

The next few sections take you through some of the more useful tasks you can perform with the Disk Management snap-in.

Assigning a Different Letter to a Disk Drive

Windows 8 assigns letters to all your PC drives. For example, the system volume is usually set up as drive C. If you also have an optical drive it might be drive D, your PC's memory card slots would be assigned letters beginning with E, and so on.

You won't have to change these drive letters very often, but we've found that it comes up every now and then, so you should know how it's done. For example, some older programs require a floppy disk drive for certain actions, and it's a rare PC that comes with a floppy drive these days. In most cases you can fool the program into thinking your system has a floppy drive by assigning drive A to a flash drive or memory card slot.

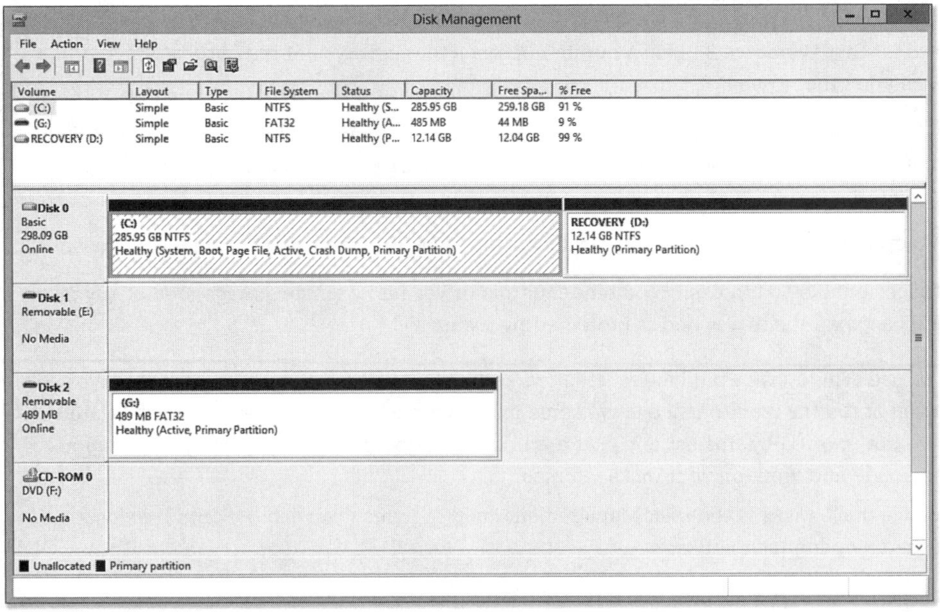

Figure 25.14
The Disk Management snap-in is your tool of choice for many disk chores.

Follow these steps to assign a different letter to a drive:

1. In the Disk Management window, right-click the drive you want to work with and then click Change Drive Letter and Paths. (Note that you can right-click the drive either in the Volume list or in the graphical display.) The Change Drive Letter and Paths dialog box appears.

2. Click Change. The Change Drive Letter or Path dialog box appears, as shown in Figure 25.15.

> 🔊 **caution**
>
> Don't try to change the drive letter assigned to your Windows 8 system volume, which is usually drive C. This drive is vital to the operation of your system, and changing its drive letter would render your PC unusable.

Figure 25.15
Use this dialog box to assign a different drive letter to the drive.

3. Select the drive letter you want to use and then click OK. Windows 8 asks you to confirm.

4. Click Yes. Windows 8 assigns the new drive letter to the disk drive.

Dividing Your Hard Drive into Two Volumes

As we mentioned earlier, most hard disks consist of just a single volume that takes up the entire disk, and that volume is almost always drive C. However, it's possible to divide a single hard disk into two (or more) volumes and assign a drive letter to each—say, C and D.

Why would you want to do such a thing? Lots of reasons, but two are by far the most common:

- You want to install a second operating system on your computer and dual-boot between them. In this case, you need to create a second volume and install the other operating system to that volume.

> For information on dual-booting, **see** "Dual- (and Multi-) Booting Windows 8." **p. 41**.

- You want to separate your data from Windows. In this case, you need to create a second volume and move your data to that volume. This is a good idea because if you ever have to reinstall Windows from scratch, you can wipe drive C: without having to worry about your data.

Creating multiple volumes on a single hard disk is sometimes called *partitioning*, because a partition is roughly equivalent to (but not quite the same as) a volume.

In Windows versions prior to Vista, partitioning a hard drive required third-party software such as Disk Director (www.acronis.com) or Partition Master (www.partition-tool.com). Windows Vista changed that by offering the welcome ability to manage volumes without extra software, and that Disk Management feature continues in Windows 8. You can reduce the size of a volume, enlarge a volume, create a new volume, and delete an existing volume.

In this section, you learn how to divide a hard drive into two volumes. You do that by first shrinking the existing volume and then creating the new volume in the freed-up disk space. Here are the steps to follow:

1. In the Disk Management window, right-click the drive you want to partition and then click Shrink Volume. Disk Management displays the Shrink *D*: dialog box (where *D* is the drive letter of the volume).

2. Use the Enter the Amount of Space to Shrink in MB text box to type the amount by which you want the volume size reduced, as shown in Figure 25.16. Keep in mind that this will be the approximate size of the new volume that you create a bit later.

---

tip

If the list of available drive letters doesn't include drive A, Windows 8 most likely believes (mistakenly, of course) that your PC has a floppy drive. You solve this problem by disabling this phantom floppy drive. Press Windows Logo+X and then click Device Manager. Open the Floppy Disk Drives branch, click Floppy Disk Drive, select Action, Disable, and then click Yes when Device Manager asks you to confirm.

---

note

You can't enter a shrink size that's larger than the shrink space you have at your disposal, which is given by the Size of Available Shrink Space value. If you're shrinking drive C, the available shrink space will be quite a bit less than the available free space because Windows reserves quite a bit of space on drive C for the paging file and other system files that may grow over time.

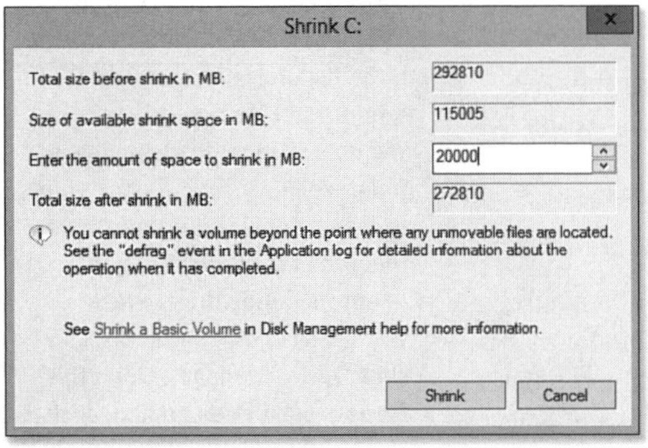

Figure 25.16
Enter the amount by which you want the existing volume reduced.

3. Click Shrink. Windows 8 shrinks the volume and displays the freed space as Unallocated, as you can see in Figure 25.17.

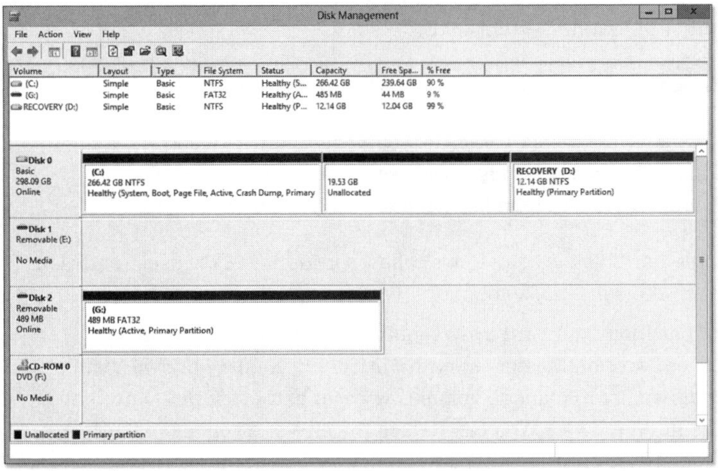

Figure 25.17
The space removed from the existing volume now appears as Unallocated in the Disk Management snap-in.

4. Right-click the Unallocated space and then click New Simple Volume. The New Simple Volume Wizard appears.

5. Click Next. The Specify Volume Size Wizard appears.

6. Make sure that the Simple Volume Size in MB text box is set to the maximum value, and then click Next. The Assign Drive Letter or Path dialog box appears.

7. Select the Assign the Following Drive Letter option, use the list to select the drive letter you want to assign to the new volume, and then click Next.

8. Select the Format This Volume with the Following Settings option, leave the settings "as is" (you might want to change the Volume Label, however), and click Next.

9. Click Finish. Windows 8 formats the volume and assigns the drive letter.

Creating a Spanned Volume

Earlier you learned about storage spaces, the new Windows 8 feature that creates a single storage pool out of multiple hard disks. This is one of the best new features in Windows 8, and there's no reason that we can think of not to use it. Still, for the sake of giving you a complete look at Disk Management, the next couple of sections show you the Disk Management tools that mimic storage spaces.

We begin with the *spanned volume*. This is a kind of virtual drive that combines two or more physical hard drives into a single storage area with two main characteristics:

- The new volume is *dynamic* because if you install more drives on the server, you can add those drives to the volume to instantly increase the storage area without losing any existing data.

- The new volume is *spanned* because data is seamlessly stored on all the physical hard drives without you having to worry about where the data is stored. If one of the hard drives fills up, Windows 8 will automatically write new data to one of the other drives in the volume.

Is there a downside to using spanned volumes? Yes, unfortunately, there is a disadvantage, and it's a big one: If one of the hard drives dies, you lose all the data stored in the spanned volume, even data that resides on the remaining functional drives.

In other words, if you go this route, we strongly recommend that you back up the spanned volume to prevent data loss.

Converting Hard Drives to Dynamic Disks

To get started, your first chore is to take the hard drives that you want to use for the spanned volume and convert them to dynamic disks:

1. In the lower half of the Disk Management pane, right-click one of the drives you want to convert to a dynamic volume. Be sure to right-click on the left side of the drive display (where you see the disk designations, such as Disk 0, Disk 1, Disk 2, and so on).

2. Click Convert to Dynamic Disk. Disk Management displays the Convert to Dynamic Disk dialog box.

3. Make sure the check box beside the disk is activated, as shown in Figure 25.18, and then click OK. Disk Management displays the Disks to Convert dialog box.

Figure 25.18
Your first task is to convert to dynamic disks those drives you want to include in the spanned volume.

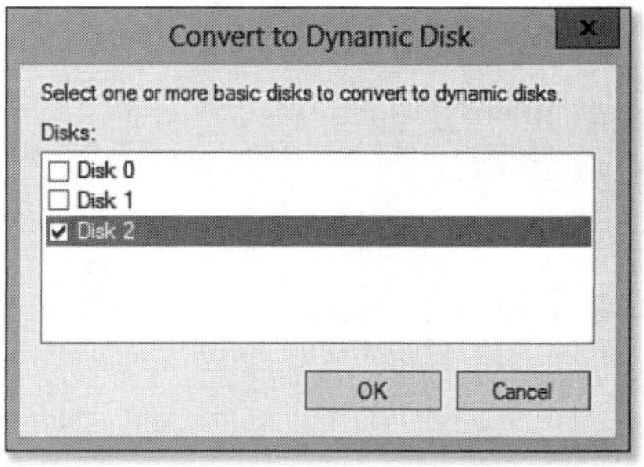

4. Click Convert. Disk Management asks you to confirm.

5. Click Yes. Disk Management converts the drive to a dynamic disk.

6. Repeat steps 1–5 to convert any other drives you want to include in the spanned volume.

Combining Dynamic Disks into a Spanned Volume

With your dynamic disks converted, you can now combine them into a spanned volume by following these steps:

1. In the list of hard drives in the lower half of the Disk Management pane, right-click one of the drives you want to include in the spanned volume. Be sure to right-click on the left side of the drive display (where you see the disk designations, such as Disk 0, Disk 1, Disk 2, and so on).

2. Click New Spanned Volume. Disk Management runs the New Spanned Volume Wizard.

3. Click Next. The Select Disks dialog box appears.

4. In the Available list, click a dynamic disk you want to include in the volume and then click Add.

5. Repeat step 4 to add any other drives you want to include in the volume. Figure 25.19 shows a spanned volume with two dynamic disks added.

note

You don't have to include the entire dynamic disk in the spanned volume. For example, you might want to set aside a portion of the dynamic disk for other storage uses. In that case, click the disk in the Selected list and then use the Select the Amount of Space in MB spin box to set the amount of space you want to assign to the spanned volume.

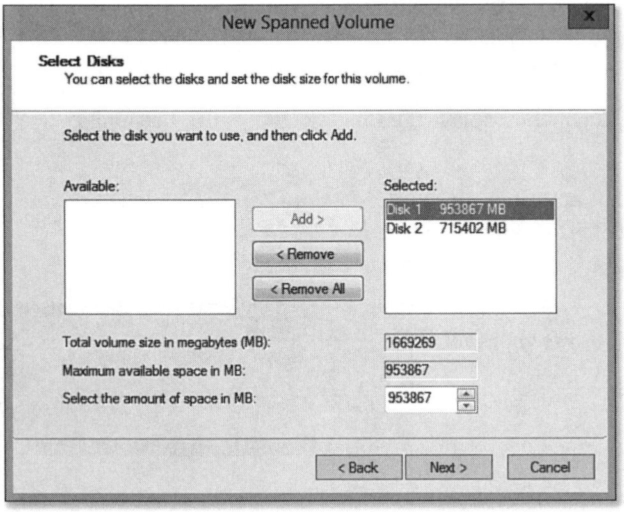

Figure 25.19
Add the dynamic drives you want to include in the new spanned volume.

6. Click Next. The Assign Drive Letter or Path dialog box appears.

7. Choose a drive letter (the default will probably be D, which is fine) and then click Next. The Format Volume dialog box appears.

8. Assign a Volume Label, if needed, leave the other options "as is," and then click Next. The last wizard dialog box appears.

9. Click Finish. Disk Management creates the spanned volume.

Figure 25.20 shows how the new spanned volume (drive D, in this case) appears in Disk Management (the top window) and in the Computer folder (bottom window).

Figure 25.20
The new spanned volume shown in the Disk Management snap-in and the Computer folder.

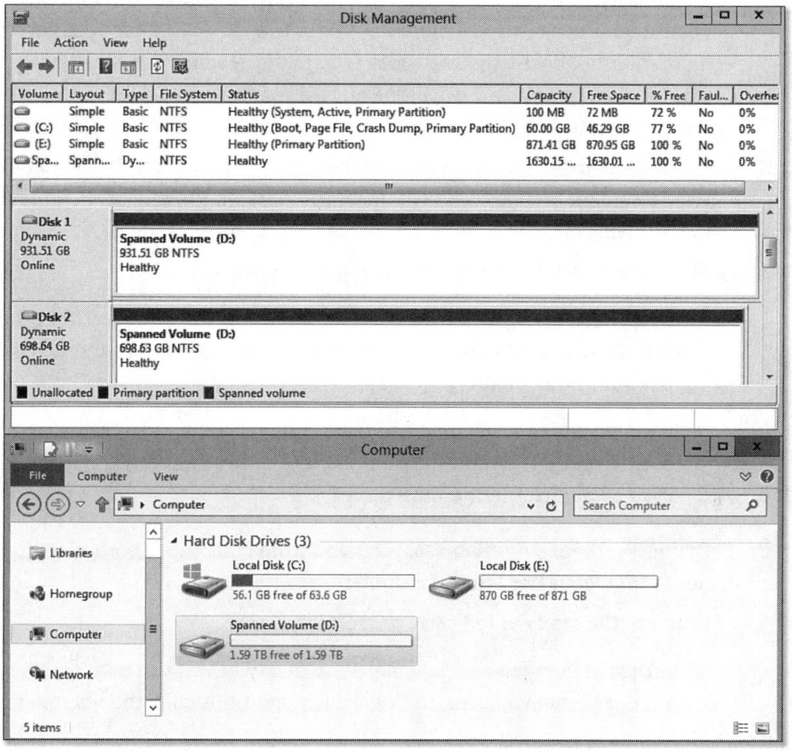

Adding Another Dynamic Disk to the Spanned Volume

If you add a new hard drive to your computer, you can add that drive to the spanned volume. Open the Disk Management snap-in and convert the new drive to a dynamic disk, as we described earlier. Now follow these steps to add the new dynamic disk to the spanned volume:

1. In the list of hard drives in the lower half of the Disk Management pane, right-click one of the disks in your current spanned volume. Be sure to right-click on the right of the drive display (where you see the spanned volume drive letter).

2. Click Extend Volume. Disk Management runs the Extend Volume Wizard.

3. Click Next. The Select Disks dialog box appears.

4. In the Available list, click the new dynamic disk and then click Add.

5. Click Next. The last wizard dialog box appears.

6. Click Finish. Disk Management adds the dynamic disk to the spanned volume.

Creating Mirrored Volumes

A spanned volume provides an easy way to set up a dynamic storage pool using multiple drives, which is great if you don't want your data needs being cramped by a single hard drive. However, what if your concerns are more about data resiliency? That is, if you want to minimize system downtime, then the best way to do that is to have a redundant set of data on another hard drive. That way, if the original hard drive goes down for the count, you can still keep the computer running off the redundant data on the other drives.

You can establish this data redundancy by setting up another volume as a mirror of the original. Windows 8 maintains exact copies of the data on the mirror drive, and if the original drive dies, the system will continue to function by using the mirrored data.

There are a couple of ways you can go about this:

- If you have a single hard drive and plan on leaving your system files and data on that drive, you can add a second hard drive of the same size (or larger) and use this new hard drive as a mirror for your original data.

- If you've added a second hard drive and are using it to store important data (such as ripped movies or recorded TV shows), you can add a third drive of the same size (or larger) and use this new drive as a mirror of the data drive.

Of course, there's nothing stopping you from combining both techniques, depending on your data needs (and your hard drive budget!).

Here are the steps to follow to mirror a volume:

1. In Disk Management, make sure the disk you want to use for the mirror has no current volumes. If it does have volumes, then for each one right-click the volume and click Delete Volume.

2. In the list of volumes in the lower half of the Disk Management window, right-click the volume you want to mirror and then click Add Mirror. The Add Mirror dialog box appears.

3. Click the disk you want to use for the mirror and then click Add Mirror. Disk Management warns you that the disk to be mirrored must be converted to a dynamic disk and asks you to confirm this conversion.

4. Click Yes. Disk Management converts the disk to dynamic and then starts mirroring the volume to the other hard drive.

5. Repeat steps 2–4 for any other volumes you also want to mirror. Figure 25.21 shows the Disk Management snap-in with two mirrors: on Disk 0, drives C and E are being mirrored to same-sized volumes on Disk 1. The original sync might take as little as a few minutes or as much as tens of hours, depending on how much data is to be mirrored.

Figure 25.21
Disk Management showing mirrors for drives C and E.

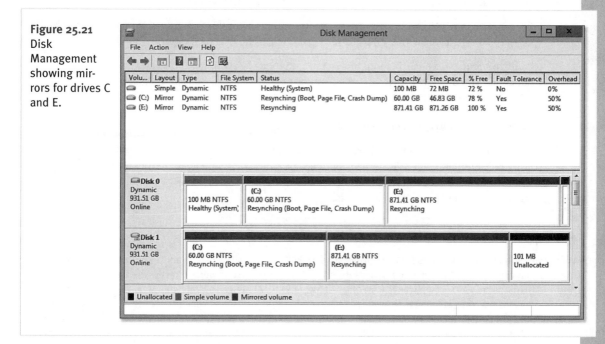

Creating a RAID 5 Volume

So far you've seen that you can mimic an expandable storage pool by creating a spanned volume that stores data in a single storage area that encompasses two or more hard drives (see "Creating a Spanned Volume"). Similarly, you saw that you can add resiliency by creating mirrored volumes that store each file and folder on two or more hard drives (see "Creating Mirrored Volumes"). These easy-to-implement techniques can be really useful, depending on your data and safety needs.

However, we want to show you a third technique that combines spanning and mirroring, and also includes a bit of load balancing (writing to a second hard drive if one hard drive is busy). This is called RAID 5, and it has the following characteristics:

- **Three drive minimum**—To implement a RAID 5 volume, you require at least three empty drives.

- **Expandable storage pool**—A RAID volume is expandable, so you can add more drives to increase the size of the storage pool. In a three-drive RAID setup, the total available storage space in the volume will be twice the size of the smallest drive, in a four-drive setup it will be three times the smallest drive, and so on. Therefore, it's best to use drives that are the same size to maximize the available storage area.

- **Data protection**—One of the RAID drives is used as a so-called *parity volume*, which monitors data integrity to prevent data corruption.

- **Data redundancy**—The other RAID drives are used to store data, with each file and folder being stored multiple times. This means that if one of the data drives fails, you don't lose any data.

- **Load balancing**—RAID monitors drive activity, and if one of the data drives is busy reading or writing data, RAID uses the other drive to perform the current read or write operation.

- **Fault tolerance**—In a RAID setup, if any hard drive goes down, the entire array remains operational and you don't lose any data. However, it's always best to replace the faulty drive as soon as possible, because if a second drive goes down, you lose everything.

Are there negatives to consider? Yes, as usual:

- **Slow**—The type of RAID we're talking about here is called *software RAID* because the entire array is maintained and utilized by a software program. Software is inherently slower than hardware, so you might see quite a performance drop when you use a RAID volume, particularly for streaming media files and similar tasks.

🌐 tip

What's the solution to slow software RAID? Speedy hardware RAID! This means that you add a RAID-dedicated hardware device to your computer, and that device manages the array. Because the device works directly with the drives (bypassing the CPU), hardware RAID is many times faster than software RAID. Although several types of hardware RAID are available, the most common solution is to insert a RAID controller card inside your computer. These cards usually come with multiple SATA ports (usually two, four, or eight) and you attach your hard drives directly to these controller card ports instead of the motherboard SATA ports. When you start your computer, you see an option to invoke the controller card setup routine, which enables you to choose the disks you want in the array and what type of RAID level you prefer.

- **Expensive**—Because RAID 5 requires a minimum of three hard drives, it can get quite expensive.

With all that in mind, if you want to implement a RAID 5 volume on your computer, follow these steps to set it up:

1. In the list of hard drives in the lower half of the Disk Management pane, right-click one of the drives you want to include in the RAID 5 volume and then click New RAID-5 Volume. Disk Management runs the New RAID-5 Volume Wizard.

2. Click Next. The Select Disks dialog box appears.

3. In the Available list, click a disk you want to include in the volume and then click Add.

4. Repeat step 3 to add any other drives you want to include in the volume. Figure 25.22 shows a RAID 5 volume with three disks added (the minimum).

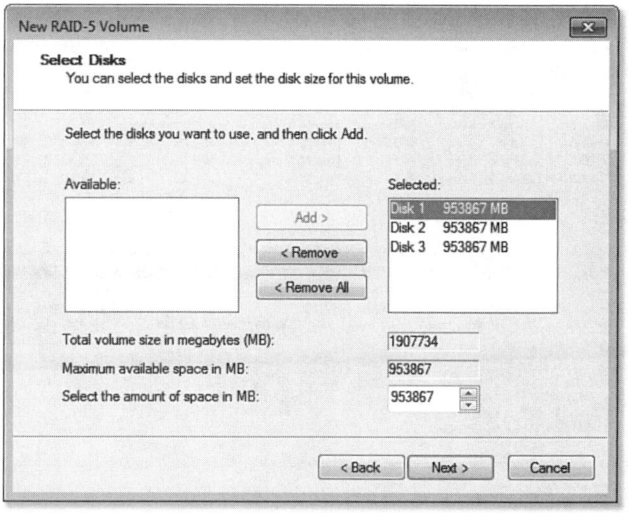

Figure 25.22
You must add at least three disks to the RAID 5 volume.

5. Click Next. The Assign Drive Letter or Path dialog box appears.

6. Choose a drive letter and then click Next. The Format Volume dialog box appears.

7. Assign a volume label, if needed, leave the other options "as is," and then click Next. The last wizard dialog box appears.

8. Click Finish. Disk Management warns you that it must convert the disks to dynamic disks and asks you to confirm.

9. Click Yes. Disk Management creates the RAID 5 volume.

Figure 25.23 shows how the new RAID 5 volume (drive R, in this case, combining Disk 1, Disk 2, and Disk 3) appears in Disk Management.

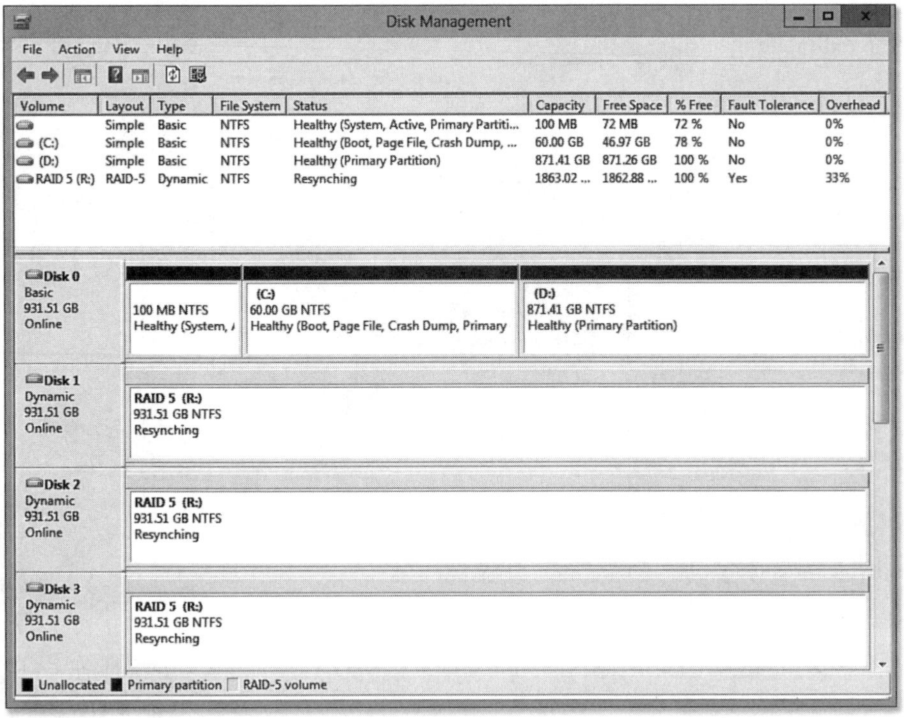

Figure 25.23
The new RAID 5 volume shown in the Disk Management snap-in.

Working with Disk Files

All the Windows 8 press focuses on the new interface and apps, but Windows 8 implements a few other new features that should have all power users leaping with joy. The ability to implement storage spaces (described earlier) is one, and the other is the ability to work directly with disk files, specifically disc images and virtual hard disks. The rest of this chapter takes you through these new and very welcome features.

Mounting an ISO File

Working with optical (CD or DVD) data discs is a bit of a hassle because you have to insert the disc and then wait for Windows 8 to recognize and mount the disc. An optical disc drive is also much slower than your hard drive, so working with disc files can be time-consuming.

You can work around all of these problems by using a *disc image*, instead, which is a precise copy of the contents of an optical disc, including the disc's file system. A disc image is an ISO (International Organization for Standardization) file that uses the .iso file extension.

When would you ever deal with such a file? They're actually becoming increasingly common. For example, some backup applications use ISO files as their archival format, and there are plenty of programs that are now distributed in the ISO format.

In Windows 7 and earlier versions of Windows, you needed a third-party program to view an ISO file or work with its contents. Most of these programs would just burn the ISO file to an optical disc, which just brings us back to the original problems inherent in using discs. Windows 8 changes all that by incorporating support for ISO files right into File Explorer. This means that you no longer need a third-party program to view and work with the contents of an ISO file. Instead, you can use File Explorer to directly mount the ISO as a virtual optical drive.

One consequence of this built-in ISO support is that you don't need to keep copies of your optical discs lying around. Instead, you can convert those discs to ISO files and then store them on your hard drive for easier and faster access.

Follow these steps to mount an ISO file:

1. In File Explorer, open the folder that contains the ISO file you want to mount.

2. Select the ISO file.

3. In the Actions tab, click Mount. Windows 8 creates a virtual disc drive for the ISO and displays the contents of the disc image, as shown in Figure 25.24.

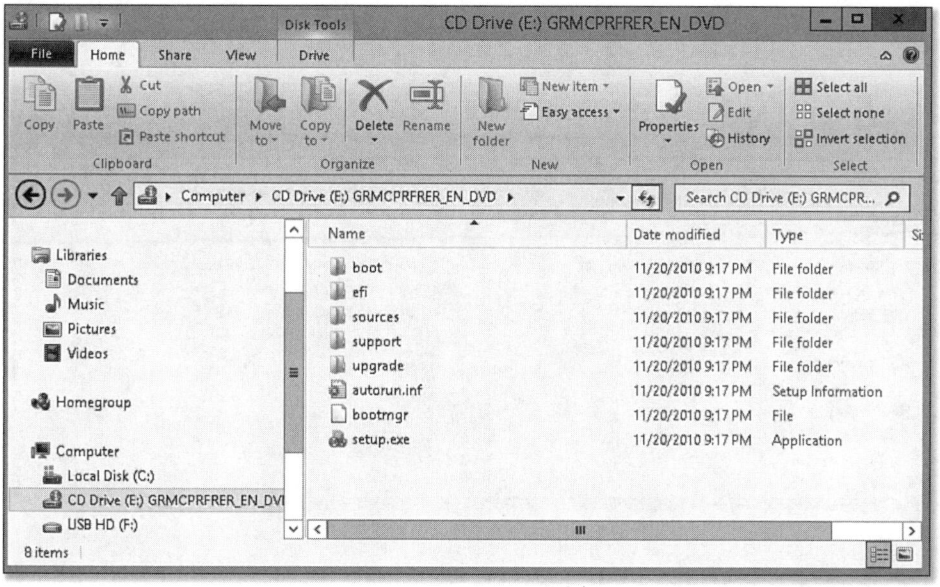

> **🔍 note**
>
> Unfortunately, File Explorer doesn't come with a feature that enables you to convert optical discs to the ISO format. However, there are third-party utilities available that can do this. Our favorite example is Free ISO Creator, which you can download from www.freeisocreator.com.

Figure 25.24 In Windows 8, Explorer lets you mount and work with ISO files directly.

Mounting a Virtual Hard Disk

In the same way that an ISO disk image file is an exact replica of an optical disc, a *virtual hard disk (VHD)* is a disk image that is an exact replica of a physical hard disk, including the file system and the hard disk's volumes, folders, and files. A virtual hard disk is stored as a VHD file that uses the .vhd file extension.

Why would you need such a thing? The most common use by far for VHDs is the hard disk for a virtual machine, especially one created using Microsoft's Hyper-V virtual machine manager.

Windows 8 bakes support for VHD files right into File Explorer, so you can easily view the contents of and copy data from a VHD file without third-party software. File Explorer accomplishes this by enabling you to mount a VHD as a virtual hard disk on your PC.

Follow these steps to mount a virtual hard disk:

1. In File Explorer, open the folder that contains the VHD file you want to mount.

2. Select the VHD file.

3. Click the Actions tab and then click Mount. Windows 8 creates a virtual hard disk for the VHD and displays the contents of the virtual hard disk, as shown in Figure 25.25.

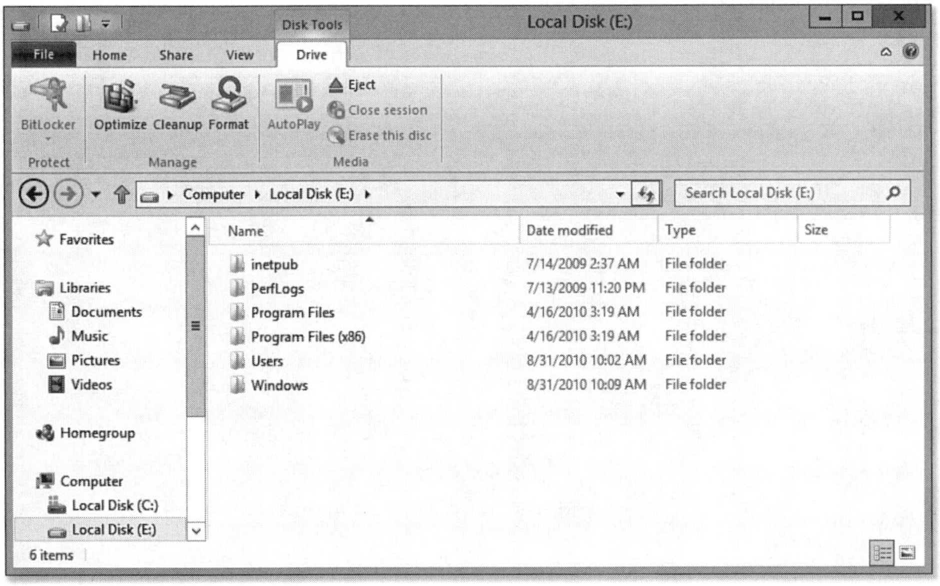

Figure 25.25
You can now use File Explorer to mount and work with virtual hard disk files.

Creating a Virtual Hard Disk

You might find that you have a need for another hard disk on your PC. For example, you might need a second drive to install another operating system and dual-boot between Windows 8 and the other OS. Or you just might want the drive to store personal files. However, what happens if your PC has no open ports for an external hard disk, and you don't have the expertise or a free drive bay to install an internal hard disk? What if you simply don't want to shell out the bucks for a new hard disk?

In all these cases, you can bypass the need for a physical hard disk by creating a virtual hard disk, instead. Windows 8 treats the VHD exactly like a physical hard disk, so whatever operations you can perform on a physical disk you can do with a virtual one. You can also encrypt a VHD using BitLocker, so a VHD is a great way to store private or sensitive files.

Follow these steps to create a virtual hard disk:

1. In the Disk Management snap-in, select Action, Create VHD. Disk Management displays the Create and Attach Virtual Hard Disk dialog box.

2. Click Browse. The Browse Virtual Disk Files dialog box appears.

3. Choose the folder you want to use to store the VHD, type a name for the VHD, and then click Save.

4. Specify the size of the VHD (in MB, GB, or TB).

5. Select the Virtual Hard Disk Format you want to use:

   - **VHD**—This format is supported by earlier versions of Windows, but can only create disks up to 2TB.

   - **VHDX**—This format is only supported by Windows 8, but it can create disks up to 16TB and is less prone to file corruption in the event of a power failure.

6. Choose Fixed Size.

7. Click OK. Disk Management creates the virtual hard disk.

Your VHD is now created, but you can't use it yet because it hasn't been configured to store files. This means that you now need to initialize the VHD and add a new simple volume to the disk. To do this, first locate the new VHD in the bottom section of the Disk Management window, right-click the VHD on the left side of the window, and then select Initialize Disk. Activate the MBR option and select OK. Now follow the instructions given earlier in this chapter to create a new simple volume on the VHD (see "Dividing Your Hard Drive into Two Volumes").

TROUBLESHOOTING AND REPAIRING PROBLEMS

A long time ago, somebody proved mathematically that it was impossible to make any reasonably complex software program problem-free. As the number of variables increase, as the interactions of subroutines and objects become more complex, and as the underlying logic of a program grows beyond the ability of a single person to grasp all at once, errors inevitably creep into the code. Given Windows 8's status as possibly the most complex software ever created, the bad news is that there are certainly problems lurking in the weeds. However, the good news is that the overwhelming majority of these problems are extremely obscure and appear only under the rarest circumstances.

This doesn't mean that you're guaranteed a glitch-free computing experience—far from it. Third-party programs and devices cause the majority of computer woes, either because they have inherent problems themselves or because they don't get along well with Windows 8. Using software, devices, and device drivers designed for Windows 8 can help tremendously, as can the maintenance program we outline in the rest of the chapters here in Part VI. But computer problems, like the proverbial death and taxes, are certainties in life, so you need to know how to troubleshoot and resolve the problems that will inevitably come your way. In this chapter, we help you do just that by showing you our favorite techniques for determining problem sources, and by taking you through all of Windows 8's recovery tools.

Troubleshooting Strategies: Determining the Source of a Problem

One of the ongoing mysteries that all Windows users experience at one time or another is what might be called the "now you see it, now you don't" problem. This is a glitch that plagues you for a while and then mysteriously vanishes without any intervention on your part. (This also tends to occur when you ask a nearby user or someone from the IT department to look at the problem. Like the automotive problem that goes away when you take the car to a mechanic, computer problems will often resolve themselves as soon as a knowledgeable user sits down at the keyboard.) When this happens, most people just shake their heads and resume working, grateful to no longer have to deal with the problem.

Unfortunately, most computer ills aren't resolved so easily. For these more intractable problems, your first order of business is to hunt down the source of the glitch. This is, at best, a black art, but it can be done if you take a systematic approach. Over the years, we've found that the best approach is to ask a series of questions designed to gather the required information or to narrow down what might be the culprit. The next few sections take you through these questions.

Did You Get an Error Message?

Unfortunately, most computer error messages are obscure and do little to help you resolve a problem directly. However, error codes and error text can help you down the road, either by giving you something to search for in an online database or by providing information to a tech support person. Therefore, you should always write down the full text of any error message that appears.

> **tip**
>
> If the error message is lengthy and you can still use other programs on your computer, don't bother writing down the full message. Instead, while the message is displayed, press Windows Logo+Print Screen to place an image of the current screen as a PNG file in your Pictures library.

Does an Error or Warning Appear in the Event Viewer Logs?

Launch the Event Viewer (press Windows Logo+W, type **event**, and then click View Event Logs), open the Windows Logs branch, and then examine the Application and System logs. In particular, look in the Level column for Error or Warning events. If you see any, double-click each one to read the event description. Figure 26.1 shows an example. Again, although the information here is obscure, the error code and error text gives you something to search for in an online database or to give to a tech support person.

> **tip**
>
> If the error message appears before Windows 8 starts, but you don't have time to write it down, press the Pause Break key to pause the startup. After you record the error, press Ctrl+Pause Break to resume the startup.

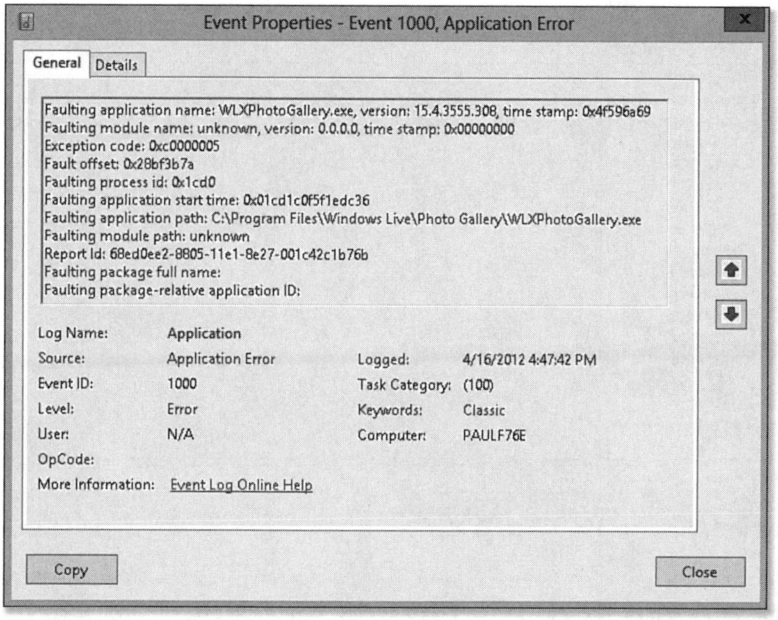

Figure 26.1
In the Event Viewer, look for Error and Warning events in the Application and System logs.

Event Properties - Event 1000, Application Error

General | Details

Faulting application name: WLXPhotoGallery.exe, version: 15.4.3555.308, time stamp: 0x4f596a69
Faulting module name: unknown, version: 0.0.0.0, time stamp: 0x00000000
Exception code: 0xc0000005
Fault offset: 0x28bf3b7a
Faulting process id: 0x1cd0
Faulting application start time: 0x01cd1c0f5f1edc36
Faulting application path: C:\Program Files\Windows Live\Photo Gallery\WLXPhotoGallery.exe
Faulting module path: unknown
Report Id: 68ed0ee2-8805-11e1-8e27-001c42c1b76b
Faulting package full name:
Faulting package-relative application ID:

Log Name:	Application
Source:	Application Error
Event ID:	1000
Level:	Error
User:	N/A
OpCode:	
More Information:	Event Log Online Help

Logged:	4/16/2012 4:47:42 PM
Task Category:	(100)
Keywords:	Classic
Computer:	PAULF76E

Copy | Close

Does an Error Appear in System Information?

In the Start screen, type **msinfo32** and then press Enter to launch the System Information utility. In the Hardware Resources branch, click the Conflicts/Sharing sub-branch for device conflicts. Also, see whether the Components/Problem Devices category lists any devices, as shown in Figure 26.2. Make note of any errors, and then either search for the error online or contact tech support and provide the engineer with the information.

Did You Recently Edit the Registry?

Improper Registry modifications can cause all kinds of mischief. If the problem occurred after editing the Registry, try restoring the changed key or setting. Ideally, if you exported a backup of the offending key, you should import the backup. We show you how to back up the Registry in Chapter 29, "Editing the Windows Registry."

 To learn how to back up a Registry key, **see** *"Backing Up the Registry Editor,"* **p. 697**.

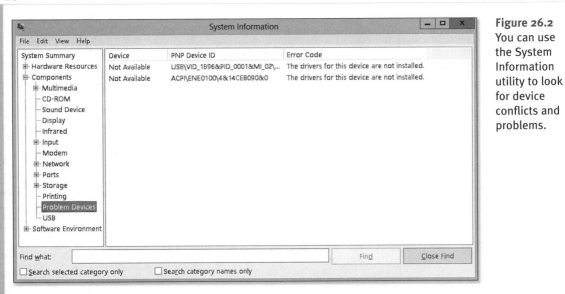

Figure 26.2
You can use the System Information utility to look for device conflicts and problems.

Did You Recently Change Any Windows Settings?

If the problem started after you changed your Windows configuration, try reversing the change. Even something as seemingly innocent as activating a screensaver can cause problems, so don't rule anything out. If you've made a number of recent changes and you're not sure about everything you did, or if it would take too long to reverse all the changes individually, use System Restore to revert your system to the most recent checkpoint before you made the changes. See "Recovering Using System Restore," later in this chapter.

Did Windows 8 "Spontaneously" Reboot?

When certain errors occur, Windows 8 will reboot itself. This apparently random behavior is actually built in to the system in the event of a system failure—also called a *stop error* or a *blue screen of death (BSOD)*. By default, Windows 8 writes an error event to the system log, dumps the contents of memory into a file, and then reboots the system. So, if your system reboots, check the Event Viewer to see what happened.

You can control how Windows 8 handles system failures by following these steps:

1. In the Start screen, press Windows Logo+W to open the Settings search pane, type **advanced system**, and then click View Advanced System Settings to open the System Properties dialog box with the Advanced tab displayed.

2. In the Startup and Recovery group, click Settings. Figure 26.3 shows the Startup and Recovery dialog box that appears.

Figure 26.3
Use the Startup and Recovery dialog box to configure how Windows 8 handles system failures.

Startup and Recovery

System startup

Default operating system:
Windows 8

☑ Time to display list of operating systems: 30   seconds
☐ Time to display recovery options when needed: 30   seconds

System failure
☑ Write an event to the system log
☑ Automatically restart
Write debugging information

Automatic memory dump

Dump file:
%SystemRoot%\MEMORY.DMP
☑ Overwrite any existing file

OK   Cancel

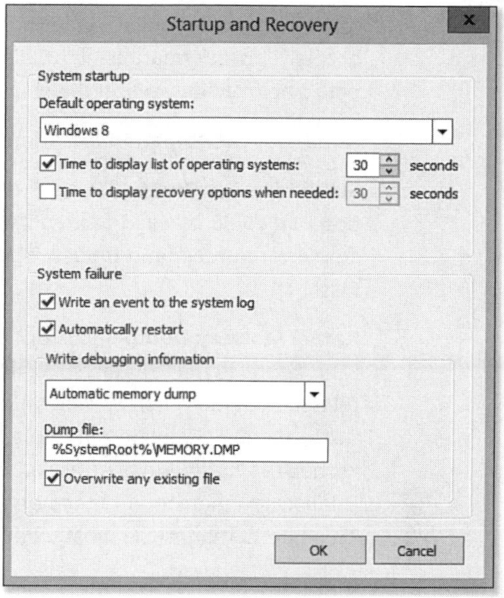

3. Configure how Windows 8 handles system failures using the following controls in the System Failure group:

   ■ **Write an Event to the System Log**—Leave this check box activated to have the system failure recorded in the system log. This enables you to view the event in the Event Viewer.

   ■ **Automatically Restart**—This is the option that, when activated, causes your system to reboot when a stop error occurs. Deactivate this check box if you want to avoid the reboot. This is useful if an error message appears briefly before Windows 8 reboots. By disabling the automatic restart, you give yourself time to read and write down the error message.

⦿ tip

If the BSOD problem occurs during startup, your computer winds up in an endless loop: you reboot, the problem occurs, the BSOD appears, and then your computer reboots. Unfortunately, the BSOD appears only fleetingly, so you never have enough time to read (much less record) the error message. If this happens, display the Advanced Startup Options menu (see "Navigating the Recovery Environment," later in this chapter) and then select the Disable Automatic Restart on System Failure item. This tells Windows 8 not to reboot after the BSOD appears, so you can then write down the error message and, hopefully, successfully troubleshoot the problem.

- **Write Debugging Information**—This list determines what information Windows 8 saves to disk (in the folder specified in the Dump file text box below the list) when a system failure occurs. This information—it's called a *memory dump*—contains data that can help a tech support employee determine the cause of the problem. You have five choices:

  None—No debugging information is written.

  Small Memory Dump (256 KB)—This option writes the minimum amount of useful information that could be used to identify what caused the stop error. This 256KB file includes the stop error number and its description, the list of running device drivers, and the processor state.

  Kernel Memory Dump—This option writes the contents of the kernel memory to the disk. (The *kernel* is the Windows 8 component that manages low-level functions for processor-related activities such as scheduling and dispatching threads, handling interrupts and exceptions, and synchronizing multiple processors.) This dump includes memory allocated to the kernel, the hardware abstraction layer, and the drivers and programs used by the kernel. Unallocated memory and memory allocated to user programs are not included in the dump. This information is the most useful for troubleshooting, so we recommend using this option.

  Complete Memory Dump—This option writes the entire contents of RAM to the disk.

  Automatic Memory Dump—This is usually the default option and it means that Windows 8 decides which of the preceding options to use when writing the debugging info. This is the way to go if you're not getting any debugging info written to the disk. Why would that happen? Windows 8 first writes the debugging information to the paging file—`Pagefile.sys` in the root folder of the `%SystemDrive%`. When you restart the computer, Windows 8 then transfers the information to the dump file. Therefore, you must have a large enough paging file to handle the memory dump. If not, you don't see the debugging data. The Automatic Memory Dump option can determine in advance whether there is enough room in the paging file and, if not, it will default to a smaller dump.

- **Overwrite Any Existing File**—When this option is activated, Windows 8 overwrites any existing dump file with the new dump information. If you deactivate this check box, Windows 8 creates a new dump file with each system failure. Note that this option is enabled only for the Kernel Memory Dump and the Complete Memory Dump (which by default write to the same file: `%SystemRoot%\Memory.dmp`).

4. Click OK in all the open dialog boxes to put the new settings into effect.

Did You Recently Change Any Application Settings?

If you've recently changed an application setting, try reversing the change to see whether doing so solves the problem. If that doesn't help, here are three other things to try:

- Check the developer's website to see whether an upgrade or patch is available.
- Run the application's Repair option (if it has one), which is often useful for fixing corrupted or missing files. To see whether a program has a Repair option, press Windows Logo+W, type **uninstall**, and then click Change or Remove a Program. In the Programs and Features window, click the problematic application and then look to see whether there is a Repair item in the taskbar (see Figure 26.4).
- Reinstall the program.

note
If a program freezes, you won't be able to shut it down using conventional methods. If you try, you might see a dialog box warning you that the program is not responding. If so, click End Now to force the program to close. If that doesn't work, right-click the taskbar and then click Task Manager. You should see your stuck application listed. Click the program and then click End Task.

Figure 26.4
In the Programs and Features window, click the program and look for a Repair option in the taskbar.

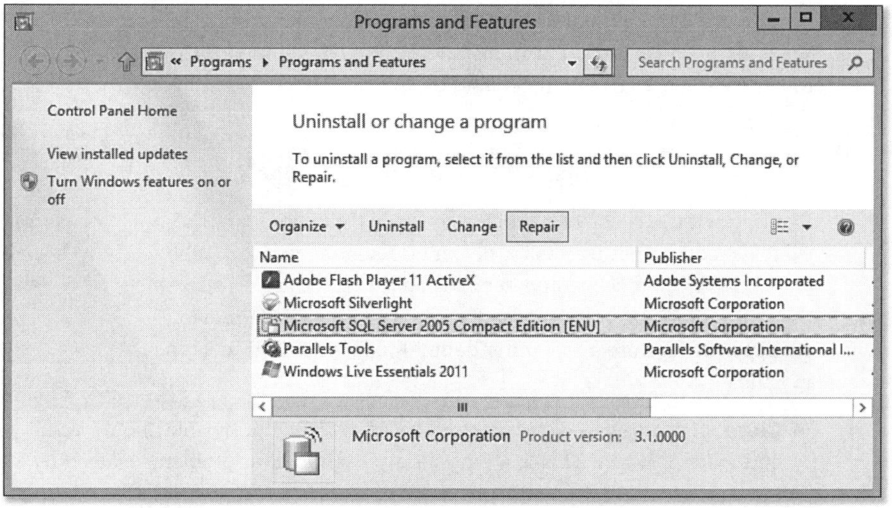
Programs and Features
« Programs ▸ Programs and Features
Search Programs and Features
Control Panel Home
View installed updates
Turn Windows features on or off
Uninstall or change a program
To uninstall a program, select it from the list and then click Uninstall, Change, or Repair.
Organize
Uninstall
Change
Repair
Name
Publisher
Adobe Flash Player 11 ActiveX
Adobe Systems Incorporated
Microsoft Silverlight
Microsoft Corporation
Microsoft SQL Server 2005 Compact Edition [ENU]
Microsoft Corporation
Parallels Tools
Parallels Software International I...
Windows Live Essentials 2011
Microsoft Corporation
Microsoft Corporation Product version: 3.1.0000

Did You Recently Install a New Program?

If you suspect a new program is causing system instability, restart Windows 8 and try operating the system for a while without using the new program. If the problem doesn't reoccur, the new program is likely the culprit. Try using the program without any other programs running.

You should also examine the program's readme file (if it has one) to look for known problems and possible workarounds. It's also a

tip
When a program crashes, Windows 8 displays a dialog box asking if you want to see whether a solution to the problem is available. You can control the behavior of this prompt. See "Checking for Solutions to Problems," later in this chapter.

good idea to check for a Windows 8–compatible version of the program. Again, you can also try the program's Repair option (if it has one) or you can reinstall the program.

Similarly, if you recently upgraded an existing program, try uninstalling the upgrade.

Did You Recently Install a New Device?

If you recently installed a new device or if you recently updated an existing device driver, the new device or driver might be causing the problem. Check Device Manager to see whether there's a problem with the device, as described later in this chapter (see "Troubleshooting Device Problems").

Did You Recently Apply an Update from Windows Update?

It's an unfortunate fact of life that occasionally updates designed to fix one problem end up causing another problem. Fortunately, Windows 8 lets you uninstall an update. Press Windows Logo+W to open the Settings search pane, type **installed**, and then click View Installed Updates. In the Installed Updates window, click the update you want to remove and then click Uninstall.

 tip

If you have Windows 8 set up to perform automatic updating, you can keep tabs on the changes made to your system by pressing Windows Logo+X, clicking Control Panel, and then selecting System and Security, Windows Update. Click the View Update History link to see a list of the installed updates, which includes the update's Name, Status (such as Successful), Importance (such as Important or Recommended), and Date Installed.

General Troubleshooting Tips

Figuring out the cause of a problem is often the hardest part of troubleshooting, but by itself it doesn't do you much good. When you know the source, you need to parlay that information into a fix for the problem. We discussed a few solutions in the previous section, but here are a few other general fixes you need to keep in mind:

- **Close all programs**—You can often fix flaky behavior by shutting down all your open programs and starting again. This is a particularly useful fix for problems caused by low memory or low system resources.

- **Log off Windows 8**—Logging off clears the RAM and thus gives you a slightly cleaner slate than merely closing all your programs.

- **Reboot the computer**—If there are problems with some system files and devices, logging off won't help because these objects remain loaded. By rebooting the system, you reload the entire system, which is often enough to solve many computer problems.

- **Turn off the computer and restart**—You can often solve a hardware problem by first shutting your machine off. Wait for 30 seconds to give all devices time to spin down, and then restart.

- **Check connections, power switches, and so on**—Some of the most common (and some of the most embarrassing) causes of hardware problems are the simple physical things. Therefore, make sure that a device is turned on, check that cable connections are secure, and ensure that insertable devices are properly connected.

More Troubleshooting Tools

Windows 8 comes with diagnostic tools—together, they're called the *Windows Diagnostic Infrastructure (WDI)*—that not only do a better job of finding the source of many common disk, memory, and network problems, but can detect impending failures and alert you to take corrective or mitigating action (such as backing up your files). The next few sections describe these tools.

Running the Windows 8 Troubleshooters

Windows Vista introduced the idea of the *troubleshooter*, a Help system component that offers a series of solutions that lead you deeper into a problem in an attempt to fix it. In Windows 7, the troubleshooters were beefed up and given their own home within the Control Panel interface, and that home remains in place in Windows 8. To see the Windows 8 troubleshooters, press Windows Logo+W, type **trouble**, and then choose Troubleshooting in the search results.

The Troubleshooting window (see Figure 26.5) is divided into several categories (Programs, Hardware and Sound, and so on), each of which offers a few links to general troubleshooting tasks. (If you see a message asking whether you want the most up-to-date troubleshooting content, be sure to click Yes.)

Figure 26.5
Windows 8's Troubleshooting window offers links to various troubleshooting categories and tasks.

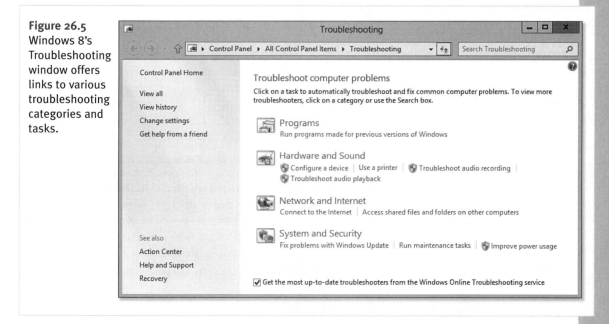

Note, too, the Get the Most Up-to-Date Troubleshooters check box at the bottom of the window. If you leave that option activated and then click a category, Windows 8 queries the Windows Online Troubleshooting service for the latest troubleshooting packs and then displays the complete list for that category. For example, Figure 26.6 shows the troubleshooters available for the Programs category as we wrote this chapter.

> **tip**
> If you want to see all the available troubleshooters, click the View All link in the Troubleshooting window.

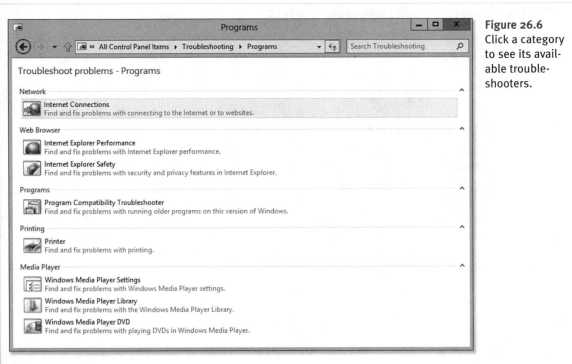

Figure 26.6
Click a category to see its available troubleshooters.

Running the Memory Diagnostics Tool

Few computer problems are as maddening as those related to physical memory defects because they tend to be intermittent and to cause problems in secondary systems, forcing you to waste time on wild goose chases all over your system.

Therefore, it is welcome news indeed that Windows 8 ships with a Windows Memory Diagnostics tool that works with Microsoft Online Crash Analysis to determine whether defective physical memory is the cause of program crashes. If so, Windows Memory Diagnostics lets you know about the problem and schedules a memory test for the next time you start your computer. If it detects actual problems, the system also marks the affected memory area as unusable to avoid future crashes.

Windows 8 also comes with a Memory Leak Diagnosis tool that's part of the Diagnostic Policy Service. If a program is leaking memory (using up increasing amounts of memory over time), this tool will diagnose the problem and take steps to fix it.

To run the Memory Diagnostics tool yourself, follow these steps:

1. Press Windows Logo+W, type **memory**, and then click Diagnose Your Computer's Memory Problems in the search results. The Windows Memory Diagnostic window appears, as shown in Figure 26.7.

Figure 26.7
Use the Windows Memory Diagnostic tool to check for memory problems.

2. Click one of the following options:

- **Restart Now and Check for Problems**—Click this option to force an immediate restart and schedule a memory test during startup. Be sure to save your work before clicking this option.

- **Check for Problems the Next Time I Start My Computer**—Click this option to schedule a memory test to run the next time you boot.

After the test runs (it takes 10 or 15 minutes, depending on how much RAM is in your system), Windows 8 restarts and you see (for a short time) the Windows Memory Diagnostic icon in the taskbar's notification area. This icon displays a notification that shows the results of the memory test.

Checking for Solutions to Problems

Microsoft constantly collects information about Windows 8 from users. When a problem occurs, Windows 8 usually asks whether you want to send information about the problem to Microsoft and, if you do, it stores these tidbits in a massive database. Engineers then tackle the "issues" (as they euphemistically call them) and hopefully come up with solutions.

One of Windows 8's most promising features is called Problem Reporting, and it's designed to make solutions available to anyone who goes looking for them. Windows 8 keeps a list of problems your computer is having, so you can tell it to go online and see whether a solution is available. If there's a solution waiting, Windows 8 will download it, install it, and fix your system.

Here are the steps to follow to check for solutions to problems:

1. Press Windows Logo+W, type **action**, and then click Action Center in the results. The Action Center window appears.

2. In the Maintenance section, click Check for Solutions. Windows 8 begins checking for solutions.

3. If you see a dialog box asking whether you want to send more information about your problems, you can click View Problem Details to see information about the problems, as shown in Figure 26.8. When you're ready to move on, click Send Information.

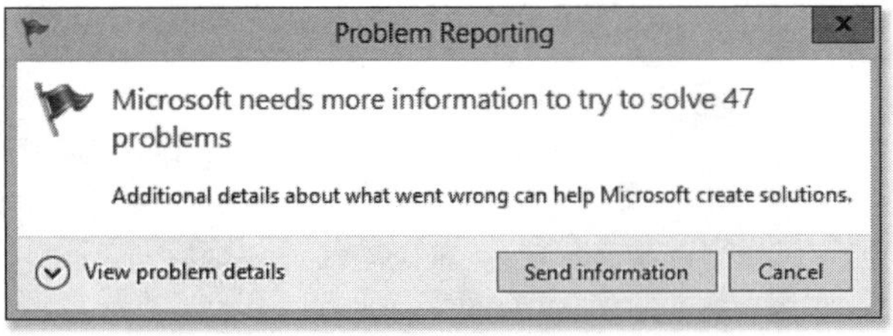

Figure 26.8
If Windows 8 tells you it needs more information, click View Problem Details to see the problems.

4. If a solution exists for your computer, you see it listed in the Maintenance section of the Action Center window. Click the solution to install it.

By default, when a problem occurs, Windows 8 does two things:

- It automatically checks for a solution to the problem.

- It asks whether you want to send more information about the problem to Microsoft.

You can control this behavior by configuring a few settings:

1. In the Action Center's Maintenance section, click Settings. The Problem Reporting Settings window appears.

2. Click Change Report Settings for All Users. The Problem Reporting dialog box appears, shown in Figure 26.9.

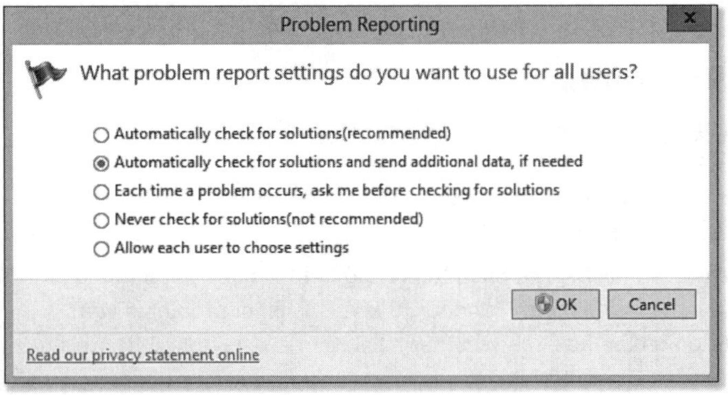

Figure 26.9
Use the Problem Reporting dialog box to configure the Problem Reporting feature.

3. To configure problem reporting, click one of the following options:

- **Automatically Check for Solutions**—Activate this option (it's the default) to have Windows 8 automatically check online for an existing solution to a problem.

- **Automatically Check for Solutions and Send Additional Data, If Needed**—Activate this option to have Windows 8 automatically check online for an existing solution to a problem and to automatically send extra information about the problem.

- **Each Time a Problem Occurs, Ask Me Before Checking for Solutions**—Activate this option to have Windows 8 prompt you to check for solutions and to send additional information about the problem.

- **Never Check for Solutions**—Activate this option if you don't want to report problems at all.

- **Allow Each User to Choose Settings**—Activate this option if your PC has multiple users and you prefer that each user to choose his or her own reporting options.

4. Click OK to put the new settings into effect.

Troubleshooting Startup

Computers are often frustrating beasts, but few things in computerdom are as maddening as a computer that won't compute, or an operating system that won't operate. After all, if your PC won't even start Windows, then Windows can't start any programs, which means *you* can't get any work done.

What you've got on your hands is a rather expensive boat anchor, not to mention a hair-pullingly, teeth-gnashingly frustrating problem that you have to fix *now*. To help save some wear and tear on your hair and teeth, this chapter outlines a few common startup difficulties and their solutions.

Some Things to Try Before Anything Else

Startup problems generally are either trivially easy to fix or are take-it-to-the-repair-shop difficult to solve. Fortunately, startup conundrums often fall into the former camp, and in many cases one of the following solutions will get your PC back on its electronic feet:

- Some boot problems mercifully fall into the Temporary Glitch category of startup woes. That is, it could be that your PC has just gone momentarily and temporarily haywire. To find out, shut down the computer and leave it turned off for at least 30 seconds to give everything time to spin down. Turn your PC back on and cross whatever parts of your body you think might help.

- There may be a setting in your computer's BIOS options that's preventing a normal startup. For example, one of us once had a PC that wouldn't boot no matter what we did. When we decided to check the BIOS, we found that the hard drive wasn't listed as the boot device! When we configured the BIOS to boot from the hard drive, all was well. Restart your PC and then press whatever key or key combination your BIOS requires to access the settings (usually the Delete key or a function key such as F2). If you don't see anything obvious (such as miscon-figured boot options), try resetting all the options to the default state.

- Every now and then a defective device will interfere with the boot process. To ensure that this isn't the case, disconnect

> **⚑ caution**
> Whatever you do, resist the temptation to fiddle with the BIOS settings willy-nilly. If you're not sure what a setting is used for, don't mess with it. If you have Internet access through another computer or device, you might be able to find an online reference for your PC's BIOS, which will let you know what each setting does.

every device that's disconnectable and then try booting your newly naked PC. If you get a successful launch, one of the devices was almost certainly the culprit. Attach the devices one by one and try rebooting each time until you find out which one is causing the boot failure. You could then reboot without the device, upgrade the device driver, and try again. If that still doesn't work, the device is probably defective and should be repaired or replaced.

- If you get no power when you flick your desktop PC's On switch, it's likely you've either got a defective power supply on your hands or one or more of the power supply connections have come loose. Check the connections or, if they're fine, replace the power supply. If nothing happens when you try to turn on your notebook or tablet PC, you might be looking at a drained battery. Connect the machine to a power source and try again.

Disabling Startup Programs

If you're having trouble getting Windows 8 off the ground, a program that launches during the system startup may be the culprit. How do you know which programs run at startup? You can find out by opening Task Manager (either press Windows Logo+X or right-click the taskbar, and then click Task Manager) and selecting the Startup tab (see Figure 26.10).

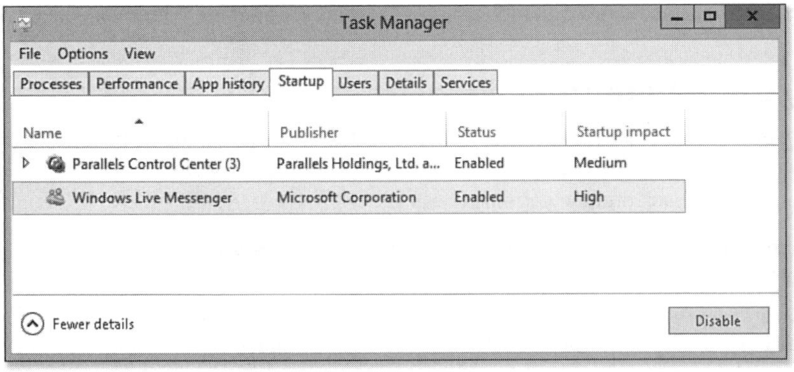

Figure 26.10
Task Manager's Startup tab lists the programs that launch during the Windows 8 startup.

This list comes from the Registry, and typically the settings are stored in the following keys:

```
HKEY_CURRENT_USER\SOFTWARE\Microsoft\Windows\CurrentVersion\Run
HKEY_LOCAL_MACHINE\SOFTWARE\Microsoft\Windows\CurrentVersion\Run
```

To find out whether one of the programs is causing Windows 8 to misfire at startup, disable the startup programs one by one (or use the method shown in the "Troubleshooting by Halves" sidebar later in this chapter) to see whether that solves the problem. To disable a startup program, click it and then click Disable.

Disabling Startup Services

If Windows 8 won't start, troubleshooting the problem usually involves trying various advanced startup options. It's almost always a time-consuming and tedious business.

However, what if Windows 8 *will* start, but you encounter problems along the way? Or what if you want to try a few different configurations to see whether you can eliminate startup items or improve Windows 8's overall performance? For these scenarios, don't bother trying out different startup configurations by hand. Instead, take advantage of Windows 8's System Configuration utility, which gives you a graphical frontend that offers precise control over how Windows 8 starts.

Launch the System Configuration utility (in the Start screen, type **msconfig** and press Enter) and display the General tab, which has three startup options:

- **Normal Startup**—This option loads Windows 8 normally.

- **Diagnostic Startup**—This option loads only those device drivers and system services that are necessary for Windows 8 to boot. This is equivalent to deactivating all the check boxes associated with the Selective Startup option, discussed next.

- **Selective Startup**—When you activate this option, the following check boxes become available (see Figure 26.11): Load System Services, Load Startup Items, and Use Original Boot Configuration. From the previous section, you already know how to work with startup items, so here our only concern is system services. The Load System Services category refers to the system services that Windows 8 loads at startup. The specific services loaded by Windows 8 are listed in the Services tab.

> **note**
>
> A *service* is a program or process that performs a specific, low-level support function for the operating system or for an installed program. For example, Windows 8's Automatic Updates feature is a service.

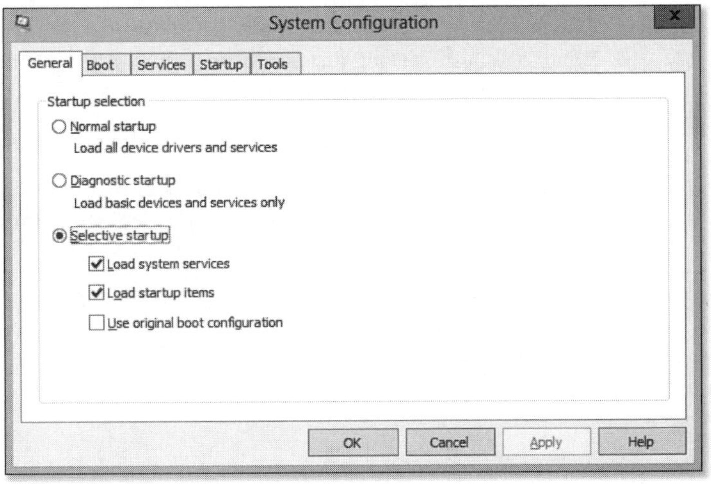

You use these check boxes to select which portions of the startup should be processed.

Figure 26.11
Use the System Configuration utility's General tab to troubleshoot the Windows 8 startup.

To control startup services, the System Configuration utility gives you two choices:

- To prevent Windows 8 from loading every nonessential service, activate Selective Startup in the General tab and then deactivate the Load System Services check box. Click OK.

- To prevent Windows 8 from loading only specific services, display the Services tab and then deactivate the check box beside the service or services you want to bypass at startup. Click OK.

A Startup Troubleshooting Procedure

Now that you know how to disable startup items and services, here's a basic procedure you can follow to use Task Manager and System Configuration to troubleshoot a startup problem:

1. In System Configuration, activate the Diagnostic Startup option, and then reboot the computer. If the problem did not occur during the restart, you know the cause lies in the system services or the startup items.

2. In System Configuration, activate the Selective Startup option.

3. In System Configuration, activate Load System Services; in Task Manager, disable all the startup programs; reboot the computer.

4. In System Configuration, deactivate Load System Services; in Task Manager enable all the startup programs; reboot the computer.

5. The problem will reoccur either during the step 3 reboot or the step 4 reboot. When this happens, you know that whatever category (services or programs) you enabled before rebooting is the source of the problem:

   - If the problem reoccurred after you activated the Load System Services check box, run System Configuration and select the Services tab.

   - If the problem reoccurred after you enabled the startup programs, run Task Manager and select the Startup tab.

6. If you're in System Configuration, click Disable All to clear all the check boxes; if you're in Task Manager, disable all the programs.

7. Activate one of the services or enable one of the programs and then reboot the computer.

8. Repeat step 7 for each of the other services or programs until the problem reoccurs. When this happens, you know that whatever item you activated or enabled just before rebooting is the source of the problem.

9. In the System Configuration utility's General tab, activate the Normal Startup option.

Troubleshooting by Halves

If you have a large number of items to test (such as in the Services tab), activating one at a time and rebooting can become very tedious very fast. A faster method is to begin by activating the first half of the check boxes and reboot. One of two things will happen:

- **The problem doesn't reoccur**—This means that one of the items represented by the deactivated check boxes is the culprit. Clear all the check boxes, activate half of the other check boxes, and then reboot.

- **The problem reoccurs**—This means that one of the activated check boxes is the problem. Activate only half of those check boxes and reboot.

Keep halving the number of activated check boxes until you isolate the offending item.

10. Fix or work around the problem:

- If the problem is a system service, you can disable the service. Press Windows Logo+W, type **services**, and then click View Local Services. Double-click the problematic service to open its property sheet. In the Startup Type list, select Disabled and then click OK.

- If the problem is a Startup item, use Task Manager to disable it. If the item is a program, consider uninstalling or reinstalling the program.

Troubleshooting Device Problems

Windows 8 has excellent support for most newer devices, and most major hardware vendors have taken steps to update their devices and drivers to run properly with Windows 8. If you use only recent, Plug and Play–compliant devices that qualify for the Designed for Windows 8 logo, you should have a trouble-free computing experience (at least from a hardware perspective). Of course, putting *trouble-free* and *computing* next to each other is just asking for trouble. Hardware is not foolproof; far from it. Things still can, and will, go wrong, and when they do, you'll need to perform some kind of troubleshooting. (Assuming, of course, that the device doesn't have a physical fault that requires a trip to the repair shop.) Fortunately, Windows 8 also has some handy tools to help you both identify and rectify hardware ills.

Troubleshooting with Device Manager

Device Manager (press Windows Logo+X and then click Device Manager) not only provides you with a comprehensive summary of your system's hardware data, it also doubles as a decent troubleshooting tool. To see what I mean, check out the Device Manager window shown in Figure 26.12. See how the Other Devices branch has an Unknown Device item that has an exclamation mark superimposed on its icon? This tells you that there's a problem with the device.

If you double-click the problem device to open its properties, as shown in Figure 26.13, the Device Status area tells you a bit more about what's wrong. As you can see in Figure 26.13, the problem here is that the device drivers aren't installed. Device Manager usually offers a suggested remedy (such as the Update Driver button shown in Figure 26.13).

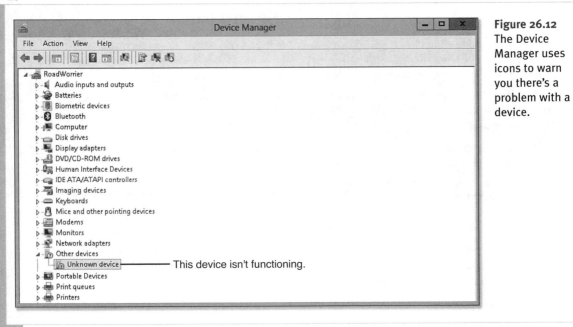

Figure 26.12
The Device Manager uses icons to warn you there's a problem with a device.

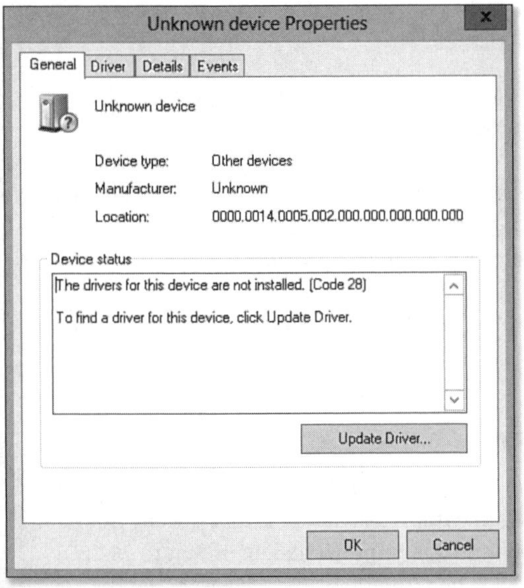

This device isn't functioning.

Figure 26.13
The Device Status area tells you if the device isn't working properly.

Device Manager uses three different icons to give you an indication of the device's current status:

- A black exclamation mark (!) on a yellow field tells you that there's a problem with the device.

- A red *X* tells you that the device is disabled or missing.

- A blue *i* on a white field tells you that the device's Use Automatic Settings check box (on the Resources tab) is deactivated and that at least one of the device's resources was selected manually. Note that the device might be working just fine, so this icon doesn't indicate a problem. If the device isn't working properly, however, the manual setting might be the cause. (For example, the device might have a DIP switch or jumper set to a different resource.)

If your system flags a device, but you don't notice any problems, you can usually get away with just ignoring the flag. I've seen lots of systems that run perfectly well with flagged devices, so this falls under the "If it ain't broke..." school of troubleshooting. The danger here is that tweaking your system to try and get rid of the flag can cause other—usually more serious—problems.

Troubleshooting Device Driver Problems

Other than problems with the hardware itself, device drivers are the cause of most device woes. This is true even if your device doesn't have one of the problem icons mentioned in the previous section. That is, if you open the device's properties sheet, Windows 8 may tell you that the device is "working properly," but all that means is that Windows 8 can establish a simple communications channel with the device. So if your device isn't working right, but Windows 8 says otherwise, suspect a driver problem. Here are a few tips and pointers for correcting device driver problems:

- **Reinstall the driver**—A driver might be malfunctioning because one or more of its files have become corrupted. You can usually solve this by reinstalling the driver. Just in case a disk fault caused the corruption, you should check the partition where the driver is installed for errors before reinstalling.

- **Upgrade to a signed driver**—Unsigned drivers—that is, device drivers that don't come with a signature from Microsoft that verifies the drivers are safe to install—are accidents waiting for a place to happen in Windows 8, so you should upgrade to a signed driver, if possible. How can you tell whether an installed driver is unsigned? Open the device's properties sheet and then display the Driver tab. Signed driver files display a name beside the Digital Signer label, whereas unsigned drivers display "Not digitally signed" instead.

- **Disable an unsigned driver**—If an unsigned driver is causing system instability and you can't upgrade the driver, try disabling it. In the Driver tab of the device's properties sheet, click Disable.

- **Use the Signature Verification tool**—This program checks your entire system for unsigned drivers. To use it, press Windows Logo+R, type **sigverif**, and click OK. In the File Signature Verification window, click Start. When the verification is complete, the program displays a list of the unsigned driver files (if any). The results for all the scanned files are written to the log file `Sigverif.txt`, which is copied to the `%SystemRoot%` folder when you close the window that shows the list of unsigned drivers. In the Status column of `Sigverif.txt`, look for files listed as "Not Signed." If you find any, consider upgrading these drivers to signed versions.

- **Try the manufacturer's driver supplied with the device**—If the device came with its own driver, either try updating the driver to the manufacturer's or try running the device's setup program.

- **Download the latest driver from the manufacturer**—Device manufacturers often update drivers to fix bugs, add new features, and tweak performance. Go to the manufacturer's website to see whether an updated driver is available.

- **Roll back a driver**—If the device stops working properly after you update the driver, try rolling it back to the old driver. (See the next section.)

Rolling Back a Device Driver

If an updated device driver is giving you problems, you have two ways to fix things:

- If updating the driver was the last action you performed on the system, restore the system to the most recent restore point.

- If you've updated other things on the system in the meantime, a restore point might restore more than you need. In that case, you need to roll back just the device driver that's causing problems.

Follow these steps to roll back a device driver:

1. Press Windows Logo+X and select Device Manager.

2. Double-click the device to open its Properties dialog box.

3. Display the Driver tab.

4. Click Roll Back Driver, and then click OK.

Recovering from a Problem

Ideally, solving a problem will require a specific tweak to the system: a Registry setting change, a driver upgrade, a program uninstall. But sometimes you need to take more of a "big picture" approach to revert your system to some previous state in the hope that you'll leap past the problem and get your system working again. Fortunately, Windows 8 comes with a boatload of tools that can help in both scenarios, and we use the rest of this chapter to tell you about these tools.

Accessing the Recovery Environment

Windows 8 offers a revamped Recovery Environment (RE) that gives you a simple, easily navigated set of screens that offer a number of troubleshooting tools and utilities. In previous versions of Windows, you could access the advanced startup options by pressing F8 during startup (after your PC completed its Power-On Self Test). That no longer works, but Windows 8 offers many other ways to get to the RE and its advanced startup options:

- Use the PC Settings app from within Windows 8.

- Use the SHUTDOWN command from within Windows 8.

- Use the boot options screen if you dual-boot Windows 8 and another operating system.

- Boot to a recovery drive.

- Boot to a system repair disc.

- Boot to your Windows 8 installation media.

The next few sections discuss each method in more detail.

Accessing the RE via PC Settings

If you're having trouble with your PC, but you can still start Windows 8, then you can use the PC Settings app to access the RE. Follow these steps to boot to the RE using the PC Settings app within Windows 8:

1. Press Windows Logo+W to open the Settings search pane.

2. Type **advanced** and then click Advanced Startup Options in the search results. Windows 8 opens the PC Settings app and displays the General tab.

3. In the Advanced Startup section, click Restart Now. The Choose an Option screen appears, as shown in Figure 26.14.

4. Click Troubleshoot.

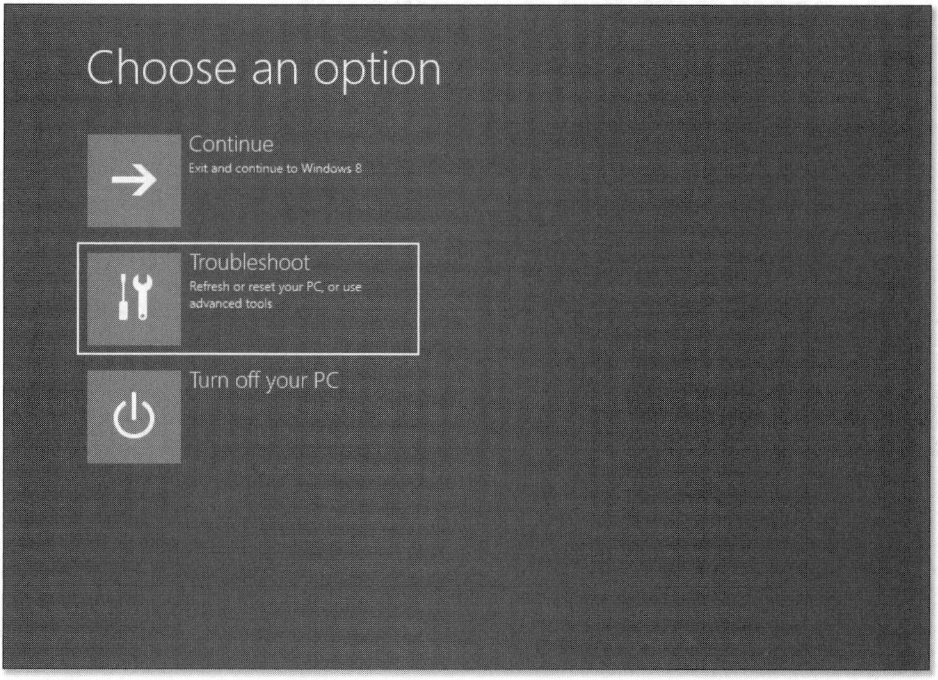

Figure 26.14 When you boot to the Choose an Option screen, click Troubleshoot to see the Recovery Environment tools.

Choose an option

→ Continue
Exit and continue to Windows 8

Troubleshoot
Refresh or reset your PC, or use advanced tools

⏻ Turn off your PC

Accessing the RE via the SHUTDOWN Command

Rather than access the RE via the convoluted PC Settings route, you can create a shortcut that runs the SHUTDOWN command-line utility with the /o switch, which restarts Windows 8 and automatically invokes the RE. Follow these steps to create the shortcut:

1. On the Start screen, click Desktop (or press Windows Logo+D).

2. Right-click the desktop and then select New, Shortcut. The Create Shortcut dialog box appears.

3. Enter the following in the Type the Location of the Item text box and press Enter:

   ```
   shutdown.exe /o /r /t 00
   ```

4. Type a name for the shortcut and click Finish.

5. Right-click the shortcut and click Properties.

6. Click Change Icon and then click OK when Windows 8 tells you the program contains no icons. Windows 8 displays the icons that come with the shell32.dll file.

7. Select an icon, click OK, and then click OK to close the Properties dialog box.

When you run this shortcut, Windows 8 reboots the system and you end up at the Choose an Option screen. Click Troubleshoot.

Accessing the RE via Boot Options

If you're having trouble starting Windows 8, but you still have access to your hard drive, you may be able to access the RE if you have already configured your system to dual-boot Windows 8 with another operating system.

 For information on setting up your system to dual-boot, **see** *"Dual-Booting Windows 8,"* **p. 42.**

If you dual-boot Windows 8 and other operating systems, follow these steps to boot to the RE:

1. Restart your computer. The Choose an Operating System screen appears.

2. Click Change Defaults or Choose Other Options. The Options screen appears.

3. Click Choose Other Options. The Choose an Option screen appears.

4. Click Troubleshoot.

Accessing the RE via a Recovery Drive

If you're having a problem with your system and are unable to start Windows 8 and can't even access your hard drive, you can still access a version of the RE if you created a recovery drive.

 To learn how to create a Windows 8 recovery drive, **see** *"Creating a Recovery Drive,"* **p. 768.**

Follow these steps to boot to the RE using the recovery drive:

1. Insert the recovery drive.

2. Restart your PC and boot to the USB flash drive:

   ■ If you have a newer PC that has a Unified Extensible Firmware Interface (UEFI), Windows 8 will recognize the flash drive automatically and display the Use a Device screen. Click your flash drive in the list that appears.

   ■ If you have an older PC that doesn't support UEFI, you will need to access your PC's BIOS settings and configure them to boot to the flash drive. Look for a message right after you turn on the PC that says something like "Press Del to access BIOS/Start settings." Press the key and then use the BIOS interface's boot options to configure your PC to boot to the USB flash drive.

3. Click a keyboard layout. The Choose an Option screen appears.

4. Click Troubleshoot.

Accessing the RE via a System Repair Disc

If some problem is preventing you from accessing Windows 8 and your hard drive, but you didn't create a recovery drive, you can still access the RE if you have a Windows 8 system repair disc.

  To learn how to create a system repair disc, **see** *"Creating a System Repair Disc,"* **p. 772.**

Follow these steps to boot to the RE using a system repair disc:

1. Insert the recovery drive.

2. Restart your PC and boot to the system repair disc. In most cases, wait until you see a message similar to "Press any key to boot from CD or DVD..." and then press a key.

3. Click a keyboard layout. The Choose an Option screen appears.

4. Click Troubleshoot.

Accessing the RE via Windows 8 Install Media

If you didn't create a recovery drive or a system repair disc, but you have your Windows 8 installation media, follow these steps to boot to the RE using the install media:

1. Insert your Windows 8 install media.

2. Restart your PC and boot to the install drive.

3. When the Windows Setup dialog box appears, click Next.

4. Click Repair Your Computer. The Choose an Option screen appears.

5. Click Troubleshoot.

tip

If your system won't boot from the Windows 8 install media (or the system repair disc), you need to adjust the system's BIOS settings to allow this. Restart the computer and look for a startup message that prompts you to press a key or key combination to modify the BIOS settings (which might be called *Setup* or something similar). Find the boot options and either enable a media drive–based boot or make sure that the option to boot from the media drive comes before the option to boot from the hard disk. If you use a USB keyboard, you may also need to enable an option that lets the BIOS recognize keystrokes after the POST but before the OS starts.

Navigating the Recovery Environment

In the previous few sections, each procedure dropped you off at the Troubleshoot screen, shown in Figure 26.15.

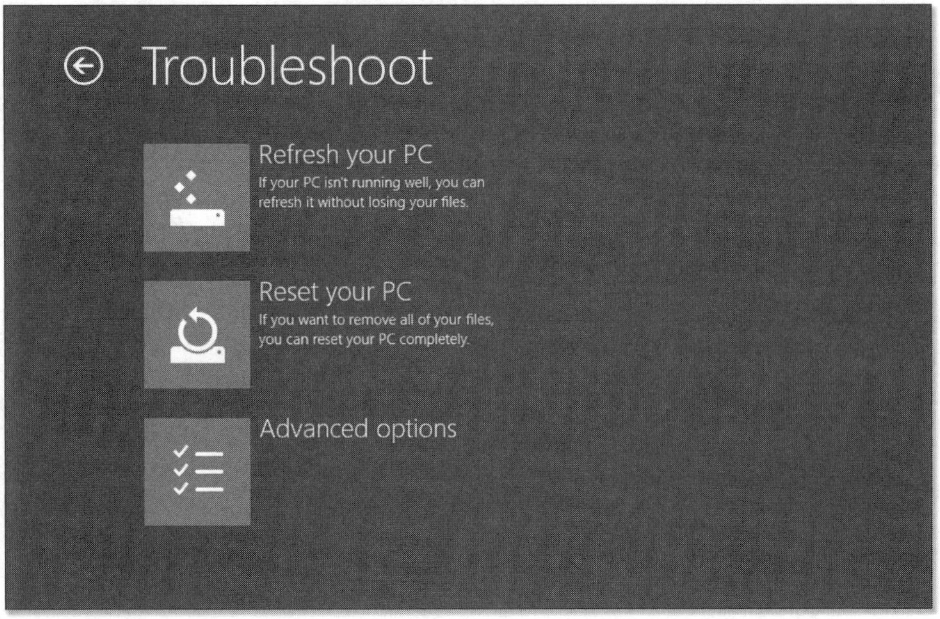

⊜ Troubleshoot

Refresh your PC
If your PC isn't running well, you can refresh it without losing your files.

Reset your PC
If you want to remove all of your files, you can reset your PC completely.

Advanced options

Figure 26.15
The new Troubleshoot screen offers a few trouble-shooting tools.

From here, you can refresh or reset your PC (we discuss these options later in this chapter; see "Refreshing Your PC" and "Resetting Your PC"). You can also click Advanced Options to display the Advanced Options screen, shown in Figure 26.16

From here, you can run System Restore (see "Recovering Using System Restore," later in this chapter), recover a system image (see "Restoring a System Image"), run an automatic repair (see "Automatically Repairing Your PC"), or access the Command Prompt to use its command-line tools.

In most cases, you can also click Startup Settings and then click Restart to access even more startup settings. (Note that you don't see the Windows Startup Settings option if you boot to a recovery drive, a system repair disc, or the Windows 8 install media.) Windows 8 restarts your PC and displays the Startup Settings screen, shown in Figure 26.17.

Figure 26.16
The new Advanced Options screen offers even more troubleshooting tools.

Advanced options
System Restore
Use a restore point recorded on your PC to restore Windows
Command Prompt
C:\
Use the Command Prompt for advanced troubleshooting
System Image Recovery
Recover Windows using a specific system image file
Startup Settings
Change Windows startup behavior
Automatic Repair
Fix problems that keep Windows from loading

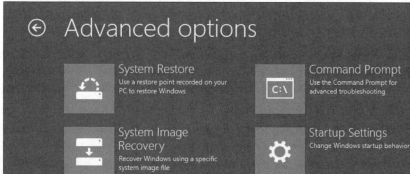

Figure 26.17
The Startup Settings screen offers several startup options.

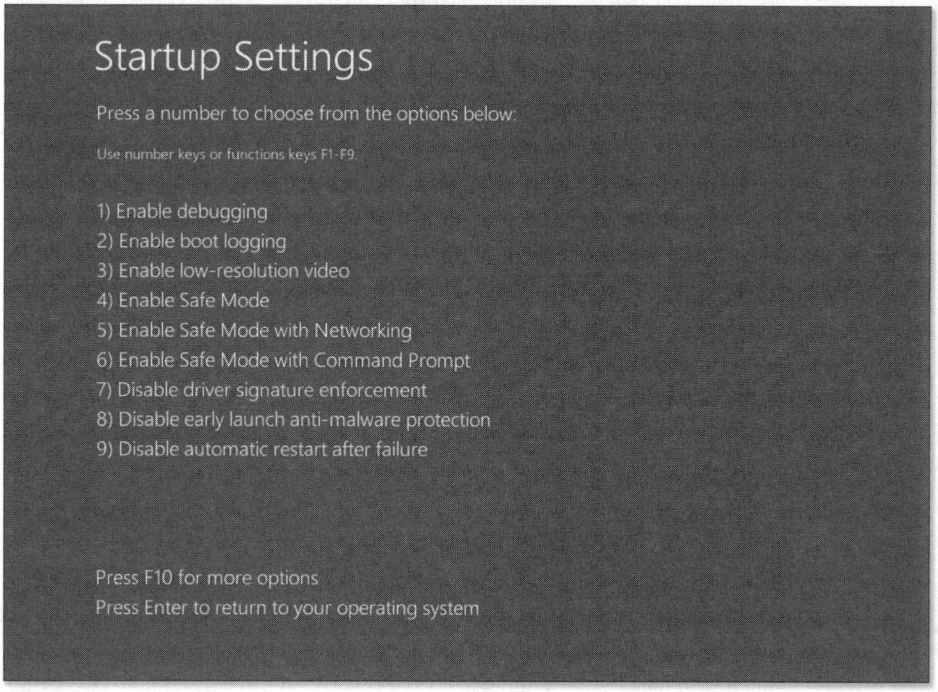
Startup Settings
Press a number to choose from the options below:
Use number keys or functions keys F1-F9.
1) Enable debugging
2) Enable boot logging
3) Enable low-resolution video
4) Enable Safe Mode
5) Enable Safe Mode with Networking
6) Enable Safe Mode with Command Prompt
7) Disable driver signature enforcement
8) Disable early launch anti-malware protection
9) Disable automatic restart after failure
Press F10 for more options
Press Enter to return to your operating system

Press Enter to load Windows 8 in the usual fashion. You can use the other options to control the rest of the startup procedure:

- **Enable Debugging**—This command enables remote debugging of the Windows 8 kernel.

- **Enable Boot Logging**—This option is the same as the Boot Normally option, except that Windows 8 logs the boot process in a text file named `ntbtlog.txt` that resides in the system root.

- **Enable Low-Resolution Video**—This option loads Windows 8 with the video display set to 640×480 and 256 colors. This is useful if your video output is garbled when you start Windows 8. For example, if your display settings are configured at a resolution that your video card can't handle, boot in the low-resolution mode and then switch to a setting supported by your video card.

- **Safe Mode**—The three Safe Mode options enable you to run a barebones version of Windows 8 for troubleshooting. See "Booting Up in Safe Mode," later in this chapter.

- **Disable Driver Signature Enforcement**—This item prevents Windows 8 from checking whether device drivers have digital signatures. Choose this option to ensure that Windows 8 loads an unsigned driver, if failing to load that driver is causing system problems.

- **Disable Early Launch Anti-Malware Driver**—This option prevents Windows 8 from scanning device drivers for malware during startup. If Windows 8 won't start, it's possible that the anti-malware scan is messing with a driver.

- **Disable Automatic Restart After Failure**—This option prevents Windows 8 from restarting automatically when the system crashes. Choose this option if you want to prevent your system from restarting so that you can read an error message or deduce other information that can help you troubleshoot the problem.

Booting Up in Safe Mode

You saw in the previous section that Windows 8's Advanced Options menu has tons of startup choices. By far the most useful of these are the various Safe Mode options, which we discuss in more detail in the next few sections.

Safe Mode

If you're having trouble with Windows 8—for example, if a corrupt or incorrect video driver is mangling your display, or if Windows 8 won't start—you can use the Safe Mode option to run a stripped-down version of Windows 8 that includes only the minimal set of device drivers that Windows 8 requires to load. Using this mode you could, for example, reinstall or roll back the offending device driver and then load Windows 8 normally.

When you start in Safe mode, Windows 8 uses the all-powerful Administrator account, which is the account to use when troubleshooting problems. However, caution is required when doing so.

When Windows 8 finally loads, as shown in Figure 26.18, the desktop reminds you that you're in Safe mode by displaying "Safe Mode" in each corner. (Also, Windows Help and Support appears with Safe mode–related information and links.)

Figure 26.18
Windows 8 in
Safe mode.

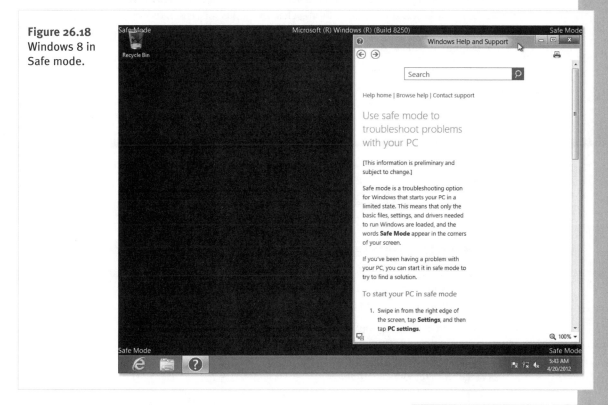

You should use the Safe mode option if one of the following conditions occurs:

- Windows 8 doesn't start after the POST ends.

- Windows 8 seems to stall for an extended period.

- You can't print to a local printer.

- Your video display is distorted and possibly unreadable.

- Your computer stalls repeatedly.

- Your computer suddenly slows down and doesn't return to normal without a reboot.

- You need to test an intermittent error condition.

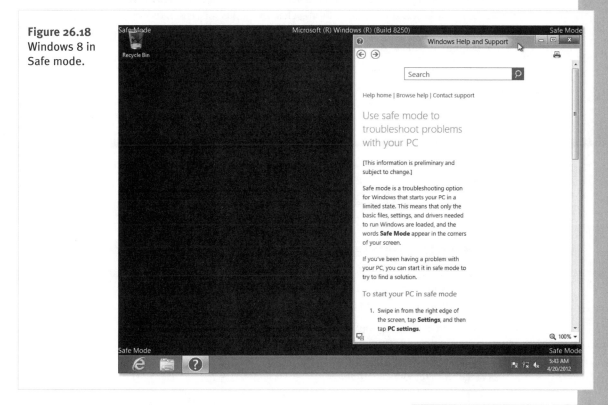

note

If you're curious to know which drivers are loaded during a Safe mode boot, see the subkeys in the following Registry key:

HKEY_LOCAL_MACHINE\SYSTEM\
CurrentControlSet\Control\
SafeBoot\Minimal\

Safe Mode with Networking

This option is identical to plain Safe mode, except that Windows 8's networking drivers are also loaded at startup. This enables you to log on to your network, which is handy if you need to access the network to load a device driver, run a troubleshooting utility, or send a tech support request. This option also gives you Internet access if you connect via a gateway on your network. This is useful if you need to download drivers or contact online tech support.

You should use the Safe Mode with Networking option if one of the following situations occurs:

- Windows 8 fails to start using any of the other Safe mode options.

- The drivers or programs you need to repair a problem exist on a shared network resource.

- You need access to email or other network-based communications for technical support.

- You need to access the Internet via your network to download device drivers or visit an online tech support site.

- Your computer is running a shared Windows 8 installation.

Safe Mode with Command Prompt

This option is the same as plain Safe mode, except that it doesn't load the Windows 8 GUI. Instead, it runs cmd.exe to load a Command Prompt session. You should use the Safe Mode with Command Prompt option if one of the following situations occurs:

- Windows 8 fails to start using any of the other Safe mode options.

- The programs you need to repair a problem must be run from the Command Prompt.

- You can't load the Windows 8 GUI.

Adding Safe Mode to the Boot Options Menu

If you find that you use Safe mode frequently, it can be a real hassle to drill down through the endless startup screens to get to the Advanced Options menu. To work around that problem, you can configure Windows 8 startup to display a boot menu that lets you choose between a regular startup and a Safe mode startup. Here are the steps to follow:

1. Press Windows Logo+W, type **command**, right-click Command Prompt, click Run as Administrator, and then enter your User Account Control credentials.

2. At the command line, type the following command and press Enter (this tells BCDEdit to write your PC's boot info to a file named boot.txt on your desktop):

   bcdedit /enum /v > %userprofile%\desktop\boot.txt

3. Leave Command Prompt open and double-click the boot.txt file on your desktop to open the file in Notepad.

4. In the Windows Boot Loader section, copy the identifier value.

5. Return to Command Prompt and type **bcdedit /copy** followed by a space.

6. Press Alt+Spacebar and then select Edit, Paste to paste the identifier value you copied in Step 4.

7. Type a space followed by **/d "Windows 8 (Safe Mode)"** and then press Enter. BCDEdit copies the boot info to the new entry.

8. Type **msconfig** and then press Enter to start the System Configuration tool.

9. In the Boot tab, click the Windows 8 (Safe Mode) boot item you just created.

10. Select the Safe Boot check box, as shown in Figure 26.19.

11. Click OK.

Figure 26.19
The Advanced Boot Options screen offers several startup options.

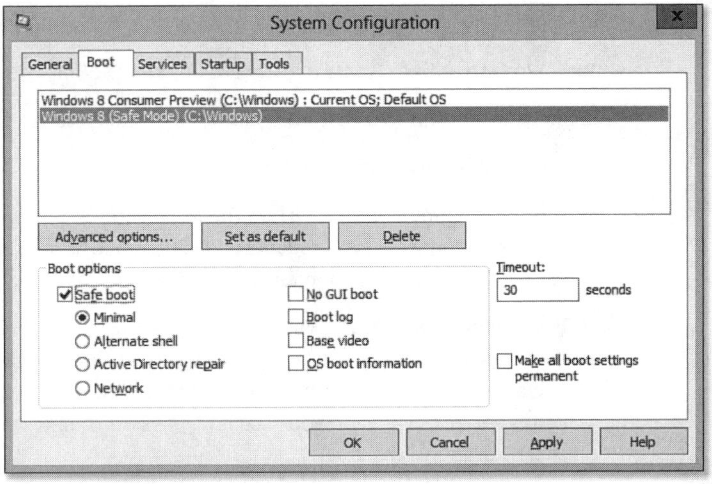

Automatically Repairing Your PC

If Windows 8 won't start normally, your first troubleshooting step is almost always to start the system in Safe mode. When you make it to Windows 8, you can investigate the problem and make the necessary changes (such as disabling or rolling back a device driver). But what if your system won't even start in Safe mode?

Your next step should be the RE's Automatic Repair option, which attempts various repair strategies that are often useful for getting a PC back on its feet. Here's how to use it:

1. Boot to the RE, as described earlier (see "Accessing the Recovery Environment").

2. Click Advanced Options. The Advanced Options screen appears.

3. Click Automatic Repair. Windows 8 reboots and Automatic Repair prompts you for your user account.

4. Click your user account. Automatic Repair prompts you for your password.

5. Type your account password and then click Continue. Automatic Repair begins the repair process.

Recovering Using System Restore

If you make a change to your system—such as adding new hardware, updating a device driver, installing a program, or modifying some settings—and then find that the system won't start or acts weirdly, it's a good bet that the change is the culprit. In that case, you can tell Windows 8 to revert to an earlier configuration that worked. (That is, a configuration that doesn't include your most recent change.) The theory is that by using the previous working configuration, you can make your problem go away because the system is bypassing the change that caused the problem.

You revert Windows 8 to an earlier configuration by using System Restore. We showed you how to use System Restore to set restore points in Chapter 32.

> *To learn how to create a restore point,* **see** *"Setting System Restore Points," p. 767.*

To revert your system to a restore point, follow these steps:

1. Launch System Restore:

- **If you can boot Windows 8**—In the Start screen, press Windows Logo+W, type **recovery**, click Recovery, click Advanced Tools, and then click Open System Restore.

- **If you can't boot Windows 8**—Boot to the RE, as described earlier (see "Accessing the Recovery Environment"), click Advanced Options, and then click System Restore. Click your user account, type your account password, and then click Continue.

 tip

System Restore is available in Safe mode. Therefore, if Windows 8 won't start properly, perform a Safe mode startup and run System Restore from there.

2. In the initial System Restore dialog box, click Next. System Restore displays a list of restore points.

3. If you don't see the restore point you want to use, click to activate the Show More Restore Points check box, which tells Windows 8 to display all the available restore points.

4. Click the restore point you want to use. There are seven common types of restore points:

- **System**—A restore point that Windows 8 creates automatically. For example, the System Checkpoint is the restore point that Windows 8 creates each day or when you boot your computer.

 note

By default, Windows 8 displays only the restore points from the previous 5 days. When you activate the Show More Restore Points check box, you tell Windows 8 to also show the restore points that are more than 5 days old.

- **Critical Update**—A restore point set prior to installing an important update.

- **Install**—A restore point set prior to installing a program or optional update.

- **Uninstall**—A restore point set prior to uninstalling a program or update.

- **Manual**—A restore point you create yourself.

- **Undo**—A restore point set prior to a previous use of System Restore to revert the system to an earlier state.

- **Unknown**—Any restore point that doesn't fit in the preceding categories.

5. Click Next. If other hard disks are available in the restore point, Windows 8 displays a list of the disks. Activate the check box beside each disk you want to include in the restore and then click Next.

6. Click Finish. Windows 8 asks you to confirm that you want your system restored.

7. Click Yes. System Restore begins reverting to the restore point. When it's done, it restarts your computer and displays a message telling you the results of the restore.

8. Click Close.

Refreshing Your PC

If the Automatic Repair and System Restore features didn't solve your problem, the next recovery step to try is Refresh Your PC. This is a new tool that reinstalls a fresh copy of Windows 8 while keeping your data, settings, and Windows 8 apps intact. When you refresh your PC, the computer boots to the RE, gathers up your data, copies it to another part of the hard drive, reinstalls Windows 8, and then restores your data.

Here's what gets saved when you refresh your PC:

- The files in your user account.

- Your personalization settings, wireless network connections, mobile broadband connections, drive letter assignments, and BitLocker settings.

- Any Windows 8 apps you've installed.

> **⚠ caution**
> Because the refresh first makes a copy of your data and settings, you must have enough free space on your hard drive to hold this data. If you don't have the space, you can't refresh your PC.

Here's what does *not* get saved during the refresh:

- All other PC settings (which are reverted to their defaults).

- Any desktop programs you installed. However, Windows 8 does generate a list of these programs for you.

Here are the steps to follow to refresh your PC:

1. Launch Refresh Your PC:

- **If you can boot Windows 8**—In the Start screen, press Windows Logo+W, type **refresh**, and then click Refresh Your PC.

- **If you can't boot Windows 8**—Boot to the RE's Troubleshoot screen, as described earlier (see "Accessing the Recovery Environment") and click Refresh Your PC. Windows 8 reboots the PC and asks you to choose your user account. Click your user account, type your account password, and then click Continue.

2. Click Next. Refresh Your PC prompts you to insert your installation media or a recovery drive.

3. Insert the media. Refresh Your PC validates the media and prompts you to start the process.

4. Click Refresh. Refresh Your PC reboots the computer and runs the refresh.

Resetting Your PC

Refreshing your PC should solve most problems. If it doesn't for some reason, or if you don't have enough room on your hard drive to perform the refresh, then your next option is to completely reset your PC. (Although first consider restoring a system image, if you have one, as described in the next section.) This procedure completely erases your data, reformats your hard drive, and then reinstalls Windows 8, so it's a fairly drastic step.

Follow these steps to reset your PC:

1. Launch Reset Your PC:

   - **If you can boot Windows 8**—In the Start screen, press Windows Logo+W, type **reset**, and then click Remove Everything and Reinstall Windows.

   - **If you can't boot Windows 8**—Boot to the RE's Troubleshoot screen, as described earlier (see "Accessing the Recovery Environment") and click Reset Your PC.

2. Click Next. Windows 8 reboots the PC and prompts you to insert your installation media or a recovery drive.

3. Insert the media. Reset Your PC asks how you want to remove your personal files.

4. Make your choice:

   - **Thoroughly**—Choose this route if you're resetting your PC to give or sell to someone else. This erases your personal data by overwriting it with random data at the sector level, but it can take a few hours to complete.

   - **Quickly**—Choose this option if you're keeping your computer and want to get it back on its feet as soon as possible.

> **note**
>
> Resetting your PC is perfect if you're going to be giving your PC to someone else or selling it. This way, you don't have to worry about the new owner seeing any of your data or programs.

> **caution**
>
> The thorough data removal option is indeed thorough, but it is *not* 100% secure. Reset Your PC erases your data with a single pass of random data, but that's not enough to prevent someone with extremely sophisticated (and expensive) equipment from recovering some of your data. The thorough option is fine for the vast majority of us, but consider more robust erasure methods if your PC contains extremely sensitive or secret data.

5. Click Reset. Reset Your PC begins the recovery. Along the way you'll need to enter your Windows 8 product key, accept the license terms, name your PC, sign in with your Microsoft account, and a few other setup chores.

Restoring a System Image

If you can't reset your PC because you don't have your Windows 8 install media or a recovery drive, you can still get your system back on its feet if you created a backup system image, as we described in Chapter 32.

 To learn how to create a system image, **see** *"Setting System Restore Points," p. 767.*

Follow these steps to restore a system image:

1. If you saved the system image to an external hard drive, connect that hard drive. If you used DVDs, insert the last DVD in the set.

2. Boot to the RE, as described earlier (see "Accessing the Recovery Environment").

3. Click Advanced Options. The Advanced Options screen appears.

4. Click System Image Recovery. Windows 8 asks you to choose a target operating system.

5. Click Windows 8. System Image Recovery prompts you to select a system image backup and offers two options:

   ▪ **Use the Latest Available System Image**—Activate this option to restore Windows 8 using the most recently created system image. This is almost always the best way to go because it means you'll restore the maximum percentage of your data and programs. If you choose this option, click Next and skip to step 8.

   ▪ **Select a System Image**—Activate this option to select from a list of restore points. This is the way to go if you saved a system image to your network, or if the most recent system image includes some change to your system that you believe is the source of your system problems. Click Next and continue with step 6.

6. Click the location of the system image and then click Next.

7. Click the system image you want to use for the restore and then click Next. If you want to use a system image saved to a network share, click Advanced and then click Search for a System Image on the Network.

8. If you replaced your hard drive, activate the Format and Repartition Disks check box.

9. Click Next. System Image Recovery displays a summary of the restore process.

10. Click Finish. System Image Recovery asks you to confirm.

11. Click Yes. System Image Recovery begins restoring your computer and then reboots to Windows 8 when the restore is complete.

MANAGING YOUR SOFTWARE

Configuring and Managing Windows Update

Microsoft is constantly working to improve Windows 8 with bug fixes, security patches, new program versions, and device driver updates. All of these new and improved components are available online, so you should check for updates and patches often.

You might think you'd have to go online to get these updates, but that's not the case. Windows 8 comes with an automatic updating feature that can download and install updates automatically.

Configuring Automatic Updates

If you prefer to know what's happening with your computer, it's possible to control the automatic updating by following these steps:

1. Press Windows Logo+X and then click Control Panel. The Control Panel window appears.

2. Select System and Security, Windows Update. (If you're viewing Control Panel using icons instead of categories, just click Windows Update directly.) This opens the Windows Update window, which shows you the current update status and enables you to view installed updates.

> **note**
>
> To view the updates installed on your computer, click the View Update History link.

3. Click the Change Settings link to display the Change Settings window, shown in Figure 27.1.

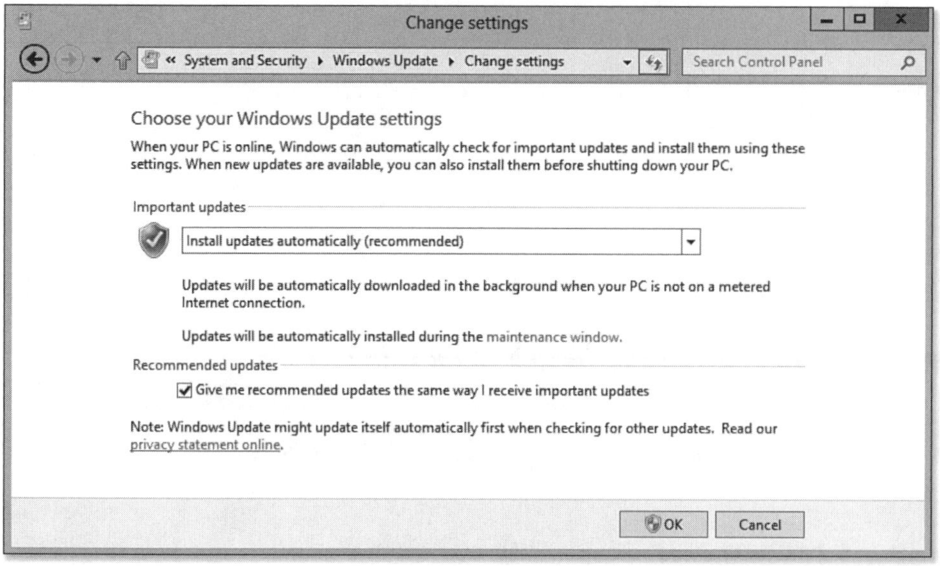

Figure 27.1
Use the Change Settings window to configure Windows 8's automatic updating.

4. In the Important Updates list, select one of the following options to determine how Windows 8 performs the updating:

- **Install Updates Automatically**—This option tells Windows 8 to download and install updates automatically. Windows 8 checks for new updates during the automatic maintenance window (see "Setting the Automatic Maintenance Schedule," next).

➡ *To learn how to set up an automatic logon,* **see** *"Just One User?,"* **p. 73**.

- **Download Updates, but Let Me Choose Whether to Install Them**—If you select this option, Windows 8 checks for new updates and then automatically downloads any updates available. Windows 8 then displays a notification to let you know that the updates are ready to install. Click the notification to see the list of updates. If you see an update that you don't want to install, deactivate its check box.

- **Check for Updates but Let Me Choose Whether to Download and Install Them**—If you select this option, Windows 8 checks for new updates and then, if any are available, displays a notification to let you know that the updates are ready to download. Click the notification to see the list of updates. If you see an update that you don't want to download, deactivate its check box. Click Start Download to initiate the

> ⚠ **caution**
> To go into effect, some updates require your computer to reboot. In such cases, if you activate the Install Updates Automatically option, Windows 8 will automatically reboot your system. This could lead to problems if you have open documents with unsaved changes or if you need a particular program to be running at all times. You can work around these problems by saving your work constantly, by setting up an automatic logon, and by setting up any programs you need running to launch automatically at startup.

download. When the download is complete, Windows 8 displays another notification to let you know that the updates are ready to install. Click the notification and then click Install to install the updates.

■ **Never Check for Updates**—Activate this option to prevent Windows 8 from checking for new updates.

5. If you only want the setting from step 3 to apply to important updates and not recommended updates, be sure to deactivate the check box in the Recommended Updates section.

6. Click OK to put the new settings into effect.

Setting the Automatic Maintenance Schedule

If you chose the Install Updates Automatically option, Windows 8 automatically checks for, downloads, and installs updates during the *maintenance window*, which is defined by default as follows:

■ Maintenance is performed each day at 3:00 a.m.

■ If you are using your computer, maintenance is postponed until you are no longer using it.

■ If your computer is in sleep mode, maintenance is postponed until the computer is awake.

■ If the maintenance server is running late, maintenance is postponed until the server is ready, as long as your computer is not being used and is awake.

Windows 8 uses the maintenance window not only to check for updates, but also to run Windows Defender security scans and to perform system diagnostics. If the default 3:00 a.m. window is inconvenient for you, you can configure the maintenance window as follows:

1. Display the Automatic Maintenance window:

■ If you have the Change Settings window onscreen, click the Maintenance Window link.

■ In the Start screen, press Windows Logo+W, type **main**, and then click Change Automatic Maintenance Settings.

2. Use the Run Maintenance Tasks Daily At list to choose the time you want Windows 8 to attempt to perform its maintenance chores.

3. If you want Windows 8 to wake your sleeping computer (as along as it's plugged in) to perform the maintenance, activate the Allow Scheduled Maintenance to Wake Up My Computer check box.

4. Click OK to put the new settings into effect.

Checking for Updates

If you chose the Never Check for Updates option, it's up to you to manually check for updates, which you should do regularly to keep your PC safe and sound. Even if you're using one of the automatic checking options, you might still want to do a manual check if you're waiting for an important security patch or some other crucial update that you'd prefer to install now rather than waiting for the automatic maintenance window.

Whatever the reason, follow these steps to perform a manual check for updates:

1. Press Windows Logo+X and then click Control Panel. The Control Panel window appears.

2. Select System and Security, Windows Update. (If you're viewing Control Panel using icons instead of categories, just click Windows Update directly.) The Windows Update window appears.

3. Click Check for Updates. Windows Update connects to the update server and checks for updates.

If Windows Update determines that one or more updates are available, it lets you know under the status. As shown in Figure 27.2, you see one link for the important updates and a second link for the optional updates, each of which tells you how many updates are available. See the next section to learn how to select the updates you want to install. Once you've done that, click Install Updates.

Figure 27.2
After you check for updates, Windows Update lets you know how many important and optional updates are available.

Selecting Updates to Install

If you configured Windows 8 to not download and install updates automatically, you can choose which updates to apply to your system. Note that, depending on your current Windows Update settings, you'll be choosing either which updates to both download and install or which updates just to install.

Here are the steps to follow to select the updates you want to install:

1. Press Windows Logo+X and then click Control Panel. The Control Panel window appears.

2. Select System and Security, Windows Update. (If you're viewing Control Panel using icons instead of categories, just click Windows Update directly.) The Windows Update window appears.

3. If you have important updates, click the X Important Updates Are Available link. The Select Updates to Install window appears.

4. If there are any important updates you don't want to install, deactivate their check boxes.

5. Click Optional. Windows Updates displays a list of the optional updates available for your system.

6. If there are any optional updates you don't want to install, deactivate their check boxes.

7. Click Install. Windows 8 installs the selected updates.

> **⚠ caution**
>
> Generally speaking, important updates are identified as important for a reason: they are designed to enhance your computer's security, stability, or performance. Therefore, we recommend that you always install all the available important updates.

Hiding and Restoring Updates

An update that you choose not to install still appears in the Select Updates to Install window. If you'd prefer not to see that update, right-click the update, click Hide Update, and then click Cancel. If you later want to unhide the update, display the Windows Update window and click the Restore Hidden Updates link. In the Restore Hidden Updates window, activate the update's check box and then click Restore.

Working with Third-Party Software

Outside of hardware woes and user errors (what IT personnel call a PEBCAK—Problem Exists Between Chair And Keyboard), most computer problems are caused by improperly installing a desktop program or installing a desktop program that doesn't mesh correctly with the system. (We're specifically referencing desktop programs here because Windows 8 apps use a standard install routine that is completely controlled by Windows 8 to ensure that each app is installed and configured correctly.) It could be that the installation makes unfortunate changes to the configuration files, or that the program replaces a crucial system file with an older version, or that the program just wasn't meant to operate on (or wasn't tested with) a machine with this configuration. Whatever the reason, you can minimize these kinds of problems by understanding the desktop installation process as it relates to user accounts and by following a few precautions before installing a new desktop software package.

Running Through a Pre-Installation Checklist

For those who enjoy working with computers, few things are as tempting as a new software package. The tendency is to just tear into the box, liberate the source disks, and let the installation program rip without further ado. That temptation is even worse in these days of downloadable software because it only takes a click or three to begin a program install.

This approach often loses its luster when, after a willy-nilly installation, your system starts to behave erratically. That's usually because the application's setup program has made adjustments to one or more important configuration files and given your system a case of indigestion in the process.

That's the hard way to learn the hazards of a haphazard installation.

To avoid such a fate, you should always look before you leap. That is, you should follow a few simple safety measures before double-clicking that `setup.exe` file. The next few sections take you through a list of things to check before you install any program.

 *To learn how to install Windows 8 apps, **see** "Installing Apps from the Windows Store," **p. 146.***

> ### note
> To avoid confusion, we'll reiterate that the discussion in this section applies only to desktop programs, not Windows 8 apps, which give you no control over the installation and always mesh properly with your system. We discuss installing Windows 8 apps in Chapter 5.

Check for Windows 8 Compatibility

Check to see whether the program is compatible with Windows 8. The easiest and safest setups occur with programs certified to work with Windows 8. In a pinch, if the program says that it's compatible with Windows 7, you should still be okay.

Set a Restore Point

The quickest way to recover from a bad installation is to restore your system to the way it was before you ran the setup program. The only way to do that is to set a system restore point just before you run the program, as we explain in Chapter 32, "Protecting your Data from Loss and Theft."

 *To learn how to create your own restore points, **see** "Setting System Restore Points," **p. 767.***

Read `Readme.txt` and Other Documentation

Although it's the easiest thing in the world to skip, you really should peruse whatever setup-related documentation the program provides. This includes the appropriate installation material in the manual, `Readme` text files found on the disc or in the download archive, and whatever else looks promising. By spending a few minutes looking over these resources, you can glean the following information:

- Any advance preparation you need to perform on your system

- What to expect during the installation

- Information you need to have on hand to complete the setup (such as a product's serial number)

- Changes the install program will make to your system or to your data files (if you're upgrading)

- Changes to the program and/or the documentation that were put into effect after the manual was printed

Virus-Check Downloaded Files

If you downloaded the application you're installing from the Internet, or if a friend or colleague sent you the installation file as an email attachment, you should scan the file using a good (and up-to-date) virus checker.

Sometimes it pays to be paranoid. You should check for viruses before installing under the following circumstances:

- You ordered the program directly from an unknown developer.

- The package was already open when you purchased it from a dealer (buying opened software packages is never a good idea).

- A friend or colleague gave you the program on a USB flash drive or recordable optical disc or sent it to you over email.

Understand the Effect on Your Data Files

Few software developers want to alienate their installed user base, so they usually emphasize upward compatibility in their upgrades. That is, the new version of the software will almost always be able to read and work with documents created with an older version. However, in the interest of progress, you often find that the data file format used by the latest incarnation of a program is different from its predecessors, and this new format is rarely *downward* compatible. That is, an older version of the software will usually gag on a data file that was created by the new version. So, you're faced with two choices:

- Continue to work with your existing documents in the old format, thus possibly foregoing any benefits that come with the new format

- Update your files and thus risk making them incompatible with the old version of the program, should you decide to uninstall the upgrade

One possible solution to this dilemma is to make backup copies of all your data files before installing the upgrade. That way, you can always restore the good copies of your documents if the upgrade causes problems or destroys some of your data. If you've already used the upgrade to make changes to some documents, but you want to uninstall the upgrade, most programs have a Save As command that enables you to save the documents in their old format.

Take Control of the Installation

Some setup programs give new meaning to the term *brain-dead*. You slip in the source disk, run `Setup.exe` (or whatever), and the program proceeds to impose itself on your hard disk without so much as a how-do-you-do. Thankfully, most installation programs are a bit more thoughtful than that. They usually give you some advance warning about what's to come, and they prompt you for information as they go along. You can use this newfound thoughtfulness to assume a certain level of control over the installation.

27

In particular, the best programs offer you a choice of installation options. Whenever possible, choose the Custom option, if one is available. This gives you maximum control over the components that are installed, including where and how they're installed.

Installing Software

After you've run through this checklist, you're ready to install the program. Here's a summary of the various methods you can use to install a program in Windows 8:

- **AutoPlay install**—If the program comes on a disc or drive that supports AutoPlay, you'll see a notification like the one shown in Figure 27.3. Click the notification to see a list of tasks you can run (see Figure 27.4) and then click Run SETUP.EXE (or whatever Windows has determined is the name of the install executable files).

- **Run** setup.exe—For most applications, the installed program is named setup.exe (sometimes it's install.exe). Use File Explorer to find the install program and then double-click it. Alternatively, press Windows Logo+R to open the Run dialog box, enter the path to the setup.exe file (such as e:\setup), and click OK.

- **Decompress downloaded files**—If you downloaded an application from the Internet, the file you receive will be either an .exe file or a .zip file. Either way, you should always store the file in an empty folder just in case it needs to extract files. You then do one of the following:

  - If it's an .exe file, double-click it; in most cases, the install program will launch. In other cases, the program will extract its files and you then launch setup.exe (or whatever).

  - If it's a .zip file, double-click it and Windows 8 will open a new compressed folder that shows the contents of the .zip file. If you see an installation program, double-click it. It's more likely, however, that you won't see an install program. Instead, the application is ready to go and all you have to do is extract the files to a folder and run the application from there.

- **Install from an** .inf **file**—Some (rare) applications install via an information (.inf) file. To install these programs, right-click the file and then click Install in the shortcut menu that appears.

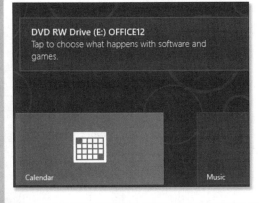

Figure 27.3
When you insert an install drive or disc, Windows 8 usually displays a notification such as the one shown here.

Figure 27.4
After you click the notification, click the option that runs the application's installation program.

DVD RW Drive (E:) OFF...

Choose what to do with software and games.

Install or run program from your media

 Run SETUP.EXE
Published by Microsoft Corporation

Other choices

Open folder to view files
Windows Explorer

Take no action

Opening the Programs and Features Window

In the Start screen, press Windows Logo+W to open the Settings search pane, type **programs**, and then click Programs and Features in the search results. This opens the Programs and Features window, shown in Figure 27.5. This operates as a kind of one-stop shop for your installed desktop applications.

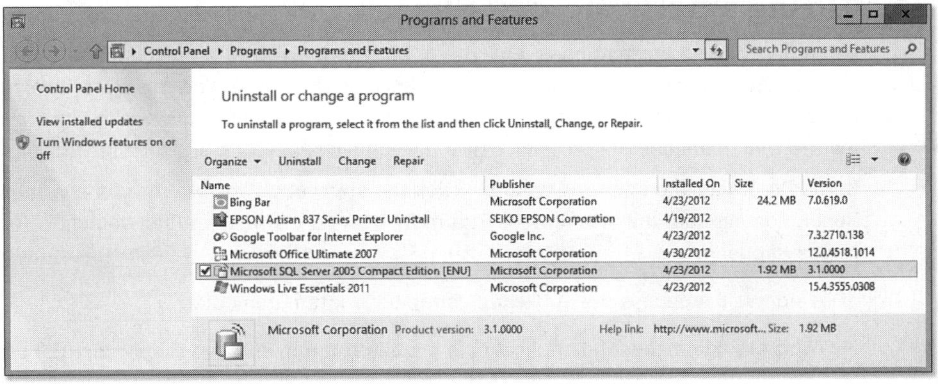

Figure 27.5
You use the Programs and Features window to modify, repair, and uninstall desktop programs.

	Programs and Features	– □ ×

↑ Control Panel ▸ Programs ▸ Programs and Features   ▾ ↻ Search Programs and Features 🔍

Control Panel Home

View installed updates

Turn Windows features on or off

Uninstall or change a program

To uninstall a program, select it from the list and then click Uninstall, Change, or Repair.

Organize ▾ Uninstall Change Repair

Name	Publisher	Installed On	Size	Version
Bing Bar	Microsoft Corporation	4/23/2012	24.2 MB	7.0.619.0
EPSON Artisan 837 Series Printer Uninstall	SEIKO EPSON Corporation	4/19/2012		
Google Toolbar for Internet Explorer	Google Inc.	4/23/2012		7.3.2710.138
Microsoft Office Ultimate 2007	Microsoft Corporation	4/30/2012		12.0.4518.1014
Microsoft SQL Server 2005 Compact Edition [ENU]	Microsoft Corporation	4/23/2012	1.92 MB	3.1.0000
Windows Live Essentials 2011	Microsoft Corporation	4/23/2012		15.4.3555.0308

Microsoft Corporation Product version: 3.1.0000   Help link: http://www.microsoft... Size: 1.92 MB

Items that can be modified or uninstalled via Programs and Features have corresponding Registry entries that come from the following Registry key:

`HKLM\SOFTWARE\Microsoft\Windows\CurrentVersion\Uninstall`

Each installed application (as well as many installed Windows components) have a subkey in the `Uninstall` key. This subkey provides the data you see in the Installed Programs window, including Name (from the `DisplayName` setting), Publisher (the `Publisher` setting), Installed On (the `InstallDate` setting), Size (the `EstimatedSize` setting), Help Link (from the Help Link at the bottom of screen), and Version (the `DisplayVersion` setting). Note that not all programs display all this information.

Changing a Software Installation

If you ran a custom version of a program's installation procedure, you might later decide that you'd now like to use some uninstalled components, or that you no longer need some installed components. Most applications that allow you to run a custom install also allow you to make changes to the installation after the fact. In the Programs and Features window, click the application you want to work with and then look for a Change command in the taskbar (refer to Figure 27.5 for an example). In some cases, the corresponding command is Uninstall/Change.

When you click Change (or Uninstall/Change), Windows 8 launches the application's install program (almost always a version that now resides on your hard drive). From there, you follow the instructions to modify the installation.

Repairing a Software Installation

If you find that an application is crashing or behaving erratically, one common cause is that one or more of the application's internal files have become corrupted. You can often resolve such problems by uninstalling and then reinstalling the application. However, some applications come with a repair feature that examines the program's files and replaces any that are corrupted or missing.

In the Programs and Features window, click the application you want to fix and then look for a Repair command in the taskbar (see Figure 27.5 for an example). When you click Repair, one of two things happens:

- Windows 8 launches the application's repair program immediately.

- Windows 8 launches the application's install program, and you then select the repair option.

Uninstalling Software

Applications, like the people we meet, fall into three categories: friends for life, acquaintances we deal with occasionally, and those we hope never to speak to again. Avoiding people we dislike is usually just a matter of avoiding contact with them—they'll get the hint after a while. Unlikable applications, however, just don't seem to get it. They keep hanging around like party guests who won't leave. If you have an application that has worn out its welcome, you need to uninstall it so that it's out of your life forever.

In the Programs and Features window, click the application you want to remove and then look for an Uninstall command in the taskbar (refer to Figure 27.5 for an example). In some cases, the corresponding command is Uninstall/Change.

When you click Uninstall (or Uninstall/Change), Windows 8 launches the application's install program and you follow the instructions to modify the installation.

Understanding Compatibility Mode

Most new software programs are certified as "Windows 8 compatible," meaning they can be installed and run without mishap on any Windows 8 system. But what about older programs that were coded before Windows 8 was released? They can be a bit more problematic. Although Microsoft takes great pains to accommodate older software, it's inevitable that some of those legacy programs will either be unstable while running under Windows 8 or they won't run at all.

> **tip**
>
> After you uninstall a program, you might find that it still appears in the Programs and Features list. To fix this, open the Registry Editor, display the Uninstall key mentioned earlier (see "Opening the Programs and Features Window"), and look for the subkey that represents the program. (If you're not sure, click a subkey and examine the DisplayName setting.) Delete that subkey, and the uninstalled program will disappear from the Programs and Features window.

Why do such incompatibilities arise? One common reason is that the programmers of a legacy application hardwired certain data into the program's code. For example, installation programs often poll the operating system for its version number. If an application is designed for, say, Windows XP, the programmers might have set things up so that the application installs if and only if the operating system returns the Windows XP version number. The program might run perfectly well under any later version of Windows, but this simplistic brain-dead version check prevents it from even installing on anything but Windows XP.

Another reason incompatibilities arise is that calls to API (application programming interface) functions return unexpected results. For example, the programmers of a very old application might have assumed that the FAT (File Allocation Table) file system would always be the standard, so when checking for free disk space before installing the program, they'd expect to receive a number that is 2GB or less (the maximum size of a FAT partition). However, FAT32 and NTFS (NT File System) partitions can be considerably larger than 2GB, so a call to the API function that returns the amount of free space on a partition could return a number that blows out a memory buffer and crashes the installation program.

These types of problems might make it seem as though getting older programs to run under Windows 8 would be a nightmare. Fortunately, that's not usually the case because the Windows 8 programmers did something very smart: because many of these application incompatibilities are predictable, the programmers gave Windows 8 the capability to make allowances for them. Therefore, many older programs are able to run under Windows 8 without modification. In Windows 8, *application compatibility* refers to a

> **caution**
>
> Although application compatibility can work wonders to give aging programs new life under Windows 8, this doesn't mean that *every* legacy program will benefit. If history is any guide, some programs simply will not run under Windows 8, no matter which compatibility rabbits you pull out of Windows 8's hat. In some of these cases you may be able to get a program to run by installing a patch from the manufacturer, so check the program's website to see if updates are available that make the program "Windows 8 friendly."

set of concepts and technologies that enables the operating system to adjust its settings or behavior to compensate for the shortcomings of legacy programs. This section shows you how to work with Windows 8's application compatibility tools.

Determining Whether a Program Is Compatible with Windows 8

One way to determine whether an application is compatible with Windows 8 is to go ahead and install it. If the program is not compatible with Windows 8, you might see a dialog box similar to the one shown in Figure 27.6.

C:\Users\paul\Downloads\HTML Writer\HTMLWRIT.EXE

The version of this program isn't compatible with the version of Windows you're running. Check your computer's system information to see whether you need a different version of the program for a 32-bit operating system, 64-bit operating system, or an ARM processor. Then see if it's available from the software publisher.

OK

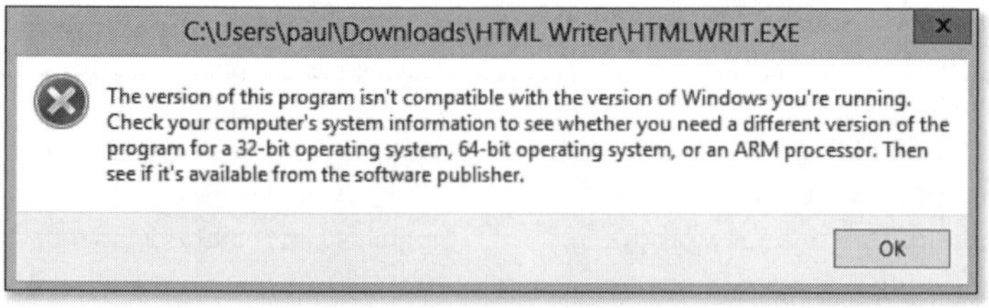

Figure 27.6
You might see a dialog box such as this if you try to install a program that isn't compatible with Windows 8.

In some cases, the dialog box gives you an opportunity to run the program anyway (by clicking Run Program or Continue), but this is a risky strategy because you can't be sure how the program will interact with Windows 8. This approach is riskiest of all when dealing with disk utilities, backup software, antivirus programs, and other software that requires low-level control of the system. It's extremely unlikely that Windows 8 would ever allow such programs to run, but you should *always* upgrade such products to Windows 8–compatible versions. A much safer route is to click Cancel to abort the installation and then visit the vendor's website to see whether a Windows 8–friendly update is available. (You can often get the company's web address by clicking the Details button.)

A better approach is to find out in advance whether the program is compatible with Windows 8. The most obvious way to do this is to look for the Designed for Windows 8 logo on the box or on the product's website. You also can check the manufacturer's website to see whether the company has made an upgrade available. Alternatively, Microsoft has a web page that enables you to search on the name of a program or manufacturer to find out compatibility information:www.microsoft.com/en-us/windows/compatibility/en-US/CompatCenter/Home

note

Where does the information in these dialog boxes come from? In the %SystemRoot%\AppPatch folder, Windows 8 has various system database (.sdb) files that contain messages such as the one shown in Figure 27.6 for all known applications that don't have compatibility fixes (discussed later in this section). The system database files aren't text files, so opening them with Notepad or WordPad will not allow you to read any of these stored messages.

Running a Program in Compatibility Mode

To help you run programs under Windows 8, especially those programs that worked properly in a previous version of Windows, Windows 8 offers a new way to run applications using *compatibility layers*. This means that Windows 8 runs the program by doing one or both of the following:

- **Running the program in a *compatibility* mode**—This involves emulating the behavior of a previous version of Windows. Windows 8 can emulate the behavior of Windows 95, Windows 98, Windows Me, Windows XP (with Service Pack 2 or Service Pack 3), Windows Vista (with Service Pack 1 or Service Pack 2), or Windows 7.

- **Temporarily changing the system's visual display so that it's compatible with the program**—There are four possibilities here: setting the color depth to 8-bit (256 colors), setting the color depth to 16-bit (65,536 colors), changing the screen resolution to 640×480, and disabling the display of scaling on high-DPI settings.

 note

Windows 8 and Microsoft often use the terms *compatibility layer* and *compatibility mode* interchangeably, depending on which compatibility tool you're using. In some cases, the emulations of previous Windows versions are called *operating system modes*.

To set up a compatibility layer, you right-click the program's executable file or a shortcut to the file, click Properties, and then display the Compatibility tab in the property sheet that appears. To set the compatibility mode, activate the Run This Program in Compatibility Mode For check box (see Figure 27.7) and then use the list to choose the Windows version the program requires. You can also use the check boxes in the Settings group to adjust the color mode that Windows 8 will switch to when you use the program.

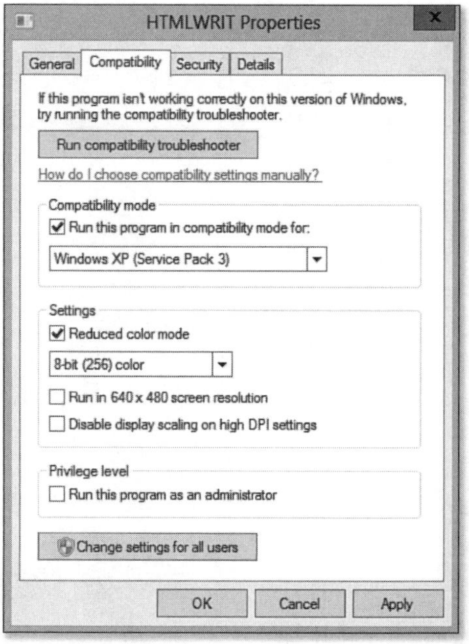

Figure 27.7
In the property sheet for an executable file, use the Compatibility tab to set the compatibility layer for the program.

If you don't feel like fiddling with these settings, you can see if Windows 8 will do the work for you. Right-click the program's executable file and then click Troubleshoot Compatibility. This launches the Program Compatibility Troubleshooter, shown in Figure 27.8. The easiest route here is to click Try Recommended Settings to see if your program runs. If not, click Troubleshoot Program to run through a series of questions that the troubleshooter uses to narrow down the problems you're having and from that suggest one or more compatibility fixes.

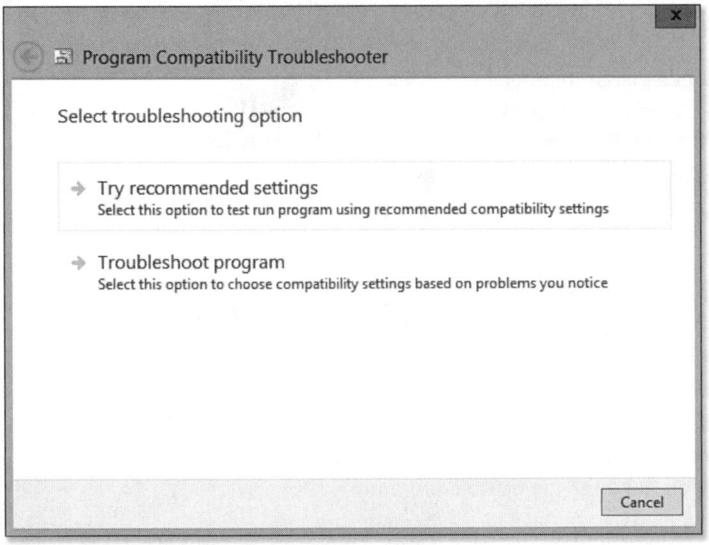

Figure 27.8
The Program Compatibility Troubleshooter may be able to get a recalcitrant legacy program running under Windows 8.

MANAGING YOUR HARDWARE

Windows 8 and Hardware

Man is a shrewd inventor, and is ever taking the hint of a new machine from his own structure, adapting some secret of his own anatomy in iron, wood, and leather, to some required function in the work of the world.

—Ralph Waldo Emerson

Emerson's concept of a "machine" was decidedly low tech ("iron, wood, and leather"), but his basic idea is still apt in these high-tech times. Man has taken yet another "secret of his own anatomy" (the brain) and used it as the "hint of a new machine" (the computer). And although even the most advanced computer is still a mere toy compared to the breathtaking complexity of the human brain, some spectacular advancements have been made in the art of hardware in recent years.

One of the hats an operating system must wear is that of an intermediary between you and your hardware. Any OS worth its salt has to translate incomprehensible "devicespeak" into something you can make sense out of, and it must ensure that devices are ready, willing, and able to carry out your commands. Given the sophistication and diversity of today's hardware market, however, that's no easy task.

The good news is that Windows 8 brings to the PC world support for a broad range of hardware, from everyday devices such as keyboards, mice, printers, monitors, as well as video, sound, memory, and network cards, to more exotic hardware fare such as multitouch input panels and the latest wireless standards. However, although this hardware support is broad, it's not all that deep, meaning that Windows 8 doesn't have built-in support for many older devices. So, even though lots of hardware vendors have taken at least some steps toward upgrading their devices and drivers, managing hardware is still one of Windows 8's trickier areas. This chapter should help as we take you through lots of practical techniques for installing, updating, and managing devices in Windows 8.

Viewing Your Devices

The simplest device-related task you can perform with Windows 8 is to view a list of the devices installed on your PC. To see this list, press Windows Logo+I to open the Settings pane, click More PC Settings, and then click Devices. (Alternatively, press Windows Logo+W, type **devices**, and then click Devices in the search results.) Figure 28.1 shows the PC Settings app's Devices tab, which is just a simple list of the attached devices and, where applicable, a device's current status. As you see a bit later in this chapter, about the only thing you can do with this list is uninstall a device and install a Bluetooth device.

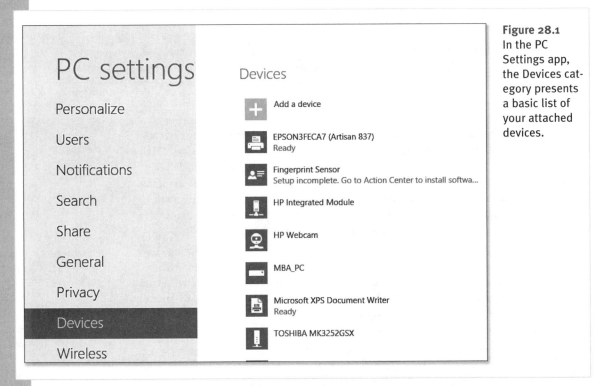

Figure 28.1
In the PC Settings app, the Devices category presents a basic list of your attached devices.

There's also a desktop feature called Devices and Printers that provides a similar list, albeit with much more functionality. To get there, press Windows Logo+W to return to the Settings search pane, type **devices** once again, but this time click Devices and Printers in the search results. Figure 28.2 shows the Devices and Printers window, which divides your devices into several categories, including Printers and Multimedia Devices. Clicking a device displays information about it in the Details pane at the bottom of the window. In many cases (particularly printers), you also see several device-related commands in the taskbar, such as Start Scan for a scanner and Eject for an optical drive. You can also double-click a device to see its properties and functions.

Figure 28.2
Control Panel's Devices and Printers window provides information and commands related to your installed devices.

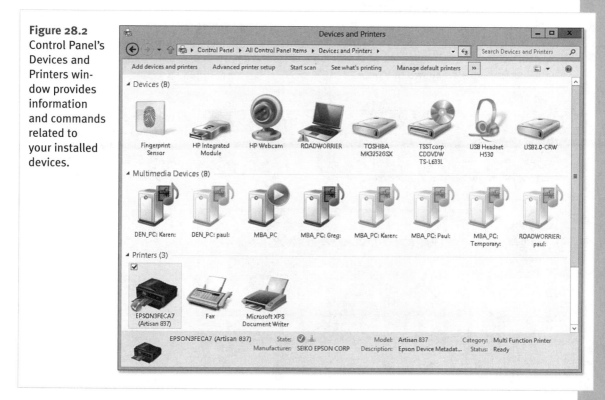

Installing Devices

Before installing a device, it's best to find out in advance whether the device is compatible with Windows 8. The easiest way to do this is to look for the Designed for Windows 8 logo on the box. For older devices, check the manufacturer's website to see whether the company tells you that the program can be run under Windows 8 or if an upgrade is available. Alternatively, Microsoft has a web page that enables you to search on the name of a device or manufacturer to find out compatibility information:

http://www.microsoft.com/en-us/windows/compatibility/en-US/CompatCenter/Home

If you see your device (and, in some cases, the correct device version) in the hardware list, you can install it secure in the knowledge that it will work properly with Windows 8.

Installing Plug and Play Devices

Computing old-timers will remember (none too fondly) the days when installing devices required flipping DIP switches, fiddling with jumpers, or fussing with various IRQ, I/O port, and DMA combinations. If, on the other hand, all the abbreviations in the previous sentence are incomprehensible to you, think yourself lucky that you live in a time when all the devices manufactured in recent years support Plug and Play, which means you simply attach the device and Windows 8 automatically recognizes it and installs the necessary drivers and other software.

How do you know this is happening? If you're on the desktop, you see the Device Setup icon appear on the taskbar, and the icon shows a green background moving in from the left. That background is actually a progress bar that's showing you the state of the device installation. Click the icon to see the install details, as shown in Figure 28.3.

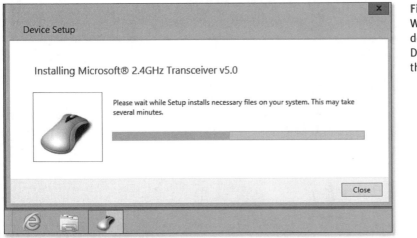

Figure 28.3
When you attach a new device, click the taskbar's Device Setup icon to watch the progress of the install.

When the install is done, the Device Setup dialog box and taskbar icon disappear, and your device is ready to go.

Using Action Center to Complete a Device Install

Plug and Play device installations almost always go off without a hitch. *Almost* always. In some cases, Windows 8 might encounter a problem or it might not have access to the necessary files to complete the install. If you open the PC Settings app's Devices tab, the status of the new device will say something like the following (see Figure 28.4):

"Setup incomplete. Go to Action Center to install software."

To rectify the situation, open Action Center (press Windows Logo+W, type **action**, and then click Action Center). In the Messages section, you'll see an "Install software for your devices" message, as shown in Figure 28.5. Click Install to complete the installation. In most cases, Windows 8 scours the Web for the needed software, downloads it, and then proceeds with the installation.

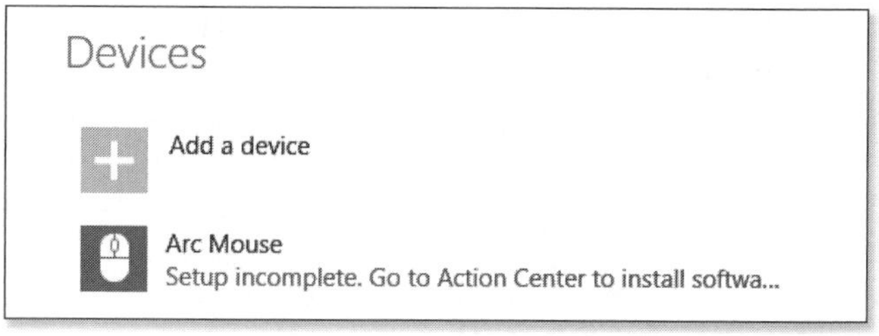

Figure 28.4
Every now and then Windows 8 fumbles an install.

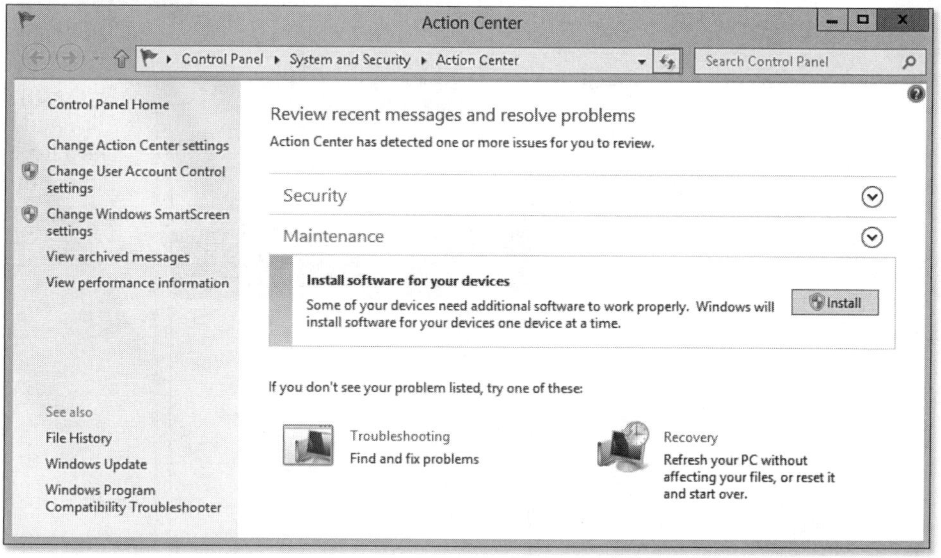

Devices

Add a device

Arc Mouse
Setup incomplete. Go to Action Center to install softwa...

Figure 28.5
You can use Action Center to complete the device installation.

Action Center

Control Panel ▸ System and Security ▸ Action Center   Search Control Panel

Control Panel Home
Change Action Center settings
Change User Account Control settings
Change Windows SmartScreen settings
View archived messages
View performance information

Review recent messages and resolve problems
Action Center has detected one or more issues for you to review.

Security

Maintenance

Install software for your devices
Some of your devices need additional software to work properly. Windows will install software for your devices one device at a time.   Install

If you don't see your problem listed, try one of these:

Troubleshooting
Find and fix problems

Recovery
Refresh your PC without affecting your files, or reset it and start over.

See also
File History
Windows Update
Windows Program Compatibility Troubleshooter

Installing a Bluetooth Device

You're probably familiar with Wi-Fi, the standard that enables you to perform networking chores without the usual network cables. Bluetooth is a similar technology in that it enables you to exchange data between two devices without any kind of physical connection between them. Bluetooth uses radio frequencies to set up a communications link between the devices. Bluetooth is a short-distance networking technology with a maximum range of about 33 feet (10 meters). If your PC has a built-in Bluetooth receiver (or you insert a USB Bluetooth receiver), you can make connections with a wide variety of devices, including mice, keyboards, headsets, and printers.

In theory, connecting Bluetooth devices should be criminally easy. You turn on each device's Bluetooth feature (in Bluetooth jargon, you make the devices *discoverable*), bring them within 33 feet of each other, and they connect without further ado. In practice, however, there's usually at least a bit of further ado (and sometimes plenty of it). That's because, as a security precaution, many Bluetooth devices do not connect automatically to a PC. This makes sense, because otherwise it means a stranger with a Bluetooth device could connect to your computer. To prevent this, most Bluetooth devices require you to enter a password before the connection is made. This is known as *pairing* the two devices.

Once you've made your Bluetooth device discoverable, you can follow these steps to pair it with your Windows 8 PC:

1. Press Windows Logo+I to open the Settings pane.

2. Click More PC Settings. The PC Settings app appears.

3. Click Devices.

4. Click Add a Device. Windows 8 begins scouring the nearby airwaves looking for discoverable Bluetooth devices, which it then displays in a list (see Figure 28.6).

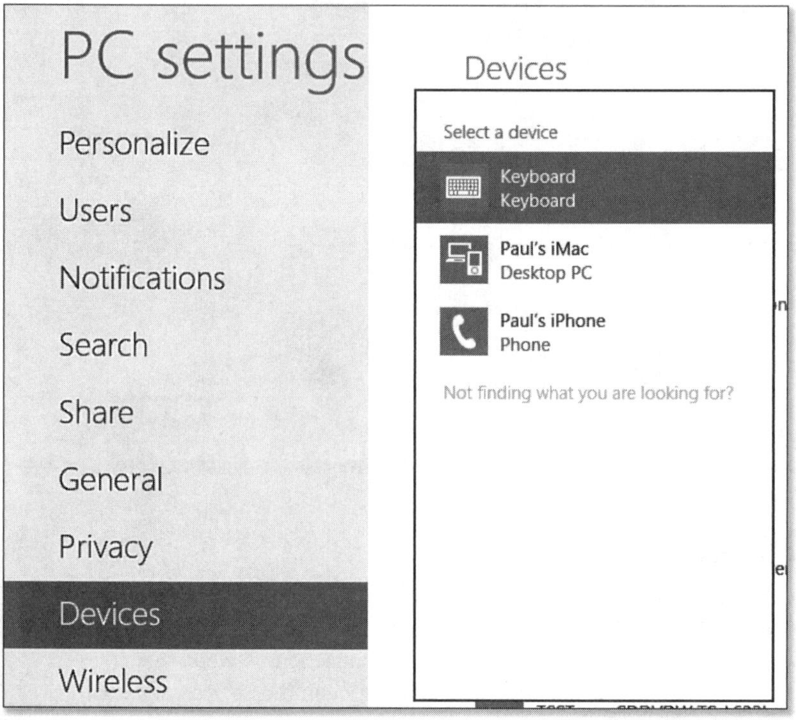

PC settings

Personalize

Users

Notifications

Search

Share

General

Privacy

Devices

Wireless

Devices

Select a device

Keyboard
Keyboard

Paul's iMac
Desktop PC

Paul's iPhone
Phone

Not finding what you are looking for?

Figure 28.6
Click Add a Device to see a list of discoverable Bluetooth devices.

5. Click your Bluetooth device. If the device requires a passcode to complete the pairing, you see a screen similar to the one shown in Figure 28.7.

6. Enter the passcode. Windows 8 pairs with the device.

Figure 28.7
If your
Bluetooth
device requires
a passcode for
pairing, you
see this screen.

Running Windows 8 with Multiple Monitors

Over the past few years, many studies have shown that you can greatly improve your productivity by doing one thing: adding a second monitor to your system. This enables you to have whatever program you are currently working with displayed on one monitor, and your reference materials, email program, or some other secondary program on the second monitor. This is more efficient because you no longer have to switch back and forth between the two programs.

To work with two monitors on a single computer, one solution is to install a second video card and attach the second monitor to it. However, most video cards now available come with multiple output ports, which can be any combination of VGA, DVI, HDMI, and DisplayPort. Also, almost all notebook PCs have at least one video output port that you can use to connect to a second monitor.

Once you have installed the new video card (if necessary) and attached the monitors, you then need to tell Windows 8 how you want to use the second monitor. You have three choices:

- Extend the screen across both monitors.

- Duplicate the screen on the second monitor.

- Use only the second monitor as your display.

The next few sections provide you with the details.

Extending the Screen to a Second Monitor

For most people, the extra expense of a second monitor is justified if it increases productivity, and you can do that by extending the Windows 8 interface across a second monitor. In this case, Windows 8 leaves the Start screen displayed on the original monitor, and it opens the Desktop app on the second monitor.

Here are the steps to follow to extend the Windows 8 screen to the second monitor:

1. Connect the second monitor to your Windows PC.

2. Press Windows Logo+K. Windows 8 displays the Devices pane.

3. Click Second Screen. The Second Screen pane appears, as shown in Figure 28.8.

4. Click Extend. Windows 8 connects to the second monitor and uses it to display the Desktop app.

> **tip**
> You can jump directly to the Second Screen pane by pressing Windows Logo+P.

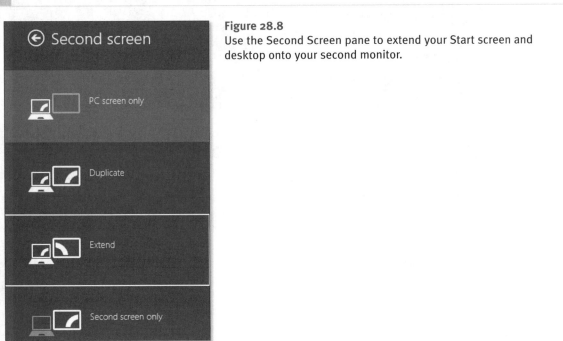

Figure 28.8
Use the Second Screen pane to extend your Start screen and desktop onto your second monitor.

Now you need to choose which monitor is the main display that shows the taskbar's notification area. This is also the display that Windows 8 uses to open desktop apps when you launch them from the Start screen. Follow these steps:

1. Press Windows Logo+W. The Settings search pane appears.

2. Type **resolution**.

3. Click Adjust Screen Resolution. The Screen Resolution window appears on the desktop, as shown in Figure 28.9.

4. Click the monitor you want to set as the main display.

5. Activate the Make This My Main Display check box.

6. Click OK.

> 🔍 **note**
>
> Ideally, you should be able to move your mouse continuously from the left monitor to the right monitor. If you find that the mouse stops at the right edge of your left monitor, it means you need to exchange the icons of the left and right monitors. To do that, click and drag the left monitor icon to the right of the other monitor icon (or vice versa).

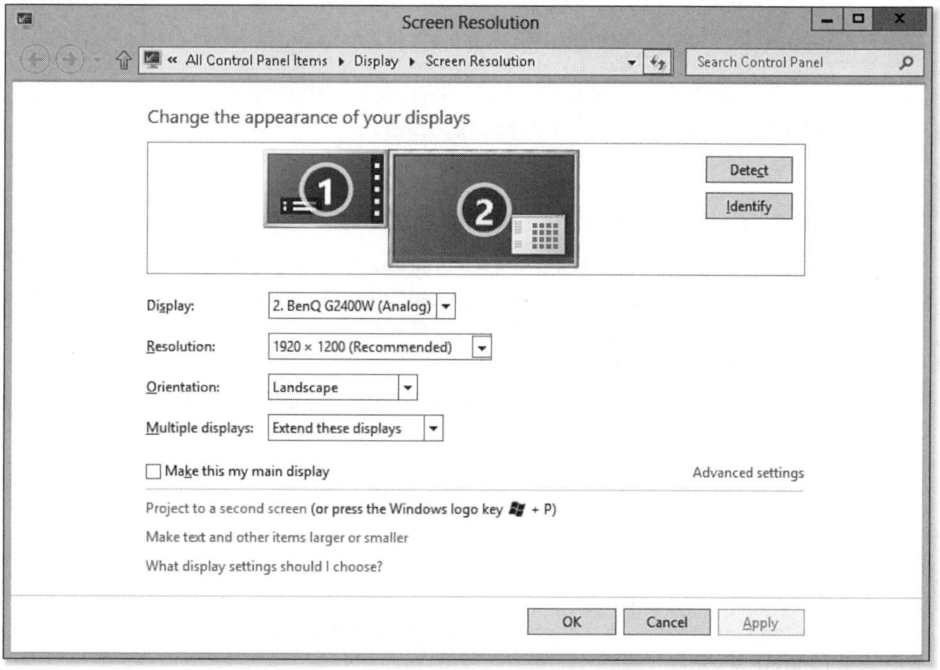

Figure 28.9
Use the Screen Resolution window to set the main display.

Duplicating the Screen on a Second Monitor

If you're making a presentation, the ideal setup is to be able to see what's on your main monitor (particularly if you're using a notebook PC), and then duplicate that same screen on the second monitor or projector. Duplicating the screen is also useful if you've connected your PC to a TV and want to control the screen from your PC but see the content on the larger screen.

Here are the steps to follow to duplicate the screen to the second monitor:

1. Connect the second monitor to your Windows PC.

2. Press Windows Logo+P. The Second Screen pane appears.

3. Click Duplicate. Windows 8 connects to the second monitor and uses it to display the same content as the main monitor.

Using Only the Second Monitor

If your second monitor is larger than your main monitor (such as a notebook PC screen) or has a higher quality image, then you might prefer to use only the second monitor as your output screen. This is also a useful scenario if your main monitor is damaged or distorted.

Follow these steps to switch your screen output to the second monitor:

1. Connect the second monitor to your Windows PC.

2. Press Windows Logo+P. The Second Screen pane appears.

3. Click Second Screen Only. Windows 8 connects to the second monitor and uses it to display the screen output.

Multiple Monitors and the Windows 8 UI

One of the nice features in Windows 8's multi-monitor support is that the techniques and gestures that apply to a single-monitor system also apply to a multiple-monitor system. Not only that, but you can use these techniques and gestures on *any* monitor:

- Move the mouse pointer to the top-right or bottom-right corner of any monitor to display the Charms menu. If both monitors support touch, you also can display the Charms menu by swiping left from the right edge of either monitor.

- Move the mouse pointer to the top-left corner of any monitor to display the most recently used running app.

- Move the mouse pointer to the top-left corner of any monitor, and then move the mouse down to display the list of running apps. For touch monitors, you can use either display to slide right from the left edge to drag the next running app, and then drag back to the left edge to see the list of running apps.

- Move the mouse pointer to the bottom-left corner of any monitor to see the Start screen thumbnail.

- To move a Windows 8 app to another monitor, press Windows Logo+Page Up (or Page Down). You can also move your mouse to the top edge of the screen (where it changes to a hand), drag down until you see the windows thumbnail, and then drag the thumbnail to another monitor.

Setting the Multi-Monitor Desktop Background

You'll likely use the Desktop app on both monitors at least some of the time, so you might want to give some thought to setting the desktop background that each monitor uses. You actually have three choices here:

- Display the same image as the desktop background on both monitors. In this case, the same image is displayed twice, once on each monitor.

- Display a different desktop background image on each monitor.

- Display a single desktop background image spanned across both monitors. In this case, the same image is displayed once, with part of the image on one monitor and the rest on the second monitor.

Here are the steps to follow:

1. Right-click the desktop, and then click Personalize. The Personalization window appears.

2. Click Desktop Background to open the Desktop Background window.

3. Select the type of background you want:

    - **The same image as the desktop background on both monitors**—This is the default setup, so you need to select only the image you want to display.

    - **A different desktop background image on each monitor**—Right-click the image you want to appear on the first monitor, and then click Set for Monitor 1; right-click the image you want to appear on the second monitor, and then click Set for Monitor 2.

    - **A single desktop background image spanned across both monitors**—Select the image you want to show on both monitors, and then use the Picture Position list to select Span.

4. Click Save Changes to put the new setting into effect.

Configuring the Taskbar for Multiple Monitors

By default, Windows 8 displays the taskbar on both monitors, and both taskbars display icons for all the running desktop apps, regardless of which monitor the apps appear on. You might want to change these defaults. For example, if you want to maximize the available screen real estate on the secondary display, you can configure Windows 8 to show the taskbar only on the main display. Similarly, you can configure the taskbars to show an icon for a running program only on the display where that program appears.

Here are the steps to follow:

1. In the Desktop app, right-click the taskbar and then click Properties. The Taskbar Properties dialog box appears.

2. If you want the taskbar to appear only on the main display, deactivate the Show Taskbar on All Displays check box, and then skip to step 4.

3. use the Show Taskbar Buttons On list to select how you want the buttons displayed:

- **All Taskbars**—This is the default, and it means that a button for every running desktop program appears on each taskbar.

- **Main Taskbar and Taskbar Where Window Is Open**—Select this option to display a button for every running desktop program on the main taskbar. If the program's window appears on another display, that display's taskbar also includes a button for the program.

- **Taskbar Where Window Is Open**—Select this option to display a button for a running program only on the taskbar in the same window.

4. Click OK to put the settings into effect.

Moving Up to Three Monitors

Rocking with two monitors is great, but let's crank things up a notch and go for not two, but *three* monitors! You could have Word on one monitor, reference materials or whatever on a second monitor, and Outlook on the third. It's almost scary how productive this setup will make you.

How does this work? The secret is that you need three output ports on your PC. Many new PCs ship with three or even four output ports—VGA, DVI, HDMI, or DisplayPort—so you just need to match these with your monitor input ports. If your PC has only two output ports, you must install a second video card on your system. However, you can't just plop any old video card in there and hope things will work. Instead, you need to use video cards that come with dual-GPU (graphics processing unit) support. Both AMD and NVIDIA offer dual-GPU technologies:

- **AMD CrossFireX**—AMD's dual-GPU technology is called CrossFireX (or CFX). To use it, you need a motherboard with a CrossFireX-compatible chipset and two free PCI Express slots that are designed for CrossFireX, as well as two CrossFireX-capable video cards from the same chipset family. Figure 28.10 shows two video cards connected with a CrossFireX bridge. To learn more about CrossFireX-compatible equipment, see http://sites.amd.com/us/game/technology/Pages/crossfirex.aspx.

> **note**
>
> Both AMD and NVIDIA now offer both *triple*-GPU and *quadruple*-GPU video cards, just in case you feel like running Windows 8 with six or even eight monitors!

- **NVIDIA SLI**—NVIDIA's dual-GPU technology is called *scalable link interface (SLI)*. To use it, you need a motherboard with an SLI-compatible chipset and two free PCI Express slots designed for SLI, as well as two SLI-capable video cards that use the same NVIDIA chipset. To learn more about SLI-compatible equipment, see http://www.geforce.com/hardware/technology/sli.

Each of these video cards has two output ports, so you have a total of four ports to use. After you get the cards installed, you run VGA or DVI cables from three of those ports (or four, if you want to go all the way and use four monitors) to the corresponding ports on your monitors. When you next start Windows, install the video card drivers.

Now you're ready to configure Windows to extend the desktop across all your monitors. Here are the steps to follow:

Figure 28.10
Two video cards connected with a CrossFireX bridge.

1. Make sure all your monitors are connected and turned on.

2. Press Windows Logo+W. The Settings search pane appears.

3. Type **resolution**.

4. Click Adjust Screen Resolution. The Screen Resolution window appears on the desktop. You now see icons for four monitors, which represent the four output ports of the video cards.

5. In the Multiple Displays list, select Extend These Displays.

6. Click and drag the monitor icons to the orientation you prefer. For example, you might want your main monitor (the monitor that holds the taskbar) in the middle and the other two monitors on either side.

7. Adjust the resolution for each monitor, as desired.

8. Click OK.

> ### tip
> If you're not sure which three of the four icons represent your actual monitors, select Identify. Windows 8 displays large numbers—1, 2, and 3—on each monitor, and the numbers correspond to the numbered icons in the Screen Resolution window.

Managing Your Hardware with Device Manager

Windows 8 stores all its hardware data in the Registry, but it provides Device Manager to give you a graphical view of the devices on your system. To display Device Manager, you have a couple of choices:

- Press Windows Logo+W, type **device**, and then click Device Manager in the search results.

- Press Windows Logo+X and then click Device Manager.

Device Manager's default display is a tree-like outline that lists various hardware types. To see the specific devices, click the plus sign (+) to the left of a device type. For example, opening the Disk Drives branch displays all the hard drives, Flash drives, and memory card slots attached to your computer, as shown in Figure 28.11.

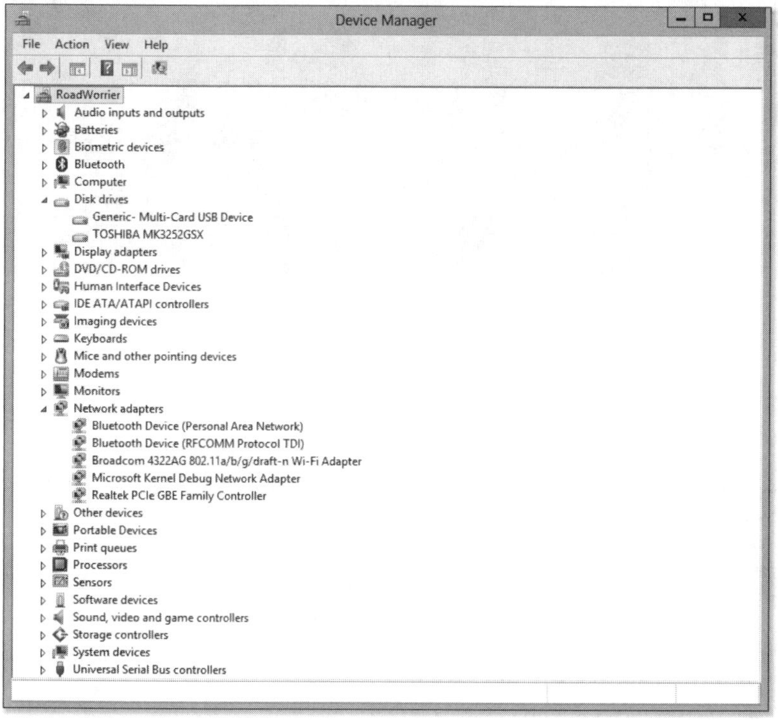

Figure 28.11
Device Manager organizes your computer's hardware in a tree-like hierarchy organized by hardware type.

Controlling the Device Display

Device Manager's default view is by hardware type, but it also offers several other views, all of which are available on the View menu:

- **Devices by Connection**—This view displays devices according to what they are connected to within your computer. For example, to see which devices connect to the PCI bus, on most systems you'd open the ACPI branch, and then the Microsoft ACPI-Compliant System branch, and finally the PCI Bus branch.

- **Resources by Type**—This view displays devices according to the *hardware resources* they require. Your computer's resources are the communications channels by which devices communicate back and forth with software. There are four types: Direct Memory Access (DMA), Input/Output (IO), Interrupt Request (IRQ), and Memory (a portion of the computer's memory that's allocated to the device and is used to store device data).

- **Resources by Connection**—This view displays the computer's allocated resources according to how they're connected within the computer.

- **Show Hidden Devices**—When you activate this command, Device Manager displays those non–Plug and Play devices that you normally don't need to adjust or troubleshoot. It also displays *nonpresent devices*, which are those that have been installed but aren't currently attached to the computer. (However, refer to "Showing Nonpresent Devices in Device Manager" to be sure you're seeing all devices.)

Viewing Device Properties

Each device listed in Device Manager has its own properties sheet. You can use these properties not only to learn more about the device (such as the resources it's currently using), but also to make adjustments to the device's resources, change the device driver, alter the device's settings (if it has any), and make other changes.

To display the properties sheet for a device, double-click the device to take you to the Properties box or right-click the device and then select Properties. The number of tabs you see depends on the hardware, but most devices have at least the following:

- **General**—This tab gives you general information such as the name of the device, its hardware type, and the manufacturer's name. The Device Status group tells you whether the device is working properly, and gives you status information if it's not.

   ➡ *For information on using Device Manager for troubleshooting, see "Troubleshooting Device Problems," p. 635.*

- **Driver**—This tab gives you information about the device driver and offers several buttons to manage the driver. See "Working with Device Drivers," later in this chapter.

- **Resources**—This tab tells you the hardware resources used by the device.

Showing Nonpresent Devices in Device Manager

I mentioned earlier that if you have any non–Plug and Play devices that you want to work with in Device Manager, you select View, Show Hidden Devices.

That works, but it doesn't mean that Device Manager is now showing all your devices. If you have any devices that you've installed in Windows, but that you regularly connect and then disconnect (such as a USB digital camera), Device Manager won't show them. (Windows describes such devices as *ghosted* devices.) That makes a bit of sense, because it might be confusing to see nonconnected hardware in Device Manager.

However, what if you're having a problem with a ghosted device? For example, suppose Windows hangs or crashes every time you connect such a device. Ideally, you'd like to use Device Manager to uninstall that device, but you can't because Windows goes belly-up whenever you connect the nasty thing. What do to?

The solution to this kind of problem is to force Device Manager to show ghosted devices. Here's how:

1. Press Windows Logo+X and then click Command Prompt. Windows 8 launches a new Command Prompt session.

2. Type the following command, and then press Enter:

   ```
   set devmgr_show_nonpresent_devices=1
   ```

3. Type the following command, and then press Enter to launch Device Manager:

   ```
   devmgmt.msc
   ```

4. In Device Manager, select View, Show Hidden Devices. Device Manager adds to the device list any ghosted devices installed on your PC.

> **note**
>
> By setting the DEVMGR_SHOW_NONPRESENT_DEVICES environment variable in your Command Prompt session, you must launch Device Manager from that session. If you just launch Device Manager in the usual way, you won't see the ghosted devices.

Working with Device Drivers

For most users, device drivers exist in the nether regions of the PC world, shrouded in obscurity and the mysteries of assembly language programming. As the middlemen brokering the dialogue between Windows 8 and our hardware, however, these complex chunks of code perform a crucial task. After all, it's just not possible to unleash the full potential of your system unless the hardware and the operating system coexist harmoniously and optimally. To that end, you need to ensure that Windows 8 is using appropriate drivers for all your hardware. You do that by updating to the latest drivers and by rolling back drivers that aren't working properly.

Tips for Downloading Device Drivers

Finding device drivers on the World Wide Web is an art in itself. We can't tell you how much of our lives we've wasted rooting around manufacturer websites trying to locate a device driver. Most hardware vendor sites seem to be optimized for sales rather than service, so although you can purchase, say, a new printer with just a mouse click or two, downloading a new driver for that printer can take a frustratingly long time. To help you avoid such frustration, here are some tips from our hard-won experience:

- If the manufacturer offers different sites for different locations (such as different countries), always use the company's "home" site. Most mirror sites aren't true mirrors, and (Murphy's law still being in effect) it's usually the driver you're looking for that a mirror site is missing.

- The temptation when you first enter a site is to use the search feature to find what you want. This works only sporadically for drivers, and the site search engines almost always return marketing or sales material first.

- Instead of the search engine, look for an area of the site dedicated to driver downloads. The good sites will have links to areas called Downloads or Drivers, but it's far more common to have to go through a Support or Customer Service area first.

- Don't try to take any shortcuts to where you *think* the driver might be hiding. Trudge through each step the site provides. For example, it's common to have to select an overall driver category, and then a device category, and then a line category, and then the specific model you have. This is tedious, but it almost always gets you where you want to go.

- If the site is particularly ornery, the preceding method might not lead you to your device. In that case, try the search engine. Note that device drivers seem to be particularly poorly indexed, so you might have to try lots of search text variations. One thing that usually works is searching for the exact filename. How can you possibly know that? A method that often works for us is to use Google (www.google.com) or Google Groups (groups.google.com) or some other web search engine to search for the driver. Chances are, someone else has looked for your file and will have the filename (or, if you're really lucky, a direct link to the driver on the manufacturer's site).

- When you get to the device's download page, be careful which file you choose. Make sure it's a Windows 8 driver, and make sure you're not downloading a utility program or some other non-driver file.

- When you finally get to download the file, be sure to save it to your computer rather than opening it. If you reformat your system or move the device to another computer, you'll be glad you have a local copy of the driver so that you don't have to wrestle with the whole download rigmarole all over again.

Checking Windows Update for Drivers

Before getting to the driver tasks that Windows 8 offers, remember that if Windows 8 can't find drivers when you initially attach a device, it automatically checks Windows Update to see whether any drivers are available. If Windows 8 finds a driver, it installs the software automatically. In most cases, this is desirable behavior because it requires almost no input from you. However, lots of people don't like to use Windows on automatic pilot all the time because doing so can lead to problems. In this case, for example, the Windows Update driver might be older than the driver available at the Windows Update site. If you've downloaded the driver you actually want to use from the manufacturer's website, you don't want whatever is on Windows Update to be installed.

To gain control over Windows Update driver downloads, follow these steps:

1. Select Start, type **systempropertieshardware**, and then press Enter. Windows 8 opens the System Properties dialog box with the Hardware tab displayed.

2. Click Device Installation Settings. Windows 8 displays the Device Installation Settings dialog box.

3. Select the No, Let Me Choose What to Do option. Windows 8 displays the options shown in Figure 28.12.

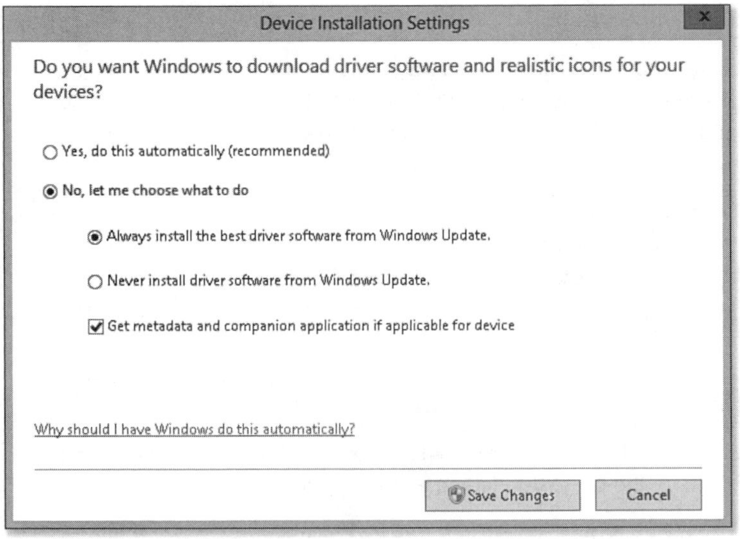

Figure 28.12
Use the Device Installation Settings dialog box to control how Windows 8 uses Windows Update to locate and install device drivers.

4. You have two choices:

   ■ **Always Install the Best Driver Software from Windows Update**—This is the default setting, and it tells Windows 8 to go ahead and locate and install Windows Update drivers each time you attach a new device.

   ■ **Never Install Driver Software from Windows Update**—Activate this option to tell Windows 8 to bypass Windows Update for all new devices. Use this option if you always use the manufacturer's device driver, whether it's on a disc that comes with the device or is downloaded via the manufacturer's website.

5. If you don't want Windows to automatically download the device program as well as the device information from the vendor, deactivate the Automatically Get the Device App and Info Provided By Your Device Manufacturer check box.

6. Click Save Changes.

Updating a Device Driver

Follow these steps to update a device driver:

1. If you have a disc with the updated driver, insert it. If you downloaded the driver from the Internet, decompress the driver file, if necessary.

2. In Device Manager, click the device with which you want to work.

3. Select Action, Update Driver Software. (You can also click the Update Driver Software button in the toolbar or open the device's properties sheet, display the Driver tab, and click Update Driver.) The Update Driver Software Wizard appears.

4. You have two choices:

   ■ **Search Automatically for Updated Driver Software**—Click this option to have Windows 8 check Windows Updates for the driver.

   ■ **Browse My Computer for Driver Software**—Click this option if you have a local device driver, whether on a disc or in a downloaded file. In the dialog box that appears, click Browse, and then select the location of the device driver.

 note

If your driver download comes packaged in a setup file, it's almost always best just to launch the setup file and let it perform the update for you.

Configuring Windows to Ignore Unsigned Device Drivers

Device drivers that meet the Designed for Windows 8 specifications have been tested for compatibility with Microsoft and are then given a digital signature. This signature tells you that the driver works properly with Windows and that it hasn't been changed since it was tested. (For example, the driver hasn't been infected by a virus or Trojan horse program.) When you're installing a device, if Windows 8 comes across a driver that has not been digitally signed, it displays a dialog box similar to the one shown in Figure 28.13.

Figure 28.13
Windows 8 displays a dialog box similar to this one when it comes across a device driver that does not have a digital signature.

If you click Don't Install This Driver Software, Windows aborts the driver installation, and you won't be able to use the device. This is the most prudent choice in this situation because an unsigned driver can cause all kinds of havoc, including lock-ups, BSODs (blue screens of death), and other system instabilities. You should check the manufacturer's website for an updated driver that's compatible with Windows 8, or you can upgrade to newer hardware that's supported by Windows 8.

However, although not installing an unsigned driver is the *prudent* choice, it's not the most *convenient* choice because, in most cases, you probably want to use the device now rather than later. The truth is that *most* of the time these unsigned drivers cause no problems and work as advertised, so as long as you obtained the driver from a source that you're certain is legitimate, it's probably safe to continue with the installation. In any case, Windows always sets a restore point prior to the installation of an unsigned driver, so you can restore your system to its previous state should anything go wrong.

> *To learn how to roll back a driver,* **see** *"Rolling Back a Device Driver," p. 638.*

By default, Windows gives you the option of either continuing or aborting the installation of the unsigned driver. You can change this behavior to automatically accept or reject all unsigned drivers by following these steps:

1. Press Windows Logo+R, type **gpedit.msc**, and press Enter to launch the Local Group Policy Object Editor.

2. Open the User Configuration\Administrative Templates\System\Driver Installation branch.

3. Double-click the Code Signing for Device Drivers policy. Windows displays the Code Signing for Device Drivers Properties dialog box.

4. Click Enable.

5. Use the When Windows Detects a Driver File Without a Digital Signature list to select one of the following items (see Figure 28.14):

   - **Ignore**—Choose this option if you want Windows 8 to install all unsigned drivers.

   - **Warn**—Choose this option if you want Windows 8 to warn you about an unsigned driver by displaying the dialog box shown earlier in Figure 28.13.

   - **Block**—Choose this option if you do not want Windows 8 to install any unsigned drivers.

6. Click OK.

> **note**
>
> Test your system thoroughly after installing the driver: use the device, open and use your most common applications, and run some disk utilities. If anything seems awry, roll back the driver, as described in Chapter 26, "Troubleshooting and Repairing Problems." If that doesn't work, use the restore point to roll back the system to its previous configuration.

> **note**
>
> If you're running a version of Windows 8 that doesn't come with the Group Policy Editor, we'll show you a bit later how to perform this tweak using the Registry.

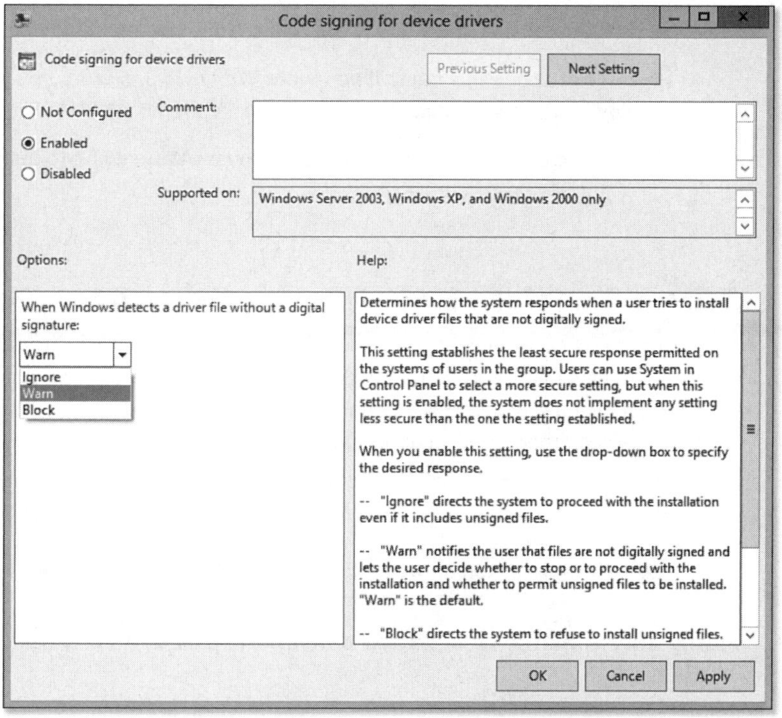

Figure 28.14
Enable the Code Signing for Device Drivers policy, and then choose what you want Windows 8 to do when it comes across an unsigned driver.

If your version of Windows 8 doesn't support the Local Group Policy Editor, follow these steps to set the driver-signing options via the Registry:

1. Press Windows Logo+R, type **regedit**, press Enter, and then enter your User Account Control credentials. Windows 8 launches the Registry Editor.

2. Navigate to the following key:

   HKCU\Software\Policies\Microsoft\

3. If you don't see a Windows NT key, select Edit, New, Key, type **Windows NT**, and click OK.

4. Select Edit, New, Key, type **Driver Signing**, and click OK.

5. Select Edit, New, DWORD, type **BehaviorOnFailedVerify**, and click OK.

6. Double-click the BehaviorOnFailedVerify setting to open it for editing.

> **tip**
>
> There are some device drivers that Windows 8 knows will cause system instabilities. Windows 8 will simply refuse to load these problematic drivers, no matter which action you choose in the Driver Signing Options dialog box. In this case, you'll see a dialog box similar to the one in Figure 28.13, except this one tells you that the driver will not be installed, and your only choice is to cancel the installation.

7. Type one of the following values:

   - **1**—(Ignore) Use this value if you want Windows 8 to install all unsigned drivers.

   - **2**—(Warn) Use this value if you want Windows 8 to warn you about an unsigned driver by displaying the dialog box shown earlier in Figure 28.13.

   - **3**—(Block) Use this value if you do not want Windows 8 to install any unsigned drivers.

8. Click OK.

Write a Complete List of Device Drivers to a Text File

There are times when you wish you had a list of all the drivers installed on your PC. For example, if your system crashes, it would be nice to have some kind of record of what drivers are in there. More likely, such a list would come in handy if you have to set up your PC from scratch and you want to know which drivers you have to update.

How do you get such a list? Oddly, Windows doesn't give you any straightforward way to do this. However, you can make your own list by using a script like the one shown in Listing 28.1.

➡ *For information on working with scripts, **see** "Windows Script Host," **p. 723**.*

Listing 28.1 A Script That Writes a Complete List of a PC's Installed Device Drivers to a Text File

```
Option Explicit
Dim strComputer, objWMI, collDrivers, objDriver, intDrivers
Dim objFSO, strFolder, objFile
'
' Change the following value to the path of the folder
' where you want to store the text file
'
strFolder = "d:\backups\"
'
' Initialize the file system object
'
Set objFSO = CreateObject("Scripting.FileSystemObject")
'
' Create the text file
'
Set objFile = objFSO.CreateTextFile(strFolder & "drivers.txt", True)
'
' Get the WMI object
'
strComputer = "."
Set objWMI = GetObject("winmgmts:\\" & strComputer)
'
' Return the collection of device drivers on the computer
```

```
'
Set collDrivers = objWMI.ExecQuery _
    ("Select * from Win32_PnPSignedDriver")
'
' Run through each item in the collection
'
intDrivers = 0
For Each objDriver in collDrivers
    '
    ' Write the driver data to the text file
    '
    objFile.WriteLine(objDriver.DeviceName)
    objFile.WriteLine("=========================================")
    objFile.WriteLine("Device Class: " & objDriver.DeviceClass)
    objFile.WriteLine("Device Description: " & objDriver.Description)
    objFile.WriteLine("Device ID: " & objDriver.DeviceID)
    objFile.WriteLine("INF Filename: " & objDriver.InfName)
    objFile.WriteLine("Driver Provider: " & objDriver.DriverProviderName)
    objFile.WriteLine("Driver Version: " & objDriver.DriverVersion)
    objFile.WriteLine("Driver Date: " & ReturnDriverDate(objDriver.DriverDate))
    objFile.WriteLine("")
    intDrivers = intDrivers + 1
Next
'
' Close the text file
'
objFile.Close
WScript.Echo "Wrote " & intDrivers & " drivers to the text file."


'
' ReturnDriverDate()
' This function takes the driver datetime value and converts
' it to a friendlier date and time format
'
Function ReturnDriverDate(dDriverDate)
    Dim eventDay, eventMonth, eventYear
    Dim eventSecond, eventMinute, eventHour
    eventYear = Left(dDriverDate, 4)
    eventMonth = Mid(dDriverDate, 5, 2)
    eventDay = Mid(dDriverDate, 7, 2)
    eventHour = Mid(dDriverDate, 9, 2)
    eventMinute = Mid(dDriverDate, 11, 2)
    eventSecond = Mid(dDriverDate, 13, 2)
    ReturnDriverDate = DateSerial(eventYear, eventMonth, eventDay) & _
                " " & TimeSerial(eventHour, eventMinute, eventSecond)
End Function
```

The script uses VBScript's FileSystemObject to connect to the PC's file system. In this case, the script uses FileSystemObject to create a new text file in the folder specified by strFolder. The script then sets up the usual Windows Management Instrumentation (WMI) object, and then uses

WMI to return the collection of installed device drivers. A `For Each...Next` loop goes through each device and writes various data to the text file, including the device name and description as well as the driver version and date.

Uninstalling a Device

When you remove a Plug and Play device, the BIOS informs Windows 8 that the device is no longer present. Windows 8, in turn, updates its device list in the Registry, and the peripheral no longer appears in the Device Manager display.

If you're removing a legacy device, however, you need to tell Device Manager that the device no longer exists. To do that, follow these steps:

1. Press Windows Logo+X, click Device Manager, and then click the device in the Device Manager tree.

2. Select Action, Uninstall. (Alternatively, click Uninstall in the toolbar or open the device's properties sheet, display the Driver tab, and click Uninstall.)

3. When Windows 8 warns you that you're about to remove the device, click OK.

Working with Device Security Policies

The Group Policy Editor offers several device-related policies. To see them, open the Group Policy Editor (press Windows Logo+R, type **gpedit.msc**, and press Enter) and select Computer Configuration, Windows Settings, Security Settings, Local Policies, Security Options. Here are the policies in the Devices category:

- **Allow Undock Without Having to Log On**—When this policy is enabled, users can undock a notebook computer without having to log on to Windows 8. (That is, they can undock the computer by pressing the docking station's eject button.) If you want to restrict who can do this, disable this policy.

- **Allowed to Format and Eject Removable Media**—Use this policy to determine the groups allowed to format floppy disks and eject CDs and other removable media.

- **Prevent Users from Installing Printer Drivers**—Enable this policy to prevent users from installing a network printer. Note that this doesn't affect the installation of a local printer.

- **Restrict CD-ROM Access to Locally**—Enable this policy to prevent network users from operating the computer's CD-ROM or DVD drive at the same time as a local user. If no local user is accessing the drive, the network user can access it.

- **Restrict Floppy Access to Locally**—Enable this policy to prevent network users from operating the computer's floppy drive at the same time as a local user. If no local user is accessing the drive, the network user can access it.

> **tip**
>
> To control who can undock the computer, display Computer Configuration, Windows Settings, Security Settings, Local Policies, User Rights Assignment. Use the Remove Computer from Docking Station policy to assign the users or groups who have this right.

EDITING THE WINDOWS REGISTRY

What Is the Registry?

The Windows Registry is a database in which Windows and application programs store configuration settings, startup information, hardware settings, user preferences, file locations, license and registration information, last-viewed file lists, and so on. The Registry holds a huge amount of information about installed program components and subcomponents (DLLs, COM objects, and so on). In addition, the Registry stores the associations between file types and the applications that create and use them. For example, the Registry holds the information that tells Windows to use Media Player when you click an MPG movie file. In the early days of DOS and Windows, programs stored this kind of information in a random collection of hundreds of files scattered all over your hard disk. Now, almost all Windows configuration information is stored in the Registry.

Most of the time the Registry does its job behind the scenes. Most Registry information is set and read by Control Panel applets, applications, Windows services, device drivers, and so on. You'll rarely if ever need to touch it directly. However, there are some settings that can only be made by manually changing Registry values, and knowing how the Registry works can help you track down viruses and annoying auto-starting programs. Therefore, it's worth knowing how the Registry is organized and how to make changes when necessary.

 tip

If you're already familiar with the Registry, you might want to skip ahead to the section "New Registry Features," where you learn how User Account Control and 64-bit Windows impact the Registry.

How the Registry Is Organized

The Registry is organized a lot like the files and folders on a hard disk. Just as a hard disk can contain partitions, the Registry contains separate sections called *top-level keys*. In each section is a list of named entries, called *keys*, which correspond to the folders on a hard disk. And just as a folder can contain files and more nested folders, a Registry key can contain *values*, which hold information such as numbers or text strings, and more nested keys. Even the way that file folders and Registry keys are described is similar: a folder might be named \Users\brian\chapter29, and a Registry key might be named \HKEY_CURRENT_USER\Control Panel\Desktop. You can see this structure in Figure 29.1. Control Panel and Desktop are the names of keys, and the Desktop key contains values, which have names like ActiveWndTrackTimeout and AutoColorization.

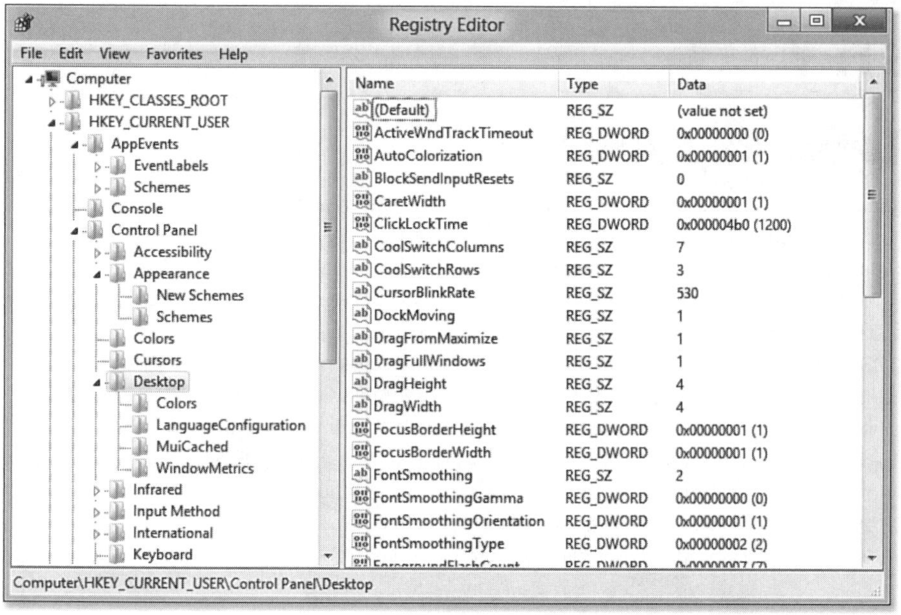

Figure 29.1
The Registry Editor screen shows keys on the left and values on the right.

The two main "top-level" keys are as follows:

- HKEY_LOCAL_MACHINE contains all the hardware and machine-specific setup information for your computer. Most values and keys under HKEY_LOCAL_MACHINE can be changed only by Administrator users running with elevated privileges. This helps protects this Registry section from malware.

Some of the primary keys in HKEY_LOCAL_MACHINE are as follows:

BDC00000000 contains system boot information. (The data in this key is actually stored in a separate partition on the boot hard drive.)

HARDWARE contains information gathered by the Plug and Play system during Windows startup.

SOFTWARE contains Windows and application information that applies to all users of the computer. Most software vendors create a subkey under SOFTWARE with their company name, with subkeys below that for each of their applications. On 64-bit systems, there is a subkey named Wow6432Node that holds information for 32-bit applications and software components. We talk about this later in the chapter under "Registry Redirection and Reflection."

SYSTEM contains information about installed services and device drivers.

- HKEY_USERS contains a key for each user account created on the computer, including the accounts used only internally by Windows services.

  The keys under HKEY_USERS are mostly named using long numeric strings that are the user account's Security Identifier (SID) number. Usually, not all accounts' keys are visible at the same time. Each account's key is loaded into the Registry when the user logs on and is unloaded a short time after the user logs out. Each user's key contains his or her personal Windows and application settings and preferences. Most entries are secured so that only the owning user can modify them.

The Registry Editor displays three other sections that look like they are separate top-level keys but that are actually views of information inside HKEY_LOCAL_MACHINE or HKEY_USERS:

- HKEY_CURRENT_USER is a shortcut to the subsection of HKEY_USERS that corresponds to the currently logged-on user. That is, when *you* run the Registry Editor, HKEY_CURRENT_USER shows *your* Windows and application preferences and settings.

  Some of the primary keys in HKEY_CURRENT_USER are as follows:

  Control Panel holds per-user preferences set by—you guessed it—Control Panel applets.

  Environment contains per-user environment variables set in the Advanced Computer Properties dialog box (sysdm.cpl).

  Network contains information about mapped network drives.

  Software, the largest section, contains per-user application preferences and configuration.

- HKEY_CURRENT_CONFIG is a shortcut to HKEY_LOCAL_MACHINE\System\CurrentControlSet\ Hardware Profiles\Current and contains hardware and device settings specific to the hardware profile used when Windows was started.

- HKEY_CLASSES_ROOT stores file associations, the information that Windows uses to link file types to applications, and a huge amount of setup information for Windows software components. It is actually a combined view of the contents of two other Registry sections: HKEY_LOCAL_MACHINE\Software\ Classes, which holds settings that are made for all users on this computer, and HKEY_CURRENT_USER\Software\Classes, which holds personal settings made just by the current user. If the same value is defined in both HKEY_CURRENT_USER\... and HKEY_LOCAL_MACHINE\..., the HKEY_CURRENT_USER value is used.

> 🔍 **note**
>
> HKEY_LOCAL_MACHINE is often abbreviated as HKLM, and HKEY_CURRENT_USER is often abbreviated as HKCU. We'll use those abbreviations in this chapter.

Registry keys have the exact same type of security settings as files and folders. In most cases, you have full control over the keys under your own account's HKCU section, unless an application explicitly removes the Modify or Delete permissions from its keys. And in general, only Administrators with elevated privileges can edit the contents of HKLM, except keys that were explicitly set to allow other users to edit it. (Some application installers do this.) We talk more about Registry security later in this chapter.

When User Account Control is active, and you are logged on as an Administrator, the Registry Editor requests elevated permissions so that you can edit HKLM keys. This is why you get a User Account Control prompt when you run it. If you are not logged on as an Administrator, the Registry Editor will run with reduced privileges unless you use the Run As Administrator option to start it. We discuss this later in the chapter, too.

New Registry Features

Windows Vista introduced some new features to the Registry: virtualization and 64/32–bit reflection. These features are also present, although somewhat changed, in Windows 8 and Windows 7, and this section gives you a brief tour. The features are called Registry virtualization, redirection, and reflection. This topic is somewhat gnarly and obscure, so on your first read, you might want to skip ahead to the section titled "Backing Up and Restoring the Registry."

Registry Virtualization

In the days before Windows security became a serious concern, many applications stored information in keys under HKLM, typically in a key named along the lines of HKLM\Software\ *ManufacturerName**ApplicationName*, so that the information could be made available to all users on the computer. Imagine a game that keeps track of the highest score achieved by any user. It has to store that high score somewhere accessible to all users, and HKLM is exactly such a place. So, versions of Windows up to XP let any application write to this key or its subkeys. This became an enormous security problem, because this also made it very easy for malware to make changes to global Windows settings affecting all users.

User Account Control, first introduced in Windows Vista, brought an end to this. Now, by default, only trusted setup programs or programs running with elevated Administrator permissions may make changes to keys and values under HKLM\Software. Application developers today are supposed to know this, and if an application really needs to store updatable information under HKLM, its developer needs to create these keys during installation and change their permission settings so that "normal" users can modify them later.

However, there are tens of thousands of older Windows applications that were designed before this change in the rules, and they would stop working if they couldn't make the Registry changes they expect to make. To get around this, Microsoft added Registry virtualization. Here's how it works: when User Account Control is enabled, if an application attempts to store information in HKEY_LOCAL_MACHINE\Software, but doesn't have permission to change information there, the information will actually get stored in HKEY_CURRENT_USER\Software\CLASSES\VirtualStore\ MACHINE\Software.

Applications still "see" the information as if it was in the intended location—this alternative key location "overlays" the original location. As a result, applications that aren't aware of the new, tighter restrictions on HKEY_LOCAL_MACHINE will run without a hitch, although their settings and data will be per-user instead of machinewide.

You need to know this so you can check the alternative locations when you're investigating problems with Registry settings in your system.

If you change an application program's preference setting that should apply to all users of the program, but it affects only you, and the setting isn't changed when other users run the application, most likely the configuration setting is stored in a Registry key under HKEY_LOCAL_MACHINE that isn't writeable by you. When you make the change, Windows virtualizes the Registry value, and only your account sees the change.

To fix this, first try to contact the software manufacturer for a workaround. If none exists, try this:

1. Locate the Registry key in which the setting is being saved. Either search the Registry for the setting value or use a Registry change-monitoring tool such as Registrar Registry Manager (or procmon from sysinternals.com) to see where the application saves your setting.

2. As an Administrator, locate the key in the left pane of the Registry Editor, right-click it, and select Permissions. Select the Users entry and check Full Control.

3. Using your account, locate the virtualized copy of the key under HKEY_CLASES_ROOT\ VirtualStore and delete it.

4. Run the application and change the setting again.

After this, everyone should share the same copy of the setting.

Virtualization doesn't occur under some circumstances. In those cases, the application simply is allowed to fail in its attempt to make changes to HKEY_LOCAL_MACHINE. These circumstances are listed here:

- If User Account Control is disabled.

- If virtualization is disabled by your network administrator, using Group Policy on a Windows domain network.

- If the application is a 64-bit or WinRT application.

- If the application program has a *manifest*, a block of data that the developer included inside the application or in a separate file to describe advanced security settings. The logic is that manifests are a relatively new construct. If an application is new enough to have a manifest, its developer should know how to cooperate with User Account Control. Almost all the applications that come with Windows—including Notepad, the Command Prompt interpreter (cmd.exe), and the Registry Editor—have manifests, so almost all Windows utilities do not see virtualized Registry settings.

- If a key is marked with a special flag that indicates that it is not to be redirected. HKEY_LOCAL_ MACHINE\Software\Microsoft\Windows\CurrentVersion\Run is marked this way so that a virus that attempts to set itself up to run at logon via this key won't be capable of doing so.

The command-line utility REG can modify the virtualization flag. Type **REG FLAGS /?** at the command-line prompt for more information.

Virtualization is seen as a stopgap measure and may be removed from some future version of Windows, once most applications either store information in HKEY_CURRENT_USER or explicitly set less restrictive permissions on their keys in HKEY_LOCAL_MACHINE when they're installed.

Registry Redirection and Reflection

The 64-bit versions of Windows support running 32-bit Windows applications. This presents a problem because many Windows subcomponents (objects and dynamic link libraries) may be present in both 32- and 64-bit versions on the same computer, and information about their file locations and configuration is stored in the Registry under keys whose names were set in stone before Microsoft considered the need to distinguish between the two flavors. To work around this, when a 32-bit application attempts to read or write information to a few specific Registry keys, Windows silently uses an alternative location. The application is none the wiser. This is called *Registry redirection*. The result is that 32-bit and 64-bit applications can both use these same, fixed key names but their information doesn't get intermingled.

Most, but *not all* of the subkeys under HKEY_LOCAL_MACHINE\Software and HKEY_CURRENT_USER\Software are subject to redirection. Those that are not redirected are considered "shared"—32-bit and 64-bit applications see the same value. For information about which specific subkeys are redirected and which are shared, go to msdn.microsoft.com and search for the article "Registry Keys Affected By Wow64." (Because the information shown under HKEY_CLASSES_ROOT is actually stored under those two Software keys, many of its keys are redirected too).

Redirected information for 32-bit applications is actually stored under HKEY_LOCAL_MACHINE\Software\WOW6432Node (for systemwide settings) and HEY_CURRENT_USER\Software\WOW6432Node (for per-user settings). When a 32-bit application requests information from a redirected key using the original location, it is fed information from below WOW6432Node.

Here's an example: a software manufacturer might decide to store the locations of its program files under the key HKEY_LOCAL_MACHINE\Software\PrettyGoodPrograms\MyFiles. A 64-bit application from this vendor will store its information in that actual location. A 32-bit application from this vendor will think it's storing and reading information there, but it will actually be fed the information from HKEY_LOCAL_MACHINE\Software\WOW6432Node\PrettyGoodPrograms\MyFiles. The 32- and 64-bit programs can thus see entirely different values from the same Registry key.

This impacts you too: when working with the Registry on a 64-bit system, you need to know to look under these two WOW6432Node entries when looking for setup information for 32-bit components. When you're tracking down configuration problems, you should usually check *both* locations.

Alternatively, you can use the 32-bit version of regedit; this presents all information in the standard locations seen by 32-bit applications. When you run regedit from the command line, you get the 64-bit version. However, if you run %systemroot%\syswow64\regedit.exe, you get the 32-bit version and can edit the values seen by 32-bit applications.

 note

You must close the 64-bit version of the Registry Editor before you can open the 32-bit version, and vice versa, unless you start the second instance of the Registry Editor with the -m command-line argument.

In that article, you will see references to the term *reflection*. Windows Vista had a feature that automatically copied some information set by 32-bit and 64-bit components and applications to *both* the 32- and 64-bit locations. This was called *Registry reflection*. Reflection was removed from Windows 7 and Windows 8. For more information, visit msdn.microsoft.com and search for the topics "Removal of Windows Registry Reflection." Also, see the Microsoft Knowledge Base article http://support.microsoft.com/kb/305097.

Backing Up and Restoring the Registry

Because the Registry is now the *one* place where all the Windows hardware and software settings are stored, it's also the one thing that Windows absolutely needs to run. If you have to use the Registry Editor to manually change Registry settings, we strongly suggest that you back up your Registry *before* you make any changes.

Backing Up the Registry

You can back up the Registry in several ways, including (in order of preference) using a third-party Registry-backup program, backing up the entire hard disk using a third-party program or File Recovery, using System Restore, and using the Registry Editor to save a key to a text file. In general, backups that include the *entire* hard disk should include the Registry, because the Registry's data is stored in ordinary files. Some backup applications have a Registry backup as an explicit option. Windows built-in System Restore feature backs up the HKLM registry section automatically.

We suggest that before you install a piece of new hardware or a significant software application or update, do a *full* disk backup, including the Registry. Alternatively, use System Restore to manually create a restore point, in case the application installer does not do this itself. These methods are discussed later in this section.

Before you manually edit the Registry for other purposes, back up the Registry by any of the means discussed in the next few sections.

Backing Up with Third-Party Registry-Backup Software

There are third-party programs that can back up and restore the Registry. See the section, "Other Registry Tools," later in this chapter.

If you're adventurous, there is also a free tool called ERUNT, which you can download from www.larshederer.homepage.t-online.de/erunt.

These programs come with instructions on backing up, restoring, repairing, and maintaining the Registry.

Backing Up the Hard Disk

You can save the Registry by performing a backup of the entire contents of the hard disk on which Windows resides. To start a backup, press Windows+X, select Control Panel, search for File Recovery, and click Back Up Now. (This assumes that you've set up File Recovery already. If not, now's the time to do it!)

Be sure that a system image is included, and that it includes the drive C.

Alternatively, use a third-party disk backup program and ensure that it's backing up the Registry. Check your backup software's manual for instructions on saving Registry and system information when you back up. We suggest that you always include the Registry in your backups.

Backing Up with System Restore

If you will be changing only entries under HKEY_LOCAL_MACHINE, you can create a restore point to back up a copy of this part of the Registry. To create a restore point, follow these steps:

1. Type Windows+X and select Control Panel, or search the Start screen for the word **control**, then select Control Panel under Settings. Search the Control Panel for the word **point,** and select Create A Restore Point.

2. Be sure that the disk volume that contains Windows (usually C) is checked and then click Create.

3. Enter a description for the restore point, such as **Before changing Registry**, and then click Create.

Now you can edit the Registry as described later in this chapter.

Backing Up with the Registry Editor

The Registry Editor has a mechanism to export a set of Registry keys and values to a text file. If you can't or won't use a more comprehensive backup system before you manually edit the Registry, at least use this editor to select and back up the key that contains all the subkeys and values you plan to modify. Remember, though, that this method cannot remove entries you added that were not in the Registry before the backup!

To back up a key and its subkeys and values, follow these steps:

1. At the Start screen, or in the Search charm, type **regedit**. Then take one of the following actions:

   - If you are an Administrator, click the regedit icon in the results list, and confirm the User Account Control (UAC) prompt.

   - If you are not an Administrator and want to back up your own keys in HKCU, follow the same procedure. There will be no UAC prompt.

caution

Be aware that the backup programs provided with Windows 8 do not provide a simple means of backing up the Registry as insurance against accidents. File Recovery is useful for Registry backups only if you create a complete system image backup, which can take a long time. Restoring from such a backup would take a long time, too. System Restore backs up only HKEY_LOCAL_MACHINE, not your own HKEY_CURRENT_ USER data. It's okay to use System Restore only if you're modifying just HKEY_LOCAL_ MACHINE settings.

note

The reason for these complicated variations is that malicious programs and email attachments can easily abuse the Registry Editor, so it's subject to UAC restrictions. The Registry Editor must be running in elevated mode to edit, restore, or modify Registry keys that are changeable only by the Administrator. By the way, there is no indication in the Registry Editor's title bar to tell whether it's running with elevated privileges—you just have to remember.

- If you are not an Administrator and need to back up HKLM keys, right-click the regedit icon in the search results and select Run As Administrator. Then enter Administrator credentials.

2. Locate and select the key you plan to modify, or a key containing all the keys you plan to modify, in the left pane.

3. Select File, Export.

4. Choose a location and filename to use to store the Registry keys. (I usually use the desktop for temporary files like this, so that I'll see them and delete them later.)

5. Select All Files from the Save As Type list and enter a name (possibly with an extension other than .reg—for example, `before.sav`).

6. Click Save. The chosen key or keys are then saved as a text file.

Restoring the Registry

If you've made Registry changes that cause problems, you can try to remember each and every change you made, reenter the original information, delete any keys you added, and thus undo the changes manually. Good luck! If you were diligent and made a backup before you started, however, you can simply restore the backup and have confidence that the recovery is complete and accurate.

Signs of Registry Problems

Registry corruption can take two forms: either the Registry's database files can be damaged by an errant disk operation, or information can be mangled by a buggy program or an overzealous regedit user. No matter what the cause, the result can be a system that won't run or one that reboots itself over and over.

These could be other signs of Registry corruption or errors:

- Drivers aren't loaded, or they give errors while Windows is booting.

- Software complains about components that aren't registered or cannot be located.

- Undesirable programs attempt to run when you log in.

- Windows does not boot, or it starts up only in Safe mode.

If you made a Registry backup using a disk or Registry backup tool, use the instructions that came with your product to restore the Registry. If you created a restore point or used Regedit, follow the steps described in the following sections.

Restoring the Registry from a Restore Point

If you created a restore point before modifying the Registry, you can back out the change by following these steps:

1. From the Start screen or in the Search charm, type **Control**. Open the Control Panel. Type **point** in its search box, and click Create a Restore Point. (Alternatively, run `sysdm.cpl` in a Command Prompt window or use Windows Logo+R and then select the System Protection tab.)

2. Locate the restore point you created. Select it and click Next; then click Finish. Windows will restart.

If the Registry problem is severe enough that Windows can't boot or get to the System Restore function, you can perform a system restore from the system recovery tools on your Windows setup DVD.

 For instructions on performing a system restore this way, **see** *"Recovering Using System Restore,"* **p. 648**.

Restoring the Registry from Regedit

If a Registry-editing session has gone awry and you need to restore the Registry from a key you saved from within Regedit, follow these steps:

1. At the Start screen or in the Search charm, type **regedit**. Then take one of the following actions:

   ▪ If you are an Administrator, click the regedit icon in the results list, and confirm the User Account Control (UAC) prompt.

   ▪ If you are not an Administrator and want to restore your own keys in HKCU, follow the same procedure. There will be no UAC prompt.

   ▪ If you are not an Administrator and need to restore HKLM keys, right-click the regedit icon in the search results and select Run As Administrator. Then enter Administrator credentials.

2. In Regedit, select File, Import.

3. Select All Files from the Files of Type list.

4. Locate the file you used to back up the Registry key or keys—for example, `before.reg`.

5. Select Open.

The saved Registry keys are then imported, replacing any changes or deletions. However, any keys or values you've added to the Registry are not removed. If they are the cause of the problem, this restore will *not* help.

 tip
If you encounter what you think are Registry problems with add-on software, your best bet is to uninstall the software, if possible, and reinstall it before attempting *any* Registry restores or repairs.

If the Registry problems persist, you can try a rather drastic measure: you can use Regedit to delete the key or keys that were changed and then import the backup file again. This time, any added keys or values are removed. We suggest that you try this approach only with keys related to add-on software, *not* for any of the Microsoft software or hardware keys.

Using Regedit

Most people never need to edit the Registry by hand because most Registry keys are set by the software that uses them. However, you might need to edit the Registry by hand if you're directed by a technical support person who's helping you fix a problem, or when you're following a published procedure to make an adjustment for which there is no Control Panel setting.

In the latter case, before going any further, we need to say this one last time, to make it absolutely clear: unless you're quite certain that you can't make a mistake, back up the Registry (or at least the section you want to change) before making any changes.

The next few sections cover the basics of the Registry Editor.

Viewing the Registry

The easiest way to run the Registry Editor is to go to the Start screen and type **regedit**. Then take one of the following actions:

- If you are logged on as an Administrator, click the regedit icon in the results list, and confirm the User Account Control (UAC) prompt. The Registry Editor will run with full elevated privileges.

- If you are not an Administrator and want to edit just your own keys in HKEY_CURRENT_USER, follow the same procedure. There will be no UAC prompt. The Registry Editor will run with reduced privileges, and you will not be able to change systemwide settings.

- If you are not an Administrator and need to edit keys in HKEY_LOCAL_MACHINE, right-click the regedit icon in the search results and select Run As Administrator. Then enter Administrator credentials.

Regedit offers a two-pane display, as shown earlier in Figure 29.1. The top-level keys, which are listed below Computer, can be expanded just like drives and folders in File Explorer. In the pane on the right are the values for each key. The name of the currently selected key appears in the status bar.

Values have names, just as the files in a folder do, and it's in the values that configuration information is finally stored. Each key has a (Default) value, which is the value of the key itself, and any number of named values. For example, Figure 29.1 shows the key HKEY_CURRENT_USER\Control Panel\Desktop. The value of HKEY_CURRENT_USER\Control Panel\Desktop itself is undefined (blank), and the value HKEY_CURRENT_USER\Control Panel\Desktop\DragFullWindows is 1.

Registry values have a data type, which is usually one of the types shown in Table 29.1. The Registry Editor display lists values by their technical names.

Table 29.1   Data Types Supported by Regedit

Technical Name	"Friendly" Name	Description
REG_SZ	String value	Textual information, a simple string of letters.
REG_BINARY	Binary value	Binary data, displayed as an arbitrary number of hexadecimal digits.
REG_DWORD	DWORD (32-bit) value	A single number displayed in hexadecimal or decimal.
REG_QWORD	QWORD (64-bit) value	A single number displayed in hexadecimal or decimal. QWORD values are used primarily by 64-bit Windows applications.
REG_MULTI_SZ	Multistring value	A string that can contain more than one line of text.
REG_EXPAND_SZ	Expandable string value	Text that can contain environment variables (such as %TEMP%).

Other data types, such as REG_DWORD_BIG_ENDIAN and REG_RESOURCE_LIST, exist, but they are obscure and rare and can't be edited with Regedit.

Searching in the Registry

You can search for a Registry entry by key name, value name, or the contents of a value string. First, select a starting point for the search in the left pane. You can select Computer to select the entire Registry, or you can limit your search to one of the top-level keys or any subordinate key. Next, select Edit, Find from the menu and enter a search string in the Find dialog box. The Find feature is not case sensitive, so it doesn't matter whether you use upper- or lowercase letters. You can check any of the Look At boxes to designate where in the Registry you expect to find the desired text: in the name of a key, in the name of a value, or in the data, the value itself.

Check Match Whole String Only to search only for items whose whole name or value is the desired string.

 note

When I search the Registry, most of the time, I check all the Look At boxes but not Match Whole String Only.

Click Find Next to start the search. The Regedit display indicates the first match to your string; by pressing F3, you can repeat the search to look for other instances.

Also remember that Windows might store information in some places you are not familiar with, as discussed previously under "New Registry Features."

tip

The search function has two limitations:

- You can't enter a backslash (\) in the search string when looking for a key or value name; Regedit won't complain, but it won't find anything, either.

- You can't search for the initial HKEY_xxx part of a key name. That's not actually part of the name; it's just the section of the Registry in which the key resides.

For example, to find a key named HKEY_CLASSES_ROOT\MIDFile\shell\Play\Command, you can't type all that in and have Find jump right to the key. If you already know the full pathname of a key, use the left pane of Regedit to browse for the key directly.

Editing Keys and Values

Regedit has no Save and Undo menu items and no Recycle Bin. Changes to the Registry happen *immediately* and *permanently*. Additions, deletions, and changes are for real. This is the reason for all the warnings to back up before you poke into the Registry.

Adding a Value

To add a value to a key, select the key in the left pane and choose Edit, New. Select the type of value to add; you can select any of the supported Registry data types, which are listed by the "friendly" names shown previously in Table 29.1. The instructions you're following indicate which type of value to add. A new value entry then appears in the right pane.

Type the new value's name and press Enter to edit the value:

- For string values, enter the text of the desired string.

- For DWORD values, choose Decimal or Hexadecimal, and enter the desired value in the chosen format.

- For binary values, enter pairs of hexadecimal characters as instructed. (You'll never be asked to do this, we promise.)

Changing a Value

If you want to change a value, double-click it in the right pane to bring up the Edit Value dialog box. Alternatively, right-click it and select Modify. Then make the desired change and click OK.

That is all you will likely ever need to do with Regedit. However, in the extremely unlikely case that you want to delete a value or add or remove a key, the following sections can help see you through these processes.

note

Many of the keys that control Windows itself have access restrictions and can be modified only by an Administrator, and only when the Registry Editor is running with elevated permissions. For instructions on running with elevated permissions, see "Viewing the Registry" in this chapter.

704   Editing the Windows Registry

Deleting a Value

If you've added a Registry value in the hope of fixing some problem and found that the change wasn't needed, or if you're instructed to delete a value by a Microsoft Knowledge Base article or other special procedure, you can delete the entry by viewing its key and locating the value on the right pane.

Select the value and choose Edit, Delete from the menu, or right-click and select Delete from the context menu. Confirm by clicking OK.

> **⚠ caution**
>
> There is no Undo command in the Registry Editor—when you delete a value, it's gone for good. Be sure you've made a Registry backup before editing or deleting Registry keys and values.

Adding or Deleting a Key

Keys must be added as subkeys of existing keys; you can't create a new top-level key. To add a key, select an existing key in the left pane and select Edit, New, Key from the menu. Alternatively, right-click the existing key and select New, Key from the context menu. A new key appears in the left pane, where you can edit its name. Press Enter after you enter the name.

You can delete a key by selecting it in the left pane and choosing Edit, Delete from the menu, or by right-clicking it and selecting Delete from the context menu. Click OK to confirm that you intend to delete the key. Deleting a key deletes its values *and all its subkeys* as well, so without the protection of Undo (or a Registry Recycling Bin), this action is serious.

> **⚠ caution**
>
> Don't attempt to rename keys without a *very good* reason—for example, because you mistyped the name of the key you were adding. If Windows can't find specific Registry keys it needs, Windows might not boot or operate correctly.

Renaming a Key

As you have probably guessed, the pattern for renaming a key follows the File Explorer model exactly: choose the key in the left pane and select Edit, Rename, or right-click the key and select Rename. Finally, enter a new name and press Enter.

Using Copy Key Name

As you have probably noticed by now, the names of Registry keys can be quite long, tortuous things. The Registry Editor offers a bit of help to finger-fatigued Registry Editors (and authors): choosing Edit, Copy Key Name puts the name of the currently selected key into the Clipboard so you can paste it elsewhere if you need to.

Editing Registry Entries for Another User

As an administrator, you might find it necessary to edit HKEY_USER entries for another user. For example, a startup program in HKEY_CURRENT_USER\Software\Windows\CurrentVersion\Run might be causing such trouble that the user can't log on. If you can't log on as that user, you can edit his HKEY_CURRENT_USER Registry keys by loading his registry data manually. You load his registry *hive* and edit it. A hive is a file that contains registry data. The registry view that you see in the registry editor is the sum total of all loaded hive files. The systemwide registry sections are loaded when Windows boots. The personal registry sections are loaded when each user logs on. If a user isn't logged on, you can manually load and edit his hive file using these steps:

1. Log on as an Administrator and run Regedit with elevated permissions, as discussed in "Viewing the Registry" in this chapter.

2. Select the HKEY_USERS window.

3. Highlight the top-level key HKEY_USERS.

4. Select File, Load Hive.

5. Browse to the profile folder for the desired user. For a local user account, this is in \Users\ *username*. (For a Windows Server domain, look in the folder used for user profiles on the domain controller.) The name of this folder might have the computer name or a domain name attached. For example, on one computer, my profile folder name is bknittel.java.

6. Type the filename NTUSER.DAT. (The file will most likely not appear in the Browse dialog box because it's *super hidden*—marked with both the Hidden and System attributes.) Click Open.

7. A dialog box appears, asking you to enter a name for the hive. HKEY_USERS normally loads user hives with a long numeric name, so we suggest that you type the user's logon name, or something like *users* key. Click OK. The user's Registry data is then loaded and can be edited, as shown in Figure 29.2.

Figure 29.2
An offline user's Registry hive is now loaded and can be edited.

Loaded Hive Appears Here

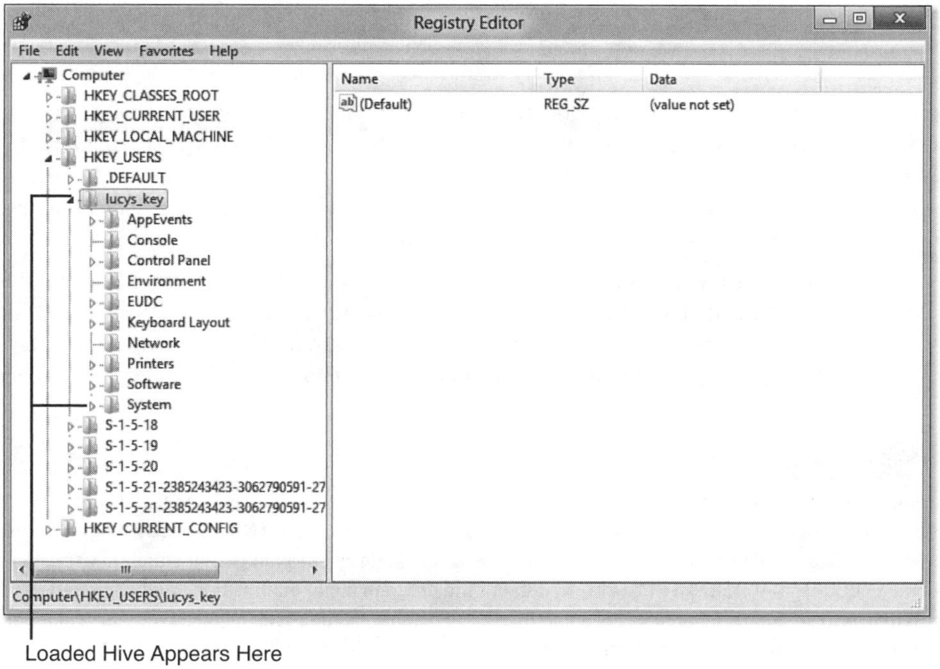

8. When you're finished editing, unload the hive. Select the key you added under HKEY_USERS (for example, lucys_key in Figure 29.2), and select File, Unload Hive. Confirm by clicking Yes on the warning dialog box.

Editing Registry Entries for Another Windows Installation

If you need to retrieve Registry entries from an installation of Windows on another hard disk or partition, perhaps one that can't boot due to a virus, rootkit, or errant driver, you can load any of that installation's hive files for editing or exporting.

To edit the other installation's Registry, you need to locate its hive files. They are usually found in the locations shown in Table 29.2.

> **🔍 note**
>
> If the other installation is on a different computer, you'll need to move its hard disk into your computer. Then, be sure that your computer boots from *your* hard disk, not the one you just added.

Table 29.2 Usual Location of Hive Files

Key	Default Location and Hive File
HKEY_LOCAL_MACHINE\SAM	\windows\system32\config\sam
HKEY_LOCAL_MACHINE\Security	\windows\system32\config\security
HKEY_LOCAL_MACHINE\Software	\windows\system32\config\software
HKEY_LOCAL_MACHINE\System	\windows\system32\config\system
HKEY_LOCAL_MACHINE\Components	\windows\system32\config\components
HKEY_USERS\.Default	\windows\system32\config\default

To edit another Windows installation's Registry, use the technique described in "Editing Registry Entries for Another User," but instead of locating a user's NTUSER.DAT file, locate the desired hive file on the other hard drive or partition. (We omitted the drive letters from Table 29.2. Find the hive file on the drive that corresponds to the other Windows installation.) Unload the hive after you've exported or corrected the desired information.

In some cases, you will find that you cannot view or modify keys loaded from another installation. This occurs if the keys are protected with security attributes that list specific users or groups defined in the other installation. In this case, you need to first take ownership of the keys and then add yourself as a user who is authorized to read or change the keys. The next section describes this.

> **🔍 note**
>
> You rarely should have to modify Registry security settings, but it does happen. The usual case is that an incorrectly designed program places information in a subkey of HKEY_LOCAL_MACHINE\Software that is intended to be shared and modified by all users running the program. Because Windows does not permit standard users to modify any keys in HKEY_LOCAL_MACHINE\Software by default, the program might malfunction. Modifying permissions so that standard users can edit the shared key is sometimes necessary to fix the problem. Microsoft also sometimes recommends modifying Registry security in emergency security bulletins.

Editing Registry Security

Just as files and folders in an NTFS-formatted disk partition have security attributes to control access based on user and group identity, Registry keys and values also have a complete set of access control attributes that determine who has rights to read, write, and modify each entry.

If you absolutely must change permissions or auditing controls, locate the desired key or value, right-click it, and select Permissions. The Permissions dialog box looks just like the comparable dialog box for files and folders (see Figure 29.3), and it lets you set read, write, and modify rights for specific groups and users. You'll find a corresponding set of audit settings.

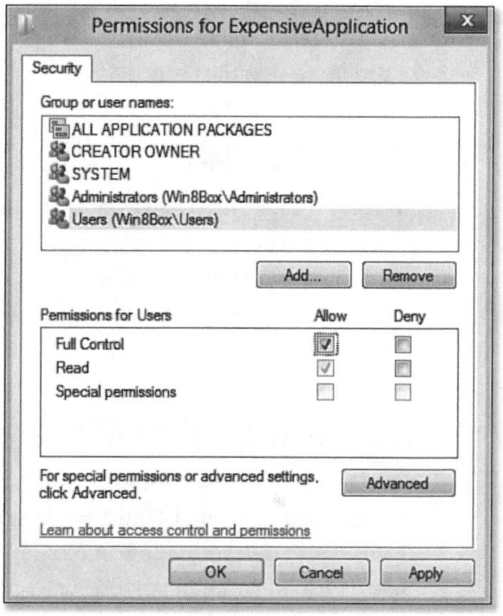

Figure 29.3
Registry key permissions control which users or groups are allowed to see or modify the Registry key and its values.

In most cases, a software vendor supplies precise instructions for making changes necessary to work around an application problem. Here, we describe a general procedure to make a given key readable and writeable by all users. You might do this to make a key capable of sharing information between users, or to repair an alternate Windows installation, as mentioned in the previous section. To set more generous permissions, follow these steps:

1. Locate and select the key in the left pane.

2. Right-click it and select Permissions.

3. Select the Users entry in the top Group or User Names section. If Users is not listed, click Add, type **Users**, and click OK.

4. In the lower section, check Allow in the Full Control row and then click Apply. If this is successful, click OK.

5. If you are unable to make the changes, even though you're running the Registry Editor as an Administrator, click Advanced and select the Owner tab.

6. If the Current Owner is listed as unknown, select Administrators in the lower list and click OK.

7. Click OK to close the Advanced Security Settings dialog box, and return to Step 3.

This is a risky procedure because it could result in another user or application being unable to access its own Registry keys. Use this as a procedure of last resort.

Other Registry Tools

You can use some third-party tools to edit the registry and adjust Windows features. Here are three of the more popular utilities.

Registry Toolkit

Registry Toolkit is a shareware Registry Editor made by Funduc software (www.funduc.com) with a nifty search-and-replace system. You can scan the Registry, changing all occurrences of one string to another, which is something most other Windows Registry Editors can't do. Its user interface isn't very comfortable or slick, but if you need to manage a lot of identical changes in the Registry, this is one cool tool. It's free to try, $25 to register, at www.funduc.com.

Registrar Registry Manager

Registrar Registry Manager is a powerful Registry-editing tool produced by Resplendence Software Projects (www.resplendence.com), with a drag-and-drop interface. It includes a Registry backup, restore, and defragmentation tool, a Registry-compare tool, an Undo capability, and many more features. The full version costs $55, and there is a free "lite" version.

Tweak-8

Tweak-8 from Totalidea Software (www.totalidea.com) combines tweaking tools with additional enhancements and plug-ins. The cost is approximately $30 for one computer, with multiple-license discounts available. Check the totalidea.com website for this and other cool Windows 8 tools.

Registry Privileges and Policies

On Windows corporate "domain"-type networks, Administrators can use the *policy* system to restrict users' ability to change their computer configuration. When you log on using a Domain user account, the policy system downloads and installs Registry settings prepared by system administrators. These Registry settings not only can help automate the setup of networking and other components, but can also restrict your ability to (mis)manage your computer.

Here's how it works: Windows looks at a boatload of Registry entries to determine what features to make available to you. For example, one value determines whether the Start menu is allowed to display the Run item; another makes the Control Panel hide the Power Management settings. Most of these values normally don't appear in the Registry at all, but they can be installed there by the policy system, and Windows security settings prevent users from changing or deleting them.

> *On a computer that's a member of a Windows Domain network, the policy system is called Group Policy. On a standalone computer, it's called Local Security Policy. For a more detailed discussion of Local Security Policy, **see** "Tightening Local Security Policy," **p. 813**.*

30

COMMAND-LINE AND AUTOMATION TOOLS

Command-Line Tools

Despite the ease of use of the Windows graphical user interface, the command-line interface remains a useful way to perform many maintenance, configuration, and diagnostic tasks. In fact, many important diagnostic tools such as ping, tracert, and nslookup are available only from the command line, unless you purchase third-party graphical add-ons to perform these functions. And although the term *batch file* might bring back uncomfortable memories of the old MS-DOS days, batch files and program scripts are still powerful tools that provide a useful way to encapsulate common management functions. Together, command-line utilities, batch files, and scripts based on Windows Script Host provide a complete set of building blocks from which you can develop high-level utilities for repetitive or complex tasks.

In this book, we give you a quick introduction to setting up and using the command-line environment. We don't have room for more than that. For much more detail, tutorials, examples, and many helpful tips on using command-line tools, check out Brian's book *Windows 7 and Vista Guide to Scripting, Automation, and Command Line Tools*, published by Que.

 tip

The command line can even help you with graphical tasks. Are you tired yet of clicking and swiping around the Windows 8 Start screen and desktop to open a control panel applet? You can open most control panels, system properties dialog boxes, and Computer Maintenance tools with just a few keystrokes. We show you how in this chapter.

The Windows 8 Command Prompt Environment

The Command Prompt window lets you type commands and review output, as shown in Figure 30.1. The quickest way to open a Command Prompt window is to press Windows Logo+X and select Command Prompt.

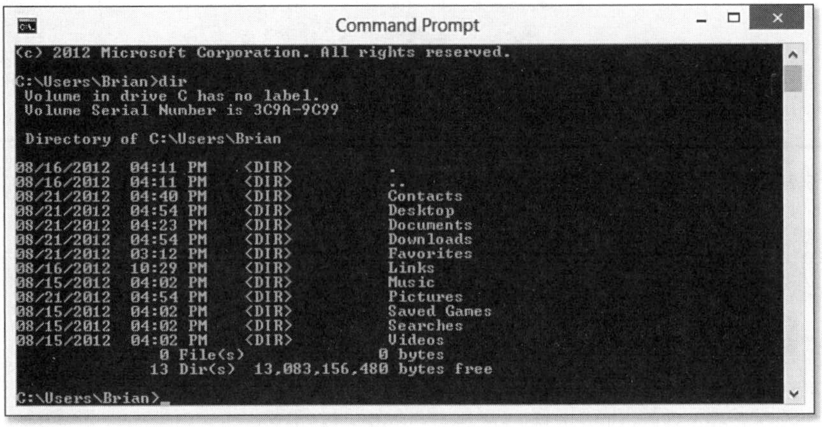

Figure 30.1
The Command Prompt window is the gateway to a world of powerful Windows management tools.

Alternatively, you could perform one of the following actions:

- Press Windows Logo+R, then type **cmd** and press Enter.

- Go to the Start screen, type **cmd**, and wait a moment. On most computers, "Command Prompt" will appear as the only search result. Press Enter to launch it.

- Right-click the Start screen, select All Apps, and locate Command Prompt in the Windows System section.

Any of these methods work equally well.

The main difference between a standard Windows application and a command-line program—which in Windows is technically called a *console program*—is that it doesn't use a graphical display or pull-down menus. Instead, you type commands into the Command Prompt window to tell Windows to do something, and the programs type information back to you. Each command line starts with the name of the program that you want to run, followed by additional information called *arguments*. Arguments tell the program what specifically you want to do.

> **tip**
>
> If you plan on using the Command Prompt window regularly, open a Command Prompt window by one of the means mentioned previously. Locate its icon in the taskbar—it has the tiny characters C:\ in white, against a black background. Right-click it and select Pin This Program to Taskbar. Now you can easily open a Command Prompt window anytime you're at the Desktop.

Changing Directories

The Command Prompt environment has a concept of a "current directory," the folder that is used for file operations if you don't specify one explicitly. You can change the current directory with the `cd` command, as in: `cd \windows`. If you want to change the default drive letter as well as the default folder, put /d on the cd command line, as in `cd /d d:\setup`.

Saving Output

The output of a command-line program usually prints out in the Command Prompt window. You can save output by redirecting it into a file, using the > character. For example, the command

```
dir >listing.txt
```

lists the files in the current directory, and stores the results in the file `listing.txt`. You could then type `notepad listing.txt` to view the results. By itself, > creates a new file or replaces an existing file. You can tack output onto the end of (append to) a file using >>, as in this example:

```
dir c:\windows >>listing.txt
```

You can also send the output of one program to another program using ¦ (the pipe character), as in

```
dir c:\windows ¦ findstr /i setup
```

which lists the contents of folder `c:\windows` and prints out only entries that contain the word `setup` somewhere in the name. One handy use of the pipe mechanism is to send output to the command `more`, which stops after it displays each screen full, so you can read through a long printout:

```
dir c:\windows ¦ more
```

When it stops printing, you press the spacebar to see the next screen.

There are more ways to redirect program input and output, which you can read about in the references at the end of this chapter.

The Search Path

When you type a command line, Windows searches a list of folders called the *search path* for a file whose name matches the program name you typed and whose name ends with any of several extensions, such as `.exe`, `.bat`, or `.vbs`. The most common program extensions are listed in Table 30.1. Windows examines the file to see what type of program it is, and then runs it. It's then the program's job to interpret any arguments you typed after the program name.

Table 30.1   Typical Executable Program Extensions

Extension	Program Type
.bat, .cmd	Batch file.
.com	Archaic MS-DOS program. (Not available on 64-bit Windows.)
.exe	Windows GUI program, console program, or MS-DOS program. (Windows determines which by examining the contents of the file.)
.js	Script file written in the JavaScript language.
.msc	Microsoft Management Console snap-in.
.vbs	Script file written in the VBScript language.

The search path is defined by a list of folder names in the PATH environment variable, and the complete list of extensions that Windows looks for is defined in the PATHEXT environment variable. The default search path includes the following folders:

```
C:\Windows\system32
C:\Windows
C:\Windows\System32\Wbem
C:\Windows\System32\WindowsPowerShell\v1.0\
```

This means that any program file, batch file, or script stored in any of these folders can be run simply by typing its name. You can start both Windows programs and command-line programs in this way. For example, you just have to type **notepad** to start the Notepad accessory.

If you create your own batch files, scripts, or programs, it's a good idea to create a separate folder to store them in, and to put that folder in the search path. We show you how to do so later in this chapter, under "Setting the PATH Environment Variable."

Running Commands with Elevated Privileges

Some command-line programs require elevated Administrator privileges (via User Account Control) to do their job correctly. To use a Command Prompt window to run a program with elevated privileges, you must run it from a Command Prompt window that is itself "elevated."

To open an elevated Command Prompt window, use one of these methods:

- Press Windows Logo+X and select Command Prompt (Admin).

- If you have pinned Command Prompt to the taskbar, right-click the taskbar icon, right-click Command Prompt, and then select Run As Administrator.

- At the Start screen, search for cmd. Right-click the Command Prompt result, or touch it and swipe down, to display the App bar. Select Run As Administrator.

⚑ caution

Be *very* careful when using an elevated Command Prompt window. Any commands you start from within this window will run with elevated privileges from the get-go, and you will receive no further UAC prompts when you start them. This includes Windows GUI programs—for example, if you type the command optional-features, you will get the Turn Windows Features On or Off dialog box, and you will not have to confirm anything before it starts.

If you want, you can set a Command Prompt shortcut or pinned taskbar icon so that it is elevated by default. Right-click the icon and select Properties. On the Shortcut tab, click the Advanced button and check Run As Administrator. Be sure to rename the shortcut so that it's clear that it opens an elevated prompt.

To be safe, do not use an elevated Command Prompt window for general-purpose work. Use it only to accomplish a specific task that requires elevated privileges; then close it.

Cutting and Pasting in the Command Prompt Window

Although you will usually use output redirection to store the output from command-line programs in files, you can also use cut and paste to move text into or out of a Command Prompt window.

To paste text into the window at the cursor location, click the window's System Menu (the upper-left corner) and select Edit, Paste. It's easier to do this without the mouse: just press Alt+Spacebar and type **E P**.

To copy text from the window to the Clipboard, click the window's System Menu and select Edit, Mark. Alternatively, press Alt+Spacebar and type **E M**. Use the mouse to highlight a rectangular area of the screen and then press Enter. This copies the text to the Clipboard.

By default, the mouse does not select text until you use the Mark sequence. This makes it easier to use MS-DOS programs that are mouse-aware. If you seldom use the mouse with MS-DOS applications, click the System Menu (or press Alt+Spacebar), select Defaults, and check Quick Edit. When Quick Edit is enabled, you can use the mouse to mark text for copying to the Clipboard without having to press Alt+Spacebar and type **E M** first.

Learning About Command-Line Programs

How do you know what programs are available and how to use them? For that, you must turn to documentation about the command-line environment. For some reason, Microsoft no longer provides this in the Help and Support system, but you can search online, and some programs can be told to display their own usage information.

To get an idea of what's available, see Appendix B, "Command-Line Utilities," at the end of this book. And you might want to check out Brian's book *Windows 7 and Vista Guide to Scripting, Automation, and Command Line Tools*.

For a general online listing, perform the Google search

```
site:microsoft.com command line a-z windows server
```

and then locate the A–Z listing for Windows Server 2008 or Windows Server 2003. Most of the programs listed there are available on Windows 8.

Many programs will print out their own usage information if you run them in a Command Prompt window, following the program name with /? as in this example:

```
dir /?
```

Running GUI Programs from the Command Line

Windows will start any program whose name it can find in the search path, whether it's a console application or a GUI program. If you know Windows programs by name, this can save you an awful lot of poking around and clicking with the mouse. Just type! Table 30.2 lists just a few GUI programs you start by typing their name into a Command Prompt window or the Windows Logo+R "Run" dialog box.

> **🔍 note**
>
> For those programs whose name ends with .msc, you can omit the .msc when you type the name into a Command Prompt window.

Table 30.2　Some GUI Program Names

Type	To Launch
appwiz.cpl	Uninstall or Change a Program
compmgmt.msc	Computer Management
control	Control Panel
devmgmt.msc	Device Manager
eventvwr	Event Viewer
explorer	File Explorer
lusrmgr.msc	Local Users and Groups
ncpa.cpl	Network Connections
notepad	Windows Notepad
powercfg.cpl	Power Plans
secpol.msc	Local Security Policy
sysdm.cpl	System Properties
taskschd.msc	Task Scheduler
timedate.cpl	Time and Date
wf.msc	Windows Firewall with Advanced Security

Setting Environment Variables

Using environment variables is one of the ways that Windows communicates information such as the location of system files and folders—as set up on your particular computer—to programs. Environment variables indicate where temporary files are stored, what folders contain Windows program files, and other settings that affect program operation and system performance. In addition, they can be used in batch files to temporarily hold information about the job at hand.

In Windows 8, the initial environment variables defined when every Command Prompt window is first opened are set up using the GUI shown in Figure 30.2.

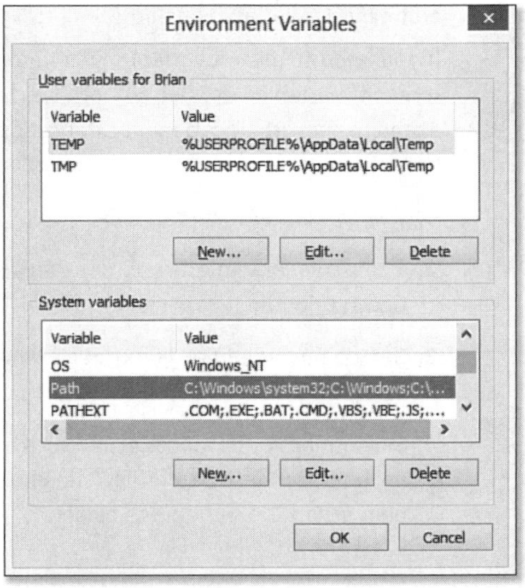

Figure 30.2
Examining the environment variables for the current user (top) and for all users of the system (bottom). The per-user list adds to or overrides the systemwide list.

This dialog box has two sections: System Variables and User Variables. The lower section, System Variables, defines the environment variables set up for every user account. The upper section, User Variables, defines additional default environment variables just for the current user account. These add to or override the variables set up in the systemwide list.

To open this dialog box, if you are a computer administrator user, use either of these two methods:

- If you have a Command Prompt window open, type the command **start sysdm.cpl** and press Enter. You might need to confirm a UAC prompt. Then, select the Advanced tab and click the Environment Variables button.

- Alternatively, click Start, type **computer**, right-click Computer in the results, and select Properties. Select Advanced System Settings. You might need to confirm a UAC prompt. Then, click the Environment Variables button.

You can now edit both the upper User Variables (personal settings) and lower System Variables (systemwide settings) lists.

If you are not a computer administrator user, it's a bit trickier. Use either of these two procedures:

- To edit the systemwide settings, you can use either of the preceding methods, but you'll have to supply an administrator password. *Don't* change the upper (personal) part of the dialog box—you will be changing settings for the wrong account.

- To edit your own personal environment variable list, you must use the following method: click Start, Control Panel, User Accounts and Family Safety, User Accounts. In the task list at the left side, click Change My Environment Variables. You will be able to edit only the upper (personal) environment variable list.

After you have the dialog box open, you can create new variables, delete variables, or highlight and edit existing variables using the corresponding buttons.

If you need to alter a variable, you must understand what happens if there's a conflict between environment variables defined in both the System Variables and User Variables lists. As a rule, Windows examines several locations for definitions, and the last definition seen wins. Windows sets variables from the following sources, in this order:

1. The systemwide variable list.

2. The personal variable list. (At this step, the PATH variable is treated specially. See the next section for details.)

3. Set commands in autoexec.nt. (This applies only for MS-DOS or Windows 3.*x* applications. See "The MS-DOS Environment" later in the chapter for more information.)

4. Subsequent definitions issued by set commands typed in a Command Prompt window or encountered in a batch file. These changes apply only to that particular window and will disappear when the window is closed.

Setting the PATH Environment Variable

If you write batch files or scripts, it's useful to put them into one folder and to add this folder name to the PATH variable so that you can run your batch files and scripts simply by typing their names.

Because mis-editing the PATH variable can prevent Windows from finding applications it needs to run, Windows gives the "personal" PATH definition special treatment:

- For the PATH variable, the User Variables definition is *added to* the end of (appended to) the System Variables definition.

- For all other environment variables, a User Variables definition *overrides* a System Variables definition.

In other words, you can enter your own personal folder(s) into the User Variables definition of PATH without worrying about copying or messing up the system definitions.

To create a folder for your own scripts and batch files, use one of these two procedures:

- If you want to use the scripts and batch files only for your own use, create a folder and put the full path to the folder into your "personal" PATH variable. For example, create a folder named c:\scripts.

  Then, add a PATH variable to the upper part of the Environment Variables dialog box (refer to Figure 30.2) with the value c:\scripts. If you need to add more than one folder to your personal PATH, put a semicolon (;) between each folder name.

- If you want to create scripts and batch files that can be used by anyone who uses your computer, create a folder and be sure that its permissions are set so that all users can read it.

  For example, create a folder named c:\scripts. Right-click the folder, select Properties, and select the Security tab. If Users does not appear under Group or User Names, click Edit, click Add, and then add "Users" to the list. Be sure that the Read & Execute permission setting is checked.

To learn more about editing permissions, **see** "Setting Security Permissions on Files and Folders," **p. 775**.

Then, carefully edit the PATH variable in the lower part of the Environment Variables dialog box (shown in Figure 30.2). Add a semicolon (;) to the end of the existing text and then add the folder name c:\scripts.

Your folder now will be part of the PATH when you open a new Command Prompt window.

The MS-DOS Environment

If you still use MS-DOS programs, you'll be glad to know that the 32-bit versions of Windows 8 still support MS-DOS programs.

The 32-bit versions of Windows run MS-DOS applications inside a program called ntvdm, which stands for *Windows NT Virtual DOS Machine*. Ntvdm is also used by the Windows 3.*x* support environment. It simulates the environment that DOS programs expect and makes them work correctly under Windows. Ntvdm runs automatically when you attempt to start an MS-DOS or 16-bit Windows program.

Editing Advanced Settings for a DOS Application

If you're experiencing difficulties while running a specific DOS program, find the program file or a shortcut to it. Right-click it and choose Properties.

Poke through each tab and use the ? (question mark) button for help on the settings. Educational and game programs will most often require you to adjust the Memory and Compatibility settings.

You can choose to further configure the MS-DOS and Windows 3.*x* environment by modifying Windows 8's equivalent of the old CONFIG.SYS and AUTOEXEC.BAT files. These files are called config.nt and autoexec.nt and are used to configure each DOS VDM when it starts up. You can edit the config.nt and autoexec.nt files with a simple text editor such as Notepad. They're protected files, however, so you must run an elevated version of Notepad, using this procedure:

1. On the Start screen, type the word **notepad**.

2. When Notepad appears as a search result under Apps, right-click it and select Run As Administrator.

> **note**
>
> The MS-DOS and 16-bit Windows subsystems are not provided with the 64-bit versions of Windows. (It's a technical limitation, not a marketing decision.) If you use a 64-bit version of Windows and still need to run MS-DOS or Windows 3.1 applications, you can set up a "virtual" computer, install a copy of MS-DOS, Windows 3.1, or a 32-bit version of Windows, and run your older applications inside the simulated environment. We talk about this in Appendix A, "Virtualization."

> **note**
>
> On 32-bit versions of Windows 8, the first time you try to run a 16-bit DOS or Windows 3.1 program, Windows will prompt you to enable the 16-bit subsystem. There is also a control panel applet that lets you turn the subsystem on or off. Search Control Panel for "16-bit Application Support." The registry value that controls the subsystem is DisallowedPolicyDefault, in key HKEY_LOCAL_MACHINE\System\CurrentControlSet\Control\WOW. On a corporate network, the network administrator may permanently enable or disable the subsystem through Group Policy.

3. Confirm the UAC prompt, or enter an Administrator password as requested. (Alternately, you can just type **notepad** in an elevated Command Prompt window.)

4. Click File, Open and browse to \windows\system32. Select autoexec.nt or config.nt, as desired.

Most of the settings used in MS-DOS 6 still work in config.nt, with some exceptions. For more information about configuring the MS-DOS environment in Windows, go to google.com and enter this search: **site:technet.microsoft.com windows xp devicehigh**. Select the result titled just "Devicehigh." The left pane will display a list of MS-DOS configuration commands.

> **◉ tip**
>
> It's usually a good idea to edit config.nt, add the line device=ansi.sys, and change the line files=40 to files=100.

Issues with DOSKEY and ANSI.SYS

The MS-DOS enhancement ANSI.SYS was used to let programs move the cursor around on the screen. It can be made available for MS-DOS programs simply by adding the line device= ansi.sys to config.nt.

Conversely, DOSKEY—which has been enhanced significantly from the old DOS days—functions only in the 32-bit Windows console environment, and even if you attempt to load it in autoexec.nt, it does not function within the MS-DOS COMMAND.COM shell.

> **🔍 note**
>
> If you make changes to autoexec.nt or config.nt after having run an MS-DOS program from a Command Prompt window, you must close the Command Prompt window and open a new one for the MS-DOS subsystem to reload and take on the new configuration.

Printing from MS-DOS Applications

Most DOS applications can print only to LPT ports. If you want to use a printer that is on a USB port or is out there somewhere on a LAN, you must share the printer (even if it's just attached to your own computer and you're not using a network) and then issue the command

```
net use lpt2: \\localhost\sharename
```

from the Command Prompt window, replacing sharename with the name you used when you shared the printer. Direct your DOS program to use LPT2. (You can use LPT1, LPT2, or LPT3, but you must select an LPT port number that does not have an associated physical LPT port in your computer.) Some MS-DOS applications know how to send output directly to networked printers using a UNC share name, so you don't need to use the LPT trick with them.

➡ *For more information about the* net use *command,* ***see*** *"Managing Network Resources Using the Command Line," **p. 484.***

Batch Files

Although Windows Script Host is the most powerful tool for creating your own helpful programs, it's also useful to know how to use the batch file language. Batch files let you take advantage of the hundreds of command-line programs supplied with Windows.

A batch file, at the simplest level, is just a list of command prompt commands that have been typed into a file whose extension is .bat or .cmd. When you enter the name of a batch file at the command prompt, Windows looks for a file with this name in the current directory and in the folders of the PATH environment variable. Windows treats each line in the batch file as a command, and runs them one after the other as if you'd typed the commands by hand. At this simplest level, then, a batch file can be a big help if you find yourself typing the same commands over and over.

Beyond this, there are several commands that you can use to write rudimentary "programs" within a batch file so that it can take different actions depending on what you type on the command line, or depending on the results of the commands it executes. These programming commands have been greatly improved since the MS-DOS days, so writing useful batch files on Windows 8 is much easier than writing them was in the old days. In particular, the IF and FOR statements have been greatly extended. You can prompt the user for input. It's possible to manipulate strings and filenames and perform arithmetic calculations. You can create subroutines within a single batch file. And there's more.

Unfortunately, I don't have room to provide coverage of batch file programming in this book, but I do in my book *Windows 7 and Vista Guide to Scripting, Automation, and Command Line Tools*, published by Que.

And some Microsoft documentation is available online. After reading this chapter, go to www.microsoft.com and search for these phrases:

```
Command Shell Overview
Environment Variables
Using Batch Parameters
Using Batch Files
Using Command Redirection Operators
Cmd
Command-Line Reference
```

Then, open a Command Prompt window and type the commands

```
help cmd
help set
help for
help if
```

and so on.

Batch File Tips

Table 30.3 lists several short batch files that I put on every computer that I use. These short command scripts let me edit files, change the path, view a folder with File Explorer, and so on, simply by typing a couple of letters followed by a folder or filename. They don't involve fancy programming, but they save me a significant amount of time when I'm working with the Command Prompt window.

If you create a `c:\scripts` folder and add it to the PATH, as discussed earlier under "Setting the PATH Environment Variable," you might want to create these same batch files in that folder for your own use.

 tip

To learn how to get the most from the batch files and the command line, get Brian's book *Windows 7 and Vista Guide to Scripting, Automation, and Command Line Tools*.

Table 30.3 Useful Tiny Batch Files

Filename	Contents and Purpose

ap.bat	`@echo off`
	`for %%p in (%path%) do if /%%p/ == /%1/ exit /b`
	`set path="%1";%path%`
	Adds the named folder to the PATH if it is not already listed. (This lasts only as long as the Command Prompt window is open.)
	Example: `ap c:\test`

bye.bat	`@logout` Logs off Windows. Example: `bye`
e.bat	`@if /%1/ == // (explorer /e,.) else explorer /e,%1` Opens File Explorer in Folder mode to view the named directory, or the current directory if no path is entered on the command line. Example: `e d:`
h.bat	`@cd /d %userprofile%` Changes the current directory to your user profile (home) directory. Example: `h`
n.bat	`@start notepad "%1"` Edits the named file with Notepad. Example: `n test.bat`
s.bat	`@cd /d c:\scripts` Makes `c:\scripts` the current directory, when you want to add or edit batch files and scripts. Example: `s`

Windows Script Host

Scripts can massage, digest, and manipulate text files and data, view and change Windows settings, and more. Scripts have an advantage over batch files in that they can perform complex calculations and can manipulate text information in powerful ways, because you write them in a full-featured programming language. In addition, scripts can enlist applications such as Microsoft Word and Excel to present information in tidy, formatted documents and charts.

Windows comes with support for two different scripting languages:

- **VBScript**—Nearly identical to the Visual Basic for Applications (VBA) macro language used in Word and Excel.

- **JScript**—Microsoft's version of the JavaScript language, which is widely used to make web pages interactive. (JavaScript, by the way, is not the same thing as Java. Java is another programming language altogether.)

In addition, you can download and install scripting support for other languages. If you have a UNIX or Linux background, for example, you might want to use the Perl, Python, or TCL scripting languages. You can get free WSH-compatible versions of these languages at www.activestate.com.

If you are already versed in one of the scripting languages mentioned here, by all means, use it. If you don't already know a scripting language, VBScript is probably the best one to start with because you can also use it to write macros for Microsoft's desktop applications. We'll use VBScript in the examples in this section.

Some Sample Scripts

We don't have room here to give you even an introductory course in VBScript programming. As mentioned, that's a topic that can fill an entire book. What we can do is give you some examples of how WSH can be used to perform useful tasks and to manage Windows. These sample scripts assume that you have set the default script environment to console mode, as opposed to windowed mode, by typing this command just once in an elevated Command Prompt window:

```
cscript //h:cscript //nologo //s
```

(Elevated Command Prompt windows were described earlier in this chapter.)

Disk and Network Management

WSH comes with tools to examine and modify drives, folders, and files. Here is an example of a VBScript script that performs a reasonably useful task:

```
set fso = CreateObject("Scripting.FileSystemObject")
set drivelist = fso.Drives
for each drv in drivelist
    if drv.IsReady then
        wscript.echo "Drive", drv.DriveLetter, "has", drv.FreeSpace, "bytes free"
    end if
next
```

It displays the amount of free space on each of your computer's drives. Type this script into a file named `freespace.vbs` in your batch file directory, and then type the command-line command **freespace**. On my computer this prints the following:

```
Drive C: has 15866540032 bytes free
Drive D: has 27937067008 bytes free
Drive F: has 335872000 bytes free
Drive H: has 460791808 bytes free
```

WSH can also work with networking features. The following VBScript script displays your computer's current network drive mappings:

```
set wshNetwork = CreateObject("WScript.Network") ' create the helper object
set maps = wshNetwork.EnumNetworkDrives          ' collection describes mapped drives
for i = 0 to maps.Length-2 step 2                ' step through collection by twos
    wscript.echo "Drive", maps.item(i), "is mapped to", maps.item(i+1)
next
```

Windows Management Instrumentation

Windows Management Instrumentation (WMI) is a system service that provides access to virtually every aspect of a Windows computer system, from the hardware components up to the highest-level system services.

The following script lists the status of each system service installed on your computer. This script file can be named `showservices.vbs`. (The underscores at the end of some of the lines are part of the script.)

```
set services = GetObject("winmgmts:{impersonationlevel=impersonate," & _
        "authenticationlevel=pkt}!" & _
        "/root/CIMV2:Win32 Service")     ' get services WMI info
for each svc in services.Instances _     ' display information for each service
    wscript.echo svc.name, "State:", svc.State, "Startup:", svc.StartMode
next
```

On my computer, the first few lines of output from this script look like this:

```
AeLookupSvc State: Stopped Startup: Manual
ALG State: Stopped Startup: Manual
AllUserInstallAgent State: Stopped Startup: Manual
AppIDSvc State: Stopped Startup: Manual
```

Remember, too, that because these are command-line programs, you can redirect the output of these scripts into a file. The command

```
showservices >listing.txt
```

puts the service list into file `listing.txt`, just as if `showservices` was a native Windows executable program.

Windows PowerShell

Microsoft developed a command-line environment called Windows PowerShell (WPS), which is installed as a standard accessory starting with Windows 7. WPS in many ways looks and acts like the familiar Command Prompt window, but it's actually a very strange animal, and it gives you access to some very powerful programming tools. We don't have room in this book to teach you much about it, but we will describe how it differs from batch file and scripts, and we'll point you to resources that will help you learn more.

We used the word *strange*. Can a computer program be strange? Definitely! For one thing, most Windows PowerShell commands (which are properly called *cmdlets*) generate streams of *objects*, not text. Objects are computer representations of real-world things. They have *properties* that describe attributes of the things they represent, and *methods* that let you manipulate the things. For example, an object that represents a specific file on your hard disk might have properties such as Name, Size, and LastWriteTime as well as methods such as Delete, Edit, and Open. Windows PowerShell works with objects in a new, unusual, and ultimately very powerful way.

Now, if you type dir in a regular Command Prompt window, the command shell interprets dir and generates a bunch of text listing the current folder's files by name. The dir command is programmed very specifically to print information about files in text form. That's all it can do.

In WPS, you can type dir and this will also print out a list of filenames, but something completely different is happening behind the scenes. In WPS, dir is a shortcut for the Get-Childitem cmdlet, which in its simplest use generates a stream of File objects; each object represents one of the files in a folder, and each object has properties and methods (for example, name and size). When an object (of any sort) lands in the WPS prompt window, WPS prints out a line of text listing the object's most important properties. For a File object, this includes the file's name, size, and the date it was created. So, when you type dir, WPS produces a stream of File objects and they end up as a nice, tabular listing of files.

The end result is the same as in the old Command Prompt environment, but it's happening in a general, more abstract way. The cmdlet doesn't know about or care about text or formatting: it simply spits out a bunch of File objects. And the WPS window will turn *any* list of objects into a nice tabular listing. Files, user accounts, hard drives, Windows services—whatever object a cmdlet throws into the WPS window turns into a nice text listing.

In addition, WPS includes a full-scale object-oriented programming language and has access to Microsoft's .NET programming platform, which means WPS scripts can perform complex computations and communicate with other computers and networked ("cloud") services.

WPS even lets you do complex things with objects without programming. You can use the familiar ¦ (pipe) symbol to direct streams of objects from one cmdlet to another, and this lets you do very complex, specific things with tools that are separately very simple and general-purpose in nature. For example, the following command will delete all files in the current folder that are more than 6 months old:

```
dir ¦ where-object { $_.LastWriteTime -lt (get-date).addmonths(-6)} ¦ remove-item
```

It looks complex at first, but it's not so bad. This command line strings three separate cmdlets together:

- `dir`—Spits out a list of all the `File` objects in the current directory. Here, they don't land in the WPS command window, so they don't make a text listing. Instead, the pipe (¦) symbol instructs WPS to pass the objects to the next command.

- `where-object`—Passes just some of the objects through, based on the "filtering" condition inside the curly brackets. In this example, it passes through only those files that have not been changed for more than 6 months (that is, whose `LastWriteTime` value is less than the date/time 6 months back). So, objects representing just the old files are piped to the next command.

- `remove-item`—Deletes the hard disk files corresponding to each of the file objects it receives.

> ### 📡 caution
>
> Don't just open a WPS window and type this command to see whether it works! You'll most likely delete a bunch of important files from your Windows profile folder. If you want to see whether it works, type just the first two parts of the command:
>
> ```
> dir ¦ where-object { $_.LastWriteTime -lt (get-date).addmonths(-6)}
> ```
>
> This will print out a list of the selected files but will not delete them.

As we said earlier, you're not limited just to using commands that you type into the WPS window. WPS has a full-scale programming language with variables, loops, subroutines, user-defined objects, and so on. You can use these at the command prompt or in script files. You also can create shortcuts (called *aliases*) for commonly used commands and scripts to make typing easier, and a bunch of aliases are predefined for you.

For more information about WPS, check out Brian's book *Windows 7 and Vista Guide to Scripting, Automation, and Command Line Tools* or *Windows PowerShell 2.0 Unleashed*.

Task Scheduler

Windows Task Scheduler is an automation tool that lets you specify programs to be run automatically at specified dates and times and on certain events such as system startup, users logging on, and even the occurrence of any event that can be logged in the Event Viewer.

What kinds of tasks would you run with Task Scheduler? As mentioned, the tasks need to run without user interaction. So, they are typically maintenance tasks such as defragmenting the hard disk, cleaning out temporary files, and so on. Windows uses Task Scheduler for this very purpose, and you'll notice that several pre-installed scheduled tasks are set up when Windows is installed to do this very sort of thing.

> ### 🔍 note
>
> When Task Scheduler runs a task as a different user than the one currently logged on, the logged-on user cannot see or interact with the program. Be sure that scheduled tasks can operate without user input and exit cleanly when they've done their work. And keep in mind that once an application or service is running, even if it was launched through a scheduled task, it will affect system performance just as if you started it manually.

> **note**
>
> Obviously, the computer must be alive to run a task, so if you expect to do a disk cleanup at 4:00 a.m., be sure to leave the computer on. If a scheduled task is missed because the computer was turned off, Windows will perform the task the next time the computer is started but the task will now be running while you're using the computer, which is probably what you were trying to avoid by having it run at night.

Task Scheduler is especially useful with batch files and scripts, because these scheduled programs can usually be designed to run without any user interaction. It's truly the ultimate automation tool because you don't even have to be there when it's working!

There are several ways to open the Task Scheduler:

- Go to the Start screen and type **taskschd**. Then, select Task Scheduler from the search results.

- Press Windows Logo+R, type **taskschd.msc**, and then press Enter.

- Press Windows+X, then select Computer Management. In the left pane, click the small arrow to the left of Task Scheduler.

Then, in the left pane, select Task Scheduler Library.

There are two types of tasks you can create in Task Scheduler:

- **Basic tasks**—Designed to be run using the current user's account and to support a single triggering event or time.

- **Tasks**—Can be run using any specified user account, and can be configured to run whether the user is logged in or not. Tasks can also be run in Windows XP or Windows Server 2003 compatibility mode, and can be configured to run with elevated priority if necessary.

To create a Basic task in Task Scheduler, follow these steps:

1. Open Task Scheduler as discussed earlier in this section. Task Scheduler displays in the top-center pane a summary list of tasks that started and/or completed during the last 24 hours, and displays a list of active tasks below that. (Here, *active* means "defined and enabled to run at the specified time or event." It doesn't necessarily mean "actively running right now.")

2. The Add Actions pane is located on the right side. Click Create Basic Task. The Create Basic Task Wizard opens.

3. Enter the name of the task and a description. Enter whatever you want, to remind you of what the tasks does. Click Next to continue.

4. On the Task Trigger screen, select when to run the task. You can choose daily, weekly, monthly, one time, when the computer starts, when you log on, or when a specific event is logged.

   You can use the When a Specific Event Is Logged option to trigger the task when a specific Event Log entry is recorded. For example, you could use this to perform some sort of notification if a disk error event occurs. You'll need to enter the event's numeric ID number.

5. Click Next.

6. Specify applicable time options, such as time of day, as required. Click Next.

7. Select what you want the task to do (open a program, send an email, or display a message). Click Next to continue.

 tip

To find an event's ID number, find an occurrence of the event in the Windows Event Log.

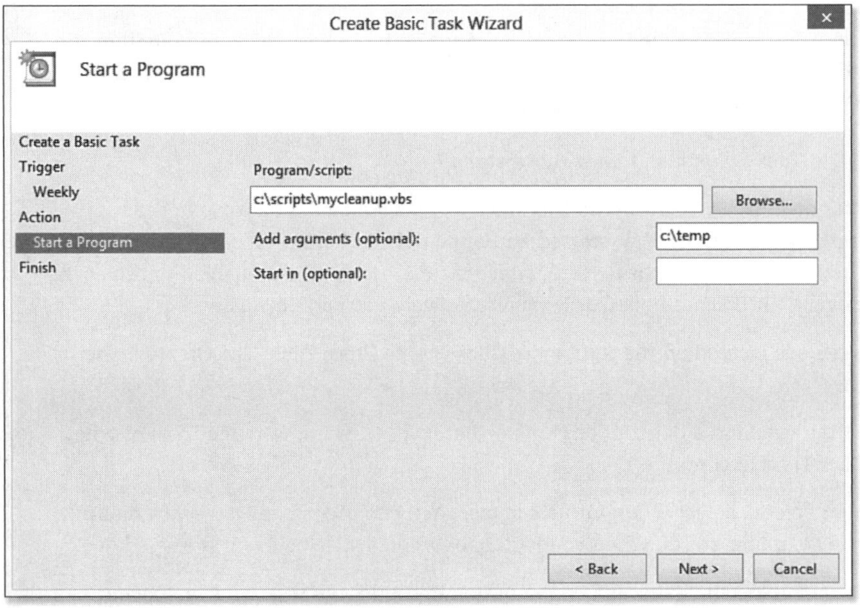

8. If you selected Start a Program, use Browse to locate the program, batch file, or script. (For Windows applications, browse in the \Windows or \Windows\ system32 folders. For third-party applications, search in the \Program Files folders. For scripts you've written yourself, browse to the folder in which you've stored the script or batch file.) Then provide any necessary command-line switches or settings, and if you want to specify a default drive and folder for the program, enter the path to the desired folder.

   If you selected Send an Email, enter the information for sender, receiver, SMTP email server, message, and so forth.

   If you selected Display a Message, enter the message title and message text. Then, click Next.

9. Review the task on the Summary screen (see Figure 30.3). If you want to set advanced options such as idle time, what to do if the computer is running on batteries, and what to do after the task completes, check Open Advanced Properties for This Task When I Click Finish. Click Finish to complete the task.

Figure 30.3
Completing the configuration of a basic task.

For more advanced scheduling, use the Create Task selection. The Create Task interface uses a multitabbed interface instead of a wizard. The General tab includes security options, whereas the Triggers tab permits you to specify multiple triggers for a task (the task will be performed whenever *any* of the triggers occurs). The Actions tab supports multiple actions in a task; the Conditions tab includes options to configure idle time, power, and network connection requirements; and the Settings tab supports conditions for running and stopping a task. Use Create Task, rather than Create Basic Task, when you need these additional settings in your task.

A Task Scheduler Conundrum

If you change the name of your computer, Scheduled Tasks might display the message, "An error has occurred for task *xxxx*. Error message: The specified account name is not valid." However, the problem task won't appear in the list of tasks, so you can't do anything about it. This happens to any scheduled task that was associated with a specific user account as the logon trigger, as the user credential for the task, and so on. The same thing happens if you delete a user account that was named in a Scheduled Task. To fix the problem, follow these steps:

1. Open File Explorer and browse to c:\windows\system32\tasks. This folder contains an XML text file for each scheduled task.

2. Delete the files for any broken tasks that you simply want to delete.

3. To repair a broken task, move the file for the broken task entry from \windows\system32\ tasks into another folder. You must *move* it, not *copy* it. You can do this using File Explorer or the move command in a Command Prompt window.

4. Open the task file in its new location using Notepad. Fix the computer name and/or account name wherever it occurs, and save the file. Repeat steps 3 and 4 for any other problem tasks.

5. Open Scheduled Tasks or, if it's already open, select Action, Refresh. There should be no error messages now because the problem task(s) were removed.

6. Under the Action menu, use the Import command to locate and import the edited task file. This will restore the scheduled task. Repeat for any other edited task files.

PROTECTING WINDOWS FROM VIRUSES AND SPYWARE

Avoiding Viruses and Spyware: The Basics

Let's begin with a look at protecting your PC from direct attacks: that is, when an unauthorized *cracker* (which we define as a hacker who has succumbed to the Dark Side of the Force) sits down at your keyboard and tries to gain access to your system. Sure, it may be unlikely that a malicious user would gain physical access to the computer in your home or office, but it's not impossible.

Crackers specialize in breaking into systems ("cracking" system security, hence the name), and at any given time, hundreds (perhaps even thousands) of crackers roam cyberspace looking for potential targets. If you're online right now, the restless and far-seeing eyes of the crackers are bound to find you eventually.

Sounds unlikely, you say? You wish. The crackers are armed with programs that automatically search through millions of IP addresses (the addresses that uniquely identify any computer or device connected to the Internet). The crackers are specifically looking for computers that aren't secure, and if they find one they'll pounce on it and crack their way into the system.

Again, if all this sounds unlikely or that it would take them forever to find you, think again. Tests have shown that new and completely unprotected systems routinely get cracked within 20 minutes of connecting to the Internet!

First, a Few Simple Precautions

So how do your thwart the world's crackers? We often joke that it's easy if you follow a simple four-prong plan:

- Don't connect to the Internet. Ever.

- Don't install programs on your computer. No, not even that one.

- Don't let anyone else work with, touch, glance at, talk about, or come within 20 feet of your computer.

- Burglar-proof your home or office.

The point here is that if you use your computer (and live your life) in an even remotely normal way, you open up your machine to security risks. That's a bleak assessment, for sure, but fortunately it doesn't take a lot of effort on your part to turn your computer into a maximum-security area. The security techniques in this chapter (and the next three chapters) will get to that goal, but first make sure you've nailed down the basics:

- **Leave User Account Control turned on**—Yes, we know UAC is a hassle, but if you're coming to Windows 8 from Windows Vista you'll find that it's *way* better now because it doesn't get in your face nearly as often. UAC is the best thing that's happened to Windows security in a long time, and it's a fact of life that your computer is much more secure when UAC has got your back. See "Making Sure User Account Control Is Turned On," later in this chapter.

- **Be paranoid**—The belief that everyone's out to get you may be a sign of trouble in the real world, but it's just common sense in the computer world. Assume someone will sit down at your desk when you're not around; assume someone will try to log on to your computer when you leave for the night; assume all uninvited email attachments are viruses; assume unknown websites are malicious; assume any offer that sounds too good to be true probably is.

- **Keep to yourself**—We all share lots of personal info online these days, but there's sharing and then there's asking-for-trouble sharing. Don't tell anybody any of your passwords. Don't put your email address online unless it's disguised in some way (for example, by writing it as *username* at *yourdomain* dot com). Don't give out sensitive personal data such as your social security number, bank account number, or even your address and phone number (unless making a purchase with a reputable vendor). Only give your credit card data to online vendors you trust implicitly; even better, get a secure PayPal account and use that instead.

- **Test the firewall**—A firewall's not much good if it leaves your computer vulnerable to attack, so you should test the firewall to make sure it's doing its job. We show you several ways to do this in Chapter 33, "Protecting Your Network from Hackers and Snoops."

➡ *For the details on using Windows Firewall,* **see** *"Configuring Windows Firewall,"* **p. 816.**

- **Take advantage of your router's firewall, too**—Why have one line of defense when in all probability you can have two! If your network has a router and that router connects to the Internet, then it, too, has an IP address that crackers can scan for vulnerabilities, particularly holes that expose your network. To prevent this, most routers come with built-in hardware firewalls that provide robust security. Access your router's setup pages, locate the firewall settings (see Figure 31.1 for an example), and then make sure the firewall is turned on.

- **Update, update, update**—Many crackers take advantage of known Windows vulnerabilities to compromise a system. To avoid this, keep your PC updated with the latest patches, fixes, and service packs, many of which are designed to plug security leaks.

> **note**
> To access the router setup pages, open a web browser, type the router address, and then press Enter. See your device documentation for the correct URL, but for most routers the address is http://192.168.1.1, http://192.168.0.1, or http://192.168.2.1. In most cases, you have to log in with a username and password, so, again, see your documentation.

➡ *To learn more about keeping your PC updated, **see** "Configuring and Managing Windows Update," **p. 653**.*

Figure 31.1
If your network has a router, make sure its firewall is turned on.

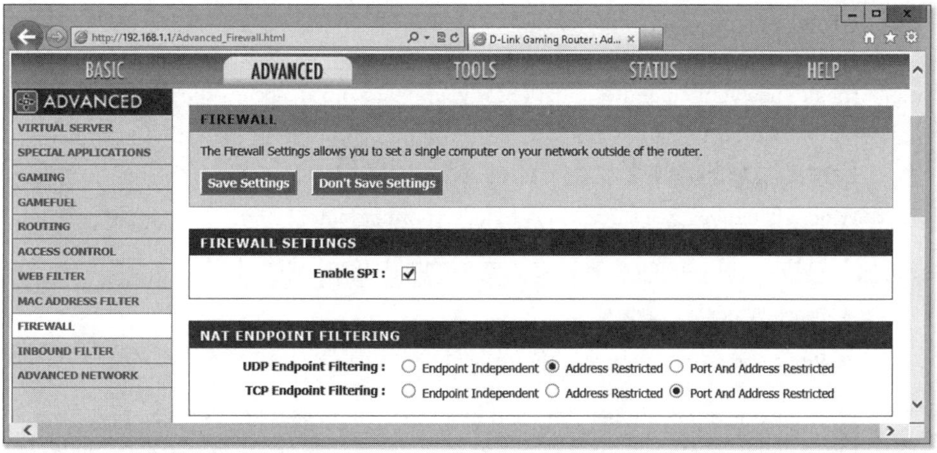

- **Assume the worst**—Back up your data regularly, keep your receipts, keep all email correspondence, and read the fine print.

Locking Your Computer

In Chapter 32, "Protecting Your Data from Loss and Theft," you learn a few more security tweaks, including important measures such as advanced file permissions and encryption. These two features are great, but they each have one small flaw: they rely on the assumption that after you've entered a legitimate username and password to log on to your Windows user account, only *you* will use your computer. This means that after you log on, you become a "trusted" user and you have full access to your files, even if they're protected by permissions and encryption.

This is certainly reasonable on the surface. After all, you wouldn't want to have to enter your account credentials every time you want to open, edit, create, or delete a document. So while you're logged on and at your desk, you get full access to your stuff.

But what happens when you leave your desk? If you remain logged on to Windows, any other person who sits down at your computer can take advantage of your trusted-user status to view and work with secure files (including copying them to a USB flash drive inserted by the snoop). This is what we mean by permissions and encryption having a flaw, and it's a potentially significant security hole in large offices where it wouldn't be hard for someone to pull up your chair while you're stuck in yet another meeting.

One way to prevent this would be to turn off your computer every time you leave your desk. That way, any would-be snoop would have to get past your login to get to your files. This, obviously, is wildly impractical and inefficient.

Is there a better solution? You bet: you can lock your system before leaving your desk. Anyone who tries to use your computer must enter your password to access the Windows desktop.

Locking Your Computer Manually

Windows 8 gives you three ways to lock your computer before heading off:

- In the Start screen, click your user account tile and then click Lock.

- Press Windows Logo+L.

- Press Ctrl+Alt+Delete and then click Lock.

Whichever method you use, you end up at the Windows 8 Lock screen. Press any key to switch to the sign-on screen, shown in Figure 31.2. Note that "Locked" is displayed under your username.

Locking Your Computer Automatically

The locking techniques from the previous section are easy enough to do, but the hard part is *remembering* to do them. If you're late for a meeting or a rendezvous, locking up your machine is probably the last thing on your mind as you dash out the door. The usual course of events in these situations is that just as you arrive at your destination you remember that you forgot to lock your PC, and you then spend the next while fretting about your defenseless computer.

Figure 31.2
You see a screen similar to this when you lock your Windows 8 computer.

To avoid the fretting (not to mention the possible intrusion), you can configure your computer to lock automatically after a period of inactivity. Here's how it's done:

1. Right-click the desktop and then click Personalize to open the Personalization window.

2. Click Screen Saver.

3. If you want to have a screensaver kick in after your PC is inactive for a while, choose one from the Screen Saver list.

4. Activate the On Resume, Display Logon Screen check box.

5. Use the Wait spin box to set the interval (in minutes) of idle time that Windows 8 waits before locking your PC.

6. Click OK.

Requiring Ctrl+Alt+Delete at Startup

Protecting your Windows 8 user account with a password, though an excellent idea, is not foolproof. Hackers are an endlessly resourceful bunch, and some of the smarter ones figured out a way to defeat the user account password system. The trick is that they install a virus or Trojan horse pro-gram—usually via an infected email message or malicious website—that loads itself when you start your computer. This program then displays a *fake* version of the Windows 8 logon screen. When you type your username and password into this dialog box, the program records it and your system security is compromised.

To thwart this clever ruse, Windows 8 enables you to configure your system so that you must press Ctrl+Alt+Delete before you can log on. This key combination ensures that the authentic logon screen appears.

To require that users must press Ctrl+Alt+Delete before they can log on, follow these steps:

1. Press Windows Logo+R to display the Run dialog box.

2. Type **control userpasswords2** and then click OK. The User Accounts dialog box appears.

3. Display the Advanced tab.

4. Activate the Require Users to Press Ctrl+Alt+Delete check box.

5. Click OK.

Checking Your Computer's Security Settings

Windows 8 comes with four security features enabled by default:

- Windows Firewall is turned on.

- Windows Defender protects your computer against spyware in real time and by scanning your PC on a schedule.

- User Account Control is turned on.

- The Administrator account is disabled.

However, even though these are the default settings, they're important enough not to be left to chance. The next four sections show you how to check that these crucial security settings really are enabled on your PC.

Making Sure Windows Firewall Is Turned On

By far the most important thing you need to do to thwart crackers is to have a software firewall run-ning on your computer. A *firewall* is a security feature that blocks unauthorized attempts to send data to your computer. The best firewalls completely hide your computer from the Internet, so those dastardly crackers don't even know you're there! Windows Firewall is turned on by default, but you should periodically check this, just to be safe:

1. Press Windows Logo+W to open the Settings search pane.

2. Type **firewall** and then click Windows Firewall in the search results. The Windows Firewall win-dow appears. Check the Windows Firewall State value. If it says On, as shown in Figure 31.3, you're fine; otherwise, continue to step 3.

Figure 31.3
In the Windows Firewall window, make sure the firewall state value is On.

3. Click Turn Windows Firewall On or Off. The Customize Settings window appears.

4. In the Private Network Location Settings section, activate the Turn On Windows Firewall option.

5. In the Public Network Location Settings section, activate the Turn On Windows Firewall option.

6. Click OK.

Making Sure Windows Defender Is Turned On

We've been troubleshooting Windows PCs for many years. It used to be that users accidentally deleting system files or making ill-advised attempts to edit the Registry or some other important configuration file caused most problems. Recent versions of Windows (particularly XP) could either prevent these kinds of PEBCAK (*Problem Exists Between Chair And Keyboard*) issues or recover from them without a lot of trouble. However, we're all too well aware of the latest menace to rise in the past few years, and it has taken over as the top cause of desperate troubleshooting calls we receive: *malware*, the generic term for malicious software such as viruses and Trojan horses.

The worst malware offender by far these days is *spyware*, a plague upon the earth that threatens to deprive a significant portion of the online world of its sanity. As often happens with new concepts, the term *spyware* has become encrusted with multiple meanings as people attach similar ideas to a convenient and popular label. However, spyware is generally defined as any program that surreptitiously monitors a user's computer activities—particularly the typing of passwords, PINs, and credit card numbers—or harvests sensitive data on the user's computer and then sends that information to an individual or a company via the user's Internet connection (the so-called *back channel*) without the user's consent.

You might think that having a robust firewall between you and the bad guys would make malware a problem of the past. Unfortunately, that's not true. These programs piggyback on other legitimate programs that users actually *want* to download, such as file-sharing programs, download managers, and screensavers. A *drive-by download* is the download and installation of a program without a user's knowledge or consent. This relates closely to a *pop-up download*—the download and installation of a program after the user clicks an option in a pop-up browser window, particularly when the option's intent is vaguely or misleadingly worded.

To make matters even worse, most spyware embeds itself deep into a system, and removing it is a delicate and time-consuming operation beyond the abilities of even experienced users. Some programs actually come with an Uninstall option, but it's nothing but a ruse, of course. The program appears to remove itself from the system, but what it actually does is a *covert reinstall*—it reinstalls a fresh version of itself when the computer is idle.

All this means that you need to buttress your firewall with an antispyware program that can watch out for these unwanted programs and prevent them from getting their hooks into your system. In versions of Windows prior to Vista, you needed to install a third-party program. However, Windows Vista came with an antispyware program named Windows Defender, and that tool remains part of Windows 8.

Windows Defender protects your computer from spyware in two ways. It can scan your system for evidence of installed spyware programs (and remove or disable those programs, if necessary), and it can monitor your system in real time to watch for activities that indicate the presence of spyware (such as a drive-by download or data being sent via a back channel).

If the real-time protection feature of Windows Defender is turned off, you usually see the Action Center message shown in Figure 31.4. Click that message to launch Windows Defender. Otherwise, switch to the Start screen, type **defender**, and then click Windows Defender in the search results.

Figure 31.4
The Windows 8 Action Center will let you know if Windows Defender isn't monitoring your system in real time for spyware.

In the Windows Defender Status bar, which appears just below the title bar, if your see "PC status: At risk," it means that Windows Defender is not actively guarding against virus and spyware activity.

Follow these steps to ensure that Windows Defender is actively monitoring your system for suspicious activity:

1. Click the Settings tab.

2. Click Real-Time Protection.

3. Activate the Turn On Real-Time Protection check box.

4. Click Save Changes.

Spyware Scanning

For the scanning portion of its defenses, Windows Defender supports three different scan types:

- **Quick Scan**—This scan checks just those areas of your system where it is likely to find evidence of spyware. This scan usually takes just a couple of minutes. This scan is the default, and you can initiate one at any time by selecting the Home tab and then clicking Scan Now.

- **Full Scan**—This scan checks for evidence of spyware in system memory, all running processes, and the system drive (usually drive C), and it performs a deep scan on all folders. This scan might take 30 minutes or more, depending on your system. To run this scan, select the Home tab, activate the Full option, and then click Scan Now.

- **Custom Scan**—This scan checks just the drives and folders you select. The length of the scan depends on the number of locations you select and the number of objects in those locations. To run this scan, select the Home tab, activate the Custom option, and then click Scan Now. This displays the dialog box shown in Figure 31.5. Activate the check boxes for the drives and folders you want scanned and then click OK to start the scan.

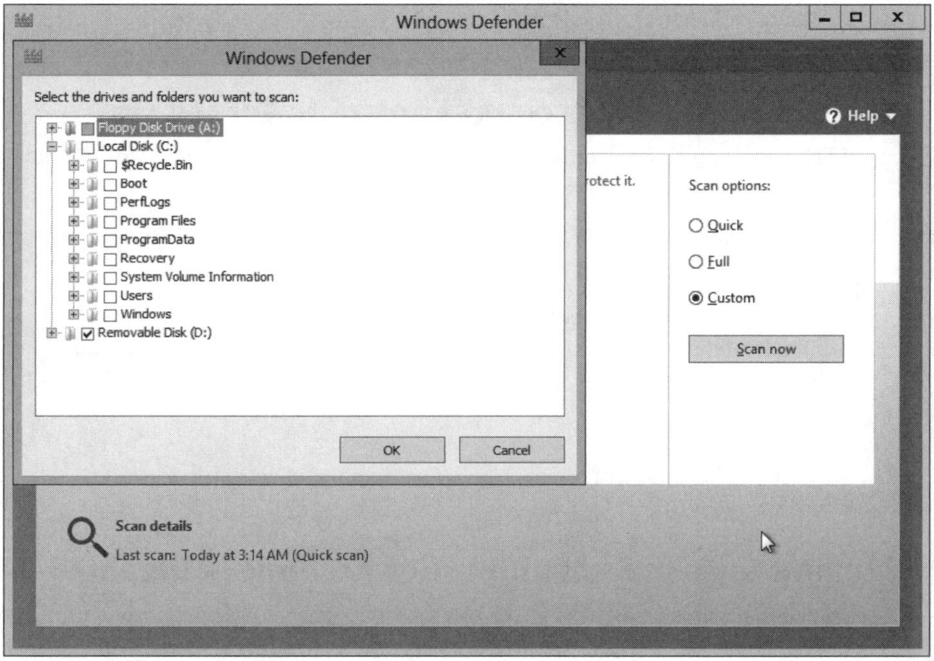

Figure 31.5
Select the Custom option and then click Scan Now to choose which drives and folders Windows Defender includes in the scan.

Windows Defender Settings

To configure Windows Defender, select the Settings tab and then work with the options in the following seven groups:

- **Real-Time Protection**—Includes a check box that toggles real-time protection on and off.

- **Excluded Files and Locations**—Use this section to specify files or folders that you don't want Windows Defender to scan.

- **Excluded File Types**—Use this section to specify file extensions that you don't want Windows Defender to scan.

- **Excluded Processes**—Use this section to specify system processes that you don't want Windows Defender to scan.

- **Advanced**—Use these options to enable scanning inside archive files and removable drives. You can also configure Windows Defender to create a restore point before handling detected items, and you can set a timeframe when quarantined items get removed from the system.

- **Microsoft Active Protection Service**—These options determine whether your PC sends information about any malware detected on your PC to a central database.

- **Administrator**—This section has a check box that toggles Windows Defender on and off.

> **tip**
>
> Windows Defender will often warn you that a program might be spyware and ask whether you want to allow the program to operate normally or to block it. If you accidentally allow an unsafe program, click the History tab, select the Allowed Items option, and then click View Details. Select the program in the Allowed Items list, and then click Remove. Similarly, if you accidentally blocked a safe program, select the Quarantined Items option, click View Details, select the program in the Quarantined Items list, and then click Restore.

Making Sure User Account Control Is Turned On

We'll be talking about User Account Control in detail later in this chapter. For now, let's just make sure it's enabled on your system:

1. Press Windows Logo+W, type **uac**, and then click Change User Account Control Settings in the search results. The User Account Control Settings dialog box appears.

2. Make sure the slider is set to anything other than Never Notify at the bottom. Again, we explain the different settings a bit later. If you're not sure what to go with, for now choose Default (second from the top).

3. Click OK.

4. Restart your computer to put the new setting into effect.

Making Sure the Administrator Account Is Disabled

One of the confusing aspects about Windows 8 is that the Administrator account seems to disappear after the setup is complete. That's because, for security reasons, Windows 8 doesn't give you access to this all-powerful account. However, there are ways to activate this account, so it pays to take a second and make sure it's still in its disabled state.

You can so this in several ways, but here's a quick look at two of them:

- **Using the Local Security Policy Editor**—In the Start screen, type **secpol.msc**, and then click secpol. In the Local Security Policy window, open the Local Policies, Security Options branch, and then double-click the Accounts: Administrator Account Status policy. Click Disabled, and then click OK.

- **Using the Local Users and Groups snap-in**—In the Start screen, type **lusrmgr.msc**, and then click lusmgr. In the Local Users and Groups snap-in, click Users and then double-click Administrator. In the Administrator Properties dialog box, activate the Account Is Disabled check box and then click OK.

These methods suffer from a serious drawback: they only work in Windows 8 Pro. Fortunately, we haven't exhausted all the ways to activate Windows 8's Administrator account. Here's a method that works with *all* versions of Windows 8:

1. Press Windows Logo+X to display the advanced tools menu.

2. Click Command Prompt (Admin). The User Account Control dialog box appears.

3. Enter your UAC credentials to continue.

4. At the command line, enter the following command:

```
net user Administrator /active:no
```

Understanding User Account Control (UAC)

Most (we're actually tempted to say the vast majority) of the security-related problems in versions of Windows prior to Vista boiled down to a single root cause: most users were running Windows with administrator-level permissions. Administrators can do *anything* to a Windows machine, including installing programs, adding devices, updating drivers, installing updates and patches, changing Registry settings, running administrative tools, and creating and modifying user accounts. This is convenient, but it leads to a huge problem: any malware that insinuates itself onto your system will also be capable of operating with administrative permissions, thus enabling the program to wreak havoc on the computer and just about anything connected to it.

Windows Vista tried to solve this problem, and its solution was called User Account Control (UAC), which used a principle called the *least-privileged user*. The idea behind this is to create an account level that has no more permissions than it requires. Again, such accounts are prevented from editing the Registry and performing other administrative tasks. However, these users can perform other day-to-day tasks:

- Install programs and updates

- Add printer drivers

- Change wireless security options (such as adding a WEP or WPA key)

The least-privileged user concept arrives in the form of a new account type called the *standard user*. This means that Windows Vista had three basic account levels:

- **Administrator account**—This built-in account can do anything to the computer.

- **Administrators group**—Members of this group (except the Administrator account) run as standard users but can elevate their privileges when required just by clicking a button in a dialog box (see the next section).

- **Standard Users group**—These are the least-privileged users, although they, too, can elevate their privileges when needed. However, they require access to an administrator password to do so.

However, if there was a problem with the UAC implementation in Vista, it was that it was a tad, well, *enthusiastic* (to put the best face on it). Any minor setting change (even changing the date or time) required elevation, and if you were a dedicated settings changer, UAC probably caused you to tear out more than a few clumps of hair in frustration.

The good (some would say great) news in Windows 7 was that Microsoft did two things to rein in UAC:

- It made UAC configurable so that you could tailor the notifications to suit your situation.

- It set up the default configuration of UAC so that it only rarely prompted you for elevation when you changed the settings on your PC. Two notable (and excusable) exceptions were when you changed the UAC configuration and when you started the Registry Editor.

Windows 8 carries on this easier implementation of UAC, but it adds two more conditions:

- It only allows a single user account in the Administrators group, which is usually the account you use to install Windows 8.

- All other accounts you create in Windows 8 are members of the Standard Users group.

This makes Windows 8 even more secure because now you only ever have to worry about a single administrator account, and that account must always have a password. (Windows 8 doesn't even show a password hint for the administrator account, like it does for the standard user accounts.)

Elevating Privileges

The idea of elevating privileges is at the heart of the UAC security model. In Windows XP, you could use the Run As command to run a task as a different user (that is, one with higher privileges). In Windows 8 (as with Windows 7 and Vista), you usually don't need to do this because Windows 8 prompts you for the elevation automatically.

With your main Windows 8 user account (which, again, is a member of the Administrators group), you run with the privileges of a standard user for extra security. When you attempt a task that requires administrative privileges, Windows 8 prompts for your consent by displaying a User Account Control dialog box similar to the one shown in Figure 31.6. Click Yes to permit the task to proceed. If this dialog box appears unexpectedly instead of in response to an action you've just taken, it's possible that a malware program is trying to perform some task that requires administrative privileges; you can thwart that task by clicking No instead.

Figure 31.6
When your main Windows 8 administrative account launches a task that requires elevated privileges, Windows 8 displays this dialog box to ask for consent.

If you're running as a standard user and attempt a task that requires administrative privileges, Windows 8 uses an extra level of protection. That is, instead of just prompting you for consent, it prompts you for the password of the main administrative account, as shown in Figure 31.7. Type the password for the main administrative account and then click Yes. Again, if this dialog box shows up unexpectedly, it might be malware, so you should click No to prevent the task from going through.

Figure 31.7
When a standard user launches a task that requires administrative privileges, Windows 8 displays this dialog box to ask for administrative credentials.

Note, too, that in both cases Windows 8 switches to secure desktop mode, which means that you can't do anything else with Windows 8 until you give your consent or credentials or cancel the operation. Windows 8 indicates the secure desktop by darkening everything on the screen except the User Account Control dialog box.

> **note**
> It's also possible to elevate your privileges for any individual program. You do this by right-clicking the program file or shortcut and then clicking Run as Administrator.

Configuring User Account Control

As we mentioned earlier, Windows 8 supports a configurable UAC so that you can set it to a level that you're comfortable with. Here's how to configure UAC in Windows 8:

1. Press Windows Logo+W, type **uac**, and then click Change User Account Control Settings in the search results. The User Account Control Settings dialog box appears, as shown in Figure 31.8.

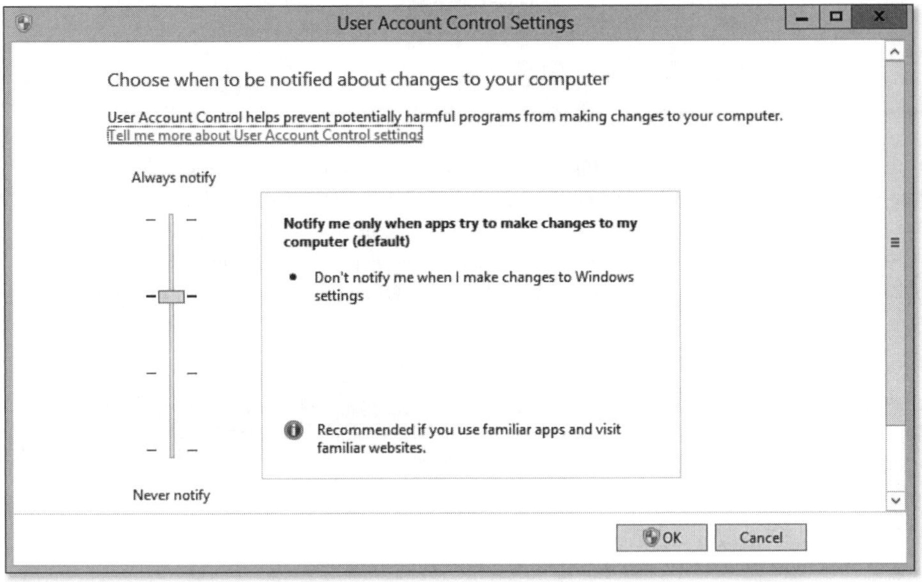

Figure 31.8
In Windows 8, you can use the User Account Control Settings dialog box to set up UAC as you see fit.

2. Use the slider to choose one of the following four UAC settings:

   ■ **Always Notify**—This is the top level, and it works much like UAC in Windows Vista in that you're prompted for elevation when you change Windows settings, and when programs try to change settings and install software.

   ■ **Default**—This is the second highest level, and it prompts you for elevation only when programs try to change settings and install software. This level uses secure desktop mode to display the UAC dialog box.

   ■ **No Secure Desktop**—This is the second lowest level, and it's the same as the Default level (that is, it only prompts you for elevation when programs try to change settings and install software), but this level doesn't use secure desktop mode when displaying the UAC dialog box.

   ■ **Never Notify**—This is the bottom level, and it turns off UAC. Of course you, as a responsible PC user, would never select this setting, right? We figured as much.

3. Click OK. The User Account Control dialog box appears.

4. Enter your UAC credentials to put the new setting into effect.

User Account Control Policies

You can customize User Account Control to a certain extent by using local group policies. In the Local Security Settings snap-in (in the Start screen, type **secpol.msc**, and then click secpol), open the Security Settings, Local Policies, Security Options branch. Here you'll find ten policies related to User Account Control:

- **User Account Control: Admin Approval Mode for the Built-in Administrator Account**—This policy controls whether the Administrator account falls under User Account Control. If you enable this policy, the Administrator account is treated like any other account in the Administrators group and the user must click Continue in the consent dialog box when Windows 8 requires approval for an action.

- **User Account Control: Allow UIAccess Applications to Prompt for Elevation Without Using the Secure Desktop**—Use this policy to enable or disable whether Windows 8 allows elevation for accessibility applications that require access to the user interface of another window without using the secure desktop mode.

- **User Account Control: Behavior of the Elevation Prompt for Administrators in Admin Approval Mode**—This policy controls the prompt that appears when the main administrative account requires elevated privileges. The default setting is Prompt for Consent for Non-Windows Binaries, where the user clicks either Yes or No. You can also choose Prompt for Credentials to force the user to type his or her password. If you choose No Prompt, the main administrative account can't elevate its privileges.

- **User Account Control: Behavior of the Elevation Prompt for Standard Users**—This policy controls the prompt that appears when a standard user requires elevated privileges. For a more detailed look at this policy, see "Preventing Elevation for All Standard Users," next.

- **User Account Control: Detect Application Installations and Prompt for Elevation**—Use this policy to enable or disable automatic privilege elevation while installing programs.

- **User Account Control: Only Elevate Executables That Are Signed and Validated**—Use this policy to enable or disable whether Windows 8 checks the security signature of any program that asks for elevated privileges.

- **User Account Control: Only Elevate UIAccess Applications That Are Installed in Secure Locations**—Use this policy to enable or disable whether Windows 8 allows elevation for accessibility applications that require access to the user interface of another window only if they are installed in a secure location (such as the %ProgramFiles% folder).

- **User Account Control: Run All Administrators in Admin Approval Mode**—Use this policy to enable or disable running the main administrative account (excluding the Administrator account) as a standard user.

- **User Account Control: Switch to the Secure Desktop When Prompting for Elevation**—Use this policy to enable or disable whether Windows 8 switches to the secure desktop when the elevation prompts appear.

- **User Account Control: Virtualize File and Registry Write Failures to Per-User Locations**—Use this policy to enable or disable file and Registry virtualization for standard users.

Preventing Elevation for All Standard Users

You saw earlier (in "Elevating Privileges") that when a standard user attempts a task that requires elevation, he or she sees a UAC dialog box that requires an administrator password, and the screen switches to secure desktop mode.

There are two problems with this:

- Standard users almost never have the proper credentials to elevate an action.

- The combination of the sudden appearance of the User Account Control dialog box and the change into secure desktop mode is confusing for many users, particularly the inexperienced.

These two problems mean that in most cases it would be better if standard users didn't get prompted to elevate their privileges. Instead, it would be better to display an Access Denied message and let the user move on from there.

You can use the Local Security Settings snap-in to set this up. Here are the steps to follow:

1. Press Windows Logo+W, type **secpol.msc**, and then click secpol. The Local Security Policy snap-in appears.

2. Open the Local Policies branch.

3. Click the Security Options branch.

4. Double-click the User Account Control: Behavior of the Elevation Prompt for Standard Users policy.

5. In the list, choose Automatically Deny Elevation Requests, as shown in Figure 31.9.

6. Click OK to put the new setting into effect.

Now when a standard user attempts something that requires elevated privileges, he or she just sees a simple dialog box like the one shown in Figure 31.10. Windows 8 doesn't switch into secure desktop mode, and the user just has to click the command button to continue.

 note

File and Registry virtualization creates virtual %SystemRoot% and %ProgramFiles% folders as well as a virtual HKEY_LOCAL_MACHINE Registry key, all of which are stored with the user's files. This enables a program installer to proceed without jeopardizing actual system files.

note

These steps require the Local Security Settings snap-in, which is available only with Windows 8 Pro. If you're not running this version, normally we'd show you how to modify the Registry to get the same effect. Unfortunately, the policy value we tweak here doesn't have a Registry equivalent for security reasons.

Figure 31.9
Open the User Account Control: Behavior of the
Elevation Prompt for Standard Users policy and choose
Automatically Deny Elevation Requests.

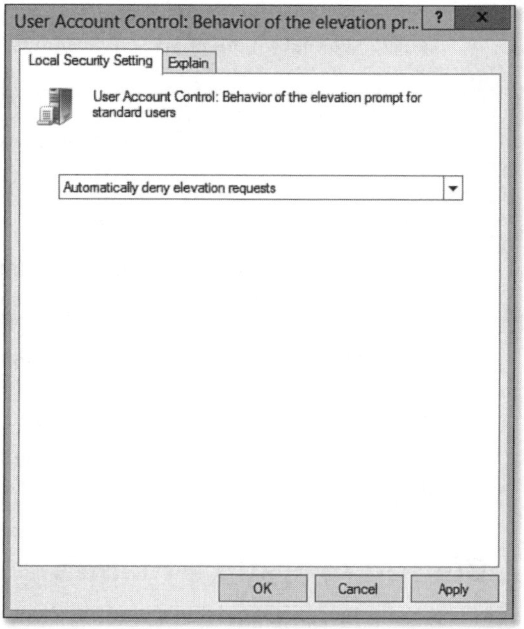

Figure 31.10
When standard users are denied elevation requests, they see a
simple dialog box when they attempt an administrator-level task.

Enhancing Your Browsing Security

As more people, businesses, and organizations establish a presence online, the world becomes an
increasingly connected place. And the more connected the world becomes, the more opportunities
arise for communicating with others, doing research, sharing information, and collaborating on projects. The flip side to this new connectedness is the increased risk of connecting with a remote user
whose intentions are less than honorable. The person at the other end of the connection could be a
fraud artist who sets up a legitimate-looking website to steal your password or credit card number,
or a cracker who breaks into your Internet account. It could be a virus programmer who sends a
Trojan horse attached to an email, or a website operator who uses web browser security holes to
run malicious code on your machine.

While all this was happening, Microsoft's operating systems seemed to become less secure. It's difficult to say whether overall operating system security got worse with each new release, but it's not hard to see that a perfect security storm was brewing:

- Thanks to the Internet, news of vulnerabilities spread quickly and efficiently.

- An increasing number of malicious users online worked to exploit those vulnerabilities.

- An increasing number of Windows users got online, most of whom didn't keep up with the latest security patches from Microsoft.

- An increasing number of online users had always-on broadband connections, which give malicious users more time to locate and break into poorly patched machines.

So, even though it might have been the case that each new version of Windows was no less secure than its predecessors, it *appeared* that Windows was becoming increasingly vulnerable to attack.

Surfing the Web may be inherently unsecure, but fortunately Internet Explorer 10 comes with lots of defensive weapons that you can deploy. The next few sections take a look at the most important ones.

Blocking Pop-Up Windows

Among the most annoying things on the Web are those ubiquitous pop-up windows that infest your screen with advertisements when you visit certain sites. (A variation on the theme is the *pop-under*, a window that opens under your current browser window, so you don't know it's there until you close the window.) Pop-up windows can also be dangerous because some unscrupulous software makers have figured out ways to use them to install software on your computer without your permission. They're nasty things, any way you look at them.

Fortunately, Microsoft has given us a way to stop most pop-ups before they start. Internet Explorer comes with a feature called the *Pop-up Blocker* that looks for pop-ups and prevents them from opening. It's not perfect (the occasional pop-under still breaks through the defenses), but it makes surfing sites much more pleasant. Follow these steps to use and configure the Pop-up Blocker:

1. In Internet Explorer, press Alt+T to open the Tools menu, then click Pop-up Blocker.

2. If you see the command Turn Off Pop-up Blocker, skip to step 3; otherwise, select Turn On Pop-up Blocker, click Yes when Internet Explorer asks you to confirm, then press Alt+T and click Pop-up Blocker.

3. Click Pop-up Blocker Settings to display the Pop-up Blocker Settings dialog box. You have the following options:

   - **Address of Web Site to Allow**—Use this option when you have a site that displays pop-ups you want to see. Type the address and then click Add.

   - **Play a Sound When a Pop-up Is Blocked**—When this check box is activated, Internet Explorer plays a brief sound each time it blocks a pop-up. In Internet Explorer 10, you can't deactivate this check box.

■ **Show Notification Bar When a Pop-up Is Blocked**—When this check box is activated, Internet Explorer displays a Notification bar message at the bottom of the window each time it blocks a pop-up so that you know it's working on your behalf.

■ **Blocking Level**—Use this list to choose how aggressively you want it to block pop-ups: High (no pop-ups get through, ever), Medium (the default level, which blocks most—but not all—pop-ups), or Low (allows pop-ups from secure sites).

4. Click Close.

With the Pop-Up Blocker on the case, it monitors your surfing and steps in front of any pop-up window that tries to disturb your peace. A Notification bar appears at the bottom of the window to let you know that Pop-up Blocker thwarted a pop-up (see Figure 31.11). The Notification bar offers the following choices:

■ **Allow Once**—Click this command to enable pop-ups on the site just this one time.

■ **Options for This Site: Always Allow**—Click this command to allow future pop-ups for the current domain.

■ **Options for This Site: More Settings**—Click this command to display the Pop-Up Blocker Settings dialog box.

Figure 31.11
When the Pop-up Blocker has your back, it displays the Notification bar each time it thwarts a pop-up.

Internet Explorer blocked a pop-up from **www.popuptest.com**. [Allow once] [Options for this site ▾] ✕

Adding and Removing Zone Sites

When implementing security for Internet Explorer, Microsoft realized that different sites have different security needs. For example, it makes sense to have stringent security for Internet sites, but you can probably scale the security back a bit when browsing pages on your corporate intranet.

To handle these different types of sites, Internet Explorer defines various *security zones*, and you can customize the security requirements for each zone. To work with zones, select Tools, Internet Options and then select the Security tab (see Figure 31.12) in the Internet Properties dialog box that appears.

The list at the top of the dialog box shows icons for the four types of zones available:

■ **Internet**—Websites that aren't in any of the other three zones. The default security level is Medium-High.

■ **Local Intranet**—Web pages on your computer and your network (intranet). The default security level is Medium-Low.

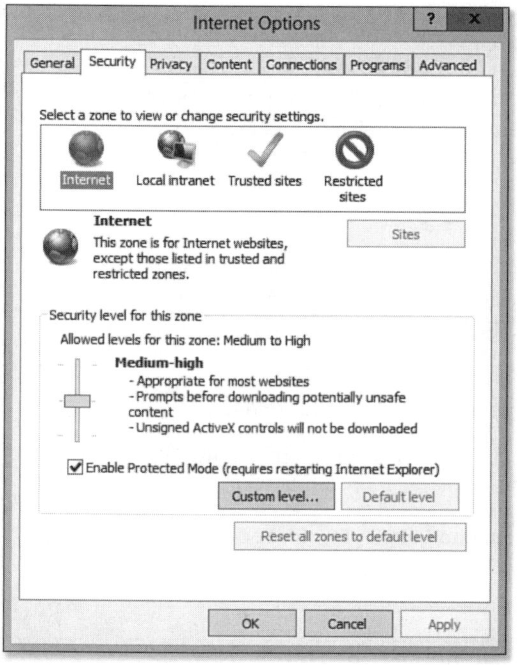

Figure 31.12
Use the Security tab to set up security zones and customize the security options for each zone.

- **Trusted Sites**—Websites that implement secure pages and that you're sure have safe content. The default security level is Medium.

- **Restricted Sites**—Websites that don't implement secure pages or that you don't trust, for whatever reason. The default security level is High.

Three of these zones—Local Intranet, Trusted Sites, and Restricted Sites—enable you to add sites. To do so, follow these steps:

1. Select the zone you want to work with and then click Sites.

2. If you selected Trusted Sites or Restricted Sites, skip to step 4. Otherwise, if you selected the Local Intranet zone, you see a dialog box with four check boxes. The Automatically Detect Intranet Network check box activates by default, and this tells Windows 8 to detect intranets automatically, which should be fine in most cases. If you want more detailed control, deactivate that check box to enable the other three:

   - **Include All Local (Intranet) Sites Not Listed in Other Zones**—When activated, this option includes all intranet sites in the zone. If you add specific intranet sites to other zones, those sites aren't included in this zone.

   - **Include All Sites That Bypass the Proxy Server**—When this check box is activated, sites that you've set up to bypass your proxy server (if you have one) are included in this zone.

■ **Include All Network Paths (UNCs)**—When this check box is activated, all network paths that use the Universal Naming Convention are included in this zone. (UNC is a standard format used with network addresses. They usually take the form *server**resource*, where *server* is the name of the network server and *resource* is the name of a shared network resource.)

3. To add sites to the Local Intranet zone, click Advanced.

4. Type the site's address in the Add This Website to the Zone text box and then click Add.

5. If you make a mistake and enter the wrong site, select it in the Websites list and then click Remove.

6. Two of these dialog boxes (Local Intranet and Trusted Sites) have a Require Server Verification (https:) for All Sites In This Zone check box. If you activate this option, each site you enter must use the secure HTTPS protocol.

7. Click Close.

> 🔍 **note**
>
> When typing an address, you can include an asterisk as a wildcard character. For example, the address http://*.microsoft.com adds every microsoft.com domain, including www.microsoft.com, support.microsoft.com, windowsupdate.microsoft.com, and so on.

Changing a Zone's Security Level

To change the security level for a zone, select the zone and then use the Security Level for This Zone slider to set the level. To set up your own security settings, click Custom Level. This displays the Security Settings dialog box shown in Figure 31.13.

Figure 31.13
Use this dialog box to set up customized security levels for the selected zone.

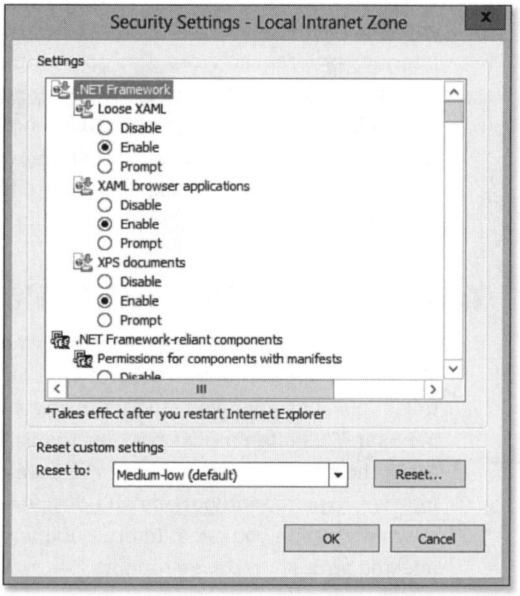

The Security Settings dialog box provides you with a long list of possible security issues, and your job is to specify how you want Internet Explorer to handle each issue. You usually have three choices:

- **Disable**—Security is on. For example, if the issue is whether to run an ActiveX control, the control does not run.

- **Enable**—Security is off. For example, if the issue is whether to run an ActiveX control, the control runs automatically.

- **Prompt**—Internet Explorer asks how you want to handle the issue (for example, whether you want to accept or reject an ActiveX control).

Protected Mode: Reducing Internet Explorer's Privileges

Because spyware often leeches onto a system through a drive-by or pop-up download, it makes sense to set up the web browser as the first line of defense. Microsoft has done just that by including *protected mode* for Internet Explorer. Protected mode builds on Windows 8's User Account Control feature. Protected Mode means that Internet Explorer runs with a privilege level that's high enough to surf the Web, but that's about it. Internet Explorer can't install software without your permission, modify the user's files or settings, add shortcuts to the Startup folder, or even change its own settings for the default home page and search engine. The Internet Explorer code is completely isolated from any other running application or process on your system. In fact, Internet Explorer can write data only to the Temporary Internet Files folder. If it needs to write elsewhere (during a file download, for example), it must get your permission. Therefore, Internet Explorer blocks any add-ons or other malware that attempt a covert install via Internet Explorer before they can even get to Windows Defender.

> ### 🔍 note
>
> If you don't want to run Internet Explorer in protected mode for some reason, you can turn it off. Select Tools, Internet Options, select the Security tab, and then click the Internet zone. Click the Enable Protected Mode check box to deactivate it, click OK, and then click OK again in the Warning! dialog box. Internet Explorer displays a message in the Notification bar telling you that your security settings are putting you at risk.

Total Security: Internet Explorer Without Add-Ons

For the ultimate in browsing security, Windows 8 ships with an alternative Internet Explorer shortcut that loads the browser without any third-party add-ons, extensions, toolbars, or ActiveX controls. This is useful if you suspect your computer is infected with spyware that has hijacked your browser. This often means not only that the spyware has changed your home page, but in many cases the spyware also prevents you from accessing antispyware or antivirus sites. By running Internet Explorer without any add-ons, you effectively disable the spyware, and you can then surf to whatever site you need. Internet Explorer without add-ons is also completely safe from being infected with spyware, so running this version of Internet Explorer is useful if you'll be surfing in darker areas of the Web where you suspect the possibility of infection is very high.

To run Internet Explorer without add-ons, follow these steps:

1. Press Windows Logo+R. The Run dialog box appears.

2. Type **iexplore -extoff**.

3. Click OK. Internet Explorer runs without loading any add-ons.

If you find yourself using this version of Internet Explorer regularly, consider creating a shortcut for it on the Start screen, as described (in a different context) in Chapter 4.

 To learn how to add a shortcut tile to the Start screen, **see** *"Adding Shutdown and Restart Tiles to the Start Screen,"* **p. 117.**

Understanding Internet Explorer's Advanced Security Options

To close our look at Windows 8's web security features, this section takes you through Internet Explorer's Advanced security options. Select Tools, Internet Options, display the Advanced tab, and then scroll down to the Security section to see the following options:

- **Allow Active Content from CDs to Run on My Computer**—Leave this check box deactivated to prevent active content such as scripts and controls located in CD-based web pages to execute on your computer. However, if you have a CD-based program that won't function, you might need to activate this check box to enable the program to work properly.

- **Allow Active Content to Run in Files on My Computer**—Leave this check box deactivated to prevent active content such as scripts and controls located in local web pages to execute on your computer. If you're testing a web page that includes active content, activate this check box so that you can test the web pages locally.

- **Allow Software to Run or Install Even If the Signature Is Invalid**—Leave this check box deactivated to avoid running or installing software that doesn't have a valid digital signature. If you can't get a program to run or install, consider activating this check box.

- **Block Unsecured Images with Other Mixed Content**—If you activate this check box, Internet Explorer looks for images that were delivered to the current secure (HTTPS) page via an unsecure (HTTP) source. If it detects such an image, it treats the entire page as unsecure. Unsecure images are not dangerous, so you shouldn't have to activate this option.

- **Check for Publisher's Certificate Revocation**—When this option is activated, Internet Explorer examines a site's digital security certificates to see whether they have been revoked.

- **Check for Server Certificate Revocation**—If you activate this option, Internet Explorer also checks the security certificate for the web page's server.

- **Check for Signatures on Downloaded Programs**—If you activate this check box, Internet Explorer checks for a digital signature on any program that you download.

- **Do Not Save Encrypted Pages to Disk**—If you activate this option, Internet Explorer won't store encrypted files in the Temporary Internet Files folder.

- **Empty Temporary Internet Files Folder When Browser Is Closed**—With this option activated, Internet Explorer removes all files from the Temporary Internet Files folder when you exit the program.

- **Enable DOM Storage**—When this check box is activated, Internet Explorer 8 stores Document Object Model (DOM) data, which is similar to cookie data, but with a much larger capacity (up to 10MB as opposed to the maximum of 10KB with cookies). Internet Explorer might not be able to save session data if you disable this option. If you're worried about Internet Explorer storing that much personal data, the data actually gets cleared automatically as soon as you close any Internet Explorer tab or window that requires that data. However, deleting cookies (as described earlier) also deletes the DOM storage.

- **Enable Enhanced Protected Mode**—If you activate this check box, Internet Explorer runs in Enhanced Protected Mode, which is Protected Mode with a few extra safety precautions thrown in. For example, it doesn't allow Internet Explorer to access your user account data.

- **Enable Integrated Windows Authentication**—With this check box activated, Internet Explorer uses Integrated Windows Authentication (formerly known as Windows NT Challenge/Response Authentication) to attempt to log on to a restricted site. This means the browser attempts to log on using the current credentials from the user's network domain logon. If this doesn't work, Internet Explorer displays a dialog box prompting the user for a username and password.

- **Enable Memory Protection to Help Mitigate Online Attacks**—This option (which you can't deactivate) enables Data Execution Prevention for Internet Explorer, which prevents malicious code from running in protected memory locations.

- **Enable Native XMLHTTP Support**—With this check box activated, Internet Explorer works properly with sites that use the XMLHTTPRequest API to transfer XML data between the browser and a server. This API is most commonly used in Ajax-powered sites. Ajax (Asynchronous JavaScript and XML) is a web development technique that creates sites that operate much like desktop programs. In particular, the XMLHTTPRequest API enables the browser to request and accept data from the server without reloading the page.

- **Enable SmartScreen Filter**—This option toggles the SmartScreen phishing filter on and off.

- **Use SSL 2.0**—This check box toggles support for the Secure Sockets Layer Level 2 security protocol on and off. This version of SSL is currently the Web's standard security protocol.

- **Use SSL 3.0**—This check box toggles support for SSL Level 3 on and off. SSL 3.0 is more secure than SSL 2.0 (it can authenticate both the client and the server), but isn't currently as popular as SSL 2.0.

- **Use TLS 1.0**—This check box toggles support for Transport Layer Security (TLS) version 1.0 on and off. TLS is the successor to SSL, and is starting to be implemented more widely, which may be why Internet Explorer 8 activates this check box by default.

- **Use TLS 1.1**—This check box toggles support for TLS version 1.1. Activate this option if you have trouble accessing a secure site (for example, if Internet Explorer displays an error telling you the site's security certificate can't be verified).

- **Use TLS 1.2**—This check box toggles support for TLS version 1.2. Activate this option if you have trouble accessing a secure site and enabling support for TSL 1.1 didn't help.

- **Warn About Certificate Address Mismatch**—When activated, this option tells Internet Explorer to display a warning dialog box if a site is using an invalid digital security certificate.

- **Warn If Changing Between Secure and Not Secure Mode**—When activated, this option tells Internet Explorer to display a warning dialog box whenever you enter and leave a secure site.

- **Warn If POST Submittal Is Redirected to a Zone That Does Not Permit Posts**—When activated, this option tells Internet Explorer to display a warning dialog box if a form submission is sent to a site other than the one hosting the form.

Protecting Yourself Against Email Viruses

Computing veterans will remember that way back when the primary method computer viruses used to propagate themselves was the floppy disk. A user with an infected machine would copy some files to a floppy, and the virus would surreptitiously add itself to the disk. When the recipient inserted the disk, the virus copy came to life and infected yet another computer.

Most of us haven't even *seen* a floppy disk in years, but that didn't stop the spread of viruses. On the contrary, the Internet's now firm foothold in the mainstream has been a boon to virus writers everywhere, who happily adapted to the new reality and soon began propagating their malware either via malicious websites or via infected program files downloaded to users' machines.

However, by far the most productive method for viruses to replicate has been the humble email message: Melissa, We Love You, BadTrans, Sircam, Klez. The list of email viruses and Trojan horses is a long one, but they all operate more or less the same way: they arrive as a message attachment, usually from someone you know. When you open the attachment, the virus infects your computer and then, without your knowledge, uses your email client and your address book to ship out messages with more copies of itself attached. The nastier versions also mess with your computer by deleting data or corrupting files.

You can avoid infection by one of these viruses by implementing a few commonsense procedures:

- Never open an attachment that comes from someone you don't know.

- Even if you know the sender, check the message: If it's vague or extremely short (or just doesn't sound like the sender), you should be immediately suspicious about the attachment. Otherwise, if the attachment isn't something you're expecting, assume that the sender's system is infected. Write back and confirm that the sender emailed the message.

- Some viruses come packaged as scripts hidden within messages that use the HTML format. This means that the virus can run just by the message being viewed! If a message looks suspicious, don't open it; just delete it. (Note that you'll need to turn off the Windows Live Mail Reading pane before deleting the message. Otherwise, when you highlight the message, it appears in the Reading pane and sets off the virus. Click the View tab, click Reading Pane, and then click Off.)

- Install a top-of-the-line antivirus program, particularly one that checks incoming email. In addition, be sure to keep your antivirus program's virus list up to date. As you read this, there are probably dozens, maybe even hundreds, of morally challenged scumnerds designing even nastier viruses. Regular updates will help you keep up. Here are some security suites to check out:

> **⚠ caution**
>
> It's particularly important to turn off the Reading pane before displaying Windows Live Mail's Junk Email folder. Because many junk messages also carry a virus payload, your chances of initiating an infection are highest when working with messages in this folder. Fortunately, Windows Live Mail is sensible enough to turn off the Reading pane by default when you open the Junk Email folder.

Norton Internet Security (www.symantec.com)

McAfee Internet Security Suite (www.mcafee.com)

Avast! Antivirus (www.avast.com)

AVG Internet Security (http://free.avg.com/)

Besides these general procedures, Windows Live Mail also comes with its own set of virus protection features. Here's how to use them:

1. In Windows Live Mail, select File, Options, Safety Options. Windows Live Mail opens the Safety Options dialog box.

2. Display the Security tab.

3. In the Virus Protection group, you have the following options:

   - **Select the Security Zone to Use**—Earlier in this chapter we described the security zone model used by Internet Explorer. From the perspective of Windows Live Mail, you use the security zones to determine whether to allow active content inside an HTML-format message to run:

     Internet Zone—If you choose this zone, active content is allowed to run.

     Restricted Sites Zone—If you choose this option, active content is disabled. This is the default setting and the one we recommend.

   - **Warn Me When Other Applications Try to Send Mail as Me**—As we mentioned earlier, it's possible for programs and scripts to send email messages without your knowledge. This happens by using *Simple MAPI* (*Messaging Application Programming Interface*) calls, which can send messages via your computer's default mail client—and it's all hidden from you. With this check box activated, Windows Live Mail displays a warning dialog box when a program or script attempts to send a message using Simple MAPI.

■ **Do Not Allow Attachments to Be Saved or Opened That Could Potentially Be a Virus**—With this check box activated, Windows Live Mail monitors attachments to look for file types that could contain viruses or destructive code. If it detects such a file, it disables your ability to open and save that file, and it displays a note at the top of the message to let you know about the unsafe attachment.

4. Click OK to put the new settings into effect.

> **⨀ tip**
>
> What do you do if you want to send a file that's on the Windows Live Mail unsafe-file list and you want to make sure that the recipient will be able to open it? The easiest workaround is to compress the file into a `.zip` file—a file type not blocked by Windows Live Mail, Outlook, or any other mail client that blocks file types.

File Types Disabled by Windows Live Mail

Internet Explorer's built-in unsafe-file list defines the file types that Windows Live Mail disables. That list includes file types associated with the following extensions: `.ad`, `.ade`, `.adp`, `.bas`, `.bat`, `.chm`, `.cmd`, `.com`, `.cpl`, `.crt`, `.exe`, `.hlp`, `.hta`, `.inf`, `.ins`, `.isp`, `.js`, `.jse`, `.lnk`, `.mdb`, `.mde`, `.msc`, `.msi`, `.msp`, `.mst`, `.pcd`, `.pif`, `.reg`, `.scr`, `.sct`, `.shb`, `.shs`, `.url`, `.vb`, `.vbe`, `.vbs`, `.vsd`, `.vss`, `.vst`, `.vsw`, `.wsc`, `.wsf`, `.wsh`.

PROTECTING YOUR DATA FROM LOSS AND THEFT

Preparing for Trouble

Computer problems, like the proverbial death and taxes, seem to be one of those constants in life. Whether it's a hard disk giving up the ghost, a power failure that trashes your files, or a virus that invades your system, the issue isn't *whether* something will go wrong, but rather *when* it will happen. Instead of waiting to deal with these difficulties after they've occurred (what we call *pound-of-cure mode*), you need to become proactive and perform maintenance on your system in advance (*ounce-of-prevention mode*). This not only reduces the chances that something will go wrong, but it also sets up your system to recover more easily from any problems that do occur.

A big part of ounce-of-prevention mode is the unwavering belief that someday something *will* go wrong with your computer. That might sound unduly pessimistic, but hey this is a *PC* we're talking about here, and it's never a question of *if* the thing will go belly up one day, but rather *when* that day will come.

With that gloomy mindset, the only sensible thing to do is prepare for that dire day so that you're ready to get your system back on its feet. So part of your Windows 8 maintenance chores should be getting a few things ready that will serve you well on the day your PC decides to go haywire on you. Besides performing a system image backup (which we describe a bit later), you should be setting system restore points and creating a system recovery disc. The next two sections cover these last two techniques.

Backing Up File Versions with File History

High-end databases have long supported the idea of the *transaction*, a collection of data modifications—inserts, deletions, updates, and so on—treated as a unit, meaning that either all the modifications occur or none of them does. For example, consider a finance database system that needs to perform a single chore: transfer a specified amount of money from one account to another. This involves two discrete steps (I'm simplifying here): debit one account by the specified amount and credit the other account for the same amount. If the database system did not treat these two steps as a single transaction, you could run into problems. For example, if the system successfully debited the first account but for some reason was unable to credit the second account, the system would be left in an unbalanced state. By treating the two steps as a single transaction, the system does not commit any changes unless both steps occur successfully. If the credit to the second account fails, the transaction is *rolled back* to the beginning, meaning that the debit to the first account is reversed and the system reverts to a stable state.

What does all this have to do with the Windows 8 file system? It's actually directly related because Windows 8 implements an interesting technology called *Transactional NTFS*, or TxF, for short. (New Technology File System [NTFS] is the default Windows 8 file system.) TxF applies the same transactional database ideas to the file system. Put simply, with TxF, if some mishap occurs to your data—it could be a system crash, a program crash, an overwrite of an important file, or even just imprudent edits to a file—Windows 8 enables you to roll back the file to a previous version. It's kind of like System Restore, except that it works not for the entire system, but for individual files and folders.

Windows 8's capability to restore previous versions of files and folders comes from two processes:

- Once an hour, Windows 8 creates a shadow copy of your user account files. A *shadow copy* is essentially a snapshot of the user account's contents at a particular point in time.

- After creating the shadow copy, Windows 8 uses transactional NTFS to intercept all calls to the file system. Windows 8 maintains a meticulous log of those calls so that it knows exactly which files and folders in your user account have changed.

Together these processes enable Windows 8 to store previous versions of files and folders, where a "previous" version is defined as a version of the object that changed after a shadow copy was created. For example, suppose that you make changes to a particular document each day. This means that you'll end up with three previous versions of the document: today's, yesterday's, and the day before yesterday's.

Taken together, these previous versions represent the document's *file history*, and you can access and work with previous versions by activating the File History feature. When you turn on File History and specify an external drive to store the data, Windows 8 begins monitoring your libraries, your desktop, your contacts, and your Internet Explorer favorites. Once an hour, Windows 8 checks to see if any of this data has changed since the last check. If it has, Windows 8 saves copies of the changed files to the external drive.

Once you have some data saved, you can then use it to restore a previous version of a file, as described later in this chapter.

Selecting the File History Drive

To get started, connect an external drive to your PC. The drive should have enough capacity to hold your user account files, so an external hard drive is probably best. Now you need to set up the external drive for use with File History.

The easiest way to do this is to look for the notification that appears a few moments after you connect the drive. Click the notification and then click Configure This Drive for Backup.

If you miss the notification, follow these steps instead:

1. In the Windows 8 Start screen, press Windows Logo+W to open the Settings search pane, type **history**, and then click File History. The File History window appears.

2. Examine the Copy Files To section of the window. If you see your external hard drive listed, as shown in Figure 32.1, you can skip the rest of these steps.

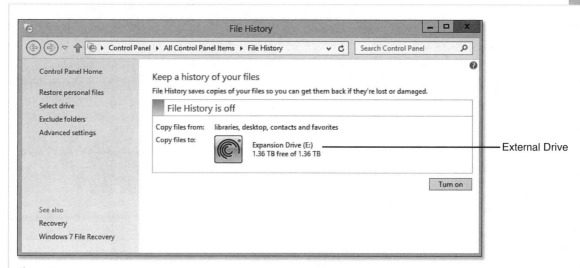

Figure 32.1
Windows 8 should recognize your external drive and add it to the File History window.

3. Click Select Drive. The Change Drive window appears.

4. Select the drive you want to use and then click OK. Windows 8 displays the external drive in the File History window.

Using a Network Share as the File History Drive

What happens if you don't have an external drive, or if your drives don't have enough capacity to store your user account files? For the latter, you can try excluding a folder or two from your file history, as we discuss in the next section. If that doesn't work, you can still use File History if you have access (and permission to write file) to a network share. Follow these steps:

1. In the Windows 8 Start screen, press Windows Logo+W to open the Settings search pane, type **history**, and then click File History. The File History window appears.

2. Click Select Drive to open the Change Drive window.

3. Click Add Network Location. Windows 8 opens the Select Folder dialog box and displays the Network folder.

4. Open the network computer you want to use, click the shared folder, and then click Select Folder. Windows 8 returns you to the Select Drive window and adds the network share to the drive list.

5. Make sure the network share is selected, and then click OK. Windows 8 displays the share in the File History window, as shown in Figure 32.2.

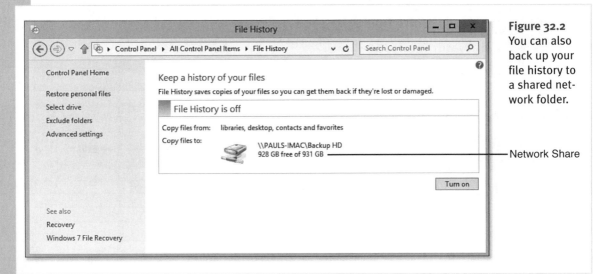

Figure 32.2
You can also back up your file history to a shared network folder.

Excluding a Folder from Your File History

By default, File History stores copies of everything in your Windows 8 libraries—including Documents, Music, Photos, and Videos—as well as your desktop items, contacts, and Internet Explorer favorites. However, there may be situations where you don't want every file to be included in your history. For example, if your external drive has a limited capacity, you might want to exclude extremely large files, such as recorded TV show or ripped movies in your Videos library.

Similarly, you might have sensitive or private files in your Documents library that you do not want copied to the external drive because that drive can easily be stolen or lost. (A similar caveat applies to storing sensitive files on a shared network folder that other people might also be able to access.)

Whatever the reason, you can configure File History to exclude a particular folder from being copied to the external drive by following these steps:

1. In the Windows 8 Start screen, press Windows Logo+W to open the Settings search pane, type **history**, and then click File History. The File History window appears.

2. Click Exclude Folders. The Exclude Folders window appears.

3. Click Add. Windows 8 displays the Select Folder dialog box.

4. Select the folder you want to exclude, and then click Select Folder. Windows 8 adds the folder to the Excluded Folders and Libraries list.

5. Repeat steps 3 and 4 to exclude any other folders you want to leave out of your file history.

6. Click Save Changes.

Configuring File History

File History uses the following default settings:

■ **File History looks for changed files every hour**—If you are particularly busy you might prefer a more frequent save interval to ensure you don't lose any data. On the hand, if you are running out of space on the external drive, you might prefer a less frequent save interval to preserve space.

■ **File History sets aside five percent of hard disk space for its offline cache**—The offline cache is a hard disk storage area that File History uses if your external drive or network share is temporarily unavailable. You can reduce the size of the offline cache if your hard disk is running low on free space, or you can increase the cache size if your backup location will be unavailable for a while.

 tip

You don't have to wait until the next scheduled backup. If File History is turned on (see "Activating File History") and you have important changes you'd prefer to save right away, open File History and then click Run Now.

■ **File History does not delete any of the file versions it saves**—To free up space on the external drive, you can configure File History to delete versions after a specified time or when space is needed on the drive.

Follow these steps to configure these settings:

1. In the Start screen, press Windows Logo+W, type **history**, and then click File History to open the File History window.

2. Click Advanced Settings to open the Advanced Settings window, shown in Figure 32.3.

3. Use the Save Copies of Files list to select a save frequency (from Every 10 Minutes to Daily).

4. Use the Size of Offline Cache list to select a cache size (from 2% of Disk Space to 20% of Disk Space).

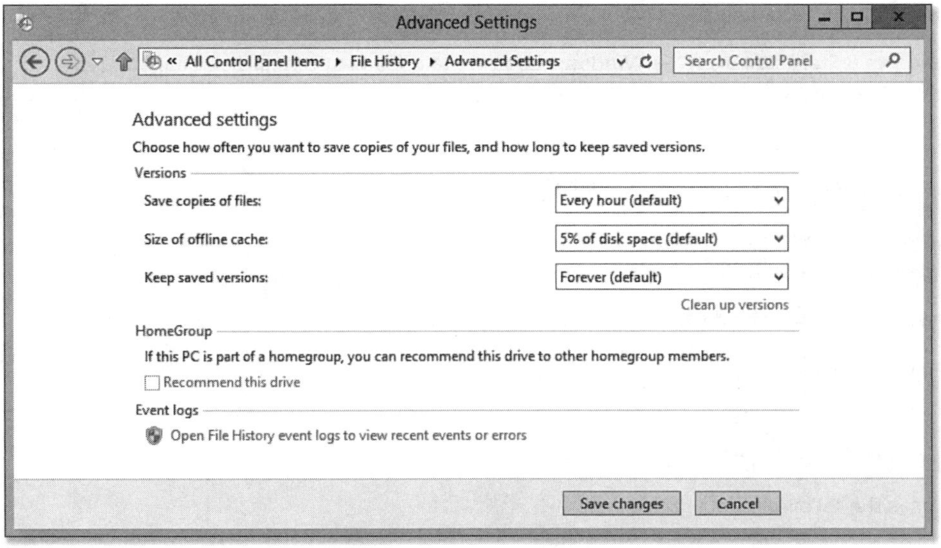

Figure 32.3
Use the Advanced Settings window to configure File History.

5. Use the Keep Saved Versions list to select when you want File History to delete old versions of files (from 1 Month to 2 Years, Until Space is Needed, or Forever).

Cleaning Up Versions to Save Disk Space

If your external drive is running low on free space, you can delete some older versions right away. Click Clean Up Versions to open the File History Cleanup dialog box, select a time frame for the file you want to remove (from Older Than 1 Month to Older Than 2 Years, or All But the Latest One), and then click Clean Up.

6. If you're using an external drive and your computer is part of a homegroup, you can activate the Recommend This Drive check box to allow other homegroup users the chance to use the same drive for their backups.

7. If you want to keep an eye on what File History is doing, click Open File History Event Logs to View Recent Events or Errors. This launches the Event Viewer and displays the File History Backup Log.

8. Click Save Changes to put the new settings into effect.

Activating File History

At long last, you're ready to start using File History. In the File History window, click Turn On. If Windows 8 asks if you want to recommend the drive to your homegroup, click Yes or No, as you see fit. File History immediately goes to work saving the initial copies of your files to the external drive or network share.

Restoring a Previous Version of a File

When you activate File History on your PC, as described earlier in this chapter, Windows 8 periodically—by default, once an hour—looks for files that have changed since the last check. If it finds a changed file, it takes a "snapshot" of that file and saves that version of the file to the external drive that you specified when you set up File History. This gives Windows 8 the capability to reverse the changes you have made to a file by reverting to an earlier state of the file. An earlier state of a file is called a *previous version*.

Why would you want to revert to a previous version of a file? One reason is that you might improperly edit the file by deleting or changing important data. In some cases, you might be able to restore that data by going back to a previous version of the file. Another reason is that the file might become corrupted if the program or Windows 8 crashes. You can get a working version of the file back by restoring a previous version.

Follow these steps to restore a previous version of a file:

1. In the Start screen, press Windows Logo+W, type **history**, and then click File History to open the File History window.

2. Click Restore Personal Files. The Home – File History window appears.

3. Double-click the library that contains the file you want to restore.

4. Open the folder that contains the file.

5. Click Previous Version (see Figure 32.4) or press Ctrl+Left Arrow until you open the version of the folder you want to use. If you'd prefer a more recent version, click Next Version or press Ctrl+Right Arrow.

6. Click the file you want to restore.

7. Click Restore to Original Location (pointed out in Figure 32.4). If the original folder has a file with the same name, File History asks what you want to do.

8. Select an option:

   ▪ **Replace the File in the Destination Folder**—Click this option to overwrite the existing file with the previous version.

   ▪ **Skip This File**—Click this option to skip the restore and do nothing.

   ▪ **Compare Info for Both Files**—Click this option to display the File Conflict dialog box (see Figure 32.5), which shows the original and the previous version side by side, along with the last modification date and time and the file size. Activate the check box beside the version you want to keep, and then click Continue. To keep both versions, activate both check boxes. File History restores the previous version with (2) appended to its filename.

> **note**
>
> If you need to remove the external drive temporarily (for example, if you need to use the port for another device), you should turn off File History before disconnecting the external drive. In the Windows 8 Start screen, press Windows Logo+W to open the Settings search pane, type **history**, and then click File History. In the File History window, click Turn Off.

> **note**
>
> Windows 8 also keeps track of previous versions of folders, which is useful if an entire folder becomes corrupted because of a system crash.

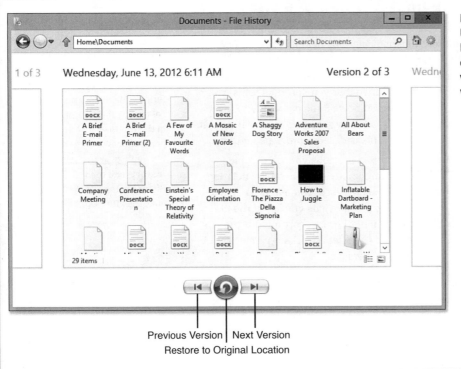

Figure 32.4
Use the Home – File History window to choose which previous version you want to restore.

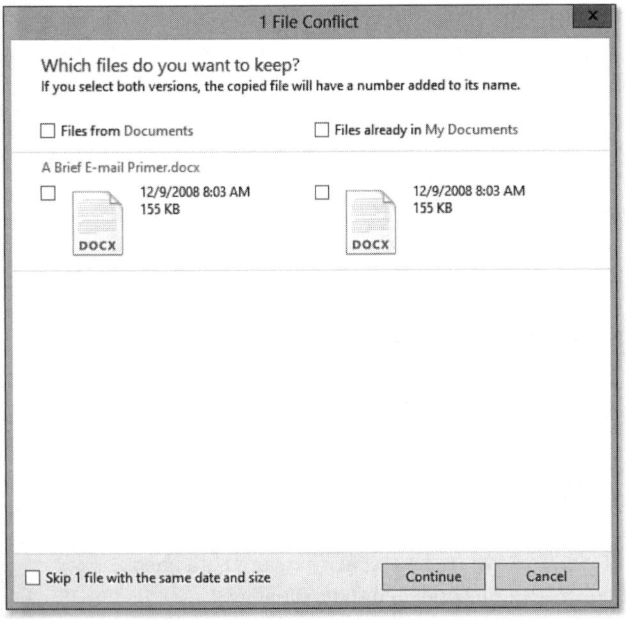

Previous Version | Next Version
Restore to Original Location

Figure 32.5
If the original folder has a file with the same name and you're not sure which one to keep, use the File Conflict dialog box to decide.

Setting System Restore Points

One of the biggest causes of Windows instability in the past was the tendency of some newly installed programs simply to not get along with Windows. The problem could be an executable file that didn't mesh with the Windows system or a Registry change that caused havoc on other programs or on Windows. Similarly, hardware installs often caused problems by adding faulty device drivers to the system or by corrupting the Registry.

To help guard against software or hardware installations that bring down the system, Windows 8 offers the System Restore feature. Its job is straightforward, yet clever: to take periodic snapshots—called *restore points* or *protection points*—of your system, each of which includes the currently installed program files, Registry settings, and other crucial system data. The idea is that if a program or device installation causes problems on your system, you use System Restore to revert your system to the most recent restore point before the installation.

System Restore automatically creates restore points under the following conditions:

- **Every week**—This is called a *system checkpoint*, and it's set once a week during the automatic maintenance window as long as your computer is running. If your computer isn't running, the system checkpoint is created the next time you start your computer, assuming that it has been at least a week hours since that previous system checkpoint was set.

- **Before installing certain applications**—Some newer applications (notably Windows Live Essentials and Office 2000 and later) are aware of System Restore and will ask it to create a restore point prior to installation.

- **Before installing a Windows Update patch**—System Restore creates a restore point before you install a patch either by hand via the Windows Update site or via the Automatic Updates feature.

- **Before installing an unsigned device driver**—Windows 8 warns you about installing unsigned drivers. If you choose to go ahead, the system creates a restore point before installing the driver.

- **Before reverting to a previous configuration using System Restore**—Sometimes reverting to an earlier configuration doesn't fix the current problem or it creates its own set of problems. In these cases, System Restore creates a restore point before reverting so that you can undo the restoration.

It's also possible to create a restore point manually using the System Protection feature. Here are the steps to follow:

1. Press Windows Logo+W to open the Settings search pane, type **restore point**, and then click Create a Restore Point in the search results. This opens the System Properties dialog box with the System Protection tab displayed, as shown in Figure 32.6.

2. By default, Windows 8 creates automatic restore points for just the system drive. If you have other drives on your system and you want to create automatic restore points for them as well, click the drive in the Protection Settings list, click Configure, turn on the System Protection option, and then click OK.

3. Click Create to display the Create a Restore Point dialog box.

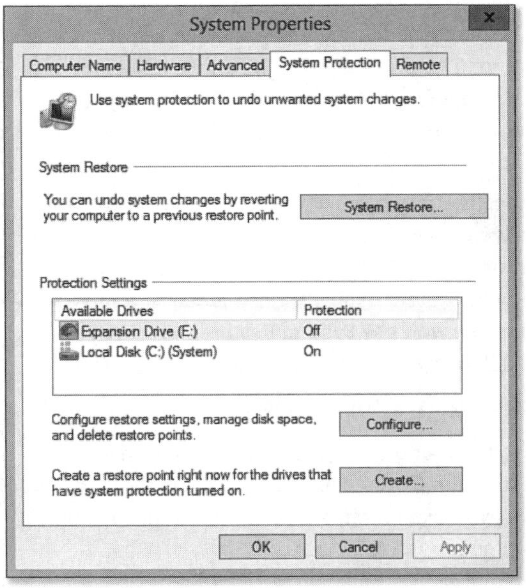

Figure 32.6
Use the System Protection tab to set a restore point.

4. Type a description for the new restore point and then click Create. System Protection creates the restore point and displays a dialog box to let you know.

5. Click Close to return to the System Properties dialog box.

6. Click OK.

➡ *To learn how to revert your PC to an earlier restore point,* **see** *"Recovering Using System Restore," p. 648.*

Creating More Room for Restore Points

By default, Windows 8 sets aside 3% of your hard disk space for restore points. When that space is used up, Windows 8 deletes the oldest restore points as new ones are added. If you use restore points frequently and you have lots of free space on your hard drive, consider increasing the amount of space allotted to restore points. Click the drive in the Protection Settings list, click Configure, and use the Max Usage slider to set the amount of disk space you want. If the hard disk is getting low on free space, you can also click the Delete button to remove all the restore points from the hard disk.

Creating a Recovery Drive

We all hope our computers operate trouble-free over their lifetimes, but we know from bitter experience that this is rarely the case. Computers are incredibly complex systems, so it is almost inevitable that a PC will develop glitches. If your hard drive is still accessible, you can boot to Windows 8 and access the recovery tools, as we described in Chapter 26, "Troubleshooting and Repairing Problems."

➡ *To learn how to boot to the Windows 8 recovery tools,* ***see*** *"Accessing the Recovery Environment," **p. 638**.*

If you can't boot your PC, however, then you must boot using some other drive. If you have your Windows 8 installation media, you can boot using that drive. If you don't have the installation media, you can still recover if you've created a USB recovery drive. This is a USB flash drive that contains the Windows 8 recovery environment, which enables you to refresh or reset your PC, use System Restore, recover a system image, and more.

Before you can boot to a recovery drive, such as a USB flash drive, you need to create the drive. Follow these steps:

1. Insert the USB flash drive you want to use. Note that the drive must have a capacity of at least 256MB. Also, Windows 8 will erase all data on the drive, so make sure it doesn't contain any files you want to keep.

2. In the Start screen, press Windows Logo+W, type **recovery**, and then click Create a Recovery Drive. User Account Control appears.

3. Click Yes or enter administrator credentials to continue. The Recovery Drive Wizard appears.

4. Click Next. The Recovery Drive Wizard prompts you to choose the USB flash drive, as shown in Figure 32.7.

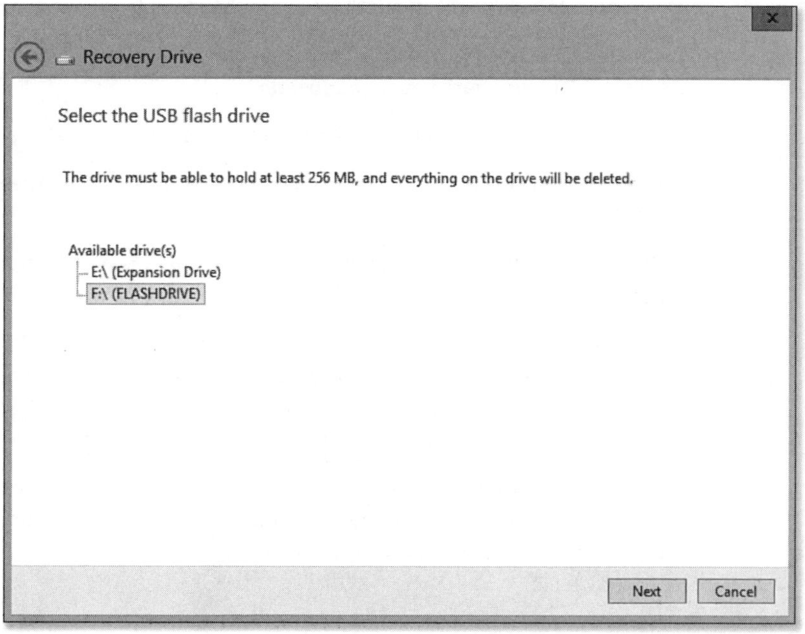

Figure 32.7
Select the flash drive that you inserted in step 1.

5. Click the drive, if it isn't selected already, and then click Next. The Recovery Drive Wizard warns you that all the data on the drive will be deleted.

6. Click Create. The wizard formats the drive and copies the recovery tools and data.

7. Click Finish.

Remove the drive, label it, and then put it someplace where you'll be able to find it later on, just in case.

Creating a System Image Backup

The worst-case scenario for PC problems is a system crash that renders your hard disk or system files unusable. Your only recourse in such a case is to start from scratch with either a reformatted hard disk or a new hard disk. This usually means that you have to reinstall Windows 8 and then reinstall and reconfigure all your applications. In other words, you're looking at the better part of a day or, more likely, a few days, to recover your system. However, Windows 8 has a feature that takes most of the pain out of recovering your system. It's called a *system image* backup, and it's part of the system recovery options that we discussed in Chapter 26.

> ➡ *To learn how to restore your PC from an image, **see** "Restoring a System Image," **p. 651**.*

The system image backup is actually a complete backup of your Windows 8 installation. It takes a long time to create a system image (at least several hours, depending on how much stuff you have), but it's worth it for the peace of mind. Here are the steps to follow to create the system image:

1. Press Windows Logo+W, type **file recovery**, and then click Windows 7 File Recovery. The Windows 7 File Recovery window appears.

2. Click Create a System Image. The Create a System Image Wizard appears.

3. The wizard asks you to specify a backup destination. You have three choices, as shown in Figure 32.8. (Click Next when you're ready to continue.)

   ■ **On a Hard Disk**—Select this option if you want to use a disk drive on your computer. If you have multiple drives, use the list to select the one you want to use.

   ■ **On One or More DVDs**—Select this option if you want to use DVDs to hold the backup. Depending on how much data your PC holds, you could be talking about using dozens of discs for this (at least!), so we don't recommend this option.

   ■ **On a Network Location**—Select this option if you want to use a shared network folder. Either type the address of the share or click Select and then click Browse to use the Browse for Folder dialog box to choose the shared network folder. Make sure it's a share for which you have permission to add data. Type a username and password for accessing the share, and then click OK.

⊛ tip

To make sure your recovery drive works properly, you should test it by booting your PC to the drive. Insert the recovery drive and then restart your PC. How you boot to the drive depends on your system. Some PCs display a menu of boot devices, and you select the USB drive from that menu. In other cases, you see a message telling you to press a key.

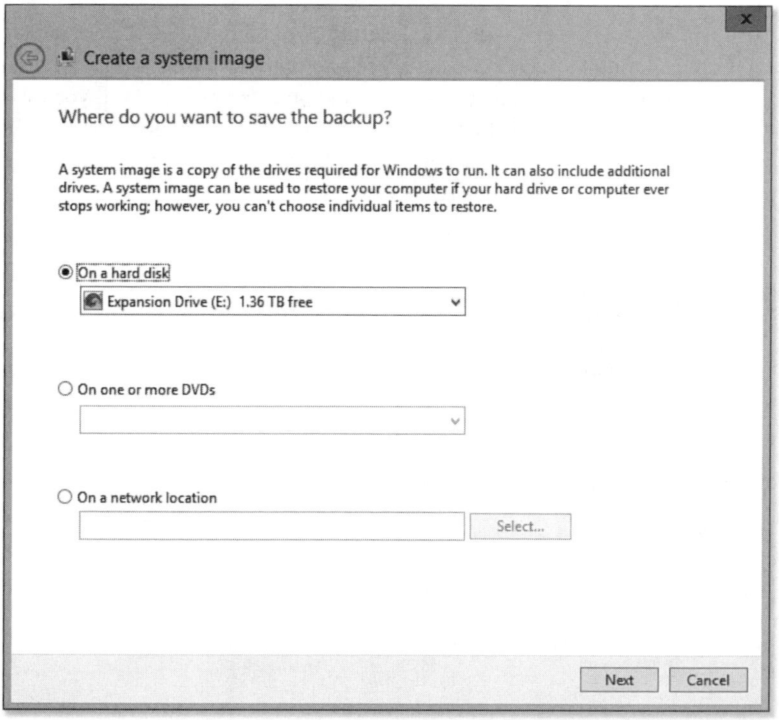

Figure 32.8
You can create the system image on a hard drive, on DVDs, or on a network share.

4. The system image backup automatically includes your internal hard disk in the system image, and you can't change that. However, if you also have external hard drives, you can add them to the backup by activating their check boxes. Click Next. Windows Backup asks you to confirm your backup settings.

5. Click Start Backup. Windows Backup creates the system image. When the backup is complete, Windows 8 asks if you want to create a system repair disc.

6. You don't need a system repair disc if you already created a recovery drive, so click No. If you don't have a recovery drive and don't have a USB flash drive to create one, click Yes and follow steps 2 to 5 in the next section.

7. Click Close.

8. Click OK.

If you used a hard drive and you have multiple external drives lying around, be sure to label the one that contains the system image so you'll be able to find it later.

> **🔔 caution**
> Many people make the mistake of creating the system image once and then ignoring it, forgetting that their systems aren't set in stone. Over the coming days and weeks you'll be installing apps, tweaking settings, and of course creating lots of new documents and other data. This means that you should periodically create a fresh system image. Should disaster strike, you'll be able to recover most of your system.

Creating a System Repair Disc

In Windows Vista, you could attempt to get a badly behaving machine up and running again by booting to the Vista install disc and then accessing the system recovery options. That was a nice feature, but only if you could find your install disc (or if you ever had one in the first place)! Windows 7 fixed that problem by giving you the option of creating your own system repair disc and, despite the more convenient feature of the USB recovery drive, Windows 8 still offers that option (although slightly deprecated as a "Windows 7 recovery tool"). Here's how you go about his:

1. Insert a blank recordable CD or DVD into your burner. If an AutoPlay notification shows up, close it.

2. Press Windows Logo+W, type **file recovery**, and then click Windows 7 File Recovery.

3. Click Create a System Repair Disc. The Create a System Repair Disc dialog box appears, as shown in Figure 32.9.

Create a system repair disc [−][□][✕]

Select a CD/DVD drive and insert a blank disc into the drive

A system repair disc can be used to boot your computer. It also contains Windows system recovery tools that can help you recover Windows from a serious error or restore your computer from a system image.

Drive: DVD Drive (D:) ⌄

[Create disc]   [Cancel]

Figure 32.9
Windows 8 still offers the system repair disc option.

4. If you have multiple burners, use the Drive list to select the one you want to use.

5. Click Create Disc. Windows 8 creates the disc (it takes a minute or two), and then displays a particularly unhelpful dialog box.

6. Click Close and then click OK.

Eject the disc, label it, and then put it someplace where you'll be able to find it later on. To learn how to use the system repair disc in the event of a real emergency, see Chapter 26, "Troubleshooting and Repairing Problems."

 *See "Accessing the RE via a System Repair Disc," **p. 641**.*

Protecting a File

Much day-to-day work in Windows 8 is required but not terribly important. Most memos, letters, and notes are run-of-the-mill and don't require extra protection. Occasionally, however, you may create or work with a file that *is* important. It could be a carefully crafted letter, a memo detailing important company strategy, or a collection of hard-won brainstorming notes. Whatever the content, such a file requires extra protection to ensure that you don't lose your work.

Making a File Read-Only

You can set advanced file permissions that can prevent a document from being changed or even deleted (see "Setting Security Permissions on Files and Folders," later in the chapter). If your only concern is preventing other people from making changes to a document, a simpler technique you can use is making the document *read-only*. This means that although other people can make changes to a document, they cannot *save* those changes (except to a new file). The following steps show you how to make a file read-only:

1. Use File Explorer to open the folder that contains the file you want to protect.

2. Click the file.

3. In the Home tab, click the top half of the Properties button. The file's Properties dialog box appears.

4. Click the General tab.

5. Activate the Read-Only check box, as shown in Figure 32.10.

6. Click OK. The file is now read-only.

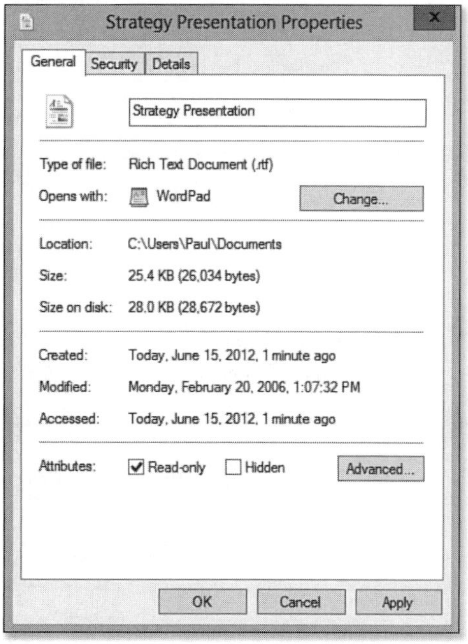

Figure 32.10
Activate the Read-Only check box to prevent a file from being changed.

To confirm that the file is protected, open it, make changes to the file, and then save it. The program displays the Save As dialog box. Click Save, and then when the programs asks if you want to overwrite the file, click Yes. Instead of overwriting the file, the program just tells you that the file is read-only.

Hiding a File

If you have a file that contains sensitive or secret data, making it read-only isn't good enough because you probably don't want unauthorized users to even *see* the contents of the file much less change them. To prevent other people from viewing a file, you can hide it so that it doesn't appear during a cursory examination of the folder's contents. Here are the steps to follow:

1. Use File Explorer to open the folder that contains the file you want to hide.

2. Click the file.

3. In the Home tab, click the top half of the Properties button. The file's Properties dialog box appears.

4. Click the General tab.

5. Activate the Hidden check box, as shown in Figure 32.11.

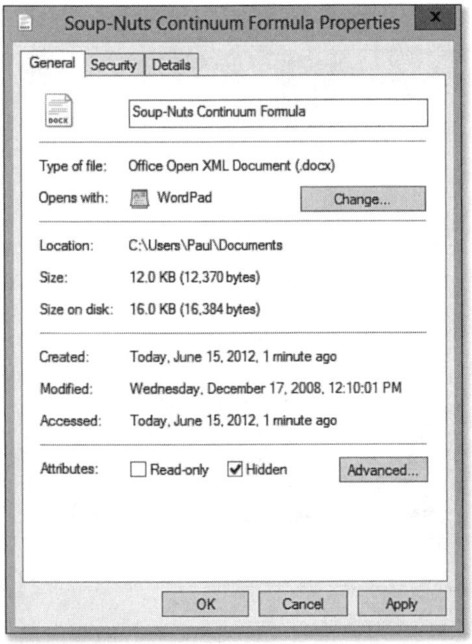

Figure 32.11
Activate the Hidden check box to prevent a file from being seen.

6. Click Advanced to open the Advanced Attributed dialog box.

7. Deactivate the Allow This File to Have Contents Indexed in Addition to File Properties check box. This is optional, but it does prevent the file's data from being found during a file search.

8. Click OK to return to the Properties dialog box.

9. Click OK. The file is now hidden.

To see a hidden file, first use File Explorer to open the folder containing the file. In the ribbon, click the View tab and then activate the Hidden Items check box.

Setting Security Permissions on Files and Folders

At the file system level, security for Windows 8 is most often handled by assigning *permissions* to a file or folder. Permissions specify whether a user or group is allowed to access a file or folder and, if access is allowed, they also specify what the user or group is allowed to do with the file or folder. For example, a user may be allowed only to read the contents of a file or folder, whereas another may be allowed to make changes to the file or folder.

Windows 8 offers a basic set of six permissions for folders, and five permissions for files:

- **Full Control**—A user or group can perform any of the actions listed. A user or group can also change permissions.

- **Modify**—A user or group can view the file or folder contents, open files, edit files, create new files and subfolders, delete files, and run programs.

- **Read and Execute**—A user or group can view the file or folder contents, open files, and run programs.

- **List Folder Contents (folders only)**—A user or group can view the folder contents.

- **Read**—A user or group can open files, but cannot edit them.

- **Write**—A user or group can create new files and subfolders as well as open and edit existing files.

There is also a long list of so-called *special permissions* that offer more fine-grained control over file and folder security. (We'll run through these special permissions a bit later; see "Assigning Special Permissions.")

Permissions are often handled most easily by using the built-in security groups. Each security group is defined with a specific set of permissions and rights, and any user added to a group is automatically granted that group's permissions and rights. There are two main security groups:

- **Administrators**—Members of this group have complete control over the computer, meaning they can access all folders and files; install and uninstall programs (including legacy programs) and devices; create, modify, and remove user accounts; install Windows updates, service packs, and fixes; use Safe mode; repair Windows; take ownership of objects; and more.

■ **Users**—Members of this group (also known as *standard users*) can access files only in their own folders and in the computer's shared folders, change their account's password and picture, and run programs and install programs that don't require administrative-level rights.

In addition to those groups, Windows 8 also defines up to a dozen others that you'll use less often (actually, most of these extra groups are of interest only to corporate IT personnel). Note that the permissions assigned to these groups are automatically assigned to members of the Administrators group. This means that if you have an Administrator account, you don't also have to be a member of any other group to perform the task's specific to that group. Here's the list of groups:

■ **Access Control Assistance Operators**—Members of this group can perform remote queries to determine the permissions assigned to a computer's resources.

■ **Backup Operators**—Members of this group can access the Backup program and use it to back up and restore folders and files, no matter what permissions are set on those objects.

■ **Cryptographic Operators**—Members of this group can perform cryptographic tasks.

■ **Distributed COM Users**—Members of this group can start, activate, and use Distributed COM (DCOM) objects.

■ **Event Log Readers**—Members of this group can access and read Windows 8's event logs.

■ **Guests**—Members of this group have the same privileges as those of the Users group. The exception is the default Guest account, which is not allowed to change its account password.

■ **HomeUsers**—Members of this group have access to resources shared using Windows 8's home-group networking feature.

■ **Hyper-V Administrators**—Members of this group have complete access to all the features of the Hyper-V virtualization software.

■ **IIS_IUSRS**—Members of this group can access an Internet Information Server website installed on the Windows 8 computer.

■ **Network Configuration Operators**—Members of this group have a subset of the administrator-level rights that enables them to install and configure networking features.

■ **Performance Log Users**—Members of this group can use the Windows Performance Diagnostic Console snap-in to monitor performance counters, logs, and alerts, both locally and remotely.

■ **Performance Monitor Users**—Members of this group can use the Windows Performance Diagnostic Console snap-in to monitor performance counters only, both locally and remotely.

■ **Power Users**—Members of this group have a subset of the Administrators group privileges. Power users can't back up or restore files, replace system files, take ownership of files, or install or remove device drivers. In addition, power users can't install applications that explicitly require the user to be a member of the Administrators group.

■ **Remote Desktop Users**—Members of this group can log on to the computer from a remote location using the Remote Desktop feature.

- **Remote Management Users**—Members of this group have access to Windows Management Instrumentation (WMI) resources using Windows management protocols such as the Windows Remote Management service. Another group—WinRMRemoteWMIUsers—offers similar access.

- **Replicator**—Members of this group can replicate files across a domain.

Assigning a User to a Security Group

The advantage of using security groups to assign permissions is that once you set the group's permissions on a file or folder, you never have to change the security again on that object. Instead, any new users you create, you assign to the appropriate security group, and they automatically inherit that group's permissions.

Here are the steps to follow to assign a user to a Windows 8 security group:

1. Press Windows Logo+R to display the Run dialog box.

2. In the Open text box, type **control userpasswords2**.

3. Click OK. Windows 8 displays the User Accounts dialog box, shown in Figure 32.12.

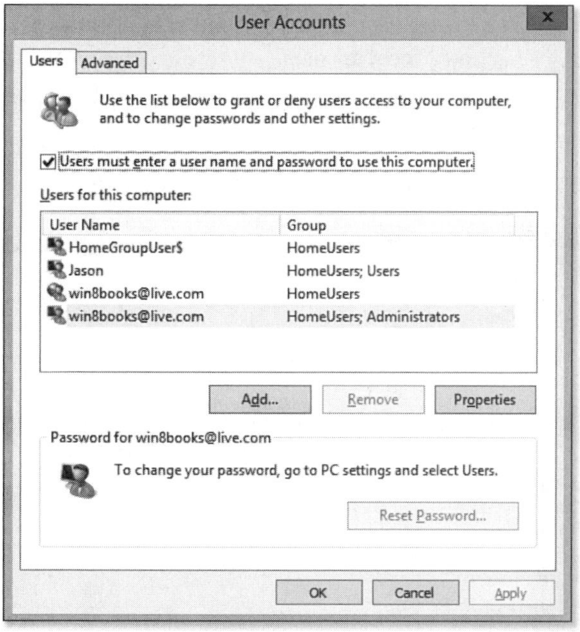

Figure 32.12
The User Accounts dialog box enables you to assign users to any Windows 8 security group.

CHAPTER

778   Protecting Your Data from Loss and Theft

32

4. Click the user you want to work with, and then click Properties. The user's property sheet appears.

5. Display the Group Membership tab.

6. Click either Standard User or Administrator. (This is a temporary change; in Windows 8, it's the only way to activate the Other list.)

7. Click the Other option.

8. Use the Other list to select the security group.

9. Click OK. Windows 8 assigns the user to the security group.

Assigning a User to Multiple Security Groups

If you want to assign a user to more than one security group, the User Account dialog box method that we ran through in the preceding section won't work. If you have Windows 8 Pro or Enterprise, you can use the Local Users and Groups snap-in to assign a user to multiple groups. Here's how:

1. At the Start screen, type `lusrmgr.msc`, and then press Enter. The Local Users and Groups snap-in appears.

2. Select the Users branch and then double-click the user you want to work with. The user's property sheet appears.

3. Display the Member Of tab, which displays the groups assigned to the user (see Figure 32.13).

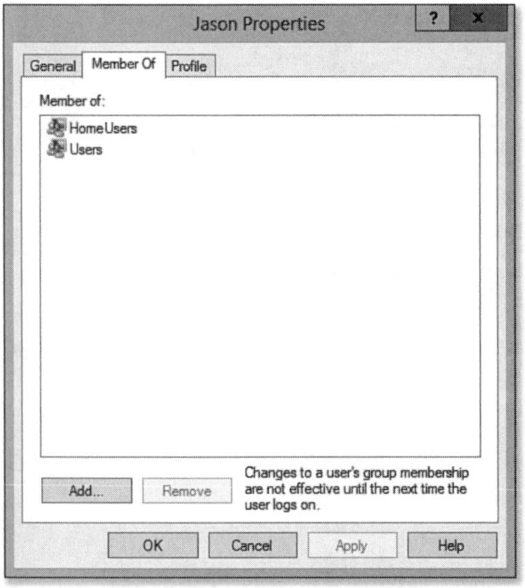

Figure 32.13
Use the Local User and Groups snap-in to assign a user to multiple security groups.

4. Click Add. Windows 8 displays the Select Groups dialog box.

5. If you know the name of the group, type it in the large text box. Otherwise, click Advanced, Find Now, and then double-click the group in the list that appears.

6. Repeat step 5 to assign the user to other groups, as needed.

7. Click OK. Windows 8 adds the groups to the Member Of tab.

8. Click OK. Windows 8 assigns the user to the security groups the next time the user logs on.

Assigning Standard Permissions

When you're ready to assign any of the standard permissions that we discussed earlier to a user or group, follow these steps:

1. In File Explorer, display the file or folder you want to secure.

2. Display the Home tab and then click the top half of the Properties button.

3. Display the Security tab.

4. Click Edit. The Permissions for *Object* dialog box appears, where *Object* is the name of the file or folder.

5. Click Add to open the Select Users or Groups dialog box.

6. If you know the name of the user or group you want to add, type it in the large text box. Otherwise, click Advanced, Find Now, and then double-click the user or group in the list that appears.

7. Click OK. Windows 8 returns you to the Permissions for *Object* dialog box with the new user or group added.

8. Use the check boxes in the Allow and Deny columns to assign the permissions you want for this user or group, as shown in Figure 32.14.

9. Click OK in all the open dialog boxes.

Assigning Special Permissions

In some situations, you might want more fine-tuned control over a user's or group's permissions. For example, you may want to allow a user to add new files to a folder, but not new subfolders. Similarly, you may want to give a user full control over a file or folder, but deny that user the ability to change permissions or take ownership of the object.

For these more specific situations, Windows 8 offers a set of 14 special permissions for folders, and 13 special permissions for files:

- **Full Control**—A user or group can perform any of the actions listed here.

- **Traverse Folder/Execute File**—A user or group can open the folder to get to another folder, or can execute a program file.

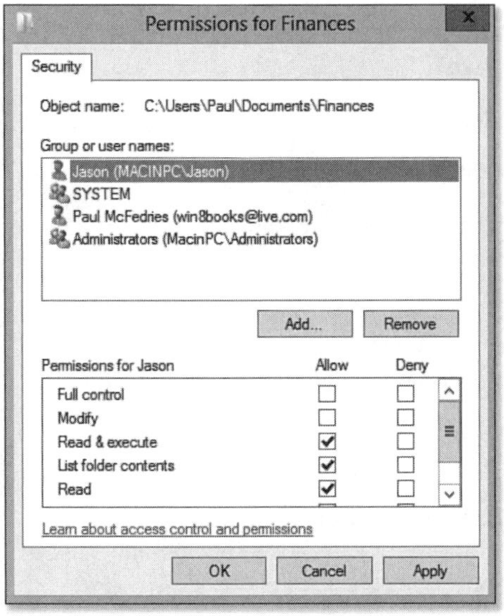

Figure 32.14
Use a file or folder's Permissions dialog box to assign standard permissions for a user or security group.

- **List Folder/Read Data**—A user or group can view the folder contents or can read the contents of a file.

- **Read Attributes**—A user or group can read the folder's or file's attributes, such as Read-Only or Hidden.

- **Read Extended Attributes**—A user or group can read the folder's or file's extended attributes. (These are extra attributes assigned by certain programs.)

- **Create File/Write Data**—A user or group can create new files within a folder, or can make changes to a file.

- **Create Folders/Append Data**—A user or group can create new subfolders within a folder, or can add new data to the end of a file (but can't change any existing file data).

- **Write Attributes**—A user or group can change the folder's or file's attributes.

- **Write Extended Attributes**—A user or group can change the folder's or file's extended attributes.

- **Delete Subfolders and Files (folders only)**—A user or group can delete subfolders and files within the folder.

- **Delete**—A user or group can delete the folders or file.

- **Read Permissions**—A user or group can read the folder's or file's permissions.

- **Change Permissions**—A user or group can edit the folder's or file's permissions.

- **Take Ownership**—A user or group can take ownership of the folder or file.

> 🔍 **note**
> To see a file's or folder's attributes, right-click the item, click Properties, and then display the General tab.

Here are the steps to follow to assign special permissions to a file or folder:

1. In File Explorer, display the file or folder you want to secure.

2. Display the Home tab and then click the top half of the Properties button.

3. Display the Security tab.

4. Click Advanced. The Advanced Security Settings for *Object* dialog box appears, where *Object* is the name of the file or folder.

5. In the Permissions tab, click Add. The Permission Entry for *Object* dialog box appears.

6. Click Select a Principal.

7. If you know the name of the user or group you want to work with, type it in the large text box. Otherwise, click Advanced, Find Now, and then double-click the user or group in the list that appears.

8. Click Show Advanced Permissions.

9. In the Type list, select either Allow or Deny.

10. Use the check boxes to assign the permissions you want for this user or group, as shown in Figure 32.15

Figure 32.15
Use a file
or folder's
Permission
Entry dialog
box to assign
special permis-
sions for a user
or security
group.

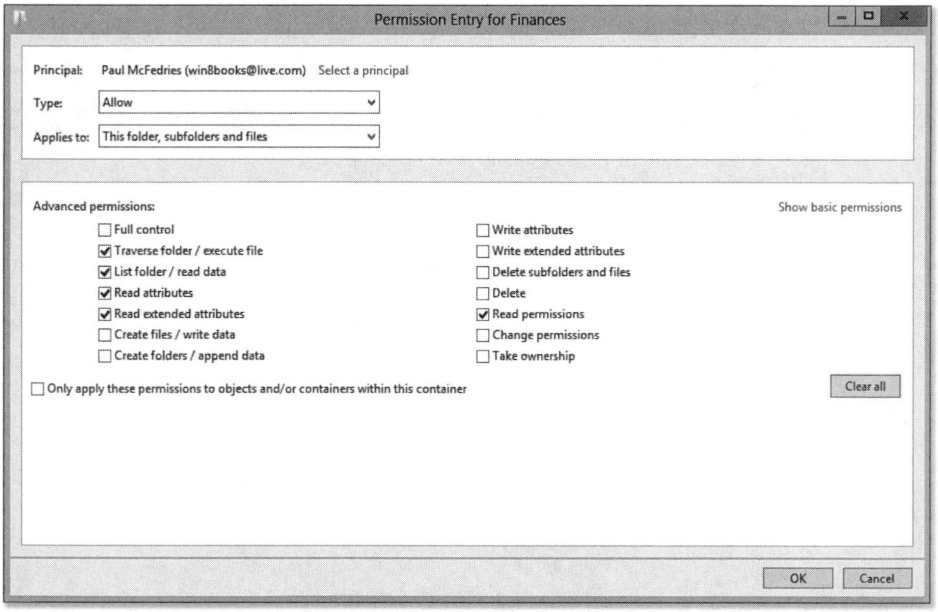

11. Click OK in all the open dialog boxes.

Fixing Permission Problems by Taking Ownership of Your Files

When you're working in Windows 8, you may have trouble with a folder (or a file) because Windows tells you that you don't have permission to edit (add to, delete, whatever) the folder. The result is often a series of annoying User Account Control dialog boxes.

You might think the solution is to give your user account Full Control permissions on the folder, but it's not as easy as that. Why not? Because you're not the owner of the folder. (If you were, you'd have the permissions you need automatically.) So the solution is to first take ownership of the folder, and then assign your user account full control permissions over the folder.

Here are the steps to follow:

1. Use File Explorer to locate the folder you want to take ownership of.

2. Display the Home tab and then click the top half of the Properties button.

3. Display the Security tab.

4. Click Advanced to open the Advanced Security Settings dialog box.

5. Display the Permissions tab.

6. Click the Change link that appears beside the current owner. The Select user or Group dialog box appears.

7. Type your username and then click OK.

8. Activate the Replace Owner on Subcontainers and Objects check box, as shown in Figure 32.16.

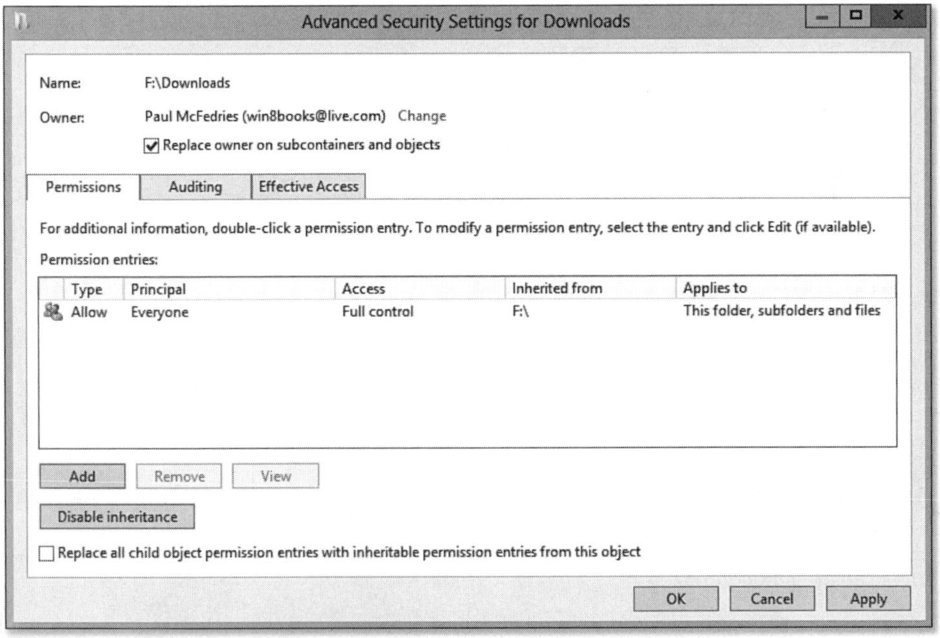

Figure 32.16
Use a folder's Advanced Security Settings dialog box to take ownership of the folder.

9. Click OK to return to the Security tab of the folder's Properties dialog box.

10. If you don't see your user account in the Group or User Names list, click Edit, click Add, type your username, and click OK.

11. Click your username.

12. Click the Full Control check box in the Allow column.

13. Click OK.

Note that, obviously, this is quite a bit of work. If you only have to do it every once in a while, it's no big thing, but if you find you have to take ownership regularly, you'll probably want an easier way to go about it. You've got it! Listing 32.1 shows a Registry Editor file that modifies the Registry in such a way that you end up with a Take Ownership command in the shortcut menu that appears if you right-click any folder and any file.

Listing 32.1 A Registry Editor File That Creates a Take Ownership Command

```
Windows Registry Editor Version 5.00

[HKEY_CLASSES_ROOT\*\shell\runas]
@="Take Ownership"
"NoWorkingDirectory"=""

[HKEY_CLASSES_ROOT\*\shell\runas\command]
@="cmd.exe /c takeown /f \"%1\" && icacls \"%1\" /grant administrators:F"
"IsolatedCommand"="cmd.exe /c takeown /f \"%1\" && icacls \"%1\" /grant
➥administrators:F"

[HKEY_CLASSES_ROOT\Directory\shell\runas]
@="Take Ownership"
"NoWorkingDirectory"=""

[HKEY_CLASSES_ROOT\Directory\shell\runas\command]
@="cmd.exe /c takeown /f \"%1\" /r /d y && icacls \"%1\" /grant administrators:F /t"
"IsolatedCommand"="cmd.exe /c takeown /f \"%1\" /r /d y && icacls \"%1\" /grant
➥administrators:F /t"
```

To use the file, double-click it and then enter your UAC credentials when prompted. As you can see in Figure 32.17, right-clicking (in this case) a folder displays a shortcut menu with a new Take Ownership command. Click that command, enter your UAC credentials, and sit back as Windows does all the hard work for you!

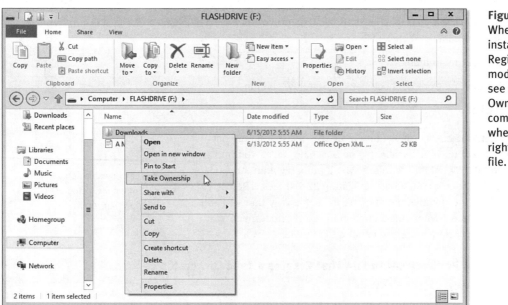

Figure 32.17
When you install the Registry mod, you see the Take Ownership command when you right-click a file.

Encrypting Files and Folders

If a snoop can't log on to your Windows PC, does that mean your data is safe? No, unfortunately, it most certainly does not. If a cracker has physical access to your PC—either by sneaking into your office or by stealing your computer—the cracker can use advanced utilities to view the contents of your hard drive. This means that if your PC contains extremely sensitive or confidential informa-tion—personal financial files, medical histories, corporate salary data, trade secrets, business plans, journals or diaries—it wouldn't be hard for the interloper to read and even copy that data.

If you're worried about anyone viewing these or other "for your eyes only" files, Windows 8 enables you to *encrypt* the file information. Encryption encodes the file to make it completely unreadable by anyone unless the person logs on to your Windows 8 account. After you encrypt your files, you work with them exactly as you did before, with no noticeable loss of performance.

note

To use file encryption, the drive must use NTFS To check the current file system, open File Explorer, click Computer, click the drive, select Computer, Properties, and then examine the file system information in the Properties dialog box. If you need to convert a drive to NTFS, press Windows Logo+X, click Command Prompt (Admin), and then click Yes when User Account Control asks you to confirm. At the command prompt, type **convert** *d***: /fs:ntfs**, where *d* is the letter of the hard drive you want to convert, and press Enter. If Windows asks to "dismount the volume," press **Y** and then Enter.

Encrypting a Folder

Follow these steps to encrypt important data:

1. Use File Explorer to display the icon of the folder containing the data that you want to encrypt.

2. In the Home tab, click the top half of the Properties button to open the folder's property sheet.

3. Click the General tab.

4. Click Advanced. The Advanced Attributes dialog box appears.

5. Click to activate the Encrypt Contents to Secure Data check box.

6. Click OK in each open dialog box. The Confirm Attribute Changes dialog box appears.

7. Click the Apply Changes to This Folder, Subfolders and Files option.

8. Click OK. Windows encrypts the folder's contents.

 tip

Although it's possible to encrypt individual files, encrypting an entire folder is easier because Windows 8 then automatically encrypts new files that you add to the folder.

tip

By default, Windows displays the names of encrypted files and folders in a green font, which helps you to differentiate these items from unencrypted files and folders. If you'd rather see encrypted filenames and folder names in the regular font, open any folder window and select View, Options. Click the View tab, click to deactivate the Show Encrypted or Compressed NTFS Files in Color check box, and then click OK.

Backing Up Your Encryption Key

When you sign on to Windows 8, it uses your credentials to access the encryption key that decrypts the folder so you can access it. This encryption key is stored on your hard disk for easy and fast access. However, like any file or folder on your hard disk, the encryption key can become corrupted. If that happens, you lose access to the encrypted data, so key corruption is a disaster waiting to happen. To avoid that disaster, you should back up the encryption key to a removable drive for safekeeping.

When you encrypt a folder for the first time, Windows 8 displays a notification suggesting you back up the encryption key, as shown in Figure 32.18. Click that notification to get started. If you miss the notification, click the Show Hidden Icons arrow in the taskbar's notification area, and then click the Encrypting File System icon.

Figure 32.18
When you first use the encrypting file system, you see this notification prompting you to back up your encryption key.

Follow these steps to back up your encryption key to a removable drive:

1. In the initial Encrypting File System dialog box, click Back Up Now. The Certificate Export Wizard appears.

2. Click Next. The Export File Format dialog box appears.

3. The default format is fine, so click Next. The Security dialog box appears and prompts you for a password to protect the encryption key.

4. Activate the Password text box, type the password in both the Password text box and then the Confirm Password text box, and then click Next. The File to Export dialog box appears.

5. Insert a removable drive, such as a USB flash drive.

6. Click Browse, click Computer, double-click the removable drive, type a filename, and then click Save.

7. Click Next.

8. Click Finish, and then click OK when the wizard tells you the export was successful.

Encrypting a Disk with BitLocker

Take Windows 8 security technologies such as the bidirectional Windows Firewall, Windows Defender, and Windows Service Hardening; throw in good patch-management policies (that is, applying security patches as soon as they're available); and add a dash of common sense. If you do so, your computer should never be compromised by malware while Windows 8 is running.

Windows Service Hardening

Windows Service Hardening is an under-the-hood Windows 8 security feature designed to limit the damage that a compromised service can wreak upon a system by implementing the following security techniques:

- All services run in a lower privilege level.

- All services have been stripped of permissions that they don't require.

- All services are assigned a security identifier (SID) that uniquely identifies each service. This enables a system resource to create its own access control list (ACL) that specifies exactly which SIDs can access the resource. If a service that's not on the ACL tries to access the resource, Windows 8 blocks the service.

- A system resource can restrict which services are allowed write permission to the resource.

- All services come with network restrictions that prevent services from accessing the network in ways not defined by the service's normal operating parameters.

However, what about when Windows 8 is *not* running? If your computer is stolen or if an attacker breaks into your home or office, your machine can be compromised in a couple of different ways:

- By booting to a removable drive and using command-line utilities to reset the administrator password

- By using a removable drive-based operating system to access your hard disk and reset folder and file permissions

Either exploit gives the attacker access to the contents of your computer. If you have sensitive data on your machine—financial data, company secrets, and so on—the results could be disastrous.

To help you prevent a malicious user from accessing your sensitive data, Windows 8 comes with a technology called BitLocker that encrypts an entire hard drive. That way, even if a malicious user gains physical access to your computer, he or she won't be able to read the drive contents. BitLocker works by storing the keys that encrypt and decrypt the sectors on a system drive in a Trusted Platform Module (TPM) 1.2 chip, which is a hardware component available on many newer machines.

> **🔍 note**
>
> To find out whether your computer has a TPM chip installed, restart the machine and then access the computer's BIOS settings (usually by pressing Delete or some other key; watch for a startup message that tells you how to access the BIOS). In most cases, look for a Security section and see if it lists a TPM entry.

Enabling BitLocker on a System with a TPM

To enable BitLocker on a system that comes with a TPM, press Windows Logo+W to open the Settings search pane, type **bit**, and then click BitLocker Drive Encryption. In the BitLocker Drive Encryption window, shown in Figure 32.19, click the Turn On BitLocker link associated with your hard drive.

Figure 32.19
Use the BitLocker Drive Encryption window to turn BitLocker on and off.

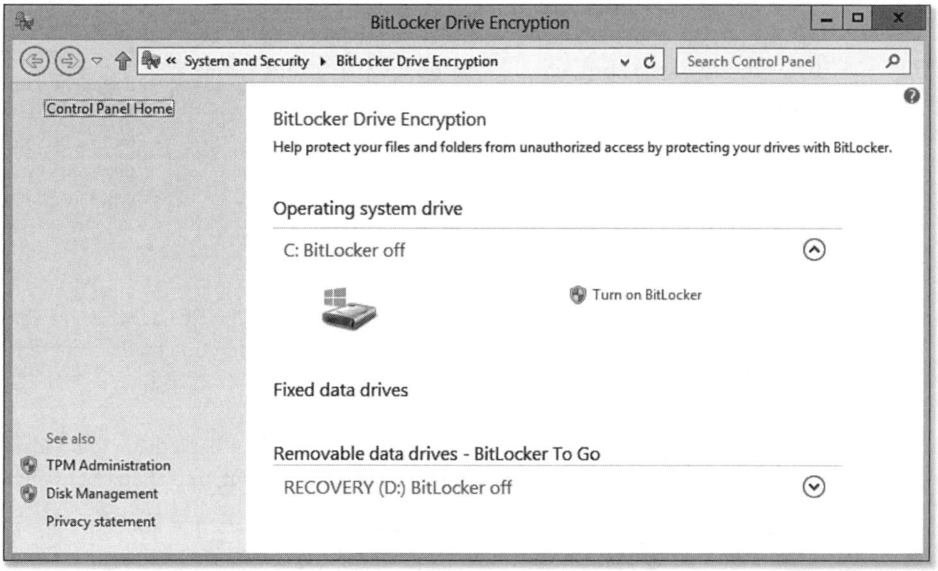

note

You can also use the Trusted Platform Module (TPM) Management snap-in to work with the TPM chip on your computer. In the Start screen, type **tpm.msc** and then press Enter. This snap-in enables you to view the current status of the TPM chip, view information about the chip manufacturer, and perform chip-management functions.

Enabling BitLocker on a System Without a TPM

If your PC doesn't have a TPM chip, you can still use BitLocker. In this case, however, you'll be forced to jump an extra hurdle when you start your computer. This hurdle will either be an extra password that you must enter or a USB flash drive that you must insert. Only by doing this will Windows 8 decrypt the drive and enable you to work with your computer in the normal way.

First you need to configure Windows 8 to allow BitLocker on a system without a TPM. Here's how it's done:

1. At the Start screen, type **gpedit.msc** and then press Enter to open the Local Group Policy Editor.

2. Open the Computer Configuration, Administrative Templates, Windows Components, BitLocker Drive Encryption, Operating System Drives branch.

3. Double-click the Require Additional Authentication at Startup policy.

4. Select Enabled.

5. Click to activate the Allow BitLocker Without a Compatible TPM check box, as shown in Figure 32.20.

6. Click OK.

7. To ensure that Windows 8 recognizes the new policy right away, return to the Start screen, type **gpupdate /force**, and press Enter.

> **note**
>
> If your version of Windows 8 doesn't offer the Local Group Policy Editor, you can still configure BitLocker to work on non-TPM systems by editing the Registry. However, this requires creating and configuring a new Registry key and a half dozen settings. To make this easier, we created a REG file that does everything automatically. You can download this file from www.mcfedries.com/ Windows8InDepth/.

You can now enable BitLocker:

1. Press Windows Logo+W to open the Settings search pane, type **bit**, and then click BitLocker Drive Encryption to open the BitLocker Drive Encryption window.

2. Click the Turn On BitLocker link beside your hard drive. The BitLocker Drive Encryption Wizard appears and asks how you want to unlock your drive when you start the system.

3. Make your choice:

   - **Insert a USB Flash Drive**—Click this option to require a flash drive to be inserted at startup. Insert the flash drive, wait until the wizard recognizes it, and then click Save.

   - **Enter a Password**—Click this option to require a password at startup. Type your password in the two text boxes, and then click Next.

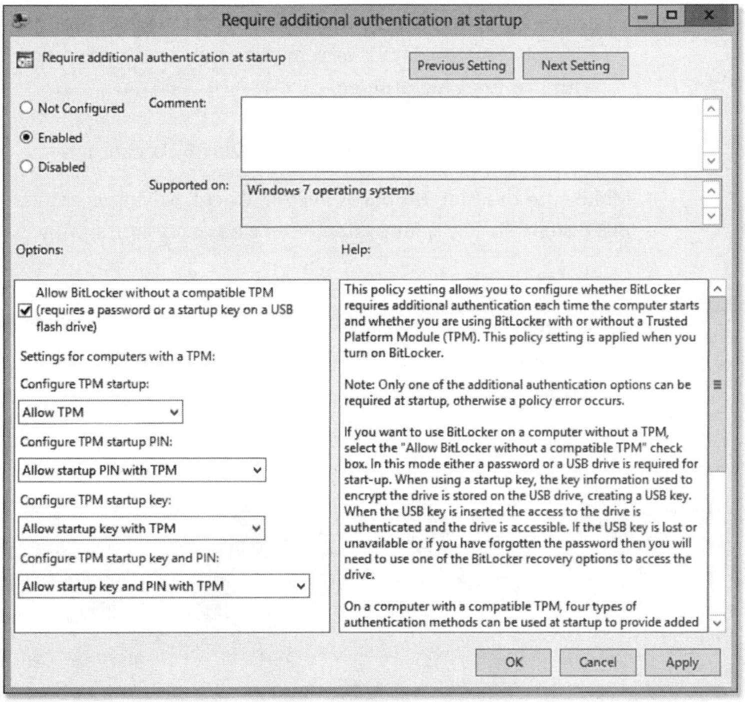

Figure 32.20
Use the Require Additional Authentication at Startup policy to configure Windows 8 to use BitLocker without a TPM.

4. The wizard now asks how you want to store your recovery key, which you'll need if you ever have trouble unlocking your PC. Click one (or more) of the following options:

- **Save to your Microsoft account**—Click this option to save the recovery key as part of your Microsoft account.

- **Save to a USB Flash Drive**—Click this option to save the recovery key to a flash drive. This is probably the best way to go because it means you can recover your files just by inserting the flash drive. Insert the flash drive, select it in the list that appears, and then click Save.

- **Save to a File**—Click this option to save the recovery key to a separate hard drive on your system. Use the Save BitLocker Key As dialog box to choose a location, and then click Save.

- **Print the Recovery Key**—Click this option to print out the recovery key. Choose your printer in the dialog box that appears, and then click Print.

5. Click Next. The wizard asks how much of your drive you want to encrypt.

6. Select an option:

- **Encrypt Used Disk Space Only**—This option only encrypts the current data on the drive; any new data you add gets encrypted automatically. This is a much faster option, but it might not give you total protection if you've been using your PC for a while.

- **Encrypt Entire Drive**—This options encrypts both the current data on the drive and the drive's empty space. This takes quite a bit longer, but it offers total security because it also encrypts deleted data that remains on the hard drive and could otherwise be read by a snoop with low-level file utilities.

7. Click Next. The wizard lets you know that BitLocker now needs to be activated.

8. Make sure the Run BitLocker System Check setting is activated and then click Continue. BitLocker tells you your system won't be encrypted until you restart.

9. Restart your PC.

10. If you chose to enter a password at startup, you see the BitLocker screen shown in Figure 32.21. Type your BitLocker password and press Enter. If you chose a flash drive startup, make sure the flash drive is inserted.

11. Sign on to Windows 8. BitLocker begins encrypting your hard drive.

Figure 32.21
If you chose to enter a password at startup, use this screen to type the password and then press Enter.

PROTECTING YOUR NETWORK FROM HACKERS AND SNOOPS

It's a Cold, Cruel World

You might be considering connecting your office or home network to the Internet, or you might have done so already. Connecting may be a bit more work than you expect (even with, or due to, our advice), but the achievement will be gratifying. And after you make just a few keystrokes, you'll be able to connect to your home computer from Italy. Millions of potential customers can reach you. You'll be one with the world.

We don't want to spoil your day, but the cruel fact is that, besides you, your customers, friends, mother, and curious, benign strangers, your computer and your LAN will also be exposed to pranksters, hackers, spammers, information bandits, thieves, and a variety of other bottom-feeders and bad guys who, like anyone else, can probe, prod, and test your system. Will your network be up to the task?

By this point in the book, you are aware that network design is foremost a task of planning. It's especially true in this case: *before* you connect to the Internet, you must plan for security, whether you have a single computer or a large local area network (LAN).

Explaining everything that you can and should do would be impossible. In this chapter, we give you an idea of what network security entails. We talk about the types of risks you'll be exposed to and the means people use to minimize this exposure; then we end with some tips and to-do lists. If you want to have

> ### 🔍 note
> You should know this: even if you don't have a network, but have just one computer that is only occasionally connected to the Internet by modem, you're still at risk. The material in this chapter applies to almost everyone!

a network or security consultant take care of implementation for you, that's great. This chapter gives you the background to understand what the consultant is doing. If you want to go it on your own, consider this chapter to be a survey course, with your assignment to continue to research, write, and implement a security plan.

> ⦿ **tip**
>
> This chapter gives you a good background on the ways that the "bad guys" can get into your computer and cause damage. If you don't want to read about this, skip ahead to "Specific Configuration Steps for Windows 8," later in the chapter. If even that's too much, we can give you the short version in one paragraph:
>
> Windows 8 has better security than previous versions of Windows right out of the box. *Don't* turn off User Account Control (UAC), Windows Firewall, or Windows Defender, no matter what anyone else tells you. *Do* back up your hard disk frequently. If you do that, and make no changes to Microsoft's default security settings, you'll be better off than 95% of the people out there.

Who Would Be Interested in My Computer?

Most of us don't give security risks a second thought. After all, who is a data thief going to target: me or the Pentagon? Who'd be interested in my computer? Well, the sad truth is that thousands of people out there would be delighted to find that they could connect to *your* computer. They might be looking for your credit card information, passwords for computers and websites, or a way to get to other computers on your LAN. Even more, they would love to find that they could install software on your computer that they could then use to send spam and probe other people's computers. They might even use your computer to launch attacks against corporate or governmental networks. *Don't doubt that this could happen to you.* Much of the spam you receive is sent from home computers that have been taken over by criminals through the conduit of an unsecured Internet connection. For a decade Microsoft shrugged off any responsibility for preventing this, but starting with Windows XP Service Pack 2, Microsoft started enabling the strictest network security settings by default instead of requiring you to take explicit steps to enable them. There were just too many Windows computers—perhaps millions—with no protection whatsoever. And with the advent of high-speed, always-on Internet connections, the risks were increasing because computers stayed connected and exposed for longer periods of time.

Starting with Windows 7, Microsoft improved things further by having Windows automatically batten the hatches down again anytime it detects that it has been connected to a new network (for example, at a Wi-Fi hotspot or a friend's home). You must explicitly open things up by telling Windows that the new network is safe. This feature is called Network Location, and we discuss it later in the chapter.

In this chapter, we explain a bit about how network attacks and defenses work. We tell you ways to prevent and prepare for recovery from a hacker attack. And most importantly, we show you what to do to make your system secure.

> 🔍 **note**
>
> If your computer is connected to a Windows domain-type network, your network administrators probably have taken care of all this for you. In fact, you might not even be able to make any changes in your computer's network or security settings. If this is the case, even if you're not too interested in this topic and don't read any other part of this chapter, you should read and carry out the steps in the section "Specific Configuration Steps for Windows 8."

If outside attacks weren't enough, in a business environment, security risks can come from *inside* a network environment as well as from outside. Inside, you might be subject to highly sophisticated eavesdropping techniques or even simple theft. I know of a company whose entire customer list and confidential pricing database walked out the door one night with the receptionist, whose significant other worked for the competition. The theft was easy; at the time, any employee could read and print any file on the company's network. Computer security is a real and serious issue. And it only helps to think about it *before* things go wrong.

Types of Attack

Before we talk about how to defend your computer against attack, let's briefly go through the types of attacks you're facing. Hackers can work their way into your computer and network using several methods. Here are some of them:

- **Password cracking**—Given a user account name, so-called "cracking" software can tirelessly try dictionary words, proper names, and random combinations in the hope of guessing a correct password. If your passwords aren't complex (that is, if they're not composed of upper- and lowercase letters, numbers, and punctuation characters), this doesn't take long to accomplish. If you make your computer(s) accessible over the Internet via Remote Desktop or if you run a public FTP, web, or email server, I can *promise* you that you will be the target of this sort of attack.

- **Address spoofing**—If you've seen the caller ID service used on telephones, you know that it can be used to screen calls: you answer the phone only if you recognize the caller. But what if telemarketers could make the device say "Mom's calling"? There's an analogy to this in networking. Hackers can send "spoofed" network commands into a network with a trusted IP address.

- **Impersonation**—By tricking Internet routers and the domain name registry system, hackers can have Internet or network data traffic routed to their own computers instead of the legitimate website server. With a fake website in operation, they can collect credit card numbers and other valuable data. This type of attack is on the rise due to vulnerabilities in the Internet's basic infrastructure.

- **Eavesdropping**—Wiretaps on your telephone or network cable, or monitoring of the radio emissions from your computer and monitor, can let the more sophisticated hackers and spies see what you're seeing and record what you're typing. This sounds like KGB/CIA-type stuff, but wireless networks, which are everywhere these days, are extremely vulnerable to eavesdropping.

- **Exploits**—It's a given that complex software has bugs. Some bugs make programs fail in such a way that part of the program itself gets replaced by data from the user. Exploiting this sort of bug, hackers can run their own programs on your computer. It sounds farfetched and unlikely, but exploits in Microsoft's products alone are reported about once a week. Add-on products such as Adobe Acrobat Viewer, Flash Player, and Oracle's Java have also been responsible for huge numbers of exploits.

  Security researchers try to stay ahead of the hackers by finding exploits and reporting them to the responsible manufacturer before they get used "in the wild," but you'll often see reports of bugs that are detected only after criminals have started to use them. These are called "zero-day" exploits, meaning, zero days elapsed between their detection and their exploitation. You can be sure that even the most up-to-date copy of Windows has exploits just waiting to be used.

- **Back doors**—Some software developers put special features into programs intended for their use only, usually to help in debugging. These back doors sometimes circumvent security features. Hackers discover and trade information on these and are only too happy to use the Internet to see if they work on your computer.

- **Open doors**—All the attack methods described previously involve direct and malicious actions to try to break into your system. But this isn't always necessary: sometimes, a computer can be left open in such a way that it just offers itself to the public. Just as leaving your front door wide open might invite burglary, leaving a computer unsecured by passwords and without proper controls on network access allows hackers to read and write your files by the simplest means. Password Protected Sharing, which we discuss later in the chapter, mitigates this risk somewhat.

- **Viruses and Trojan horses**—The ancient Greeks came up with the idea 3,200 years ago, and the Trojan horse trick is still alive and well today. Shareware programs used to be the favored way to distribute disguised attack software, but today email attachments and websites are the favored method. Most email providers automatically strip out obviously executable email attachments, so the current trend is for viruses to send their payloads in ZIP file attachments. File- and music-sharing programs, Registry cleanup tools, and other "free" software utilities are another great source of unwanted add-ons commonly called *spyware*, *adware*, and *malware*. You may also hear the term *rootkit*, which refers to a virus that burrows so deeply into the operating system that it can prevent you from detecting its presence when you list files or active running programs. Another source of viruses are hacked or malicious websites that use Internet Explorer or media player exploits to install malware just by viewing the site. Sometimes legitimate, high-volume websites get hacked to do this, or links to these sites are sent in spam and phishing email.

- **Phishing and social engineering**—A more subtle approach than brute-force hacking is to simply call or email someone who has useful information and ask for it. One variation on this approach is called *phishing*, where the criminals send email that purports to come from a bank or other service provider, saying there was some sort of account glitch and asking the user to reply with his or her password and Social Security number so the glitch can be fixed. P. T. Barnum said there's a sucker born every minute. Sadly, this works out to 1,440 suckers per day, or more than half a million per year, and it's not too hard to reach a lot of them with one bulk email. For more information about phishing, see Chapter 34, "Protecting Yourself from Fraud and Spam."

- **Denial of service (DoS)**—Every hacker is interested in your credit cards or business secrets. Some are just plain vandals, however, and it's enough for them to know that you can't get your work done. They might erase your hard drive or, more subtly, crash your server or tie up your Internet connection with a torrent of meaningless data. In any case, you're inconvenienced.

- **Identity theft**—Hackers often attempt to steal personal information, such as your name, date of birth, address, credit card, and Social Security number. Armed with this, they can proceed to open credit card and bank accounts, redirect your mail, take you're your email and social networking accounts, obtain services, purchase goods, obtain employment, and so on, all without your knowledge. This is one of the most vicious attacks and can have a profound and lasting effect on victims. Computers can expose you to identity theft in several ways: you might provide personal information to a phishing scheme or to an unscrupulous online seller yourself. Hackers can break into your computer or that of an online seller and steal your information stored there. Criminals can even tap into your home or business network, a wireless network in a public space, or even the wiring at an Internet service provider and capture unencrypted information flowing through the network there.

If all this makes you nervous about connecting to the Internet, we've done our job well. Before you pull the plug, though, read on.

Your Lines of Defense

Making your computer and network completely impervious to all these forms of attack is quite impossible, if for no other reason than that there is always a human element that you cannot control, and there are always bugs and exploits not yet anticipated.

You *can* do a great deal, however, if you plan ahead. Furthermore, as new software introduces new features and risks, and as existing flaws are identified and repaired, you have to keep on top of things to maintain your defenses. The most important part of the process is that you spend some time thinking about security.

The following sections delve into the four main lines of computer defense:

- Preparation

- Active defense

- Testing, logging, and monitoring

- Disaster planning

You can omit any of these measures, of course, if you weigh what you have at risk against what these efforts will cost you, and decide that the benefit isn't worth the effort.

What we're describing sounds like a lot of work, and it can be if you take full-fledged measures in a business environment. Nevertheless, even if you're a home user, we encourage you to consider each of the following steps and to put them into effect with as much diligence as you can muster.

Preparation: Network Security Basics

Preparation involves eliminating unnecessary sources of risk before they can be attacked. You should take the following steps:

- Invest time in planning and policies. If you want to be really diligent about security, for each of the strategies we describe in this chapter, outline how you plan to implement each one.

- Structure your network to restrict unauthorized access. Do you really need to allow users to use their own modems to connect to the Internet? Do you want to permit access from the Internet directly into your network, indirectly via a virtual private network (VPN), Remote Desktop, or not at all? Eliminating points of access reduces risk but also convenience. You have to decide where to strike the balance.

- If you're concerned about unauthorized in-house access to your computers, be sure that every user account is set up with a good password—one with letters and numbers and punctuation. You must also ensure that an effective firewall is in place between your LAN and the Internet. We show you how to use Windows Firewall later in this chapter.

- Install only needed services. The less network software you have installed, the less you'll have to maintain through updates, and the fewer potential openings you'll offer to attackers. For example, don't install SNMP or Internet Information Services (IIS) unless you really need them. Don't install the optional Simple TCP Services network service; it provides no useful function, only archaic services that make great DoS attack targets.

- Use software known to be secure and (relatively) bug-free. Use the Windows Automatic Updates feature. Update your software promptly when fixes become available. Be *very* wary of shareware and freeware, unless you can be sure of its pedigree and safety.

- Install an antivirus program and keep it updated. You can buy a third-party product, get a free third-party product, or use Microsoft's free Windows Security Essentials. Whichever program you select, be sure to keep it up to date.

- Properly configure your computers, file systems, software, and user accounts to maintain appropriate access control. We discuss this in detail later in the chapter.

- Hide from the outside world as much information about your systems as possible. Don't give hackers any assistance by revealing user account or computer names, if you can help it. For example, if you set up your own Internet domain, put as little information into DNS as you can get away with. Don't install SNMP unless you need it, and be sure to block it at your Internet firewall.

 tip

The most important program to keep up to date is Windows itself. We suggest that you keep up to date on Windows 8 bugs and fixes through the Automatic Updates feature *and* through independent watchdogs. Configure Windows to notify you of critical updates. Subscribe to the security bulletin mailing lists at www.microsoft.com/security and www.sans.org. I personally also check my computer with http://browsercheck.qualys.com every few weeks. This web-based tool examines Windows and applications, and lets you know if you're not up to date.

If you use Microsoft IIS to host a website, pay particular attention to announcements regarding Internet Explorer and IIS. Internet Explorer and IIS together account for the lion's share of Windows security problems.

Security is partly a technical issue and partly a matter of organizational policy. No matter how you've configured your computers and network, one user with a modem and a lack of responsibility can open a door into the best-protected network.

You should decide which security-related issues you want to leave to your users' discretion and which you want to mandate as a matter of policy. On a Windows domain network, the operating system enforces some of these points, but if you don't have a domain server, you might need to rely on communication and trust alone. The following are some issues to ponder:

- Do you trust users to create and protect their own shared folders, or should this be done by management only?

- Do you want to let users run a web server, an FTP server, or other network services, each of which provides benefits but also increases risk?

- Are your users allowed to create simple alphabetic passwords without numbers or punctuation? (You can enforce more complex passwords using a Windows security policy setting.)

- Are users allowed to send and receive personal email from the network?

- Are users allowed to install software they obtain themselves?

- Are users allowed to share access to their desktops with Remote Desktop, Remote Assistance, GoToMyPC, LogMeIn, VNC, PCAnywhere, or other remote-control software?

Make public your management and personnel policies regarding network security and appropriate use of computer resources.

If your own users don't respect the integrity of your network, you don't stand a chance against the outside world. A crucial part of any effective security strategy is making up the rules in advance and ensuring that everyone knows them.

Active Defense

Active defense means actively resisting known methods of attack. Active defenses include these:

- Firewalls and gateways to block dangerous or inappropriate Internet traffic as it passes between your network and the Internet at large

- Encryption and authentication to limit access based on some sort of credentials (such as a password)

- Efforts to keep up to date on security and risks, especially with respect to Windows 8

- Antivirus programs to detect and delete malware that makes it through your other defenses.

When your network is in place, your next job is to configure it to restrict access as much as possible. This task involves blocking network traffic that is known to be dangerous and configuring network protocols to use the most secure communications protocols possible.

Firewalls and NAT (Connection-Sharing) Devices

Using a firewall is an effective way to secure your network. From the viewpoint of design and maintenance, it is also the most efficient tool because you can focus your efforts on one critical place—the interface between your internal network and the Internet.

A *firewall* is a program or piece of hardware that intercepts all data that passes between two networks—for example, between your computer or LAN and the Internet. The firewall inspects each incoming and outgoing data packet and permits only certain packets to pass. Generally, a firewall is set up to permit traffic for safe protocols such as those used for email and web browsing. It blocks packets that carry file-sharing or computer administration commands.

Network Address Translation (NAT), the technology behind Internet Connection Sharing and connection-sharing routers, insulates your network from the Internet by funneling all of your LAN's network traffic through one IP address—the Internet analog of a telephone number. Like an office's switchboard operator, NAT lets all your computers place outgoing connections at will, but it intercepts all incoming connection attempts. If an incoming data request was anticipated, it's forwarded to one of your computers, but all other incoming network requests are rejected or ignored. Microsoft's Internet Connection Sharing and hardware Internet Connection Sharing routers all use a NAT scheme.

➡ *To learn more about this topic,* **see** *"NAT and Internet Connection Sharing,"* **p. 418**.

The use of either NAT or a firewall, or both, can protect your network by letting you specify exactly how much of your network's resources you expose to the Internet.

Windows Firewall

One of Windows 8's most important security features is the built-in Windows Firewall software.

Windows Firewall is enabled on every hard-wired, wireless, or dial-up network connection. On those connections that lead directly to the Internet, it blocks virtually all attempts by outside computers to reach your computer, so it prevents computers on the Internet from accessing your shared files, Remote Desktop, Remote Administration, and other "sensitive" functions.

On an Internet-facing connection, Window Firewall by default blocks all attempts by other computers to reach your computer, except in response to communications that you initiate yourself. For example, if you try to view a web page, your computer starts the process by connecting to a web server out on the Internet. Windows Firewall knows that the returning data is in response to your request, so it allows the reply to return to your computer. However, someone "out there" who tries to view your shared files will be rebuffed. Any unsolicited, incoming connection will simply be ignored.

This type of network haughtiness is generally a good thing, except that it would also prevent you from sharing your computer with people who you do want to share with. For example, it would block file and printer sharing, Remote Assistance, and other desirable services. So, Windows Firewall can make *exceptions* that permit incoming connections from other computers on a case-by-case basis. By that, we mean that it can differentiate connections based on the software involved (which is discerned by the connection's *port number*) by the remote computer's *network address*, which lets Windows know whether the request comes from a computer on your own network or from a computer "out there" on the Internet. And in Windows 8 and 7, Windows Firewall uses a third criterion for judging incoming requests: the "public" or "private" label attached to the particular network adapter through which a request comes.

This is a *huge* improvement over Windows XP and Vista, and here's why: when you're at home, the other computers on your network share a common network address scheme (just as most telephone numbers in a neighborhood start with the same area code and prefix digits). Those computers can be trusted to share your files and printers. However, if you take your computer to a hotel or coffee shop, the computers on your local network should *not* be trusted, even though they will share the same network addressing scheme. With Windows Vista and earlier versions, you had to reconfigure

Windows Firewall every time you moved your computer from one network to another, so that you didn't inadvertently expose your shared files to unknown people.

On Windows 8 and 7, this is automatic. When you connect your computer to a network for the first time, Windows asks you whether the network is private or public. As you might guess, a public network is one where you don't trust the other connected computers. This would be an appropriate choice in a coffee shop or hotel, or for a connection from your computer directly to a DSL or cable modem. A private network is one where you trust the other computers that are directly attached. This network might connect to the Internet through a router, but you can still consider it private, because your local trusted computers can be distinguished by sharing a common network address.

> **🔍 note**
>
> Windows Firewall has the advantage that it can permit incoming connections for programs such as Remote Assistance. On the other hand, it's part of the very operating system it's trying to protect, and if either Windows *or* Windows Firewall gets compromised, your computer's a goner.

Windows Firewall is enabled by default when you install Windows. You can also enable or disable it manually by selecting the Change Settings task on the Windows Firewall window. (We tell you how to do this later in the chapter, under "Specific Configuration Steps for Windows 8.") You also can tell Windows Firewall whether you want it to permit incoming requests for specific services. If you have a web server installed in your computer, for example, you need to tell Windows Firewall to permit incoming HTTP data.

If you have an external firewall device—such as a commercial firewall server or a connection-sharing router with filter rules—this device will perform firewall duties for you. But, even with this, there is no good reason to disable Windows Firewall. You're better off using *both*.

Packet Filtering

If you use a hardware Internet Connection Sharing router (also called a *residential gateway*) or a full-fledged network router for your Internet service, you can instruct it to block data that carries services you don't want exposed to the Internet. This is called *packet filtering*. You can set this up in addition to NAT, to provide an additional layer of protection.

Filtering works like this: each Internet data packet contains identifying numbers that indicate the protocol type (such as TCP or UDP) and the IP address for the source and destination computers. Some protocols also have an additional number called a *port*, which identifies the program that is to receive the packet. The WWW service, for example, expects TCP protocol packets addressed to port 80. A domain name server listens for UDP packets on port 53.

A packet that arrives at the firewall from either side is examined; then it is either passed on or discarded, according to a set of rules that lists the protocols and ports permitted or prohibited for each direction. A prohibited packet can be dropped silently, or the router can reject the packet with an error message returned to the sender indicating that the requested network service is unavailable. If possible, specify the silent treatment. (Why tell hackers that a desired service is present, even if it's unavailable to them? In security, silence is golden.) Some routers can also make a log entry or send an alert indicating that an unwanted connection was attempted.

Configuring routers for filtering is beyond the scope of this book, but Table 33.1 lists some relevant protocols and ports. If your router lets you block incoming requests separately from outgoing requests, you should block incoming requests for all the services listed, unless you are *sure* you want to enable access to them. If you have a basic gateway router that doesn't provide separate incoming and outgoing filters, you probably want to filter only those services that are marked with an asterisk (*).

Table 33.1   Services That You Might Want to Block

Protocol	Port(s)	Associated Service
TCP	20–21	FTP—File Transfer Protocol.
TCP	22	SSH—Secure Shell protocol, an encrypted version of Telnet.
TCP*	23	Telnet—Clear-text passwords are sent by this remote terminal service, which also is used to configure routers.
TCP	53	DNS—Domain name service. Block only TCP mode "zone" transfers, which reveal machine names.
TCP+UDP	67	BOOTP—Bootstrap protocol (similar to DHCP). Unnecessary.
TCP+UDP*	69	TFTP—Trivial File Transfer Protocol. No security.
TCP	110	POP3—Post Office Protocol.
TCP+UDP*	137–139	NetBIOS—These ports are used by Microsoft File Sharing.
UDP*	161–2	SNMP—Simple Network Monitoring Protocol. Reveals too much information and can be used to reconfigure the router.
TCP*	445	SMB—Windows File Sharing can use port 445 as well as ports 137–139.
TCP	515	LPD—UNIX printer-sharing protocol supported by Windows.
UDP, TCP	1900, 5000	Universal Plug and Play—Can be used to reconfigure routers.

As stated earlier, if you use a hardware router to connect to the Internet, we can't show you the specifics for your device. We can give you a couple of examples, though. My Linksys cable/DSL–sharing router uses a web browser for configuration, and there's a page for setting up filters, as shown in Figure 33.1. In this figure, I've blocked the ports for Microsoft file-sharing services.

If you use routed DSL Internet service, your ISP might have provided a router manufactured by Flowpoint, Cisco, Netopia, or another manufacturer. These are complex devices, and your ISP will help you set up yours. Insist that your ISP install filters for ports 137, 138, 139, and 445, at the very least.

Figure 33.1
Configuring packet filters in a typical Internet Connection Sharing router.

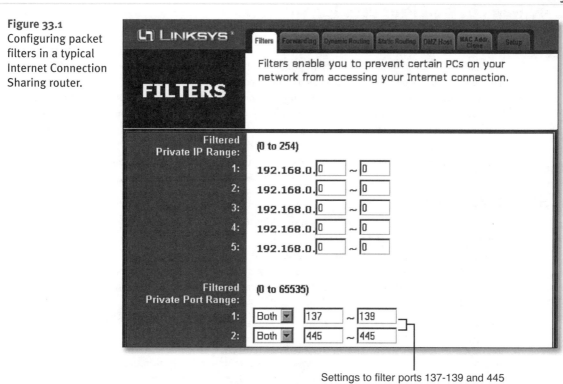

Settings to filter ports 137-139 and 445

Using NAT or Internet Connection Sharing

By either name, Network Address Translation (NAT) has two big security benefits. First, it can be used to hide an entire network behind one IP address. Then, while it transparently passes connections from you out to the Internet, it rejects all incoming connection attempts except those that you explicitly direct to waiting servers inside your LAN. Packet filtering isn't absolutely necessary with NAT, although it can't hurt to add it.

➡ *To learn more about NAT,* ***see*** *"NAT and Internet Connection Sharing," p. 418*.

You learned how to configure Windows Internet Connection Sharing in Chapter 19, "Connecting Your Network to the Internet," so we won't repeat that information here.

If you have built a network with another type of router or connection-sharing device, you must follow the manufacturer's instructions or get help from your ISP to set it up.

> ## ⚡ caution
> Microsoft's Internet Connection Sharing (ICS) blocks incoming access to other computers on the LAN, but unless Windows Firewall is also enabled, it does *not* protect the computer that is sharing the Internet connection. If you use ICS, you *must* enable Windows Firewall on the same connection, or you must use a third-party software firewall application.

Add-on Firewall Products for Windows

Commercial products called *personal firewalls are* designed for use on PCs. These types of products—Norton Internet Security (www.symantec.com), for instance—range in price from free to about $80. Now that Windows includes an integral firewall, and Microsoft offers a free antivirus program, add-on products might no longer be necessary, and I personally don't think that it's worth paying for a software firewall program alone. Windows Firewall is good enough, it's free, and it's built in. It's *far* more important that you keep Windows and all of your add-on applications up to date, and use Windows Security Essentials or a third-party antivirus/antispyware program. On the other hand, some of the third-party firewalls do monitor *outgoing* Internet connections, and this can let them detect a virus that slipped by an antivirus program, due to the virus' activity. That's pretty cool.

Secure Your Router

If you use a router for your Internet connection and rely on it to provide network protection, you *must* make it require a secure password. If your router doesn't require a password, *anyone* can connect to it across the Internet and delete the filters you've set up. (As configured by the manufacturers and ISPs, connection-sharing routers are set up with the same password. Usually it's `password`. On the plus side, they typically won't accept configuration commands from the Internet, but only from your own network.)

To lock down your router, you have to follow procedures for your specific router. You'll want to do the following:

- Change the router's administrative password to a combination of letters, numbers, and punctuation. Be sure to write it down somewhere, and keep it in a secure place. (I usually write the password on a sticky label and attach it to the bottom of the router.)

- If the router supports the SNMP protocol, change the read-only and read-write community names (which are, in effect, passwords) to a secret word or a very long random string of random characters; or better yet, prohibit write access via SNMP or disable SNMP entirely.

- If the router supports the Telnet protocol, change all Telnet login passwords, whether administrative or informational.

If your ISP supplied your router and you change the password yourself, be sure to give the new password to your ISP.

Configure Passwords and File Sharing

Windows 8 supports password-protected and passwordless file sharing. Before we explain this, we need to give you some background. In the original Windows NT workgroup network security model, when you attempted to use a network resource shared by another computer, Windows would see if your username and password matched an account on that remote computer. One of four things would happen:

- If the username and password exactly matched an account defined on the remote computer, you got that user's privileges on the remote machine for reading and writing files.

- If the username matched but the password didn't, you were prompted to enter the correct password.

- If the username didn't match any predefined account, or if you failed to supply the correct password, you got the privileges accorded to the Guest account, *if* the Guest account was enabled.

- If the Guest account was disabled—and it usually was—you were denied access.

The problem with this system is that it required you to create user accounts on each computer you wanted to reach over the network. Multiply, say, five users by five computers, and you had 25 user accounts to configure. What a pain! (People pay big bucks for a Windows Server–based domain network to eliminate this very hassle.) Because it was so much trouble, people usually enabled the Guest account.

Windows 8 and 7 have a feature called the HomeGroup that provides a way around the headaches of managing lots of user accounts and passwords. When you make a Windows 8 or 7 computer a member of a homegroup, it uses a built-in user account named HomeGroupUser$ when it accesses shared resources on other computers in the group. The member computers all have this same account name set up, with the same password (which is derived from the homegroup's password in some way), so that all member computers can use any shared resource. When you share a library, folder, or printer with the homegroup, Windows gives the user account HomeGroupUser$ permission to read or to read/write the files in that folder. It's a simple, convenient scheme, but only Windows 8 and 7 computers can take advantage of it.

Another way to avoid password headaches is to entirely disable the use of passwords for network resources. If you disable Password Protected Sharing, the contents of the Public folder and all other shared folders are accessible to everyone on the network, even if they don't have a user account and password on your computer, and regardless of the operating system they're using. This is ideal if you want to share everything in your Public folder and do not need to set sharing permissions for individuals.

From a security perspective, only a few folders are accessible when Password Protected Sharing is disabled, and although anybody with access to the network can access them, the damage an intruder can do is limited to stealing or modifying just the files in a few folders that are known to be public.

If you do disable Password Protected Sharing, it's *crucial* that you have a firewall in place. Otherwise, everyone on the Internet will have the same rights in your shared folders as you.

> **🔍 note**
>
> When you disable Password Protected Sharing, you get what was called Simple File Sharing on Windows XP, but with a twist: on XP, when Simple File Sharing was in effect, every network accessed shared resources using the Guest account, no matter what username and password they supplied. On Windows 8 and 7, if the remote user's username matches a user account and the account has a password set, they'll be able to access the shared resources using that account's privileges. The Guest account is used only when the remote user's account doesn't match one on the Windows computer, or if the matching account has no password.
>
> If your computer is a member of a Windows domain network, you cannot disable Password Protected Sharing.

By default, Windows 8 has Password Protected Sharing enabled, which limits access to the Public folder and all other shared folders to users with a user account and password on your computer, or to member computers in a homegroup.

If you want to make the Public folder accessible to everyone on your network without having to create for each person an account on every computer, you have four choices:

- If you are on a home or small office network and you have only (or mostly) Windows 8 and 7 computers, you can enable the HomeGroup networking feature, as discussed in Chapter 18, "Creating a Windows Network."

- You can set up accounts for every user on your computer, so that everyone will access the shared folder using their own account. You'll need to be sure that everyone uses the same password on every computer.

- You can create a special user account, for example, named "share," and give people you trust the password to this account. Everyone can use this same username and password to access the shared folder on your computer.

- You can disable Password Protected Sharing. To do this, go to the desktop. Right-click the network icon at the right end of the taskbar and select Open Network and Sharing Center. (Alternatively, open File Explorer, select Network at the left, and click Open Network and Sharing Center in the ribbon.)

  Select Change Advanced Sharing Options. Under All Networks, locate Password Protected Sharing, click Turn Off Password Protected Sharing, and then click Save Changes.

Set Up Restrictive Access Controls

Possibly the most important and difficult step you can take is to limit access to shared files, folders, and printers. You can use the guidelines shown in Table 33.2 to help organize a security review of every machine on your network.

Table 33.2   Restricting Access Controls

Access Point	Controls
File Sharing	Don't share your computers' entire hard drives. Share only folders that need to be shared. Use Password Protected Sharing.
Passwords	Set up *all* accounts to require passwords. You can configure your computers to require long passwords if you want to enforce good internal security. We show you how to do this later in the chapter.
Partitions	If you install IIS and want to make a website or FTP site available to the Internet, set up a separate NTFS partition on your hard drive *just* for website files.
Access Control	Don't disable User Account Control. In fact, even with UAC in place, you can elect not to use a Computer Administrator account for your day-to-day work. Instead, create a Standard user account for yourself, and type in an Administrator password when you're prompted to.

Access Point	Controls
FTP	If you install a public FTP server, do not let FTP share a FAT-formatted drive or partition. In addition, you must prevent anonymous FTP users from writing to your hard drive.
SMTP	Configuring an email system is beyond the scope of this book. But if you operate an email server, consider storing incoming mail in a separate partition, to avoid getting overrun with too much mail. Also, you *must* prohibit "relaying" from outside SMTP servers to outside domains, lest your server be used as a spam relay site.
HTTP (Web)	Don't enable both Script/Execute permission and Write permission on the same folder. Enabling both permissions would permit outside users to install and run arbitrary programs on your computer. You should manually install any needed scripts or CGI programs. (The WebDAV/FrontPage extensions can publish scripts to protected directories, but they perform strong user authentication before doing so.)
SNMP	This network-monitoring option is a useful tool for large networks, but it also poses a security risk. If installed, it could be used to modify your computer's network settings and, at the very least, will happily reveal the names of all the user accounts on your computer. Don't install SNMP unless you need it, and if you do, change the "community name" from public to something confidential and difficult to guess. Block SNMP traffic through your Internet connection with filtering.

Testing, Logging, and Monitoring

Testing, logging, and monitoring involve testing your defense strategies and detecting breaches. It's tedious, but who would you rather have be the first to find out that your system is hackable: you or "them"? Your testing steps should include these:

- Testing your defenses before you connect to the Internet

- Detecting and recording suspicious activity on the network and in application software

You can't second-guess what 100 million potential "visitors" might do to your computer or network, but you should at least be sure that all your roadblocks stop the traffic you were expecting them to stop.

Test Your Defenses

Some companies hire expert hackers to attempt to break into their networks. You can do this, too, or you can try to be your own hacker. Before you connect to the Internet, and periodically thereafter, try to break into your own system. Find its weaknesses.

Go through each of your defenses and each of the security policy changes you made, and try each of the things you thought they should prevent.

> **note**
>
> If you're on a corporate network, contact your network manager before trying this. If your company uses intrusion monitoring, this probe might set off alarms and get you in hot water.

First, connect to the Internet, visit www.grc.com, and view the ShieldsUP page. (Its author, Steve Gibson, is a very bright guy and has lots of interesting things to say, but be forewarned that some of it is a bit hyperbolic.) This website attempts to connect to Microsoft Networking and TCP/IP services on your computer to see whether any are accessible from the outside world. Click the File Sharing and Common Ports buttons to see whether this testing system exposes any vulnerabilities. Don't worry if the only test your computer fails is the ping test. This is a great tool!

As a second test, find out what your public IP address is. An easy way to find out is to open www.whatismyip.com in Internet Explorer. Then, enlist the help of a friend or go to a computer that is *not* on your site but connected to the Internet some other way. At the desktop, Open Windows Explorer (*not* Internet Explorer) and, in the Address box, type *1.2.3.4*, but in place of *1.2.3.4*, type the IP address that you recorded earlier. This attempts to connect to your computer for file sharing. You should not be able to see any shared folders, and you shouldn't even be prompted for a username and/or password. If you have more than one public IP address, test *all* of them.

Shared Folders Are Visible to the Internet

First, be sure Windows Firewall is enabled on all of your network's computers. You should also enable filtering on your Internet connection. At the very least, you must block TCP/UDP ports 137–139 and 445. Don't leave this unfixed.

If you have several computers connected to a cable modem with just a hub and no connection-sharing router, you should read Chapter 19 for alternative ways to share your cable Internet connection.

If you have installed a web or FTP server, attempt to view any protected pages *without* using the correct username or password. With FTP, try using the login name anonymous and the password guest. Try to copy files to the FTP site while connected as anonymous—you shouldn't be able to.

Sensitive Web Pages or FTP Folders Are Visible to the Internet

When you access your self-hosted website from the Internet using a web browser or anonymous FTP and can view folders that you thought were private and protected, be sure that the shared folders are not on a FAT-formatted disk partition. FAT disks don't support user-level file protection. Share only folders from NTFS-formatted disks.

Then, check the folder's NTFS permissions to be sure that anonymous access is not permitted. Locate the folders in File Explorer on the computer running IIS. View the folders' Properties page and view the Security tab. Be sure that none of the following users or groups is granted access to the folder: *Everyone, IUSR_XXXX* (where *XXXX* is your computer name), IUSR, or IIS_IUSRS. On the folders you wish to protect, grant read and write privileges only to authorized users. In the IIS management console, you can also explicitly disable anonymous access to the website's folder or a specific folder.

Use network-testing utilities to attempt to connect to any other of the network services you think you have blocked, such as SNMP.

Network Services Are Not Being Blocked

If you can connect to your computer across the Internet with remote administration tools such as the Registry editor, with SNMP viewers, or with other tools that use network services, network services are not being blocked.

Look up the protocol type (for example, UDP or TCP) and port numbers of the unblocked services, and configure filters in your router to block these services. Your ISP might be able to help you with this problem. You also might have disabled Windows Firewall by mistake.

Attempt to use Telnet to connect to your router, if you have one. If you are prompted for a login, try the factory default login name and password listed in the router's manual. If you've blocked Telnet with a packet filter setting, you should not be prompted for a password. If you are prompted, be sure the factory default password does not work, because you should have changed it.

More advanced port-scanning tools are available to perform many of these tests automatically. We caution you to use these sorts of tools in addition to, not instead of, the other tests listed here.

Monitor Suspicious Activity

If you use Windows Firewall, you can configure it to keep a record of rejected connection attempts. Here's how:

1. Log on using a Computer Administrator account and go to the Start screen. If you don't have a keyboard, open the Search charm.

2. Type the word **firewall**, at the right select Settings, then select Windows Firewall. Select Advanced Settings.

3. Right-click Windows Firewall with Advanced Security in the left pane and select Properties. Select one of the available profile tabs (Private Profile, in most cases) and click the Customize button within the Logging area. Set Log Dropped Packets to Yes.

4. Take note of the location of the log file, and then click OK. By default, the log file is \windows\system32\LogFiles\Firewall\pfirewall.log.

You can enable this setting for all profiles if you wish. Inspect the log file periodically by viewing it with Notepad.

Disaster Planning: Preparation for Recovery After an Attack

Disaster planning should be a key part of your security strategy. The old saying "Hope for the best and prepare for the worst" certainly applies to network security. Murphy's Law predicts that if you don't have a way to recover from a network or security disaster, you'll soon need one. If you're prepared, you can recover quickly and may even be able to learn something useful from the experience. Here are some suggestions to help you prepare for the worst:

- Make permanent, archived "baseline" backups of exposed computers *before* they're connected to the Internet and anytime system software is changed.

- Make frequent backups once online.

- Prepare written, thorough, and *tested* computer restore procedures.

- Write and maintain documentation of your software and network configuration.

- Prepare an incident plan.

A little planning now will go a long way toward helping you through this situation. The key is having a good backup of all critical software. Each of the points discussed in the preceding list is covered in more detail in the following sections.

Make a Baseline Backup Before You Go Online

You should make a permanent "baseline" backup of your computer before you connect with the Internet for the first time so that you know it doesn't have any virus infections. Make this backup onto a removable disk or tape that can be kept separate from your computer, and keep this backup permanently. You can use it as a starting point for recovery if your system is compromised.

➡ To learn more about making backups, **see** "Creating a System Image Backup," **p. 770**.

Make Frequent Backups When You're Online

We hate to sound like a broken record on this point, but you should have a backup plan and stick to it. Make backups at some sensible interval and always after a session of extensive or significant changes (for example, after installing new software or adding users). In a business setting, you might want to have your backup program schedule a backup every day automatically. (You *do* have to remember to change the backup media, even if the backups are automatic.) In a business setting, backup media should be rotated offsite to prevent against loss from theft or fire. You may want to do this even for home backups—take an external hard drive or DVD backup to a friend's house for safekeeping.

Online backup services such as Carbonite and SOS Online Backup are great tools, too. They usually don't back up Windows and applications, but they do frequently back up your personal files.

Write and Test Server Restore Procedures

We can tell you from personal experience that the only feeling more sickening than losing your system is finding out that the backups you've been diligently making are unreadable. Whatever your backup scheme is, be sure it works!

This step is difficult to take, but we urge you to try to completely rebuild a system after an imaginary break-in or disk failure. Use a sacrificial computer, of course, not your main computer, and allow yourself a whole day for this exercise. Go through all the steps: reformat hard disks, reinstall Windows or use the image feature, reinstall backup software (if you use a third-party product), and restore the most recent backups. You will find this a very enlightening experience, well worth the cost in time and effort. Finding the problem with your system *before* you need the backups is much better than finding it afterward.

Also be sure to document the whole restoration process so that you can repeat it later. After a disaster, you'll be under considerable stress, so you might forget a step or make a mistake. Having a clear, written, tested procedure goes a long way toward making the recovery process easier and more likely to succeed.

Write and Maintain Documentation

It's in your own best interest to maintain a log of all software installed on your computers, along with software settings, hardware types and settings, configuration choices, network address information, and so on. (Do you vaguely remember some sort of ordeal when you installed your wireless router last year? How *did* you resolve that problem, anyway?)

In businesses, this information is often part of the "oral tradition," but a written record is an important insurance policy against loss due to memory lapses or personnel changes. Record all installation and configuration details.

Then *print a copy* of this documentation so you'll be able to refer to it if your computer crashes.

Make a library of software DVDs and CD-ROMs, repair disks, startup disks, utility disks, backup disks, tapes, manuals, and notebooks that record your configurations and observations. Keep them together in one place and locked up, if possible.

> **tip**
>
> Windows has no utilities to print the configuration settings for software and network systems. You can use Alt+PrntScrn to record the configurations for each program and network component and then paste the images into WordPad or Microsoft Word.

Prepare an Incident Plan

A system crash, virus infection, or network intrusion is a highly stressful event. A written plan of action made now will help you keep a clear head when things go wrong. The actual event probably won't go as you imagined, but at least you'll have some good first steps to follow while you get your wits about you.

If you know a break-in has been successful, you must take immediate action. First, immediately disconnect your network from the Internet. Then find out what happened.

Unless you have an exact understanding of what happened and can fix the problem, you should clean out your system entirely. This means that you should reformat your hard drive, install Windows and all applications from CDs/DVDs or pristine disks, and make a clean start. Then you can look at recent backups to see whether you have any you know aren't compromised, restore them, and then go on.

But most of all, have a plan. The following are some steps to include in your incident plan:

- Write down exactly how to properly shut down computers and servers.

- Make a list of people to notify, including company officials, your computer support staff, your ISP, an incident response team, your therapist, and anyone else who will be involved in dealing with the aftermath.

- If you had a hacker break-in at your business, check www.first.org to see whether you are eligible for assistance from one of the many FIRST response teams around the world. The FIRST (Forum of Incident Response and Security Teams) Secretariat can tell you which agencies might best be able to help you in the event of a security incident; call 301-975-3359.

  Alternatively, the CERT-CC (Computer Emergency Response Team Coordination Center) might also be able to help you, or at least can get information from your break-in to help protect others. Check www.cert.org. In an emergency, call 412-268-7090.

- You can find a great deal of general information on effective incident response planning at www.cert.org. CERT offers training seminars, libraries, security (bug) advisories, and technical tips as well.

Specific Configuration Steps for Windows 8

Many of the points mentioned in this chapter so far are general, conceptual ideas that should be helpful in planning a security strategy, but perhaps not specific enough to directly implement. The following sections provide some specific instructions to tighten security on your Windows 8 computer or LAN. These instructions are for a single Windows 8 computer or a workgroup without a Windows Server. Windows Server offers more powerful and integrated security tools than are available with Windows alone (and happily for you, it's the domain administrator's job to set everything up).

Windows 8's Security Features

Right out of the box, Windows 8 has better security tools built in than previous versions of Windows. If you do nothing else but let these tools do their job, you'll be better off than most people, and certainly far better off than anyone still running Windows XP. These are the built-in security features:

- **User Account Control**—UAC makes sure that programs don't have the ability to change important Windows settings without you giving your approval. This helps prevent virus programs from taking over your computer and disabling your computer's other security features.

- **Protected Mode Internet Explorer**—Internet Explorer is the primary gateway for bad software to get into your computer. You don't even have to deliberately install the bad stuff or go to shady websites to get it—hackers take over well-known, legitimate websites and modify the sites' pages so that just viewing them pulls virus and Trojan horse software into your computer. This risk is so great that Internet Explorer was modified to run with such low privileges that these bad programs can't do much damage. (They *can* impair your web browsing, though, and if you inadvertently grant malware permission to modify your system via a User Account Control prompt, anything goes).

- **Windows Firewall**—Windows Firewall blocks other computers on the Internet from connecting to your computer.

- **Windows Defender**—Defender is an antispyware program that scans your hard disk and monitors your Internet downloads for certain categories of malicious software. It's preinstalled on Windows 8 in most cases. It's not a full antivirus program, but it does help.

- **Microsoft Security Essentials**—If some time goes by and you don't install a third-party antivirus program, Windows Update will offer to install Microsoft Security Essentials, a free, full-scale antivirus program. You can also download it directly.

These features are all good at their jobs. Together, they're even better. The best bit of security advice we can give you is this: *do not disable any of them.* In particular, don't disable UAC. If you find that any of the security features cause some problems with one of your applications, fix the problem *just for that application* instead of disabling the security feature outright. For example, if you have a program that doesn't work well under UAC, use the Run As Administrator setting on that application's shortcut to let *just that program* bypass UAC.

If you just follow that advice, you'll be in pretty good shape. If you want to ratchet up your defenses another notch or two, read on.

If You Have a Windows 8 Computer Without a LAN

If you have a Windows 8 computer that connects directly to the Internet but doesn't connect to a home or office LAN, it's still part of a network. (A really big one). You need to take only a few steps to be sure you're safe when browsing the Internet:

- Enable Macro Virus Protection in your Microsoft Office applications.

- Be sure that Windows Defender is turned on and up to date—or, better yet, install Microsoft Security Essentials or a third-party antivirus/antispyware program.

- When you connect to the Internet, be sure to stay connected long enough for Windows Update to download needed updates.

> 🔍 **note**
>
> Unfortunately, the Windows Automatic Updates pop-up appears only when you are logged in using a Computer Administrator account. Unless you've configured Windows Automatic Updates to allow all users to install updates, or to automatically install the updates, you need to log on as an administrator at least once every week or two to see if anything new has been downloaded.

- Be very wary of viruses and Trojan horses in email attachments and downloaded software. Install a virus scan program, and discard unsolicited email with attachments without opening it. If you use Outlook or Windows Mail, you can disable the preview pane that automatically displays email. Several viruses have exploited this open-without-asking feature.

- Keep your system up to date with Windows Update, service packs, application software updates, and virus scanner updates. Check for updates every couple weeks, at the very least. View http://browsercheck.qualys.com every few weeks.

- If you use Microsoft Office or other Microsoft applications, go to the Windows Update web page and, next to Get Updates for Other Microsoft Products, click Find Out More. Follow the instructions to install Microsoft Update. This will let Windows automatically download updates and security fixes for Office as well as Windows.

- Make the Security Policy changes suggested later in this chapter under "Tightening Local Security Policy."

- Use strong passwords on each of your accounts, including the Administrator account. For all passwords, use uppercase letters *and* lowercase letters *and* numbers *and* punctuation; don't use your name or other simple words.

> **note**
>
> Local Security Policy settings are not available on the basic Windows 8 versions, only on Windows 8 Pro and Enterprise.

- Be absolutely certain that Windows Firewall is enabled on a network adapter that connects to a Broadband modem and on any dial-up connection icons.

If You Have a LAN

If your computer is connected to others through a LAN, follow the suggestions from the list in the preceding section. Make the Security Policy changes on *each* computer.

In addition, if you use a wireless network, you *must* use encryption to protect your network. Otherwise, thanks to passwordless file sharing, random people passing by could have the same access to your shared files as you do. Use WPA2 encryption if all of your computers and routers support it; otherwise, see whether you can use WPA. Use WEP only if you have devices that don't support WPA.

Keep Up to Date

New bugs in major operating systems and applications software are found every week, and patches and updates are issued almost as frequently. Even Microsoft's own public servers have been taken out by virus software.

Software manufacturers, including Microsoft, have become quite forthcoming with information about security risks, bugs, and the like. It wasn't always the case; they mostly figured that if they kept the problems a secret, fewer bad guys would find out about them, so their customers would be better off (and it saved them the embarrassment of admitting the seriousness of their bugs). Information is shared so quickly among the bad guys now that it has become essential for companies to inform users of security problems as soon as a defensive strategy can be devised.

I personally like to visit http://browsercheck.qualys.com every few weeks. This web page checks your computer for software that is known to have security bugs.

For more detailed information, you can subscribe to the Microsoft Email Updates security bulletin service at www.microsoft.com/security. The following are some other places to check out:

> www.sans.org
> www.cert.org
> www.first.org
> www.cerias.purdue.edu/coast
> www.greatcircle.com
> Usenet newsgroups: comp.security.*, comp.risks

Some of these sites point you toward security-related mailing lists. You should subscribe to Microsoft Security Advisor Bulletins at least. Forewarned is forearmed.

Tightening Local Security Policy

You should set your machine's own (local) security policy whether you have a standalone computer or are on a LAN. The Local Security Policy lets Windows enforce some commonsense security rules, such as requiring a password of a certain minimum length or requiring users to change their passwords after a certain number of days. This tool is available only on Windows 8 Pro and Enterprise, however. The more basic Windows 8 versions have to settle for default security policies.

If your computer is part of a Windows domain-type network, your Local Security Policy settings will almost certainly be superseded by policies set by your domain administrator, but you should set them anyway so that you're protected if your domain administrator doesn't specify a so-called global policy. To configure Local Security Policy, log in as a computer administrator. In the Start screen, press Windows Logo+R, type **secpol.msc**, and press Enter. This opens the Local Security Policy editor, as shown in Figure 33.2. If you don't have a keyboard, or you want to take the long road, follow these steps:

1. Go to the Start screen and open the Search charm.

2. Type the word **policy**, at the right select Settings, and then select Edit Group Policy.

3. When the Local Group Policy Editor window opens, drill down into Local Computer Policy, Computer Configuration, Windows Settings, Security Settings. You'll have these extra layers to dig through to get to the settings shown in Figure 33.2.

To change the settings, select the policy categories from the left pane and double-click one of the policy names listed in the right pane. A Properties dialog box will appear in which you can change the setting.

You don't need to change all the policies; we list the important ones in the following sections.

Account Policies

Account policies can be used to enforce long, difficult, frequently changed passwords and make it hard for users to recycle the same passwords when forced to change. You should lock out accounts that fail several login attempts, locally or over the LAN. In the Local Security Policy window's left pane, open the list under Account Policies and select Password Policy or Account Lockout Policy to see the available settings. Table 33.3 shows the Password Policy changes we suggest you make, and Table 33.4 shows the options at your disposal for locking out an account if someone is attempting to guess passwords.

Table 33.3   Password Policy Settings

Password Policy	Local Setting
Enforce password history	10 passwords remembered
Minimum password length	8 characters
Passwords must meet complexity requirements	Enabled
Store password using reversible encryption	Disabled

Table 33.4   Account Lockout Policy Settings

Account Lockout Policy	Local Setting
Account lockout duration	30 minutes
Account lockout threshold	5 invalid logon attempts
Reset account lockout counter after	30 minutes

Local Policies

You should have Windows make an entry in the Event Log whenever someone oversteps his or her bounds. Table 33.5 shows the recommended audit policy changes.

Table 33.5   Audit Policy Settings

Audit Policy	Local Setting
Audit account logon events	Failure
Audit account management	Failure
Audit directory service access	Failure
Audit logon events	Failure
Audit policy change	Success, Failure
Audit system events	Failure

No changes are necessary in the User Rights Assignment section, but you might want to view these entries to see what sorts of permission restrictions Windows uses.

Finally, go through the security options, as listed in Table 33.6. Security options are used to restrict what users can do with system options.

> **note**
>
> If you're interested in how Windows regulates the operation of your computer, take a look at the settings under User Rights Assignment and Security Options. You'll probably never need to change any of these settings, but these two sections are the heart of Windows' security controls.

Table 33.6   Security Options Settings

Security Option	Local Setting
Interactive logon: Message text	You can display a sort of "Posted: No Trespassing" warning for users attempting to log on with this entry.
Devices: Prevent users from	Disabled by default. If you want to prevent users from installing printer drivers or installing potentially untested printer and hardware drivers, check out the options for these settings.
Audit: Shut down system	A common hacker trick is to fill up audit logs with junk immediately if unable to log messages and then break in. If you want, you can have security audits shut down Windows when the Security Event Log fills. The downside is that it makes your security system a denial-of-service risk.

When you log out and back in, the new restrictive security policies will take effect.

Configuring Windows Firewall

The purpose of Windows Firewall is to examine all incoming network data, looking for attempts to connect to your computer. Windows Firewall maintains a list of networking services for which incoming connections should be permitted, within a given range of network addresses. For example, by default, on a private network, Windows Firewall permits file-sharing connections only from computers on the same "subnet" or LAN as your computer. Attempts by users outside your immediate network to contact your computer are rebuffed. This prevents Internet users from examining your shared files. (Outgoing requests, attempts by your computer to connect to others, are not restricted.)

Windows Firewall also monitors application programs and system services that announce their willingness to receive connections through the network. These are compared against a list of authorized programs. If an unexpected program sets itself up to receive incoming network connections, Windows Firewall displays a pop-up message similar to the one shown in Figure 33.3, giving you the opportunity to either prevent the program from receiving any network traffic (Cancel) or add the program to the authorized list (Allow Access). This gives you a chance to prevent "spyware" and Trojan horses from doing their dirty work. (The installers for some applications such as Windows Messenger instruct Windows Firewall to unblock their data connections at the time they're installed, so you might not always get this prompt with a new networked application.)

> **note**
>
> You might ask, why don't the spyware programs do the same thing? Good question. They will certainly try. However, UAC ensures that unless you give them permission, they won't have the privileges necessary to open up the firewall. Most application setup programs are run with elevated privileges, so they do have the opportunity to configure Windows Firewall as part of the setup process. You will be shown a UAC prompt before such a setup program runs.

If you don't recognize the program listed in a Windows Firewall pop-up, click Cancel. This is a break from the way Windows programs usually work: Cancel here doesn't mean "don't do anything now." In this case it actually does make an entry in the firewall's program list, and the entry is set up to block the program.

Figure 33.3
Windows Firewall displays a pop-up message if a previously unauthorized program asks to receive network connections.

As mentioned previously in this chapter, Windows Firewall has separate settings for each application based on whether your computer is connected to a public or private network. In most cases, it's best to allow a program to receive connections on private networks, but not public. This is certainly the case for file and printer sharing and Windows management functions. The exceptions to this principle would be programs that are meant to work with other Internet users, such as chat and telephony programs.

The remainder of this section discusses the various setup options for Windows Firewall.

> 🔍 **note**
>
> On a corporate network, your network manager might enforce or prevent the use of Windows Firewall, and may restrict your capability to change its settings while your computer is connected to the network.

Enabling and Disabling Windows Firewall

To configure Windows Firewall, go to the Start screen, and if you don't have a keyboard, open the Search charm. Type the word **firewall**, and at the right select Settings. Then, select Windows Firewall. (As a shortcut you can just press Windows Logo+R, type `firewall.cpl`, and press Enter.) The firewall's current settings are listed in the right pane, as shown in Figure 33.4.

It should not ever be necessary to change the firewall's default settings. However, if you do have to make a change, click one of the left pane tasks, which are described in turn in the following sections.

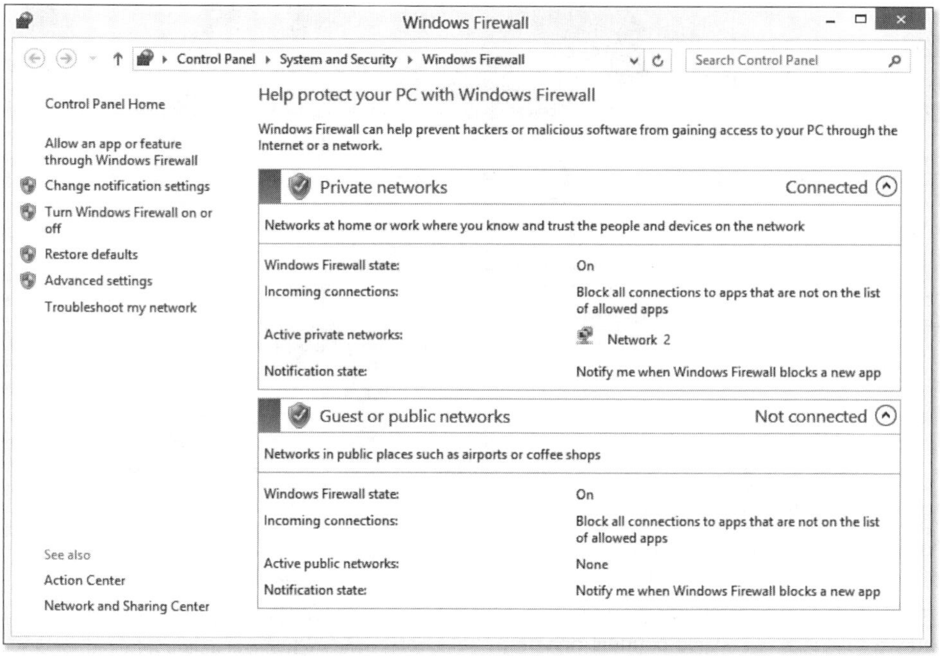

Figure 33.4
Windows
Firewall displays its current settings
in the right
pane. To configure it, click
a task in the
left pane.

Allow an App or Feature Through Windows Firewall

If you use a program that has to receive incoming network connections, its setup program should configure Windows Firewall to permit incoming connections; failing that, the first time you run it you should see a pop-up notification like that shown in Figure 33.3. If you handle that pop-up incorrectly, or want to change the setting, select the Allow an App or Feature Through Windows Firewall task to bring up the dialog box shown in Figure 33.5. Then, click Change Settings.

To entirely prevent a program from connecting through the network and to the Internet, find it in the list and uncheck the box to the *left* of its name.

To enable a program's connections, find it in the list and check the box to the left of its name. Then, check either or both of the boxes to the right, to permit it to receive connections through a private network and/or a public network.

To make a new entry for a specific program, so that it can receive connections, click Allow Another App. Then, click Browse, locate the program file (.exe file), and click OK. Click Add. In the new list entry, review the Private and Public check boxes to make sure that they are set correctly.

To open the firewall for specific network port numbers, rather than whole applications, you'll have to use the Advanced Settings task, which is discussed shortly.

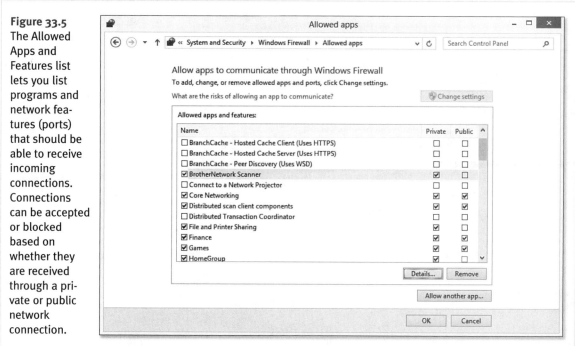

Figure 33.5
The Allowed Apps and Features list lets you list programs and network features (ports) that should be able to receive incoming connections. Connections can be accepted or blocked based on whether they are received through a private or public network connection.

Change Notification Settings, Turn Windows Firewall On or Off

Both of these tasks bring up the same screen, shown in Figure 33.6. From there, you can turn Windows Firewall on or off. You can also check a box that blocks *all* incoming connections regardless of any entries in the Allowed Apps list. (This corresponds to the Block All Incoming Connections and Don't Allow Exceptions check boxes in Windows Vista and XP, respectively.) Finally, you can enable or disable the pop-up that occurs when a new application wants to receive incoming connections. If you disable notification, newly discovered applications will be blocked silently.

In Windows Vista and previous versions, it was necessary to disable all firewall exceptions when you brought your computer to a public location, but on Windows 8 and 7, as mentioned previously, this is not necessary.

Restore Defaults

This task restores Windows Firewall to its default settings, and clears out any additions you've made to the Allowed Apps list. This may cause networking applications such as instant messaging programs and remote control programs like VNC to stop working until you reinstall them, but it will re-secure your computer and restore the functioning of standard services such as file and print sharing.

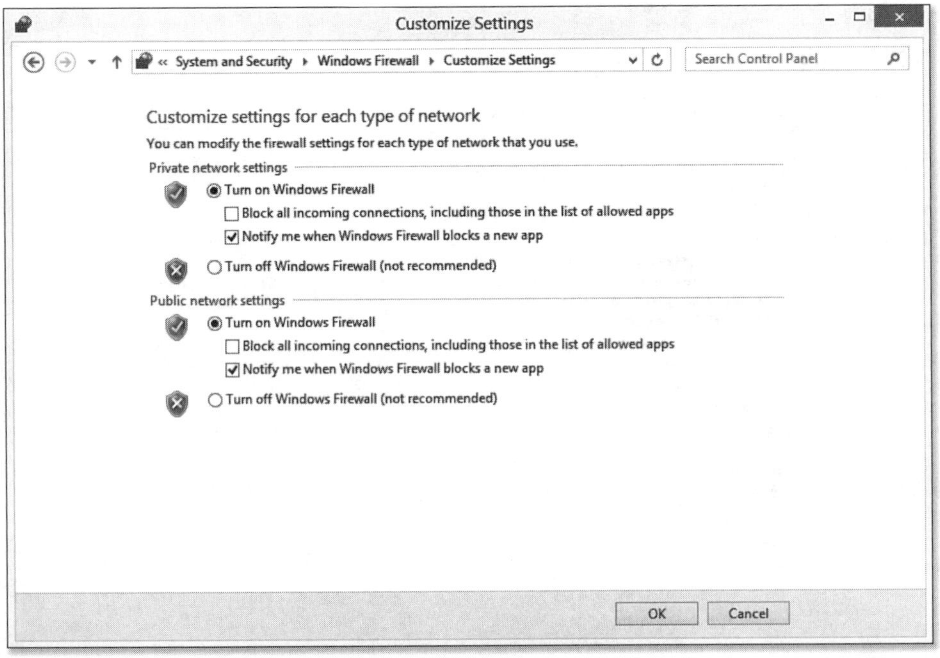
Customize Settings
« System and Security ▸ Windows Firewall ▸ Customize Settings
Search Control Panel
Customize settings for each type of network
You can modify the firewall settings for each type of network that you use.
Private network settings
Turn on Windows Firewall
Block all incoming connections, including those in the list of allowed apps
Notify me when Windows Firewall blocks a new app
Turn off Windows Firewall (not recommended)
Public network settings
Turn on Windows Firewall
Block all incoming connections, including those in the list of allowed apps
Notify me when Windows Firewall blocks a new app
Turn off Windows Firewall (not recommended)
OK
Cancel

Figure 33.6 The Change Notification Settings task lets you turn Windows Firewall on or off and configure its pop-up notification.

Advanced Settings

This task brings up the Windows Firewall with Advanced Security administrative program, shown in Figure 33.7. You will need to use this program if you want to open the firewall for a network service based on its port number, because the basic firewall Allowed Apps list does not let you do this. To open an exception for a TCP or UDP network port, follow these steps:

1. In the left pane, click Inbound Rules.
2. In the Actions list to the right, select New Rule.
3. Select Port and click Next.
4. Select TCP or UDP, and then select Specific Local Ports. Enter the port number or a port number range, and then click Next. (To open an exception for both TCP and UDP, you must enter two separate rules.)
5. Select Allow the Connection and click Next.
6. Select the types of networks from which the connection should be accepted: Domain (corporate), Private, and/or Public. Click Next.
7. Enter a name and description for the network service, and click Next.

Figure 33.7
The Windows
Firewall with
Advanced
Security pro-
gram lets you
open excep-
tions for a
network service
based on a port
number.

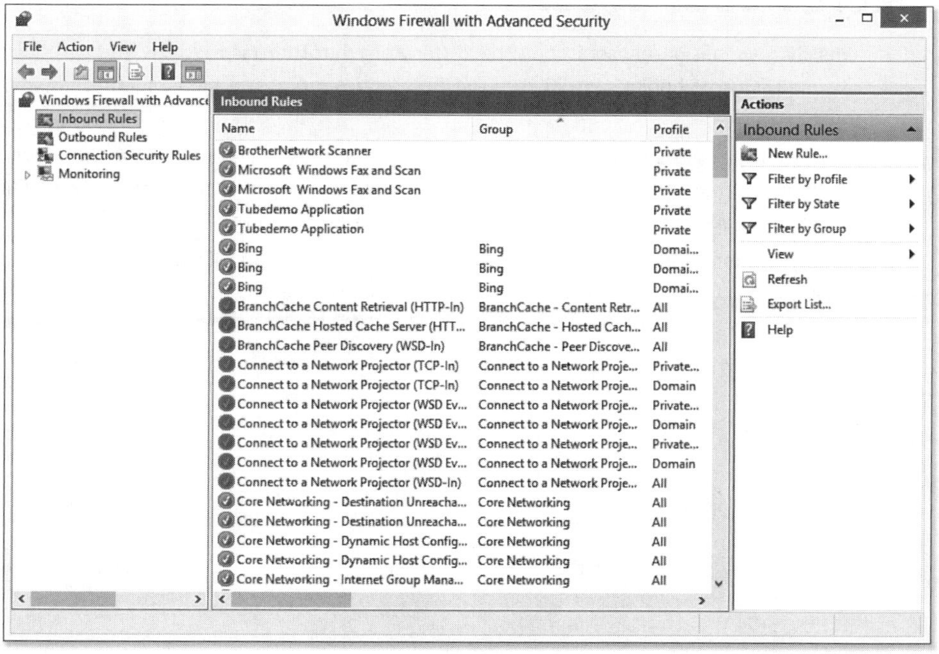

[Figure 33.7: Screenshot of the Windows Firewall with Advanced Security program window showing the Inbound Rules panel with a list of rules including BrotherNetwork Scanner, Microsoft Windows Fax and Scan, Tubedemo Application, Bing, BranchCache rules, Connect to a Network Projector rules, and Core Networking rules, along with the Actions panel on the right.]

tip

Are you curious to know what programs and services on your computer are listening for incoming network connections? Just follow these convoluted steps:

1. Press Windows Logo+X and select Command Prompt. (If you have no keyboard, go to the Start screen, open the search charm, type **cmd**, and then select Command Prompt.)

2. When the Command Prompt window opens, type the command `netstat -ab > x` and press Enter. This might take quite a long time to run. When the prompt reappears, type **notepad x** and press Enter. This will display a list of open ports along with the names of the programs that are using them.

An even better way to view this information is to download and run the program at http://live.sysinternals.com/tcpview.exe.

If you don't recognize a listed program's name, use Google to see if it's discussed on any web pages; this might help you determine whether it's a legitimate Windows program or some sort of malware.

You can also use this tool to open an exception for a protocol other than TCP or UDP, and you can filter based on the remote IP address and port number; we won't describe this other than to suggest that at step 3, select Custom. It can also provide outbound connection filtering, but that is outside the scope of this book and is rarely necessary.

More About Security

This chapter just barely scratched the surface of what there is to know and do about network security. Lots of great books have been published on the topic, and we've mentioned several of them in this chapter.

You also can get lots of information on the Web. First, as we mentioned earlier, www.sans.org and www.cert.org are great places to start looking into the security community. Steve Gibson has plenty to say about security at www.grc.com—it's educational and entertaining.

Finally, you might look into additional measures you can take to protect your computer and your network. You can configure networks in many ways. For example, it's common to keep public web or email servers separate from the rest of your LAN.

In any case, we're glad you're interested enough in security to have read to the end of the chapter.

PROTECTING YOURSELF FROM FRAUD AND SPAM

Phishing for Information

Some years ago, before the Internet was commonly available to home users, America Online was an innovative service accessed by dial-up modems. It was appealing, but not cheap. Some people figured out that obtaining free access was as simple as using a program to generate a fake credit card number and using that to open an AOL account. It took AOL a few weeks to figure out that the credit card number was no good, after which another fake number got the ball rolling again.

AOL eventually put a stop to this, so, naturally, even more reprehensible practices ensued. A program called AOHell emerged. It could send a barrage of instant messages to subscribers, posing as an AOL representative, luring them into providing personal account information. Voila, free credit card numbers. The program's creator referred to this practice as *phishing*, a play on the earlier term *phone phreaking*, in which people tricked the telephone system into connecting free long-distance calls.

AOHell has been retired, but the basic concept is still used by thieves around the world: the use of diffuse targets (a broad swath of victims), social engineering (a plausible story), and technology to gather the information volunteered. This is the essence of phishing.

By all accounts, phishing is prevalent and highly successful. Studies done on human susceptibility to specific, concocted phishing scams have varied greatly in results, with anywhere from 3% to 70% of the message recipients being susceptible. But if even if just one person in a hundred falls prey, with the number of people online today, the number of potential victims is astounding.

Common Types of Fraud

You are certain to run into many categories of online fraud, of which classic "phishing" is just one. We'll list a few of them. Regardless of the con, the criminals are after one of the following things:

- **Your personal and financial information**—You'll give it to them, and they'll use it to go on a spending spree, or will sell it to other criminals.

- **Your money**—You'll send them money, and get nothing in return.

- **Your computer**—You'll follow a link to a bogus website, or even a legitimate website that's been hacked. Your computer will get infected with a virus just by viewing the web page, in what's called a *drive-by attack*. The criminals will record your keystrokes to get your password and banking information, or they'll use your computer to commit any number of online crimes: sending spam, collecting information stolen by phishing, launching denial-of-service attacks, breaking codes and passwords, committing "click fraud".... The list goes on and on.

It's pretty ugly stuff. The following sections detail a few of the techniques criminals use to lure you in.

Classic Phishing

An email arrives seemingly from an organization or business that you're actually affiliated with. The email says something significant has happened. There is endless variety to the messages used, but the goal is always to arouse your curiosity, your concern, or both. Here are some examples:

- Your account was suspended due to suspicious activity. You need to respond immediately to restore your account.

- A sum of money was posted to your account, can you confirm it?

- An expensive online purchase you made is on its way to you.

- Someone tried to change the password on your account. Click the link if it wasn't you. (This is a clever one. It seems like it might be safe to confirm that you *didn't* do anything.)

There are instructions for you to log on to a website to confirm or deny the activity. It's a phony website, decked out to look just like the real one, and you'll be asked to provide personal information to log on. Of course, this scam only works if you actually have an account with the purported sender. They don't know if *you* do or not. But that doesn't matter. They send millions of these emails, so they'll hit plenty of actual customers just due to the numbers.

The Stranded Friend

You get an email, Facebook message, or other online message from a friend who's traveling and has lost his wallet and passport. He is apologetic but desperate, and needs you to wire some money urgently. The message really is coming from your friend's account, which has been taken over by a criminal who bought the username and password online from other criminals who use software to guess passwords.

> ### 🌐 tip
>
> If you don't want your email or social networking account used to try to con your friends, don't use the same password on multiple websites. If hackers break into one poorly protected website and steal the username and password list, they'll use it to break into your accounts on other websites. Most people use the same password everywhere, so this pays off in a big way. They get your password by hacking into some poorly protected, little online business site you visited once (or, from Yahoo! Mail, which inadvertently gave up 400,000 passwords to thieves in 2012, oops), and they use it to get into your Facebook account.

Advance Fee Fraud

You are invited into an exchange in which someone will send you money, and you're to send them less money back. For example, you post something for sale on Craigslist, usually something for which you're asking at least several hundred dollars. Someone wants you to ship the item to them, and it's quite a distance. They offer to pay with a cashier's check or money order made out for the amount of the item plus *plenty* more to cover whatever shipping will cost, and you're supposed to send the leftover money back to them. The money order or cashier's check will turn out to be phony, but you won't find out until after you've sent them the change.

"Nigerian Letter" Scam

There is a large sum of money in an account in a distant foreign country. A very respectable, high-ranking person is looking for help getting it out of that country into yours, and he found *you*. He will split the sum with you in return for your help. If you respond, it will turn out that you will have to wire him money to help cover his expenses in getting the process started. (I got one of these letters by postal mail once, actually from Nigeria. I kept the stamp. It was beautiful.)

Lottery Scams

It's your lucky day: you won the lottery, airplane tickets, a chance to be on a TV show, a magazine subscription, a mail-order bride.... Well, whatever it is, it's free, valuable, rare, and exciting. You'll just have to provide a credit card number to cover shipping and handling.

There really is no end to the inventive means that criminals come up with to part you from your money. Most seem laughably obvious—the bad grammar and spelling, the incorrect information, the implausible scenario.... However, I promise you that one day, one will slip by your internal BS detector. It has happened to me and it will happen to you. You won't even think about it. You'll just click and....

You can just hope that before you type in your banking password, or your credit card number, you'll have a second thought and will want to find out if the thing is real or not. That can take a bit of investigation, as we discuss in the next section.

Live Phish: A Real-World Example

A typical phishing email tends to report that some activity has taken place in your account with a specific organization with which you're affiliated: a password was changed, a deposit or withdrawal was made, money was transferred, a shipment was made, or an important message is waiting. The email requires that you click a web link to attend to the matter immediately, to confirm the activity, or to deny that you initiated it. Now, you'll know right away it's phony if you aren't actually affiliated with the bank or company in question. But if you are affiliated, you might not know whether it's a fraud, at least not right away. You have to look deeper.

Figure 34.1 shows an example of a rather sad attempt I found in my inbox earlier this year.

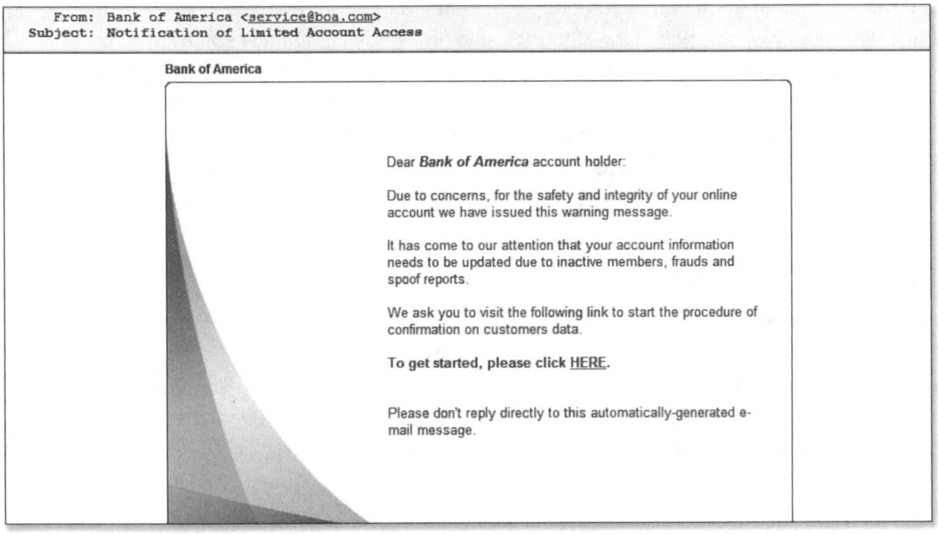

From: Bank of America <service@boa.com>
Subject: Notification of Limited Account Access

Bank of America

Dear *Bank of America* account holder:

Due to concerns, for the safety and integrity of your online account we have issued this warning message.

It has come to our attention that your account information needs to be updated due to inactive members, frauds and spoof reports.

We ask you to visit the following link to start the procedure of confirmation on customers data.

To get started, please click HERE.

Please don't reply directly to this automatically-generated e-mail message.

Figure 34.1
Phishing email from... well, it's not really from Bank of America.

On the surface, it appears my bank is worried about frauds and spoof reports (whatever that means), so they want me to sign on to confirm my password and banking information. I don't think so! This one is a pretty bad job: the language is peculiar and the bank's logo is missing. No legitimate corporation would let an email go out so badly written and with the wrong graphics.

So, this one is pretty clearly a fake, but some phishing letters are actually pretty good. Let's see what other clues there might be to tell us this letter isn't legitimate.

> **caution**
>
> The phishing lure's aim is to trick you first into opening the email and then clicking a web link and divulging your banking password. In other cases, criminals exploit bugs in web browsers, PDF viewers, and media players to create websites that put viruses and spyware onto visitors' computers just by opening the site. These are technically called *drive-bys*, because you get hit just for being to the wrong place, without even typing anything. We talk about these more in Chapter 31, "Protecting Windows from Viruses and Spyware." The take-away message is, it's best never to even click a link in an email if you have even the slightest suspicion about it.

The main clue that this email is not the real deal lies in the web link. The word HERE is innocuous, and in most phishing emails the links look absolutely legitimate. It doesn't matter either way; the displayed text is not the actual "active" address inside the link. It doesn't matter what *any* blue underlined text says, because the text you see is just an arbitrary description of the underlying actual URL. Before you click a link in any email that seems even the least bit suspicious, look to see where any link it contains would take you. Here's how to check:

1. If you're using the Windows 8–style app version of Internet Explorer, press Windows Logo+Z , right-click the bottom of the screen or swipe up from the bottom, then click the wrench (Page Tools) icon, and select View On the Desktop.

2. In the Desktop version of Internet Explorer, hover the mouse over the link, and then look in the status bar in the lower-left part of the browser. A URL should be displayed there. If the URL looks bogus, it *is* bogus. Stop! But, this text can be easily forged. If the URL looks reasonable, don't trust it yet. Instead, proceed to step 3.

3. Right-click the link and select Properties. If the link is too long to fit in two lines, you might not see it entirely, but if you click and drag over the link, it will scroll to display the entire link.

   Alternatively, right-click the link, select Copy Shortcut, and paste the copied text into Notepad or Word.

   If the URL display says something like `onclick();` rather than a recognizable URL, the link's target is determined by script programming inside the email, or web page, and you can't easily or reliably determine where it leads. If you see this, treat the email as very suspicious.

   If the actual URL doesn't look like it leads to the organization you expected, stop! Even if it looks reasonable, you should examine it carefully, as we will explain.

In my sample phishing email, I found that the real link was this:

> http://bofamerica.online.tc/sitekey/

The bofamerica part does seem plausible, but look at the domain name, the part between // and the first /. Start at the *end* of the domain name and work backward. The .tc at the end is a dead give-away. Tc is the country code for the Turks and Caicos Islands. Bank of America isn't based there!

A domain name that is clearly invalid is a dead giveaway that this email is bogus. An all-numeric addresses like http://64.101.32.1012/bankfamerica.com would also have been a sign of an invalid site location. Secure websites *never* use numeric addresses.

Finally, notice that the link starts with *http:* instead of *https:*, so it's not a secure web page. *No* truly secure login page starts with http:.

So this phishing email gave itself away as a fraud; however, some are not so easy to spot. Sometimes the email's language and formatting are perfect, and only by looking at the URL do you see a clue.

tip

The commonly recognized site names that end with suffixes such as .com, .org, and .gov should be immediately preceded by the core organization name and immediately followed by a slash (if anything). For example, good URLs include the following:

http://www.mybanksite.com

https://accounts.mybanksite.com/mainpage.asp

Here are some potential phishing URLs:

http://www.myba.nksite.com/

http://www.mybanksite.com.elsewhere.com/

http://www.mybanksite.com.*xx*/, where *xx* is not your country code

http://202.12.29.20/mybanksite.com/

Don't enter account, password, or personal information into a webpage that uses the http: prefix. If it doesn't start with https:, consider it suspicious. And a legitimate corporate domain name is owned by the corresponding company. See "Whois Database" at the end of this chapter for a way to find out who actually owns a domain name.

Although the astute observer might not fall for the particular phishing email I got, it's highly possible that a bleary-eyed, unsuspecting computer user who has not yet had morning coffee might miss its warning signs. This is where Internet Explorer's SmartScreen Filter comes in. Figure 34.2 shows what is presented when the link is clicked.

Figure 34.2
The Internet Explorer SmartScreen Filter at work.

When IE's SmartScreen Filter is enabled, Internet Explorer sends every URL you click to Microsoft for screening against a list of known fraudulent or virus-infested websites. In the case of this phishing email, Internet Explorer has communicated in no uncertain terms that it is a known dangerous site. It provides the option to continue to the web page, if desired, but it explicitly states that clicking the link to proceed is absolutely not recommended.

To use the SmartScreen Filter, go to the Desktop, open Internet Explorer, click the Safety button on the IE toolbar, and select SmartScreen Filter. (If the Safety button is not present, press and release the Alt key and then click Tools, SmartScreen Filter.)

If the menu selection says Turn Off SmartScreen Filter, it's currently on, and you don't need to do anything. Just press Esc or click outside the IE window. Otherwise, select Turn On SmartScreen Filter.

As stated earlier, when the filter is enabled, every URL you view is sent to Microsoft for checking against a list of known bad sites. This list is built up by feedback from users, information gathered from spam, and presumably is verified by Microsoft staff. When a site is under investigation, Internet Explorer might prompt you to "vote" on your feeling about the site's safety.

> **🔍 note**
>
> Does SmartScreen slow down your web surfing? Not by much, if at all. When you browse to a website, Internet Explorer starts downloading the site's content, and it sends the URL to Microsoft's SmartScreen servers at the same time. The amount of information exchanged is very small, and IE continues to download content while SmartScreen is checking. If the response from SmartScreen is delayed, IE may still decide—based on its analysis of the web page content itself—to go ahead and display the page, so you don't have to worry that if Microsoft's servers go down, you'll be stuck.

Viewing a Site That Was Flagged Incorrectly

If the SmartScreen filter flags a site that you *know* is safe, click the down arrow next to More Information in the warning screen. You can tell Microsoft that you think the site is legitimate by clicking Report That This Site Does Not Contain Threats. You can continue past the warning to view the site by clicking Disregard and Continue.

Flagging a Fraudulent Site

If you find that the SmartScreen filter fails to flag a site that you feel is fraudulent, or if it does flag a site that you know is safe, you can report the error back to Microsoft. This will help other IE users.

Here's how to report an error:

1. If you're using the Windows 8–style version of Internet Explorer, pause for a moment. If you're reporting a site that wants to install malicious software (that is, the site brought up a message from an antivirus program or from Windows Defender), just close the page and stop. Don't proceed.

2. If you want to report phishing, press Windows Logo+Z or swipe up from the bottom, click the wrench (Page Tools) icon, and select View On the Desktop.

3. In the Desktop version of Internet Explorer, click the Safety button on the IE toolbar and select SmartScreen Filter. (If the Safety button is not present, press and release the Alt key, and then click Tools, SmartScreen Filter.)

4. Click Report Unsafe Website. Check the relevant boxes, and enter the "captcha" letters at the bottom of the page, which proves that you are a human being and not software that is trying to scam Microsoft. Click Submit.

Sacrificing Privacy for Security

If you feel that this feature sounds good but also a little bit creepy, I agree with you. On the one hand, it's nice to have this sort of protection available, because a lot of people just don't have the time to sort out where every email link leads. On the other hand, the filter doesn't just monitor links from fraudulent emails; it communicates data about every web page you visit and every web search you perform. Microsoft states that the information is transmitted in encrypted form and that it has "taken steps to help ensure that no personally identifiable information is retained or used for purposes other than improving online safety"—that is, neither your IP address nor the URLs you visit are archived.

However, in the United States at least, the national security environment is such that (a) it's conceivable that your data could still be captured and scanned by, oh, say, a large government agency with a huge secret budget, and (b) it would be illegal for Microsoft to tell you that this was occurring, if they even knew. Personally, I leave SmartScreen Filter turned on. I'm just suggesting that you treat corporate privacy policies as skeptically as you do emails from random banks.

☎ caution

Internet Explorer's SmartScreen Filter tries to make educated guesses about the validity of URLs, but in reality, it's only as good as Microsoft's list of known phishing sites. *Don't rely on it entirely!* Be very skeptical. If you suspect that an email allegedly from one of your financial institutions or organizations is not legitimate, *don't click any links in the email*. Instead, visit the organization's website directly, by typing its URL yourself, or call your bank and ask if the email is legitimate.

More Help from Internet Explorer

In addition to the SmartScreen Filter, Microsoft displays a lock icon when you are viewing a site whose data is encrypted in transit, and whose identity is at least reasonably assured. The lock icon is displayed right next to the URL it describes, as shown in Figure 34.3.

You can view the site's certificate information by clicking the lock icon, and it will show up against a red background if there is anything odd about the site's certificate.

The entire address bar is shaded green if the site's identity is (reasonably) assured with Extended Validation (previously High Assurance SSL) certificates. This indicates that the site has submitted to a rigorous identification process and has paid for the new certificate type.

☎ caution

On the other hand, IE and the Web in general now support something that will make bad URLs harder to spot: internationalized domain names (IDNs). Until recently, you had to worry about only your native alphabet or character set in the URL bar, but now you can get international character sets that could look similar to something in your native language yet be a different site entirely. Would you think it was safe to visit http://www.päypal.com? Use a keen eye to watch for accent marks and oddly shaped characters!

Figure 34.3
The lock icon indicates an encrypted website. Click the lock to display the site's certificate information.

Lock Icon

Protecting Yourself on a Public Computer

If you use a public computer, for example, a computer in a library, an Internet cafe, or even a friend's house for that matter, you should be concerned that the computer might be infected with viruses that may monitor your activity and steal your information. Never use a public computer to conduct banking or work with sensitive information. Think twice even about checking your email or social networking account; your logon name and password might be recorded and collected by criminals before you even sign out.

If you *do* use a public computer to conduct personal business, consider using InPrivate Browsing, discussed in Chapter 15, "Using Internet Explorer 10." Close Internet Explorer when you're done.

If InPrivate Browsing doesn't work with the site you're using and you have to use Internet Explorer in its normal mode, be absolutely *sure* to sign out of any website you logged on to. And when you're finished, clean up Internet Explorer's cache of retained information before you walk away, using these steps. We'll give the instructions for Windows 8. (Previous versions of Windows and other web browsers have similar tools. You'll have to hunt for them.)

- If you're using the Windows 8–style version of Internet Explorer, bring up the charms with Windows Logo+C or by swiping in from the right edge of the screen. Select Settings, Internet Options and then click the Delete button under Delete Browsing History.

- If you're using the Desktop version of IE, click the Safety button on the toolbar and select Delete Browsing History. If the Safety button is not displayed, press and release the Alt key and then click Tools, Delete Browsing History. By default, Temporary Internet Files and Website Files, Cookies and Website Data and History are checked. Check Form Data and Passwords as well, then click Delete.

Two-Way Authentication

Authentication is the process of proving that you are who you claim to be. The frequent use of bogus websites demonstrates the need not only for the users to prove their identity to a site, but also for a site to prove its identity to the users. One way to accomplish this type of two-way authentication is for the user to choose a secret symbol, such as a small picture of a tropical sunset, which is known only between the user and the site. Henceforth, whenever that user visits the site, that tropical sunset picture is displayed alongside the rest of the site information. A malicious site replica will not know which symbol to produce, so even if a user is tricked into visiting one, it will be clear that the site is not authentic. Sounds like an improvement, and it is. Many financial institutions are using this system now, and you may already have seen it in action.

The system works by placing a unique signature on the user's computer. When the customer visits the site and provides a valid account, the site verifies that the computer is the right one. If it is, the picture of the sunset (for example) is displayed along with the password prompt. The customer will recognize the picture, know it's the right site, and type in the password. Nice plan. But what if you are at a computer that you don't usually use? In that case, in addition to your username and password, you have to provide the answer to another security question before the site displays the secret symbol.

Two-Factor Authentication

The most pervasive example of single-factor authentication is having a password to prove that you are who you say you are. Two-factor authentication involves both something you know and something you have. A password or PIN is something you know. Something you have can come in many different forms but is usually either an electronic token of some sort or a biological property, such as your fingerprint or retina, that can be used to identify you. Using two factors to prove who you are is much better than using a password alone: whereas a password can be electronically stolen, obtaining both a password and a unique physical device—or a finger, for that matter—is substantially more difficult.

One challenge with two-factor authentication is that the computer must be capable of validating the "something you have." That usually means extra, specialized hardware. For example, to scan your finger for authentication, the computer must be equipped with a fingerprint reader. To use a special electronic token, you need a piece of equipment that can validate the token. When you consider that some institutions have millions of customers, the cost of extra hardware adds up.

Windows 8 includes built-in support for new and better two-factor security devices such as biometric readers, so hopefully the use of this sort of equipment will increase.

Identity-Management Software

Because no centralized or standard system exists for managing usernames and passwords across different websites, users are forced to improvise solutions for managing their various electronic identities. The most rudimentary solutions to this problem involve using the same or similar usernames and passwords for different sites, using usernames and passwords based on some type of mnemonic system, or even cutting and pasting the information from a Word document.

All these solutions leave much to be desired and become unwieldy as the number of identities increases. Identity is a tricky subject. Just ask any philosopher or information systems architect. The computer industry is still wrestling with this problem. Several solutions are on the table—some that are relatively simple and direct, and others that attempt to address the system as a whole.

A detailed discussion about the identity problem in the information systems world is way too big for this chapter, but satisfying workarounds available today run independently on Windows 8. Password-management programs keep track of all your various usernames and passwords, and store them in a safe, encrypted format. They often have browser-integrated features that, with your permission, automatically fill in your credentials by site. These programs help circumvent keystroke loggers because there are no keystrokes. If you were ever in the habit of clicking the Remember My Password on This Computer check box at any number of websites, that bad habit can be alleviated by using a password manager. Programs such as Roboform, LastPass, and 1Password provide one-click logons and enable you to use diverse and more complex usernames and passwords because you don't have to remember them. It's nice to know that with so many people focused on making life difficult with malware, innovative and pragmatic software developers are making life on the Web easier.

Fighting Spam

Email users of the world are no doubt nostalgic for a time when Spam was just a tasty pork product. Now it is the scourge of email systems throughout the world, as unsolicited email messages from an ever-increasing number of junk-mail senders congest mail systems and take up space on our computers. Spam is such a problem because, on the scale of subversive electronic activities, it is fairly easy to do, fairly difficult to be caught, and very inexpensive for the sender. Despite ridiculously low response rates, spammers continue to dupe shady advertisers into paying for it.

Although the most important cost involved with spam is in human time—time spent reading, deleting, and devising ways to fight it—there's actually a huge environmental cost as well: to filter out the estimated 95 trillion junk emails sent in 2010, computers burned through enough electricity to generate more than 28 million metric tons of CO_2 emissions.

Thankfully, antispam technology continues to get better, and there are several practical things you can do to both make spam less of a nuisance and reduce the risk that it will lead to even more serious problems, such as email-borne viruses or information theft.

> **tip**
>
> To make it more challenging for spam tools to guess an email address, use uncommon combinations instead of common naming conventions. Although it's less intuitive than john_doe@myemail.com, using initials and meaningful (to you) combinations of numbers, such as jhdo213@myemail.com, makes you a more difficult spam target.

To avoid spam, it helps to understand a bit about how you get targeted in the first place. Spammers generally find email addresses by harvesting them from public sources, such as message boards or web pages. They buy them from website operators who aren't above selling email addresses they've collected from visitors, registration pages, or guestbooks. They may distribute virus software that steals email address books from victims' computers. They also use special programs called *spambots* to methodically crawl the Web for email addresses wherever they might be. Then, because they're not above scamming their own customers, they pad their lists with a huge percentage of email addresses they just make up using common names and domain suffixes. Because little cost or penalty is associated with sending spam to the wrong email address, spammers trade and compile enormous email lists, with many incorrect and probably some legitimate addresses as well. If your email address ends up on one of these lists, it will probably stay there, so the best defense is to keep your email address off the list in the first place.

Protect Your Email Address

The best way to avoid getting on spammers' lists is to share your email address only when necessary and only with the trusted few. One of the simplest ways that information is inadvertently shared is bad email etiquette. When a single email is sent to multiple people, it's best to use the Bcc field and keep the names out of the To and Cc lines. The exception to this rule is when you are on a private network, such as a corporate email system, where the email will not generally travel over the Internet unprotected.

Another way to reduce spam is to use multiple email addresses for different purposes. One email address could be a primary address for trusted friends or merchants, and another could be for sites that are less familiar, or for times you need to register with a site for a one-time use. Keeping one address for important communications and another for "junk email" not only is effective at reducing spam, but also can help protect you in other ways. In the phishing example earlier in this chapter, an email arrived from PayPal at my junk email address, yet I knew I had provided PayPal with my trusted email address, so it was a clear red flag. This works even better if you have yet more-specific email addresses for important lines of communication. Free email address services abound. Many of them have good spam-filtering capabilities, so they make good choices for a junk email address.

Better yet, some email systems let you add a suffix to your email address. For example, if my address is brian@myisp.com, I can also use brian+paypal@myisp.com and brian+amazon@myisp.com; in fact, I can use brian+*anything*@myisp.com. If you have such a service, make up a distinct email address every time you register your email address on a website. Then, if one of these appears in a spam list, you can block just that address and never be bothered by it again. (And send a nastygram to the website owner while you're at it.)

> **note**
>
> Here's an unsolicited plug: in my experience, the spam filtering provided by Google's Gmail and the related Google Apps mail service for organizations is absolutely amazing, filtering out about 99.98% of the 1,000 or so spams targeted at my email address each day. About 900 of these are refused outright—that is, the Gmail email server recognizes that the email sender is a virus or known spam program, and won't even allow it into their system. Of the remainder, all but about one per day are automatically categorized as spam and filed accordingly.
>
> In the past year, only about 30 of my legitimate emails were incorrectly categorized as spam, and only one was a "personal" email; the rest were legal, bulk mailings from companies that I've done business with. That's an incredible success rate and it's far better than any of the other online email services I use.

Use Spam Filtering

Despite good faith and antispam tactics, an email address *will* eventually receive some spam. Spammers might be innovative, but equally innovative people are at work preventing spam from taking valuable time away from your life. Spam filters analyze email and relegate spam to a "junk mail" folder or the like. They use various methods, including some similar to other antimalware programs, to detect and get rid of spam before it hits your inbox. All online email service providers, such as Yahoo! Mail, Gmail, Hotmail, and so on, provide free spam filtering as a matter of their own survival as much as for good customer service. Filtering spam at the server level is actually more effective than filtering it in your own computer, because servers will typically receive the same spam email for thousands of customers at once, giving it a higher profile.

Windows Live Mail, the free download discussed in Chapter 16, "Windows 8 Internet Communications," has a built-in junk mail filter and some powerful tools for dealing with spam. Microsoft Outlook, which is part of the Office productivity suite, includes spam filtering. Most third-party email programs offer spam filtering as well.

You may also install an aftermarket spam filter as an add-on. It will insert itself between your email program and the Internet. There are even some plug-in hardware devices that protect from spam at the network level.

Avoid Spammers' Tricks

Spammers have hundreds or maybe thousands of tricks up their grimy sleeves to bypass filters. Still, there are plenty of simple things to do to limit exposure and reduce junk email in its various forms.

Some spammers appear repentantly courteous. That is, they have violated your inbox by being there uninvited, but now that they have your attention, please don't be offended, because you can simply click this link to opt out of receiving any more spam from them. Honest.

Do not reply to spam that claims to provide an "opt out" link. By clicking the link in an attempt to stop receiving spam, you are confirming that your email address is good. You are just increasing your value as a spam target, and your spam level likely will increase. In fact, it's a good idea to never respond to spam, especially to buy anything. Although it is possible some well-intentioned but ill-advised vendors are using spam to sell legitimate products, all purveyors of spam are suspect simply because of the insidious nature of the communication: unsolicited, unauthorized, unwelcome, and often illegal. Avoid spam like the plague it is. If you suspect an email message is spam, you're probably right. Don't opt out. Don't even open it; just delete it.

Read the terms of use and privacy policies when you register with a website, to make sure they will not sell or share your information. Often at the end of the form are preselected check boxes indicating that you'd love to receive email from them, their sponsors, their affiliates, and so on. Clicking those boxes is considered opting in and permits them to legally bombard you with spam. Many spammers disregard the law anyway, but it's never a good idea to give them carte blanche with your inbox.

The right way for an upstanding website to manage an email list is called *confirmed opt-in*, and you've probably used it before. Good citizens of the Internet will not start sending email to you until they have confirmed, by receiving email from your email address, that you actually want it. Without such confirmation, anyone could type your email address into a hundred different Send Me

Mail forms, some of which are perhaps distasteful, and every day you'd have an inbox full of junk. This is such an important premise that, in general, if it's not a confirmed opt-in, it might as well be spam.

Junk email can come from the most unlikely sources. Well-intentioned relatives bent on protecting their loved ones from syringes on movie seats, international kidney thieves, or cancer-causing agents in shampoo are responsible for a type of spam that's hard to avoid because, although it might be tempting, you don't want to filter *everything* that comes from them. And if you feel the urge to forward a tantalizing or tender tidbit, before asking others to spend time reading the message, take a moment to search and make sure it's true.

> 🔍 **note**
>
> Several Internet sites have evolved to fight electronic chain letters, spam, and especially urban legends that compel so many people to send massive amounts of ultimately groundless email. Snopes.com has emerged as an excellent source to determine whether an email is fact or fiction. Use it often. Your friends and relatives will thank you.

Take Action Against Email Abuse

So far, this chapter has taken the Aikido route to spam and fraud defense: avoidance and being "like water." Among our many techniques, we sidestep dangerous links, make email addresses slippery to spambots, and use identity management software to leave would-be keyloggers with nothing. These are useful defensive techniques, but sometimes an offensive approach to vanquishing online foes is more effective and satisfying. Some spammers can be identified and extinguished. Once discovered, phishing sites can be quickly put out of business.

Many commercial Internet sites provide readily available tools to report suspicious activity. For example, eBay and PayPal request that you forward suspected fake emails to spoof@ebay.com or spoof@paypal.com, respectively. They will quickly take appropriate action. Responsible sites display security or fraud-related links on the front page, so it's easy to find their preferred mode of communication. If you suspect a phishing scam, take a moment to find the right email address and report it. You may save someone else a lot of heartache, and will validate your own "sleuthiness." If you stumble upon a suspected phishing site with Internet Explorer, report the site using the SmartScreen Filter tool discussed under "Flagging a Fraudulent Site," earlier in this chapter.

Reporting spam can be easy, too. Free email services used with a web browser often provide a "report spam" button that can automatically notify the provider to take action. This removes the message from your inbox and can help eliminate thousands of other copies in other peoples' inboxes.

If you prefer to use a separate email program, such as Windows Mail, there are a plethora of add-ons that can help report and eliminate most spam. Some of the most interesting and effective ones use collaborative networks. Like the free email services that have potentially millions of users, these add-ons are based on the premise that humans can filter spam better than any algorithm alone. When a number of users identify a particular message as spam, the other members of the network can be spared the trouble. It's a successful strategy used by companies such as Cloudmark, and there are other successful strategies as the field continues to evolve to provide convenient, active ways to fight spam.

On the other hand, there are not-quite-so-convenient yet more active ways for those who desire to "get medieval" on spammers. With a little practice, it's not difficult to track down email headers using publicly available Internet resources. You can often identify the service provider whose network was used to send spam, and they can opt to shut down the spammer's Internet access if enough complaints are received. Additionally, the Federal Trade Commission encourages you to forward spam to spam@uce.gov. The FTC may not respond to individual complaints, but they will go after the worst spammers. Every so often you hear of an arrest, followed by a distinct downturn in the daily worldwide volume of spam.

Whois Database

Anyone registering an Internet domain name is required to file contact information with a domain registry. This is public information, and you can use it to find out whether a domain is owned by the company it purports to be, and how to contact the owners of a domain whose customers have sent spam mail or with whom you have other concerns.

Finding the registrar for a given domain name can be cumbersome. You can find the registrar information for any .aero, .arpa, .biz, .com, .coop, .edu, .info, .int, .museum, .net, or .org domain via the following web page: www.internic.net/whois.html.

The search results from this page indicate the URL of the whois lookup page for the associated domain registrar. Enter the domain name again on that page, and you should see the contact information.

It's a bit harder to find the registrar associated with two-letter country code domains ending in, for example, .au, .de, .it, and so on. The InterNIC site recommends searching through www.uwhois.com.

You can find the owner of an IP address (for example, the address from which an email arrived) through a similar lookup at www.arin.net/whois. Enter an IP address to find the owner of the block of IP addresses from which the specific address was allocated. This is usually an ISP or, in some cases, an organization that has had IP addresses assigned to it directly. You might have to visit www.apnic.net or another registry.

WINDOWS 8 ON MOBILE DEVICES

Windows 8 on Tablets and Mobile Devices

Apple's iPad was not the first tablet-format computer. Between the tablet's debut on TV in *Star Trek* in 1966 and the release of the iPad in 2010, there were many attempts to produce a usable computer in the tablet format, with the power of a PC in a digital version of the venerable yellow steno pad.

There were small versions, notably the pioneering Apple Newton and the incredibly successful Palm Pilot, followed by a host of similar devices called Personal Digital Assistants (PDAs). This name captured the essence of these devices: they were personal, they were digital, and they did assist you. But they weren't close in power to a personal computer. They never really grew up.

There were also many attempts to make PCs "grow down," with early tablet or "slate" formats appearing in the late 1980s, and convertibles, which are laptops whose display cover can hinge back or turn around, so that it lays flat but open on the case. This got us something close to today's tablet. However, several things conspired to keep them either slow or thick and heavy, but in any case rare. Every few years starting in the 1980s someone gave a keynote speech at the huge Comdex consumer electronics show, saying that tablet computers with pen input devices would soon be taking off, but they never did.

Most of the limitations were technological: with the available microprocessor CPUs, you could have either fast or low power, but not both. With the available battery technologies, it look *pounds* of batteries to power a fast CPU long enough to get any reasonable amount of work done. Early liquid crystal display screens were thick, usually monochrome, and expensive. (My first color LCD monitor was 15" diagonal and cost nearly $1000!)

Over time, the technologies improved dramatically. Screamingly fast low-power CPUs emerged. Lithium Polymer technology gave us batteries the size of a matchbook that deliver power like little nuclear reactors. LCD display costs fell so much that CRT monitors aren't even manufactured anymore. And advances in touch screen technology has made the finger a viable and fairly precise input device; odd little styli, which are easily lost, are no longer necessary.

The final missing ingredient was imagination, and that was something that Steve Jobs and the team at Apple had in breathtaking abundance. What they brought to the tablet was an insistence on perfection, simplicity, performance, and perfect smoothness both literally and figuratively. Many companies could have produced the iPad before Apple did, but nobody did, because nobody but Steve Jobs believed that something could be that good. (And it turns out that people really do want things that are that good. In the fourth quarter of 2011, Apple's revenues from iPhones and iPads exceeded Microsoft's revenues from *everything* they do and sell.)

With the secret out, tablets are now everywhere. The software on them has been, until Windows 8, essentially smartphone software: Apple's iOS and Google's Android. It's a perfect fit, because these tiny operating systems grew up in a very power-, CPU-, and memory-constrained environment, and got good while still sticking to a very lean diet.

Two years after the debut of the iPad, an operating system as complex as Windows 8 can now run in a tablet environment. For this to happen, Windows had to learn how to run lean, and processors and batteries and Flash memory had to advance enough to meet Windows in the middle.

Windows RT Versus Windows 8

At the time this was written, Microsoft has developed two tablet computers of its own, called Microsoft Surface. The Pro version has an Intel processor that executes the same instruction set that's used on desktop PCs. It runs Windows 8 Pro in its entirety.

The entry-level tablet uses an ARM microprocessor embedded in an NVIDIA system-on-a-chip combination CPU/graphics processor. ARM processors are notable for low power consumption but a high performance/power ratio. The ARM-based tablet runs some core components of Windows 8—but not the whole enchilada—recompiled for the ARM instruction set. This version of the operating system is named Windows RT to distinguish it from Windows 8. Windows RT can run Windows 8–style apps written in HTML and JavaScript, apps written in programming languages compiled to Microsoft's IL (Intermediate Language) instruction set and using the .NET application programming interface (API), and apps written in languages compiled directly to ARM instructions and using the Windows Runtime (WinRT) API.

Officially, Microsoft says that Windows RT does not include support for the Win32 API that underlies traditional desktop Windows applications. However, Windows RT comes with Microsoft Office desktop applications preinstalled, and the Office programs are Win32 applications. Therefore, Microsoft has indeed recompiled for ARM at least as much of the Win32 API code as Office applications need (but probably no more), and what they meant to say is that they won't let anyone *else* run Win32 applications on Windows RT. This has ruffled some developers' feathers, but it makes perfect sense. If Microsoft officially supported software vendors in creating Win32-on-ARM applications, it would undermine Microsoft's contention that Windows 8–style apps are the way to go, they'd have to spend an *enormous* amount of money on full-fledged development and support, it still wouldn't add much value to Windows RT, and they'd make nothing in return. Win32-on-ARM was simply an expedient way to save the huge expense of re-creating Word and Excel in a new programming environment.

By the time you're reading this, there are sure to be a plethora of other Windows RT and Windows 8 tablets to choose from.

For the most part, Windows 8 and RT tablets can be used and managed like any Windows 8 desktop computer. Internet connectivity and power management are discussed in Chapter 14, "Getting Connected," and Chapter 37, "Computing on the Road," respectively. In this chapter, we focus on tablet input techniques. And although this book doesn't explicitly cover Windows RT, much of the discussion of input techniques applies to Windows RT as well as Windows 8.

Tablet Input Methods

Although the Microsoft Surface tablets include a keyboard built into the cover, not all tablets include a keyboard, and you'll find that you can actually do reasonably well without one. In the following sections, we discuss how to enter text and graphics using alternative input methods. Even with a keyboard there will be times when you may want to use some of the following five methods:

- Use the Windows 8 Touch Keyboard

- Use the On Screen Keyboard

- Use your fingers on a multitouch screen

- Use a stylus or pen to draw

- Use your fingers or a pen with handwriting recognition

Each technique receives some special assists from Windows, as you'll see.

Touch Keyboard

Windows 8 has a nifty on screen keyboard called the Touch Keyboard. It was designed *specifically* for use with your fingers on a tablet or other mobile device's touch screen. Whenever text input is possible (that is, when the vertical bar cursor is displayed in a window or in an entry field that can accept text), you can use the Touch Keyboard.

You can also use a mouse or stylus with the Touch Keyboard. Several physical layouts are available for the Touch Keyboard. You can change layouts by touching or clicking the keyboard icon at the bottom right of the Touch Keyboard, as shown in Figure 35.1. The layout options are as follows:

> **note**
>
> If the Touch Keyboard doesn't appear when the cursor is in an input field, open the Settings charm, select Keyboard, and then select Touch Keyboard and Handwriting Panel.

- **Default Layout**—This layout has large, widely spaced keys. It's nice on a tablet-sized screen. There is a numeric keypad with the numbers arranged as on a telephone (1 at top). Microsoft did extensive research and testing to come up with this layout and they're justifiably proud of it.

- **Split Layout**—This keyboard shifts the left- and right-hand keys to the edges of the screen. It's appropriate for thumb typing on a phone-sized screen.

- **Handwriting Input**—This isn't a keyboard as such; instead, it lets you enter and edit text using a stylus or pen (or mouse or finger, in a pinch). Handwriting input is discussed under "Using Handwriting Recognition," later in this chapter.

- **Standard Layout**—This layout uses the familiar standard IBM PC keyboard layout. It's the only Touch Keyboard layout that lets you enter the Windows Logo key. You can use this, for example, to type Windows Logo+X to bring up a helpful menu of Windows management tools.

Figure 35.1
The keyboard icon on the Touch Keyboard lets you select a keyboard layout or the Handwriting Input panel.

The Standard layout isn't available by default. To enable it, open the Settings charm and then select Change PC Settings, General. Scroll down to the end of the Touch Keyboard section and slide Make the Standard Keyboard Layout Available to the right.

The On Screen Keyboard

Besides the Touch Keyboard that's new in Windows 8, you can also use the On Screen Keyboard (OSK) that has been brought forward through several previous Windows versions. It's one of the Accessibility Tools discussed in Chapter 8.

You can't have both the Touch Keyboard and the OSK on the screen at the same time. Opening one closes the other. However, you can use either one with both desktop and Windows 8–style apps.

Multitouch Input and Gestures

A touch interface is adequate for text entry, but where it really shines is in interacting with software: Selecting and moving things around, turning and resizing them, and so on. Windows 8 recognizes a number of specific fingertip movements and you need to know them to get the most out of any Windows 8 computer that has touch input, whether it's a tablet or a desktop computer with a touch screen. The visual response to your physical gestures is quite pleasing somehow, and this is one of the reasons that people are so enthusiastic about tablet computers.

> *We give you a quick run-through of the most important touch gestures in "The Touch Tour,"* ***p. 62,*** *and we also cover touch input and gestures under "Navigating the Start Screen with a Touch Interface,"* ***p. 102.***

Pen and Stylus Input

Pens or styli were included with most early "slate"-type portable computers, and stylus input devices are commonly available today as add-on products such as the Wacom "Bamboo" series of pen devices. Artists, designers, and kids find them useful and fun.

Windows 8 has special entry modes for pens and styli. These have evolved as part of Microsoft's long-term interest in "pen computing," which was demonstrated by their first pen-input software release in 1991 and continues to this day. (Remember earlier in the chapter when we referred to those recurrent "The Tablet Is Coming" keynote speeches at Comdex? Bill Gates was giving them as far back as 1994.) Windows interacts with pens in two ways: through Pen Flicks, where Windows 8 recognizes some specific pen gestures, and handwriting recognition, where handwritten letters are turned into typewritten characters. We discuss these in the following sections. Pen Flicks will only be available if your computer has an input device that Windows recognizes as a pen or stylus device.

You also might want to check out the note-taking tool called Windows Journal. It's a great of example how useful pen technology can be. It's covered in Chapter 8, "Accessories and Accessibility," in the section titled "Windows Journal."

> **⚠ caution**
>
> You can use a pen or stylus with most touch-screen devices, although you must take care to use one designed specifically for your screen. The wrong kind of tip may either not work at all, or may scratch or damage the screen's transparent electronic layers.

Configuring Touch and Pen Input

Several settings affect touch and pen input. We describe them briefly here:

- **To tell Windows whether you're left or right handed**—Go to the Start screen or open the Search charm, type **tablet**, and under Settings select Tablet PC Settings. Select the Other tab and set your handedness preference. This tells Windows to display balloon notifications where you can see them, not underneath your pen or hand.

- **If your pen or finger can't move the cursor to the full extremes of your screen**—Go to the Start screen or open the Search charm, type **tablet**, and under Settings select Tablet PC Settings. Select the Display tab and click or touch Calibrate.

- **To set the direction that your screen rotates**—If your device has a button that changes the screen orientation, view the Display tab as described in the previous item and select Go To Orientation

- **To change what your tablet's buttons do**—Go to the Start screen or open the Search charm, type **tablet**, and under Settings select Set Tablet Buttons to Perform Certain Tasks.

- **To select the pen gestures that equate to single-, double-, and right-clicks**—Go to the Start screen or open the Search charm, type **tablet**, and under Settings select Pen and Touch. Change entries in the Pen Actions section.

We discuss other settings such as Pen Flicks in subsequent sections of this chapter.

Pen Flicks

If your computer has a touch-sensitive screen or pad that identifies itself to Windows as a pen input device, Windows should enable the recognition of a set of gestures called *Pen Flicks* that can control Windows and edit your input. Some tablet computers include a stylus, and their screens are identified by the manufacturer as pen devices. You can also purchase external pen and stylus input devices, such as the Wacom Bamboo. These should come with Windows 8–compatible drivers that are recognized as pen devices.

> **note**
>
> If your pen can't move the cursor to the full extremes of your screen, your input device needs to be recalibrated. We discuss how to calibrate a pen later in this chapter.

To enable and configure Pen Flicks, go to the Start screen or the Search charm and type **flick**. Under Settings, select Set Flicks to Perform Certain Tasks. There you can entirely enable or disable Pen Flicks, and you can elect to have the pen perform navigation only or both navigation and editing. Figure 35.2(a) shows Flicks set to perform both functions.

To perform a Flick, press the pen to your screen or input tablet and quickly snap it a short distance up, down, left, or right, with the pen rising off the surface at the end of the gesture. Flick as if you were trying to brush away a spot of dirt on the screen. If you've enabled Navigational and Editing Flicks, you can flick diagonally as well, giving you eight possible flick gestures. In the Pen and Touch dialog, you can select Practice Using Flicks to bring up a tutorial window that teaches you how to reliably perform a Flick gesture.

In the Pen and Touch dialog, you can also click Customize to change the interpretation of the four or eight Flicks. The Customize Flicks dialog is shown in Figure 35.2(b).

The default functions are as follows:

Direction	Action
Up	Drag (slide) the active window up
Down	Drag (slide) the active window down
Left	Scroll the active window down (forward)
Right	Scroll the active window up (back)
Up Left	Delete the last character or the selected text or object
Down Left	Undo
Up Right	Copy
Down Right	Paste

(a) Pen and Touch Dialog Box   (b) Customize Flicks Dialog Box

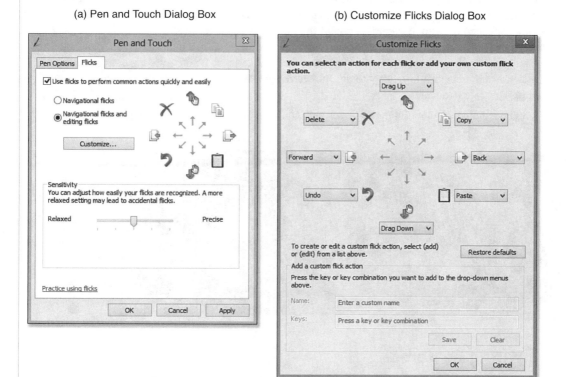

Figure 35.2
You can have the pen perform navigation or both navigation and editing using the Pen and Touch dialog (left).
You can also customize what the Flicks do (right).

You can change the meaning of these Flicks to any of the 20 predefined actions, such as Cut, Open, or Save, or you can map a flick to a keystroke, such as Alt+M or Ctrl+Ins.

The manufacturer of your stylus screen or pen device may have added additional functions not described here. Check its documentation, or you can open the Control Panel, select View By: Small Icons, and look for a nonstandard control panel item added by the device's manufacturer. For example, the Wacom device mentioned earlier adds a control panel applet named Bamboo Preferences.

Using Handwriting Recognition

If you have a tablet computer that includes a stylus input device, or if you have an add-on writing or drawing tablet or pen, you may want to use these devices to handwrite text input rather than typing or using the Touch Keyboard. (You can also write with the mouse or your finger, although it's not quite as convenient as with a pen.)

To write, open the Touch Keyboard, touch or click the keyboard icon, and select the Handwriting Input icon shown previously in Figure 35.1. The Handwriting Input panel appears as shown in Figure 35.3. Simply write in the upper half of the input box using either separate (block) letters or cursive, which, amazingly, Windows does a very good job of recognizing. It does this by looking up likely words in an internal dictionary of your local language, so if you write a word that isn't in the dictionary, it is much less likely to get the word right. You can train it to recognize new words, though, as described shortly.

If you have more text than fits in the upper half, continue in the lower half of the panel.

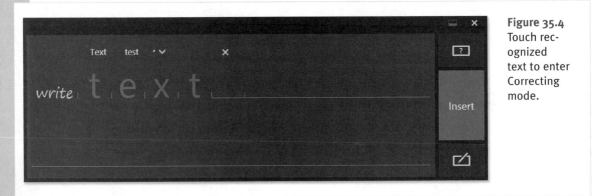

Figure 35.3
The Handwriting Input panel lets you write text by hand, and easily edit it if necessary.

Handwriting Gestures

You can edit recognized text displayed in the Handwriting Input panel using simple pen gestures:

- **Correcting**—To change entered text, tap the pen (or mouse or your finger) on the converted text. The letters slide apart, as shown in Figure 35.4. You can replace the selected word by choosing an alternative spelling from the word displayed above the letters. The v-shaped symbol lets you add an unrecognized word to the dictionary. The x-shaped × symbol ends correction mode. You can also remove and add letters using the deleting, splitting, and joining gestures.

Figure 35.4
Touch recognized text to enter Correcting mode.

- **Deleting**—To delete a word, draw a line backward through it. To delete one or more individual characters, tap a character to expand into Correcting mode and then draw a line backward through the letters you wish to delete. Be sure to draw across the full width of the characters you wish to delete.

- **Splitting**—To insert a space between letters and possibly insert more text, draw a vertical line downward between the two letters.

- **Joining**—To join two separate words, draw a line backward along the baseline of the words, from the beginning of the second word back to the end of the first word, curving a little down and back up. In other words, make a little smile linking the two words.

The deleting, splitting, and joining gestures are illustrated in Figure 35.5.

Figure 35.5
You can edit handwritten text using these pen gestures.

Deleting

Splitting

Joining

The ? button displays a menu that lets you select four brief, very well-done animations that demonstrate these editing gestures.

When you're finished writing, or to add characters that aren't easy to draw, touch or click the Insert box. This moves any entered text to your app, clears the Handwriting Input panel, and displays buttons for Backspace, Tab, Enter, left and right cursor movements, and the spacebar. The button labeled &123 displays a keyboard of numbers and common symbols.

Training the Handwriting Recognizer

Windows does a pretty good job of recognizing standard English written in generic block or cursive form. If you start to use handwriting input a lot, though, you'll find that it has trouble with some of the details and quirks of your own handwriting.

Windows will slowly learn to accommodate those quirks on its own if you use the Correcting mode described in the previous section to choose the alternate spellings that Windows suggests, or to add new words to the dictionary. You can speed the learning process up considerably by doing a little one-on-one training with the handwriting system.

As of the time this was written, Microsoft hadn't done a good job of making the training wizard accessible. In your copy of Windows, try this: go to the Start screen or open the Search charm, type **touch**, and under Settings select Pen and Touch. If there is a Handwriting tab, select it and see if there is a link or button that indicates that it might lead to the Handwriting Training Wizard.

If there is no such option, open File Explorer and browse into the following folders: Computer, Local Disk C:, Program Files, Common Files, Microsoft Shared, Ink. Scroll down and double-click the ShapeCollector application (.exe) file.

The Handwriting Personalization Wizard appears. You can perform any or all of the following training exercises:

- **To run through a standardized training session**—Click Teach the Recognizer Your Handwriting Style, Sentences. Write the requested sentences and symbols in your own, most comfortable writing style. This takes a while. There are 50 sentences to write!

  After the arduous Sentences session, if you want Windows to learn to recognize your handwritten numbers and other symbols, click Teach the Recognizer Your Handwriting Style, Symbols and Letters.

- **To teach Windows to recognize a specific word that it has trouble with**—Click Target Specific Recognition Errors, Character or Word You Specify.

- **To help Windows distinguish between similar letter forms**—Select Target Specific Recognition Errors, Characters with Similar Shapes.

WIRELESS NETWORKING

Wireless Networking in Windows 8

Wireless (Wi-Fi) and cellular data networks are everywhere. From home to work to just about everywhere on the road, it seems like you can fire up a wireless-capable device and get connected no matter where you are. Wireless networks are popular for several reasons, including low costs to get started and, more important, ease of configuration and use.

With the rapid growth of wireless networking has come evolving standards. The 802.11 series of standards was created by the networking industry to ensure hardware and software interoperability among wireless networking vendors. The current state-of-the-art standard 802.11n was an important step forward for wireless performance and reliability, and we're sure that network industry gurus are hard at work at whatever's coming next.

And while people have been using cellular telephone networks to get data service for mobile devices for some time, the software for making and managing these connections was vendor specific and could be cumbersome to use. Today (thanks largely to Apple's iPhones and iPads), consumers have come to expect seamless, effortless, and ubiquitous data service, and so Microsoft has integrated cellular data into the built-in, native networking stack in Windows 8. If you use cellular (3G or 4G) data service on your Windows 8 device, you'll be able to manage it using the same control panels we describe in this chapter. Configuration may still be vendor specific, but your vendor will help with this, and it's not something you'll have to do on a day-to-day basis.

Types of Wi-Fi Networks

Most Wi-Fi (wireless data) networks use a wireless router, base station, or access point. These are called *infrastructure networks*; all communications on the network are between the computers and the access point. You can also tie a group of computers together without an access point; this is called an *ad hoc network*. In this type of network, the computers talk directly to each other. A common scenario for using an ad hoc network is where a group of business people connect together at a conference table in order to share files and information, or to *tether* other devices to one device that has an Internet connection.

This chapter shows you how to use infrastructure networks that have already been set up. We also discuss joining an ad hoc network for quick file sharing between a group of computers at, for example, a meeting.

 For information on setting up a new wireless network for your home or office, **see** *"Installing a Wireless Network," **p. 392**.*

Take Care When You Share

Wireless networking is just another network connection type as far as Windows is concerned, so file and printer sharing is also available. Other wireless users can work with your shared folders, files, and printers, just as if you and they were connected to a wired network. This might be just what you want in your home or office, but when you're at a public location or are using an unsecured, unencrypted wireless network, everyone else who connects to the network, whether you know and trust them or not, might also be able to get to your same shared folders, files, and printers.

To prevent random, unknown people from seeing your shared resources, the Network Location feature keeps track of the identities of various networks to which you attach, and lets you designate whether each one is safe for file sharing. There are actually three location "types": Public network, Private network, and Domain (corporate) network. In more detail, the standard types are as follows:

- **Public network**—A network where other computers and users can't be trusted. The Public network location should be selected for any network link that is directly connected to the Internet without an intervening router or hardware firewall; a network in a cafe, airport, university, or other public location; or a home or office that you are visiting. When you designate a network as a Public network, Windows file and printer sharing is blocked to protect your computer.

- **Private network**—A network at home or work that is trusted to be secure. Either it has no Internet connection or its Internet connection is protected by an external firewall or a connection-sharing router. In addition, you trust all the users and the other computers on the network to access files and printers shared by your computer (with or without a password, depending on the Password Protected Sharing setting in the Network and Sharing Center window). Examples of Private networks are home and business networks managed by you or someone you trust.

> **⚑ caution**
>
> Be sure to select the appropriate network location when Windows prompts you after you've connected to a new network. If in doubt, select Public. You can always change it to a less restrictive setting later if you find that you can't use the network services you need.

■ **Domain network**—A network that is managed by one or more computers running a Windows Server OS. This is a trusted network, and the security of the network and its member computers is managed by network administrators.

The first time you connect to a given network, Windows should prompt you to select the appropriate network location. Windows can take up to a couple of minutes to prompt you after you've connected to a new network for the first time. For whatever reason, you can't hurry the process along. During this time, it will treat the network as a public network, and file sharing will be disabled. Wait a minute or so for Windows to prompt you.

You can view the current setting through the Network and Sharing Center. On Domain networks, this location is not changeable, but it can be changed for the other types of networks.

If you need to change a network's location type, bring up the list of networks by clicking the network icon in the desktop's taskbar, or open the charms, select Settings, and then click the network icon at the bottom of the panel. Right-click a network name and select Turn Sharing On or Off. To specify a Public network, click No, Don't Turn On Sharing. To specify a safe, Private network, click Yes, Turn On Sharing.

Several settings that affect the security of the computer are changed automatically by Windows when you connect to these various types of networks. On Domain networks, Group Policy configures the settings for network discovery and file and printer sharing alike. When you connect to a Public network, Windows disables network discovery and file and printer sharing.

> 🔍 **note**
>
> Windows determines each network's identity by examining the physical network adapter (MAC) address of the network's gateway IP address. If you are on a network with no gateway address set (that is, no router and no shared Internet connection), Windows will permanently label the network an "Unknown Network," will not prompt you to select a location, and will not let you manually change the network location. It will be stuck as Public. (For information about dealing with the Unknown Network problem, *see* "File and Printer Sharing without a Router," *p. 407*.)

After connecting, you can change these default settings, but you really should *not* enable file and printer sharing when you're connected to a network that might contain computers that are unknown to you or are not under your control.

Joining a Wireless Network

Windows 8's new Networks panel makes connecting to a wireless network easier than ever. This section shows you how to connect to wireless networks in some common—but distinctly different—scenarios.

The basic steps are the same in each case:

1. Open the charms, select Settings, and then click the Network icon at the bottom. Alternatively, at the desktop, click the network icon at the right end of the taskbar.

2. The Networks panel opens, as shown in Figure 36.1. Windows displays a list of the names (SSIDs) of the wireless networks that it "hears."

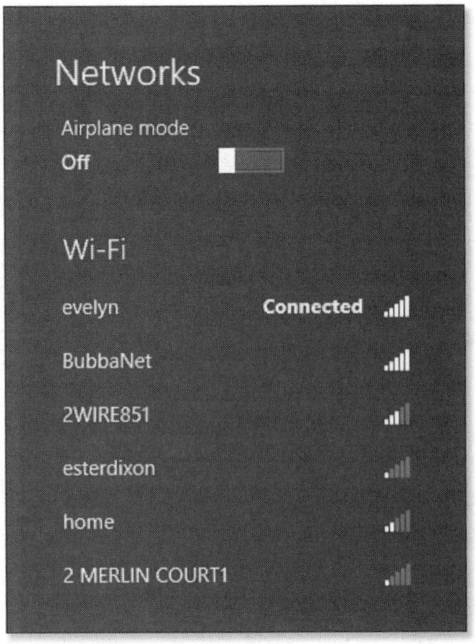

Networks

Airplane mode

Off

Wi-Fi

evelyn   **Connected** .ıll

BubbaNet   .ıll

2WIRE851   .ıll

esterdixon   .ıll

home   .ıll

2 MERLIN COURT1   .ıll

Figure 36.1
Open the Windows 8–style Networks panel and then select the
wireless network you wish to use.

Click or touch a network name. If you want to use this network whenever you're in its range, check Connect Automatically. If you are connecting to the network only temporarily, and you're in range of another network that you would normally prefer to use, uncheck Connect Automatically. Then, select Connect.

3. Windows determines what type of security the network is using. If the network is encrypted, it prompts you to enter the network key. Enter the passphrase or the 10- or 26-digit hexadecimal key that was used when the network was set up. The network's owner will have to tell you what this is.

4. When the connection has been established, Windows should ask you to select a network location: Public or Private. It is very important that you make the right selection.

Windows will save the password you enter, so the next time you return to this location you can reconnect without having to reenter it. You can change other connections as described later in this chapter under "Managing Wireless Network Connections."

The following sections tell you how to proceed to protect your privacy, depending on the type of network you've chosen: corporate, your home/small office, someone else's home or office, or a public place.

Windows Is Unable to Find Any Networks

If you are using a laptop and the list of available wireless networks is empty, check to see whether your laptop has an on/off switch for the wireless adapter (this is put there to let you save battery power when you're not using the network). Be sure the switch is turned on. If there is an Airplane Mode setting in the Networks panel, be sure it's set to Off.

Also, be sure the wireless network adapter is enabled in software. Right-click the network icon in the taskbar, select Open Network and Sharing Center, Change Adapter Settings, and see if the wireless network connection icon is labeled "Disabled." If so, right-click it and select Enable.

If that's not it, there is a chance that your computer isn't within range of any wireless access point. I've been in hotel rooms where the wireless signal is almost nonexistent in one room but excellent in a nearby room. Radio interference is just one of the causes of weak and nonexistent signals when connecting to a wireless network. Unfortunately, there is little that can be done about this problem aside from moving closer to the access point—or in the case of interference, removing the source of the interference.

Unable to Connect to Wireless Network

Sometimes when you attempt to connect to a wireless network, you are not asked to enter a key, or the connection never completes.

For several reasons, you might not be able to connect to a wireless network, even though Windows says that the network is otherwise in range and available. With anything from poor signal strength, an incorrectly typed encryption key, to problems with the wireless access point or DHCP server, the range of problems that can arise when connecting to a wireless network seems limitless.

The Networks panel that appears when you click the taskbar's network icon indicates signal strength next to each wireless network, as a series of white bars. If all or most of the bars are gray, the signal might be too weak to use. You might get a better signal if you move somewhere closer to the network router.

If the network appears to connect you but Windows displays "Limited Access" next to the connection name in the Networks panel, the router to which you've connected may have lost its Internet connection. It's also possible that Windows was unable to actually complete the connection and has gotten stuck in negotiating the connection. Right-click the connection's name in the Networks panel, select Forget This Network, and start over. Try this once; it might fix the connection.

In the Corporate Environment

Wireless networks in a business setting are frequently configured using automated means. For large enterprises, your computer will be preloaded with a certificate, a sort of digital fingerprint that identifies your computer as being authorized to use the corporate network, and the wireless network will be configured for you. Wireless network clients can now be configured via Group Policy (in other words, *by other people*—and there's nothing you can do about it) as well as through the command line using `netsh` commands for wireless adapters, as shown later in this chapter.

At Your Home or Small Office

A wireless network at your home or small office usually doesn't have the same configuration needs as in a large enterprise setting. Wireless networks are configured manually in these environments, using an inexpensive access point or router. Some Internet service providers offer a preconfigured wireless router as standard equipment.

Within a minute of connecting for the first time, Windows should ask you if you want to enable file and printer sharing on the network. If the network is private, under your control, and you trust the other users and computers on the network, you can select Yes, Turn On Sharing and Connect to Devices. If the network is a place where you can't trust every other computer and user, select No, Don't Turn On Sharing or Connect to Devices. *If in doubt, click No. You can always turn sharing on later.*

> **tip**
>
> Always be sure to change the default management password on any access points or routers that you own. Even if it means writing the password on a piece of paper and taping it to the bottom of the device, this is still more secure than leaving the default password in place.

In Someone Else's Home or Office

When you're away from home or the home office, you might find yourself connecting to another person's wireless network. A common scenario is when you visit an office and need to access files on their network, or people on that network need to access files on your computer.

Make the connection as described in the previous section, but be sure you're not inadvertently making the contents of your computer available to other people on the network. Follow these precautionary steps:

1. When you make the connection, if you're asked if you want to enable file sharing and device discovery, click No, and you're done.

2. If you aren't prompted about file sharing, after you make the connection, bring the Networks panel back up again and locate the name of the network to which you just connected. The word *Connected* will appear next to it. Right-click it (or touch and hold), select Turn Sharing On or Off, and then select No, Don't Turn On Sharing or Connect to Devices.

Even with sharing turned off, you can still use network resources shared by others on the network. They just won't be able to get into *your* computer.

If for some reason you *do* need to let someone there use files or printers shared by your computer, open the Networks panel, right-click the network name, select Turn Sharing On or Off, and then select Yes, Turn On Sharing and Connect to Devices. Create a user account just for the person who needs access to your computer (see Chapter 3) and create a password for it. Right-click the network icon in the taskbar and click Open Network and Sharing Center. In the Network and Sharing Center, click Change Advanced Sharing Settings, scroll down, open the All Networks section, and select Turn On Password Protected Sharing, as shown in Figure 36.2. Click Save Changes. Right-click a folder you want the other user to access, select Share With, and then click Specific People to open the File Sharing dialog box. Enter the account name, click Add, and then Share. You can later remove the user account or change its password.

For information on creating a new user account, *see* "Setting Up User Accounts," *p. 68*.

Figure 36.2
In the Advanced Sharing Settings window, select the Turn On Password Protected Sharing option.

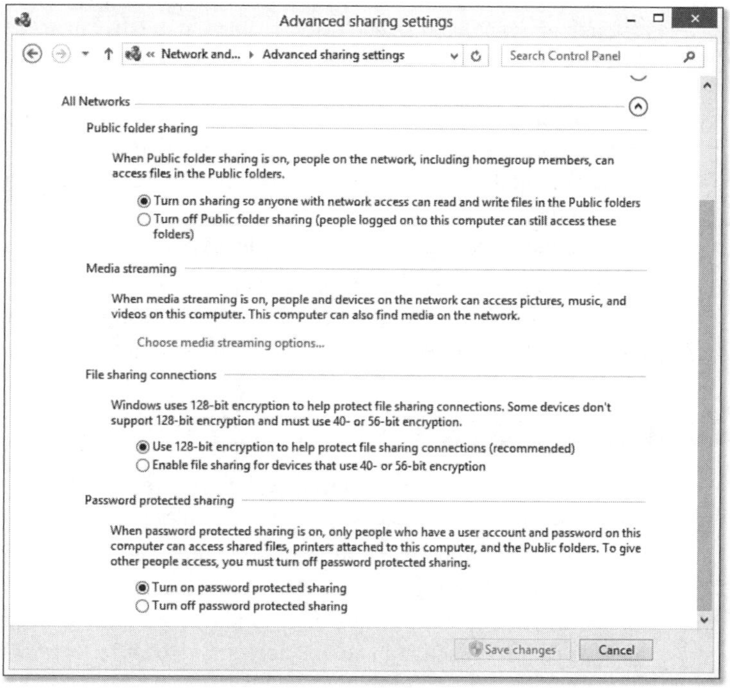

For additional information on sharing files safely, *see* Chapter 21, "Using a Windows Network."

At a Public Hot Spot

Public wireless network hot spots (also called *Wi-Fi hot spots*) are quite helpful when you're on the road and need to check email, get travel information, or just surf the Web. But public hot spots can also be places for would-be attackers to find easy victims.

One path for attack at a public hot spot is through files that client computers accidentally share. When you connect, follow these steps:

1. When you make the connection, if you're asked if you want to enable file sharing and device discovery, click No, and you're set.

2. If you aren't prompted about file sharing, after you make the connection, bring the Networks panel back up again and locate the name of the network to which you just connected. The word *Connected* will appear next to it. Right-click it (or touch and hold) and select Turn Sharing On or Off. Then, select No, Don't Turn On Sharing or Connect to Devices.

 tip

On a public wireless network, it's best to avoid using an email program that uses the POP or SMTP server protocol, and to avoid using FTP (File Transfer Protocol) with a username and password, unless you are certain that the client programs use an encrypted connection.

On open, unsecured public hot spots, it's possible for eavesdroppers to listen in on other people's wireless traffic. Even if the network is secured with encryption, it's possible for eavesdroppers to listen to traffic if they can break the encryption scheme. It can take them mere seconds to break WEP encryption, for example.

Therefore, at a public location, you should be *very* careful when you use websites that display sensitive information or that require you to enter a password. If the URL of the website starts with *https:*, your data will be protected. If the URL starts with just *http:*, think twice about signing in.

Ad Hoc Networks and Meetings

Earlier in the chapter, we discussed joining a wireless infrastructure network where devices rely on a base station called an *access point* or a *wireless router*.

Computers, laptops, and tablets can also communicate with each other directly, without an access point or router. This is called an *ad hoc* wireless network. You might use an ad hoc network so that you can share files with another person in a meeting without requiring any additional hardware. Another common use for an ad hoc network is to let one computer share a direct Internet connection with other devices. For example, you may have a laptop that has a cellular data modem and want to share this Internet connection with another device. This is called *tethering*.

One computer needs to "create" the ad hoc network. Then, users of various types of devices can join it just as they do any other wireless network, by choosing the network's name from a list of available networks.

Windows 8 can *join* an existing ad hoc wireless network, but unfortunately Microsoft removed from the ability to easily *create* one. There is, however, a way you might be able to create one manually, *if* your wireless adapter supports it. You can try these steps:

1. Press Windows Logo+X or right-click the very bottom-left corner of the screen and then select Command Prompt (Admin). Confirm the User Account Control prompt.

2. Type the command **netsh wlan show drivers** and press Enter. Look for the line "Hosted Network Supported." You may need to scroll up to see it. If that line says No, you're out of luck; Windows can't work with your wireless adapter's driver to create an ad hoc network. If it says Yes, you can proceed.

3. Type the two commands

```
netsh wlan set hostednetwork mode=allow ssid=networkname key=passkey
netsh wlan start hostednetwork
```

but substitute the name you'd like to give your network for *networkname* and enter a passphrase of your own devising, using eight or more letters and numbers, for *passkey*. Press Enter after typing each line.

4. Go to the desktop and right-click the network icon in the taskbar. Select Open Network and Sharing Center. Select Change Adapter Settings. You will see a new icon that corresponds to the ad hoc network you just created. Make note of its name. (It might be something like "Wireless 2.")

5. In the Network and Sharing Center, locate the Connections link icon that corresponds to your Internet connection (for example, your Ethernet or cellular modem connection) and click it. Click Properties, select the Sharing tab, and check Allow Other Network Users to Connect Through This Computer's Internet Connection. In the Home Networking drop-down list, select the ad hoc network device you noted in the previous step. Click OK.

Other devices should now be able to see the network you created, and they'll have Internet connectivity through your computer.

If you want to enable file and printer sharing on the ad hoc network, go to the desktop and click the network icon in the taskbar (or open the charms, select Settings, and select the network icon). Right-click the entry for your ad hoc network, select Turn Sharing On or Off, and then select Yes.

To delete the ad hoc network, follow these steps:

1. At the desktop, right-click the network icon in the taskbar, select Open the Network and Sharing Center, click the Connections link that corresponds to your Internet connection, select the Sharing tab, uncheck Share This Connection..., and click OK.

2. Type Windows Logo+X or right-click the very bottom-left corner of the screen, select Command Prompt (Admin), type **netsh wlan stop hostednetwork**, and press Enter.

Managing Wireless Network Connections

If you travel and connect to different networks, Windows will collect a list of several known networks.

When Windows is not currently connected to any wireless network, it scans through its list of known networks, in order. If any is in range, and you have enabled automatic connection, Windows selects the one it thinks you're most likely to want to use and then connects. (Previous versions of Windows let you manually prioritize the list of known networks. Windows 8 guesses based on your past usage, and lets you change the networks if it guesses wrong.)

In most cases, this system works without any adjustments, but there are ways to change the preferences if necessary, as we discuss in the next few sections.

Changing Wireless Settings

If you have to change the security information for an existing wireless connection, use one of these methods:

- Click the network icon in the taskbar or in the Settings charm. Right-click the wireless network, and then click View Connection Properties. The wireless network's Properties dialog box appears with the Security tab displayed.

- Right-click the taskbar's Network icon, click Open Network and Sharing Center, click Change Adapter Settings, right-click the wireless adapter, click Status, click Wireless Properties, and then click the Security tab.

Either way, you can now use the Security tab to change the security type and security key.

Setting Up Preferred Wireless Networks

Once you successfully connect to any new network, Windows remembers the network's details as a *profile*, which is a collection of settings for a given network. By default, Windows keeps profiles for all networks to which you've previously attached, and—unless you've disabled automatic connection—reconnects when one becomes available. This lets you move from place to place, while Windows automatically connects to whatever network is appropriate.

If you are in an area where your computer can receive signals from two or more known networks—that is, networks to which you've previously connected—at the same time, you may want to tell Windows which one to use in preference to the others. One might have faster download speeds. Or, you may want to connect to your neighbor's network when yours is out of reach, but, if both are available, you want to use yours.

How does Windows know which to use? In previous versions of Windows, you could sort the list of known networks into your own preferred order. Windows would use whatever available network was topmost in the list.

Windows 8 doesn't let you manually sort the list of networks, but it does let you switch between available networks, and it keeps track of which network you end up actually using, if more than one is available. To train Windows, you must manually switch networks, using these steps:

1. View the list of available networks by clicking the network icon in the taskbar, or by clicking the network icon in the Settings charm.

   If you are currently connected to a network, it will be labeled Connected.

2. If you want to connect to a different network, click or touch its name and then select Connect.

Windows should remember your preference of one over the other for future connections.

You can also give hints to Windows by changing a network's connection properties. You can put each network into one of three priority categories. To set these categories, open the Networks panel, right-click (or touch and hold) a network name, select View Connection Properties, select the Connection tab, and then designate how you want Windows to treat the network. Here's the list of options (see Figure 36.3):

- **This is a top-choice network. I'm happy to use this one anytime. Stick with this network until the signal is lost**—Check Connect Automatically When This Network Is in Range, and uncheck Look for Other Wireless Networks While Connected to This Network.

- **This is a backup network. Use it if necessary, but if a top-choice network becomes available, switch over**—Check Connect Automatically... and then check Look for Other Wireless Networks....

- **This is a special-purpose network or a last resort. Connect to it only when I tell you to**— Uncheck Connect Automatically....

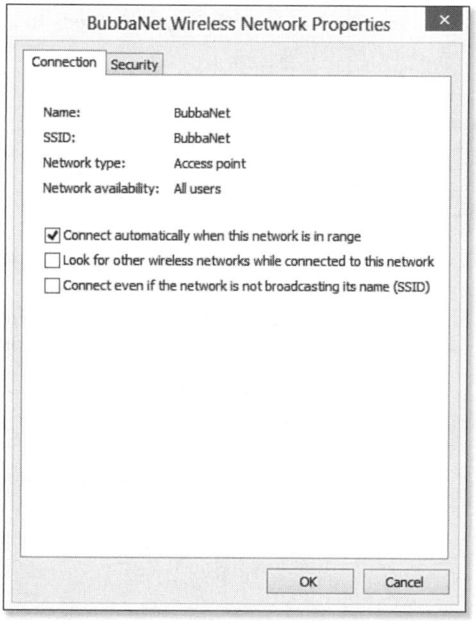

Figure 36.3
In the wireless network's Properties dialog box, use the Connection tab to specify how you want Windows 8 to treat the wireless network.

Adding a Network Manually

Some people instruct their wireless routers not to advertise their network name (SSID), as a sort of security measure. The thinking is, if the network is invisible, people won't try to use it.

This doesn't really make them secure, just difficult for you to connect to. A network that does not broadcast its network name (SSID) usually will not appear in the list of available networks. (Although, it might, if Windows overhears network traffic that includes the name.) To connect to such a hidden network, you must enter its connection information manually. Follow these steps:

> **note**
>
> Just so you know, a hacker can find such "invisible" networks without any problem. For your own networks, if you really want to secure them, encrypt them with WPA2.

1. Go to the taskbar and right-click the network icon. Then click Open Network and Sharing Center.

2. Select Set Up a New Connection or Network, Manually Connect to a Wireless Network, and then click Next.

3. Enter the network's name (SSID), set the security type, and enter the key, if required.

4. For a network that does not broadcast its SSID (a choice the network's owner made in a futile attempt to hide his network from hackers), check Connect Even If the Network Is Not Broadcasting. This network will now always appear in the list of (potentially) available connections. You should *not* check Start This Connection Automatically. If you do, *your* computer will frequently broadcast the name of the network it's looking for, which makes you vulnerable to being tricked. (A hacker could have his computer say "Yes, here I am, connect to me.")

5. Click Next, and then click Close to save the new profile.

To later connect to a network with a hidden SSID when you're in range, open the list of available networks, click the name of the network, and click Connect.

Deleting Wireless Profiles

To remove wireless network profiles—to unclutter the list after traveling, or so that Windows will not automatically connect to them in the future—follow these steps:

1. From the desktop, click the network icon in the taskbar. Alternatively, bring up the charms, select Settings, and then select the network icon at the bottom of Settings.

2. Right-click or touch-and-hold the network name you want to remove and then select Forget This Network.

If no right-click options appear for the network name you selected, it means that this is a network to which you've never connected, so there is no memorized information to delete. The network is just listed because Windows is picking up its signal.

COMPUTING ON THE ROAD

Windows Unplugged: Mobile and Remote Computing

Some people predict that one day a global Internet will cover every inch of the earth's surface, giving us an always-on, always-available stream of data they call the "Evernet." We're not quite there yet, but today the Internet is available in pretty much any city you might visit, and it has become easy to stay in touch with home while you're traveling. It really is starting to matter less and less where you are because your data, services, and online life are now present everywhere you go.

Windows 8 supports you when you're away from home or the office with some pretty spiffy portability and networking features, including these features that are covered in other chapters:

- SkyDrive, Microsoft ("online") accounts, and other cloud services ensure that your account preferences, passwords, data, and apps are available no matter where you are and what device you're using. This topic is covered in Chapter 5, "Windows 8 Apps and the Windows Store."

- Portable device features such as power management, handwriting input, and touch are covered in Chapter 35, "Windows 8 on Mobile Devices."

- Wireless networking support lets Windows stay connected when you're on the go. This is covered in Chapter 36, "Wireless Networking."

- Windows 8 Pro makes it easier to use a portable or laptop computer to make business or school presentations. Presentations are covered in Chapter 38, "Meetings, Conferencing, and Collaboration."

- Windows has a nifty Remote Desktop feature that lets you use your own home-based computer from somewhere else, over the Internet. This is covered in Chapter 39, "Remote Desktop and Remote Access."

This chapter covers several other Windows 8 features, which are mostly related to getting the most out of mobile (portable, laptop, notebook, or tablet) computers while you're working away from home or the office:

- For laptops, the Windows Mobility Center puts a bunch of important settings in one window so you can manage your computer's display, power consumption, and networking features.

- Dial-up and Virtual Private Network (VPN) networking let you access a remote network when you're traveling, and you can even set up remote access to your own home or office network.

- The Offline Files feature lets you automatically keep up-to-date personal copies of the files stored in network folders, so you really can "take them with you."

Let's start by discussing the Mobility Center.

Managing Mobile Computers

Portable computers come in an ever-increasing variety and go by many names: laptops, notebooks, netbooks, slates, pads, and tablets. They are no longer an expensive perk provided only to jet-setting executives. They're now standard equipment for most people who work at least part time away from their office, and consumers now buy more portable computers than desktops for home and personal use. Consequently, portables have become powerful and inexpensive, and support for their special needs by Windows has grown considerably.

> **note**
>
> Tablet devices are available that use the ARM microprocessor and run a version of Windows called Windows RT. The entry-level Microsoft Surface devices fall into this category. Although many of the Windows 8-style features and settings we discuss in this chapter should apply to Windows RT devices, this chapter addresses mobile computers running Windows 8 on an Intel-compatible processor.

Airplane Mode

When you're not using your device's Wi-Fi or cellular data connection, you can extend the device's battery life (and avoid a confrontation with a flight attendant) by turning on Airplane mode, which disables the data radio. To turn Airplane mode on or off, open the Settings charm and select the network icon at the bottom. The Airplane Mode switch is at the top of the Networks panel, but only on mobile devices such as laptops and tablets.

Windows Mobility Center

If you have a mobile computer running Windows 8, you'll find that Windows provides a tool called Windows Mobility Center, a special control panel that desktop computers don't have. To open the Mobility Center, shown in Figure 37.1, use one of these methods:

- Type Windows Logo+X and select Mobility Center.

- If your computer has a mouse or trackpad, right-click the very bottom-left corner of the screen and select Mobility Center.

- Go to the Start screen, and if you don't have a keyboard, open the Search charm. Type in **mobil**, select Settings at the right, and then select Windows Mobility Center.

- Open the charms and select Settings, Control Panel, Hardware and Sound, Windows Mobility Center.

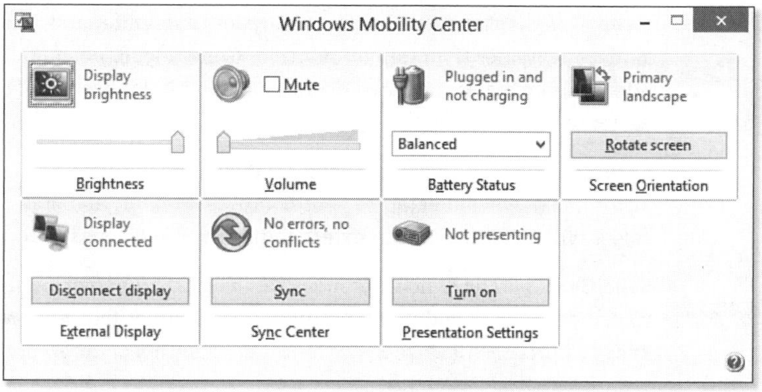

Figure 37.1
Windows Mobility Center has tools for quickly changing settings on mobile computers.

The Mobility Center is designed to bring together in one window most of the settings you'll want to change while using your portable computer remotely. The settings pertain mostly to power management (so you can make your device's battery last as long as possible) and display management, because many people use laptops to make business and school presentations. Your computer's Mobility Center may display some or all of the following controls:

- **Brightness**—The slider lets you increase or decrease your screen's backlight brightness. A lower setting should make your computer run longer on a battery charge. Windows remembers separate brightness settings for battery and AC-powered operation, stores them as part of a power profile, and resets the brightness when the power status changes. You can fine-tune the setting with this control. (There is also a brightness control in the Settings charm.)

- **Volume**—The slider controls your computer's speaker volume, and the Mute check box lets you instantly shut the sound off. This may be useful, for example, if you're in a meeting and someone keeps sending you noisy IM pop-ups. (And again, there is also a volume control in the Settings charm.)

- **Battery Status**—The icon shows you whether you are running on AC or battery-only power. (The power plug in the icon shown in Figure 37.1 indicates that the computer is on AC power.) The battery icon and the text tell you the battery's charge level. The drop-down list lets you select a power profile.
Power profiles let you choose a balance between lower power consumption and greater performance. We discuss power profiles in more detail in the next section, "Getting the Most Out of Your Battery."

tip

If you used the Windows Logo+X keyboard shortcut in Windows 7 or Vista to open the Mobility Center, you'll find that on Windows 8 this shortcut brings up a list of administrative tools (handy, but not what you were after). Mobility Center is in this list. Just click it.

If you want to pin the Mobility Center to the desktop's taskbar, bring it up, right-click its icon in the taskbar, and select Pin This Program To Taskbar.

Oddly, it's difficult to pin it to the Start screen. To do that, you have to search for **mblctr**, select Apps, right-click mblctr, and select Pin to Start. It works, but what you get is the Mobility Center's program filename, not its longer descriptive name from the control panel.

- **Screen Orientation**—On tablet PCs, this control lets you switch the display between portrait (taller than wide) and landscape (wider than tall) orientation. Generally, in portrait orientation it's easier to read documents, and in landscape it's easier to watch movies.

> **note**
>
> Your computer manufacturer may have added additional controls not listed here.

- **External Display**—When an external display monitor or projector has been connected to your computer's external display connector, this control lets you select what appears on the external display. We discuss External Display in detail in Chapter 38.

- **Sync Center**—The Sync Center is used to copy files to or from an external device such as a smartphone, or to update copies of network server files that you've obtained using the Offline Files feature. We discuss Sync Center later in this chapter, under "Offline Files."

- **Presentation Settings**—When you turn Presentation Settings on, Windows suppresses some behaviors that could disrupt your presentation. We discuss Presentation Settings in Chapter 38.

In addition, the Hardware and Sound section in the Control Panel has some sections that are especially helpful to know about if you have a mobile PC. Here are some of the settings you might want to remember:

- **Power Options**—Lets you select a power profile. We discuss this in the next section.

- **Change What the Power Buttons Do (under Power Options)**—Lets you choose whether the computer shuts down or goes into Sleep or Hibernate mode when you press your portable computer's power button or close its lid while it's running. We discuss this, too, in the next section.

- **Adjust Settings Before Giving a Presentation**—Lets you specify the types of interruptions you want to prevent during presentations. This is discussed in Chapter 38.

Getting the Most Out of Your Battery

The central processing unit (CPU) chip and graphical processor unit (GPU) chip can be the two biggest energy guzzlers in a computer, but in most cases, they spend little of their time actually working. For example, as I type this chapter, my computer's CPU takes less than a millisecond to react to each keystroke and update the display. The CPU and display processor might be occupied with useful work much less than 0.1% of the time. Processors that can take advantage of the relatively long lulls by slowing their processing speed or *clock speed* way down between bursts of activity significantly reduce power consumption. This extends battery life on portables (and can make desktop PCs quieter, because their CPU fans can be slowed down).

Additionally, laptops can conserve energy by dimming the backlight lamp that illuminates the display, and by turning off hardware devices such as the disk drive, DVD or CD drive, network adapter, and modem when they are not actively being used. Even these devices' interface electronics can be shut off.

Of course, when you're watching a movie (which requires a lot of processor effort to decode the DVD's data into millions of pixels per second) or performing heavy-duty calculations, power consumption can go way up.

You can adjust how Windows manages hardware power consumption, and how fast the processor is allowed to run, by creating *power profiles*, which are collections of settings that can be applied in different situations. Out of the box, Windows 8 enables you to choose between three profiles:

- **Balanced**—Select this profile to strike a fair balance between power savings and performance. You'll still get full processing power when it's needed.

- **Power Saver**—Select this profile when you want to extend the battery life as long as possible, even if it noticeably slows the processor. Windows may also eliminate some graphical effects.

- **High Performance**—Select this profile when you want maximum speed even when your computer is running on battery power.

To view the power profiles, use one of these methods:

- Press Windows Logo+X and select Power Options.

- If your computer has a mouse or trackpad, right-click the very bottom-left corner of the screen and select Power Options.

- Go to the Desktop, open the charms and select Settings, Control Panel, Hardware and Sound, Power Options.

note

If you have a scenario that's begging for its own profile, you can add a new one to this list. To do so, click Create a Power Plan in the left pane.

This will display the Power Options screen, which lets you select the profile you want to use at any given time.

To select what settings are put into effect by each profile, click the phrase Change Plan Settings next to a profile name. This displays the window shown in Figure 37.2. Here, you can select how long Windows should wait before darkening the screen and putting the computer to sleep when idle, under AC power and battery power. You can use the slider at the bottom to adjust the screen brightness for battery-powered operation.

If you rarely stop while you are actually working, but tend to leave for a while when you do stop, you might gain additional battery life by reducing the time before turning off the display or shutting down when on battery power. Dimming the display can help, too, if you're not working outdoors.

To really change the speed-versus-power compromise, click Change Advanced Power Settings to get the dialog box shown in Figure 37.3. Here, you can change quite a number of power-related delays and rates. Each setting has two values: one to use when on AC power, and another to use when on battery power. Start by clicking Change Settings That Are Currently Unavailable to gain access to the entire list of settings.

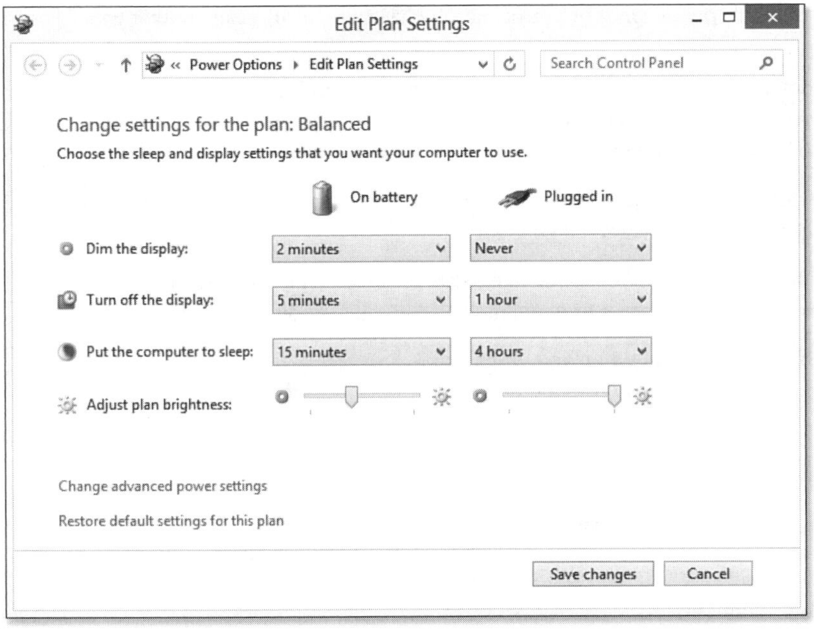

Figure 37.2
On the Edit Plan Settings page, you can adjust various power-saving timers.

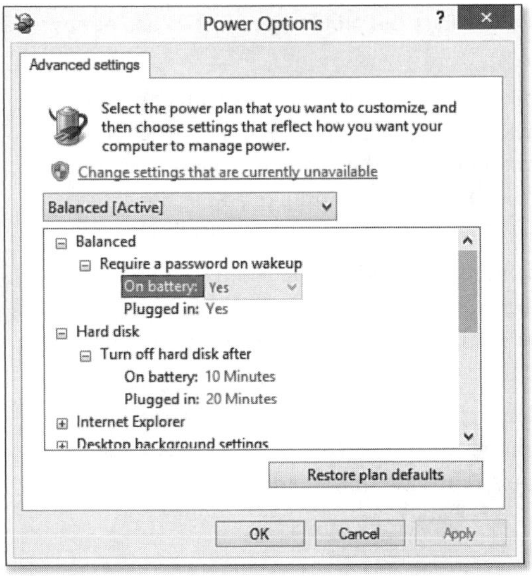

Figure 37.3
The Power Options Advanced Settings dialog box lets you adjust power management settings for a large number of specific devices.

If you really do love tweaking, you might want to look at some of the more interesting advanced settings:

- **Hard Disk**—Set the time that the disk is allowed to spin after being used. The default time on battery is 10 minutes. If your usage pattern usually spins the disk right back up just after it shuts down, you might increase this time. If your device has a solid state disk (SSD), this setting is not relevant.

- **Wireless Adapter Settings**—You can choose any of four settings, from Maximum Performance to Maximum Power Saving (and presumably slower and less reliable data transfer). If your wireless access point is nearby, Maximum Power Saving might help extend battery life. (And as mentioned earlier in the chapter, you can use the Airplane Mode switch on the Networks panel to completely turn off your device's data radio.)

- **Sleep**—Hybrid Sleep is a mode in which Windows will wake the computer up after a certain time in Sleep mode (the Hibernate After time) and perform a full hibernate. You can extend battery life by reducing the Hibernate After time. The trade-off is that Windows takes longer to start up after hibernating.

- **Processor Power Management**—You can set the lowest and highest processor states (speeds) in terms of % of maximum speed. Setting a low minimum speed increases battery life without costing much in performance. Reducing the maximum speed helps battery life but also takes a bite out of performance.

- **Multimedia Settings**—If you use Windows Media Sharing, this setting can prevent Windows from going to sleep while it's sharing media. Sleep cuts off your remote players.

- **Battery**—You can select the battery percentage levels at which Windows takes action to warn you about power loss or shutdown, and what actions to take at low and critically low power levels. You should not select Sleep as the Critical Battery Action, because Windows might not be able to keep system RAM alive when the battery level falls even further. If the battery dies in Sleep mode, you may lose unsaved data.

> **🔍 note**
>
> When Hybrid Sleep is enabled (the default setting), the shutdown options on the Start menu and in the Change What the Power Buttons Do control panel applet list Sleep as a choice but not Hibernate, because hibernating is automatic in this case. If you want to manually control when Windows sleeps and when it hibernates, you must disable Hybrid Sleep. Then, the Start menu's shutdown button and the power button setup applet will offer Hibernate as an option. If you disable Hybrid Sleep, you must remember to manually shut down or hibernate your computer if you're not going to be using it for an extended time; otherwise, you risk losing data if the device loses power.

VPN and Dial-Up Networking

Windows can connect to a remote Windows network via a dial-up modem, or via a protected connection called a Virtual Private Network (VPN) that's routed through the Internet. Using these services, all file sharing, printing, and directory services are available just as if you were directly connected to the remote network (albeit much slower in some cases). You can connect, open shared folders, transfer files, and use email as if you were "there," and then disconnect when you're finished.

The receiving end of a VPN or a dial-up networking connection is usually handled by the Remote Access Services (RAS) provided by Windows Server or third-party remote connection devices manufactured by networking companies such as Cisco and Lucent. But Windows 8 comes with a stripped-down version of RAS so you can set up your own Windows computer to receive a single incoming modem or VPN connection. You can use this, for example, to get access to your office computer and LAN from home, provided that your company's security policies permit this.

You learn how to allow incoming connections later in the chapter.

Virtual Private Networking

Most of us are familiar with using a modem to connect a computer to the Internet. Establishing a dial-up networking or VPN connection is no different; the remote network is just a bit smaller than the Internet.

Virtual private networking deserves a bit more explanation. In a nutshell, a VPN lets you connect to a remote network in a secure way. A VPN creates what is effectively a *tunnel* between your computer and a remote network, a tunnel that can pass data freely and securely through potentially hostile intermediate territory like the Internet. Authorized data is encapsulated in special packets that are passed through your computer's firewall and the remote network's firewall. These are inspected by a VPN server before being released to the protected network.

Figure 37.4 illustrates the concept, showing a VPN connection between a computer out on the Internet and a server on a protected network. The computer sends your data (1) through a VPN connection that encapsulates it (2) and transmits it over the Internet (3). A firewall (4) passes VPN packets but blocks all others. The VPN server verifies the authenticity of the data, extracts it (5), and transmits the original packet (6) on to the desired remote server. The encapsulation process allows for encryption of your data, and allows "private" IP addresses to be used as the endpoints of the network connection.

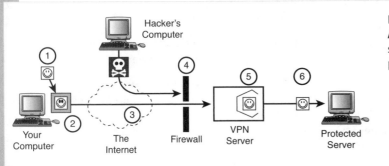

Figure 37.4
A virtual private network encapsulates and encrypts data that is passed over the Internet.

🔍 **note**

Several companies manufacture VPN software and hardware solutions, some of which are faster and provide better management tools than Microsoft's VPN system. If your organization uses a VPN product purchased from a company such as Juniper Networks, CheckPoint Software Technologies, or Cisco Systems, you'll have to follow their instructions for installing and using their VPN software.

Smaller-scale alternatives include a series of Internet Connection Sharing routers made by Linksys (Cisco) that have VPN capabilities built in, and a software product called Hamachi made by logmein.com. If you're interested in setting up a permanent VPN between locations you use, you might want to check out these solutions.

VPN connections work like dial-up connections. After you have an Internet connection established (via modem or a dedicated service), Windows establishes the link between your computer and a VPN server on the remote network. After it's connected, in effect, you are a part of the distant LAN. The connection won't be as fast as a direct LAN connection, but a VPN can be very useful for copying files and securely accessing Remote Desktop connections.

Both desktop and Server versions of Windows come with VPN software built in. In the next section, we describe how to use Microsoft's VPN system.

Setting Up a VPN or Dial-Up Networking Connection

To create a VPN or dial-up connection to a remote network or computer, you need a working Internet connection or modem, respectively. You learned how to install both of these in Chapter 14, "Getting Connected," so if you haven't done so already, start there to install and configure your modem and Internet connection.

You also must obtain or confirm the information shown in Table 37.1 from the remote network's or computer's manager.

Table 37.1 Information Needed for a VPN or RAS Dial-Up Connection

Information	Reason
For Dial-Up	
Telephone number	You must know the receiving modem's telephone number, including area code.
Modem compatibility	You must confirm that your modem is compatible with the modems used by the remote network; check which modem protocols are supported (V.90, V.32, and so on).
For VPN	
VPN server	You need either the hostname or IP address of the remote VPN server computer.
For Either	
Protocols in use	The remote network must support TCP/IP. Windows 8 does not support networking with the IPX/SPX or NetBEUI protocol.
TCP/IP configuration	You should confirm that the Remote Access Server assigns TCP/IP information automatically (dynamically) via DHCP. Usually, the answer is yes.
Mail servers	You might need to obtain the IP addresses or names of SMTP, POP, Exchange, Lotus Notes, or Microsoft Mail servers if you want to use these applications while connected to the remote network.
User ID and password	You must be ready to supply a username and password to the remote server. If you're calling into a Windows workstation or server, use the same Windows username and password you use on that remote network.

Armed with this information, you're ready to create a connection to the remote network. To do so, follow these steps:

1. Go to the desktop, right-click the network icon in the taskbar, and select Open Network and Sharing Center. (Alternatively, go to the desktop, open the charms, and select Settings, Control Panel, View Network Status and Tasks.)

2. In the middle of the window, under Change Your Networking Settings, select Set Up a New Connection or Network.

3. Select Connect to a Workplace and then click Next.

4. Select No, Create a New Connection and then click Next.

If you're setting up a VPN collection, continue with these steps:

5. Select Use My Internet Connection (VPN).

6. Enter the hostname or the IP address of the remote VPN server. Change the Destination Name field to something meaningful to you, such as "VPN to Big Client."

   If your network uses smartcard authentication (your network administrator will tell you so), check Use a Smart Card.

7. Finally, click Create.

Alternatively, if you are setting up a dial-up connection, continue with these steps:

5. Select Dial Directly.

6. Enter the telephone number of the remote computer, including area code, in the appropriate format. For telephone numbers in the North American Numbering Plan, the format is (###)###-####, where # represents a digit. Then, click Dialing Rules to double-check that your current location and area code are set correctly. Change these, if necessary, and click OK.

   Change the Destination Name field to something meaningful to you, such as "Dial-up office network."

   Check Don't Connect Now; Just Set It Up So I Can Use It Later. Then, click Next.

7. Enter the username and password that you use when logging on to the remote computer, or use the name and password assigned by your network administrator. If this is a Windows domain logon, enter the domain name in the Domain (Optional) field. You can check Show Characters if you want to be sure you typed the password correctly.

   If you want to have Windows remember the password so that you can connect without having to type it every time, check Remember This Password. However, if earlier you checked Allow Other People to Use This Connection, this would let others connect using your network credentials, so think carefully whether you want to allow that.

8. Finally, click Create.

Now, you'll see the Windows 8 Networks panel. You can select the name of the VPN or dial-up connection you just created to make the connection. To bring this panel up at any time, take one of the following actions:

- Go to the desktop and select the network icon in the taskbar.

- Go to the Start screen, search for **connect**, select Settings, and then select Connect to a Network.

Before you connect for the first time, you may want to check the new connection's settings, as described in the next section.

Setting a VPN or Dial-Up Connection's Properties

To edit the properties of a VPN or dial-up connection, open the Networks panel as described at the end of the previous section. Right-click a dial-up or VPN connection name and select View Connection Properties. (Alternatively, if you have the Network and Sharing Center open, select Change Adapter settings, right-click a connection icon, and select Properties.)

A connection's properties dialog box has five tabs and a heap o' parameters. Most of the time, the default settings will work correctly, but you might need to change some of them. The most important parameters are listed in Table 37.2.

Table 37.2   Important Dial-Up Connection Properties

Tab	Property	Description
General (VPN)	Host Name or IP Address	Contact information for the VPN server.
	Dial Another Connection First	Check this box and select a dial-up or PPPoE connection if you need to establish an Internet connection before attempting the VPN connection.
General (Dial-up)	Area Code, Phone Number, Country/ Region Code	Set the appropriate dialing information here. If the remote server has more than one phone number (or more than one hunt group), you can click Alternates to specify alternate telephone numbers.
	Use Dialing Rules	Check to have Windows determine when to dial prefixes and area codes. If you want to use this, enter the area code and phone number in their separate fields. This feature is useful if you will be calling the same number from several locations with different dialing properties.
Options	Prompt for Name and Password	Check to have Windows allow you to change previously stored credentials.
	Include Windows Logon Domain	Check if you are connecting to a Windows Server computer.
	Idle Time Before Hanging Up	You can change how long the phone stays connected if you don't transmit data for a while. This can save you on toll charges.

Table 37.2 Continued

Tab	Property	Description
Security		Your network administrator may instruct you to change these settings; otherwise, the default settings should work. Be sure to leave Data Encryption set to Require Encryption.
	Automatically Use My Windows Logon Name and Password	Check this box if you have an account on the computer to which you're connecting that has the same logon name and password (and domain name, if you are on an enterprise network) that you're using now, *and* if you want to let the connection be made without having to reenter your password.
Networking		Usually, all protocols and services should be checked except File and Printer Sharing, which should be disabled so remote network users cannot use your computer's shared folders and printers. If you really do want to let the remote network's users see your shares, check File and Printer Sharing.
	Internet Protocol Version 4 (TCP/IP)	Normally, a Remote Access Server automatically assigns your connection the proper IP and DNS addresses. In the very unlikely event that the network administrator tells you that you must set TCP/IP parameters yourself, select Internet Protocol Version 4 (TCP/IP) from the Components list and then click Properties. Enter the required IP address and DNS addresses there.

If you are connecting to a small network that has only one subnet (one range of network addresses), and if you want to browse the Internet while you're also using the dial-up or VPN connection, you can change the connection's gateway setting so that Windows won't route connections to Internet-based hosts through the VPN or dial-up connection—this will speed up web browsing considerably. To change the gateway setting, follow these steps:

1. Open the connection's properties as described in the previous section.

2. Select the Networking tab, select Internet Protocol Version 4, and choose Properties. Then click the Advanced button.

3. Uncheck Use Default Gateway on Remote Network.

You can make this change on more complex networks as well, but you'll have to add routing information so that Windows knows which network addresses are reached through the VPN connection and which are reached directly on the Internet. We explain how to make routing entries later in the chapter under "Advanced Routing for Remote Networks."

After you've finished making any needed changes to the connection's options, click OK.

Now, to establish the connection, view the Networks panel, select the connection icon, and select Connect.

Managing Dial-Up Connections from Multiple Locations

As you've seen already, Windows lets you enter your current telephone area code and dialing prefix requirements so that when you're making modem calls, Windows uses the customs and prefixes appropriate for your local phone system. This capability is great if you use a portable computer. For example, at home, you might be in area code 415. At the office, you might be in area code 707 and have to dial 9 to get an outside telephone line. When you're visiting Indianapolis, you're in area code 317 and might need to use a telephone company calling card when making long-distance calls.

Windows offers great support for these variations by letting you define "locations," each with a separate local area code and dialing rules. As long as you've told Windows your current location, it will automatically apply the correct set of rules when making a dial-up connection.

 For instructions on establishing locations and dialing rules, **see** *"Adjusting Dial-Up Connection Properties," p. 288.*

If your ISP has access points in various cities, or your company has different local access numbers in various regions, you'll find that this "locations" system does not let you associate a different dial-up number with each location. It would be great if it did, but no such luck. If you use different "local" dial-up numbers for the various locations you visit with your computer, set up a separate Network Connections icon for each access number and use the appropriate icon when making a connection at each location.

Here's how to do this easily: set up and test the first access number you need. Then, when you need to add a new access number, view the Network and Sharing Center, select Change Adapter Settings, right-click the original dial-up connection icon, and select Create Copy. Click Rename This Connection at the top of the screen and then click the new name to bring up the Properties box. Change its telephone number. I name my icons based on the location of the local access number: Office-Berkeley, Office-Seattle, and so on. When you travel and need to make a dial-up connection, select the appropriate dial-up icon and be *sure* to set your current Dialing Rules location before you click Dial.

> ## tip
>
> If you travel, you'll find that having your Internet Options set to dial a particular connection automatically is not a great idea. It would dial the chosen connection no matter where you were (and remember, if there's a 50-50 chance of things going wrong, nine times out of ten they will). So, if you travel with your computer, you might want to open the desktop version of Internet Explorer, press and release the Alt key, then click Tools, Internet Options. Select the Connections tab and choose Never Dial a Connection. This way, you won't be blindsided by an inadvertent call to Indiana while you're in India.

Establishing a VPN or Dial-Up Connection

Making a remote network dial-up or VPN connection is no more difficult than connecting to the Internet.

Dial-Up Only: Check Your Current Location

If you're making a dial-up connection and you've changed area codes or phone systems since the last time you made a modem connection, check your location setting by following these steps before dialing into the network:

1. At the Start screen, type **modem**, select Settings, and then select Set Up Dialing Rules.

2. Check your current location in the list of configured dialing locations on the Dialing Rules tab. Click New if you need to add a new location.

3. Click OK to close the dialog box.

Windows should now use the correct area code and dialing prefixes.

Make the Connection

To connect to a remote network, follow these steps:

1. Click the network icon in your taskbar (alternatively, from the Start screen type the word **connect**, select Settings, then select Connect to a Network). Then, click the name of the connection you wish to establish and click Connect.

2. Windows will open a dialog box or a panel to let you enter your login name, password, and (if appropriate) your account's Windows domain name. Figure 37.5 shows the VPN version on the left and the dial-up version on the right.

VPN Prompt

Dial-Up Prompt

Figure 37.5
When you start a VPN or dial-up connection, Windows will prompt you for your username and password on the remote computer or network.

Enter the login name, password, and Windows domain name (if appropriate) for your account on the remote computer or network. If you do have a domain login name, you can enter it in the form myusername@mydomainname.

However, if you are connecting to a Windows 8 computer and you have a Microsoft account, you can't enter your account in myname@domain.com format. You must use the local account name, which the remote computer owner can tell you (they saw it when they set up incoming VPN access). This is described later in the chapter.

For a dial-up connection, you can select Properties to adjust the connection's telephone number or dialing properties. The Dialing From choice appears only if you checked Use Dialing Rules and have defined more than one dialing location.

3. Click OK or Dial. Windows shows you the progress of your connection as it dials or contacts the remote server, verifies your username and password, and registers your computer on the remote network.

If the connection fails, unless you dialed the wrong number, you'll most likely get a reasonable explanation: the password or account name was invalid, the remote system is not accepting calls, and the like. If you entered an incorrect username or password, you are usually given two more chances to reenter the information before the other end hangs up on you.

If the connection completes successfully, and you hover your mouse over the taskbar's network icon, a small balloon will appear showing the active network connections. If you click the network icon, you'll see the active dial-up or VPN connection in the list of active connections. To disconnect, just click the name and then click Disconnect.

In most cases, the remote network will be a corporate network or a network you control, so if Windows prompts you for a network location, select Private.

If it doesn't prompt you for a location the first time you connect, right-click the network icon in the taskbar and select Open the Network and Sharing Center. If the VPN or dial-up connection's entry in the Active Connections list says "Public Network," as it probably will, click the network icon in the taskbar to view the network panel again, right-click the connection icon, select Turn Sharing On or Off, and then select Yes, Turn On Sharing.

You can now use the remote network's resources, as discussed next.

VPN Connection Fails with Error Number 720 or 629

If you are trying to make a VPN connection to a computer you set up yourself to receive incoming connections, and the connection fails with error 720 or 629, most likely the computer you are using to establish the connection has an active LAN connection in the same network address range as the computer to which you're connecting—even though the networks aren't physically attached. It's just an unfortunate coincidence. You must fix this at the VPN host computer. Right-click the Incoming Connections icon and select Properties. Select the Networking tab, highlight Internet Protocol Version 4, and select Properties. Uncheck Allow Callers to Access My Local Area Network and then check Select IP Addresses. Set the From value to **192.168.111.2** and the To value to **192.168.111.20**.

> ### VPN Connection Fails Without Certificate
>
> If you receive the message "Unable to negotiate the encryption you requested without a certifi-
> cate" when you attempt to make a VPN connection, you are trying to connect to a VPN server
> with a higher level of encryption than your computer or the other computer is configured to carry
> out. Contact your network administrator to get the appropriate certificate installed.

Using Remote Network Resources

When you're connected, you can use network resources exactly as if you were physically on the network. The Network folder, shared folders, and network printers all function as if you were directly
connected.

The following are some tips for effective remote networking:

- Don't try to run application software that is installed on the remote network itself. Starting it
  could take quite a long time! (However, if you have previously connected directly to the network,
  and the Offline Files system is in use, you might have a cached copy of the application on your
  hard disk. Your network manager will set this up for you if it's a reasonable thing to use.)

- If you get disconnected while you are editing a document that was originally stored on the
  remote network, immediately use Save As to save it on your local hard disk the moment you
  notice that the connection has been disrupted. Then, when the connection is reestablished, save
  it back to its original location. This will help you avoid losing your work.

- You can place shortcuts to network folders on your desktop or in other folders for quick access.

- If the remote LAN has Internet access, you should be able to browse the Internet while you're
  connected to the LAN, although it can be slower to do so because data from Internet sites goes
  first to the remote network and then through the VPN connection to you. See "Setting a VPN or
  Dial-Up Connection's Properties" in this chapter for information about an option that can speed
  up Internet browsing.

- If you use a standalone email program, you might have trouble sending mail while you're connected through the VPN. Your ISP may not accept outgoing mail because your connection
  appears to be coming from the "wrong" network. We discuss this in the next section.

Email and Network Connections

If you use your computer with remote LANs as well as the Internet, or if you use different ISPs in
different situations, you might need to be careful with the email programs you use. Most email programs don't make it easy for you to associate different mail servers with different connections.

Although most email servers allow you to *retrieve* your mail from anywhere on the Internet, most
are very picky about whom they let *send* email. Generally, to use an SMTP server to send mail out,
you must be using a computer whose IP address is known by the server as belonging to its own

network, or you must provide a username and password to the outgoing mail server (that is, you must *authenticate*).

If your ISP lets you (or requires you) to use authenticated SMTP (that is, if you set your email program to supply a username and password to the outgoing mail server), there should be no problem sending mail.

If you can't use authenticated SMTP, see if your favorite email program can configure separate "identities," each with associated incoming and outgoing servers. Set up a separate identity for each network you use, and configure each identity to use the correct outgoing SMTP server for its associated network. When you make a dial-up or VPN network connection, set your email program to use the corresponding identity.

Monitoring and Ending a VPN or Dial-Up Connection

To check the status of a dial-up or VPN connection, click the network icon in the taskbar, right-click the connection name, and select View Network Status. This will display a dialog box showing the number of bytes sent and received.

To end a connection, click the network icon in the taskbar, click the connection name, and then click Disconnect. Poof! It's gone.

Advanced Routing for Remote Networks

As discussed previously, if you use dial-up or Virtual Private Networking to connect to a remote network with more than one subnet, you usually must let Windows set the default gateway to be the remote network. Otherwise, Windows won't know which network hosts must be reached through the VPN or dial-up connection and which should be reached through your Internet connection. Unfortunately, all your Internet traffic will travel through the tunnel, too, thus slowing you down. The remote network might not even permit outgoing Internet access.

The alternative is to disable the use of the default gateway and then manually add routes to all subnets known to belong to the private network.

To disable the default gateway, follow the steps under "Setting a VPN or Dial-Up Connection's Properties" in this chapter.

To add routes manually, you have to work in a Command Prompt window with elevated privileges. Type Windows Logo+X, or right-click in the very bottom-left corner of the screen, select Command Prompt (Admin), and then confirm the UAC prompt.

To add information about remote network subnets, use the route command, which looks like this:

route add *subnet* **mask** *netmask gateway*

The *subnet* and *netmask* arguments are the addresses for additional networks that can be reached through the gateway address *gateway*. To add a route, you must know the gateway address for the VPN as well as the IP address and mask information for each subnet on the remote network.

You must get the subnet information from the network administrator at the remote end. You can find the VPN gateway address from your own computer. Connect to the remote VPN and in the

Command Prompt window, type **ipconfig** and press Enter. One of the connections printed should be labeled PPP Adapter, SSTP Adapter, or L2TP Adapter. Note the gateway IP address listed. This address can be used as the gateway address to send packets destined for all subnets on the remote network. For example, if you're connected to a dial-up networking host through a connection named Client Net and you find the connection addresses

```
PPP adapter Client Net:
   IP Address. . . . . . . 192.168.5.226
   Subnet Mask . . . . . . 255.255.255.255
   Default Gateway . . . . 192.168.5.226
```

the gateway address is 192.168.5.226. Now, suppose you know that there are two additional subnets on the remote network: 192.168.10.0 mask 255.255.255.0 and 192.168.15.0 mask 255.255.255.0. You can reach these two networks by typing two route commands:

```
route add 192.168.10.0 mask 255.255.255.0 192.168.5.226
route add 192.168.15.0 mask 255.255.255.0 192.168.5.226
```

Each route command ends with the IP address of the remote gateway address (it's called the *next hop*).

Check your work by typing **route print** and looking at its output. In the IPv4 Route Table section, you should see only one destination labeled 0.0.0.0; if you see two, you forgot to disable the use of the default gateway on the remote network. Verify that the two routes you added are shown.

When you disconnect the VPN connection, Windows removes the added routes automatically.

To avoid having to type all this every time you connect, you can use another neat trick: create a batch file that will automatically establish the VPN or dial-up connection and then make the route changes. You'll need to find out from the remote network's administrator the real next-hop "gateway" address used for incoming dial-up or VPN connections. In the example we've been using, it might 192.168.5.1.

For the example, I would open Windows Notepad (one of the Accessories apps) and type the following:

```
@echo off
rasphone -d "VPN to Office"
route add 192.168.10.0 mask 255.255.255.0 192.168.5.1
route add 192.168.15.0 mask 255.255.255.0 192.168.5.1
```

Then I would save this to the Desktop with the name openvpn.bat. If you do this yourself, use your connection's actual name, rather than VPN to Office, and type your network's address information.

Now, to open the connection, right-click the openvpn icon and select Run As Administrator. This will establish the link and then run the route commands.

Incoming VPN and Dial-Up Access

Windows has a stripped-down Remote Access Server (RAS) built in, and you can use it to connect to your computer by modem, or through the Internet, from another location using any computer running Windows. After you're connected, you can access your computer's shared files and printers just as you can on your home or office network. To use this feature, your computer must have a modem and/or a dedicated, always-on Internet connection. At most, one remote user can connect at a time.

Setting up a modem to receive calls is straightforward: just connect your modem to a phone line, and you can dial in from anywhere. Setting up an incoming Internet (VPN) connection is substantially more difficult because you need an always-on Internet connection, whose external IP address you know and can reach from the Internet at large. We talk about ways to establish an Internet hostname using static addressing or dynamic DNS providers in Chapter 39, so we won't repeat that discussion here. Besides a discoverable IP address, you will also have to configure your Internet router or Windows Internet Connection sharing service to forward VPN data through the firewall to the computer you're going to set up to receive VPN connections. We'll discuss this in more detail shortly, under "Enabling Incoming VPN Connections with NAT." We will tell you right up front that very few hardware-connection sharing routers can be set up to forward VPN connections.

The process for enabling VPN access is the same as for enabling dial-in access. Let's walk through that process now.

Setting Up VPN and Dial-Up Access

To enable VPN or dial-up access, follow these steps:

1. Go to the desktop, right-click the network icon in the taskbar, and select Open Network and Sharing Center. (Alternatively, go to the desktop, open the charms, and select Settings, Control Panel, View Network Status and Tasks.) Then, click Change Adapter Settings.

2. If the standard menu bar (File, Edit, View, Tools, Advanced, Help) isn't displayed, press and release the Alt key. Then click File, New Incoming Connection and confirm the UAC prompt.

3. Select the user accounts that will be permitted to access your computer remotely. This step is very important: check only the names of those users to whom you really want and need to give access. The fewer accounts you enable, the less likely that someone might accidentally break into your computer.

> **🔍 note**
>
> Setting up your computer to receive Microsoft VPN connections is fairly complex, as you can see from the following instructions, and may not even be possible if you use an Internet Connection Sharing router. If you want to make VPN connections to your own computer or home network, you might want to check out Hamachi, an alternative "zero configuration" VPN system, available at www.logmeinhamachi.com.

> **🔍 note**
>
> Windows Firewall doesn't have to be told to permit incoming VPN connections, because it knows to let them in.

> **⚠ caution**
>
> Permitting remote access opens up security risks. Before you try to enable incoming access on a computer at work, be sure that your company permits it. In some companies, you could be fired for violating the security policies.

Note that if you have any users who have Microsoft accounts, they will appear in this list with usernames along the lines of brian_000. They will need to use these "local" names, and their Microsoft password, when they connect to your computer.

Under no circumstances should you check Guest, HomeGroupUser$, or a name that looks like IUSR_*xxx* or IWAM_*xxx*.

4. After selecting users, click Next. Then select the means that you will use for remote access. Check Through the Internet to enable incoming VPN connections, and/or Through a Dial-Up Modem to enable dial-up access. If you enable dial-up access, you must also select the modem that is to be used. Then click Next.

5. Windows displays a list of network protocols and services that will be made available to the dial-up connection. Select the Internet Protocol Version 4 (TCP/IP) entry and then click Properties. Select Specify an IP Address and then set the From value to **192.168.111.2** and the To value to **192.168.111.20**. Then, click OK.

6. Make sure that Internet Protocol Version 4 (TCP/IP) is checked and that Internet Protocol Version 6 (TCP/IP) is unchecked. Then click Allow Access. When the final window appears, click Close.

> **note**
>
> The Add Someone button lets you create a username and password that someone can use to connect remotely but not log on directly at the computer. A user added this way will only be able to use the network resources available to Everyone unless you explicitly grant this account access rights to the resources. You can only delete such an account using the Computer Management Local Users and Groups tool.

> **note**
>
> If you enable dial-up access, the selected modem will answer all incoming calls on its telephone line.

When the incoming connection information has been entered, a new Incoming Connection icon appears in your Network Connections window.

When someone connects to your computer, a second icon appears in the Network Connections folder showing their username, as shown in Figure 37.6. If necessary, you can right-click this to disconnect them.

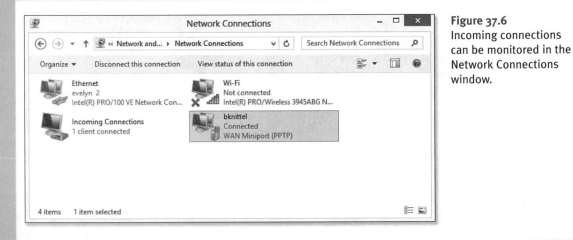

Figure 37.6
Incoming connections can be monitored in the Network Connections window.

Enabling Incoming VPN Connections with NAT

Microsoft's Internet Connection Sharing (ICS) and DSL/cable-sharing routers use an IP-addressing trick called Network Address Translation (NAT) to serve an entire LAN with only one public IP address. Thus, incoming connections, such as from a VPN client to a VPN host, have to be directed to a single host computer on the internal network.

If you use a shared Internet connection, only one computer can be designated as the recipient of incoming VPN connections. If you use Microsoft's ICS, that one computer must be the one sharing its connection. It will receive and properly handle VPN requests.

If you use a hardware-sharing router, the VPN server can be any computer you want to designate. Your router must be set up to forward the following packet types to the designated computer:

> TCP port 1723
> GRE (protocol 47—not the same as port 47!)

Unfortunately, most inexpensive commercial DSL/cable connection-sharing routers don't have a way to explicitly forward GRE packets. There are several ways around this:

- Some routers know about Microsoft's Point-to-Point Tunneling Protocol (PPTP) and you can specify the computer that is to receive incoming VPN connections.

   To learn more about forwarding network requests on a shared Internet connection, ***see*** *"Enabling Access with a Sharing Router," **p. 430**.*

- If the option doesn't work, someone might suggest that you designate the VPN computer as a DMZ host so that it receives *all* unrecognized incoming packets. This is a bad idea because that computer becomes vulnerable to hacker attacks. You would have to designate the computer's network location as Public to protect it, and this means it could not participate in sharing files or printers, which is what you wanted to do with the VPN to start with. Therefore, we don't recommend that you do this. If you do, you must at least configure your router to block Microsoft File Sharing packets on TCP and UDP ports 137 through 139 and port 445. A better idea follows.

- As an alternative to using Microsoft's VPN software, you can use a connection-sharing router that has the ability to receive incoming VPN connections; Linksys makes some. You have to use their routers at all of your locations, however. You might also investigate Hamachi at logmein.com. This is a software VPN solution.

Disabling Incoming Connections

To disable incoming dial-up connections so that your modem will not answer the phone whenever it rings, or to disable incoming VPN connections, follow these steps:

1. Right-click the network icon in the taskbar and select Open Network and Sharing Center. Then, click Change Adapter Settings.

2. To temporarily disable incoming connections, right-click the Incoming Connections icon and select Properties. Uncheck the modem entry and/or the Virtual Private Networking check box and then click OK.

3. To completely disable incoming connections, right-click the Incoming Connections icon and select Delete.

Offline Files

You might recognize the "Offline" problem: if you have a portable computer that you sometimes use with your office network, and sometimes use out in the field, you probably make copies of important "online" documents—documents stored on the network server—on your laptop. But, if you make changes to one of your "offline" copies, the network's copy will be out of date. Likewise, if someone updates the original on the network, your copy will be out of date. And, trying to remember where the originals came from and who has the most recent version of a given file is a painful job. I admit that more than once I've accidentally overwritten a file I'd worked on with an older copy—or worse, overwritten somebody else's work—because I wasn't paying attention to the files' date and time stamps.

Windows 8 has a solution to this housekeeping problem: Offline Files and the Sync Center. Here's how it works: when you use a network folder and tell Windows to make it available for offline use, Windows stashes away a copy (*caches*) of the folder's files somewhere on your hard drive, but all you see is the original network folder on your screen. When you disconnect, the shared file folder remains on your screen, with its files intact. You can still add, delete, and edit the files. For all intents and purposes, Windows makes it look like you're still connected to the network. Meanwhile, network users continue to work with the original, online copies. When you reconnect later, Windows will set everything right again thanks to a program called the Sync Center. Files you've modified will be copied to the network, and files others have modified will refresh old copies in your offline cache.

> **note**
>
> Offline Files is available only on Windows 8 Professional and Enterprise editions. The Sync Center is present on all Windows 8 versions, though, because it can also work with handheld devices such as PDAs and cell phones. If your version of Windows doesn't support Offline Files (or even if it does), you should know about Microsoft's Sync Toy tool, which is a free program you can download from Microsoft.com (search for **Synctoy**; you want version 2.0 or later). Sync Toy can do a pretty good job of copying new and updated files back and forth between a network location and a folder on your portable computer. It's not quite as seamless as Offline Files, but it can do just as good a job.

You'll find that the Offline Files system works really well, and is more powerful than it seems at first glance. The following are some of the potential applications:

- Maintaining an up-to-date copy of a set of shared files on both a server (or desktop computer) and a remote or portable computer. If you keep a project's files in a file folder marked for offline use, Windows keeps the copies up to date on all your computers.

- "Pushing" application software or data from a network to a portable computer. If software or data is kept in an offline file, your portable computer can update itself whenever you connect or dock to the LAN.

- Automatically backing up important files from your computer to an alternative location. Your computer can connect to a dial-up or network computer on a timer and refresh your offline files and folders automatically.

It's easy to make folders available offline, as you'll see in the next section.

Identifying Files and Folders for Offline Use

You can mark specific files, subfolders, or even entire shared folders from a "remote" server for offline use.

While you're connected to the remote network, view the desired items in File Explorer. If you've mapped a drive letter to the shared folder, you can select the mapped drive in the Computer section; otherwise, you can see it in the Network section.

When you find the mapped drive, file, folder, or folders you want to use while offline, select it (or them), right-click, and select Always Available Offline.

(You can also select a file or folder in File Explorer's *right* pane—that is, the contents window rather than the left pane tree listing—and use the ribbon's Easy Access button to select Always Available Offline. The ribbon only works on items you select in the right pane, not the left pane.)

Be cautious about marking entire shared drives or folders available offline, though, unless you're sure how much data they contain, and you're sure you want it all. You could end up with gigabytes of stuff you don't need. (Remember, all of this stuff will be copied to your own hard drive.)

 note

The server we're talking about might be in the next room, which isn't very "remote" at all, but that's what we'll call it for simplicity's sake. In this section, a "remote" server refers to some other computer that you access via networking.

note

Before you mark a folder for offline use, check to make sure you don't have any of its files open in Word, Excel, or so on. Open files can't be copied.

Can't Make File Available Offline

If Always Available Offline isn't displayed as an option when you right-click a file or folder, several things could be wrong. You must be using Windows 8 Pro or Enterprise—plain Windows 8 doesn't have this feature. Also, you can't enable Offline access by right-clicking an entry in the Favorites list in File Explorer. It's not available there. To make an entire shared folder available offline, open a remote computer's entry under Network and right-click the folder there, or map a drive letter to the shared folder and right-click the drive letter.

The feature might also be disabled. To check, go to the Start screen and search for **sync**. Select Settings, Sync Center, Manage Offline Files, and then view the General tab. If there is a button labeled Enable Offline Files, click it. Another cause could be that your network manager might have disabled Offline Files via group policy, in which case you're out of luck.

Files of This Type Cannot Be Made Available Offline

If you mark files or folders for offline use, you might receive the error "Files of This Type Cannot Be Made Available Offline." Some file types (for example, Microsoft Access MDB database files) usually should not be available offline because such files are generally used by multiple LAN users simultaneously, and there's no way to reconcile changes made by offline and online users. Your network manager might have designated one or more files as being unavailable for offline for this reason. Ask your network manager to check Group Policy entry `Computer Configuration\ Administrative Templates\ Network\ Offline Files\ Files not cached`.

The first time you mark a file or folder for offline use, Windows copies it (and all its contents) from the network location to a hidden folder on your hard drive. This may take a while if there is a lot to copy or if your network connection is slow. If any files cannot be copied, you can click the Sync Center link to see their names and the reasons for the problem.

When the file, folder, or folders have been copied, you will be able to use the network folders whether you're connected to the network or not.

Using Files While Offline

When you've marked a file, folder, or mapped network drive as Always Available Offline, a small green Sync Center icon appears on the topmost folder or file marked for offline use, as shown in Figure 37.7. If you select any item inside an offline folder, the text at the bottom of the File Explorer window shows the item's status.

When files or folders are marked for offline use, you can click Easy Access, Work Offline in the File Explorer ribbon bar to treat all offline files and folders as if you were disconnected from the network, even if you are still connected. This lets you make changes to these files locally, without actually changing the network copies. You can later sync them to the network.

Once files and folders are marked for offline use, when you disconnect from the network or use the Work Offline button, the marked files and folders will remain in the File Explorer display.

> **note**
>
> The most common reason a file can't be copied is that it is open and in use by an application. If this is the case for any of your files, close the application and perform another sync, as discussed later in this section. Another common problem is that `thumbs.db`, a hidden file Windows creates in folders that contain pictures, is sometimes in use by File Explorer and can't be copied. You can ignore problems with `thumbs.db`—right-click the file's name in the Sync Results window and select Ignore.

> **caution**
>
> If the files that you're copying from your network contain sensitive information, you may want to ask Windows to encrypt the copies stored on your computer. To see how to do this, skip ahead to "Managing and Encrypting Offline Files," later in this chapter.

Figure 37.7
When a folder or network drive is Always Available Offline, a Sync Center icon is displayed on the top-level folder, and the status bar shows the sync status of any item inside.

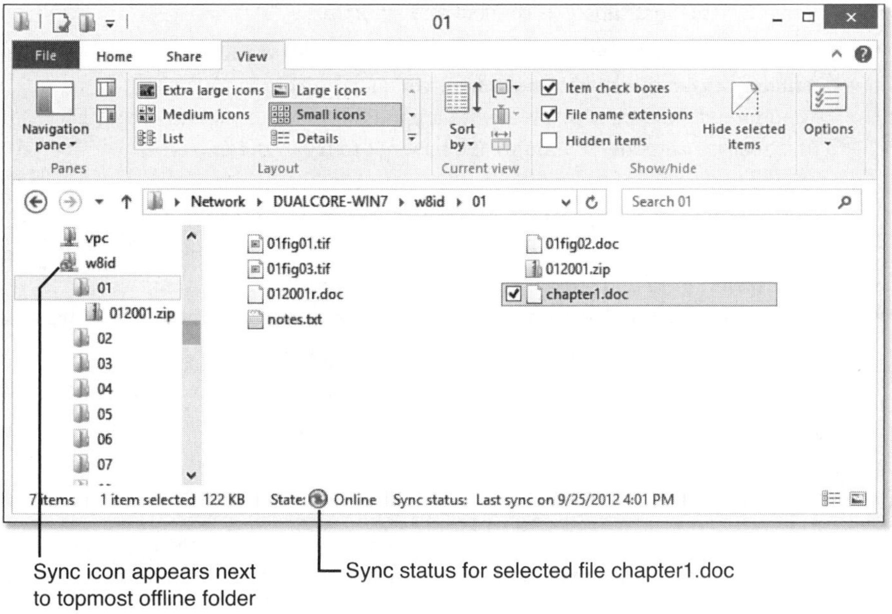

Sync icon appears next to topmost offline folder

Sync status for selected file chapter1.doc

 tip

If your network or VPN connection is unreliable, you may find that your applications sometimes hang when you're trying to save your work to a network folder. If this happens to you frequently, the Work Offline button is your new best friend. With it you can *force* Windows to use a local, cached copy of a document while you edit it, then sync it back up after you've saved your changes. Here's how to do it: locate a network folder in File Explorer. Mark it Always Available Offline. Open the folder and click the Work Offline button. Edit the file(s) you need to edit and then click Work Online. This should run the Sync Center and copy your changes back to the network.

While offline, you can add new files, delete files, or edit files in a folder that you marked Always Available Offline. If you had mapped a drive letter to the network folder, the drive letter still functions. Folders and/or files that were *not* marked Always Available Offline will disappear from the display when you disconnect from the network.

Offline Files Are Missing

If you can't find files or folders you know you clearly marked for offline use, you might not have synchronized after marking the file, its folder, or a containing folder for offline use. The solution is to go back online and synchronize. Then check the Sync Conflicts page to see if Windows says that it couldn't copy your file for some reason.

You can also rename files, and the network copy of the file will be renamed the next time you connect and sync up.

However, in most cases, you cannot rename a folder while it is offline. On some corporate networks, you may be able to rename "redirected" folders if your network administrator has enabled this feature. In general, though, it's best not to try to rename an offline folder while you're offline.

Overall the Offline Files system works very well. You can happily work away as if you were really still connected to the network. All network files and folders stay right where you're used to them being. The only difference is that your changes won't be visible to others on the network until you reconnect.

When you do reconnect, you should promptly synchronize your offline files and folders with the network folders so that both sets will be up to date.

> **📡 caution**
>
> If you delete a file from a network folder, while you are either offline *or* online, it will be deleted from your computer immediately and permanently. Files stored on a network are *not* saved in the Recycle Bin when you delete them!

Sync Center

You can synchronize files anytime you are connected to the network that contains the original shared folder, whether you connect by LAN, modem, or VPN. You can start a synchronization in any of several ways:

- At the Start screen, type **sync**, select Settings, select Sync Center, then click Sync All.

- In File Explorer, right-click a specific shared file or folder and select Sync, Sync Selected Offline Files.

- If you have a portable computer, click the Sync Settings button in the Windows Mobility Center and then click Sync All.

Synchronization can also occur automatically:

- When you reconnect to the network and Windows is idle.

- When you click Work Online in the folder view.

- When you log on and off.

- At specified times and days of the week. For a scheduled synchronization, Windows can even automatically make a dial-up connection.

The Sync Center has the job of reconciling changes made to the online and offline copies of the files.

Reconciling Changes

The Sync Center will automatically copy new or changed files from your computer to the network, and vice versa. However, three situations exist in which it will need some help:

- If both you and another user have changed the same file, you'll have to pick which version to keep.

- If you deleted a file while you were disconnected, you'll have to decide if you want to also delete the network's copy.

- If a network user deleted a file while you were disconnected, you'll have to confirm that you want to delete your copy.

If any problems occur while syncing files, the Sync Center icon in the notification area on your taskbar will display a yellow warning triangle. Double-click the Sync Center icon to display the Sync Center and then click View Sync Conflicts in the tasks list. This displays the Conflicts page, as shown in Figure 37.8.

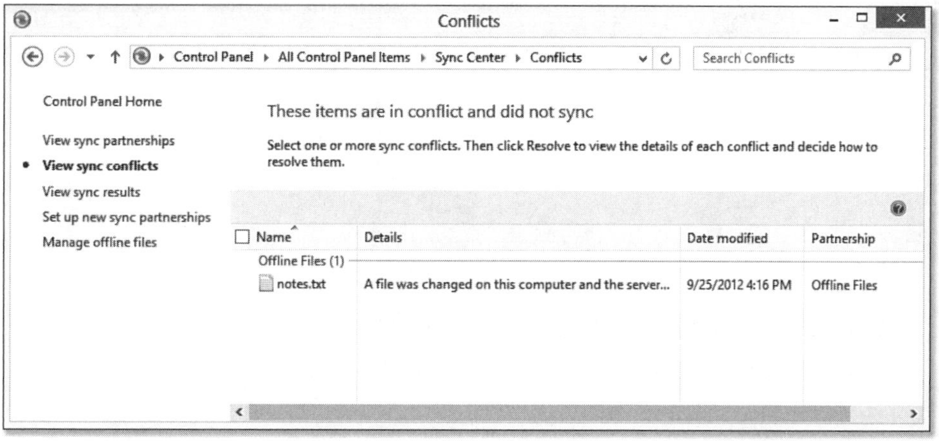

Figure 37.8
The Conflicts page lists files that cannot be reconciled without help.

Double-click the first listed file. This displays an explanation of why Sync Center can't update the file, and you see a selection of choices to resolve the issue. For example, if both you and a network user modified the same file while you were disconnected, the dialog box will look like the one shown in Figure 37.9.

> **caution**
> If the sync process fails because a file is in use, you should repeat the synchronization when no one is editing files in the shared folder; otherwise, you might lose changes to some files.

Continue through the conflict list to resolve each problem.

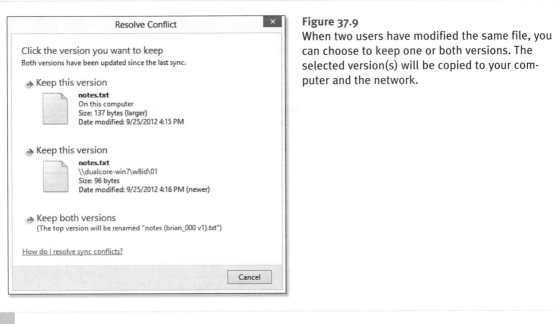

Figure 37.9
When two users have modified the same file, you can choose to keep one or both versions. The selected version(s) will be copied to your computer and the network.

Managing and Encrypting Offline Files

To manage the Offline Files feature, go to the Start screen and type **sync**. Select Settings, then Sync Center. In the left pane, click Manage Offline Files. There are four tabs in the Offline Files dialog box:

- **General**—Here you can enable or disable the Offline Files feature entirely. You can also see a list of all files that have been copied to your hard disk for offline use.

- **Disk Usage**—This tab lets you monitor or limit the amount of disk space used by offline file copies.

- **Encryption**—Here you can select to encrypt the network files that are stored on your hard disk. This makes them safe from theft should your computer fall into the wrong hands.

  ➡ *If you enable encryption and your computer is not joined to a corporate network, **see** "Backing Up Your Encryption Key," **p. 785**.*

- **Network**—If Windows detects that you have a slow network connection (dial-up, for instance), Windows can automatically elect to work with offline copies and will sync them up periodically while you continue to work.

Finally, remember that you can uncheck Always Available Offline on a file or folder anytime to remove it from the cached file list. This will delete the cached copies of the files in that folder.

Making Your Shared Folders Available for Offline Use by Others

When you've marked a network file for offline use, Windows makes a copy of the file on your hard disk. Windows can use your local copy of the file even while you're still connected to the network; this could really save time, for example, if you are running an application from a network folder. On the other hand, this would not be appropriate for files that change frequently or for database files that are used by multiple users concurrently.

Therefore, Windows has to know whether or not it's appropriate to serve up cached copies for online use, and it leaves the choice up to the person who *shares*, not uses, a given network folder. So, when you share a folder on your computer, you can specify the way Windows will make this folder available for offline use by others.

Normally, Windows will not give users a cached copy of a file if the network copy is available. It's useful to change this default setting if you are sharing a folder that has "read-only" documents that don't change often, or a folder that contains application programs. In this case, you may be able to give users faster access by following these steps:

1. Use File Explorer or Computer to locate the folder you're sharing. Right-click it and select Properties.

2. View the Sharing tab. Click the Advanced Sharing button. If Share This Folder is not checked, check it now.

3. Click the Caching button.

4. Select one of the following caching options:

   - **Only the files and programs that users specify are available offline**—Lets users make the choice of whether or not to make the folder contents available offline. This is the default setting.

   - **No files or programs from the share are available offline**—Prevents users from making the folder's contents available offline.

   - **All files and programs that users open from the share are automatically available offline**—Causes other computers to automatically make the contents of any file opened from the folder available for use offline. Furthermore, even while connected, if the user runs an application program from the network folder, their computer will use their cached copy for speedier performance. This is automatic for Windows 8, 7, and Vista computers. Check Optimize for Performance to let Windows XP computers do this as well.

5. Click OK to close the Offline Settings dialog box, and then click OK to close the Advanced Sharing dialog box.

The amount of disk space allocated to "automatically" available offline files is limited to an amount set on the Disk Usage tab in the Sync Center's Manage Offline Files dialog box.

Multiple LAN Connections

Most desktop computers sit where they are installed, gathering dust until they're obsolete (or in some cases, long afterwards—a neighbor recently asked if I had a Windows 95 repair disc). But portable computer users often carry their computers from office to office, docking or plugging in to several LANs. Although Windows makes it very easy for you to manage different dial-up and VPN connections, it's difficult to manage connections to different LANs if the network configuration settings are manually set.

IP settings are the difficult ones. If all of your networks are set up to use DHCP for automatic TCP/IP configuration, you won't encounter any problems; your computer will absorb the local information each time you connect.

If your TCP/IP settings are set manually, things aren't so simple. Microsoft has come up with a partial solution called Alternate Configuration. You can configure your computer for automatic IP address assignment on most networks and manual assignment on one. The way this works is that Windows looks for a DHCP server when it boots up, and if it doesn't find one it uses the Alternate Configuration. This can be a static IP address, or the default setting Automatic Private IP Address, whereby Windows chooses a random address in the 169.254 subnet.

This means that your computer can automatically adjust itself to multiple networks, at most one of which requires manual IP address settings.

To set up Alternate Configuration, open the Network and Sharing Center, select Change Adapter Settings, right-click your LAN connection icon (usually named Ethernet or Wireless), and select Properties. Double-click Internet Protocol Version 4 (TCP/IP). Be sure the General tab uses the Obtain an IP Address Automatically setting—if not, this discussion doesn't apply to your computer. View the Alternate Configuration tab and choose User Configured to enter the static LAN's information.

If you need to commute between multiple networks that require manual configuration, you'll have to change the General settings each time you connect to a different network. We suggest that you stick a 3-by-5-inch card with the settings for each network in your laptop carrying case for handy reference.

MEETINGS, CONFERENCING, AND COLLABORATION

Windows 8 Plays Well with Others

Today's computers are no longer seen as tools used in isolation. They've become portals through which people can communicate and work just as easily from across the globe as from across the room. Business users and students are increasingly relying on computers to make presentations and give reports (making them at least more colorful, if not more interesting).

In this chapter, we'll cover several Windows features that make it easier for you to work with others:

- When you use your laptop or tablet computer to display a business or class presentation, the Presentation Settings feature lets you tell Windows not to disrupt your presentation with messages, noises, or the screen saver.

- If you use a laptop computer, the External Display tool makes it easy to control an external monitor or a projector.

- If you need help with your computer, or if you want to demonstrate some computer task or application to others using their computer, Remote Assistance may be just what you need.

We'll start by looking at Windows 8's support for making presentations.

Making Presentations with a Mobile Computer

If you use a mobile (laptop or tablet) computer, Windows 8 has two features that make giving presentations smoother and easier. The features are Presentation Settings and External Display, part of the Windows Mobility Center discussed in Chapter 37, "Computing on the Road." External Display lets you manage an external monitor or a projector, and Presentation Settings keeps Windows from interrupting your presentation.

Adjusting Presentation Settings

One the more thoughtful features of Windows 8 Pro is the Presentation Settings section in Windows Mobility Center. When you indicate that you are making a presentation, Windows takes steps to keep itself out of your way. (This feature is part of Windows 8 Pro, but not plain Windows 8). Presentation Settings can make the following accommodations:

- Display a screen background chosen to minimize distraction or promote your company logo.

- Disable the screen saver, so that if you leave the computer alone for a few minutes, it doesn't treat the audience to an animated aquarium or a slide show that includes pictures of you dressed for a Halloween party in really bad drag.

- Disable pop-up notifications and reminders from Windows services.

- Set the speaker volume so that you aren't bothered by sounds associated with events such as mouse clicks, Window resizing, and the like.

- Disable automatic shutdown so that your computer won't go to sleep while you're talking. (There is unfortunately no corresponding setting for the audience.)

🔍 note

Presentation Settings and the Windows Mobility Center are available only if you are using a mobile (laptop or tablet) computer. However, there is a Registry hack you can use to enable it on a desktop computer: using the Registry editor (covered in Chapter 29, "Editing the Windows Registry"), select the key HKEY_CURRENT_USER\Software\ Microsoft and create the key MobilePC. Select this new key, create the key AdaptableSettings, and within that create a DWORD value named SkipBatteryCheck with a value of 1. Then, select the key MobilePC again. Create another new key named MobilityCenter, and within it a DWORD value named RunOnDesktop with a value of 1. Once that's done, to open the Mobility Center, press Windows Logo+R, type **mblctr**, and press Enter. This can get tiresome, so you may want to pin it to your taskbar.

To tell Windows how to behave when you're making a presentation, bring up the Windows Mobility Center, using these steps:

1. If you have a keyboard, type Windows Logo+X and select Mobility Center.

   If you don't have a keyboard, go to the Start screen, open the Search charm, type **mobil**, select Settings, and then select Windows Mobility Center. (You can also get to the Mobility Center through the Control Panel under Hardware and Sound, but it's a more cumbersome process.) You might want to pin it to your taskbar.

2. In the Presentation Settings tile, click the small icon that looks like a video projector. The Presentation Settings dialog box appears, as shown in Figure 38.1.

Figure 38.1
Presentation Settings lets you tell Windows how you want it to appear during a presentation.

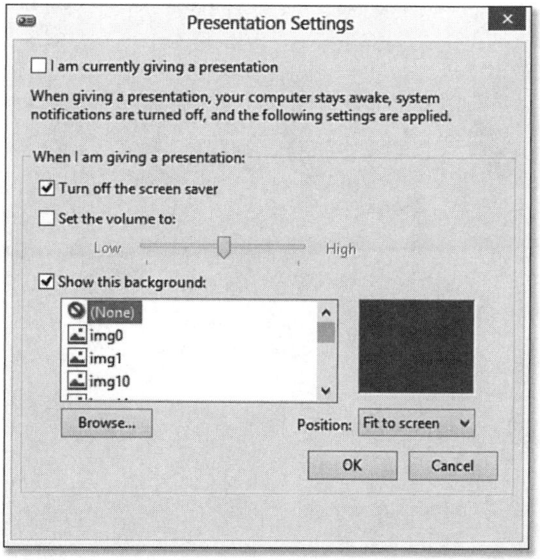

3. Set the check boxes next to the desired accommodations, and preselect the sound volume and set a desktop background if desired. Save your presentation Settings Preferences by clicking OK.

Whenever you are making a presentation, bring up the Windows Mobility Center by following steps 1 and 2 again. Then, in the Presentation Settings tile, click Turn On. You can use the other tiles to adjust the volume and display.

You can later change the presentation options, if need be, by clicking the small icon in the Presentation Settings tile again.

tip

If you used the Windows Logo+X keyboard shortcut in Windows 7 or Vista, you'll find that this shortcut now brings up a list of administrative tools. Mobility Center is in there; just click it. If you make a lot of presentations, you can pin the Mobility Center to the taskbar. Bring it up, right-click its icon in the taskbar, and select Pin to Taskbar.

Controlling An External Display

The External Display tile on the Windows Mobility Center lets you control what appears on any connected external display or monitor attached to your laptop or tablet computer.

To start, attach your external monitor or projector, or connect to a network-attached projector as described in the next section. Then, take one of the following actions:

- Press Windows Logo+P to bring up the External Display tile, shown in Figure 38.2.

- On the Start screen, display Charms, select Devices, and select Second Screen.

- If you have the Windows Mobility Center open, as discussed in the previous section, click the Connect Display or Disconnect Display button in the External Display tile.

The External Display tile lets you choose how to use the added screen real estate.

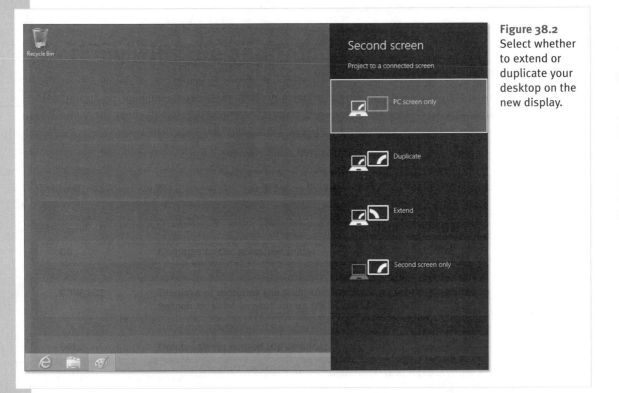

Figure 38.2
Select whether to extend or duplicate your desktop on the new display.

Then select one of the four display options:

- **PC Screen Only**—The external display will be blacked out.

- **Duplicate**—The same display will appear on both monitors. Use this setting if you need to see your own presentation and can't see the external display.

- **Extend**—The Windows desktop will be spread across both displays. You could put your notes on one display and a program for the audience on the other. I tried this once for a presentation and found it awkward; it was like trying to pat my head and rub my belly at the same time. Maybe that was just me.

- **Second Screen Only**—The computer's internal display will be shut off and only the attached display will be used.

note

If you select the Duplicate option, your screen's resolution might be reduced. Windows will use the highest reasonable screen resolution supported by both monitors. If both displays don't have the same shape, the external display might look pinched or stretched. If this happens, right-click the desktop, select Screen Resolution, click in the Resolution box, and adjust the resolution slider that appears to find a more acceptable setting. Click Apply after making each adjustment. You'll have to find a compromise because you can't select different resolutions for the two monitors when the Duplicate setting is in effect.

Later, when you disconnect the external display, Windows should automatically reset your laptop's screen resolution to its original setting. If it doesn't, follow the preceding instructions and move the Resolution slider to the laptop display's native resolution—usually the topmost position.

Click one of the icons or press Enter to save the setting. You can press Windows Logo+P to change it back later.

 To learn about Windows 8's other accessories for mobile computers, ***see*** *"Windows Mobility Center,"* ***p. 862***.

 For more information about managing external displays, ***see*** *"Running Windows 8 with Multiple Monitors,"* ***p. 673***.

Connecting to Network Projectors

Windows 8 includes support for connecting to video projectors that are reached over a network, rather than requiring them to be attached directly to your computer. You might find a network-attached projector in a corporate conference room.

To use a network-attached projector, follow these steps:

1. Go to the Start screen, and if you don't have a keyboard, open the Search charm. Type **project**.

   If Connect to a Network Projector does not appear under Apps, change your search term from **project** to **features**, select the Settings section, and select Turn Windows Features On and Off. Check Network Projection, click OK, and then search for **project** again.

2. Select Connect to a Network Projector.

3. If Windows asks for permission to allow the network projector to communicate through Windows Firewall, click Yes. You might need to confirm a User Account Control (UAC) prompt.

4. Click Search for a Projector. If the projector appears in the list of available devices, select its name and click Connect. If the projector can't be found, click the Back button (the left arrow in the upper-left corner of the window) and then click Enter the Projector Address. Type in the projector's network path, as provided by the network administrator. Enter the projector's password, if a password is required. Then click Connect.

Next, follow any additional prompts to direct your presentation output to the connected projector. You can press Windows Logo+P to change the way your laptop and the external display are configured, as discussed in the previous section.

Remote Assistance

Remote Assistance lets two people work collaboratively on one Windows computer—one at the computer and one remotely, over the Internet. Remote Assistance is designed to let a person get technical assistance from someone else at a remote location. It's not so much a "let's all work together" tool as a "let me help you with this" tool. Some computer manufacturers advertise that they'll use Remote Assistance to help you with your computer after you purchase it, although, to be honest, most companies are switching to one of the online services listed in Chapter 39, "Remote Desktop and Remote Access," under "Third-Party Remote Control Tools," and you may well want to give them a try yourself. At the end of this chapter, we also discuss some programs that you can use to connect three or more people.

Remote Assistance is based on the same technology as the Remote Desktop feature we discuss in Chapter 39. There are similarities and significant differences between the two:

- Remote Assistance is available on all versions of Windows 8, 7, Vista, and XP, whereas Remote Desktop is available only on the higher-end Windows versions: Windows 8 Pro and Enterprise, Windows 7 Professional, Enterprise, and Ultimate, Windows Vista Business, Enterprise, and Ultimate, and Windows XP Professional.

- With Remote Assistance, both the local and remote users see the same screen at the same time, and both can move the mouse, type on the keyboard, and so forth. With Remote Desktop, when a remote user is working, the computer's monitor can only display the Welcome screen.

- Remote Assistance doesn't make the local computer's hard drives available, nor does it transmit sound, as Remote Desktop does.

- Remote Assistance connections can't be made *ad lib*. One Windows user must invite another through email or Windows [Live] Messenger. Alternatively, one user can offer assistance to another using Messenger. In any case, the procedure requires the simultaneous cooperation of users at both ends of the connection.

- Remote Assistance allows you to use a text chat window or voice chat while the desktop session is active.

A big plus with Remote Assistance on Windows 8, 7, and Vista is that it should work even if you are using a shared Internet connection. This is a big improvement over Remote Assistance on Windows XP, which rarely worked over a shared connection. The reason is that Remote Assistance can now use Internet Protocol Version 6 and Teredo tunneling to correctly pass data through Internet Connection Sharing routers and firewalls.

> **note**
>
> To take advantage of the new, more reliable connection method, both you and the person who is helping you—or the person you are helping—must be using Windows 8, 7, or Vista, *and* you must change a setting, as described in the next section. Any user running Windows Vista must have Vista Service Pack 1 installed, or any later service pack.

Enabling Remote Assistance

Remote Assistance is usually enabled by default when you install Windows, but before you try to use it to get help, you should confirm that it is enabled. Furthermore, if you want to use the new, more reliable connection method to work with another Windows 8, 7, or Vista user, you must change a setting by following these steps:

1. Go to the Start screen, and if you don't have a keyboard, open the Search charm. Type **remote**. Select Settings at the right and then select Allow Remote Access to Your Computer.

2. If a UAC prompt appears, enter an Administrator account and password, as requested.

3. This brings up the System Properties dialog box. In the Remote tab, check to be sure that Allow Remote Assistance Connections to This Computer is checked. If it isn't, check it.

4. Click the Advanced button.

5. If you use an Internet connection sharing router, check Create Invitations That Can Only Be Used from Computers Running Windows Vista or Later. You will only be able to invite other Windows 8, 7, or Vista users to help you, not XP users, but at least it will work.

   If you uncheck Allow This Computer to Be Controlled Remotely, people you invite to connect will be able to view but not control your screen.

6. Click OK to save your changes.

Requesting Remote Assistance

To invite a friend or colleague to work with you on your computer, you both must have a working Internet connection. First, contact your friend and confirm that she is ready to work with you.

Then, follow these steps:

1. If the other person is using Windows 8 or 7, skip to step 2.

   If the other person is using Windows Vista, use the instructions in the previous section to check the box labeled Create Invitations That Can Only Be Used from Computers Running Windows Vista or Later.

   If your friend is using Windows XP, use the instructions in the previous section to *uncheck* the box labeled Create Invitations That Can Only Be Used from Computers Running Windows Vista or Later. However, if you are using an Internet Connection Sharing router, or if you are on a business network that uses a firewall, the odds of your friend's computer being able to connect to yours are fairly slim. You're better off trying one of the third-party tools mentioned in Chapter 39 under "Third-Party Remote Control Tools," or at the end of this chapter.

2. Go to the Start screen, and if you don't have a keyboard, open the Search charm. Type in **help**, at the right select Settings, and then select Invite Someone to Connect to Help You or Offer to Help Someone Else (the icon you want says all that). Then, click Invite Someone You Trust to Help You.

3. Windows needs to send an "invitation" to your friend. Use one of these methods:

- If you have previously worked with this friend, her name might be listed and you can click the name to repeat the previous invitation.

- If the other person is using Windows 8 or 7, click Use Easy Connect.

- If you chat with your friend using Windows Live Messenger, start a chat session with your friend and click Actions, Request Remote Assistance. When she accepts your request, Windows will pop up a password, as described in step 4. You can give her this password over the phone or through the Chat window. Your friend should type the password using upper-case letters.

- If you have an email application installed in your computer, select Use Email to Send an Invitation.

- Otherwise, if you use a web-based email program, select Save This Invitation As a File. Choose a location to save the invitation file, and make note of it. You'll have to send this file as an email attachment later on, or get the file to your friend some other way.

> **note**
>
> If your friend uses Windows Vista or XP, tell her to be sure to type the password in uppercase.

4. Windows will display a password composed of 12 letters and digits. The password is shown with three groups of letters shaded in different colors to make it easier to read; the shading isn't important. Write the password down and give it to the person who you are inviting to help, by phone text message, email, or whatever means you have available.

5. If you selected Use Easy Connect, just wait for your friend to start up Remote Assistance (using the steps in the next section) and type in the password you gave to her.

(If your friend's computer initially says that Easy Connect is not available, have her click Cancel and try again. I've seen it take two tries.)

If you selected Use Email to Send an Invitation, your default email program will pop up with an email ready to address and send. Enter your friend's email address and send the email. The important part is the attachment, which is a file named something along the lines of `Invitation.MsRcIncident`. Don't delete the attachment!

If you selected Save This Invitation as a File, use your web-based email system to send the invitation file you created in step 4 to your friend as an attachment. The file has a name along the lines of `Invitation.MsRcIncident`. Alternatively, get the invitation file to your friend by other means, such as a flash drive or a network folder.

> **note**
>
> If you use a dial-up Internet connection or a DSL service that requires you to sign on, your Internet IP address changes every time you connect. The Remote Assistance invitation uses this address to tell the other person's computer how to contact you, so it will work only if you stay connected from the time you send the invitation to the time your friend responds. If you have a fixed (static) IP address, this won't be a problem.

6. Windows will display a window that says "Waiting for an Incoming Connection." Leave this window alone until your friend receives the invitation and responds.

If you sent the request by email, it could be some time before the other party receives and reads it.

When your friend responds to your request for assistance, a dialog box will appear on your screen, asking if it's okay for her to connect. Click Yes, and after a short while—perhaps a minute or so—a window will appear with which you can control the Remote Assistance session, as shown in Figure 38.3.

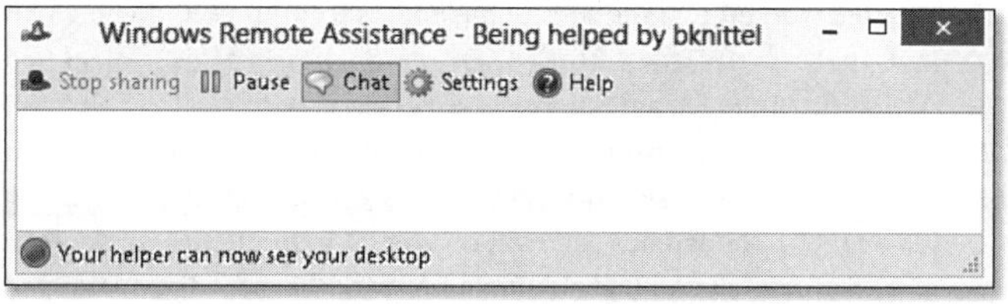

Figure 38.3
When your "remote assistant" has connected, use this window to chat and control the connection.

At this point, your friend can see your screen and can watch what you do with it, but she can't actually do anything with your computer. She first has to ask to take control, and you have to consent. Then, either of you can type, move the mouse, and otherwise poke around and use your computer.

When a friend asks to take control of your computer, a request will pop up on your screen. If she's just going to work with normal Windows applications such as Word, just click Yes to let her take control. However, if she needs to manage Windows itself, you have to decide who is going to handle the UAC prompts that might appear. By default, your friend won't be able to see or respond to them. You have two options:

- If you want to respond to all UAC prompts yourself, just click Yes to let her connect. If she performs an action that requires security confirmation, her screen will go black for a moment, and you'll have to respond to the UAC prompt.

- If you want to let her change Windows settings without your intervention, check Allow *Username* to Respond to User Account Control Prompts, then click Yes. You will be asked to confirm a UAC prompt yourself at this point.

🔍 **note**

If you don't completely trust the person who's helping you, make this setting change right away: click Settings, check Use ESC Key to Stop Sharing Control, and then click OK. This way, after you've given the person control, if you don't like what they're doing, you can press the Esc key, and they'll immediately be locked out. Unfortunately, if they press Esc while they're working, the same thing will happen, so you'll have to grant them access again. This can get irritating, but it does let you control what they're doing.

> **note**
>
> If you don't have Administrator privileges on your computer, you won't be able to give your friend permission to perform administrative actions that require a UAC confirmation, either. There are two ways to work around this.
>
> If your friend knows an Administrator password and will tell you what it is, check Allow *Username* to Respond to User Account Control Prompts and click Yes. When the prompt appears, select the account and enter the password she gave you.
>
> The second workaround requires some advance setup before you use Remote Assistance, and an Administrator has to do it. Here are the steps: at the Start screen, type **policy**. Select Settings at the right; then in Settings, select Edit Group Policy. Under Local Computer Policy, browse into Computer Configuration, Windows Settings, Security Settings, Local Policies, Security Options. In the right pane, open User Account Control: Allow UIAccess Applications to Prompt for Elevation Without Using the Secure Desktop and select Enabled. Click OK and then restart Windows. With this option enabled, the remote user will be able to respond to UAC prompts even if the logged-on user doesn't know an Administrator password. (On a domain network this setting can be made through Group Policy.)

Now your friend should be able to work your keyboard and mouse, and help you.

The Windows Remote Assistance toolbar has a few other features that you will find useful:

- If you want a moment of privacy, perhaps to read email or look at a sensitive file, click Pause. This will black out the other person's view of your screen without disconnecting that person. Click Continue to restore the view.

- To communicate with your friend via text messaging, click Chat. The Remote Assistance toolbar will enlarge. Type your comments into the lower box on the window and press Enter (or click Send), and your friend will see what you type. You'll see your friend's responses in the upper part of the window. Click the Chat button again to shrink the toolbar back to its original size.

- To take control away from your friend, click Stop Sharing. Your friend will still be able to see your screen, but can only watch. She has to request control again to do anything.

When you're finished, click Disconnect to end the Remote Assistance session.

Responding to an Assistance Request

A friend, colleague, or customer can invite you to provide Remote Assistance in one of several ways: using Easy Connect, Windows Live Messenger, or an invitation email or file. Use one of the following procedures to respond to their request.

Responding with Easy Connect

If both you and your friend are using Windows 8 or 7 (or perhaps some future version), you can use Easy Connect. Your friend will use Easy Connect to invite you. To respond, follow these steps:

1. Go to the Start screen, and if you don't have a keyboard, open the Search charm. Type in **help**, at the right select Settings, and then select Invite Someone to Connect to Help You or Offer to Help Someone Else. Then, click Help Someone Who Has Invited You.

If you have helped this person previously, his name might be listed, and you can simply click it to accept the new invitation.

2. Select Help Someone Who Has Invited You. Then select Use Easy Connect.

3. Type in the password your friend gave you. It consists of 12 letters and numbers and is not case sensitive (upper- and lowercase don't matter). Then, press Enter.

When the connection is established, skip ahead to "Working with Remote Assistance."

Responding Through Windows Live Messenger

If you and your friend are both chatting with Windows Live Messenger, your friend's invitation will appear in a pop-up window. Just click Accept to begin the connection, follow the instructions, and skip ahead to "Working with Remote Assistance."

Responding to an Invitation Email or File

Your friend might send you an email with an attachment containing an invitation file named something like `Invitation.MsRcIncident`. Alternatively, he might send you the file through a network or a portable drive.

To accept an email invitation, open the message's attachment. (How you do that depends on your email program. If you use web-based email, you might have to download the attachment separately.) Opening the attachment should activate the Remote Assistance connection. If you receive the invitation as a file, just double-click the file's icon.

You will be asked to enter the password associated with the invitation. The person who invited you will have to tell you what it is.

> **note**
>
> If your friend is using Windows Vista or XP, you must type the password exactly as he did—that is, upper- and lowercase matter. If he is using Windows 8 or 7, the password consists of 12 letters and numbers. Upper- and lowercase don't matter.

Working with Remote Assistance

After you've responded to the assistance invitation, it can take more than a minute for the required software to load and for the other user's desktop to appear on your screen, as shown in Figure 38.4.

Across the top is a menu of controls. The choices are as follows:

- **Request Control**—Click to begin using the other computer's mouse and keyboard. The remote user will have to grant permission. After you have control of the other computer, both of you can use your mouse and keyboard.

> **note**
>
> If Windows is unable to establish a connection to the person who invited you, ask him what operating system he's using. If it's XP and it doesn't work the first time, the chances that it's ever going to work are slim. If he's using Windows 8 or 7, ask him to check the box labeled Create Invitations That Can Only Be Used from Computers Running Windows 7 or Later, as described in the "Enabling Remote Assistance" section, earlier in this chapter. Then have him send you a new invitation.

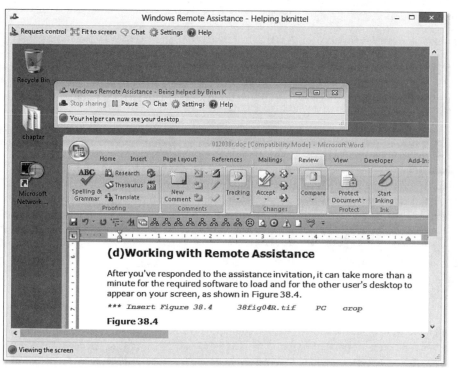

Figure 38.4

Figure 38.4
The Remote
Assistance screen
has a control
panel at the
top and a view
of the remote
user's screen
underneath. Click
Request Control
if you want to
manipulate the
remote computer.

- **Actual Size**—Click to make the size of the Remote Assistance window exactly match the other person's screen. You might have to scroll around to see all of his desktop. This choice alternates with Fit to Screen.

- **Fit to Screen**—Click to shrink the view of the other computer's screen so that it fits perfectly in your Remote Assistance window. You won't have to use the scrollbars to see the far corners anymore, but the text might be tiny. Maximize your Remote Assistance window to improve the display.

- **Chat**—Click to open a text chat panel in the left side of the Remote Assistance window. Type your messages into the small box at the bottom of the Chat area.

- **Settings**—Click to turn off the recording of the remote session that Windows makes by default.

- **Help**—Click to display online help for Remote Assistance.

If your friend clicks the Stop Sharing button, you'll lose control of the remote screen. Just click Request Control again to ask for permission to resume working.

Using Third-Party Tools

If you want to help someone remotely, Remote Assistance is great tool, and it's preinstalled with Windows, but it sometimes refuses to work. Luckily, several third-party tools are as good as or better than Remote Assistance (and Remote Desktop), and most of them work even when Remote Assistance and Remote Desktop won't. We talk more about these tools in Chapter 39 in the section "Third-Party Remote Control Tools," and at the end of this chapter, so we won't repeat those discussions here. I'll just mention that the free version of LogMeIn (http://secure.logmein.com) has saved the day for many of my friends and clients.

You might also try one of the online meeting tools described in the next section. They're typically designed to let a group of people work together on a common project, but most of them could also let two people work together to solve a problem with Windows.

Online Meeting Tools

When groups of people work together on a common project in diverse locations, having a shared, common computer screen can be a great tool. One person makes a change, say, in a Word file or a PowerPoint presentation, and everyone sees the results in real time.

Remote Assistance, described in the previous section, is a fine tool for this when just two people want to collaborate—if it works. And whereas previous versions of Windows included NetMeeting and Windows Meeting Space, collaboration tools that were designed to let *more* than two people work together, Microsoft has retired these programs and they're no longer available. Microsoft SharedView, formerly available for download, has also been removed from service.

Therefore, for alternative collaboration tools, you'll need to look to other vendors. In the section "Third-Party Remote Control Tools" of Chapter 39, we discuss alternate remote control programs that can let *two* people work together. Table 38.1 lists additional tools that you can use when you want to connect three or more people. Several of them offer a free trial, discounts for annual subscriptions, and meeting access on Macs, iOS, and Android devices.

Table 38.1   Third-Party Collaboration Tools

Program and URL	Comments
Adobe Connect www.adobe.com/products/adobeconnect	$55/month for up to 25 participants. Can include videoconferencing.
Central Desktop www.centraldesktop.com	$99/month and up. Includes file sharing and other services.
Cisco WebEx MeetMe Center www.webex.com	Free for up to three participants, $24/month for up to eight, and up from there. Optional voice conferencing by telephone.
GoToMeeting www.gotomeeting.com	From the GoToMyPC people. $49/month for up to 25 participants.

Table 38.1   Continued

Program and URL	Comments
Join.me join.me	From the LogMeIn people. Free for one "presenter." Paid subscription required to share control.
Mikogo www.mikogo.com	$13/month for up to three participants, and up from there.
TeamViewer www.teamviewer.com	Free for personal use. One-time purchase for business licenses.
Vyew www.vyew.com	Free version has advertising and allows up to 20 participants. You can pay to increase participants and reduce the amount of advertising.
Yugma www.yugma.com	Free version "broadcasts" your desktop; $10/month and up for versions that share keyboard and mouse control.

More such tools are appearing all the time, so you might want to supplement this list with some Google searching. You might search the Store app too.

REMOTE DESKTOP AND REMOTE ACCESS

Using Your Computer Remotely

With today's global availability of the Internet, you expect to be able to access the websites that hold your email and data from anywhere, anytime. You can store documents in the cloud for global access. But what about stuff that you didn't remember to—or don't want to—store "out there"? Why can't you have the same global access to your own private data on your computer at home? Well, as it turns out, you can, through features that are built into Windows, and also through some third-party products. We describe these in this chapter.

If your computer runs Windows 8 Pro or Enterprise edition, your computer has a spiffy feature called Remote Desktop that lets it accept connections from another computer. When you travel, you can see your home computer's screen, move its mouse and type on its keyboard, open files, and even print, just as if you were really sitting in front of it. The neat part is that you can do this from any computer that runs Windows or Mac OS X, and even iOS and Android devices.

If you have the basic version of Windows 8, you can still get remote access to your computer using a third-party program such as logmein, which we discuss at the end of the chapter.

Whatever program you use, Figure 39.1 shows how it works. Your keystrokes, mouse, and touch movements get sent from one computer to your own computer, wherever it is. The remote computer's display, sound, and print output travel back to you and appear on the local computer.

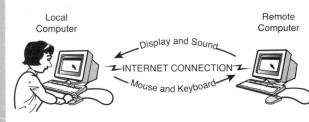

Local Computer

Remote Computer

Display and Sound

INTERNET CONNECTION

Mouse and Keyboard

Figure 39.1
You can use any computer running Windows or Macintosh OS X to connect to and control your computer.

This is just what you need when you're out of town and need to read a file you left on the computer back home, or if you want to read your office email from home. I've been using this feature since it first appeared in Windows XP Professional, and I love it.

You also can use the Remote Desktop Client program to attach to computers running Windows Server to access applications or for administration and maintenance. The *client* part of Remote Desktop, which lets you connect *to* other computers, runs on any version of Windows.

The Remote Desktop *service*, which lets a computer be controlled *by* a remote connection, is available only on some Windows versions:

- Windows 8 Pro and Enterprise

- Windows 7 Professional, Ultimate, and Enterprise

- Windows Vista Professional, Ultimate, and Enterprise

- Windows XP Professional

- All versions of Windows Server since Windows 2000 Server

> **note**
> You don't have to be miles away to take advantage of Remote Desktop, either. You can also use it to access other computers in your home or office, using your local area network (LAN). For instance, you can use it to start a lengthy computing or printing job on someone else's computer without leaving your own desk.

If you have plain Windows 8, or one of the earlier "Home" editions, you can't set your computer up to accept Remote Desktop connections. However, you can still use one of the options discussed later in this chapter in the "Third-Party Remote Control Tools" section.

In fact, even if your computer does have Remote Desktop capability, you may want to check out the third-party tools. We recommend reading about both options before you decide to use one or the other. Here are the tradeoffs:

- Remote Desktop can be considerably harder to set up than the third-party programs if you want access through the Internet.

- There is better support for the third-party programs on iOS and Android devices than for Remote Desktop.

- Remote Desktop won't let you collaborate with or assist someone who's sitting at the remote computer, because it blanks out the remote screen while you're connected from afar. (You would instead have to use Remote Assistance, discussed in Chapter 38, "Meetings, Conferencing, and Collaboration," for that.) Third-party tools *will* let you work with someone who's at the remote computer.

- Remote Desktop may offer better security. The third-party options that provide access over the Internet all open a data connection between your computer and the host company's servers. They keep a "pipeline" open into your computer from their facilities at all times. You have to trust that they'll never get hacked themselves; otherwise, criminals could conceivably snoop into your computer from their facilities. (On the other hand, third-party vendors will block access to someone who's trying to guess passwords. Remote Desktop will happily let someone test passwords all day.)

- Remote Desktop works well between computers on a home or office LAN, and on a LAN that isn't connected to the Internet. Most of the third-party products require Internet access, so they won't work on a disconnected LAN.

- Remote Desktop automatically transmits sound and lets you print from the home (host) computer to your remote location. Third-party programs don't all do this, at least in their free versions.

You'll have to decide for yourself whether you're more concerned about convenience or privacy. Over the past few years, I've switched from Remote Desktop to a third-party program for remote access to my own personal computer, but I still use only Remote Desktop for business networks.

This chapter consists of three sections. The first part shows you how to set up your computer so that you can access it remotely. The second part shows you how to connect to another computer using the Remote Desktop Client. The third part discusses third-party alternatives.

By the way, Remote Desktop is a scaled-down version of Windows Terminal Services, a component of the Windows Server versions that lets multiple users run programs on one central server. By "scaled down," we mean that only one person is allowed to connect to a Windows 8 computer at a time, either remotely or with the regular monitor and keyboard. So if you connect remotely, a local user is temporarily kicked out to the Welcome screen. And if a user logs on at the home computer while you're connected remotely, *you'll* be disconnected. You won't lose your work—you can reconnect later and pick up where you left off—but the bottom line is that only one person at a time is allowed to use a Windows 8 computer.

Setting Up Access to Your Own Computer

This first section tells you how to set up remote access into your own computer.

If you want to use the Remote Desktop Connection client to access *another* computer, skip ahead to "Connecting to Other Computers with Remote Desktop," later in this chapter.

As mentioned previously, incoming Remote Desktop connections are only available on Windows 8 Pro and Enterprise (corporate) versions. If you want to set up remote access into your computer but it runs plain vanilla Windows 8, see the last section in this chapter, which discusses third-party options.

Across a LAN (that is, between computers in your home or office), Remote Desktop works right "out of the box"—you just have to enable the feature. However, if you want to use Remote Desktop to reach your computer over the Internet, you have to set up several other things in advance. The procedure might sound complex as you read it, but it really isn't that bad. Just go through the process step by step. You can go about this in other ways, of course, but what we give you here is a procedure that's suitable for a home or small office user with Windows 8 Pro.

Again, there are web-based programs that do much the same thing as Remote Desktop. Several of them are free, and most of them require very little setup work—in particular, they completely bypass the networking issues we'll discuss shortly. If the instructions in this section sound too difficult, or if the setup doesn't work for you, check out the section "Third-Party Remote Control Tools" at the end of the chapter.

Enabling Remote Desktop Access to Your Computer

To be sure that incoming Remote Desktop connections are enabled on your computer, follow these steps:

1. At the Start screen, type **remote**, select Settings at the right, and then select Allow Remote Access to Your Computer.

   Alternatively, right-click the very bottom-left corner of the screen, select System, and select Remote Settings. Or, just type **sysdm.cpl** at a Command Prompt and then select the Remote tab.

2. In the bottom half of the dialog box, select Allow Remote Connections to This Computer, and uncheck Allow Connections Only from...Recommended. (The "more secure" version works only on corporate networks using IPSec security and doesn't work for home/small office users.)

3. By default, all Administrator-level accounts will be allowed to connect to the computer. If you want to grant Remote Desktop access to any Standard users, click Select Users, Add, Advanced, Find Now, and then locate the desired name in the Search Results section. Double-click the name. To add another name, click Advanced and Find Now again.

4. Click OK to close all the dialog boxes.

> **note**
>
> A password *must* be set on a user's account before that user can connect to the computer using Remote Desktop. Users without passwords will not be allowed to log in remotely even if they appear in the list of permitted users.

If your computer is set to go to sleep when it sits unused for a while, and you want the computer to be available for incoming connections at all times, you'll have to disable automatic sleep. To do this, go to the Start screen. Type **sleep**, select Settings at the right, and select Change When the Computer Sleeps. If Put the Computer to Sleep is one of the options, select Never. Then click Save Changes.

Now, confirm that Remote Desktop connections are correctly set up to be allowed through the Windows Firewall. At the Start screen, type **firewall**. Select Settings at the right, and select Allow an App Through Windows Firewall. Scroll down the list of Allowed Apps and Features and locate Remote Desktop. Be sure it's checked under both Private and Public. If it isn't, click Change Settings and then check the boxes. Click OK.

If you just want to use Remote Desktop within your home or office network, you're finished, and can skip ahead to the "Connecting to Other Computers with Remote Desktop" section. However, if you want to reach your computer through the Internet, you have more work to do.

Establishing 24×7 Access

Because you won't be there at your home or office to turn on your computer and establish an Internet connection, you have to set things up so that your computer and connection are always working.

First, you need to be sure that your computer will turn itself back on if the power goes out while you're not there. You do this from the computer's BIOS setup screen. Restart Windows and wait for the screen to go black. Press the BIOS setup hotkey. The screen should tell you what to press; it's usually the Delete or F2 key. Then, look for the Power Management settings. Find an entry titled AC Power Recovery, or something similar. Some computers have an option labeled Last Setting, which turns the computer on only if it was already on when the power failed. If it's available, you can select that. Otherwise, select the setting that turns your computer on whenever the AC power comes on. Then save the BIOS settings and restart Windows.

Besides a 24×7 computer, you need a 24×7 Internet connection. If you have cable Internet service or a type of DSL service that does not require you to enter a username or password, you already have an always-on Internet connection and can skip ahead to the next section. Otherwise, if you have Internet service that is connection-based, you need to take one of the following actions:

- See if your DSL provider can upgrade your service to provide a static IP address and always-on service. This *might* be inexpensive enough to make it worthwhile.

> **caution**
> Be sure that every user account that can be reached via Remote Desktop (that is, every Administrator account and any Standard accounts that you select in step 4) has a strong password. This means a password with uppercase letters *and* lowercase letters *and* one or more numbers or punctuation, and at least eight characters in length. I like to use two-word passwords like this: **autumn/ robot**.

> **note**
> If you are using an add-on third-party firewall product, configure it to permit incoming Remote Desktop connections on TCP port 3389.

- Use a hardware connection-sharing router. If you don't have a router already, buying one is a worthwhile investment. They cost between $0 (after rebate) and $75, and can also provide wireless networking capability for your home or office. Chapter 19, "Connecting Your Network to the Internet," tells how to set up a router for DSL service. Be sure to enable the router's "keepalive" feature so that your connection is kept going all the time.

- If you use the Internet Connection Sharing built into Windows, you can add a third-party program to force Windows to keep the connection open all the time. The DynDNS Updater program (which we discuss later) can do this for you.

Next, you must make sure you can locate your computer from out on the Internet.

Setting Up Dynamic DNS

All Internet connections are established on the basis of a number called an *IP address*, which is to your Internet connection what your telephone number is to your phone. When you're somewhere else, you'll need a way to let Windows find your home computer's IP address so that Remote Desktop can establish a connection back to it.

🔍 note

Many DDNS providers exist, and some of them offer free services. You can find them easily enough by doing a Google search for "free DDNS service." Here we give you step-by-step instructions for setting up DynDNS Pro service at Dyn.com because it's directly supported by many hardware connection-sharing routers. If your router doesn't support it, you can install their IP address updating program on your computer. The company name has changed from DynDNS.com to Dyn.com, and the price has unfortunately gone from free to $20/year, but it's still a great product.

To be clear, if you have a static IP address, you can use any DNS service to map your IP address to a hostname+domain name. If you have a connection-based Internet service, you can use any Dynamic DNS service; however, the process for installing and configuring it will be different than what we describe here.

The solution to this problem is to use a dynamic domain name service (DDNS). You'll use the service to give your computer a name, such as `brian.likes-pie.com`. (Seriously.) Add-on software in your computer will keep the service updated whenever your computer's address changes.

To set up dynamic DNS service at Dyn.com, follow these steps:

1. Open Internet Explorer and go to www.dyn.com/dns. In the list of products, click Remote Access/ DynDNS Pro. Scroll to the bottom of the page and click the link DynDNS Pro Free Trial. Then, click Start the Trial.

2. Enter a hostname that you can easily remember, and select a domain name from the pull-down list. (I entered hostname `brian` and selected domain `likes-pie.com`. This gives my computer the Internet name `brian.likes-pie.com`.) Under the IP Address box, click Your Current Location's IP Address Is. If someone else has claimed the name you chose, change the name or domain and try again until you succeed. Be sure to write down the hostname and domain name that you eventually select.

(At the time we wrote this, the hostname entered here ends up not actually getting registered, but you have to go through this exercise anyway.)

Leave Wildcard unchecked and Service Type set to Host with IP Address. Click the link Your Current Location's IP Address Is... to record that address. Then, click Add to Cart.

3. You should have DynDNSPro Trial (14 days) and a Dynamic DNS Hostname in the cart. Complete the rest of the registration process. You'll have to click a link in a confirmation email. This will take you to a payment page, where you'll need to supply credit card information.

   (If you cancel the service before 14 days elapse, you will not be charged and you will still be allowed one free registered dynamic hostname; however, it could get deleted if its address is not updated at least once a month.)

4. After the order has been processed, at the left click My Services, then under that click DynDNS Pro/Hosts. If your desired hostname is listed, you're good to go. Otherwise, click +Add New Hostname and reenter what you entered in step 2, clicking Activate when done.

Next, set up a DNS client program so that changes to your IP address are sent to Dyn.com. There are two ways to do this. If you have a hardware Internet router, it may be able to automatically update your IP address. There is support information on Dyn.com that may help you do this.

Alternatively, install a Dynamic DNS updating tool on the computer you're enabling for Remote Desktop access. This is a software service that will periodically determine your network's public IP address and will update your name-to-address mapping in Dyn.com's server.

Here's how to do this on the computer you're enabling for Remote Desktop access:

1. Log on as a Computer Administrator. Open Internet Explorer and go to www.dyn.com/support. At the left, click Dyn Update Clients, Download Now, Run. Approve the User Account Control prompt.

2. Step through the installation screens, using the default settings (except uncheck Enable Dyn Internet Guide on This PC).

3. When the program starts, enter the Dyn.com account username and password that you created previously. In the list of hosts, click the check box for the hostname you created for this computer and then click OK.

The Dyn Updater service will now keep your hostname updated with your public IP address whenever it changes. (This is a true Windows service and runs whenever your computer is turned on, whether or not you are logged in.)

To be sure that the service is working, right-click the very bottom-left corner of the screen and select Command Prompt. Type the command **ping** followed by the hostname and domain name you chose for your computer; for example, `ping brian.likes-pie.com`. Press Enter and be sure that the command finds your IP address, and doesn't print "Could not find host."

Now your registered hostname will always point to your computer, even when your IP address changes. After a change, it might take up to an hour for the update to occur, but changes should be infrequent.

Configuring Port Forwarding

The last setup step is to make sure that incoming Remote Desktop connections from the Internet make it to the right computer. If your computer connects directly to your cable or DSL modem, you can skip this step. Otherwise, you have to instruct your sharing computer or router to forward Remote Desktop data through to your computer. To be precise, you have to set up your sharing computer or router to forward incoming requests on TCP port 3389 to the computer you want to reach by Remote Desktop.

The procedure depends on whether you are using the ICS service built into Windows or a hardware-sharing router. Use one of the procedures described in the next two sections.

Port Forwarding with a Router

If you are using a hardware connection-sharing router, setup is somewhat difficult but is worth-while. We give you an overview of the process here. To learn more about forwarding network requests on a shared Internet connection, see "Enabling Access with a Sharing Router" in Chapter 19.

First, because your router doesn't know your computers by their names, you have to set up a fixed IP address on the computer that you will be using via Remote Desktop, using these steps:

1. Right-click the very bottom-left corner of the screen and select Command Prompt. Type the command **ipconfig /all** and press Enter. Locate the Local Area Connection part of the printout, which will look something like this:

   ```
   Ethernet adapter Local Area Connection:
           Connection-specific DNS Suffix  . : somewhere.com
           Description . . . . . . . . . . . : NVIDIA nForce Networking Controller
           Physical Address. . . . . . . . . : 00-53-8F-D2-CA-5F
           Dhcp Enabled. . . . . . . . . . . : Yes
           Autoconfiguration Enabled . . . . : Yes
           IP Address. . . . . . . . . . . . : 192.168.0.102
           Subnet Mask . . . . . . . . . . . : 255.255.255.0
           Default Gateway . . . . . . . . . : 192.168.0.1
           DHCP Server . . . . . . . . . . . : 192.168.0.1
           DNS Servers . . . . . . . . . . . : 200.123.45.6
                                               200.123.67.8
   ```

   The important information is bold. (On your computer, the numbers will be different—use your numbers, not these!)

   If the entry Dhcp Enabled says No, you don't have to change anything here. Just note the IP Address entry, skip steps 2 through 8, and configure your router.

2. At the desktop, right-click the network icon at the right end of the taskbar and select Open Network and Sharing Center. Select Change Adapter Settings.

3. Right-click the icon that represents your LAN connection (most likely Ethernet or Wireless) and select Properties.

4. Select the Internet Protocol Version 4 (TCP/IPv4) entry and click Properties.

5. Check Use the Following IP Address. Enter the first three parts of your original IP address exactly as you see it in your Command Prompt window, but replace the last part with **250** (for example, 192.168.0.250). The first three sets of digits might be different on your network.

6. For the subnet mask and default gateway, enter the same numbers that were displayed in the Command Prompt window.

7. Check Use the Following DNS Server Addresses. Enter the one or two DNS Server addresses that were displayed in the Command Prompt window.

8. Click OK.

(If you need to set up any other computers to have fixed IP addresses, use the same procedure but use addresses ending in .249, .248, .247, and so on, counting backward from .250.)

Now you have to instruct your router to forward Remote Desktop connections to this computer. Open Internet Explorer and enter **http://** followed by the Default Gateway address you noted in step 1 (for example, http://192.168.0.1). Then press Enter. Every router uses a slightly different scheme, but Figure 39.2 shows a typical router. You need to find the router's setup screen and enable its Port Forwarding feature, which some routers call Virtual Server or Applications and Gaming.

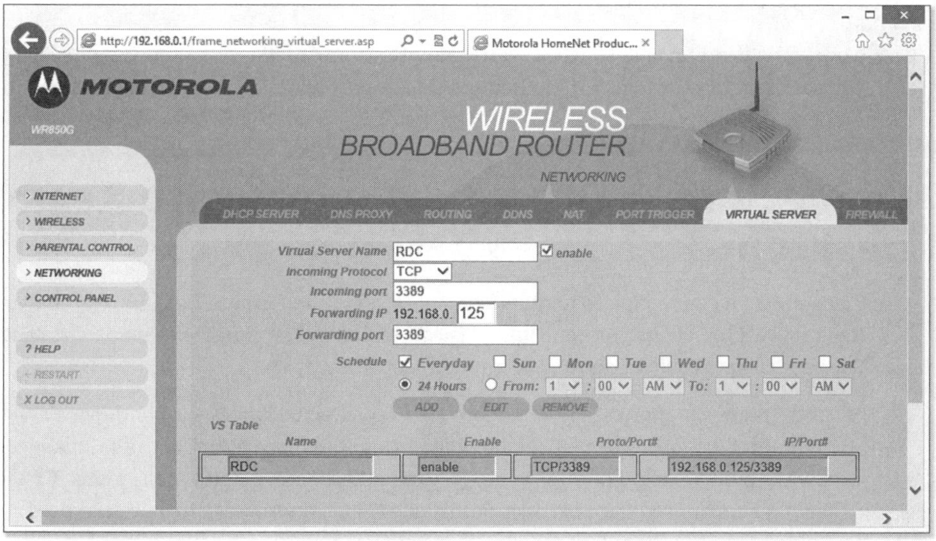

Figure 39.2
Use your router's setup system to forward TCP port 3389 to your computer.

On the router, you need to enter the fixed IP address that you assigned to your computer, and tell the router to forward connections on TCP port 3389 to this address. If a range of port numbers is required, or if external and internal numbers are entered separately, enter **3389** in all fields.

Now you should be able to reach your computer from anywhere on the Internet using the hostname you set up on Dyn.com.

Port Forwarding with Internet Connection Sharing

If you use the built-in Windows ICS service to share an Internet connection on one computer with the rest of your LAN, the forwarding procedure is pretty straightforward using these steps:

1. Go to the computer that is sharing its connection (whether or not it's the one you want to reach via Remote Desktop) and log on as a Computer Administrator.

2. View the Properties dialog box for the local area connection that corresponds to the Internet connection itself. On Windows 8, go to the desktop, right-click the network icon in the taskbar, and Open Network and Sharing Center. In the Tasks list, select Change Adapter Settings.

3. Locate the connection icon that goes to your Internet service. It will have the word *Shared* under or next to it. Right-click the icon, select Properties, and view the Sharing tab.

4. Click Settings and, under Services, check Remote Desktop. In the Service Settings dialog box, enter the name of the computer that you want to make available via Remote Desktop and click OK. (To find the name of the computer, view its System or System Properties screen.)

5. When you're finished, click OK to close all the dialog boxes.

Now you should be able to reach your computer from anywhere on the Internet using the hostname you set up on Dyn.com using the Remote Desktop Connection client program described in the next section.

Connecting to Other Computers with Remote Desktop

To establish a connection to another computer using the Remote Desktop system, you need a Remote Desktop client program, which is sometimes called Remote Desktop Connection or Terminal Services Client. You can get this program in several ways:

- On Windows 8, there are two Remote Desktop clients. There is a Windows 8-style version named "Remote Desktop" that you can download from the Store app. The traditional desktop client is always preinstalled. For either one, go to the Start screen and type **remote**. To use the Windows 8-style version, see the next section. To use the desktop version, select Remote Desktop Connection. We describe both clients in this chapter. You can also run the desktop version by typing **mstsc**.

On Windows 7 and Vista, click Start, All Programs, Accessories, Remote Desktop Connection. This is the traditional version.

On Windows XP, click Start, All Programs, Accessories, Communications, Remote Desktop Connection.

The version that came with XP lacks support for multiple monitors and plug-and-play devices. You can upgrade the version on XP by downloading and installing the new version, as described in the next paragraph.

- You can download it from www.microsoft.com/download. Search for "Remote Desktop Connection" and get the latest version available for your operating system. There are versions there for Windows and Mac OS X.

- If you have an iOS device such as an iPad, you can get the PocketCloud app made by Citrix from the iTunes store. I've found it somewhat buggy, but acceptable for emergency use. You might search for "RDC" to see if there are other credible Remote Desktop clients. Because you will be letting the app have your Windows password, you should only get a Remote Desktop app from a known, large corporation that you trust.

In the next two sections, we discuss the Windows 8–style and traditional desktop client programs. The traditional Remote Desktop client has more keyboard, display, sound, and printing options than the Windows 8–style version. Try them both and see which you prefer.

Using the Windows 8–Style Remote Desktop Client

To start a connection to a remote computer from a Windows 8 computer using the Windows 8–style client, go to the Start screen and type **remote**. If Remote Desktop appears, select it. If it does not appear under Apps, go to the Store app and download it.

When the Remote Desktop app opens, you can do one of the following things:

- If you want to connect to a computer you've used previously and it appears in the list of recent connection icons, just click the icon.

- You can right-click a recent connection icon and delete or edit it. The Edit option lets you customize its connection settings or delete a saved credential (password) stored for the connection.

- At the bottom of the app, type in the name of a remote computer, such as the one set up in the first part of this chapter (`brian.likes-pie.com`) and press Enter to start the connection process. You can also type the name of a computer on your own LAN.

- Display the charms (Alt+C or swipe in from the right) and select Settings to change settings, as shown in Figure 39.3.

> **🔍 note**
>
> To download the Remote Desktop app, go to the Start screen, type **store**, and select the Store app. Bring up the charms. Select the Search charm and type **remote desktop**. Select and install the Remote Desktop app published by Microsoft. It's free.

Figure 39.3
The Windows 8-style Remote Desktop client displays icons for recent connections and has a Settings panel that you can reach from the charms.

- Click Access RemoteApp and Desktop Connections to connect to a corporate app server. (Instructions for using this feature would be provided by a network administrator.) Once connected, you can use the Windows 8–style client as discussed in this section.

On the Settings panel, under Connection Settings you can change the following:

- **Appearance**—Determines how visual effects such as transparency, fade-ins, and so on are handled. These are impacted by slow network speeds. By default, Windows determines which effects to use and which to suppress to save bandwidth.

- **Devices**—Lets the remote computer (the one you're connecting *to*) use devices on the local computer (the one you're connecting *from*). If you enable the printer, for example, you can have remote applications print on the computer at your current location.

- **Remote Desktop Gateway**—Specifies an Internet-facing computer that serves as a gateway to protected Remote Desktop servers on a corporate network. Information about this would be supplied to you by a network administrator.

- **Advanced**—Controls whether images from the remote session can be stored and displayed on your local computer. Disable Thumbnails and Persistent Caching if you will be viewing sensitive information on the remote computer, such as banking or personal information, that you would not want to be stored as images in temporary files on the computer you're using locally.

On the Settings panel under Permissions, you can control access to devices on your computer such as cameras and microphones. Apps running on a remote Windows 8 computer can access some local devices as if they were connected there. Conceivably, a program on the remote computer might surreptitiously watch you or listen in on you, so this has privacy implications. Such hardware must be enabled both under Devices *and* under Permissions.

When you've entered a computer name or selected a recent connection, the application connects to the remote computer and prompts you for your username and password.

If the computer is not on a secured network, you will be warned that the computer to which you're connecting might not be the one you expect. If you trust that the hostname you entered really does lead to the computer you want to use, click Connect Anyway.

Once the connection is made, you can use the remote computer as if you were sitting there.

The keyboard and mouse control the *remote* computer. The Windows Logo keyboard shortcuts, in particular, are sent to the remote computer and act there. Only the Ctrl+Alt+Del key combination acts locally; you can type Ctrl+Alt+End to send this to the remote computer.

On the other hand, Windows 8 multitouch gestures—the ones that open the charms, display app commands, and scroll between apps—act on the *local* computer. If you have touch only, and no keyboard, you'll need to use the Remote Desktop app's app commands to perform these actions on a remote Windows 8 computer.

> **⊛ tip**
>
> If you're connecting to a Windows 8 computer, and you're used to a touch screen at home, but the computer you're using to connect has just a keyboard and mouse, check out the Windows 8 shortcut keys listed in Table 4.1 on page 101.

To display the app commands, slide your finger up from the bottom center of the screen. Alternatively, touch the top center of the screen, and touch the box that contains the name of the remote computer. You can use a mouse to do this too.

The app commands appear as shown in Figure 39.4. Not all of the icons will appear if the remote computer is not running Windows 8. The panels let you control the connection as follows:

- **The + symbol (at the top of the screen)**—Opens an additional connection to another computer. The icons here let you select from a number of concurrent connections to remote computers. Click the icon's X to close the connection. You will remain logged in on the remote computer if you disconnect this way. We show another way to disconnect shortly.

- **Home**—Returns to the Remote Desktop home screen, which you can use as another way to open an additional connection.

- **Connection**—Displays the condition of the network connection to the remote computer.

- **Zoom**—Opens the Magnifier tool on the remote computer.

- **Start**—Returns the remote computer to its Start screen.

- **Switch Apps**—Lets you select between different running apps on the remote computer.

- **App Commands**—Displays the remote computer's current app's command panel; equivalent to a touch swipe up from the bottom of the screen.

- **Charms**—Displays the Remote Computer's charms.

Figure 39.4
If you click the name of the remote computer at the top of the screen, you can control the remote connection.

When you are finished working remotely, to disconnect from the remote computer and leave it signed in, running your apps, use the computer name title at the top of the screen, and then close the connection's icon by clicking its **X**. (The Power button in the remote computer's Settings charm also disconnects, leaving you logged on.)

To sign off entirely, go to the remote computer's Start screen and sign out by selecting your name at the top. Select Sign Out. This logs you out and closes the connection.

Using the Standard Remote Desktop Client

To run the desktop Remote Desktop client from Windows 8, go to the Start screen and type **remote**, then select Remote Desktop Connection. (We list the ways to run it from earlier versions of Windows in the section "Connecting to Other Computers with Remote Desktop," earlier in this chapter.) If you're using the Remote Desktop client on any earlier version of Windows, or on a Mac or other device, this is the type of client you'll be using.

Two Monitors Are Better Than One

If the computer you're using to establish the remote connection has two or more monitors, you might be able to use them all for the remote connection.

If you're connecting from a computer that is running Windows 8 or 7, when you start the traditional Remote Desktop Client, click the Options button, select the Display tab, and select Use All of My Monitors for the Remote Session. When you connect to the remote computer, set the Display size to Full Screen. (This works only with the Remote Desktop Connection client version 7.0 or higher, as provided with Windows 8 and 7, or downloaded from Microsoft.com.)

If you are connecting *from* a computer that is running Windows Vista, *and* both of its monitors have the same height (that is, the same vertical resolution) *and* are aligned side by side, follow this procedure: click Start and, in the Windows Search box, type `mstsc /span`. Press Enter. When you connect to the remote computer, set the Display size to Full Screen. (This works only with Remote Desktop Connection client version 6.1 or higher, as provided with Windows Vista and later, or downloaded from Microsoft.com. If this indeed works well for you, you can create a shortcut containing this command.)

When you run the Remote Desktop Client, you'll see the Remote Desktop Connection dialog box (see Figure 39.5).

Figure 39.5
The Remote Desktop Connection dialog box enables you to configure the connection and select the remote computer to use.

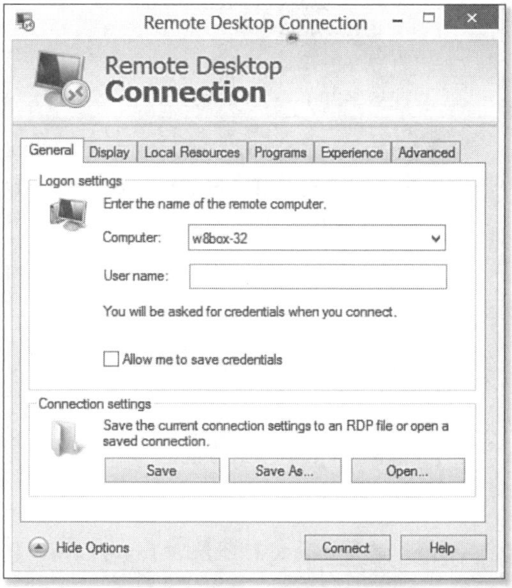

Enter the IP address or registered DNS name of the computer you want to use. If you have set up a DDNS hostname, as described in the first part of this chapter, the name might look something like `brian.likes-pie.com`. If you're connecting to a computer on your own home or office network, it's enough just to type its computer name.

At this point, you can select options that control how the remote connection is made, how large a window to use, and so on.

Connection Options

In the Remote Desktop Connection dialog box, you can set several connection options. In most cases, you can use the default settings and simply click Connect to start the connection, but several of the options can be quite useful.

To view the option categories, click the Show Options button. The dialog box expands to show six tabs, as shown in Figure 39.5, which you can select by clicking the tab names across the top. You will rarely need to adjust any of these settings. However, some situations might require you to change settings before making a Remote Desktop connection. Table 39.1 lists these situations.

Table 39.1   Some Reasons to Change Remote Desktop Settings

Situation	Setting Change
You always connect across the Internet and/or your remote computer is not on a secure corporate LAN.	On the Advanced tab, set Authentication Options to Connect and Don't Warn Me.
You are using a dial-up Internet connection.	On the Experience tab, change the Connection Speed to Modem (56K). On the Local Resources tab, click Settings and set audio playback to Do Not Play.
The remote computer has a slow Internet upload speed.	Most home Internet service has a fast download connection but a slow upload speed, often less than 500Kbps. If you're connecting to a computer that has a slow upload speed and the screen updates sluggishly, disconnect, and on the Experience tab, set the Performance setting to Low-Speed Broadband. Then try again.
You need to work with the local and remote screens simultaneously.	On the Display tab, change the resolution to a size smaller than your local screen, perhaps 800×600.
You need to see as much of the remote computer's screen as possible.	On the Display tab, change the resolution to Full Screen. If the remote computer runs Windows 7 and you have multiple monitors on your local computer, check Use All My Monitors for the Remote Session.
You need to be able to print from the applications on the remote computer and get the printouts where you are working.	On the Local Resources tab, check Printers.
You don't need to print while connected.	On the Local Resources tab, uncheck Printers.

Situation	Setting Change
You want remote applications to be able to access files on the computer where you are working.	On the Local Resources tab, click More, expand the Drives list, and then click the boxes next to the drive letter(s) you want to be made visible to the remote computer.
You need to use an application that uses a device attached to a COM port (for example, a Palm Pilot).	On the Local Resources tab, click More, and then check Ports.
You want the Windows key to be sent to the remote computer even when your remote connection isn't in Full Screen mode.	On the Local Resources tab, set Apply Windows Key Combinations to On the Remote Computer.

The Full Screen setting is very useful if you have serious work to do on the remote computer because it gives you the maximum amount of desktop space on which to work. (It also helps when you're connecting to a Windows 8 computer, because the Windows key will be sent to the remote computer, rather than acting on the local computer.) Although the resulting connection will fill your local computer's screen, you can still switch back and forth between remote and local work, as described in the next section.

When you have made the necessary settings, you might want to save them as the default settings for future connections. To do this, select the General tab and click Save.

Finally, after you have made any necessary option settings, click Connect to begin the connection. Windows prompts you to enter your username and password before it establishes the connection.

tip

If you routinely make connections to different computers using different settings, you can set up Remote Desktop Connection files with the computer name and all options preset. To do this, make the settings, click Save As, and select a filename. You can create shortcuts to the saved files and put them on your desktop, put them in your Start page, or pin them to your taskbar.

note

If you are connecting to a Windows Server Domain computer, you usually will enter your domain logon in the form domainname\username. If you need to specify a local machine account, enter *machinename\username*, as in mycomputer\Administrator.

The program prompts you to enter a username and password. Type the username and password you use on the *remote* computer, the one to which you're connecting. Entering the password is optional and, in most cases, not entering it here is safer. Let the remote system prompt you for your password.

caution

Do *not* check Remember My Credentials if you are using a computer in a public place, or one that is not your own or is not secure, because otherwise anyone who has access to the account you're using will be able to connect to the remote computer using your logon.

If you want the logon name and password to be stored (relatively securely) in the local computer so that future connections can be automatic, enter the password and check Remember My Credentials.

Finally, click OK to begin the connection.

Logon Is Denied

If the remote computer connects but will not let you sign on, the account you tried to use might have a blank password or might be a Standard account that was not entered as an account authorized to connect remotely. See "Enabling Remote Desktop Access to Your Computer," earlier in the chapter, for instructions on authorizing accounts. An account must have a password set before you can use it remotely, even if it's authorized.

If Network Level Authentication is being used and the connection to the remote computer does not use the IPSec network security protocol, you might get a warning that the remote computer's identity cannot be validated. (Thus, you *could* end up giving your password to a counterfeit computer.) In most cases, this is not a problem, so you can click Yes. You can also check Don't Prompt Me Again for Connections to This Computer, or you can use the Advanced tab in the connection options, as described earlier, to prevent this warning from reoccurring.

Using the Remote Connection

When you're logged on, you'll see the remote computer's desktop, and you can use it as if you were actually sitting in front of it. In a full-screen connection, the title bar at the top of the screen tells you that you're viewing the remote computer's screen. The title bar might slide up out of view, but you can hover the mouse near the top of the screen to bring it back. You can also click the Minimize button to hide the remote screen, or you can click the Maximize button to switch between a windowed or full-screen view.

The keyboard, mouse, display, and sound (unless you disabled it) should be fully functional. It all works quite well—and it can even be difficult to remember which computer you're actually using!

If you elected to connect to the local computer's disk drives in the connection options dialog box, the local computer's drives appear when you open File Explorer on the remote computer. Access to these drives is fairly slow and annoying. Still, you can take advantage of this to copy files between the local and remote computers.

In addition, any printers attached to your local computer will appear as choices if you print from applications on the remote computer, as long as a compatible printer driver is available on the *remote* computer. Printers might not work if you are connecting from a Mac or a computer that is running an older version of Windows.

> **tip**
>
> If the computer to which you're connecting has more than one monitor or a larger monitor than the one you're currently using, when you start an application, its window might not be visible. The problem is that when the application was last used, its window was placed on a secondary monitor and its position is now completely off the Remote Desktop screen. To make it visible, hover the mouse over the program's icon in the taskbar. When the preview window appears, right-click it and select Move (or Restore, then Move). Then press and hold the arrow keys to slide the window into view. Press Enter when it's visible, then finish positioning it with your mouse.

Keyboard Shortcuts

While you're connected, you might want to use keyboard shortcuts such as Alt+Tab to switch between applications and Windows Logo+R to run a command. This can confuse Windows, which won't know whether to switch applications on the local computer or the remote computer. There are three ways to make the Alt and Windows special functions act on the remote computer:

- Put the remote connection window into Full Screen mode. Then, all Windows keys will be sent to the remote computer, except Ctrl+Alt+Del. To send Ctrl+Alt+Del, press Ctrl+Alt+End.

- Before you make the connection, view the Local Resources options page and set Apply Windows Key Combinations to On the Remote Computer. (And, as before, this fixes all but Ctrl+Alt+Del.)

- Memorize and use the alternate key combinations listed in Table 39.2. These replacement keystrokes don't work, by the way, if you are using either of the preceding two alternatives.

Table 39.2 shows the alternate keyboard shortcuts that can be used if the window isn't in Full Screen mode and you haven't selected to send all Windows key combinations to the remote computer.

Table 39.2   Some Remote Desktop Keyboard Shortcuts

Use These Keys:	To Transmit This to the Remote Computer:
Alt+PgUp, Alt+PgDn	Alt+Tab (to switch programs)
Alt+End	Ctrl+Alt+Del (to open Task Monitor)
Alt+Home	Ctrl+Esc (to display the Start Screen on Windows 8, and the Start Menu on earlier versions)
Alt+Del	Alt+Space (to display a window's System menu)
Ctrl+Alt+Break	Alt+Enter (to toggle Full Screen)
Ctrl+Alt+Plus on numeric pad	Alt+PrntScrn (to print the screen to the Clipboard)
Ctrl+Alt+End	Ctrl+Alt+Del (to display Task Manager)

When you've finished using the remote computer, log off using the normal means for the remote version of Windows. (On Windows 8, click your name in the upper-right corner of the Start screen.) If you want to leave yourself logged on with applications running, use the remote computer's normal Shutdown option, which will say Disconnect instead. (On Windows 8, open the Settings charm and click Power, as shown in Figure 39.6, or just close the Remote Desktop connection window.) You can later reconnect via Remote Desktop or by signing on at the remote computer itself.

I use Remote Desktop to use my work computer from home, and I've found that I save a lot of time by never logging off entirely. When I finish at work, I just press Windows Logo+L to switch out to the Welcome screen. Then I can reconnect from home and pick up where I left off. Likewise, at home, when I'm finished, I simply disconnect, so I never actually log off.

Figure 39.6
Use the Logout or Disconnect choice to end your remote session. Disconnect leaves you logged in on the remote computer.

One User at a Time

Windows 8 permits only one person to use each computer. If you attempt to connect to a computer with Remote Desktop while another user is logged on, you will have the choice of disconnecting yourself or forcing that user to the Welcome (logon) screen. And, if Fast User Switching is not enabled on the remote computer, they are summarily logged off and lose any work in process.

If you log on using the same username as the local user, though, you simply take over the desktop without forcing a logoff.

If someone else logs on to the remote computer while you're connected from afar, your session is disconnected. Again, if Fast User Switching is enabled on the remote computer, you can simply reconnect later and pick up where you left off. Otherwise, the same deal applies: if it is a different user, your applications are shut down.

If you're using Remote Desktop to use your own computer, this probably won't matter to you because you'll probably never see what happens on the other screen. But if you use Remote Desktop to work on someone else's computer, let that person know what will happen before starting; otherwise, the two of you could get into a tussle, repeatedly kicking the other person off the computer, with neither of you knowing that the other person is there trying to get something done.

Third-Party Remote Control Tools

If you don't want to set up Remote Desktop, you might want to consider using one of several third-party remote control tools. A bunch of web-based products have emerged that work very well. Many of them have free versions, and most have some advantages over Remote Desktop: they work with any version of Windows, and they require almost no setup, even if you have a router on your Internet connection. Here are some products to check out:

- **LogMeIn**—Available in free and Pro versions. Pro gets you file transfer, sound, and printing. Mac and Windows versions are available. No network setup is necessary. Find information at www. logmein.com. I use this program myself and I *really* like it. The iOS and Android client is called LogMeIn Ignition. It's superb.

- **TeamViewer**—Available free for personal, noncommercial use, TeamViewer requires no network setup and can even make your LAN available to the remote client computer through a built-in VPN service. Both Windows and Mac clients and hosts are available. Check out www.teamviewer.com.

- **I'm InTouch**—Another no-network-setup remote access product. The remote client is Java based, so you could access your PC from your Blackberry. There are iOS and Android clients, too. Check out www.01com.com.

- **BeAnywhere**—Another subscription-based remote access product, requiring no network setup. Check it out at www.beanywhere.com.

- **LapLink Everywhere (formerly Carbon Copy)**—Requires no network setup. Clients are available for iOS and PocketPCs as well as PCs. Information can be found at www.laplink.com.

- **GoToMyPC**—A commercial subscription-based product that offers remote access through any web browser. Information can be found at www.gotomypc.com. You can access your computer from Windows, OS X, Android, and iOS.

- **Radmin**—A low-cost remote control program. Information can be found at www.radmin.com. Requires network setup.

- **VNC**—A free, open-source program initially developed by AT&T. A big plus for VNC is that both host and client programs are available for virtually every OS. There are several VNC versions available, with TightVNC and RealVNC being the most popular. For information, check out www.tightvnc.com and www.realvnc.com. VNC products require network setup and do not encrypt their data, so they are *not safe* for connecting directly over the Internet. They are fine to use on a home or business LAN or over a VPN connection.

> **note**
>
> The products that require network setup can also access a computer across a LAN or corporate network. If you want to access a remote computer via a dial-up modem, though, you must use one of the old-school programs, such as Symantec PCAnywhere. Alternatively, you can set up an incoming dial-up networking connection for your computer and use Remote Desktop or a network-based remote control program such as VNC.

A

VIRTUALIZATION

A *virtual machine (VM)* program simulates the hardware functions of a computer within an application running on another computer. It lets you run an entire operating system as an application program, so that you can work in various operating systems without rebooting. Virtualization has been used on big mainframe computers since the 1960s, and it is now also used on PCs and PC-type server computers. If you use Windows 8, you could conceivably have Windows XP, Windows Vista, Windows 7, Windows 8, various versions of Windows Server and Linux, and other operating systems all running at once, on your desktop. You can also run a copy of Windows inside a virtual computer on a machine running Linux, Mac OS X, or other versions of Windows.

Virtualization is a handy way for individuals and organizations to run multiple operating systems without having to set up dual- or multi-boot environments or purchase additional hardware. IT departments use virtualization to test software updates and patches before rolling them out to end users, and developers use virtualization when creating, testing, and documenting software programs. End users most commonly use virtualization to run applications that require an older version of Windows on a computer that has a newer version of Windows.

In virtualization vocabulary, the *host* operating system is the one that runs the physical computer. A *guest* operating system runs inside the virtual machine system provided by the host. In this appendix, we'll talk about Windows 8 as both host and guest.

Windows 8 as a Host: Running Other Operating Systems Inside Windows 8

> **🔍 note**
>
> You can install a virtualization host program so that you can run other operating systems inside Windows 8. Microsoft's Hyper-V product is included with the 64-bit versions of Windows 8 Professional and Windows 8 Enterprise editions. Hyper-V is Microsoft's industrial-strength VM system used across the Windows Server product line. In this section, we show you how to activate Hyper-V (which by default is not enabled), how to create new virtual machines (VMs), and how to convert an existing physical installation of Windows into a VM that you can then run inside Windows 8.
>
> If you want to run virtual machines inside plain Windows 8, or on a 32-bit version of Windows 8, you'll have to use a different virtual machine manager, such as VirtualBox (free, from virtualbox.org), Parallels Workstation ($79, from parallels.com), or VMWare Workstation ($199, from vmware.com). I used VirtualBox extensively while writing this book and found it completely adequate. There are some screen-refreshing issues at times (which were annoying but not deal-killers), but there are frequent bug-fix updates to the program, and I would not be surprised if the display issues get fixed soon.
>
> Microsoft's previous virtualization offerings, Microsoft Virtual PC and Windows Virtual PC, do not work on Windows 8. The Windows XP Mode system—a preconfigured, virtualized copy of Windows XP that Microsoft offered to Windows 7 Professional, Ultimate, and Enterprise users—is also not available on Windows 8. We talk about converting existing Virtual PC and XP Mode virtual machines for Hyper-V later in this section.

The version of Hyper-V provided with Windows 8 is called Client Hyper-V, and it's is almost exactly the same VM manager used on the industrial-strength Windows Server operating systems. When Hyper-V is installed and you start your computer, Hyper-V actually loads first, and Windows 8 loads on top of it as a sort of half-client/half-partner. Your copy of Windows 8 won't be running on the "bare metal" exactly, but it's also not as restricted as a regular virtual machine would be—and there's almost no performance hit. Windows 8 runs as what's called Hyper-V's Management Operating System, and it has direct access to the computer's hardware. You can see this in the Device Manager, which shows that Windows 8 still "sees" your computer's real hardware devices, not the simulated Intel network adapter and video adapter that a regular Hyper-V VM sees.

Installing and Configuring Hyper-V

To install Hyper-V on Windows 8, press Windows Logo+X and select Control Panel. Select Programs and then select Turn Windows Features On or Off. Check the Hyper-V box and click OK. Windows will need to restart once or twice.

When you log back on, at the Start screen select Hyper-V Manager. Once this opens on the desktop, you may wish to right-click its icon in the taskbar and select Pin This Program to Taskbar.

The next step is to create a virtual network switch (network hub) that your virtual computer will use to connect to your LAN and to the Internet. To do this, in the Actions panel, select Virtual Switch Manager. Select New Virtual Switch. In the list of switch types, select External and click Next. This will let your virtual machines connect to your LAN through your computer's network adapter. Click

Create Virtual Switch. Change the name to Shared Network Switch. If your computer has more than one network adapter, under External Network select the adapter that leads to your LAN and to the Internet. Be sure to keep Allow Management Operating System to Share This Network Adapter checked—the Management Operating System is your copy of Windows 8 and you don't want to disconnect it from the network adapter.

Finally, click OK to close the Virtual Switch Manager.

(You can also use the Virtual Switch Manager to create private networks that connect only virtual machines, or a network that contains only VMs and your own computer, but that's beyond the scope of this book.)

Creating Virtual Machine Instances

To create a new virtual computer, follow these steps:

1. At the Start screen, select Hyper-V Manager, shown in Figure A.1.

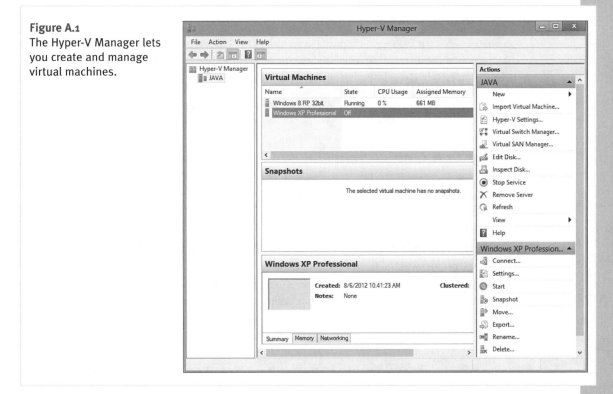

Figure A.1
The Hyper-V Manager lets you create and manage virtual machines.

2. In the right pane, select New, Virtual Machine and then Click Next.

3. Enter a name for the new VM and click Next.

4. Enter the amount of RAM the VM should see. If your computer has 8GB of RAM or more, you can probably be somewhat generous, offering 2GB to 4GB, or more, but be aware that a 32-bit operating system won't be able to use any more than 3GB. Check Use Dynamic Memory to let Windows automatically manage the partitioning of your computer's physical RAM between the VMs and your applications. Then, click Next.

5. To give the VM access to your network, select the Shared Network Switch that you created when you installed Hyper-V. Click Next.

6. Unless you have an existing virtual hard disk you want to use, select Create a Virtual Hard Disk, type in a name for it that ends with .vhdx, and set a *maximum* size for its contents. Windows won't preallocate a file of this size, but the disk file could grow to this size.

   If, instead, you want to use the .vhd format so that the file will be compatible with other virtualization programs, in the Action pane select New, Hard Disk and use the wizard to create a new .vhd hard disk. Then, back in the Connect Virtual Hard Disk dialog box, select Use an Existing Virtual Hard Disk and then browse to the file you created.

   Then, click Next.

7. If you want to attach a physical or virtual (.iso file) CD or DVD to the virtual machine when it boots for the first time, so that you can install an operating system, make this selection on the Installation Options screen. Click Next and then Finish.

The virtual machine is now ready to start. The first time you boot it up, install the Integration Services, as described in the next section.

Running and Connecting to a VM

Hyper-V runs virtual machines entirely outside of Windows 8. They're not desktop applications as they were with Virtual PC. To "see" a virtual machine, you use the Hyper-V Virtual Machine Connection program, which is a version of the Remote Desktop connection program that knows how to find VMs on your own computer or other computers.

It's easiest to start from the Hyper-V Manager, which you can run from the Start screen (or if you pinned it to the taskbar, from the desktop).

In the Virtual Machines list, select the VM that you want to start, and from the Actions menu or in the section below the left Actions panel, select Connect. This will display a Remote Desktop–like window that shows that the computer is turned off. Now, from the Actions menu or from the Actions panel, select Start.

From this point, you can start, stop, pause, and take "snapshots" of the virtual machine's current configuration using the Hyper-V manager window, and you interact with the VM through the Virtual Machine Connection window, as shown in Figure A.2.

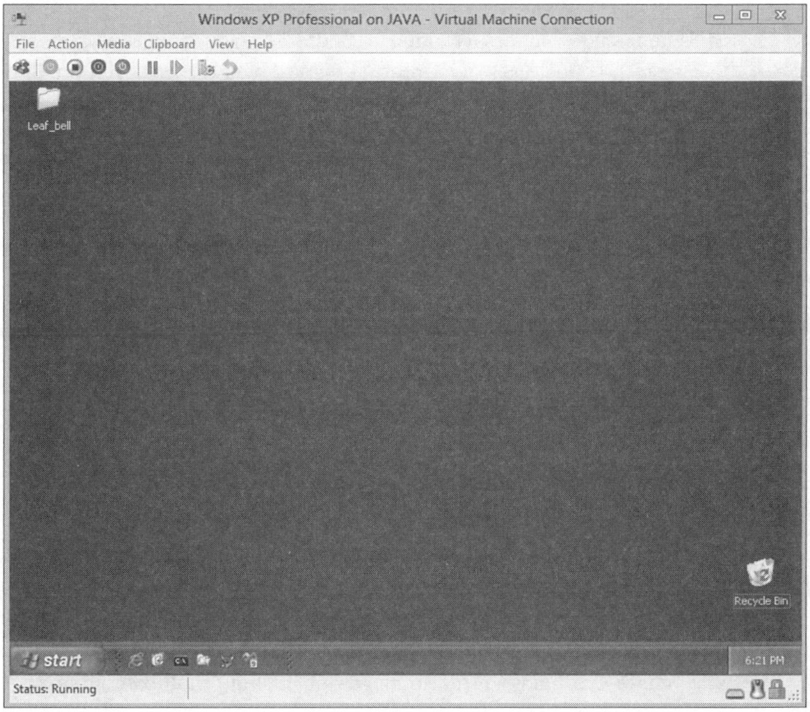

Figure A.2
The Virtual Machine Connection program lets you view and interact with a virtual machine.

Here are some tips for interacting with the VM:

- Once you have an operating system installed and running, try to install the Hyper-V Integration Services (IS) inside the VM. There are versions for Windows and Linux. This installs modified disk, network, and mouse drivers inside the VM that "know" about the Hyper-V environment and communicate directly with your real disk, network, and mouse without going through the overhead of working with simulated hardware. For Windows operating systems, IS lets you cut and paste between the host and guest operating systems, and it makes the mouse smoothly cross in and out of the Virtual Machine Connection window.

  To install Integration Services, in the Virtual Machine Connection window select Action, Insert Integration Services Setup Disk. This attaches a CD image file to the VM, and from there Autorun should run the IS installer. If the installer doesn't start automatically, locate the CD drive inside the VM and run the setup program manually.

- Until you install the Integration Services, you have to click the mouse inside the Virtual Machine Connection window for the guest OS to see it, and once you do, the guest "captures" the mouse. It won't leave the connection window. Press Ctrl+Alt+Left Arrow to release it back to Windows 8.

- Use the Media menu item to select CD, DVD, and floppy disk images to mount inside the VM.

- When you're finished working with the VM, you have several choices: you can shut it down using the guest OS's own internal menus; you can click Action, Shut Down to send the signal the VM would get if you pressed a real computer's Power button; or you can click Action, Save to store a copy of the VM's current state to your hard disk. You can resume it later. (This is like hibernation, except it happens outside rather than inside the guest OS.)

- If you simply close the Virtual Machine Connection window, the guest OS *does not stop running*. You won't see anything saying that it's running even in the Task Manager. Only the Hyper-V Manager shows that it's still active. You must reconnect to the VM or use the Hyper-V Manager to shut it down.

There is plenty more to using Hyper-V. You can find lots of information online at technet.microsoft.com.

Converting a Physical Computer to a VM

If you're like me, you probably have one or two old computers that you rarely use anymore, but you keep around because of *one* application you use once or twice a year, and some files you *might* want to get to someday. If so, you may be able to vacuum up the contents of its hard disk into a virtual machine, so that you can run the old computer anytime you want, right from within Windows 8. Older computers often have hard disks that are fairly small by today's standards—under 300GB in most cases, with most of that unused—so copying their contents into a single file on your new hard disk isn't that unreasonable.

We'll give you the procedure for Hyper-V. Other products such as VMware have their own tools for converting physical-to-virtual tools. This procedure isn't guaranteed to work, but it's worth a shot.

First, prepare the old machine for imaging. Clean up anything you can think of cleaning up: run the Disk Cleanup Wizard, delete temporary Internet files, and so on. If you feel daring, run Device Manager to delete the installed network and display adapters, but this step is optional. Remove any huge files you're certain you don't want. Remove any unwanted startup programs (live.sysinternals. com/autoruns.exe is great for this). Then, empty the Recycle Bin.

The next step is to capture an image of the hard disk in the old computer. You can temporarily install the old disk in your new computer, or you can perform the imaging step on the old computer and then either save the image file on a detachable USB hard drive or save it across the network to your Windows 8 computer. To create the image, download and run Disk2VHD from sysinternals. com (this site is owned by Microsoft, by the way, so it's safe). Follow Disk2VHD's instructions to create an image of the old disk. Don't check Prepare for Use on Virtual PC. Either save the VHD image file directly to your Windows 8 computer, or transport it on a removable drive and then copy it to your Windows 8 computer. Put the VHD file on your Windows 8 system in `c:\users\Public\ Documents\Hyper-V\Virtual Hard Disks`.

Now, on Windows 8, run the Hyper-V Manager and create a new VM using the steps described earlier in this appendix, but with these changes:

- At the Connect Virtual Hard Disk Step, select Use an Existing Virtual Hard Disk and then browse to the VHD file you created in the previous step.

- Under Installation Options, select Install an Operating System Later.

- When you boot the machine for the first time, install the Integration Options.

Windows XP Mode Virtual Machines

If you used Windows XP Mode under Windows 7, you have a fully bootable VHD file containing Windows XP that has your old Windows applications and data already set up, and you might want to continue to use it under Windows 8. This copy of Windows XP is not licensed to be used on Windows 8, and if you try to do so, Windows product activation enforces the license restriction. You technically can move a Windows XP Mode virtual machine to Hyper-V, but once you start it up, Windows XP detects the new environment and initiates a product activation cycle that you can't complete.

You can, however, keep the XP Mode virtual hard disk and the files it contains. Use the DISK2VHD application described in the previous section to create a snapshot of the disk as seen inside the copy of XP. Copy this file to your Windows 8 computer. On Windows 8, you can double-click to mount and view the contents of the virtual hard disk file.

Windows 8 as a Guest: Running Windows 8 Inside Other Operating Systems

You can run Windows 8 as a guest operating system in some virtual machine host systems. It runs well in Hyper-V, so you can run a Windows 8 guest inside a Windows 8 host. (Why would someone do that? A couple reasons could be: for sandboxing, that is, testing software in an environment where it can't do any damage, and to test software on all of the various editions in both 32-bit and 64-bit versions). You may also want to work with Windows 8 on a computer that happens to run Mac OS X, Linux, or an older version of Windows as its primary OS.

If the host OS runs a 64-bit operating system, you should be able to install and run both the 32-bit and 64-bit versions of Windows 8. If the host runs as a 32-bit operating system, you will only be able to run the 32-bit versions of Windows 8.

At the time this was written, and as we mentioned earlier, the following products could run Windows 8 as a guest: VirtualBox, Parallels Workstation, and VMWare Workstation. By the time you read this, other VM software vendors might have made their products able to run Windows 8. These products are available for Windows XP through Windows 8, Mac OS X, and Linux, so you can run Windows 8 within any of these host operating systems.

Unfortunately, neither Microsoft Virtual PC nor Windows Virtual PC can run Windows 8 as a guest OS. These programs were available as free downloads for Windows 7, Vista, and XP. You can run Windows 8 on these older versions of Windows using one of the

> 🔍 **note**
>
> Be sure to check the licensing terms for your copy of Windows 8 to see if you can install it in a virtual machine. Generally, the OEM licenses for a copy of Windows 8 that comes preinstalled on a new computer are tied to the computer itself. You may be able to run your copy of Windows 8 in a VM on the same computer. (This can be useful, as we mentioned earlier, for testing and sandboxing). To run Windows 8 on a different computer, you would need an additional license.

aforementioned third-party VM applications. Windows 8 runs well in VirtualBox, but it works only if the CPU in the host computer has hardware virtualization support.

Booting a VHD File on Hardware

If you have Windows 7 Ultimate or Enterprise, or Windows 8 Professional or Enterprise, your computer can physically boot and run a copy of either of these operating systems stored in a VHD virtual disk file. You can take advantage of this to physically boot a Windows 8 or 7 virtual machine on real hardware. We'd recommend making a backup copy of the VHD file before you try this.

To set up a new boot option, you can use a third-party GUI boot manager tool such as EasyBCD (www.neosmart.net), or you can use the BCDEDIT command-line tool provided with Windows. Follow these steps:

1. Open an elevated Command Prompt window. To do this on Windows 8, press Windows Logo+X and then select Command Prompt (Admin).

2. Type the command

   ```
   bcdedit /copy {default} /d "New Name"
   ```

   replacing New Name with the name you'd like to give the new boot option—something like **Windows 7 Ultimate 32bit VHD**. This will print a new globally unique identifier (GUID), something like {e88fb488-e1a9-11dd-8a96-a967342a44b3}.

3. Press Alt+Space and type **E K**. Then use the mouse to select the new GUID, including its curly brackets, and press Enter.

4. Type the following three commands, replacing {*guid*} with the identifier you just copied. Press Alt+Space and type **E P** to paste it in. Type the actual path to your bootable VHD file in place of [C:]*path**filename*. In these commands, the square brackets don't mean that the drive letter is optional, they really have to be typed in literally, as shown.

```
bcdedit /set {guid} device vhd="[C:]\path\filename.vhd"
bcdedit /set {guid} osdevice vhd="[C:]\path\filename.vhd"
bcdedit /set {guid} detecthal on
```

Now you should be able to restart and select the new OS entry from the boot menu.

When the VHD copy of Windows starts, it will see your computer's physical hardware for the first time, and should install the appropriate devices. You *should* be able to switch back and forth between booting it on real hardware and booting it inside Hyper-V or another VM manager. There could conceivably be some complaining by Windows Product Activation; however, a license that covers a VM installation should cover bare-metal execution of the same OS installation as well, because it's all installed on the exact same hardware and CPU. (The OS may *see* different hardware due to virtualization, but it's running on the same system in both cases.)

B

COMMAND-LINE UTILITIES

Working with Disk Management Tools

Windows 8 comes with a large collection of command-line disk management tools that enable you to check disks or partitions for errors, as well as defragment, format, partition, and convert disks. Table B.1 lists the disk management tools you can use with Windows 8.

> **note**
>
> If you need a refresher on accessing and using the command line, see Chapter 30, "Command-Line and Automation Tools."

> **note**
>
> In this section, we use the word *volume* to refer to any disk, partition, or mount point.

Table B.1 Windows 8's Command-Line Disk Management Tools

Tool	Description
CHKDSK	Checks a specified volume for errors.
CHKNTFS	Configures automatic disk checking.
CONVERT	Converts a specified volume to a different file system.
DEFRAG	Defragments a specified volume.
DISKCOMP	Compares the contents of two floppy disks. (This tool does not compare hard disks or other types of removable media, such as memory cards.)
DISKCOPY	Copies the contents of one floppy disk to another. (This tool does not copy hard disks or other types of removable media, such as memory cards.)
DISKPART	Enables you to list, create, select, delete, and extend disk partitions.
EXPAND	Extracts one or more files from a compressed file such as a .cab file found on some installation discs.
FORMAT	Formats the specified volume.
FSUTIL	Performs a number of file system tasks.
LABEL	Changes or deletes the name of a specified volume.
MOUNTVOL	Creates, displays, or deletes a mount point.
VOL	Displays the name and serial number of a specified volume.

The next three sections give you more detailed coverage of the CHKDKS, CHKNTFS, and DEFRAG tools.

CHKDSK: **Checking for Hard Disk Errors**

In Chapter 25, "Managing Hard Disks and Storage Spaces," you learned how to use the Check Disk utility to check a hard disk for errors. Check Disk also comes with a command-line version called CHKDSK that you can run in a Command Prompt window.

Here's the syntax for CHKDSK:

CHKDSK [*volume* [*filename*]] [/F] [/V] [/R] [/B] [/X] [/I] [/C] [/L:[*size*]]

volume	The drive letter (followed by a colon) or mount point.
filename	On FAT16 and FAT32 disks, the name of the file to check. Include the path if the file isn't in the current folder.
/F	Tells CHKDSK to automatically fix errors. This is the same as running the Check Disk GUI with the Automatically Fix File System Errors option activated.
/V	Runs CHKDSK in verbose mode. On FAT16 and FAT32 drives, CHKDSK displays the path and name of every file on the disk; on NTFS drives, CHKDSK displays cleanup messages, if any.

/R	Tells CHKDSK to scan the disk surface for bad sectors and recover data from the bad sectors, if possible. (The /F switch is implied.) This is the same as running the Check Disk GUI with the Scan For and Attempt Recovery of Bad Sectors option activated.
/B	Tells CHKDSK to clear the list of bad sectors on the disk and then recheck the entire disk. Including this parameter is the same as also including the /R parameter.
/X	On NTFS nonsystem disks that have open files, forces the volume to dismount, invalidates the open file handles, and then runs the scan. (The /F switch is implied.)
/I	On NTFS disks, tells CHKDSK to check only the file system's index entries.
/C	On NTFS disks, tells CHKDSK to skip the checking of cycles within the folder structure. This is a rare error, so using /C to skip the cycle check can speed up the disk check.
/L:[*size*]	On NTFS disks, tells CHKDSK to set the size of its log file to the specified number of kilobytes. The default size is 65,536, which is plenty big enough for most systems, so you should never need to change the size. Note that if you include this switch without the *size* parameter, Check Disk tells you the current size of the log file.
/scan	On NTFS disks, scans the volume for errors while leaving the volume online.
/forceofflinefix	On NTFS disks, forces CHKDSK to queue all volume errors for offline repair, even errors that can be fixed while the volume is online. The /scan parameter must also be included.
/perf	On NTFS disks, requests more system resources to increase scan performance. The /scan parameter must also be included.
/spotfix	On NTFS disks, spot fixes the volume.
/offlinescanandfix	On NTFS disks, takes the volume offline and runs a scan and repair on the volume.

For example, to run a read-only check—that is, a check that doesn't repair errors—on the C: drive, you enter the following command:

```
chkdsk c:
```

Note that when you use the /F switch to fix errors, CHKDSK must lock the volume to prevent running processes from using the volume during the check. If you use the /F switch on the %SystemDrive%, which is the drive where Windows 8 is installed (usually drive C:), CHKDSK can't lock the drive, and you see the following message:

```
Cannot lock current drive.

Chkdsk cannot run because the volume is in use by another
process. Would you like to schedule this volume to be
checked the next time the system restarts? (Y/N)
```

If you press Y and Enter, CHKDSK schedules a check for drive C: to run the next time you reboot Windows 8.

CHKNTFS: **Scheduling Automatic Disk Checks**

You saw in the preceding section that CHKDSK prompts you to schedule an automatic disk check during the next reboot if you run CHKDSK /F on the system drive (usually drive C: in Windows 8).

If you press Y and Enter at these prompts, CHKDSK adds the AUTOCHK utility to the following Registry setting:

```
HKLM\SYSTEM\CurrentControlSet\Control\Session Manager\BootExecute
```

This setting specifies the programs that Windows 8 should run at boot time when the Session Manager is loading. AUTOCHK is the automatic version of CHKDSK that runs at system startup.

Windows 8 also comes with a command-line tool named CHKNTFS that enables you to cancel pending automatic disk checks, schedule boot-time disk checks without using CHKDSK, and set the time that AUTOCHK counts down before running the automatic disk checks.

Here's the syntax for CHKNTFS:

```
CHKNTFS [volume ][/C volume:] [/X volume:] [/D] [/T:[time]]
```

volume	A drive letter (followed by a colon) or mount point.
/C *volume*	Tells CHKNTFS to schedule an automatic startup disk check for the specified volume. You can specify multiple volumes (separated by spaces).
/X *volume*	Tells CHKNTFS to exclude the specified volume from an automatic startup disk check. You can specify multiple volumes (separated by spaces).
/D	Tells CHKNTFS to exclude all volumes from an automatic startup disk check.
/T:[*time*]	Specifies the time that AUTOCHK counts down before starting the automatic disk checks.

When you run CHKNTFS with just a volume name, you see one of the following:

- If the volume is not scheduled for a startup disk check, you see the volume's file system:

  ```
  The type of the file system is NTFS.
  ```

- If the volume is scheduled for a startup disk check, you see the following message:

  ```
  Chkdsk has been scheduled manually to run on next reboot.
  ```

- If Windows 8's Storage Manager has detected an error on the volume, it marks the volume as *dirty*, so in this case you see the following message (using drive C: as an example):

  ```
  C: is dirty. You may use the /C option to schedule chkdsk for this drive.
  ```

This last message is confusing because Windows 8 *always* performs an automatic startup disk check of any volume that's marked as dirty. What you can do with CHKNTFS is bypass the automatic startup disk check of any volume that is marked as dirty. To do that, run CHKNTFS with the /X switch, as in this example:

```
chkntfs /x c:
```

If a volume isn't already marked as dirty, you can force CHKDSK to check a volume at startup by running CHKNTFS with the /C switch. For example, the following command sets up an automatic start check for the D: drive:

```
chkntfs /c d:
```

Note that the /C switch is cumulative, meaning that if you run it multiple times and specify a different volume each time, CHKNTFS adds each new volume to the list of volumes to check at startup. Instead of running multiple commands, however, you can specify multiple volumes in a single command, like so:

```
chkntfs /c c: d:
```

If you know a volume has been scheduled for a startup check, but you want to cancel that check, run CHKNTFS with the /X switch, as in this example:

```
chkntfs /x d:
```

You can also specify multiple volumes, if needed:

```
chkntfs /x c: d:
```

If you know that multiple volumes are scheduled for automatic startup checks, you can cancel all the checks by running CHKNTFS with the /D switch:

```
chkntfs /d
```

If you've scheduled a startup check for one or more volumes, or if a volume is marked as dirty, the next time you reboot Windows 8, you see a message similar to the following (which uses drive C: as an example):

```
Checking file system on C:
The type of the file system is NTFS.
Volume label is SYS.

One of your disks needs to be checked for consistency. You
may cancel the disk check, but it is strongly recommended
that you continue.
To skip disk checking, press any key within 10 second(s).
```

> **note**
>
> To manually mark a volume as dirty, use the FSUTIL DIRTY SET *volume* command, where *volume* is the drive you want to work with. For example, the following command marks drive C: as dirty:
>
> ```
> fsutil dirty set c:
> ```
>
> If you're not sure whether a drive is dirty, either run CHKNTFS *volume* or run FSUTIL DIRTY QUERY *volume*, as in this example:
>
> ```
> fsutil dirty query c:
> ```
>
> Note, however, that FSUTIL doesn't give you any way to unmark a drive as dirty.

The number of seconds in the last line counts down to 0. If you press a key before the countdown ends, Windows 8 skips the disk check; otherwise, it continues with CHKDSK.

You can change the initial countdown value by running CHKNTFS with the /T switch, followed by the number of seconds you want to use for the countdown. For example, the following command sets the countdown to 30 seconds:

> ⚡ **caution**
>
> Pressing any key to skip the disk check usually only works with wired keyboards. On most wireless keyboards, pressing a key has no effect.

```
chkntfs /t:30
```

Note that if you run the command CHKNTFS /T (that is, you don't specify a countdown value), CHKNTFS returns the current countdown value.

DEFRAG: Defragmenting the System Drive

In Chapter 25, you learned how to defragment a volume using Windows 8's Disk Defragmenter program. If you want to schedule a defragment or perform this chore from a batch file, you have to use the DEFRAG command-line tool. Here's the syntax:

```
DEFRAG disks [task(s)] [/A] [/C] [/E] [/F] [/H] [/M] [/O] [/R] [/T] [/U] [/V]
```

disks	Specifies the drive letter (followed by a colon) of each disk you want to defragment (separate multiple drives with a space).
task(s)	As this book went to press, Microsoft had not provided any information on this new parameter.
/A	Tells DEFRAG only to analyze the disk.
/C	Tells DEFRAG to defragment all the system's drives.
/D	Tells DEFRAG to run a traditional optimization (that is, one that does not include the *tasks(s)* parameter; this is the default switch, meaning that this is the type of optimization that DEFRAG runs if you don't specify any switches).
/E	Tells DEFRAG to defragment all the system's drives except those specified with the *disks* parameter.
/F	Forces DEFRAG to defragment the disk, even if it doesn't need defragmenting or if the disk has less than 7% free space. (DEFRAG normally requires at least that much free space because it needs an area in which to sort the files.)
/H	Runs DEFRAG with a higher program priority for better performance.
/M	Tells DEFRAG to defragment all the specified drives at the same time (in parallel).
/O	Tells DEFRAG to perform.
/T	Tells DEFRAG to show the progress of an already running defrag.
/U	Tells DEFRAG to show the progress of the defrag.
/V	Runs DEFRAG in verbose mode, which displays both the analysis report and the defragmentation report.
/X	Consolidates the free space on the volume.

For example, to get an analysis report of the fragmentation of drive C:, enter the following command:

```
defrag c: /a
```

If the volume isn't too fragmented, you see a report similar to this:

```
Post Defragmentation Report:

        Volume Information:
                Volume size             = 116.49 GB
                Free space              = 106.89 GB
                Total fragmented space  = 1%
                Largest free space size = 56.49 GB


        Note: File fragments larger than 64MB are not
        included in the fragmentation statistics.

        You do not need to defragment this volume.
```

However, if the drive is quite fragmented, you see a report similar to the following:

```
Post Defragmentation Report:

        Volume Information:
                Volume size             = 397.12 GB
                Free space              = 198.32 GB
                Total fragmented space  = 9%
                Largest free space size = 158.43 GB


        Note: File fragments larger than 64MB are not
        included in the fragmentation statistics.

It is recommended that you defragment this volume.
```

If you try to defragment a volume that is running low on disk space, DEFRAG displays the following message:

```
Volume DATA has only 9% free space available for use by Disk Defragmenter.
To run effectively, Disk Defragmenter requires at least 15% usable free space.
There is not enough disk space to properly complete the operation.
Delete some unneeded files on your hard disk, and then try again.
```

If you can't delete files from the volume (for example, if this is a Windows 8 data partition), you can try running DEFRAG with the -f switch to force the operation:

```
defrag d: -f
```

> **note**
>
> To run the DEFRAG utility, you must use an administrator Command Prompt session. Press Windows Logo+X and then click Command Prompt (Admin).

> **note**
>
> Forcing the defrag operation shouldn't cause problems in most cases. With less free space in which to work, DEFRAG just takes quite a bit longer to defragment the volume, and there may be parts of the volume that it simply can't defragment.

Working with File and Folder Management Tools

File Explorer is the GUI tool of choice for most file and folder operations. However, Windows 8 comes with an impressive collection of command-line file and folder tools that let you perform all the standard operations, such as renaming, copying, moving, and deleting, as well as more interesting chores, such as changing file attributes and comparing the contents of two files. Table B.2 lists the file management tools you can use with Windows 8.

Table B.2 Windows 8's Command-Line File and Folder Management Tools

Tool	Description
ATTRIB	Displays, applies, or removes attributes for the specified file or folder.
CD	Changes to the specified folder.
COMP	Compares the contents of two specified files, byte by byte.
COMPACT	Displays or modifies the compression settings for the specified file or folder (which must be located on an NTFS partition).
COPY	Creates a copy of the specified file or folder in another location.
DEL	Deletes the specified file or folder.
DIR	Displays a directory listing for the current folder or for the specified file or folder.
FC	Compares the content of two specified files.
FIND	Searches for and displays all the instances of a specified string in a file.
FINDSTR	Uses a regular expression to search for and display all the instances of a specified string in a file.
MKDIR	Creates the specified folder.
MOVE	Moves the specified file or folder to another location.
REN	Changes the name of the specified file or folder.
REPLACE	Replaces files in the destination folder with files in the source folder that have the same name.
RMDIR	Deletes the specified folder.
SORT	Sorts the specified file and then displays the results.
SFC	Runs the System File Checker, which scans and verifies the protected Windows 8 files.
TAKEOWN	Enables an administrator to take ownership of the specified file.

Tool	Description
TREE	Displays a graphical tree diagram showing the subfolder hierarchy of the current folder or the specified folder.
WHERE	Searches for and displays all the files that match a specified pattern in the current folder and in the PATH folders.
XCOPY	Creates a copy of the specified file or folder in another location. This tool offers many more options than the COPY command.

The next few sections take a closer look at a half dozen of these tools: ATTRIB, FIND, REN, REPLACE, SORT, and XCOPY.

Before getting to the tools, we should mention that most of the file and folder management tools work with the standard wildcard characters: ? and *. In a file or folder specification, you use ? to substitute for a single character, and you use * to substitute for multiple characters. Here are some examples:

File Specification	Matches
Budget201?.xlsx	Budget2012.xlsx, Budget2013.xlsx, and so on
Memo.doc?	Memo.doc, Memo.docx, Memo.docm, and so on
*.txt	ReadMe.txt, log.txt, to-do.txt, and so on
*201?.pptx	Report2011.pptx, Budget2012.pptx, Conference2013.pptx, and so on
.	Every file

ATTRIB: **Modifying File and Folder Attributes**

A file's *attributes* are special codes that indicate the status of the file. There are seven attributes you can work with:

- **Archive**—When this attribute is turned on, it means the file has been modified since it was last backed up.

- **Hidden**—When this attribute is turned on, it means the file doesn't show up in a DIR listing and isn't included when you run most command-line tools. For example, if you run DEL *.* in a folder, Windows 8 deletes all the files in that folder, except the hidden files.

- **Integrity**—When this attribute is set, it means the volume is configured with *integrity*, where data is stored in such a way that it is protected from certain types of file errors. Although technically available in Windows 8, this attribute only works with Windows 8 Server volumes formatted with the ReFS file system.

- **No scrub**—When this attribute is set, the file is skipped by the scrubber, which is a background service that identifies and (if possible) fixes certain types of file errors. Again, this attribute only works with Windows 8 Server volumes formatted with the ReFS file system.

- **Not content indexed**—When this attribute is set, the file's contents will not be indexed for searching.

- **Read-only**—When this attribute is turned on, it means the file can't be modified or erased.

- **System**—When this attribute is turned on, it means the file is an operating system file (that is, a file that was installed with Windows 8).

The `ATTRIB` command lets you turn these attributes on or off. Here's the syntax:

```
ATTRIB [+A ¦ -A] [+H ¦ -H] [+I ¦ -I] [+R ¦ -R] [+S ¦ -S] filename [/S [/D] [/L]]
```

+A	Sets the archive attribute.
-A	Clears the archive attribute.
+H	Sets the hidden attribute.
-H	Clears the hidden attribute.
+I	Sets the not content indexed attribute.
-I	Clears the not content indexed attribute.
+R	Sets the read-only attribute.
-R	Clears the read-only attribute.
+S	Sets the system attribute.
-S	Clears the system attribute.
+X	Sets the integrity attribute.
-X	Clears the integrity attribute.
filename	The file or files you want to work with.
/S	Applies the attribute change to the matching files in the current folder and all of its subfolders.
/D	Applies the attribute change only to the current folder's subfolders. You must use this switch in conjunction with /S.
/L	Applies the command to a symbolic link (that is, an NTFS file system object that points to another file system object, which is called the *target*) rather than the target of the symbolic link.

For example, if you want to hide all the DOCX files in the current directory, use the following command:

```
attrib +h *.docx
```

As another example, if you've ever tried to delete or edit a file and got the message Access denied, the file is likely read-only. You can turn off the read-only attribute by running ATTRIB with the -R switch, as in this example:

```
attrib -r readonly.txt
```

You can also use ATTRIB for protecting important or sensitive files. When you hide a file, it doesn't show up in a listing produced by the DIR command. Out of sight is out of mind, so someone taking a casual glance at your files won't see the hidden ones and, therefore, won't be tempted to display or erase them.

> **note**
>
> If you want to check out a file's attributes, use the DIR command's /A switch. Use /AA to see files with their archive attribute set; /AH for hidden files; /AI for not content indexed files; /AR for read-only files; /AS for system files; and /AX for integrity files.

Although a hidden file is invisible, it's not totally safe. Someone who knows the name of the file can attempt to modify the file by opening it with the appropriate program. As an added measure of safety, you can also set the file's read-only attribute. When you do this, the file can't be modified. You can set both attributes with a single command:

```
attrib +h +r payroll.xlsx
```

FIND: **Locating a Text String in a File**

You use the FIND command to search for a string inside a file. Here's the syntax:

```
FIND [/C] [/I] [/N] [/V] "string" filename
```

/C	Displays the number of times that *string* appears in *filename*.
/I	Performs a case-insensitive search.
/N	Displays each match of *string* in *filename* with the line number in *filename* where each match occurs.
/V	Displays the lines in *filename* that don't contain *string*.
string	The string you want to search for.
filename	The file you want to search in. (Note that you can't use wildcards with the FIND command.) If the filename contains one or more spaces, surround it with double quotation marks.

For example, to find the string *Xbox* in a file named WishList.txt, you use the following command:

```
find "Xbox" WishList.txt
```

If the string you want to find contains double quotation marks, you need to place two quotation marks in the search string. For example, to find the phrase *Dave "The Hammer" Schultz* in the file players.doc, use the following command:

```
find "Dave ""The Hammer"" Schultz" players.doc
```

> **note**
>
> The FIND command doesn't work with the Office 2007 and later XML-based file formats. However, it works fine with most documents created in earlier versions of Office.

🌐 tip

The FIND command doesn't accept wildcard characters in the filename parameter. That's too bad, because it's often useful to search multiple files for a string. Fortunately, you can work around this limitation by using a FOR loop where the command you run on each file is FIND. Here's the general syntax to use:

```
FOR %f IN (filespec) DO FIND "string" %f
```

Replace filespec with the file specification you want to use, and string with the string you want to search for. For example, the following command runs through all the .doc files in the current folder and searches each file for the string *Thanksgiving*:

```
FOR %f IN (*.doc) DO FIND "Thanksgiving" %f
```

If the file specification will match files with spaces in their names, you need to surround the last %f parameter with quotation marks, like so:

```
FOR %f IN (*.doc) DO FIND "Thanksgiving" "%f"
```

One of the most common uses of the FIND command is as a filter in pipe operations. In this case, instead of a filename, you pipe the output of another command through FIND. In this case, FIND searches this input for a specified string and, if it finds a match, displays the line that contains the string.

For example, the last line of a DIR listing tells you the number of bytes free on the current drive. Rather than wade through the entire DIR output just to get this information, use this command instead:

```
dir ¦ find "free"
```

You'll see something like the following:

```
2 Dir(s) 28,903,331,184 bytes free
```

FIND scours the DIR listing piped to it and looks for the word *free*. You can use this technique to display specific lines from, say, a CHKDSK report. For example, searching for *bad* finds the number of bad sectors on the disk.

REN: **Renaming a File or Folder**

You use the REN (or RENAME) command to change the name of one or more files and folders. Here's the syntax:

```
REN old_filename1 new_filename
```

old_filename	The original filename
new_filename	The new filename

For example, the following command renames `Budget 2012.xlsx` to `Budget 2013.xlsx`:

```
ren "Budget 2012.xlsx" "Budget 2013.xlsx"
```

A simple file or folder rename such as this probably isn't something you'll ever fire up a command-line session to do because renaming a single object is faster and easier in File Explorer. However, the real power of the REN command is that it accepts wildcards in the file specifications. This enables you to rename several files at once, something you can't do in File Explorer.

For example, suppose you have a folder full of files, many of which contain `2012` somewhere in the filename. To rename all those files by changing `2012` to `2013`, you'd use the following command:

```
ren *2012* *2013*
```

Similarly, if you have a folder full of files that use the `.htm` extension and you want to change each extension to `.asp`, you use the following command:

```
ren *.htm *.asp
```

Note that for these multiple-file renames to work, in most cases the original filename text and the new filename text must be the same length. For example, digital cameras often supply photos with names such as `img_1234.jpg` and `img_5678.jpg`. If you have a number of related photos in a folder, you might want to give them more meaningful names. If the photos are from a vacation in Rome, you might prefer names such as `Rome_Vacation_1234.jpg` and `Rome_Vacation_5678.jpg`. Unfortunately, the REN command can't handle this. However, it can rename the files to `Rome_1234.jpg` and `Rome_5678.jpg`:

```
ren img_* Rome*
```

The exception to the same-length rule is if the replacement occurs at the end of the filenames. For example, the following command renames all files with the `.jpeg` extension to `.jpg`:

```
ren *.jpeg *.jpg
```

REPLACE: **Smarter File Copying**

If there was such a thing as a Most Underrated Command award, REPLACE would win it hands down. This command, which you almost never hear about, can do three *very* useful (and very different) things:

- It copies files, but only if their names match those in the target directory.

- It copies files, but only if their names don't exist in the target directory.

- It copies files, but only if their names match those in the target directory and the matching files in the target directory are older than the files being copied.

Here's the syntax:

```
REPLACE source_files target /A /U /P /R /S /W
```

source_files	The path and file specification of the files you want to copy.
target	The folder to which you want to copy the files.
/A	Copies only new files to the *target* folder. You can't use this switch in conjunction with /S or /U.
/U	Copies files that have the same name in the *target* folder and that are newer than the matching files in the *target* folder. You can't use this switch in conjunction with /A.
/P	Prompts you for confirmation before replacing files.
/R	Replaces read-only files.
/S	Replaces files in the *target* folder's subfolders. You can't use this switch in conjunction with /A.
/W	Waits for you to insert a disk before starting.

If you don't specify switches, REPLACE copies a file from the source folder to the target folder if and only if it finds a file with a matching name in the target.

More useful is the REPLACE command's updating mode, where it copies a file from the source folder to the target folder if and only if it finds a file with a matching name in the target and that target file is older than the source file. A good example where updating comes in handy is when you copy some files to a disk or memory card so that you can use them on another machine (such as taking files from your computer at work to use them at home). When you need to copy the files back to the first machine, the following REPLACE command does the job. (This assumes the disk or memory card is in the G: drive.)

```
replace g:*.* %UserProfile% /s /u
```

For each file on the G: drive, REPLACE looks for matching filenames anywhere in the %UserProfile% folder and its subfolders (thanks to the /S switch) and replaces only the ones that are newer (the /U switch).

What if you created some new files on the other computer? To copy those to the first machine, use the /A switch, as follows:

```
replace g:*.* %UserProfile%\Documents /a
```

In this case, REPLACE only copies a file from the G: drive if it doesn't exist in the %UserProfile%\Documents folder. (You have to specify a target folder because you can't use the /S switch with /A.)

SORT: **Sorting the Contents of a File**

When you obtain a file from the Internet or some other source, the data in the file may not appear in the order you want. What we usually do in such cases is import the file into Word or Excel and then use the program's Sort feature. This sometimes involves extra steps (such as converting text to a table in Word), so it's not always an efficient way to work.

If the file is text, it's often easier and faster to run the SORT command-line tool. By default, SORT takes the content of the file, sorts it in ascending alphanumeric order (0 to 9, then a to z, and then A to Z) starting at the beginning of each line in the file, and then displays the sorted results. You can also run descending order sorts, write the results to the same file or another file, and more. Here's the syntax:

```
SORT [input_file] [/+n] [/R] [/L locale] [/M kilobytes] [/REC characters]
➥[/T temp_folder] [/O output_file]
```

input_file	The file you want to sort.
/+n	Specifies the starting character position (*n*) of the sort. The default is 1 (that is, the first character on each line in the file).
/R	Sorts the file in descending order (Z to A, then z to a, and then 9 to 0).
/L locale	Specifies a *locale* for sorting other than the default system locale. Your only choice here is to use "C" to sort the file using the binary values for each character.
/M kilobytes	Specifies the amount of memory, in kilobytes, that SORT uses during the operation. If you don't specify this value, SORT uses a minimum of 160KB and a maximum of 90% of available memory.
/REC characters	Specifies the maximum length, in characters, of each line in the file. The default value is 4,096 characters, and the maximum value is 65,535 characters.
/T temp_folder	Specifies the folder that SORT should use to hold the temporary files it uses during the sort.
/O output_file	Specifies the file that SORT should create to store the results of the sort. You can specify a different file or the *input file*.

For example, the following SORT command sorts the data in `records.txt` and stores the results in `sorted_records.txt`:

```
sort records.txt sorted_records.txt
```

XCOPY: **Advanced File Copying**

The XCOPY command is one of the most powerful of the file management command-line tools, and you can use it for some fairly sophisticated file copying operations. Here's the syntax for XCOPY:

```
XCOPY source destination [/A ¦ /M] [/C] [/D[:mm-dd--yyyy]]
➡[/EXCLUDE:file1[+file2[+file3]]] [/F] [/G] [/H] [/I] [/K] [/L] [/N]
➡[/O] [/P] [/Q] [/R] [/S [/E]] [/T] [/U] [/V] [/W] [/X] [/Y ¦ -Y] [/Z]
```

source	The path and names of the files you want to copy.
destination	The location where you want the *source* files copied.
[/A]	Tells XCOPY to only copy those *source* files that have their archive attribute turned on. The archive attribute is not changed. If you use /A, you can't also use /M.
[/M]	Tells XCOPY to only copy those *source* files that have their archive attribute turned on. The archive attribute is turned off. If you use /M, you can't also use /A.
[/C]	Tells XCOPY to ignore any errors that occur during the copy operation. Otherwise, XCOPY aborts the operation if an error occurs.
[/D[:*mm-dd-yyyy*]]	Copies only those *source* files that changed on or after the date specified by *mm-dd-yyyy*. If you don't specify a date, using /D tells XCOPY to copy those *source* files that are newer than *destination* files that have the same name.
[/EXCLUDE: *file1* [+*file2*[+*file3*]]]	Tells XCOPY to not copy the files or file specification given by *file1*, *file2*, *file3*, and so on.
[/F]	Displays the *source* and *destination* filename during the copy operation.
[/G]	Creates decrypted copies of encrypted *source* files.
[/H]	Tells XCOPY to include in the copy operation any hidden and system files in the *source* folder.
[/I]	Tells XCOPY to create the *destination* folder. For this to work, the *source* value must be a folder or a file specification with wildcards.
[/K]	For each *source* file that has its read-only attribute set, tells XCOPY to maintain the read-only attribute on the corresponding *destination* file.
[/L]	Displays a list of the files that XCOPY will copy. (No files are copied if you use /L.)
[/N]	Tells XCOPY to use 8.3 filenames in the *destination* folder. Use this switch if the *destination* folder is a FAT partition that doesn't support long filenames.
[/O]	Tells XCOPY to also copy ownership and discretionary access control list data to the *destination*.
[/P]	Prompts you to confirm each file copy.
[/Q]	Tells XCOPY not to display messages during the copy.

[/R]	Includes read-only files in the copy.
[/S]	Tells XCOPY to also include the *source* folder's subfolders in the copy.
[/E]	Tells XCOPY to include empty subfolders in the copy if you specify the /S or /T switch.
[/T]	Tells XCOPY to copy the *source* folder subfolder structure. (No files are copied, just the subfolders.)
[/U]	Only copies those *source* files that exist in the *destination* folder.
[/V]	Tells XCOPY to verify that each *destination* copy is identical to the original *source* file.
[/W]	Displays the message Press any key to begin copying file(s) before copying. You must press a key to launch the copy (or press Ctrl+C to cancel).
[/X]	Tells XCOPY to also copy file audit settings and system access control list data to the *destination*. (This switch implies /O.)
[/Y]	Tells XCOPY not to ask you whether you want to overwrite existing files in the *destination*.
[/-Y]	Tells XCOPY to ask you whether you want to overwrite existing files in the *destination*. Use this switch if you've set the %COPYCMD% environment variable to /Y, which suppresses overwrite prompts for XCOPY, COPY, and MOVE.
[/Z]	If you're copying to a network *destination*, this switch tells XCOPY to restart to the copy if the network connection goes down during the operation.

In its basic form, XCOPY works just like COPY. So, for example, to copy all the .doc files in the current folder to a folder called Documents in the G: drive, use the following command:

```
xcopy *.doc g:\documents
```

Besides being faster, XCOPY also contains a number of features not found in the puny COPY command. Think of it as COPY on steroids. (The X in XCOPY means that it's an extended COPY command.) For example, suppose you want to copy all the .doc files in the current folder and all the .doc files in any attached subfolders to G:\Documents. With COPY, you first have to create the appropriate folders on the destination partition and then perform separate COPY commands for each folder, which is not very efficient, to say the least. With XCOPY, all you do is add a single switch:

```
xcopy *.doc g:\documents /s
xcopy *.bat d:\batch /s
```

The /S switch tells XCOPY to copy the current folder and all nonempty subfolders, and to create the appropriate folders in the destination, as needed. (If you want XCOPY to copy empty subfolders, include the /E switch as well.)

Another useful feature of XCOPY is the ability to copy files by date. This is handy for performing incremental backups of files that you modified on or after a specific date. For example, suppose you keep your word processing documents in %UserProfile%\Documents and you want to make backup copies in your Windows 8 user share of all the .doc files that have changed since August 23, 2010. You can do this with the following command:

```
xcopy %userprofile%\documents\*.doc \\server\users\%Username%\ /d:08-23-2010
```

It's common to use XCOPY in batch files, but take care to handle errors. For example, what if a batch file tries to use XCOPY, but there's not enough memory? Or what if the user presses Ctrl+C during the copy? It might seem impossible to check for these kinds of errors; yet it is not only possible, it's really quite easy.

When certain commands finish, they always file a report on the progress of the operation. This report, or *exit code*, is a number that specifies how the operation went. For example, Table B.3 lists the exit codes that the XCOPY command uses.

Table B.3 XCOPY Exit Codes

Exit Code	What It Means
0	Everything's okay; the files were copied.
1	Nothing happened because no files were found to copy.
2	The user pressed Ctrl+C to abort the copy.
4	The command failed because there wasn't enough memory or disk space or because something was wrong with the command's syntax or an invalid drive name was entered.
5	The command failed because of a disk error.

What does all this mean for your batch files? You can use a variation of the IF command—IF ERRORLEVEL—to test for these exit codes. For example, here's a batch file that uses some of the XCOPY exit codes to check for errors:

```
@ECHO OFF
XCOPY %1 %2
IF ERRORLEVEL 4 GOTO ERROR
IF ERRORLEVEL 2 GOTO CTRL+C
IF ERRORLEVEL 1 GOTO NO_FILES
GOTO DONE
:ERROR
ECHO Bad news! The copy failed because there wasn't
ECHO enough memory or disk space or because there was
ECHO something wrong with your file specs . . .
GOTO DONE
:CTRL+C
ECHO Hey, what gives? You pressed Ctrl+C to abort . . .
```

```
GOTO DONE
:NO_FILES
ECHO Bad news! No files were found to copy . . .
:DONE
```

As you can see, the ERRORLEVEL conditions check for the individual exit codes and then use GOTO to jump to the appropriate label.

One of the most important things to know about the IF ERRORLEVEL test is how Windows 8 interprets it. For example, consider the following IF command:

```
IF ERRORLEVEL 2 GOTO CTRL+C
```

Windows 8 interprets this command as "If the exit code from the last command is equal to or greater than 2, jump to the CTRL+C label." This has two important consequences for your batch files:

> **note**
>
> How does a batch file know what a command's exit code was? When Windows 8 gets an exit code from a command, it stores it in a special data area set aside for exit code information. When Windows 8 sees the IF ERRORLEVEL command in a batch file, it retrieves the exit code from the data area so that it can be compared to whatever is in the IF condition.

- The test IF ERRORLEVEL 0 doesn't tell you much because it's always true. If you just want to find out whether the command failed, use the test IF NOT ERRORLEVEL 0.

- To get the correct results, always test the *highest* ERRORLEVEL first and then work your way down.

Working with System Management Tools

System management is one of those catch-all terms that encompasses a wide range of tasks, from simple adjustments such as changing the system date and time to more complex tweaks such as modifying the Registry. Windows 8's command-line system management tools also enable you to monitor system performance, shut down or restart the computer, and even modify the huge Windows Management Instrumentation (WMI) interface. Table B.4 lists the system management command-line tools that apply to Windows 8.

Table B.4 Windows 8's Command-Line System Management Tools

Tool	Description
BCDEDIT	Displays or modifies the Boot Manager startup parameters
CHCP	Displays or changes the number of active console code pages
DATE	Displays or sets the system date
EVENTCREATE	Creates a custom event in an event log
REG	Adds, modifies, displays, and deletes Registry keys and settings
REGSVR32	Registers dynamic link library (DLL) files as command components in the Registry
SHUTDOWN	Shuts down or restarts Windows 8 or a remote computer

Table B.4 Continued

Tool	Description
SYSTEMINFO	Displays a wide range of detailed configuration information about the computer
TIME	Displays or sets the system time
TYPEPERF	Monitors a performance counter
WHOAMI	Displays information about the current user, including the domain name (not applicable to Windows 8), computer name, username, security group membership, and security privileges
WMIC	Operates the Windows Management Instrumentation command-line tool that provides command-line access to the WMI interface

The next few sections take more detailed looks at five of these command-line tools: REG, SHUTDOWN, SYSTEMINFO, TYPEPERF, and WHOAMI.

REG: **Working with Registry Keys and Settings**

In Chapter 29, "Editing the Windows Registry," you learned how to view, add, and modify Registry keys and settings using the Registry Editor. That's the easiest and safest way to make Registry changes. However, there may be some settings that you change quite often. In such cases, it can become burdensome to be frequently launching the Registry Editor and changing the settings. A better idea is to create a shortcut or batch file that uses the REG command-line tool to make your Registry changes for you.

REG actually consists of 11 subcommands, each of which enables you to perform different Registry tasks:

REG ADD	Adds new keys or settings to the Registry. You can also use this command to modify existing settings.
REG QUERY	Displays the current values of one or more settings in one or more keys.
REG COMPARE	Compares the values of two Registry keys or settings.
REG COPY	Copies Registry keys or settings to another part of the Registry.
REG DELETE	Deletes a key or setting.
REG EXPORT	Exports a key to a .reg file.
REG IMPORT	Imports the contents of a .reg file.
REG SAVE	Copies Registry keys or settings to a hive (.hiv) file.
REG RESTORE	Writes a hive file into an existing Registry key. The hive file must be created using REG SAVE.
REG LOAD	Loads a hive file into a new Registry key. The hive file must be created using REG SAVE.
REG UNLOAD	Unloads a hive file that was loaded using REG LOAD.

We won't go through all of these commands. Instead, we'll focus on the three most common Registry tasks: viewing, adding, and modifying Registry data.

To view the current value of the Registry setting, you use the REG QUERY command:

```
REG QUERY KeyName [/V SettingName ¦ /VE] [/C] [/D] [/E] [/F data] [/K ¦ [/S]
➥[/SE separator] [/T type] [/Z]
```

KeyName	The Registry key that contains the setting or settings you want to view. The *KeyName* must include a root key value: HKCR, HKCU, HKLM, HKU, or HKCC. Place quotation marks around key names that include spaces.
/V *ValueName*	The Registry setting in *KeyName* that you want to view.
/VE	Tells REG to look for empty settings (that is, settings with a null value).
/F data	Specifies the *data* that REG should match in the *KeyName* settings.
/C	Runs a case-sensitive query.
/E	Returns only exact matches.
/K	Queries only key names, not settings.
/S	Tells REG to query the subkeys of *KeyName*.
/SE *separator*	Defines the *separator* to search for in REG_MULTI_SZ settings.
/T *type*	Specifies the setting type or types to search: REG_SZ, REG_MULTI_SZ, REG_EXPAND_SZ, REG_DWORD, REG_BINARY, or REG_NONE.
/Z	Tells REG to include the numeric equivalent of the setting type in the query results.

For example, if you want to know the current value of the RegisteredOwner setting in HKLM\Software\Microsoft\Windows NT\CurrentVersion, run the following command:

```
reg query "hklm\software\microsoft\windows nt\currentversion" registeredowner
```

The Registry Editor has a Find command that enables you to look for text within the Registry. However, it would occasionally be useful to see a list of the Registry keys and settings that contains a particular bit of text. You can do this using the /F switch. For example, suppose you want to see a list of all the HKLM keys and settings that contain the text *Windows Defender*. Here's a command that will do this:

```
reg query hklm /f "Windows Defender" /s
```

To add a key or setting to the Registry, use the REG ADD command:

```
REG ADD KeyName [/V SettingName ¦ /VE] [/D data] [/F ¦ [/S separator] [/T type]
```

KeyName	The Registry key that you want to add or to which you want to add a setting. The *KeyName* must include a root key value: HKCR, HKCU, HKLM, HKU, or HKCC. Place quotation marks around key names that include spaces.
/V *ValueName*	The setting you want to add to *KeyName*.
/VE	Tells REG to add an empty setting.
/D *data*	Specifies the *data* that REG should use as the value for the new setting.
/F	Modifies an existing key or setting without prompting to confirm the change.
/S *separator*	Defines the *separator* to use between multiple instances of data in a new REG_MULTI_SZ setting.
/T *type*	Specifies the setting type: REG_SZ, REG_MULTI_SZ, REG_EXPAND_SZ, REG_DWORD, REG_DWORD_BIG_ENDIAN, REG_DWORD_LITTLE_ENDIAN, REG_BINARY, or REG_LINK.

For example, the following command adds a key named MySettings to the HKCU root key:

```
reg add hkcu\MySettings
```

Here's another example that adds a setting named CurrentProject to the new MySettings key and sets the value of the new setting to Win 8 In Depth:

```
reg add hkcu\MySettings /v CurrentProject /d "Win 8 In Depth"
```

If you want to make changes to an existing setting, run REG ADD on the setting. For example, to change the HKCU\MySettings\CurrentProject setting to Windows 8 In Depth, you run the following command:

```
reg add hkcu\MySettings /v CurrentProject /d "Windows 8 In Depth"
```

Windows 8 responds with the following prompt:

```
Value CurrentProject exists, overwrite (Yes/No)?
```

To change the existing value, press Y and press Enter.

 tip
To avoid being prompted when changing existing settings, add the /F switch to the REG ADD command.

SHUTDOWN: **Shutting Down or Restarting the System**

You can use the SHUTDOWN command to restart or shut down your computer (or a remote computer on your network). Here's the full syntax:

```
SHUTDOWN [[/R] ¦ [/S] ¦ [/L] ¦ [/H] ¦ [/I] ¦ [/P] ¦ [/E] ¦ [/A]] [/F ¦
➥[/T seconds] [/D [P:]xx:yy] [/M \\ComputerName] [/C "comment"]
```

/R	Restarts the computer.
/S	Shuts down the computer.
/L	Logs off the current user immediately.
/H	Puts the computer into hibernation, if the computer supports hibernation mode.
/I	Displays the Remote Shutdown dialog box, which enables you to specify many of the options provided by these switches.
/P	Turns off the local computer immediately (that is, without the usual warning interval).
/E	Enables you to document the reason for an unexpected shutdown.
/A	Cancels the pending restart or shutdown.
/F	Forces all running programs on the target computer to shut down without warning. This, obviously, is dangerous and should be used only as a last resort.

/D
[P:]*major:minor*

Specifies the reason for the shutdown. Include P: to indicate the shutdown is planned. Use values between 0 and 255 for *major* and between 0 and 65535 for *minor*. Windows also defines a number of predefined values for the *major* and *minor* parameters:

major	*minor*	Reason
0	0	Other (Planned)
0	5	Other Failure: System Unresponsive
1	1	Hardware: Maintenance (Unplanned)
1	1	Hardware: Maintenance (Planned)
1	2	Hardware: Installation (Unplanned)
1	2	Hardware: Installation (Planned)
2	3	Operating System: Upgrade (Planned)
2	4	Operating System: Reconfiguration (Unplanned)
2	4	Operating System: Reconfiguration (Planned)
2	16	Operating System: Service Pack (Planned)
2	17	Operating System: Hot Fix (Unplanned)
2	17	Operating System: Hot Fix (Planned)
2	18	Operating System: Security Fix (Unplanned)
2	18	Operating System: Security Fix (Planned)
4	1	Application: Maintenance (Unplanned)
4	1	Application: Maintenance (Planned)
4	2	Application: Installation (Planned)
4	5	Application: Unresponsive

4	6	Application: Unstable
5	15	System Failure: Stop Error
5	19	Security Issue
5	19	Security Issue
5	19	Security Issue
5	20	Loss of Network Connectivity (Unplanned)
6	11	Power Failure: Cord Unplugged
6	12	Power Failure: Environment
7	0	Legacy API Shutdown

/M *ComputerName* Specifies the remote computer you want to shut down.

/T *seconds* Specifies the number of seconds after which the computer is shut down. The default is 30 seconds, and you can specify any number up to 600.

/C "*comment*" The *comment* text (which can be a maximum of 127 characters) appears in the dialog box and warns the user of the pending shutdown. This comment text also appears in the shutdown event that is added to the System log in Event Viewer. (Look for an Event ID of 1074.)

For example, to restart your computer immediately, use the following command:

```
shutdown /r /t 0
```

If you've launched a restart or shutdown using some nonzero value for /T, and you need to cancel the pending shutdown, run SHUTDOWN with the /A switch before the timeout interval is over:

```
shutdown /a
```

SYSTEMINFO: Returning System Configuration Data

If you want to get information about various aspects of your computer, a good place to start is the SYSTEMINFO command-line tool, which displays data about the following aspects of your system:

- The operating system name, version, and configuration type
- The registered owner and organization
- The original install date
- The system boot time
- The computer manufacturer, make, and model
- The system processors

- The BIOS version

- The total and available physical memory

- The paging file's maximum size, available size, in-use value, and location

- The installed hotfixes

- The network interface card data, such as the name, connection, DHCP status, and IP address (or addresses)

You can see all this data (and more), as well as control the output, by running SYSTEMINFO with the following syntax:

```
SYSTEMINFO [/S computer] [/U [domain]\username] [/P password]
➡[/FO format] [/NH]
```

/S computer	The name of the remote computer for which you want to view the system configuration.
/U [domain]\username	The *username* and, optionally, the *domain* of the account under which you want to run the SYSTEMINFO command.
/P password	The *password* of the account you specified with /U.
/FO format	The output format, where *format* is one of the following values:
	table—The output is displayed in a row-and-column format, with headers in the first row and values in subsequent rows.
	list—The output is displayed in a two-column list, with the headers in the first column and values in the second column.
	csv—The output is displayed with headers and values separated by commas. The headers appear on the first line.
/NH	Tells SYSTEMINFO not to include column headers when you use the /FO switch with either table or csv.

The output of SYSTEMINFO is quite long, so pipe it through the MORE command to see the output one screen at a time:

```
systeminfo ¦ more
```

If you want to examine the output in another program or import the results into Excel or Access, redirect the output to a file and use the appropriate format. For example, Excel can read .csv files, so you can redirect the SYSTEMINFO output to a .csv file while using csv as the output format:

```
systeminfo /fo csv > systeminfo.csv
```

TYPEPERF: **Monitoring Performance**

In Chapter 23, "Windows Management Tools," you learned how to use the Performance Monitor utility to track the real-time performance of counters in various categories such as processor and memory.

➡️ *For the details on the Performance Monitor utility,* ***see*** *"Using the Performance Monitor," **p. 554**.*

You can get the same benefit without the Performance Monitor GUI by using the powerful TYPEPERF command-line tool. Here's the syntax:

```
TYPEPERF [counter1 [counter2 ...]] [-CF file] [-O file] [-F format]
➥[-SI interval] [-SC samples] [-Q [object]] [-QX [object]]
➥[-CONFIG file] [-S computer]
```

counter1 *counter2...]*	Specifies the path of the performance counter to monitor. If you want to track multiple counters, separate each counter path with a space. If any path includes spaces, surround the path with quotation marks.
-CF *file*	Loads the counters from *file*, where *file* is a text file that lists the counter paths on separate lines.
-O *file*	Specifies the path and name of the file that will store the performance data.
-F *format*	Specifies the format for the output file format given by the /O switch, where *format* is one of the following values:
	csv The output is displayed with each counter separated by a comma and each sample on its own line. This is the default output format.
	tsv The output is displayed with each counter separated by a tab and each sample on its own line.
	bin The output is displayed in binary format.
-SI *interval*	Specifies the time interval between samples. The *interval* parameter uses the form [mm:] ss. The default interval is 1 second.
-SC *samples*	Specifies the number of samples to collect. If you omit this switch, TYPEPERF samples continuously until you press Ctrl+C to cancel.
-Q [*object*]	Lists the available counters for *object* without instances.
-QX [*object*]	Lists the available counters for *object* with instances.
-CONFIG *file*	Specifies the pathname of the settings file that contains the TYPEPERF parameters you want to run.
-S *computer*	Specifies that the performance counters should be monitored on the PC named *computer* if no computer name is specified in the counter path.
-Y	Answers yes to any prompts generated by TYPEPERF.

The official syntax of a counter path looks like this:

`[\\Computer]\Object([Parent/][Instance][#Index])\Counter`

Computer	The computer on which the counter is to be monitored. If you omit a computer name, TYPEPERF monitors the counter on the local computer.
Object	The performance object—such as `Processor`, `Memory`, or `PhysicalDisk`—that contains the counter.
Parent	The container instance of the specified *Instance*.
Instance	The instance of the *Object*, if it has multiple instances. For example, in a two- (or dual-core) processor system, the instances are `0` (for the first processor), `1` (for the second processor), and `Total` (for both processors combined). You can also use an asterisk (*) to represent all the instances in *Object*.
Index	The index number of the specified *Instance*.
Counter	The name of the performance counter. You can also use an asterisk (*) to represent all the counters in *Object(Instance)*.

In practice, however, you rarely use the *Computer*, *Parent*, and *Index* parts of the path, so most counter paths use one of the following two formats:

`\Object\Counter`
`\Object(Instance)\Counter`

For example, here's the path for the `Memory` object's `Available MBytes` counter:

`\Memory\Available MBytes`

Here's a TYPEPERF command that displays five samples of this counter:

`typeperf "\Memory\Available Mbytes" -sc 5`

Similarly, here's the path for the `Processor` object's `% Processor Time` counter, using the first processor instance:

`\Processor(0)\% Processor Time`

Here's a TYPEPERF command that displays ten samples of this counter every 3 seconds, and saves the results to a file named `ProcessorTime.txt`:

`typeperf "\Processor(0)\% Processor Time" -sc 10 -si 3 -o ProcessorTime.txt`

To use the -CONFIG parameter with TYPEPERF, you need to create a text file that stores the command-line parameters you want to use. This configuration file consists of a series of parameter/value pairs that use the following general format:

```
[Parameter]
Value
```

Here, *Parameter* is text that specifies a TYPEPERF parameter—such as F for the -F parameter and S for the -S parameter. Use C to specify one or more counter paths, and *Value* is the value you want to assign to the parameter.

For example, consider the following command:

```
typeperf "\PhysicalDisk(_Total)\% Idle Time" -si 5 -sc 10 -o idletime.txt
```

To run the same command using the -CONFIG parameter, you first need to create a file with the following text:

```
[c]
\PhysicalDisk(_Total)\% Idle Time
[si]
5
[sc]
10
[o]
idletime.txt
```

If this file is named IdleTimeCounter.txt, you can run it at any time with the following command (assuming IdleTimeCounter.txt resides in the current folder):

```
typeperf -config IdleTimeCounter.txt
```

WHOAMI: Getting Information About the Current User

The WHOAMI command gives you information about the user who is currently logged on to the computer:

```
WHOAMI [/UPN ¦ /FQDN ¦ LOGONID] [/USER ¦ /GROUPS ¦ /CLAIMS ¦ /PRIV] [/ALL]
➥[/FO Format]
```

/UPN	(Domains only) Returns the current user's name using the user principal name (UPN) format.
/FQDN	(Domains only) Returns the current user's name using the fully qualified domain name (FQDN) format.
/LOGONID	Returns the current user's security identifier (SID).

/USER	Returns the current username using the *computer\user* format.
/GROUPS	Returns the groups of which the current user is a member.
/CLAIMS	(Domains only) Returns the current user's claims.
/PRIV	Returns the current user's privileges.
/ALL	Returns the current user's SID, username, groups, and privileges.
/FO format	The output format, where *format* is one of the following values:

	table	The output is displayed in a row-and-column format, with headers in the first row and values in subsequent rows.
	list	The output is displayed in a two-column list, with the headers in the first column and values in the second column.
	csv	The output is displayed with headers and values separated by commas. The headers appear on the first line.

You probably won't use this command often on the Windows 8 computer because you'll almost always be logged on as administrator. However, WHOAMI is useful when you're working on a client computer and you're not sure who is currently logged on.

For example, the following command redirects the current user's SID, username, groups, and privileges to a file named whoami.txt using the list format:

```
whoami /all /fo list > whoami.txt
```

Working with Users, Groups, and Shares

You can script your user and group chores by taking advantage of the NET USER and NET LOCALGROUP commands. These commands enable you to add users, change passwords, modify accounts, add users to groups, and remove users from groups. Note that you must run these commands under the Administrator account, so press Windows Logo+X, click Command Prompt (Admin), and then enter your User Account Control credentials.

NET USER: Working with Users

You use the NET USER command to add users, set account passwords, disable accounts, set account options (such as the times of day the user is allowed to log on), and remove accounts. For local users, the NET USER command has the following syntax:

```
NET USER [username [password ¦ * ¦ /RANDOM] [/ADD] [/DELETE] [options]]
```

username   The name of the user you want to add or work with. If you run NET USER with only the name of an existing user, the command displays the user's account data.

password   The password you want to assign to the user. If you use *, Windows 8 prompts you for the password; if you use the /RANDOM switch, Windows 8 assigns a random password (containing eight characters, consisting of a random mix of letters, numbers, and symbols), and then displays the password on the console.

/ADD   Creates a new user account.

/DELETE   Deletes the specified user account.

options   These are optional switches you can append to the command:

/ACTIVE:{YES ¦ NO}—Specifies whether the account is active or disabled.

/EXPIRES:{*date* ¦ NEVER}—The date (expressed in the system's Short Date format) on which the account expires.

/HOMEDIR:*path*—The home folder for the user, which should be a subfolder within %SystemDrive%\Users (make sure that the folder exists).

/PASSWORDCHG:{YES ¦ NO}—Specifies whether the user is allowed to change his password.

/PASSWORDREQ:{YES ¦ NO}—Specifies whether the user is required to have a password.

/PROFILEPATH:*path*—The folder that contains the user's profile.

/SCRIPTPATH:*path*—The folder that contains the user's logon script.

/TIMES:{*times* ¦ ALL}—Specifies the times that the user is allowed to log on to the system. Use single days or day ranges (for example, Sa or M-F). For times, use 24-hour notation or 12-hour notation with am or pm. Separate the day and time with a comma, and separate day/time combinations with semicolons. Here are some examples:

```
M-F,9am-5pm
M,W,F,08:00-13:00
Sa,12pm-6pm;Su,1pm-5pm
```

Note, too, that if you execute NET USER without any parameters, it displays a list of the local user accounts.

> ## ⚠ caution
> If you use the /RANDOM switch to create a random password, be sure to make a note of the new password so that you can communicate it to the new user.

〰 tip

If you want to force a user to log off when his logon hours expire, open the Local Group Policy Editor and select Computer Configuration, Windows Settings, Security Settings, Local Policies, Security Options. In the Network Security category, enable the Force Logoff When Logon Hours Expire policy.

NET LOCALGROUP: **Working with Groups**

You use the NET LOCALGROUP command to add users to and remove users from a specified security group. NET LOCALGROUP has the following syntax:

```
NET LOCALGROUP [group name1 [name2 ...] {/ADD ¦ /DELETE}
```

group	This is the name of the security group with which you want to work.
name1 [*name2* ...]	One or more usernames you want to add or delete, separated by spaces.
/ADD	Adds the user or users to the group.
/DELETE	Removes the user or users from the group.

NET USE: **Mapping Folders**

You can also map a network folder to a local drive letter by using a Command Prompt session and the NET USE command. Although you probably won't use this method very often, it's handy to know how it works, just in case. Here's the basic syntax:

```
NET USE [drive] [share] [password] [/USER:user]
➥[/PERSISTENT:[YES ¦ NO]] ¦ /DELETE]
```

drive	The drive letter (following by a colon) of the local drive to which you want the network folder mapped.
share	The network address of the folder.
password	The password required to connect to the shared folder (that is, the password associated with the username, specified next).
/USER:*user*	The username you want to use to connect to the shared folder.
/PERSISTENT:	Add YES to reconnect the mapped network drive the next time you log on.
/DELETE	Deletes the existing mapping that's associated with *drive*.

For example, the following command maps the shared folder \\PAULSPC\Paul\Writing\Books to the Z: drive:

```
net use z: \\paulspc\paul\writing\books \persistent:yes
```

Working with Network Troubleshooting Tools

Windows 8 TCP/IP comes with a few command-line utilities you can use to review your TCP/IP settings and troubleshoot problems. Here's a list of the available utilities:

- **ARP** — This utility displays (or modifies) the IP-to-Ethernet or IP-to-Token Ring address translation tables used by the Address Resolution Protocol (ARP) in TCP/IP. Enter the command arp -? for the syntax.

- **NBTSTAT** — This utility displays the protocol statistics and the current TCP/IP connections using NBT (NetBIOS over TCP/IP). Enter nbtstat -? for the syntax.

- **NETSTAT** — This utility displays the protocol statistics and current TCP/IP connections. The command netstat -? displays the syntax.

- **PING** — This utility can check a network connection to a remote computer. This is one of the most commonly used TCP/IP diagnostic tools, so we describe it more detail in the next section.

- **ROUTE** — This utility can be used to manipulate a network routing table (LMHOSTS). Enter route -? for the syntax.

- **TRACERT** — This utility can check the route taken to a remote host. We explain this valuable diagnostic command in more detail later.

- **IPCONFIG** — This utility displays the current TCP/IP network configuration. If you run the command ipconfig without any switches, the utility returns your system's current IP address, subnet mask, and default gateway. If you run the command ipconfig /all, the utility returns more detailed information, as shown here:

```
Windows IP Configuration

   Host Name . . . . . . . . . . . . : MediaPC
   Primary Dns Suffix  . . . . . . . :
   Node Type . . . . . . . . . . . . : Hybrid
   IP Routing Enabled. . . . . . . . : No
   WINS Proxy Enabled. . . . . . . . : No
   DNS Suffix Search List. . . . . . : phub.net.cable.rogers.com

Ethernet adapter Local Area Connection:

   Connection-specific DNS Suffix  . : phub.net.cable.rogers.com
   Description . . . . . . . . . . . : Atheros L1 Gigabit Ethernet 10/100/
   1000Base-T Controller
   Physical Address. . . . . . . . . : 00-1E-8C-7D-97-3A
   DHCP Enabled. . . . . . . . . . . : Yes
   Autoconfiguration Enabled . . . . : Yes
   Link-local IPv6 Address . . . . . : fe80::452f:6db7:eaf2:3112%11(Preferred)
   IPv4 Address. . . . . . . . . . . : 192.168.0.84(Preferred)
   Subnet Mask . . . . . . . . . . . : 255.255.0.0
```

```
Lease Obtained. . . . . . . . . : Wednesday, October 24, 2012 10:38:42 AM
Lease Expires . . . . . . . . . : Thursday, October 25, 2012 2:07:16 PM
Default Gateway . . . . . . . . : 192.168.1.1
DHCP Server . . . . . . . . . . : 192.168.1.1
DHCPv6 IAID . . . . . . . . . . : 234888844
DHCPv6 Client DUID. . . . . . . : 00-01-00-01-11-52-C4-05-00-1E-8C-7D-97-3A
DNS Servers . . . . . . . . . . : 192.168.1.1
NetBIOS over Tcpip. . . . . . . : Enabled

Tunnel adapter isatap.phub.net.cable.rogers.com:

Media State . . . . . . . . . . : Media disconnected
Connection-specific DNS Suffix  . : phub.net.cable.rogers.com
Description . . . . . . . . . . : Microsoft ISATAP Adapter
Physical Address. . . . . . . . : 00-00-00-00-00-00-00-E0
DHCP Enabled. . . . . . . . . . : No
Autoconfiguration Enabled . . . . : Yes

Tunnel adapter Teredo Tunneling Pseudo-Interface:

Connection-specific DNS Suffix  . :
Description . . . . . . . . . . : Teredo Tunneling Pseudo-Interface
Physical Address. . . . . . . . : 00-00-00-00-00-00-00-E0
DHCP Enabled. . . . . . . . . . : No
Autoconfiguration Enabled . . . . : Yes
IPv6 Address. . . . . . . . . . : 2001:0:4137:9e50:3032:38c1:3f57:ffab
(Preferred)
Link-local IPv6 Address . . . . . : fe80::3032:38c1:3f57:ffab%13(Preferred)
Default Gateway . . . . . . . . : ::
NetBIOS over Tcpip. . . . . . . : Disabled

Tunnel adapter Reusable ISATAP Interface {D767BCA8-D27E-404C-9A50-CD680EF507C0}:

Media State . . . . . . . . . . : Media disconnected
Connection-specific DNS Suffix  . :
Description . . . . . . . . . . : Microsoft ISATAP Adapter #2
Physical Address. . . . . . . . : 00-00-00-00-00-00-00-E0
DHCP Enabled. . . . . . . . . . : No
Autoconfiguration Enabled . . . . : Yes
```

Here's a basic procedure you can run through to troubleshoot networking problems using the command-line tools:

1. Release the current DHCP lease by running the following command:

   ```
   ipconfig /release
   ```

2. Renew the DHCP lease by running the following command:

   ```
   ipconfig /renew
   ```

note

A *DHCP lease* is a guarantee that the Dynamic Host Control Protocol (DHCP) client computer will have the IP address supplied by the DHCP server for a specified period of time. To avoid lease expiration, the DHCP client usually sends a request—a DHCPREQUEST message—for lease renewal to the original DHCP server after 50% of the lease time has expired. If 87.5% of its lease time has expired, the DHCP client sends a lease renewal request to all available DHCP servers.

3. Flush the ARP cache. The ARP handles the conversion of an IP address to a physical address of a network adapter. (To see the physical address of your adapter, open the connection's Status dialog box, display the Support tab, and click Details.) To improve performance, Windows 8 stores resolved addresses in the *ARP cache* for a short time. Some networking problems are caused by ARP cache entries that are obsolete or incomplete. The cache is normally flushed regularly, but to force a flush, run the following command:

```
arp -d
```

tip

To see the contents of the ARP cache, run the following command:arp -a

You'll see output similar to the following:

```
Interface: 192.168.1.101 --- 0x2
  Internet Address      Physical Address      Type
  192.168.1.1           00-12-17-8c-48-88     dynamic
  192.168.1.100         00-11-24-1a-7a-fc     dynamic
  192.168.1.103         00-11-11-be-c7-78     dynamic
```

4. Flush the NetBIOS name cache. NetBIOS handles the conversion between the network names of computers and their IP addresses. To improve performance, Windows 8 stores resolved names in the *NetBIOS name cache*. To solve problems caused by NetBIOS name cache entries that are obsolete or bad, this step clears the cache. Run the following command:

```
nbtstat -r
```

5. Re-register the computer with the network's WINS server. That is, you ask the WINS server to release the computer's NetBIOS names that are registered with the server and then re-register them. This is useful if you're having problems connecting to other computers using their network names. Run the following command:

```
nbtstat -rr
```

6. Flush the DNS cache. DNS handles the conversion of domain names to IP addresses. To improve performance, Windows 8 stores resolved domain names in the *DNS cache*. To solve problems

caused by DNS cache entries that are obsolete or bad, clear the cache by running the following command:

```
ipconfig /flushdns
```

7. Re-register the computer with the DNS server. This is useful if you're having trouble resolving domain names or if you're having trouble with a dynamic DNS server. Run the following command:

```
ipconfig /registerdns
```

PING: **Checking Connectivity**

As you might know, a submarine can detect a nearby object by using sonar to send out a sound wave and then seeing whether the wave is reflected. This is called *pinging* an object.

Windows 8 has a PING command that performs a similar function. PING sends out a special type of IP packet—called an *Internet Control Message Protocol (ICMP) echo packet*—to a remote location. This packet requests that the remote location send back a response packet. PING then tells you whether the response was received. In this way, you can check your network configuration to see whether your computer can connect with a remote host.

To use PING, first open a command-line session by selecting Start, All Programs, Accessories, Command Prompt. Here's a simplified version of the PING syntax:

```
ping [-t] [-n count]  target_name
```

-t	Pings the specified *target_name* until you interrupt the command.
-n *count*	Sends the number of echo packets specified by *count*. The default is 4.
target_name	Specifies either the IP address or the hostname (a fully qualified domain name) of the remote host you want to ping.

Here's an example that uses PING on the Google.com domain:

```
C:\Users\Paul>ping google.com

Pinging google.com [64.233.187.99] with 32 bytes of data:

Reply from 64.233.187.99: bytes=32 time=43ms TTL=240
Reply from 64.233.187.99: bytes=32 time=42ms TTL=239
Reply from 64.233.187.99: bytes=32 time=43ms TTL=239
Reply from 64.233.187.99: bytes=32 time=42ms TTL=240

Ping statistics for 64.233.187.99:
    Packets: Sent = 4, Received = 4, Lost = 0 (0% loss),A
Approximate round trip times in milli-seconds:
    Minimum = 42ms, Maximum = 43ms, Average = 42ms
```

Here you see that each echo packet received a reply. If you can't connect to the remote host, PING returns a Request timed out message for each packet.

If you can't connect to a remote host, here are some notes on using PING to troubleshoot problems:

- First, check to see whether you can use PING successfully on the loopback address:

  ping 127.0.0.1.

  The only reason this PING would fail is if your computer doesn't have the Internet Protocol installed. However, all Windows 8 machines have IP installed, and the option to uninstall it is disabled, so pinging the loopback address will almost certainly work. The only reason to include it in your troubleshooting is that if it doesn't work, it means you have a serious problem with your machine. Either revert to a working configuration, reinstall Windows 8, or take your machine to a computer repair professional.

- Try using PING on your computer's IP address. (If you're using DHCP, run the IPCONFIG utility to get your current IP address.) If you don't get a successful echo, your NIC may not be inserted properly or the device drivers may not be installed.

- Now PING another computer on your network. If PING fails, check your cable or wireless connections.

- The next test you should run is on your default gateway (that is, your router). If you can't successfully PING the router's internal IP address, you won't be able to access remote Internet sites. In this case, check the IP address you entered for the gateway, check the cable connections, and make sure the router is turned on. You may need to power cycle the router.

- If you get this far, try using PING on the remote host you're trying to contact. If you're unsuccessful, check to make sure you're using the correct IP address for the host. Try power cycling your broadband modem.

TRACERT: Tracking Packets

If you can't PING a remote host, it could be that your echo packets are getting held up along the way. To find out, you can use the TRACERT (trace route) command:

tracert [-d] [-h *maximum_hops*] [-j *host-list*] [-w *timeout*] *target_name*

-d	Specifies not to resolve IP addresses to hostnames.
-h *maximum_hops*	Specifies the maximum number of hops to search for the *target_name*. (The default is 30.)
-j *host-list*	Specifies loose source route along the *host-list*.
-w *timeout*	Waits the number of milliseconds specified by *timeout* for each reply.
target_name	Specifies the hostname of the destination computer.

TRACERT operates by sending ICMP echo packets with varying TTL values. Recall that TTL places a limit on the number of hops that a packet can take. Each host along the packet's route decrements the TTL value until, when the TTL value is 0, the packet is discarded (assuming that it hasn't reached its destination by then).

In TRACERT, the ICMP packets specify that whichever host decrements the echo packet to 0 should send back a response. So, the first packet has a TTL value of 1, the second has a TTL value of 2, and so on. TRACERT keeps sending packets with incrementally higher TTL values until either a response is received from the remote host or a packet receives no response. Here's an example of a TRACERT command in action:

```
C:\>tracert google.com

Tracing route to google.com [216.239.57.99]
over a maximum of 30 hops:

 1     <1 ms     <1 ms     <1 ms   192.168.1.1
 2      8 ms      8 ms      8 ms   64.230.197.178
 3      6 ms      6 ms      6 ms   64.230.221.201
 4      6 ms      6 ms      6 ms   64.230.234.249
 5      8 ms      6 ms      7 ms   64.230.233.93
 6     17 ms     17 ms     16 ms   core1-chicago23-pos0-0.in.bellnexxia.net
  ➥[206.108.103.130]
 7     17 ms     17 ms     17 ms   bx2-chicago23-pos11-0.in.bellnexxia.net
  ➥[206.108.103.138]
 8     17 ms     17 ms     17 ms   so-4-3-3.cr1.ord2.us.above.net [208.184.233.185]
 9     18 ms     17 ms     18 ms   so-0-0-0.cr2.ord2.us.above.net [64.125.29.186]
10     36 ms     36 ms     36 ms   so-5-2-0.cr1.dca2.us.above.net [64.125.30.225]
11     47 ms     46 ms     46 ms   so-4-1-0.mpr2.atl6.us.above.net [64.125.29.41]
12     48 ms     48 ms     48 ms   64.124.229.173.google.com [64.124.229.173]
13     48 ms     48 ms     48 ms   216.239.48.23
14     49 ms     49 ms     49 ms   216.239.46.44
15    100 ms    100 ms    100 ms   216.239.47.129
16     99 ms     99 ms     99 ms   216.239.49.250
17     99 ms     99 ms     99 ms   66.249.95.65
18     99 ms     99 ms     99 ms   66.249.94.27
19    102 ms    101 ms    101 ms   216.239.49.97
20     99 ms    100 ms     99 ms   216.239.57.99

Trace complete.
```

The first column is the hop number (that is, the TTL value set in the packet). Notice that, in my case, it took 20 hops to get to Google.com. The next three columns contain round-trip times for an attempt to reach the destination with that TTL value. (Asterisks indicate that the attempt timed out.) The last column contains the hostname (if it was resolved) and the IP address of the responding system.

Changing the Default TTL Value

One of the reasons your packets might not be getting to their destination is that the default TTL value used by Windows 8 might be set too low. This is actually very unlikely because the default is 128, which should be more than enough. However, you *can* increase this value if you want. Start the Registry Editor and highlight the following key:

```
HKLM\System\CurrentControlSet\Services\Tcpip\Parameters
```

Select Edit, New, DWORD Value. Type **DefaultTTL** and then press Enter. Change the value of this new setting to any decimal value between 0 and 255 (0 to FF in hexadecimal).

INDEX

two-way, 832

wireless networks, 392, 393

authorization, People, 352

Authorization Manager, 530

autoanswer, faxes, 259

AUTOCHK tool, 938

Auto-Hide the Taskbar option, 578

Automatic Maintenance window, 655

Automatic Memory Dump, 624

automating

automatic document feeders. *See* ADFs

command-line tools, 727

See also command-line tools

components, installing, 55

disk checks, 938-940

Disk Cleanup, 596

dual-booting, 41

email, viewing, 339

faxes, receiving, 263-264

hibernation, 82

locking, 734-735

Mail check, 337

maintenance, 591, 655

repair to PCs, 647-648

restarting, 623

System Restore points, 767

tools, 711

updates, configuring, 653-655

Windows Boot Manager, 43

AutoPlay, 34, 509

See also playing

imaging devices, connecting, 240

third-party applications, 660

WMP, 214

availability

DSL, 281

network services, 428-431

Avast! Antivirus, 756

AVG Internet Security, 756

Axentra, 434

B

back doors, 794

backgrounds

Lock screens, customizing, 120

multiple monitors, 677

slide shows, formatting, 232

Start screens, customizing, 118

tabs, opening web pages in, 306

backing up

See also saving

baselines, 808

BCD stores, 53

computers on networks, 469

email, 346

encryption keys, 785-786

files, 32, 760-765

Registry, 697-698

hard disks, 697-698

Registry Editor, 698

System Restore, 698

scheduling, 763

system images, 33-34, 770-771

Backup Operators group, 776

Balanced profile, 865

balancing headphones, 271-273

bars

Address

entering URLs, 302

optimizing, 304-305

Favorites, 302

baseline backups, 808

basic Mail account settings, 332-333

C

for email, 337

existing adapters, 384-385

free space, 593-595

hard disks, 32, 936-938

networks, configuring, 498-501

security, settings, 736-741

system requirements, 32

for updates, 655-656, 683

checklists, installing, 31-34

chimes, 274

See also sounds

CHKDSK tool, 935-938

installation, running at, 32

CHKNTFS tool, 935, 938-940

circuits, telephones, 386

cleaning

layouts, 127

out inboxes, 345

See also maintaining

up hard disks, 32

versions to save disk space, 764

clearing

Address bar lists, 304

tile notifications, 113

ClearType Tuner tool, 75

clients

networks, troubleshooting, 488

Remote Desktop Connection, 907, 914, 918-920

Samba, 441

clocks, viewing multiple time zones, 585

closing

applications, 107

tabs, 307

tiles, 113, 117-118

UDF sessions, 250-251

Windows 8, 81-82

cloud services, 8-9

CLSID subkey, 151

clusters, 157

.cmd files, 713

cmdlets, 726

codes, Type and Creator, 445

collaboration, 891

Color Management, 509

colors

backgrounds, formatting, 232

calendars, modifying, 129

Internet Explorer, 320

schemes, 119

columns, sizing, 571

COM (Component Object Model), 507

Remote Desktop, 921

.com files, 713

combining

dynamic disks into spanned volumes, 608-609

multiple drives, 603

Command Prompt window

commands, running, 714

cutting/pasting, 714

directories, modifying, 713

environmental variable settings, 716-719

GUIs, 716

MS-DOS, 719-720

navigating, 712-716

opening, 498

output, saving, 713

resources, 714-716

searching, 713-714

Command Type dialog box, 535

command-line tools, 711, 935

batch files, 721-722

chkdsk, 590

How can we make this index more useful? Email us at indexes@quepublishing.com

How can we make this index more useful? Email us at indexes@quepublishing.com

How can we make this index more useful? Email us at indexes@quepublishing.com

How can we make this index more useful? Email us at indexes@quepublishing.com

G

How can we make this index more useful? Email us at indexes@quepublishing.com

How can we make this index more useful? Email us at indexes@quepublishing.com

M

slide shows, customizing, 231-232

TV shows, archiving, 233-237

Media Player. *See* **WMP**

Media Streaming

Options window, 221

settings, 492

meetings, 129, 856-857, 891, 903

memory, 668

cards

accessing media on, 242

inserting, 214, 242

devices, viewing, 681

dumps, 624

Memory Diagnostics tool, 629

performance monitoring, 550

system requirements, 28-29

values, 552

video, 225

Memory Diagnostics tool, running, 628-629

Memory (RAM) metric, 548

Memory Sticks, 242

menus

Charms, 97-98

Print, 185, 191

Send To, customizing, 159

Start

See also Start screens

accessing items from taskbars, 123-124

navigating without, 24-25

Message Rules dialog box, 347

messages

deleting, 338

DHCPREQUEST, 968

email, 331, 340-345

See also email

errors, 620

Event Log, 497

formatting, 340

forwarding, 338

indenting, 344

Mail, 133

See also Mail

moving, 337, 346

People, 353

Presentation Settings feature, 891

printing, 338

processing, 337-338

read options, 338-339

rules, 347-349

searching, 349-351

store databases, compacting, 347

Windows Firewall, 817, 820

Messaging, 136

metadata

files, managing, 162-164

searching, 166

tags, adding, 248

metering Internet usage, 24

methods

input, mobile devices, 841-843

StartService, 544

StopService, 544

transfer, 79

metrics, performance monitoring, 547

Metro app, 10

See also interfaces; navigating; Windows 8

Microphone Setup Wizard, 275

microphones, configuring, 275

microprocessors

ARM, 840

limitations of, 840

Microsoft accounts, 68-69

Microsoft Active Protection Service, 740

Microsoft Management Console. *See* **MMC**

Microsoft Office, 840

Microsoft Security Advisory 2719662, 194

Microsoft Security Essentials, 811

N

How can we make this index more useful? Email us at indexes@quepublishing.com

How can we make this index more useful? Email us at indexes@quepublishing.com

How can we make this index more useful? Email us at indexes@quepublishing.com

S

T

How can we make this index more useful? Email us at indexes@quepublishing.com

How can we make this index more useful? Email us at indexes@quepublishing.com

U

How can we make this index more useful? Email us at indexes@quepublishing.com

How can we make this index more useful? Email us at indexes@quepublishing.com

Z

Windows 8

IN DEPTH

que

Brian Knittel and Paul McFedries

Safari
Books Online

FREE
Online Edition

Your purchase of *Windows 8 In Depth* includes access to a free online edition for 45 days through the **Safari Books Online** subscription service. Nearly every Que book is available online through **Safari Books Online**, along with thousands of books and videos from publishers such as Addison-Wesley Professional, Cisco Press, Exam Cram, IBM Press, O'Reilly Media, Prentice Hall, Sams, and VMware Press.

Safari Books Online is a digital library providing searchable, on-demand access to thousands of technology, digital media, and professional development books and videos from leading publishers. With one monthly or yearly subscription price, you get unlimited access to learning tools and information on topics including mobile app and software development, tips and tricks on using your favorite gadgets, networking, project management, graphic design, and much more.

Activate your FREE Online Edition at
informit.com/safarifree

STEP 1: Enter the coupon code: ZWEWOEH.

STEP 2: New Safari users, complete the brief registration form.
Safari subscribers, just log in.

If you have difficulty registering on Safari or accessing the online edition,
please e-mail customer-service@safaribooksonline.com